Reason and Responsibility

REASON AND RESPONSIBILITY

Readings in Some Basic Problems of Philosophy

Tenth Edition

Edited by

Joel Feinberg
University of Arizona

Russ Shafer-Landau
University of Kansas

Wadsworth Publishing Company

I(T)P® An International Thomson Publishing Company

Belmont, CA • Albany, NY • Boston • Cincinnati • Johannesburg • London • Madrid • Melbourne
Mexico City • New York • Pacific Grove, CA • Scottsdale, AZ • Singapore • Tokyo • Toronto

Philosophy Editor: Peter Adams
Assistant Editor: Kerri Abdinoor
Editorial Assistant: Kelly Bush
Marketing Manager: Dave Garrison
Project Editor: Jerry Holloway
Print Buyer: Stacey Weinberger
Permissions Editor: Robert Kauser
Production: Matrix Productions Inc.
Copy Editor: Judy Winthrop
Cover Design: Ross Carron
Compositor: Thompson Type
Printer: R. R. Donnelley & Sons

This book is printed on acid-free recycled paper.

Printed in the United States of America
1 2 3 4 5 6 7 8 9 10

For more information, contact Wadsworth Publishing Company, 10 Davis Drive, Belmont, CA 94002, or electronically at http://www.wadsworth.com

International Thomson Publishing Europe
Berkshire House
168-173 High Holborn
London, WC1V 7AA, England

International Thomson Editores
Seneca, 53
Colonia Polanco
11560 México D.F. México

Nelson ITP, Australia
102 Dodds Street
South Melbourne
Victoria 3205, Australia

International Thomson Publishing Asia
60 Albert Street #15-01
Albert Complex
Singapore 189969

Nelson Canada
1120 Birchmount Road
Scarborough, Ontario
Canada M1K 5G4

International Thomson Publishing Japan
Hirakawa-cho Kyowa Building, 3F
2-2-1 Hirakawa-cho, Chiyoda-ku
Tokyo 102, Japan

International Thomson Publishing Southern Africa
Building 18, Constantia Park
138 Sixteenth Road, P.O. Box 2459
Halfway House, 1685 South Africa

Library of Congress Cataloging-in-Publication Data

Reason and responsibility : readings in some basic problems of philosophy / edited by Joel Feinberg and Russ Shafer-Landau. — 10th ed.
p. cm.
ISBN 0-534-54351-0
1. Philosophy. I. Feinberg, Joel, . II. Shafer-Landau, Russ.
B29.R367 1998
100—dc21 98-15744

Contents

Preface

The conviction underlying this volume is that introducing the college student to philosophy by means of a few representative problems examined in great detail is far preferable to offering a "little bit of everything," with each "branch" of philosophy, each major "ism," and each major historical period represented with scrupulous impartiality, even though the articles may have little relevance to one another. Accordingly, we have selected articles from both classical and contemporary sources on such topics as religion, mind, personal identity, death, freedom, responsibility, duty, justice, and selfishness. The problems that concern philosophers under these headings are not mere idle riddles, but rather questions of vital interest to any reflective person. Each set of problems is plumbed in considerable depth in essays expressing different, often opposing, views. Our hope is that exposure to this argumentative give-and-take will encourage students to take part in the process themselves, and through this practice to develop their powers of philosophical reasoning.

I am fortunate indeed to have persuaded so able a philosopher and pedagogue as Russ Shafer-Landau of the University of Kansas to be my co-editor. He has also contributed an article on ethical subjectivism to this edition of *Reason and Responsibility.*

This tenth edition of *Reason and Responsibility* has been improved by the addition of fourteen new selections. Plato's dialogue *Euthyphro* has been replaced by another of his dialogues, the *Crito,* as an initial exercise in philosophical argumentation. The latter work is a typical piece of Platonic reasoning. As such, while it appears in Part Five of this volume, there is no reason why the *Crito* cannot lead off the whole collection if the instructor so wishes. In addition, several articles in this collection appear in an edited form that will make it easier for undergraduate students to understand them. That is true of the Lycan and Schlesinger article in Part One, and the Chisholm and Pollock pieces in Part Two.

The greatest changes, however, are in Part Five—"The Claims of Morality and Justice"—where we include nine new articles and a new subsection on distributive justice. Under the subsection "Proposed Standards of Right Conduct," three new articles appear: Russ Shafer-Landau's "Ethical Subjectivism"; selections from Thomas Hobbes's *Leviathan;* and Onora O'Neill's "Kantian Approaches to Some Famine Problems." Our revised subsection on "Justice and Law" now includes Plato's *Crito* and new articles by both John Rawls and Joel Feinberg on civil disobedience. Finally, the section on distributive justice includes new selections from Robert Nozick and John Stuart Mill, and an expanded excerpt from John Rawls' *A Theory of Justice.*

Similarly significant revisions can be found in Part Four—"Determinism, Free Will, and Responsibility"—where three new articles appear and there is one new subsection ("Freedom and Moral Responsibility"). We have included Walter Stace's article on reconciling free will and determinism, and Roderick Chisholm's article that tries to show why no such reconciliation can take place. Also new to this edition is Harry Frankfurt's piece that criticizes a thought deeply embedded in our ordinary views on freedom and responsibility. Most of us think freedom requires an ability to do otherwise—if we can't do anything other than what we actually do, then we cannot be responsible for our choices or conduct—and Frankfurt takes direct aim at this thought. His widely discussed views are complemented in this new section by Thomas Nagel's justly famous discussion of moral luck, and Susan Wolf's penetrating attempt to show how genuine moral responsibility is compatible with our characters and choices having been determined by events that occurred even before we were born.

Part One, "The Existence and Nature of God," now includes an article, written by Deborah Mathieu specially for this volume, that explores patriarchal conceptions of religious belief. We also include Peter van Inwagen's subtle views on how theists might best reconcile the existence of evil with the existence of an all-good, omnipotent god. Finally, Part Three, "Mind and Its Place in Nature," has been strengthened by inclusion of Frank Jackson's provocative article defending the claim that what goes on in the mind is not identical with what goes on in the brain.

This volume currently contains eight classics: three that are complete (Descartes' *Meditations,* Berkeley's *Dialogues,* and Plato's *Crito*); one that is presented in virtual totality (Hume's *Dialogues*); and four that appear in very substantial sections (Hume's *Inquiry,* Mill's *Utilitarianism,* Kant's *Foundations,* and Plato's *Republic*). The text can be used to teach an introductory course based solidly on a reading of these classics; more recent articles can be seen as a kind of dividend. The book contains many articles by contemporary philosophers, including nine that are addressed specifically to beginning students and that were written expressly for this book by William Rowe, Wesley Salmon, John Perry, William Lycan and George Schlesinger, Colin Allen, Deborah Mathieu, and both editors.

We do not presume to dictate that there is one "necessary and natural" order of sequence in which to read these materials. The book begins with the philosophy of religion because many beginners are familiar with its problems. But it is just as "natural" to begin with Part Two, because the question of our knowledge of God presupposes the question of the "grounds and limits of human knowledge" generally. Similarly, there is no reason why one could not begin with the mind-body problem (Part Three) or the problem of determinism and free will (Part Four). Indeed, many professors have told me that they prefer to begin with ethics (Part Five) and work their way toward the front of the book.

In selecting the materials for this tenth edition, we have been helped by the advice, positive and negative, of the following critics: John Bricke, University of Kansas; Joseph Keim Campbell, Washington State University; Earl Conee, University of Rochester; Charles Crittenden, California State University; Daniel Howard-Snyder, Seattle Pacific University; Kathie Jenni, University of Redlands; Stephen Laurence, London School of Economics; David Newman, Western Michigan University; Jacob Pinnolis, University of Florida; Thomas Senor, University of Arkansas; and Jim Stone, University of New Orleans. I am grateful for their help and also for that of Kristen Hessler, my research assistant, who not only did the many useful but relatively rote tasks of an assistant—typing, photocopying, finding obscure journals and books, etc.—but also handled the permissions requests and dealt with the problems they inevitably raise.

Joel Feinberg

Reason and Responsibility

Part I

Reason and Religious Belief

WHAT CAN REASON TELL US about such vast topics as the origin of the universe and the existence and nature of God? Most of us have beliefs about these matters—beliefs derived from religious authorities or based on faith; but is there any way to demonstrate that these beliefs are reasonable or unreasonable? This question provides the unifying theme for the readings in Part 1.

Traditional arguments for the existence of God are often divided into two groups: those whose premises are justified **a posteriori** (based on experience) and those whose premises are known **a priori** (independently of experience). In fact, however, only one mode of argument has ever purported to be wholly independent of experience, namely, the **ontological argument,** invented by St. Anselm in the eleventh century and defended in one form or another by Descartes, Spinoza, and Leibniz in the seventeenth century. (For Descartes' version of the argument, see his fifth Meditation, p. 170.) According to this argument, the very concept of God (or definition of the word *God*) entails that God must exist. If the argument is correct, anyone who has an idea of God—even if that person has no knowledge whatever of the kind derived from sense experience—has conclusive rational grounds for believing that God exists. The ontological argument still has defenders among philosophers of religion today, but among those who reject it, there is little agreement over precisely what is wrong with the argument. One recent discussion of the argument is included here. William L. Rowe's essay sets forth Anselm's argument clearly, step-by-step (including steps that are only implicit in Anselm's own formulation), summarizes the three most important objections to the argument, and then presents his own criticism. Rowe concludes that the ontological argument is defective but that it is nevertheless a "work of genius," which, despite its apparent simplicity, raises philosophical questions about the nature of existence that are subtle and fascinating in their own right.

Other arguments for God's existence are often called a priori, but these always contain at least one premise that asserts some simple experiential fact. Factual premises summarizing some facet of our experience are found in the various versions of the **cosmological argument**—illustrated in this section by the selections from St. Thomas Aquinas and Samuel Clarke. For the first three of his "Five Ways," Aquinas begins each argument by citing a familiar fact of experience: Some things are in motion; there are causes and effects; things are generated and corrupted. He then tries to show that this fact can be explained only by the existence of God because alternative explanations lead to logical absurdities. In his second article in this section, Rowe examines the cosmological argument in the form given it by Samuel Clarke and other seventeenth- and eighteenth-century philosophers. Put simply, the argument goes as follows:

1. Every being (that exists or ever did exist) is either a dependent being or self-existent being.
2. Not every being can be a dependent being.
3. Therefore, there exists a self-existent being.

The argument clearly is valid; that is, *if* its premises are true, then its conclusion is true. But the premises, especially the second, are highly controversial. Rowe reviews the dialectic of the debate, pro and con, over the truth of the second premise, before cautiously concluding that the premise has not yet been conclusively shown to be true.

Both the ontological and the cosmological arguments are **deductive** in form; that is, they purport to demonstrate that if their premises are true, then their conclusions must necessarily be true. It is logically impossible for a valid deductive argument to have both true premises and false conclusion. The **teleological argument** (more commonly called "the argument from design") for God is more modest. It argues not that its conclusion follows necessarily from its premises, but only that its premises establish a probability that the conclusion is true. It is therefore what logicians call an **inductive argument.** The famous argument from design, which is given classic formulations in William Paley's *Natural Theology* (1802) and by Cleanthes, a character in David Hume's *Dialogues Concerning Natural Religion* (1779), has the **inductive** form. More precisely, it is an argument by analogy, with the following form:

1. *a, b, c,* and *d* all have properties *P* and *Q.*
2. *a, b,* and *c* all have property *R* as well.
3. Therefore, *d* has property *R* too (probably).

The closer the similarity between *d* and *a, b,* and *c,* the more probable is the conclusion. Cleanthes' argument can be rendered as follows:

1. Boats, houses, watches, and the whole experienced world have such properties as "mutual adjustment of parts to whole" and "curious adapting of means to ends."
2. Boats, houses, and watches have the further property of having been produced by design.
3. Therefore, it is probable that the universe also has this further property, that it too was produced by design.

The conclusion of this argument, that a designer of the world exists, has the same logical role as a scientific hypothesis designed to explain the facts of experience and must be accepted or rejected according to whether it meets the criteria of adequacy by which hypotheses are appraised in science and in everyday life.

In Hume's *Dialogues,* the case against the argument from design is stated with great force and ingenuity by Philo, probably speaking for Hume himself. The analogies cited by the argument, he claims, are weak, partly because we know only one small part of the universe and cannot with confidence infer from it the nature of the whole. Moreover, he argues, there are other equally plausible ways of accounting for the observed order in the world. One of these alternative explanations, called by Philo in Part VII of the "Epicurean Hypothesis," bears striking resemblance to the Darwinian theory that biological adaptations are the result of chance variations and the survival of the fittest. In his essay "The Panda's Thumb," Stephen Jay Gould describes animal and plant adaptation as it appears to evolutionary biologists: not perfect, once-and-for-all "design" but rather a kind of makeshift patchwork. The circumstances and needs of animals change continuously, so that the successful species are those that contrive *new* "designs" out of the materials at hand that they are "stuck with."

Parts X and XI of the *Dialogues* contain one of the most famous discussions of "**the problem of evil,**" so central to religious belief. Here Philo concedes that if the existence of God has already been established by some a priori argument, then perhaps one can account for the appearance of evil in the world. But, he goes on to argue, one cannot infer the existence of an all-good and all-powerful being from the appearance of evil; that is, the former can hardly be an *explanation* of the latter.

In the later subsection devoted entirely to the problem of evil, the great Russian novelist Fyodor Dostoevsky dramatically sets the stage for the philosophical discussion that follows by showing how the problem can arise in human experience. J. L. Mackie and Peter van Inwagen approach the problem of evil in different ways. Van Inwagen approaches the problem from the Christian standpoint, but he does not underestimate the difficulty for Christian belief posed by the undeniable fact of human suffering. **Moral evil** (wickedness), according to a predominant strain of Christian teaching, is a necessary concomitant of human free will, indeed the price we pay for freedom; and it is **logically impossible,** in this line of thought, for God to have created perfectly free and perfectly (always) good creatures. (This is the point at which Mackie's attack is mainly aimed.) **Impersonal evil,** like the suffering that comes from natural disasters, may be thought to be harder to reconcile with God's **omnipotence** and perfect goodness than human-caused moral evil (wickedness) is. Some Christian philosophers still follow the suggestions of the great seventeenth-century philosopher G. F. Leibniz that what *appears* evil from our finite perspectives is not the genuine evil that would appear as such from the infinite standpoint from which God understands such matters.

In contrast, Mackie uses the traditional problem of evil to launch a stronger attack even than Hume's against belief in a God with the attributes traditionally ascribed to Him by the Western monotheistic religions. Mackie argues that those attributes, specifically, omnipotence and perfect benevolence, are inconsistent with the existence of evil, even with human-caused wickedness, arguing that there is no logical contradiction in the conception of a deity who creates people who always freely choose to do what is right. Numerous philosophers, on both sides of the issue, agree that the coherence of this description—"created so as always to freely choose what is right"—is at the root of the problem of evil. It may be useful to the student who is especially interested in the problem of evil to read the materials on free will in Part 4.

What if it should turn out (as many philosophers now believe) that all traditional arguments for the existence of God are defective, or at least inconclusive? Would it follow that religious belief is unreasonable? Not necessarily. Some believers have claimed that the grounds of their belief have nothing to do with argument but rather derive from a direct experience of deity (a "mystic experience"). These believers cannot prove that God exists, but they cannot prove that *they themselves* exist either. In both cases, they claim to know directly, by immediate confrontation, that something exists, and further proof is unnecessary.

Although they have nothing to do with argument, mystical experiences might nevertheless be considered a kind of "evidence" for their attendant beliefs. The question posed by the final subsection of this chapter, however, is whether beliefs based on no evidence at all can nonetheless be, in some circumstances, reasonable. W. K. Clifford argues emphatically for the negative and affirms his own rationalistic "ethic of belief," namely, that "it is wrong always, everywhere, and for anyone to believe anything upon insufficient evidence." The seventeenth-century mathematician-philosopher Blaise Pascal had argued for the reasonableness of a kind of "bet" on God's existence even in the absence of all evidence, urging that it costs little to believe in God and act accordingly even if God in fact does not exist, whereas there is an infinite amount to lose by not believing if in fact God exists. Many

Christian **fideists** (those whose belief is based on faith rather than argument), including William James, have found the unveiled appeal to self-interest in Pascal's "wager" to be a kind of embarrassment; but two contemporary writers, William Lycan and George Schlesinger, have contributed to this section a thorough, reasoned defense of Pascal. William James, in his famous "The Will to Believe," disowns Pascal but goes on to explain in his own way why belief in the absence of evidence can in some circumstances be reasonable. (Careful readers might well ask themselves, however, whether James's strict conditions for the proper exercise of "the will to believe" are in fact ever satisfied.) If there is one thing that James, the nineteenth-century Protestant, has in common with Pascal, the seventeenth-century Catholic, it is the conviction that the primary function of religious belief is not simply to allay philosophical curiosity about things. Both writers are aware that, to many, religious belief is a vital practical need, and each in his own way urges this to be taken into account when the reasonableness of belief is assessed.

The god whose existence philosophers have tried to prove over the centuries bears little resemblance to the God of ordinary worshipers. The God of the simple believer, though vastly greater than us in all relevant ways, is nonetheless a *person,* that is, a being who can perceive, communicate, understand, intend, love, become angry, and so on. Insofar as the God of the philosophers is but a "necessary being," or "a ground of all contingency," or "an unmoved mover," or "the being than whom a more perfect being cannot be conceived," He is too abstract to be easily identified with the being worshipped in churches, mosques, and synagogues, unless a supplementary personal character be ascribed to Him.

In contrast, the God of the ordinary believer seems to have many traits that bring Him closer to us and make both religious stories and such religious attitudes and practices as worship and prayer more fitting. Not least among these traits is *gender.* While very few educated persons would insist on affirming as a literal truth that an infinitely perfect being would have a sexual identity, ordinary believers tend to think of God as a wise and loving *person,* and none of us has ever seen a genuine person who was not either a he or a she. In the tradition of the major Western religions—Judaism, Christianity, and Islam—God is always spoken of as He, and the legends and myths that give God a dramatic role typically make Him a King, a warrior (Lord of Hosts), or a land- and slave-owning nobleman—all once exclusively male political roles. Moreover, prayers are directed to God the father, God the shepherd, and God the supreme judge, again exploiting analogies to roles once reserved for men. Assignments of those roles to God, of course, are frequently interpreted as mere metaphors, not literal truths. Still, even if that is so, it remains to explain why the metaphors are not based on analogies to traditional female roles, like motherhood. Until recently, almost everyone thought that the various conceptions of God expressed in simile and metaphor were mere symbols, necessary for poetic usage, and for converting what would otherwise be an impersonal "force" into a being with whom we can stand in personal relationships, but having no particular *philosophical* significance. But with the spread of philosophical feminism and women's liberation movements, more and more people now take it to be an important *philosophical* question to ask why God must be a He and not a She or an It. Deborah Mathieu, in a provocative article written expressly for this volume, takes religious symbols seriously, and she argues that in our traditionally patriarchal culture, sexist symbolism has been harmful to the integrity of religious thought. "Mere symbols," rather than being insignificantly decorative appendages to religious discourse, are centrally important to an understanding of the form and function of that discourse. Moreover, associating God with the symbols of male power and governance supports the assignment of women to a subordinate place in a male-dominated world. And if *that* has been an essential function of the major religions of our time, then it is surely a part of the philosophy of religion to deal with it.

The Existence and Nature of God

The Ontological Argument, from *Proslogium**

SAINT ANSELM

Saint Anselm (1033–1109) was Archbishop of Canterbury.

CHAPTER II

Truly there is a God, although the fool hath said in his heart, There is no God.

AND SO, LORD, do thou, who dost give understanding to faith, give me, so far as thou knowest it to be profitable, to understand that thou art as we believe; and that thou art that which we believe. And, indeed, we believe that thou art a being than which nothing greater can be conceived. Or is there no such nature, since the fool hath said in his heart, there is no God? (Psalms xiv. 1). But, at any rate, this very fool, when he hears of this being of which I speak—a being than which nothing greater can be conceived—understands what he hears, and what he understands is in his understanding; although he does not understand it to exist.

For, it is one thing for an object to be in the understanding, and another to understand that the object exists. When a painter first conceives of what he will afterwards perform, he has it in his understanding, but he does not yet understand it to be, because he has not yet performed it. But after he has made the painting, he both has it in his understanding, and he understands that it exists, because he has made it.

Hence, even the fool is convinced that something exists in the understanding, at least, than which nothing greater can be conceived. For, when he hears of this, he understands it. And whatever is understood, exists in the understanding. And assuredly that, than which nothing greater can be conceived, cannot exist in the understanding alone. For, suppose it exists in the understanding alone: then it can be conceived to exist in reality; which is greater.

Therefore, if that, than which nothing greater can be conceived, exists in the understanding alone, the very being, than which nothing greater can be conceived, is one, than which a greater can be conceived. But obviously this is impossible. Hence, there is no doubt that there exists a being, than which nothing greater can be conceived, and it exists both in the understanding and in reality.

**From* St. Anselm: Basic Writings, *trans. S. N. Deane, with an Introduction by Charles Hartshorne (La Salle, Ill.: Open Court, 1961). Reprinted by permission of the publisher.*

CHAPTER III

God cannot be conceived not to exist.—God is that, than which nothing greater can be conceived.—That which can be conceived not to exist is not God.

And it assuredly exists so truly, that it cannot be conceived not to exist. For, it is possible to conceive of a being which cannot be conceived not to exist; and this is greater than one which can be conceived not to exist. Hence, if that, than which nothing greater can be conceived, can be conceived not to exist, it is not that than which nothing greater can be conceived. But this is an irreconcilable contradiction. There is, then, so truly a being than which nothing greater can be conceived to exist, that it cannot even be conceived not to exist; and this being thou art, O Lord, our God.

So truly, therefore, dost thou exist, O Lord, my God, that thou canst not be conceived not to exist; and rightly. For, if a mind could conceive of a being better than thee, the creature would rise above the Creator; and this is most absurd. And, indeed, whatever else there is, except thee alone, can be conceived not to exist. To thee alone, therefore, it belongs to exist more truly than all other beings, and hence in a higher degree than all others. Why, then, has the fool said in his heart, there is no God (Psalms xiv. 1), since it is so evident, to a rational mind, that thou dost exist in the highest degree of all? Why, except that he is dull and a fool?

CHAPTER IV

How the fool has said in his heart what cannot be conceived.—A thing may be conceived in two ways: (1) when the word signifying it is conceived; (2) when the thing itself is understood. As far as the word goes God can be conceived not to exist; in reality he cannot.

But how has the fool said in his heart what he could not conceive; or how is it that he could not conceive what he said in his heart? since it is the same to say in the heart, and to conceive.

But, if really, nay, since really, he both conceived, because he said in his heart; and did not say in his heart, because he could not conceive; there is more than one way in which a thing is said in the heart or conceived. For, in one sense, an object is conceived, when the word signifying it is conceived; and in another, when the very entity, which the object is, is understood.

In the former sense, then, God can be conceived not to exist; but in the latter, not at all. For no one who understands what fire and water are can conceive fire to be water, in accordance with the nature of the facts themselves, although this is possible according to the words. So, then, no one who understands what God is can conceive that God does not exist; although he says these words in his heart, either without any, or with some foreign signification. For, God is that than which a greater cannot be conceived. And he who thoroughly understands this, assuredly understands that this being so truly exists, that not even in concept can it be nonexistent. Therefore, he who understands that God so exists, cannot conceive that he does not exist.

I thank thee, gracious Lord, I thank thee; because what I formerly believed by thy bounty, I now so understand by thine illumination, that if I were unwilling to believe that thou dost exist, I should not be able not to understand this to be true.

CHAPTER V

God is whatever it is better to be than not to be; and he, as the only self-existent being, creates all things from nothing.

What art thou, then, Lord God, than whom nothing greater can be conceived? But what art thou, except that which, as the highest of all beings, alone exists through itself, and creates all other things from nothing? For, whatever is not this is less than a thing which can be conceived of. But this cannot be conceived of thee. What good, therefore, does the supreme Good lack, through which every good is? Therefore, thou art just, truthful, blessed, and whatever it is better to be than not to be. For it is better to be just than not just; better to be blessed than not blessed.

The Ontological Argument*

WILLIAM L. ROWE

William L. Rowe (1931–) teaches philosophy at Purdue University. He is a distinguished authority in the philosophy of religion.

ARGUMENTS FOR THE EXISTENCE of God are commonly divided into a posteriori and a priori arguments. An a posteriori argument depends on a principle or premise that can be known only by means of our experience of the world. An a priori argument, on the other hand, purports to rest on principles which can be known independently of our experience of the world, just by reflecting on and understanding them. Of the three major arguments for the existence of God—the Cosmological, Teleological, and Ontological—only the last is entirely a priori. In the Cosmological argument one starts from some simple fact about the world, such as the fact that it contains things which are caused to exist by other things. In the Teleological argument a somewhat more complicated fact about the world serves as a starting point: the fact that the world exhibits order and design. In the Ontological argument, however, one begins simply with a concept of God.

I

It is perhaps best to think of the Ontological argument as a family of arguments, each member of which begins with a concept of God, and by appealing only to a priori principles, endeavors to establish that God actually exists. Within this family of arguments the most important historically is the argument set forth by Anselm in the second chapter of his *Proslogium* (A Discourse).[1] Indeed, the Ontological argument begins with chapter II of Anselm's *Proslogium*. In an earlier work, *Monologium* (A Soliloquy), Anselm had endeavored to establish the existence and nature of God by weaving together several versions of the Cosmological argument. In the Preface to *Proslogium* Anselm remarks that after the publication of *Monologium* he began to search for a single argument which alone would establish the existence and nature of God. After much strenuous but unsuccessful effort, he reports that he sought to put the project out of his mind in order to turn to more fruitful tasks. The idea, however, continued to haunt him until one day the proof he had so strenuously sought became clear to his mind. Anselm sets forth this proof in the second chapter of *Proslogium*.

Before discussing Anselm's argument in step-by-step fashion, there are certain concepts that will help us understand some of the central ideas of the argument. Suppose we draw a vertical line in our imagination and agree that on the left side of our line are all the things which exist, while on the right side of the line are all the things which don't exist. We might then begin to make a list of some of the things on both sides of our imaginary line, as follows:

Things Which Exist	*Things Which Don't Exist*
The Empire State Building	The Fountain of Youth
Dogs	Unicorns
The planet Mars	The Abominable Snowman

Now each of the things (or sorts of things) listed thus far has (have) the following feature: it (they) logically might have been on the other side of the line. The Fountain of Youth, for example, is on the right side of the line, but *logically* there is no absurdity in the idea that it might have been on the left side of the line. Similarly, although dogs do exist, we surely can imagine without logical absurdity that they might not have existed, that they might have been on the right side of the line. Let us then record this feature of the things thus far listed by introducing the idea of a *contingent thing* as a thing that logically might have been on the other side of the line from the side it actually is on. The planet Mars and the Abominable Snowman are contingent things, even though the former happens to exist and the latter does not.

Suppose we add to our list the phrase "the object which is completely round and completely square at the same time" on the right side of our line. The round square, however, unlike the other things thus far listed on the right side of our line, is something that *logically could not* have been on the left side of the line. Noting this, let us introduce the idea of an *impossible thing* as a thing that is on the right side of the line and logically could not have been on the left side of the line.

Looking again at our list, we wonder if there is anything on the left side of our imaginary line which, unlike the things thus far listed on the left side, *logically could not* have been on the right side of the line. At this point we don't have to answer this question, but it is useful to have a concept to apply to any such things, should there be any. Accordingly, let us say that a *necessary thing* is a thing on the left side of our imaginary line and logically could not have been on the right side of the line.

Finally, a *possible thing* is any thing that is either on the left side of our imaginary line or logically might have been on the left side of the line. Possible things, then, will be all those things that are not impossible things—that is, all those things that are either contingent or necessary. If there are no necessary things, then all possible things will be contingent and all contingent things will be possible. If there is a necessary thing, however, then there will be a possible thing which is not contingent.

Armed with these concepts, we can clarify certain important distinctions and ideas in Anselm's thought. The first of these is his distinction between *existence in the understanding* and *existence in reality.* Anselm's notion of existence in reality is the same as our notion of existence; that is, being on the left side of our imaginary line. Since the Fountain of Youth is on the right side of the line, it does not exist in reality. The things which exist are, to use Anselm's phrase, the things which exist in reality. Anselm's notion of existence in the understanding, however, is not the same as any idea we normally employ. When we think of a certain thing, say the Fountain of Youth, then that thing, on Anselm's view, exists in the understanding. Also, when we think of an existing thing like the Empire State Building, it, too, exists in the understanding. So some of the things on both sides of our imaginary line exist in the understanding, but only those on the left side of our line exist in reality. Are there any things that don't exist in the understanding? Undoubtedly there are, for there are things, both existing and non-existing, of which we have not really thought. Now suppose I assert that the Fountain of Youth does not exist. Since to meaningfully deny the existence of something I have to have that thing in mind, I have to think of it, it follows on Anselm's view that whenever someone asserts that some thing does not exist, that thing *does* exist in the understanding.[2] So in asserting that the Fountain of Youth does not exist, I imply that the Fountain of Youth does exist in the understanding. And in asserting that it does not exist I have asserted (on Anselm's view) that it does not exist in reality. This means that my simple assertion amounts to the somewhat more complex claim that the Fountain of Youth exists in the understanding but does not exist in reality—in short, that the Fountain of Youth exists *only* in the understanding.

We can now understand why Anselm insists that anyone who hears of God, thinks about God, or even denies the existence of God is, nevertheless, committed to the view that God exists in the understanding. Also, we can understand why Anselm treats what he calls "the fool's claim" that God does not exist as the claim that God exists *only* in the understanding—that is, that God exists in the understanding but does not exist in reality.

In *Monologium* Anselm sought to prove that among those beings which do exist there is one which is the greatest, highest, and the best. But in *Proslogium* he undertakes to prove that among those beings which exist there is one which is not just the greatest among existing beings, but is such that no conceivable being is greater. We need to distinguish these two ideas: (1) a being than which *no existing being* is greater, and (2) a being than which *no conceivable being* is greater. If the only things in existence were a stone, a frog, and a man, the last of these would satisfy our first idea but not our second—for we can conceive of a being (an angel or God) greater than a man. Anselm's idea of God, as he expresses it in *Proslogium* II, is the same as (2) above; it is the idea of "a being than which nothing greater can be conceived." It will facilitate our understanding of Anselm's argument if we make two slight changes in the way he has expressed his idea of God. For his phrase I shall substitute the following: "*the* being than which none greater *is possible*."[3] This idea says that if a certain being is God then no *possible being* can be greater than it, or conversely, if a certain being is such that it is even *possible* for there to be a being greater than it, then that being is not God. What Anselm proposes to prove, then, is that the being than which none greater is possible exists in reality. If he proves this he will have proved that God, as he conceives of Him, exists in reality.

But what does Anselm mean by "greatness"? Is a building, for example, greater than a man? In *Monologium,* chapter II, Anselm remarks: "But I do not mean physically great, as a material object is great, but that which, the greater it is, is the better or the more worthy—wisdom, for instance." Contrast wisdom with size. Anselm is saying that wisdom is something that contributes to the greatness of a thing. If a thing comes to have more wisdom than it did before then (given that its other characteristics remain the same), that thing has become a greater, better, more worthy thing than it was. Wisdom, Anselm is saying, is a great-making quality. However, the mere fact that something increases in size (physical greatness) does not make that thing a better thing than it was before so size is not a great-making quality. By "greater than" Anselm means "better than," "superior to," or "more worthy than," and he believes that some characteristics, like wisdom and moral goodness, are great-making characteristics in that anything which has them is a *better thing* than it would be (other characteristics of it remaining the same) were it to lack them.

We come now to what we may call the *key idea* in Anselm's Ontological argument. Anselm believes that *existence in reality is a great-making quality.* Does Anselm mean that anything that exists is a greater thing than anything that doesn't? Although he does not ask or answer the question, it is perhaps reasonable to believe that Anselm did not mean this. When he discusses wisdom as a great-making quality he is careful not to say that any wise thing is better than any unwise thing—for he recognizes that a just but unwise man might be a better being than a wise but unjust man.[4] I suggest that what Anselm means is that anything that doesn't exist but might have existed (is on the right side of our line but might have been on the left) would have been a greater thing if it had existed (if it had been on the left side of our line). He is not comparing two different things (one existing and one not existing) and saying that the first is therefore greater than the second. Rather, he is talking about *one* thing and pointing out that if it does not exist but might have existed, then *it* would have been a greater thing if it had existed. Using Anselm's distinction between existence in the understanding and existence in reality, we may express the key idea in Anselm's reasoning as follows: If something exists only in the understanding but might have existed in reality, then it might have been greater than it is. Since the Fountain of Youth, for example, exists only in the understanding but (unlike the round square) might have existed in reality, it follows by Anselm's principle that the Fountain of Youth might have been a greater thing than it is.

II

We can now consider the step-by-step development of Anselm's Ontological argument. I shall use the term "God" in place of the longer phrase "the being than which none greater is possible"—wherever the term "God" appears we are to think of it as simply an abbreviation of the longer phrase.

1. God exists in the understanding.

As we have noted, anyone who hears of the being than which none greater is possible is, on Anselm's view, committed to premise (1).

2. God might have existed in reality (God is a possible being).

Anselm, I think, assumes the truth of (2) without making it explicit in his reasoning. By asserting (2) I do not mean to imply that God does not exist in reality, but that, unlike the round square, God is a possible being.

3. If something exists only in the understanding and might have existed in reality, then it might have been greater than it is.

As we noted, this is the key idea in Anselm's Ontological argument. It is intended as a general principle, true of anything whatever.

Steps (1)–(3) constitute the basic premises of Anselm's Ontological argument. From these three items, Anselm believes, it follows that God exists in reality. But how does Anselm propose to convince us that if we accept (1)–(3) we are committed by the rules of logic to accept his conclusion that God exists in reality? Anselm's procedure is to offer what is called a *reductio ad absurdum* proof of his conclusion. Instead of showing directly that the existence of God follows from steps (1)–(3), Anselm invites us to *suppose* that God does not exist (i.e., that the conclusion he wants to establish is false) and then shows how this supposition, when conjoined with steps (1)–(3), leads to an absurd result, a result that couldn't possibly be true because it is contradictory. Since the supposition that God does not exist leads to an absurdity, that supposition must be rejected in favor of the conclusion that God does exist.

Does Anselm succeed in reducing the "fool's belief" that God does not exist to an absurdity? The best way to answer this question is to follow the steps of his argument.

4. Suppose God exists only in the understanding.

This supposition, as we saw earlier, is Anselm's way of expressing the belief that God does not exist.

5. God might have been greater than He is. (2, 4, and 3)[5]

Step (5) follows from steps (2), (4), and (3). Since (3), if true, is true of anything whatever, it will be true of God. Therefore, (3) implies that if God exists only in the understanding and might have existed in reality, then God might have been greater than He is. If so, then given (2) and (4), (5) must be true. For what (3) says when applied to God is that given (2) and (4), it follows that (5).

6. God is a being than which a greater is possible. (5)

Surely if God is such that He logically might have been greater, then He is such than which a greater is possible.

We can now appreciate Anselm's *reductio* argument. He has shown that if we accept steps (1)–(4), we must accept step (6). But (6) is unacceptable; it is the absurdity Anselm was after. By replacing "God" in (6) with the longer phrase it abbreviates, we see that (6) amounts to the absurd assertion:

7. The being than which none greater is possible is a being than which a greater is possible.

Now since steps (1)–(4) have led us to an obviously false conclusion, and if we accept Anselm's basic premises (1)–(3) as true, then (4), the supposition that God exists only in the understanding, must be rejected as false. Thus we have shown that:

8. It is false that God exists only in the understanding.

But since premise (1) tells us that God does exist in the understanding and (8) tells us that God does not exist only there, we may infer that

9. God exists in reality as well as in the understanding. (1, 8)

III

Most of the philosophers who have considered this argument have rejected it because of a basic conviction that from the logical analysis of a certain idea or concept we can never determine that there exists in reality anything answering to that idea or concept. We may examine and analyse, for example, the idea of an elephant or the idea of a unicorn, but it is only by our experience of the world that we can determine that there exist things answering to our first idea and not to the second. Anselm, however, believes that the concept of God is utterly unique—from an analysis of this concept he believes that it can be determined that there exists in reality a being which answers to it. Moreover, he presents us with an argument to show that it can be done in the case of the idea of God. We can, of course, simply reject Anselm's argument on the grounds that it violates the basic conviction noted above. Many critics, however, have sought to prove more directly that it is a bad argument and to point out the particular step that is mistaken. Next we shall examine the three major objections that have been advanced by the argument's critics.

The first criticism was advanced by a contemporary of Anselm's, a monk named "Gaunilo," who wrote a response to Anselm entitled, "On Behalf of the Fool."[6] Gaunilo sought to prove that Anselm's reasoning is mistaken by applying it to things other than God, things which we know don't exist. He took as his example the island than which none greater is possible. No such island really exists. But, argues Gaunilo, if Anselm's reasoning were correct we could show that such an island really does exist. For since it is greater to exist than not to exist, if the island than which none greater is possible doesn't exist then it is an island than which a greater is possible. But it is impossible for the island than which none greater is possible to be an island than which a greater is possible. Therefore, the island than which none greater is possible must exist. About this argument Gaunilo remarks:

> If a man should try to prove to me by such reasoning that this island truly exists, and that its existence should no longer be doubted, either I should believe that he was jesting, or I know not which I ought to regard as the greater fool: myself, supposing I should allow this proof; or him, if he should suppose that he had established with any certainty the existence of this island.[7]

Gaunilo's strategy is clear: by using the very same reasoning Anselm employs in his argument, we can prove the existence of things we know don't exist. Therefore, Anselm's reasoning in his proof of the existence of God must be mistaken. In reply to Gaunilo, Anselm insisted that his reasoning applies only to God and cannot be used to establish the existence of things other than God. Unfortunately, Anselm did not explain just why his reasoning cannot be applied to things like Gaunilo's island.

In defense of Anselm against Gaunilo's objection, there are two difficulties in applying Anselm's reasoning to things like Gaunilo's island. The first derives from the fact that Anselm's principle that existence is a great-making quality was taken to mean that if something does not exist then it is not as great *a thing* (being) as it would have been had it existed. Now if we use precisely this principle in Gaunilo's argument, all we will prove is that if Gaunilo's island does not exist then the island than which none greater is possible is an island than which *a greater thing* is possible. But this statement is not an absurdity. For the island than which no greater *island* is possible can be something than which *a greater thing* is possible—an unsurpassable island may be a surpassable thing. (A perfect man might be a greater thing than a perfect island.) Consequently, if we follow Anselm's reasoning exactly, it does not appear that we can derive an absurdity from the supposition that the island than which none greater is possible does not exist.

A second difficulty in applying Anselm's reasoning to Gaunilo's island is that we must accept the premise that Gaunilo's island is a possible thing. But this seems to require us to believe that some finite, limited thing (an island) might have unlimited perfections. It is not at all clear that this is possible. Try to think, for example, of a hockey player than which none greater is possible. How fast would he have to skate? How many goals would he have to score in a game? How fast would he have to shoot the puck? Could he ever fall down, be checked, or receive a penalty? Although the phrase, "the hockey player than which none greater is possible," seems meaningful, as soon as we try to get a clear idea of what such a being would be like we discover that we can't form a coherent idea of it all.

For we are being invited to think of some limited, finite thing—a hockey player or an island—and then to think of it as exhibiting unlimited, infinite perfections. Perhaps, then, since Anselm's reasoning applies only to possible things, Anselm can reject its application to Gaunilo's island on the grounds that the island than which none greater is possible is, like the round square, an impossible thing.

By far the most famous objection to the Ontological argument was set forth by Immanuel Kant in the eighteenth century. According to this objection the mistake in the argument is its claim, implicit in premise (3), that existence is a quality or predicate that adds to the greatness of a thing. There are two parts to this claim: (1) existence is a quality or predicate, and (2) existence, like wisdom and unlike physical size, is a great-making quality or predicate. Someone might accept (1) but object to (2); the objection made famous by Kant, however, is directed at (1). According to this objection, existence is not a predicate at all. Therefore, since in its third premise Anselm's argument implies that existence *is* a predicate, the argument must be rejected.

The central point in the philosophical doctrine that existence is not a predicate concerns what we do when we ascribe a certain quality or predicate to something: for example, when we say of a man next door that he is intelligent, six feet tall, or fat. In each case we seem to assert or presuppose that there *exists* a man next door and then go on to ascribe to him a certain predicate—"intelligent," "six feet tall," or "fat." And many proponents of the doctrine that existence is not a predicate claim that this is a *general feature* of predication. They hold that when we ascribe a quality or predicate to anything we assert or presuppose that the thing exists and then ascribe the predicate to it. Now if this is so, then it is clear that existence cannot be a predicate which we may ascribe to or deny of something. For if it were a predicate, then when we assert of some thing (things) that it (they) exists (exist) we would be asserting or presupposing that it (they) exists (exist) and then going on to predicate existence of it (them). For example, if existence were a predicate, then in asserting "tigers exist" we would be asserting or presupposing that tigers exist and then going on to predicate existence of them. Furthermore, in asserting "dragons do not exist" we would be asserting or presupposing, if existence were a predicate, that dragons do exist and then going on to deny that existence attaches to them. In short, if existence were a predicate, the affirmative existential statement "tigers exist" would be a redundancy and the negative existential statement "dragons do not exist" would be contradictory. But clearly "tigers exist" is not a redundancy; and "dragons do not exist" is true and, therefore, not contradictory. What this shows, according to the proponents of Kant's objection, is that existence is not a genuine predicate.

According to the proponents of the above objection, when we assert that tigers exist and that dragons do not we are not saying that certain things (tigers) have and certain other things (dragons) do not have a peculiar predicate, *existence;* rather, we are saying something about the *concept* of a tiger and the *concept* of a dragon. We are saying that the concept of a tiger applies to something in the world and that the concept of a dragon does not apply to anything in the world.

Although this objection to the Ontological argument has been widely accepted, it is doubtful that it provides us with a conclusive refutation of the argument. It may be true that existence is not a predicate, that in asserting the existence of something we are not ascribing a certain predicate or attribute to that thing. But the arguments presented for this view seem to rest on mistaken or incomplete claims about the nature of predication. For example, the argument which we stated earlier rests on the claim that when we ascribe a predicate to anything we assert or presuppose that that thing exists. But this claim appears to be mistaken. In asserting that Dr. Doolittle is an animal lover I seem to be ascribing the predicate "animal lover" to Dr. Doolittle, but in doing so I certainly am not asserting or presupposing that Dr. Doolittle actually exists. Dr. Doolittle doesn't exist, but it is nevertheless true that he is an animal lover. The plain fact is that we can talk about and ascribe predicates to many things which do not exist and never did. Merlin, for example, no less than Houdini, was a magician, although Houdini existed but Merlin did not.

If, as these examples suggest, the claim that whenever we ascribe a predicate to something we assert or presuppose that the thing exists is a false claim, then we will need a better argument for the doctrine that existence is not a predicate. There is some question, however, whether anyone has succeeded in giving a really conclusive argument for this doctrine.[8]

A third objection against the Ontological argument calls into question the premise that God might have existed in reality (God is a possible being). As we saw, this premise claims that the being than which none greater is possible is not an impossible object. But is this true? Consider the series of positive integers: 1, 2, 3, 4, etc. We know that any integer in this series, no matter how large, is such that a larger integer than it is possible. Therefore, the positive integer than which none larger is possible is an impossible object. Perhaps this is also true of the being than which none greater is possible. That is, perhaps no matter how great a being may be, it is possible for there to be a being greater than it. If this were so, then, like the integer than which none larger is possible, Anselm's God would not be a possible object. The mere fact that there are degrees of greatness, however, does not entitle us to conclude that Anselm's God is like the integer than which none larger is possible. There are, for example, degrees of size in angles—one angle is larger than another—but it is not true that no matter how large an angle is it is possible for there to be an angle larger than it. It is logically impossible for an angle to exceed four right angles. The notion of an angle, unlike the notion of a positive integer, implies a degree of size beyond which it is impossible to go. Is Anselm's God like a largest integer, and therefore impossible, or like a largest angle, and therefore possible? Some philosophers have argued that Anselm's God is impossible,[9] but the arguments for this conclusion are not very compelling. Perhaps, then, this objection is best construed not as proving that Anselm's God is impossible, but as raising the question whether any of us is in a position to know that the being than which none greater is possible is a possible object. For Anselm's argument cannot be a successful proof of the existence of God unless its premises are not just true but are really ***known*** to be true. Therefore, if we do not know that Anselm's God is a possible object, then his argument cannot prove the existence of God to us, cannot enable us to know that God exists.

IV

Finally, I want to present a somewhat different critique of Anselm's argument, a critique suggested by the basic conviction noted earlier; namely that from the mere logical analysis of a certain idea or concept we can never determine that there exists in reality anything answering to that idea or concept.

Suppose someone comes to us and says:

> I propose to define the term "God" as *an existing, wholly perfect being.* Now since it can't be true that an existing, wholly perfect being does not exist, it can't be true that God, as I've defined Him, does not exist. Therefore, God must exist.

His argument appears to be a very simple Ontological argument. It begins with a particular idea or concept of God and ends by concluding that God, so conceived, must exist. What can we say in response? We might start by objecting to his definition, claiming: (1) that only predicates can be used to define a term, and (2) that existence is not a predicate. But suppose he is not impressed by this response—either because he thinks that no one has fully explained what a predicate is or proved that existence isn't one, or because he thinks that anyone can define a word in whatever way he pleases. Can we allow him to define the word "God" in any way he pleases and still hope to convince him that it will not follow from that definition that there actually exists something to which his concept of God applies? I think we can. Let us first invite him, however, to consider some concepts other than his peculiar concept of God.

Earlier we noted that the term "magician" may be applied both to Houdini and Merlin, even though the former existed and the latter did not. Noting that our friend has used "existing" as part of his definition of "God," suppose we agree with him that we can define a word in any way we please, and, accordingly, introduce the following definitions:

> A "magican" is defined as *an existing magician.*
> A "magico" is defined as *a non-existing magician.*

Here we have introduced two words and used "existing" or "non-existing" in their definitions. Now something of interest follows from the fact that "existing" is part of our definition of a "magican." For while it is true that Merlin was a *magician,* it is not true that Merlin was a *magican.* And something of interest follows from our including "non-existing" in the definition of a "magico"—it is true that Houdini was a *magician,* but it is not true that Houdini was a *magico.* Houdini was a *magician* and a *magican,* but not a *magico;* Merlin was a *magician* and a *magico,* but not a *magican.*

We have just seen that introducing "existing" or "non-existing" into the definition of a concept has a very important implication. If we introduce "existing" into the definition of a concept, it follows that no non-existing thing can exemplify that concept. And if we introduce "non-existing" into the definition of a concept, it follows that no existing thing can exemplify that concept. No non-existing thing can be a *magican,* and no existing thing can be a *magico.*

But must some existing thing exemplify the concept "magican"? No! From the fact that "existing" is included in the definition of "magican" it does not follow that some existing thing is a magican—all that follows is that no non-existing thing is a magican. If there were no magicans in existence there would be nothing to which the term "magican" would apply. This being so, it clearly does not follow merely from our definition of "magican" that some existing thing is a magician. Only if magicians exist will it be true that some existing thing is a magican.

We are now in a position to help our friend see that the mere fact that "God" is defined as an existing, wholly perfect being it will not follow that some existing being is God. Something of interest does follow from his definition; namely that no non-existing being can be God. But whether some existing thing is God will depend entirely on whether some existing thing is a wholly perfect being. If no wholly perfect being exists there will be nothing to which his concept of God can apply. This being so, it clearly does not follow merely from his definition of "God" that some existing thing is God. Only if a wholly perfect being exists will it be true that God, as he conceives of Him, exists.

The implications of these considerations for Anselm's ingenious argument can now be traced. Anselm conceives of God as a being than which none greater is possible. He then claims that existence is a great-making quality and something that has it is greater than it would have been had it lacked existence. Clearly then, no non-existing thing can exemplify Anselm's concept of God. For if we suppose that some non-existing thing exemplifies Anselm's concept of God and also suppose that that non-existing thing might have existed in reality (is a possible thing) then we are supposing that that non-existing thing (1) might have been a greater thing, and (2) is, nevertheless, a thing than which a greater is not possible. Thus far Anselm's reasoning is, I believe, impeccable. But what follows from it? All that follows from it is that no non-existing thing can be God (as Anselm conceives of God). All that follows is that given Anselm's concept of God, the proposition, "Some non-existing thing is God," cannot be true. But, as we saw earlier, this is also the case with the proposition, "Some non-existing thing is a magican." What remains to be shown is that some existing thing exemplifies Anselm's concept of God. What really does follow from his reasoning is that the only thing that logically could exemplify his concept of God is something which actually exists. And this conclusion is not without interest. But from the mere fact that nothing but an existing thing could exemplify Anselm's concept of God, it does not follow that some existing thing actually does exemplify his concept of God—no more than it follows from the mere fact that no non-existing thing can be a magican that some existing thing is a magican.[10]

There is, however, one major difficulty in this critique of Anselm's argument. This difficulty arises when we take into account Anselm's implicit claim that God is a possible thing. To see just what this difficulty is, let us return to the idea of a possible thing, which is any thing that either is on the left side of our imaginary line or logically might have been on the left side of the line. Possible things, then, will be all those things that, unlike the round square, are not impossible things. Suppose we concede to Anselm that God, as he conceives of Him, is a possible thing. Now, of course, the mere knowledge that something is a possible thing does not enable us to conclude that that thing is an existing thing. Many possible things, like the Fountain of Youth, do not exist. But if something is a possible thing then it is either an existing thing or a non-existing thing. The set of possible things can be exhaustively divided into those possible things which actually exist and those possible things which do not exist. Therefore, if Anselm's God is a possible thing it is either an existing thing or a non-existing thing. We have concluded, however, that no non-existing thing can be Anselm's God; therefore, it seems we must conclude with Anselm that some actually existing thing does exemplify his concept of God.

To see the solution to this major difficulty we need to return to an earlier example. Let us consider again the idea of a "magican," an existing magician. It so happens that some magicians have existed—Houdini, the Great Blackstone, etc. But, of course, it might have been otherwise. Suppose, for the moment that no magicians have ever existed. The concept "magician" would still have application, for it would still be true that Merlin was a magician. But would any possible object be picked out by the concept of a "magican"? No, for no non-existing thing could exemplify the concept "magican." And on the supposition that no magicians ever existed, no existing thing would exemplify the concept "magican."[11] We then would have a coherent concept "magican" which would not be exemplified by any possible object at all. For if all the possible objects which are magicians are non-existing things, none of them would be a magican and, since no possible objects which exist are magicians, none of them would be a magican. Put in this way, our result seems paradoxical. We are inclined to think that only contradictory concepts like "the round square" are not exemplified by any possible things. The truth is, however, that when "existing" is included in or implied by a certain concept, it may be the case that no possible object does in fact exemplify that concept. For no possible object that doesn't exist will exemplify a concept like "magican" in which "existing" is included; and if there are no existing things which exemplify the other features included in the concept—for example, "being a magician" in the case of the concept "magican"—then no possible object that exists will exemplify the concept. Put in its simplest terms, if we ask whether any possible thing is a magican the answer will depend entirely on whether any existing thing is a magician. If no existing things are magicians then no possible things are magicans. Some possible object is a magican just in the case some actually existing thing is a magician.

Applying these considerations to Anselm's argument, we can find the solution to our major difficulty. Given Anselm's concept of God and his principle that existence is a great-making quality, it really does follow that the only thing that logically could exemplify his concept of God is something which actually exists. But, we argued, it doesn't follow from these considerations alone that God actually exists, that some existing thing exemplifies Anselm's concept of God. The difficulty we fell into, however, is that when we add the premise that God is a possible thing, that some possible object exemplifies his concept of God, it really does follow that God actually exists, that some actually existing thing exemplifies Anselm's concept of God. For if some possible object exemplifies his concept of God, that object is either an existing thing or a non-existing thing. But since no non-existing thing could exemplify Anselm's concept of God, it follows that the possible object which exemplifies his concept of God must be a possible object that actually exists. Therefore, given (1) Anselm's concept of God, (2) his principle that existence is a great-making quality, and (3) the premise that God, as conceived by Anselm, is a possible thing, it really does follow that Anselm's God actually exists. But we now can see that in granting Anselm the premise that God is a possible thing we have granted far more than we intended. All we thought we were conceding is that Anselm's concept of God, unlike the concept of a round square, is not contradictory or incoherent. But without realizing it we were in fact granting much more than this, as became apparent when we considered the idea of a magican. There is nothing contradictory in the idea of a magican, an existing magician. But in asserting that a magican is a possible thing we are, as we saw, directly implying that some existing thing is a magician. For if no existing thing is a magician, the concept of a magican will apply to no possible object whatever. The same point holds with respect to Anselm's God. Since Anselm's concept of God logically cannot apply to some non-existing thing, the only possible objects to which it could apply are possible objects which actually exist. Therefore, in granting that Anselm's God is a possible thing we are conceding far more than that his idea of God isn't incoherent or contradictory. Suppose, for example, that every existing being has some defect which it might not have had. Without realizing it we were denying this when we granted that Anselm's God is a possible being. If every existing being has a defect it might not have had, then every existing being might have been greater. But if every existing being might have been greater, then Anselm's concept of God will apply to no possible object whatever. Therefore, if we allow Anselm his concept of God and his principle that existence is a great-making quality, then in granting that God, as Anselm conceives of Him, is a possible being we will be granting much more than that his concept of God is not contradictory. We will be conceding, for example, that some existing thing is as perfect as it can be. The fact is that Anselm's God is a possible thing only if some *existing* thing is as perfect as it can be.

Our final critique of Anselm's argument is simply this. In granting that Anselm's God is a possible thing we are in fact granting that Anselm's God actually exists. But since the purpose of the argument is to prove to us that Anselm's God exists, we cannot be asked to grant as a premise a statement which is virtually equivalent to the conclusion that is to be proved. Anselm's concept of God may be coherent and his principle that existence is a great-making quality may be true. But all that follows from this is that no non-existing thing can be Anselm's God. If we add to all of this the premise that God is a possible thing it will follow that God actually exists. But the additional premise claims more than that Anselm's concept of God isn't incoherent or contradictory. It amounts to the assertion that some existing being is supremely great. And since this is, in part, the point the argument endeavors to prove, the argument begs the question: it assumes the point it is supposed to prove.

If the above critique is correct, Anselm's argument fails as a proof of the existence of God. This is not to say, however, that the argument is not a work of genius. Perhaps no other argument in the history of thought has raised so many basic philosophical questions and stimulated so much hard thought. Even if it fails as a proof of the existence of God, it will remain as one of the high achievements of the human intellect.

NOTES

1. Some philosophers believe that Anselm sets forth a different and more cogent argument in chapter III of his *Proslogium.* For this viewpoint see Charles Hartshorne, *Anselm's Discovery* (LaSalle, Ill.: Open Court Publishing Co., 1965); and Norman Malcolm, "Anselm's Ontological Arguments," *The Philosophical Review* LXIX, No. 1 (January 1960): 41–62. For an illuminating account both of Anselm's intentions in *Proslogium II* and *III* and of recent interpretations of Anselm see Arthur C. McGill's essay "Recent Discussions of Anselm's Argument" in *The Many-faced Argument,* ed. John Hick and Arthur C. McGill (New York: The Macmillan Co., 1967), pp. 33–110.

2. Anselm does allow that someone may assert the sentence "God does not exist" without having in his understanding the object or idea for which the word 'God' stands (see *Proslogium,* chapter IV). But when a person does understand the object for which a word stands, then when he uses that word in a sentence denying the existence of that object he must have that object in his understanding. It is doubtful, however, that Anselm thought that incoherent or contradictory expressions like "the round square" stand for objects which may exist in the understanding.

3. Anselm speaks of "a being" rather than "the being" than which none greater can be conceived. His argument is easier to present if we express his idea of God in terms of "the being." Secondly, to avoid the psychological connotations of "can be conceived" I have substituted "possible."

4. See *Monologium,* chapter XV.

5. The numbers in parentheses refer to the earlier steps in the argument from which the present step is derived.

6. Gaunilo's brief essay, Anselm's reply, and several of Anselm's major works, as translated by S. N. Deane, are collected in *Saint Anselm: Basic Writings* (LaSalle, Ill.: Open Court Publishing Co., 1962).

7. *Saint Anselm: Basic Writings,* p. 151.

8. Perhaps the most sophisticated presentation of the objection that existence is not a predicate is William P. Alston's "The Ontological Argument Revisited" in *The Philosophical Review* 69 (1960): 452–474.

9. See, for example, C. D. Broad's discussion of the Ontological Argument in *Religion, Philosophy, and Psychical Research* (New York: Harcourt, Brace & World, 1953).

10. An argument along the lines just presented may be found in J. Shaffer's illuminating essay "Existence, Predication and the Ontological Argument," *Mind* 71 (1962): 307–325.

11. I am indebted to Professor William Wainwright for bringing this point to my attention.

The Five Ways, from *Summa Theologica**

SAINT THOMAS AQUINAS

Saint Thomas Aquinas (1225–1274) is the philosopher and theologian whose teachings are most favored by the Roman Catholic Church.

[Part I, Question 2, Article 3]

THE EXISTENCE OF GOD can be proved in five ways.

The first and more manifest way is the argument from motion. It is certain, and evident to our senses, that in the world some things are in motion. Now whatever is moved is moved by another, for nothing can be moved except it is in potentiality to that towards which it is moved; whereas a thing moves inasmuch as it is in act. For motion is nothing else than the reduction of something from potentiality to actuality. But nothing can be reduced from potentiality to actuality, except by something in a state of actuality. Thus that which is actually hot, as fire, makes wood, which is potentially hot, to be actually hot, and thereby moves and changes it. Now it is not possible that the same thing should be at once in actuality and potentiality in the same respect, but only in different respects. For what is actually hot cannot simultaneously be potentially hot; but it is simultaneously potentially cold. It is therefore impossible that in the same respect and in the same way a thing should be both mover and moved, *i.e.,* that it should move itself. Therefore, whatever is moved must be moved by another. If that by which it is moved be itself moved, then this also must needs be moved by another, and that by another again. But this cannot go on to infinity, because then there would be no first mover, and consequently no other mover, seeing that subsequent movers move only inasmuch as they are moved by the first mover; as the staff moves only

**From* The Basic Writings of Saint Thomas Aquinas, *ed. Anton C. Pegis (New York: Random House; London: Burns & Oates, 1945), pp. 22–23.*

because it is moved by the hand. Therefore it is necessary to arrive at a first mover, moved by no other; and this everyone understands to be God.

The second way is from the nature of efficient cause. In the world of sensible things we find there is an order of efficient causes. There is no case known (neither is it, indeed, possible) in which a thing is found to be the efficient cause of itself; for so it would be prior to itself, which is impossible. Now in efficient causes it is not possible to go on to infinity, because in all efficient causes following in order, the first is the cause of the intermediate cause, and the intermediate is the cause of the ultimate cause, whether the intermediate cause be several, or one only. Now to take away the cause is to take away the effect. Therefore, if there be no first cause among efficient causes, there will be no ultimate, nor any intermediate, cause. But if in efficient causes it is possible to go on to infinity, there will be no first efficient cause, neither will there be an ultimate effect, nor any intermediate efficient causes; all of which is plainly false. Therefore it is necessary to admit a first efficient cause, to which everyone gives the name of God.

The third way is taken from possibility and necessity, and runs thus. We find in nature things that are possible to be and not to be, since they are found to be generated, and to be corrupted, and consequently, it is possible for them to be and not to be. But it is impossible for these always to exist, for that which can not-be at some time is not. Therefore, if everything can not-be, then at one time there was nothing in existence. Now if this were true, even now there would be nothing in existence, because that which does not exist begins to exist only through something already existing. Therefore, if at one time nothing was in existence, it would have been impossible for anything to have begun to exist; and thus even now nothing would be in existence—which is absurd. Therefore, not all beings are merely possible, but there must exist something the existence of which is necessary. But every necessary thing either has its necessity caused by another, or not. Now it is impossible to go on to infinity in necessary things which have their necessity caused by another, as has been already proved in regard to efficient causes. Therefore we cannot but admit the existence of some being having of itself its own necessity, and not receiving it from another, but rather causing in others their necessity. This all men speak of as God.

The fourth way is taken from the gradation to be found in things. Among beings there are some more and some less good, true, noble, and the like. But *more* and *less* are predicated of different things according as they resemble in their different ways something which is the maximum, as a thing is said to be hotter according as it more nearly resembles that which is hottest; so that there is something which is truest, something best, something noblest, and, consequently, something which is most being, for those things that are greatest in truth are greatest in being, as it is written in *Metaph.* ii.[1] Now the maximum in any genus is the cause of all in that genus, as fire, which is the maximum of heat, is the cause of all hot things, as is said in the same book.[2] Therefore there must also be something which is to all beings the cause of their being, goodness, and every other perfection; and this we call God.

The fifth way is taken from the governance of the world. We see that things which lack knowledge, such as natural bodies, act for an end, and this is evident from their acting always, or nearly always, in the same way, so as to obtain the best result. Hence it is plain that they achieve their end, not fortuitously, but designedly. Now whatever lacks knowledge cannot move towards an end, unless it be directed by some being endowed with knowledge and intelligence; as the arrow is directed by the archer. Therefore some intelligent being exists by whom all natural things are directed to their end; and this being we call God.

NOTES

1. [Aquinas refers here to Aristotle's *Metaphysics,* Ia 1 (993b30).]

2. [*Metaphysics,* Ia 1 (993b25).]

A Modern Formulation of the Cosmological Argument*

SAMUEL CLARKE

Samuel Clarke (1675–1729), English theologian and philosopher, was one of the first to be greatly influenced by Isaac Newton's physics.

THERE HAS EXISTED *from eternity some one unchangeable and independent being.* For since something must needs have been from eternity; as hath been already proved, and is granted on all hands: either there has always existed one unchangeable and *independent* Being, from which all other beings that are or ever were in the universe, have received their original; or else there has been an infinite succession of changeable and *dependent* beings, produced one from another in an endless progression, without any original cause at all: which latter supposition is so very absurd, that tho' all atheism must in its account of most things (as shall be shown hereafter) terminate in it, yet I think very few atheists ever were so weak as openly and directly to defend it. For it is plainly impossible and contradictory to itself. I shall not argue against it from the supposed impossibility of infinite succession, *barely and absolutely considered in itself;* for a reason which shall be mentioned hereafter: but, if we consider such an infinite progression, as *one* entire endless *series* of *dependent* beings; 'tis plain this whole *series* of beings can have no cause *from without,* of its existence; because in it are supposed to be included *all things* that are or ever were in the universe: and 'tis plain it can have no reason *within itself,* of its existence; because no one being in this infinite succession is supposed to be self-existent or *necessary* (which is the only ground or reason of existence of any thing, that can be imagined *within the thing itself,* as will presently more fully appear), but every one *dependent* on the foregoing: and where *no part* is necessary, 'tis manifest *the whole* cannot be necessary; absolute necessity of existence, not being an outward, relative, and accidental determination; but an inward and essential property of the nature of the thing which so exists. An infinite succession therefore of merely *dependent* beings, without any original independent cause; is a *series* of beings, that has neither necessity nor cause, nor any reason *at all* of its existence, neither *within itself* nor *from without:* that is, 'tis an express contradiction and impossibility; 'tis a supposing *something* to be *caused,* (because it's granted in every one of its stages of succession, not to be necessary and from itself); and yet that in the whole it is caused *absolutely by nothing:* Which every man knows is a contradiction to be done *in time;* and because duration in this case makes no difference, 'tis equally a contradiction to suppose it done from eternity: And consequently there must *on the contrary,* of necessity have existed from eternity, *some one* immutable and *independent* Being: Which, what it is, remains in the next place to be inquired.

**From Samuel Clarke,* A Demonstration of the Being and Attributes of God *(1705), Part II.*

The Cosmological Argument*

WILLIAM L. ROWE

SINCE ANCIENT TIMES thoughtful people have sought to justify their religious beliefs. Perhaps the most basic belief for which justification has been sought is the belief that there is a God. The effort to justify belief in the existence of God has generally started either from facts available to believers and nonbelievers alike or from facts, such as the experience of God, normally available only to believers. . . . We shall consider some major attempts to justify belief in God by appealing to facts supposedly available to any rational person, whether religious or not. By starting from such facts theologians and philosophers have developed arguments for the existence of God, arguments which, they have claimed, prove beyond reasonable doubt that there is a God.

STATING THE ARGUMENT

Arguments for the existence of God are commonly divided into *a posteriori* arguments and *a priori* arguments. An *a posteriori* argument depends on a principle or premise that can be known only by means of our experience of the world. An *a priori* argument, on the other hand, purports to rest on principles all of which can be known independently of our experience of the world, by just reflecting on and understanding them. Of the three major arguments for the existence of God—the Cosmological, the Teleological, and the Ontological—only the last of these is entirely *a priori*. In the Cosmological Argument one starts from some simple fact about the world, such as that it contains things which are caused to exist by other things. In the Teleological Argument a somewhat more complicated fact about the world serves as a starting point, the fact that the world exhibits order and design. In the Ontological Argument, however, one begins simply with a concept of God. In this chapter we shall consider the Cosmological Argument. . . .

Before we state the Cosmological Argument itself, we shall consider some rather general points about the argument. Historically, it can be traced to the writings of the Greek philosophers, Plato and Aristotle, but the major developments in the argument took place in the thirteenth and in the eighteenth centuries. In the thirteenth century, Aquinas put forth five distinct arguments for the existence of God, and of these, the first three are versions of the Cosmological Argument.[1] In the first of these he started from the fact that there are things in the world undergoing change and reasoned to the conclusion that there must be some ultimate cause of change that is itself unchanging. In the second he started from the fact that there are things in the world that clearly are caused to exist by other things and reasoned to the conclusion that there must be some ultimate cause of existence whose own existence is itself uncaused. And in the third argument he started from the fact that there are things in the world which need not have existed at all, things which do exist but which we can easily imagine might not, and reasoned to the conclusion that there must be some being that had to be, that exists and could not have failed to exist. Now it might be objected that even if Aquinas' arguments do prove beyond doubt the existence of an unchanging changer, an uncaused cause, and a being that could not have failed to exist, the arguments fail to prove the existence of the theistic God. For the theistic God, as we saw, is supremely good, omnipotent, omniscient, and creator of but separate from and

**From William L. Rowe,* Philosophy of Religion *(Belmont, Calif.: Wadsworth Publishing Co., 1978), pp. 16–30. Reprinted by permission of the publisher and the author.*

independent of the world. How do we know, for example, that the unchanging changer isn't evil or slightly ignorant? The answer to this objection is that the Cosmological Argument has two parts. In the first part the effort is to prove the existence of a special sort of being, for example, a being that could not have failed to exist, or a being that causes change in other things but is itself unchanging. In the second part of the argument the effort is to prove that the special sort of being whose existence has been established in the first part has, and must have, the features—perfect goodness, omnipotence, omniscience, and so on—which go together to make up the theistic idea of God. What this means, then, is that Aquinas' three arguments are different versions of only the first part of the Cosmological Argument. Indeed, in later sections of his *Summa Theologica* Aquinas undertakes to show that the unchanging changer, the uncaused cause of existence, and the being which had to exist are one and the same being and that this single being has all of the attributes of the theistic God.

We noted above that a second major development in the Cosmological Argument took place in the eighteenth century, a development reflected in the writings of the German philosopher, Gottfried Leibniz (1646–1716), and especially in the writings of the English theologian and philosopher, Samuel Clarke (1675–1729). In 1704 Clarke gave a series of lectures, later published under the title *A Demonstration of the Being and Attributes of God.* These lectures constitute, perhaps, the most complete, forceful, and cogent presentation of the Cosmological Argument we possess. The lectures were read by the major skeptical philosopher of the century, David Hume (1711–1776), and in his brilliant attack on the attempt to justify religion in the court of reason, his *Dialogues Concerning Natural Religion,* Hume advanced several penetrating criticisms of Clarke's arguments, criticisms which have persuaded many philosophers in the modern period to reject the Cosmological Argument. In our study of the argument we shall concentrate our attention largely on its eighteenth-century form and try to assess its strengths and weaknesses in the light of the criticisms which Hume and others have advanced against it.

The first part of the eighteenth-century form of the Cosmological Argument seeks to establish the existence of a self-existent being. The second part of the argument attempts to prove that the self-existent being is the theistic God, that is, has the features which we have noted to be basic elements in the theistic idea of God. We shall consider mainly the first part of the argument, for it is against the first part that philosophers from Hume to Russell have advanced very important objections.

In stating the first part of the Cosmological Argument we shall make use of two important concepts, the concept of a *dependent being* and the concept of a *self-existent being.* By "a dependent being" we mean a *being whose existence is accounted for by the causal activity of other things.* Recalling Anselm's division into the three cases: "explained by another," "explained by nothing," and "explained by itself," it's clear that a dependent being is a being whose existence is explained by another. By "a self-existent being" we mean *a being whose existence is accounted for by its own nature.* This idea . . . is an essential element in the theistic concept of God. Again, in terms of Anselm's three cases, a self-existent being is a being whose existence is explained by itself. Armed with these two concepts, the concept of a dependent being and the concept of a self-existent being, we can now state the first part of the Cosmological Argument.

1. Every being (that exists or ever did exist) is either a dependent being or a self-existent being.
2. Not every being can be a dependent being.

Therefore,

3. There exists a self-existent being.

Deductive Validity

Before we look critically at each of the premises of this argument, we should note that this argument is, to use an expression from the logician's vocabulary, ***deductively valid.*** To find out whether an argument is deductively valid we need only ask the question: If its premises were true would its conclusion have to be true? If the answer is yes, the argument is deductively valid. If the answer is no, the argument is deductively invalid. Notice that the question of the validity of an argument is entirely different from the question of whether its premises are in fact true. The following argument is made up entirely of false statements, but it is deductively valid.

1. Babe Ruth is the President of the U.S.
2. The President of the U.S. is from Indiana.
Therefore,
3. Babe Ruth is from Indiana.

The argument is deductively valid because even though its premises are false, if they were true its conclusion would have to be true. Even God, Aquinas would say, cannot bring it about that the premises of this argument are true and yet its conclusion is false, for God's power extends only to what is possible, and it is an absolute impossibility that Babe Ruth be the President, the President be from Indiana, and yet Babe Ruth not be from Indiana.

The Cosmological Argument (that is, its first part) is a deductively valid argument. If its premises are or were true its conclusion would have to be true. It's clear from our example about Babe Ruth, however, that the fact that an argument is deductively valid is insufficient to establish the truth of its conclusion. What else is required? Clearly that we know or have rational grounds for believing that the premises are true. If we know that the Cosmological Argument is deductively valid and can establish that its premises are true, we shall thereby have proved that its conclusion is true. Are, then, the premises of the Cosmological Argument true? To this more difficult question we must now turn.

PSR and The First Premise

At first glance the first premise might appear to be an obvious or even trivial truth. But it is neither obvious nor trivial. And if it appears to be obvious or trivial, we must be confusing the idea of a self-existent being with the idea of a being that is not a dependent being. Clearly, it is obviously true that any being is either a dependent being (explained by other things) or it is not a dependent being (not explained by other things). But what our premise says is that any being is either a dependent being (explained by other things) or it is a self-existent being (explained by itself). Consider again Anselm's three cases.

a. explained by another
b. explained by nothing
c. explained by itself

What our first premise asserts is that each being that exists (or ever did exist) is either of sort *a* or of sort *c*. It denies that any being is of sort *b*. And it is this denial that makes the first premise both significant and controversial. The obvious truth we must not confuse it with is the truth that any being is either of sort *a* or not of sort *a*. While this is true it is neither very significant nor controversial.

Earlier we saw that Anselm accepted as a basic principle that whatever exists has an explanation of its existence. Since this basic principle denies that any thing of sort *b* exists or ever did exist, it's clear that Anselm would believe the first premise of our Cosmological Argument. The eighteenth-century proponents of the argument also were convinced of the truth of the basic principle we attributed to Anselm. And because they were convinced of its truth, they readily accepted the first premise of the Cosmological Argument. But by the eighteenth century, Anselm's basic principle had been more fully elaborated and had received a name, "the Principle of Sufficient Reason." Since this principle (PSR, as we shall call it) plays such an important role in justifying the premises of the Cosmological Argument, it will help us to consider it for a moment before we continue our enquiry into the truth or falsity of the premises of the Cosmological Argument.

The Principle of Sufficient Reason (PSR), as it was expressed by both Leibniz and Samuel Clarke, is a very general principle and is best understood as having two parts. In its first part it is simply a restatement of Anselm's principle that there must be an explanation of the *existence* of any being whatever. Thus if we come upon a man in a room, PSR implies that there must be an explanation of the fact that that particular man exists. A moment's reflection, however, reveals that there are many facts about the man other than the mere fact that he exists. There is the fact that the man in question is in the room he's in, rather than somewhere else, the fact that he is in good health, and the fact that he is at the moment thinking of Paris, rather than, say, London. Now the purpose of the second part of PSR is to require an explanation of these facts as well. We may state PSR, therefore, as the principle that *there must be an explanation (a) of the existence of any being, and (b) of any positive fact whatever.* We are now in a position to study the role this very important principle plays in the Cosmological Argument.

Since the proponent of the Cosmological Argument accepts PSR in both its parts, it is clear that he will appeal to its first part, PSRa, as justification for the first premise of the Cosmological Argument. Of course, we can and should enquire into the deeper question of whether the proponent of the argument is rationally justified in accepting PSR itself. But we shall put this question aside for the moment. What we need to see first is whether he is correct in thinking that *if* PSR is true then both of the premises of the Cosmological Argument are true. And what we have just seen is that if only the first part of PSR, that is, PSRa, is true, the first premise of the Cosmological Argument will be true. But what of the second premise of the Argument? For what reasons does the proponent think that it must be true?

The Second Premise

According to the second premise, not every being that exists can be a dependent being, that is, can have the explanation of its existence in some other being or beings. Presumably, the proponent of the argument thinks there is something fundamentally wrong with the idea that every being that exists is dependent, that each existing being was caused by some other being which in turn was caused by some other being, and so on. But just what does he think is wrong with it? To help us in understanding his thinking, let's simplify things by supposing that there exists only one thing now, A_1, a living thing perhaps, that was brought into existence by something else A_2, which perished shortly after it brought A_1 into existence. Suppose further that A_2 was brought into existence in similar fashion some time ago by A_3, and A_3 by A_4, and so forth back into the past. Each of these beings is a *dependent* being, it owes its existence to the preceding thing in the series. Now if nothing else ever existed but these beings, then what the second premise says would not be true. For if every being that exists or ever did exist is an *A* and was produced by a preceding *A*, then every being that exists or ever did exist would be dependent and, accordingly, premise two of the Cosmological Argument would be false. If the proponent of the Cosmological Argument is correct there must, then, be something wrong with the idea that every being that exists or did exist is an *A* and that they form a causal series, A_1 caused by A_2, A_2 caused by A_3, A_3 caused by A_4, . . . A_n caused by A_{n+1}. How does the proponent of the Cosmological Argument propose to show us that there is something wrong with this view?

A popular but mistaken idea of how the proponent tries to show that something is wrong with the view that every being might be dependent is that he uses the following argument to reject it.

1. There must be a *first being* to start any causal series.
2. If every being were dependent there would be no *first being* to start the causal series.

Therefore,

3. Not every being can be a dependent being.

Although this argument is deductively valid and its second premise is true, its first premise overlooks the distinct possibility that a causal series might be *infinite,* with no first member at all. Thus if we go back to our series of *A* beings, where each *A* is dependent, having been produced by the preceding *A* in the causal series, it's clear that if the series existed it would have no first member, for every *A* in the series there would be a preceding *A* which produced it, *ad infinitum.* The first premise of the argument just given assumes that a causal series must stop with a first member somewhere in the distant past. But there seems to be no good reason for making that assumption.

The eighteenth-century proponents of the Cosmological Argument recognized that the causal series of dependent beings could be infinite, without a first member to start the series. They rejected the idea that every being that is or ever was is dependent not because there would then be no first member to the series of dependent beings, but because there would then be no explanation for the fact that there are and have always been dependent beings. To see their reasoning let's return to our simplification of the supposition that the only things that exist or ever did exist are dependent beings. In our simplification of that supposition only one of the dependent beings exists at a time, each one perishing as it produces the next in the series. Perhaps the first thing to note about this supposition is that there is no individual *A* in the causal series of dependent beings whose existence is unexplained—A_1 is explained by A_2, A_2 by A_3, and A_n by A_{n+1}. So the first part of PSR, PSRa, appears to be satisfied. There is no particular being whose existence lacks an explanation. What, then, is it that lacks an explanation, if every particular *A* in the causal series of dependent beings has an explanation? It is the *series itself* that lacks an explanation. Or, as I've chosen to express it, *the fact that there are and have always been dependent beings.* For suppose we ask why it is that there are and have always been *A*s in existence. It won't do to say that *A*s have always been producing other *A*s—we can't explain why there have always been *A*s by saying there always have been *A*s. Nor, on the supposition that only *A*s have ever existed, can we explain the fact that there have always been *A*s by appealing to something other than an *A*—for no such thing would have existed. Thus the supposition that the only things that exist or ever existed are dependent things leaves us with a fact for which there can be no explanation; namely, the fact that there are and have always been dependent beings.

Questioning the Justification of the Second Premise

Critics of the Cosmological Argument have raised several important objections against the claim that if every being is dependent the series or collection of those beings would have no explanation. Our understanding of the Cosmological Argument, as well as of its strengths and weaknesses, will be deepened by a careful consideration of these criticisms.

The first criticism is that the proponent of the Cosmological Argument makes the mistake of treating the collection or series of dependent beings as though it were itself a dependent being, and, therefore, requires an explanation of its existence. But, so the objection goes, the collection of dependent beings is not itself a dependent being any more than a collection of stamps is itself a stamp.

A second criticism is that the proponent makes the mistake of inferring that because each member of the collection of dependent beings has a cause the collection itself must have a cause. But, as Bertrand Russell noted, such reasoning is as fallacious as to infer that the human race (that is, the collection of human beings) must have a mother because each member of the collection (each human being) has a mother.

A third criticism is that the proponent of the argument fails to realize that for there to be an explanation of a collection of things is nothing more than for there to be an explanation of each of the things making up the collection. Since in the infinite collection (or series) of dependent beings, each being in the collection does have an explanation—by virtue of having been caused by some preceding member of the collection—the explanation of the collection, so the criticism goes, has already been given. As David Hume remarked, "Did I show you the particular causes of each individual in a collection of twenty particles of matter, I should think it very unreasonable, should you afterwards ask me, what was the cause of the whole twenty. This is sufficiently explained in explaining the cause of the parts."[2]

Finally, even if the proponent of the Cosmological Argument can satisfactorily answer these objections, he must face one last objection to his ingenious attempt to justify premise two of the Cosmological Argument. For someone may agree that if nothing exists but an infinite collection of dependent beings, the infinite collection will have no explanation of its existence, and still refuse to conclude from this that there is something wrong with the idea that every being is a dependent being. Why, he might ask, should we think that everything has to have an explanation? What's wrong with admitting that the fact that there are and have always been dependent beings is a *brute fact,* a fact having no explanation whatever? Why does everything have to have an explanation anyway? We must now see what can be said in response to these several objections.

Responses to Criticism

It is certainly a mistake to think that a collection of stamps is itself a stamp, and very likely a mistake to think that the collection of dependent beings is itself a dependent being. But the mere fact that the proponent of the argument thinks that there must be an explanation not only for each member of the collection of dependent beings but for the collection itself is not sufficient grounds for concluding that he must view the collection as itself a dependent being. The collection of human beings, for example, is certainly not itself a human being. Admitting this, however, we might still seek an explanation of why there is a collection of human beings, of why there are such things as human beings at all. So the mere fact that an explanation is demanded for the collection of dependent beings is no proof that the person who demands the explanation must be supposing that the collection itself is just another dependent being.

The second criticism attributes to the proponent of the Cosmological Argument the following bit of reasoning:

1. Every member of the collection of dependent beings has a cause or explanation.

Therefore,

2. The collection of dependent beings has a cause or explanation.

As we noted in setting forth this criticism, arguments of this sort are often unreliable. It would be a mistake to conclude that a collection of objects is light in weight simply because each object in the collection is light in weight, for if there were many objects in the collection it might be quite heavy. On the other hand, if we know that each marble weighs more than one ounce we could infer validly that the collection of marbles weighs more than an ounce. Fortunately, however, we don't need to decide whether the inference from (1) to (2) is valid or invalid. We need not decide this question because the proponent of the Cosmological Argument need not use this inference to establish that there must be an explanation of the collection of dependent beings. He need not use this inference because he has in PSR a principle from which it follows immediately that the collection of dependent beings has a cause or explanation. For according to PSR every positive fact must have an explanation. If it is a fact that there exists a collection of dependent beings then, according to PSR, that fact too must have an explanation. So it is PSR that the proponent of the Cosmological Argument appeals to in concluding that there must be an explanation of the collection of dependent beings, and not some dubious inference from the premise that each member of the collection has an explanation. It seems, then, that neither of the first two criticisms is strong enough to do any serious damage to the reasoning used to support the second premise of the Cosmological Argument.

The third objection contends that to explain the existence of a collection of things is the same thing as to explain the existence of each of its members. If we consider a collection of dependent beings where each being in the collection is explained by the preceding member which caused it, it's clear that no member of the collection will lack an explanation of its existence. But, so the criticism goes, if we've explained the existence of every member of a collection we've explained the existence of the collection—there's nothing left over to be explained. This forceful criticism, originally advanced by David Hume, has gained considerable support in the modern period. But the criticism rests on an assumption that the proponent of the Cosmological Argument would not accept. The assumption is that to explain the existence of a collection of things it is *sufficient* to explain the existence of every member in the collection. To see what is wrong with this assumption is to understand the basic issue in the reasoning by which the proponent of the Cosmological Argument seeks to establish that not every being can be a dependent being.

In order for there to be an explanation of the existence of the collection of dependent beings, it's clear that the eighteenth-century proponents would require that the following two conditions be satisfied:

C1. There is an explanation of the existence of each of the members of the collection of dependent beings.
C2. There is an explanation of why there are *any* dependent beings.

According to the proponents of the Cosmological Argument if every being that exists or ever did exist is a dependent being—that is, if the whole of reality consists of nothing more than a collection of dependent beings—C1 will be satisfied, but C2 will not be satisfied. And since C2 won't be satisfied there will be no explanation of the collection of dependent beings. The third criticism, therefore, says in effect that if C1 is satisfied C2 will be satisfied, and, since in a collection of dependent beings each member will have an explanation in whatever it was that produced it, C1 will be satisfied. So, therefore, C2 will be satisfied and the collection of dependent beings will have an explanation.

Although the issue is a complicated one, I think it is possible to see that the third criticism rests on a mistake: the mistake of thinking that if C1 is satisfied C2 must also be satisfied. The mistake is a natural one to make for it is easy to imagine circumstances in which if C1 is satisfied C2 also will be satisfied. Suppose, for example, that the whole of reality includes not just a collection of dependent beings but also a self-existent being. Suppose further that instead of each dependent being having been produced by some other dependent being every dependent being was produced by the self-existent being. Finally, let us consider both the possibility that the collection of dependent beings is finite in time and has a first member and the possibility that the collection of dependent beings is infinite in past time, having no first member. Using "G" for the self-existent being, the first possibility may be diagrammed as follows:

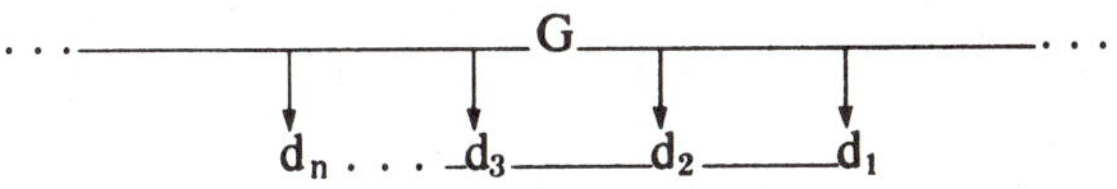

G, we shall say, has always existed and always will. We can think of d_1 as some presently existing dependent being, d_2, d_3, and so forth as dependent beings that existed at some time in the past, and d_n as the first dependent being to exist. The second possibility may be portrayed as follows:

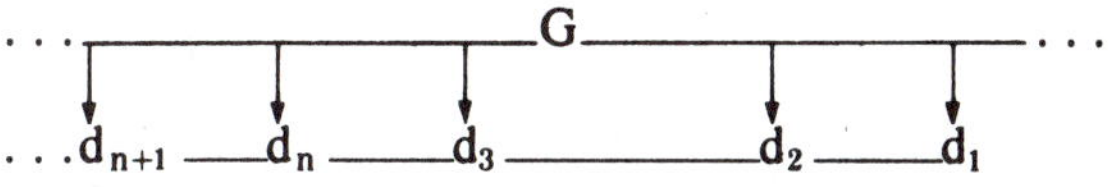

On this diagram there is no first member of the collection of dependent beings. Each member of the infinite collection, however, is explained by reference to the self-existent being G which produced it. Now the interesting point about both these cases is that the explanation that has been provided for the members of the collection of dependent beings carries with it, at least in part, an answer to the question of why there are any dependent beings at all. In both cases we may explain why there are dependent beings by pointing out that there exists a self-existent being that has been engaged in producing them. So once we have learned that the existence of each member of the collection of dependent beings has its existence explained by the fact that G produced it, we have already learned why there are dependent beings.

Someone might object that we haven't really learned why there are dependent beings until we also learn *why* G has been producing them. But, of course, we could also say that we haven't really explained the existence of a particular dependent being, say d_3, until we also learn not just that G produced it but *why* G produced it. The point we need to grasp, however, is that once we admit that every dependent being's existence is explained by G, we must admit that the fact that there are dependent beings has also been explained. So it is not unnatural that someone should think that to explain the existence of the collection of dependent beings is nothing more than to explain the existence of its members. For, as we've seen, to explain the collection's existence is to explain each member's existence and to explain why there are any dependent beings at all. And in the examples we've considered, in doing the one (explaining why each dependent being exists) we've already done the other (explained why there are any dependent beings at all).

We must now see, however, that on the supposition that the whole of reality consists *only* of a collection of dependent beings, to give an explanation of each member's existence is not to provide an explanation of why there are dependent beings.

In the examples we've considered we have gone *outside* of the collection of dependent beings in order to explain the members' existence. But if the only beings that exist or ever existed are dependent beings then each dependent being will be explained by some other dependent being, ad infinitum. This does not mean that there will be some particular dependent being whose existence is unaccounted for. Each dependent being has an explanation of its existence; namely, in the dependent being which preceded it and produced it. So C1 is satisfied: there is an explanation of the existence of each member of the collection of dependent beings. Turning to C2, however, we can see that it will not be satisfied. We cannot explain why there are (or have ever been) dependent beings by appealing to all the members of the infinite collection of dependent beings. For if the question to be answered is why there are (or have ever been) any dependent beings at all, we cannot answer that question by noting that there always have been dependent beings, each one accounting for the existence of some other dependent being. Thus on the supposition that every being is dependent it seems there will be no explanation of why there are dependent beings. C2 will not be satisfied. Therefore, on the supposition that every being is dependent there will be no explanation of the existence of the collection of dependent beings.

The Truth of PSR

We come now to the final criticism of the reasoning supporting the second premise of the Cosmological Argument. According to this criticism, it is admitted that the supposition that every being is dependent implies that there will be a *brute fact* in the universe, a fact, that is, for which there can be no explanation whatever. For there will be no explanation of the fact that dependent beings exist and have always been in existence. It is this brute fact that the proponents of the argument were describing when they pointed out that if every being is dependent the series or collection of dependent beings would lack an explanation of *its* existence. The final criticism asks what is wrong with admitting that the universe contains such a brute, unintelligible fact. In asking this question the critic challenges the fundamental principle, PSR, on which the Cosmological Argument rests. For, as we've seen, the first premise of the argument denies that there exists a being whose existence has no explanation. In support of this premise the proponent appeals to the first part of PSR. The second premise of the argument claims that not every being can be dependent. In support of this premise the proponent appeals to the second part of PSR, the part which states that there must be an explanation of any positive fact whatever.

The proponent reasons that if every being were a dependent being then although the first part of PSR would be satisfied—every being would have an explanation—the second part would be violated, there would be no explanation for the positive fact that there are and have always been dependent beings. For first, since every being is supposed to be dependent, there would be nothing outside of the collection of dependent beings to explain the collection's existence. Second, the fact that each member of the collection has an explanation in some other dependent being is insufficient to explain why there are and have always been dependent beings. And, finally, there is nothing about the collection of dependent beings that would suggest that it is a self-existent collection. Consequently, if every being were dependent, the fact that there are and have always been dependent beings would have no explanation. But this violates the second part of PSR. So the second premise of the Cosmological Argument must be true, not every being can be a dependent being. This conclusion, however, is no better than the principle, PSR, on which it rests. And it is the point of the final criticism to question the truth of PSR. Why, after all, should we accept the idea that every being and every positive fact must have an explanation? Why, in short, should we believe PSR? These are important questions, and any final judgment of the Cosmological Argument depends on how they are answered.

Most of the theologians and philosophers who accept PSR have tried to defend it in either of two ways. Some have held that PSR is (or can be) known *intuitively* to be true. By this they mean that if we fully understand and reflect on what is said by PSR we can see that it must be true. Now, undoubtedly, there are statements which are known intuitively to be true. "Every triangle has exactly three angles" or "No physical object can be in two different places in space at one and the same time" are examples of statements whose truth we can apprehend just by understanding and reflecting on them. The difficulty with the claim that PSR is intuitively true, however, is that a number of very able philosophers fail to apprehend its truth, and some even claim that the principle is false. It is doubtful, therefore, that many of us, if any, know intuitively that PSR is true.

The second way philosophers and theologians who accept PSR have sought to defend it is by claiming that although it is not known to be true, it is, nevertheless, a presupposition of reason, a basic assumption that rational people make, whether or not they reflect sufficiently to become aware of the assumption. It's probably true that there are some assumptions we all make about our world, assumptions which are so basic that most of us are unaware of them. And, I suppose, it might be true that PSR is such an assumption. What bearing would this view of PSR have on the Cosmological Argument? Perhaps the main point to note is that even if PSR is a presupposition we all share, the premises of the Cosmological Argument could still be false. For PSR itself could still be false. The fact, if it is a fact, that all of us *presuppose* that every existing being and every positive fact has an explanation does not imply that no being exists, and no positive fact obtains, without an explanation. Nature is not bound to satisfy our presuppositions. As the American philosopher, William James, once remarked in another connection, "In the great boarding house of nature, the cakes and the butter and the syrup seldom come out so even and leave the plates so clear."

Our study of the first part of the Cosmological Argument has led us to the fundamental principle on which its premises rest, the Principle of Sufficient Reason. Since we do not seem to know that PSR is true we cannot reasonably claim to know that the premises of the Cosmological Argument are true. They might be true. But unless we do know them to be true they cannot *establish* for us the conclusion that there exists a being that has the explanation of its existence within its own nature. If it were shown, however, that even though we do not *know* that PSR is true we all, nevertheless, *presuppose* PSR to be true, then, whether PSR is true or not, to be consistent we should accept the Cosmological Argument. For, as we've seen, its premises imply its conclusion and its premises do seem to follow from PSR. But no one has succeeded in *showing* that PSR is an assumption that most or all of us share. So our final conclusion must be that although the Cosmological Argument might be a *sound* argument (valid with true premises), it does not provide us with good rational grounds for believing that among those beings that exist there is one whose existence is accounted for by its own nature. Having come to this conclusion we may safely put aside the second part of the argument. For even if it succeeded in showing that a self-existent being would have the other attributes of the theistic God, the Cosmological Argument would still not provide us with good rational grounds for belief in God, having failed in its first part to provide us with good rational grounds for believing that there is a self-existent being.

NOTES

1. See St. Thomas Aquinas, *Summa Theologica,* 1a. 2, 3.

2. David Hume, *Dialogues Concerning Natural Religion,* Part IX, ed. H. D. Aiken (New York: Hafner Publishing Company, 1948), pp. 59–60.

The Argument from Design*

WILLIAM PALEY

William Paley (1743–1805) was an English philosopher of religion and ethics.

CHAPTER ONE: STATE OF THE ARGUMENT

IN CROSSING A HEATH, suppose I pitched my foot against a *stone* and were asked how the stone came to be there, I might possibly answer that for anything I knew to the contrary it had lain there forever; nor would it, perhaps, be very easy to show the absurdity of this answer. But suppose I had found a *watch* upon the ground, and it should be inquired how the watch happened to be in that place, I should hardly think of the answer which I had before given, that for anything I knew the watch might have always been there. Yet why should not this answer serve for the watch as well as for the stone? Why is it not as admissible in the second case as in the first? For this reason, and for no other, namely, that when we come to inspect the watch, we perceive—what we could not discover in the stone—that its several parts are framed and put together for a purpose, e.g., that they are so formed and adjusted as to produce motion, and that motion so regulated as to point out the hour of the day; that if the different parts had been differently shaped from what they are, of a different size from what they are, or placed after any other manner or in any other order than that in which they are placed, either no motion at all would have been carried on in the machine, or none which would have answered the use that is now served by it. To reckon up a few of the plainest of these parts and of their offices, all tending to one result; we see a cylindrical box containing a coiled elastic spring, which, by its endeavor to relax itself, turns round the box. We next observe a flexible chain—artificially wrought for the sake of flexure—communicating the action of the spring from the box to the fusee. We then find a series of wheels, the teeth of which catch in and apply to each other, conducting the motion from the fusee to the balance and from the balance to the pointer, and at the same time, by the size and shape of those wheels, so regulating that motion as to terminate in causing an index, by an equable and measured progression, to pass over a given space in a given time. We take notice that the wheels are made of brass, in order to keep them from rust; the springs of steel, no other metal being so elastic; that over the face of the watch there is placed a glass, a material employed in no other part of the work, but in the room of which, if there had been any other than a transparent substance, the hour could not be seen without opening the case. This mechanism being observed—it requires indeed an examination of the instrument, and perhaps some previous knowledge of the subject, to perceive and understand it; but being once, as we have said, observed and understood—the inference we think is inevitable, that the watch must have had a maker—that there must have existed, at some time and at some place or other, an artificer or artificers who formed it for the purpose which we find it actually to answer, who comprehended its construction and designed its use.

I. Nor would it, I apprehend, weaken the conclusion, that we had never seen a watch made—that we had never known an artist capable of making one—that we were altogether incapable of executing such a piece of workmanship ourselves, or of

**From* Natural Theology *(1800).*

understanding in what manner it was performed; all this being no more than what is true of some exquisite remains of ancient art, of some lost arts, and, to the generality of mankind, of the more curious productions of modern manufacture. Does one man in a million know how oval frames are turned? Ignorance of this kind exalts our opinion of the unseen and unknown artist's skill, if he be unseen and unknown, but raises no doubt in our minds of the existence and agency of such an artist, at some former time and in some place or other. Nor can I perceive that it varies at all the inference, whether the question arise concerning a human agent or concerning an agent of a different species, or an agent possessing in some respects a different nature.

II. Neither, secondly, would it invalidate our conclusion, that the watch sometimes went wrong or that it seldom went exactly right. The purpose of the machinery, the design, and the designer might be evident, and in the case supposed, would be evident, in whatever way we accounted for the irregularity of the movement, or whether we could account for it or not. It is not necessary that a machine be perfect in order to show with what design it was made: still less necessary, where the only question is whether it were made with any design at all.

III. Nor, thirdly, would it bring any uncertainty into the argument, if there were a few parts of the watch, concerning which we could not discover or had not yet discovered in what manner they conduced to the general effect; or even some parts, concerning which we could not ascertain whether they conduced to that effect in any manner whatever. For, as to the first branch of the case, if by the loss, or disorder, or decay of the parts in question, the movement of the watch were found in fact to be stopped, or disturbed, or retarded, no doubt would remain in our minds as to the utility or intention of these parts, although we should be unable to investigate the manner according to which, or the connection by which, the ultimate effect depended upon their action or assistance; and the more complex is the machine, the more likely is this obscurity to arise. Then, as to the second thing supposed, namely, that there were parts which might be spared without prejudice to the movement of the watch, and that we had proved this by experiment, these superfluous parts, even if we were completely assured that they were such, would not vacate the reasoning which we had instituted concerning other parts. The indication of contrivance remained, with respect to them, nearly as it was before.

IV. Nor, fourthly, would any man in his senses think the existence of the watch with its various machinery accounted for, by being told that it was one out of possible combinations of material forms; that whatever he had found in the place where he found the watch, must have contained some internal configuration or other; and that this configuration might be the structure now exhibited, namely, of the works of a watch, as well as a different structure.

V. Nor, fifthly, would it yield his inquiry more satisfaction, to be answered that there existed in things a principle of order, which had disposed the parts of the watch into their present form and situation. He never knew a watch made by the principle of order; nor can he even form to himself an idea of what is meant by a principle of order distinct from the intelligence of the watchmaker.

VI. Sixthly, he would be surprised to hear that the mechanism of the watch was no proof of contrivance, only a motive to induce the mind to think so:

VII. And not less surprised to be informed that the watch in his hand was nothing more than the result of the laws of *metallic* nature. It is a perversion of language to assign any law as the efficient, operative cause of any thing. A law presupposes an agent, for it is only the mode according to which an agent proceeds: it implies a power, for it is the order according to which that power acts. Without this agent, without this power, which are both distinct from itself, the *law* does nothing, is nothing. The expression, "the law of metallic nature," may sound strange and harsh to a philosophic ear; but it seems quite as justifiable as some others which are more familiar to him, such as "the law of vegetable nature," "the law of animal nature," or, indeed, as "the law of nature" in general, when assigned as the cause of phenomena, in exclusion of agency and power, or when it is substituted into the place of these.

VIII. Neither, lastly, would our observer be driven out of his conclusion or from his confidence in its truth by being told that he knew nothing at all about the matter. He knows enough for his argument; he knows the utility of the end; he knows the subserviency and adaptation of the means to the end. These points being known, his ignorance of other points, his doubts concerning other points affect not the certainty of his reasoning. The consciousness of knowing little need not beget a distrust of that which he does know.

CHAPTER TWO: STATE OF THE ARGUMENT CONTINUED

Suppose, in the next place, that the person who found the watch should after some time discover that, in addition to all the properties which he had hitherto observed in it, it possessed the unexpected property of producing in the course of its movement another watch like itself—the thing is conceivable; that it contained within it a mechanism, a system of parts—a mold, for instance, or a complex adjustment of lathes, files, and other tools—evidently and separately calculated for this purpose; let us inquire what effect ought such a discovery to have upon his former conclusion.

I. The first effect would be to increase his admiration of the contrivance, and his conviction of the consummate skill of the contriver. Whether he regarded the object of the contrivance, the distinct apparatus, the intricate, yet in many parts intelligible mechanism by which it was carried on, he would perceive in this new observation nothing but an additional reason for doing what he had already done—for referring the construction of the watch to design and to supreme art. If that construction *without* this property, or, which is the same thing, before this property had been noticed, proved intention and art to have been employed about it, still more strong would the proof appear when he came to the knowledge of this further property, the crown and perfection of all the rest.

II. He would reflect, that though the watch before him were, *in some sense,* the maker of the watch, which, was fabricated in the course of its movements, yet it was in a very different sense from that in which a carpenter, for instance, is the maker of a chair—the author of its contrivance, the cause of the relation of its parts to their use. With respect to these, the first watch was no cause at all to the second; in no such sense as this was it the author of the constitution and order, either of the parts which the new watch contained, or of the parts by the aid and instrumentality of which it was produced. We might possibly say, but with great latitude of expression, that a stream of water ground corn; but no latitude of expression would allow us to say, no stretch of conjecture could lead us to think that the stream of water built the mill, though it were too ancient for us to know who the builder was. What the stream of water does in the affair is neither more nor less than this: by the application of an unintelligent impulse to a mechanism previously arranged, arranged independently of it and arranged by intelligence, an effect is produced, namely, the corn is ground. But the effect results from the arrangement. The force of the stream cannot be said to be the cause or author of the effect, still less of the arrangement. Understanding and plan in the formation of the mill were not the less necessary for any share which the water has in grinding the corn; yet is this share the same as that which the watch would have contributed to the production of the new watch, upon the supposition assumed in the last section. Therefore,

III. Though it be now no longer probable that the individual watch which our observer had found was made immediately by the hand of an artificer, yet does not this alteration in anyway affect the inference that an artificer had been originally employed and concerned in the production. The argument from design remains as it was. Marks of design and contrivance are no more accounted for now than they were before. In the same thing, we may ask for the cause of different properties. We may ask for the cause of the color of a body, of its hardness, of its heat; and these causes may be all different. We are now asking for the cause of that subserviency to a use, that relation to an end, which we have remarked in the watch before us. No answer is given to this question by telling us that a preceding watch produced it. There cannot be design without a designer; contrivance without a contriver; order without choice; arrangement without anything capable of arranging; subserviency and relation to a purpose without that which could intend a purpose; means suitable to an end, and executing their office in accomplishing that end, without the end ever having been contemplated or the means accommodated to it. Arrangement, disposition of parts, subserviency of means to an end, relation of instruments to a use imply the presence of intelligence and mind. No one, therefore, can rationally believe that the insensible, inanimate watch, from which the watch before us issued, was the proper cause of the mechanism we so much admire in it—could be truly said to have constructed the instrument, disposed its parts, assigned their office, determined their order, action, and mutual dependency, combined their several motions into one result, and that also a result connected with the utilities of other beings. All these properties, therefore, are as much unaccounted for as they were before.

IV. Nor is anything gained by running the difficulty farther back, that is, by supposing the watch before us to have been produced from another watch, that from a former, and so on indefinitely. Our going back ever so far brings us no nearer to the least degree of satisfaction upon the subject. Contrivance is still unaccounted for. We still want a contriver. A designing mind is neither supplied by this supposition nor dispensed with. If the difficulty were diminished the farther we went back, by going back indefinitely we might exhaust it. And this is the only case to which this sort of reasoning applies. Where there is a tendency, or, as we increase the number of terms, a continual approach toward a limit, *there,* by supposing the number of terms to be what is called infinite, we may conceive the limit to be attained; but where there is no such tendency or approach, nothing is effected by lengthening the series. There is no difference as to the point in question, whatever there may be as to many points, between one series and another—between a series which is finite and a series which is infinite. A chain composed of an infinite number of links, can no more support itself, than a chain composed of a finite number of links. And of this we are assured, though we never *can* have tried the experiment; because, by increasing the number of links, from ten, for instance, to a hundred, from a hundred to a thousand, etc., we make not the smallest approach, we observe not the smallest tendency toward self-support. There is no difference in this respect—yet there may be a great difference in several respects—between a chain of a greater or less length, between one chain and another, between one that is finite and one that is infinite. This very much resembles the case before us. The machine which we are inspecting demonstrates, by its construction, contrivance and design. Contrivance must have had a contriver, design a designer, whether the machine immediately proceeded from another machine or not. That circumstance alters not the case. That other machine may, in like manner, have proceeded from a former machine: nor does that alter the case; contrivance must have had a contriver. That former one from one preceding it: no alteration still; a contriver is still necessary. No tendency is perceived, no approach toward a diminution of this necessity. It is the same with any and every succession of these machines—a succession of ten, of a hundred, of a thousand; with one series, as with another—a series which is finite, as with a series which is infinite. In whatever other respects they may differ, in this they do not. In all equally, contrivance and design are unaccounted for.

The question is not simply, How came the first watch into existence? which question, it may be pretended, is done away by supposing the series of watches thus produced from one another to have been infinite, and consequently to have had no such *first* for which it was necessary to provide a cause. This, perhaps, would have been nearly the state of the question, if nothing had been before us but an unorganized, unmechanized substance, without mark or indication of contrivance. It might be difficult to show that such substance could not have existed from eternity, either in succession—if it were possible, which I think it is not, for unorganized bodies to spring from one another—or by individual perpetuity. But that is not the question now. To suppose it to be so is to suppose that it made no difference whether he had found a watch or a stone. As it is, the metaphysics of that question have no place; for, in the watch which we are examining are seen contrivance, design, an end, a purpose, means for the end, adaptation to the purpose. And the question which irresistibly presses upon our thoughts is, whence this contrivance and design? The thing required is the intending mind, the adapting hand, the intelligence by which that hand was directed. This question, this demand is not shaken off by increasing a number or succession of substances destitute of these properties; nor the more, by increasing that number to infinity. If it be said that, upon the supposition of one watch being produced from another in the course of that other's movements and by means of the mechanism within it, we have a cause for the watch in my hand, namely, the watch from which it proceeded; I deny that for the design, the contrivance, the suitableness of means to an end, the adaptation of instruments to a use, all of which we discover in the watch, we have any cause whatever. It is in vain, therefore, to assign a series of such causes or to allege that a series may be carried back to infinity; for I do not admit that we have yet any cause at all for the phenomena, still less any series of causes either finite or infinite. Here is contrivance but no contriver; proofs of design, but no designer.

V. Our observer would further also reflect that the maker of the watch before him was in truth and reality the maker of every watch produced from it: there being no difference, except that the latter manifests a more exquisite skill, between the making of another watch with his own hands, by the mediation of files, lathes, chisels, etc., and the disposing, fixing, and inserting of these instruments, or of others equivalent to them, in the body of the watch already made, in such a manner as to form a new watch in the course of the movements which he had given to the old one. It is only working by one set of tools instead of another.

The conclusion which the *first* examination of the watch, of its works, construction, and movement, suggested, was that it must have had, for cause and author of that construction, an artificer who understood its mechanism and designed its use. This conclusion is invincible. A *second* examination presents us with a new discovery. The watch is found, in the course of its movement, to produce another watch similar to itself; and not only so, but we perceive in it a system of organization separately calculated for that purpose. What effect would this discovery have or ought it to have upon our former inference? What, as has already been said, but to increase beyond measure our admiration of the skill which had been employed in the formation of such a machine? Or shall it, instead of this, all at once turn us round to an opposite conclusion, namely, that no art or skill whatever has been concerned in the business, although all other evidences of art and skill remain as they were, and this last and supreme piece of art be now added to the rest? Can this be maintained without absurdity? Yet this is atheism. . . .

CHAPTER FIVE: APPLICATION OF THE ARGUMENT CONTINUED

Every observation which was made in our first chapter concerning the watch may be repeated with strict propriety concerning the eye, concerning animals, concerning plants, concerning, indeed, all the organized parts of the works of nature. As,

I. When we are inquiring simply after the *existence* of an intelligent Creator, imperfection, inaccuracy, liability to disorder, occasional irregularities may subsist in a considerable degree without inducing any doubt into the question; just as a watch may frequently go wrong, seldom perhaps exactly right, may be faulty in some parts, defective in some, without the smallest ground of suspicion from thence arising that it was not a watch, not made, or not made for the purpose ascribed to it. When faults are pointed out, and when a question is started concerning the skill of the artist or dexterity with which the work is executed, then, indeed, in order to defend these qualities from accusation, we must be able either to expose some intractableness and imperfection in the materials or point out some invincible difficulty in the execution, into which imperfection and difficulty the matter of complaint may be resolved; or, if we cannot do this, we must adduce such specimens of consummate art and contrivance proceeding from the same hand as may convince the inquirer of the existence, in the case before him, of impediments like those which we have mentioned, although, what from the nature of the case is very likely to happen, they be unknown and unperceived by him. This we must do in order to vindicate the artist's skill, or at least the perfection of it; as we must also judge of his intention and of the provisions employed in fulfilling that intention, not from an instance in which they fail but from the great plurality of instances in which they succeed. But, after all, these are different questions from the question of the artist's existence; or, which is the same, whether the thing before us be a work of art or not; and the questions ought always to be kept separate in the mind. So likewise it is in the works of nature. Irregularities and imperfections are of little or no weight in the consideration when that consideration relates simply to the existence of a Creator. When the argument respects His attributes, they are of weight; but are then to be taken in conjunction—the attention is not to rest upon them, but they are to be taken in conjunction with the unexceptionable evidence which we possess of skill, power, and benevolence displayed in other instances; which evidences may, in strength, number, and variety, be such and may so overpower apparent blemishes as to induce us, upon the most reasonable ground, to believe that these last ought to be referred to some cause, though we be ignorant of it, other than defect of knowledge or of benevolence in the author. . . .

The Panda's Thumb*

STEPHEN JAY GOULD

Stephen Jay Gould (1941–) teaches biology, geology, and the history of science at Harvard University. He writes a regular column for *Natural History Magazine*.

FEW HEROES LOWER their sights in the prime of their lives; triumph leads inexorably on, often to destruction. Alexander wept because he had no new worlds to conquer; Napoleon, overextended, sealed his doom in the depth of a Russian winter. But Charles Darwin did not follow the *Origin of Species* (1859) with a general defense of natural selection or with its evident extension to human evolution (he waited until 1871 to publish *The Descent of Man*). Instead, he wrote his most obscure work, a book entitled: *On the Various Contrivances by Which British and Foreign Orchids Are Fertilized by Insects* (1862).

Darwin's many excursions into the minutiae of natural history—he wrote a taxonomy of barnacles, a book on climbing plants, and a treatise on the formation of vegetable mold by earthworms—won him an undeserved reputation as an old-fashioned, somewhat doddering describer of curious plants and animals, a man who had one lucky insight at the right time. A rash of Darwinian scholarship has laid this myth firmly to rest during the past twenty years (see essay 2). Before then, one prominent scholar spoke for many ill-informed colleagues when he judged Darwin as a "poor joiner of ideas . . . a man who does not belong with the great thinkers."

In fact, each of Darwin's books played its part in the grand and coherent scheme of his life's work—demonstrating the fact of evolution and defending natural selection as its primary mechanism. Darwin did not study orchids solely for their own sake.

**Reprinted from* The Panda's Thumb: More Reflections in Natural History, *by Stephen Jay Gould, by permission of W. W. Norton & Company, Inc. Copyright © 1980 by Stephen Jay Gould.*

Michael Ghiselin, a California biologist who finally took the trouble to read all of Darwin's books (see his *Triumph of the Darwinian Method*), has correctly identified the treatise on orchids as an important episode in Darwin's campaign for evolution.

Darwin begins his orchid book with an important evolutionary premise: continued self-fertilization is a poor strategy for long-term survival, since off-spring carry only the genes of their single parent, and populations do not maintain enough variation for evolutionary flexibility in the face of environmental change. Thus, plants bearing flowers with both male and female parts usually evolve mechanisms to ensure cross-pollination. Orchids have formed an alliance with insects. They have evolved an astonishing variety of "contrivances" to attract insects, guarantee that sticky pollen adheres to their visitor, and ensure that the attached pollen comes in contact with female parts of the next orchid visited by the insect.

Darwin's book is a compendium of these contrivances, the botanical equivalent of a bestiary. And, like the medieval bestiaries, it is designed to instruct. The message is paradoxical but profound. Orchids manufacture their intricate devices from the common components of ordinary flowers, parts usually fitted for very different functions. If God had designed a beautiful machine to reflect his wisdom and power, surely he would not have used a collection of parts generally fashioned for other purposes. Orchids were not made by an ideal engineer; they are jury-rigged from a limited set of available components. Thus, they must have evolved from ordinary flowers.

Thus, the paradox, and the common theme of this trilogy of essays: Our textbooks like to illustrate evolution with examples of optimal design—nearly perfect mimicry of a dead leaf by a butterfly or of a poisonous species by a palatable relative. But ideal design is a lousy argument for evolution, for it mimics the postulated action of an omnipotent creator. Odd arrangements and funny solutions are the proof of evolution—paths that a sensible God would never tread but that a natural process, constrained by history, follows perforce. No one understood this better than Darwin. Ernst Mayr has shown how Darwin, in defending evolution, consistently turned to organic parts and geographic distributions that make the least sense. Which brings me to the giant panda and its "thumb."

Giant pandas are peculiar bears, members of the order Carnivora. Conventional bears are the most omnivorous representatives of their order, but pandas have restricted this catholicity of taste in the other direction—they belie the name of their order by subsisting almost entirely on bamboo. They live in dense forests of bamboo at high elevations in the mountains of western China. There they sit, largely unthreatened by predators, munching bamboo ten to twelve hours each day.

As a childhood fan of Andy Panda, and former owner of a stuffed toy won by some fluke when all the milk bottles actually tumbled at the county fair, I was delighted when the first fruits of our thaw with China went beyond ping pong to the shipment of two pandas to the Washington zoo. I went and watched in appropriate awe. They yawned, stretched, and ambled a bit, but they spent nearly all their time feeding on their beloved bamboo. They sat upright and manipulated the stalks with their forepaws, shedding the leaves and consuming only the shoots.

I was amazed by their dexterity and wondered how the scion of a stock adapted for running could use its hands so adroitly. They held the stalks of bamboo in their paws and stripped off the leaves by passing the stalks between an apparently flexible thumb and the remaining fingers. This puzzled me. I had learned that a dexterous, opposable thumb stood among the hallmarks of human success. We had maintained, even exaggerated, this important flexibility of our primate forebears, while most mammals had sacrificed it in specializing their digits. Carnivores run, stab, and scratch. My cat may manipulate me psychologically, but he'll never type or play the piano.

So I counted the panda's other digits and received an even greater surprise: there were five, not four. Was the "thumb" a separately evolved sixth finger? Fortunately, the giant panda has its bible, a monograph by D. Dwight Davis, late curator of vertebrate anatomy at Chicago's Field Museum of Natural History. It is probably the greatest work of modern evolutionary comparative anatomy, and it contains more than anyone would ever want to know about pandas. Davis had the answer, of course.

The panda's "thumb" is not, anatomically, a finger at all. It is constructed from a bone called the radial sesamoid, normally a small component of the wrist. In pandas, the radial sesamoid is greatly enlarged and elongated until it almost equals the metapodial bones of the true digits in length. The radial sesamoid underlies a pad on the panda's forepaw; the five digits form the framework of another pad, the palmar. A shallow furrow separates the two pads and serves as a channelway for bamboo stalks.

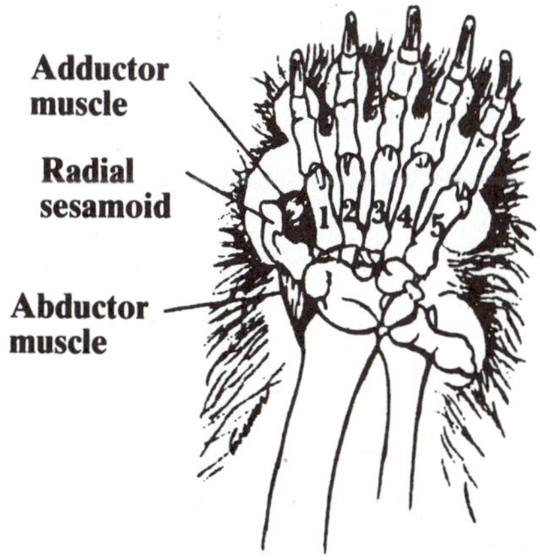

D. L. CRAMER

The panda's thumb comes equipped not only with a bone to give it strength but also with muscles to sustain its agility. These muscles, like the radial sesamoid bone itself, did not arise *de novo*. Like the parts of Darwin's orchids, they are familiar bits of anatomy remodeled for a new function. The abductor of the radial sesamoid (the muscle that pulls it away from the true digits) bears the formidable name *abductor pollicis longus* ("the long abductor of the thumb"—*pollicis* is the genitive of *pollex*, Latin for "thumb"). Its name is a giveaway. In other carnivores, this muscle attaches to the first digit, or true thumb. Two shorter muscles run between the radial sesamoid and the pollex. They pull the sesamoid "thumb" towards the true digits.

Does the anatomy of other carnivores give us any clue to the origin of this odd arrangement in pandas? Davis points out that ordinary bears and raccoons, the closest relatives of giant pandas, far surpass all other carnivores in using their forelegs for manipulating objects in feeding. Pardon the backward metaphor, but pandas, thanks to their ancestry, began with a leg up for evolving greater dexterity in feeding. Moreover, ordinary bears already have a slightly enlarged radial sesamoid.

In most carnivores, the same muscles that move the radial sesamoid in pandas attach exclusively to the base of the pollex, or true thumb. But in ordinary bears, the long abductor muscle ends in two tendons: one inserts into the base of the thumb as in most carnivores, but the other attaches to the radial sesamoid. The two shorter muscles also attach, in part, to the radial sesamoid in bears. "Thus," Davis concludes, "the musculature for operating this remarkable new mechanism—functionally a new digit—required no intrinsic change from conditions already present in the panda's closest relatives, the bears. Furthermore, it appears that the whole sequence of events in the musculature follows automatically from simple hypertrophy of the sesamoid bone."

The sesamoid thumb of pandas is a complex structure formed by marked enlargement of a bone and an extensive rearrangement of musculature. Yet Davis argues that the entire apparatus arose as a mechanical response to growth of the radial sesamoid itself. Muscles shifted because the enlarged bone blocked them short of their original sites. Moreover, Davis postulates that the enlarged radial sesamoid may have been fashioned by a simple genetic change, perhaps a single mutation affecting the timing and rate of growth.

In a panda's foot, the counterpart of the radial sesamoid, called the tibial sesamoid, is also enlarged, although not so much as the radial sesamoid. Yet the tibial sesamoid supports no new digit, and its increased size confers no advantage, so far as we know Davis argues that the coordinated increase of both bones, in response to natural selection upon one alone, probably reflects a simple kind of genetic change. Repeated parts of the body are not fashioned by the action of individual genes—there is no gene "for" your thumb, another for your big toe, or a third for your pinky. Repeated parts are coordinated in development; selection for a change in one element causes a corresponding modification in others. It may be genetically more complex to enlarge a thumb and *not* to modify a big toe, than to increase both together. (In the first case, a general coordination must be broken, the thumb favored separately, and correlated increase of related structures suppressed. In the second, a single gene may increase the rate of growth in a field regulating the development of corresponding digits.)

The panda's thumb provides an elegant zoological counterpart to Darwin's orchids. An engineer's best solution is debarred by history. The panda's true thumb is committed to another role, too specialized for a different function to become an opposable, manipulating digit. So the panda must use parts on hand and settle for an enlarged wrist bone and a somewhat clumsy, but quite workable, solution. The sesamoid thumb wins no prize in an engineer's derby. It is, to use Michael Ghiselin's phrase, a contraption, not a lovely contrivance. But it does its job and excites our imagination all the more because it builds on such improbable foundations.

Darwin's orchid book is filled with similar illustrations. The marsh Epipactus, for example, uses its labellum—an enlarged petal—as a trap. The labellum is divided into two parts. One, near the flower's base, forms a large cup filled with nectar—the object of an insect's visit. The other, near the flower's edge, forms a sort of landing stage. An insect alighting on this runway depresses it and thus gains entrance to the nectar cup beyond. It enters the cup, but the runway is so elastic that it instantly springs up, trapping the insect within the nectar cup. The insect must then back out through the only available exit—a path that forces it to brush against the pollen masses. A remarkable machine but all developed from a conventional petal, a part readily available in an orchid's ancestor.

Darwin then shows how the same labellum in other orchids evolves into a series of ingenious devices to ensure cross-fertilization. It may develop a complex fold that forces an insect to detour its proboscis around and past the pollen masses in order to reach nectar. It may contain deep channels or guiding ridges that lead insects both to nectar and pollen. The channels sometimes form a tunnel, producing a tubular flower. All these adaptations have been built from a part that began as a conventional petal in some ancestral form. Yet nature can do so

Marsh *Epipactis,* lower sepals removed

a. Runway of labellum depressed after insect lands.

D. L. CRAMER

b. Runway of labellum raised after insect crawls into cup below.

D. L. CRAMER

much with so little that it displays, in Darwin's words, "a prodigality of resources for gaining the very same end, namely, the fertilization of one flower by pollen from another plant."

Darwin's metaphor for organic form reflects his sense of wonder that evolution can fashion such a world of diversity and adequate design with such limited raw material:

> Although an organ may not have been originally formed for some special purpose, if it now serves for this end we are justified in saying that it is specially contrived for it. On the same principle, if a man were to make a machine for some special purpose, but were to use old wheels, springs, and pulleys, only slightly altered, the whole machine, with all its parts, might be said to be specially contrived for that purpose. Thus throughout nature almost every part of each living being has probably served, in a slightly modified condition, for diverse purposes, and has acted in the living machinery of many ancient and distinct specific forms.

We may not be flattered by the metaphor of refurbished wheels and pulleys, but consider how well we work. Nature is, in biologist François Jacob's words, an excellent tinkerer, not a divine artificer. And who shall sit in judgment between these exemplary skills?

Senseless Signs of History*

STEPHEN JAY GOULD

WORDS PROVIDE CLUES about their history when etymology does *not* match current meaning. Thus, we suspect that emoluments were once fees paid to the local miller (from the Latin *molere*, to grind), while disasters must have been blamed upon evil stars.

Evolutionists have always viewed linguistic change as a fertile field for meaningful analogies. Charles Darwin, advocating an evolutionary interpretation for such vestigial structures as the human appendix and the embryonic teeth of whalebone whales, wrote: "Rudimentary organs may be compared with the letters in a word, still retained in the spelling, but become useless in the pronunciation, but which serve as a clue in seeking for its derivation." Both organisms and languages evolve.

This essay masquerades behind a list of curious facts, but it is really an abstract discourse on method—or, rather, on a particular method widely used but little appreciated by scientists. In the stereotyped image, scientists rely upon experiment and logic. A middle-aged man in a white coat (most stereotypes are sexist), either shyly reticent, but burning with an inner zeal for truth, or else ebullient and eccentric, pours two chemicals together and watches his answer emerge in a flask. Hypotheses, predictions, experiments, and answers: the scientific method.

But many sciences do not and cannot work this way. As a paleontologist and evolutionary biologist, my trade is the reconstruction of history. History is unique and complex. It cannot be reproduced in a

---

**From* The Panda's Thumb: More Reflections in Natural History *(New York: W. W. Norton & Company, 1989), pp. 27–29. Reprinted by permission of the publisher.*

flask. Scientists who study history, particularly an ancient and unobservable history not recorded in human or geological chronicles, must use inferential rather than experimental methods. They must examine *modern results* of historical processes and try to reconstruct the path leading from ancestral to contemporary words, organisms, or landforms. Once the path is traced, we may be able to specify the causes that led history to follow this, rather than another, route. But how can we infer pathways from modern results? In particular, how can we be sure that there was a pathway at all? How do we know that a modern result is the product of alteration through history and not an immutable part of a changeless universe?

This is the problem that Darwin faced, for his creationist opponents did view each species as unaltered from its initial formation. How did Darwin prove that modern species are the products of history? We might suppose that he looked toward the most impressive results of evolution, the complex and perfected adaptations of organisms to their environments: the butterfly passing for a dead leaf, the bittern for a branch, the superb engineering of a gull aloft or a tuna in the sea.

Paradoxically, he did just the opposite. He searched for oddities and imperfections. The gull may be a marvel of design; if one believes in evolution beforehand, then the engineering of its wing reflects the shaping power of natural selection. But you cannot demonstrate evolution with perfection because perfection need not have a history. After all, perfection of organic design had long been the favorite argument of creationists, who saw in consummate engineering the direct hand of a divine architect. A bird's wing, as an aerodynamic marvel, might have been created exactly as we find it today.

But, Darwin reasoned, if organisms have a history, then ancestral stages should leave *remnants* behind. Remnants of the past that don't make sense in present terms—the useless, the odd, the peculiar, the incongruous—are the signs of history. They supply proof that the world was not made in its present form. When history perfects, it covers its own tracks.

Why should a general word for monetary compensation refer literally to a profession now virtually extinct, unless it once had some relation with grinding and grain? And why should the fetus of a whale make teeth in its mother's womb only to resorb them later and live a life sifting krill on a whalebone filter, unless its ancestors had functional teeth and these teeth survive as a remnant during a stage when they do no harm?

No evidence for evolution pleased Darwin more than the presence in nearly all organisms of rudimentary or vestigial structures, "parts in this strange condition, bearing the stamp of unutility," as he put it. "On my view of descent with modification, the origin of rudimentary organs is simple," he continued. They are bits of useless anatomy, preserved as remnants of functional parts in ancestors.

The general point extends both beyond rudimentary structures and beyond biology to any historical science. Oddities in current terms are the signs of history. The first essay . . . raised the same subject in a different context. The panda's "thumb" demonstrates evolution *because* it is clumsy and built from an odd part, the radial sesamoid bone of the wrist. The true thumb had been so shaped in its ancestral role as the running and clawing digit of a carnivore that it could not be modified into an opposable grasper for bamboo in a vegetarian descendant. . . .

Dialogues Concerning Natural Religion*

DAVID HUME

David Hume (1711–1776) was a leading philosopher of the Enlightenment, the author of a famous history of England, and the tutor of Adam Smith in political economy. He spent most of his life in Edinburgh.

PART II

I MUST OWN, Cleanthes, said Demea, that nothing can more surprise me than the light in which you have all along put this argument. By the whole tenor of your discourse, one would imagine that you were maintaining the Being of a God against the cavils of atheists and infidels, and were necessitated to become a champion for that fundamental principle of all religion. But this, I hope, is not by any means a question among us. No man, no man at least of common sense, I am persuaded, ever entertained a serious doubt with regard to a truth so certain and self-evident. The question is not concerning the *being* but the *nature* of God. This I affirm, from the infirmities of human understanding, to be altogether incomprehensible and unknown to us. The essence of that supreme Mind, his attributes, the manner of his existence, the very nature of his duration—these and every particular which regards so divine a Being are mysterious to men. Finite, weak, and blind creatures, we ought to humble ourselves in his august presence, and, conscious of our frailties, adore in silence his infinite perfections which eye hath not seen, ear hath not heard, neither hath it entered into the heart of man to conceive. They are covered in a deep cloud from human curiosity; it is profaneness to attempt penetrating through these sacred obscurities, and, next to the impiety of denying his existence, is the temerity of prying into his nature and essence, decrees and attributes.

But lest you should think that my *piety* has here got the better of my *philosophy*, I shall support my opinion, if it needs any support, by a very great authority. I might cite all the divines, almost from the foundation of Christianity, who have ever treated of this or any other theological subject; but I shall confine myself, at present, to one equally celebrated for piety and philosophy. It is Father Malebranche who, I remember, thus expresses himself.[1] "One ought not so much," says he, "to call God a spirit in order to express positively what he is, as in order to signify that he is not matter. He is a Being infinitely perfect—of this we cannot doubt. But in the same manner as we ought not to imagine, even supposing him corporeal, that he is clothed with a human body, as the anthropomorphites asserted, under colour that that figure was the most perfect of any, so neither ought we to imagine that the spirit of God has human ideas or bears any resemblance to our spirit, under colour that we know nothing more perfect than a human mind. We ought rather to believe that as he comprehends the perfections of matter without being material . . . he comprehends also the perfections of created spirits without being spirit, in the manner we conceive spirit: that his true name is *He that is,* or, in other words, Being without restriction, All Being, the Being infinite and universal."

After so great an authority, Demea, replied Philo, as that which you have produced, and a thousand more which you might produce, it would appear ridiculous in me to add my sentiment or ex-

**First published in 1779.*

press my approbation of your doctrine. But surely, where reasonable men treat these subjects, the question can never be concerning the *being* but only the *nature* of the Deity. The former truth, as you well observe, is unquestionable and self-evident. Nothing exists without a cause; and the original cause of this universe (whatever it be) we call God, and piously ascribe to him every species of perfection. Whoever scruples this fundamental truth deserves every punishment which can be inflicted among philosophers, to wit, the greatest ridicule, contempt, and disapprobation. But as all perfection is entirely relative, we ought never to imagine that we comprehend the attributes of this divine Being, or to suppose that his perfections have any analogy or likeness to the perfections of a human creature. Wisdom, thought, design, knowledge—these we justly ascribe to him because these words are honourable among men, and we have no other language or other conceptions by which we can express our adoration of him. But let us beware lest we think that our ideas anywise correspond to his perfections, or that his attributes have any resemblance to these qualities among men. He is infinitely superior to our limited view and comprehension, and is more the object of worship in the temple than of disputation in the schools.

In reality, Cleanthes, continued he, there is no need of having recourse to that affected scepticism so displeasing to you in order to come at this determination. Our ideas reach no further than our experience. We have no experience of divine attributes and operations. I need not conclude my syllogism, you can draw the inference yourself. And it is a pleasure to me (and I hope to you, too) that just reasoning and sound piety here concur in the same conclusion, and both of them establish the adorably mysterious and incomprehensible nature of the Supreme Being.

Not to lose any time in circumlocutions, said Cleanthes, addressing himself to Demea, much less in replying to the pious declamations of Philo, I shall briefly explain how I conceive this matter. Look round the world, contemplate the whole and every part of it: you will find it to be nothing but one great machine, subdivided into an infinite number of lesser machines, which again admit of subdivisions to a degree beyond what human senses and faculties can trace and explain. All these various machines, and even their most minute parts, are adjusted to each other with an accuracy which ravishes into admiration all men who have ever contemplated them. The curious adapting of means to ends, throughout all nature, resembles exactly, though it much exceeds, the productions of human contrivance—of human design, thought, wisdom, and intelligence. Since therefore the effects resemble each other, we are led to infer, by all the rules of analogy, that the causes also resemble, and that the Author of nature is somewhat similar to the mind of man, though possessed of much larger faculties, proportioned to the grandeur of the work which he has executed. By this argument *a posteriori,* and by this argument alone, do we prove at once the existence of a Deity and his similarity to human mind and intelligence.

I shall be so free, Cleanthes, said Demea, as to tell you that from the beginning I could not approve of your conclusion concerning the similarity of the Deity to men, still less can I approve of the mediums by which you endeavour to establish it. What! No demonstration of the Being of God! No abstract arguments! No proofs *a priori!* Are these which have hitherto been so much insisted on by philosophers all fallacy, all sophism? Can we reach no farther in this subject than experience and probability? I will not say that this is betraying the cause of a Deity; but surely, by this affected candour, you give advantages to atheists which they never could obtain by the mere dint of argument and reasoning.

What I chiefly scruple in this subject, said Philo, is not so much that all religious arguments are by Cleanthes reduced to experience, as that they appear not to be even the most certain and irrefragable of that inferior kind. That a stone will fall, that fire will burn, that the earth has solidity, we have observed a thousand and a thousand times; and when any new instance of this nature is presented, we draw without hesitation the accustomed inference. The exact similarity of the cases gives us a perfect assurance of a similar event, and a stronger evidence is never desired nor sought after. But wherever you depart, in the least, from the similarity of the cases, you diminish proportionably the evidence, and may at last bring it to a very weak *analogy*, which is confessedly liable to error and uncertainty. After having experienced the circulation of the blood in human creatures, we make no doubt that it takes place in Titius and Maevius; but from its circulation in frogs and fishes it is only a presumption, though a strong one, from analogy that it takes place in men and other animals. The analogical reasoning is much weaker when we infer the circulation of the sap in vegetables from our experience that the blood circulates in animals; and those who hastily followed that imperfect analogy are found, by more accurate experiments, to have been mistaken.

If we see a house, Cleanthes, we conclude, with the greatest certainty, that it had an architect or builder because this is precisely that species of effect which we have experienced to proceed from that species of cause. But surely you will not affirm that the universe bears such a resemblance to a house that we can with the same certainty infer a similar cause, or that the analogy is here entire and perfect. The dissimilitude is so striking that the utmost you can here pretend to is a guess, conjecture, a presumption concerning a similar cause; and how that pretension will be received in the world, I leave you to consider.

It would surely be very ill received, replied Cleanthes; and I should be deservedly blamed and detested did I allow that the proofs of Deity amounted to no more than a guess or conjecture. But is the whole adjustment of means to ends in a house and in the universe so slight a resemblance? the economy of final causes? the order, proportion, and arrangement of every part? Steps of a stair are plainly contrived that human legs may use them in mounting; and this inference is certain and infallible. Human legs are also contrived for walking and mounting; and this inference, I allow, is not altogether so certain because of the dissimilarity which you remark; but does it, therefore, deserve the name only of presumption or conjecture?

Good God! cried Demea, interrupting him, where are we? Zealous defenders of religion allow that the proofs of a Deity fall short of perfect evidence! And you, Philo, on whose assistance I depended in proving the adorable mysteriousness of the Divine Nature, do you assent to all these extravagant opinions of Cleanthes? For what other name can I give them? or, why spare my censure when such principles are advanced, supported by such an authority, before so young a man as Pamphilus?

You seem not to apprehend, replied Philo, that I argue with Cleanthes in his own way, and, by showing him the dangerous consequences of his tenets, hope at last to reduce him to our opinion. But what sticks most with you, I observe, is the representation which Cleanthes has made of the argument *a posteriori;* and, finding that the argument is likely to escape your hold and vanish into air, you think it so disguised that you can scarcely believe it to be set in its true light. Now, however much I may dissent, in other respects, from the dangerous principle of Cleanthes, I must allow that he has fairly represented that argument, and I shall endeavour so to state the matter to you that you will entertain no further scruples with regard to it.

Were a man to abstract from everything which he knows or has seen, he would be altogether incapable, merely from his own ideas, to determine what kind of scene the universe must be, or to give the preference to one state or situation of things above another. For as nothing which he clearly conceives could be esteemed impossible or implying a contradiction, every chimera of his fancy would be upon an equal footing; nor could he assign any just reason why he adheres to one idea or system, and rejects the others which are equally possible.

Again, after he opens his eyes and contemplates the world as it really is, it would be impossible for him at first to assign the cause of any one event, much less of the whole of things, or of the universe. He might set his fancy a rambling, and she might bring him in an infinite variety of reports and representations. These would all be possible, but, being all equally possible, he would never of himself give a satisfactory account for his preferring one of them to the rest. Experience alone can point out to him the true cause of any phenomenon.

Now, according to this method of reasoning, Demea, it follows (and is, indeed, tacitly allowed by Cleanthes himself) that order, arrangement, or the adjustment of final causes, is not of itself any proof of design, but only so far as it has been experienced to proceed from that principle. For aught we can know *a priori,* matter may contain the source or spring of order originally within itself, as well as mind does; and there is no more difficulty in conceiving that the several elements, from an internal unknown cause, may fall into the most exquisite arrangement, than to conceive that their ideas, in the great universal mind, from a like internal unknown cause, fall into that arrangement. The equal possibility of both these suppositions is allowed. But, by experience, we find (according to Cleanthes) that there is a difference between them. Throw several pieces of steel together, without shape or form, they will never arrange themselves so as to compose a watch. Stone and mortar and wood, without an architect, never erect a house. But the ideas in a human mind, we see, by an unknown, inexplicable economy, arrange themselves so as to form the plan of a watch or house. Experience, therefore, proves that there is an original principle of order in mind, not in matter. From similar effects we infer similar causes. The adjustment of means to ends is alike in the universe, as in a machine of human contrivance. The causes, therefore, must be resembling.

I was from the beginning scandalized, I must own, with this resemblance which is asserted between the Deity and human creatures, and must conceive it to imply such a degradation of the Supreme Being as no sound theist could endure. With your assistance, therefore, Demea, I shall endeavour to defend what you justly call the adorable mysteriousness of the Divine Nature, and shall refute this reasoning of Cleanthes, provided he allows that I have made a fair representation of it.

When Cleanthes had assented, Philo, after a short pause, proceeded in the following manner.

That all inferences, Cleanthes, concerning fact are founded on experience, and that all experimental reasonings are founded on the supposition that similar causes prove similar effects, and similar effects similar causes, I shall not at present much dispute with you. But observe, I entreat you, with what extreme caution all just reasoners proceed in the transferring of experiments to similar cases. Unless the cases be exactly similar, they repose no perfect confidence in applying their past observation to any particular phenomenon. Every alteration of circumstances occasions a doubt concerning the event; and it requires new experiments to prove certainly that the new circumstances are of no moment or importance. A change in bulk, situation, arrangement, age, disposition of the air, or surrounding bodies—any of these particulars may be attended with the most unexpected consequences. And unless the objects be quite familiar to us, it is the highest temerity to expect with assurance, after any of these changes, an event similar to that which before fell under our observation. The slow and deliberate steps of philosophers here, if anywhere, are distinguished from the precipitate march of the vulgar, who, hurried on by the smallest similitude, are incapable of all discernment or consideration.

But can you think, Cleanthes, that your usual phlegm and philosophy have been preserved in so wide a step as you have taken when you compared to the universe houses, ships, furniture, machines, and, from their similarity in some circumstances, inferred a similarity in their causes? Thought, design, intelligence, such as we discover in men and other animals, is no more than one of the springs and principles of the universe, as well as heat or cold, attraction or repulsion, and a hundred others which fall under daily observation. It is an active cause by which some particular parts of nature, we find, produce alterations on other parts. But can a conclusion, with any propriety, be transferred from parts to the whole? Does not the great disproportion bar all comparison and inference? From observing the growth of a hair, can we learn anything concerning the generation of a man? Would the manner of a leaf's blowing, even though perfectly known, afford us any instruction concerning the vegetation of a tree?

But allowing that we were to take the *operations* of one part of nature upon another for the foundation of our judgment concerning the *origin* of the whole (which never can be admitted), yet why select so minute, so weak, so bounded a principle as the reason and design of animals is found to be upon this planet? What peculiar privilege has this little agitation of the brain which we call *thought,* that we must thus make it the model of the whole universe? Our partiality in our own favour does indeed present it on all occasions, but sound philosophy ought carefully to guard against so natural an illusion.

So far from admitting, continued Philo, that the operations of a part can afford us any just conclusion concerning the origin of the whole, I will not allow any one part to form a rule for another part if the latter be very remote from the former. Is there any reasonable ground to conclude that the inhabitants of other planets possess thought, intelligence, reason, or anything similar to these faculties in men? When nature has so extremely diversified her manner of operation in this small globe, can we imagine that she incessantly copies herself throughout so immense a universe? And if thought, as we may well suppose, be confined merely to this narrow corner and has even there so limited a sphere of action, with what propriety can we assign it for the original cause of all things? The narrow views of a peasant who makes his domestic economy the rule for the government of kingdoms is in comparison a pardonable sophism.

But were we ever so much assured that a thought and reason resembling the human were to be found throughout the whole universe, and were its activity elsewhere vastly greater and more commanding than it appears in this globe, yet I cannot see why the operations of a world constituted, arranged, adjusted, can with any propriety be extended to a world which is in its embryo state, and is advancing towards that constitution and arrangement. By observation we know somewhat of the economy, action, and nourishment of a finished animal, but we must transfer with great caution that observation to the growth of a foetus in the womb, and still more to the formation of an animalcule in the loins of its male parent. Nature, we find, even from our limited experience, possesses an infinite number of springs and principles which incessantly discover themselves on every change of her position and situation. And what new and unknown principles would actuate her in so new and unknown a situation as that of the formation of a universe, we cannot, without the utmost temerity, pretend to determine.

A very small part of this great system, during a very short time, is very imperfectly discovered to us; and do we thence pronounce decisively concerning the origin of the whole?

Admirable conclusion! Stone, wood, brick, iron, brass, have not, at this time, in this minute globe of earth, an order or arrangement without human art and contrivance; therefore, the universe could not originally attain its order and arrangement without something similar to human art. But is a part of nature a rule for another part very wide of the former? Is it a rule for the whole? Is a very small part a rule for the universe? Is nature in one situation a certain rule for nature in another situation vastly different from the former?

And can you blame me, Cleanthes, if I here imitate the prudent reserve of Simonides, who, according to the noted story, being asked by Hiero, *What God was?* desired a day to think of it, and then two days more; and after that manner continually prolonged the term, without ever bringing in his definition or description? Could you even blame me if I had answered, at first, *that I did not know,* and was sensible that this subject lay vastly beyond the reach of my faculties? You might cry out sceptic and raillier, as much as you pleased; but, having found in so many other subjects much more familiar the imperfections and even contradictions of human reason, I never should expect any success from its feeble conjectures in a subject so sublime and so remote from the sphere of our observation. When two *species* of objects have always been observed to be conjoined together, I can *infer,* by custom, the existence of one wherever I *see* the existence of the other; and this I call an argument from experience. But how this argument can have place where the objects, as in the present case, are single, individual, without parallel or specific resemblance, may be difficult to explain. And will any man tell me with a serious countenance that an orderly universe must arise from some thought and art like the human because we have experience of it? To ascertain this reasoning it were requisite that we had experience of the origin of worlds; and it is not sufficient, surely, that we have seen ships and cities arise from human art and contrivance.

Philo was proceeding in this vehement manner, somewhat between jest and earnest, as it appeared to me, when he observed some signs of impatience in Cleanthes, and then immediately stopped short. What I had to suggest, said Cleanthes, is only that you would not abuse terms, or make use of popular expressions to subvert philosophical reasonings. You know that the vulgar often distinguish reason from experience, even where the question relates only to matter of fact and existence, though it is found, where that *reason* is properly analyzed, that it is nothing but a species of experience. To prove by experience the origin of the universe from mind is not more contrary to common speech than to prove the motion of the earth from the same principle. And a caviller might raise all the same objections to the Copernican system which you have urged against my reasonings. Have you other earths, might he say, which you have seen to move? Have . . .

Yes! cried Philo, interrupting him, we have other earths. Is not the moon another earth, which we see to turn around its centre? Is not Venus another earth, where we observe the same phenomenon? Are not the revolutions of the sun also a confirmation, from analogy, of the same theory? All the planets, are they not earths which revolve about the sun? Are not the satellites moons which move round Jupiter and Saturn, and along with these primary planets round the sun? These analogies and resemblances, with others which I have not mentioned, are the sole proofs of the Copernican system; and to you it belongs to consider whether you have any analogies of the same kind to support your theory.

In reality, Cleanthes, continued he, the modern system of astronomy is now so much received by all inquirers, and has become so essential a part even of our earliest education, that we are not commonly very scrupulous in examining the reasons upon which it is founded. It is now become a matter of mere curiosity to study the first writers of that subject who had the full force of prejudice to encounter, and were obliged to turn their arguments on every side in order to render them popular and convincing. But if we peruse Galileo's famous *Dialogues* concerning the system of the world, we shall find that that great genius, one of the sublimest that ever existed, first bent all his endeavours to prove that there was no foundation for the distinction commonly made between elementary and celestial substances. The schools, proceeding from the illusions of sense, had carried this distinction very far; and had established the latter substances to be ingenerable, incorruptible, unalterable, impassible; and had assigned all the opposite qualities to the former. But Galileo, beginning with the moon, proved its similarity in every particular to the earth: its convex figure, its natural darkness when not illuminated, its density, its distinction into solid and liquid, the variations of its phases, the mutual illuminations of the earth and moon, their mutual eclipses, the inequalities of the lunar surface, etc. After many instances of this kind, with regard to all the planets, men plainly saw that these bodies became proper objects of experience, and that the similarity of their nature enabled us to extend the same arguments and phenomena from one to the other.

In this cautious proceeding of the astronomers you may read your own condemnation, Cleanthes, or rather may see that the subject in which you are engaged exceeds all human reason and inquiry. Can you pretend to show any such similarity between the fabric of a house and the generation of a universe? Have you ever seen nature in any such situation as resembles the first arrangement of the elements? Have worlds ever been formed under your eye, and have you had leisure to observe the whole progress of the phenomenon, from the first appearance of order to its final consummation? If you have, then cite your experience and deliver your theory.

PART III

How the most absurd argument, replied Cleanthes, in the hands of a man of ingenuity and invention, may acquire an air of probability! Are you not aware, Philo, that it became necessary for Copernicus and his first disciples to prove the similarity of the terrestrial and celestial matter because several philosophers, blinded by old systems and supported by some sensible appearances, had denied this similarity? But that it is by no means necessary that theists should prove the similarity of the works of *nature* to those of *art* because this similarity is self-evident and undeniable? The same matter, a like form; what more is requisite to show an analogy between their causes, and to ascertain the origin of all things from a divine purpose and intention? Your objections, I must freely tell you, are no better than the abstruse cavils of those philosophers who denied motion, and ought to be refuted in the same manner—by illustrations, examples, and instances rather than by serious argument and philosophy.

Suppose, therefore, that an articulate voice were heard in the clouds, much louder and more melodious than any which human art could ever reach; suppose that this voice were extended in the same instant over all nations and spoke to each nation in its own language and dialect; suppose that the words delivered not only contain a just sense and meaning, but convey some instruction altogether worthy of a benevolent Being superior to mankind—could you possibly hesitate a moment concerning the cause of this voice, and must you not instantly ascribe it to some design or purpose? Yet I cannot see but all the same objections (if they merit that appellation) which lie against the system of theism may also be produced against this inference.

Might you not say that all conclusions concerning fact were founded on experience; that, when we hear an articulate voice in the dark and thence infer a man, it is only the resemblance of the effects which leads us to conclude that there is a like resemblance in the cause; but that this extraordinary voice, by its loudness, extent, and flexibility to all languages, bears so little analogy to any human voice that we have no reason to suppose any analogy in their causes; and, consequently, that a rational, wise, coherent speech proceeded, you know not whence, from some accidental whistling of the winds, not from any divine reason or intelligence? You see clearly your own objections in these cavils, and I hope too you see clearly that they cannot possibly have more force in the one case than in the other.

But to bring the case still nearer the present one of the universe, I shall make two suppositions which imply not any absurdity or impossibility. Suppose that there is a natural, universal, invariable language, common to every individual of the human race, and that books are natural productions which perpetuate themselves in the same manner with animals and vegetables, by descent and propagation. Several expressions of our passions contain a universal language: all brute animals have a natural speech, which, however limited, is very intelligible to their own species. And as there are infinitely fewer parts and less contrivance in the finest composition of eloquence than in the coarsest organized body, the propagation of an *Iliad* or *Aeneid* is an easier supposition than that of any plant or animal.

Suppose, therefore, that you enter into your library thus peopled by natural volumes containing the most refined reason and most exquisite beauty; could you possibly open one of them and doubt that its original cause bore the strongest analogy to mind and intelligence? When it reasons and discourses; when it expostulates, argues, and enforces its views and topics; when it applies sometimes to the pure intellect, sometimes to the affections; when it collects, disposes, and adorns every consideration suited to the subject; could you persist in asserting that all this, at the bottom, had really no meaning, and that the first formation of this volume in the loins of its original parent proceeded not from thought and design? Your obstinacy, I know, reaches not that degree of firmness; even your sceptical play and wantonness would be abashed at so glaring an absurdity.

But if there be any difference, Philo, between this supposed case and the real one of the universe, it is all to the advantage of the latter. The anatomy of an animal affords many stronger instances of design than the perusal of Livy or Tacitus; and any objection which you start in the former case, by carrying me back to so unusual and extraordinary a scene as the first formation of worlds, the same objection has place on the supposition of our vegetating library. Choose, then, your party, Philo, without ambiguity or evasion; assert either that a rational volume is no proof of a rational cause or admit of a similar cause to all the works of nature.

Let me here observe, too, continued Cleanthes, that this religious argument, instead of being weakened by that scepticism so much affected by you, rather acquires force from it and becomes more firm and undisputed. To exclude all argument or reasoning of every kind is either affectation or madness. The declared profession of every reasonable sceptic is only to reject abstruse, remote, and refined arguments; to adhere to common sense and the plain instincts of nature; and to assent, wherever any reasons strike him with so full a force that he cannot, without the greatest violence, prevent it. Now the arguments for natural religion are plainly of this kind; and nothing but the most perverse, obstinate metaphysics can reject them. Consider, anatomize the eye, survey its structure and contrivance, and tell me, from your own feeling, if the idea of a contriver does not immediately flow in upon you with a force like that of sensation. The most obvious conclusion, surely, is in favour of design; and it requires time, reflection, and study, to summon up those frivolous though abstruse objections which can support infidelity. Who can behold the male and female of each species, the correspondence of their parts and instincts, their passions and whole course of life before and after generation, but must be sensible that the propagation of the species is intended by nature? Millions and millions of such instances present themselves through every part of the universe, and no language can convey a more intelligible irresistible meaning than the curious adjustment of final causes. To what degree, therefore, of blind dogmatism must one have attained to reject such natural and such convincing arguments?

Some beauties in writing we may meet with which seem contrary to rules, and which gain the affections and animate the imagination in opposition to all the precepts of criticism and to the authority of the established masters of art. And if the argument for theism be, as you pretend, contradictory to the principles of logic, its universal, its irresistible influence proves clearly that there may be arguments of a like irregular nature. Whatever cavils may be urged, an orderly world, as well as a coherent, articulate speech, will still be received as an incontestable proof of design and intention.

It sometimes happens, I own, that the religious arguments have not their due influence on an ignorant savage and barbarian, not because they are obscure and difficult, but because he never asks himself any question with regard to them. Whence arises the curious structure of an animal? From the copulation of its parents. And these whence? From *their* parents? A few removes set the objects at such a distance that to him they are lost in darkness and confusion; nor is he actuated by any curiosity to trace them farther. But this is neither dogmatism nor scepticism, but stupidity: a state of mind very different from your sifting, inquisitive disposition, my ingenious friend. You can trace causes from effects; you can compare the most distant and remote objects; and your greatest errors proceed not from barrenness of thought and invention, but from too luxuriant a fertility which suppresses your natural good sense by a profusion of unnecessary scruples and objections.

Here I could observe, Hermippus, that Philo was a little embarrassed and confounded; but, while he hesitated in delivering an answer, luckily for him, Demea broke in upon the discourse and saved his countenance.

Your instance, Cleanthes, said he, drawn from books and language, being familiar, has, I confess, so much more force on that account; but is there not some danger, too, in this very circumstance, and may it not render us presumptuous, by making us imagine we comprehend the Deity and have some adequate idea of his nature and attributes? When I read a volume, I enter into the mind and intention of the author; I become him, in a manner, for the instant, and have an immediate feeling and conception of those ideas which revolved in his imagination while employed in that composition. But so near an approach we never surely can make to the Deity. His ways are not our ways, his attributes are perfect but incomprehensible. And this volume of nature contains a great and inexplicable riddle, more than any intelligible discourse or reasoning.

The ancient Platonists, you know, were the most religious and devout of all the pagan philosophers, yet many of them, particularly Plotinus, expressly declare that intellect or understanding is not to be ascribed to the Deity, and that our most perfect worship of him consists, not in acts of veneration, reverence, gratitude, or love, but in a certain mysterious self-annihilation or total extinction of all our faculties. These ideas are, perhaps, too far stretched, but still it must be acknowledged that, by representing the Deity as so intelligible and comprehensible, and so similar to a human mind, we are guilty of the grossest and most narrow partiality, and make ourselves the model of the whole universe.

All the *sentiments* of the human mind, gratitude, resentment, love, friendship, approbation, blame, pity, emulation, envy, have a plain reference to the state and situation of man, and are calculated for preserving the existence and promoting the activity of such a being in such circumstances. It seems, therefore, unreasonable to transfer such sentiments to a supreme existence or to suppose him actuated by them; and the phenomena, besides, of the universe will not support us in such a theory. All our *ideas* derived from the senses are confessedly false and illusive, and cannot therefore be supposed to have place in a supreme intelligence. And as the ideas of internal sentiment, added to those of the external senses, composed the whole furniture of human understanding, we may conclude that none of the *materials* of thought are in any respect similar in the human and in the divine intelligence. Now, as to the *manner* of thinking, how can we make any comparison between them or suppose them anywise resembling? Our thought is fluctuating, uncertain, fleeting, successive, and compounded; and were we to remove these circumstances, we absolutely annihilate its essence, and it would in such a case be an abuse of terms to apply to it the name of thought or reason. At least, if it appear more pious and respectful (as it really is) still to retain these terms when we mention the Supreme Being, we ought to acknowledge that their meaning, in that case, is totally incomprehensible, and that the infirmities of our nature do not permit us to reach any ideas which in the least correspond to the ineffable sublimity of the Divine attributes.

PART IV

It seems strange to me, said Cleanthes, that you, Demea, who are so sincere in the cause of religion, should still maintain the mysterious, incomprehensible nature of the Deity, and should insist so strenuously that he has no manner of likeness or resemblance to human creatures. The Deity, I can readily allow, possesses many powers and attributes of which we can have no comprehension; but, if our ideas, so far as they go, be not just and adequate and correspondent to his real nature, I know not what there is in this subject worth insisting on. Is the name, without any meaning, of such mighty importance? Or how do you mystics, who maintain the absolute incomprehensibility of the Deity, differ from sceptics or atheists, who assert that the first cause of all is unknown and unintelligible? Their temerity must be very great if, after rejecting the production by a mind—I mean a mind resembling the human (for I know of no other)—they pretend to assign, with certainty, any other specific intelligible cause; and their conscience must be very scrupulous, indeed, if they refuse to call the universal unknown cause a God or Deity, and to bestow on him as many sublime eulogies and unmeaning epithets as you shall please to require of them.

Who could imagine, replied Demea, that Cleanthes, the calm philosophical Cleanthes, would attempt to refute his antagonists by affixing a nickname to them, and, like the common bigots and inquisitors of the age, have recourse to invective and declamation instead of reasoning? Or does he not perceive that these topics are easily retorted, and that *anthropomorphite* is an appellation as invidious, and implies as dangerous consequences, as the epithet of *mystic* with which he has honoured us? In reality, Cleanthes, consider what it is you assert when you represent the Deity as similar to the human mind and understanding. What is the soul of man? A composition of various faculties, passions, sentiments, ideas—united, indeed, into one self or person, but still distinct from each other. When it reasons, the ideas which are the parts of its discourse arrange themselves in a certain form or order which is not preserved entire for a moment, immediately gives place to another arrangement. New opinions, new passions, new affections, new feelings arise which continually diversify the mental scene and produce in it the greatest variety and most rapid succession imaginable. How is this compatible with that perfect immutability and simplicity which all true theists ascribe to the Deity? By the same act, say they, he sees past, present, and future; his love and hatred, his mercy and justice, are one individual operation; he is entire in every point of space, and complete in every instant of duration. No succession, no change, no acquisition, no diminution. What he is implies not in it any shadow of distinction or diversity. And what he is this moment he ever has been and ever will be, without any new judgment, sentiment, or operation. He stands fixed in one simple, perfect state; nor can you ever say, with any propriety, that this act of his is different from that other, or that this judgment or idea has been lately formed and will give place, by succession, to any different judgment or idea.

I can readily allow, said Cleanthes, that those who maintain the perfect simplicity of the Supreme Being, to the extent in which you have explained it, are complete mystics, and chargeable with all the consequences which I have drawn from their opinion. They are, in a word, atheists, without knowing it. For though it be allowed that the Deity possesses attributes of which we have no comprehension, yet ought we never to ascribe to him any attributes which are absolutely incompatible with that intelligent nature essential to him. A mind whose acts and sentiments and ideas are not distinct and successive, one that is wholly simple and totally immutable, is a mind which has no thought, no reason, no will, no sentiment, no love, no hatred; or, in a word, is no mind at all. It is an abuse of terms to give it that appellation, and we may as well speak of limited extension without figure, or of number without composition.

Pray consider, said Philo, whom you are at present inveighing against. You are honouring with the appellation of *atheist* all the sound, orthodox divines, almost, who have treated of this subject; and you will at last be, yourself, found, according to your reckoning, the only sound theist in the world. But if idolaters be atheists, as, I think, may justly be asserted, and Christian theologians the same, what becomes of the argument, so much celebrated, derived from the universal consent of mankind?

But, because I know you are not much swayed by names and authorities, I shall endeavor to show you, a little more distinctly, the inconveniences of that anthropomorphism which you have embraced, and shall prove that there is no ground to suppose a plan of the world to be formed in the Divine mind, consisting of distinct ideas, differently arranged, in the same manner as an architect forms in his head the plan of a house which he intends to execute.

It is not easy, I own, to see what is gained by this supposition, whether we judge of the matter by *reason* or by *experience*. We are still obliged to mount higher in order to find the cause of this cause which you had assigned as satisfactory and conclusive.

If *reason* (I mean abstract reason derived from inquiries *a priori*) be not alike mute with regard to all questions concerning cause and effect, this sentence at least it will venture to pronounce: that a mental world or universe of ideas requires a cause as much as does a material world or universe of objects, and, if similar in its arrangement, must require a similar cause. For what is there in this subject which should occasion a different conclusion or inference? In an abstract view, they are entirely alike; and no difficulty attends the one supposition which is not common to both of them.

Again, when we will needs force *experience* to pronounce some sentence, even on these subjects which lie beyond her sphere, neither can she perceive any material difference in this particular between those two kinds of worlds, but finds them to be governed by similar principles, and to depend upon an equal variety of causes in their operations. We have specimens in miniature of both of them. Our own mind resembles the one; a vegetable or animal body the other. Let experience, therefore, judge from these samples. Nothing seems more delicate, with regard to its causes, than thought; and as these causes never operate in two persons after the same manner, so we never find two persons who think exactly alike. Nor indeed does the same person think exactly alike at any two different periods of time. A difference of age, of the disposition of his body, of weather, of food, of company, of books, of passions—any of these particulars, or others more minute, are sufficient to alter the curious machinery of thought and communicate to it very different movements and operations. As far as we can judge, vegetables and animal bodies are not more delicate in their motions, nor depend upon a greater variety or more curious adjustment of springs and principles.

How, therefore, shall we satisfy ourselves concerning the cause of that Being whom you suppose the Author of nature, or, according to your system of anthropomorphism, the ideal world into which you trace the material? Have we not the same reason to trace that ideal world into another ideal world or new intelligent principle? But if we stop and go no farther, why go so far? Why not stop at the material world? How can we satisfy ourselves without going on *in infinitum?* And, after all, what satisfaction is there in that infinite progression? Let us remember the story of the Indian philosopher and his elephant. It was never more applicable than to the present subject. If the material world rests upon a similar ideal world, this ideal world must rest upon some other, and so on without end. It were better, therefore, never to look beyond the present material world. By supposing it to contain the principle of its order within itself, we really assert it to be God: and the sooner we arrive at that Divine Being, so much the better. When you go one step beyond the mundane system, you only excite an inquisitive humour which it is impossible ever to satisfy.

To say that the different ideas which compose the reason of the Supreme Being fall into order of themselves and by their own nature is really to talk without any precise meaning. If it has a meaning, I would fain know why it is not as good sense to say that the parts of the material world fall into order of themselves and by their own nature. Can the one opinion be intelligible, while the other is not so?

We have, indeed, experience of ideas which fall into order of themselves and without any *known* cause. But, I am sure, we have a much larger experience of matter which does the same, as in all instances of generation and vegetation where the accurate analysis of the cause exceeds all human comprehension. We have also experience of particular systems of thought and of matter which have no order; of the first in madness, of the second in corruption. Why, then, should we think that order is more essential to one than the other? And if it requires a cause in both, what do we gain by your system, in tracing the universe of objects into a similar universe of ideas? The first step which we make leads us on for ever. It were, therefore, wise in us to limit all our inquiries to the present world, without looking farther. No satisfaction can ever be attained by these speculations which so far exceed the narrow bounds of human understanding.

It was usual with the Peripatetics, you know, Cleanthes, when the cause of any phenomenon was demanded, to have recourse to their *faculties* or *occult qualities,* and to say, for instance, that bread nourished by its nutritive faculty, and senna purged by its purgative. But it has been discovered that this subterfuge was nothing but the disguise of ignorance, and that these philosophers, though less ingenuous, really said the same thing with the sceptics or the vulgar who fairly confessed that they knew not the cause of these phenomena. In like manner, when it is asked, what cause produced order in the ideas of the Supreme Being, can any other reason be assigned by you, anthropomorphites, than that it is a *rational* faculty, and that such is the nature of the Deity? But why a similar answer will not be equally satisfactory in accounting for the order of the world, without having recourse to any such intelligent creator as you insist on, may be difficult to determine. It is only to say that *such* is the nature of material objects, and that they are all originally possessed of a *faculty* of order and proportion. These are only more learned and elaborate ways of confessing our ignorance; nor has the one hypothesis any real advantage above the other, except in its greater conformity to vulgar prejudices.

You have displayed this argument with great emphasis, replied Cleanthes: You seem not sensible how easy it is to answer it. Even in common life, if I assign a cause for any event, is it any objection, Philo, that I cannot assign the cause of that cause, and answer every new question which may incessantly be started? And what philosophers could possibly submit to so rigid a rule?—philosophers who confess ultimate causes to be totally unknown, and are sensible that the most refined principles into which they trace the phenomena are still to them as inexplicable as these phenomena themselves are to the vulgar. The order and arrangement of nature, the curious adjustment of final causes, the plain use and intention of every part and organ—all these bespeak in the clearest language an intelligent cause or author. The heavens and the earth join in the same testimony: The whole chorus of nature raises one hymn to the praises of its Creator. You alone, or almost alone, disturb this general harmony. You start abstruse doubts, cavils, and objections; you ask me what is the cause of this cause? I know not; I care not; that concerns not me. I have found a Deity; and here I stop my inquiry. Let those go farther who are wiser or more enterprising.

I pretend to be neither, replied Philo; and for that very reason I should never, perhaps, have attempted to go so far, especially when I am sensible that I must at last be contented to sit down with the same answer which, without further trouble, might have satisfied me from the beginning. If I am still to remain in utter ignorance of causes and can absolutely give an explication of nothing, I shall never esteem it any advantage to shove off for a moment a difficulty which you acknowledge must immediately, in its full force, recur upon me. Naturalists indeed very justly explain particular effects by more general causes, though these general causes themselves should remain in the totally inexplicable, but they never surely thought it satisfactory to explain a particular effect by a particular cause which was no more to be accounted for than the effect itself. An ideal system, arranged of itself, without a precedent design, is not a whit more explicable than a material one which attains its order in a like manner; nor is there any more difficulty in the latter supposition than in the former.

PART V

But to show you still more inconveniences, continued Philo, in your anthropomorphism, please to take a new survey of your principles. *Like effects prove like causes.* This is the experimental argument; and this, you say too, is the sole theological argument. Now it is certain that the liker the effects are which are seen and the liker the causes which are inferred, the stronger is the argument. Every departure on either side diminishes the probability and renders the experiment less conclusive. You cannot doubt of the principle; neither ought you to reject its consequences.

All the new discoveries in astronomy which prove the immense grandeur and magnificence of the works of nature are so many additional arguments for a Deity, according to the true system of theism; but, according to your hypothesis of experimental theism, they become so many objections, by removing the effect still farther from all resemblance to the effects of human art and contrivance. For if Lucretius, even following the old system of the world, could exclaim:

> Quis regere immensi summam, quis habere profundi
> Indu manu validas potis est moderanter habenas?
> Quis pariter coelos omnes convertere? et omnes
> Ignibus aetheriis terras suffire feraces?
> Omnibus inque locis esse omni tempore praesto?[2]
> [The English translation is in the end note.]

If Tully [Cicero] esteemed this reasoning so natural as to put it into the mouth of his Epicurean:

> Quibus enim oculis animi intueri potuit vester Plato fabricam illam tanti operis, qua construi a Deo atque aedificari mundum facit? quae molitio? quae ferramenta? qui vectes? quae machinae? qui ministri tanti muneris fuerunt? quemadmodum autem obedire et parere voluntati architecti aer, ignis, aqua, terra potuerunt?[3]
> [The English translation is in the end note.]

If this argument, I say, had any force in former ages, how much greater must it have at present when the bounds of Nature are so infinitely enlarged and such a magnificent scene is opened to us? It is still more unreasonable to form our idea of so unlimited a cause from our experience of the narrow productions of human design and invention.

The discoveries by microscopes, as they open a new universe in miniature, are still objections, according to you, arguments, according to me. The further we push our researches of this kind, we are still led to infer the universal cause of all to be vastly different from mankind, or from any object of human experience and observation.

And what say you to the discoveries in anatomy, chemistry, botany? . . . These surely are no objections, replied Cleanthes; they only discover new instances of art and contrivance, it is still the image of mind reflected on us from innumerable objects. Add a mind *like the human,* said Philo. I know of no other, replied Cleanthes. And the liker, the better, insisted Philo. To be sure, said Cleanthes.

Now, Cleanthes, said Philo, with an air of alacrity and triumph, mark the consequences. *First,* by this method of reasoning you renounce all claim to infinity in any of the attributes of the Deity. For, as the cause ought only to be proportioned to the effect, and the effect, so far as it falls under our cognizance, is not infinite, what pretensions have we, upon your suppositions, to ascribe that attribute to the Divine Being? You will still insist that, by removing him so much from all similarity to human creatures, we give in to the most arbitrary hypothesis, and at the same time weaken all proofs of his existence.

Secondly, you have no reason, on your theory, for ascribing perfection to the Deity, even in his finite capacity, or for supposing him free from every error, mistake, or incoherence, in his undertakings. There are many inexplicable difficulties in the works of nature which, if we allow a perfect author to be proved *a priori,* are easily solved, and become only seeming difficulties from the narrow capacity of man, who cannot trace infinite relations. But according to your method of reasoning, these difficulties become all real, and, perhaps, will be insisted on as new instances of likeness to human art and contrivance. At least, you must acknowledge that it is impossible for us to tell, from our limited views, whether this system contains any great faults or deserves any considerable praise if compared to other possible and even real systems. Could a peasant, if the *Aeneid* were read to him, pronounce that poem to be absolutely faultless, or even assign to it its proper rank among the productions of human wit, he who had never seen any other production?

But were this world ever so perfect a production, it must still remain uncertain whether all the excellences of the work can justly be ascribed to the workman. If we survey a ship, what an exalted idea must we form of the ingenuity of the carpenter who framed so complicated, useful, and beautiful a machine? And what surprise must we feel when we find him a stupid mechanic who imitated others, and copied an art which, through a long succession of ages, after multiplied trials, mistakes, corrections, deliberations, and controversies, had been gradually improving? Many worlds might have been botched and bungled, throughout an eternity, ere this system was struck out; much labour lost, many fruitless trials made, and a slow but continued improvement carried on during infinite ages in the art of world-making. In such subjects, who can determine where the truth, nay, who can conjecture where the probability lies, amidst a great number of hypotheses which may be proposed, and a still greater which may be imagined?

And what shadow of an argument, continued Philo, can you produce from your hypothesis to prove the unity of the Deity? A great number of men join in building a house or ship, in rearing a city, in framing a commonwealth; why may not several deities combine in contriving and framing a world? This is only so much greater similarity to human affairs. By sharing the work among several, we may so much further limit the attributes of each, and get rid of that extensive power and knowledge which must be supposed in one deity, and which, according to you, can only serve to weaken the proof of his existence. And if such foolish, such vicious creatures as man can yet often unite in framing and executing one plan, how much more those deities or demons, whom we may suppose several degrees more perfect!

To multiply causes without necessity is indeed contrary to true philosophy, but this principle applies not to the present case. Were one deity antecedently proved by your theory who were possessed of every attribute requisite to the production of the universe, it would be needless, I own (though not absurd) to suppose any other deity existent. But while it is still a question whether all these attributes are united in one subject or dispersed among several independent beings, by what phenomena in nature can we pretend to decide the controversy? Where we see a body raised in a scale, we are sure that there is in the opposite scale, however concealed from sight, some counterpoising weight equal to it; but it is still allowed to doubt whether that weight be an aggregate of several distinct bodies or one uniform united mass. And if the weight requisite very much exceeds anything which we have ever seen conjoined in any single body, the former supposition becomes still more probable and natural. An intelligent being of such vast power and capacity as is necessary to produce the universe, or, to speak in the language of ancient philosophy, so prodigious an animal exceeds all analogy and even comprehension.

But further, Cleanthes: Men are mortal, and renew their species by generation; and this is common to all living creatures. The two great sexes of male and female, says Milton, animate the world. Why must this circumstance, so universal, so essential, be excluded from those numerous and limited deities? Behold, then, the theogeny of ancient times brought back upon us.

And why not become a perfect anthropomorphite? Why not assert the deity or deities to be corporeal, and to have eyes, a nose, mouth, ears, etc.? Epicurus maintained that no man had ever seen reason but in a human figure; therefore, the gods must have a human figure. And this argument, which is deservedly so much ridiculed by Cicero, becomes, according to you, solid and philosophical.

In a word, Cleanthes, a man who follows your hypothesis is able, perhaps, to assert or conjecture that the universe sometime arose from something like design; but beyond that position he cannot ascertain one single circumstance, and is left afterwards to fix every point of his theology by the utmost license of fancy and hypothesis. This world, for aught he knows, is very faulty and imperfect, compared to a superior standard, and was only the first rude essay of some infant deity who afterwards abandoned it, ashamed of his lame performance; it is the work only of some dependent, inferior deity, and is the object of derision to his superiors; it is the production of old age and dotage in some superannuated deity, and ever since his death has run on at adventures, from the first impulse and active force which it received from him. You justly give signs of horror, Demea, at these strange suppositions; but these, and a thousand more of the same kind, are Cleanthes' suppositions, not mine. From the moment the attributes of the Deity are supposed finite, all these have place. And I cannot, for my part, think that so wild and unsettled a system of theology is, in any respect, preferable to none at all.

These suppositions I absolutely disown, cried Cleanthes: they strike me, however, with no horror, especially when proposed in that rambling way in which they drop from you. On the contrary, they give me pleasure when I see that, by the utmost indulgence of your imagination, you never get rid of the hypothesis of design in the universe, but are obliged at every turn to have recourse to it. To this concession I adhere steadily; and this I regard as a sufficient foundation for religion.

PART VI

It must be a slight fabric, indeed, said Demea, which can be erected on so tottering a foundation. While we are uncertain whether there is one deity or many, whether the deity or deities, to whom we owe our existence, be perfect or imperfect, subordinate or supreme, dead or alive, what trust or confidence can we repose in them? What devotion or worship address to them? What veneration or obedience pay them? To all the purposes of life the theory of religion becomes altogether useless; and even with regard to speculative consequences its uncertainty, according to you, must render it totally precarious and unsatisfactory.

To render it still more unsatisfactory, said Philo, there occurs to me another hypothesis which must acquire an air of probability from the method of reasoning so much insisted on by Cleanthes. That like effects arise from like causes—this principle he supposes the foundation of all religion. But there is another principle of the same kind, no less certain and derived from the same source of experience, that, where several known circumstances are observed to be similar, the unknown will also be found similar. Thus, if we see the limbs of a human body, we conclude that it is also attended with a human head, though hid from us. Thus, if we see, through a chink in a wall, a small part of the sun, we conclude that were the wall removed we should see the whole body. In short, this method of reasoning is so obvious and familiar that no scruple can ever be made with regard to its solidity.

Now, if we survey the universe, so far as it falls under our knowledge, it bears a great resemblance to an animal or organized body, and seems actuated with a like principle of life and motion. A continual circulation of matter in it produces no disorder; a continual waste in every part is incessantly repaired; the closest sympathy is perceived throughout the entire system; and each part or member, in performing its proper offices, operates both to its own preservation and to that of the whole. The world, therefore, I infer, is an animal; and the Deity is the *soul* of the world, actuating it, and actuated by it.

You have too much learning, Cleanthes, to be at all surprised at this opinion which, you know, was maintained by almost all the theists of antiquity, and chiefly prevails in their discourses and reasonings. For though, sometimes, the ancient philosophers reason from final causes, as if they thought the world the workmanship of God, yet it appears rather their favourite notion to consider it as his body whose organization renders it subservient to him. And it must be confessed that, as the universe resembles more a human body than it does the works of human art and contrivance, if our limited analogy could ever, with any propriety, be extended to the whole of nature, the inference seems juster in favour of the ancient than the modern theory.

There are many other advantages, too, in the former theory which recommended it to the ancient theologians. Nothing more repugnant to all their notions because nothing more repugnant to common experience than mind without body, a mere spiritual substance which fell not under their senses nor comprehension, and of which they had not observed one single instance throughout all nature. Mind and body they knew because they felt both; an order, arrangement, organization, or internal machinery, in both they likewise knew, after the same manner; and it could not but seem reasonable to transfer this experience to the universe, and to suppose the divine mind and body to be also coeval and to have, both of them, order and arrangement naturally inherent in them and inseparable from them.

Here, therefore, is a new species of *anthropomorphism,* Cleanthes, on which you may deliberate, and a theory which seems not liable to any considerable difficulties. You are too much superior, surely, to *systematical prejudices* to find any more difficulty in supposing an animal body to be, originally, of itself or from unknown causes, possessed of order and organization, than in supposing a similar order to belong to mind. But the *vulgar prejudice* that body and mind ought always to accompany each other ought not, one should think, to be entirely neglected; since it is founded on *vulgar experience,* the only guide which you profess to follow in all these theological inquiries. And if you assert that our limited experience is an unequal standard by which to judge of the unlimited extent of nature, you entirely abandon your own hypothesis, and must thenceforward adopt our mysticism, as you call it, and admit of the absolute incomprehensibility of the Divine Nature.

This theory, I own, replied Cleanthes, has never before occurred to me, though a pretty natural one; and I cannot readily, upon so short an examination and reflection, deliver any opinion with regard to it. You are very scrupulous, indeed, said Philo. Were I to examine any system of yours, I should not have acted with half that caution and reserve in stating objections and difficulties to it. However, if anything occur to you, you will oblige us by proposing it.

Why then, replied Cleanthes, it seems to me that, though the world does, in many circumstances, resemble an animal body, yet is the analogy also defective in many circumstances the most material: no organs of sense; no seat of thought or reason; no one precise origin of motion and action. In short, it seems to bear a stronger resemblance to a vegetable than to an animal, and your inference would be so far inconclusive in favour of the soul of the world.

But, in the next place, your theory seems to imply the eternity of the world; and that is a principle which, I think, can be refuted by the strongest reasons and probabilities. I shall suggest an argument to this purpose which, I believe, has not been insisted on by any writer. Those who reason from the late origin of arts and sciences, though their inference wants not force, may perhaps be refuted by considerations derived from the nature of human society, which is in continual revolution between ignorance and knowledge, liberty and slavery, riches and poverty; so that it is impossible for us, from our limited experience, to foretell with assurance what events may or may not be expected. Ancient learning and history seem to have been in great danger of entirely perishing after the inundation of the barbarous nations; and had these convulsions continued a little longer or been a little more violent, we should not probably have now known what passed in the world a few centuries before us. Nay, were it not for the superstition of the popes, who preserved a little jargon of Latin in order to support the appearance of an ancient and universal church, that tongue must have been utterly lost; in which case the Western world, being totally barbarous, would not have been in a fit disposition for receiving the Greek language and learning, which was conveyed to them after the sacking of Constantinople. When learning and books had been extinguished, even the mechanical arts would have fallen considerably to decay; and it is easily imagined that fable or tradition might ascribe to them a much later origin than the true one. This vulgar argument, therefore, against the eternity of the world seems a little precarious.

But here appears to be the foundation of a better argument. Lucullus was the first that brought cherry-trees from Asia to Europe, though that tree thrives so well in many European climates that it grows in the woods without any culture. Is it possible that, throughout a whole eternity, no European had ever passed into Asia and thought of transplanting so delicious a fruit into his own country? Or if the tree was once transplanted and propagated, how could it ever afterwards perish? Empires may rise and fall, liberty and slavery succeed alternately, ignorance and knowledge give place to each other; but the cherry-tree will still remain in the woods of Greece, Spain, and Italy, and will never be affected by the revolutions of human society.

It is not two thousand years since vines were transplanted into France, though there is no climate in the world more favourable to them. It is not three centuries since horses, cows, sheep, swine, dogs, corn, were known in America. Is it possible that during the revolutions of a whole eternity there never arose a Columbus who might open the communication between Europe and that continent? We may as well imagine that all men would wear stockings for ten thousand years, and never have the sense to think of garters to tie them. All these seem convincing proofs of the youth or rather infancy of the world, as being founded on the operation of principles more constant and steady than those by which human society is governed and directed. Nothing less than a total convulsion of the elements will ever destroy all the European animals and vegetables which are now to be found in the Western world.

And what argument have you against such convulsions? replied Philo. Strong and almost incontestable proofs may be traced over the whole earth that every part of this globe has continued for many ages entirely covered with water. And though order were supposed inseparable from matter, and inherent in it, yet may matter be susceptible of many and great revolutions, through the endless periods of eternal duration. The incessant changes to which every part of it is subject seem to intimate some such general transformations; though, at the same time, it is observable that all the changes and corruptions of which we have ever had experience are but passages from one state of order to another; nor can matter ever rest in total deformity and confusion. What we see in the parts, we may infer in the whole; at least, that is the method of reasoning on which you rest your whole theory. And were I obliged to defend any particular system of this nature, which I never willingly should do, I esteem none more plausible than that which ascribes an eternal inherent principle of order to the world, though attended with great and continual revolutions and alterations. This at once solves all difficulties; and if the solution, by being so general, is not entirely complete and satisfactory, it is at least a theory that we must sooner or later have recourse to, whatever system we embrace. How could things have been as they are, were there not an original inherent principle of order somewhere, in thought or in matter? And it is very indifferent to which of these we give the preference. Chance has no place, on any hypothesis, sceptical or religious. Everything is surely governed by steady, inviolable laws. And were the inmost essence of things laid open to us, we should then discover a scene of which, at present, we can have no idea. Instead of admiring the order of natural beings, we should clearly see that it was absolutely impossible for them, in the smallest article, ever to admit of any other disposition.

Were anyone inclined to revive the ancient pagan theology which maintained, as we learned from Hesiod, that this globe was governed by 30,000 deities, who arose from the unknown powers of nature, you would naturally object. Cleanthes, that nothing is gained by this hypothesis; and that it is as easy to suppose all men animals, beings more numerous but less perfect, to have sprung immediately from a like origin. Push the same inference a step further, and you will find a numerous society of deities as explicable as one universal deity who possesses within himself the powers and perfections of the whole society. All these systems, then, of Scepticism, Polytheism, and Theism, you must allow, on your principles, to be on a like footing, and that no one of them has any advantage over the others. You may thence learn the fallacy of your principles.

PART VII

But here, continued Philo, in examining the ancient system on the soul of the world there strikes me, all of a sudden, a new idea which, if just, must go near to subvert all your reasoning, and destroy even your first inferences on which you repose such confidence. If the universe bears a greater likeness to animal bodies and to vegetables than to the works of human art, it is more probable that its cause resembles the cause of the former than that of the latter, and its origin ought rather to be ascribed to generation or vegetation than to reason or design. Your conclusion, even according to your own principles, is therefore lame and defective.

Pray open up this argument a little further, said Demea, for I do not rightly apprehend it in that concise manner in which you have expressed it.

Our friend Cleanthes, replied Philo, as you have heard, asserts that, since no question of fact can be proved otherwise than by experience, the existence of a Deity admits not of proof from any other medium. The world, says he, resembles the works of human contrivance; therefore its cause must also resemble that of the other. Here we may remark that the operation of one very small part of nature, to wit, man, upon another very small part, to wit, that inanimate matter lying within his reach, is the rule by which Cleanthes judges of the origin of the whole; and he measures objects, so widely disproportioned, by the same individual standard. But to waive all objections drawn from this topic, I affirm that there are other parts of the universe (besides the machines of human invention) which bear still a greater resemblance to the fabric of the world, and which, therefore, afford a better conjecture concerning the universal origin of this system. These parts are animals and vegetables. The world plainly resembles more an animal or a vegetable than it does a watch or a knitting-loom. Its cause, therefore, it is more probable, resembles the cause of the former. The cause of the former is generation or vegetation. The cause, therefore, of the world we may infer to be something similar or analogous to generation or vegetation.

But how is it conceivable, said Demea, that the world can arise from anything similar to vegetation or generation?

Very easily, replied Philo. In like manner as a tree sheds its seed into the neighboring fields and produces other trees, so the great vegetable, the world, or this planetary system, produces within itself certain seeds which, being scattered into the surrounding chaos, vegetate into new worlds. A comet, for instance, is the seed of a world; and after it has been fully ripened, by passing from sun to sun, and star to star, it is, at last, tossed into the unformed elements which everywhere surround this universe, and immediately sprouts up into a new system.

Or if, for the sake of variety (for I see no other advantage), we should suppose this world to be an animal: a comet is the egg of this animal; and in like manner as an ostrich lays its egg in the sand, which, without any further care, hatches the egg and produces a new animal, so . . . I understand you, says Demea. But what wild, arbitrary suppositions are these! What *data* have you for such extraordinary conclusions? And is the slight, imaginary resemblance of the world to a vegetable or an animal sufficient to establish the same inference with regard to both? Objects which are in general so widely different, ought they to be a standard for each other?

Right, cries Philo: This is the topic on which I have all along insisted. I have still asserted that we have no *data* to establish any system of cosmogony. Our experience, so imperfect in itself and so limited both in extent and duration, can afford us no probable conjecture concerning the whole of things. But if we must needs fix on some hypothesis, by what rule, pray, ought we to determine our choice? Is there any other rule than the greater similarity of the objects compared? And does not a plant or an animal, which springs from vegetation or generation, bear a stronger resemblance to the world than does any artificial machine, which arises from reason and design?

But what is this vegetation and generation of which you talk? said Demea. Can you explain their operations, and anatomize that fine internal structure on which they depend?

As much, at least, replied Philo, as Cleanthes can explain the operations of reason, or anatomize that internal structure on which it depends. But without any such elaborate disquisitions, when I see an animal, I infer that it sprang from generation; and that with as great certainty as you conclude a house to have been reared by design. These words *generation, reason* mark only certain powers and energies in nature whose effects are known, but whose essence is incomprehensible; and one of these principles, more than the other, has no privilege for being made a standard to the whole of nature.

In reality, Demea, it may reasonably be expected that the larger the views are which we take of things, the better will they conduct us in our conclusions concerning such extraordinary and such magnificent subjects. In this little corner of the world alone, there are four principles, *reason, instinct, generation, vegetation,* which are similar to each other, and are the causes of similar effects. What a number of other principles may we naturally suppose in the immense extent and variety of the universe could we travel from planet to planet, and from system to system, in order to examine each part of this mighty fabric? Any one of these four principles above mentioned (and a hundred others which lie open to our conjecture) may afford us a theory by which to judge of the origin of the world; and it is a palpable and egregious partiality to confine our view entirely to that principle by which our own minds operate. Were this principle more intelligible on that account, such a partiality might be somewhat excusable; but reason, in its internal fabric and structure, is really as little known to us as instinct or vegetation; and, perhaps, even that vague, undeterminate word *nature,* to which the vulgar refer everything is not at the bottom more inexplicable. The effects of these principles are all known to us from experience; but the principles themselves and their manner of operation are totally unknown; nor is it less intelligible or less conformable to experience to say that the world arose by vegetation, from a seed shed by another world, than to say that it arose from a divine reason or contrivance, according to the sense in which Cleanthes understands it.

But methinks, said Demea, if the world had a vegetative quality and could sow the seeds of new worlds into the infinite chaos, this power would be still an additional argument for design in its author. For whence could arise so wonderful a faculty but from design? Or how can order spring from anything which perceives not that order which it bestows?

You need only look around you, replied Philo, to satisfy yourself with regard to this question. A tree bestows order and organization on that tree which springs from it, without knowing the order; an animal in the same manner on its offspring; a bird on its nest; and instances of this kind are even more frequent in the world than those of order which arise from reason and contrivance. To say that all this order in animals and vegetables proceeds ultimately from design is begging the question; nor can that great point be ascertained otherwise than by proving, *a priori,* both that order is, from its nature, inseparably attached to thought and that it can never of itself or from original unknown principles belong to matter.

But further, Demea, this objection which you urge can never be made use of by Cleanthes, without renouncing a defense which he has already made against one of my objections. When I inquired concerning the cause of that supreme reason and intelligence into which he resolves everything, he told me that the impossibility of satisfying such inquiries could never be admitted as an objection in any species of philosophy. *We must stop somewhere,* says he; *nor is it ever within the reach of human capacity to explain ultimate causes or show the last connections of any objects. It is sufficient if any steps, as far as we go, are supported by experience and observation.* Now that vegetation and generation, as well as reason, are experienced to be principles of order in nature is undeniable. If I rest my system of cosmogony on the former, preferably to the latter, it is at my choice. The matter seems entirely arbitrary. And when Cleanthes asks me what is the cause of my great vegetative or generative faculty, I am equally entitled to ask him the cause of his great reasoning principle. These questions we have agreed to forbear on both sides; and it is chiefly his interest on the present occasion to stick to this agreement. Judging by our limited and imperfect experience, generation has some privileges above reason; for we see every day the latter arise from the former, never the former from the latter.

Compare, I beseech you, the consequences on both sides. The world, say I, resembles an animal; therefore it is an animal, therefore it arose from generation. The steps, I confess, are wide, yet there is some small appearance of analogy in each step. The world, says Cleanthes, resembles a machine; therefore it is a machine, therefore it arose from design. The steps are here equally wide, and the analogy less striking. And if he pretends to carry on *my* hypothesis a step further, and to infer design or reason from the great principle of generation on which I insist, I may, with better authority, use the same freedom to push further *his* hypothesis, and infer a divine generation or theogony from his principle of reason. I have at least some faint shadow of experience, which is the utmost that can ever be attained in the present subject. Reason, in innumerable instances, is observed to arise from the principle of generation, and never to arise from any other principle.

Hesiod and all the ancient mythologists were so struck with this analogy that they universally explained the origin of nature from an animal birth, and copulation. Plato, too, so far as he is intelligible, seems to have adopted some such notion in his *Timaeus*.

The Brahmins assert that the world arose from an infinite spider, who spun this whole complicated mass from his bowels, and annihilates afterwards the whole or any part of it, by absorbing it again and resolving it into his own essence. Here is a species of cosmogony which appears to us ridiculous because a spider is a little contemptible animal whose operations we are never likely to take for a model of the whole universe. But still here is a new species of analogy, even in our globe. And were there a planet wholly inhabited by spiders (which is very possible), this inference would there appear as natural and irrefragable as that which in our planet ascribes the origin of all things to design and intelligence, as explained by Cleanthes. Why an orderly system may not be spun from the belly as well as from the brain, it will be difficult for him to give a satisfactory reason.

I must confess, Philo, replied Cleanthes, that, of all men living, the task which you have undertaken, of raising doubts and objections, suits you best and seems, in a manner, natural and unavoidable to you. So great is your fertility of invention than I am not ashamed to acknowledge myself unable, on a sudden, to solve regularly such out-of-the-way difficulties as you incessantly start upon me, though I clearly see, in general, their fallacy and error. And I question not, but you are yourself, at present, in the same case, and have not the solution so ready as the objection, while you must be sensible that common sense and reason are entirely against you, and that such whimsies as you have delivered may puzzle but never can convince us.

PART VIII

What you ascribe to the fertility of my invention, replied Philo, is entirely owing to the nature of the subject. In subjects adapted to the narrow compass of human reason there is commonly but one determination which carries probability or conviction with it; and to a man of sound judgment all other suppositions but that one appear entirely absurd and chimerical. But in such questions as the present, a hundred contradictory views may preserve a kind of imperfect analogy, and invention has here full scope to exert itself. Without any great effort of thought, I believe that I could, in an instant, propose other systems of cosmogony which would have some faint appearance of truth, though it is a thousand, a million to one if either yours or any one of mine be the true system.

For instance, what if I should revive the old Epicurean hypothesis? This is commonly, and I believe justly, esteemed the most absurd system that has yet been proposed; yet I know not whether, with a few alterations, it might not be brought to bear a faint appearance of probability. Instead of supposing matter infinite, as Epicurus did, let us suppose it finite. A finite number of particles is only susceptible of finite transpositions; and it must happen, in an eternal duration, that every possible order or position must be tried an infinite number of times. This world, therefore, with all its events, even the most minute, has before been produced and destroyed, and will again be produced and destroyed, without any bounds and limitations. No one who has a conception of the powers of infinite, in comparison of finite, will ever scruple this determination.

But this supposes, said Demea, that matter can acquire motion without any voluntary agent or first mover.

And where is the difficulty, replied Philo, of that supposition? Every event, before experience, is equally difficult and incomprehensible; and every event, after experience, is equally easy and intelligible. Motion, in many instances, from gravity, from elasticity, from electricity, begins in matter, without any known voluntary agent; and to suppose always, in these cases, an unknown voluntary agent is mere hypothesis and hypothesis attended with no advantages. The beginning of motion in matter itself is as conceivable *a priori* as its communication from mind and intelligence.

Besides, why may not motion have been propagated by impulse through all eternity, and the same stock of it, or nearly the same, be still upheld in the universe? As much is lost by the composition of motion, as much is gained by its resolution. And whatever the causes are, the fact is certain that matter is and always has been in continual agitation, as far as human experience or tradition reaches. There is not probably, at present, in the whole universe, one particle of matter at absolute rest.

And this very consideration, too, continued Philo, which we have stumbled on in the course of the argument, suggests a new hypothesis of cosmogony that is not absolutely absurd and improbable. Is there a system, an order, an economy of things, by which matter can preserve that perpetual agitation which seems essential to it, and yet maintain a constancy in the forms which it produces? There certainly is such an economy, for this is actually the case with the present world. The continual motion of matter, therefore, in less than infinite transpositions, must produce this economy or order, and by its very nature, that order, when once established, supports itself for many ages if not to eternity. But wherever matter is so poised, arranged, and adjusted, as to continue in perpetual motion, and yet preserve a constancy in the forms, its situation must, of necessity, have all the same appearance of art and contrivance which we observe at present. All the parts of each form must have a relation to each other and to the whole; and the whole itself must have a relation to the other parts of the universe, to the element in which the form subsists, to the materials with which it repairs its waste and decay, and to every other form which is hostile or friendly. A defect in any of these particulars destroys the form, and the matter of which it is composed is again set loose, and is thrown into irregular motions and fermentations till it unite itself to some other regular form. If no such form be prepared to receive it, and if there be a great quantity of this corrupted matter in the universe, the universe itself is entirely disordered, whether it be the feeble embryo of a world in its first beginnings that is thus destroyed or the rotten carcase of one languishing in old age and infirmity. In either case, a chaos ensues till finite though innumerable revolutions produce, at last, some forms whose parts and organs are so adjusted as to support the forms amidst a continued succession of matter.

Suppose (for we shall endeavour to vary the expression) that matter were thrown into any position by a blind, unguided force; it is evident that this first position must, in all probability, be the most confused and most disorderly imaginable, without any resemblance to those works of human contrivance which, along with a symmetry of parts, discover an adjustment of means to ends and a tendency to self-preservation. If the actuating force cease after this operation, matter must remain for ever in disorder and continue an immense chaos, without any proportion or activity. But suppose that the actuating force, whatever it be, still continues in matter, this first position will immediately give place to a second which will likewise, in all probability, be as disorderly as the first, and so on through many successions of changes and revolutions. No particular order or position ever continues a moment unaltered. The original force, still remaining in activity, gives a perpetual restlessness to matter. Every possible situation is produced and instantly destroyed. If a glimpse or dawn of order appears for a moment, it is instantly hurried away and confounded by that never-ceasing force which actuates every part of matter.

Thus the universe goes on for many ages in a continued succession of chaos and disorder. But is it not possible that it may settle at last, so as not to lose its motion and active force (for that we have supposed inherent in it), yet so as to preserve an uniformity of appearance, amidst the continual motion and fluctuation of its parts? This we find to be the case with the universe at present. Every individual is perpetually changing, and every part of every individual; and yet the whole remains, in appearance, the same. May we not hope for such a position or rather be assured of it from the eternal revolutions of unguided matter; and may not this account for all the appearing wisdom and contrivance which is in the universe? Let us contemplate the subject a little, and we shall find that this adjustment if attained by matter of a seeming stability in the forms, with a real and perpetual revolution or motion of parts, affords a plausible, if not a true, solution of the difficulty.

It is in vain, therefore, to insist upon the uses of the parts in animals or vegetables, and their curious adjustment to each other. I would fain know how an animal could subsist unless its parts were so adjusted? Do we not find that it immediately perishes whenever this adjustment ceases, and that its matter, corrupting, tries some new form? It happens indeed that the parts of the world are so well adjusted that some regular form immediately lays claim to this corrupted matter; and if it were not so, could the world subsist? Must it not dissolve, as well as the animal, and pass through new positions and situations till in great but finite succession it fall, at last, into the present or some such order?

It is well, replied Cleanthes, you told us that this hypothesis was suggested on a sudden, in the course of the argument. Had you had leisure to examine it, you would soon have perceived the insuperable objections to which it is exposed. No form, you say, can subsist unless it possess those powers and organs requisite for its subsistence; some new order or economy must be tried, and so on, without intermission, till at last some order which can support and maintain itself is fallen upon. But according to this hypothesis, whence arise the many conveniences and advantages which men and all animals possess? Two eyes, two ears are not absolutely necessary for the subsistence of the species. The human race might have been propagated and preserved without horses, dogs, cows, sheep, and those innumerable fruits and products which serve to our satisfaction and enjoyment. If no camels had been created for the use of man in the sandy deserts of Africa and Arabia, would the world have been dissolved? If no loadstone had been framed to give that wonderful and useful direction to the needle, would human society and the human kind have been immediately extinguished? Though the maxims of nature be in general very frugal, yet instances of this kind are far from being rare; and any one of them is a sufficient proof of design—and of a benevolent design—which gave rise to the order and arrangement of the universe.

At least, you may safely infer, said Philo, that the foregoing hypothesis is so far incomplete and imperfect, which I shall not scruple to allow. But can we ever reasonably expect greater success in any attempts of this nature? Or can we ever hope to erect a system of cosmogony that will be liable to no exceptions, and will contain no circumstance repugnant to our limited and imperfect experience of the analogy of nature? Your theory itself cannot surely pretend to any such advantage, even though you have run into *anthropomorphism*, the better to preserve a conformity to common experience. Let us once more put it to trial. In all instances which we have ever seen, ideas are copied from real objects, and are ectypal, not archetypal, to express myself in learned terms. You reverse this order and give thought the precedence. In all instances which we have ever seen, thought has no influence upon matter except where that matter is so conjoined with it as to have an equal reciprocal influence upon it. No animal can move immediately anything but the members of its own body; and, indeed, the equality of action and reaction seems to be an universal law of nature; but your theory implies a contradiction to this experience. These instances, with many more which it were easy to collect (particularly the supposition of a mind or system of thought that is eternal or, in other words, an animal ingenerable and immortal)—these instances, I say, may teach all of us sobriety in condemning each other, and let us see that as no system of this kind ought ever to be received from a slight analogy, so neither ought any to be rejected on account of a small incongruity. For that is an inconvenience from which we can justly pronounce no one to be exempted.

All religious systems, it is confessed, are subject to great and insuperable difficulties. Each disputant triumphs in his turn, while he carries on an offensive war, and exposes the absurdities, barbarities, and pernicious tenets of his antagonist. But all of them, on the whole, prepare a complete triumph for the *sceptic,* who tells them that no system ought ever to be embraced with regard to such subjects: for this plain reason that no absurdity ought ever to be assented to with regard to any subject. A total suspense of judgment is here our only reasonable resource. And if every attack, as is commonly observed, and no defence among theologians is successful, how complete must be *his* victory who remains always, with all mankind, on the offensive, and has himself no fixed station or abiding city which he is ever, on any occasion, obliged to defend?

PART IX

But if so many difficulties attend the argument *a posteriori,* said Demea, had we not better adhere to that simple and sublime argument *a priori* which, by offering to us infallible demonstration, cuts off at once all doubt and difficulty? By this argument, too, we may prove the *infinity* of the Divine attributes, which, I am afraid, can never be ascertained with certainty from any other topic. For how can an effect which either is finite or, for aught we know, may be so—how can such an effect, I say, prove an infinite cause? The unity, too, of the Divine Nature it is very difficult, if not absolutely impossible, to deduce merely from contemplating the works of nature; nor will the uniformity alone of the plan, even were it allowed, give us any assurance of that attribute. Whereas the argument *a priori*. . . .

You seem to reason, Demea, interposed Cleanthes, as if those advantages and conveniences in the abstract argument were full proofs of its solidity. But it is first proper, in my opinion, to determine what argument of this nature you choose to insist on; and we shall afterwards, from itself, better than from its *useful* consequences, endeavour to determine what value we ought to put upon it.

The argument, replied Demea, which I would insist on is the common one. Whatever exists must have a cause or reason of its existence, it being absolutely impossible for anything to produce itself or be the cause of its own existence. In mounting up, therefore, from effects to causes, we must either go on in tracing an infinite succession, without any ultimate cause at all, or must at last have recourse to some ultimate cause that is *necessarily* existent. Now that the first supposition is absurd may be thus proved. In the infinite chain or succession of causes and effects, each single effect is determined to exist by the power and efficacy of that cause which immediately preceded; but the whole eternal chain or succession, taken together, is not determined or caused by anything, and yet it is evident that it requires a cause or reason, as much as any particular object which begins to exist in time. The question is still reasonable why this particular succession of causes existed from eternity, and not any other succession or no succession at all. If there be no necessarily existent being, any supposition which can be formed is equally possible; nor is there any more absurdity in *nothing's* having existed from eternity than there is in that succession of causes which constitutes the universe. What was it, then, which determined *something* to exist rather than *nothing,* and bestowed being on a particular possibility, exclusive of the rest? *External causes,* there are supposed to be none. *Chance* is a word without a meaning. Was it *nothing*? But that can never produce anything. We must, therefore, have recourse to a necessarily existent Being who carries the *reason* of his existence in himself, and who cannot be supposed not to exist, without an express contradiction. There is, consequently, such a Being—that is, there is a Deity.

I shall not leave it to Philo, said Cleanthes, though I know that the starting objections is his chief delight, to point out the weakness of this metaphysical reasoning. It seems to me so obviously ill-grounded, and at the same time of so little consequence to the cause of true piety and religion, that I shall myself venture to show the fallacy of it.

I shall begin with observing that there is an evident absurdity in pretending to demonstrate a matter of fact, or to prove it by arguments *a priori.* Nothing is demonstrable unless the contrary implies a contradiction. Nothing that is distinctly conceivable implies a contradiction. Whatever we conceive as existent, we can also conceive as non-existent. There is no being, therefore, whose non-existence implies a contradiction. Consequently there is no being whose existence is demonstrable. I propose this argument as entirely decisive, and am willing to rest the whole controversy upon it.

It is pretended that the Deity is a necessarily existent being; and this necessity of his existence is attempted to be explained by asserting that, if we knew his whole essence or nature, we should perceive it to be as impossible for him not to exist, as for twice two not to be four. But it is evident that this can never happen, while our faculties remain the same as at present. It will still be possible for us, at any time, to conceive the nonexistence of what we formerly conceived to exist; nor can the mind ever lie under a necessity of supposing any object to remain always in being; in the same manner as we lie under a necessity of always conceiving twice two to be four. The words, therefore, *necessary existence* have no meaning or, which is the same thing, none that is consistent.

But further, why may not the material universe be the necessarily existent Being, according to this pretended explication of necessity? We dare not affirm that we know all the qualities of matter; and, for aught we can determine, it may contain some qualities which, were they known, would make its non-existence appear as great a contradiction as that twice two is five. I find only one argument employed to prove that the material world is not the necessarily existent Being; and this argument is derived from the contingency both of the matter and the form of the world. "Any particle of matter," it is said, "may be *conceived* to be annihilated, and any form may be *conceived* to be altered. Such an annihilation or alteration, therefore, is not impossible."[4] But it seems a great partiality not to perceive that the same argument extends equally to the Deity, so far as we have any conception of him, and that the mind can at least imagine him to be nonexistent or his attributes to be altered. It must be some unknown, inconceivable qualities which can make his non-existence appear impossible or his attributes unalterable; and no reason can be assigned why these qualities may not belong to matter. As they are altogether unknown and inconceivable, they can never be proved incompatible with it.

Add to this that in tracing an eternal succession of objects it seems absurd to inquire for a general cause or first author. How can anything that exists from eternity have a cause, since that relation implies a priority in time and a beginning of existence?

In such a chain, too, or succession of objects, each part is caused by that which preceded it, and causes that which succeeds it. Where then is the difficulty? But the *whole,* you say, wants a cause. I answer that the uniting of these parts into a whole, like the uniting of several distinct countries into one kingdom, or several distinct members into one body is performed merely by an arbitrary act of the mind, and has no influence on the nature of things. Did I show you the particular causes of each individual in a collection of twenty particles of matter, I should think it very unreasonable should you afterwards ask me what was the cause of the whole twenty. This is sufficiently explained in explaining the cause of the parts.

Though the reasonings which you have urged, Cleanthes, may well excuse me, said Philo, from starting any further difficulties, yet I cannot forbear insisting still upon another topic. It is observed by arithmeticians that the products of 9 compose always either 9 or some lesser product of 9 if you add together all the characters of which any of the former products is composed. Thus, of 18, 27, 36, which are products of 9, you make 9 by adding 1 to 8, 2 to 7, 3 to 6. Thus 369 is a product also of 9; and if you add 3, 6, and 9, you make 18, a lesser product of 9.[5] To a superficial observer so wonderful a regularity may be admired as the effect either of chance or design; but a skillful algebraist immediately concludes it to be the work of necessity, and demonstrates that it must for ever result from the nature of these numbers. Is it not probable, I ask, that the whole economy of the universe is conducted by a like necessity, though no human algebra can furnish a key which solves the difficulty? And instead of admiring the order of natural beings, may it not happen that, could we penetrate into the intimate nature of bodies, we should clearly see why it was absolutely impossible they could ever admit of any other disposition? So dangerous is it to introduce this idea of necessity into the present question! and so naturally does it afford an inference directly opposite to the religious hypothesis!

But dropping all these abstractions, continued Philo, and confining ourselves to more familiar topics, I shall venture to add an observation that the argument *a priori* has seldom been found very convincing, except to people of a metaphysical head who have accustomed themselves to abstract reasoning, and who, finding from mathematics that the understanding frequently leads to truth through obscurity, and contrary to first appearances, have transferred the same habit of thinking to subjects where it ought not to have place. Other people, even of good sense and the best inclined to religion, feel always some deficiency in such arguments, though they are not perhaps able to explain distinctly where it lies—a certain proof that men ever did and ever will derive their religion from other sources than from this species of reasoning.

PART X

It is my opinion, I own, replied Demea, that each man feels, in a manner, the truth of religion within his own breast, and, from a consciousness of his imbecility and misery rather than from any reasoning, is led to seek protection from that Being on whom he and all nature is dependent. So anxious or so tedious are even the best scenes of life that futurity is still the object of all our hopes and fears. We incessantly look forward and endeavour, by prayers, adoration, and sacrifice, to appease those unknown powers whom we find, by experience, so able to afflict and oppress us. Wretched creatures that we are! What resource for us amidst the innumerable ills of life did not religion suggest some methods of atonement, and appease those terrors with which we are incessantly agitated and tormented?

I am indeed persuaded, said Philo, that the best and indeed the only method of bringing everyone to a due sense of religion is by just representations of the misery and wickedness of men. And for that purpose a talent of eloquence and strong imagery is more requisite than that of reasoning and argument. For is it necessary to prove what everyone feels within himself? It is only necessary to make us feel it, if possible, more intimately and sensibly.

The people, indeed, replied Demea, are sufficiently convinced of this great and melancholy truth. The miseries of life, the unhappiness of man, the general corruptions of our nature, the unsatisfactory enjoyment of pleasures, riches, honours—these phrases have become almost proverbial in all languages. And who can doubt of what all men declare from their own immediate feeling and experience?

In this point, said Philo, the learned are perfectly agreed with the vulgar; and in all letters, *sacred* and *profane,* the topic of human misery has been insisted on with the most pathetic eloquence that sorrow and melancholy could inspire. The poets, who speak from sentiment, without a system, and whose testimony has therefore the more authority, abound in images of this nature. From Homer down to Dr. Young, the whole inspired tribe have ever been sensible that no other representation of things would suit the feeling and observation of each individual.

As to authorities, replied Demea, you need not seek them. Look round this library of Cleanthes. I shall venture to affirm that, except authors of particular sciences, such as chemistry or botany, who have no occasion to treat of human life, there is scarce one of those innumerable writers from whom the sense of human misery has not, in some passage or other, extorted a complaint and confession of it. At least, the chance is entirely on that side; and no one author has ever, so far as I can recollect, been so extravagant as to deny it.

There you must excuse me, said Philo: Leibniz has denied it, and is perhaps the first[6] who ventured upon so bold and paradoxical an opinion; at least, the first who made it essential to his philosophical system.

And by being the first, replied Demea, might he not have been sensible of his error? For is this a subject in which philosophers can propose to make discoveries especially in so late an age? And can any man hope by a simple denial (for the subject scarcely admits of reasoning) to bear down the united testimony of mankind, founded on sense and consciousness?

And why should man, added he, pretend to an exemption from the lot of all other animals? The whole earth, believe me, Philo, is cursed and polluted. A perpetual war is kindled amongst all living creatures. Necessity, hunger, want stimulate the strong and courageous; fear, anxiety, terror agitate the weak and infirm. The first entrance into life gives anguish to the new-born infant and to its wretched parent; weakness, impotence, distress attend each stage of that life, and it is, at last finished in agony and horror.

Observe, too, says Philo, the curious artifices of nature in order to embitter the life of every living being. The stronger prey upon the weaker and keep them in perpetual terror and anxiety. The weaker, too, in their turn, often prey upon the stronger, and vex and molest them without relaxation. Consider that innumerable race of insects, which either are bred on the body of each animal or, flying about, infix their stings in him. These insects have others still less than themselves which torment them. And thus on each hand, before and behind, above and below, every animal is surrounded with enemies which incessantly seek his misery and destruction.

Man alone, said Demea, seems to be, in part, an exception to this rule. For by combination in society he can easily master lions, tigers, and bears, whose greater strength and agility naturally enable them to prey upon him.

On the contrary, it is here chiefly, cried Philo, that the uniform and equal maxims of nature are most apparent. Man, it is true, can, by combination, surmount all his *real* enemies and become master of the whole animal creation; but does he not immediately raise up to himself *imaginary* enemies, the demons of his fancy, who haunt him with superstitious terrors and blast every enjoyment of life? His pleasure, as he imagines, becomes in their eyes a crime; his food and repose give them umbrage and offence; his very sleep and dreams furnish new materials to anxious fear; and even death, his refuge from every other ill, presents only the dread of endless and innumerable woes. Nor does the wolf molest more the timid flock than superstition does the anxious breast of wretched mortals.

Besides, consider, Demea: This very society by which we surmount those wild beasts, our natural enemies, what new enemies does it not raise to us? What woe and misery does it not occasion? Man is the greatest enemy of man. Oppression, injustice, contempt, contumely, violence, sedition, war, calumny, treachery, fraud—by these they mutually torment each other, and they would soon dissolve that society which they had formed were it not for the dread of still greater ills which must attend their separation.

But though these external insults, said Demea, from animals, from men, from all the elements, which assault us from a frightful catalogue of woes, they are nothing in comparison of those which arise within ourselves, from the distempered condition of our mind and body. How many lie under the lingering torment of diseases? Hear the pathetic enumeration of the great poet.

> Intestine stone and ulcer, colic-pangs,
> Demoniac frenzy, moping melancholy,
> And moon-struck madness, pining atrophy
> Marasmus, and wide-wasting pestilence.
> Dire was the tossing, deep the groans: *Despair*
> Tended the sick, busiest from couch to couch
> And over them triumphant *Death* his dart
> Shook: but delay'd to strike, though oft invok'd
> With vows, as their chief good and final hope.[7]

The disorders of the mind, continued Demea, though more secret, are not perhaps less dismal and vexatious. Remorse, shame, anguish, rage, disappointment, anxiety, fear, dejection, despair—who has ever passed through life without cruel inroads from these tormentors? How many have scarcely ever felt any better sensations? Labour and poverty, so abhorred by everyone, are the certain lot of the far greater number; and those few privileged persons who enjoy ease and opulence never reach contentment or true felicity. All the goods of life united would not make a very happy man, but all the ills united would make a wretch indeed; and any one of them almost (and who can be free from every one?), nay, often the absence of one good (and who can possess all?) is sufficient to render life ineligible.

Were a stranger to drop on a sudden into this world, I would show him, as a specimen of its ills, an hospital full of diseases, a prison crowded with malefactors and debtors, a field of battle strewed with carcases, a fleet floundering in the ocean, a nation languishing under tyranny, famine, or pestilence. To turn the gay side of life to him and give him a notion of its pleasures—whither should I conduct him? To a ball, to an opera, to court? He might justly think that I was only showing him a diversity of distress and sorrow.

There is no evading such striking instances, said Philo, but by apologies which still further aggravate the charge. Why have all men, I ask, in all ages, complained incessantly of the miseries of life? . . . They have no just reason, says one: these complaints proceed only from their discontented, repining, anxious disposition. . . . And can there possibly, I reply, be a more certain foundation of misery than such a wretched temper?

But if they were really as unhappy as they pretend, says my antagonist, why do they remain in life? . . .

> Not satisfied with life, afraid of death—

This is the secret chain, say I, that holds us. We are terrified, not bribed to the continuance of our existence.

It is only a false delicacy, he may insist, which a few refined spirits indulge, and which has spread these complaints among the whole race of mankind. . . . And what is this delicacy, I ask, which you blame? Is it anything but a greater sensibility to all the pleasures and pains of life? And if the man of a delicate, refined temper, by being so much more alive than the rest of the world, is only so much more unhappy, what judgment must we form in general of human life?

Let men remain at rest, says our adversary, and they will be easy. They are willing artificers of their own misery. . . . No! reply I: an anxious languor follows their repose; disappointment, vexation, trouble, their activity and ambition.

I can observe something like what you mention in some others, replied Cleanthes, but I confess I feel little or nothing of it in myself, and hope that it is not so common as you represent it.

If you feel not human misery yourself, cried Demea, I congratulate you on so happy a singularity. Others, seemingly the most prosperous, have not been ashamed to vent their complaints in the most melancholy strains. Let us attend to the great, the fortunate emperor, Charles V, when tired with human grandeur, he resigned all his extensive dominions into the hands of his son. In the last harangue which he made on that memorable occasion, he publicly avowed *that the greatest prosperities which he had ever enjoyed had been mixed with so many adversities that he might truly say he had never enjoyed any satisfaction or contentment.* But did the retired life in which he sought for shelter afford him any greater happiness? If we may credit his son's account, his repentance commenced the very day of his resignation.

Cicero's fortune, from small beginnings, rose to the greatest lustre and renown; yet what pathetic complaints of the ills of life do his familiar letters, as well as philosophical discourses, contain? And suitably to his own experience, he introduces Cato, the great, the fortunate Cato protesting in his old age that had he a new life in his offer he would reject the present.

Ask yourself, ask any of your acquaintance, whether they would live over again the last ten or twenty years of their life. No! but the next twenty, they say, will be better:

> And from the dregs of life, hope to receive
> What the first sprightly running could not give.[8]

Thus, at last, they find (such is the greatness of human misery, it reconciles even contradictions) that they complain at once of the shortness of life and of its vanity and sorrow.

And is it possible, Cleanthes, said Philo, that after all these reflections, and infinitely more which might be suggested, you can still persevere in your anthropomorphism, and assert the moral attributes of the Deity, his justice, benevolence, mercy, and rectitude, to be of the same nature with these virtues in human creatures? His power, we allow, is infinite; whatever he wills is executed; but neither man nor any other animal is happy; therefore, he does not will their happiness. His wisdom is infinite; he is never mistaken in choosing the means to any end; but the course of nature tends not to human or animal felicity; therefore, it is not established for that purpose. Through the whole compass of human knowledge there are no inferences more certain and infallible than these. In what respect, then, do his benevolence and mercy resemble the benevolence and mercy of men?

Epicurus' old questions are yet unanswered.

Is he willing to prevent evil, but not able? then is he impotent. Is he able, but not willing? then is he malevolent. Is he both able and willing? whence then is evil?

You ascribe, Cleanthes (and I believe justly), a purpose and intention to nature. But what, I beseech you, is the object of that curious artifice and machinery which she has displayed in all animals—the preservation alone of individuals, and propagation of the species? It seems enough for her purpose, if such a rank be barely upheld in the universe, without any care or concern for the happiness of the members that compose it. No resource for this purpose: no machinery in order merely to give pleasure or ease; no fund of pure joy and contentment; no indulgence without some want or necessity accompanying it. At least, the few phenomena of this nature are over-balanced by opposite phenomena of still greater importance.

Our sense of music, harmony, and indeed beauty of all kinds, gives satisfaction, without being absolutely necessary to the preservation and propagation of the species. But what racking pains, on the other hand, arise from gouts, gravels, megrims, toothaches, rheumatisms, where the injury to the animal machinery is either small or incurable? Mirth, laughter, play, frolic seem gratuitous satisfactions which have no further tendency; spleen, melancholy, discontent, superstition are pains of the same nature. How then does the Divine benevolence display itself, in the sense of you anthropomorphites? None but we mystics, as you were pleased to call us, can account for this strange mixture of phenomena, by deriving it from attributes infinitely perfect but incomprehensible.

And have you, at last, said Cleanthes smiling, betrayed your intentions, Philo? Your long agreement with Demea did indeed a little surprise me, but I find you were all the while erecting a concealed battery against me. And I must confess that you have now fallen upon a subject worthy of your noble spirit of opposition and controversy. If you can make out the present point, and prove mankind to be unhappy or corrupted, there is an end at once of all religion. For to what purpose establish the natural attributes of the Deity, while the moral are still doubtful and uncertain?

You take umbrage very easily, replied Demea, at opinions the most innocent and the most generally received, even amongst the religious and devout themselves; and nothing can be more surprising than to find a topic like this—concerning the wickedness and misery of man—charged with no less than atheism and profaneness. Have not all pious divines and preachers who have indulged their rhetoric on so fertile a subject, have they not easily, I say, given a solution of any difficulties which may attend it? This world is but a point in comparison of the universe; this life but a moment in comparison of eternity. The present evil phenomena, therefore, are rectified in other regions, and in some future period of existence. And the eyes of men, being then opened to larger views of things, see the whole connection of general laws, and trace, with adoration, the benevolence and rectitude of the Deity through all the mazes and intricacies of his providence.

No! replied Cleanthes, no! These arbitrary suppositions can never be admitted, contrary to matter of fact, visible and uncontroverted. Whence can any cause be known but from its known effects? Whence can any hypothesis be proved but from the apparent phenomena? To establish one hypothesis upon another is building entirely in the air; and the utmost we ever attain by these conjectures and fictions is to ascertain the bare possibility of our opinion, but never can we, upon such terms, establish its reality.

The only method of supporting Divine benevolence—and it is what I willingly embrace—is to deny absolutely the misery and wickedness of man. Your representations are exaggerated; your melancholy views mostly fictitious; your inferences contrary to fact and experience. Health is more common than sickness; pleasure than pain; happiness than misery. And for one vexation which we meet with, we attain, upon computation, a hundred enjoyments.

Admitting your position, replied Philo, which yet is extremely doubtful, you must at the same time allow that, if pain be less frequent than pleasure, it is infinitely more violent and durable. One hour of it is often able to outweigh a day, a week, a month of our common insipid enjoyments; and how many days, weeks, and months are passed by several in the most acute torments? Pleasure, scarcely in one instance, is ever able to reach ecstasy and rapture; and in no one instance can it continue for any time at its highest pitch and altitude. The spirits evaporate, the nerves relax, the fabric is disordered, and the enjoyment quickly degenerates into fatigue and uneasiness. But pain often, good God, how often! rises to torture and agony; and the longer it continues, it becomes still more genuine agony and torture. Patience is exhausted, courage languishes, melancholy seizes us, and nothing terminates our misery but the removal of its cause or another event which is the sole cure of all evil, but which, from our natural folly, we regard with still greater horror and consternation.

But not to insist upon these topics, continued Philo, though most obvious, certain, and important, I must use the freedom to admonish you, Cleanthes, that you have put the controversy upon a most dangerous issue, and are unawares introducing a total scepticism into the most essential articles of natural and revealed theology. What! no method of fixing a just foundation for religion unless we allow the happiness of human life, and maintain a continued existence even in this world, with all our present pains, infirmities, vexations, and follies, to be eligible and desirable! But this is contrary to everyone's feeling and experience; it is contrary to an authority so established as nothing can subvert. No decisive proofs can ever be produced against this authority; nor is it possible for you to compute, estimate, and compare all the pains and all the pleasures in the lives of all men and of all animals; and thus, by your resting the whole system of religion on a point which, from its very nature, must for ever be uncertain, you tacitly confess that that system is equally uncertain.

But allowing you what never will be believed, at least, what you never possibly can prove, that animal or, at least, human happiness in this life exceeds its misery, you have yet done nothing; for this is not, by any means, what we expect from infinite power, infinite wisdom, and infinite goodness. Why is there any misery at all in the world? Not by chance, surely. From some cause then. Is it from the intention of the Deity? But he is perfectly benevolent. Is it contrary to his intention? But he is almighty. Nothing can shake the solidity of this reasoning, so short, so clear, so decisive, except we assert that these subjects exceed all human capacity, and that our common measures of truth and falsehood are not applicable to them—a topic which I have all along insisted on, but which you have, from the beginning, rejected with scorn and indignation.

But I will be contented to retire still from this intrenchment, for I deny that you can ever force me in it. I will allow that pain or misery in man is *compatible* with infinite power and goodness in the Deity, even in your sense of these attributes: what are you advanced by all these concessions? A mere possible compatibility is not sufficient. You must *prove* these pure, unmixt, and uncontrollable attributes from the present mixt and confused phenomena, and from these alone. A hopeful undertaking! Were the phenomena ever so pure and unmixt, yet, being finite, they would be insufficient for that purpose. How much more, where they are also so jarring and discordant!

Here, Cleanthes, I find myself at ease in my argument. Here I triumph. Formerly, when we argued concerning the natural attributes of intelligence and design, I needed all my sceptical and metaphysical subtilty to elude your grasp. In many views of the universe and of its parts, particularly the latter, the beauty and fitness of final causes strike us with such irresistible force that all objections appear (what I believe they really are) mere cavils and sophisms; nor can we then imagine how it was ever possible for us to repose any weight on them. But there is no view of human life or of the condition of mankind from which, without the greatest violence, we can infer the moral attributes or learn that infinite benevolence, conjoined with infinite power and infinite wisdom, which we must discover by the eyes of faith alone. It is your turn now to tug the labouring oar, and to support your philosophical subtilties against the dictates of plain reason and experience.

PART XI

I scruple not to allow, said Cleanthes, that I have been apt to suspect the frequent repetition of the word *infinite,* which we meet with in all theological writers, to savour more of panegyric than of philosophy, and that any purposes of reasoning, and even of religion, would be better served were we to rest contented with more accurate and more moderate expressions. The terms *admirable, excellent, superlatively great, wise,* and *holy*—these sufficiently fill the imaginations of men, and anything beyond, besides that it leads into absurdities, has no influence on the affections or sentiments. Thus, in thy present subject, if we abandon all human analogy, as seems your intention, Demea, I am afraid we abandon all religion and retain no conception of the great object of our adoration. If we preserve human analogy, we must forever find it impossible to reconcile any mixture of evil in the universe with infinite attributes; much less can we ever prove the latter from the former. But supposing the Author of nature to be finitely perfect, though far exceeding mankind, a satisfactory account may then be given of natural and moral evil, and every untoward phenomenon be explained and adjusted. A less evil may then be chosen in order to avoid a greater; inconveniences be submitted to in order to reach a desirable end; and, in a word, benevolence, regulated by wisdom and limited by necessity, may produce just such a world as the present. You, Philo, who are so prompt at starting views and reflections and analogies, I would gladly hear, at length, without interruption, your opinion of this new theory; and if it deserve our attention, we may afterwards, at more leisure, reduce it into form.

My sentiments, replied Philo, are not worth being made a mystery of; and, therefore, without any ceremony, I shall deliver what occurs to me with regard to the present subject. It must, I think, be allowed that, if a very limited intelligence whom we shall suppose utterly unacquainted with the universe were assured that it were the production of a very good, wise, and powerful Being, however finite, he would, from his conjectures, form *beforehand* a different notion of it from what we find it to be by experience; nor would he ever imagine, merely from these attributes of the cause of which he is informed, that the effect could be so full of vice and misery and disorder, as it appears in this life. Supposing now that this person were brought into the world, still assured that it was the workmanship of such a sublime and benevolent Being, he might, perhaps, be surprised at the disappointment, but would never retract his former belief if founded on any very solid argument, since such a limited intelligence must be sensible of his own blindness and ignorance, and must allow that there may be many solutions of those phenomena which will for ever escape his comprehension. But supposing, which is the real case with regard to man, that this creature is not antecedently convinced of a supreme intelligence, benevolent, and powerful, but is left to gather such a belief from the appearances of things—this entirely alters the case, nor will he ever find any reason for such a conclusion. He may be fully convinced of the narrow limits of his understanding, but this will not help him in forming an inference concerning the goodness of superior powers, since he must form that inference from what he knows, not from what he is ignorant of. The more you exaggerate his weakness and ignorance, the more diffident you render him, and give him the greater suspicion that such subjects are beyond the reach of his faculties. You are obliged, therefore, to reason with him merely from the known phenomena, and to drop every arbitrary supposition or conjecture.

Did I show you a house or palace where there was not one apartment convenient or agreeable, where the windows, doors, fires, passages, stairs, and the whole economy of the building were the source of noise, confusion, fatigue, darkness, and the extremes of heat and cold, you would certainly blame the contrivance, without any further examination. The architect would in vain display his subtilty, and prove to you that, if this door or that window were altered, greater ills would ensue. What he says may be strictly true: the alteration of one particular, while the other parts of the building remain, may only augment the inconveniences. But still you would assert in general that, if the architect had had skill and good intentions, he might have formed such a plan of the whole, and might have adjusted the parts in such a manner as would have remedied all or most of these inconveniences. His ignorance, or even your own ignorance of such a plan, will never convince you of the impossibility of it. If you find any inconveniences and deformities in the building, you will always, without entering into any detail, condemn the architect.

In short, I repeat the question: Is the world, considered in general and as it appears to us in this life, different from what a man or such a limited being would, *beforehand,* expect from a very powerful, wise, and benevolent Deity? It must be strange prejudice to assert the contrary. And from thence I conclude that, however consistent the world may be, allowing certain suppositions and conjectures with the idea of such a Deity, it can never afford us an inference concerning his existence. The consistency is not absolutely denied, only the inference. Conjectures, especially where infinity is excluded from the Divine attributes, may perhaps be sufficient to prove a consistency, but can never be foundations for any inference.

There seem to be *four* circumstances on which depend all or the greatest part of the ills that molest sensible creatures; and it is not impossible but all these circumstances may be necessary and unavoidable. We know so little beyond common life, or even of common life, that, with regard to the economy of a universe, there is no conjecture, however wild, which may not be just, nor any one, however plausible, which may not be erroneous. All that belongs to human understanding, in this deep ignorance and obscurity, is to be sceptical or at least cautious, and not to admit of any hypothesis whatever, much less of any which is supported by no appearance of probability. Now this I assert to be the case with regard to all the causes of evil and the circumstances on which it depends. None of them appear to human reason in the least degree necessary or unavoidable, nor can we suppose them such, without the utmost license of imagination.

The *first* circumstance which introduces evil is that contrivance or economy of the animal creation by which pains, as well as pleasures, are employed to excite all creatures to action, and make them vigilant in the great work of self-preservation. Now pleasure alone, in its various degrees, seems to human understanding sufficient for this purpose. All animals might be constantly in a state of enjoyment; but when urged by any of the necessities of nature, such as thirst, hunger, weariness, instead of pain, they might feel a diminution of pleasure by which they might be prompted to seek that object which is necessary to their subsistence. Men pursue pleasure as eagerly as they avoid pain; at least, they might have been so constituted. It seems, therefore, plainly possible to carry on the business of life without any pain. Why then is any animal ever rendered susceptible of such a sensation? If animals can be free from it an hour, they might enjoy a perpetual exemption from it, and it required as particular a contrivance of their organs to produce that feeling as to endow them with sight, hearing, or any of the senses. Shall we conjecture that such a contrivance was necessary, without any appearance of reason, and shall we build on that conjecture as on the most certain truth?

But a capacity of pain would not alone produce pain were it not for the *second* circumstance, viz., the conducting of the world by general laws; and this seems nowise necessary to a very perfect Being. It is true, if everything were conducted by particular volitions, the course of nature would be perpetually broken, and no man could employ his reason in the conduct of life. But might not other particular volitions remedy this inconvenience? In short, might not the Deity exterminate all ill, wherever it were to be found, and produce all good, without any preparation or long progress of causes and effects?

Besides, we must consider that, according to the present economy of the world, the course of nature, though supposed exactly regular, yet to us appears not so, and many events are uncertain, and many disappoint our expectations. Health and sickness, calm and tempest, with an infinite number of other accidents whose causes are unknown and variable, have a great influence both on the fortunes of particular persons and on the prosperity of public societies; and indeed all human life, in a manner, depends on such accidents. A being, therefore, who knows the secret springs of the universe might easily, by particular volitions, turn all these accidents to the good of mankind and render the whole world happy, without discovering himself in any operation. A fleet whose purposes were salutary to society might always meet with a fair wind. Good princes enjoy sound health and long life. Persons born to power and authority be framed with good tempers and virtuous dispositions. A few such events as these, regularly and wisely conducted, would change the face of the world, and yet would no more seem to disturb the course of nature or confound human conduct than the present economy of things where the causes are secret and variable and compounded. Some small touches given to Caligula's brain in his infancy might have converted him into a Trajan. One wave, a little higher than the rest, by burying Caesar and his fortune in the bottom of the ocean, might have restored liberty to a considerable part of mankind. There may, for aught we know, be good reasons why Providence interposes not in this manner, but they are unknown to us; and, though the mere supposition that such reasons exist may be sufficient to *save* the conclusion concerning the Divine attributes, yet surely it can never be sufficient to *establish* that conclusion.

If everything in the universe be conducted by general laws, and if animals be rendered susceptible of pain, it scarcely seems possible but some ill must arise in the various shocks of matter and the various concurrence and opposition of general laws; but this ill would be very rare were it not for the *third* circumstance which I proposed to mention, viz., the great frugality with which all powers and faculties are distributed to every particular being. So well adjusted are the organs and capacities of all animals, and so well fitted to their preservation, that, as far as history or tradition reaches, there appears not to be any single species which has yet been extinguished in the universe. Every animal has the requisite endowments, but these endowments are bestowed with so scrupulous an economy that any considerable diminution must entirely destroy the creature. Wherever one power is increased, there is a proportional abatement in the others. Animals which excel in swiftness are commonly defective in force. Those which possess both are either imperfect in some of their senses or are oppressed with the most craving wants. The human species, whose chief excellence is reason and sagacity, is of all others the most necessitous, and the most deficient in bodily advantages, without clothes, without arms, without food, without lodging, without any convenience of life, except what they owe to their own skill and industry. In short, nature seems to have formed an exact calculation of the necessities of her creatures, and, like a *rigid master,* has afforded them little more powers or endowments than what are strictly sufficient to supply those necessities. An *indulgent parent* would have bestowed a large stock in order to guard against accidents, and secure the happiness and welfare of the creature in the most unfortunate concurrence of circumstances. Every course of life would not have been so surrounded with precipices that the least departure from the true path, by mistake or necessity, must involve us in misery and ruin. Some reserve, some fund, would have been provided to ensure happiness, nor would the powers and the necessities have been adjusted with so rigid an economy. The Author of nature is inconceivably powerful; his force is supposed great, if not altogether inexhaustible, nor is there any reason, as far as we can judge, to make him observe this strict frugality in his dealings with his creatures. It would have been better, were his power extremely limited, to have created fewer animals, and to have endowed these with more faculties for their happiness and preservation. A builder is never esteemed prudent who undertakes a plan beyond what his stock will enable him to finish.

In order to cure most of the ills of human life, I require not that man should have the wings of the eagle, the swiftness of the stag, the force of the ox, the arms of the lion, the scales of the crocodile or rhinoceros; much less do I demand the sagacity of an angel or cherubim. I am contented to take an increase in one single power or faculty of his soul. Let him be endowed with a greater propensity to industry and labour, a more vigorous spring and activity of mind, a more constant bent to business and application. Let the whole species possess naturally an equal diligence with that which many individuals are able to attain by habit and reflection, and the most beneficial consequences, without any allay of ill, is the immediate and necessary result of this endowment. Almost all the moral as well as natural evils of human life arise from idleness; and were our species, by the original constitution of their frame, exempt from this vice or infirmity, the perfect cultivation of land, the improvement of arts and manufactures, the exact execution of every office and duty, immediately follow; and men at once may fully reach that state of society which is so imperfectly attained by the best regulated government. But as industry is a power, and the most valuable of any, nature seems determined, suitably to her usual maxims, to bestow it on man with a very sparing hand, and rather to punish him severely for his deficiency in it than to reward him for his attainments. She has so contrived his frame that nothing but the most violent necessity can oblige him to labour; and she employs all his other wants to overcome, at least in part, the want of diligence, and to endow him with some share of a faculty of which she has thought fit naturally to bereave him. Here our demands may be allowed very humble, and therefore the more reasonable. If we required the endowments of superior penetration and judgment, of a more delicate taste of beauty, of a nicer sensibility to benevolence and friendship, we might be told that we impiously pretend to break the order of nature, that we want to exalt ourselves into a higher rank of being, that the presents which we require, not being suitable to our state and condition, would only be pernicious to us. But it is hard, I dare to repeat it, it is hard that, being placed in a world so full of wants and necessities, where almost every being and element is either our foe or refuses its assistance . . . we should also have our own temper to struggle with, and should be deprived of that faculty which can alone fence against these multiplied evils.

The *fourth* circumstance whence arises the misery and ill of the universe is the inaccurate workmanship of all the springs and principles of the great machine of nature. It must be acknowledged that there are few parts of the universe which seem not to serve some purpose, and whose removal would not produce a visible defect and disorder in the whole. The parts hang all together, nor can one be touched without affecting the rest, in a greater or less degree. But at the same time, it must be observed that none of these parts or principles, however useful, are so accurately adjusted as to keep precisely within those bounds in which their utility consists; but they are, all of them, apt, on every occasion, to run into the one extreme or the other. One would imagine that this grand production had not received the last hand of the maker—so little finished is every part, and so coarse are the strokes with which it is executed. Thus the winds are requisite to convey the vapours along the surface of the globe, and to assist men in navigation; but how often, rising up to tempests and hurricanes, do they become pernicious? Rains are necessary to nourish all the plants and animals of the earth; but how often are they defective? how often excessive? Heat is requisite to all life and vegetation, but is not always found in the due proportion. On the mixture and secretion of the humours and juices of the body depend the health and prosperity of the animal; but the parts perform not regularly their proper function. What more useful than all the passions of the mind, ambition, vanity, love, anger? But how often do they break their bounds and cause the greatest convulsions in society? There is nothing so advantageous in the universe but what frequently becomes pernicious, by its excess or defect; nor has nature guarded, with the requisite accuracy, against all disorder or confusion. The irregularity is never perhaps so great as to destroy any species, but is often sufficient to involve the individuals in ruin and misery.

On the concurrence, then, of these *four* circumstances does all or the greatest part of natural evil depend. Were all living creatures incapable of pain, or were the world administered by particular volitions, evil never could have found access into the universe; and were animals endowed with a large stock of powers and faculties, beyond what strict necessity requires, or were the several springs and principles of the universe so accurately framed as to preserve always the just temperament and medium, there must have been very little ill in comparison of what we feel at present. What then shall we pronounce on this occasion? Shall we say that these circumstances are not necessary, and that they might easily have been altered in the contrivance of the universe? This decision seems too presumptuous for creatures so blind and ignorant. Let us be more modest in our conclusions. Let us allow that, if the goodness of the Deity (I mean a goodness like the human) could be established on any tolerable reasons *a priori,* these phenomena, however untoward, would not be sufficient to subvert that principle, but might easily, in some unknown manner, be reconcilable to it. But let us still assert that, as this goodness is not antecedently established but must be inferred from the phenomena, there can be no grounds for such an inference while there are so many ills in the universe, and while these ills might so easily have been remedied, as far as human understanding can be allowed to judge on such a subject. I am sceptic enough to allow that the bad appearances, notwithstanding all my reasonings, may be compatible with such attributes as you suppose, but surely they can never prove these attributes. Such a conclusion cannot result from scepticism, but must arise from the phenomena, and from our confidence in the reasonings which we deduce from these phenomena.

Look round this universe. What an immense profusion of beings, animated and organized, sensible and active! You admire this prodigious variety and fecundity. But inspect a little more narrowly these living existences, the only beings worth regarding. How hostile and destructive to each other! How insufficient all of them for their own happiness! How contemptible or odious to the spectator! The whole presents nothing but the idea of a blind nature, impregnated by a great vivifying principle, and pouring forth from her lap, without discernment or parental care, her maimed and abortive children!

Here the Manichaean system occurs as a proper hypothesis to solve the difficulty; and, no doubt, in some respects it is very specious and has more probability than the common hypothesis, by giving a plausible account of the strange mixture of good and ill which appears in life. But if we consider, on the other hand, the perfect uniformity and agreement of the parts of the universe, we shall not discover in it any marks of the combat of a malevolent with a benevolent being. There is indeed an opposition of pains and pleasures in the feelings of sensible creatures; but are not all the operations of nature carried on by an opposition of principles, of hot and cold, moist and dry, light and heavy? The true conclusion is that the original Source of all things is entirely indifferent to all these principles, and has no more regard to good above ill than to heat above cold, or to drought above moisture, or to light above heavy.

There may *four* hypotheses be framed concerning the first causes of the universe: that they are endowed with perfect goodness; that they have perfect malice; that they are opposite and have both goodness and malice; that they have neither goodness nor malice. Mixed phenomena can never prove the two former unmixed principles; and the uniformity and steadiness of general laws seem to oppose the third. The fourth, therefore, seems by far the most probable.

What I have said concerning natural evil will apply to moral with little or no variation; and we have no more reason to infer that the rectitude of the Supreme Being resembles human rectitude than that his benevolence resembles the human. Nay, it will be thought that we have still greater cause to exclude from him moral sentiments, such as we feel them, since moral evil, in the opinion of many, is much more predominant above moral good than natural evil above natural good.

But even though this should not be allowed, and though the virtue which is in mankind should be acknowledged much superior to the vice, yet, so long as there is any vice at all in the universe, it will very much puzzle you anthropomorphites how to account for it. You must assign a cause for it, without having recourse to the first cause. But as every effect must have a cause, and that cause another, you must either carry on the progression *in infinitum* or rest on that original principle, who is the ultimate cause of all things. . . .

Hold! hold! cried Demea: Whither does your imagination hurry you? I joined in alliance with you in order to prove the incomprehensible nature of the Divine Being, and refute the principles of Cleanthes, who would measure everything by human rule and standard. But I now find you running into all the topics of the greatest libertines and infidels, and betraying that holy cause which you seemingly espoused. Are you secretly, then, a more dangerous enemy than Cleanthes himself?

And are you so late in perceiving it? replied Cleanthes. Believe me, Demea, your friend Philo, from the beginning, has been amusing himself at both our expense; and it must be confessed that the injudicious reasoning of our vulgar theology has given him but too just a handle of ridicule. The total infirmity of human reason, the absolute incomprehensibility of the Divine Nature, the great and universal misery, and still greater wickedness of men—these are strange topics, surely, to be so fondly cherished by orthodox divines and doctors. In ages of stupidity and ignorance, indeed, these principles may safely be espoused; and perhaps no views of things are more proper to promote superstition than such as encourage the blind amazement, the diffidence, and melancholy of mankind. But at present. . . .

Blame not so much, interposed Philo, the ignorance of these reverend gentlemen. They know how to change their style with the times. Formerly, it was a most popular theological topic to maintain that human life was vanity and misery, and to exaggerate all the ills and pains which are incident to men. But of late years, divines, we find, begin to retract this position and maintain, though still with some hesitation, that there are more goods than evils, more pleasures than pains, even in this life. When religion stood entirely upon temper and education, it was thought proper to encourage melancholy, as, indeed, mankind never have recourse to superior powers so readily as in that disposition. But as men have now learned to form principles and to draw consequences, it is necessary to change the batteries, and to make use of such arguments as will endure at least some scrutiny and examination. This variation is the same (and from the same causes) with that which I formerly remarked with regard to scepticism.

Thus Philo continued to the last his spirit of opposition, and his censure of established opinions. But I could observe that Demea did not at all relish the latter part of the discourse; and he took occasion soon after, on some pretence or other, to leave the company.

NOTES

1. *Recherche de la Verité,* liv. 3, cap. 9.
2. *De Rerum Natura,* lib. XI [II], 1094. (Who can rule the sum, who hold in his hand with controlling force the strong reins, of the immeasurable deep? Who can at once make all the different heavens to roll and warm with ethereal fires all the fruitful earths, or be present in all places at all times?)—(Translation by H. A. J. Munro, G. Bell & Sons, 1920.)
3. *De Natura Deorum,* lib. I [cap. VIII]. (For with what eyes could your Plato see the construction of so vast a work which, according to him, God was putting together and building? What materials, what tools, what bars, what machines, what servants were employed in such gigantic work? How could the air, fire, water, and earth pay obedience and submit to the will of the architect?)
4. Dr. Clarke [Samuel Clarke, the rationalist theologian (1675–1729)].
5. *Republique des Lettres,* Aut 1685.
6. That sentiment had been maintained by Dr. King and some few others before Leibniz, though by none of so great fame as that German philosopher.
7. Milton: *Paradise Lost,* Bk. XI.
8. John Dryden, *Aureng-Zebe,* Act IV, sc. 1.

Male-Chauvinist Religion*

DEBORAH MATHIEU

Deborah Mathieu teaches philosophy and political science at the University of Arizona.

Man for the field and woman for the hearth
Man for the sword and for the needle she
Man with the head and woman with the heart
Man to command and woman to obey
All else confusion.

ALFRED, LORD TENNYSON[1]

ALL FUNCTIONING SOCIETIES rely on a division of labor: some individuals raise children, some produce food, some construct roads, some adjudicate disputes, and so on. Occasionally these tasks overlap, but often they do not. How do societies decide who does what? How, in other words, are rights and responsibilities allocated?

There is no one universally accepted method of determining which people will perform which roles, and often a given society will employ several methods. One common distributive standard is age: no one over a certain age or under a certain age may perform certain functions. Another distributive standard is ability: an intelligent person with a sense of fairness may adjudicate disputes, for instance, while a brawny person willing to work hard may construct roads. Yet another common standard is gender: males perform one set of tasks while females perform another. There are other allocative standards as well: race, religion, family, class, education, and so on.

The United States has employed all of these (and more) to determine who does what. Most of the criteria are unfair most of the time: your family name, for instance, should be irrelevant to your career (unless you work in the family business), as should your theology (unless you work as a religious official). But I am not concerned with all unfair standards, just with one: gender. If positions are allocated according to gender, then no female—regardless of her talents, her education, her aspirations—may perform those tasks assigned to males.

During the many decades in which the United States used gender as a principle method of distribution, a woman could wash clothes but she could not shine shoes, she could be a barmaid but not a bartender, she could raise children but could not hold public office. Women could not be lawyers, serve on juries, operate elevators, or mine coal. Indeed, it was once illegal in this country for women to perform *most* jobs outside the home.[2] This type of occupational gender segregation, of course, is very common around the world. One result is that work traditionally performed by women—rearing children, cleaning house, teaching grammar school—though necessary and often arduous, is usually undervalued and underpaid.[3]

The separation of tasks according to gender typically means that males act in the public sphere of politics and paid work while females stay in the private sphere of the home. But why would an intelligent woman with a robust sense of fairness concede that she should spend her time cleaning

**Reprinted by permission of the author.*

house instead of refereeing disputes? Why would any woman acquiesce to any sort of gender stereotyping, especially when the results are harmful to her?

The answer is simple and somewhat frightening: she believes that only certain narrowly defined roles are appropriate for her. Why would she believe that? Because every facet of her society—the media, her schools, her books, her friends, her parents, even her toys—have conspired to convince her that it is so.

One of the most powerful tools in this respect is religion, for it tells people not only what is proper and good, but what is holy and unholy, natural and unnatural. Having certain activities branded by a sacred text as unholy or unnatural when performed by females certainly helps ensure that females will avoid those activities. Equally inhibiting are declarations from religious leaders. Public declarations by a few Islamic *ulama* that women may not drive automobiles, for instance, surely have more clout than the private remonstrations of a multitude of husbands. In short, when important distinctions are made along gender lines, religious doctrines and practices are valuable instruments of indoctrination.

Of the many male-chauvinist religions, three have been especially successful in relegating females to inferior positions: Christianity, Islam, and Judaism. In addition to the institutionalization of patriarchal, even misogynistic, mores and practices, these familiar religions have much in common: belief in one and only one supreme being, identification of one book as a record of its god's words and deeds, characterization of its god as male, emphasis on compassion, and status as a major world religion. The relationship among these factors is fascinating, especially the roles they have played in the subjugation of females.

MISOGYNY ON HIGH

The practices of Christianity, Islam, and Judaism originated when males and females were assigned different social roles in life: males in the public sphere, females in the private.[4] Because the males' role included designing the rules, they designed the rules to favor themselves. One of the most important rules, of course, was that only males could craft the rules.

This separation of roles extended to religion, so the males designed the rules there as well: they formulated the beliefs and practices, they created the institutions, they controlled the rituals. It should be no surprise, then, that the resulting religions explicitly reinforced the belief that males are superior to females and endorsed a set of social relations in which males controlled females.[5]

Religious practices demonstrated this message constantly. Females could not be religious leaders, and they could be religious participants only from a distance. They were not permitted near the holy sanctuaries, allowed to speak (or sing) in the church/mosque/synagogue, or even allowed to read the holy books. Of course the religious teachings were often harshly judgmental of females. A leader of the early Christian church, for instance, went so far as to blame human sin and suffering on females:

> The sentence of God on this sex of yours lives in this age: the guilt must of necessity live too. You are the Devil's gateway; you are the first deserter of the divine law; you are she who persuaded him whom the devil was not valiant enough to attack. You so carelessly destroyed man, God's image. On account of your desert, even the Son of God had to die.[6]

Indeed, all facets of the religions could be used to dishonor females, even prayer. Every morning, for instance, the Jewish man was expected to thank God: "Blessed art thou, O Lord our God, King of the Universe, who has not made me a woman."

And yet, despite their malice toward the female sex, these three religions flourished. How could this be? How could a theology that demeaned females become a significant religion throughout the world? How could something so blatantly one-sided and unfair gain such legitimacy? It is easy to imagine the existence of a few all-male cults built around the idea (and it is just an idea) of male superiority. But why would millions of sensible women support three worldwide religions based on that idea? How could reasonable women believe in these gods?

CO-OPTING FEMALES

The first part of the explanation relates to the high value all three religions place on compassion and equality. All virtuous people are equal in the sight of God, the holy books proclaim. To honor each other is to honor God, the books declare, so be kind to each other, show concern for the vulnerable, help those less fortunate, be fair in all your dealings. No doubt females heard these words and believed them, despite the mountains of evidence to the contrary.

The second, and less comforting, reason females accepted these religions is related to the need of those who wield power to justify that status quo to themselves and to others. Men claiming such inordinate power needed to mollify any misgivings the advantaged might have and to gain the acquiescence of the disadvantaged. The benefits of this to those who make and enforce the rules are obvious: if people believe that the status quo is the best system, they will not fight against it, and the privileged can maintain their position (relatively) peacefully.

Therefore males used their religion to brainwash females into accepting the theory of male superiority as fact. The technique has been effective because of its multi-faceted approach: it appeals to the female's intellect as well as her emotions.

The crux of the male's argument for supremacy over females is inherent in all three religions: the contention that the one and only true god is male. Thus the very cores of all three theologies were deployed to subjugate females. The results were devastatingly successful, as well as successfully devastating.

The basic deductive argument is built around two simple syllogisms of the following classic form:

If P, Then Q.
P
______
Therefore Q.

The first part of the argument goes like this:

If god is male, then human males are more like god than human females are.
God is male.
______
Therefore human males are more like god than human females are.

The second part of the argument is:

If human males are more like god than human females are, then human males are superior to human females.
Human males are more like god than human females are.
______
Therefore human males are superior to human females.

The argument is not a sound one. But it still has power, for if you accept the premises, then the conclusions follow inevitably and indisputably.

Those conclusions have led to the disenfranchisement of females, especially within the religions themselves. Why couldn't Christian women be priests? Because a priest impersonates (the male) Christ during Eucharist. Why must Jewish women sit behind a screen in the synagogue, away from the sanctuary? Because they are too flawed to be near the holy objects. Why must Islamic women cover their entire bodies even though Allah commanded only that they dress modestly? Because the (male) *ulama* interpret Allah otherwise, and they know better. Why were women prevented from conducting the religious ceremonies, setting the rules, designing the practices? Because of their inherent inferiority to the men who do. And why is a woman's labor rewarded less than a man's? Need we ask?

It is curious that the deductive arguments noted above could ever be persuasive, for under scrutiny they collapse. Both syllogisms suffer from the same flaw: they rely on premises that are open to dispute. The first shaky premise is the assertion that god is male. It need not be so. Indeed, there are other, equally plausible alternatives: god may be female, or neither male nor female, or both male and female. In short, one may believe in the existence of god and yet deny that god is male.[7] This seems a sound approach for religious females to take, especially as it is to their advantage to do so.

Feminist theologians have staunchly advocated this approach. But this is a very recent development; for thousands of years women agreed that god was male, and many women still do. Why? Because that contention enjoys powerful support: the holy books of the three religions. According to the Jewish *Tenakh,* the Christian *Bible,* and the Islamic *Qur'an,* god is male. Yahweh, Christ, and Allah all have male attributes and male sobriquets: Lord of Hosts, God the Father, God the Son, King of the Universe, He who gives life and death, He who exalts. If you accept any of these books as literally true, then you are likely to view your god as male.

But if females believe that their god is male, and therefore refuse to challenge that part of the argument, they still may challenge another, equally shaky premise: the contention that, if human males are more like god than human females are, then human males are superior to human females. Other plausible options are available here, too. If the god is an inferior one, for instance, then being similar to him may not be an asset; perhaps being similar to god in some way makes one, not better than another, but more vulnerable. Perhaps being different (i.e., female) makes someone more, not less, fit to rule.

Of course the holy books can be used to rebut this challenge as well. God is magnificent, omnipotent, omniscient, wonderful in every way, the three books declare. To be like him, then, is to have positive attributes. And to be unlike him is to have negative attributes. It follows that because males are like god and females are not, males must be superior to females. And surely superior beings should rule inferior ones.

This argument could be broken down into a set of syllogisms, each of which would have at least one shaky premise. But the response would be the same as above: an appeal could be made to any of the three holy books to attest to the inevitability, the undeniability, the universality of female subordinacy. In short, if god is male, then females are in trouble. It is that simple.

This brings us to the second component of religious brainwashing: the appeal to emotions. The religious ceremonies and teachings were designed to make females feel both accepted (if they conform to certain standards) and unacceptable (because of their inherent unworthiness). They were designed, as well, to make the females doubt themselves.

Imagine how a woman might feel as she listened to St. Paul's Letter to the Ephesians read as part of the day's religious ceremony:

> Wives, submit yourselves unto your own husbands, as unto the Lord. For the husband is the head of the wife, even as Christ is the head of the church, and he is the savior of the body. Therefore, as the church is subject unto Christ, so let the wives be to their own husbands in every thing. (Eph 5:22–24)[8]

How would a female feel, seated in the back of the synagogue behind a screen during every religious service of her life? How would she feel when her presence in the synagogue is not even counted toward the quorum needed for a service? How would she feel, covered in black from head to foot in the blazing sun of a desert summer? Would she be angry? Would she be offended? Or might she instead feel inferior, inadequate?

And how might she feel when she realizes that all meaningful choices in life are denied to her? How might she feel when she is told—in school, at home, and in her place of worship—that males are superior to females? Might she come to believe that her want of options, as well as her lack of power, was natural? On what basis might she think otherwise?

And if she believes that everyone else accepts the proposition that she is second-rate, simply because she is female, is she likely to rebel? Is she even likely to question the system? Or is she more apt to question her own feelings, to distrust her ability to understand? If no one else believes that she is intelligent, or even rational, is she likely to presume it? If no one else believes she is capable of performing anything other than the most routine, mundane tasks, will she? Probably not.

So what is the result? Is she likely to be brimming with confidence and self-respect, eager to strike out on her own to make her way in the world? Is she likely to question the foundations of the dominant religion, to argue forcefully against the unfairness of the system? Or is she more likely to be someone who is fearful and insecure, someone who is subservient to others?

The answer is obvious: she behaves as you would expect someone who has been marginalized all her life would behave. She does what she is told, she acquiesces to the system, she accepts her fate. Perhaps she suffers from low self-esteem, perhaps she is passive and dependent and anxious. She behaves, in other words, like an unempowered female. After all, the whole system is designed to make her this way.

In short, males have heavy-handedly used these three religions to advance their own interests and to justify their having the upper hand. It can even be argued that the basic features of the religions—belief in one and only one supreme being, identification of one book as a record of the god's words and deeds, and characterization of its god as male—were designed to augment male domination over female members of his species. Perhaps even the purported emphasis on compassion and equality was merely a smokescreen hiding the truth, a cruel hoax played on females to entice them to acquiesce in their own destruction.

MISOGYNY AND MONOTHEISM

The question is, then, how important is male chauvinism to these religions? Is the misogyny, in other words, as integral a part as the monotheism?

Four responses to this question merit discussion:

1. "anatomy is destiny"[9]
2. god is a male chauvinist
3. the religious images should be taken symbolically
4. sexism has always been superfluous to these religions.

I will explain each in turn and also offer a rebuttal to each.

1. Anatomy is Destiny

The contention here is that the three religions accurately reflect the fact that males and females are different types of beings. Males are rational while females are emotional; males are rule-oriented while females are relationship-oriented; males are domineering while females are submissive; males are properly heads of households while females are their helpmeets; males belong in the public sphere while females belong in the private sphere. It has been this way since time immemorial. It has been this way, not because males have unfairly dominated females, but because it is the natural course of life. This is the way the world was designed, it is the way the world works, and all reasonable people recognize it. To fight this natural order is to invite disaster.

We have heard declarations like these for centuries; but all of them are wrong, terribly, tragically wrong. A female is not by nature someone who stays home to raise children, wash clothes, and bake bread. Nor is she by nature subservient to males. She becomes that type of person by adopting a certain gender role, a view of what is acceptable for her to do/say/think as a female. Gender roles are social constructions that begin at birth, not biological determinates beginning at conception.

There is one question everyone asks when told of a birth: Is it a boy or a girl? We ask because it makes a difference to us; we need to know how to treat this new being. We dress a male differently from a female; we address a male differently from a female; we expect different behaviors from a male than from a female. The children, of course, internalize these differences, and behave accordingly. They tend to repeat behaviors we have rewarded and reinforced, just as they tend to avoid behaviors we have punished and discouraged. They learn gender differences in other ways as well: from observation, for instance, and by generalizing from one type of experience to another.

These patterns continue throughout their lives, as males and females adapt to the dissimilar social expectations and mores imposed on them. The interplay of their behaviors with variations in treatment by others creates different life experiences. And these different life experiences form different sorts of people—people with the characteristics of distinct genders—with different feelings, beliefs, and skills. This, then, is how gender is constructed. And because gender roles are social constructs, they vary from culture to culture, and may even vary within a culture over time.

This is not to say that there are no biological differences between male and female humans; of course there are. The contrasts are sometimes obvious (such as their dramatically dissimilar reproductive organs), sometimes less noticeable (the two X chromosomes of a typical female, versus the one X chromosome and one Y of a typical male). The point is, rather, that these biological differences are less significant than the cultural ones in determining the ways males and females operate in the world. In other words, in the nature/nurture debate, I am arguing that the evidence indicates that more weight should be given to nurture than nature when it comes to gender differences.[10]

It is difficult, though, to convince skeptics of the validity of an ambiguous stance like this: it is true that there are innate differences between males and females *and* that gender is a largely social construct. In contrast, positions on the outside boundaries of the debate offer the comfort of firm absolutes. At one end are the postmodernists, who reject grand explanatory theories in general and theories of innate human traits in particular; all of our options and preferences, they argue, are the result of cultural influences. And at the other end are their arch-enemies, the sociobiologists, who argue that myriad human traits are genetically based. I am suggesting, instead, that the truth lies somewhere between the two; that, while genes exert a probabalistic influence on human behavior, their influence is muted dramatically by the environment.

This is not the place, however, to engage at length in the contentious nature/nurture debate that has raged across disciplines for years (and which shows no signs of abating). Suffice it to say that it seems clear to me that anatomy is not destiny (at least with regard to most gender differences), that females are not inherently inferior to males, and that cultural conditioning shapes most gender roles.

2. *God is a Male Chauvinist*

Nothing about the nature of god follows from my criticisms of these three religions. And I offer no propositions about the true nature of god, or even about the existence of god. Instead, let us assume for the sake of argument that these three religions are correct: god exists and he is a male chauvinist. In this case, it does not matter whether males and females are inherently different because god has designated separate social roles for them. And if we wish to obey god's will, then we will treat males and females as different. If one result is that the members of one gender wield most of the power, then so be it.

This position raises a fundamental question about the response of females to god. Would a male chauvinist god be likely to inspire love in females? Would a biased, unfair god inspire awe? Or devotion? Or would such a being inspire some other reaction in females: something closer to wrath, perhaps, or resentment?

When confronted with a god who consigns you to a drab, dull existence, wouldn't you be angry? When told during religious services that you are base and inferior, simply because of the design of your genitalia, wouldn't you be indignant? Or perhaps Nelle Morton illustrates the proper tone for a female to adopt:

> No one is wise enough to know why God made female reproductive organs compact and internal so that woman is physically free to move about unencumbered and take her natural place of leadership in the world of womankind. Or why God made a male's organs external and exposed, so that he would demand sheltering and protection from the outside in order that he may be kept for reproducing the race.[11]

Surely Morton is correct that the situation calls for at least a little irony. Maybe even a good dose of sarcasm. But not love, certainly not love. Fear might be appropriate perhaps, given the unsavory outcomes for females, but not love. And not awe.

After all, there is nothing splendid about a sexist god. And should we even consider such a limited being to be a god?

But females did not spurn the gods of these three religions, at least not generally. Nor were anger, indignation, and irony the typical responses of females to these gods or their religions. Instead, Christianity, Islam, and Judaism became powerful in part because of their female adherents.

That is because attitudes such as irony and indignation are possible only if you are able to step back from the god, to view the religion clearly. Females were prevented from doing precisely that. One successful method was to deny them access to education (so they could not read the holy books themselves) as well as access to any decision-making processes. Another, equally effective method was to prey on their emotions, to make them believe they were somehow inadequate, even irrational.

But today these techniques are not nearly so widespread nor so effective. And misogyny is no longer so much in vogue. Eventually, as sexist social systems disappear, so will sexist religions. And as our mores change, so must our gods.

3. The Religious Images Should be Taken Symbolically, not Literally

One way to save these three religions from the charge of unfair sexism is to deny that the holy books are literally true. The religious images, it is argued, should be understood as metaphors, as devices for expounding profound truths too difficult for the average person to describe (or understand) in the abstract. And abstractions are too impersonal and cold to instill the deeply emotional responses that religious faith requires. It seems more natural, for instance, to love and honor the particularized image of Jesus—a god who became a man in order to die for all human sin—than an abstruse concept of forgiveness.

So religious stories use familiar objects to create images we can grasp and to which we are likely to react with reverence and awe. These images are so powerful that we often forget that they are mere symbols. But that is our failing, not the fault of the holy books. We need to remind ourselves that religious discourse was meant to be taken figuratively, that, for instance, Yahweh's promise in Genesis to deliver his chosen people into a "land flowing with milk and honey" is not a contract at all, and certainly not one guaranteeing a future awash in sweetened dairy products; it is, instead, a reassurance of a brighter future, an exhortation to be hopeful.

It should not be surprising, the argument continues, that some of these images are couched in misogynistic language, given the low status of women at the time the religious works were compiled. But this sexism is only a contingent feature of the religions; the religious tenets can be expressed in nonsexist, even nongendered, language. Thus God need not be seen as a male, but understood instead as a perfect nongendered being, "the being than whom a more perfect being cannot be conceived." In short, we should be able to see beyond these time-bound images to appreciate the deeper truths they contain; we should be able to proceed beyond the sexist language of these ancient works to understand the universalist metaphors they express.

As compelling as this argument appears, it is persuasive only if one is willing to deny reality. Among its many weaknesses, three are worth noting here. The first problem is that even the sophisticated have difficulty being abstract. Can you really imagine what it means to be "the being than whom a more perfect being cannot be conceived" or "a ground of all contingency"? Most people cannot. And that is why religious literature continues to maintain a gendered image of god. Even those who seek to expunge sexism from religious practices find it impossible to erase gender altogether. Take, for instance, the Society for the Promotion of Christian Knowledge, Britain's oldest publisher of religious books, which touts its new, nonsexist prayer book. In it, Christianity's most often recited prayer, the Lord's Prayer, has been cleansed of its male chauvinist overtones. Retitled the "Prayer of Jesus," it now appeals not to a male god or an ungendered god but to an androgynous god. Thus where the prayer once began, "Our father, who art in heaven, hallowed be thy name," it now begins: "Beloved, our father and mother, in whom is heaven, hallowed be your name."[12] The new prayer book has met, of course, with considerable resistance. "I think it's heretical," the Archdeacon of York recently said. "I would walk out of a service if that was read."[13] This attitude is reflected in many places, including the Catholic Mass, which still features the centuries-old Nicene Creed:

> We believe in one God, the Father, Almighty, maker of heaven and earth, of all that is seen and unseen. We believe in one Lord, Jesus Christ, the only Son of God, eternally begotten of the Father. . . .

It seems clear that, while change is coming, it is slow and halting, and leaves untouched millions of lives.

A second and related problem is that one may adopt the theoretical principle that religious images are to be taken symbolically yet fail to accept that precept on an emotional level. It often is the case that "images function powerfully long after they have been repudiated intellectually."[14] Thus we find ourselves making declarations on an intellectual level that we simply do not accept on an emotional level. With religious images tending to honor males and dishonor females, we may find ourselves unconsciously doing the same.

Finally, there is the woeful fact that for thousands of years these images were used to subjugate women. Suggesting that the interpretations may have been mistaken, or that we should understand them figuratively, is insufficient; the sexist language is there, and it has caused terrible harm by marginalizing generations of females. And it continues to do so.

4. Male Chauvinism Is and Always Has Been Superfluous to Christianity, Islam, and Judaism

The holy books of all three religions acknowledge the profound value of females: the account of creation in the *Qur'an* describes the common origin of men and women, as does one of the versions of creation in the *Tenakh,* while the Gospels of the *New Testament* indicate that Christ treated females with respect and compassion. Indeed, all of the holy books give the impression that, in ultimate spiritual terms, males and females are equal.[15] Thus the fact that these religions may have been used by males to subjugate females shows only that males will manipulate anything and everything in order to maintain power; it does not show that these religions are necessarily sexist.

This is both the strongest and the weakest of the countervailing considerations. It is the strongest because it is accurate: I have shown only that male chauvinism is a major part of these three religions, I have not demonstrated that it is an essential part. Nor could I. A few Christian sects (such as Christian Scientists and Quakers) have always treated females as the equals of males; the largest Islamic group, Sunni Muslims, believe that females are as competent as males to perform some religious rites; and there have been Jewish female (reform) rabbis since 1972. Surely these are powerful counterexamples to my arguments.

Yes and no. Yes, they demonstrate that these three religions can exist intact minus a certain degree of misogyny. But no, they are not powerful enough to do the job; the examples are too few, and are overwhelmed by the countless instances of raw sexism. Indeed, many religious sects remain robustly male chauvinist, continuing to justify their stance by reference to their sacred texts and customs. The Catholic Church, for instance, declared as recently as 1995 that women may not be priests, not now, not ever.[16] This is to be expected; in the traditional forms of these religious, men continue to keep most of the interesting and influential roles for themselves.

The contention that the male chauvinism of these religions is only contingently a part of them—that they could exist intact without it—is a serious indictment against those who are unwilling to relinquish it. To hold tight to tradition is to embrace patriarchy. And that is not a pretty picture: it conserves an unfair and damaging conception of what it means to be female; it supports a one-sided power grab, allowing males to monopolize key roles; and it may even, as Mary Daly charges, sustain a hoax, "a front for men's plans and a cover for inadequacy, ignorance, and evil."[17]

The traditional forms of these religions are opting, in short, to cast doubt on the nature and value of religion itself. They are opting, as well, to cast doubt on the existence of an infinitely powerful yet benevolent god, for their disgraceful treatment of females raises the same demanding question posed by all great evils: what kind of god would allow this to happen?

NOTES

1. Alfred Lord Tennyson, *The Princess: A Medley.* William J. Rolfe, ed. (Cambridge, MA: Riverside Press 1884), lines 437–441.

2. See D. M. Stetson, *Women's Rights in the U.S.A.* (Belmont, CA: Wadsworth, 1991); Carol Hymowitz and Michaele Weissman, *A History of Women in America* (N.Y.: Bantam Books, 1978).

3. See Pamela K. Brubaker, *Women Don't Count* (Atlanta: Scholars Press, 1994); *The State of the World's Women, 1985* (Oxford: New International Publications, 1985).

4. For a thoughtful history of the evolution of these three religions, see Karen Armstrong, *A History of God* (N.Y.: Ballentine Books, 1993).

5. Rachel Biale, *Women and Jewish Law* (N.Y.: Schocken, 1986); Mary Daly, *Beyond God the Father* (Boston: Beacon Press, 1973); Alice L. Hageman, ed., *Sexist Religion and Women in the Church* (N.Y.: Association Press, 1974); John S. Hawley, *Fundamentalism and Gender* (N.Y.: Oxford University Press, 1994); Jean Holm, ed. *Women in Religion* (N.Y.: Pinter, 1994); Rosemary R. Ruether, ed. *Images of Women in the Jewish and Christian Traditions* (N.Y.: Simon and Schuster, 1973).

6. Tertullian, *On Female Dress,* I, i. Tertullian, a North African theologian, lived about a hundred years after the death of Christ.

Note as well the male chauvinist writings of other well-known Christian writers: Augustine, Cyprian, Jerome, Aquinas, Karl Barth, Dietrich Bonhoeffer, and Reinhold Niebuhr.

7. You may also dispute the premise by claiming that there is no god, or at least not one that matters much. Two directions are then possible: you can reject all religious belief, or you can choose a system of spiritual thought with no central god. You may discover, though, that the second alternative contains its own set of sexist elements. Consider, for instance, Buddhism, a non-theistic religion which emphasizes the human roots of suffering. Although the details of Buddhism change with every culture into which it is introduced, a core set of "Noble Truths" is embraced by nearly all Buddhists: suffering is universal, suffering is a result of desire, to eliminate suffering you must eliminate desire, a path can be followed to achieve freedom from desire and suffering. These tenets are gender-neutral and apply to all, without exception. Yet Buddhism is still tainted by misogyny. According to Buddha himself, for instance, the most senior nun must defer to the most junior monk. And in the system of reincarnation, rebirth as a female is generally considered unfortunate compared to rebirth as a male.

8. See also the words ascribed to Paul in 1 Tim. 2: 12: "But I suffer not a woman to teach, nor to usurp authority over the man, but to be in silence." Interestingly, many contemporary scholars agree that Paul never made any of these sexist remarks, that they were appended later to his letters. See, e.g., Robin Scroggs, "Paul and the Eschatological Woman," *Journal of the American Academy of Religion* 40: 283–303, 1972.

9. Freud said this, earning the enmity of feminists. Sigmund Freud, *On Sexuality: Three Essays on the Theory of Sexuality and Other Works,* James Strachey, cn. (London: Penguin, 1991).

10. For more on gender socialization see: Pierre Bourdieu, *The Logic of Practice* (Stanford, CA: Stanford University Press, 1990); R. W. Connell, *Gender and Power* (Stanford, CA: Stanford University Press, 1987); Michelle H. Garskof, ed. *Roles Women Play* (Belmont, CA: Belmont/Cole, 1971); Eleanor E. Maccoby, ed. *The Development of Sex Differences* (Stanford, CA: Stanford University Press, 1966); Dorothy E. Smith, *The Everyday World as Problematic* (Toronto: University of Toronto Press, 1987).

11. Nelle Morton, "Preaching the Word," in Alice L. Hageman, ed. *Sexist Religion and Women in the Church* (N.Y.: Association Press, 1974), pp. 30–31.

12. *Including Women: A Non-Sexist Prayer Book* is published by the Society for the Promotion of Christian Knowledge, and has been adopted by some Church of England congregations since 1991.

13. "Equal-opportunity Prayers." *Maclean's* August 5, 1991.

14. Morton, *op. cit.,* p. 32.

15. The *Qur'an* even gave women legal rights of inheritance and divorce, rights most Western women would not gain for over a thousand years.

16. Pope John Paul II issued an apostolic letter in 1994 declaring that the Catholic Church may not ordain women; in 1995 the Vatican's Congregation for the Doctrine of the Faith confirmed that this conclusion was infallible and irrevocable.

17. Mary Daly, *op cit.,* p. 30.

The Problem of Evil

Rebellion*

FYODOR DOSTOEVSKY

Fyodor Dostoevsky (1821–1881) was one of the great Russian novelists of the nineteenth century.

"I MUST MAKE YOU ONE CONFESSION," Ivan began. "I could never understand how one can love one's neighbors. It's just one's neighbors, to my mind, that one can't love, though one might love those at a distance. I once read somewhere of John the Merciful, a saint, that when a hungry, frozen beggar came to him, he took him into his bed, held him in his arms, and began breathing into his mouth, which was putrid and loathsome from some awful disease. I am convinced that he did that from 'self-laceration,' from the self-laceration of falsity, for the sake of the charity imposed by duty, as a penance laid on him. For any one to love a man, he must be hidden, for as soon as he shows his face, love is gone."

"Father Zossima has talked of that more than once," observed Alyosha, "he, too, said that the face of a man often hinders many people not practiced in love, from loving him. But yet there's a great deal of love in mankind, and almost Christ-like love. I know that myself, Ivan."

"Well, I know nothing of it so far, and can't understand it, and the innumerable mass of mankind are with me there. The question is, whether that's due to men's bad qualities or whether it's inherent in their nature. To my thinking, Christ-like love for men is a miracle impossible on earth. He was God. But we are not gods. Suppose I, for instance, suffer intensely. Another can never know how much I suffer, because he is another and not I. And what's more, a man is rarely ready to admit another's suffering (as though it were a distinction). Why won't he admit it, do you think? Because I smell unpleasant, because I have a stupid face, because I once trod on his foot. Besides there is suffering and suffering; degrading, humiliating suffering such as humbles me—hunger, for instance—my benefactor will perhaps allow me; but when you come to higher suffering—for an idea, for instance—he will very rarely admit that, perhaps because my face strikes him as not at all what he fancies a man should have who suffers for an idea. And so he deprives me instantly of his favor, and not at all from badness of heart. Beggars, especially genteel beggars, ought never to show themselves, but to ask for charity through the newspapers. One can love one's neighbors in the abstract, or even at a distance, but at close quarters it's almost impossible. If it were as on the stage, in the ballet, where if beggars come in they wear silken rags and tattered lace and beg for alms dancing gracefully, then one might like looking at them. But even then we should not love them. But enough of that. I simply wanted to show you my point of view. I meant to speak of the suffering of mankind generally, but we had better confine ourselves to the sufferings of the children. That reduces the scope of my argument to the tenth of what it would be. Still we'd better keep to the chil-

*From The Brothers Karamazov, *C. Garnett, trans., Book V, Chap. 4 (New York: Modern Library, Inc., 1950).*

dren, though it does weaken my case. But, in the first place, children can be loved even at close quarters, even when they are dirty, even when they are ugly (I fancy, though, children never are ugly). The second reason why I won't speak of grown-up people is that, besides being disgusting and unworthy of love, they have a compensation—they've eaten the apple and know good and evil, and they have become 'like god.' They go on eating it still. But the children haven't eaten anything, and are so far innocent. Are you fond of children, Alyosha? I know you are, and you will understand why I prefer to speak of them. If they, too, suffer horribly on earth, they must suffer for their fathers' sins, they must be punished for their fathers, who have eaten the apple; but that reasoning is of the other world and is incomprehensible for the heart of man here on earth. The innocent must not suffer for another's sins, and especially such innocents! You may be surprised at me, Alyosha, but I am awfully fond of children, too. And observe, cruel people, the violent, the rapacious, the Karamazovs are sometimes very fond of children. Children while they are quite little—up to seven, for instance—are so remote from grown-up people; they are different creatures, as it were, of a different species. I knew a criminal in prison who had, in the course of his career as a burglar, murdered whole families, including several children. But when he was in prison, he had a strange affection for them. He spent all his time at his window, watching the children playing in the prison yard. He trained one little boy to come up to his window and made great friends with him . . . You don't know why I am telling you all this, Alyosha? My head aches and I am sad."

"You speak with a strange air," observed Alyosha uneasily, "as though you were not quite yourself."

"By the way, a Bulgarian I met lately in Moscow," Ivan went on, seeming not to hear his brother's words, "told me about the crimes committed by Turks and Circassians in all parts of Bulgaria through fear of a general rising of the Slavs. They burn villages, murder, outrage women and children, they nail their prisoners by the ears to the fences, leave them so till morning, and in the morning they hang them—all sorts of things you can't imagine. People talk sometimes of bestial cruelty, but that's a great injustice and insult to the beasts; a beast can never be so cruel as a man, so artistically cruel. The tiger only tears and gnaws, that's all he can do. He would never think of nailing people by the ears, even if he were able to do it. These Turks took a pleasure in torturing children, too; cutting the unborn child from the mother's womb, and tossing babies up in the air and catching them on the points of their bayonets before their mother's eyes. Doing it before the mother's eyes was what gave zest to the amusement. Here is another scene that I thought very interesting. Imagine a trembling mother with her baby in her arms, a circle of invading Turks around her. They've planned a diversion; they pet the baby, laugh to make it laugh. They succeed, the baby laughs. At that moment a Turk points a pistol four inches from the baby's face. The baby laughs with glee, holds out its little hands to the pistol, and he pulls the trigger in the baby's face and blows out its brains. Artistic, wasn't it? By the way, Turks are particularly fond of sweet things, they say."

"Brother, what are you driving at?" asked Alyosha.

"I think if the devil doesn't exist, but man has created him, he has created him in his own image and likeness."

"Just as he did God, then?" observed Alyosha.

"'It's wonderful how you can turn words,' as Polonius says in *Hamlet,*" laughed Ivan. "You turn my words against me. Well, I am glad. Yours must be a fine God, if man created Him in His image and likeness. You asked just now what I was driving at. You see, I am fond of collecting certain facts, and, would you believe, I even copy anecdotes of a certain sort from newspapers and books, and I've already got a fine collection. The Turks, of course, have gone into it, but they are foreigners. I have specimens from home that are even better than the Turks. You know we prefer beating—rods and scourges—that's our national institution. Nailing ears is unthinkable for us, for we are, after all, Europeans. But the rod and scourge we have always with us and they cannot be taken from us. Abroad now they scarcely do any beating. Manners are more humane, or laws have been passed, so that they don't dare to flog men now. But they make up for it in another way just as national as ours. And so national that it would be practically impossible among us, though I believe we are being inoculated with it, since the religious movement began in our aristocracy. I have a charming pamphlet, translated from the French, describing how, quite recently, five years ago, a murderer, Richard, was executed—a young man, I believe, of three and twenty, who repented and was converted to the Christian faith at the very scaffold. This Richard was an illegitimate child who was given as a child of six by his parents to some shepherds on the Swiss mountains. They brought him up to work for them. He grew up like a little wild beast among them. The shepherds taught him nothing, and scarcely fed or clothed him, but sent him out at seven to herd the flock in cold and wet, and no one hesitated or scrupled to treat him so. Quite the contrary, they thought they had every right, for Richard had been given to them as a chattel, and they did not even see the necessity of feeding him. Richard himself describes how in those years, like the Prodigal Son in the Gospel, he longed to eat of the mash given to the pigs, which were fattened for sale. But they wouldn't even give him that, and beat him when he stole from the pigs. And that was how he spent all his childhood and his youth, till he grew up and was strong enough to go away and be a thief. The savage began to earn his living as a day laborer in Geneva. He drank what he earned, he lived like a brute, and finished by killing and robbing an old man. He was caught, tried, and condemned to death. They are no sentimentalists there. And in prison he was immediately surrounded by pastors, members of Christian brotherhoods, philanthropic ladies, and the like. They taught him to read and write in prison, and expounded the Gospel to him. They exhorted him, worked upon him, drummed at him incessantly, till at last he confessed his crime. He was converted. He wrote to the court himself that he was a monster, but that in the end God had vouch-safed him light and shown grace. All Geneva was in excitement about him—all philanthropic and religious Geneva. All the aristocratic and well-bred society of the town rushed to the prison, kissed Richard and embraced him: 'You are our brother, you have found grace.' And Richard does nothing but weep with emotion, 'Yes, I've found grace! All my youth and childhood I was glad to have pigs' food, but now even I have found grace. I am dying in the Lord.' 'Yes, Richard, die in the Lord; you have shed blood and must die. Though it's not your fault that you knew not the Lord, when you coveted the pigs' food and were beaten for stealing it (which was very wrong of you, for stealing is forbidden); but you've shed blood and you must die.' And on the last day, Richard, perfectly limp, did nothing but cry and repeat every minute: 'This is my happiest day. I am going to the Lord.' 'Yes,' cry the pastors and the judges and philanthropic ladies. 'This is the happiest day of your life, for you are going to the Lord!' They all walk or drive to the scaffold in procession behind the prison van. At the scaffold they call to Richard: 'Die, brother, die in the Lord, for even thou hast found grace!' And so, covered with his brothers' kisses, Richard is dragged onto the scaffold, and led to the guillotine. And they chopped off his head in brotherly fashion, because he had found grace. Yes, that's characteristic. That pamphlet is translated into Russian by some Russian philanthropists of aristocratic rank and evangelical aspirations, and has been distributed gratis for the enlightenment of the people. The case of Richard is interesting because it's national. Though to us it's absurd to cut off a man's head, because he has become our brother and has found grace, yet we have our own specialty, which is all but worse. Our historical pastime is the direct satisfaction of inflicting pain. There are lines in Nekrassov describing how a peasant lashes a horse on the eyes, 'on its meek eyes'; everyone must have seen it. It's peculiarly Russian. He describes how a feeble little nag had foundered under too heavy a load and cannot move. The peasant beats it, beats it savagely, beats it at last not knowing what he is doing in the intoxication of cruelty, thrashes it mercilessly over and over again. 'However weak you are, you must pull, if you die for it.' The nag strains, and he begins lashing the poor defenseless creature on its weeping, on its 'meek eyes.' The frantic beast tugs and draws the load, trembling all over, gasping for breath, moving sideways, with a sort of unnatural spasmodic action—it's awful in Nekrassov. But that's only a horse, and God has given horses to be beaten. So the Tatars have taught us, and they left us the knout as a remembrance of it. But men, too, can be beaten. A well-educated, cultured gentleman and his wife beat their own child with a birch-rod, a girl of seven. I have an exact account of it. The papa was glad that the birch was covered with twigs. 'It stings more,' said he, and so he began stinging his daughter. I know for a fact there are people who at every blow are worked up to sensuality, to literal sensuality, which increases progressively at every blow they inflict. They beat for a minute, for five minutes, for ten minutes, more often and more savagely. The child screams. At last the child cannot scream, it gasps, 'Daddy! daddy!' By some diabolical unseemly chance the case was brought into court. A counsel was engaged. The Russian people have long called a barrister 'a conscience for hire.' The counsel protests in his client's defense. 'It's such a simple thing,' he says, 'an everyday domestic event. A father corrects his child. To our shame be it said, it is brought into court.' The jury, convinced by him, gives a favorable verdict. The public roars with delight that the torturer is acquitted. Ah, pity I wasn't there! I would have proposed to raise a subscription in his honor! . . . Charming pictures.

"But I've still better things about children. I've collected a great, great deal about Russian children, Alyosha. There was a little girl of five who was hated by her father and mother, 'most worthy and respectable people, of good education and breeding.' You see, I must repeat again, it is a peculiar characteristic of many people, this love of torturing children, and children only. To all other types of humanity these torturers behave mildly and benevolently like cultivated and humane Europeans; but they are very fond of tormenting children, even fond of children themselves in that sense. It's just their defenselessness that tempts the tormentor, just the angelic confidence of the child who has no refuge and no appeal that sets his vile blood on fire. In every man, of course, a demon lies hidden—the demon of rage, the demon of lustful heat at the screams of the tortured victim, the demon of lawlessness let off the chain, the demon of diseases that follow on vice, gout, kidney disease, and so on.

"This poor child of five was subjected to every possible torture by those cultivated parents. They beat her, thrashed her, kicked her for no reason till her body was one bruise. Then, they went to greater refinements of cruelty—shut her up all night in the cold and frost in a privy, and because she didn't ask to be taken up at night (as though a child of five sleeping its angelic, sound sleep could be trained to wake and ask), they smeared her face and filled her mouth with excrement, and it was her mother, her mother did this. And that mother could sleep, hearing the poor child's groans! Can you understand why a little creature, who can't even understand what's done to her, should beat her little aching heart with her tiny fist in the dark and the cold, and weep her meek unresentful tears to dear, kind God to protect her? Do you understand that, friend and brother, you pious and humble novice? Do you understand why this infamy must be and is permitted? Without it, I am told, man could not have existed on earth, for he could not have known good and evil. Why should he know that diabolical good and evil when it costs so much? Why, the whole world of knowledge is not worth that child's prayer to 'dear, kind God'! I say nothing of the sufferings of grown-up people, they have eaten the apple, damn them, and the devil take them all! But these little ones! I am making you suffer, Alyosha, you are not yourself. I'll leave off it if you like."

"Never mind. I want to suffer too," muttered Alyosha.

"One picture, only one more, because it's so curious, so characteristic, and I have only just read it in some collection of Russian antiquities. I've forgotten the name. I must look it up. It was in the darkest days of serfdom at the beginning of the century, and long live the Liberator of the People! There was in those days a general of aristocratic connections, the owner of great estates, one of those men—somewhat exceptional, I believe, even then—who, retiring from the service into a life of leisure, are convinced that they've earned absolute power over the lives of the subjects. There were such men then. So our general, settled on his property of two thousand souls, lives in pomp, and domineers over his poor neighbors as though they were dependents and buffoons. He has kennels of hundreds of hounds and nearly a hundred dog-boys—all mounted, and in uniform. One day a serf boy, a little child of eight, threw a stone in play and hurt the paw of the general's favorite hound. 'Why is my favorite dog lame?' He is told that the boy threw a stone that hurt the dog's paw. 'So you did it.' The general looked the child up and down. 'Take him.' He was taken—taken from his mother and kept shut up all night. Early that morning the general comes out on horseback, with the hounds, his dependents, dog-boys, and huntsmen, all mounted around him in full hunting parade. The servants are summoned for their edification, and in front of them all stands the mother of the child. The child is brought from the lockup. It's a gloomy, cold, foggy autumn day, a capital day for hunting. The general orders the child to be undressed; the child is stripped naked. He shivers, numb with terror, not daring to cry . . . 'Make him run,' commands the general. 'Run! run!' shout the dog-boys. The boy runs . . . 'At him!' yells the general, and he sets the whole pack of hounds on the child. The hounds catch him, and tear him to pieces before his mother's eyes! . . . I believe the general was afterwards declared incapable of administering his estates. Well—what did he deserve? To be shot? To be shot for the satisfaction of our moral feelings? Speak, Alyosha!"

"To be shot," murmured Alyosha, lifting his eyes to Ivan with a pale, twisted smile.

"Bravo!" cried Ivan delighted. "If even you say so . . . You're a pretty monk! So there is a little devil sitting in your heart, Alyosha Karamazov!"

"What I said was absurd, but—"

"That's just the point that 'but'!" cried Ivan. "Let me tell you, novice, that the absurd is only too necessary on earth. The world stands on absurdities, and perhaps nothing would have come to pass in it without them. We know what we know!"

"What do you know?"

"I understand nothing," Ivan went on, as though in delirium. "I don't want to understand anything now. I want to stick to the fact. I made up my mind long ago not to understand. If I try to understand anything, I shall be false to the fact and I have determined to stick to the fact."

"Why are you trying me?" Alyosha cried, with sudden distress. "Will you say what you mean at last?"

"Of course, I will; that's what I've been leading up to. You are dear to me, I don't want to let you go, and I won't give you up to your Zossima [priest, Father]."

Ivan for a minute was silent, his face became all at once very sad.

"Listen! I took the case of children only to make my case clearer. Of the other tears of humanity with which the earth is soaked from its crust to its center, I will say nothing. I have narrowed my subject on purpose, I am a bug, and I recognize in all humility that I cannot understand why the world is arranged as it is. Men are themselves to blame, I suppose; they were given paradise, they wanted freedom, and stole fire from heaven, though they knew they would become unhappy, so there is no need to pity them. With my pitiful, earthly, Euclidean understanding, all I know is that there is suffering and that there are none guilty; that cause follows effect, simply and directly; that everything flows and finds its level—but that's only Euclidean nonsense, I know that, and I can't consent to live by it! What comfort is to me that there are none guilty and that cause follows effect simply and directly, and that I know it—I must have justice, or I will destroy myself. And not justice in some remote infinite time and space, but here on earth, and that I could see myself. I have believed in it. I want to see it, and if I am dead by then, let me rise again, for if it all happens without me, it will be too unfair. Surely I haven't suffered, simply that I, my crimes and my sufferings, may manure the soil of the future harmony for somebody else. I want to see with my own eyes the hind lie down with the lion and the victim rise up and embrace his murderer. I want to be there when everyone suddenly understands what it has all been for. All the religions of the world are built on this longing, and I am a believer. But there are the children, and what am I to do about them? That's a question I can't answer. For the hundredth time I repeat, there are numbers of questions, but I've only taken the children, because in their case what I mean is so unanswerably clear. Listen! If all must suffer to pay for the eternal harmony, what have children to do with it, tell me, please? It's beyond all comprehension why they should suffer, and why they should pay for the harmony. Why should they, too, furnish material to enrich the soil for the harmony of the future? I understand solidarity in sin among men. I understand solidarity in retribution, too; but there can be no such solidarity with children. And if it is really true that they must share responsibility for all their father's crimes, such a truth is not of this world and is beyond my comprehension. Some jester will say, perhaps, that the child would have grown up and have sinned, but you see he didn't grow up, he was torn to pieces by the dogs, at eight years old. Oh, Alyosha, I am not blaspheming! I understand, of course, what an upheaval of the universe it will be, when everything in heaven and earth blends in one hymn of praise and everything that lives and has lived cries aloud: 'Thou art just, O Lord, for Thy ways are revealed.' When the mother embraces the fiend who threw her child to the dogs, and all three cry aloud with tears, 'Thou are just, O Lord!' then, of course, the crown of knowledge will be reached and all will be made clear. But what pulls me up here is that I can't accept that harmony. And while I am on earth, I make haste to take my own measures. You see, Alyosha, perhaps it really may happen that if I live to that moment, or rise again to see it, I, too, perhaps, may cry aloud with the rest, looking at the mother embracing the child's torturer, 'Thou are just, O Lord!' but I don't want to cry aloud then. While there is still time, I hasten to protect myself and so I renounce the higher harmony altogether. It's not worth the tears of that one tortured child who beat itself on the breast with its little fist and prayed in its stinking outhouse with an unexpiated tear to 'dear, kind God'! It's not worth it, because those tears are unatoned for. They must be atoned for, or there can be no harmony. But how? How are you going to atone for them? Is it possible? By their being avenged? But what do I care for avenging them? What do I care for a hell for oppressors? What good can hell do, since those children have already been tortured? And what becomes of harmony, if there is hell? I want to forgive. I want to embrace. I don't want more suffering. And if the sufferings of children go to swell the sum of sufferings which was necessary to pay for truth, then I protest that the truth is not worth such a price. I don't want the mother to embrace the oppressor who threw her son to the dogs! She dare not forgive him! Let her forgive him for herself, if she will, let her forgive the torturer for the immeasurable suffering of her mother's heart. But the sufferings of her tortured child she has no right to forgive; she dare not forgive the torturer, even if the child were to forgive him! And if that is so, if they dare not forgive, what becomes of harmony? Is there in the whole world a being who would have the right to forgive and could forgive? I don't want harmony. From love for humanity I don't want it. I would rather be left with the unavenged suffering. I would rather remain with my unavenged suffering and unsatisfied indignation, *even if I were wrong*. Besides, too high a price is asked for harmony; it's beyond our means to pay so much to enter on it. And so I hasten to give back my entrance ticket, and if I am an honest man I am bound to give it back as soon as possible. And that I am doing. It's not God that I don't accept, Alyosha, only I most respectfully return Him the ticket."

"That's rebellion," murmured Alyosha, looking down.

"Rebellion? I am sorry you call it that," said Ivan earnestly. "One can hardly live in rebellion, and I want to live. Tell me yourself, I challenge you—answer. Imagine that you are creating a fabric of human destiny with the object of making men happy in the end, giving them peace and rest at last, but that it was essential and inevitable to torture to death only one tiny creature—that baby beating its breast with its fist, for instance—and to found that edifice on its unavenged tears, would you consent to be the architect on those conditions? Tell me, and tell the truth."

"No, I wouldn't consent," said Alyosha softly. . . .

Evil and Omnipotence*

J. L. MACKIE

J. L. Mackie (1917–1983) taught philosophy at University College, Oxford.

THE TRADITIONAL ARGUMENTS for the existence of God have been fairly thoroughly criticized by philosophers. But the theologian can, if he wishes, accept this criticism. He can admit that no rational proof of God's existence is possible. And he can still retain all that is essential to his position, by holding that God's existence is known in some other, nonrational way. I think, however, that a more telling criticism can be made by way of the traditional problem of evil. Here it can be shown, not that religious beliefs lack rational support, but that they are positively irrational, that the several parts of the essential theological doctrine are inconsistent with one another, so that the theologian can maintain his position as a whole only by a much more extreme rejection of reason than in the former case. He must now be prepared to believe, not merely what cannot be proved, but what can be *disproved* from other beliefs that he also holds.

The problem of evil, in the sense in which I shall be using the phrase, is a problem only for someone who believes that there is a God who is both omnipotent and wholly good. And it is a logical problem, the problem of clarifying and reconciling a number of beliefs: it is not a scientific problem that might be solved by further observations, or a practical problem that might be solved by a decision or an action. These points are obvious; I mention them only because they are sometimes ignored by theologians, who sometimes parry a statement of the problem with such remarks as "Well, can you solve the problem yourself?" or "This is a mystery which may be revealed to us later" or "Evil is something to be faced and overcome, not to be merely discussed."

In its simplest form the problem is this: God is omnipotent; God is wholly good; and yet evil exists. There seems to be some contradiction between these three propositions, so that if any two of them were true the third would be false. But at the same time all three are essential parts of most theological positions: the theologian, it seems, at once *must* adhere and *cannot consistently* adhere to all three. (The problem does not arise only for theists, but I shall discuss it in the form in which it presents itself for ordinary theism.)

However, the contradiction does not arise immediately; to show it we need some additional premises, or perhaps some quasi-logical rules connecting the terms "good," "evil," and "omnipotent." These additional principles are that good is opposed to evil, in such a way that a good thing always eliminates evil as far as it can, and that there are no limits to what an omnipotent thing can do. From these it follows that a good omnipotent thing eliminates evil completely, and then the propositions that a good omnipotent thing exists, and that evil exists, are incompatible.

ADEQUATE SOLUTIONS

Now once the problem is fully stated it is clear that it can be solved, in the sense that the problem will not arise if one gives up at least one of the proposi-

**From* Mind, *Vol. LXIV, No. 254 (1955). Reprinted by permission of the author and Basil Blackwell, Publisher.*

tions that constitute it. If you are prepared to say that God is not wholly good, or not quite omnipotent, or that evil does not exist, or that good is not opposed to the kind of evil that exists, or that there are limits to what an omnipotent thing can do, then the problem of evil will not arise for you.

There are, then, quite a number of adequate solutions of the problem of evil, and some of these have been adopted, or almost adopted, by various thinkers. For example, a few have been prepared to deny God's omnipotence, and rather more have been prepared to keep the term "omnipotence" but severely to restrict its meaning, recording quite a number of things that an omnipotent being cannot do. Some have said that evil is an illusion, perhaps because they held that the whole world of temporal, changing things is an illusion, and that what we call evil belongs only to this world, or perhaps because they held that although temporal things *are* much as we see them, those that we call evil are not really evil. Some have said that what we call evil is merely the privation of good, that evil in a positive sense, evil that would really be opposed to good, does not exist. Many have agreed with Pope that disorder is harmony not understood, and that partial evil is universal good. Whether any of these views is *true* is, of course, another question. But each of them gives an adequate solution of the problem of evil in the sense that if you accept it this problem does not arise for you, though you may, of course, have *other* problems to face.

But often enough these adequate solutions are only *almost* adopted. The thinkers who restrict God's power, but keep the term "omnipotence," may reasonably be suspected of thinking, in other contexts, that his power is really unlimited. Those who say that evil is an illusion may also be thinking, inconsistently, that this illusion is itself an evil. Those who say that "evil" is merely privation of good may also be thinking, inconsistently, that privation of good is an evil. . . . If Pope meant what he said in the first line of his couplet, that "disorder" is only harmony not understood, the "partial evil" of the second line must, for consistency, mean "that which, taken in isolation, falsely appears to be evil," but it would more naturally mean "that which, in isolation, really is evil." The second line, in fact, hesitates between two views, that "partial evil" isn't really evil, since only the universal quality is real, and that "partial evil" is really an evil, but only a little one.

In addition, therefore, to adequate solutions, we must recognize unsatisfactory inconsistent solutions, in which there is only a half-hearted or temporary rejection of one of the propositions which together constitute the problem. In these, one of the constituent propositions is explicitly rejected, but it is covertly reasserted or assumed elsewhere in the system.

FALLACIOUS SOLUTIONS

Besides these half-hearted solutions, which explicitly reject but implicitly assert one of the constituent propositions, there are definitely fallacious solutions which explicitly maintain all the constituent propositions, but implicitly reject at least one of them in the course of the argument that explains away the problem of evil.

There are, in fact, many so-called solutions which purport to remove the contradiction without abandoning any of its constituent propositions. These must be fallacious, as we can see from the very statement of the problem, but it is not so easy to see in each case precisely where the fallacy lies. I suggest that in all cases the fallacy has the general form suggested above: in order to solve the problem one (or perhaps more) of its constituent propositions is given up, but in such a way that it appears to have been retained, and can therefore be asserted without qualification in other contexts. Sometimes there is a further complication: the supposed solution moves to and fro between, say, two of the constituent propositions, at one point asserting the first of these but covertly abandoning the second, at another point asserting the second but covertly abandoning the first. These fallacious solutions often turn upon some equivocation with the words "good" and "evil," or upon some vagueness about the way in which good and evil are opposed to one another, or about how much is meant by "omnipotence." I propose to examine some of these so-called solutions, and to exhibit their fallacies in detail. Incidentally, I shall also be considering whether an adequate solution could be reached by a minor modification of one or more of the constituent propositions, which would, however, still satisfy all the essential requirements of ordinary theism.

1. "Good cannot exist without evil" or "Evil is necessary as a counterpart to good."

It is sometimes suggested that evil is necessary as a counterpart to good, that if there were no evil there could be no good either, and that this solves the problem of evil. It is true that it points to an answer to the question "Why should there be evil?" But it does so only by qualifying some of the propositions that constitute the problem.

First, it sets a limit to what God can do, saying that God *cannot* create good without simultaneously creating evil, and this means either that God is not omnipotent or that there are *some* limits to what an omnipotent thing can do. It may be replied that these limits are always presupposed, that omnipotence has never meant the power to do what is logically impossible, and on the present view the existence of good without evil would be a logical impossibility. This interpretation of omnipotence may, indeed, be accepted as a modification of our original account which does not reject anything that is essential to theism, and I shall in general assume it in the subsequent discussion. It is, perhaps, the most common theistic view, but I think that some theists at least have maintained that God can do what is logically impossible. Many theists, at any rate, have held that logic itself is created or laid down by God, that logic is the way in which God arbitrarily chooses to think. (This is, of course, parallel to the ethical view that morally right actions are those which God arbitrarily chooses to command, and the two views encounter similar difficulties.) And *this* account of logic is clearly inconsistent with the view that God is bound by logical necessities—unless it is possible for an omnipotent being to bind himself, an issue which we shall consider later, when we come to the Paradox of Omnipotence. This solution of the problem of evil cannot, therefore, be consistently adopted along with the view that logic is itself created by God.

But, secondly, this solution denies that evil is opposed to good in our original sense. If good and evil are counterparts, a good thing will not "eliminate evil as far as it can." Indeed, this view suggests that good and evil are not strictly qualities of things at all. Perhaps the suggestion is that good and evil are related in much the same way as great and small. Certainly, when the term "great" is used relatively as a condensation of "greater than so-and-so," and "small" is used correspondingly, greatness and smallness are counterparts and cannot exist without each other. But in this sense greatness is not a quality, not an intrinsic feature of anything; and it would be absurd to think of a movement in favor of greatness and against smallness in this sense. Such a movement would be self-defeating, since relative greatness can be promoted only by a simultaneous promotion of relative smallness. I feel sure that no theists would be content to regard God's goodness as analogous to this—as if what he supports were not the *good* but the *better,* and as if he had the paradoxical aim that all things should be better than other things.

This point is obscured by the fact that "great" and "small" seem to have an absolute as well as a relative sense. I cannot discuss here whether there is absolute magnitude or not, but if there is, there could be an absolute sense for "great," it could mean of at least a certain size, and it would make sense to speak of all things getting bigger, of a universe that was expanding all over, and therefore it would make sense to speak of promoting greatness. But in *this* sense great and small are not logically necessary counterparts: either quality could exist without the other. There would be no logical impossibility in everything's being small or in everything's being great.

Neither in the absolute nor in the relative sense, then, of "great" and "small" do these terms provide an analogy of the sort that would be needed to support this solution of the problem of evil. In neither case are greatness and smallness *both* necessary counterparts *and* mutually opposed forces or possible objects for support and attack.

It may be replied that good and evil are necessary counterparts in the same way as any quality and its logical opposite: redness can occur, it is suggested, only if nonredness also occurs. But unless evil is merely the privation of good, they are not logical opposites, and some further argument would be needed to show that they are counterparts in the same way as genuine logical opposites. Let us assume that this could be given. There is still doubt of the correctness of the metaphysical principle that a quality must have a real opposite: I suggest that it is not really impossible that everything should be, say, red, that the truth is merely that if everything were red we should not notice redness, and so we should have no word "red"; we observe and give names to qualities only if they have real opposites. If so, the principle that a term must have an opposite would belong only to our language or to our thought, and would not be an ontological principle, and, correspondingly, the rule that good cannot exist without evil would not state a logical necessity of a sort that God would just have to put up with. God might have made everything good, though *we* should not have noticed it if he had.

But, finally, even if we concede that this *is* an ontological principle, it will provide a solution for the problem of evil only if one is prepared to say, "Evil exists, but only just enough evil to serve as the counterpart of good." I doubt whether any theist will accept this. After all, the *ontological* requirement that nonredness should occur would be satisfied even if all the universe, except for a minute speck, were red, and, if there were a corresponding requirement for evil as a counterpart to good, a minute dose of evil would presumably do. But theists are not usually willing to say, in all contexts, that all the evil that occurs is a minute and necessary dose.

2. "Evil is necessary as a means to good."

It is sometimes suggested that evil is necessary for good not as a counterpart but as a means. In its simple form this has little plausibility as a solution of the problem of evil, since it obviously implies a severe restriction of God's power. It would be a *causal* law that you cannot have a certain end without a certain means, so that if God has to introduce evil as a means to good, he must be subject to at least some causal laws. This certainly conflicts with what a theist normally means by omnipotence. This view of God as limited by causal laws also conflicts with the view that causal laws are themselves made by God, which is more widely held than the corresponding view about the laws of logic. This conflict would, indeed, be resolved if it were possible for an omnipotent being to bind himself, and this possibility has still to be considered. Unless a favorable answer can be given to this question, the suggestion that evil is necessary as a means to good solves the problem of evil only by denying one of its constituent propositions, either that God is omnipotent or that "omnipotent" means what it says.

3. "The universe is better with some evil in it than it could be if there were no evil."

Much more important is a solution which at first seems to be a mere variant of the previous one, that evil may contribute to the goodness of a whole in which it is found, so that the universe as a whole is better as it is, with some evil in it, than it would be if there were no evil. This solution may be developed in either of two ways. It may be supported by an aesthetic analogy, by the fact that contrasts heighten beauty, that in a musical work, for example, there may occur discords which somehow add to the beauty of the work as a whole. Alternatively, it may be worked out in connection with the notion of progress, that the best possible organization of the universe will not be static, but progressive, that the gradual overcoming of evil by good is really a finer thing than would be the eternal unchallenged supremacy of good.

In either case, this solution usually starts from the assumption that the evil whose existence gives rise to the problem of evil is primarily what is called physical evil, that is to say, pain. In Hume's rather half-hearted presentation of the problem of evil, the evils that he stresses are pain and disease, and those who reply to him argue that the existence of pain and disease makes possible the existence of sympathy, benevolence, heroism, and the gradually successful struggle of doctors and reformers to overcome these evils. In fact, theists often seize the opportunity to accuse those who stress the problem of evil of taking a low, materialistic view of good and evil, equating these with pleasure and pain, and of ignoring the more spiritual goods which can arise in the struggle against evils.

But let us see exactly what is being done here. Let us call pain and misery "first order evil" or "evil (1)." What contrasts with this, namely, pleasure and happiness, will be called "first order good" or "good (1)." Distinct from this is "second order good" or "good (2)" which somehow emerges in a complex situation in which evil (1) is a necessary component—logically, not merely causally, necessary. (Exactly *how* it emerges does not matter: in the crudest version of this solution good (2) is simply the heightening of happiness by the contrast with misery, in other versions it includes sympathy with suffering, heroism in facing danger, and the gradual decrease of first order evil and increase of first order good.) It is also being assumed that second order good is more important than first order good or evil, in particular that it more than outweighs the first order evil it involves.

Now this is a particularly subtle attempt to solve the problem of evil. It defends God's goodness and omnipotence on the ground that (on a sufficiently long view) this is the best of all logically possible worlds because it includes the important second order goods, and yet it admits that real evils, namely first order evils, exist. But does it still hold that good and evil are opposed? Not, clearly, in the sense that we set out originally: good does not tend to eliminate evil in general. Instead, we have a modified, a more complex pattern. First order good (e.g., happiness) *contrasts with* first order evil (e.g., misery): these two are opposed in a fairly mechanical way; some second order goods (e.g., benevolence) try to maximize first order good and minimize first order evil; but God's goodness is not this, it is rather the will to maximize *second* order good. We might, therefore, call God's goodness an example of a third order goodness, or good (3). While this account is different from our original one, it might well be held to be an improvement on it, to give a more accurate description of the way in which good is opposed to evil, and to be consistent with the essential theist position.

There might, however, be several objections to this solution.

First, some might argue that such qualities as benevolence—and *a fortiori* the third order goodness which promotes benevolence—have a merely derivative value, that they are not higher sorts of good, but merely means to good (1), that is, to happiness, so that it would be absurd for God to keep misery in existence in order to make possible the virtues of benevolence, heroism, etc. The theist who adopts the present solution must, of course, deny this, but he can do so with some plausibility, so I should not press this objection.

Secondly, it follows from this solution that God is not in our sense benevolent or sympathetic: he is not concerned to minimize evil (1), but only to promote good (2); and this might be a disturbing conclusion for some theists.

But, thirdly, the fatal objection is this. Our analysis shows clearly the possibility of the existence of a *second* order evil, an evil (2) contrasting with good (2) as evil (1) contrasts with good (1). This would include malevolence, cruelty, callousness, cowardice, and states in which good (1) is decreasing and evil (1) increasing. And just as good (2) is held to be the important kind of good, the kind that God is concerned to promote, so evil (2) will, by analogy, be the important kind of evil, the kind which God, if he were wholly good and omnipotent, would eliminate. And yet evil (2) plainly exists, and indeed most theists (in other contexts) stress its existence more than that of evil (1). We should, therefore, state the problem of evil in terms of second order evil, and against this form of the problem the present solution is useless.

An attempt might be made to use this solution again, at a higher level, to explain the occurrence of evil (2): indeed the next main solution that we shall examine does just this, with the help of some new notions. Without any fresh notions, such a solution would have little plausibility: for example, we could hardly say that the really important good was a good (3), such as the increase of benevolence in proportion to cruelty, which logically required for its occurrence the occurrence of some second order evil. But even if evil (2) could be explained in this way, it is fairly clear that there would be third order evils contrasting with this third order good: and we should be well on the way to an infinite regress, where the solution of a problem of evil, stated in terms of evil (n), indicated the existence of an evil ($n + 1$), and a further problem to be solved.

4. "Evil is due to human free will."

Perhaps the most important proposed solution of the problem of evil is that evil is not to be ascribed to God at all, but to the independent actions of human beings, supposed to have been endowed by God with freedom of the will. This solution may be combined with the preceding one: first order evil (e.g., pain) may be justified as a logically necessary component in second order good (e.g., sympathy) while second order evil (e.g., cruelty) is not *justified,* but is so ascribed to human beings that God cannot be held responsible for it. This combination evades my third criticism of the preceding solution.

The free-will solution also involves the preceding solution at a higher level. To explain why a wholly good God gave men free will although it would lead to some important evils, it must be argued that it is better on the whole that men should act freely, and sometimes err, than that they should be innocent automata, acting rightly in a wholly determined way. Freedom, that is to say, is now treated as a third order good, and as being more valuable than second order goods (such as sympathy and heroism) would be if they were deterministically produced, and it is being assumed that second order evils, such as cruelty, are logically necessary accompaniments of freedom, just as pain is a logically necessary pre-condition of sympathy.

I think that this solution is unsatisfactory primarily because of the incoherence of the notion of freedom of the will: but I cannot discuss this topic adequately here, although some of my criticisms will touch upon it.

First I should query the assumption that second order evils are logically necessary accompaniments of freedom. I should ask this: if God has made men such that in their free choices they sometimes prefer what is good and sometimes what is evil, why could he not have made men such that they always freely choose the good? If there is no logical impossibility in a man's freely choosing the good on one, or on several occasions, there cannot be a logical impossibility in his freely choosing the good on every occasion. God was not, then, faced with a choice between making innocent automata and making beings who, in acting freely, would sometimes go wrong: there was open to him the obviously better possibility of making beings who would act freely but always go right. Clearly, his failure to avail himself of this possibility is inconsistent with his being both omnipotent and wholly good.

If it is replied that this objection is absurd, that the making of some wrong choices is logically necessary for freedom, it would seem that "freedom" must here mean complete randomness or indeterminacy, including randomness with regard to the alternatives good and evil, in other words that men's choices and consequent actions can be "free" only if they are not determined by their characters. Only on this assumption can God escape the responsibility for men's actions; for if he made them as they are, but did not determine their wrong choices, this can only be because the wrong choices are not determined by men as they are. But then if freedom is randomness, how can it be a characteristic of *will?* And, still more, how can it be the most important good? What value or merit would there be in free choices if these were random actions which were not determined by the nature of the agent?

I conclude that to make this solution plausible two different senses of "freedom" must be confused, one sense which will justify the view that freedom is a third order good, more valuable than other goods would be without it, and another sense, sheer randomness, to prevent us from ascribing to God a decision to make men such that they sometimes go wrong when he might have made them such that they would always freely go right.

This criticism is sufficient to dispose of this solution. But besides this there is a fundamental difficulty in the notion of an omnipotent God creating men with free will, for if men's wills are really free this must mean that even God cannot control them, that is, that God is no longer omnipotent. It may be objected that God's gift of freedom to men does not mean that he *cannot* control their wills, but that he always *refrains* from controlling their wills. But why, we may ask, should God refrain from controlling evil wills? Why should he not leave men free to will rightly, but intervene when he sees them beginning to will wrongly? If God could do this, but does not, and if he is wholly good, the only explanation could be that even a wrong free act of will is not really evil, that its freedom is a value which outweighs its wrongness, so that there would be a loss of value if God took away the wrongness and the freedom together. But this is utterly opposed to what theists say about sin in other contexts. The present solution of the problem of evil, then, can be maintained only in the form that God has made men so free that he *cannot* control their wills.

This leads us to what I call the Paradox of Omnipotence: can an omnipotent being make things which he cannot subsequently control? Or, what is practically equivalent to this, can an omnipotent being make rules which then bind himself? (These are practically equivalent because any such rules could be regarded as setting certain things beyond his control, and *vice versa.*) The second of these formulations is relevant to the suggestions that we have already met, that an omnipotent God creates the rules of logic or causal laws, and is then bound by them.

It is clear that this is a paradox: the questions cannot be answered satisfactorily either in the affirmative or in the negative. If we answer "Yes," it follows that if God actually makes things which he cannot control, or makes rules which bind himself, he is not omnipotent once he has made them: there are *then* things which he cannot do. But if we answer "No," we are immediately asserting that there are things which he cannot do, that is to say that he is already not omnipotent.

It cannot be replied that the question which sets this paradox is not a proper question. It would make perfectly good sense to say that a human mechanic has made a machine which he cannot control: if there is any difficulty about the question it lies in the notion of omnipotence itself.

This, incidentally, shows that although we have approached this paradox from the free-will theory, it is equally a problem for a theological determinist. No one thinks that machines have free will, yet they may well be beyond the control of their makers. The determinist might reply that anyone who makes anything determines its ways of acting, and so determines its subsequent behavior: even the human mechanic does this by his *choice* of materials and structure for his machine, though he does not know all about either of these: the mechanic thus determines, though he may not foresee, his machine's actions. And since God is omniscient, and since his creation of things is total, he both determines and foresees the ways in which his creatures will act. We may grant this, but it is beside the point. The question is not whether God *originally* determined the future actions of his creatures, but whether he can *subsequently* control their actions, or whether he was able in his original creation to put things beyond his subsequent control. Even on determinist principles the answers "Yes" and "No" are equally irreconcilable with God's omnipotence.

Before suggesting a solution of this paradox, I would point out that there is a parallel Paradox of Sovereignty. Can a legal sovereign make a law restricting its own future legislative power? For example, could the British parliament make a law forbidding any future parliament to socialize banking, and also forbidding the future repeal of this law itself? Or could the British parliament, which was legally sovereign in Australia in, say, 1899, pass a valid law, or series of laws, which made it no longer sovereign in 1933? Again, neither the affirmative nor the negative answer is really satisfactory. If we were to answer "Yes," we should be admitting the validity of a law which, if it were actually made, would mean that parliament was no longer sovereign. If we were to answer "No," we should be admitting that there is a law, not logically absurd, which parliament cannot validly make, that is, that parliament is not now a legal sovereign. This paradox can be solved in the following way. We should distinguish between first order laws, that is, laws governing the actions of individuals and bodies other than the legislature, and second order laws, that is, laws about laws, laws governing the actions of the legislature itself. Correspondingly, we should distinguish two orders of sovereignty, first order sovereignty (sovereignty [1]) which is unlimited authority to make first order laws, and second order sovereignty (sovereignty [2]) which is unlimited authority to make second order laws. If we say that parliament is sovereign we might mean that any parliament at any time has sovereignty (1), or we might mean that parliament has both sovereignty (1) and sovereignty (2) at present, but we cannot without contradiction mean both that the present parliament has sovereignty (2) and that every parliament at every time has sovereignty (1), for if the present parliament has sovereignty (2) it may use it to take away the sovereignty (1) of later parliaments. What the paradox shows is that we cannot ascribe to any continuing institution legal sovereignty in an inclusive sense.

The analogy between omnipotence and sovereignty shows that the paradox of omnipotence can be solved in a similar way. We must distinguish between first order omnipotence (omnipotence [1]), that is, unlimited power to act, and second order omnipotence (omnipotence [2]), that is, unlimited power to determine what powers to act things shall have. Then we could consistently say that God all the time has omnipotence (1), but if so no beings at any time have powers to act independently of God. Or we could say that God at one time had omnipotence (2), and used it to assign independent powers to act to certain things, so that God thereafter did not have omnipotence (1). But what the paradox shows is that we cannot consistently ascribe to any continuing being omnipotence in an inclusive sense.

An alternative solution of this paradox would be simply to deny that God is a continuing being, that any times can be assigned to his actions at all. But on this assumption (which also has difficulties of its own) no meaning can be given to the assertion that God made men with wills so free that he could not control them. The paradox of omnipotence can be avoided by putting God outside time, but the free-will solution of the problem of evil cannot be saved in this way, and equally it remains impossible to hold that an omnipotent God *binds himself* by causal or logical laws.

CONCLUSION

Of the proposed solutions of the problem of evil which we have examined, none has stood up to criticism. There may be other solutions which require examination, but this study strongly suggests that there is no valid solution of the problem which does not modify at least one of the constituent propositions in a way which would seriously affect the essential core of the theistic position.

Quite apart from the problem of evil, the paradox of omnipotence has shown that God's omnipotence must in any case be restricted in one way or another, that unqualified omnipotence cannot be ascribed to any being that continues through time. And if God and his actions are not in time, can omnipotence, or power of any sort, be meaningfully ascribed to him?

The Magnitude, Duration and Distribution of Evil: A Theodicy*

PETER VAN INWAGEN

Peter van Inwagen has written works in metaphysics and the philosophy of religion. He teaches at the University of Notre Dame.

**From* Philosophical Topics *vol. 16, 1988. Reprinted by permission.*

I

IT IS GENERALLY, but not universally, conceded by Christians that the existence of evil has something to do with free will. The theodicy I shall present is of the "free will" type. That is to say, it proceeds by extending and elaborating the following story:

> God made the world and it was very good. An important part of its goodness was that it contained creatures made in His own image—that is, created beings capable of understanding (to some degree) their own nature and their place in the scheme of things entire; creatures, moreover, that were fit to be loved by God and to love Him in return and to love one another. But love implies freedom: for A to love B is for A freely to choose to be united to B in a certain way. Now even an omnipotent being cannot *insure* that some other being *freely* choose *x* over *y*. For God to create beings capable of loving Him, therefore, it was necessary for Him to take a risk: to risk the possibility that the beings He created would freely choose to withhold their love from Him.
>
> To love God and to desire to submit to His will are very closely related—at least as closely as the love of one's offspring and the desire to nurture and protect and raise them. God's free creatures—or some of them—, instead of loving Him and submitting to His will, chose to turn away from Him and "to follow instead the devices and desires of their own hearts." It was thus that evil entered the world. A husband and father who turns away from his wife and children and suppresses his natural desire to live with and to love and protect them, and chooses instead to indulge a desire for fame or sexual adventure or "self-realization," turns himself into something unnatural and harmful. Likewise, a creature who turns away from God turns himself into something unnatural and harmful. Having turned away from God, His creatures laid violent hands on the created world. They snatched it out of His grasp, and turned it to their own purposes. We are now living with the catastrophic consequences of that act.

This is the beginning of our theodicy. At its heart is what is a familiar "move" in discussions of the problem of evil, the insistence that even an omnipotent being cannot insure that someone *freely* do one thing rather than some contemplated alternative. Some philosophers have said that the proposition

> An omnipotent being cannot insure that a creature who has a free choice between *x* and *y* choose *x* rather than *y*

is false. . . . The issues raised by this contention have been extensively debated, and I have nothing new to say about them. I shall simply assume that this proposition is true.

I proceed now to elaborate the above very sketchy narrative of the origin of evil. It is obvious that this must be done. As it stands, the narrative accounts for the existence of only, as we might say, "some evil or other." It says nothing about evil of the kinds or in the amounts we actually observe, or anything about its duration—thousands upon thousands of years—or anything about the fact that its worst effects are distributed apparently at random and certainly without regard for desert. I shall elaborate this narrative with certain propositions drawn from Christian theology. All Christian theologians who could lay any claim to the titles "orthodox," "Catholic," or "traditional" would accept the following theses:

- *All* evil is the result of the primordial act of turning away from God; there is no source of evil other than creaturely rebellion.
- The creatures who committed the initial act of rebellion received sufficient warning that their act would lead to disaster. While they may have been unlike us in many ways, they were not children and were at least as intelligent as we; they fully understood the warning and the wisdom and authority of its Source.
- Among the creatures who rebelled were an entire generation of human beings, all of the human beings who were alive at some particular moment. [In my view, it was the *first* generation of human beings. But I shall not build this into our theodicy because (a) it is not nec-

essary, and (b) to argue that the proposition that there *was* a first generation of human beings is compatible with what we know about our evolutionary history would require a lengthy digression. The digression would involve the removal of two sorts of misunderstanding: misunderstandings about what it would be for there to be a first generation of human beings, and misunderstandings about what scientific study of the evolutionary history of our species has actually shown.] Before this rebellion, there was no evil—or at any rate none that affected human beings.

- In turning away from God, our ancestors ruined themselves; they became unable to turn back to Him of their own power, as someone who ignores a warning not to go too near the edge of a pit may fall into it, injure himself, and be unable to climb out. Thus, the act of rebellion, or its immediate consequences, may be called "the Fall."
- Their ruin was in some way inherited by all of their descendants. [This does not necessarily mean that their genes were altered by the Fall. I believe that it is possible to construct models of the Fall according to which its hereditary aspect is due to the effects of unaltered genes operating under conditions for which they were not "designed"—namely, conditions attendant upon separation from God. But I will not argue for this here.] Thus, evil is a persisting and—by any natural means—unalterable fact of history.
- God has not left His creatures to their misery—not, at any rate, His human creatures. He has inaugurated a plan whose workings will one day eventuate in the Atonement (at-one-ment) of His human creatures with Himself. (Or, at least, the Atonement of some of His human creatures with Himself. It may be that some of His creatures will, by their own free choice, resist Atonement forever.) In order to achieve Atonement with God, a ruined creature must turn to God and ask for His help and accept that help. The undoing of creaturely ruin must be a cooperative endeavor. The creature cannot accomplish it for himself, and even an omnipotent being cannot effect the required sort of regeneration of a creature if the creature refuses to be regenerate. Any aspect of the creatures' environment that would tend to discourage them from turning to Him and asking for His help would therefore be an obstacle to the completion of His plan.
- Every human being has an eternal future (and, therefore, the human species has an eternal future). We are now living, and have been living, throughout the archaeologically accessible past, within a temporary aberration in human history, an aberration that is a finite part of an eternal whole. When God's plan of Atonement comes to fruition, there will never again be undeserved suffering or any other sort of evil. The "age of evil" will eventually be remembered as a sort of transient "flicker" at the very beginning of human history.

I have said that I have drawn these points from Christian theology. But I have stated them so abstractly that, I think, at least some Jews and Muslims would agree with most of them. . . .

I added the above flesh to the skeleton provided by the standard "free-will" account of the origin of evil because it was clear that that skeleton was no theodicy. The skeleton, however, will require more flesh than this. We have still not got a finished theodicy. If we claimed that we had, a sceptic might, quite properly, respond along the following lines.

"God, you say, has set in motion a plan of Atonement. But why is it taking so long for His plan to work out? It's all very well to tell a tale that represents 'the age of evil' as a 'transient flicker at the very beginning of human history.' But every finite period is a mere flicker in Eternity. Nothing has been said to challenge the obvious proposition that God would not allow 'the age of evil' to go on any longer than necessary. Why, then, is 'this long' necessary?

"And why is there so *much* evil at any given time? Evil may be, as you say, the result of the creaturely abuse of free will. But the amount of evil could have been far less. For example, God, without in any way diminishing Cain's free will, could have warned Abel not to turn his back on him. If the implied general policy had been put into effect, a vast amount of evil would have been avoided.

"And why does God allow evil to be so unfairly distributed? Why is it so often the innocent—small children, for example—who suffer? Why is it so often the wicked who prosper?

"And what about 'physical' or 'natural' evil? How can the effects of the Bubonic Plague or the Lisbon earthquake be a result of creaturely free will?

"To roll all of these questions into one, Why has it been for thousands and thousands of years that enormous numbers of uncomprehending children have died as a result of epidemic disease and famine and natural disaster—while many a tyrant has died in bed? How could evil of such types and quantity and duration and distribution be necessary to God's plan of Atonement? Or, if all this evil is *not* necessary to God's plan, why does He not eliminate most of it, and make do with that residue of evil that is really necessary?"

II

I will continue to flesh out our skeletal theodicy by attending to the questions posed by our imaginary sceptic. I will address the last of them first.

The question presupposes that if there are evils that are not required by God's plan of Atonement, then there is such a thing as "that residue of evil that is really necessary," the minimum of evil that is required for God's plan to succeed. But this is not a very plausible thesis. It is not very plausible to suppose that there is a way in which evil could be distributed such that (i) that distribution of evil would serve God's purposes as well as any distribution could and (ii) God's purposes would be less well served by *any* distribution involving less evil. (One might as well suppose that if God's purposes require an impressively tall prophet to appear at a certain place and time, there is a minimum height such a prophet could have.) But if there is no minimum of evil that would serve God's purposes, then one cannot argue that God is unjust or cruel for not "getting by with less evil"—any more than one can argue that a law that fines motorists $25.00 for illegal parking is unjust or cruel owing to the fact that a fine of $24.99 would have an identical deterrent effect. The same point can be made in relation to time. If there is a purpose that is served by allowing "the age of evil" to have a certain duration, doubtless the same purpose would be served if the age of evil were cut short by a day or a year or even a century. But we would not call a judge unjust or cruel for imposing on a criminal a sentence of ten years on the ground—doubtless *true*—that a sentence of ten years less a day would have served as well whatever end the sentence was designed to serve. It is obvious that if, for any amount of evil that would have served God's purposes, slightly less evil would have served His purposes just as well—a very plausible assumption—, then the principle that God should have got by with less evil, if less would have served, entails the (*ex hypothesi* false) conclusion that God should have got by with no evil at all. . . .

The important things to recognize about these two points are, first, that they are valid and that to ignore them is to court confusion, and, secondly, that, valid though they be, they do not really meet the essence of the difficulty perceived by the sceptic, the difficulty that prompts him to ask, Why so much?, Why so long? To revert to our legal and judicial analogy, there may be no minimum appropriate fine for illegal parking, but (most of us would agree) if a fine of $25.00 would serve whatever purposes a fine for illegal parking is supposed to serve—deterrence, presumably—, then it would be wrong to set the fine at five thousand dollars. Similarly, if an "age of evil" of twenty years' duration, an age during which there were a few dozen broken bones and a score or so of very bad cases of influenza, would have served God's ends as well as the actual evil of human history serves them, then the enormity of His achieving these same ends by allowing the existence of "actual evil" passes all possibility of adequate description.

What the theodicist must do, given the facts of history, is to say what contribution—what essential contribution—to God's plan of Atonement is made by the facts about the types, magnitude, duration, and distribution of evil that are made known to us by historians and journalists (not to mention our own experience).

It will be useful to divide this problem facing the theodicist—and why not call it simply the problem of evil?—into several sub-problems. One division of the problem of evil is well known: the division of the problem into "the problem of moral evil" and "the problem of natural evil." A second division, one that will be particularly useful in our project of fleshing out our skeletal theodicy so as to meet the questions of the imaginary sceptic, cuts across the first. It divides the problem into three:

- the problem of the magnitude of evil
- the problem of the duration of evil
- the problem of the distribution of evil.

III

I assume that we already have an adequate answer to the problem of moral evil. I am not much interested in treating the problem of natural evil; my main interest in the present paper is the sub-problems generated by the second division. I shall, accordingly, treat the problem of natural evil in a rather perfunctory way. I shall suggest the broadest outlines of a solution, and leave the details for another time—or another writer. (But some of the things said in the course of our later discussion of the distribution problem will have some relevance to questions about the role in God's plan of natural evil.)

Natural evil is often cited as a special problem for those who say that evil entered the world through the creaturely abuse of free will, since tornadoes and earthquakes are obviously not caused by the acts—free or unfree—of human beings. The evil that results from tornadoes and earthquakes must nevertheless be treated in any theodicy of the "free will" type as somehow stemming from creaturely free will. One notorious way of doing this is to postulate that tornadoes and earthquakes are caused by malevolent non-human creatures. Another way (the way I shall take) proceeds from the observation that it is not earthquakes and tornadoes *per se* that are evil, but rather the suffering and death that they cause. Consider the following tale.

"Earthquakes all occur in one particular region called Earthquake Country, a region that was uninhabited (because everyone knew about the earthquakes and had no reason to go there) until twenty years ago. At that time, gold was discovered on the borders of Earthquake Country and the geological indications were that there was much more inside. Motivated solely by a desire to get rich, many people—people by no means in want—moved to Earthquake Country to prospect for gold. Many took their families with them. Some of them got rich, but many of them were killed or maimed by earthquakes."

This tale may not be true, but it demonstrates that earthquakes need not be caused by the actions of creatures for the suffering and death caused by earthquakes to be a result of the actions of those creatures.

Our theodicy, as we have so far stated it, entails that at one time—before the Fall—our ancestors lived in a world without evil. This, I suppose, entails that they were not subject to the baleful effects of earthquakes and tornadoes. But why not? Well, for the purposes of a *perfunctory* treatment of the problem of natural evil, we need assume only that there was *some* reason for this, a reason that became inoperative when our ancestors separated themselves from God. We *might* suppose, for example, that the old tradition (it is without Biblical warrant) that Adam and Eve possessed "preternatural powers" is substantially correct, and that these powers included certain cognitive powers; we might suppose that our unfallen ancestors knew (and pretty far in advance) whether an earthquake or tornado would strike a particular spot—and when. And we might suppose that their being able to know such things depended on their union with God and was lost as a natural consequence of their separating themselves from God. We must remember that, according to Christianity, human beings were designed for union with God, in the same sense as that in which they are designed to live in community with one another and to use language. A "feral child" is a ruined human being—though he is no less our brother than is Homer or Leonardo—and his ruin entails a grave diminution of his cognitive powers. According to Christianity, we have all been ruined by our separation from God, just as the feral child has been ruined by his separation from the human community. (The feral child's ruin is thus a ruin within a ruin, a second, individual ruin of an already ruined common human nature.) And the ruin of human nature consequent on our separation from God may have involved a grave diminution of our cognitive powers. According to the "just-so story" I am telling, we were designed by God to be able to protect ourselves from earthquakes and tornadoes—if you think that it would be possible to design a planet, and a universe to contain it, that was both capable of supporting human life and contained no earthquakes or tornadoes, I can only point out that you have never tried—and that the loss of this power is as natural a consequence of our ancestors' separation from God as is the loss of the capacity to acquire language a natural consequence of the feral child's separation from the human community. (Expansion of this just-so story to cover tigers and droughts and epidemic disease and so on is left as an exercise for the reader.) Doubtless we could tell many tales of speculative theological fiction having the feature that our being subject to the destructive forces of nature is ultimately a consequence of the creaturely abuse of free will. For our purposes, as I have said, it will suffice to assume that one of the tales that fits this abstract description is true.

This is all I have to say about natural evil, but I wish to remind the reader that if all human beings were wise and good, our sufferings would be vastly less than they are; and it is probably not true that we should be much better off for a complete elimination of natural evil. Doubtless there would be human beings more than willing to take up the slack. Our ancestral ruin is *primarily* a moral, as opposed to a cognitive, ruin. But ruins we are. If two explorers—who have never seen such a thing—come upon a ruined temple in the jungle, and if one of them thinks that it is a natural geological formation and the other that it is a building that is just as it was designed to be, neither will understand its shape. From the Christian point of view, it is impossible for one to understand humanity if one thinks of a human being as either a product of natural forces behind which there is no Mind or as the work that a Mind intended to produce. Both naturalism and deism (Christianity holds) go wrong about our nature right at the outset, and neither can yield an understanding of that nature.

We thus have some basis for understanding both "moral" and "natural" evil. (In a sense, the theodicy I am proposing entails that there is no fundamental distinction between them: natural evil is a special category of moral evil.) That is, we have a basis for understanding why God would allow such things to come to be. (This is a very abstract statement. Remember, we have not yet said anything about the magnitude, duration, or distribution of either sort of evil.) We may, to sum up, add the following statement to our theodicy.

> Our unfallen ancestors were somehow able to protect themselves from earthquakes and tornadoes and wild beasts and disease and so on. This ability depended on their union with God, and was lost when they separated themselves from Him.

I now turn to my primary interests in offering a theodicy: The magnitude, duration, and distribution of evil.

IV

"Our ancestors turned away from God and ruined themselves both morally and intellectually—and thus they began to harm one another and they lost their aboriginal power to protect themselves from the potentially destructive forces of non-human nature. This condition—their wickedness and helplessness—has persisted through all the generations, being somehow hereditary. But God has set a chain of events in motion that will eventually bring this state of affairs to an end."

The theodicist who wishes to add to this story elements that will account for evil as we actually find it must consider the questions about the magnitude, duration, and distribution of evil that we have put into the mouth of our imaginary sceptic. It will aid my order of exposition—and not, I think, unfairly modify the sceptic's case—if we recast the sceptic's three questions as four questions. The first and third have to do with the duration of evil, the second with its magnitude, and the fourth with its distribution.

Question 1. Why didn't God immediately restore His fallen creatures to their original union with Him?

Question 2. Why doesn't God protect His fallen creatures from the worst effects of their separation from Him: the horrible pain and suffering?

Question 3. Why has God allowed "the age of evil" to persist for thousands and thousands of years?

Question 4. Why do the innocent suffer and the wicked prosper?

Question 1

What would doing that actually have involved? Suppose that two brothers quarrel. Suppose that the quarrel becomes violent and then bitter and that finally they come to hate each other. Suppose that their mother prays to God that He restore their mutual love—and not by any gradual process, but immediately, right on the spot. What is she asking God to do? I can think of only one thing: to grant her request, God would have to wipe away all memory of everything that had happened between them since just before the moment they quarreled. Any philosopher worth his salt will probably be able to think of several grave conceptual difficulties that would attend this plan, but (assuming they could be overcome by omnipotence) God would not do such a thing, because, as Descartes has pointed out, God is not a deceiver, and such an act would constitute a grave deception about the facts of history. . . . I cannot see how God could simply, by sheer fiat, immediately have restored fallen humanity other than by a similar grave deception. And, we may add, if He did, what would happen next? What would prevent the Fall from immediately recurring?

V

Question 2

Consider the parable of the Prodigal Son. (Those whose memory of this story is dim will find it in the Gospel According to St. Luke, 15:11–32.) Suppose the father of the Prodigal had foreseen the probable effects of his son's rash use of his patrimony, and had hired actors to represent themselves as gamblers and deliberately to lose substantial sums to the Prodigal; and suppose that he had further arranged for his agents to bribe prostitutes to tell the Prodigal that they had fallen in love with him and wanted to give him all their earnings (following which declaration they are to pass on to him monies provided by his father); and suppose that the father's agents, on his instructions, had followed the Prodigal about in secret to protect him from the dangers attendant on the night life of the ancient Middle East.

What would have been the effects of this fatherly solicitude? Certainly the son could have continued to squander his substance indefinitely and with impunity. But here the word impunity must be understood in a rather superficial sense: for the son will be living a life of illusion (and that is a misfortune), and it is hard to see what could ever induce him to consider returning to his father (and I am inclined to think that that would also be a misfortune).

This modification of the story of the Prodigal Son suggests why it is that God does not simply "cancel"—by an almost continuous series of miracles—the pain and suffering that our separation of ourselves from Him has led to. First, if He did so, He would be, no less than in the case of the deleted memories, a deceiver. If He did so, we should be living in a world of illusion. Our lives would be invisibly "propped up" by God, but we should—justifiably—think that we were living successfully simply by the exercise of our native powers. This, it seems to me, would reduce our existence to something worse than meaningless: We should be, every one of us, *comic* figures. (If there were a novel whose plot was the "revised" life of the Prodigal Son sketched above, he could not be its hero or even a sympathetic character. The novel would be a low comedy and he would be the butt of the joke.) Now illusion of this sort is a bad thing in itself, but it would have consequences even worse than its intrinsic badness. If God did what is proposed, we should all be satisfied with our existence—or at least a lot closer to being satisfied than most of us are now. And if we are satisfied with our existence, why should we even consider turning to God and asking for His help? An essential and important component of God's plan of Atonement—this constitutes an addition to our theodicy—is to make us *dissatisfied* with our state of separation from Him; and not by miraculously altering our values or by subjecting us to illusion or by causing us suffering that has no natural connection with our separation, but simply by allowing us to "live with" the natural consequences of this separation, and by making it as difficult as possible for us to delude ourselves about the kind of world we live in: a hideous world, much of whose hideousness is quite plainly traceable to the inability of human beings to govern themselves or to order their own lives. Let us expand our theodicy:

> An essential part of God's plan of Atonement for separated humanity is for human beings to perceive that a natural consequence of human beings' attempting to order their own lives is a hideous world—a world that is hideous not only by His standards, but by the very standards they themselves accept.

Why is it important for human beings to perceive the hideousness of the world? Well, first, because that's how things are. That's what "man on his own" *means.* Look at the world around you—the world of violence, starvation, hatred, the world of the death camps and the Gulag and (quite possibly) thermonuclear or ecological catastrophe. (These are not the worst features of separated human life in the eyes of God, for these are all finite evils, and He can see quite plainly that each of us daily risks an infinite evil, the loss of the end for which he was made. But they really are hideous and they are recognizable as hideous by almost everyone, no matter what his beliefs and values may be.) These are natural effects of our living to ourselves, just as a literally feral existence is a natural effect of an infant's separation from the human community.

People who do not believe in God do not, of course, see our living to ourselves as a result of a prehistoric separation from God. But they can be aware—and it is a part of God's plan of Atonement that they *should* be aware—that something is pretty wrong and that this wrongness is a consequence of the intrinsic inability of human beings to devise a manner of life that is anything but hideous. (They *can* be aware. Few are. Part of the reason is that various myths have been invented for the purpose of obscuring the intrinsic incapacity of human beings to live successfully even by their own standards. The myths of Enlightenment, Progress, and the Revolution are the most prominent of these. Such myths in the end refute themselves by leading to ever deeper human misery; but, unfortunately, only in the end.) The broad psychological outlines of this feature of the plan that our theodicy ascribes to God are not hard to fathom. The realization that undirected human life is bound to be a failure even in secular terms may possibly set people to wondering whether there may not be some direction somewhere. But people who still think that the obvious hideousness of our world is caused by some accidental feature of human life—superstition, technological backwardness, primitive economic organization—, one that we shall presently get round to altering, are probably not going even to consider turning to God. It is a commonplace that religious belief is more common in South America and the Middle East and Africa than in the English-speaking countries and Western Europe. One possible explanation of this fact is that miserable and uneducated people turn to religious institutions as a man with a painful and incurable illness turns to quacks (and he is all the more likely to fall prey to quacks if he is uneducated). Here is another possible explanation. In the relatively prosperous and well-ordered West, people—middle-class people, anyway—are subject to an illusion about human nature and the conditions of human life. Although the prosperity and order in their lives is due to a special, fragile, and transient set of circumstances, they foolishly regard the kind of life they lead as the sort of thing human nature can be trusted to produce. The "wretched of the earth," on the other hand, see human nature as it really is. Many of them may be uneducated, in the sense of lacking the cognitive skills necessary to construct and operate a machine-based civilization, but they are far better educated than middle-class Europeans and Americans as regards the most general and important features of human nature. If an analogy involving medical quackery is wanted, we may say that a typical "post-religious" American or European is like a desperately sick man who has got his hands on some temporary panacea and who, as a consequence, has decided that the doctors who attempted to impress upon him the gravity of his condition are all quacks.

God's refusal to "cancel" the suffering that is a natural consequence of the Fall by providing separated humanity with a vast set of miraculous and invisible props can (according to the theodicy I propose) be understood on the model of a doctor who refuses to prescribe a pain-killer (say, for angina), on the ground that he knows that his patient will curtail some beloved but self-destructive activity—long-distance running, say—only if the patient continues to experience the pain that his condition signals. Now this sort of behavior on the part of a *doctor* may well be morally objectionable. The doctor is the patient's fellow adult and fellow citizen, and, or so it can plausibly be argued, it would be presumptuous of him to act in such a paternalistic way. One might even say that in so acting the doctor would be "playing God." But we can hardly accuse *God* of playing God. God is justifiably paternalistic because He is our Father and because He is perfect in knowledge and wisdom and because, or so I would argue, He has certain rights over us. These rights, as I see it, derive from the following facts: He made up the very idea of there being creatures like us out of the thought of His own mind, and He made us out of nothing to meet the specifications contained in that idea; everything we have—including the intellectual and moral faculties by means of which we make judgments about paternalism—we have received from Him; He made us for a certain purpose (to glorify Him and to enjoy Him forever) and we threaten to prevent that purpose from being fulfilled.

I have suggested that the initial stage of God's plan of Atonement essentially involves His separated creatures' being aware of the hideousness of their condition and of its being a natural result of their attempting to order their own lives. I would also suggest that the *outcome* of His plan of Atonement, the unending union of creatures with Himself, will essentially involve the *memory* of that hideousness. . . .

Let us formally add these ideas to our theodicy:

> The perception by human beings of their incapacity to "live to themselves" is essential to God's plan of Atonement because, first, without this perception few if any human beings would consider turning to God. (If, therefore, God were miraculously to "cancel" the natural consequences of separation from Himself, He would not only be a deceiver but would remove the only motivation fallen human beings have for turning to Him.) And because, secondly, memory of the hideousness of separated human life will be an important, perhaps an essential, component of the final state of restored humanity. Among the natural consequences of separation from God is the vast quantity of pain and suffering that we observe.

VI

Question 3

I am uncertain about what to say about the duration of the "age of evil." I suggest some speculations that seem to me to be plausible.

—Perhaps God wants the final community of those in union with Him to be rather *large.* (Couldn't God allow an increase in the human population to occur *after* His plan of Atonement has been completed? Well, there is certainly the point to be considered that people born after the completion of God's plan would not remember the "age of evil" and thus would be just as liable to sin as their remote ancestors in Paradise; and it might be, as I have speculated, that memory of a world separated from God will be an essential part of the final condition of restored humanity.)

—Perhaps God wants the final community of those in union with Him to be rather *diverse.* It seems plausible to suppose that if God had brought the age of evil to an end in, say, 1000 A.D., the final human community would have been very unlike what it would be if He brought that age to an end tomorrow. In the latter case the final community would contain men and women whose cast of mind and world-view were radically unlike those of the members of any earlier age or culture. One might speculate that the members of a community composed of people born in diverse periods and cultures would be able to perceive and to communicate to one another aspects of the Divine Nature that the members of a community of less heterogeneous cultural origins would have been blind to.

Various important stages in God's plan of Atonement may require particular levels of social and cultural development. The unhappy first generation of separated human beings must have been in a truly miserable state, having lost the smoothly functioning behavioral instincts of their purely animal ancestors, but without the learned social organization, custom and tradition by which human beings—as we know them—maintain themselves in an environment indifferent to their welfare. (Perhaps they were even without an actual language: a population of feral children, as it were. I suppose no one claims to know what would happen to a closed population of feral children over many generations?) Or even if they were never wholly without a culture and social organization, we can hardly suppose them to have had anything but a tribal culture. It may well be that God's plan of Atonement requires that at certain points in history some people belong to a more "advanced" culture than a tribal culture. If we consider the Christian account of God's plan of Atonement, for example, we shall see that it is evident that the ministry of Jesus (an essential part of God's plan) could not have taken place in a culture much different from that of first-century Palestine; certainly it could not have taken place in a tribal culture, or in a "normal" culture of the ancient Mediterranean world, a pagan polytheism. A "specialized" culture like that of ancient Judaism cannot appear overnight. Even if one does not believe the Biblical account of God's long interaction with Israel, one must grant that the Hebrew culture of two thousand years ago embodied a long history. (God doubtless had the power to "raise up children for Abraham from these stones," but if He had exercised that power He would have been a deceiver; vivid and detailed memories of the long history of their people were an essential part of the reaction of Jesus' Hebrew audience to His preaching.) And, of course, the rapid and accurate spread of the news about Jesus (also an essential part of God's plan, according to Christians) could hardly have happened except within the setting of a vast, cosmopolitan empire.

—Creatures like ourselves, sunk deep in self-will, take a long time to respond to any sort of guidance, particularly if it appeals to considerations higher than power and wealth. It may be hard to kick against the goad, but it is certainly done.

Question 4

Let us not discuss cases of the suffering of the innocent that depend on human wickedness or folly or corrupt institutions. Let us instead examine cases in which there are no oppressors but only victims. These would seem to raise all of the difficulties for the theodicist that are raised by cases in which an oppressor is present, and to be amenable to a smaller class of solutions; they are not, for example, amenable to any solution that involves a concern for the ultimate spiritual welfare of the oppressor or respect for his free will or anything of that sort.

A young mother dies of leukemia. A school bus full of children is crushed by a landslide. A child is born without limbs. A wise and good man in the prime of life suffers brain damage and spends the remaining thirty years of his life in a coma. I do not know of a good general term for such events. Journalists often call them tragedies. But this word is properly applied only to events that are in some sense meaningful, and I know of no reason to think that such events *always* have a "meaning." I will call them *horrors*.

Why do horrors happen? I want to suggest that horrors happen for no reason at all, that when, e.g., a child is born without limbs, the only answer to the question, "Why did that happen?" is "There is no reason or explanation; it just happened." Or, at any rate, I want to suggest that this is sometimes the case. (Whether some horrors are brought about by God for special purposes is a question I shall not attempt to answer. If *some* horrors are brought about by God, and thus have a purpose and a meaning known to God but not to us, I have no opinion as to what percentage of the whole they might constitute.) But are not *all* events ordered by God, and must not *all* events therefore have some sort of meaning? Christians and other theists are, I believe, committed to the truth of the following proposition:

> God is the maker of all things, visible and invisible (other than Himself); He sustains all created things in existence from moment to moment,

> and continuously supplies them with their causal powers.

In a previous paper, in which I presented an account of God's action in the world, I argued that this proposition is consistent with the proposition that there are events having the following feature: If one asks concerning one of these events, "Why did that happen?," the only answer to one's question is, "There is no reason or explanation for that event. God did not cause it to happen or intend it to happen. It is not a part of God's plan for the world or anyone else's plan for anything. It just happened, and that's all there is to say about it." (Let us say of such events that they are *due to chance.*) I will not reproduce my arguments. Interested readers may turn to the earlier paper, to which the present paper is a sequel (although I have tried to make it self-contained). Now to say that there is no answer to the question, Why did X occur? is not to say that there is no answer to such questions as Why did God allow X to occur? or Why did God not prevent X? I ended the earlier paper with these words:

> If what I have said is true, it yields a moral for students of the Problem of Evil: Do not attempt any solution to this problem that entails that every particular evil has a purpose, or that, with respect to every individual misfortune, or every devastating earthquake, or every disease, God has some special reason for allowing it. Concentrate rather on the problem of what sort of reasons a loving and providential God might have for allowing His creatures to live in a world in which many of the evils that happen to them happen to them for no reason at all.

I will now take my own advice and present my solution to this problem. God's reason for allowing His creatures to live in such a world is that their living in such a world is a natural consequence of their separation from Him. Consider again our earlier sketchy account of natural evil: in separating ourselves from God, we have somehow deprived ourselves of our primordial defenses against such potentially destructive things as tigers and landslides and tornadoes. But if, by our rebellion and folly, we have allowed the destructive potential of these things to become actual, how shall we expect the effects of that actuality to be distributed? At random, surely? That is, with no correlation between these things and the innocence or wickedness of the people they impinge on—since the operations of these things in no way depend upon the moral qualities of the people they interact with? In fact, there is little correlation between the manner in which these things operate and *any* factor under human control (although civilization does what it can to try to induce correlations of this type).

Suppose that a certain man chooses, of his own free will, to stand at spot x at time t. His arrival at that place at that time converges with the arrival of an avalanche. Let us suppose that God did not miraculously cause the avalanche, and that He did not "move" the man to be at that place at that time. And let us also suppose that neither the man's arrival at x at t nor the avalanche's arrival at x at t was determined by the laws of nature and the state of the world, say, one hundred years earlier. (This is a plausible assumption on scientific grounds. Quantum mechanics has the following astounding consequence: Imagine a billiard table, one not subject to external influence other than constant, uniform gravitation, on which there are rolling perfectly spherical and perfectly elastic balls that—somehow—do not lose energy to the walls of the table in collision or to its surface in friction; the position of the balls a minute or so in the future is not even approximately determined by the laws of nature and the present physical state of the balls. This example strongly suggests that the precise moment at which an avalanche occurs is not determined a hundred years in advance.)

The man's death in the avalanche would seem to be in every sense due to chance, even though (the theist must suppose) God knew in advance that he would be killed by the avalanche and could have prevented it. In fact, the theist must suppose that, during the course of that event, God held all of the particles that composed the man and the moving mass of snow and ice in existence and continuously decreed the operation of the laws of nature by which those particles interacted with one another.

Why did God not miraculously save the man? We have seen the answer to this question already. He might very well have. Perhaps He sometimes does miraculously save people in such situations. But if He *always* did so, He would be a deceiver. If He always saved people about to be destroyed by a chance encounter with a violent phenomenon of nature, He would engender an illusion with the following propositional content:

> It is possible for human beings to live apart from God and not be subject to destruction by chance.

To live under this illusion would be a bad thing in itself, but, more importantly, it would have harmful effects. This illusion would be, as it were, a tributary of illusion feeding into a great river of illusion whose content was, "Human beings can live successfully in separation from God."

In our current state of separation from God, we are continually blundering into "lines of causation" (the descent of an avalanche; the evolution of the AIDS virus; the building up of tension along a geological fault) that perhaps have no purpose at all and certainly have no purpose in relation to us. (It is simply a part of the mechanics of nature that intrinsically harmless but potentially destructive things like avalanches or viruses or earthquakes should exist. As I remarked above, if you think that you can design a world that does not contain such things and which can also serve as a home for human beings, you have never tried. Such things are a part of God's design in the sense that the ticking sound made by a clock is a part of the watchmaker's design: not intended, necessitated by what *is* intended, foreseen, and allowed for. What is not in any sense a part of God's design is *this* avalanche, *this* virus, and *this* earthquake. These are—sometimes, at any rate—due to chance.) If we had never separated ourselves from God, we should have been able to avoid such blunders. No longer to be able to avoid them is a natural consequence of the Fall. It is as if God had had—for some purpose—to cover the earth with a certain number of deep pits. These pits (we may stipulate) were not dangerous, since they could easily be seen and avoided; but we frustrated God's Providence in this matter by deliberately making ourselves blind; and now we complain that some of us—quite often the good and wise and innocent—fall into the pits. God's response to this complaint, according to the theodicy I propose, is this: "You are the ones who made yourselves blind. If you make yourselves blind, some of you will fall into the pits, and, moreover, *who* falls into a pit and *when* will be wholly a matter of chance. Goodness and wisdom and innocence have no bearing on this matter. That's part of what being blind means." Or, rather, this is what we might imagine God's response to be in our simple "world of pits." In the real world, we should have to picture God as saying something more complex, something like the following.

"Even I can't make a world that is suitable for human beings but which contains no phenomena that would harm human beings *if* they were in the wrong place at the wrong time. The reasons for this are complicated, but they turn on the fact that the molecular bonds that hold you human beings together must be weaker by many orders of magnitude than the disruptive potential of the surges of energy that must happen here and there in a structurally and nomologically coherent world [i.e., a world governed by stable laws of physics] complex enough to contain you. My Providence dealt with this fact by endowing you with the power never to be in the wrong place at the wrong time, a power you lost when you ruined yourselves by turning away from Me. That is why horrors happen to some of you: you simply blunder into things. If I were to protect you from the consequences of your blindness by guiding you away from potentially destructive phenomena by an unending series of miracles—and I remind you that for all you know I *sometimes* do guide you out of harm's way—I should be deceiving you about the meaning of your separation from Me and seriously weakening the only motivation you have for returning to Me."

We may add the following proposition to our theodicy:

> Among the natural consequences of the Fall is the following evil state of affairs: Horrors happen to people without any relation to desert [i.e., what people deserve]. They happen simply as a matter of chance. It is a part of God's plan of Atonement that we realize that a natural con-

sequence of our living to ourselves is our living in a world that has that feature.

This completes my presentation of the theodicy I propose. I have fleshed out the well-known story about how evil entered the world through the abuse of the divine gift of free will; I have fleshed it out in such a way as to provide plausible—at any rate, I find them plausible—answers to four pointed questions about the magnitude, duration, and distribution of evil. But in a sense it is not possible effectively to present a theodicy in a single piece of work by one author. Various elements in any proposed theodicy are bound to be thought false or felt to be implausible by some people. An essential part of presenting a theodicy is meeting the objections of those who have difficulties with it, or perhaps refining it in the face of their objections. A theodicy is a dialectical enterprise. The present paper, therefore, is best regarded as the "opening move" in such an enterprise, rather than a finished product. In closing, I wish to answer one objection to the theodicy I have presented, an objection that has been raised in conversation and correspondence by Eleonore Stump. Professor Stump objects that the theodicy I have presented represents God as allowing people to suffer misfortunes that do not (even in the long run) benefit *them.* An example may make the point of this objection clear. Suppose that God allows a horrible, disfiguring accident to happen to Alice (a true accident, an event due entirely to chance, but one that God foresaw and could have prevented). And suppose that the only good that is brought out of this accident is embodied in the following state of affairs and certain of its remote consequences: The accident, together with an enormous number of similar horrors, causes various people to realize that one feature of a world in which human beings live to themselves is that in such a world horrors happen to people for no reason at all. But suppose that Alice herself did not need to realize this; suppose that she was already fully aware of this consequence of separation from God. And suppose that many of the people who do come to realize this partly as the result of Alice's accident manage (owing mainly to luck) to get through life without anything very bad happening to them. According to Stump, these suppositions—and it is pretty certain that there *are* cases like this if our theodicy is correct—represent God as violating the following moral principle:

> It is wrong to allow something bad to happen to X—without X's permission—in order to secure some benefit for others (and no benefit for X).

I do not find this principle particularly appealing—not as a *universal* moral principle, one that is supposed to apply with equal rigor to all possible moral agents in all possible circumstances. The circumstances in which it seems most doubtful are these: The agent is in a position of lawful authority over both X and the "others" and is responsible for their welfare (consider, for example, a mother and her children or the state and its citizens); the good to be gained by the "others" is considerably greater than the evil suffered by X; there is no way in which the good for the "others" can be achieved except by allowing the evil in question to happen to X or to someone else no more deserving of it than X; the agent knows these things to be true. By way of example, we might consider cases of quarantine or of the right of eminent domain. Is it not morally permissible for the state to restrict my freedom of movement and action if I am the carrier of a contagious disease, or to force me to move if my house stands in the way of a desperately needed irrigation canal (one that will not benefit *me* in any way)? It is not to the point to protest that these cases are not much like cases involving an omnipotent God, who can cure diseases or provide water by simple fiat. They are counterexamples to the above moral principle, and, therefore, that moral principle is false. What is required of anyone who alleges that the theodicy I have proposed represents God as violating some (correct) moral principle is a careful statement of that moral principle. When we have examined that carefully stated moral principle, and have satisfied ourselves that it is without counterexample, we can proceed with the argument.

Reason and Faith

The Ethics of Belief*

W. K. CLIFFORD

W. K. Clifford (1845–1879) was an English mathematician and philosopher.

A SHIPOWNER WAS about to send to sea an emigrant-ship. He knew that she was old, and not overwell built at the first; that she had seen many seas and climes, and often had needed repairs. Doubts had been suggested to him that possibly she was not seaworthy. These doubts preyed upon his mind, and made him unhappy; he thought that perhaps he ought to have her thoroughly overhauled and refitted, even though this should put him to great expense. Before the ship sailed, however, he succeeded in overcoming these melancholy reflections. He said to himself that she had gone safely through so many voyages and weathered so many storms that it was idle to suppose she would not come safely home from this trip also. He would put his trust in Providence, which could hardly fail to protect all these unhappy families that were leaving their fatherland to seek for better times elsewhere. He would dismiss from his mind all ungenerous suspicions about the honesty of builders and contractors. In such ways he acquired a sincere and comfortable conviction that his vessel was thoroughly safe and seaworthy; he watched her departure with a light heart, and benevolent wishes for the success of the exiles in their strange new home that was to be; and he got his insurance-money when she went down in mid-ocean and told no tales.

What shall we say of him? Surely this, that he was verily guilty of the death of those men. It is admitted that he did sincerely believe in the soundness of his ship; but the sincerity of his conviction can in no wise help him, because *he had no right to believe on such evidence as was before him.* He had acquired his belief not by honestly earning it in patient investigation, but by stifling his doubts. And although in the end he may have felt so sure about it that he could not think otherwise, yet inasmuch as he had knowingly and willingly worked himself into that frame of mind, he must be held responsible for it.

Let us alter the case a little, and suppose that the ship was not unsound after all; that she made her voyage safely, and many others after it. Will that diminish the guilt of her owner? Not one jot. When an action is once done, it is right or wrong for ever; no accidental failure of its good or evil fruits can possibly alter that. The man would not have been innocent, he would only have been not found out. The question of right or wrong has to do with the origin of his belief, not the matter of it; not what it was, but how he got it; not whether it turned out to be true or false, but whether he had a right to believe on such evidence as was before him.

There was once an island in which some of the inhabitants professed a religion teaching neither the doctrine of original sin nor that of eternal punishment. A suspicion got abroad that the professors of this religion had made use of unfair means to get their doctrines taught to children. They were accused of wresting the laws of their country in such a way as to remove children from the care of their natural and legal guardians; and even of stealing

---

**From W. K. Clifford,* Lectures and Essays *(1879).*

them away and keeping them concealed from their friends and relations. A certain number of men formed themselves into a society for the purpose of agitating the public about this matter. They published grave accusations against individual citizens of the highest position and character, and did all in their power to injure these citizens in the exercise of their professions. So great was the noise they made, that a Commission was appointed to investigate the facts; but after the Commission had carefully inquired into all the evidence that could be got, it appeared that the accused were innocent. Not only had they been accused on insufficient evidence, but the evidence of their innocence was such as the agitators might easily have obtained, if they had attempted a fair inquiry. After these disclosures the inhabitants of that country looked upon the members of the agitating society, not only as persons whose judgment was to be distrusted, but also as no longer to be counted honourable men. For although they had sincerely and conscientiously believed in the charges they had made, yet *they had no right to believe on such evidence as was before them.* Their sincere convictions, instead of being honestly earned by patient inquiring, were stolen by listening to the voice of prejudice and passion.

Let us vary this case also, and suppose, other things remaining as before, that a still more accurate investigation proved the accused to have been really guilty. Would this make any difference in the guilt of the accusers? Clearly not; the question is not whether their belief was true or false, but whether they entertained it on wrong grounds. They would no doubt say, "Now you see that we were right after all; next time perhaps you will believe us." And they might be believed, but they would not thereby become honourable men. They would not be innocent, they would only be not found out. Every one of them, if he chose to examine himself *in foro conscientiae,* would know that he had acquired and nourished a belief, when he had no right to believe on such evidence as was before him; and therein he would know that he had done a wrong thing.

It may be said, however, that in both of these supposed cases it is not the belief which is judged to be wrong, but the action following upon it. The shipowner might say, "I am perfectly certain that my ship is sound, but still I feel it my duty to have her examined, before trusting the lives of so many people to her." And it might be said to the agitator, "However convinced you were of the justice of your cause and the truth of your convictions, you ought not to have made a public attack upon any man's character until you had examined the evidence on both sides with the utmost patience and care."

In the first place, let us admit that, so far as it goes, this view of the case is right and necessary; right, because even when a man's belief is so fixed that he cannot think otherwise, he still has a choice in regard to the action suggested by it, and so cannot escape the duty of investigating on the ground of the strength of his convictions; and necessary, because those who are not yet capable of controlling their feelings and thoughts must have a plain rule dealing with overt acts.

But this being premised as necessary, it becomes clear that it is not sufficient, and that our previous judgment is required to supplement it. For it is not possible so to sever the belief from the action it suggests as to condemn the one without condemning the other. No man holding a strong belief on one side of a question, or even wishing to hold a belief on one side, can investigate it with such fairness and completeness as if he were really in doubt and unbiased; so that the existence of a belief not founded on fair inquiry unfits a man for the performance of this necessary duty.

Nor is that truly a belief at all which has not some influence upon the actions of him who holds it. He who truly believes that which prompts him to an action has looked upon the action to lust after it, he has committed it already in his heart. If a belief is not realized immediately in open deeds, it is stored up for the guidance of the future. It goes to make a part of that aggregate of beliefs which is the link between sensation and action at every moment of all our lives, and which is so organized and compacted together that no part of it can be isolated from the rest, but every new addition modifies the structure of the whole. No real belief, however trifling and fragmentary it may seem, is ever truly insignificant; it prepares us to receive more of its like, confirms those which resembled it before, and weakens others; and so gradually it lays a stealthy train in our inmost thoughts, which may someday explode into overt action, and leave its stamp upon our character for ever.

And no one man's belief is in any case a private matter which concerns himself alone. Our lives are guided by that general conception of the course of things which has been created by society for social purposes. Our words, our phrases, our forms and processes and modes of thought, are common property, fashioned and perfected from age to age; an heirloom which every succeeding generation inherits as a precious deposit and a sacred trust to be handed on to the next one, not unchanged but enlarged and purified, with some clear marks of its proper handiwork. Into this, for good or ill, is woven every belief of every man who has speech of his fellows. An awful privilege, and an awful responsibility, that we should help to create the world in which posterity will live.

In the two supposed cases which have been considered, it has been judged wrong to believe on insufficient evidence, or to nourish belief by suppressing doubts and avoiding investigation. The reason of this judgment is not far to seek: it is that in both these cases the belief held by one man was of great importance to other men. But forasmuch as no belief held by one man, however seemingly trivial the belief, and however obscure the believer, is ever actually insignificant or without its effect on the fate of mankind, we have no choice but to extend our judgment to all cases of belief whatever. Belief, that sacred faculty which prompts the decisions of our will, and knits into harmonious working all the compacted energies of our being, is ours not for ourselves, but for humanity. It is rightly used on truths which have been established by long experience and waiting toil, and which have stood in the fierce light of free and fearless questioning. Then it helps to bind men together, and to strengthen and direct their common action. It is desecrated when given to unproved and unquestioned statements, for the solace and private pleasure of the believer; to add a tinsel splendour to the plain straight road of our life and display a bright mirage beyond it; or even to drown the common sorrows of our kind by a self-deception which allows them not only to cast down, but also to degrade us. Whoso would deserve well of his fellows in this matter will guard the purity of his belief with a very fanaticism of jealous care, lest at any time it should rest on an unworthy object, and catch a stain which can never be wiped away.

It is not only the leader of men, statesman, philosopher, or poet, that owes this bounden duty to mankind. Every rustic who delivers in the village alehouse his slow, infrequent sentences, may help to kill or keep alive the fatal superstitions which clog his race. Every hard-worked wife of an artisan may transmit to her children beliefs which shall knit society together, or rend it in pieces. No simplicity of mind, no obscurity of station, can escape the universal duty of questioning all that we believe.

It is true that this duty is a hard one, and the doubt which comes out of it is often a very bitter thing. It leaves us bare and powerless where we thought that we were safe and strong. To know all about anything is to know how to deal with it under all circumstances. We feel much happier and more secure when we think we know precisely what to do, no matter what happens, than when we have lost our way and do not know where to turn. And if we have supposed ourselves to know all about anything, and to be capable of doing what is fit in regard to it, we naturally do not like to find that we are really ignorant and powerless, that we have to begin again at the beginning, and try to learn what the thing is and how it is to be dealt with—if indeed anything can be learnt about it. It is the sense of power attached to a sense of knowledge that makes men desirous of believing, and afraid of doubting.

This sense of power is the highest and best of pleasures when the belief on which it is founded is a true belief, and has been fairly earned by investigation. For then we may justly feel that it is common property, and hold good for others as well as for ourselves. Then we may be glad, not that *I* have learned secrets by which I am safer and stronger, but that *we men* have got mastery over more of the world; and we shall be strong, not for ourselves, but in the name of Man and in his strength. But if the belief has been accepted on insufficient evidence, the pleasure is a stolen one. Not only does it deceive ourselves by giving us a sense of power which we do not really possess, but it is sinful, because it is stolen in defiance of our duty to mankind. That duty is to guard ourselves from such beliefs as from a pestilence, which may shortly master our own body and then spread to the rest of the town. What would be thought of one who, for the sake of a sweet fruit, should deliberately run the risk of bringing a plague upon his family and his neighbours?

And, as in other such cases, it is not the risk only which has to be considered; for a bad action is always bad at the time when it is done, no matter what happens afterwards. Every time we let ourselves believe for unworthy reasons, we weaken our powers of self-control, of doubting, of judicially and fairly weighing evidence. We all suffer severely enough from the maintenance and support of false beliefs and the fatally wrong actions which they lead to, and the evil born when one such belief is entertained is great and wide. But a greater and wider evil arises when the credulous character is maintained and supported, when a habit of believing for unworthy reasons is fostered and made permanent. If I steal money from any person, there may be no harm done by the mere transfer of possession; he may not feel the loss, or it may prevent him from using the money badly. But I cannot help doing this great wrong towards Man, that I make myself dishonest. What hurts society is not that it should lose its property, but that it should become a den of thieves, for then it must cease to be society. This is why we ought not to do evil, that good may come; for at any rate this great evil has come, that we have done evil and are made wicked thereby. In like manner, if I let myself believe anything on insufficient evidence, there may be no great harm done by the mere belief; it may be true after all, or I may never have occasion to exhibit it in outward acts. But I cannot help doing this great wrong towards Man, that I make myself credulous. The danger to society is not merely that it should believe wrong things, though that is great enough; but that it should become credulous, and lose the habit of testing things and inquiring into them; for then it must sink back into savagery.

The harm which is done by credulity in a man is not confined to the fostering of a credulous character in others, and consequent support of false beliefs. Habitual want of care about what I believe leads to habitual want of care in others about the truth of what is told to me. Men speak the truth to one another when each reveres the truth in his own mind and in the other's mind; but how shall my friend revere the truth in my mind when I myself am careless about it, when I believe things because I want to believe them, and because they are comforting and pleasant? Will he not learn to cry, "Peace," to me, when there is no peace? By such a course I shall surround myself with a thick atmosphere of falsehood and fraud, and in that I must live. It may matter little to me, in my cloud-castle of sweet illusions and darling lies; but it matters much to Man that I have made my neighbours ready to deceive. The credulous man is father to the liar and the cheat; he lives in the bosom of this his family, and it is no marvel if he should become even as they are. So closely are our duties knit together, that whoso shall keep the whole law, and yet offend in one point, he is guilty of all.

To sum up: it is wrong always, everywhere, and for anyone, to believe anything upon insufficient evidence.

If a man, holding a belief which he was taught in childhood or persuaded of afterwards, keeps down and pushes away any doubts which arise about it in his mind, purposely avoids the reading of books and the company of men that call in question or discuss it, and regards as impious those questions which cannot easily be asked without disturbing it—the life of that man is one long sin against mankind.

If this judgment seems harsh when applied to those simple souls who have never known better, who have been brought up from the cradle with a horror of doubt, and taught that their eternal welfare depends on *what* they believe, then it leads to the very serious question, *Who hath made Israel to sin?*

It may be permitted me to fortify this judgment with the sentence of Milton[1]—

> A man may be a heretic in the truth; and if he believe things only because his pastor says so, or the assembly so determine, without knowing

other reason, though his belief be true, yet the very truth he holds becomes his heresy.

And with this famous aphorism of Coleridge[2]—

He who begins by loving Christianity better than Truth, will proceed by loving his own sect or Church better than Christianity, and end in loving himself better than all.

Inquiry into the evidence of a doctrine is not to be made once for all, and then taken as finally settled. It is never lawful to stifle a doubt; for either it can be honestly answered by means of the inquiry already made, or else it proves that the inquiry was not complete.

"But," says one, "I am a busy man; I have no time for the long course of study which would be necessary to make me in any degree a competent judge of certain questions, or even able to understand the nature of the arguments."

Then he should have no time to believe.

NOTES

1. *Areopagitica.*
2. *Aids to Reflections.*

The Wager*

BLAISE PASCAL

Blaise Pascal (1623–1662) was a mathematician, scholar, and theologian of great distinction.

INFINITY—NOTHING. Our soul is cast into the body where it finds number, time, dimensions; it reasons about these things and calls them natural, or necessary, and can believe nothing else.

Unity added to infinity does not increase it at all, any more than a foot added to an infinite measurement: the finite is annihilated in the presence of the infinite and becomes pure nothingness. So it is with our mind before God, with our justice before divine justice. There is not so great a disproportion between our justice and God's as between unity and infinity.

God's justice must be as vast as his mercy. Now his justice towards the damned is less vast and ought to be less startling to us than his mercy towards the elect.

We know that the infinite exists without knowing its nature, just as we know that it is untrue that numbers are finite. Thus it is true that there is an infinite number, but we do not know what it is. It is untrue that it is even, untrue that it is odd, for by adding a unit it does not change its nature. Yet it is a number, and every number is even or odd. (It is true that this applies to every finite number.)

Therefore we may well know that God exists without knowing what he is.

Is there no substantial truth, seeing that there are so many true things which are not truth itself?

**Blaise Pascal,* Pensées, *translated by A. J. Krailsheimer (Baltimore and Harmondsworth: Penguin Books, 1966), pp. 149–155. Reprinted by permission of Penguin Books. Ltd.*

Thus we know the existence and nature of the finite because we too are finite and extended in space.

We know the existence of the infinite without knowing its nature, because it too has extension but unlike us no limits.

But we do not know either the existence or the nature of God, because he has neither extension nor limits.

But by faith we know his existence, through glory we shall know his nature.

Now I have already proved that it is quite possible to know that something exists without knowing its nature.

Let us now speak according to our natural lights.

If there is a God, he is infinitely beyond our comprehension, since, being indivisible and without limits, he bears no relation to us. We are therefore incapable of knowing either what he is or whether he is. That being so, who would dare to attempt an answer to the question? Certainly not we, who bear no relation to him.

Who then will condemn Christians for being unable to give rational grounds for their belief, professing as they do a religion for which they cannot give rational grounds? They declare that it is a folly, *stultitiam,* in expounding it to the world, and then you complain that they do not prove it. If they did prove it they would not be keeping their word. It is by being without proof that they show they are not without sense. "Yes, but although that excuses those who offer their religion as such, and absolves them from the criticism of producing it without rational grounds, it does not absolve those who accept it." Let us then examine this point, and let us say: "Either God is or he is not." But to which view shall we be inclined? Reason cannot decide this question. Infinite chaos separates us. At the far end of this infinite distance a coin is being spun which will come down heads or tails. How will you wager? Reason cannot make you choose either, reason cannot prove either wrong.

Do not then condemn as wrong those who have made a choice, for you know nothing about it. "No, but I will condemn them not for having made this particular choice, but any choice, for, although the one who calls heads and the other one are equally at fault, the fact is that they are both at fault: the right thing is not to wager at all."

Yes, but you must wager. There is no choice, you are already committed. Which will you choose then? Let us see: since a choice must be made, let us see which offers you the least interest. You have two things to lose: the true and the good; and two things to stake: your reason and your will, your knowledge and your happiness; and your nature has two things to avoid: error and wretchedness. Since you must necessarily choose, your reason is no more affronted by choosing one rather than the other. That is one point cleared up. But your happiness? Let us weigh up the gain and the loss involved in calling heads that God exists. Let us assess the two cases: if you win you win everything, if you lose you lose nothing. Do not hesitate then; wager that he does exist. "That is wonderful. Yes, I must wager, but perhaps I am wagering too much." Let us see: since there is an equal chance of gain and loss, if you stood to win only two lives for one you could still wager, but supposing you stood to win three?

You would have to play (since you must necessarily play) and it would be unwise of you, once you are obliged to play, not to risk your life in order to win three lives at a game in which there is an equal chance of losing and winning. But there is an eternity of life and happiness. That being so, even though there were an infinite number of chances, of which only one were in your favour, you would still be right to wager one in order to win two; and you would be acting wrongly, being obliged to play, in refusing to stake one life against three in a game, where out of an infinite number of chances there is one in your favour, if there were an infinity of infinitely happy life to be won. But here there is an infinity of infinitely happy life to be won, one chance of winning against a finite number of chances of losing, and what you are staking is finite. That leaves no choice; wherever there is infinity, and where there are not infinite chances of losing against that of winning, there is no room for hesitation, you must give everything. And thus, since you are obliged to play, you must be renouncing reason if you hoard your life rather than risk it for an infinite gain, just as likely to occur as a loss amounting to nothing.

For it is no good saying that it is uncertain whether you will win, that it is certain that you are taking a risk, and that the infinite distance between the certainty of what you are risking and the uncertainty of what you may gain makes the finite good you are certainly risking equal to the infinite good that you are not certain to gain. This is not the case. Every gambler takes a certain risk for an uncertain gain, and yet he is taking a certain finite risk for an uncertain finite gain without sinning against reason. Here there is no infinite distance between the certain risk and the uncertain gain: that is not true. There is, indeed, an infinite distance between the certainty of winning and the certainty of losing, but the proportion between the uncertainty of winning and the certainty of what is being risked is in proportion to the chances of winning or losing. And hence if there are as many chances on one side as on the other you are playing for even odds. And in that case the certainty of what you are risking is equal to the uncertainty of what you may win; it is by no means infinitely distant from it. Thus our argument carries infinite weight, when the stakes are finite in a game where there are even chances of winning and losing and an infinite prize to be won.

This is conclusive and if men are capable of any truth this is it.

"I confess, I admit it, but is there really no way of seeing what the cards are?"—"Yes. Scripture and the rest, etc."—"Yes, but my hands are tied and my lips are sealed; I am being forced to wager and I am not free; I am being held fast and I am so made that I cannot believe. What do you want me to do then?"—"That is true, but at least get it into your head that, if you are unable to believe, it is because of your passions, since reason impels you to believe and yet you cannot do so. Concentrate then not on convincing yourself by multiplying proofs of God's existence but by diminishing your passions. You want to find faith and you do not know the road. You want to be cured of unbelief and you ask for the remedy: learn from those who were once bound like you and who now wager all they have. These are people who know the road you wish to follow, who have been cured of the affliction of which you wish to be cured: follow the way by which they began. They behaved just as if they did believe, taking holy water, having masses said, and so on. That will make you believe quite naturally, and will make you more docile."[1]—"But that is what I am afraid of."—"But why? What have you to lose? But to show you that this is the way, the fact is that this diminishes the passions which are your great obstacles. . . ."

End of this address.

"Now what harm will come to you from choosing this course? You will be faithful, honest, humble, grateful, full of good works, a sincere, true friend. . . . It is true you will not enjoy noxious pleasures, glory and good living, but will you not have others?

"I tell you that you will gain even in this life, and that at every step you take along this road you will see that your gain is so certain and your risk so negligible that in the end you will realize that you have wagered on something certain and infinite for which you have paid nothing."

"How these words fill me with rapture and delight!—"

"If my words please you and seem cogent, you must know that they come from a man who went down upon his knees before and after to pray this infinite and indivisible being, to whom he submits his own, that he might bring your being also to submit to him for your own good and for his glory: and that strength might thus be reconciled with lowliness."

Custom is our nature. Anyone who grows accustomed to faith believes it, and can no longer help fearing hell, and believes nothing else.

Anyone accustomed to believe that the king is to be feared. . . .

Who then can doubt that our soul, being accustomed to see number, space, movement, believes in this and nothing else?

"Do you believe that it is impossible for God to be infinite and indivisible?"—"Yes."—"Very well, I will show you something infinite and indivisible: it is a point moving everywhere at an infinite speed.

"For it is one and the same everywhere and wholly present in every place. From this natural phenomenon which previously seemed impossible to you you should realize that there may be others which you do not yet know. Do not conclude from your apprenticeship that there is nothing left for you to learn, but that you still have an infinite amount to learn."

It is untrue that we are worthy to be loved by others. It is unfair that we should want such a thing. If we were born reasonable and impartial, with a knowledge of ourselves and others, we should not give our wills this bias. However, we are born with it, and so we are born unfair.

For everything tends towards itself: this is contrary to all order.

The tendency should be towards the general, and the bias towards self is the beginning of all disorder, in war, politics, economics, in man's individual body.

The will is therefore depraved. If the members of natural and civil communities tend to the good of the whole body, the communities themselves should tend towards another more general body of which they are members. We should therefore tend towards the general. Thus we are born unfair and depraved.

No religion except our own has taught that man is born sinful, no philosophical sect has said so, so none has told the truth.

No sect and no religion has always existed on earth except Christianity.

We are greatly indebted to those who point out our faults, for they mortify us, they teach us that we have incurred contempt, but they do not prevent us incurring it in the future, for we have plenty of other faults to deserve it. They prepare us for the exercise of correcting and eradicating a given fault.

The heart has its reasons of which reason knows nothing: we know this in countless ways.

I say that it is natural for the heart to love the universal being or itself, according to its allegiance, and it hardens itself against either as it chooses. You have rejected one and kept the other. Is it reason that makes you love yourself?

It is the heart which perceives God and not the reason. That is what faith is: God perceived by the heart, not by the reason.

The only knowledge which is contrary alike to common sense and human nature is the only one always to have existed among men.

Only Christianity makes men both happy and lovable: the code of the gentleman does not allow you to be both happy and lovable.

NOTES

1. *abêtira.* That is, the unbeliever will act unthinkingly and mechanically, and in this become more like the beasts, from whom man was differentiated, according to contemporary philosophy, by his faculty of reason.

You Bet Your Life: Pascal's Wager Defended*

WILLIAM G. LYCAN AND GEORGE N. SCHLESINGER

William G. Lycan (1945–) and George N. Schlesinger (1925–) both teach philosophy at The University of North Carolina, Chapel Hill.

PASCAL'S FAMOUS WAGER is often mentioned in introductory philosophy classes and very occasionally addressed in the professional literature, but never favorably on the whole. It is considered an amusing bonbon and an entertaining early (mis)application of decision theory, but it is hardly thought convincing or even intellectually respectable. We maintain, to the contrary, that the Wager is seriously defensible and that the stock objections to it can be answered, even if there are more sophisticated criticisms to be made of Pascal's argument. We are inclined to think that the Wager is rational, and we propose to defend it here.

1. THE ORIGINAL ARGUMENT

We shall concentrate on the standard expected-utility version of the Wager. Pascal supposed that the relevant alternatives are either that God exists or that God does not exist, and, at least for the sake of argument, that both options are equally likely to be true, since

> [r]eason can decide nothing here. There is an infinite chaos which separates us. A game is being played at the extremity of this infinite distance where heads or tails will turn up. What will you wager?[1]

The relevant *choices* are to believe in God and adopt a reverent and devout lifestyle, or not to believe and to behave however one otherwise would.[2] Since the Christian God, at least, promises eternal joy and blissful union with Himself to those who do truly believe, and damnation (on some accounts eternal torment) to those who have heard but do not believe, the expected payoffs are as follows:

	God exists	God doesn't exist
Believe	∞	-20
Don't	$-\infty$	20

The two nonfinite payoffs represent (respectively) the eternal joy granted to the believer if God does exist, and the infinite suffering one will undergo if God exists and one chooses not to believe in Him. "-20" somewhat arbitrarily represents the inconvenience of living a devout and continent life when one doesn't have to, and "20" represents the fun one would have if totally released from religious hangups. (We assume for the moment that sin is fun; if not, so much the better for Pascal's argument.) The expected utility (EU) of theism is thus $.5(\infty) + .5(-20) = \infty$; the EU of agnosticism or atheism is $.5(-\infty) + .5(20) = -\infty$.[3] According to Pascal, this doesn't even leave room for discussion; one would have to be demented to pass up such an offer. Whatever inconveniences may attend the devout and unpolluted life, they pale beside the hope of eternal joy and the fear of damnation.

Pascal is not, of course, arguing for the existence of God; he affects to think that no such argument

*An edited version of William Lycan and George Schlesinger, "You Bet Your Life: Pascal's Wager Defended." *

can be given and that the balance of evidence favors agnosticism. He is contending that despite the epistemic irrationality of theism, if you like, it is *prudentially* rational—i.e., in one's interest—to believe in God regardless of the balance of evidence.

2. MISGUIDED OBJECTIONS

Just to get a better feel for the Wager, let us very quickly run through a few preliminary objections, before coming to the two which we consider serious.

(i) "But my beliefs are not under my control; if I don't believe, then I can't believe, any more than I can believe there to be a live swordfish in front of me just because someone offers me $1,000 if I can get myself to believe that." *Reply:* In the long run, most people's beliefs *are* under their control; as Pascal himself emphasized, behavior therapy is remarkably effective even upon intellectuals. Start going to church and observing its rituals; associate with intelligent and congenial religious people; stop reading philosophy and associating with cynics and logical positivists. To quote William James's pungent paraphrase of Pascal,[4] "Go then and take holy water, and have masses said; belief will come and stupefy your scruples." It may be that some people, of an indefatigably analytical and uncredulous temperament, simply cannot let themselves neglect the evidence and acquiesce in faith, just as some people simply cannot let themselves be hypnotized. But this is no reflection on the prudential rationality of the Wager; many people are psychologically incapable of doing what is demonstrably in their interest and known by them to be in their interest.[5]

(ii) "The Wager is cynical and mercenary; God wouldn't reward a "believer' who makes it." *Reply:* Of course He wouldn't, just like that. Pascal's claim is rather that our interest lies in leaving our cynicism behind and eventually *becoming* believers, if we can. There is no particular reason to think that God would punish a truly sincere and devout believer just because of the historical origins of his/her belief. People are reportedly saved as a result of deathbed conversions, even after lives of the most appalling corruption, if their new belief is sincere and authentic.

(iii) "Pascal is wrong in conjecturing that the probability of theism is as high as 50%. It isn't; it's miniscule." *Reply:* That doesn't matter; even if the probability of theism is one in a thousand, the expected payoffs are still infinite. "All right, then, the probability is *zero*. I'm *certain* there is no God." *Reply:* How certain? And on what grounds? We would need to see a very convincing argument that no God of even roughly the traditional sort *could* exist, and it would have to be better than most philosophical arguments. (How many philosophical arguments do we know that confer probability *1* [i.e., absolute certainty] on their conclusions??)

(iv) "But if I bet on theism and in fact there is no God, my life will have been based on a lie." *Reply:* But if one bets on atheism and in fact there is a God, one's life will have been based on a lie. (And one's *after*life will be based on the worm that dieth not and the fire that is not quenched.) "But Pascal is telling us, brazenly, to form a firm belief that is unsupported by evidence and may even go directly against the evidence. That is an epistemic vice, the shirking of an epistemic obligation. As a professional philosopher I couldn't live with myself knowing I had done that." *Reply:* Epistemic obligation is not moral obligation. No one suffers if (in this sort of case) one violates an epistemic norm. No one could possibly care except (a) academic philosophers, (b) self-righteous textbook slaves, and (c) God Himself. As history abundantly shows, the first two of these may safely be ignored; the third is ultimately to be counted on Pascal's side (see the reply to objection [ii]). What does an epistemic peccadillo matter, compared to infinite joy or damnation?

(v) "What do you mean, '−20'? I *love* sin! And we're not talking about just a few Sunday mornings here, but proposing to bet an entire lifestyle." *Reply:* Does anyone *really* love sin so much as to be *rationally and without AKRASIA* [weakness of will] willing to risk eternal damnation for it? That cannot be true of many people. Indeed (to make a slightly different point), a survey would probably show that religious people are on the average happier and more satisfied with their lives than are nonreligious people[6] (whether this happiness is an *opiate* in some objectionable sense is a vexed question, resting on mixed empirical issues and philosophical concerns). How bad could a devout life be, compared to the (possible) alternative?

Actually, we are forced to agree, the devout life *could* be very bad indeed. The strictly correct answer to our rhetorical question leads directly to the first of the two objections to Pascal's argument that we are inclined to take more seriously. (After addressing it, we will turn to the second, *viz.*, the celebrated Many-Gods problem.)

3. THE TWO SERIOUS OBJECTIONS

We need not dwell on the potential intolerability of time-consuming weekly devotions and of even more frequent abstinence from sin; for many leading religions, including Christianity and particularly Islam, require potentially far more: specifically, *martyrdom.* If political conditions are inimical, you or I might be faced with the choice of denying our faith or being put very horribly to death. Now, even if we grant that a few Sunday mornings and even a fully reverent Christian lifestyle of the 1980's are an eminently good bet *sub specie aeternitatis,* what if we were suddenly faced with real martyrdom? Would Pascal counsel beheading for anyone in Thomas More's position? Should we be willing, *just in virtue of making the Wager,* to be cast into the Coliseum and wait patiently for the biggest lion?

A first and sensible reply would be that most of us who are reading this paper have excellent (though hardly conclusive) grounds for thinking that we will never in fact be called upon to martyr ourselves; and if so, then the Wager remains reasonable at least *for us* until such time as we are presented with ominous new contrary evidence. But this is too simple. For in order to attain the *genuinely* religious life, as is required for salvation, we must achieve a condition in which we *would* gladly martyr ourselves if called upon to do so, even though we could not rationally want this in our present agnostic state. Could it possibly be reasonable for us, now, in our *present* circumstances and state of mind, to embark on a procedure that we fully intend will brainwash us into accepting a potentially disastrous course of action?—Is this any more rational than (for money) taking a pill that will make us into suicidal depressives or lunatic daredevils?

Yes, of course it is. The expected payoff is still infinite. For death, even horrible and very painful death, is still only finitely disutile [harmful]. There are fates worse than death, as is evidenced by the plain fact that countless human beings *have* willingly and not irrationally chosen death before dishonor, death rather than drastic indignity, death to save a loved one, death in service of a cherished cause, or the like. In that sense one's life is one's own, and is available as a stake among other stakes in a gamble, though such a gamble must be a desperate one.

If this is right, then our instinctive recoil from martyrdom is just that—instinctive recoil. Of course we shrink from violent death, and of course the prospect of immediate rending and shredding would very likely cause us (quickly) to rethink the Wager. But this does nothing *argumentatively* to show that the Wager is not still in fact rational. At best it shows that visceral fear drives out sound argument, and we knew that anyway. . . .

Let us turn at last to the Many-Gods problem. Pascal assumes a very specific sort of god—roughly a Christian god who rewards His own partisans with infinite bliss and who perhaps sentences opponents and even neutrals to damnation of one truly awful sort or another. But logical space contains countless possible gods of very different natures—all infinite, if you like—and if we can know nothing of infinitude then we cannot have reason to prefer any one of these gods to another. Unfortunately, their respective expected payoffs are diverse and conflicting: What if instead of the Christian God there is a Baal, a Moloch, a Wotan, or a Zeus, who prepares a particularly nasty fate for devout Christians? What if there is a very shy and reclusive god who does not want to be believed in and who enforces this desire by damning all believers to eternal torment? Etc., etc. Pascal assumed that *his* God has a .50% probability of existing, but this is grossly presumptuous in the face of all the other gods who cannot be ruled out *a priori.* Either Pascal's Christian God must take His place equiprobably alongside the indefinitely many other possible deities, in which case the probability of His existence is negligible, or Pascal's argument could be reiterated for every other god who offers infinite payoffs, in which case it proves too much and leads directly to contradiction due to incompatibly jealous gods.

4. A FIRST ANSWER TO THE MANY-GODS OBJECTION

A natural response is to say that for one reason or another all the various possible gods are *not* equiprobable. Intuitively, it is far more likely that the Christian God, the God of the Jews, or Allah exists, than that there is a vindictively shy god or a god who rewards all and only those who do not shave themselves or a god who wears pink bowties that light up. For here, we believe, empirical evidence is relevant to a certain extent. There is *some* empirical reason for thinking that the Christian God or the God of Israel—or even Allah—exists, in the form of partially checkable scriptures, historical reports (made by ostensibly intelligent and impartial observers) of divine manifestations, and the like, even if this evidence is pathetically far from convincing; while there is simply no reason of any sort for thinking that there is a reclusive god or a divine rewarder of non-self-shaving or whatever. (We also think that the ability of a particular religion to attract and sustain millions of adherents over thousands of years is epistemically a mark in its favor, even if a very weak one.) . . .

There is still another powerful objection . . . to this initial response: . . . how are we to choose between the gods of the major religions? Why should we believe in the Christian God rather than Yahweh? (These deities may well be considered identical by theorists, but their worship is not; they respectively require incompatible conduct.) For that matter, why should we believe in either of those rather than in Allah, or in one or more of the Hindu gods? There are probably more Muslims and more Hindus than there are genuinely religious Christians or Jews, so consensus is of no help in the present regard.

Here some fine-tuning is in order, though we cannot pursue the question in any detail. (i) Empirical indications are still germane. If one looks carefully, one may find that history provides more respectable evidence (however imperfect) for one of the major gods than for another. (ii) One must attend to the details of the respective payoffs; other things being equal, one should go for the deity that offers the more attractive afterlife and/or the nastiest form of damnation. (More on this shortly.) (iii) Given the facts taken account of in (i) and (ii), one must try for the lowest common denominator in terms of tolerance: that is, one must keep one's faith as ecumenical as one dares. Some gods are more jealous than others, of course; some deny salvation to any but the adherents of some crackpot sect, while others grant it to anyone who has led the right sort of life and had an appropriately respectful attitude toward something or other. So, overall, one must balance considerations (i), (ii) and (iii) against each other for each particular case and see how the resulting EUs come out. This is a very tricky but not completely unfeasible bit of comparison shopping. Of course, we may get it wrong and back the wrong god. In fact, given the multiplicity of major deities and the narrow tolerances involved in our attempt at judicious ecumenism, we *probably will* get it wrong. But a significant chance of infinite success offset by a greater chance of infinite failure is still better odds than *no* chance of success supplemented by a *still* greater chance of failure. . . .

5. A SECOND ANSWER TO THE MANY-GODS OBJECTION

A deeper and more authentic approach would take into account the special nature of the reward on which one is bid to wager. First, we are to realize that what Pascal is urging is for the gambler to set his eyes upon a prize of a sort entirely different from the "poisonous pleasures" Pascal advises him to abandon. The gratification to be pursued by the religious seeker is not something extrinsic to the devout life, but an organic outgrowth of it. It does not differ in kind from the seeking, as if one were to be handed a new IBM color-graphics monitor as a prize for having won the Carrboro Marathon, but is the natural fruit of one's way of life. Theists in every age have anticipated the dissolving of their narrow selves in the ecstasy of a God-centered life here on earth and, more to Pascal's point, their eventual smooth translation into a disembodied existence in holy felicity—an eternal love of the Divine. A human being becomes capable of this kind of love only after he/she has grasped the idea of God. Maimonides puts it as follows:

> What is the proper love of God? It is the love of the Lord with a great and very strong love so that one's soul shall be tied to the love of the Lord, and one should be continually enraptured by it, like a love-sick individual, whose mind is at no time free from his passion for a particular woman, the thought of her filling his heart at all times, when sitting down or rising up, even when he is eating or drinking. Still more intense should be the love of God in the hearts of those who love Him.[7]

According to classical theologians, one who has spent one's life as a passionate servant of the Lord will have developed and perfected one's soul adequately to have acquired the capacity to partake in the transmundane bliss that awaits in the afterlife. The suitably groomed soul, when released from its earthly fetters, will bask in the radiance of the Divine presence and delight in the adoring communion with a loving God (if this is a multiply mixed metaphor, it doesn't matter).

It is appropriate at this point to comment again upon objection (ii) considered in sec. 2 above, the complaint that because of its calculating and mercenary character, the Wager is both morally repugnant and inefficacious, and incompatible with the spirit of any genuine religion. Many people would recoil from a Wagerer just as they would from a hypocrite who went out of his way to brighten the mood of an enfeebled (but wealthy) elderly person for no loftier reason than to increase his chance of being mentioned in that person's will. Such misgivings could not easily be dismissed if Pascal had had in mind a pie-in-the-sky, anthropocentric sort of heaven such as that which Heinrich Heine sardonically claimed to be reserved for the righteous. According to Heine's mouth-watering description, Heaven is a place where roast geese fly around with gravy boats in their bills and there are brooks of boullion and champagne and everyone revels in eternal feasting and carousing. It would and should be hard to admire anyone who pursued a godly, righteous and sober life mainly in the hope of gaining admission to that kind of paradise. But we are considering the Wager in the context of an infinitely more exalted afterlife. Suppose that we have always had great admiration for Smith because of the noteworthy humanitarian works he has performed, and that lately we have heard of further truly heroic acts of benevolence on his part that make his previous accomplishments pale into insignificance. Then we should hardly be condemned for making efforts to discover more information concerning Smith's further laudable deeds—even if we are fully conscious of the sentiments of Thomas Carlyle, who wrote, "Does not every true man feel that he is himself made higher by doing reverence to what is really above him?"[8] Most people would find our conduct neither ignoble nor stupid, even if our efforts to discover the grounds of Smith's greatly intensified worthiness were done explicitly for the sake of feeling ourselves made higher by doing reverence to a more exalted personage. . . .

It is the crux of our problem that for more than one deity there is an eternal and hence infinite payoff. Still, the very nature of the sublime gratification the believer aspires to ensures that its quality will vary with the character of the deity he/she bets on. When Carlyle spoke of the self-enhancement resulting from doing reverence to what is above oneself, he had in mind an entirely worldly context. But when the object of one's homage is a divine being, the uplift is immeasurably greater. Pascal wagered on the ecstasy to be derived from exalting a supereminent being and basking in its radiance, and naturally, the more glorious and sublime the being, the greater that worshipful ecstasy would be. Thus, Pascal's argument leads us to maximize religious benefit by positing that superbeing which is the very most worthy of worship, *viz.*, the absolutely perfect being, which we take to be the God of Judeo-Christian theism and of some other, non-Western religions as well, minus some of the tendentious if traditional special features ascribed to Him by sectarian practitioners of those religions.

6. CONCLUSION

If one does not already incline toward theism, or perhaps even if one does so incline, there is still a temptation—a powerful one—to refuse to take the Wager seriously. How, again, can one listen to all this stuff about grooming one's soul, absolute perfection, infinite ecstasy, and the like, if one (as things are) *simply does not* believe in any god and regards theism of any sort as being on an equal epistemic footing with belief in the Easter Bunny?

To this we say: Consider the arguments fairly. We maintain that the *standard* and ubiquitous intuitive rejection of the Wager by philosophers is grounded in a confused conflation of the objections we have already addressed, particularly: the feeling that one could not do anything about one's beliefs even if one tried, the feeling that theism has probability zero, and the feeling that any failure to proportion one's belief to the evidence is a shameful if secret vice. But once these various misgivings have been separated and cast explicitly in the form of objections, they are seen to have little rational force. If one wishes to decline the Wager one will have to think of more subtle criticisms than those which have appeared in the literature to date.

We do not claim that our case is conclusive, or that the Wager is now dictated by reason. We do contend that at the present stage of investigation Pascal's argument is unrefuted and not unreasonable.

Let us pray.

NOTES

1. Blaise Pascal, "The Wager," reprinted in this volume, pp. 114–117.

2. Of course there are degrees of belief in between, including a significant range of agnosticism. The possibility of metaphysical agnosticism accompanied by a selflessly beneficent—even saintly—life is a piquant one, and much debated by some major religions, but we shall neglect it here.

3. Expected utility refers to the likely good or harm one can expect from choosing one option over another. We determine expected utility as follows. First, identify the relevant alternatives. (In the wager, this refers to belief or lack of belief in god's existence.) Then identify and assign a numerical value to all of the outcomes ("payoffs") associated with each alternative. In the wager, the payoffs associated with belief are either infinite happiness or a so-so life of religious propriety. Lycan and Schelsinger value this latter payoff as −20. The payoffs associated with nonbelief are infinite misery or a decent life of secular satisfactions. The authors value this last payoff as 20. Now determine the probability or likelihood that each of the outcomes will occur. Pascal claims that there is a 50% chance of God's existing, so there is a 50% probability that any one of the payoffs will be generated. Now you need to do a little math. Start by focusing on one alternative (say, belief in God). In the wager, theism is associated with two outcomes or payoffs. Multiply each payoff (infinite happiness, −20) by the probability that it will be realized (fifty percent). Then add the products together. This (infinite happiness) is the expected utility of belief in god. Work through the same steps to figure out the expected utility of nonbelief in god. To decide what best serves one's interests (i.e., what it is *prudent* to do), compare the relevant alternatives (here, belief or nonbelief in god) and opt for the one with the greatest expected utility. If Pascal is right, this is an easy call. [Eds.]

4. William James, "The Will to Believe," extract reprinted in this volume, 124–132.

5. Someone experiences an ominous medical symptom, and does not—cannot—go to the doctor because he is paralyzed with fear. He ends up dead. Someone else does not—cannot—make Pascal's Wager because he is paralyzed with textbook rationality. He ends up dead. Permanently.

6. Actual demographic surveys do show at least that religious people fare better with respect to divorce, suicide, and other indicators of troubled personal lives.

7. Maimonides, *Mishneh Torah,* Hilkhot Teshuvah X.

8. Thomas Carlyle, *On Heroes, Hero-Worship and the Heroic in History* (London: J. Fraser, 1841), p. 1.

The Will to Believe*

WILLIAM JAMES

William James (1842–1910) spent his career teaching philosophy and the new science of psychology at Harvard.

IN THE RECENTLY published *Life* by Leslie Stephen of his brother, Fitz-James, there is an account of a school to which the latter went when he was a boy. The teacher, a certain Mr. Guest, used to converse with his pupils in this wise, "Gurney, what is the difference between justification and sanctification?—Stephen, prove the omnipotence of God!" etc. In the midst of our Harvard freethinking and indifference we are prone to imagine that here at your good old orthodox College conversation continues to be somewhat upon this order; and to show you that we at Harvard have not lost all interest in these vital subjects, I have brought with me tonight something like a sermon on justification by faith to read to you,—I mean an essay in justification *of* faith, a defence of our right to adopt a believing attitude in religious matters, in spite of the fact that our merely logical intellect may not have been coerced. "The Will to Believe," accordingly, is the title of my paper.

I have long defended to my own students the lawfulness of voluntarily adopted faith; but as soon as they have got well imbued with the logical spirit, they have as a rule refused to admit my contention to be lawful philosophically, even though in point of fact they were personally all the time chock-full of some faith or other themselves. I am all the while, however, so profoundly convinced that my own position is correct, that your invitation has seemed to me a good occasion to make my statements more clear. Perhaps your minds will be more open than those with which I have hitherto had to deal. I will be as little technical as I can, though I must begin by setting up some technical distinctions that will help us in the end.

I

Let us give the name of hypothesis to anything that may be proposed to our belief; and just as the electricians speak of live and dead wires, let us speak of any hypothesis as either *live* or *dead*. A live hypothesis is one which appeals as a real possibility to him to whom it is proposed. If I ask you to believe in the Mahdi, the notion makes no electric connection with your nature—it refuses to scintillate with any credibility at all. As an hypothesis it is completely dead. To an Arab, however (even if he be not one of the Mahdi's followers), the hypothesis is among the mind's possibilities: It is alive. This shows that deadness and liveness in an hypothesis are not intrinsic properties, but relations to the individual thinker. They are measured by his willingness to act. The maximum of liveness in an hypothesis means willingness to act irrevocably. Practically, that means belief; but there is some believing tendency wherever there is willingness to act at all.

Next, let us call the decision between two hypotheses an *option*. Options may be of several kinds. They may be first, *living* or *dead;* secondly, *forced* or *avoidable;* thirdly, *momentous* or *trivial;* and for our purposes we may call an option a *genuine* option when it is of the forced, living, and momentous kind.

This essay, originally an address delivered before the Philosophical Clubs of Yale and Brown Universities, was first published in 1896.

1. A living option is one in which both hypotheses are live ones. If I say to you: "Be a theosophist or be a Mohammedan," it is probably a dead option, because for you neither hypothesis is likely to be alive. But if I say: "Be an agnostic or be a Christian," it is otherwise: trained as you are, each hypothesis makes some appeal, however small, to your belief.

2. Next, if I say to you: "Choose between going out with your umbrella or without it," I do not offer you a genuine option, for it is not forced. You can easily avoid it by not going out at all. Similarly, if I say, "Either love me or hate me," "Either call my theory true or call it false," your option is avoidable. You may remain indifferent to me, neither loving nor hating, and you may decline to offer any judgment as to my theory. But if I say, "Either accept this truth or go without it," I put on you a forced option, for there is no standing place outside of the alternative. Every dilemma based on a complete logical disjunction, with no possibility of not choosing, is an option of this forced kind.

3. Finally, if I were Dr. Nansen and proposed to you to join my North Pole expedition, your option would be momentous; for this would probably be your only similar opportunity, and your choice now would either exclude you from the North Pole sort of immortality altogether or put at least the chance of it into your hands. He who refuses to embrace a unique opportunity loses the prize as surely as if he tried and failed. *Per contra,* the option is trivial when the opportunity is not unique, when the stake is insignificant, or when the decision is reversible if it later prove unwise. Such trivial options abound in the scientific life. A chemist finds an hypothesis live enough to spend a year in its verification: he believes in it to that extent. But if his experiments prove inconclusive either way, he is quit for his loss of time, no vital harm being done.

It will facilitate our discussion if we keep all these distinctions well in mind.

II

The next matter to consider is the actual psychology of human opinion. When we look at certain facts, it seems as if our passional and volitional nature lay at the root of all our convictions. When we look at others, it seems as if they could do nothing when the intellect had once said its say. Let us take the latter facts up first.

Does it not seem preposterous on the very face of it to talk of our opinions being modifiable at will? Can our will either help or hinder our intellect in its perceptions of truth? Can we, by just willing it, believe that Abraham Lincoln's existence is a myth, and that the portraits of him in *McClure's Magazine* are all of some one else? Can we, by any effort of our will, or by any strength of wish that it were true, believe ourselves well and about when we are roaring with rheumatism in bed, or feel certain that the sum of the two one-dollar bills in our pocket must be a hundred dollars? We can *say* any of these things, but we are absolutely impotent to believe them; and of just such things is the whole fabric of the truths that we do believe in made up—matters of fact, immediate or remote, as Hume said, and relations between ideas, which are either there or not there for us if we see them so, and which if not there cannot be put there by any action of our own.

In Pascal's *Thoughts* there is a celebrated passage known in literature as Pascal's wager. In it he tries to force us into Christianity by reasoning as if our concern with truth resembled our concern with the stakes in a game of chance. Translated freely his words are these: You must either believe or not believe that God is—which will you do? Your human reason cannot say. A game is going on between you and the nature of things which at the day of judgment will bring out either heads or tails. Weigh what your gains and your losses would be if you should stake all you have on heads, or God's existence: if you win in such case, you gain eternal beatitude; if you lose, you lose nothing at all. If there were an infinity of chances, and only one for God in this wager, still you ought to stake your all on God; for though you surely risk a finite loss by this procedure, any finite loss is reasonable, even a certain one is reasonable, if there is but the possibility of infinite gain. Go, then, and take holy water, and have masses said; belief will come and stupefy your scruples. . . . Why should you not? At bottom, what have you to lose?

You probably feel that when religious faith expresses itself thus, in the language of the gaming-table, it is put to its last trumps. Surely Pascal's own personal belief in masses and holy water had far other springs; and this celebrated page of his is but an argument for others, a last desperate snatch at a weapon against the hardness of the unbelieving heart. We feel that a faith in masses and holy water adopted wilfully after such a mechanical calculation would lack the inner soul of faith's reality; and if we were ourselves in the place of the Deity, we should probably take particular pleasure in cutting off believers of this pattern from their infinite reward. It is evident that unless there be some preexisting tendency to believe in masses and holy water, the option offered to the will by Pascal is not a living option. Certainly no Turk ever took to masses and holy water on its account; and even to us Protestants these means of salvation seem such foregone impossibilities that Pascal's logic, invoked for them specifically, leaves us unmoved. As well might the Mahdi write to us, saying, "I am the Expected One whom God has created in his effulgence. You shall be infinitely happy if you confess me; otherwise you shall be cut off from the light of the sun. Weigh, then, your infinite gain if I am genuine against your finite sacrifice if I am not!" His logic would be that of Pascal; but he would vainly use it on us, for the hypothesis he offers us is dead. No tendency to act on it exists in us to any degree.

The talk of believing by our volition seems, then, from one point of view, simply silly. From another point of view it is worse than silly, it is vile. When one turns to the magnificent edifice of the physical sciences, and sees how it was reared; what thousands of disinterested moral lives of men lie buried in its mere foundations; what patience and postponement, what choking down of preference, what submission to the icy laws of outer fact are wrought into its very stones and mortar; how absolutely impersonal it stands in its vast augustness—then how besotted and contemptible seems every little sentimentalist who comes blowing his voluntary smoke-wreaths, and pretending to decide things from out of his private dream! Can we wonder if those bred in the rugged and manly school of science should feel like spewing such subjectivism out of their mouths? The whole system of loyalties which grow up in the schools of science go dead against its toleration; so that it is only natural that those who have caught the scientific fever should pass over to the opposite extreme, and write sometimes as if the incorruptibly truthful intellect ought positively to prefer bitterness and unacceptableness to the heart in its cup.

It fortifies my soul to know
That though I perish, Truth is so

sings Clough, while Huxley exclaims: "My only consolation lies in the reflection that, however bad our posterity may become, so far as they hold by the plain rule of not pretending to believe what they have no reason to believe, because it may be to their advantage so to pretend [the word 'pretend' is surely here redundant], they will not have reached the lowest depth of immorality." And that delicious *enfant terrible* Clifford writes: "Belief is desecrated when given to unproved and unquestioned statements for the solace and private pleasure of the believer. . . . Whoso would deserve well of his fellows in this matter will guard the purity of his belief with a very fanaticism of jealous care, lest at any time it should rest on an unworthy object, and catch a stain which can never be wiped away. . . . If [a] belief has been accepted on insufficient evidence [even though the belief be true, as Clifford on the same page explains] the pleasure is a stolen one. . . . It is sinful because it is stolen in defiance of our duty to mankind. That duty is to guard ourselves from such beliefs as from a pestilence which may shortly master our own body and then spread to the rest of the town. . . . It is wrong always, everywhere, and for every one, to believe anything upon insufficient evidence."

III

All this strikes one as healthy, even when expressed, as by Clifford, with somewhat too much of robustious pathos in the voice. Free will and simple wishing do seem, in the matter of our credences, to be only fifth wheels to the coach. Yet if any one should thereupon assume that intellectual insight is what remains after wish and will and sentimental preference have taken wing, or that pure reason is what then settles our opinions, he would fly quite as directly in the teeth of the facts.

It is only our already dead hypotheses that our willing nature is unable to bring to life again. But what has made them dead for us is for the most part a previous action of our willing nature of an antagonistic kind. When I say "willing nature," I do not mean only such deliberate volitions as may have set up habits of belief that we cannot now escape from—I mean all such factors of belief as fear and hope, prejudice and passion, imitation and partisanship, the circumpressure of our caste and set. As a matter of fact we find ourselves believing, we hardly know how or why. Mr. Balfour gives the name of "authority" to all those influences, born of the intellectual climate, that make hypotheses possible or impossible for us, alive or dead. Here in this room, we all of us believe in molecules and the conservation of energy, in democracy and necessary progress, in Protestant Christianity and the duty of fighting for "the doctrine of the immortal Monroe," all for no reasons worthy of the name. We see into these matters with no more inner clearness, and probably with much less, than any disbeliever in them might possess. His unconventionality would probably have some grounds to show for its conclusions; but for us, not insight, but the *prestige* of the opinions, is what makes the spark shoot from them and light up our sleeping magazines of faith. Our reason is quite satisfied, in nine hundred and ninety-nine cases out of every thousand of us, if it can find a few arguments that will do to recite in case our credulity is criticized by some one else. Our faith is faith in some one else's faith, and in the greatest matters this is the most the case. . . .

Evidently, then, our non-intellectual nature does influence our convictions. There are passional tendencies and volitions which run before and others which come after belief, and it is only the latter that are too late for the fair; and they are not too late when the previous passional work has been already in their own direction. Pascal's argument, instead of being powerless, then seems a regular clincher, and is the last stroke needed to make our faith in masses and holy water complete. The state of things is evidently far from simple; and pure insight and logic, whatever they might do ideally, are not the only things that really do produce our creeds.

IV

Our next duty, having recognized this mixed-up state of affairs, is to ask whether it be simply reprehensible and pathological, or whether, on the contrary, we must treat it as a normal element in making up our minds. The thesis I defend is, briefly stated, this: *Our passional nature not only lawfully may, but must, decide an option between propositions, whenever it is a genuine option that cannot by its nature be decided on intellectual grounds; for to say, under such circumstances, "Do not decide, but leave the question open," is itself a passional decision—just like deciding yes or no—and is attended with the same risk of losing the truth. . . .*

VII

One more point, small but important, and our preliminaries are done. There are two ways of looking at our duty in the matter of opinion—ways entirely different, and yet ways about whose difference the theory of knowledge seems hitherto to have shown very little concern. *We must know the truth;* and *we must avoid error*—these are our first and great commandments as would-be knowers; but they are not two ways of stating an identical commandment, they are two separable laws. Although it may indeed happen that when we believe the truth A, we escape as an incidental consequence from believing the falsehood B, it hardly ever happens that by merely disbelieving B we necessarily believe A. We may in escaping B fall into believing other falsehoods, C or D, just as bad as B; or we may escape B by not believing anything at all, not even A.

Believe truth! Shun error!—these, we see, are two materially different laws; and by choosing between them we may end by coloring differently our whole intellectual life. We may regard the chase for truth as paramount, and the avoidance of error as secondary; or we may, on the other hand, treat the avoidance of error as more imperative, and let truth take its chance. Clifford, in the instructive passage which I have quoted, exhorts us to the latter course. Believe nothing, he tells us, keep your mind in suspense forever, rather than by closing it on insufficient evidence incur the awful risk of believing lies.

You, on the other hand, may think that the risk of being in error is a very small matter when compared with the blessings of real knowledge, and be ready to be duped many times in your investigation rather than postpone indefinitely the chance of guessing true. I myself find it impossible to go with Clifford. We must remember that these feelings of our duty about either truth or error are in any case only expressions of our passional life. Biologically considered, our minds are as ready to grind out falsehood as veracity, and he who says, "Better go without belief forever than believe a lie!" merely shows his own preponderant private horror of becoming a dupe. He may be critical of many of his desires and fears, but this fear he slavishly obeys. He cannot imagine any one questioning its binding force. For my own part, I have also a horror of being duped; but I can believe that worse things than being duped may happen to a man in this world: so Clifford's exhortation has to my ears a thoroughly fantastic sound. It is like a general informing his soldiers that it is better to keep out of battle forever than to risk a single wound. Not so are victories either over enemies or over nature gained. Our errors are surely not such awfully solemn things. In a world where we are so certain to incur them in spite of all our caution, a certain lightness of heart seems healthier than this excessive nervousness on their behalf. At any rate, it seems the fittest thing for the empiricist philosopher.

VIII

And now, after all this introduction, let us go straight at our question. I have said, and now repeat it, that not only as a matter of fact do we find our passional nature influencing us in our opinions, but that there are some options between opinions in which this influence must be regarded both as an inevitable and as a lawful determinant of our choice.

I fear here that some of you my hearers will begin to scent danger, and lend an inhospitable ear. Two first steps of passion you have indeed had to admit as necessary—we must think so as to avoid dupery, and we must think so as to gain truth; but the surest path to those ideal consummations, you will probably consider, is from now onwards to take no further passional step.

Well, of course, I agree as far as the facts will allow. Wherever the option between losing truth and gaining it is not momentous, we can throw the chance of *gaining truth* away, and at any rate save ourselves from any chance of *believing falsehood,* by not making up our minds at all till objective evidence has come. In scientific questions, this is almost always the case; and even in human affairs in general, the need of acting is seldom so urgent that a false belief to act on is better than no belief at all. Law courts, indeed, have to decide on the best evidence attainable for the moment, because a judge's duty is to make law as well as to ascertain it, and (as a learned judge once said to me) few cases are worth spending much time over: the great thing is to have them decided on *any* acceptable principle, and got out of the way. But in our dealings with objective nature we obviously are recorders, not makers, of the truth; and decisions for the mere sake of deciding promptly and getting on to the next business would be wholly out of place. Throughout the breadth of physical nature facts are what they are quite independently of us, and seldom is there any such hurry about them that the risks of being duped by believing a premature theory need be faced. The questions here are always trivial options, the hypotheses are hardly living (at any rate not living for us spectators), the choice between believing truth or falsehood is seldom forced. The attitude of sceptical balance is therefore the absolutely wise one if we would escape mistakes. What difference, indeed, does it make to most of us whether we have or have not a theory of the Röntgen rays, whether we believe or not in mind-stuff, or have a conviction about the causality of conscious states? It makes no difference. Such options are not forced on us. On every account it is better not to make them, but still keep weighing reasons *pro et contra* with an indifferent hand.

I speak, of course, here of the purely judging mind. For purposes of discovery such indifference is to be less highly recommended, and science would be far less advanced than she is if the passionate desires of individuals to get their own faiths confirmed had been kept out of the game. See for example the sagacity which Spencer and Weismann now display. On the other hand, if you want an absolute duffer in an investigation, you must, after all, take the man who has no interest whatever in its results: he is the warranted incapable, the positive fool. The most useful investigator, because the most sensitive observer, is always he whose eager interest in one side of the question is balanced by an equally keen nervousness lest he become deceived.[1] Science has organized this nervousness into a regular *technique,* her so-called method of verification; and she has fallen so deeply in love with the method that one may even say she has ceased to care for truth by itself at all. It is only truth as technically verified that interests her. The truth of truths might come in merely affirmative form, and she would decline to touch it. Such truth as that, she might repeat with Clifford, would be stolen in defiance of her duty to mankind. Human passions, however, are stronger than technical rules. "*Le coeur a ses raisons,*" as Pascal says, "*que la raison ne connait pas*";[2] and however indifferent to all but the bare rules of the game the umpire, the abstract intellect, may be, the concrete players who furnish him the materials to judge of are usually, each one of them, in love with some pet "live hypothesis" of his own. Let us agree, however, that wherever there is no forced option, the dispassionately judicial intellect with no pet hypothesis, saving us, as it does, from dupery at any rate, ought to be our ideal.

The question next arises: Are there not somewhere forced options in our speculative questions, and can we (as men who may be interested at least as much in positively gaining truth as in merely escaping dupery) always wait with impunity till the coercive evidence shall have arrived? It seems *a priori* improbable that the truth should be so nicely adjusted to our needs and powers as that. In the great boardinghouse of nature, the cakes and the butter and the syrup seldom come out so even and leave the plates so clean. Indeed, we should view them with scientific suspicion if they did.

IX

Moral questions immediately present themselves as questions whose solution cannot wait for sensible proof. A moral question is a question not of what sensibly exists, but of what is good, or would be good if it did exist. Science can tell us what exists; but to compare the *worths,* both of what exists and of what does not exist, we must consult not science, but what Pascal calls our heart. . . .

Turn now from these wide questions of good to a certain class of questions of fact, questions concerning personal relations, states of mind between one man and another. *Do you like me or not?*—for example. Whether you do or not depends, in countless instances, on whether I meet you halfway, am willing to assume that you must like me, and show you trust and expectation. The previous faith on my part in your liking's existence is in such cases what makes your liking come. But if I stand aloof, and refuse to budge an inch until I have objective evidence, until you shall have done something apt, as the absolutists say, *ad extorquendum assensum meum,* ten to one your liking never comes. How many women's hearts are vanquished by the mere sanguine insistence of some man that they *must* love him! He will not consent to the hypothesis that they cannot. The desire for a certain kind of truth here brings about that special truth's existence; and so it is in innumerable cases of other sorts. . . . *And where faith in a fact can help create the fact,* that would be an insane logic which should say that faith running ahead of scientific evidence is the "lowest kind of immorality" into which a thinking being can fall. Yet such is the logic by which our scientific absolutists pretend to regulate our lives!

X

In truths dependent on our personal action, then, faith based on desire is certainly a lawful and possibly an indispensable thing.

But now, it will be said, these are all childish human cases, and have nothing to do with great cosmical matters, like the question of religious faith. Let us then pass on to that. Religions differ so much in their accidents that in discussing the religious question we must make it very generic and broad. What then do we now mean by the religious hypothesis? Science says things are; morality says some things are better than other things; and religion says essentially two things.

First, she says that the best things are the more eternal things, the overlapping things, the things in the universe that throw the last stone, so to speak, and say the final word. "Perfection is eternal"—this phrase of Charles Secrétan seems a good way of putting this first affirmation of religion, an affirmation which obviously cannot yet be verified scientifically at all.

The second affirmation of religion is that we are better off even now if we believe her first affirmation to be true.

Now, let us consider what the logical elements of this situation are *in case the religious hypothesis in both its branches be really true.* (Of course, we must admit that possibility at the outset. If we are to discuss the question at all, it must involve a living option. If for any of you religion be a hypothesis that cannot, by any living possibility, be true, then you need go no farther. I speak to the "saving remnant" alone.) So proceeding, we see, first, that religion offers itself as a *momentous* option. We are supposed to gain, even now, by our belief, and to lose by our non-belief, a certain vital good. Secondly, religion is a *forced* option, so far as that good goes. We cannot escape the issue by remaining sceptical and waiting for more light, because, although we do avoid error in that way *if religion be untrue,* we lose the good, *if it be true,* just as certainly as if we positively chose to disbelieve. It is as if a man should hesitate indefinitely to ask a certain woman to marry him because he was not perfectly sure that she would prove an angel after he brought her home. Would he not cut himself off from that particular angel-possibility as decisively as if he went and married some one else? Scepticism, then, is not avoidance of option; it is option of a certain particular kind of risk. *Better risk loss of truth than chance of error*—that is your faith-vetoer's exact position. He is actively playing his stake as much as the believer is; he is backing the field against the religious hypothesis, just as the believer is backing the religious hypothesis against the field. To preach scepticism to us as a duty until "sufficient evidence" for religion be found, is tantamount therefore to telling us, when in presence of the religious hypothesis, that to yield to our fear of its being error is wiser and better than to yield to our hope that it may be true. It is not intellect against all passions, then; it is only intellect with one passion laying down its law. And by what, forsooth, is the supreme wisdom of this passion warranted? Dupery for dupery, what proof is there that dupery through hope is so much worse than dupery through fear? I, for one, can see no proof; and I simply refuse obedience to the scientist's command to imitate his kind of option, in a case where my own stake is important enough to give me the right to choose my own form of risk. If religion be true and the evidence for it be still insufficient, I do not wish, by putting your extinguisher upon my nature (which feels to me as if it had after all some business in this matter), to forfeit my sole chance in life of getting upon the winning side—that chance depending, of course, on my willingness to run the risk of acting as if my passional need of taking the world religiously might be prophetic and right.

All this is on the supposition that it really may be prophetic and right, and that, even to us who are discussing the matter, religion is a live hypothesis which may be true. Now, to most of us religion comes in a still further way that makes a veto on our active faith even more illogical. The more perfect and more eternal aspect of the universe is represented in our religions as having personal form. The universe is no longer a mere *It* to us, but a *Thou,* if we are religious; and any relation that may be possible from person to person might be possible here. For instance, although in one sense we are passive portions of the universe, in another we show a curious autonomy, as if we were small active centers on our own account. We feel, too, as if the appeal of religion to us were made to our own active good-will, as if evidence might be forever withheld from us unless we met the hypothesis halfway to take a trivial illustration: just as a man who in a company of gentlemen made no advances, asked a warrant for every concession, and believed no one's word without proof, would cut himself off by such churlishness from all the social rewards that a more trusting spirit would earn—so here, one who should shut himself up in snarling logicality and try to make the gods extort his recognition willy-nilly, or not get it at all, might cut himself off forever from his only opportunity of making the gods' acquaintance. This feeling, forced on us we know not whence that by obstinately believing that there are gods (although not to do so would be so easy both for our logic and our life) we are doing the universe the deepest service we can, seems part of the living essence of the religious hypothesis. If the hypothesis *were* true in all its parts, including this one, then pure intellectualism, with its veto on our making willing advances, would be an absurdity; and some participation of our sympathetic nature would be logically required. I therefore, for one, cannot see my way to accepting the agnostic rules for truth-seeking, or wilfully agree to keep my willing nature out of the game. I cannot do so for this plain reason, that *a rule of thinking which would absolutely prevent me from acknowledging certain kinds of truth if those kinds of truth were really there, would be an irrational rule.* That for me is the long and short of the formal logic of the situation, no matter what the kinds of truth might materially be.

I confess I do not see how this logic can be escaped. But sad experience makes me fear that some of you may still shrink from radically saying with me, *in abstracto,* that we have the right to believe at our own risk any hypothesis that is live enough to tempt our will. I suspect, however, that if this is so, it is because you have got away from the abstract logical point of view altogether, and are thinking (perhaps without realizing it) of some particular religious hypothesis which for you is dead. The freedom to "believe what we will" you apply to the case of some patent superstition; and the faith you think of is the faith defined by the schoolboy when he said, "Faith is when you believe something that you know ain't true." I can only repeat that this is misapprehension. *In concreto,* the freedom to believe can only cover living options which the intellect of the individual cannot by itself resolve; and living options never seem absurdities to him who has them to consider. When I look at the religious question as it really puts itself to concrete men, and when I think of all the possibilities which both practically and theoretically it involves, then this command that we shall put a stopper on our heart, instincts, and courage, and *wait*—acting of course meanwhile more or less as if religion were *not* true[3]—till doomsday, or till such time as our intellect and senses working together may have raked in evidence enough—this command, I say, seems to me the queerest idol ever manufactured in the philosophic cave. Were we scholastic absolutists, there might be more excuse. If we had an infallible intellect with its objective certitudes, we might feel ourselves disloyal to such a perfect organ of knowledge in not trusting to it exclusively, in not waiting for its releasing word. But if we are empiricists, if we believe that no bell in us tolls to let us know for certain when truth is in our grasp, then it seems a piece of idle fantasticality to preach so solemnly our duty of waiting for the bell. Indeed we *may* wait if we will—I hope you do not think that I am denying that—but if we do so, we do so at our peril as much as if we believed. In either case we *act,* taking our life in our hands. No one of us ought to issue vetoes to the other, nor should we bandy words of abuse. We ought, on the contrary, delicately and profoundly to respect one another's mental freedom: then only shall we bring about the intellectual republic; then only shall we have that spirit of inner tolerance without which all our outer tolerance is soulless, and which is empiricism's glory; then only shall we live and let live, in speculative as well as in practical things.

I began by a reference to Fitz-James Stephen; let me end by a quotation from him. "What do you think of yourself? What do you think of the world? . . . These are questions with which all must deal as it seems good to them. They are riddles of the Sphinx, and in some way or other we must deal with them. . . . In all important transactions of life we have to take a leap in the dark. . . . If we decide to leave the riddles unanswered, that is a choice; if we waver in our answer, that, too, is a choice: but whatever choice we make, we make it at our peril. If a man chooses to turn his back altogether on God and the future, no one can prevent him; no one can show beyond reasonable doubt that he is mistaken. If a man thinks otherwise and acts as he thinks, I do not see that any one can prove that *he* is mistaken. Each must act as he thinks best; and if he is wrong, so much the worse for him. We stand on a mountain pass in the midst of whirling snow and blinding mist, through which we get glimpses now and then of paths which may be deceptive. If we stand still we shall be frozen to death. If we take the wrong road we shall be dashed to pieces. We do not certainly know whether there is any right one. What must we do? 'Be strong and of a good courage.' Act for the best, hope for the best, and take what comes. . . . If death ends all, we cannot meet death better."[4]

NOTES

1. Compare Wilfrid Ward's Essay "The Wish to Believe," in his *Witnesses to the Unseen* (Macmillan & Co., 1893).

2. "The heart has its reasons which reason does not know." Editor's Trans.

3. Since belief is measured by action, he who forbids us to believe religion to be true, necessarily also forbids us to act as we should if we did believe it to be true. The whole defence of religious faith hinges upon action. If the action required or inspired by the religious hypothesis is in no way different from that dictated by the naturalistic hypothesis, then religious faith is a pure superfluity, better pruned away, and controversy about its legitimacy is a piece of idle trifling, unworthy of serious minds. I myself believe, of course, that the religious hypothesis gives to the world an expression which specifically determines our reactions, and makes them in a large part unlike what they might be on a purely naturalistic scheme of belief.

4. *Liberty, Equality, Fraternity*, p. 353, 2d edition (London, 1874).

Part II

Human Knowledge: Its Grounds and Limits

DURING THE GREAT GOLDEN AGE OF PHILOSOPHY, in the seventeenth and eighteenth centuries, problems about the nature of human knowledge divided philosophers into two schools; and despite changing idioms and increased understanding of the methods of science, the division to a large degree persists. On the one hand, the **empiricists,** whose leading thinkers were John Locke (1632–1704), George Berkeley (1685–1753), and David Hume (1711–1776), held that all our ideas come from experience and that no proposition about any matter of fact can be known to be true independently of experience. On the other hand, the **rationalists,** whose most important representatives were René Descartes (1596–1650), Baruch Spinoza (1632–1677), and Gottfried Leibniz (1646–1716), maintained that there are **innate ideas** and that certain general propositions (usually called *necessary* or *a priori* propositions) can be known to be true in advance of, or in the absence of, empirical verification.[1]

Advocates of the theory of innate ideas did not, of course, hold that we are born literally thinking certain thoughts, but rather that we are born with inherited dispositions to have thoughts of a certain form and structure. Just as dehydrated milk has the disposition to become milk when water is added to it, so the mind, on this theory, has from birth the disposition to acquire the concepts of being, substance, duration—even infinitude and God—once a certain amount of experience is "added to it." Thus, rationalism holds that there can be in the mind ideas and truths that were not first present in experience but only later activated by experience. For the empiricist, on the other hand, the mind is (as Locke put it) like a tablet on which nothing has been written (a ***tabula rasa***) until experience writes its message on it.

The writings of René Descartes, a leading mathematician, man of science, and philosopher, are a clear example not only of the rationalistic doctrine and method but also of the rationalistic temper of mind. In the autobiographical *Discourse on Method,* Descartes compares the state of the sciences and philosophy to an ancient European town, grown helter-skelter from an older village, with crooked streets, random walls, and poor sanitation. Of course, we are not accustomed to rip down whole cities in order to start from scratch the task of rational redesign; but individuals can without arrogance or absurdity think of ripping down and rebuilding their own homes:

> . . . and the same I thought was true of any similar project for reforming the body of the Sciences, or the order of teaching them established in the Schools: but as for the opinions which up to that time I had embraced, I thought that I could not do better than resolve at once to sweep them wholly away, that I might afterwards be in a position to admit either others more correct, or even perhaps the same ones when they had undergone the scrutiny of reason. I firmly believed that in this way I should

[1] It should be noted that both the rationalist and the empiricist are "rationalists" in the wider sense of the term—that is, as opposed to fideism, romanticism, or irrationalism. Both can support rational inquiry as the sole road to truth, but they differ in their conceptions of what rational inquiry is, particularly regarding the role that sense experience plays in it.

> much better succeed in the conduct of my life, than if I built only upon old foundations, and leaned upon principles which, in my youth, I had taken upon trust.

Thus, Descartes begins his dramatic quest for new "foundations," doubting everything that can be doubted until he finds a solid basis for reconstruction in the indubitable fact of his own existence as a "thinking substance." What makes the argument for his own existence so convincing, Descartes decides, is its "clearness and distinctness." Hence, he has a working criterion of truth to use in the voyage away from his skeptical starting point: Whatever he conceives clearly and distinctly is true.

In his third Meditation, Descartes finds in himself the idea of an infinite God. The idea, he argues, could not be his own invention, nor could it be derived from merely finite experience. Its only possible cause must be the actually existing deity. He then goes on to prove that this deity is no deceiver. Therefore, (a) because God has given us a powerful disposition to believe in the existence of material objects (such as human bodies), (b) because God would be a deceiver if no such objects existed, and (c) because God is not a deceiver, it follows that such objects do exist and that human knowledge is reliable. Intellectual error, then, when it occurs, springs from a kind of hasty willfulness in ourselves and not from God.

Although many philosophers today would quarrel with particular steps in Descartes' arguments, there is no denying that his general method has left its mark on most of his successors. For three centuries, philosophers have tried to give a rational reconstruction of our knowledge, beginning with the relatively indubitable and building on it, taking very seriously as they work the nagging claims of imaginary **skeptics** that what we think we know with certainty we may not really know at all.

Admitting some minimal possibility that hitherto undoubted and apparently indubitable belief might yet be false is for most of us just a matter of make-believe. It will be simply feigning a doubt for the purposes of some irksome riddle or pointless intellectual game that some people find it fun to play. In order fully to appreciate how important it was to seventeenth and eighteenth century philosophers to "refute the skeptic," however, one must be able *genuinely* to doubt, to "doubt with conviction," if you will, to *honestly* believe that previously undoubted beliefs might yet be false, and to take that real possibility to heart, not just as a move in a game, but as a troublesome disturbance in one's network of convictions and indeed in one's orientation to the world. Imaginative teachers of philosophy often try to give examples from science fiction of what such a frame of mind would be like. The late Charles L. Stevenson, for example, used to introduce Descartes to his beginning students at the University of Michigan with a simple story of his own invention:

> Imagine a neurosurgeon whose expertise on the human brain and whose knowledge of daily events are such that he can, with probes, dictate a subject's experiences. After he has implanted electrodes in the brain of a certain male volunteer, the surgeon causes him to experience the removal of the probes, although they are still in place; then to experience going home through the rain, spending the night with his wife, receiving a call from the surgeon in the morning asking him to return to the laboratory, and returning—all this while he is, in fact, still on the operating table.
>
> The next day, the surgeon does actually remove the electrodes and sends the subject home, whereupon his wife inquires indignantly, "Where were you last night?" "Right here with you," the man replies. "Oh, no, you weren't," she rejoins, "and I can prove it. I had the whole neighborhood out searching for you."

> Then the enlightened husband smiles and says, "Ah, now I see. That surgeon fooled me. He made me *think* I came home. But I was on the operating table the whole time."
>
> His smile quickly fades, however, never to return, because from that point forward the poor fellow can never be certain he is not still on the operating table.[2]

A similar story with more dramatic detail is told by John Pollock in the selection that leads off Part 2, which is renamed here "A Brain in a Vat." Pollock's illustration of real doubt taken to heart then leads into his introduction to a course in **epistemology.**

There are various ways of introducing a student to an academic discipline that is new to her, and all of them have their merits. One can organize the introduction historically, and take the student back to the great books that are the original sources, or the more naturally engaging sources, of the problems that define for the student the discipline that is new to her. In the case of epistemology, that source is Descartes' *Meditations,* here included in its entirety. Roderick Chisholm, one of the twentieth century's leading epistemologists, gives us a rare example of a different kind of introduction. His remarkable essay, "The Problem of the Criterion," confronts head on what is perhaps the most basic epistemological problem, namely our apparent inability to separate true from false beliefs until we have a criterion for distinguishing them, and our parallel inability to recognize an adequate criterion until we see whether it succeeds in distinguishing true from false beliefs correctly. But that test of criteria in turn presupposes that we already know which of our beliefs are true and which are false, and that in turn requires that we have an adequate criterion, and so on, around the circle forever. Chisholm does not, however, abandon the field to the skeptic. Instead, he makes a strong case for a "particularist" solution to his puzzle, which aligns him with the so-called "Common Sense Scottish School of Philosophy" and its leading spokesman, Thomas Reid (1710–1796).

Skeptical doubts are especially likely to torment the empiricist philosopher. Because empiricism holds that the sole source ultimately of our knowledge of things external to us is sense experience, it is a matter of importance to empiricists to explain just how that knowledge is derived from the "impressions" made upon our various sense organs. John Locke rested a great part of his theory upon a crucial distinction first used in antiquity and then revived by Galileo—namely, the distinction between *primary* and *secondary qualities* of physical objects. **Primary qualities** are intrinsic characteristics of the object itself—characteristics such as solidity, extension in space (size), figure (shape), motion or rest, and number. These are qualities that the objects would continue to possess even if there were no perceiving beings in the world. **Secondary qualities,** on the other hand (such qualities as color, taste, smell, sound, warmth, and cold), exist only when actually sensed and then only "in the mind" of the one who senses them. Primary qualities are inseparable from the material object and are found in every part of it, no matter how small. Every conceivable unit of matter, from a celestial body to an atom, must have some size and shape. (On the other hand, no mere atom could have color.)

Locke also contributed to the terminology of subsequent empiricists the technical term "idea" to stand for "whatever is the object of the understanding when a man thinks" or,

[2] From Arthur W. Burks, "Preface," *Values and Morals, Essays in Honor of William Frankena, Charles Stevenson, and Richard Brandt,* edited by Alvin I. Goldman and Jaegwon Kim (Dordrecht: D. Reidel Publishing Co., 1978), p. xiii.

more generally, for any direct object of awareness or consciousness.[3] And, again, the "ideas" that result from our perception of primary qualities are different from our "ideas" of secondary qualities. When we perceive a primary quality, according to Locke, our "idea" of this quality exactly resembles the corresponding primary quality in the material object itself. In contrast, when we perceive a secondary quality, our "idea" of this quality has no resemblance to a corresponding property of the thing itself. That is, our "idea" of, for instance, color or odor in an object is produced in us by virtue of the object's "power" to reflect and absorb light waves of certain frequencies or to emit molecules in certain degrees of vibration. Because of these capacities or "powers" of material objects, color and odor can come into existence. Yet without eyes, there could be no color; without noses, no odor; and without minds, no "secondary qualities" at all.

Locke's theory of perception, then, does seem to have strong support from scientifically sophisticated common sense. It is often contrasted with another possible theory of perception (a theory held by no reputable philosopher), which is sometimes ascribed (quite unfairly) to the scientifically unsophisticated common sense of "the ordinary person." According to the latter theory, called **naive realism,** the qualities that Locke called "primary" and those he called "secondary" are both strictly part of physical objects, and both can exist quite independently of perceiving minds.[4] It follows from naive realism that a world without perceiving minds might yet be a colorful, clamorous, and smelly place. Locke's view, in contrast, is that physical substances and their primary qualities can exist independently of sentient minds and only the secondary qualities are mind-dependent. This theory can be called **sophisticated realism:** "sophisticated" because it seems to accord with what science tells us about secondary qualities; "realism" because it allows that material objects have a real existence independent of minds. Locke's view is often called **representative realism** because of the tenet that ideas ("in the mind") faithfully mirror or "represent" material objects to us in perception, even though the material objects and the "ideas" by which we come to know them are quite distinct entities. The textbooks also call Locke's view the **causal theory of perception** because of the tenet that material objects are the causes of the ideas, or appearances, or sense data we have of them. The material substance itself is distinct from its own qualities, even from its own primary qualities, and, not being directly perceivable, must simply be posited as an unknowable "**substratum**" for its powers and properties. (Locke's conception of substance was rejected by most later empiricists, who preferred to think of a material thing as a mere "bundle of attributes," not as a mysterious entity "underlying" or "possessing" its own attributes.)

The realism of Locke, roughly sketched in the preceding paragraphs, must be understood as the primary target of the arguments of George Berkeley, Bishop of Cloyne. Locke would have approved of Berkeley's systematic demonstration that secondary qualities are mental. Berkeley argues for the conclusion in two ways. First of all, he maintains that extreme degrees of each secondary quality are inseparable in our consciousness from pain.

[3] David Hume's usage was somewhat narrower. In the *Treatise of Human Nature,* his earlier more formal exposition of the views included here. Hume explains that he will use the word "impression" to mean "all our sensations, passions, and emotions, as they make their first appearance in the soul." By "ideas" he means "the faint images of these in thinking and reasoning."

[4] The Spanish-American philosopher George Santayana (*Winds of Doctrine* [London: J. M. Dent and Sons, New York: Charles Scribner's Sons, 1940], p. 146) once lampooned a similar view about the ethical characteristic "goodness" by likening it to the claim that whiskey is "intoxicating in itself, without reference to any animal; that it is pervaded, as it were, by an inherent intoxication, and stands dead drunk in its bottle!"

Hence, if it is absurd to imagine that pain is, for example, *in* or *part of* the stove, then it is equally absurd to imagine that the heat is literally in the stove. Berkeley's second argument is the famous "argument from the relativity of perception." If I put one ice-chilled hand and one warm hand into a tub of tepid water, the water will feel hot to my cold hand and cold to my hot hand; but the water itself cannot be both hot and cold. Hence, both heat and cold must be "in the mind" only.

But Berkeley then turns the tables on Locke by arguing in quite similar ways for the necessarily mental status of *primary qualities* too. If the supporter of Locke accepts these latter arguments, there is nothing left of his conception of an external object beyond that of an unknowable "substratum." Berkeley easily disposes of the concept of a substratum as theoretically superfluous and unintelligible. He is left then with a world in which only perceiving minds ("subjects") and their "ideas" (the appearances of primary and secondary qualities) exist. Hence, the universe is through and through mental. This theory of reality bears the name **subjective idealism.** (Perhaps *ideaism* would be less misleading because the theory has nothing whatever to do with ideals.)

Berkeley was as concerned as Descartes or Locke to find a solid alternative to skepticism. As an empiricist, he was resolved to show that all of our ideas, insofar as they are genuine (not merely confused), are derived from experience. What, then, of our idea of corporeal objects such as trees, tables, bodies? Berkeley was driven by his logic and his empiricist startings to conclude that physical objects, insofar as we have any clear idea of them at all, are simply collections of sense impressions. Those **corporeal** substances, of which Descartes was at last able to form a "clear and distinct idea," turn out on analysis to be the figments of muddled thought.

Has empiricism then truly reconstructed our knowledge of the world, if this is its conclusion? Doesn't Berkeley's conception of a world "through and through mental" give a violent jolt to common sense? Not so, replies Berkeley's spokesman Philonous. Berkeley's idealism implies that tables and trees and bodies are just exactly what they seem—colored, shaped, hard, and so on. There is indeed nothing to these things except the qualities they seem to have. Moreover, it is not true that tables "vanish" or "pop out of existence" the moment we turn our backs on them (that *would* be repugnant to common sense); for God is always perceiving them, and therefore they continue to exist as ideas in His mind. To many later empiricists, this use of God seemed a desperate expedient to save Berkeley's theory from embarrassment. John Stuart Mill (1806–1873) was typical of later empiricists (often called **phenomenalists**) who found ways to make the rejection of "corporeal substance" more palatable to common sense without invoking a ***deus ex machina.*** According to Mill, if we say that the table continues to exist when unperceived, all we can mean by this is that *if* someone were to look in a certain place, then he would have sense impressions of a certain (table-like) kind; for material objects are not simply bundles of actual sense impressions but are rather to be understood as "permanent possibilities of sensation," and this conception exhausts whatever clear idea we have of them. Some writers have suggested that phenomenalism (the view of David Hume as well as of Mill) can be thought of as "Berkeley's view without Berkeley's God."

David Hume in the eighteenth century applied the empiricist philosophy not only to the concept of a material substance but to other basic concepts as well, with results that even he called skeptical. Unlike Berkeley, who regarded skepticism as a charge to be rebutted, Hume thought of it as a position to be reluctantly adopted. In the selections included here, he examines the concept of causation and finds no more sense in the idea of a "necessary connection" between cause and effect (when we drop a stone, it *must* fall—so we think) than Berkeley did in the idea of "corporeal substance." We may continue to talk, as Hume himself does, of one thing's causing another, but all we can *mean* is that events of the first kind are in fact constantly conjoined with events of the second kind; and the so-called necessity that the second follow the first is simply the reflection of our habitual expectation. Hume would not have us deny the plain reports of our senses or the fruits of our mathematical deductions; he merely points out that there is no logically infallible method of achieving truth about matters of fact, and indeed no method at all for reasoning about matters that lie beyond all experience. But this kind of skepticism need not force us into a permanent suspension of judgment about all things, even in the practical affairs of life; for we will (as Hume elsewhere puts it) continue to leave buildings by the first-floor door rather than the upstairs window, and "Nature will always maintain her rights and prevail in the end over any abstract reasoning whatever."

The article "An Encounter with David Hume" was written specifically for the third edition of this volume by Wesley C. Salmon, now of the University of Pittsburgh. It is meant to show the beginning student of philosophy and science ("Physics 1a") how natural Hume's doubts can seem to one who ponders the methods and results of the exact sciences and how important it is to our conception of scientific knowledge to come to terms with those doubts. In particular, Salmon discusses such scientific notions as causation, inductive inference, probability, laws of nature, the regularity of nature, necessity, and predictability, in the light of Hume's empiricism. Salmon's essay views these matters through the eyes of a sensitive undergraduate student of physics who comes to wonder whether all science rests ultimately on a kind of "faith" in the uniformity of nature that cannot be rationally demonstrated to be correct. If this is so, he asks (with a certain amount of anguish), how can physics be shown to be a more reliable guide to knowledge of the future than, say, astrology or crystal gazing? These questions pose in a very rough way what has come to be called "the problem of induction" or "Hume's riddle of induction." Salmon concludes by sketching the main strategies that have been proposed by philosophers for coming to terms with Hume's skeptical doubts about scientific method.

The theory of knowledge comes by its interest in the philosophy of science quite naturally, since the methods of science have been the most reliable—some philosophers say the *only* reliable—producers of knowledge. The first question epistemologists should ask about science, of course is: When are investigative methods properly called "scientific"? A full answer to the question "What is science?", however, will describe what job is assigned to science either in its crude or developed state and contrast that task with that of other cultural activities that could be, and often are, confused with it. John Maynard Smith, in his contribution to this section, contrasts science with what he calls "Myth." Myth functions in every society, including our modern "post-industrial" society, to impart and celebrate the fundamental shared values that make an aggregation of individuals into a community. Maynard Smith argues that it is a mistake to expect science to do the job of myth, just as it is a mistake to demand of myth that it do the job of science. It does not discredit the story of Genesis to point out all of its "mistakes" about geology, astronomy, and so on. Properly understood the function of myth is not to teach us about such matters as velocity, mass, and gravitation. Its job is to impart moral teachings via parables and stories, and to inspire people to achieve the excellence of great exemplars. Its role then is not one that puts it in competition with science. Any society needs both, and both are intellectually legitimate.

In the 1980s, in the aftermath of a number of state statutes requiring "equal time" in public school biology courses for bible-based "creation science" (that is, a place in the high school curriculum equal to that allotted to the prevailing evolutionary approach to biology), discussion of the nature of science and its role in the production of knowledge spread through the philosophical, scientific, and legal communities. Professor James M. Smith explains why: "The demand that creation science be taught in science classes as a (scientific) alternative to evolutionary theory has resulted in legislation and subsequent court tests of the legislation. When the Arkansas state legislature passed a law requiring equal time for creation science in science classes, the ACLU and several churches and individuals filed suit. They alleged that creation science is not a science but a religious doctrine. Thus, the law requiring equal time violated the provision in the U.S. Constitution prohibiting the government from establishing religion." Judge William R. Overton heard testimony from the leaders of the Creation Science movement and from leading scientists and philosophers of science before writing his opinion, an excerpt from which is reprinted here. The most important question he had to decide was whether Creation Science was truly science or simply religious doctrine in disguise. The question was not whether it was good science or bad science, good theology or bad theology, but *only* whether it was any kind of science at all. That, of course, led Judge Overton to the writings and the testimony of philosophers and the criteria they have proposed for distinguishing science from other forms of inquiry. The result was the judicial opinion reprinted here.

The final selections in this part of the book are by Charles Sanders Peirce whose theory of belief, meaning, and truth he called **pragmatism,** the one distinctively American contribution, some have said, to Western philosophy. To believe a proposition, Peirce held, is to be disposed to act or to feel in certain ways in certain kinds of situations. Without these practical dispositions, there is nothing left to identify with the belief. The meaning of the proposition that we believe must make some difference to our experience. If the practical consequences of its being true were no different from the practical consequences of its being false, then it would have no genuine meaning at all. The philosophical procedure invented by Descartes and presupposed to some degree by most of the writers in this section, which requires us to begin our philosophical inquiries by raising doubts about everything that *can* be doubted, according to Peirce, is fundamentally misguided. The aim of philosophy is to cope with (remove) only real and living doubts and in that manner to "fix belief." Cartesian doubt, as opposed to the actual doubts we sometimes are led to experience by practical frustrations in the world of action, is "a mere self-deception" and make-believe. Philosophy should not aim at speculative beliefs that are beyond all possible doubt, but rather at beliefs that *work* by rendering coherent the beliefs with which we begin and can be relied upon as guides to our practical expectations.

Philosophical Doubts

A Brain in a Vat*

JOHN POLLOCK

John Pollock (1940–), of the University of Arizona, has written important books on the theory of knowledge, the philosophy of mind, and cognitive science.

IT ALL BEGAN THAT COLD WEDNESDAY NIGHT. I was sitting alone in my office watching the rain come down on the deserted streets outside, when the phone rang. It was Harry's wife, and she sounded terrified. They had been having a late supper alone in their apartment when suddenly the front door came crashing in and six hooded men burst into the room. The men were armed and they made Harry and Anne lie face down on the floor while they went through Harry's pockets. When they found his driver's license one of them carefully scrutinized Harry's face, comparing it with the official photograph and then muttered, "It's him all right." The leader of the intruders produced a hypodermic needle and injected Harry with something that made him lose consciousness almost immediately. For some reason they only tied and gagged Anne. Two of the men left the room and returned with a stretcher and white coats. They put Harry on the stretcher, donned the white coats, and trundled him out of the apartment, leaving Anne lying on the floor. She managed to squirm to the window in time to see them put Harry in an ambulance and drive away.

By the time she called me, Anne was coming apart at the seams. It had taken her several hours to get out of her bonds, and then she called the police. To her consternation, instead of uniformed officers, two plain clothed officials arrived and, without even looking over the scene, they proceeded to tell her that there was nothing they could do and if she knew what was good for her she would keep her mouth shut. If she raised a fuss they would put out the word that she was a psycho and she would never see her husband again.

Not knowing what else to do, Anne called me. She had had the presence of mind to note down the number of the ambulance, and I had no great difficulty tracing it to a private clinic at the outskirts of town. When I arrived at the clinic I was surprised to find it locked up like a fortress. There were guards at the gate and it was surrounded by a massive wall. My commando training stood me in good stead as I negotiated the 20 foot wall, avoided the barbed wire, and silenced the guard dogs on the other side. The ground floor windows were all barred, but I managed to wriggle up a drainpipe and get in through a second story window that someone had left ajar. I found myself in a laboratory. Hearing muffled sounds next door I peeked through the keyhole and saw what appeared to be a complete operating room and a surgical team laboring over Harry. He was covered with a sheet from the neck down and they seemed to be connecting tubes and wires to him. I stifled a gasp when I realized that they had removed the top of Harry's skull. To my considerable consternation, one of the surgeons reached into the open top of Harry's head and

**From John Pollock,* Contemporary Theories of Knowledge *(Savage, MD: Rowman & Littlefield, 1986), pp. 1–4.*

eased his brain out, placing it in a stainless steel bowl. The tubes and wires I had noted earlier were connected to the now disembodied brain. The surgeons carried the bloody mass carefully to some kind of tank and lowered it in. My first thought was that I had stumbled on a covey of futuristic Satanists who got their kicks from vivisection. My second thought was that Harry was an insurance agent. Maybe this was their way of getting even for the increases in their malpractice insurance rates. If they did this every Wednesday night, their rates were no higher than they should be!

My speculations were interrupted when the lights suddenly came on in my darkened hidey hole and I found myself looking up at the scariest group of medical men I had ever seen. They manhandled me into the next room and strapped me down on an operating table. I thought, "Oh, oh, I'm for it now!" The doctors huddled at the other end of the room, but I couldn't turn my head far enough to see what they were doing. They were mumbling among themselves, probably deciding my fate. A door opened and I heard a woman's voice. The deferential manner assumed by the medical malpractitioners made it obvious who was boss. I strained to see this mysterious woman but she hovered just out of my view. Then, to my astonishment, she walked up and stood over me and I realized it was my secretary, Margot. I began to wish I had given her that Christmas bonus after all.

It was Margot, but it was a different Margot than I had ever seen. She was wallowing in the heady wine of authority as she bent over me. "Well Mike, you thought you were so smart, tracking Harry here to the clinic," she said. Even now she had the sexiest voice I have ever heard, but I wasn't really thinking about that. She went on, "It was all a trick just to get you here. You saw what happened to Harry. He's not really dead, you know. These gentlemen are the premier neuroscientists in the world today. They have developed a surgical procedure whereby they remove the brain from the body but keep it alive in a vat of nutrient. The Food and Drug Administration wouldn't approve the procedure, but we'll show them. You see all the wires going to Harry's brain? They connect him up with a powerful computer. The computer monitors the output of his motor cortex and provides input to the sensory cortex in such a way that everything appears perfectly normal to Harry. It produces a fictitious mental life that merges perfectly into his past life so that he is unaware that anything has happened to him. He thinks he is shaving right now and getting ready to go to the office and stick it to another neurosurgeon. But actually, he's just a brain in a vat."

"Once we have our procedure perfected we're going after the head of the Food and Drug Administration, but we needed some experimental subjects first. Harry was easy. In order to really test our computer program we need someone who leads a more interesting and varied life—someone like you!" I was starting to squirm. The surgeons had drawn around me and were looking on with malevolent gleams in their eyes. The biggest brute, a man with a pockmarked face and one beady eye staring out from under his stringy black hair, was fondling a razor sharp scalpel in his still-bloody hands and looking as if he could barely restrain his excitement. But Margot gazed down at me and murmured in that incredible voice, "I'll bet you think we're going to operate on you and remove your brain just like we removed Harry's, don't you? But you have nothing to worry about. We're not going to remove your brain. We already did—three months ago!"

With that they let me go. I found my way back to my office in a daze. For some reason, I haven't told anybody about this. I can't make up my mind. I am racked by the suspicion that I am really a brain in a vat and all this I see around me is just a figment of the computer. After all, how could I tell? If the computer program really works, no matter what I do, everything will seem normal. Maybe nothing I see is real. It's driving me crazy. I've even considered checking into that clinic voluntarily and asking them to remove my brain just so that I can be sure. . . .

The Problem of the Criterion*

RODERICK M. CHISHOLM

Roderick M. Chisholm (1916–), one of America's most distinguished epistemologists, spent his entire career at Brown University.

1

"THE PROBLEM OF THE CRITERION" seems to me to be one of the most important and one of the most difficult of all the problems of philosophy. I am tempted to say that one has not begun to philosophize until one has faced this problem and has recognized how unappealing, in the end, each of the possible solutions is. . . .

2

What is the problem, then? It is the ancient problem of "the diallelus"—the problem of "the wheel" or "the vicious circle." It was put very neatly by Montaigne in his *Essays.* So let us begin by paraphrasing his formulation of the puzzle. To know whether things really are as they seem to be, we must have a *procedure* for distinguishing appearances that are true from appearances that are false. But to know whether our procedure is a good procedure, we have to know whether it really *succeeds* in distinguishing appearances that are true from appearances that are false. And we cannot know whether it does really succeed unless we already know which appearances are *true* and which ones are *false.* And so we are caught in a circle.[1]

Let us try to see how one gets into a situation of this sort.

The puzzles begin to form when you ask yourself, "What can I really know about the world?" We are all acquainted with people who think they know a lot more than in fact they do know. I'm thinking of fanatics, bigots, mystics, various types of dogmatists. And we have all heard of people who claim at least to know a lot less than what in fact they do know. I'm thinking of those people who call themselves "skeptics" and who like to say that people cannot know what the world is really like. People tend to become skeptics, temporarily, after reading books on popular science: the authors tell us we cannot know what things are like really (but they make use of a vast amount of knowledge, or a vast amount of what is claimed to be knowledge, to support this skeptical conclusion). And as we know, people tend to become dogmatists, temporarily, as a result of the effects of alcohol, or drugs, or religious and emotional experiences. Then they claim to have an inside view of the world and they think they have a deep kind of knowledge giving them a key to the entire workings of the universe.

If you have a healthy common sense, you will feel that something is wrong with both of these extremes and that the truth is somewhere in the middle: we can know far more than the skeptic says we can know and far less than the dogmatist or the mystic says that he can know. But how are we to decide these things?

3

How do we decide, in any particular case, whether we have a genuine item of knowledge? Most of us are ready to confess that our beliefs far transcend

**An edited version of "The Problem of The Criterion," from Roderick M. Chisholm,* The Foundations of Knowing *(Sussex: Harvester Press, 1982), pp. 61–75. Reprinted by permission of Marquette University Press.*

what we really know. There are things we believe that we don't in fact know. And we can say of many of these things that we know that we don't know them. I believe that Mrs. Jones is honest, say, but I don't know it, and I know that I don't know it. There are other things that we don't know, but they are such that we don't know that we don't know them. Last week, say, I thought I knew that Mr. Smith was honest, but he turned out to be a thief. I didn't know that he was a thief, and, moreover, I didn't know that I didn't know that he was a thief; I thought I knew that he was honest. And so the problem is: How are we to distinguish the real cases of knowledge from what only seem to be cases of knowledge? Or, as I put it before, how are we to decide in any particular case whether we have genuine items of knowledge?

What would be a satisfactory solution to our problem? Let me quote in detail what Cardinal Mercier says:

> If there is any knowledge which bears the mark of truth, if the intellect does have a way of distinguishing the true and the false, in short, *if* there *is* a criterion of truth, then this criterion should satisfy three conditions: it should be *internal, objective,* and *immediate.*
>
> It should be *internal.* No reason or rule of truth that is provided by an *external authority* can serve as an ultimate criterion. For the reflective doubts that are essential to criteriology can and should be applied to this authority itself. The mind cannot attain to certainty until it has found *within itself* a sufficient reason for adhering to the testimony of such an authority.
>
> The criterion should be *objective.* The ultimate reason for believing cannot be a merely *subjective* state of the thinking subject. A man is aware that he can reflect upon his psychological states in order to control them. Knowing that he has this ability, he does not, so long as he has not made use of it, have the right to be sure. The ultimate ground of certitude cannot consist in a subjective feeling. It can be found only in that which, objectively, produces this feeling and is adequate to reason.
>
> Finally, the criterion must be *immediate.* To be sure, a certain conviction may rest upon many different reasons some of which are subordinate to others. But if we are to avoid an infinite regress, then we must find a ground of assent that presupposes no other. We must find an *immediate* criterion of certitude.
>
> Is there a criterion of truth that satisfies these three conditions? If so, what is it?[2]

4

To see how perplexing our problem is, let us consider a figure that Descartes had suggested and that Coffey takes up in his dealings with the problem of the criterion.[3] Descartes' figure comes to this.

Let us suppose that you have a pile of apples and you want to sort out the good ones from the bad ones. You want to put the good ones in a pile by themselves and throw the bad ones away. This is a useful thing to do, obviously, because the bad apples tend to infect the good ones and then the good ones become bad, too. Descartes thought our beliefs were like this. The bad ones tend to infect the good ones, so we should look them over very carefully, throw out the bad ones if we can, and then—or so Descartes hoped—we would be left with just a stock of good beliefs on which we could rely completely. But how are we to do the sorting? If we are to sort out the good ones from the bad ones, then, of course, we must have a way of recognizing the good ones. Or at least we must have a way of recognizing the bad ones. And—again, of course—you and I do have a way of recognizing good apples and also of recognizing bad ones. The good ones have their own special feel, look, and taste, and so do the bad ones.

But when we turn from apples to beliefs, the matter is quite different. In the case of the apples, we have a method—a criterion—for distinguishing the good ones from the bad ones. But in the case of the beliefs, we do not have a method or a criterion for distinguishing the good ones from the bad ones. Or, at least, we don't have one yet. The question we started with was: How *are* we to tell the good ones from the bad ones? In other words, we were asking: What is the proper method for deciding which are the good beliefs and which are the bad ones—which beliefs are genuine cases of knowledge and which beliefs are not?

And now, you see, we are on the wheel. First, we want to find out which are the good beliefs and which are the bad ones. To find this out we have to have some way—some method—of deciding which are the good ones and which are the bad ones. But there are good and bad methods—good and bad ways—of sorting out the good beliefs from the bad ones. And so we now have a new problem: How are we to decide which are the good methods and which are the bad ones?

If we could fix on a good method for distinguishing between good and bad methods, we might be all set. But this, of course, just moves the problem to a different level. How are we to distinguish between a good and a bad method for choosing good methods? If we continue in this way, of course, we are led to an infinite regress and we will never have the answer to our original question.

What do we do in fact? We do know that there are fairly reliable ways of sorting out good beliefs from bad ones. Most people will tell you, for example, that if you follow the procedures of science and common sense—if you tend carefully to your observations and if you make use of the canons of logic, induction, and the theory of probability—you will be following the best possible procedure for making sure that you will have more good beliefs than bad ones. This is doubtless true. But how do we know that it is? How do we know that the procedures of science, reason, and common sense are the best methods that we have?

If we do know this, it is because we know that these procedures work. It is because we know that these procedures do in fact enable us to distinguish the good beliefs from the bad ones. We say: "See—these methods turn out good beliefs." But *how* do we know that they do? It can only be that we already know how to tell the difference between the good beliefs and the bad ones.

And now you can see where the skeptic comes in. He'll say this: "You said you wanted to sort out the good beliefs from the bad ones. Then to do this, you apply the canons of science, common sense, and reason. And now, in answer to the question, 'How do you know that that's the right way to do it?', you say "Why, I can see that the ones it picks out are the good ones and the ones it leaves behind are the bad ones.' But if you can *see* which ones are the good ones and which ones are the bad ones, why do you think you need a general method for sorting them out?"

5

We can formulate some of the philosophical issues that are involved here by distinguishing two pairs of questions. These are:

A) "*What* do we know? What is the *extent* of our knowledge?"

B) "How are we to decide *whether* we know? What are the *criteria* of knowledge?"

If you happen to know the answers to the first of these pairs of questions, you may have some hope of being able to answer the second. Thus, if you happen to know which are the good apples and which are the bad ones, then maybe you could explain to some other person how he could go about deciding whether or not he has a good apple or a bad one. But if you don't know the answer to the first of these pairs of questions—if you don't know what things you know or how far your knowledge extends—it is difficult to see how you could possibly figure out an answer to the second.

On the other hand, *if,* somehow, you already know the answers to the second of these pairs of questions, then you may have some hope of being able to answer the first. Thus, if you happen to have a good set of directions for telling whether apples are good or bad, then maybe you can go about finding a good one—assuming, of course, that there are some good apples to be found. But if you don't know the answer to the second of these pairs of questions—if you don't know how to go about deciding whether or not you know, if you don't know what the criteria of knowing are—it is difficult to see how you could possibly figure out an answer to the first.

And so we can formulate the position of *the skeptic* on these matters. He will say: "You cannot answer question A until you have answered question B.

And you cannot answer question B until you have answered question A. Therefore you cannot answer either question. You cannot know what, if anything, you know, and there is no possible way for you to decide in any particular case." Is there any reply to this?

6

Broadly speaking, there are at least two other possible views. So we may choose among three possibilities.

There are people—philosophers—who think that they do have an answer to B and that, given their answer to B, they can then figure out their answer to A. And there are other people—other philosophers—who have it the other way around: they think that they have an answer to A and that, given their answer to A, they can then figure out the answer to B.

There don't seem to be any generally accepted names for these two different philosophical positions. (Perhaps this is just as well. There are more than enough names, as it is, for possible philosophical views.) I suggest, for the moment, we use the expressions "methodists" and "particularists." By "methodists," I mean, not the followers of John Wesley's version of Christianity, but those who think they have an answer to B, and who then, in terms of it, work out their answer to A. By "particularists" I mean those who have it the other way around.

7

Thus John Locke was a methodist—in our present, rather special sense of the term. He was able to arrive—somehow—at an answer to B. He said, in effect: "The way you decide whether or not a belief is a good belief—that is to say, the way you decide whether a belief is likely to be a genuine case of knowledge—is to see whether it is derived from sense experience, to see, for example, whether it bears certain relations to your sensations." Just what these relations to our sensations might be is a matter we may leave open, for present purposes. The point is: Locke felt that if a belief is to be credible, it must bear certain relations to the believer's sensations—but he never told us *how* he happened to arrive at this conclusion. This, of course, is the view that has come to be known as "empiricism." David Hume followed Locke in this empiricism and said that empiricism gives us an effective criterion for distinguishing the good apples from the bad ones. You can take this criterion to the library, he said. Suppose you find a book in which the author makes assertions that do not conform to the empirical criterion. Hume said: "Commit it to the flames: for it can contain nothing but sophistry and illusion."

8

Empiricism, then, was a form of what I have called "methodism." The empiricist—like other types of methodist—begins with a criterion and then he uses it to throw out the bad apples. There are two objections, I would say, to empiricism. The first—which applies to every form of methodism (in our present sense of the word)—is that the criterion is very broad and far-reaching and at the same time completely arbitrary. How can one *begin* with a broad generalization? It seems especially odd that the empiricist—who wants to proceed cautiously, step by step, from experience—begins with such a generalization. He leaves us completely in the dark so far as concerns what *reasons* he may have for adopting this particular criterion rather than some other. The second objection applies to empiricism in particular. When we apply the empirical criterion—at least, as it was developed by Hume, as well as by many of those in the nineteenth and twentieth centuries who have called themselves "empiricists"—we seem to throw out, not only the bad apples but the good ones as well, and we are left, in effect, with just a few parings or skins with no meat behind them. Thus Hume virtually conceded that, if you are going to be empiricist, the only matters of fact that you can really know about pertain to the existence of sensations. "'Tis vain," he said, "To ask whether there be body." He meant you cannot know whether any physical things exist—whether there are trees, or houses, or bodies, much less whether there are atoms or other such microscopic particles. All you can know is that there are and have been certain sensations. You cannot know whether there is any you who experiences those sensations—much less whether any other people exist who experience sensations. And I think, if he had been consistent in his empiricism, he would also have said you cannot really be sure whether there have been any sensations in the past; you can know only that certain sensations exist here and now.

9

The great Scottish philosopher, Thomas Reid, reflected on all this in the eighteenth century. He was serious about philosophy and man's place in the world. He finds Hume saying things implying that we can know only of the existence of certain sensations here and now. One can imagine him saying: "Good Lord! What kind of nonsense is this?" What he did say, among other things, was this: "A traveler of good judgment may mistake his way, and be unawares led into a wrong track; and while the road is fair before him, he may go on without suspicion and be followed by others but, when it ends in a coal pit, it requires no great judgment to know that he hath gone wrong, nor perhaps to find out what misled him."[4]

Thus Reid, as I interpret him, was not an empiricist; nor was he, more generally, what I have called a "methodist." He was a "particularist." That is to say, he thought that he had an answer to question A, and in terms of the answer to question A, he then worked out kind of an answer to question B.[5] An even better example of a "particularist" is the great twentieth century English philosopher, G. E. Moore.

Suppose, for a moment, you were tempted to go along with Hume and say "The only thing about the world I can really know is that there are now sensations of a certain sort. There's a sensation of a man, there's the sound of a voice, and there's a feeling of bewilderment or boredom. But that's all I can really know about." What would Reid say? I can imagine him saying something like this: "Well, you can talk that way if you want to. But you know very well that it isn't true. You know that you are there, that you have a body of such and such a sort and that other people are here, too. And you know about this building where you were this morning and all kinds of other things as well." G. E. Moore would raise his hand at this point and say: "I know very well this is a hand, and so do you. If you come across some philosophical theory that implies that you and I cannot know that this is a hand, then so much the worse for the theory." I think that Reid and Moore are right, myself, and I'm inclined to think that the "methodists" are wrong.

Going back to our questions A and B, we may summarize the three possible views as follows: there is skepticism (you cannot answer either question without presupposing an answer to the other, and therefore the questions cannot be answered at all); there is "methodism" (you begin with an answer to B); and there is "particularism" (you begin with an answer to A). I suggest that the third possibility is the most reasonable.

10

I would say—and many reputable philosophers would disagree with me—that, to find out whether you know such a thing as that this is a hand, you don't have to apply any test or criterion. Spinoza has it right. "In order to know," he said, "there is no need to know that we know, much less to know that we know that we know."[6]

This is part of the answer, it seems to me, to the puzzle about the diallelus. There are many things that quite obviously, we do know to be true. If I report to you the things I now see and hear and feel—or, if you prefer, the things I now think I see and hear and feel—the chances are that my report will be correct; I will be telling you something I know. And so, too, if you report the things that you think you now see and hear and feel. To be sure, there are hallucinations and illusions. People often think they see or hear or feel things that in fact they do not see or hear or feel. But from this fact—that our senses do sometimes deceive us—it hardly follows that your senses and mine are deceiving you and me right now. One may say similar things about what we remember.

Having these good apples before us, we can look them over and formulate certain criteria of goodness. Consider the senses, for example. One important criterion—one epistemological principle—was formulated by St. Augustine. It is more reasonable, he said, to trust the senses than to distrust them. Even though there have been illusions and hallucinations, the wise thing, when everything seems all right, is to accept the testimony of the senses. I say "when everything seems all right." If on a particular occasion something about *that* particular occasion makes you suspect that particular report of the senses, if, say, you seem to remember having been drugged or hypnotized, or brainwashed, then perhaps you should have some doubts about what you think you see, or hear, or feel, or smell. But if nothing about this particular occasion leads you to suspect what the senses report on this particular occasion, then the wise thing is to take such a report at its face value. In short the senses should be regarded as innocent until there is some positive reason, on some particular occasion, for thinking that they are guilty on that particular occasion.

One might say the same thing of memory. If, on any occasion, you think you remember that such-and-such an event occurred, then the wise thing is to assume that that particular event did occur—unless something special about this particular occasion leads you to suspect your memory.

We have then a kind of answer to the puzzle about the diallelus. We start with particular cases of knowledge and then from those we generalize and formulate criteria of goodness—criteria telling us what it is for a belief to be epistemologically respectable. . . .

CONCLUSION

So far as our problem of the criterion is concerned, the essential thing to note is this. In formulating such principles we will simply proceed as Aristotle did when he formulated his rules for the syllogism. As "particularists" in our approach to the problem of the criterion, we will fit our rules to the cases—to the apples we know to be good and to the apples we know to be bad. Knowing what we do about ourselves and the world, we have at our disposal certain instances that our rules or principles should countenance, and certain other instances that our rules or principles should rule out or forbid. And, as rational beings, we assume that by investigating these instances we can formulate criteria that any instance must satisfy if it is to be countenanced and we can formulate other criteria that any instance must satisfy if it is to be ruled out or forbidden.

If we proceed in this way we will have satisfied Cardinal Mercier's criteria for a theory of evidence or, as he called it, a theory of certitude. He said that any criterion, or any adequate set of criteria, should be internal, objective, and immediate. The type of criteria I have referred to are certainly *internal,* in his sense of the term. We have not appealed to any external authority as constituting the ultimate test of evidence. (Thus we haven't appealed to "science" or to "the scientists of our culture circle" as constituting the touchstone of what we know.) I would say that our criteria are *objective.* We have formulated them in terms of the concept of epistemic preferability—where the location "p is epistemically preferable to q for S" is taken to refer to an objective relation that obtains independently of the actual preferences of any particular subject. The criteria that we formulate, if they are adequate, will be principles that are necessarily true. And they are also *immediate.* Each of them is such that, if it is applicable at any particular time, then the fact that it is then applicable is capable of being directly evident to that particular subject at that particular time.

But in all of this I have presupposed the approach I have called "particularism." The "methodist" and the "skeptic" will tell us that we have started in the wrong place. If now we try to reason with them, then, I am afraid, we will be back on the wheel.

What few philosophers have had the courage to recognize is this: we can deal with the problem only by begging the question. It seems to me that, if we do recognize this fact, as we should, then it is unseemly for us to try to pretend that it isn't so.

One may object: "Doesn't this mean, then, that the skeptic is right after all?" I would answer: "Not at all. His view is only one of the three possibilities and in itself has no more to recommend it than the others do. And in favor of our approach there is the fact that we *do* know many things, after all."

NOTES

1. The quotation is a paraphrase. What Montaigne wrote was: "Pour juger des apparences que nous recevons des subjects, il nous faudroit un instrument judicatoire; pour verifier cet instrument, il nous y faut de la demonstration; pour verifier la demonstration, un instrument; nous voylà au rouet. Puisque les sens ne peuvent arrester notre dispute, éstans pleins euxmesmes d'incertitude, il faut que se soit la raison; aucune raison s'establira sans une autre raison: nous voylà à reculons jusques à l'infiny." The passage appears in book 2, chapter 12 ("An Apologie of Raymond Sebond"); it may be found on page 544 of the Modern Library edition of *The Essays of Montaigne.*

2. Cardinal D. J. Mercier, *Critériologie Générale ou Théorie Générale de la Certitude,* 8th Edition (Louvain, 1923), p. 234.

3. See the reply to the VIIth set of Objections and Coffey, vol. 1, p. 127.

4. Thomas Reid, *Inquiry into the Human Mind,* chap. 1, sec. 8.

5. Unfortunately Cardinal Mercier takes Reid to be what I have called a "methodist." He assumes, incorrectly I think, that Reid defends certain principles (principles that Reid calls principles of "common sense") on the ground that these principles happen to be the deliverance of a faculty called "common sense." See Mercier, pp. 179–81.

6. *On Improvement of the Understanding,* in *Chief Works of Benedict de Spinoza,* vol. 2, trans. R. H. M. Elwes, rev. ed. (London: George Bell and Sons, 1898), p. 13.

Our Knowledge of the External World

Meditations on First Philosophy*

RENÉ DESCARTES

René Descartes (1596–1650) is commonly said to be the founder of modern philosophy. Among his other achievements was the invention of analytical geometry.

SYNOPSIS OF THE SIX FOLLOWING MEDITATIONS

In the first Meditation I set forth the reasons for which we may, generally speaking, doubt about all things and especially about material things, at least so long as we have no other foundations for the sciences than those which we have hitherto possessed. But although the utility of a Doubt which is so general does not at first appear, it is at the same time very great, inasmuch as it delivers us from every kind of prejudice, and sets out for us a very simple way by which the mind may detach itself from the senses; and finally it makes it impossible for us ever to doubt those things which we have once discovered to be true.

In the second Meditation, mind, which making use of the liberty which pertains to it, takes for granted that all those things of whose existence it has the least doubt, are non-existent, recognises that it is however absolutely impossible that it does not itself exist. This point is likewise of the greatest

**René Descartes,* Meditations on First Philosophy, *trans. Elizabeth Haldane and G. R. T. Ross (London: Cambridge University Press, 1931). Reprinted by permission of the publisher. First published in Latin in 1641.*

moment, inasmuch as by this means a distinction is easily drawn between the things which pertain to mind—that is to say to the intellectual nature—and those which pertain to body.

But because it may be that some expect from me in this place a statement of the reasons establishing the immortality of the soul, I feel that I should here make known to them that having aimed at writing nothing in all this Treatise of which I do not possess very exact demonstrations, I am obliged to follow a similar order to that made use of by the geometers, which is to begin by putting forward as premises all those things upon which the proposition that we seek depends, before coming to any conclusion regarding it. Now the first and principal matter which is requisite for thoroughly understanding the immortality of the soul is to form the clearest possible conception of it, and one which will be entirely distinct from all the conceptions which we may have of body; and in this Meditation this has been done. In addition to this it is requisite that we may be assured that all the things which we conceive clearly and distinctly are true in the very way in which we think them; and this could not be proved previously to the Fourth Meditation. Further we must have a distinct conception of corporeal nature, which is given partly in this Second, and partly in the Fifth and Sixth Meditations. And finally we should conclude from all this, that those things which we conceive clearly and distinctly as being diverse substances, as we regard mind and body to be, are really substances essentially distinct one from the other; and this is the conclusion of the Sixth Meditation. This is further confirmed in this same Meditation by the fact that we cannot conceive of body excepting in so far as it is divisible, while the mind cannot be conceived of excepting as indivisible. For we are not able to conceive of the half of a mind as we can do of the smallest of all bodies; so that we see that not only are their natures different but even in some respects contrary to one another. I have not however dealt further with this matter in this Treatise, both because what I have said is sufficient to show clearly enough that the extinction of the mind does not follow from the corruption of the body, and also to give men the hope of another life after death, as also because the premises from which the immortality of the soul may be deduced depend on an elucidation of a complete system of Physics. This would mean to establish in the first place that all substances generally—that is to say all things which cannot exist without being created by God—are in their nature incorruptible, and that they can never cease to exist unless God, in denying to them his concurrence, reduce them to nought; and secondly that body, regarded generally, is a substance, which is the reason why it also cannot perish, but that the human body, inasmuch as it differs from other bodies, is composed only of a certain configuration of members and of other similar accidents, while the human mind is not similarly composed of any accidents, but is a pure substance. For although all the accidents of mind be changed, although, for instance, it think certain things, will others, perceive others, etc., despite all this it does not emerge from these changes another mind: the human body on the other hand becomes a different thing from the sole fact that the figure or form of any of its portions is found to be changed. From this it follows that the human body may indeed easily enough perish, but the mind [or soul of man (I make no distinction between them)] is owing to its nature immortal.

In the third Meditation it seems to me that I have explained at sufficient length the principal argument of which I make use in order to prove the existence of God. But none the less, because I did not wish in that place to make use of any comparisons derived from corporeal things, so as to withdraw as much as I could the minds of readers from the senses, there may perhaps have remained many obscurities which, however, will, I hope, be entirely removed by the Replies which I have made to the Objections which have been set before me. Amongst others there is, for example, this one, 'How the idea in us of a being supremely perfect possesses so much objective reality [that is to say participates by representation in so many degrees of being and perfection] that it necessarily proceeds from a cause which is absolutely perfect.' This is illustrated in these Replies by the comparison of a very perfect machine, the idea of which is found in the mind of some workman. For as the objective contrivance of this idea must have some cause, i.e. either the science of the workman or that of some other from whom he has received the idea, it is similarly impossible that the idea of God which is in us should not have God himself as its cause.

In the fourth Meditation it is shown that all these things which we very clearly and distinctly perceive are true, and at the same time it is explained in what the nature of error or falsity consists. This must of necessity be known both for the confirmation of the preceding truths and for the better comprehension of those that follow. (But it must meanwhile be remarked that I do not in any way there treat of sin—that is to say of the error which is committed in the pursuit of good and evil, but only of that which arises in the deciding between the true and the false. And I do not intend to speak of matters pertaining to the Faith or the conduct of life, but only of those which concern speculative truths, and which may be known by the sole aid of the light of nature.)

In the fifth Meditation corporeal nature generally is explained, and in addition to this the existence of God is demonstrated by a new proof in which there may possibly be certain difficulties also, but the solution of these will be seen in the Replies to the Objections. And further I show in what sense it is true to say that the certainty of geometrical demonstrations is itself dependent on the knowledge of God.

Finally in the Sixth I distinguish the action of the understanding [*intellectio*] from that of the imagination [*imaginatio*]; the marks by which this distinction is made are described. I here show that the mind of man is really distinct from the body, and at the same time that the two are so closely joined together that they form, so to speak, a single thing. All the errors which proceed from the senses are then surveyed, while the means of avoiding them are demonstrated, and finally all the reasons from which we may deduce the existence of material things are set forth. Not that I judge them to be very useful in establishing that which they prove, to wit, that there is in truth a world, that men possess bodies, and other such things which never have been doubted by anyone of sense; but because in considering these closely we come to see that they are neither so strong nor so evident as those arguments which lead us to the knowledge of our mind and of God; so that these last must be the most certain and most evident facts which can fall within the cognizance of the human mind. And this is the whole matter that I have tried to prove in these Meditations, for which reason I here omit to speak of many other questions with which I dealt incidentally in this discussion.

MEDITATION I

Of the things which may be brought within the sphere of the doubtful.

It is now some years since I detected how many were the false beliefs that I had from my earliest youth admitted as true, and how doubtful was everything I had since constructed on this basis; and from that time I was convinced that I must once for all seriously undertake to rid myself of all the opinions which I had formerly accepted, and commence to build anew from the foundation, if I wanted to establish any firm and permanent structure in the sciences. But as this enterprise appeared to be a very great one, I waited until I had attained an age so mature that I could not hope that at any later date I should be better fitted to execute my design. This reason caused me to delay so long that I should feel that I was doing wrong were I to occupy in deliberation the time that yet remains to me for action. To-day, then, since very opportunely for the plan I have in view I have delivered my mind from every care [and am happily agitated by no passions] and since I have procured for myself an assured leisure in a peaceable retirement, I shall at last seriously and freely address myself to the general upheaval of all my former opinions.

Now for this object it is not necessary that I should show that all of these are false—I shall perhaps never arrive at this end. But inasmuch as reason already persuades me that I ought no less carefully to withhold my assent from matters which are not entirely certain and indubitable than from those which appear to me manifestly to be false, if I am able to find in each one some reason to doubt, this will suffice to justify my rejecting the whole. And for that end it will not be requisite that I should examine each in particular, which would be an endless undertaking; for owing to the fact that the destruction of the foundations of necessity brings with it the downfall of the rest of the edifice, I shall only in the first place attack those principles upon which all my former opinions rested.

All that up to the present time I have accepted as most true and certain I have learned either from the senses or through the senses; but it is sometimes proved to me that these senses are deceptive, and it is wiser not to trust entirely to any thing by which we have once been deceived.

But it may be that although the senses sometimes deceive us concerning things which are hardly perceptible, or very far away, there are yet many others to be met with as to which we cannot reasonably have any doubt, although we recognize them by their means. For example, there is the fact that I am here, seated by the fire, attired in a dressing gown, having this paper in my hands and other similar matters. And how could I deny that these hands and this body are mine, were it not perhaps that I compare myself to certain persons, devoid of sense, whose cerebella are so troubled and clouded by the violent vapours of black bile, that they constantly assure us that they think they are kings when they are really quite poor, or that they are clothed in purple when they are really without covering, or who imagine that they have an earthenware head or are nothing but pumpkins or are made of glass. But they are mad, and I should not be any the less insane were I to follow examples so extravagant.

At the same time I must remember that I am a man, and that consequently I am in the habit of sleeping, and in my dreams representing to myself the same things or sometimes even less probable things, than do those who are insane in their waking moments. How often has it happened to me that in the night I dreamt that I found myself in this particular place, that I was dressed and seated near the fire, whilst in reality I was lying undressed in bed! At this moment it does indeed seem to me that it is with eyes awake that I am looking at this paper; that this head which I move is not asleep, that it is deliberately and of set purpose that I extend my hand and perceive it; what happens in sleep does not appear so clear nor so distinct as does all this. But in thinking over this I remind myself that on many occasions I have in sleep been deceived by similar illusions, and in dwelling carefully on this reflection I see so manifestly that there are no certain indications by which we may clearly distinguish wakefulness from sleep that I am lost in astonishment. And my astonishment is such that it is almost capable of persuading me that I now dream.

Now let us assume that we are asleep and that all these particulars, e.g. that we open our eyes, shake our head, extend our hands, and so on, are but false delusions; and let us reflect that possibly neither our hands nor our whole body are such as they appear to us to be. At the same time we must at least confess that the things which are represented to us in sleep are like painted representations which can only have been formed as the counterparts of something real and true, and that in this way those general things at least, i.e. eyes, a head, hands, and a whole body, are not imaginary things, but things really existent. For, as a matter of fact, painters, even when they study with the greatest skill to represent sirens and satyrs by forms the most strange and extraordinary, cannot give them natures which are entirely new, but merely make a certain medley of the members of different animals; or if their imagination is extravagant enough to invent something so novel that nothing similar has ever before been seen, and that then their work represents a thing purely fictitious and absolutely false, it is certain all the same that the colours of which this is composed are necessarily real. And for the same reason, although these general things, to wit, [a body], eyes, a head, hands, and such like, may be imaginary, we are bound at the same time to confess that there are at least some other objects yet more simple and more universal, which are real and true; and of these just in the same way as with certain real colours, all these images of things which dwell in our thoughts, whether true and real or false and fantastic, are formed.

To such a class of things pertains corporeal nature in general, and its extension, the figure of extended things, their quantity or magnitude and number, as also the place in which they are, the time which measures their duration, and so on.

That is possibly why our reasoning is not unjust when we conclude from this that Physics, Astronomy, Medicine and all other sciences which have as their end the consideration of composite things, are very dubious and uncertain; but that Arithmetic, Geometry and other sciences of that kind which only treat of things that are very simple and very general, without taking great trouble to ascertain whether they are actually existent or not, contain some measure of certainty and an element of the indubitable. For whether I am awake or asleep, two and three together always form five, and the square can never have more than four sides, and it does not seem possible that truths so clear and apparent can be suspected of any falsity [or uncertainty].

Nevertheless I have long had fixed in my mind the belief that an all-powerful God existed by whom I have been created such as I am. But how do I know that He has not brought it to pass that there is no earth, no heaven, no extended body, no magnitude, no place, and that nevertheless [I possess the perceptions of all these things and that] they seem to me to exist just exactly as I now see them? And, besides, as I sometimes imagine that others deceive themselves in the things which they think they know best, how do I know that I am not deceived every time that I add two and three, or count the sides of a square, or judge of things yet simpler, if anything simpler can be imagined? But possibly God has not desired that I should be thus deceived, for He is said to be supremely good. If, however, it is contrary to His goodness to have made me such that I constantly deceive myself, it would also appear to be contrary to His goodness to permit me to be sometimes deceived, and nevertheless I cannot doubt that He does permit this.

There may indeed be those who would prefer to deny the existence of a God so powerful, rather than believe that all other things are uncertain. But let us not oppose them for the present, and grant that all that is here said of a God is a fable; nevertheless in whatever way they suppose that I have arrived at the state of being that I have reached—whether they attribute it to fate or to accident, or make out that it is by a continual succession of antecedents, or by some other method—since to err and deceive oneself is a defect, it is clear that the greater will be the probability of my being so imperfect as to deceive myself ever, as is the Author to whom they assign my origin the less powerful. To these reasons I have certainly nothing to reply, but at the end I feel constrained to confess that there is nothing in all that I formerly believed to be true, of which I cannot in some measure doubt, and that not merely through want of thought or through levity, but for reasons which are very powerful and maturely considered; so that henceforth I ought not the less carefully refrain from giving credence to these opinions than to that which is manifestly false, if I desire to arrive at any certainty [in the sciences].

But it is not sufficient to have made these remarks, we must also be careful to keep them in mind. For these ancient and commonly held opinions still revert frequently to my mind, long and familiar custom having given them the right to occupy my mind against my inclination and rendered them almost masters of my belief; nor will I ever lose the habit of deferring to them or of placing my confidence in them, so long as I consider them as they really are, i.e. opinions in some measure, doubtful, as I have just shown, and at the same time highly probable, so that there is much more reason to believe in than to deny them. That is why I consider that I shall not be acting amiss, if, taking of set purpose a contrary belief, I allow myself to be deceived, and for a certain time pretend that all these opinions are entirely false and imaginary, until at last, having thus balanced my former prejudices with my latter [so that they cannot divert my opinions more to one side than to the other], my judgment will no longer be dominated by bad usage or turned away from the right knowledge of the truth. For I am assured that there can be neither peril nor error in this course, and that I cannot at present yield too much to distrust, since I am not considering the question of action, but only of knowledge.

I shall then suppose, not that God who is supremely good and the fountain of truth, but some evil genius not less powerful than deceitful, has employed his whole energies in deceiving me; I shall consider that the heavens, the earth, colours, figures, sound, and all other external things are nought but the illusions and dreams of which this genius has availed himself in order to lay traps for my credulity; I shall consider myself as having no hands, no eyes, no flesh, no blood, nor any senses, yet falsely believing myself to possess all these things; I shall remain obstinately attached to this idea, and if by this means it is not in my power to arrive at the knowledge of any truth, I may at least do what is in my power [i.e. suspend my judgment], and with firm purpose avoid giving credence to any false thing, or being imposed upon by this arch deceiver, however powerful and deceptive he may be. But this task is a laborious one, and insensibly a certain lassitude leads me into the course of my ordinary life. And just as a captive who in sleep enjoys an imaginary liberty, when he begins to suspect that his liberty is but a dream, fears to awaken, and conspires with these agreeable illusions that the deception may be prolonged, so insensibly of my own accord I fall back into my former opinions, and I dread awakening from this slumber, lest the laborious wakefulness which would follow the tranquility of this repose should have to be spent not in daylight, but in the excessive darkness of the difficulties which have just been discussed.

MEDITATION II

Of the Nature of the Human Mind; and that it is more easily known than the Body.

The Meditation of yesterday filled my mind with so many doubts that it is no longer in my power to forget them. And yet I do not see in what manner I can resolve them; and, just as if I had all of a sudden fallen into very deep water, I am so disconcerted that I can neither make certain of setting my feet on the bottom, nor can I swim and so support myself on the surface. I shall nevertheless make an effort and follow anew the same path as that on which I yesterday entered, i.e. I shall proceed by setting aside all that in which the least doubt could be supposed to exist, just as if I had discovered that it was absolutely false; and I shall ever follow in this road until I have met with something which is certain, or at least, if I can do nothing else, until I have learned for certain that there is nothing in the world that is certain. Archimedes, in order that he might draw the terrestrial globe out of its place, and transport it elsewhere, demanded only that one point should be fixed and immovable; in the same way I shall have the right to conceive high hopes if I am happy enough to discover one thing only which is certain and indubitable.

I suppose, then, that all the things that I see are false; I persuade myself that nothing has ever existed of all that my fallacious memory represents to me. I consider that I possess no senses; I imagine that body, figure, extension, movement and place are but the fictions of my mind. What, then, can be esteemed as true? Perhaps nothing at all, unless that there is nothing in the world that is certain.

But how can I know there is not something different from those things that I have just considered, of which one cannot have the slightest doubt? Is there not some God, or some other being by whatever name we call it, who puts these reflections into my mind? That is not necessary, for is it not possible that I am capable of producing them myself? I myself, am I not at least something? But I have already denied that I had senses and body. Yet I hesitate, for what follows from that? Am I so dependent on body and senses that I cannot exist without these? But I was persuaded that there was nothing in all the world, that there was no heaven, no earth, that there were no minds, nor any bodies: was I not then likewise persuaded that I did not exist? Not at all; of a surety I myself did exist since I persuaded myself of something [or merely because I thought of something]. But there is some deceiver or other, very powerful and very cunning, who ever employs his ingenuity in deceiving me. Then without doubt I exist also if he deceives me, and let him deceive me as much as he will, he can never cause me to be nothing so long as I think that I am something. So that after having reflected well and carefully examined all things, we must come to the definite conclusion that this proposition: I am, I exist, is necessarily true each time that I pronounce it, or that I mentally conceive it.

But I do not yet know clearly enough what I am, I who am certain that I am; and hence I must be careful to see that I do not imprudently take some other object in place of myself, and thus that I do not go astray in respect of this knowledge that I hold to be the most certain and most evident of all that I have formerly learned. That is why I shall now consider anew what I believed myself to be before I embarked upon these last reflections; and of my former opinions I shall withdraw all that might even in a small degree be invalidated by the reasons which I have just brought forward, in order that there may be nothing at all left beyond what is absolutely certain and indubitable.

What then did I formerly believe myself to be? Undoubtedly I believed myself to be a man. But what is a man? Shall I say a reasonable animal? Certainly not; for then I should have to inquire what an animal is, and what is reasonable; and thus from a single question I should insensibly fall into an infinitude of others more difficult; and I should not wish to waste the little time and leisure remaining to me in trying to unravel subtleties like these. But I shall rather stop here to consider the thoughts which of themselves spring up in my mind, and which were not inspired by anything beyond my own nature alone when I applied myself to the consideration of my being. In the first place, then, I considered myself as having a face, hands, arms, and all that system of members composed of bones and flesh as seen in a corpse which I designated by the name of body. In addition to this I considered that I was nourished, that I walked, that I felt, and that I thought, and I referred all these actions to the soul: but I did not stop to consider what the soul was, or if I did stop, I imagined that it was something extremely rare and subtle like a wind, a flame, or an ether, which was spread throughout my grosser parts. As to body I had no manner of doubt about its nature, but thought I had a very clear knowledge of it; and if I had desired to explain it according to the notions that I had then formed of it, I should have described it thus: By the body I understand all that which can be defined by a certain figure: something which can be confined in a certain place, and which can fill a given space in such a way that every other body will be excluded from it; which can be perceived either by touch, or by sight, or by hearing, or by taste, or by smell: which can be moved in many ways not, in truth, by itself, but by something which is foreign to it, by which it is touched [and from which it receives impressions]: for to have the power of self-movement, as also of feeling or of thinking, I did not consider to appertain to the nature of body: on the contrary, I was rather astonished to find that faculties similar to them existed in some bodies.

But what am I, now that I suppose that there is a certain genius which is extremely powerful, and, if I may say so, malicious, who employs all his powers in deceiving me? Can I affirm that I possess the least of all those things which I have just said pertain to the nature of body? I pause to consider, I revolve all these things in my mind, and I find none of which I can say that it pertains to me. It would be tedious to stop to enumerate them. Let us pass to the attributes of soul and see if there is any one which is in me? What of nutrition or walking [the first mentioned]? But if it is so that I have no body it is also true that I can neither walk nor take nourishment. Another attribute is sensation. But one cannot feel without body, and besides I have thought I perceived many things during sleep that I recognised in my waking moments as not having been experienced at all. What of thinking? I find here that thought is an attribute that belongs to me; it alone cannot be separated from me. I am, I exist, that is certain. But how often? Just when I think; for it might possibly be the case if I ceased entirely to think, that I should likewise cease altogether to exist. I do not now admit anything which is not necessarily true: to speak accurately I am not more than a thing which thinks, that is to say a mind or a soul, or an understanding, or a reason, which are terms whose significance was formerly unknown to me. I am, however, a real thing and really exist; but what thing? I have answered: a thing which thinks.

And what more? I shall exercise my imagination [in order to see if I am not something more]. I am not a collection of members which we call the human body: I am not a subtle air distributed through these members, I am not a wind, a fire, a vapour, a breath, nor anything at all which I can imagine or conceive; because I have assumed that all these were nothing. Without changing that supposition I find that I only leave myself certain of the fact that I am somewhat. But perhaps it is true that these same things which I supposed were non-existent because they are unknown to me, are really not different from the self which I know. I am not sure about this, I shall not dispute about it now; I can only give judgment on things that are known to me. I know that I exist, and I inquire what I am, I whom I know to exist. But it is very certain that the knowledge of my existence taken in its precise significance does not depend on things whose existence is not yet known to me; consequently it does not depend on those which I can feign in imagination. And indeed the very term *feign* in imagination proves to me my error, for I really do this if I image myself a something, since to imagine is nothing else than to contemplate the figure or image of a corporeal thing. But I already know for certain that I am, and that it may be that all these images, and, speaking generally, all things that relate to the nature of body are nothing but dreams [and chimeras]. For this reason I see clearly that I have as little reason to say, 'I shall stimulate my imagination in order to know more distinctly what I am,' than if I were to say, 'I am now awake, and I perceive somewhat that is real and true: but because I do not yet perceive it distinctly enough, I shall go to sleep of express purpose, so that my dreams may represent the perception with greatest truth and evidence.' And, thus, I know for certain that nothing of all that I can understand by means of my imagination belongs to this knowledge which I have of myself, and that it is necessary to recall the mind from this mode of thought with the utmost diligence in order that it may be able to know its own nature with perfect distinctness.

But what then am I? A thing which thinks. What is a thing which thinks? It is a thing which doubts, understands, [conceives], affirms, denies, wills, refuses, which also imagines and feels.

Certainly it is no small matter if all these things pertain to my nature. But why should they not so pertain? Am I not that being who now doubts nearly everything, who nevertheless understands certain things, who affirms that one only is true, who denies all the others, who desires to know more, is averse from being deceived, who imagines many things, sometimes indeed despite his will, and who perceives many likewise, as by the intervention of the bodily organs? Is there nothing in all this which is as true as it is certain that I exist, even though I should always sleep and though he who has given me being employed all his ingenuity in deceiving me? Is there likewise any one of these attributes which can be distinguished from my thought, or which might be said to be separated from myself? For it is so evident of itself that it is I who doubts, who understands, and who desires, that there is no reason here to add anything to explain it. And I have certainly the power of imagining likewise; for although it may happen (as I formerly supposed) that none of the things which I imagine are true, nevertheless this power of imagining does not cease to be really in use, and it forms part of my thought. Finally, I am the same who feels, that is to say, who perceives certain things, as by the organs of sense, since in truth I see light, I hear noise, I feel heat. But it will be said that these phenomena are false and that I am dreaming. Let it be so; still it is at least quite certain that it seems to me that I see light, that I hear noise and that I feel heat. That cannot be false; properly speaking it is what is in me called feeling; and used in this precise sense that is no other thing than thinking.

From this time I begin to know what I am with a little more clearness and distinction than before; but nevertheless it still seems to me, and I cannot prevent myself from thinking, that corporeal things, whose images are framed by thought, which are tested by the senses, are much more distinctly known than that obscure part of me which does not come under the imagination. Although really it is very strange to say that I know and understand more distinctly these things whose existence seems to me dubious, which are unknown to me, and which do not belong to me, than others of the truth of which I am convinced, which are known to me and which pertain to my real nature, in a word, than myself. But I see clearly how the case stands: my mind loves to wander, and cannot yet suffer itself to be retained within the just limits of truth. Very good, let us once more give it the freest rein, so that, when afterwards we seize the proper occasion for pulling up, it may the more easily be regulated and controlled.

Let us begin by considering the commonest matters, those which we believe to be the most distinctly comprehended, to wit, the bodies which we touch and see; not indeed bodies in general, for these general ideas are usually a little more confused, but let us consider one body in particular. Let us take, for example, this piece of wax: it has been taken quite freshly from the hive, and it has not yet lost the sweetness of the honey which it contains; it still retains somewhat of the odour of the flowers from which it has been culled; its colour, its figure, its size are apparent; it is hard, cold, easily handled, and if you strike it with the finger, it will emit a sound. Finally all the things which are requisite to cause us distinctly to recognise a body, are met with in it. But notice that while I speak and approach the fire what remained of the taste is exhaled, the smell evaporates, the colour alters, the figure is destroyed, the size increases, it becomes liquid, it heats, scarcely can one handle it, and when one strikes it, no sound is emitted. Does the same wax remain after this change? We must confess that it remains; none would judge otherwise. What then did I know so distinctly in this piece of wax? It could certainly be nothing of all that the senses brought to my notice, since all these things which fall under taste, smell, sight, touch, and hearing, are found to be changed, and yet the same wax remains.

Perhaps it was what I now think, viz, that this wax was not that sweetness of honey, nor that agreeable scent of flowers, nor that particular whiteness, nor that figure, nor that sound, but simply a body which a little while before appeared to me as perceptible under these forms, and which is now perceptible under others. But what, precisely, is it that I imagine when I form such conceptions? Let us attentively consider this, and, abstracting from all that does not belong to the wax, let us see what remains. Certainly nothing remains excepting a certain extended thing which is flexible and movable. But what is the meaning of flexible and movable? Is it not that I imagine that this piece of wax being round is capable of becoming square and of passing from a square to a triangular figure? No, certainly it is not that, since I imagine it admits of an infinitude of similar changes, and I nevertheless do not know how to compass the infinitude by my imagination, and consequently this conception which I have of the wax is not brought about by the faculty of imagination. What now is this extension? Is it not also unknown? For it becomes greater when the wax is melted, greater when it is boiled, and greater still when the heat increases; and I should not conceive [clearly] according to truth what wax is, if I did not think that even this piece that we are considering is capable of receiving more variations in extension than I have ever imagined. We must then grant that I could not even understand through the imagination what this piece of wax is, and that it is my mind alone which perceives it. I say this piece of wax in particular, for as to wax in general it is yet clearer. But what is this piece of wax which cannot be understood excepting by the [understanding or] mind? It is certainly the same that I see, touch, imagine, and finally it is the same which I have always believed it to be from the beginning. But what must particularly be observed is that its perception is neither an act of vision, nor of touch, nor of imagination, and has never been such although it may have appeared formerly to be so, but only an intuition of the mind, which may be imperfect and confused as it was formerly, or clear and distinct as it is at present, according as my attention is more or less directed to the elements which are found in it, and of which it is composed.

Yet in the meantime I am greatly astonished when I consider [the great feebleness of mind] and its proneness to fall [insensibly] into error; for although without giving expression to my thoughts I consider all this in my own mind, words often impede me and I am almost deceived by the terms of ordinary language. For we say that we see the same wax, if it is present, and not that we simply judge that it is the same from its having the same colour and figure. From this I should conclude that I knew the wax by means of vision and not simply by the intuition of the mind; unless by chance I remember that, when looking from a window and saying I see men who pass in the street, I really do not see them, but infer that what I see is men, just as I say that I see wax. And yet what do I see from the window but hats and coats which may cover automatic machines? Yet I judge these to be men. And similarly solely by the faculty of judgment which rests in my mind, I comprehend that which I believed I saw with my eyes.

A man who makes it his aim to raise his knowledge above the common should be ashamed to derive the occasion for doubting from the forms of speech invented by the vulgar; I prefer to pass on and consider whether I had a more evident and perfect conception of what the wax was when I first perceived it, and when I believed I knew it by means of the external senses or at least by the common sense as it is called, that is to say by the imaginative faculty, or whether my present conception is clearer now that I have most carefully examined what it is, and in what way it can be known. It would certainly be absurd to doubt as to this. For what was there in this first perception which was distinct? What was there which might not as well have been perceived by any of the animals? But when I distinguish the wax from its external forms, and when, just as if I had taken from it its vestments, I consider it quite naked, it is certain that although some error may still be found in my judgment, I can nevertheless not perceive it thus without a human mind.

But finally what shall I say of this mind, that is, of myself, for up to this point I do not admit in myself anything but mind? What then, I who seem to perceive this piece of wax so distinctly, do I not know myself, not only with much more truth and certainty, but also with much more distinctness and clearness? For if I judge that the wax is or exists from the fact that I see it, it certainly follows much more clearly that I am or that I exist myself from the fact that I see it. For it may be that what I see is not really wax, it may also be that I do not possess eyes with which to see anything; but it cannot be that when I see, or (for I no longer take account of the distinction) when I think I see, that I myself who think am nought. So if I judge that the wax exists from the fact that I touch it, the same thing will follow, to wit, that I am; and if I judge that my imagination, or some other cause, whatever it is, persuades me that wax exists, I shall still conclude the same. And what I have here remarked of wax may be applied to all other things which are external to me [and which are met with outside of me]. And further, if the [notion or] perception of wax has seemed to me clearer and more distinct, not only after the sight or the touch, but also after many other causes have rendered it quite manifest to me, with how much more [evidence] and distinctness must it be said that I now know myself, since all the reasons which contribute to the knowledge of wax, or any other body whatever, are yet better proofs of the nature of my mind! And there are so many other things in the mind itself which may contribute to the elucidation of its nature, that those which depend on body such as these just mentioned, hardly merit being taken into account.

But finally here I am, having insensibly reverted to the point I desired, for, since it is now manifest to me that even bodies are not properly speaking known by the senses or by the faculty of imagination, but by the understanding only, and since they are not known from the fact that they are seen or touched, but only because they are understood, I see clearly that there is nothing which is easier for me to know than my mind. But because it is difficult to rid oneself so promptly of an opinion to which one was accustomed for so long, it will be well that I should halt a little at this point, so that by the length of my meditation I may more deeply imprint on my memory this new knowledge.

MEDITATION III

Of God: that He exists.

I shall now close my eyes, I shall stop my ears, I shall call away all my senses, I shall efface even from my thoughts all the images of corporeal things, or at least (for that is hardly possible) I shall esteem them as vain and false; and thus holding converse only with myself and considering my own nature, I shall try little by little to reach a better knowledge of and a more familiar acquaintanceship with myself. I am a thing that thinks, that is to say, that doubts, affirms, denies, that knows a few things, that is ignorant of many [that loves, that hates], that wills, that desires, that also imagines and perceives; for as I remarked before, although the things which I perceive and imagine are perhaps nothing at all apart from me and in themselves, I am nevertheless assured that these modes of thought that I call perceptions and imaginations, inasmuch only as they are modes of thought, certainly reside [and are met with] in me.

And in the little that I have just said, I think I have summed up all that I really know, or at least all that hitherto I was aware that I knew. In order to try to extend my knowledge further, I shall now look around more carefully and see whether I cannot still discover in myself some other things which I have not hitherto perceived. I am certain that I am a thing which thinks; but do I not then likewise know what is requisite to render me certain of a truth? Certainly in this first knowledge there is nothing that assures me of its truth, excepting the clear and distinct perception of that which I state, which would not indeed suffice to assure me that what I say is true, if it could ever happen that a thing which I conceived so clearly and distinctly could be false; and accordingly it seems to me that already I can establish as a general rule that all things which I perceive very clearly and very distinctly are true.

At the same time I have before received and admitted many things to be very certain and manifest, which yet I afterwards recognised as being dubious. What then were these things? They were the earth, sky, stars and all other objects which I apprehended by means of the senses. But what did I clearly [and distinctly] perceive in them? Nothing more than that the ideas or thoughts of these things were presented to my mind. And not even now do I deny that these ideas are met with in me. But there was yet another thing which I affirmed, and which, owing to the habit which I had formed of believing it, I thought I perceived very clearly, although in truth I did not perceive it at all, to wit, that there were objects outside of me from which these ideas proceeded, and to which they were entirely similar. And it was in this that I erred, or, if perchance my judgment was correct, this was not due to any knowledge arising from my perception.

But when I took anything very simple and easy in the sphere of arithmetic or geometry into consideration, e.g. that two and three together made five, and other things of the sort, were not these present to my mind so clearly as to enable me to affirm that they were true? Certainly if I judged that since such matters could be doubted, this would not have been so for any other reason than that it came into my mind that perhaps a God might have endowed me with such a nature that I may have been deceived even concerning things which seemed to me most manifest. But every time that this preconceived opinion of the sovereign power of a God presents itself to my thought, I am constrained to confess that it is easy to Him, if He wishes it, to cause me to err, even in matters in which I believe myself to have the best evidence. And, on the other hand, always when I direct my attention to things which I believe myself to perceive very clearly, I am so persuaded of their truth that I let myself break out into words such as these: Let who will deceive me, He can never cause me to be nothing while I think that I am, or some day cause it to be true to say that I have never been, it being true now to say that I am, or that two and three make more or less than five, or any such thing in which I see a manifest contradiction. And, certainly, since I have no reason to believe that there is a God who is a deceiver, and as I have not yet satisfied myself that there is a God at all, the reason for doubt which depends on this opinion alone is very slight, and so to speak metaphysical. But in order to be able altogether to remove it, I must inquire whether there is a God as soon as the occasion presents itself; and if I find that there is a God, I must also inquire whether He may be a deceiver; for without a knowledge of these two truths I do not see that I can ever be certain of anything.

And in order that I may have an opportunity of inquiring into this in an orderly way [without interrupting the order of meditation which I have proposed to myself, and which is little by little to pass from the notions which I find first of all in my mind to those which I shall later on discover in it] it is requisite that I should here divide my thoughts into certain kinds, and that I should consider in which of these kinds there is, properly speaking, truth or error to be found. Of my thoughts some are, so to speak, images of the things, and to these alone is the title 'idea' properly applied; examples are my thought of a man or of a chimera, of heaven, of an angel, or [even] of God. But other thoughts possess other forms as well. For example in willing, fearing, approving, denying, though I always perceive something as the subject of the action of my mind; yet by this action I always add something else to the idea which I have of that thing; and of the thoughts of this kind some are called volitions or affections, and others judgments.

Now as to what concerns ideas, if we consider them only in themselves and do not relate them to anything else beyond themselves, they cannot properly speaking be false; for whether I imagine a goat or a chimera, it is no less true that I imagine the one than the other. We must not fear likewise that falsity can enter into will and into affections, for although I may desire evil things, or even things that never existed, it is not the less true that I desire them. Thus there remains no more than the judgments which we make, in which I must take the greatest care not to deceive myself. But the principal error and the commonest which we may meet with in them, consists in my judging that the ideas which are in me are similar or conformable to the things which are outside me; for without doubt if I considered the ideas only as certain modes of my thoughts, without trying to relate them to anything beyond, they could scarcely give me material for error.

But among these ideas, some appear to me to be innate, some adventitious, and others to be formed [or invented] by myself; for, as I have the power of understanding what is called a thing, or a truth, or a thought, it appears to me that I hold this power from no other source than my own nature. But if I now hear some sound, if I see the sun, or feel heat, I have hitherto judged that these sensations proceeded from certain things that exist outside of me; and finally it appears to me that sirens, hippogryphs, and the like, are formed out of my own mind. But again I may possibly persuade myself that all these ideas are of the nature of those which I term adventitious, or else that they are all innate, or all fictitious: for I have not yet clearly discovered their true origin.

And my principal task in this place is to consider, in respect to those ideas which appear to me to proceed from certain objects that are outside me, what are the reasons which cause me to think them similar to these objects. It seems indeed in the first place that I am taught this lesson by nature; and, secondly, I experience in myself that these ideas do not depend on my will nor therefore on myself—for they often present themselves to my mind in spite of my will. Just now, for instance, whether I will or whether I do not will, I feel heat, and thus I persuade myself that this feeling, or at least this idea of heat, is produced in me by something which is different from me, i.e. by the heat of the fire near which I sit. And nothing seems to me more obvious than to judge that this object imprints its likeness rather than anything else upon me.

Now I must discover whether these proofs are sufficiently strong and convincing. When I say that I am so instructed by nature, I merely mean a certain spontaneous inclination which impels me to believe in this connection, and not a natural light which makes me recognise that it is true. But these two things are very different; for I cannot doubt that which the natural light causes me to believe to be true, as, for example, it has shown me that I am from the fact that I doubt, or other facts of the same kind. And I possess no other faculty whereby to distinguish truth from falsehood, which can teach me that what this light shows me to be true is not really true, and no other faculty that is equally truthworthy. But as far as [apparently] natural impulses are concerned, I have frequently remarked, when I had to make active choice between virtue and vice, that they often enough led me to the part that was worse; and this is why I do not see any reason for following them in what regards truth and error.

And as to the other reason, which is that these ideas must proceed from objects outside me, since they do not depend on my will, I do not find it any the more convincing. For just as these impulses of which I have spoken are found in me, notwithstanding that they do not always concur with my will, so perhaps there is in me some faculty fitted to produce these ideas without the assistance of any external things, even though it is not yet known by me; just as, apparently, they have hitherto always been found in me during sleep without the aid of any external objects.

And finally, though they did proceed from objects different from myself, it is not a necessary consequence that they should resemble these. On the contrary, I have noticed that in many cases there was a difference between the object and its idea. I find, for example, two completely diverse ideas of the sun in my mind; the one derives its origin from the senses, and should be placed in the category of adventitious ideas; according to this idea the sun seems to be extremely small; but the other is derived from astronomical reasonings, i.e. is elicited from certain notions that are innate in me, or else it is formed by me in some other manner; in accordance with it the sun appears to be several times greater than the earth. These two ideas cannot, indeed, both resemble the same sun, and reason makes me believe that the one which seems to have originated directly from the sun itself, is the one which is most dissimilar to it.

All this causes me to believe that until the present time it has not been by a judgment that was certain [or premeditated], but only by a sort of blind impulse that I believed that things existed outside of, and different from me, which, by the organs of my senses, or by some other method whatever it might be, conveyed these ideas or images to me [and imprinted on me their similitudes].

But there is yet another method of inquiring whether any of the objects of which I have ideas within me exist outside of me. If ideas are only taken as certain modes of thought, I recognize amongst them no difference or inequality, and all appear to proceed from me in the same manner; but when we consider them as images, one representing one thing and the other another, it is clear that they are very different one from the other. There is no doubt that those which represent to me substances are something more, and contain so to speak more objective reality within them [that is to say, by representation participate in a higher degree of being or perfection] than those that simply represent modes or accidents; and that idea again by which I understand a supreme God, eternal, infinite, [immutable], omniscient, omnipotent, and Creator of all things which are outside of Himself, has certainly more objective reality in itself than those ideas by which finite substances are represented.

Now it is manifest by the natural light that there must at least be as much reality in the efficient and total cause as in its effect. For, pray, whence can the effect derive its reality, if not from its cause? And in what way can this cause communicate this reality to it, unless it possessed it in itself? And from this it follows, not only that something cannot proceed from nothing, but likewise that what is more perfect—that is to say, which has more reality within itself—cannot proceed from the less perfect. And this is not only evidently true of those effects which possess actual or formal reality, but also of the ideas in which we consider merely what is termed objective reality. To take an example, the stone which has not yet existed not only cannot now commence to be unless it has been produced by something which possesses within itself, either formally or eminently, all that enters into the composition of the stone [i.e. it must possess the same things or other more excellent things than those which exist in the stone] and heat can only be produced in a subject in which it did not previously exist by a cause that is of an order [degree or kind] at least as perfect as heat, and so in all other cases. But further, the idea of heat, or of a stone, cannot exist in me unless it has been placed within me by some cause which possesses within it at least as much reality as that which I conceive to exist in the heat or the stone. For although this cause does not transmit anything of its actual or formal reality to my idea, we must not for that reason imagine that it is necessarily a less real cause; we must remember that [since every idea is a work of the mind] its nature is such that it demands of itself no other formal reality than that which it borrows from my thought, of which it is only a mode [i.e. a manner or way of thinking]. But in order that an idea should contain some one certain objective reality rather than another, it must without doubt derive it from some cause in which there is at least as much formal reality as this idea contains of objective reality. For if we imagine that something is found in an idea which is not found in the cause, it must then have been derived from nought; but however imperfect may be this mode of being by which a thing is objectively [or by representation] in the understanding by its idea, we cannot certainly say that this mode of being is nothing, nor, consequently, that the idea derives its origin from nothing.

Nor must I imagine that, since the reality that I consider in these ideas is only objective, it is not essential that this reality should be formally in the causes of my ideas, but that it is sufficient that it should be found objectively. For just as this mode of objective existence pertains to ideas by their proper nature, so does the mode of formal existence pertain to the causes of those ideas (this is at least true of the first and principal) by the nature peculiar to them. And although it may be the case that one idea gives birth to another idea, that cannot continue to be so indefinitely; for in the end we must reach an idea whose cause shall be so to speak an archetype, in which the whole reality [or perfection] which is so to speak objectively [or by representation] in these ideas is contained formally [and really]. Thus the light of nature causes me to know clearly that the ideas in me are like [pictures or] images which can, in truth, easily fall short of the perfection of the objects from which they have been derived, but which can never contain anything greater or more perfect.

And the longer and the more carefully that I investigate these matters, the more clearly and distinctly do I recognise their truth. But what am I to conclude from it all in the end? It is this, that if the objective reality of any one of my ideas is of such a nature as clearly to make me recognise that it is not in me either formally or eminently, and that consequently I cannot myself be the cause of it, it follows of necessity that I am not alone in the world, but that there is another being which exists, or which is the cause of this idea. On the other hand, had no such an idea existed in me, I should have had no sufficient argument to convince me of the existence of any being beyond myself; for I have made very careful investigation everywhere and up to the present time have been able to find no other ground.

But of my ideas, beyond that which represents me to myself, as to which there can here be no difficulty, there is another which represents a God, and there are others representing corporeal and inanimate things, others angels, other animals, and others again which represent to me men similar to myself.

As regards the ideas which represent to me other men or animals, or angels, I can however easily conceive that they might be formed by an admixture of the other ideas which I have of myself, of corporeal things, and of God, even although there were apart from me neither men nor animals, nor angels, in all the world.

And in regard to the ideas of corporeal objects, I do not recognise in them anything so great or so excellent that they might not have possibly proceeded from myself; for if I consider them more closely, and examine them individually, as I yesterday examined the idea of wax, I find that there is very little in them which I perceive clearly and distinctly. Magnitude or extension in length, breadth, or depth, I do so perceive; also figure which results from a termination of this extension, the situation which bodies of different figure preserve in relation to one another, and movement or change of situation; to which we may also add substance, duration and number. As to other things such as light, colours, sounds, scents, tastes, heat, cold and the other tactile qualities, they are thought by me with so much obscurity and confusion that I do not even know if they are true or false, i.e. whether the ideas which I form of these qualities are actually the ideas of real objects or not [or whether they only represent chimeras which cannot exist in fact]. For although I have before remarked that it is only in judgments that falsity, properly speaking, or formal falsity, can be met with, a certain material falsity may nevertheless be found in ideas, i.e. when these ideas represent what is nothing as though it were something. For example, the ideas which I have of cold and heat are so far from clear and distinct that by their means I cannot tell whether cold is merely a privation of heat, or heat a privation of cold, or whether both are real qualities, or are not such. And inasmuch as [since ideas resemble images] there cannot be any ideas which do not appear to represent some things, if it is correct to say that cold is merely a privation of heat, the idea which represents it to me as something real and positive will not be improperly termed false, and the same holds good of other similar ideas.

To these it is certainly not necessary that I should attribute any author other than myself. For if they are false, i.e. if they represent things which do not exist, the light of nature shows me that they issue from nought, that is to say, that they are only in me in so far as something is lacking to the perfection of my nature. But if they are true, nevertheless because they exhibit so little reality to me that I cannot even clearly distinguish the thing represented from non-being, I do not see any reason why they should not be produced by myself.

As to the clear and distinct idea which I have of corporeal things, some of them seem as though I might have derived them from the idea which I possess of myself, as those which I have of substance, duration, number, and such like. For [even] when I think that a stone is a substance, or at least a thing capable of existing of itself, and that I am a substance also, although I conceive that I am a thing that thinks and not one that is extended, and that the stone on the other hand is an extended thing which does not think, and that thus there is a notable difference between the two conceptions—they seem, nevertheless, to agree in this, that both represent substances. In the same way, when I perceive that I now exist and further recollect that I have in former times existed, and when I remember that I have various thoughts of which I can recognize the number, I acquire ideas of duration and number which I can afterwards transfer to any object that I please. But as to all the other qualities of which the ideas of corporeal things are composed, to wit, extension, figure, situation and motion, it is true that they are not formally in me, since I am only a thing that thinks; but because they are merely certain modes of substance [and so to speak the vestments under which corporeal substance appears to us] and because I myself am also a substance, it would seem that they might be constrained in me eminently.

Hence there remains only the idea of God, concerning which we must consider whether it is something which cannot have proceeded from me myself. By the name God I understand a substance that is infinite [eternal, immutable], independent, all-knowing, all-powerful, and by which I myself and everything else, if anything else does exist, have been created. Now all these characteristics are such that the more diligently I attend to them, the less do they appear capable of proceeding from me alone; hence, from what has been already said, we must conclude that God necessarily exists.

For although the idea of substance is within me owing to the fact that I am substance, nevertheless I should not have the idea of an infinite substance—since I am finite—if it had not proceeded from some substance which was veritably infinite.

Nor should I imagine that I do not perceive the infinite by a true idea, but only by the negation of the finite, just as I perceive repose and darkness by the negation of movement and of light; for, on the contrary, I see that there is manifestly more reality in infinite substance than in finite, and therefore that in some way I have in me the notion of the infinite earlier than the finite—to wit, the notion of God before that of myself. For how would it be possible that I should know that I doubt and desire, that is to say, that something is lacking to me, and that I am not quite perfect, unless I had within me some idea of a Being more perfect than myself, in comparison with which I should recognize the deficiencies of my nature?

And we cannot say that this idea of God is perhaps materially false and that consequently I can derive it from nought [i.e. that possibly it exists in me because I am imperfect], as I have just said is the case with ideas of heat, cold and other such things; for, on the contrary, as this idea is very clear and distinct and contains within it more objective reality than any other, there can be none which is of itself more true, nor any in which there can be less suspicion of falsehood. The idea, I say, of this Being who is absolutely perfect and infinite, is entirely true; for although, perhaps, we can imagine that such a Being does not exist, we cannot nevertheless imagine that His idea represents nothing real to me, as I have said of the idea of cold. This idea is also very clear and distinct; since all that I conceive clearly and distinctly of the real and the true, and of what conveys some perfection, is in its entirety contained in this idea. And this does not cease to be true although I do not comprehend the infinite, or though in God there is an infinitude of things which I cannot comprehend, nor possibly even reach in any way by thought; for it is of the nature of the infinite that my nature, which is finite and limited, should not comprehend it; and it is sufficient that I should understand this, and that I should judge that all things which I clearly perceive and in which I know that there is some perfection, and possibly likewise an infinitude of properties of which I am ignorant, are in God formally or eminently, so that the idea which I have of Him may become the most true, most clear, and most distinct of all the ideas that are in my mind.

But possibly I am something more than I suppose myself to be, and perhaps all those perfections which I attribute to God are in some way potentially in me, although they do not yet disclose themselves, or issue in action. As a matter of fact I am already sensible that my knowledge increases [and perfects itself] little by little, and I see nothing which can prevent it from increasing more and more into infinitude; nor do I see, after it has thus been increased [or perfected], anything to prevent my being able to acquire by its means all the other perfections of the Divine nature; nor finally why the power I have of acquiring these perfections, if it really exists in me, shall not suffice to produce the ideas of them.

At the same time I recognize that this cannot be. For, in the first place, although it were true that every day my knowledge acquired new degrees of perfection, and that there were in my nature many things potentially which are not yet there actually, nevertheless these excellences do not pertain to [or make the smallest approach to] the idea which I have of God in whom there is nothing merely potential [but in whom all is present really and actually]; for it is an infallible token of imperfection in my knowledge that it increases little by little. And further, although my knowledge grows more and more, nevertheless I do not for that reason believe that it can ever be actually infinite, since it can never reach a point so high that it will be unable to attain to any greater increase. But I understand God to be actually infinite, so that He can add nothing to His supreme perfection. And finally I perceive that the objective being of an idea cannot be produced by a being that exists potentially only, which properly speaking is nothing, but only a being which is formal or actual.

To speak the truth, I see nothing in all that I have just said which by the light of nature is not manifest to anyone who desires to think attentively on the subject; but when I slightly relax my attention, my mind, finding its vision somewhat obscured and so to speak blinded by the images of sensible objects, I do not easily recollect the reason why the idea that I possess of a being more perfect than I, must necessarily have been placed in me by a being which is really more perfect; and this is why I wish here to go on to inquire whether I, who have this idea, can exist if no such being exists.

And I ask, from whom do I then derive my existence? Perhaps from myself or from my parents, or from some other source less perfect than God; for we can imagine nothing more perfect than God, or even as perfect as He is.

But [were I independent of every other and] were I myself the author of my being, I should doubt nothing and I should desire nothing, and finally no perfection would be lacking to me; for I should have bestowed on myself every perfection of which I possessed any idea and should thus be God. And it must not be imagined that those things that are lacking to me are perhaps more difficult of attainment than those which I already possess; for, on the contrary, it is quite evident that it was a matter of much greater difficulty to bring to pass that I, that is to say, a thing or a substance that thinks, should emerge out of nothing, than it would be to attain to the knowledge of many things of which I am ignorant, and which are only the accidents of this thinking substance. But it is clear that if I had of myself possessed this greater perfection of which I have just spoken [that is to say, if I had been the author of my own existence], I should not at least have denied myself the things which are the more easy to acquire [to wit, many branches of knowledge of which my nature is destitute]; nor should I have deprived myself of any of the things contained in the idea which I form of God, because there are none of them which seem to me specially difficult to acquire: and if there were any that were more difficult to acquire, they would certainly appear to me to be such (supposing I myself were the origin of the other things which I possess) since I should discover in them that my powers were limited.

But though I assumed that perhaps I have always existed just as I am at present, neither can I escape the force of this reasoning, and imagine that the conclusion to be drawn from this is, that I need not seek for any author of my existence. For all the course of my life may be divided into an infinite number of parts, none of which is in any way dependent on the other; and thus from the fact that I was in existence a short time ago it does not follow that I must be in existence now, unless some cause at this instant, so to speak, produces me anew, that is to say, conserves me. It is as a matter of fact perfectly clear and evident to all those who consider with attention the nature of time, that, in order to be conserved in each moment in which it endures, a substance has need of the same power and action as would be necessary to produce and create it anew, supposing it did not yet exist, so that the light of nature shows us clearly that the distinction between creation and conservation is solely a distinction of the reason.

All that I thus require here is that I should interrogate myself, if I wish to know whether I possess a power which is capable of bringing it to pass that I who now am shall still be in the future; for since I am nothing but a thinking thing, or at least since thus far it is only this portion of myself which is precisely in question at present, if such a power did reside in me, I should certainly be conscious of it. But I am conscious of nothing of the kind, and by this I know clearly that I depend on some being different from myself.

Possibly, however, this being on which I depend is not that which I call God, and I am created either by my parents or by some other cause less perfect than God. This cannot be, because, as I have just said, it is perfectly evident that there must be at least as much reality in the cause as in the effect; and thus since I am a thinking thing, and possess an idea of God within me, whatever in the end be the cause assigned to my existence, it must be allowed that it is likewise a thinking thing and that it possesses in itself the idea of all the perfections which I attribute to God. We may again inquire whether this cause derives its origin from itself or from some other thing. For if from itself, it follows by the reasons before brought forward, that this cause must itself be God; for since it possesses the virtue of self-existence, it must also without doubt have the power of actually possessing all the perfections of which it has the idea, that is, all those which I conceive as existing in God. But if it derives its existence from some other cause than itself, we shall again ask, for the same reason, whether this second cause exists by itself or through another, until from one step to another, we finally arrive at an ultimate cause, which will be God.

And it is perfectly manifest that in this there can be no regression into infinity, since what is in question is not so much the cause which formerly created me, as that which conserves me at the present time.

Nor can we suppose that several causes may have concurred in my production, and that from one I have received the idea of one of the perfections which I attribute to God, and from another the idea of some other, so that all these perfections indeed exist somewhere in the universe, but not as complete in one unity which is God. On the contrary, the unity, the simplicity or the inseparability of all things which are in God is one of the principal perfections which I conceive to be in Him. And certainly the idea of this unity of all Divine perfections cannot have been placed in me by any cause from which I have not likewise received the ideas of all the other perfections; for this cause could not make me able to comprehend them as joined together in an inseparable unity without having at the same time caused me in some measure to know what they are [and in some way to recognise each one of them].

Finally, so far as my parents [from whom it appears I have sprung] are concerned, although all that I have ever been able to believe of them were true, that does not make it follow that it is they who conserve me, nor are they even the authors of my being in any sense, in so far as I am a thinking being; since what they did was merely to implant certain dispositions in that matter in which the self—i.e. the mind, which alone I at present identify with myself—is by me deemed to exist. And thus there can be no difficulty in their regard, but we must of necessity conclude from the fact alone that I exist, or that the idea of a Being supremely perfect—that is of God—is in me, that the proof of God's existence is grounded on the highest evidence.

It only remains to me to examine into the manner in which I have acquired this idea from God; for I have not received it through the senses, and it is never presented to me unexpectedly, as is usual with the ideas of sensible things when these things present themselves, or seem to present themselves, to the external organs of my senses; nor is it likewise a fiction of my mind, for it is not in my power to take from or to add anything to it; and consequently the only alternative is that it is innate in me, just as the idea of myself is innate in me.

And one certainly ought not to find it strange that God, in creating me, placed this idea within me to be like the mark of the workman imprinted on his work; and it is likewise not essential that the mark shall be something different from the work itself. For from the sole fact that God created me it is most probable that in some way he has placed his image and similitude upon me, and that I perceive this similitude (in which the idea of God is contained) by means of the same faculty by which I perceive myself—that is to say, when I reflect on myself I not only know that I am something [imperfect], incomplete and dependent on another, which incessantly aspires after something which is better and greater than myself, but I also know that He on whom I depend possesses in Himself all the great things towards which I aspire [and the ideas of which I find within myself], and that not indefinitely or potentially alone, but really, actually and infinitely; and that thus He is God. And the whole strength of the argument which I have here made use of to prove the existence of God consists in this, that I recognise that it is not possible that my nature should be what it is, and indeed that I should have in myself the idea of a God, if God did not veritably exist—a God, I say, whose idea is in me, i.e. who possesses all those supreme perfections of which our mind may indeed have some idea but without understanding them all, who is liable to no errors or defect [and who has none of all those marks which denote imperfection]. From this it is manifest that He cannot be a deceiver, since the light of nature teaches us that fraud and deception necessarily proceed from some defect.

But before I examine this matter with more care, and pass on to the consideration of other truths which may be derived from it, it seems to me right to pause for a while in order to contemplate God Himself, to ponder at leisure His marvellous attributes, to consider, and admire, and adore, the beauty of this light so resplendent, at least as far as the strength of my mind, which is in some measure dazzled by the sight, will allow me to do so. For just as faith teaches us that the supreme felicity of the other life consists only in this contemplation of the Divine Majesty, so we continue to learn by experience that a similar meditation, though incomparably less perfect, causes us to enjoy the greatest satisfaction of which we are capable in this life.

MEDITATION IV

Of the True and the False.

I have been well accustomed these past days to detach my mind from my senses, and I have accurately observed that there are very few things that one knows with certainty respecting corporeal objects, that there are many more which are known to us respecting the human mind, and yet more still regarding God Himself; so that I shall now without any difficulty abstract my thoughts from the consideration of [sensible or] imaginable objects, and carry them to those which, being withdrawn from all contact with matter, are purely intelligible. And certainly the idea which I possess of the human mind inasmuch as it is a thinking thing, and not extended in length, width and depth, nor participating in anything pertaining to body, is incomparably more distinct than is the idea of any corporeal thing. And when I consider that I doubt, that is to say, that I am an incomplete and dependent being, the idea of a being that is complete and independent, that is of God, presents itself to my mind with so much distinctness and clearness—and from the fact alone that this idea is found in me, or that I who possess this idea exist, I conclude so certainly that God exists, and that my existence depends entirely on Him in every moment of my life—that I do not think that the human mind is capable of knowing anything with more evidence and certitude. And it seems to me that I now have before me a road which will lead us from the contemplation of the true God (in whom all the treasures of science and wisdom are contained) to the knowledge of the other objects of the universe.

For, first of all, I recognise it to be impossible that He should ever deceive me; for in all fraud and deception some imperfection is to be found, and although it may appear that the power of deception is a mark of subtilty or power, yet the desire to deceive without doubt testifies to malice or feebleness, and accordingly cannot be found in God.

In the next place I experienced in myself a certain capacity for judging which I have doubtless received from God, like all the other things that I possess; and as He could not desire to deceive me, it is clear that He has not given me a faculty that will lead me to err if I use it aright.

And no doubt respecting this matter could remain, if it were not that the consequence would seem to follow that I can thus never be deceived; for if I hold all that I possess from God, and if He has not placed me in the capacity for error, it seems as though I could never fall into error. And it is true that when I think only of God [and direct my mind wholly to Him], I discover [in myself] no cause of error, or falsity; yet directly afterwards, when recurring to myself, experience shows me that I am nevertheless subject to an infinitude of errors, as to which, when we come to investigate them more closely, I notice that not only is there a real and positive idea of God or of a Being of supreme perfection present to my mind, but also, so to speak, a certain negative idea of nothing, that is, of that which is infinitely removed from any kind of perfection; and that I am in a sense something intermediate between God and nought, i.e. placed in such a manner between the supreme Being and non-being, that there is in truth nothing in me that can lead to error in so far as a sovereign Being has formed me; but that, as I in some degree participate likewise in nought or in non-being, i.e. in so far as I am not myself the supreme Being, and as I find myself subject to an infinitude of imperfections, I ought not to be astonished if I should fall into error. Thus do I recognise that error, in so far as it is such, is not a real thing depending on God, but simply a defect; and therefore, in order to fall into it, that I have no need to possess a special faculty given me by God for this very purpose, but that I fall into error from the fact that the power given me by God for the purpose of distinguishing truth from error is not infinite.

Nevertheless this does not quite satisfy me; for error is not a pure negation [i.e. is not the simple defect or want of some perfection which ought not to be mine], but it is a lack of some knowledge which it seems that I ought to possess. And on considering the nature of God it does not appear to me possible that He should have given me a faculty which is not perfect of its kind, that is, which is wanting in some perfection due to it. For if it is true that the more skillful the artisan, the more perfect is the work of his hands, what can have been produced by this supreme Creator of all things that is not in all its parts perfect? And certainly there is no doubt that God could have created me so that I could never have been subject to error; it is also certain that He ever wills what is best; is it then better that I should be subject to err than that I should not?

In considering this more attentively, it occurs to me in the first place that I should not be astonished if my intelligence is not capable of comprehending why God acts as He does; and that there is thus no reason to doubt of His existence from the fact that I may perhaps find many other things besides this as to which I am able to understand neither for what reason nor how God has produced them. For, in the first place, knowing that my nature is extremely feeble and limited, and that the nature of God is on the contrary immense, incomprehensible, and infinite, I have no further difficulty in recognising that there is an infinitude of matters in His power, the causes of which transcend my knowledge; and this reason suffices to convince me that the species of cause termed final, finds no useful employment in physical [or natural] things; for it does not appear to me that I can without temerity seek to investigate the [inscrutable] ends of God.

It further occurs to me that we should not consider one single creature separately, when we inquire as to whether the works of God are perfect, but should regard all his creations together. For the same thing which might possibly seem very imperfect with some semblance of reason if regarded by itself, is found to be very perfect if regarded as part of the whole universe; and although, since I resolved to doubt all things, I as yet have only known certainly my own existence and that of God, nevertheless since I have recognised the infinite power of God, I cannot deny that He may have produced many other things, or at least that He has the power of producing them, so that I may obtain a place as a part of a great universe.

Whereupon, regarding myself more closely, and considering what are my errors (for they alone testify to there being any imperfection in me), I answer that they depend on a combination of two causes, to wit, on the faculty of knowledge that rests in me, and on the power of choice or of free will—that is to say, of the understanding and at the same time of the will. For by the understanding alone I (neither assert nor deny anything, but] apprehend the ideas of things as to which I can form a judgment. But no error is properly speaking found in it, provided the word error is taken in its proper signification; and though there is possibly an infinitude of things in the world of which I have no idea in my understanding, we cannot for all that say that it is deprived of these ideas [as we might say of something which is required by its nature], but simply it does not possess these; because in truth there is no reason to prove that God should have given me a greater faculty of knowledge than He has given me; and however skillful a workman I represent Him to be, I should not for all that consider that He was bound to have placed in each of His works all the perfections which He may have been able to place in some. I likewise cannot complain that God has not given me a free choice or a will which is sufficient, ample and perfect, since as a matter of fact I am conscious of a will so extended as to be subject to no limits. And what seems to me very remarkable in this regard is that of all the qualities which I possess there is no one so perfect and so comprehensive that I do not very clearly recognise that it might be yet greater and more perfect. For, to take an example, if I consider the faculty of comprehension which I possess, I find that it is of very small extent and extremely limited, and at the same time I find the idea of another faculty much more ample and even infinite, and seeing that I can form the idea of it, I recognise from this very fact that it pertains to the nature of God. If in the same way I examine the memory, the imagination, or some other faculty, I do not find any which is not small and circumscribed, while in God it is immense [or infinite]. It is free will alone or liberty of choice which I find to be so great in me that I can conceive no other idea to be more great; it is indeed the case that it is for the most part this will that causes me to know that in some manner I bear the image and similitude of God. For although the power of will is incomparably greater in God than in me, both by reason of the knowledge and the power which, conjoined with it, render it stronger and more efficacious, and by reason of its object, inasmuch as in God it extends to a great many things; it nevertheless does not seem to me greater if I consider it formally and precisely in itself: for the faculty of will consists alone in our having the power of choosing to do a thing or choosing not to do it (that is, to affirm or deny, to pursue or to shun it), or rather it consists alone in the fact that in order to affirm or deny, pursue or shun those things placed before us by the understanding, we act so that we are unconscious that any outside force constrains us in doing so. For in order that I should be free it is not necessary that I should be indifferent as to the choice of one or the other of two contraries; but contrariwise the more I lean to the one—whether I recognise clearly that the reasons of the good and true are to be found in it, or whether God so disposes my inward thought—the more freely do I choose and embrace it. And undoubtedly both divine grace and natural knowledge, far from diminishing my liberty, rather increase it and strengthen it. Hence this indifference which I feel, when I am not swayed to one side rather than to the other by lack of reason, is the lowest grade of liberty, and rather evinces a lack or negation in knowledge than a perfection of will: for if I always recognised clearly what was true and good, I should never have trouble in deliberating as to what judgment or choice I should make, and then I should be entirely free without ever being indifferent.

From all this I recognise that the power of will which I have received from God is not of itself the source of my errors—for it is very ample and very perfect of its kind—any more than is the power of understanding; for since I understand nothing but by the power which God has given me for understanding, there is no doubt that all that I understand, I understand as I ought, and it is not possible that I err in this. Whence then come my errors? They come from the sole fact that since the will is much wider in its range and compass than the understanding, I do not restrain it within the same bounds, but extend it also to things which I do not understand: and as the will is of itself indifferent to these, it easily falls into error and sin, and chooses the evil for the good, or the false for the true.

For example, when I lately examined whether anything existed in the world, and found that from the very fact that I considered this question it followed very clearly that I myself existed, I could not prevent myself from believing that a thing I so clearly conceived was true: not that I found myself compelled to do so by some external cause, but simply because from great clearness in my mind there followed a great inclination of my will; and I believed this with so much the greater freedom or spontaneity as I possessed the less indifference towards it. Now, on the contrary, I not only know that I exist, inasmuch as I am a thinking thing, but a certain representation of corporeal nature is also presented to my mind; and it comes to pass that I doubt whether this thinking nature which is in me, or rather by which I am what I am, differs from this corporeal nature, or whether both are not simply the same thing; and I here suppose that I do not yet know any reason to persuade me to adopt the one belief rather than the other. From this it follows that I am entirely indifferent as to which of the two I affirm or deny, or even whether I abstain from forming any judgment in the matter.

And this indifference does not only extend to matters as to which the understanding has no knowledge, but also in general to all those which are not apprehended with perfect clearness at the moment when the will is deliberating upon them: for, however probable are the conjectures which render me disposed to form a judgment respecting anything, the simple knowledge that I have that those are conjectures alone and not certain and indubitable reasons, suffices to occasion me to judge the contrary. Of this I have had great experience of late when I set aside as false all that I had formerly held to be absolutely true, for the sole reason that I remarked that it might in some measure be doubted.

But if I abstain from giving my judgment on any thing when I do not perceive it with sufficient clearness and distinctness, it is plain that I act rightly and am not deceived. But if I determine to deny or affirm, I no longer make use as I should of my free will, and if I affirm what is not true, it is evident that I deceive myself; even though I judge according to truth, this comes about only by chance, and I do not escape the blame of misusing my freedom; for the light of nature teaches us that the knowledge of the understanding should always precede the determination of the will. And it is in the misuse of the free will that the privation which constitutes the characteristic nature of error is met with. Privation, I say, is found in the act, in so far as it proceeds from me, but it is not found in the faculty which I have received from God, nor even in the act in so far as it depends on Him.

For I have certainly no cause to complain that God has not given me an intelligence which is more powerful, or a natural light which is stronger than that which I have received from Him, since it is proper to the finite understanding not to comprehend a multitude of things, and it is proper to a created understanding to be finite; on the contrary, I have every reason to render thanks to God who owes me nothing and who has given me all the perfections I possess, and I should be far from charging Him with injustice, and with having deprived me of, or wrongfully withheld from me, these perfections which He has not bestowed upon me.

I have further no reason to complain that He has given me a will more ample than my understanding, for since the will consists only of one single element, and is so to speak indivisible, it appears that its nature is such that nothing can be abstracted from it [without destroying it]; and certainly the more comprehensive it is found to be, the more reason I have to render gratitude to the giver.

And, finally, I must also not complain that God concurs with me in forming the acts of the will, that is, the judgment in which I go astray, because these acts are entirely true and good, inasmuch as they depend on God; and in a certain sense more perfection accrues to my nature from the fact that I can form them, than if I could not do so. As to the privation in which alone the formal reason of error or sin consists, it has no need of any concurrence from God, since it is not a thing [or an existence], and since it is not related to God as to a cause, but should be termed merely a negation [according to the significance given to these words in the Schools]. For in fact it is not an imperfection in God that He has given me the liberty to give or withhold my assent from certain things as to which He has not placed a clear and distinct knowledge in my understanding; but it is without doubt an imperfection in me not to make a good use of my freedom, and to give my judgment readily on matters which I only understand obscurely. I nevertheless perceive that God could easily have created me so that I never should err, although I still remained free, and endowed with a limited knowledge, viz, by giving to my understanding a clear and distinct intelligence of all things as to which I should ever have to deliberate; or simply by His engraving deeply in my memory the resolution never to form a judgment on anything without having a clear and distinct understanding of it, so that I could never forget it. And it is easy for me to understand that, in so far as I consider myself alone, and as if there were only myself in the world, I should have been much more perfect than I am, if God had created me so that I could never err. Nevertheless I cannot deny that in some sense it is a greater perfection in the whole universe that certain parts should not be exempt from error as others are than that all parts should be exactly similar. And I have no right to complain if God, having placed me in the world, has not called upon me to play a part that excels all others in distinction and perfection.

And further I have reason to be glad on the ground that if He has not given me the power of never going astray by the first means pointed out above, which depends on a clear and evident knowledge of all the things regarding which I can deliberate, He has at least left within my power the other means, which is firmly to adhere to the resolution never to give judgment on matters whose truth is not clearly known to me; for although I notice a certain weakness in my nature in that I cannot continually concentrate my mind on one single thought, I can yet, by attentive and frequently repeated meditation, impress it so forcibly on my memory that I shall never fail to recollect it whenever I have need of it, and thus acquire the habit of never going astray.

And inasmuch as it is in this that the greatest and principal perfection of man consists, it seems to me that I have not gained little by this day's Meditation, since I have discovered the source of falsity and error. And certainly there can be no other source than that which I have explained; for as often as I so restrain my will within the limits of my knowledge that it forms no judgment except on matters which are clearly and distinctly represented to it by the understanding, I can never be deceived; for every clear and distinct conception is without doubt something, and hence cannot derive its origin from what is nought, but must of necessity have God as its author—God, I say, who being supremely perfect, cannot be the cause of any error; and consequently we must conclude that such a conception [or such a judgment] is true. Nor have I only learned to-day what I should avoid in order that I may not err, but also how I should act in order to arrive at a knowledge of the truth; for without doubt I shall arrive at this end if I devote my attention sufficiently to those things which I perfectly understand; and if I separate from these that which I only understand confusedly and with obscurity. To these I shall henceforth diligently give heed.

MEDITATION V

Of the essence of material things, and, again, of God that He exists.

Many other matters respecting the attributes of God and my own nature or mind remain for consideration; but I shall possibly on another occasion resume the investigation of these. Now (after first noting what must be done or avoided, in order to arrive at a knowledge of the truth) my principal task is to endeavour to emerge from the state of doubt into which I have these last days fallen, and to see whether nothing certain can be known regarding material things.

But before examining whether any such objects as I conceive exist outside of me, I must consider the ideas of them in so far as they are in my thought, and see which of them are distinct and which confused.

In the first place, I am able distinctly to imagine that quantity which philosophers commonly call continuous, or the extension in length, breadth, or depth, that is in this quantity, or rather in the object to which it is attributed. Further, I can number in it many different parts, and attribute to each of its parts many sorts of size, figure, situation and local movements, and, finally, I can assign to each of these movements all degrees of duration.

And not only do I know these things with distinctness when I consider them in general, but, likewise [however little I apply my attention to the matter], I discover an infinitude of particulars respecting numbers, figures, movements, and other such things, whose truth is so manifest, and so well accords with my nature, that when I begin to discover them, it seems to me that I learn nothing new, or recollect what I formerly knew—that is to say, that I for the first time perceive things which were already present to my mind, although I had not as yet applied my mind to them.

And what I here find to be most important is that I discover in myself an infinitude of ideas of certain things which cannot be esteemed as pure negations, although they may possibly have no existence outside of my thought, and which are not framed by me, although it is within my power either to think or not to think them, but which possess natures which are true and immutable. For example, when I imagine a triangle, although there may nowhere in the world be such a figure outside my thought, or ever have been, there is nevertheless in this figure a certain determinate nature, form, or essence, which is immutable and eternal, which I have not invented, and which in no wise depends on my mind, as appears from the fact that diverse properties of that triangle can be demonstrated, viz, that its three angles are equal to two right angles, that the greatest side is subtended by the greatest angle, and the like, which now, whether I wish it or do not wish it, I recognise very clearly as pertaining to it, although I never thought of the matter at all when I imagined a triangle for the first time, and which therefore cannot be said to have been invented by me.

Nor does the objection hold good that possibly this idea of a triangle has reached my mind through the medium of my senses, since I have sometimes seen bodies triangular in shape; because I can form in my mind an infinitude of other figures regarding which we cannot have the least conception of their ever having been objects of sense, and I can nevertheless demonstrate various properties pertaining to their nature as well as to that of the triangle, and these must certainly all be true since I conceive them clearly. Hence they are something, and not pure negation; for it is perfectly clear that all that is true is something, and I have already fully demonstrated that all that I know clearly is true. And even although I had not demonstrated this, the nature of my mind is such that I could not prevent myself from holding them to be true so long as I conceive them clearly; and I recollect that even when I was still strongly attached to the objects of sense, I counted as the most certain those truths which I conceived clearly as regards figures, numbers, and the other matters which pertain to arithmetic and geometry, and, in general, to pure and abstract mathematics.

But now, if just because I can draw the idea of something from my thought, it follows that all which I know clearly and distinctly as pertaining to this object does really belong to it, may I not derive from this an argument demonstrating the existence of God? It is certain that I no less find the idea of God, that is to say, the idea of a supremely perfect Being, in me, than that of any figure or number whatever it is; and I do not know any less clearly and distinctly that an [actual and] eternal existence pertains to this nature than I know that all that which I am able to demonstrate of some figure or number truly pertains to the nature of this figure or number, and therefore, although all that I concluded in the preceding Meditations were found to be false, the existence of God would pass with me as at least as certain as I have ever held the truths of mathematics (which concern only numbers and figures) to be.

This indeed is not at first manifest, since it would seem to present some appearance of being a sophism. For being accustomed in all other things to make a distinction between existence and essence,

I easily persuade myself that the existence can be separated from the essence of God, and that we can thus conceive God as not actually existing. But, nevertheless, when I think of it with more attention, I clearly see that existence can no more be separated from the essence of God than can its having its three angles equal to two right angles be separated from the essence of a [rectilinear] triangle, or the idea of a mountain from the idea of a valley; and so there is not any less repugnance to our conceiving a God (that is, a Being supremely perfect) to whom existence is lacking (that is to say, to whom a certain perfection is lacking), than to conceive of a mountain which has no valley.

But although I cannot really conceive of a God without existence any more than a mountain without a valley, still from the fact that I conceive of a mountain with a valley, it does not follow that there is such a mountain in the world; similarly although I conceive of God as possessing existence, it would seem that it does not follow that there is a God which exists; for my thought does not impose any necessity upon things, and just as I may imagine a winged horse, although no horse with wings exists, so I could perhaps attribute existence to God, although no God existed.

But a sophism is concealed in this objection; for from the fact that I cannot conceive a mountain without a valley, it does not follow that there is any mountain or any valley in existence, but only that the mountain and the valley, whether they exist or do not exist, cannot in any way be separated one from the other. While from the fact that I cannot conceive God without existence, it follows that existence is inseparable from Him, and hence that He really exists; not that my thought can bring this to pass, or impose any necessity on things, but, on the contrary, because the necessity which lies in the thing itself, i.e. the necessity of the existence of God determines me to think in this way. For it is not within my power to think of God without existence (that is of a supremely perfect Being devoid of a supreme perfection) though it is in my power to imagine a horse either with wings or without wings.

And we must not here object that it is in truth necessary for me to assert that God exists after having presupposed that He possesses every sort of perfection, since existence is one of these, but that as a matter of fact my original supposition was not necessary, just as it is not necessary to consider that all quadrilateral figures can be inscribed in the circle; for supposing I thought this, I should be constrained to admit that the rhombus might be inscribed in the circle since it is a quadrilateral figure, which, however, is manifestly false. [We must not, I say, make any such allegations because] although it is not necessary that I should at any time entertain the notion of God, nevertheless whenever it happens that I think of a first and a sovereign Being, and, so to speak, derive the idea of Him from the storehouse of my mind, it is necessary that I should attribute to Him every sort of perfection, although I do not get so far as to enumerate them all, or to apply my mind to each one in particular. And this necessity suffices to make me conclude (after having recognised that existence is a perfection) that this first and sovereign Being really exists; just as though it is not necessary for me ever to imagine any triangle, yet, whenever I wish to consider a rectilinear figure composed only of three angles, it is absolutely essential that I should attribute to it all those properties which serve to bring about the conclusion that its three angles are not greater than two right angles, even although I may not then be considering this point in particular. But when I consider which figures are capable of being inscribed in the circle, it is in no wise necessary that I should think that all quadrilateral figures are of this number; on the contrary, I cannot even pretend that this is the case, so long as I do not desire to accept anything which I cannot conceive clearly and distinctly. And in consequence there is a great difference between the false suppositions such as this, and the true ideas born within me, the first and principal of which is that of God. For really I discern in many ways that this idea is not something factitious, and depending solely on my thought, but that it is the image of a true and immutable nature; first of all, because I cannot conceive anything but God himself to whose essence existence [necessarily] pertains; in the second place because it is not possible for me to conceive two or more Gods in this same position; and, granted that there is one such God who now exists, I see clearly that it is necessary that

He should have existed from all eternity, and that He must exist eternally; and finally, because I know an infinitude of other properties in God, none of which I can either diminish or change.

For the rest, whatever proof or argument I avail myself of, we must always return to the point that it is only those things which we conceive clearly and distinctly that have the power of persuading me entirely. And although amongst the matters which I conceive of in this way, some indeed are manifestly obvious to all, while others only manifest themselves to those who consider them closely and examine them attentively; still, after they have once been discovered, the latter are not esteemed as any less certain than the former. For example, in the case of every right-angled triangle, although it does not so manifestly appear that the square of the base is equal to the squares of the two other sides as that this base is opposite to the greatest angle; still, when this has once been apprehended, we are just as certain of its truth as of the truth of the other. And as regards God, if my mind were not pre-occupied with prejudices, and if my thought did not find itself on all hands diverted by the continual pressure of sensible things, there would be nothing which I could know more immediately and more easily than Him. For is there anything more manifest than that there is a God, that is to say, a Supreme Being, to whose essence alone existence pertains?

And although for a firm grasp of this truth I have need of a strenuous application of mind, at present I not only feel myself to be as assured of it as of all that I hold as most certain, but I also remark that the certainty of all other things depends on it so absolutely, that without this knowledge it is impossible ever to know anything perfectly.

For although I am of such a nature that as long as I understand anything very clearly and distinctly, I am naturally impelled to believe it to be true, yet because I am also of such a nature that I cannot have my mind constantly fixed on the same object in order to perceive it clearly, and as I often recollect having formed a past judgment without at the same time properly recollecting the reasons that led me to make it, it may happen meanwhile that other reasons present themselves to me, which would easily cause me to change my opinion, if I were ignorant of the facts of the existence of God, and thus I should have no true and certain knowledge, but only vague and vacillating opinions. Thus, for example, when I consider the nature of a [rectilinear] triangle, I who have some little knowledge of the principles of geometry recognise quite clearly that the three angles are equal to two right angles, and it is not possible for me not to believe this so long as I apply my mind to its demonstration; but so soon as I abstain from attending to the proof, although I still recollect having clearly comprehended it, it may easily occur that I come to doubt its truth, if I am ignorant of there being a God. For I can persuade myself of having been so constituted by nature that I can easily deceive myself even in those matters which I believe myself to apprehend with the greatest evidence and certainty, especially when I recollect that I have frequently judged matters to be true and certain which other reasons have afterwards impelled me to judge to be altogether false.

But after I have recognised that there is a God—because at the same time I have also recognised that all things depend upon Him, and that He is not a deceiver, and from that have inferred that what I perceive clearly and distinctly cannot fail to be true—although I no longer pay attention to the reasons for which I have judged this to be true, provided that I recollect having clearly and distinctly perceived it, no contrary reason can be brought forward which could ever cause me to doubt of its truth; and thus I have a true and certain knowledge of it. And this same knowledge extends likewise to all other things which I recollect having formerly demonstrated, such as the truths of geometry and the like; for what can be alleged against them to cause me to place them in doubt? Will it be said that my nature is such as to cause me to be frequently deceived? But I already know that I cannot be deceived in the judgment whose grounds I know clearly. Will it be said that I formerly held many things to be true and certain which I have afterwards recognised to be false? But I had not had any clear and distinct knowledge of these things, and not as yet knowing the rule whereby I assure myself of the truth, I had been impelled to give my assent from reasons which I have since recognised to be less strong than I had at the time imagined them to be. What further objection can then be raised? That possibly I am dreaming (an objection I myself made a little while ago), or that all the thoughts which I now have are no more true than the phantasies of my dreams? But even though I slept the case would be the same, for all that is clearly present to my mind is absolutely true.

And so I very clearly recognise that the certainty and truth of all knowledge depends alone on the knowledge of the true God, in so much that, before I knew Him, I could not have a perfect knowledge of any other thing. And now that I know Him I have the means of acquiring a perfect knowledge of an infinitude of things, not only of those which relate to God Himself and other intellectual matters, but also of those which pertain to corporeal nature in so far as it is the object of pure mathematics [which have no concern with whether it exists or not].

MEDITATION VI

Of the Existence of Material Things, and of the real distinction between the Soul and Body of Man.

Nothing further now remains but to inquire whether material things exist. And certainly I at least know that these may exist in so far as they are considered as the objects of pure mathematics, since in this aspect I perceive them clearly and distinctly. For there is no doubt that God possesses the power to produce everything that I am capable of perceiving with distinctness, and I have never deemed that anything was impossible for Him, unless I found a contradiction in attempting to conceive it clearly. Further, the faculty of imagination which I possess, and of which, experience tells me, I make use when I apply myself to the consideration of material things, is capable of persuading me of their existence; for when I attentively consider what imagination is, I find that it is nothing but a certain application of the faculty of knowledge to the body which is immediately present to it, and which therefore exists.

And to render this quite clear, I remark in the first place the difference that exists between the imagination and pure intellection [or conception]. For example, when I imagine a triangle, I do not conceive it only as a figure comprehended by three lines, but I also apprehend these three lines as present by the power and inward vision of my mind, and this is what I call imagining. But if I desire to think of a chiliagon, I certainly conceive truly that it is a figure composed of a thousand sides, just as easily as I conceive of a triangle that it is a figure of three sides; but I cannot in any way imagine the thousand sides of a chiliagon [as I do the three sides of a triangle], nor do I, so to speak, regard them as present [with the eyes of my mind]. And although in accordance with the habit I have formed of always employing the aid of my imagination when I think of corporeal things, it may happen that in imagining a chiliagon I confusedly represent to myself some figure, yet it is very evident that this figure is not a chiliagon, since it in no way differs from that which I represent to myself when I think of a myriagon or any other many-sided figure; nor does it serve my purpose in discovering the properties which go to form the distinction between a chiliagon and other polygons. But if the question turns upon a pentagon, it is quite true that I can conceive its figure as well as that of a chiliagon without the help of my imagination; but I can also imagine it by applying the attention of my mind to each of its five sides, and at the same time to the space which they enclose. And thus I clearly recognise that I have need of a particular effort of mind in order to effect the act of imagination, such as I do not require in order to understand, and this particular effort of mind clearly manifests the difference which exists between imagination and pure intellection.

I remark besides that this power of imagination which is in one, inasmuch as it differs from the power of understanding, is in no wise a necessary element in my nature, or in [my essence, that is to say, in] the essence of my mind; for although I did not possess it I should doubtless ever remain the same as I now am, from which it appears that we might conclude that it depends on something which differs from me. And I easily conceive that if some body exists with which my mind is conjoined and united in such a way that it can apply itself to consider it when it pleases, it may be that by this means it can imagine corporeal objects; so that this mode of thinking differs from pure intellection only inasmuch as mind in its intellectual activity in some manner turns on itself, and considers some of the ideas which it possesses in itself; while in imagining it turns towards the body, and there beholds in it something conformable to the idea which it has either conceived of itself or perceived by the senses. I easily understand, I say, that the imagination could be thus constituted if it is true that body exists; and because I can discover no other convenient mode of explaining it, I conjecture with probability that body does exist; but this is only with probability, and although I examine all things with care, I nevertheless do not find that from this distinct idea of corporeal nature, which I have in my imagination, I can derive any argument from which there will necessarily be deduced the existence of body.

But I am in the habit of imagining many other things besides this corporeal nature which is the object of pure mathematics, to wit, the colours, sounds, scents, pain, and other such things, although less distinctly. And inasmuch as I perceive these things much better through the senses, by the medium of which, and by the memory, they seem to have reached my imagination, I believe that, in order to examine them more conveniently, it is right that I should at the same time investigate the nature of sense perception, and that I should see if from the ideas which I apprehend by this mode of thought, which I call feeling, I cannot derive some certain proof of the existence of corporeal objects.

And first of all I shall recall to my memory those matters which I hitherto held to be true, as having perceived them through the senses, and the foundations on which my belief has rested; in the next place I shall examine the reasons which have since obliged me to place them in doubt; in the last place I shall consider which of them I must now believe.

First of all, then, I perceived that I had a head, hands, feet, and all other members of which this body—which I considered as a part, or possibly even as the whole, of myself—is composed. Further I was sensible that this body was placed amidst many others, from which it was capable of being affected in many different ways, beneficial and hurtful, and I remarked that a certain feeling of pleasure accompanied those that were beneficial, and pain those which were harmful. And in addition to this pleasure and pain, I also experienced hunger, thirst, and other similar appetites, as also certain corporeal inclinations towards joy, sadness, anger, and other similar passions. And outside myself, in addition to extension, figure, and motions of bodies, I remarked in them hardness, heat, and all other tactile qualities, and, further, light and colour, and scents and sounds, the variety of which gave me the means of distinguishing the sky, the earth, the sea, and generally all the other bodies, one from the other. And certainly, considering the ideas of all these qualities which presented themselves to my mind, and which alone I perceived properly or immediately, it was not without reason that I believed myself to perceive objects quite different from my thought, to wit, bodies from which those ideas proceeded; for I found by experience that these ideas presented themselves to me without my consent being requisite, so that I could not perceive any object, however desirous I might be, unless it were present to the organs of sense; and it was not in my power not to perceive it, when it was present. And because the ideas which I receive through the senses were much more lively, more clear, and even, in their own way, more distinct than any of those which I could of myself frame in meditation, or than those I found impressed on my memory, it appeared as though they could not have proceeded from my mind, so that they must necessarily have been produced in me by some other things. And having no knowledge of those objects excepting the knowledge which the ideas themselves gave me, nothing was more likely to occur to my mind than that the objects were similar to the ideas which were caused. And because I likewise remembered that I had formerly made use of my senses rather than my reason, and recognised that the ideas which I formed of myself were not so distinct as those which I perceived through the senses, and that they were most frequently even composed of portions of these last, I persuaded myself easily that I had no idea in my mind which had not formerly come to me through the senses. Nor was it without some reason that I believed that this body (which by a certain special right I call my own) belonged to me more properly and more strictly than any other; for in fact I could never be separated from it as from other bodies; I experienced in it and on account of it all my appetites and affections, and finally I was touched by the feeling of pain and titillation of pleasure in its parts, and not in the parts of other bodies which were separated from it. But when I inquired, why, from some, I know not what, painful sensation, there follows sadness of mind, and from the pleasurable sensation there arises joy, or why this mysterious pinching of the stomach which I call hunger causes me to desire to eat, and dryness of throat causes a desire to drink, and so on, I could give no reason excepting that nature taught me so; for there is certainly no affinity (that I at least can understand) between the craving of the stomach and the desire to eat, any more than between the perception of whatever causes pain and the thought of sadness which arises from this perception. And in the same way it appeared to me that I had learned from nature all the other judgments which I formed regarding the objects of my senses, since I remarked that these judgments were formed in me before I had the leisure to weigh and consider any reasons which might oblige me to make them.

But afterwards many experiences little by little destroyed all the faith which I had rested in my senses; for I from time to time observed that those towers which from afar appeared to me to be round, more closely observed seemed square, and that colossal statues raised on the summit of these towers, appeared as quite tiny statues when viewed from the bottom; and so in an infinitude of other cases I found error in judgments founded on the external senses. And not only in those founded on the external senses, but even in those founded on the internal as well; for is there anything more intimate or more internal than pain? And yet I have learned from some persons whose arms or legs have been cut off, that they sometimes seemed to feel pain in the part which had been amputated, which made me think that I could not be quite certain that it was a certain member which pained me, even although I felt pain in it. And to those grounds of doubt I have lately added two others, which are very general; the first is that I never have believed myself to feel anything in waking moments which I cannot also sometimes believe myself to feel when I sleep, and as I do not think that these things which I seem to feel in sleep, proceed from objects outside of me, I do not see any reason why I should have this belief regarding objects which I seem to perceive while awake. The other was that being still ignorant, or rather supposing my self to be ignorant, of the author of my being, I saw nothing to prevent me from having been so constituted by nature that I might be deceived even in matters which seemed to me to be most certain. And as to the grounds on which I was formerly persuaded of the truth of sensible objects, I had not much trouble in replying to them. For since nature seemed to cause me to lean towards many things from which reason repelled me, I did not believe that I should trust much to the teachings of nature. And although the ideas which I receive by the senses do not depend on my will, I did not think that one should for that reason conclude that they proceeded from things different from myself, since possibly some faculty might be discovered in me—though hitherto unknown to me—which produced them.

But now that I begin to know myself better, and to discover more clearly the author of my being, I do not in truth think that I should rashly admit all the matters which the senses seem to teach us, but, on the other hand, I do not think that I should doubt them all universally.

And first of all, because I know that all things which I apprehend clearly and distinctly can be created by God as I apprehend them, it suffices that I am able to apprehend one thing apart from another clearly and distinctly in order to be certain that the one is different from the other, since they may be made to exist in separation at least by the omnipotence of God; and it does not signify by what power this separation is made in order to compel me to judge them to be different: and, therefore, just because I know certainly that I exist, and that meanwhile I do not remark that any other thing necessarily pertains to my nature or essence, excepting that I am a thinking thing, I rightly conclude that my essence consists solely in the fact that I am a thinking thing [or a substance whose whole essence or nature is to think]. And although possibly (or rather certainly, as I shall say in a moment) I possess a body with which I am very intimately conjoined, yet because, on the one side, I have a clear and distinct idea of myself inasmuch as I am only a thinking and unextended thing, and as, on the other, I possess a distinct idea of body, inasmuch as it is only an extended and unthinking thing, it is certain that this I [that is to say, my soul by which I am what I am], is entirely and absolutely distinct from my body, and can exist without it.

I further find in myself faculties employing modes of thinking peculiar to themselves, to wit, the faculties of imagination and feeling, without which I can easily conceive myself clearly and distinctly as a complete being; while, on the other hand, they cannot be so conceived apart from me, that is, without an intelligent substance in which they reside, for [in the notion we have of these faculties, or, to use the language of the Schools] in their formal concept, some kind of intellection is comprised, from which I infer that they are distinct from me as its modes are from a thing. I observe also in me some other faculties such as that of change of position, the assumption of different figures and such like, which cannot be conceived, any more than can the preceding, apart from some substance to which they are attached, and consequently cannot exist without it; but it is very clear that these faculties, if it be true that they exist, must be attached to some corporeal or extended substance and not to an intelligent substance, since in the clear and distinct conception of these there is some sort of extension found to be present, but no intellection at all. There is certainly further in me a certain passive faculty of perception, that is, of receiving and recognising the ideas of sensible things, but this would be useless to me [and I could in no way avail myself of it], if there were not either in me or in some other thing another active faculty capable of forming and producing these ideas. But this active faculty cannot exist in me [inasmuch as I am a thing that thinks] seeing that it does not presuppose thought, and also that those ideas are often produced in me without my contributing in any way to the same, and often even against my will; it is thus necessarily the case that the faculty resides in some substance different from me in which all the reality which is objectively in the ideas that are produced by this faculty is formally or eminently contained, as I remarked before. And this substance is either a body, that is, a corporeal nature in which there is contained formally [and really] all that which is objectively [and by representation] in those ideas, or it is God Himself, or some other creature more noble than body in which that same is contained eminently. But since God is no deceiver, it is very manifest that He does not communicate to me these ideas immediately and by Himself, nor yet by the intervention of some creature in which their reality is not formally, but only eminently, contained. For since He has given me no faculty to recognise that this is the case, but, on the other hand, a very great inclination to believe [that they are sent to me or] that they are conveyed to me by corporeal objects, I do not see how He could be defended from the accusation of deceit if these ideas were produced by causes other than corporeal objects. Hence we must allow that corporeal things exist. However, they are perhaps not exactly what we perceive by the senses, since this comprehension by the senses is in many instances very obscure and confused; but we must at least admit that all things which I conceive in them clearly and distinctly, that is to say, all things which, speaking generally, are comprehended in the object of pure mathematics, are truly to be recognised as external objects.

As to other things, however, which are either particular only, as, for example, that the sun is of such and such a figure, etc., or which are less clearly and distinctly conceived, such as light, sound, pain and the like, it is certain that although they are very dubious and uncertain, yet on the sole ground that God is not a deceiver, and that consequently He has not permitted any falsity to exist in my opinion which He has not likewise given me the faculty of correcting, I may assuredly hope to conclude that I have within me the means of arriving at the truth even here. And first of all there is no doubt that in all things which nature teaches me there is some truth contained; for by nature, considered in general, I now understand no other thing than either God Himself or else the order and disposition which God has established in created things; and by my nature in particular I understand no other thing than the complexus of all the things which God has given me.

But there is nothing which this nature teaches me more expressly [nor more sensibly] than that I have a body which is adversely affected when I feel pain, which has need of food or drink when I experience the feelings of hunger and thirst, and so on; nor can I doubt there being some truth in all this.

Nature also teaches me by the sensations of pain, hunger, thirst, etc., that I am not only lodged in my body as a pilot in a vessel, but that I am very closely united to it, and so to speak so intermingled with it that I seem to compose with it one whole. For if that were not the case, when my body is hurt, I, who am merely a thinking thing, should not feel pain, for I should perceive this wound by the understanding only, just as the sailor perceives by sight when something is damaged in his vessel; and when my body has need of drink or food, I should clearly understand the fact without being warned of it by confused feelings of hunger and thirst. For all these sensations of hunger, thirst, pain, etc. are in truth none other than certain confused modes of thought which are produced by the union and apparent intermingling of mind and body.

Moreover, nature teaches me that many other bodies exist around mine, of which some are to be avoided, and others sought after. And certainly from the fact that I am sensible of different sorts of colours, sounds, scents, tastes, heat, hardness, etc., I very easily conclude that there are in the bodies from which all these diverse sense-perceptions proceed certain variations which answer to them, although possibly these are not really at all similar to them. And also from the fact that amongst these different sense-perceptions some are very agreeable to me and others disagreeable, it is quite certain that my body (or rather myself in my entirety, inasmuch as I am formed of body and soul) may receive different impressions agreeable and disagreeable from the other bodies which surround it.

But there are many other things which nature seems to have taught me, but which at the same time I have never really received from her, but which have been brought about in my mind by a certain habit which I have of forming inconsiderate judgments on things; and thus it may easily happen that these judgments contain some error. Take, for example, the opinion which I hold that all space in which there is nothing that affects [or makes an impression on] my senses is void; that in a body which is warm there is something entirely similar to the idea of heat which is in me; that in a white or green body there is the same whiteness or greenness that I perceive; that in a bitter or sweet body there is the same taste, and so on in other instances; that the stars, the towers, and all other distant bodies are of the same figure and size as they appear from far off to our eyes, etc. But in order that in this there should be nothing which I do not conceive distinctly, I should define exactly what I really understand when I say that I am taught somewhat by nature. For here I take nature in a more limited signification than when I term it the sum of all the things given me by God, since in this sum many things are comprehended which only pertain to mind (and to these I do not refer in speaking of nature) such as the notion which I have of the fact that what has once been done cannot ever be undone and an infinitude of such things which I know by the light of nature [without the help of the body]; and seeing that it comprehends many other matters besides which only pertain to body, and are no longer here contained under the name of nature, such as the quality of weight which it possesses and the like, with which I also do not deal; for in talking of nature I only treat of those things given by God to me as a being composed of mind and body. But the nature here described truly teaches me to flee from things which cause the sensation of pain, and seek after the things which communicate to me the sentiment of pleasure and so forth; but I do not see that beyond this it teaches me that from those diverse sense-perceptions we should ever form any conclusion regarding things outside of us, without having [carefully and maturely] mentally examined them beforehand. For it seems to me that it is mind alone, and not mind and body in conjunction, that is requisite to a knowledge of the truth in regard to such things. Thus, although a star makes no larger an impression on my eye than the flame of a little candle there is yet in me no real or positive propensity impelling me to believe that it is not greater than that flame; but I have judged it to be so from my earliest years, without any rational foundation. And although in approaching fire I feel heat, and in approaching it a little too near I even feel pain, there is at the same time no reason in this which could persuade me that there is in the fire something resembling this heat any more than there is in it something resembling the pain; all that I have any reason to believe from this is, that there is something in it, whatever it may be, which excites in me these sensations of heat or of pain. So also, although there are spaces in which I find nothing which excites my senses, I must not from that conclude that these spaces contain no body; for I see in this, as in other similar things, that I have been in the habit of perverting the order of nature, because these perceptions of sense having been placed within me by nature merely for the purpose of signifying to my mind what things are beneficial or hurtful to the composite whole of which it forms a part, and being up to that point sufficiently clear and distinct, I yet avail myself of them as though they were absolute rules by which I immediately determine the essence of the bodies which are outside me, as to which, in fact, they can teach me nothing but what is most obscure and confused.

But I have already sufficiently considered how, notwithstanding the supreme goodness of God, falsity enters into the judgments I make. Only here a new difficulty is presented—one respecting those things the pursuit or avoidance of which is taught me by nature, and also respecting the internal sensations which I possess, and in which I seem to have sometimes detected error [and thus to be directly deceived by my own nature]. To take an example, the agreeable taste of some food in which poison has been intermingled may induce me to partake of the poison, and thus deceive me. It is true, at the same time, that in this case nature may be excused, for it only induces me to desire food in which I find a pleasant taste, and not to desire poison which is unknown to it; and thus I can infer nothing from this fact, except that my nature is not omniscient, at which there is certainly no reason to be astonished, since man, being finite in nature, can only have knowledge the perfectness of which is limited.

But we not unfrequently deceive ourselves even in those things to which we are directly impelled by nature, as happens with those who when they are sick desire to drink or eat things hurtful to them. It will perhaps be said here that the cause of their deceptiveness is that their nature is corrupt, but that does not remove the difficulty, because a sick man is none the less truly God's creature than he who is in health; and it is therefore as repugnant to God's goodness for the one to have a deceitful nature as it is for the other. And as a clock composed of wheels and counterweights no less exactly observes the laws of nature when it is badly made, and does not show the time properly, than when it entirely satisfies the wishes of its maker, and as, if I consider the body of a man as being a sort of machine so built up and composed of nerves, muscles, veins, blood and skin, that though there were no mind in it at all, it would not cease to have the same motions as at present, exception being made of those movements which are due to the direction of the will, and in consequence depend upon the mind [as opposed to those which operate by the disposition of its organs], I easily recognise that it would be as natural to this body, supposing it to be, for example, dropsical, to suffer the parchedness of the throat which usually signifies to the mind the feeling of thirst, and to be disposed by this parched feeling to move the nerves and other parts in the way requisite for drinking, and thus to augment its malady and do harm to itself, as it is natural to it, when it has no indisposition, to be impelled to drink for its good by a similar cause. And although, considering the use to which the clock has been destined by its maker, I may say that it deflects from the order of its nature when it does not indicate the hours correctly; and as, in the same way, considering the machine of the human body as having been formed by God in order to have in itself all the movements usually manifested there, I have reason for thinking that it does not follow the order of nature when, if the throat is dry, drinking does harm to the conservation of health, nevertheless I recognise at the same time that this last mode of explaining nature is very different from the other. For this is but a purely verbal characterisation depending entirely on my thought, which compares a sick man and a badly constructed clock with the idea which I have of a healthy man and a well made clock, and it is hence extrinsic to the things to which it is applied; but according to the other interpretation of the term nature I understand something which is truly found in things and which is therefore not without some truth.

But certainly although in regard to the dropsical body it is only so to speak to apply an extrinsic term when we say that its nature is corrupted, inasmuch as apart from the need to drink, the throat is parched; yet in regard to the composite whole, that is to say, to the mind or soul united to this body, it is not a purely verbal predicate, but a real error of nature, for it to have thirst when drinking would be hurtful to it. And thus it still remains to inquire how the goodness of God does not prevent the nature of man so regarded from being fallacious.

In order to begin this examination, then, I here say, in the first place, that there is a great difference between mind and body, inasmuch as body is by nature always divisible, and the mind is entirely indivisible. For, as a matter of fact, when I consider the mind, that is to say, myself inasmuch as I am only a thinking thing, I cannot distinguish in myself any parts, but apprehend myself to be clearly one and entire; and although the whole mind seems to be united to the whole body, yet if a foot, or an arm, or some other part, is separated from my body, I am aware that nothing has been taken away from my mind. And the faculties of willing, feeling, conceiving, etc. cannot be properly speaking said to be its parts, for it is one and the same mind which employs itself in willing and in feeling and understanding. But it is quite otherwise with corporeal or extended objects, for there is not one of these imaginable by me which my mind cannot easily divide into parts, and which consequently I do not recognise as being divisible; this would be sufficient to teach me that the mind or soul of man is entirely different from the body, if I had not already learned it from other sources.

I further notice that the mind does not receive the impressions from all parts of the body immediately, but only from the brain, or perhaps even from one of its smallest parts, to wit, from that in which the common sense is said to reside, which, whenever it is disposed in the same particular way, conveys the same thing to the mind, although meanwhile the other portions of the body may be differently disposed, as is testified by innumerable experiments which it is unnecessary here to recount.

I notice, also, that the nature of body is such that none of its parts can be moved by another part a little way off which cannot also be moved in the same way by each one of the parts which are between the two, although this more remote part does not act at all. As, for example, in the cord *ABCD* [which is in tension] if we pull the last part *D*, the first part *A* will not be moved in any way differently from what would be the case if one of the intervening parts *B* or *C* were pulled, and the last part *D* were to remain unmoved. And in the same way, when I feel pain in my foot, my knowledge of physics teaches me that this sensation is communicated by means of nerves dispersed through the foot, which, being extended like cords from there to the brain, when they are contracted in the foot, at the same time contract the inmost portions of the brain which is their extremity and place of origin, and then excite a certain movement which nature has established in order to cause the mind to be affected by a sensation of pain represented as existing in the foot. But because these nerves must pass through the tibia, the thigh, the loins, the back and the neck, in order to reach from the leg to the brain, it may happen that although their extremities which are in the foot are not affected, but only certain ones of their intervening parts [which pass by the loins or the neck], this action will excite the same movement in the brain that might have been excited there by a hurt received in the foot, in consequence of which the mind will necessarily feel in the foot the same pain as if it had received a hurt. And the same holds good of all the other perceptions of our senses.

I notice finally that since each of the movements which are in the portion of the brain by which the mind is immediately affected brings about one particular sensation only, we cannot under the circumstances imagine anything more likely than that this movement, amongst all the sensations which it is capable of impressing on it, causes mind to be affected by that one which is best fitted and most generally useful for the conservation of the human body when it is in health. But experience makes us aware that all the feelings with which nature inspires us are such as I have just spoken of; and there is therefore nothing in them which does not give testimony to the power and goodness of the God [who has produced them]. Thus, for example, when the nerves which are in the feet are violently or more than usually moved, their movement, passing through the medulla of the spine to the inmost parts of the brain, gives a sign to the mind which makes it feel somewhat, to wit, pain, as though in the foot, by which the mind is excited to do its utmost to remove the cause of the evil as dangerous and hurtful to the foot. It is true that God could have constituted the nature of man in such a way that this same movement in the brain would have conveyed something quite different to the mind; for example, it might have produced consciousness of itself either in so far as it is in the brain, or as it is in the foot, or as it is in some other place between the foot and the brain, or it might finally have produced consciousness of anything else whatsoever; but none of all this would have contributed so well to the conservation of the body. Similarly, when we desire to drink, a certain dryness of the throat is produced which moves its nerves, and by their means the internal portions of the brain; and this movement causes in the mind the sensation of thirst, because in this case there is nothing more useful to us than to become aware that we have need to drink for the conservation of our health; and the same holds good in other instances.

From this it is quite clear that, notwithstanding the supreme goodness of God, the nature of man, inasmuch as it is composed of mind and body, cannot be otherwise than sometimes a source of deception. For if there is any cause which excites, not in the foot but in some part of the nerves which are extended between the foot and the brain, or even in the brain itself, the same movement which usually is produced when the foot is detrimentally affected, pain will be experienced as though it were in the foot, and the sense will thus naturally be deceived; for since the same movement in the brain is capable of causing but one sensation in the mind, and this sensation is much more frequently excited by a cause which hurts the foot than by another existing in some other quarter, it is reasonable that it should convey to the mind pain in the foot rather than in any other part of the body. And although the parchedness of the throat does not always proceed, as it usually does, from the fact that drinking is necessary for the health of the body, but sometimes comes from quite a different cause, as is the case with dropsical patients, it is yet much better that it should mislead on this occasion than if, on the other hand, it were always to deceive us when the body is in good health; and so on in similar cases.

And certainly this consideration is of great service to me, not only in enabling me to recognise all the errors to which my nature is subject, but also in enabling me to avoid them or to correct them more easily. For knowing that all my senses more frequently indicate to me truth than falsehood respecting the things which concern that which is beneficial to the body, and being able almost always to avail myself of many of them in order to examine one particular thing, and, besides that, being able to make use of my memory in order to connect the present with the past, and of my understanding which already has discovered all the causes of my errors, I ought no longer to fear that falsity may be found in matters every day presented to me by my senses. And I ought to set aside all the doubts of these past days as hyperbolical and ridiculous, particularly that very common uncertainty respecting sleep, which I could not distinguish from the waking state; for at present I find a very notable difference between the two, inasmuch as our memory can never connect our dreams one with the other, or with the whole course of our lives, as it unites events which happen to us while we are awake. And, as a matter of fact, if someone, while I was awake, quite suddenly appeared to me and disappeared as fast as do the images which I see in sleep, so that I could not know from whence the form came nor whither it went, it would not be without reason that I should deem it a spectre or a phantom formed by my brain [and similar to those which I form in sleep], rather than a real man. But when I perceive things as to which I know distinctly both the place from which they proceed, and that in which they are, and the time at which they appeared to me; and when, without any interruption, I can connect the perceptions which I have of them with the whole course of my life, I am perfectly assured that these perceptions occur while I am waking and not during sleep. And I ought in no wise to doubt the truth of such matters, if, after having called up all my senses, my memory, and my understanding, to examine them, nothing is brought to evidence by any one of them which is repugnant to what is set forth by the others. For because God is in no wise a deceiver, it follows that I am not deceived in this. But because the exigencies of action often oblige us to make up our minds before having leisure to examine matters carefully, we must confess that the life of man is very frequently subject to error in respect to individual objects, and we must in the end acknowledge the infirmity of our nature.

The Causal Theory of Perception*

JOHN LOCKE

John Locke (1632–1704) was one of the greatest of English philosophers. His empiricist theory of knowledge and natural rights political theory have had lasting influence.

1. CONCERNING THE SIMPLE IDEAS of Sensation, it is to be considered,—that whatsoever is so constituted in nature as to be able, by affecting our senses, to cause any perception in the mind, doth thereby produce in the understanding a simple idea; which, whatever be the external cause of it, when it comes to be taken notice of by our discerning faculty, it is by the mind looked on and considered there to be a real positive idea in the understanding, as much as any other whatsoever; though, perhaps, the cause of it be but a privation of the subject.

2. Thus the ideas of heat and cold, light and darkness, white and black, motion and rest, are equally clear and positive ideas in the mind; though, perhaps, some of the causes which produce them are barely privations, in those subjects from whence our senses derive those ideas. These the understanding, in its view of them, considers all as distinct positive ideas, without taking notice of the causes that produce them: which is an inquiry not belonging to the idea, as it is in the understanding, but to the nature of the things existing without us. These are two very different things, and carefully to be distinguished; it being one thing to perceive and know the idea of white or black, and quite another to examine what kind of particles they must be, and how ranged in the superficies, to make any object appear white or black. . . .

7. To discover the nature of our *ideas* the better, and to discourse of them intelligibly, it will be convenient to distinguish them *as they are ideas or perceptions in our minds;* and *as they are modifications of matter in the bodies that cause such perceptions in us:* that so we may not think (as perhaps usually is done) that they are exactly the images and resemblances of something inherent in the subject; most of those of sensation being in the mind no more the likeness of something existing without us, than the names that stand for them are the likeness of our ideas, which yet upon hearing they are apt to excite in us.

8. Whatsoever the mind perceives *in itself,* or is the immediate object of perception, thought, or understanding, that I call *idea;* and the power to produce any idea in our mind, I call *quality* of the subject wherein that power is. Thus a snowball having the power to produce in us the ideas of white,

**Reprinted from* An Essay Concerning Human Understanding *Book II, Chapter VIII; Book IV, Chapter XI, first published 1690.*

cold, and round,—the power to produce those ideas in us, as they are in the snowball, I call qualities; and as they are sensations or perceptions in our understandings, I call them ideas; which *ideas,* if I speak of sometimes as in the things themselves, I would be understood to mean those qualities in the objects which produce them in us.

9. [Qualities thus considered in bodies are,

First, such as are utterly inseparable from the body, in what state soever it be;] and such as in all the alterations and changes it suffers, all the force can be used upon it, it constantly keeps; and such as sense constantly finds in every particle of matter which has bulk enough to be perceived; and the mind finds inseparable from every particle of matter, though less than to make itself singly be perceived by our senses; e.g. Take a grain of wheat, divide it into two parts; each part has still solidity, extension, figure, and mobility: divide it again, and it retains still the same qualities; and so divide it on, till the parts become insensible; they must retain still each of them all those qualities. For division (which is all that a mill, or pestle, or any other body, does upon another, in reducing it to insensible parts) can never take away either solidity, extension, figure, or mobility from any body, but only makes two or more distinct separate masses of matter, of that which was but one before; all which distinct masses, reckoned as so many distinct bodies, after division, make a certain number. [These I call *original* or *primary qualities* of body, which I think we may observe to produce simple ideas in us, viz. solidity, extension, figure, motion or rest, and number.

10. *Secondly,* such qualities which in truth are nothing in the objects themselves but powers to produce various sensations in us by their primary qualities, i.e. by the bulk, figure, texture, and motion of their insensible parts, as colours, sounds, tastes, &c. These I call *secondary qualities.* To these might be added *a third* sort, which are allowed to be barely powers; though they are as much real qualities in the subject as those which I, to comply with the common way of speaking, call qualities, but for distinction, secondary qualities. For the power in fire to produce a new colour, or consistency, in *wax* or *clay,*—by its primary qualities, is as much a quality in fire, as the power it has to produce in *me* a new idea or sensation of warmth or burning, which I felt not before,—by the same primary qualities, viz. the bulk, texture, and motion of its insensible parts.]

11. [The next thing to be considered is, how bodies produce ideas in us; and that is manifestly by impulse, the only way which we can conceive bodies to operate in.]

12. If then external objects be not united to our minds when they produce ideas therein; and yet we perceive these *original* qualities in such of them as singly fall under our senses, it is evident that some motion must be thence continued by our nerves, or animal spirits, by some parts of our bodies, to the brains or the seat of sensation, there to produce in our minds the particular ideas we have of them. And since the extension, figure, number, and motion of bodies of an observable bigness, may be perceived at a distance by the sight, it is evident some singly imperceptible bodies must come from them to the eyes, and therby convey to the brain some motion; which produces these ideas which we have of them in us.

13. After the same manner that the ideas of these original qualities are produced in us, we may conceive that the ideas of *secondary* qualities are also produced, viz. by the operation of insensible particles on our senses. For, it being manifest that there are bodies and good store of bodies, each whereof are so small, that we cannot by any of our senses discover either their bulk, figure, or motion,—as is evident in the particles of the air and water, and others extremely smaller than those; perhaps as much smaller than the particles of air and water, as the particles of air and water are smaller than peas or hail-stones;—let us suppose at present that the different motions and figures, bulk and number, of such particles, affecting the several organs of our senses, produce in us those different sensations which we have from the colours and smells of bodies; e.g. that a violet, by the impulse of such insensible particles of matter, of peculiar figures and bulks, and in different degrees and modifications of their motions, causes the ideas of the blue colour, and sweet scent of that flower to be produced in our minds. It being no more impossible to conceive

that God should annex such ideas to such motions, with which they have no similitude, than that he should annex the idea of pain to the motion of a piece of steel dividing our flesh, with which that idea hath no resemblance.

14. What I have said concerning colours and smells may be understood also of tastes and sounds, and other the like sensible qualities; which, whatever reality we by mistake attribute to them, are in truth nothing in the objects themselves, but powers to produce various sensations in us, and depend on those primary qualities, viz. bulk, figure, texture, and motion of parts [as I have said].

15. From whence I think it easy to draw this observation,—that the ideas of primary qualities of bodies are resemblances of them, and their patterns do really exist in the bodies themselves, but the ideas produced in us by these secondary qualities have no resemblance of them at all. There is nothing like our ideas, existing the bodies themselves. They are, in the bodies we denominate from them, only a power to produce those sensations in us: and what is sweet, blue, or warm in idea, is but the certain bulk, figure, and motion of the insensible parts, in the bodies themselves, which we call so.

16. Flame is denominated hot and light; snow, white and cold; and manna, white and sweet, from the ideas they produce in us. Which qualities are commonly thought to be the same in those bodies that those ideas are in us, the one the perfect resemblance of the other, as they are in a mirror, and it would by most men be judged very extravagant if one should say otherwise. And yet he that will consider that the same fire that, at one distance produces in us the sensation of warmth, does, at a nearer approach, produce in us the far different sensation of pain, ought to bethink himself what reason he has to say—that this idea of warmth, which was produced in him by the fire, is *actually in the fire;* and his idea of pain, which the same fire produced in him the same way, is *not* in the fire. Why are whiteness and coldness in snow, and pain not, when it produces the one and the other idea in us; and can do neither, but by the bulk, figure, number, and motion of its solid parts?

17. The particular bulk, number, figure, and motion of the parts of fire or snow are really in them,—whether any one's senses perceive them or no: and therefore they may be called *real* qualities, because they really exist in those bodies. But light, heat, whiteness, or coldness, are no more really in them than sickness or pain is in manna. Take away the sensation of them; let not the eyes see light or colours, nor the ears hear sounds; let the palate not taste, nor the nose smell, and all colours, tastes, odours, and sounds, *as they are such particular ideas,* vanish and cease, and are reduced to their causes, i.e. bulk, figure, and motion of parts.

18. A piece of manna of a sensible bulk is able to produce in us the idea of a round or square figure; and by being removed from one place to another, the idea of motion. This idea of motion represents it as it really is in manna moving: a circle or square are the same, whether in idea or existence, in the mind or in the manna. And this, both motion and figure, are really in the manna, whether we take notice of them or no: this everybody is ready to agree to. Besides, manna, by the bulk, figure, texture, and motion of its parts, has a power to produce the sensations of sickness, and sometimes of acute pains or gripings in us. That these ideas of sickness and pain are *not* in the manna, but effects of its operations on us, and are nowhere when we feel them not; this also every one readily agrees to. And yet men are hardly to be brought to think that sweetness and whiteness are not really in manna; which are but the effects of the operations of manna, by the motion, size, and figure of its particles, on the eyes and palate: as the pain and sickness caused by manna are confessedly nothing but the effects of its operations on the stomach and guts, by the size, motion, and figure of its insensible parts, (for by nothing else can a body operate, as has been proved): as if it could not operate on the eyes and palate, and thereby produce in the mind particular distinct ideas, which in itself it has not, as well as we allow it can operate on the guts and stomach, and thereby produce distinct ideas, which in itself it has not. These ideas, being all effects of the operations of manna on several parts of our bodies, by the size, figure, number, and motion of its parts;—why those produced by the eyes and palate should rather be thought to be really in the manna, than those produced by the stomach and guts; or why the pain and sickness,

ideas that are the effect of manna, should be thought to be nowhere when they are not felt; and yet the sweetness and whiteness, effects of the same manna on other parts of the body, by ways equally as unknown, should be thought to exist in the manna, when they are not seen or tasted, would need some reason to explain.

19. Let us consider the red and white colours in porphyry. Hinder light from striking on it, and its colours vanish; it no longer produces any such ideas in us: upon the return of light it produces these appearances on us again. Can any one think any real alterations are made in the porphyry by the presence or absence of light; and that those ideas of whiteness and redness are really in porphyry in the light, when it is plain *it has no colour in the dark?* It has, indeed, such a configuration of particles, both night and day, as are apt, by the rays of light rebounding from some parts of that hard stone, to produce in us the idea of redness, and from others the idea of whiteness; but whiteness or redness are not in it at any time, but such a texture that hath the power to produce such a sensation in us.

20. Pound an almond, and the clear white colour will be altered into a dirty one, and the sweet taste into an oily one. What real alteration can the beating of the pestle make in any body, but an alteration of the texture of it?

21. Ideas being thus distinguished and understood, we may be able to give an account how the same water, at the same time, may produce the idea of cold by one hand and of heat by the other: whereas it is impossible that the same water, if those ideas were really in it, should at the same time be both hot and cold. For, if we imagine *warmth,* as it is in our hands, to be nothing but a certain sort and degree of motion in the minute particles of our nerves or animal spirits, we may understand how it is possible that the same water may, at the same time, produce the sensations of heat in one hand and cold in the other; which yet *figure* never does, that never producing the idea of a square by one hand which has produced the idea of a globe by another. But if the sensation of heat and cold be nothing but the increase or diminution of the motion of the minute parts of our bodies, caused by the corpuscles of any other body, it is easy to be understood, that if that motion be greater in one hand than in the other; if a body be applied to the two hands, which has in its minute particles a greater motion than in those of one of the hands, and a less than in those of the other, it will increase the motion of the one hand and lessen it in the other; and so cause the different sensations of heat and cold that depend thereon.

22. I have in what just goes before been engaged in physical inquiries a little further than perhaps I intended. But, it being necessary to make the nature of sensation a little understood; and to make the difference between the *qualities* in bodies, and the *ideas* produced by them in the mind, to be distinctly conceived, without which it were impossible to discourse intelligibly of them;—I hope I shall be pardoned this little excursion into natural philosophy; it being necessary in our present inquiry to distinguish the *primary* and *real* qualities of bodies, which are always in them (viz. solidity, extension, figure, number, and motion, or rest, and are sometimes perceived by us, viz. when the bodies they are in are big enough singly to be discerned), from those *secondary* and *imputed* qualities, which are but the powers of several combinations of those primary ones, when they operate without being distinctly discerned;—whereby we may also come to know what ideas are, and what are not, resemblances of something really existing in the bodies we denominate from them.

23. The qualities, then, that are in bodies, rightly considered, are of three sorts:—

First, The bulk, figure, number, situation, and motion or rest of their solid parts. Those are in them, whether we perceive them or not; and when they are of that size that we can discover them, we have by these an idea of the thing as it is in itself; as is plain in artificial things. These I call *primary qualities.*

Secondly, The power that is in any body, by reason of its insensible primary qualities, to operate after a peculiar manner on any of our senses, and thereby produce in *us* the different ideas of several colours, sounds, smells, tastes, &c. These are usually called *sensible qualities.*

Thirdly, The power that is in any body, by reason of the particular constitution of its primary qualities, to make such a change in the bulk, figure, texture, and motion of *another body,* as to make it operate on our senses differently from what it did before. Thus the sun has a power to make wax white, and fire to make lead fluid. [These are usually called *powers.*]

The first of these, as has been said, I think may be properly called real, original, or primary qualities; because they are in the things themselves, whether they are perceived or not: and upon their different modifications it is that the secondary qualities depend.

The other two are only powers to act differently upon other things: which powers result from the different modifications of those primary qualities.

24. But, though the two latter sorts of qualities are powers barely, and nothing but powers, relating to several other bodies, and resulting from the different modifications of the original qualities, yet they are generally otherwise thought of. For the *second* sort, viz. the powers to produce several ideas in us, by our senses, are looked upon as real qualities in the things thus affecting us: but the *third* sort are called and esteemed barely powers, e.g., The idea of heat or light, which we receive by our eyes, or touch, from the sun, are commonly thought real qualities existing in the sun, and something more than mere powers in it. But when we consider the sun in reference to wax, which it melts or blanches, we look on the whiteness and softness produced in the wax, not as qualities in the sun, but effects produced by powers in it. Whereas, if rightly considered, these qualities of light and warmth, which are perceptions in me when I am warmed or enlightened by the sun, are no otherwise in the sun, than the changes made in the wax, when it is blanched or melted, are in the sun. They are all of them equally *powers in the sun, depending on its primary qualities;* whereby it is able, in the one case, so to alter the bulk, figure, texture, or motion of some of the insensible parts of my eyes or hands, as thereby to produce in me the idea of light or heat; and in the other, it is able so to alter the bulk, figure, texture, or motion of the insensible parts of the wax, as to make them fit to produce in me the distinct ideas of white and fluid.

25. The reason why the one are ordinarily taken for real qualities, and the other only for bare powers, seems to be, because the ideas we have of distinct colours, sounds, &c., containing nothing at all in them of bulk, figure, or motion, we are not apt to think them the effects of these primary qualities; which appear not, to our senses, to operate in their production, and with which they have not any apparent congruity or conceivable connexion. Hence it is that we are so forward to imagine, that those ideas are the resemblances of something really existing in the objects themselves: since sensation discovers nothing of bulk, figure, or motion of parts in their production; nor can reason show how bodies, *by their bulk, figure, and motion,* should produce in the mind the ideas of blue or yellow, &c. But, in the other case, in the operations of bodies changing the qualities one of another, we plainly discover that the quality produced hath commonly no resemblance with anything in the thing producing it; wherefore we look on it as a bare effect of power. For, through receiving the idea of heat or light from the sun, we are apt to think *it* is a perception and resemblance of such a quality in the sun; yet when we see wax, or a fair face, receive change of colour from the sun, we cannot imagine *that* to be the reception or resemblance of anything in the sun, because we find not those different colours in the sun itself. For, our senses being able to observe a likeness or unlikeness of sensible qualities in two different external objects, we forwardly enough conclude the production of any sensible quality in any subject to be an effect of bare power, and not the communication of any quality which was really in the efficient, when we find no such sensible quality in the thing that produced it. But our senses, not being able to discover any unlikeness between the idea produced in us, and the quality of the object producing it, we are apt to imagine that our ideas are resemblances of something in the objects, and not the effects of certain powers placed in the modification of their primary qualities, with which primary qualities the ideas produced in us have no resemblance.

26. To conclude. Beside those before-mentioned primary qualities in bodies, viz. bulk, figure, extension, number; and motion of their solid parts; all the rest, whereby we take notice of bodies, and distinguish them one from another, are nothing else but several powers in them, depending on those

primary qualities; whereby they are fitted, either by immediately operating on our bodies to produce several different ideas in us; or else, by operating on other bodies, so to change their primary qualities as to render them capable of producing ideas in us different from what before they did. The former of these, I think, may be called secondary qualities *immediately perceivable:* the latter, secondary qualities, *mediately perceivable.*

OF OUR KNOWLEDGE OF THE EXISTENCE OF OTHER THINGS

1. The knowledge of our own being we have by intuition. The existence of a God, reason clearly makes known to us, as has been shown.

The knowledge of the existence of *any other thing* we can have only by *sensation:* for there being no necessary connexion of real existence with any *idea* a man hath in his memory; nor of any other existence but that of God with the existence of any particular man: no particular man can know the existence of any other being, but only when, by actual operating upon him, it makes itself perceived by him. For, the having the idea of anything in our mind, no more proves the existence of that thing, than the picture of a man evidences his being in the world, or the visions of a dream make thereby a true history.

2. It is therefore the *actual receiving* of ideas from without that gives us notice of the existence of other things, and makes us know, that something doth exist at that time without us, which causes that idea in us; though perhaps we neither know nor consider how it does it. For it takes not from the certainty of our senses, and the ideas we receive by them, that we know not the manner wherein they are produced: e.g. whilst I write this, I have, by the paper affecting my eyes, that idea produced in my mind, which, whatever object causes, I call *white;* by which I know that that quality or accident (i.e. whose appearance before my eyes always causes that idea) doth really exist, and hath a being without me. And of this, the greatest assurance I can possibly have, and to which my faculties can attain, is the testimony of my eyes, which are the proper and sole judges of this thing; whose testimony I have reason to rely on as so certain, that I can no more doubt, whilst I write this, that I see white and black, and that something really exists that causes that sensation in me, than that I write or move my hand; which is a certainty as great as human nature is capable of, concerning the existence of anything, but a man's self alone, and of God.

3. The notice we have by our senses of the existing of things without us, though it be not altogether so certain as our intuitive knowledge, or the deductions of our reason employed about the clear abstract ideas of our own minds; yet it is an assurance that deserves the name of *knowledge*. If we persuade ourselves that our faculties act and inform us right concerning the existence of those objects that affect them, it cannot pass for an ill-grounded confidence: for I think nobody can, in earnest, be so sceptical as to be uncertain of the existence of those things which he sees and feels. At least, he that can doubt so far, (whatever he may have with his own thoughts,) will never have any controversy with me; since he can never be sure I say anything contrary to his own opinion. As to myself, I think God has given me assurance enough of the existence of things without me: since, by their different application, I can produce in myself both pleasure and pain, which is one great concernment of my present state. This is certain: the confidence that our faculties do not herein deceive us, is the greatest assurance we are capable of concerning the existence of material beings. For we cannot act anything but by our faculties; nor talk of knowledge itself, but by the help of those faculties which are fitted to apprehend even what knowledge is.

But besides the assurance we have from our senses themselves, that they do not err in the information they give us of the existence of things without us, when they are affected by them, we are further confirmed in this assurance by other concurrent reasons:—

4. I. It is plain those perceptions are produced in us by exterior causes affecting our senses: because those that want the *organs* of any sense, never can have the ideas belonging to that sense produced in their minds. This is too evident to be doubted: and therefore we cannot but be assured that they come in by the organs of that sense, and no other way. The organs themselves, it is plain, do not produce

them: for then the eyes of a man in the dark would produce colours, and his nose smell roses in the winter: but we see nobody gets the relish of a pineapple, till he goes to the Indies, where it is, and tastes it.

5. II. Because sometimes I find that *I cannot avoid the having those ideas produced in my mind.* For though, when my eyes are shut, or windows fast, I can at pleasure recall to my mind the ideas of light, or the sun, which former sensations had lodged in my memory; so I can at pleasure lay by *that* idea, and take into my view that of the smell of a rose, or taste of sugar. But, if I turn my eyes at noon towards the sun, I cannot avoid the ideas which the light or sun then produces in me. So that there is a manifest difference between the ideas laid up in my memory, (over which, if they were there only, I should have constantly the same power to dispose of them, and lay them by at pleasure,) and those which force themselves upon me, and I cannot avoid having. And therefore it must needs be some exterior cause, and the brisk acting of some objects without me, whose efficacy I cannot resist, that produces those ideas in my mind, whether I will or no. Besides, there is nobody who doth not perceive the difference in himself between contemplating the sun, as he hath the idea of it in his memory, and actually looking upon it: of which two, his perception is so distinct, that few of his ideas are more distinguishable one from another. And therefore he hath certain knowledge that they are not *both* memory, or the actions of his mind, and fancies only within him; but that actual seeing hath a cause without.

6. III. Add to this, that many of those ideas are *produced in us with pain,* which afterwards we remember without the least offence. Thus, the pain of heat or cold, when the idea of it is revived in our minds, gives us no disturbance; which, when felt, was very troublesome; and is again, when actually repeated: which is occasioned by the disorder the external object causes in our bodies when applied to them: and we remember the pains of hunger, thirst, or the headache, without any pain at all; which would either never disturb us, or else constantly do it, as often as we thought of it, were there nothing more but ideas floating in our minds, and appearances entertaining our fancies, without the real existence of things affecting us from abroad. The same may be said of *pleasure,* accompanying several actual sensations. And though mathematical demonstration depends not upon sense, yet the examining them by diagrams gives great credit to the evidence of our sight, and seems to give it a certainty approaching to that of demonstration itself. For, it would be very strange, that a man should allow it for an undeniable truth, that two angles of a figure, which he measures by lines and angles of a diagram, should be bigger one than the other, and yet doubt of the existence of those lines and angles, which by looking on he makes use of to measure that by.

7. IV. Our *senses* in many cases *bear witness to the truth of each other's report,* concerning the existence of sensible things without us. He that *sees* a fire, may, if he doubt whether it be anything more than a bare fancy, *feel* it too; and be convinced, by putting his hand in it. Which certainly could never be put into such exquisite pain by a bare idea or phantom, unless that the pain be a fancy too: which yet he cannot, when the burn is well, by raising the idea of it, bring upon himself again.

Thus I see, whilst I write this, I can change the appearance of the paper; and by designing the letters, tell *beforehand* what new idea it shall exhibit the very next moment, by barely drawing my pen over it: which will neither appear (let me fancy as much as I will) if my hands stand still; or though I move my pen, if my eyes be shut: nor, when those characters are once made on the paper, can I choose afterwards but see them as they are; that is, have the ideas of such letters as I have made. Whence it is manifest, that they are not barely the sport and play of my own imagination, when I find that the characters that were made at the pleasure of my own thoughts, do not obey them; nor yet cease to be, whenever I shall fancy it, but continue to affect my senses constantly and regularly, according to the figures I made them. To which if we will add, that the sight of those shall, from another man, draw such sounds as I beforehand design they shall stand for, there will be little reason left to doubt that those words I write do really exist without me, when they cause a long series of regular sounds to affect my ears, which could not be the effect of my imagination, nor could my memory retain them in that order.

8. But yet, if after all this any one will be so sceptical as to distrust his senses, and to affirm that all we see and hear, feel and taste, think and do, during our whole being, is but the series and deluding appearances of a long dream, whereof there is no reality; and therefore will question the existence of all things, or our knowledge of anything: I must desire him to consider, that, if all be a dream, then he doth but dream that he makes the question, and so it is not much matter that a waking man should answer him. But yet, if he pleases, he may dream that I make him this answer, That the certainty of things existing in *rerum natura* when we have the testimony of our senses for it is not only as great as our frame can attain to, but as our condition needs. For, our faculties being suited not to the full extent of being, nor to a perfect, clear, comprehensive knowledge of things free from all doubt and scruple; but to the preservation of us, in whom they are; and accommodated to the use of life: they serve to our purpose well enough, if they will but give us certain notice of those things, which are convenient or inconvenient to us. For he that sees a candle burning, and hath experimented the force of its flame by putting his finger in it, will little doubt that this is something existing without him, which does him harm, and puts him to great pain: which is assurance enough, when no man requires greater certainty to govern his actions by than what is as certain as his actions themselves. And if our dreamer pleases to try whether the glowing heat of a glass furnace be barely a wandering imagination in a drowsy man's fancy, by putting his hand into it, he may perhaps be wakened into a certainty greater than he could wish, that it is something more than bare imagination. So that this evidence is as great as we can desire, being as certain to us as our pleasure or pain, i.e. happiness or misery; beyond which we have no concernment, either of knowing or being. Such an assurance of the existence of things without us is sufficient to direct us in the attaining the good and avoiding the evil which is caused by them, which is the important concernment we have of being made acquainted with them.

9. In fine, then, when our senses do actually convey into our understandings any idea, we cannot but be satisfied that there doth something *at that time* really exist without us, which doth affect our senses, and by them give notice of itself to our apprehensive faculties, and actually produce that idea which we then perceive: and we cannot so far distrust their testimony, as to doubt that such *collections* of simple ideas as we have observed by our senses to be united together, do really exist together. But this knowledge extends as far as the present testimony of our senses, employed about particular objects that do then affect them, and no further. For if I saw such a collection of simple ideas as is wont to be called *man*, existing together one minute since, and am now alone, I cannot be certain that the same man exists now, since there is no *necessary connexion* of his existence a minute since with his existence now: by a thousand ways he may cease to be, since I had the testimony of my senses for his existence. And if I cannot be certain that the man I saw last to-day is now in being, I can less be certain that he is so who hath been longer removed from my senses, and I have not seen since yesterday, or since the last year: and much less can I be certain of the existence of men that I never saw. And, therefore, though it be highly probable that millions of men do now exist, yet, whilst I am alone, writing this, I have not that certainty of it which we strictly call knowledge; though the great likelihood of it puts me past doubt, and it be reasonable for me to do several things upon the confidence that there are men (and men also of my acquaintance, with whom I have to do) now in the world: but this is but probability, not knowledge.

10. Whereby yet we may observe how foolish and vain a thing it is for a man of a narrow knowledge, who having reason given him to judge of the different evidence and probability of things, and to be swayed accordingly; how vain, I say, it is to expect demonstration and certainty in things not capable of it; and refuse assent to very rational propositions, and act contrary to very plain and clear truths, because they cannot be made out so evident, as to surmount every the least (I will not say reason, but) pretence of doubting. He that, in the ordinary affairs of life, would admit of nothing but direct

plain demonstration, would be sure of nothing in this world, but of perishing quickly. The wholesomeness of his meat or drink would not give him reason to venture on it: and I would fain know what it is he could do upon such grounds as are capable of no doubt, no objection.

Three Dialogues between Hylas and Philonous*

GEORGE BERKELEY

George Berkeley (1685–1753), the Anglican Bishop of Cloyne, was born in Ireland.

THE FIRST DIALOGUE

PHILONOUS. Good morning, Hylas. I did not expect to find you abroad so early.

Hylas. It is indeed something unusual; but my thoughts were so taken up with a subject I was discoursing of last night that, finding I could not sleep, I resolved to rise and take a turn in the garden.

Phil. It happened well, to let you see what innocent and agreeable pleasures you lose every morning. Can there be a pleasanter time of the day or a more delightful season of the year? That purple sky, those wild but sweet notes of birds, the fragrant bloom upon the trees and flowers, the gentle influence of the rising sun—these and a thousand nameless beauties of nature inspire the soul with secret transports; its faculties, too, being at this time fresh and lively, are fit for those meditations which the solitude of a garden and tranquility of the morning naturally dispose us to. But I am afraid I interrupt your thoughts, for you seemed very intent on something.

Hyl. It is true, I was, and shall be obliged to you if you will permit me to go on in the same vein; not that I would by any means deprive myself of your company, for my thoughts always flow more easily in conversation with a friend than when I am alone; but my request is that you would suffer me to impart my reflections to you.

Phil. With all my heart, it is what I should have requested myself if you had not prevented me.

Hyl. I was considering the old fate of those men who have in all ages, through an affectation of being distinguished from the vulgar, or some unaccountable turn of thought, pretended either to believe nothing at all or to believe the most extravagant things in the world. This, however, might be borne if their paradoxes and skepticism did not draw after them some consequences of general disadvantage to mankind. But the mischief lies here: that when men of less leisure see them who are supposed to have spent their whole time in the pursuits of knowledge professing an entire ignorance of all things or advancing such notions as are repugnant to plain and commonly received principles, they will be tempted to entertain suspicions concerning the most important truths, which they had hitherto held sacred and unquestionable.

Phil. I entirely agree with you as to the ill tendency of the affected doubts of some philosophers and fantastical conceits of others. I am even so far gone of late in this way of thinking that I have quitted several of the sublime notions I had got in their schools for vulgar opinions. And I give it you

**First published in 1713.*

on my word, since this revolt from metaphysical notions to the plain dictates of nature and common sense, I find my understanding strangely enlightened, so that I can now easily comprehend a great many things which before were all mystery and riddle.

Hyl. I am glad to find there was nothing in the accounts I heard of you.

Phil. Pray, what were those?

Hyl. You were represented in last night's conversation as one who maintained the most extravagant opinion that ever entered into the mind of man, to wit, that there is no such thing as "material substance" in the world.

Phil. That there is no such thing as what philosophers call "material substance," I am seriously persuaded; but if I were made to see anything absurd or skeptical in this, I should then have the same reason to renounce this that I imagine I have now to reject the contrary opinion.

Hyl. What! Can anything be more fantastical, more repugnant to common sense or a more manifest piece of skepticism than to believe there is no such thing as matter?

Phil. Softly, good Hylas. What if it should prove that you, who hold there is, are, by virtue of that opinion, a greater skeptic and maintain more paradoxes and repugnances to common sense than I who believe no such thing?

Hyl. You may as soon persuade me the part is greater than the whole, as that, in order to avoid absurdity and skepticism, I should ever be obliged to give up my opinion in this point.

Phil. Well then, are you content to admit that opinion for true which, upon examination, shall appear most agreeable to common sense and remote from skepticism?

Hyl. With all my heart. Since you are for raising disputes about the plainest things in nature, I am content for once to hear what you have to say.

Phil. Pray, Hylas, what do you mean by a "skeptic"?

Hyl. I mean what all men mean, one that doubts of everything.

Phil. He then who entertains no doubt concerning some particular point, with regard to that point cannot be thought a skeptic.

Hyl. I agree with you.

Phil. Whether does doubting consist in embracing the affirmative or negative side of a question?

Hyl. In neither; for whoever understands English cannot but know that *doubting* signifies a suspense between both.

Phil. He then that denies any point can no more be said to doubt of it than he who affirms it with the same degree of assurance.

Hyl. True.

Phil. And, consequently, for such his denial is no more to be esteemed a skeptic than the other.

Hyl. I acknowledge it.

Phil. How comes it to pass then, Hylas, that you pronounce me a skeptic because I deny what you affirm, to wit, the existence of matter? Since, for aught you can tell, I am as peremptory in my denial as you in your affirmation.

Hyl. Hold, Philonous, I have been a little out in my definition; but every false step a man makes in discourse is not to be insisted on. I said indeed that a "skeptic" was one who doubted of everything, but I should have added: or who denies the reality and truth of things.

Phil. What things? Do you mean the principles and theorems of sciences? But these you know are universal intellectual notions, and consequently independent of matter; the denial therefore of this does not imply the denying them.

Hyl. I grant it. But are there no other things? What think you of distrusting the senses, of denying the real existence of sensible things, or pretending to know nothing of them. Is not this sufficient to denominate a man a skeptic?

Phil. Shall we therefore examine which of us it is that denies the reality of sensible things or professes the greatest ignorance of them, since, if I take you rightly, he is to be esteemed the greatest skeptic?

Hyl. That is what I desire.

Phil. What mean you by "sensible things"?

Hyl. Those things which are perceived by the senses. Can you imagine that I mean anything else?

Phil. Pardon me, Hylas, if I am desirous clearly to apprehend your notions, since this may much shorten our inquiry. Suffer me then to ask you this further question. Are those things only perceived by the senses which are perceived immediately? Or may those things properly be said to be "sensible" which are perceived mediately, or not without the intervention of others?

Hyl. I do not sufficiently understand you.

Phil. In reading a book, what I immediately perceive are the letters, but mediately, or by means of these, are suggested to my mind the notions of God, virtue, truth, etc. Now, that the letters are truly sensible things, or perceived by sense, there is no doubt; but I would know whether you take the things suggested by them to be so too.

Hyl. No, certainly; it were absurd to think God or virtue sensible things, though they may be signified and suggested to the mind by sensible marks with which they have an arbitrary connection.

Phil. It seems, then, that by "sensible things" you mean those only which can be perceived immediately by sense.

Hyl. Right.

Phil. Does it not follow from this that, though I see one part of the sky red, and another blue, and that my reason does thence evidently conclude there must be some cause of that diversity of colors, yet that cause cannot be said to be a sensible thing or perceived by the sense of seeing?

Hyl. It does.

Phil. In like manner, though I hear variety of sounds, yet I cannot be said to hear the causes of those sounds?

Hyl. You cannot.

Phil. And when by my touch I perceive a thing to be hot and heavy, I cannot say, with any truth or propriety, that I feel the cause of its heat or weight?

Hyl. To prevent any more questions of this kind, I tell you once for all that by "sensible things" I mean those only which are perceived by sense, and that in truth the senses perceive nothing which they do not perceive immediately, for they make no inferences. The deducing therefore of causes or occasions from effects and appearances, which alone are perceived by sense, entirely relates to reason.

Phil. This point then is agreed between us—that *sensible things are those only which are immediately perceived by sense.* You will further inform me whether we immediately perceive by sight anything besides light and colors and figures; or by hearing, anything but sounds; by the palate, anything besides tastes; by the smell, besides odors; or by the touch, more than tangible qualities.

Hyl. We do not.

Phil. It seems, therefore, that if you take away all sensible qualities, there remains nothing sensible?

Hyl. I grant it.

Phil. Sensible things therefore are nothing else but so many sensible qualities or combinations of sensible qualities?

Hyl. Nothing else.

Phil. Heat is then a sensible thing?

Hyl. Certainly.

Phil. Does the reality of sensible things consist in being perceived, or is it something distinct from their being perceived, and that bears no relation to the mind?

Hyl. To *exist* is one thing, and to be *perceived* is another.

Phil. I speak with regard to sensible things only; and of these I ask, whether by their real existence you mean a subsistence exterior to the mind and distinct from their being perceived?

Hyl. I mean a real absolute being, distinct from and without any relation to their being perceived.

Phil. Heat therefore, if it be allowed a real being, must exist without the mind?

Hyl. It must.

Phil. Tell me, Hylas, is this real existence equally compatible to all degrees of heat, which we perceive, or is there any reason why we should attribute it to some and deny it to others? And if there be, pray, let me know that reason.

Hyl. Whatever degree of heat we perceive by sense, we may be sure the same exists in the object that occasions it.

Phil. What! the greatest as well as the least?

Hyl. I tell you, the reason is plainly the same in respect of both: they are both perceived by sense; nay, the greater degree of heat is more sensibly perceived; and consequently, if there is any difference, we are more certain of its real existence than we can be of the reality of a lesser degree.

Phil. But is not the most vehement and intense degree of heat a very great pain?

Hyl. No one can deny it.

Phil. And is any unperceiving thing capable of pain or pleasure?

Hyl. No, certainly.

Phil. Is your material substance a senseless being or a being endowed with sense and perception?

Hyl. It is senseless, without doubt.

Phil. It cannot, therefore, be the subject of pain?

Hyl. By no means.

Phil. Nor, consequently, of the greatest heat perceived by sense, since you acknowledge this to be no small pain?

Hyl. I grant it.

Phil. What shall we say then of your external object: is it a material substance, or no?

Hyl. It is a material substance with the sensible qualities inhering in it.

Phil. How then can a great heat exist in it, since you own it cannot in a material substance? I desire you would clear this point.

Hyl. Hold, Philonous, I fear I was out in yielding intense heat to be a pain. It should seem rather that pain is something distinct from heat, and the consequence or effect of it.

Phil. Upon putting your hand near the fire, do you perceive one simple uniform sensation or two distinct sensations?

Hyl. But one simple sensation.

Phil. Is not the heat immediately perceived?

Hyl. It is.

Phil. And the pain?

Hyl. True.

Phil. Seeing therefore they are both immediately perceived at the same time, and the fire affects you only with one simple or uncompounded idea, it follows that this same simple idea is both the intense heat immediately perceived and the pain; and, consequently, that the intense heat immediately perceived is nothing distinct from a particular sort of pain.

Hyl. It seems so.

Phil. Again, try in your thoughts, Hylas, if you can conceive a vehement sensation to be without pain or pleasure.

Hyl. I cannot.

Phil. Or can you frame to yourself an idea of sensible pain or pleasure, in general, abstracted from every particular idea of heat, cold, tastes, smells?

Hyl. I do not find that I can.

Phil. Does it not therefore follow that sensible pain is nothing distinct from those sensations or ideas—in an intense degree?

Hyl. It is undeniable; and, to speak the truth, I begin to suspect a very great heat cannot exist but in a mind perceiving it.

Phil. What! are you then in that *skeptical* state of suspense, between affirming and denying?

Hyl. I think I may be positive in the point. A very violent and painful heat cannot exist without the mind.

Phil. It has not therefore, according to you, any real being?

Hyl. I own it.

Phil. Is it therefore certain that there is no body in nature really hot?

Hyl. I have not denied there is any real heat in bodies. I only say there is no such thing as an intense real heat.

Phil. But did you not say before that all degrees of heat were equally real, or, if there was any difference, that the greater were more undoubtedly real than the lesser?

Hyl. True; but it was because I did not then consider the ground there is for distinguishing between them, which I now plainly see. And it is this: because intense heat is nothing else but a particular kind of painful sensation, and pain cannot exist but in a perceiving being, it follows that no intense heat can really exist in an unperceiving corporeal substance. But this is no reason why we should deny heat in an inferior degree to exist in such a substance.

Phil. But how shall we be able to discern those degrees of heat which exist only in the mind from those which exist without it?

Hyl. That is no difficult matter. You know the least pain cannot exist unperceived; whatever, therefore, degree of heat is a pain exists only in the mind. But as for all other degrees of heat nothing obliges us to think the same of them.

Phil. I think you granted before that no unperceiving being was capable of pleasure any more than of pain.

Hyl. I did.

Phil. And is not warmth, or a more gentle degree of heat than what causes uneasiness, a pleasure?

Hyl. What then?

Phil. Consequently, it cannot exist without the mind in an unperceiving substance, or body.

Hyl. So it seems.

Phil. Since, therefore, as well those degrees of heat that are not painful, as those that are, can exist only in a thinking substance, may we not conclude that external bodies are absolutely incapable of any degree of heat whatsoever?

Hyl. On second thoughts, I do not think it is so evident that warmth is a pleasure as that a great degree of heat is a pain.

Phil. I do not pretend that warmth is as great a pleasure as heat is a pain. But if you grant it to be even a small pleasure, it serves to make good my conclusion.

Hyl. I could rather call it an "indolence." It seems to be nothing more than a privation of both pain and pleasure. And that such a quality or state as this may agree to an unthinking substance, I hope you will not deny.

Phil. If you are resolved to maintain that warmth, or a gentle degree of heat, is no pleasure, I know not how to convince you otherwise than by appealing to your own sense. But what think you of cold?

Hyl. The same that I do of heat. An intense degree of cold is a pain; for to feel a very great cold is to perceive a great uneasiness; it cannot therefore exist without the mind; but a lesser degree of cold may, as well as a lesser degree of heat.

Phil. Those bodies, therefore, upon whose application to our own we perceive a moderate degree of heat must be concluded to have a moderate degree of heat or warmth in them; and those upon whose application we feel a like degree of cold must be thought to have cold in them.

Hyl. They must.

Phil. Can any doctrine be true that necessarily leads a man into an absurdity?

Hyl. Without doubt it cannot.

Phil. Is it not an absurdity to think that the same thing should be at the same time both cold and warm?

Hyl. It is.

Phil. Suppose now one of your hands is hot, and the other cold, and that they are both at once put into the same vessel of water, in an intermediate state, will not the water seem cold to one hand, and warm to the other?

Hyl. It will.

Phil. Ought we not therefore, by your principles, to conclude it is really both cold and warm at the same time, that is, according to your own concession, to believe an absurdity?

Hyl. I confess it seems so.

Phil. Consequently, the principles themselves are false, since you have granted that no true principle leads to an absurdity.

Hyl. But, after all, can anything be more absurd than to say, *there is no heat in the fire?*

Phil. To make the point still clearer; tell me whether, in two cases exactly alike, we ought not to make the same judgment?

Hyl. We ought.

Phil. When a pin pricks your finger, does it not rend and divide the fibres of your flesh?

Hyl. It does.

Phil. And when a coal burns your finger, does it any more?

Hyl. It does not.

Phil. Since, therefore, you neither judge the sensation itself occasioned by the pin, nor anything like it to be in the pin, you should not, conformably to what you have now granted, judge the sensation occasioned by the fire, or anything like it, to be in the fire.

Hyl. Well, since it must be so, I am content to yield this point and acknowledge that heat and cold are only sensations existing in our minds. But there still remain qualities enough to secure the reality of external things.

Phil. But what will you say, Hylas, if it shall appear that the case is the same with regard to all other sensible qualities, and that they can no more be supposed to exist without the mind than heat and cold?

Hyl. Then, indeed, you will have done something to the purpose; but that is what I despair of seeing proved.

Phil. Let us examine them in order. What think you of tastes—do they exist without the mind, or no?

Hyl. Can any man in his senses doubt whether sugar is sweet or wormwood bitter?

Phil. Inform me, Hylas. Is a sweet taste a particular kind of pleasure or pleasant sensation, or is it not?

Hyl. It is.

Phil. And is not bitterness some kind of uneasiness or pain?

Hyl. I grant it.

Phil. If therefore, sugar and wormwood are unthinking corporeal substances existing without the mind, how can sweetness and bitterness, that is, pleasure and pain, agree to them?

Hyl. Hold, Philonous. I now see what it was [that] deluded me all this time. You asked whether heat and cold, sweetness and bitterness, were not particular sorts of pleasure and pain; to which I answered simply that they were. Whereas I should have thus distinguished: those qualities as perceived by us are pleasures or pains, but not as existing in the external objects. We must not therefore conclude absolutely that there is no heat in the fire or sweetness in the sugar, but only that heat or sweetness, as perceived by us, are not in the fire or sugar. What say you to this?

Phil. I say it is nothing to the purpose. Our discourse proceeded altogether concerning sensible things, which you defined to be "the things we immediately perceive by our senses." Whatever other qualities, therefore, you speak of, as distinct from these, I know nothing of them, neither do they at all belong to the point in dispute. You may, indeed, pretend to have discovered certain qualities which you do not perceive and assert those insensible qualities exist in fire and sugar. But what use can be made of this to your present purpose, I am at a loss to conceive. Tell me then once more, do you acknowledge that heat and cold, sweetness and bitterness (meaning those qualities which are perceived by the senses), do not exist without the mind?

Hyl. I see it is to no purpose to hold out, so I give up the cause as to those mentioned qualities, though I profess it sounds oddly to say that sugar is not sweet.

Phil. But, for your further satisfaction, take this along with you: that which at other times seems sweet shall, to a distempered palate, appear bitter, and nothing can be plainer than that divers persons perceive different tastes in the same food, since that which one man delights in, another abhors. And how could this be if the taste was something really inherent in the food?

Hyl. I acknowledge I know not how.

Phil. In the next place, odors are to be considered. And with regard to these I would fain know whether what has been said of tastes does not exactly agree to them? Are they not so many pleasing or displeasing sensations?

Hyl. They are.

Phil. Can you then conceive it possible that they should exist in an unperceiving thing?

Hyl. I cannot.

Phil. Or can you imagine that filth and ordure affect those brute animals that feed on them out of choice with the same smells which we perceive in them?

Hyl. By no means.

Phil. May we not therefore conclude of smells, as of the other forementioned qualities, that they cannot exist in any but a perceiving substance or mind?

Hyl. I think so.

Phil. Then as to sounds, what must we think of them, are they accidents really inherent in external bodies or not?

Hyl. That they inhere not in the sonorous bodies is plain from hence; because a bell struck in the exhausted receiver of an air-pump sends forth no sound. The air, therefore, must be thought the subject of sound.

Phil. What reason is there for that, Hylas?

Hyl. Because, when any motion is raised in the air, we perceive a sound greater or lesser, in proportion to the air's motion; but without some motion in the air we never hear any sound at all.

Phil. And granting that we never hear a sound but when some motion is produced in the air, yet I do not see how you can infer from thence that the sound itself is in the air.

Hyl. It is this very motion in the external air that produces in the mind the sensation of sound. For, striking on the drum of the ear, it causes a vibration which by the auditory nerves being communicated to the brain, the soul is thereupon affected with the sensation called "sound."

Phil. What! is sound then a sensation?

Hyl. I tell you, as perceived by us it is a particular sensation in the mind.

Phil. And can any sensation exist without the mind?

Hyl. No, certainly.

Phil. How then can sound, being a sensation, exist in the air if by the "air" you mean a senseless substance existing without the mind?

Hyl. You must distinguish, Philonous, between sound as it is perceived by us, and as it is in itself; or (which is the same thing) between the sound we immediately perceive and that which exists without us. The former, indeed, is a particular kind of sensation, but the latter is merely a vibrative or undulatory motion in the air.

Phil. I thought I had already obviated that distinction by the answer I gave when you were applying it in a like case before. But, to say no more of that, are you sure then that sound is really nothing but motion?

Hyl. I am.

Phil. Whatever, therefore, agrees to real sound may with truth be attributed to motion?

Hyl. It may.

Phil. It is then good sense to speak of "motion" as of a thing that is *loud, sweet, acute,* or *grave.*

Hyl. I see you are resolved not to understand me. Is it not evident those accidents or modes belong only to sensible sound, or sound in the common acceptation of the word, but not to sound in the real and philosophic sense, which, as I just now told you, is nothing but a certain motion of the air?

Phil. It seems then there are two sorts of sound—the one vulgar, or that which is heard, the other philosophical and real?

Hyl. Even so.

Phil. And the latter consists in motion?

Hyl. I told you so before.

Phil. Tell me, Hylas, to which of the senses, think you, the idea of motion belongs? To the hearing?

Hyl. No, certainly; but to the sight and touch.

Phil. It should follow then that, according to you, real sounds may possibly be *seen* or *felt,* but never *heard.*

Hyl. Look you, Philonous, you may, if you please, make a jest of my opinion, but that will not alter the truth of things. I own, indeed, the inferences you draw me into sound something oddly, but common language, you know, is framed by, and for the use of, the vulgar. We must not therefore wonder if expressions adapted to exact philosophic notions seem uncouth and out of the way.

Phil. Is it come to that? I assure you I imagine myself to have gained no small point since you make so light of departing from common phrases and opinions, it being a main part of our inquiry to examine whose notions are widest of the common road and most repugnant to the general sense of the world. But can you think it no more than a philosophical paradox to say that "real sounds are never heard," and that the idea of them is obtained by some other sense? And is there nothing in this contrary to nature and the truth of things?

Hyl. To deal ingenuously, I do not like it. And, after the concessions already made, I had as well grant that sounds, too, have no real being without the mind.

Phil. And I hope you will make no difficulty to acknowledge the same of colors.

Hyl. Pardon me; the case of colors is very different. Can anything be plainer than that we see them on the objects?

Phil. The objects you speak of are, I suppose, corporeal substances existing without the mind?

Hyl. They are.

Phil. And have true and real colors inhering in them?

Hyl. Each visible object has that color which we see in it.

Phil. How! is there anything visible but what we perceive by sight?

Hyl. There is not.

Phil. And do we perceive anything by sense which we do not perceive immediately?

Hyl. How often must I be obliged to repeat the same thing? I tell you, we do not.

Phil. Have patience, good Hylas, and tell me once more whether there is anything immediately perceived by the senses except sensible qualities. I know you asserted there was not; but I would now be informed whether you still persist in the same opinion.

Hyl. I do.

Phil. Pray, is your corporeal substance either a sensible quality or made up of sensible qualities?

Hyl. What a question that is! Who ever thought it was?

Phil. My reason for asking was, because in saying "each visible object has that color which we see in it," you make visible objects to be corporeal substances, which implies either that corporeal substances are sensible qualities or else that there is something besides sensible qualities perceived by sight; but as this point was formerly agreed between us, and is still maintained by you, it is a clear consequence that your corporeal substance is nothing distinct from sensible qualities.

Hyl. You may draw as many absurd consequences as you please and endeavor to perplex the plainest things, but you shall never persuade me out of my senses. I clearly understand my own meaning.

Phil. I wish you would make me understand it, too. But, since you are unwilling to have your notion of corporeal substance examined, I shall urge that point no further. Only be pleased to let me know whether the same colors which we see exist in external bodies or some other.

Hyl. The very same.

Phil. What! are then the beautiful red and purple we see on yonder clouds really in them? Or do you imagine they have in themselves any other form than that of a dark mist or vapor?

Hyl. I must own, Philonous, those colors are not really in the clouds as they seem to be at this distance. They are only apparent colors.

Phil. "Apparent" call you them? How shall we distinguish these apparent colors from real?

Hyl. Very easily. Those are to be thought apparent which, appearing only at a distance, vanish upon a nearer approach.

Phil. And those, I suppose, are to be thought real which are discovered by the most near and exact survey.

Hyl. Right.

Phil. Is the nearest and exactest survey made by the help of a microscope or by the naked eye?

Hyl. By a microscope, doubtless.

Phil. But a microscope often discovers colors in an object different from those perceived by the unassisted sight. And, in case we had microscopes magnifying to any assigned degree, it is certain that no object whatsoever, viewed through them, would appear in the same color which it exhibits to the naked eye.

Hyl. And what will you conclude from all this? You cannot argue that there are really and naturally no colors on objects because by artificial managements they may be altered or made to vanish.

Phil. I think it may evidently be concluded from your own concessions that all the colors we see with our naked eyes are only apparent as those on the clouds, since they vanish upon a more close and accurate inspection which is afforded us by a microscope. Then, as to what you say by way of prevention: I ask you whether the real and natural state of an object is better discovered by a very sharp and piercing sight or by one which is less sharp?

Hyl. By the former without doubt.

Phil. Is it not plain from dioptrics that microscopes make the sight more penetrating and represent objects as they would appear to the eye in case it were naturally endowed with a most exquisite sharpness?

Hyl. It is.

Phil. Consequently, the microscopical representation is to be thought that which best sets forth the real nature of the thing, or what it is in itself. The colors, therefore, by it perceived are more genuine and real than those perceived otherwise.

Hyl. I confess there is something in what you say.

Phil. Besides, it is not only possible but manifest that there actually are animals whose eyes are by nature framed to perceive those things which by reason of their minuteness escape our sight. What think you of those inconceivably small animals perceived by glasses? Must we suppose they are all stark blind? Or, in case they see, can it be imagined their sight has not the same use in preserving their bodies from injuries which appears in that of all other animals? And if it has, is it not evident they must see particles less than their own bodies, which will present them with a far different view in each object from that which strikes our senses? Even our own eyes do not always represent objects to us after the same manner. In the jaundice everyone knows that all things seem yellow. Is it not therefore highly probable those animals in whose eyes we discern a very different texture from that of ours, and whose bodies abound with different humors, do not see the same colors in every object that we do? From all which should it not seem to follow that all colors are equally apparent, and that none of those which we perceive are really inherent in any outward object?

Hyl. It should.

Phil. The point will be past all doubt if you consider that, in case colors were real properties or affections inherent in external bodies, they could admit of no alteration without some change wrought in the very bodies themselves; but is it not evident from what has been said that, upon the use of microscopes, upon a change happening in the humors of the eye, or a variation of distance, without any manner of real alteration in the thing itself, the colors of any object are either changed or totally disappear? Nay, all other circumstances remaining the same, change but the situation of some objects and they shall present different colors to the eye. The same thing happens upon viewing an object in various degrees of light. And what is more known than that the same bodies appear differently colored by candlelight from what they do in the open day? Add to these the experiment of a prism which, separating the heterogeneous rays of light alters the color of any object and will cause the whitest to appear of a deep blue or red to the naked eye. And now tell me whether you are still of opinion that every body has its true real color inhering in it; and if you think it has, I would fain know further from you what certain distance and position of the object, what peculiar texture and formation of the eye, what degree or kind of light is necessary for ascertaining that true color and distinguishing it from apparent ones.

Hyl. I own myself entirely satisfied that they are all equally apparent and that there is no such thing as color really inhering in external bodies, but that it is altogether in the light. And what confirms me in this opinion is that in proportion to the light colors are still more or less vivid; and if there be no light, then are there no colors perceived. Besides, allowing there are colors on external objects, yet, how is it possible for us to perceive them? For no external body affects the mind unless it acts first on our organs of sense. But the only action of bodies is motion, and motion cannot be communicated otherwise than by impulse. A distant object, therefore, cannot act on the eye, nor consequently make itself or its properties perceivable to the soul. Whence it plainly follows that it is immediately some contiguous substance which, operating on the eye, occasions a perception of colors; and such is light.

Phil. How! is light then a substance?

Hyl. I tell you, Philonous, external light is nothing but a thin fluid substance whose minute particles, being agitated with a brisk motion and in various manners reflected from the different surfaces of outward objects to the eyes, communicate different motions to the optic nerves; which, being propagated to the brain, cause therein various impressions, and these are attended with the sensations of red, blue, yellow, etc.

Phil. It seems, then, the light does no more than shake the optic nerves.

Hyl. Nothing else.

Phil. And, consequent to each particular motion of the nerves, the mind is affected with a sensation which is some particular color.

Hyl. Right.

Phil. And these sensations have no existence without the mind.

Hyl. They have not.

Phil. How then do you affirm that colors are in the light, since by "light" you understand a corporeal substance external to the mind?

Hyl. Light and colors, as immediately perceived by us, I grant cannot exist without the mind. But in themselves they are only the motions and configurations of certain insensible particles of matter.

Phil. Colors, then, in the vulgar sense, or taken for the immediate objects of sight, cannot agree to any but a perceiving substance.

Hyl. That is what I say.

Phil. Well then, since you give up the point as to those sensible qualities which are alone thought colors by all mankind besides, you may hold what you please with regard to those invisible ones of the philosophers. It is not my business to dispute about them; only I would advise you to bethink yourself whether, considering the inquiry we are upon, it be prudent for you to affirm—*the red and blue which we see are not real colors, but certain unknown mo-*

tions and figures which no man ever did or can see are truly so. Are not these shocking notions, and are not they subject to as many ridiculous inferences as those you were obliged to renounce before in the case of sounds?

Hyl. I frankly own, Philonous, that it is in vain to stand out any longer. Colors, sounds, tastes, in a word, all those termed "secondary qualities," have certainly no existence without the mind. But by this acknowledgment I must not be supposed to derogate anything from the reality of matter or external objects; seeing it is no more than several philosophers maintain, who nevertheless are the farthest imaginable from denying matter. For the clearer understanding of this you must know sensible qualities are by philosophers divided into "primary" and "secondary." The former are extension, figure, solidity, gravity, motion, and rest. And these they hold exist really in bodies. The latter are those above enumerated, or, briefly, all sensible qualities besides the primary, which they assert are only so many sensations or ideas existing nowhere but in the mind. But all this, I doubt not, you are apprised of. For my part I have been a long time sensible there was such an opinion current among philosophers, but was never thoroughly convinced of its truth until now.

Phil. You are still then of opinion that *extension* and *figures* are inherent in external unthinking substances?

Hyl. I am.

Phil. But what if the same arguments which are brought against secondary qualities will hold good against these also?

Hyl. Why then I shall be obliged to think they too exist only in the mind.

Phil. Is it your opinion the very figure and extension which you perceive by sense exist in the outward object or material substance?

Hyl. It is.

Phil. Have all other animals as good grounds to think the same of the figure and extension which they see and feel?

Hyl. Without doubt, if they have any thought at all.

Phil. Answer me, Hylas. Think you the senses were bestowed upon all animals for their preservation and well-being in life? Or were they given to men alone for this end?

Hyl. I make no question but they have the same use in all other animals.

Phil. If so, is it not necessary they should be enabled by them to perceive their own limbs and those bodies which are capable of harming them?

Hyl. Certainly.

Phil. A mite therefore must be supposed to see his own foot, and things equal or even less than it, as bodies of some considerable dimension, though at the same time they appear to you scarce discernible or at best at so many visible points?

Hyl. I cannot deny it.

Phil. And to creatures less than the mite they will seem yet larger?

Hyl. They will.

Phil. Insomuch that what you can hardly discern will to another extremely minute animal appear as some huge mountain?

Hyl. All this I grant.

Phil. Can one and the same thing be at the same time in itself of different dimensions?

Hyl. That were absurd to imagine.

Phil. But from what you have laid down it follows that both the extension by you perceived and that perceived by the mite itself, as likewise all those perceived by lesser animals, are each of them the true extension of the mite's foot; that is to say, by your own principles you are led into an absurdity.

Hyl. There seems to be some difficulty in the point.

Phil. Again, have you not acknowledged that no real inherent property of any object can be changed without some change in the thing itself?

Hyl. I have.

Phil. But, as we approach to or recede from an object, the visible extension varies, being at one distance ten or a hundred times greater than at another. Does it not therefore follow from hence likewise that it is not really inherent in the object?

Hyl. I own I am at a loss what to think.

Phil. Your judgment will soon be determined if you will venture to think as freely concerning this quality as you have done concerning the rest. Was it not admitted as a good argument that neither heat nor cold was in the water because it seemed warm to one hand and cold to the other?

Hyl. It was.

Phil. Is it not the very same reasoning to conclude there is no extension or figure in an object because to one eye it shall seem little, smooth, and round, when at the same time it appears to the other great, uneven, and angular?

Hyl. The very same. But does this latter fact ever happen?

Phil. You may at any time make the experiment by looking with one eye bare and with the other through a microscope.

Hyl. I know not how to maintain it, and yet I am loath to give up *extension;* I see so many odd consequences following upon such a concession.

Phil. Odd, say you? After the concessions already made, I hope you will stick at nothing for its oddness. [But,[1] on the other hand, should it not seem very odd if the general reasoning which includes all other sensible qualities did not also include extension? If it be allowed that no idea nor anything like an idea can exist in an unperceiving substance, then surely it follows that no figure or mode of extension, which we can either perceive or imagine, or have any idea of, can be really inherent in matter, not to mention the peculiar difficulty there must be in conceiving a material substance, prior to and distinct from extension, to be the *substratum* of extension. Be the sensible quality what it will—figure or sound or color—it seems alike impossible it should subsist in that which does not perceive it.]

Hyl. I give up the point for the present, reserving still a right to retract my opinion in case I shall hereafter discover any false step in my progress to it.

Phil. That is a right you cannot be denied. Figures and extension being dispatched, we proceed next to *motion.* Can a real motion in any external body be at the same time both very swift and very slow?

Hyl. It cannot.

Phil. Is not the motion of a body swift in a reciprocal proportion to the time it takes up in describing any given space? Thus a body that describes a mile in an hour moves three times faster than it would in case it described only a mile in three hours.

Hyl. I agree with you.

Phil. And is not time measured by the succession of ideas in our minds?

Hyl. It is.

Phil. And is it not possible ideas should succeed one another twice as fast in your mind as they do in mine, or in that of some spirit of another kind?

Hyl. I own it.

Phil. Consequently, the same body may to another seem to perform its motion over any space in half the time that it does to you. And the same reasoning will hold as to any other proportion; that is to say, according to your principles (since the motions perceived are both really in the object) it is possible one and the same body shall be really moved the same way at once, both very swift and very slow. How is this consistent either with common sense or with what you just now granted?

Hyl. I have nothing to say to it.

Phil. Then as for *solidity;* either you do not mean any sensible quality by that word, and so it is beside our inquiry; or if you do, it must be either hardness or resistance. But both the one and the other are plainly relative to our senses: it being evident that what seems hard to one animal may appear soft to another who has greater force and firmness of limbs. Nor is it less plain that the resistance I feel is not in the body.

Hyl. I own the very sensation of resistance, which is all you immediately perceive, is not in the *body,* but the cause of that sensation is.

Phil. But the causes of our sensations are not things immediately perceived, and therefore not sensible. This point I thought had been already determined.

Hyl. I own it was; but you will pardon me if I seem a little embarrassed; I know not how to quit my old notions.

Phil. To help you out, do but consider that if *extension* be once acknowledged to have no existence without the mind, the same must necessarily be granted of motion, solidity, and gravity, since they all evidently suppose extension. It is therefore superfluous to inquire particularly concerning each of them. In denying extension, you have denied them all to have any real existence.

Hyl. I wonder, Philonous, if what you say be true, why those philosophers who deny the secondary qualities any real existence should yet attribute it to the primary. If there is no difference between them, how can this be accounted for?

Phil. It is not my business to account for every opinion of the philosophers. But, among other reasons which may be assigned for this, it seems probable that pleasure and pain being rather annexed to the former than the latter may be one. Heat and cold, tastes and smells have something more vividly pleasing or disagreeable than the ideas of extension, figure, and motion affect us with. And, it being too visibly absurd to hold that pain or pleasure can be in an unperceiving substance, men are more easily weaned from believing the external existence of the secondary than the primary qualities. You will be satisfied there is something in this if you recollect the difference you made between an intense and more moderate degree of heat, allowing the one a real existence while you denied it to the other. But, after all, there is no rational ground for that distinction, for surely an indifferent sensation is as truly a *sensation* as one more pleasing or painful, and consequently should not any more than they be supposed to exist in an unthinking subject.

Hyl. It is just come into my head, Philonous, that I have somewhere heard of a distinction between *absolute* and *sensible* extension. Now though it be acknowledged that *great* and *small*, consisting merely in the relation which other extended beings have to the parts of our own bodies, do not really inhere in the substances themselves, yet nothing obliges us to hold the same with regard to *absolute* extension, which is something abstracted from *great* and *small*, from this or that particular magnitude or figure. So likewise as to motion: *swift* and *slow* are altogether relative to the succession of ideas in our own minds. But it does not follow, because those modifications of motion exist not without the mind, that therefore absolute motion abstracted from them does not.

Phil. Pray what is it that distinguishes one motion, or one part of extension, from another? Is it not something sensible, as some degree of swiftness or slowness, some certain magnitude or figure peculiar to each?

Hyl. I think so.

Phil. These qualities, therefore, stripped of all sensible properties, are without all specific and numerical differences, as the schools call them.

Hyl. They are.

Phil. That is to say, they are extension in general, and motion in general.

Hyl. Let it be so.

Phil. But it is a universally received maxim that *everything which exists is particular.* How then can motion in general, or extension in general, exist in any corporeal substance?

Hyl. I will take time to solve your difficulty.

Phil. But I think the point may be speedily decided. Without doubt you can tell whether you are able to frame this or that idea. Now I am content to put our dispute on this issue. If you can frame in your thoughts a distinct abstract idea of motion or extension divested of all those sensible modes as swift and slow, great and small, round and square, and the like, which are acknowledged to exist only in the mind, I will then yield the point you contend for. But if you cannot, it will be unreasonable on your side to insist any longer upon what you have no notion of.

Hyl. To confess ingenuously, I cannot.

Phil. Can you even separate the ideas of extension and motion from the ideas of all those qualities which they who make the distinction term "secondary"?

Hyl. What! is it not an easy matter to consider extension and motion by themselves, abstracted from all other sensible qualities? Pray how do the mathematicians treat of them?

Phil. I acknowledge, Hylas, it is not difficult to form general propositions and reasonings about those qualities without mentioning any other, and, in this sense, to consider or treat of them abstractedly. But how does it follow that, because I can pronounce the word "motion" by itself, I can form the idea of it in my mind exclusive of body? Or because theorems may be made of extension and figures, without any mention of *great* or *small*, or any other sensible mode or quality, that therefore it is possible such an abstract idea of extension, without any particular size or figure or sensible quality, should be distinctly formed and apprehended by the mind? Mathematicians treat of quantity without regarding what other sensible qualities it is attended with, as being altogether indifferent to their demonstrations. But when, laying aside the words, they contemplate the bare ideas, I believe you will find they are not the pure abstracted ideas of extension.

Hyl. But what say you to *pure intellect?* May not abstracted ideas be framed by that faculty?

Phil. Since I cannot frame abstract ideas at all, it is plain I cannot frame them by the help of pure intellect, whatsoever faculty you understand by those words. Besides, not to inquire into the nature of pure intellect and its spiritual objects, as *virtue, reason, God,* or the like, thus much seems manifest that sensible things are only to be perceived by sense or represented by the imagination. Figures, therefore, and extension, being originally perceived by sense, do not belong to pure intellect; but, for your further satisfaction, try if you can frame the idea of any figure abstracted from all particularities of size or even from other sensible qualities.

Hyl. Let me think a little—I do not find that I can.

Phil. And can you think it possible that [an idea] should really exist in nature which implies a repugnancy in its conception?

Hyl. By no means.

Phil. Since therefore it is impossible even for the mind to disunite the ideas of extension and motion from all other sensible qualities, does it not follow that where the one exist there necessarily the other exist likewise?

Hyl. It should seem so.

Phil. Consequently, the very same arguments which you admitted as conclusive against the secondary qualities are, without any further application of force, against the primary, too. Besides, if you will trust your senses, is it not plain all sensible qualities coexist, or to them appear as being in the same place? Do they ever represent a motion or figure as being divested of all other visible and tangible qualities?

Hyl. You need say no more on this head. I am free to own, if there be no secret error or oversight in our proceedings hitherto, that all sensible qualities are alike to be denied existence without the mind. But my fear is that I have been too liberal in my former concessions, or overlooked some fallacy or other. In short, I did not take time to think.

Phil. For that matter, Hylas, you may take what time you please in reviewing the progress of our inquiry. You are at liberty to recover any slips you might have made, or offer whatever you have omitted which makes for your first opinion.

Hyl. One great oversight I take to be this—that I did not sufficiently distinguish the *object* from the *sensation.* Now, though this latter may not exist without the mind, yet it will not thence follow that the former cannot.

Phil. What object do you mean? The object of the senses?

Hyl. The same.

Phil. It is then immediately perceived?

Hyl. Right.

Phil. Make me to understand the difference between what is immediately perceived and a sensation.

Hyl. The sensation I take to be an act of the mind perceiving; besides which there is something perceived, and this I call the "object." For example, there is red and yellow on that tulip. But then the act of perceiving those colors is in me only, and not in the tulip.

Phil. What tulip do you speak of? Is it that which you see?

Hyl. The same.

Phil. And what do you see besides color, figure, and extension?

Hyl. Nothing.

Phil. What you would say then is that the red and yellow are coexistent with the extension; is it not?

Hyl. That is not all; I would say they have a real existence without the mind, in some unthinking substance.

Phil. That the colors are really in the tulip which I see is manifest. Neither can it be denied that this tulip may exist independent of your mind or mine; but that any immediate object of the senses—that is, any idea, or combination of ideas—should exist in an unthinking substance, or exterior to all minds, is in itself an evident contradiction. Nor can I imagine how this follows from what you said just now, to wit, that the red and yellow were on the tulip *you saw,* since you do not pretend to *see* that unthinking substance.

Hyl. You have an artful way, Philonous, of diverting our inquiry from the subject.

Phil. I see you have no mind to be pressed that way. To return then to your distinction between *sensation* and *object;* if I take you right, you distinguish in every perception two things, the one an action of the mind, the other not.

Hyl. True.

Phil. And this action cannot exist in, or belong to, any unthinking thing, but whatever besides is implied in a perception may?

Hyl. That is my meaning.

Phil. So that if there was a perception without any act of the mind, it were possible such a perception should exist in an unthinking substance?

Hyl. I grant it. But it is impossible there should be such a perception.

Phil. When is the mind said to be active?

Hyl. When it produces, puts an end to, or changes anything.

Phil. Can the mind produce, discontinue, or change anything but by an act of the will?

Hyl. It cannot.

Phil. The mind therefore is to be accounted *active* in its perceptions so far forth as *volition* is included in them?

Hyl. It is.

Phil. In plucking this flower I am active, because I do it by the motion of my hand, which was consequent upon my volition; so likewise in applying it to my nose. But is either of these smelling?

Hyl. No.

Phil. I act, too, in drawing the air through my nose, because my breathing so rather than otherwise is the effect of my volition. But neither can this be called "smelling," for if it were I should smell every time I breathed in that manner?

Hyl. True.

Phil. Smelling then is somewhat consequent to all this?

Hyl. It is.

Phil. But I do not find my will concerned any further. Whatever more there is—as that I perceive such a particular smell, or any smell at all—this is independent of my will, and therein I am altogether passive. Do you find it otherwise with you, Hylas?

Hyl. No, the very same.

Phil. Then, as to seeing, is it not in your power to open your eyes or keep them shut, to turn them this or that way?

Hyl. Without doubt.

Phil. But does it in like manner depend on your will that in looking on this flower you perceive *white* rather than any other color? Or, directing your open eyes toward yonder part of the heaven, can you avoid seeing the sun? Or is light or darkness the effect of your volition?

Hyl. No, certainly.

Phil. You are then in these respects altogether passive?

Hyl. I am.

Phil. Tell me now whether *seeing* consists in perceiving light and colors or in opening and turning the eyes?

Hyl. Without doubt, in the former.

Phil. Since, therefore, you are in the very perception of light and colors altogether passive, what is become of that action you were speaking of as an ingredient in every sensation? And does it not follow from your own concessions that the perception of light and colors, including no action in it, may exist in an unperceiving substance? And is not this a plain contradiction?

Hyl. I know not what to think of it.

Phil. Besides, since you distinguish the *active* and *passive* in every perception, you must do it in that of pain. But how is it possible that pain, be it as little active as you please, should exist in an unperceiving substance? In short, do but consider the point and then confess ingenuously whether light and colors, tastes, sounds, etc., are not all equally passions or sensations in the soul. You may indeed call them "external objects" and give them in words what subsistence you please. But examine your own thoughts and then tell me whether it be not as I say?

Hyl. I acknowledge, Philonous, that, upon a fair observation of what passes in my mind, I can discover nothing else but that I am a thinking being affected with variety of sensations; neither is it possible to conceive how a sensation should exist in an unperceiving substance. But then, on the other hand, when I look on sensible things in a different view, considering them as so many modes and qualities, I find it necessary to suppose a material *substratum,* without which they cannot be conceived to exist.

Phil. "Material substratum" call you it? Pray, by which of your senses came you acquainted with that being?

Hyl. It is not itself sensible; its modes and qualities only being perceived by the senses.

Phil. I presume then it was by reflection and reason you obtained the idea of it?

Hyl. I do not pretend to any proper positive idea of it. However, I conclude it exists because qualities cannot be conceived to exist without a support.

Phil. It seems then you have only a relative notion of it, or that you conceive it not otherwise than by conceiving the relation it bears to sensible qualities?

Hyl. Right.

Phil. Be pleased, therefore, to let me know wherein that relation consists.

Hyl. Is it not sufficiently expressed in the term "substratum" or "substance"?

Phil. If so, the word "substratum" should import that it is spread under the sensible qualities or accidents?

Hyl. True.

Phil. And consequently under extension?

Hyl. I own it.

Phil. It is therefore somewhat in its own nature distinct from extension?

Hyl. I tell you extension is only a mode, and matter is something that supports modes. And is it not evident the thing supported is different from the thing supporting?

Phil. So that something distinct from, and exclusive of, extension is supposed to be the *substratum* of extension?

Hyl. Just so.

Phil. Answer me, Hylas, can a thing be spread without extension, or is not the idea of extension necessarily included in *spreading?*

Hyl. It is.

Phil. Whatsoever therefore you suppose spread under anything must have in itself an extension distinct from the extension of that thing under which it is spread?

Hyl. It must.

Phil. Consequently, every corporeal substance being the *substratum* of extension must have in itself another extension by which it is qualified to be a *substratum,* and so on to infinity? And I ask whether this be not absurd in itself and repugnant to what you granted just now, to wit, that the *substratum* was something distinct from and exclusive of extension?

Hyl. Aye, but, Philonous, you take me wrong. I do not mean that matter is *spread* in a gross literal sense under extension. The word "substratum" is used only to express in general the same thing with "substance."

Phil. Well then, let us examine the relation implied in the term "substance." Is it not that it stands under accidents?

Hyl. The very same.

Phil. But that one thing may stand under or support another, must it not be extended?

Hyl. It must.

Phil. Is not therefore this supposition liable to the same absurdity with the former?

Hyl. You still take things in a strict literal sense; that is not fair, Philonous.

Phil. I am not for imposing any sense on your words; you are at liberty to explain them as you please. Only, I beseech you, make me understand something by them. You tell me matter supports or stands under accidents. How! is it as your legs support your body?

Hyl. No; that is the literal sense.

Phil. Pray let me know any sense, literal or not literal, that you understand it in.—How long must I wait for an answer, Hylas?

Hyl. I declare I know not what to say. I once thought I understood well enough what was meant by matter's supporting accidents. But now, the more I think on it, the less can I comprehend it; in short, I find that I know nothing of it.

Phil. It seems then you have no idea at all, neither relative nor positive, of matter? you know neither what it is in itself nor what relation it bears to accidents?

Hyl. I acknowledge it.

Phil. And yet you asserted that you could not conceive how qualities or accidents should really exist without conceiving at the same time a material support of them?

Hyl. I did.

Phil. That is to say, when you conceive the real existence of qualities, you do withal conceive something which you cannot conceive?

Hyl. It was wrong I own. But still I fear there is some fallacy or other. Pray, what think you of this? It is just come into my head that the ground of all our mistake lies in your treating of each quality by itself. Now I grant that each quality cannot singly subsist without the mind. Color cannot without extension, neither can figure without some other sensible quality. But, as the several qualities united or blended together form entire sensible things, nothing hinders why such things may not be supposed to exist without the mind.

Phil. Either, Hylas, you are jesting or have a very bad memory. Though, indeed, we went through all the qualities by name one after another, yet my arguments, or rather your concessions, nowhere tended to prove that the secondary qualities did not subsist each alone by itself, but that they were not *at all* without the mind. Indeed, in treating of figure and motion we concluded they could not exist without the mind, because it was impossible even in thought to separate them from all secondary qualities, so as to conceive them existing by themselves. But then this was not the only argument made use of upon that occasion. But (to pass by all that has been hitherto said and reckon it for nothing, if you will have it so) I am content to put the whole upon this issue. If you can conceive it possible for any mixture or combination of qualities, or any sensible object whatever, to exist without the mind, then I will grant it actually to be so.

Hyl. If it comes to that the point will soon be decided. What more easy than to conceive a tree or house existing by itself, independent of, and unperceived by, any mind whatsoever? I do at this present time conceive them existing after that manner.

Phil. How say you, Hylas, can you see a thing which is at the same time unseen?

Hyl. No, that were a contradiction.

Phil. Is it not as great a contradiction to talk of *conceiving* a thing which is *unconceived?*

Hyl. It is.

Phil. The tree or house, therefore, which you think of is conceived by you?

Hyl. How should it be otherwise?

Phil. And what is conceived is surely in the mind?

Hyl. Without question, that which is conceived is in the mind.

Phil. How then came you to say you conceived a house or tree existing independent and out of all minds whatsoever?

Hyl. That was I own an oversight, but stay, let me consider what let me into it.—It is a pleasant mistake enough. As I was thinking of a tree in a solitary place where no one was present to see it, methought that was to conceive a tree as existing unperceived or unthought of, not considering that I myself conceived it all the while. But now I plainly see that all I can do is to frame ideas in my own mind. I may indeed conceive in my own thoughts the idea of a tree, or a house, or a mountain, but that is all. And this is far from proving that I can conceive them *existing out of the minds of all spirits.*

Phil. You acknowledge then that you cannot possibly conceive how any one corporeal sensible thing should exist otherwise than in a mind?

Hyl. I do.

Phil. And yet you will earnestly contend for the truth of that which you cannot so much as conceive?

Hyl. I profess I know not what to think; but still there are some scruples remain with me. Is it not certain I see things at a distance? Do we not perceive the stars and moon, for example, to be a great way off? Is not this, I say, manifest to the senses?

Phil. Do you not in a dream, too, perceive those or the like objects?

Hyl. I do.

Phil. And have they not then the same appearance of being distant?

Hyl. They have.

Phil. But you do not thence conclude the apparitions in a dream to be without the mind?

Hyl. By no means.

Phil. You ought not therefore to conclude that sensible objects are without the mind, from their appearance or manner wherein they are perceived.

Hyl. I acknowledge it. But does not my sense deceive me in those cases?

Phil. By no means. The idea or thing which you immediately perceive, neither sense nor reason informs you that it actually exists without the mind. By sense you only know that you are affected with such certain sensations of light, colors, etc. And these you will not say are without the mind.

Hyl. True, but, beside all that, do you not think the sight suggests something of *outness* or *distance?*

Phil. Upon approaching a distant object, do the visible size and figure change perpetually or do they appear the same at all distances?

Hyl. They are in a continual change.

Phil. Sight, therefore, does not suggest or any way inform you that the visible object you immediately perceive exists at a distance,[2] or will be perceived when you advance farther onward, there being a continued series of visible objects succeeding each other during the whole time of your approach.

Hyl. It does not; but still I know, upon seeing an object, what object I shall perceive after having passed over a certain distance: no matter whether it be exactly the same or no, there is still something of distance suggested in the case.

Phil. Good Hylas, do but reflect a little on the point, and then tell me whether there be any more in it than this. From the ideas you actually perceive by sight, you have by experience learned to collect what other ideas you will (according to the standing order of nature) be affected with, after such a certain succession of time and motion.

Hyl. Upon the whole, I take it to be nothing else.

Phil. Now is it not plain that if we suppose a man born blind was on a sudden made to see, he could at first have no experience of what may be suggested by sight?

Hyl. It is.

Phil. He would not then, according to you, have any notion of distance annexed to the things he saw, but would take them for a new set of sensations existing only in his mind?

Hyl. It is undeniable.

Phil. But to make it more plain: is not *distance* a line turned endwise to the eye?

Hyl. It is.

Phil. And can a line so situated be perceived by sight?

Hyl. It cannot.

Phil. Does it not therefore follow that distance is not properly and immediately perceived by sight?

Hyl. It should seem so.

Phil. Again, is it your opinion that colors are at a distance?

Hyl. It must be acknowledged they are only in the mind.

Phil. But do not colors appear to the eye as coexisting in the same place with extension and figures?

Hyl. They do.

Phil. How can you then conclude from sight that figures exist without, when you acknowledge colors do not; the sensible appearances being the very same with regard to both?

Hyl. I know not what to answer.

Phil. But allowing that distance was truly and immediately perceived by the mind, yet it would not thence follow it existed out of the mind. For whatever is immediately perceived is an idea; and can any *idea* exist out of the mind?

Hyl. To suppose that were absurd; but, inform me, Philonous, can we perceive or know nothing besides our ideas?

Phil. As for the rational deducing of causes from effects, that is beside our inquiry. And by the senses you can best tell whether you perceive anything which is not immediately perceived. And I ask you whether the things immediately perceived are other than your own sensations or ideas? You have indeed more than once, in the course of this conversation, declared yourself on those points, but you seem, by this last question, to have departed from what you then thought.

Hyl. To speak the truth, Philonous, I think there are two kinds of objects: the one perceived immediately, which are likewise called "ideas"; the other are real things or external objects, perceived by the mediation of ideas which are their images and representations. Now I own ideas do not exist without the mind, but the latter sort of objects do. I am sorry I did not think of this distinction sooner; it would probably have cut short your discourse.

Phil. Are those external objects perceived by sense or by some other faculty?

Hyl. They are perceived by sense.

Phil. How! is there anything perceived by sense which is not immediately perceived?

Hyl. Yes, Philonous, in some sort there is. For example, when I look on a picture or statue of Julius Caesar, I may be said, after a manner, to perceive him (though not immediately) by my senses.

Phil. It seems then you will have our ideas, which alone are immediately perceived, to be pictures of external things: and that these also are perceived by sense inasmuch as they have a conformity or resemblance to our ideas?

Hyl. That is my meaning.

Phil. And in the same way that Julius Caesar, in himself invisible, is nevertheless perceived by sight, real things, in themselves imperceptible, are perceived by sense.

Hyl. In the very same.

Phil. Tell me, Hylas, when you behold the picture of Julius Caesar, do you see with your eyes any more than some colors and figures, with a certain symmetry and composition of the whole?

Hyl. Nothing else.

Phil. And would not a man who had never known anything of Julius Caesar see as much?

Hyl. He would.

Phil. Consequently, he has his sight and the use of it in as perfect a degree as you?

Hyl. I agree with you.

Phil. Whence comes it then that your thoughts are directed to the Roman emperor, and his are not? This cannot proceed from the sensations or ideas of sense by you then perceived, since you acknowledge you have no advantage over him in that respect. It should seem therefore to proceed from reason and memory, should it not?

Hyl. It should.

Phil. Consequently, it will not follow from that instance that anything is perceived by sense which is not immediately perceived. Though I grant we may, in one acceptation, be said to perceive sensible things mediately by sense—that is, when, from a frequently perceived connection, the immediate perception of ideas by one sense suggest to the mind others, perhaps belonging to another sense, which are wont to be connected with them. For instance, when I hear a coach drive along the streets, immediately I perceive only the sound; but from the experience I have had that such a sound is connected with a coach, I am said to hear the coach. It is nevertheless evident that, in truth and strictness, nothing can be *heard* but *sound:* and the coach is not then properly perceived by sense, but suggested from experience. So likewise when we are said to see a red-hot bar of iron; the solidity and heat of the iron are not the objects of sight, but suggested to the imagination by the color and figure which are properly perceived by that sense. In short, those things alone are actually and strictly perceived by any sense which would have been perceived in case that same sense had then been first conferred on us. As for other things, it is plain they are only suggested to the mind by experience grounded on former perceptions. But, to return to your comparison of Caesar's picture, it is plain, if you keep to that, you must hold the real things or archetypes of our ideas are not perceived by sense, but by some internal faculty of the soul, as reason or memory. I would, therefore, fain know what arguments you can draw from reason for the existence of what you call "real things" or "material objects," or whether you remember to have seen them formerly as they are in themselves, or if you have heard or read of anyone that did.

Hyl. Philonous, you are disposed to raillery; but that will never convince me.

Phil. My aim is only to learn from you the way to come at the knowledge of "material beings." Whatever we perceive is perceived either immediately or mediately—by sense, or by reason and reflection. But, as you have excluded sense, pray show me what reason you have to believe their existence, or what *medium* you can possibly make use of to prove it, either to mine or your own understanding.

Hyl. To deal ingenuously, Philonous, now [that] I consider the point, I do not find I can give you any good reason for it. But thus much seems pretty plain, that it is at least possible such things may really exist. And as long as there is no absurdity in supposing them, I am resolved to believe as I did, till you bring good reasons to the contrary.

Phil. What! is it come to this, that you only believe the existence of material objects, and that your belief is founded barely on the possibility of its being true? Then you will have me bring reasons against it, though another would think it reasonable the proof should lie on him who holds the affirmative. And, after all, this very point which you are now resolved to maintain, without any reason, is in effect what you have more than once during this discourse seen good reason to give up. But to pass over all this—if I understand you rightly, you say our ideas do not exist without the mind, but that they are copies, images, or representations of certain originals that do?

Hyl. You take me right.

Phil. They are then like external things?

Hyl. They are.

Phil. Have those things a stable and permanent nature, independent of our senses, or are they in a perpetual change, upon our producing any motions in our bodies, suspending, exerting, or altering our faculties or organs of sense?

Hyl. Real things, it is plain, have a fixed and real nature, which remains the same notwithstanding any change in our senses or in the posture and motion of our bodies; which indeed may affect the ideas in our minds, but it were absurd to think they had the same effect on things existing without the mind.

Phil. How then is it possible that things perpetually fleeting and variable as our ideas should be copies or images of anything fixed and constant? Or, in other words, since all sensible qualities, as size, figure, color, etc., that is, our ideas, are continually changing upon every alteration in the distance, medium, or instruments of sensation—how can any determinate material objects be properly represented or painted forth by several distinct things each of which is so different from and unlike the rest? Or, if you say it resembles some one only of our ideas, how shall we be able to distinguish the true copy from all the false ones?

Hyl. I profess, Philonous, I am at a loss. I know not what to say to this.

Phil. But neither is this all. Which are material objects in themselves—perceptible or imperceptible?

Hyl. Properly and immediately nothing can be perceived but ideas. All material things, therefore, are in themselves insensible and to be perceived only by our ideas.

Phil. Ideas then are sensible, and their archetypes or originals insensible?

Hyl. Right.

Phil. But how can that which is sensible be like that which is insensible? Can a real thing, in itself *invisible,* be like a *color,* or a real thing which is not *audible* be like a *sound?* In a word, can anything be like a sensation or idea, but another sensation or idea?

Hyl. I must own, I think not.

Phil. Is it possible there should be any doubt on the point? Do you not perfectly know your own ideas?

Hyl. I know them perfectly, since what I do not perceive or know can be no part of my idea.

Phil. Consider, therefore, and examine them, and then tell me if there be anything in them which can exist without the mind, or if you can conceive anything like them existing without the mind?

Hyl. Upon inquiry I find it impossible for me to conceive or understand how anything but an idea can be like an idea. And it is most evident that *no idea can exist without the mind.*

Phil. You are, therefore, by your principles forced to deny the reality of sensible things, since you made it to consist in an absolute existence exterior to the mind. That is to say, you are a downright skeptic. So I have gained my point, which was to show your principles led to skepticism.

Hyl. For the present I am, if not entirely convinced, at least silenced.

Phil. I would fain know what more you would require in order to a perfect conviction. Have you not had the liberty of explaining yourself all manner of ways? Were any little slips in discourse laid hold and insisted on? Or were you not allowed to retract or reinforce anything you had offered, as best served your purpose? Has not everything you could say been heard and examined with all the fairness imaginable? In a word, have you not in every point been convinced out of your own mouth? And, if you can at present discover any flaw in any of your former concessions, or think of any remaining subterfuge, any new distinction, color, or comment whatsoever, why do you not produce it?

Hyl. A little patience, Philonous. I am at present so amazed to see myself ensnared, and as it were imprisoned in the labyrinths you have drawn me into, that on the sudden it cannot be expected I should find my way out. You must give me time to look about me and recollect myself.

Phil. Hark; is not this the college bell?

Hyl. It rings for prayers.

Phil. We will go in then, if you please, and meet here again tomorrow morning. In the meantime, you may employ your thoughts on this morning's discourse and try if you can find any fallacy in it, or invent any new means to extricate yourself.

Hyl. Agreed.

THE SECOND DIALOGUE

Hylas. I beg your pardon, Philonous, for not meeting you sooner. All this morning my head was so filled with our late conversation that I had not leisure to think of the time of the day, or indeed of anything else.

Philonous. I am glad you were so intent upon it, in hopes if there were any mistakes in your concessions, or fallacies in my reasonings from them, you will now discover them to me.

Hyl. I assure you I have done nothing ever since I saw you but search after mistakes and fallacies, and, with that [in] view, have minutely examined the whole series of yesterday's discourse; but all in vain, for the notions it led me into, upon review, appear still more clear and evident; and the more I consider them, the more irresistibly do they force my assent.

Phil. And is not this, think you, a sign that they are genuine, that they proceed from nature and are conformable to right reason? Truth and beauty are in this alike, that the strictest survey sets them both off to advantage, while the false luster of error and disguise cannot endure being reviewed or too nearly inspected.

Hyl. I own there is a great deal in what you say. Nor can anyone be more entirely satisfied of the truth of those odd consequences so long as I have in view the reasonings that lead to them. But when these are out of my thoughts, there seems, on the other hand, something so satisfactory, so natural and intelligible in the modern way of explaining things that I profess I know not how to reject it.

Phil. I know not what way you mean.

Hyl. I mean the way of accounting for our sensations or ideas.

Phil. How is that?

Hyl. It is supposed the soul makes her residence in some part of the brain, from which the nerves take their rise, and are then extended to all parts of the body; and that outward objects, by the different impressions they make on the organs of sense, communicate certain vibrative motions to the nerves, and these, being filled with spirits, propagate them to the brain or seat of the soul, which, according to the various impressions or traces thereby made in the brain, is variously affected with ideas.

Phil. And call you this an explication of the manner whereby we are affected with ideas?

Hyl. Why not, Philonous; have you anything to object against it?

Phil. I would first know whether I rightly understand your hypothesis. You make certain traces in the brain to be the causes or occasions of our ideas. Pray tell me whether by the "brain" you mean any sensible thing.

Hyl. What else think you I could mean?

Phil. Sensible things are all immediately perceivable; and those things which are immediately perceivable are ideas, and these exist only in the mind. This much you have, if I mistake not, long since agreed to.

Hyl. I do not deny it.

Phil. The brain therefore you speak of, being a sensible thing, exists only in the mind. Now I would fain know whether you think it reasonable to suppose that one idea or thing existing in the mind occasions all other ideas. And if you think so, pray how do you account for the origin of that primary idea or brain itself?

Hyl. I do not explain the origin of our ideas by that brain which is perceivable to sense, this being itself only a combination of sensible ideas, but by another which I imagine.

Phil. But are not things imagined as truly *in the mind* as things perceived?

Hyl. I must confess they are.

Phil. It comes, therefore, to the same thing; and you have been all this while accounting for ideas by certain motions or impressions of the brain, that is, by some alteration in an idea, whether sensible or imaginable it matters not.

Hyl. I begin to suspect my hypothesis.

Phil. Besides spirits, all that we know or conceive are our own ideas. When, therefore, you say all ideas are occasioned by impressions in the brain, do you conceive this brain or no? If you do, then you talk of ideas imprinted in an idea causing that same idea, which is absurd. If you do not conceive it, you talk unintelligibly, instead of forming a reasonable hypothesis.

Hyl. I now clearly see it was a mere dream. There is nothing in it.

Phil. You need not be much concerned at it, for, after all, this way of explaining things, as you called it, could never have satisfied any reasonable man. What connection is there between a motion in the nerves and the sensations of sound or color in the mind? Or how is it possible these should be the effect of that?

Hyl. But I could never think it had so little in it as now it seems to have.

Phil. Well then, are you at length satisfied that no sensible things have a real existence, and that you are in truth an arrant *skeptic?*

Hyl. It is too plain to be denied.

Phil. Look! are not the fields covered with a delightful verdure? Is there not something in the woods and groves, in the rivers and clear springs, that soothes, that delights, that transports the soul? At the prospect of the wide and deep ocean, or some huge mountain whose top is lost in the clouds, or of an old gloomy forest, are not our minds filled with a pleasing horror? Even in rocks and deserts is there not an agreeable wildness? How sincere a pleasure is it to behold the natural beauties of the earth! To preserve and renew our relish for them, is not the veil of night alternately drawn over her face, and does she not change her dress with the seasons? How aptly are the elements disposed! What variety and use in the meanest productions of nature! What delicacy, what beauty, what contrivance in animal and vegetable bodies! How exquisitely are all things suited, as well to their particular ends as to constitute apposite parts of the whole! And while they mutually aid and support, do they not also set off and illustrate each other? Raise now your thoughts from this ball of earth to all those glorious luminaries that adorn the high arch of heaven. The motion and situation of the planets, are they not admirable for use and order? Were those (miscalled "erratic") globes ever known to stray in their repeated journeys through the pathless void? Do they not measure areas round the sun ever proportioned to the times? So fixed, so immutable are the laws by which the unseen Author of nature actuates the universe. How vivid and radiant is the luster of the fixed stars! How magnificent and rich that negligent profusion with which they appear to be scattered throughout the whole azure vault! Yet, if you take the telescope, it brings into your sight a new host of stars that escape the naked eye. Here they seem contiguous and minute, but to a nearer view, immense orbs of light at various distances, far sunk in the abyss of space. Now you must call imagination to your aid. The feeble narrow sense cannot descry innumerable worlds revolving round the central fires, and in those worlds the energy of an all-perfect Mind displayed in endless forms. But neither sense nor imagination are big enough to comprehend the boundless extent with all its glittering furniture. Though the laboring mind exert and strain each power to its utmost reach, there still stands out ungrasped a surplusage immeasurable. Yet all the vast bodies that compose this mighty frame, how distant and remote soever, are by some secret mechanism, some divine art and force, linked in a mutual dependence and intercourse with each other, even with this earth, which was almost slipt from my thoughts and lost in the crowd of worlds. Is not the whole system immense, beautiful, glorious beyond expression and beyond thought! What treatment, then, do those philosophers deserve who would deprive these noble and delightful scenes of all reality? How should those principles be entertained that lead us to think all the visible beauty of the creation a false imaginary glare? To be plain, can you expect this skepticism of yours will not be thought extravagantly absurd by all men of sense?

Hyl. Other men may think as they please, but for your part you have nothing to reproach me with. My comfort is you are as much a skeptic as I am.

Phil. There, Hylas, I must beg leave to differ from you.

Hyl. What! have you all along agreed to the premises, and do you now deny the conclusion and leave me to maintain those paradoxes by myself which you led me into? This surely is not fair.

Phil. I deny that I agreed with you in those notions that led to skepticism. You indeed said the *reality* of sensible things consisted in an *absolute existence* out of the minds of spirits, or distinct from their being perceived. And, pursuant to this notion of reality, you are obliged to deny sensible things any real existence; that is, according to your own definition, you profess yourself a skeptic. But I neither said nor thought the reality of sensible things was to be defined after that manner. To me it is evident, for the reasons you allow of, that sensible things cannot exist otherwise than in a mind or spirit. Whence I conclude, not that they have no real existence, but that, seeing they depend not on my thought and have an existence distinct from being perceived by me, *there must be some other mind wherein they exist.* As sure, therefore, as the sensible world really exists, so sure is there an infinite omnipresent Spirit, who contains and supports it.

Hyl. What! this is no more than I and all Christians hold; nay, and all others, too, who believe there is a God and that He knows and comprehends all things.

Phil. Aye, but here lies the difference. Men commonly believe that all things are known or perceived by God, because they believe the being of a God; whereas I, on the other side, immediately and necessarily conclude the being of a God, because all sensible things must be perceived by him.

Hyl. But so long as we all believe the same thing, what matter is it how we come by that belief?

Phil. But neither do we agree in the same opinion. For philosophers, though they acknowledge all corporeal beings to be perceived by God, yet they attribute to them an absolute subsistence distinct from their being perceived by any mind whatever, which I do not. Besides, is there no difference between saying, *there is a God, therefore He perceives all things,* and saying, *sensible things do really exist; and if they really exist, they are necessarily perceived by an infinite mind: therefore there is an infinite mind, or God?* This furnishes you with a direct and immediate demonstration, from a most evident principle, of the *being of a God.* Divines and philosophers had proved beyond all controversy, from the beauty and usefulness of the several parts of the creation, that it was the workmanship of God. But that—setting aside all help of astronomy and natural philosophy, all contemplation of the contrivance, order and adjustment of things—an infinite mind should be necessarily inferred from the bare *existence* of the sensible world is an advantage to them only who have made this easy reflection, that the sensible world is that which we perceive by our several senses; and that nothing is perceived by the senses beside ideas; and that no idea or archetype of an idea can exist otherwise than in a mind. You may now, without any laborious search into the sciences, without any subtelty of reason or tediuous length of discourse, oppose and baffle the most strenuous advocate for atheism, those miserable refuges, whether in an eternal succession of unthinking causes and effects or in a fortuitous concourse of atoms; those wild imaginations of Vanini, Hobbes, and Spinoza: in a word, the whole system of atheism, is it not entirely overthrown by this single reflection on the repugnancy included in supposing the whole or any part, even the most rude and shapeless, of the visible world to exist without a mind? Let any one of those abettors of impiety but look into his own thoughts, and there try if he can conceive how so much as a rock, a desert, a chaos, or confused jumble of atoms, how anything at all, either sensible or imaginable, can exist independent of a mind, and he need go no further to be convinced of his folly. Can anything be fairer than to put a dispute on such an issue and leave it to a man himself to see if he can conceive, even in thought, what he holds to be true in fact, and from a notional to allow it a real existence?

Hyl. It cannot be denied there is something highly serviceable to religion in what you advance. But do you not think it looks very like a notion entertained by some eminent moderns, of *seeing all things in God?*

Phil. I would gladly know that opinion; pray explain it to me.

Hyl. They conceive that the soul, being immaterial, is incapable of being united with material things so as to perceive them in themselves, but that she perceives them by her union with the substance of God, which, being spiritual, is therefore purely intelligible, or capable of being the immediate object of a spirit's thought. Besides, the divine essence contains in it perfections correspondent to each created being, and which are, for that reason, proper to exhibit or represent them to the mind.

Phil. I do not understand how our ideas, which are things altogether passive and inert, can be the essence or any part (or like any part) of the essence or substance of God, who is an impassive, indivisible, purely active being. Many more difficulties and objections there are which occur at first view against this hypothesis; but I shall only add that it is liable to all the absurdities of the common hypothesis, in making a created world exist otherwise than in the mind of a Spirit. Beside all which it has this peculiar to itself that it makes that material world serve to no purpose. And if it pass for a good argument against other hypotheses in the sciences that they suppose nature or the divine wisdom to make something in vain, or do that by tedious roundabout methods which might have been performed in a much more easy and compendious way, what shall we think of that hypothesis which supposes the whole world made in vain?

Hyl. But what say you, are not you too of opinion that we see all things in God? If I mistake not, what you advance comes near it.

Phil. [Few men think, yet all have opinions. Hence men's opinions are superficial and confused. It is nothing strange that tenets which in themselves are ever so different should nevertheless be confounded with each other by those who do not consider them attentively. I shall not therefore be surprised if some men imagine that I run into the enthusiasm of Malebranche, though in truth I am very remote from it. He builds on the most abstract general ideas, which I entirely disclaim. He asserts an absolute external world, which I deny. He maintains that we are deceived by our senses and know not the real natures or the true forms and figures of extended beings; of all which I hold the direct contrary. So that upon the whole there are no principles more fundamentally opposite than his and mine. It must be owned that,][3] I entirely agree with what the holy Scripture says, "That in God we live and move and have our being." But that we see things in His essence, after the manner above set forth, I am far from believing. Take here in brief my meaning: It is evident that the things I perceive are my own ideas, and that no idea can exist unless it be in a mind. Nor is it less plain that these ideas or things by me perceived, either themselves or their archetypes, exist independently of my mind; since I know myself not to be their author, it being out of my power to determine at pleasure what particular ideas I shall be affected with upon opening my eyes or ears. They must therefore exist in some other mind, whose will it is they should be exhibited to me. The things, I say, immediately perceived are ideas or sensations, call them which you will. But how can any idea or sensation exist in, or be produced by, anything but a mind or spirit? This indeed is inconceivable; and to assert that which is inconceivable is to talk nonsense, is it not?

Hyl. Without doubt.

Phil. But, on the other hand, it is very conceivable that they should exist in and be produced by a spirit, since this is no more than I daily experience in myself, inasmuch as I perceive numberless ideas, and, by an act of my will, can form a great variety of them and raise them up in my imagination; though, it must be confessed, these creatures of the fancy are not altogether so distinct, so strong, vivid, and permanent as those perceived by my senses, which latter are called "real things." From all which I conclude, *there is a Mind which affects me every moment with all the sensible impressions I perceive.* And from the variety, order, and manner of these I conclude the Author of them to be *wise, powerful, and good beyond comprehension.* Mark it well; I do not say I see things by perceiving that which represents them in the intelligible Substance of God. This I do not understand; but I say the things by me perceived are known by the understanding and produced by the will of an infinite Spirit. And is not all this most plain and evident? Is there any more in it than what a little observation of our own minds, and that which passes in them, not only enables us to conceive but also obliges us to acknowledge?

Hyl. I think I understand you very clearly and own the proof you give of a Deity seems no less evident than surprising. But allowing that God is the supreme and universal cause of all things, yet may there not be still a third nature besides spirits and ideas? May we not admit a subordinate and limited cause of our ideas? In a word, may there not for that be *matter?*

Phil. How often must I inculcate the same thing? You allow the things immediately perceived by sense to exist nowhere without the mind; but there is nothing perceived by sense which is not perceived immediately: therefore there is nothing sensible that exists without the mind. The matter, therefore, which you still insist on is something intelligible, I suppose something that may be discovered by reason, and not by sense.

Hyl. You are in the right.

Phil. Pray let me know what reasoning your belief of matter is grounded on, and what this matter is in your present sense of it.

Hyl. I find myself affected with various ideas whereof I know I am not the cause; neither are they the cause of themselves or of one another, or capable of subsisting by themselves, as being altogether inactive, fleeting, dependent beings. They have therefore some cause distinct from me and them, of which I pretend to know no more than that it is *the cause of my ideas.* And this thing, whatever it be, I call "matter."

Phil. Tell me, Hylas, has everyone a liberty to change the current proper signification attached to a common name in any language? For example, suppose a traveler should tell you that in a certain country men pass unhurt through the fire; and, upon explaining himself, you found he meant by the word "fire" that which others call "water"; or, if he should assert that there are trees that walk upon two legs, meaning men by the term "trees." Would you think this reasonable?

Hyl. No, I should think it very absurd. Common custom is the standard of propriety in language. And for any man to affect speaking improperly is to pervert the use of speech, and can never serve to a better purpose than to protract and multiply disputes where there is no difference in opinion.

Phil. And does not "matter," in the common current acceptation of the word, signify an extended, solid, movable, unthinking, inactive substance?

Hyl. It does.

Phil. And has it not been made evident that no such substance can possibly exist? And though it should be allowed to exist, yet how can that which is *inactive* be a *cause,* or that which is *unthinking* be a *cause of thought?* You may, indeed, if you please, annex to the word "matter" a contrary meaning to what is vulgarly received, and tell me you understand by it an unextended, thinking, active being which is the cause of our ideas. But what else is this than to play with words and run into that very fault you just now condemned with so much reason? I do by no means find fault with your reasoning, in that you collect a cause from the phenomena; but I deny that the cause deducible by reason can properly be termed "matter."

Hyl. There is indeed something in what you say. But I am afraid you do not thoroughly comprehend my meaning. I would by no means be thought to deny that God, or an infinite Spirit, is the Supreme Cause of all things. All I contend for is that, subordinate to the Supreme Agent, there is a cause of a limited and inferior nature which concurs in the production of our ideas, not by any act of will or spiritual efficiency, but by that kind of action which belongs to matter, viz., motion.

Phil. I find you are at every turn relapsing into your old exploded conceit, of a movable and consequently an extended substance existing without the mind. What! have you already forgotten you were convinced, or are you willing I should repeat what has been said on that head? In truth, this is not fair dealing in you still to suppose the being of that which you have so often acknowledged to have no being. But, not to insist further on what has been so largely handled, I ask whether all your ideas are not perfectly passive and inert, including nothing of action in them.

Hyl. They are.

Phil. And are sensible qualities anything else but ideas?

Hyl. How often have I acknowledged that they are not.

Phil. But is not motion a sensible quality?

Hyl. It is.

Phil. Consequently, it is no action?

Hyl. I agree with you. And indeed it is very plain that when I stir my finger it remains passive, but my will which produced the motion is active.

Phil. Now I desire to know, in the first place, whether, motion being allowed to be no action, you can conceive any action besides volition; and, in the second place, whether to say something and conceive nothing be not to talk nonsense; and, lastly, whether, having considered the premises, you do not perceive that to suppose any efficient or active cause of our ideas other than *spirit* is highly absurd and unreasonable?

Hyl. I give up the point entirely. But, though matter may not be a cause, yet what hinders its being an *instrument* subservient to the Supreme Agent in the production of our ideas?

Phil. An instrument say you; pray what may be the figure, springs, wheels, and motions of that instrument?

Hyl. Those I pretend to determine nothing of, both the substance and its qualities being entirely unknown to me.

Phil. What! You are then of opinion it is made up of unknown parts, that it has unknown motions and an unknown shape?

Hyl. I do not believe that it has any figure or motion at all, being already convinced that no sensible qualities can exist in an unperceiving substance.

Phil. But what notion is it possible to frame of an instrument void of all sensible qualities, even extension itself?

Hyl. I do not pretend to have any notion of it.

Phil. And what reason have you to think this unknown, this inconceivable somewhat does exist? Is it that you imagine God cannot act as well without it, or that you find by experience the use of some such thing when you form ideas in your own mind?

Hyl. You are always teasing me for reasons of my belief. Pray what reasons have you not to believe it?

Phil. It is to me a sufficient reason not to believe the existence of anything if I see no reason for believing it. But, not to insist on reasons for believing, you will not so much as let me know what it is you would have me believe, since you say you have no manner of notion of it. After all, let me entreat you to consider whether it be like a philosopher, or even like a man of common sense, to pretend to believe you know not what, and you know not why.

Hyl. Hold, Philonous. When I tell you matter is an *instrument,* I do not mean altogether nothing. It is true I know not the particular kind of instrument, but, however, I have some notion of *instrument in general,* which I apply to it.

Phil. But what if it should prove that there is something, even in the most general notion of *instrument,* as taken in a distinct sense from *cause,* which makes the use of it inconsistent with the divine attributes?

Hyl. Make that appear and I shall give up the point.

Phil. What mean you by the general nature or notion of instrument?

Hyl. That which is common to all particular instruments composes the general notion.

Phil. Is it not common to all instruments that they are applied to the doing those things only which cannot be performed by the mere act of our wills? Thus, for instance, I never use an instrument to move my finger, because it is done by a volition. But I should use one if I were to remove part of a rock or tear up a tree by the roots. Are you of the same mind? Or can you show any example where an instrument is made use of in producing an effect immediately depending on the will of the agent?

Hyl. I own I cannot.

Phil. How, therefore, can you suppose that an all-perfect Spirit, on whose will all things have an absolute and immediate dependence, should need an instrument in his operations or, not needing it, make use of it? Thus it seems to me that you are obliged to own the use of a lifeless inactive instrument to be incompatible with the infinite perfection of God, that is, by your own confession, to give up the point.

Hyl. It does not readily occur what I can answer you.

Phil. But methinks you should be ready to own the truth when it has been fairly proved to you. We, indeed, who are beings of finite powers, are forced to make use of instruments. And the use of an instrument shows the agent to be limited by rules of another's prescription, and that he cannot obtain his end but in such a way and by such conditions. Whence it seems a clear consequence that the Supreme Unlimited Agent uses no tool or instrument at all. The will of an Omnipotent Spirit is no sooner exerted than executed, without the application of means, which, if they are employed by inferior agents, it is not upon account of any real efficacy that is in them, or necessary aptitude to produce any effect, but merely in compliance with the laws of nature or those conditions prescribed to them by the First Cause, who is Himself above all limitation or prescription whatsoever.

Hyl. I will no longer maintain that matter is an instrument. However, I would not be understood to give up its existence neither, since, notwithstanding what has been said, it may still be an *occasion*.

Phil. How many shapes is your matter to take? Or how often must it be proved not to exist before you are content to part with it? But to say no more of this (though by all the laws of disputation I may justly blame you for so frequently changing the signification of the principal term), I would fain know what you mean by affirming that matter is an "occasion," having already denied it to be a cause. And when you have shown in what sense you understand occasion, pray, in the next place, be pleased to show me what reason induces you to believe there is such an occasion of our ideas?

Hyl. As to the first point: by "occasion" I mean an inactive unthinking being, at the presence whereof God excites ideas in our minds.

Phil. And what may be the nature of that inactive unthinking being?

Hyl. I know nothing of its nature.

Phil. Proceed then to the second point and assign some reason why we should allow an existence to this inactive, unthinking, unknown thing.

Hyl. When we see ideas produced in our minds after an orderly and constant manner, it is natural to think they have some fixed and regular occasions at the presence of which they are excited.

Phil. You acknowledge then God alone to be the cause of our ideas, and that He causes them at the presence of those occasions.

Hyl. That is my opinion.

Phil. Those things which you say are present to God, without doubt He perceives.

Hyl. Certainly; otherwise they could not be to Him an occasion of acting.

Phil. Not to insist now on your making sense of this hypothesis, or answering all the puzzling questions and difficulties it is liable to: I only ask whether the order and regularity observable in the series of our ideas, or the course of nature, be not sufficiently accounted for by the wisdom and power of God; and whether it does not derogate from those attributes to suppose He is influenced, directed, or put in mind, when and what He is to act, by an unthinking substance? And, lastly, whether, in case I granted all you contend for, it would make anything to your purpose, it not being easy to conceive how the external or absolute existence of an unthinking substance, distinct from its being perceived, can be inferred from my allowing that there are certain things perceived by the mind of God which are to Him the occasion of producing ideas in us?

Hyl. I am perfectly at a loss what to think, this notion of occasion seeming now altogether as groundless as the rest.

Phil. Do you not at length perceive that in all these different acceptations of matter you have been only supposing you know not what, for no manner of reason and to no kind of use?

Hyl. I freely own myself less fond of my notions since they have been so accurately examined. But still, methinks, I have some confused perception that there is such a thing as matter.

Phil. Either you perceive the being of matter immediately or mediately. If immediately, pray inform me by which of the senses you perceive it. If mediately, let me know by what reasoning it is inferred from those things which you perceive immediately. So much for the perception. Then for the matter itself, I ask whether it is object, substratum, cause, instrument, or occasion? You have already pleaded for each of these, shifting your notions and making matter to appear sometimes in one shape, then in another. And what you have offered has been disapproved and rejected by yourself. If you have anything new to advance I would gladly hear it.

Hyl. I think I have already offered all I had to say on those heads. I am at a loss what more to urge.

Phil. And yet you are loath to part with your old prejudice. But to make you quit it more easily, I desire that, besides what has been hitherto suggested, you will further consider whether, upon supposition that matter exists, you can possibly conceive how you should be affected by it? Or, supposing it did not exist, whether it be not evident you might for all that be affected with the same ideas you now are, and consequently have the very same reason to believe its existence that you now can have?

Hyl. I acknowledge it is possible we might perceive all things just as we do now, though there was no matter in the world; neither can I conceive, if there be matter, how it should produce any idea in our minds. And I do further grant you have entirely satisfied me that it is impossible there should be such a thing as matter in any of the foregoing acceptations. But still I cannot help supposing that there is *matter* in some sense or other. What that is I do not indeed pretend to determine.

Phil. I do not expect you should define exactly the nature of that unknown being. Only be pleased to tell me whether it is a substance—and if so, whether you can suppose a substance without accidents; or in case you suppose it to have accidents or qualities, I desire you will let me know what those qualities are, at least what is meant by "matter's supporting them"?

Hyl. We have already argued on those points. I have no more to say to them. But, to prevent any further questions, let me tell you I at present understand by "matter" neither substance nor accident, thinking nor extended being, neither cause, instrument, nor occasion, but something entirely unknown, distinct from all these.

Phil. It seems then you include in your present notion of matter nothing but the general abstract idea of *entity.*

Hyl. Nothing else, save only that I superadd to this general idea the negation of all those particular things, qualities, or ideas that I perceive, imagine, or in anywise apprehend.

Phil. Pray where do you suppose this unknown matter to exist?

Hyl. Oh Philonous! now you think you have entangled me; for if I say it exists in place, then you will infer that it exists in the mind, since it is agreed that place or extension exists only in the mind; but I am not ashamed to own my ignorance. I know not where it exists; only I am sure it exists not in place. There is a negative answer for you. And you must expect no other to all the questions you put for the future about matter.

Phil. Since you will not tell me where it exists, be pleased to inform me after what manner you suppose it to exist, or what you mean by its "existence"?

Hyl. It neither thinks nor acts, neither perceives nor is perceived.

Phil. But what is there positive in your abstracted notion of its existence?

Hyl. Upon a nice observation, I do not find I have any positive notion or meaning at all. I tell you again, I am not ashamed to own my ignorance. I know not what is meant by its existence or how it exists.

Phil. Continue, good Hylas, to act the same ingenuous part and tell me sincerely whether you can frame a distinct idea of entity in general, prescinded from and exclusive of all thinking and corporeal beings, all particular things whatsoever.

Hyl. Hold, let me think a little—I profess, Philonous, I do not find that I can. At first glance methought I had some dilute and airy notion of pure entity in abstract, but, upon closer attention, it has quite vanished out of sight. The more I think on it, the more am I confirmed in my prudent resolution of giving none but negative answers and not pretending to the least degree of any positive knowledge or conception of matter, its *where,* its *how,* its *entity,* or anything belonging to it.

Phil. When, therefore, you speak of the existence of matter, you have not any notion in your mind?

Hyl. None at all.

Phil. Pray tell me if the case stands not thus: at first, from a belief of material substance, you would have it that the immediate objects existed without the mind; then, that they are archetypes; then, causes; next, instruments; then, occasions: lastly, *something in general,* which being interpreted proves *nothing.* So matter comes to nothing. What think you, Hylas, is not this a fair summary of your whole proceeding?

Hyl. Be that as it will, yet I still insist upon it, that our not being able to conceive a thing is no argument against its existence.

Phil. That from a cause, effect, operation, sign, or other circumstance there may reasonably be inferred the existence of a thing not immediately perceived; and that it were absurd for any man to argue against the existence of that thing, from his having no direct and positive notion of it, I freely own. But where there is nothing of all this, where neither reason nor revelation induces us to believe the existence of a thing, where we have not even a relative notion of it, where an abstraction is made from perceiving and being perceived, from spirit and idea, lastly, where there is not so much as the most inadequate or faint idea pretended to, I will not, indeed, thence conclude against the reality of any notion or existence of anything; but my inference shall be that you mean nothing at all, that you employ words to no manner of purpose, without any design or signification whatsoever. And I leave it to you to consider how mere jargon should be treated.

Hyl. To deal frankly with you, Philonous, your arguments seem in themselves unanswerable, but they have not so great an effect on me as to produce that entire conviction, that hearty acquiescence, which attends demonstration. I find myself still relapsing into an obscure surmise of I know not what—*matter.*

Phil. But are you not sensible, Hylas, that two things must concur to take away all scruple and work a plenary assent in the mind? Let a visible object be set in never so clear a light, yet, if there is any imperfection in the sight, or if the eye is not directed towards it, it will not be distinctly seen. And though a demonstration be never so well grounded and fairly proposed, yet, if there is withal a stain of prejudice or a wrong bias on the understanding, can it be expected on a sudden to perceive clearly and adhere firmly to the truth? No, there is need of time and pains: the attention must be awakened and detained by a frequent repetition of the same thing placed oft in the same, oft in different lights. I have said it already, and find I must still repeat and inculcate, that it is an unaccountable license you take in pretending to maintain you know not what, for you know not what reason, to you know not what purpose. Can this be paralleled in any art or science, any sect or profession of men? Or is there anything so barefacedly groundless and unreasonable to be met with even in the lowest of common conversation? But, perhaps, you will still say, matter may exist, though at the same time you neither know what is meant by "matter" or by its "existence." This indeed is surprising, and the more so because it is altogether voluntary, you not being led to it by any one reason, for I challenge you to show me that thing in nature which needs matter to explain or account for it.

Hyl. The reality of things cannot be maintained without supposing the existence of matter. And is not this, think you, a good reason why I should be earnest in its defense?

Phil. The reality of things! What things, sensible or intelligible?

Hyl. Sensible things.

Phil. My glove, for example?

Hyl. That or any other thing perceived by the senses.

Phil. But to fix on some particular thing, is it not a sufficient evidence to me of the existence of this *glove* that I see it and feel it and wear it? Or, if this will not do, how is it possible I should be assured of the reality of this thing which I actually see in this place by supposing that some unknown thing, which I never did or can see, exists after an unknown manner, in an unknown place, or in no place at all? How can the supposed reality of that which is intangible be a proof that anything tangible really exists? Or of that which is invisible, that any visible thing or, in general, of anything which is imperceptible, that a perceptible exists? Do but explain this and I shall think nothing too hard for you.

Hyl. Upon the whole, I am content to own the existence of matter is highly improbable; but the direct and absolute impossibility of it does not appear to me.

Phil. But granting matter to be possible, yet, upon that account merely, it can have no more claim to existence than a golden mountain or a centaur.

Hyl. I acknowledge it, but still you do not deny it is possible; and that which is possible, for aught you know, may actually exist.

Phil. I deny it to be possible; and have, if I mistake not, evidently proved, from your own concessions, that it is not. In the common sense of the word "matter," is there any more implied than an extended, solid, figured, movable substance existing without the mind? And have not you acknowledged, over and over, that you have seen evident reason for denying the possibility of such a substance?

Hyl. True, but that is only one sense of the term "matter."

Phil. But is it not the only proper genuine received sense? And if matter in such a sense be proved impossible, may it not be thought with good grounds absolutely impossible? Else how could anything be proved impossible? Or, indeed, how could there be any proof at all one way or other to a man who takes the liberty to unsettle and change the common signification of words?

Hyl. I thought philosophers might be allowed to speak more accurately than the vulgar, and were not always confined to the common acceptation of a term.

Phil. But this now mentioned is the common received sense among philosophers themselves. But, not to insist on that, have you not been allowed to take matter in what sense you pleased? And have you not used this privilege in the utmost extent, sometimes entirely changing, at others leaving out or putting into the definition of it whatever, for the present, best served your design, contrary to all the known rules of reason and logic? And has not this shifting, unfair method of yours spun out our dispute to an unnecessary length, matter having been particularly examined and by your own confession refuted in each of those senses? And can any more be required to prove the absolute impossibility of a thing than the proving it impossible in every particular sense that either you or anyone else understands it in?

Hyl. But I am not so thoroughly satisfied that you have proved the impossibility of matter in the last most obscure abstracted and indefinite sense.

Phil. When is a thing shown to be impossible?

Hyl. When a repugnancy is demonstrated between the ideas comprehended in its definition.

Phil. But where there are no ideas, there no repugnancy can be demonstrated between ideas?

Hyl. I agree with you.

Phil. Now, in that which you call the obscure indefinite sense of the word "matter," it is plain, by your own confession, there was included no idea at all, no sense except an unknown sense, which is the same thing as none. You are not, therefore, to expect I should prove a repugnancy between ideas where there are no ideas, or the impossibility of matter taken in an *unknown* sense, that is, no sense at all. My business was only to show you meant *nothing;* and this you were brought to own. So that, in all your various senses, you have been shown either to mean nothing at all or, if anything, an absurdity. And if this be not sufficient to prove the impossibility of a thing, I desire you will let me know what is.

Hyl. I acknowledge you have proved that matter is impossible, nor do I see what more can be said in defense of it. But, at the same time that I give up this, I suspect all my other notions. For surely none could be more seemingly evident than this once was; and yet it now seems as false and absurd as ever it did true before. But I think we have discussed the point sufficiently for the present. The remaining part of the day I would willingly spend in running over in my thoughts the several heads of this morning's conversation, and tomorrow shall be glad to meet you here again about the same time.

Phil. I will not fail to attend you.

THE THIRD DIALOGUE

Philonous. Tell me, Hylas, what are the fruits of yesterday's meditation? Has it confirmed you in the same mind you were in at parting, or have you since seen cause to change your opinion?

Hylas. Truly my opinion is that all our opinions are alike vain and uncertain. What we approve today, we condemn tomorrow. We keep a stir about knowledge and spend our lives in pursuit of it, when, alas! we know nothing all the while; nor do I think it possible for us ever to know anything in this life. Our faculties are too narrow and too few. Nature certainly never intended us for speculation.

Phil. What! say you we can know nothing, Hylas?

Hyl. There is not that single thing in the world whereof we can know the real nature, or what it is in itself.

Phil. Will you tell me I do not really know what fire or water is?

Hyl. You may indeed know that fire appears hot, and water fluid; but this is no more than knowing what sensations are produced in your own mind upon the application of fire and water to your organs of sense. Their internal constitution, their true and real nature, you are utterly in the dark as to *that.*

Phil. Do I not know this to be a real stone that I stand on, and that which I see before my eyes to be a real tree?

Hyl. Know? No, it is impossible you or any man alive should know it. All you know is that you have such a certain idea or appearance in your own mind. But what is this to the real tree or stone? I tell you that color, figure, and hardness, which you perceive, are not the real natures of those things, or in the least like them. The same may be said of all other real things or corporeal substances which compose the world. They have, none of them, anything in themselves, like those sensible qualities by us perceived. We should not, therefore, pretend to affirm or know anything of them, as they are in their own nature.

Phil. But surely, Hylas, I can distinguish gold, for example, from iron; and how could this be if I knew not what either truly was?

Hyl. Believe me, Philonous, you can only distinguish between your own ideas. That yellowness, that weight, and other sensible qualities, think you they are really in the gold? They are only relative to the senses and have no absolute existence in nature. And in pretending to distinguish the species of real things by the appearances in your mind, you may perhaps act as wisely as he that should conclude two men were of a different species because their clothes were not of the same color.

Phil. It seems, then, we are altogether put off with the appearances of things, and those false ones, too. The very meat I eat, and the cloth I wear, have nothing in them like what I see and feel.

Hyl. Even so.

Phil. But is it not strange the whole world should be thus imposed on and so foolish as to believe their senses? And yet I know not how it is, but men eat, and drink, and sleep, and perform all the offices of life as comfortably and conveniently as if they really knew the things they are conversant about.

Hyl. They do so; but you know ordinary practice does not require a nicety of speculative knowledge. Hence the vulgar retain their mistakes, and for all that make a shift to bustle through the affairs of life. But philosophers know better things.

Phil. You mean they know that they *know nothing.*

Hyl. That is the very top and perfection of human knowledge.

Phil. But are you all this while in earnest, Hylas; and are you seriously persuaded that you know nothing real in the world? Suppose you are going to write, would you not call for pen, ink, and paper, like another man; and do you not know what it is you call for?

Hyl. How often must I tell you that I know not the real nature of any one thing in the universe? I may indeed upon occasion make use of pen, ink, and paper. But what any one of them is in its own true nature, I declare positively I know not. And the same is true with regard to every other corporeal thing. And what is more, we are not only ignorant of the true and real nature of things, but even of their existence. It cannot be denied that we perceive such certain appearances or ideas, but it cannot be concluded from thence that bodies really exist. Nay, now I think on it, I must, agreeably to my former concessions, further declare that it is impossible any real corporeal thing should exist in nature.

Phil. You amaze me. Was ever anything more wild and extravagant than the notions you now maintain? And is it not evident you are led into all these extravagances by the belief of *material substance?* This makes you dream of those unknown natures in everything. It is this occasions your distinguishing between the reality and sensible appearances of things. It is to this you are indebted for being ignorant of what everybody else knows perfectly well. Nor is this all: you are not only ignorant of the true nature of everything, but you know not whether any thing really exists or whether there are any true natures at all, forasmuch as you attribute to your material beings an absolute or external existence wherein you suppose their reality consists. And as you are forced in the end to acknowledge such an existence means either a direct repugnancy or nothing at all, it follows that you are obliged to pull down your own hypothesis of material substance and positively to deny the real existence of any part of the universe. And so you are plunged into the deepest and most deplorable skepticism that ever man was. Tell me, Hylas, is it not as I say?

Hyl. I agree with you. "Material substance" was no more than a hypothesis, and a false and groundless one, too. I will no longer spend my breath in defense of it. But whatever hypothesis you advance or whatever scheme of things you introduce in its stead, I doubt not it will appear every whit as false; let me but be allowed to question you upon it. That is, suffer me to serve you in your own kind, and I warrant it shall conduct you through as many perplexities and contradictions to the very same state of skepticism that I myself am in at present.

Phil. I assure you, Hylas, I do not pretend to frame any hypothesis at all. I am of a vulgar cast, simple enough to believe my senses and leave things as I find them. To be plain, it is my opinion that the real things are those very things I see and feel, and perceive by my senses. These I know and, finding they answer all the necessities and purposes of life, have no reason to be solicitous about any other unknown beings. A piece of sensible bread, for instance, would stay my stomach better than ten thousand times as much of that insensible, unintelligible real bread you speak of. It is likewise my opinion that colors and other sensible qualities are on the objects. I cannot for my life help thinking that snow is white, and fire hot. You, indeed, who by "snow" and "fire" mean certain external, unperceived, unperceiving substances are in the right to deny whiteness or heat to be affections inherent in them. But I who understand by those words the things I see and feel am obliged to think like other folks. And as I am no skeptic with regard to the nature of things, so neither am I as to their existence. That a thing should be really perceived by my senses and at the same time not really exist is to me a plain contradiction, since I cannot prescind or abstract, even in thought, the existence of a sensible thing from its being perceived. Wood, stones, fire, water, flesh, iron, and the like things which I name and discourse of are things that I know. And I should not have known them but that I perceived them by my senses; and things perceived by the senses are immediately perceived; and things immediately perceived are ideas; and ideas cannot exist without the mind; their existence therefore consists in being perceived; when, therefore, they are actually perceived, there can be no doubt of their existence. Away then with all that skepticism, all those ridiculous philosophical doubts. What a jest is it for a philosopher to question the existence of sensible things till he has it proved to him from the veracity of God, or to pretend our knowledge in this point falls short of intuition or demonstration! I might as well doubt of my own being as of the being of those things I actually see and feel.

Hyl. Not so fast, Philonous: You say you cannot conceive how sensible things should exist without the mind. Do you not?

Phil. I do.

Hyl. Supposing you were annihilated, cannot you conceive it possible that things perceivable by sense may still exist?

Phil. I can, but then it must be in another mind. When I deny sensible things an existence out of the mind, I do not mean my mind in particular, but all minds. Now it is plain they have an existence exterior to my mind, since I find them by experience to be independent of it. There is therefore some other mind wherein they exist during the intervals between the times of my perceiving them, as likewise they did before my birth, and would do after my supposed annihilation. And as the same is true with regard to all other finite created spirits, it necessarily follows there is an *omnipresent external Mind* which knows and comprehends all things, and exhibits them to our view in such a manner and according to such rules as He Himself has ordained and are by us termed the "laws of nature."

Hyl. Answer me, Philonous. Are all our ideas perfectly inert beings? Or have they any agency included in them?

Phil. They are altogether passive and inert.

Hyl. And is not God an agent, a being purely active?

Phil. I acknowledge it.

Hyl. No idea, therefore, can be like unto or represent the nature of God.

Phil. It cannot.

Hyl. Since, therefore, you have no idea of the mind of God, how can you conceive it possible that things should exist in His mind? Or, if you can conceive the mind of God without having an idea of it, why may not I be allowed to conceive the existence of matter, notwithstanding I have no idea of it?

Phil. As to your first question: I own I have properly no *idea* either of God or any other spirit; for these, being active, cannot be represented by things perfectly inert as our ideas are. I do nevertheless know that I, who am a spirit or thinking substance, exist as certainly as I know my ideas exist. Further, I know what I mean by the terms "I" and "myself"; and I know this immediately or intuitively, though I do not perceive it as I perceive a triangle, a color, or a sound. The mind, spirit, or soul is that indivisible unextended thing which thinks, acts, and perceives. I say "indivisible," because unextended; and "unextended," because extended, figured, movable things are ideas; and that which perceives ideas, which thinks and wills, is plainly itself no idea, nor like an idea. Ideas are things inactive and perceived. And spirits a sort of beings altogether different from them. I do not therefore say my soul is an idea, or like an idea. However, taking the word "idea" in a large sense, my soul may be said to furnish me with an idea, that is, an image or likeness of God, though indeed extremely inadequate. For all the notion I have of God is obtained by reflecting on my own soul, heightening its powers, and removing its imperfections. I have, therefore, though not an inactive idea, yet in *myself* some sort of an active thinking image of the Deity. And though I perceive Him not by sense, yet I have a notion of Him, or know Him by reflection and reasoning. My own mind and my own ideas I have an immediate knowledge of; and, by the help of these, do mediately apprehend the possibility of the existence of other spirits and ideas. Further, from my own being, and from the dependency I find in myself and my ideas, I do, by an act of reason, necessarily infer the existence of a God and of all created things in the mind of God. So much for your first question. For the second: I suppose by this time you can answer it yourself. For you neither perceive matter objectively, as you do an inactive being or idea, nor know it, as you do yourself by a reflex act; neither do you mediately apprehend it by similitude of the one or the other, nor yet collect it by reasoning from that which you know immediately. All which makes the case of *matter* widely different from that of the *Deity.*

[*Hyl.*[4] You say your own soul supplies you with some sort of an idea or image of God. But, at the same time, you acknowledge you have, properly speaking, no idea of your own soul. You even affirm that spirits are a sort of beings altogether different from ideas. Consequently, that no idea can be like a spirit. We have, therefore, no idea of any spirit. You admit nevertheless that there is spiritual substance, although you have no idea of it, while you deny there can be such a thing as material substance, because you have no notion or idea of it. Is this fair dealing? To act consistently, you must either admit matter or reject spirit. What say you to this?

Phil. I say, in the first place, that I do not deny the existence of material substance merely because I have no notion of it, but because the notion of it is inconsistent, or, in other words, because it is repugnant that there should be a notion of it. Many things, for aught I know, may exist whereof neither I nor any other man has or can have any idea or notion whatsoever. But then those things must be possible, that is, nothing inconsistent must be included in their definition. I say, secondly, that, although we believe things to exist which we do not perceive, yet we may not believe that any particular thing exists without some reason for such belief; but I have no reason for believing the existence of matter. I have no immediate intuition thereof, neither can I immediately from my sensations, ideas, notions, actions, or passions infer an unthinking, unperceiving, inactive substance, either by probable deduction or necessary consequence. Whereas the being of my self, that is, my own soul, mind, or thinking principle, I evidently know by reflection. You will forgive me if I repeat the same things in answer to the same objections. In the very notion or definition of "material substance" there is included a manifest repugnance and inconsistency. But this cannot be said of the notion of spirit. That ideas should exist in what does not perceive, or be produced by what does not act, is repugnant. But it is no repugnancy to say that a perceiving thing should be the subject of ideas, or an active thing the cause of them. It is granted we have neither an immediate evidence nor a demonstrative knowledge of the existence of other finite spirits, but it will not thence follow that such spirits are on a foot with material substances, if to suppose the one be inconsistent, and it be not inconsistent to suppose the other; if the one can be inferred by no argument, and there is a probability for the other; if we see signs and effects indicating distinct finite agents like ourselves, and see no sign or symptom whatever that leads to a rational belief of matter. I say, lastly, that I have a notion of spirit, though I have not, strictly speaking, an idea of it. I do not perceive it as an idea, or by means of an idea, but know it by reflection.

Hyl. Notwithstanding all you have said, to me it seems that, according to your own way of thinking, and in consequence of your own principles, it should follow that you are only a system of floating ideas without any substance to support them. Words are not to be used without a meaning. And, as there is no more meaning in *spiritual* substance than in *material* substance, the one is to be exploded as well as the other.

Phil. How often must I repeat that I know or am conscious of my own being, and that I *myself* am not my ideas, but somewhat else, a thinking, active principle that perceives, knows, wills, and operates about ideas. I know that I, one and the same self, perceive both colors and sounds, that a color cannot perceive a sound, nor a sound a color, that I am therefore one individual principle distinct from color and sound, and, for the same reason, from all other sensible things and inert ideas. But I am not in like manner conscious either of the existence or essence of matter. On the contrary, I know that nothing inconsistent can exist, and that the existence of matter implies an inconsistency. Further, I know what I mean when I affirm that there is a spiritual substance or support of ideas, that is, that a spirit knows and perceives ideas. But I do not know what is meant when it is said that an unperceiving substance has inherent in it and supports either ideas or the archetypes of ideas. There is, therefore, upon the whole no parity of case between spirit and matter.]

Hyl. I own myself satisfied in this point. But do you in earnest think the real existence of sensible things consists in their being actually perceived? If so, how comes it that all mankind distinguish between them? Ask the first man you meet, and he shall tell you, "to be perceived" is one thing, and "to exist" is another.

Phil. I am content, Hylas, to appeal to the common sense of the world for the truth of my notion. Ask the gardener why he thinks yonder cherry tree exists in the garden, and he shall tell you, because he sees and feels it; in a word, because he perceives it by his senses. Ask him why he thinks an orange tree not to be there, and he shall tell you, because he does not perceive it. What he perceives by sense, that he terms a real being and says it "is" or "exists"; but that which is not perceivable, the same, he says, has no being.

Hyl. Yes, Philonous, I grant the existence of a sensible thing consists in being perceivable, but not in being actually perceived.

Phil. And what is perceivable but an idea? And can an idea exist without being actually perceived? These are points long since agreed between us.

Hyl. But be your opinion never so true, yet surely you will not deny it is shocking and contrary to the common sense of men. Ask the fellow whether yonder tree has an existence out of his mind; what answer think you he would make?

Phil. The same that I should myself, to wit, that it does exist out of his mind. But then to a Christian it cannot surely be shocking to say, the real tree, existing without his mind, is truly known and comprehended by (that is, *exists in*) the infinite mind of God. Probably he may not at first glance be aware of the direct and immediate proof there is of this, inasmuch as the very being of a tree, or any other sensible thing, implies a mind wherein it is. But the point itself he cannot deny. The question between the materialists and me is not whether things have a *real* existence out of the mind of this or that person, but, whether they have an *absolute* existence, distinct from being perceived by God, and exterior to all minds. This, indeed, some heathens and philosophers have affirmed, but whoever entertains notions of the Deity suitable to the Holy Scriptures will be of another opinion.

Hyl. But, according to your notions, what difference is there between real things and chimeras formed by the imagination or the visions of a dream, since they are all equally in the mind?

Phil. The ideas formed by the imagination are faint and indistinct; they have, besides, an entire dependence on the will. But the ideas perceived by sense, that is, real things, are more vivid and clear, and, being imprinted on the mind by a spirit distinct from us, have not the like dependence on our will. There is, therefore, no danger of confounding these with the foregoing, and there is as little of confounding them with the visions of a dream, which are dim, irregular, and confused. And though they should happen to be never so lively and natural, yet, by their not being connected and of a piece with the preceding and subsequent transaction of our lives, they might easily be distinguished from realities. In short, by whatever method you distinguish *things* from *chimeras* on your own scheme, the same, it is evident, will hold also upon mine. For it must be, I presume, by some perceived difference, and I am not for depriving you of any one thing that you perceive.

Hyl. But still, Philonous, you hold there is nothing in the world but spirits and ideas. And this you must needs acknowledge sounds very oddly.

Phil. I own the word "idea," not being commonly used for "thing," sounds something out of the way. My reason for using it was because a necessary relation to the mind is understood to be implied by the term; and it is now commonly used by philosophers to denote the immediate objects of the understanding. But however oddly the proposition may sound in words, yet it includes nothing so very strange or shocking in its sense, which in effect amounts to no more than this, to wit, that there are only things perceiving and things perceived, or that every unthinking being is necessarily, and from the very nature of its existence, perceived by some mind, if not by any finite created mind, yet certainly by the infinite mind of God, in whom "we live, and move, and have our being." Is this as strange as to say the sensible qualities are not on the object or that we cannot be sure of the existence of things, or know anything of their real natures, though we both see and feel them and perceive them by all our senses?

Hyl. And, in consequence of this, must we not think there are no such things as physical or corporeal causes, but that a spirit is the immediate cause of all the *phenomena* in nature? Can there be anything more extravagant than this?

Phil. Yes, it is infinitely more extravagant to say a thing which is inert operates on the mind, and which is unperceiving is the cause of our perceptions. Besides, that which to you I know not for what reason seems so extravagant is no more than the Holy Scriptures assert in a hundred places. In them God is represented as the sole and immediate Author of all those effects which some heathens and philosophers are wont to ascribe to Nature, Matter, Fate, or the like unthinking principle. This is so much the constant language of Scripture that it were needless to confirm it by citations.

Hyl. You are not aware, Philonous, that, in making God the immediate Author of all the motions in nature, you make Him the Author of murder, sacrilege, adultery, and the like heinous sins.

Phil. In answer to that I observe, first, that the imputation of guilt is the same whether a person commits an action with or without an instrument. In case, therefore, you suppose God to act by the mediation of an instrument or occasion called "matter," you as truly make Him the Author of sin as I, who think Him the immediate agent in all those operations vulgarly ascribed to Nature. I further observe that sin or moral turpitude does not consist in the outward physical action or motion, but in the internal deviation of the will from the laws of reason and religion. This is plain, in that the killing an enemy in a battle or putting a criminal legally to death is not thought sinful, though the outward act be the very same with that in the case of murder. Since, therefore, sin does not consist in the physical action, the making God an immediate cause of all such actions is not making Him the

Author of sin. Lastly, I have nowhere said that God is the only agent who produces all the motions in bodies. It is true I have denied there are any other agents besides spirits, but this is very consistent with allowing to thinking rational beings, in the production of motions, the use of limited powers, ultimately, indeed, derived from God but immediately under the direction of their own wills, which is sufficient to entitle them to all the guilt of their actions.

Hyl. But the denying matter, Philonous, or corporeal substance, there is the point. You can never persuade me that this is not repugnant to the universal sense of mankind. Were our dispute to be determined by most voices, I am confident you would give up the point without gathering the votes.

Phil. I wish both our opinions were fairly stated and submitted to the judgment of men who had plain common sense, without the prejudices of a learned education. Let me be represented as one who trusts his senses, who thinks he knows the things he sees and feels, and entertains no doubts of their existence; and you fairly set forth with all your doubts, your paradoxes, and your skepticism about you, and I shall willingly acquiesce in the determination of any indifferent person. That there is no substance wherein ideas can exist besides spirit is to me evident, and that the objects immediately perceived are ideas is on all hands agreed. And that sensible qualities are objects immediately perceived no one can deny. It is therefore evident there can be no *substratum* of those qualities but spirit, in which they exist, not by way of mode or property, but as a thing perceived in that which perceives it. I deny, therefore, that there is any unthinking *substratum* of the objects of sense, and in that acceptation that there is any material substance. But if by "material substance" is meant only sensible body, that which is seen and felt (and the unphilosophical part of the world, I dare say, mean no more), then I am more certain of matter's existence than you or any other philosopher pretend to be. If there be anything which makes the generality of mankind averse from the notions I espouse, it is a misapprehension that I deny the reality of sensible things; but as it is you who are guilty of that and not I, it follows that in truth their aversion is against your notions and not mine. I do therefore assert that I am as certain as of my own being that there are bodies or corporeal substances (meaning the things I perceive by my senses), and that, granting this, the bulk of mankind will take no thought about, nor think themselves at all concerned in the fate of, those unknown natures and philosophical quiddities which some men are so fond of.

Hyl. What say you to this? Since, according to you, men judge of the reality of things by their senses, how can a man be mistaken in thinking the moon a plain lucid surface, about a foot in diameter, or a square tower, seen at a distance, round, or an oar, with one end in the water, crooked?

Phil. He is not mistaken with regard to the ideas he actually perceives, but in the inferences he makes from his present perceptions. Thus, in the case of the oar, what he immediately perceives by sight is certainly crooked, and so far he is in the right. But if he thence conclude that upon taking the oar out of the water he shall perceive the same crookedness, or that it would affect his touch as crooked things are wont to do, in that he is mistaken. In like manner, if he shall conclude, from what he perceives in one station, that, in case he advances toward the moon or tower, he should still be affected with the like ideas, he is mistaken. But his mistake lies not in what he perceives immediately and at present (it being a manifest contradiction to suppose he should err in respect of that), but in the wrong judgment he makes concerning the ideas he apprehends to be connected with those immediately perceived, or, concerning the ideas, that from what he perceives at present he imagines would be perceived in other circumstances. The case is the same with regard to the Copernican system. We do not here perceive any motion of the earth, but it were erroneous thence to conclude that, in case we were placed at as great a distance from that as we are now from the other planets, we should not then perceive its motion.

Hyl. I understand you and must needs own you say things plausible enough, but give me leave to put you in mind of one thing. Pray, Philonous, were you not formerly as positive that matter existed as you are now that it does not?

Phil. I was. But here lies the difference. Before, my positiveness was founded, without examination, upon prejudice, but now, after inquiry, upon evidence.

Hyl. After all, it seems our dispute is rather about words than things. We agree in the thing, but differ in the name. That we are affected with ideas from without is evident; and it is no less evident that there must be (I will not say archetypes, but) powers without the mind corresponding to those ideas. And as these powers cannot subsist by themselves, there is some subject of them necessarily to be admitted, which I call "matter," and you call "spirit." This is all the difference.

Phil. Pray, Hylas, is that powerful being, or subject of powers, extended?

Hyl. It has not extension, but it has the power to raise in you the idea of extension.

Phil. It is therefore itself unextended?

Hyl. I grant it.

Phil. Is it not also active?

Hyl. Without doubt; otherwise, how could we attribute powers to it?

Phil. Now let me ask you two questions: *First,* whether it be agreeable to the usage either of philosophers or others to give the name "matter" to an unextended active being? And, secondly, whether it be not ridiculously absurd to misapply names contrary to the common use of language?

Hyl. Well then, let it not be called "matter," since you will have it so, but some "third nature," distinct from matter and spirit. For what reason is there why you should call it spirit? Does not the notion of spirit imply that it is thinking as well as active and unextended?

Phil. My reason is this: because I have a mind to have some notion or meaning in what I say, but I have no notion of any action distinct from volition, neither can I conceive volition to be anywhere but in a spirit; therefore, when I speak of an active being I am obliged to mean a spirit. Besides, what can be plainer than that a thing which has no ideas in itself cannot impart them to me; and, if it has ideas, surely it must be a spirit. To make you comprehend the point still more clearly, if it be possible: I assert as well as you that, since we are affected from without, we must allow powers to be without, in a being distinct from ourselves. So far we are agreed. But then we differ as to the kind of this powerful being. I will have it to be spirit, you matter or I know not what (I may add, too, you know not what) third nature. Thus I prove it to be spirit. From the effects I see produced I conclude there are actions; and because actions, volitions; and because there are volitions, there must be a will. Again, the things I perceive must have an existence, they or their archetypes, out of my mind; but, being ideas, neither they nor their archetypes can exist otherwise than in an understanding, there is therefore an understanding. But will and understanding constitute in the strictest sense a mind or spirit. The powerful cause, therefore, of my ideas is in strict propriety of speech a *spirit.*

Hyl. And now I warrant you think you have made the point very clear, little suspecting that what you advance leads directly to a contradiction. Is it not an absurdity to imagine any imperfection in God?

Phil. Without a doubt.

Hyl. To suffer pain is an imperfection?

Phil. It is.

Hyl. Are we not sometimes affected with pain and uneasiness by some other being?

Phil. We are.

Hyl. And have you not said that being is a spirit, and is not that spirit God?

Phil. I grant it.

Hyl. But you have asserted that whatever ideas we perceive from without are in the mind which affects us. The ideas, therefore, of pain and uneasiness are in God, or, in other words, God suffers pain; that is to say, there is an imperfection in the divine nature, which, you acknowledge, was absurd. So you are caught in a plain contradiction.

Phil. That God knows or understands all things, and that He knows, among other things, what pain is, even every sort of painful sensation, and what it is for His creatures to suffer pain, I make no question. But that God, though He knows and sometimes causes painful sensations in us, can Himself suffer pain I positively deny. We, who are limited and dependent spirits, are liable to impressions of sense, the effects of an external agent, which, being produced against our wills, are sometimes painful and uneasy. But God, whom no external being can affect, who perceives nothing by sense as we do, whose will is absolute and independent, causing all things, and liable to be thwarted or resisted by nothing, it is evident such a Being as this can suffer nothing, nor be affected with any painful sensation or, indeed, any sensation at all. We are chained to a body; that is to say, our perceptions are connected with corporeal motions. By the law of our nature we are affected upon every alteration in the nervous parts of our sensible body; which sensible body, rightly considered, is nothing but a complexion of such qualities or ideas as have no existence distinct from being perceived by a mind; so that this connection of sensations with corporeal motions means no more than a correspondence in the order of nature between two sets of ideas, or things immediately perceivable. But God is a pure spirit, disengaged from all such sympathy or natural ties. No corporeal motions are attended with the sensations of pain or pleasure in His mind. To know everything knowable is certainly a perfection, but to endure or suffer or feel anything by sense is an imperfection. The former, I say, agrees to God, but not the latter. God knows or has ideas, but His ideas are not conveyed to Him by sense, as ours are. Your not distinguishing where there is so manifest a difference makes you fancy you see an absurdity where there is none.

Hyl. But all this while you have not considered that the quantity of matter has been demonstrated to be proportional to the gravity of bodies. And what can withstand demonstration?

Phil. Let me see how you demonstrate that point.

Hyl. I lay it down for a principle that the moments or quantities of motion in bodies are in a direct compounded reason of the velocities and quantities of matter contained in them. Hence, where the velocities are equal, it follows the moments are directly as the quantity of matter in each. But it is found by experience that all bodies (bating the small inequalities arising from the resistance of the air) descend with an equal velocity; the motion therefore of descending bodies, and consequently their gravity, which is the cause or principle of that motion, is proportional to the quantity of matter, which was to be demonstrated.

Phil. You lay it down as a self-evident principle that the quantity of motion in any body is proportional to the velocity and matter taken together; and this is made use of to prove a proposition from whence the existence of matter is inferred. Pray is not this arguing in a circle?

Hyl. In the premise I only mean that the motion is proportional to the velocity, jointly with the extension and solidity.

Phil. But allowing this to be true, yet it will not thence follow that gravity is proportional to matter in your philosophic sense of the word, except you take it for granted that unknown *substratum,* or whatever else you call it, is proportional to those sensible qualities which to suppose is plainly begging the question. That there is magnitude and solidity or resistance perceived by sense I readily grant, as likewise, that gravity may be proportional to those qualities I will not dispute. But that either these qualities as perceived by us, or the powers producing them, do exist in a *material substratum*—this is what I deny, and you, indeed, affirm but, notwithstanding your demonstration, have not yet proved.

Hyl. I shall insist no longer on that point. Do you think, however, you shall persuade me the natural philosophers have been dreaming all this while? Pray what becomes of all their hypotheses and explications of the phenomena which suppose the existence of matter?

Phil. What mean you, Hylas, by the "phenomena"?

Hyl. I mean the appearances which I perceive by my senses.

Phil. And the appearances perceived by sense, are they not ideas?

Hyl. I have told you so a hundred times.

Phil. Therefore, to explain the phenomena is to show how we come to be affected with ideas in that manner and order wherein they are imprinted on our senses. Is it not?

Hyl. It is.

Phil. Now, if you can prove that any philosopher has explained the production of any one idea in our minds by the help of *matter*, I shall forever acquiesce and look on all that has been said against it as nothing; but if you cannot, it is vain to urge the explication of phenomena. That a being endowed with knowledge and will should produce or exhibit ideas is easily understood. But that a being which is utterly destitute of these faculties should be able to produce ideas, or in any sort to affect an intelligence, this I can never understand. This I say, though we had some positive conception of matter, though we knew its qualities and could comprehend its existence, would yet be so far from explaining things that it is itself the most inexplicable thing in the world. And yet, for all this, it will not follow that philosophers have been doing nothing; for by observing and reasoning upon the connection of ideas, they discover the laws and methods of nature, which is a part of knowledge both useful and entertaining.

Hyl. After all, can it be supposed God would deceive all mankind? Do you imagine He would have induced the whole world to believe the being of matter if there was no such thing?

Phil. That every epidemical opinion arising from prejudice, or passion, or thoughtlessness may be imputed to God, as the Author of it, I believe you will not affirm. Whatsoever opinion we father on Him, it must be either because He has discovered it to us by supernatural revelation or because it is so evident to our natural faculties, which were framed and given us by God, that it is impossible we should withhold our assent from it. But where is the revelation? Or where is the evidence that extorts the belief of matter? Nay, how does it appear that matter, taken for something distinct from what we perceive by our senses is thought to exist by all mankind, or, indeed, by any except a few philosophers who do not know what they would be at? Your question supposes these points are clear; and, when you have cleared them, I shall think myself obliged to give you another answer. In the meantime let it suffice that I tell you I do not suppose God has deceived mankind at all.

Hyl. But the novelty, Philonous, the novelty! There lies the danger. New notions should always be discountenanced; they unsettle men's minds, and nobody knows where they will end.

Phil. Why the rejecting a notion that has no foundation, either in sense or in reason or in Divine authority, should be thought to unsettle the belief of such opinions as are grounded on all or any of these, I cannot imagine. That innovations in government and religion are dangerous and ought to be discountenanced, I freely own. But is there the like reason why they should be discouraged in philosophy? The making anything known which was unknown before is an innovation in knowledge; and if all such innovations had been forbidden, men would [not] have made a notable progress in the arts and sciences. But it is none of my business to plead for novelties and paradoxes. That the qualities we perceive are not on the objects, that we must not believe our senses, that we know nothing of the real nature of things and can never be assured even of their existence, that real colors and sounds are nothing but certain unknown figures and motions, that motions are in themselves neither swift nor slow, that there are in bodies absolute extensions without any particular magnitude or figure, that a thing stupid, thoughtless, and inactive operates on a spirit, that the least particle of a body contains innumerable extended parts—these are the novelties, these are the strange notions which shock the genuine uncorrupted judgment of all mankind, and, being once admitted, embarrass the mind with endless doubts and difficulties. And it is against these and the like innovations I endeavor to vindicate Common Sense. It is true, in doing this I may, perhaps, be obliged to use some ambages and ways of speech not common. But if my notions are once thoroughly understood, that which is most singular in them will, in effect, be found to amount to no more than this—that it is absolutely impossible and a plain contradiction to suppose any unthinking being should exist without being perceived by a mind. And if this notion be singular, it is a shame it should be so at this time of day and in a Christian country.

Hyl. As for the difficulties other opinions may be liable to, those are out of the question. It is your business to defend your own opinion. Can anything be plainer than that you are for changing all things into ideas? You, I say, who are not ashamed to charge me with skepticism. This is so plain, there is no denying it.

Phil. You mistake me. I am not for changing things into ideas but rather ideas into things, since those immediate objects of perception, which, according to you, are only appearances of things, I take to be the real things themselves.

Hyl. Things! you may pretend what you please; but it is certain you leave us nothing but the empty forms of things, the outside only which strikes the senses.

Phil. What you call the empty forms and outside of things seem to me the very things themselves. Nor are they empty or incomplete otherwise than upon your supposition that matter is an essential part of all corporeal things. We both, therefore, agree in this, that we perceive only sensible forms; but herein we differ: you will have them to be empty appearances, I real beings. In short, you do not trust your senses, I do.

Hyl. You say you believe your senses, and seem to applaud yourself that in this you agree with the vulgar. According to you, therefore, the true nature of a thing is discovered by the senses. If so, whence comes that disagreement? Why, is not the same figure, and other sensible qualities, perceived all manner of ways? And why should we use a microscope the better to discover the true nature of a body, if it were discoverable to the naked eye?

Phil. Strictly speaking, Hylas, we do not see the same object that we feel; neither is the same object perceived by the microscope which was by the naked eye. But in case every variation was thought sufficient to constitute a new kind of individual, the endless number or confusion of names would render language impracticable. Therefore, to avoid this as well as other inconveniences which are obvious upon a little thought, men combine together several ideas, apprehended by divers senses, or by the same sense at different times or in different circumstances, but observed, however, to have some connection in nature, either with respect to coexistence or succession; all which they refer to one name and consider as one thing. Hence it follows that when I examine by my other senses a thing I have seen, it is not in order to understand better the same object which I had perceived by sight, the object of one sense not being perceived by the other senses. And when I look through a microscope, it is not that I may perceive more clearly what I perceived already with my bare eyes, the object perceived by the glass being quite different from the former. But in both cases my aim is only to know what ideas are connected together; and the more a man knows of the connection of ideas, the more he is said to know of the nature of things. What, therefore, if our ideas are variable, what if our senses are not in all circumstances affected with the same appearances? It will not thence follow they are not to be trusted or that they are inconsistent either with themselves or anything else, except it be with your preconceived notion of (I know not what) one single, unchanged, unperceivable, real nature, marked by each name; which prejudice seems to have taken its rise from not rightly understanding the common language of men speaking of several distinct ideas as united into one thing by the mind. And, indeed, there is cause to suspect several erroneous conceits of the philosophers are owing to the same original: while they began to build their schemes not so much on notions as words which were framed by the vulgar merely for convenience and dispatch in the common actions of life, without any regard to speculation.

Hyl. Methinks I apprehend your meaning.

Phil. It is your opinion the ideas we perceive by our senses are not real things, but images or copies of them. Our knowledge, therefore, is no further real than as our ideas are the true representations of those originals. But as these supposed originals are in themselves unknown, it is impossible to know how far our ideas resemble them, or whether they resemble them at all. We cannot, therefore, be sure we have any real knowledge. Further, as our ideas are perpetually varied, without any change in the supposed real things, it necessarily follows they cannot all be true copies of them, if some are and others are not, it is impossible to distinguish the former from the latter. And this plunges us yet deeper in uncertainty. Again, when we consider the point, we cannot conceive how any idea, or anything like an idea, should have an absolute existence out of a mind, nor consequently, according to you, how there should be any real thing in nature. The result of all which is that we are thrown into the most hopeless and abandoned skepticism. Now give me leave to ask you, *first,* whether your referring ideas to certain absolutely existing unperceived substances, as their originals, be not the source of all this skepticism? *Secondly,* whether you are informed, either by sense or reason, of the existence of those unknown originals? And in case you are not, whether it be not absurd to suppose them? *Thirdly,* whether, upon inquiry, you find there is anything distinctly conceived or meant by the "absolute or external existence of unperceiving substances"; *Lastly,* whether, the premises considered, it be not the wisest way to follow nature, trust your senses, and, laying aside all anxious thought about unknown natures or substances, admit with the vulgar those for real things which are perceived by the senses?

Hyl. For the present I have no inclination to the answering part. I would much rather see how you can get over what follows. Pray, are not the objects perceived by the senses of one likewise perceivable to others present? If there were a hundred more here, they would all see the garden, the trees and flowers, as I see them. But they are not in the same manner affected with the ideas I frame in my imagination. Does not this make a difference between the former sort of objects and the latter?

Phil. I grant it does. Nor have I ever denied a difference between the objects of sense and those of imagination. But what would you infer from thence? You cannot say that sensible objects exist unperceived because they are perceived by many.

Hyl. I own I can make nothing of that objection, but it has led me into another. Is it not your opinion that by our senses we perceive only the ideas existing in our minds?

Phil. It is.

Hyl. But the same idea which is in my mind cannot be in yours or in any other mind. Does it not, therefore, follow from your principles that no two can see the same thing? And is not this highly absurd?

Phil. If the term "same" be taken in the vulgar acceptation, it is certain (and not at all repugnant to the principles I maintain) that different persons may perceive the same thing, or the same thing or idea exist in different minds. Words are of arbitrary imposition; and since men are used to apply the word "same" where no distinction or variety is perceived, and I do not pretend to alter their perceptions, it follows that, as men have said before, *several saw the same thing,* so they may, upon like occasions, still continue to use the same phrase without any deviation either from propriety of language or the truth of things. But if the term "same" be used in the acceptation of philosophers who pretend to an abstracted notion of identity, then, according to their sundry definitions of this notion (for it is not yet agreed wherein that philosophic identity consists), it may or may not be possible for divers persons to perceive the same thing. But whether philosophers shall think fit to call a thing the "same" or no is, I conceive, of small importance. Let us suppose several men together, all endued with the same faculties, and consequently affected in like sort by their senses, and who had yet never known the use of language; they would without question agree in their perceptions. Though perhaps, when they came to the use of speech, some regarding the uniformness of what was perceived might call it the "same" thing; others, especially regarding the diversity of persons who perceived, might choose the denomination of "different" things. But who sees not that all the dispute is about a word, to wit, whether what is perceived by different persons may yet have the term "same" applied to it? Or suppose a house whose walls or outward shell remaining unaltered, the chambers are all pulled down, and new ones built in their place, and that you should call this the "same," and I should say it was not the "same," house—would we not, for all this, perfectly agree in our thoughts of the house considered in itself? And would not all the difference consist in a sound? If you should say we differed in our notions, for that you superadded to your idea of the house the simple abstracted idea of identity, whereas I did not, I would tell you I know not what you mean by that "abstracted idea of identity," and should desire you to look into your own thoughts and be sure you understood yourself.—Why so silent, Hylas? Are you not yet satisfied men may dispute about identity and diversity without any real difference in their thoughts and opinions abstracted from names? Take this further reflection with you—that, whether matter be allowed to exist or no, the case is exactly the same as to the point in hand. For the materialists themselves acknowledge what we immediately perceive by our senses to be our own ideas. Your difficulty, therefore, that no two see the same thing makes equally against the materialists and me.

Hyl. But they suppose an external archetype to which referring their several ideas they may truly be said to perceive the same thing.

Phil. And (not to mention your having discarded those archetypes) so may you suppose an external archetype on my principles; *external,* I mean, to your own mind, though, indeed, it must be supposed to exist in that mind which comprehends all things; but then, this serves all the ends of *identity,* as well as if it existed out of a mind. And I am sure you yourself will not say it is less intelligible.

Hyl. You have indeed clearly satisfied me either that there is no difficulty at bottom in this point or, if there be, that it makes equally against both opinions.

Phil. But that which makes equally against two contradictory opinions can be a proof against neither.

Hyl. I acknowledge it. But, after all, Philonous, when I consider the substance of what you advance against skepticism, it amounts to no more than this: we are sure that we really see, hear, feel, in a word, that we are affected with sensible impressions.

Phil. And how are we concerned any further? I see this cherry, I feel it, I taste it, and I am sure *nothing* cannot be seen or felt or tasted; it is therefore *real.* Take away the sensations of softness, moisture, redness, tartness, and you take away the cherry. Since it is not a being distinct from sensations, a cherry, I say, is nothing but a congeries of sensible impressions, or ideas perceived by various senses, which ideas are united into one thing (or have one name given them) by the mind because they are observed to attend each other. Thus, when the palate is affected with such a particular taste, the sight is affected with a red color, the touch with roundness, softness, etc. Hence, when I see and feel and taste in sundry certain manners, I am sure the cherry exists or is real, its reality being in my opinion nothing abstracted from those sensations. But if by the word "cherry" you mean an unknown nature distinct from all those sensible qualities, and by its "existence" something distinct from its being perceived, then, indeed, I own neither you nor I, nor anyone else, can be sure it exists.

Hyl. But what would you say, Philonous, if I should bring the very same reasons against the existence of sensible things in a mind which you have offered against their existing in a material *substratum?*

Phil. When I see your reasons, you shall hear what I have to say to them.

Hyl. Is the mind extended or unextended?

Phil. Unextended, without doubt.

Hyl. Do you say the things you perceive are in your mind?

Phil. They are.

Hyl. Again, have I not heard you speak of sensible impressions?

Phil. I believe you may.

Hyl. Explain to me now, O Philonous! how is it possible there should be room for all those trees and houses to exist in your mind. Can extended things be contained in that which is unextended? Or are we to imagine impressions made on a thing void of all solidity? You cannot say objects are in your mind, as books in your study, or that things are imprinted on it, as the figure of a seal upon wax. In what sense, therefore, are we to understand those expressions? Explain me this if you can, and I shall then be able to answer all those queries you formerly put to me about my *substratum.*

Phil. Look you, Hylas, when I speak of objects as existing in the mind or imprinted on the senses, I would not be understood in the gross literal sense—as when bodies are said to exist in a place or a seal to make an impression upon wax. My meaning is only that the mind comprehends or perceives them, and that it is affected from without or by some being distinct from itself. This is my explication of your difficulty; and how it can serve to make your tenet of an unperceiving material *substratum* intelligible, I would fain know.

Hyl. Nay, if that be all, I confess I do not see what use can be made of it. But are you not guilty of some abuse of language in this?

Phil. None at all. It is no more than common custom, which you know is the rule of language, has authorized, nothing being more usual than for philosophers to speak of the immediate objects of the understanding as things existing in the mind. Nor is there anything in this but what is conformable to the general analogy of language; most part of the mental operations being signified by words borrowed from sensible things, as is plain in the terms "comprehend," "reflect," "discourse," etc., which, being applied to the mind, must not be taken in their gross original sense.

Hyl. You have, I own, satisfied me in this point. But there still remains one great difficulty which I know not how you will get over. And, indeed, it is of such importance that if you could solve all others without being able to find a solution for this, you must never expect to make me a proselyte to your principles.

Phil. Let me know this mighty difficulty.

Hyl. The Scripture account of the creation is what appears to me utterly irreconcilable with your notions. Moses tells us of a creation—a creation of what? of ideas? No, certainly, but of things, of real things, solid corporeal substances. Bring your principles to agree with this and I shall perhaps agree with you.

Phil. Moses mentions the sun, moon, and stars, earth and sea, plants and animals. That all these do really exist and were in the beginning created by God, I make no question. If by "ideas" you mean fictions and fancies of the mind, then these are no ideas. If by "ideas" you mean immediate objects of the understanding, or sensible things which cannot exist unperceived, or out of a mind, then these things are ideas. But whether you do or do not call them "ideas," it matters little. The difference is only about a name. And whether that name be retained or rejected, the sense, the truth, and reality of things continues the same. In common talk, the objects of our senses are not termed "ideas" but "things." Call them so still, provided you do not attribute to them any absolute external existence, and I shall never quarrel with you for a word. The creation, therefore, I allow to have been a creation of things, of *real* things. Neither is this in the least inconsistent with my principles, as is evident from what I have now said; and would have been evident to you without this if you had not forgotten what had been so often said before. But as for solid corporeal substances, I desire you to show where Moses makes any mention of them; and if they should be mentioned by him or any other inspired writer, it would still be incumbent on you to show those words were not taken in the vulgar acceptation for things falling under our senses, but in the philosophic acceptation for matter or an unknown quiddity with an absolute existence. When you have proved these points, then (and not till then) may you bring the authority of Moses into our dispute.

Hyl. It is in vain to dispute about a point so clear. I am content to refer it to your own conscience. Are you not satisfied there is some peculiar repugnancy between the Mosaic account of the creation and your notions?

Phil. If all possible sense which can be put on the first chapter of Genesis may be conceived as consistently with my principles as any other, then it has no peculiar repugnancy with them. But there is no sense you may not as well conceive, believing as I do. Since, besides spirits, all you conceive are ideas, and the existence of these I do not deny. Neither do you pretend they exist without the mind.

Hyl. Pray let me see any sense you can understand it in.

Phil. Why, I imagine that if I had been present at the creation, I should have seen things produced into being—that is become perceptible—in the order prescribed by the sacred historian. I ever before believed the Mosaic account of the creation, and now find no alteration in my manner of believing it. When things are said to begin or end their existence, we do not mean this with regard to God, but His creatures. All objects are eternally known by God, or, which is the same thing, have an eternal existence in His mind; but when things, before imperceptible to creatures, are, by a decree of God, made perceptible to them, then are they said to begin a relative existence with respect to created minds. Upon reading therefore the Mosaic account of the creation, I understand that the several parts of the world became gradually perceivable to finite spirits endowed with proper faculties, so that, whoever such were present, they were in truth perceived by them. This is the literal obvious sense suggested to me by the words of the Holy Scripture, in which is included no mention or thought either of *substratum,* instrument, occasion, or absolute existence. And, upon inquiry, I doubt not it will be found that most plain honest men who believe the creation never think of those things any more than I. What metaphysical sense you may understand it in, you only can tell.

Hyl. But, Philonous, you do not seem to be aware that you allow created things in the beginning only a relative and consequently hypothetical being; that is to say, upon supposition there were men to perceive them, without which they have no actuality of absolute existence wherein creation might terminate. Is it not, therefore, according to you, plainly impossible the creation of any inanimate creatures should precede that of man? And is not this directly contrary to the Mosaic account?

Phil. In answer to that, I say, *first,* created beings might begin to exist in the mind of other created intelligences besides men. You will not, therefore, be able to prove any contradiction between Moses and my notions unless you first show there was no other order of finite created spirits in being before man. I say further, in case we conceive the creation as we should at this time a parcel of plants or vegetables of all sorts produced by an invisible power in a desert where nobody was present—that this way of explaining or conceiving it is consistent with my principles, since they deprive you of nothing, either sensible or imaginable; that it exactly suits with the common, natural, and undebauched notions of mankind; that it manifests the dependence of all things on God, and consequently has all the good effect or influence, which it is possible that important article of our faith should have in making men humble, thankful, and resigned to their Creator. I say, moreover, that, in this naked conception of things, divested of words, there will not be found any notion of what you call the "actuality of absolute existence." You may indeed raise a dust with those terms and so lengthen our dispute to no purpose. But I entreat you calmly to look into your own thoughts and then tell me if they are not a useless and unintelligible jargon.

Hyl. I own I have no very clear notion annexed to them. But what say you to this? Do you not make the existence of sensible things consist in their being in a mind? And were not all things externally in the mind of God? Did they not therefore exist from all eternity, according to you? And how could that which was eternal be created in time? Can anything be clearer or better connected than this?

Phil. And are not you too of opinion that God knew all things from eternity?

Hyl. I am.

Phil. Consequently, they always had a being in the Divine intellect.

Hyl. This I acknowledge.

Phil. By your own confession, therefore, nothing is new, or begins to be, in respect of the mind of God. So we are agreed in that point.

Hyl. What shall we make then of the creation?

Phil. May we not understand it to have been entirely in respect of finite spirits, so that things, with regard to us, may properly be said to begin their existence, or be created, when God decreed they should become perceptible to intelligent creatures in that order and manner which He then established and we now call the laws of nature? You may call this a "relative," or "hypothetical existence," if you please. But so long as it supplies us with the most natural, obvious, and literal sense of the Mosaic history of the creation, so long as it answers all the religious ends of that great article, in a word, so long as you can assign no other sense or meaning in its stead, why should we reject this? Is it to comply with a ridiculous skeptical humor of making everything nonsense and unintelligible? I am sure you cannot say it is for the glory of God. For allowing it to be a thing possible and conceivable that the corporeal world should have an absolute existence extrinsical to the mind of God, as well as to the minds of all created spirits, yet how could this set forth either the immensity or omniscience of the Deity or the necessary and immediate dependence of all things on Him? Nay, would it not rather seem to derogate from those attributes?

Hyl. Well, but as to this decree of God's for making things perceptible, what say you, Philonous, is it not plain God did either execute that decree from all eternity or at some certain time began to will what He had not actually willed before, but only designed to will? If the former, then there could be no creation or beginning of existence in finite things. If the latter, then we must acknowledge something new to befall the Deity, which implies a sort of change; and all change argues imperfection.

Phil. Pray consider what you are doing. Is it not evident this objection concludes equally against a creation in any sense, nay, against every other act of the Deity discoverable by the light of nature? None of which can we conceive otherwise than as performed in time and having a beginning. God is a Being of transcendent and unlimited perfections; His Nature, therefore, is incomprehensible to finite spirits. It is not, therefore, to be expected that any man, whether *materialist* or *immaterialist,* should have exactly just notions of the Deity, His attributes, and ways of operation. If then you would infer anything against me, your difficulty must not be drawn from the inadequateness of our conceptions of the Divine nature, which is unavoidable on any scheme, but from the denial of matter, of which there is not one word, directly or indirectly, in what you have now objected.

Hyl. I must acknowledge the difficulties you are concerned to clear are such only as arise from the nonexistence of matter and are peculiar to that notion. So far you are in the right. But I cannot by any means bring myself to think there is no such peculiar repugnancy between the creation and your opinion, though, indeed, where to fix it I do not distinctly know.

Phil. What would you have? Do I not acknowledge a two-fold state of things, the one ectypal or nature, the other archetypal and eternal? The former was created in time, the latter existed from everlasting in the mind of God. Is not this agreeable to the common notions of divines? Or is any more than this necessary in order to conceive the creation? But you suspect some peculiar repugnancy, though you know not where it lies. To take away all possibility of scruple in the case, do but consider this one point: either you are not able to conceive the creation on any hypothesis whatsoever, and if so, there is no ground for dislike or complaint against my particular opinion on that score; or you are able to conceive it, and if so, why not on my principles, since thereby nothing conceivable is taken away? You have all along been allowed the full scope of sense, imagination, and reason. Whatever, therefore, you could before apprehend, either immediately or mediately by your senses, or by ratiocination from your senses, whatever you could perceive, imagine, or understand, remains still with you. If, therefore, the notion you have of the creation by other principles be intelligible, you have it still upon mine; if it be not intelligible, I conceive it to be no notion at all, and so there is no loss of it. And, indeed, it seems to me very plain that the supposition of matter, that is, a thing perfectly unknown and inconceivable, cannot serve to make us conceive anything. And I hope it need not be proved to you that if the existence of matter does not make the creation conceivable, the creation's being without it inconceivable can be no objection against its nonexistence.

Hyl. I confess, Philonous, you have almost satisfied me in this point of the creation.

Phil. I would fain know why you are not quite satisfied. You tell me indeed of a repugnancy between the Mosaic history and immaterialism, but you know not where it lies. Is this reasonable, Hylas? Can you expect I should solve a difficulty without knowing what it is? But, to pass by all that, would not a man think you were assured there is no repugnancy between the received notions of materialists and the inspired writings?

Hyl. And so I am.

Phil. Ought the historical part of Scripture to be understood in a plain obvious sense or in a sense which is metaphysical and out of the way?

Hyl. In the plain sense, doubtless.

Phil. When Moses speaks of herbs, earth, water, etc., as having been created by God, think you not the sensible things commonly signified by those words are suggested to every unphilosophical reader?

Hyl. I cannot help thinking so.

Phil. And are not all ideas, or things perceived by sense, to be denied a real existence by the doctrine of the materialists?

Hyl. This I have already acknowledged.

Phil. The creation, therefore, according to them, was not the creation of things sensible, which have only a relative being, but of certain unknown natures which have an absolute being wherein creation might terminate?

Hyl. True.

Phil. Is it not, therefore, evident the assertors of matter destroy the plain obvious sense of Moses, with which their notions are utterly inconsistent, and instead of it obtrude on us I know not what, something equally unintelligible to themselves and me?

Hyl. I cannot contradict you.

Phil. Moses tells us of a creation. A creation of what? of unknown quiddities, of occasions, or *substratum?* No, certainly, but of things obvious to the senses. You must first reconcile this with your notions if you expect I should be reconciled to them.

Hyl. I see you can assault me with my own weapons.

Phil. Then as to *absolute existence,* was there ever known a more jejune notion than that? Something it is so abstracted and unintelligible that you have frankly owned you could not conceive it, much less explain anything by it. But allowing matter to exist and the notion of absolute existence to be as clear as light, yet, was this ever known to make the creation more credible? Nay, has it not furnished the atheists and infidels of all ages with the most plausible arguments against a creation? That a corporeal substance which has an absolute existence without the minds of spirits should be produced out of nothing, by the mere will of a spirit, has been looked upon as a thing so contrary to all reason, so impossible and absurd, that not only the most celebrated among the ancients, but even divers modern and Christian philosophers have thought matter coeternal with the Deity. Lay these things together and then judge you whether materialism disposes men to believe the creation of things.

Hyl. I own, Philonous, I think it does not. This of the creation is the last objection I can think of; and I must needs own it has been sufficiently answered as well as the rest. Nothing now remains to be overcome but a sort of unaccountable backwardness that I find in myself toward your notions.

Phil. When a man is swayed, he knows not why, to one side of a question, can this, think you, be anything else but the effect of prejudice, which never fails to attend old and rooted notions? And, indeed, in this respect I cannot deny the belief of matter to have very much the advantage over the contrary opinion with men of a learned education.

Hyl. I confess it seems to be as you say.

Phil. As a balance, therefore, to this weight of prejudice, let us throw into the scale the great advantages that arise from the belief of immaterialism, both in regard to religion and human learning. The being of a God and incorruptibility of the soul, those great articles of religion, are they not proved with the clearest and most immediate evidence? When I say the being of a *God,* I do not mean an obscure general cause of things whereof we have no conception, but *God* in the strict and proper sense of the word, a Being whose spirituality, omnipresence, providence, omniscience, infinite power, and goodness are as conspicuous as the existence of sensible things, of which (notwithstanding the fallacious pretenses and affected scruples of skeptics) there is no more reason to doubt than of our own being. Then, with relation to human sciences: in Natural Philosophy, what intricacies, what obscurities, what contradictions has the belief of matter led men into! To say nothing of the numberless disputes about its extent, continuity, homogeneity, gravity, divisibility, etc.—do they not pretend to explain all things by bodies operating on bodies, according to the laws of motion? And yet, are they able to comprehend how any one body should move another? Nay, admitting there was no difficulty in reconciling the notion of an inert being with a cause, or in conceiving how an accident might pass from one body to another, yet, by all their strained thoughts and extravagant suppositions, have they been able to reach the mechanical production of any one animal or vegetable body? Can they account, by the laws of motion, for sounds, tastes, smells, or colors, or for the regular course of things? Have they accounted, by physical principles, for the aptitude and contrivance even of the most inconsiderable parts of the universe? But laying aside matter and corporeal causes and admitting only the efficiency of an All-perfect Mind, are not all the effects of nature easy and intelligible? If the *phenomena* are nothing else but *ideas,* God is a *spirit,* but matter an unintelligent, unperceiving being. If they demonstrate an unlimited power in their cause, God is active and omnipotent, but matter an inert mass. If the order, regularity, and usefulness of them can never be sufficiently admired, God is infinitely wise and provident, but matter destitute of all contrivance and design. These surely are great advantages in physics. Not to mention that the apprehension of a distant Deity naturally disposes men to a negligence of their moral actions, which they would be more cautious of, in case they thought him immediately present and acting on their minds without the interposition of matter or unthinking second causes. Then in metaphysics: what difficulties concerning entity in abstract, substantial forms, hylarchic principles, plastic natures, substance and accident, principle of individuation, possibility of matter's thinking, origin of ideas, the manner how two independent substances so widely different as *spirit* and *matter* should mutually operate on each other? What difficulties, I say, and endless disquisitions concerning these and innumerable other the like points do we escape by supposing only spirits and ideas? Even the mathematics themselves, if we take away the absolute existence of extended things, become much more clear and easy, the most shocking paradoxes and intricate speculations in those sciences depending on the infinite divisibility of finite extension, which depends on that supposition. But what need is there to insist on the particular sciences? Is not that opposition to all science whatsoever, that frenzy of the ancient and modern skeptics, built on the same foundation? Or can you produce so much as one argument against the reality of corporeal things or in behalf of that avowed utter ignorance of their natures which does not suppose their reality to consist in an external absolute existence? Upon this supposition, indeed, the objections from the change of colors in a pigeon's neck, or the appearance of the broken oar in the water, must be allowed to have weight. But these and the like objections vanish if we do not maintain the being of absolute external originals, but place the reality of things in ideas, fleeting, indeed, and changeable; however, not changed at random, but according to the fixed order of nature. For herein consists that constancy and truth of things which secures all the concerns of life, and distinguishes that which is real from the irregular visions of the fancy.

Hyl. I agree to all you have now said and must own that nothing can incline me to embrace your opinion more than the advantages I see it is attended with. I am by nature lazy, and this would be a mighty abridgment in knowledge. What doubts, what hypotheses, what labyrinths of amusement, what fields of disputation, what an ocean of false learning may be avoided by that single notion of *immaterialism!*

Phil. After all, is there anything further remaining to be done? You may remember you promised to embrace that opinion which upon examination should appear most agreeable to common sense and remote from skepticism. This, by your own confession, is that which denies matter or the absolute existence of corporeal things. Nor is this all; the same notion has been proved several ways, viewed in different lights, pursued in its consequences, and all objections against it cleared. Can there be a greater evidence of its truth? Or is it possible it should have all the marks of a true opinion and yet be false?

Hyl. I own myself entirely satisfied for the present in all respects. But what security can I have that I shall still continue the same full assent to your opinion and that no unthought-of objection or difficulty will occur hereafter?

Phil. Pray, Hylas, do you in other cases, when a point is once evidently proved, withhold your assent on account of objections or difficulties it may be liable to? Are the difficulties that attend the doctrine of incommensurable quantities, of the angle of contact, of the asymptotes to curves, or the like, sufficient to make you hold out against mathematical demonstration? Or will you disbelieve the Providence of God because there may be some particular things which you know not how to reconcile with it? If there are difficulties attending immaterialism, there are at the same time direct and evident proofs of it. But for the existence of matter there is not one proof, and far more numerous and insurmountable objections lie against it. But where are those mighty difficulties you insist on? Alas! you know not where or what they are; something which may possibly occur hereafter. If this be a sufficient pretense for withholding your full assent, you should never yield it to any proposition, how free soever from exceptions, how clearly and solidly soever demonstrated.

Hyl. You have satisfied me, Philonous.

Phil. But to arm you against all future objections, do but consider that which bears equally hard on two contradictory opinions can be proof against neither. Whenever, therefore, any difficulty occurs, try if you can find a solution for it on the hypothesis of the materialists. Be not deceived by words, but sound your own thoughts. And in case you cannot conceive it easier by the help of materialism, it is plain it can be no objection against immaterialism. Had you proceeded all along by this rule, you would probably have spared yourself abundance of trouble in objecting, since of all your difficulties I challenge you to show one that is explained by matter, nay, which is not more unintelligible with than without that supposition, and consequently makes rather *against* than *for* it. You should consider, in each particular, whether the difficulty arises from the *nonexistence of matter.* If it does not, you might as well argue from the infinite divisibility of extension against the Divine prescience as from such a difficulty against immaterialism. And yet, upon recollection, I believe you will find this to have been often if not always the case. You should likewise take heed not to argue on a *petitio principii.* One is apt to say the unknown substances ought to be esteemed real things rather than the ideas in our minds; and who can tell but the unthinking external substance may concur as a cause or instrument in the productions of our ideas? But is not this proceeding on a supposition that there are such external substances? And to suppose this, is it not begging the question? But above all things, you should beware of imposing on yourself by that vulgar sophism which is called *ignoratio elenchi.* You talked often as if you thought I maintained the nonexistence of sensible things, whereas in truth no one can be more thoroughly assured of their existence than I am; and it is you who doubt, I should have said, positively deny it. Everything that is seen, felt, heard, or any way perceived by the senses is, on the principles I embrace, a real being, but not on yours. Remember, the matter you contend for is an unknown somewhat (if indeed it may be termed "somewhat"), which is quite stripped of all sensible qualities, and can neither be perceived by sense, nor apprehended by the mind. Remember, I say that it is not any object which is hard or soft, hot or cold, blue or white, round or square, etc.—for all these things I affirm do exist. Though, indeed, I deny they have an existence distinct from being perceived, or that they exist out of all minds whatsoever. Think on these points; let them be attentively considered and still kept in view. Otherwise you will not comprehend the state of the question, without which your objections will always be wide of the mark and, instead of mine, may possibly be directed (as more than once they have been) against your own notions.

Hyl. I must needs own, Philonous, nothing seems to have kept me from agreeing with you more than this same *mistaking the question.* In denying matter, at first glimpse I am tempted to imagine you deny the things we see and feel, but, upon reflection, find there is no ground for it. What think you, therefore, of retaining the name "matter" and applying it to *sensible things*? This may be done without any change in your sentiments; and, believe me, it would be a means of reconciling them to some persons who may be more shocked at an innovation in words than in opinion.

Phil. With all my heart; retain the word "matter" and apply it to the objects of sense, if you please, provided you do not attribute to them any subsistence distinct from their being perceived. I shall never quarrel with you for an expression. "Matter" or "material substance" are terms introduced by philosophers, and, as used by them, imply a sort of independence, or a subsistence distinct from being perceived by a mind; but are never used by common people, or, if ever, it is to signify the immediate objects of sense. One would think, therefore, so long as the names of all particular things with the terms "sensible," "substance," "body," "stuff," and the like, are retained, the word "matter" should be never missed in common talk. And in philosophical discourses it seems the best way to leave it quite out, since there is not, perhaps, any one thing that has more favored and strengthened the depraved bent of the mind toward atheism than the use of that general confused term.

Hyl. Well, but, Philonous, since I am content to give up the notion of an unthinking substance exterior to the mind, I think you ought not to deny me the privilege of using the word "matter" as I please, and annexing it to a collection of sensible qualities subsisting only in the mind. I freely own there is no other substance, in a strict sense, than spirit. But I have been so long accustomed to the term "matter" that I know not how to part with it. To say there is no matter in the world is still shocking to me. Whereas to say there is no matter if by that term be meant an unthinking substance existing without the mind, but if by matter is meant some sensible thing whose existence consists in being perceived, then there is matter—this distinction gives it quite another turn; and men will come into your notions with small difficulty when they are proposed in that manner. For, after all, the controversy about matter in the strict acceptation of it lies altogether between you and the philosophers, whose principles, I acknowledge, are not near so natural or so agreeable to the common sense of mankind and Holy Scripture as yours. There is nothing we either desire or shun but as it makes, or is apprehended to make, some part of our happiness or misery. But what has happiness or misery, joy or grief, pleasure or pain to do with absolute existence or with unknown entities abstracted from all relation to us? It is evident things regard us only as they are pleasing or displeasing; and they can please or displease only so far forth as they are perceived. Further, therefore, we are not concerned; and thus far you leave things as you found them. Yet still there is something new in this doctrine. It is plain, I do not now think with the philosophers, nor yet altogether with the vulgar. I would know how the case stands in that respect, precisely what you have added to or altered in my former notions.

Phil. I do not pretend to be a setter-up of new notions. My endeavors tend only to unite and place in a clearer light that truth which was before shared between the vulgar and the philosophers, the former being of opinion that *those things they immediately perceive are the real things,* and the latter, that *the things immediately perceived are ideas which exist only in the mind.* Which two notions put together do, in effect, constitute the substance of what I advance.

Hyl. I have been a long time distrusting my senses; methought I saw things by a dim light and through false glasses. Now the glasses are removed and a new light breaks in upon my understanding. I am clearly convinced that I see things in their native forms and am no longer in pain about their *unknown natures* or *absolute existence.* This is the state I find myself in at present, though, indeed, the course that brought me to it I do not yet thoroughly comprehend. You set out upon the same principles that Academics, Cartesians, and the like sects usually do, and for a long time it looked as if you were advancing their philosophical skepticism; but, in the end, your conclusions are directly opposite to theirs.

Phil. You see, Hylas, the water of yonder fountain, how it is forced upwards, in a round column, to a certain height, at which it breaks and falls back into the basin from whence it rose, its ascent as well as descent proceeding from the same uniform law or principle of gravitation. Just so, the same principles which, at first view, lead to skepticism, pursued to a certain point, bring men back to common sense.

NOTES

1. [The remainder of the present paragraph did not appear in the first and second editions.]
2. [See Berkeley's *An Essay Towards a New Theory of Vision* (1709) and *The Theory of Vision Vindicated and Explained* (1733).]
3. [The bracketed portion of this paragraph did not appear in the first and second editions.]
4. [The four paragraphs following did not appear in the first and second editions.]

Skepticism and the Methods of Science

An Inquiry Concerning Human Understanding*

DAVID HUME

SECTION II. OF THE ORIGIN OF IDEAS

EVERYONE WILL READILY ALLOW that there is a considerable difference between the perceptions of the mind when a man feels the pain of excessive heat or the pleasure of moderate warmth, and when he afterwards recalls to his memory this sensation or anticipates it by his imagination. These faculties may mimic or copy the perceptions of the senses, but they never can entirely reach the force and vivacity of the original sentiment. The utmost we say of them, even when they operate with greatest vigor, is that they represent their object in so lively a manner that we could *almost* say we feel or see it. But, except the mind be disordered by disease or madness, they never can arrive at such a pitch of vivacity as to render these perceptions altogether undistinguishable. All the colors of poetry, however splendid, can never paint natural objects in such a manner as to make the description be taken for a real landscape. The most lively thought is still inferior to the dullest sensation.

We may observe a like distinction to run through all the other perceptions of the mind. A man in a fit of anger is actuated in a very different manner from one who only thinks of that emotion. If you tell me that any person is in love, I easily understand your meaning and form a just conception of his situation, but never can mistake that conception for the real disorders and agitations of the passion. When we reflect on our past sentiments and affections, our thought is a faithful mirror and copies its objects truly, but the colors which it employs are faint and dull in comparison of those in which our original perceptions were clothed. It requires no nice discernment or metaphysical head to mark the distinction between them.

Here, therefore, we may divide all the perceptions of the mind into two classes or species, which are distinguished by their different degrees of force and vivacity. The less forcible and lively are commonly denominated "thoughts" or "ideas." The other species want a name in our language, and in most others; I suppose, because it was not requisite for any but philosophical purposes to rank them under a general term or appellation. Let us, therefore, use a little freedom and call them "impressions," employing that word in a sense somewhat different from the usual. By the term "impression," then, I mean all our more lively perceptions, when we hear, or see, or feel, or love, or hate, or desire, or will. And impressions are distinguished from ideas, which are the less lively perceptions of which we are conscious when we reflect on any of those sensations or movements above mentioned.

Nothing, at first view, may seem more unbounded than the thought of man, which not only escapes all human power and authority, but is not even restrained within the limits of nature and reality. To form monsters and join incongruous shapes and appearances costs the imagination no more trouble than to conceive the most natural and familiar objects. And while the body is confined to one planet, along which it creeps with pain and dif-

David Hume, An Inquiry Concerning Human Understanding. *Sections II, IV–VII. First published in 1748.*

ficulty, the thought can in an instant transport us into the most distant regions of the universe, or even beyond the universe into the unbounded chaos where nature is supposed to lie in total confusion. What never was seen or heard of, may yet be conceived, nor is anything beyond the power of thought except what implies an absolute contradiction.

But though our thought seems to possess this unbounded liberty, we shall find upon a nearer examination that it is really confined within very narrow limits, and that all this creative power of the mind amounts to no more than the faculty of compounding, transposing, augmenting, or diminishing the materials afforded us by the senses and experience. When we think of a golden mountain, we only join two consistent ideas, "gold" and "mountain," with which we were formerly acquainted. A virtuous horse we can conceive, because, from our own feeling, we can conceive virtue; and this we may unite to the figure and shape of a horse, which is an animal familiar to us. In short, all the materials of thinking are derived either from our outward or inward sentiment; the mixture and composition of these belongs alone to the mind and will, or, to express myself in philosophical language, all our ideas or more feeble perceptions are copies of our impressions or more lively ones.

To prove this, the two following arguments will, I hope, be sufficient. *First,* when we analyze our thoughts or ideas, however compounded or sublime, we always find that they resolve themselves into such simple ideas as were copied from a precedent feeling or sentiment. Even those ideas which at first view seem the most wide of this origin are found, upon a nearer scrutiny, to be derived from it. The idea of God, as meaning an infinitely intelligent, wise, and good Being, arises from reflecting on the operations of our own mind and augmenting, without limit, those qualities of goodness and wisdom. We may prosecute this inquiry to what length we please; where we shall always find that every idea which we examine is copied from a similar impression. Those who would assert that this position is not universally true, nor without exception, have only one, and that an easy, method of refuting it by producing that idea which, in their opinion, is not derived from this source. It will then be incumbent on us, if we would maintain our doctrine, to produce the impression or lively perception which corresponds to it.

Secondly, if it happen, from a defect of the organ, that a man is not susceptible of any species of sensation, we always find that he is as little susceptible of the correspondent ideas. A blind man can form no notion of colors, a deaf man of sounds. Restore either of them that sense in which he is deficient by opening this new inlet for his sensations, you also open an inlet for the ideas, and he finds no difficulty in conceiving these objects. The case is the same if the object proper for exciting any sensation has never been applied to the organ. A Laplander . . . has no notion of the relish of wine. And though there are few or no instances of a like deficiency in the mind where a person has never felt or is wholly incapable of a sentiment or passion that belongs to his species, yet we find the same observation to take place in a less degree. A man of mild manners can form no idea of inveterate revenge or cruelty, nor can a selfish heart easily conceive the heights of friendship and generosity. It is readily allowed that other beings may possess many senses of which we can have no conception, because the ideas of them have never been introduced to us in the only manner by which an idea can have access to the mind, to wit, by the actual feeling and sensation.

There is, however, one contradictory phenomenon which may prove that it is not absolutely impossible for ideas to arise independent of their correspondent impressions. I believe it will readily be allowed that the several distinct ideas of color, which enter by the eye, or those of sound, which are conveyed by the ear, are really different from each other, though at the same time resembling. Now, if this be true of different colors, it must be no less so of the different shades of the same color; and each shade produces a distinct idea, independent of the rest. For if this should be denied, it is possible, by the continual gradation of shades, to run a color insensibly into what is most remote from it; and if you will not allow any of the means to be different, you cannot, without absurdity, deny the extremes to be the same. Suppose, therefore, a person to have enjoyed his sight for thirty years and to have become perfectly acquainted with colors of all kinds, except one particular shade of blue, for instance, which it never has been his fortune to meet with; let all the different shades of that color, except that single one, be placed before him, descending gradually from the deepest to the lightest, it is plain that he will perceive a blank where that shade is wanting, and will be sensible that there is a greater distance in that place between the contiguous colors than in any other. Now I ask whether it be possible for him, from his own imagination, to supply this deficiency and raise up to himself the idea of that particular shade, though it had never been conveyed to him by his senses? I believe there are few but will be of opinion that he can; and this may serve as a proof that the simple ideas are not always, in every instance, derived from the correspondent impressions, though this instance is so singular that it is scarcely worth our observing, and does not merit that for it alone we should alter our general maxim.

Here, therefore, is a proposition which not only seems in itself simple and intelligible, but, if a proper use were made of it, might render every dispute equally intelligible, and banish all that jargon which has so long taken possession of metaphysical reasonings and drawn disgrace upon them. All ideas, especially abstract ones, are naturally faint and obscure. The mind has but a slender hold of them. They are apt to be confounded with other resembling ideas; and when we have often employed any term, though without a distinct meaning, we are apt to imagine it has a determinate idea annexed to it. On the contrary, all impressions, that is, all sensations either outward or inward, are strong and vivid. The limits between them are more exactly determined, nor is it easy to fall into any error or mistake with regard to them. When we entertain, therefore, any suspicion that a philosophical term is employed without any meaning or idea (as is but too frequent), we need but inquire, *from what impression is that supposed idea derived?* And if it be impossible to assign any, this will serve to confirm our suspicion. By bringing ideas in so clear a light, we may reasonably hope to remove all dispute which may arise concerning their nature and reality.[1]

SECTION IV. SKEPTICAL DOUBTS CONCERNING THE OPERATIONS OF THE UNDERSTANDING

Part I

All the objects of human reason or inquiry may naturally be divided into two kinds, to wit, "Relations of Ideas," and "Matters of Fact." Of the first kind are the sciences of Geometry, Algebra, and Arithmetic, and, in short, every affirmation which is either intuitively or demonstratively certain. *That the square of the hypotenuse is equal to the square of the two sides* is a proposition which expresses a relation between these figures. *That three times five is equal to the half of thirty* expresses a relation between these numbers. Propositions of this kind are discoverable by the mere operation of thought, without dependence on what is anywhere existent in the universe. Though there never were a circle or triangle in nature, the truths demonstrated by Euclid would forever retain their certainty and evidence.

Matters of fact, which are the second objects of human reason, are not ascertained in the same manner, nor is our evidence of their truth, however great, of a like nature with the foregoing. The contrary of every matter of fact is still possible, because it can never imply a contradiction and is conceived by the mind with the same facility and distinctness as if ever so conformable to reality. *That the sun will not rise tomorrow* is no less intelligible a proposition and implies no more contradiction than the affirmation *that it will rise.* We should in vain, therefore, attempt to demonstrate its falsehood. Were it demonstratively false, it would imply a contradiction and could never be distinctly conceived by the mind.

It may, therefore, be a subject worthy of curiosity to inquire what is the nature of that evidence which assures us of any real existence and matter of fact beyond the present testimony of our senses or the records of our memory. This part of philosophy, it is observable, had been little cultivated either by the ancients or moderns; and, therefore, our doubts and errors in the prosecution of so important an inquiry may be the more excusable while we march through such difficult paths without any guide or direction. They may even prove useful by exciting curiosity and destroying that implicit faith and security which is the bane of all reasoning and free inquiry. The discovery of defects in the common philosophy, if any such there be, will not, I presume, be a discouragement, but rather an incitement, as is usual, to attempt something more full and satisfactory than has yet been proposed to the public.

All reasonings concerning matter of fact seem to be founded on the relation of *cause* and *effect*. By means of that relation alone we can go beyond the evidence of our memory and senses. If you were to ask a man why he believes any matter of fact which is absent, for instance, that his friend is in the country or in France, he would give you a reason, and this reason would be some other fact: as a letter received from him or the knowledge of his former resolutions and promises. A man finding a watch or any other machine in a desert island would conclude that there had once been men in that island. All our reasonings concerning fact are of the same nature. And here it is constantly supposed that there is a connection between the present fact and that which is inferred from it. Were there nothing to bind them together, the inference would be entirely precarious. The hearing of an articulate voice and rational discourse in the dark assures us of the presence of some person. Why? Because these are the effects of the human make and fabric, and closely connected with it. If we anatomize all the other reasonings of this nature, we shall find that they are founded on the relation of cause and effect, and that this relation is either near or remote, direct or collateral. Heat and light are collateral effects of fire, and the one effect may justly be inferred from the other.

If we would satisfy ourselves, therefore, concerning the nature of that evidence which assures us of matters of fact, we must inquire how we arrive at the knowledge of cause and effect.

I shall venture to affirm, as a general proposition which admits of no exception, that the knowledge of this relation is not, in any instance, attained by reasonings *a priori*, but arises entirely from experience, when we find that any particular objects are constantly conjoined with each other. Let an object be presented to a man of ever so strong natural reason and abilities—if that object be entirely new to him, he will not be able, by the most accurate examination of its sensible qualities, to discover any of its causes or effects. Adam, though his rational faculties be supposed, at the very first, entirely perfect, could not have inferred from the fluidity and transparency of water that it would suffocate him, or from the light and warmth of fire that it would consume him. No object ever discovers, by the qualities which appear to the senses, either the causes which produced it or the effects which will arise from it; nor can our reason, unassisted by experience, ever draw any inference concerning real existence and matter of fact.

This proposition, *that causes and effects are discoverable, not by reason, but by experience,* will readily be admitted with regard to such objects as we remember to have once been altogether unknown to us, since we must be conscious of the utter inability which we then lay under of foretelling what would arise from them. Present two smooth pieces of marble to a man who has no tincture of natural philosophy; he will never discover that they will adhere together in such a manner as to require great force to separate them in a direct line, while they make so small a resistance to a lateral pressure. Such events as bear little analogy to the common course of nature are also readily confessed to be known only by experience, nor does any man imagine that the explosion of gunpowder or the attraction of a loadstone could ever be discovered by arguments *a priori*. In like manner, when an effect is supposed to depend upon an intricate machinery or secret structure of parts, we make no difficulty in attributing all our knowledge of it to experience. Who will assert that he can give the ultimate reason why milk or bread is proper nourishment for a man, not for a lion or tiger?

But the same truth may not appear at first sight to have the same evidence with regard to events which have become familiar to us from our first appearance in the world, which bear a close analogy to the whole course of nature, and which are supposed to depend on the simple qualities of objects without any secret structure of parts. We are apt to imagine that we could discover these effects by the mere operation of our reason without experience. We fancy that, were we brought on a sudden into this world, we could at first have inferred that one billiard ball would communicate motion to another upon impulse, and that we needed not to have waited for the event in order to pronounce with certainty concerning it. Such is the influence of custom that where it is strongest it not only covers our natural ignorance but even conceals itself, and seems not to take place, merely because it is found in the highest degree.

But to convince us that all the laws of nature and all the operations of bodies without exception are known only by experience, the following reflections may perhaps suffice. Were any object presented to us, and were we required to pronounce concerning the effect which will result from it without consulting past observation, after what manner, I beseech you, must the mind proceed in this operation? It must invent or imagine some event which it ascribes to the object as its effect; and it is plain that this invention must be entirely arbitrary. The mind can never possibly find the effect in the supposed cause by the most accurate scrutiny and examination. For the effect is totally different from the cause, and consequently can never be discovered in it. Motion in the second billiard ball is quite a distinct event from motion in the first, nor is there anything in the one to suggest the smallest hint of the other. A stone or piece of metal raised into the air and left without any support immediately falls. But to consider the matter *a priori*, is there anything we discover in this situation which can beget the idea of a downward rather than an upward or any other motion in the stone or metal?

And as the first imagination or invention of a particular effect in all natural operations is arbitrary where we consult not experience, so must we also esteem the supposed tie or connection between the cause and effect which binds them together and renders it impossible that any other effect could result from the operation of that cause. When I see, for instance, a billiard ball moving in a straight line toward another, even suppose motion in the second ball should by accident be suggested to me as the result of their contact or impulse, may I not conceive that a hundred different events might as well follow from that cause? May not both these balls remain at absolute rest? May not the first ball return in a straight line or leap off the second in any line or direction? All these suppositions are consistent and conceivable. Why, then, should we give the preference to one which is no more consistent or conceivable than the rest? All our reasonings *a priori* will never be able to show us any foundation for this preference.

In a word, then, every effect is a distinct event from its cause. It could not, therefore, be discovered in the cause, and the first invention or conception of it *a priori*, must be entirely arbitrary. And even after it is suggested, the conjunction of it with the cause must appear equally arbitrary, since there are always many other effects which, to reason, must seem fully as consistent and natural. In vain, therefore, should we pretend to determine any single event or infer any cause or effect without the assistance of observation and experience.

Hence we may discover the reason why no philosopher who is rational and modest has ever pretended to assign the ultimate cause of any natural operation, or to show distinctly the action of that power which produces any single effect in the universe. It is confessed that the utmost effort of human reason is to reduce the principles productive of natural phenomena to a greater simplicity, and to resolve the many particular effects into a few general causes, by means of reasonings from analogy, experience, and observation. But as to the causes of these general causes, we should in vain attempt their discovery, nor shall we ever be able to satisfy ourselves by any particular explication of them. These ultimate springs and principles are totally shut up from human curiosity and inquiry. Elasticity, gravity, cohesion of parts, communication of motion by impulse—these are probably the ultimate causes and principles which we ever discover in nature; and we may esteem ourselves sufficiently happy if, by accurate inquiry and reasoning, we can trace up the particular phenomena to, or near to, these general principles. The most perfect philosophy of the natural kind only staves off our ignorance a little longer, as perhaps the most perfect philosophy of the moral or metaphysical kind serves only to discover larger portions of it. Thus the observation of human blindness and weakness is the result of all philosophy, and meets us, at every turn, in spite of our endeavors to elude or avoid it.

Nor is geometry, when taken into the assistance of natural philosophy, ever able to remedy this defect or lead us into the knowledge of ultimate causes by all that accuracy of reasoning for which it is so justly celebrated. Every part of mixed mathematics proceeds upon the supposition that certain laws are established by nature in her operations, and abstract reasonings are employed either to assist experience in the discovery of these laws or to determine their influence in particular instances where it depends upon any precise degree of distance and quantity. Thus it is a law of motion, discovered by experience, that the moment or force of any body in motion is in the compound ratio or proportion of its solid contents and its velocity, and, consequently, that a small force may remove the greatest obstacle or raise the greatest weight if by any contrivance or machinery we can increase the velocity of that force so as to make it an overmatch for its antagonist. Geometry assists us in the application of this law by giving us the just dimensions of all the parts and figures which can enter into any species of machine, but still the discovery of the law itself is owing merely to experience; and all the abstract reasonings in the world could never lead us one step toward the knowledge of it. When we reason *a priori* and consider merely any object or cause as it appears to the mind, independent of all observation, it never could suggest to us the notion of any distinct object, such as its effect, much less show us the inseparable and inviolable connection between them. A man must be very sagacious who could discover by reasoning that crystal is the effect of heat, and ice of cold, without being previously acquainted with the operation of these qualities.

Part II

But we have not yet attained any tolerable satisfaction with regard to the question first proposed. Each solution still gives rise to a new question as difficult as the foregoing and leads us on to further inquiries. When it is asked, *What is the nature of all our reasonings concerning matter of fact?* the proper answer seems to be, That they are founded on the relation of cause and effect. When again it is asked, *What is the foundation of all our reasonings and conclusions concerning that relation?* it may be replied in one word, *experience.* But if we still carry on our sifting humor and ask, *What is the foundation of all conclusions from experience?* this implies a new question which may be of more difficult solution and explication. Philosophers that give themselves airs of superior wisdom and sufficiency have a hard task when they encounter persons of inquisitive dispositions, who push them from every corner to which they retreat, and who are sure at last to bring them to some dangerous dilemma. The best expedient to prevent this confusion is to be modest in our pretensions and even to discover the difficulty ourselves before it is objected to us. By this means we may make a kind of merit of our very ignorance.

I shall content myself in this section with an easy task and shall pretend only to give a negative answer to the question here proposed. I say, then, that even after we have experience of the operations of cause and effect, our conclusions from that experience are *not* founded on reasoning or any process of understanding. This answer we must endeavor both to explain and to defend.

It must certainly be allowed that nature has kept us at a great distance from all her secrets and has afforded us only the knowledge of a few superficial qualities of objects, while she conceals from us those powers and principles on which the influence of these objects entirely depends. Our senses inform us of the color, weight, and consistency of bread, but neither sense nor reason can ever inform us of those qualities which fit it for the nourishment and support of the human body. Sight or feeling conveys an idea of the actual motion of bodies, but as to that wonderful force or power which would carry on a moving body forever in a continued change of place, and which bodies never lose but by communicating it to others, of this we cannot form the most distant conception. But notwithstanding this ignorance of natural powers[2] and principles, we always presume when we see like sensible qualities that they have like secret powers, and expect that effects similar to those which we have experienced will follow from them. If a body of like color and consistence with that bread which we have formerly eaten be presented to us, we make no scruple of repeating the experiment and foresee with certainty like nourishment and support. Now this is a process of the mind or thought of which I would willingly know the foundation. It is allowed on all hands that there is no known connection between the sensible qualities and the secret powers, and, consequently, that the mind is not led to form such a conclusion concerning their constant and regular conjunction by anything which it knows of their nature. As to past *experience*, it can be allowed to give *direct* and *certain* information of those precise objects only, and that precise period of time which fell under its cognizance: But why this experience should be extended to future times and to other objects which, for aught we know, may be only in appearance similar, this is the main question on which I would insist. The bread which I formerly ate nourished me; that is, a body of such sensible qualities was, at that time, endued with such secret powers. But does it follow that other bread must also nourish me at another time, and that like sensible qualities must always be attended with like secret powers? The consequence seems nowise necessary. At least, it must be acknowledged that there is here a consequence drawn by the mind, that there is a certain step taken, a process of thought, and an inference which wants to be explained. These two propositions are far from being the same: *I have found that such an object has always been attended with such an effect,* and *I foresee that other objects which are in appearance similar will be attended with similar effects.* I shall allow, if you please, that the one proposition may justly be inferred from the other: I know, in fact, that it always is inferred. But if you insist that the inference is made by a chain of reasoning, I desire you to produce that reasoning. The connection between these propositions is not intuitive. There is required a medium which may enable the mind to draw such an inference, if indeed it be drawn by reasoning and argument. What that medium is I must confess passes my comprehension; and it is incumbent on those to produce it who assert that it really exists and is the origin of all our conclusions concerning matter of fact.

This negative argument must certainly, in process of time, become altogether convincing if many penetrating and able philosophers shall turn their inquiries this way, and no one be ever able to discover any connecting proposition or intermediate step which supports the understanding in this conclusion. But as the question is yet new, every reader may not trust so far to his own penetration as to conclude, because an argument escapes his inquiry, that therefore it does not really exist. For this reason it may be requisite to venture upon a more difficult task, and, enumerating all the branches of human knowledge, endeavor to show that none of them can afford such an argument.

All reasonings may be divided into two kinds, namely, demonstrative reasoning, or that concerning relations of ideas, and moral reasoning, or that concerning matter of fact and existence. That there are no demonstrative arguments in the case seems evident, since it implies no contradiction that the course of nature may change and that an object, seemingly like those which we have experienced, may be attended with different or contrary effects. May I not clearly and distinctly conceive that a body, falling from the clouds and which in all other respects resembles snow, has yet the taste of salt or feeling of fire? Is there any more intelligible proposition than to affirm that all the trees will flourish in December and January, and will decay in May and June? Now, whatever is intelligible and can be distinctly conceived implies no contradiction and can never be proved false by any demonstrative argument or abstract reasoning *a priori.*

If we be, therefore, engaged by arguments to put trust in past experience and make it the standard of our future judgment, these arguments must be probable only, or such as regard matter of fact and real existence, according to the division above mentioned. But that there is no argument of this kind must appear if our explication of that species of reasoning be admitted as solid and satisfactory. We have said that all arguments concerning existence are founded on the relation of cause and effect, that our knowledge of that relation is derived entirely from experience, and that all our experimental conclusions proceed upon the supposition that the future will be conformable to the past. To endeavor, therefore, the proof of this last supposition by probable arguments, or arguments regarding existence, must be evidently going in a circle and taking that for granted which is the very point in question.

In reality, all arguments from experience are founded on the similarity which we discover among natural objects, and by which we are induced to expect effects similar to those which we have found to follow from such objects. And though none but a fool or madman will ever pretend to dispute the authority of experience or to reject that great guide of human life, it may surely be allowed a philosopher to have so much curiosity at least as to examine the principle of human nature which gives this mighty authority to experience and makes us draw advantage from that similarity which nature has placed among different objects. From causes which appear similar, we expect similar effects. This is the sum of our experimental conclusions. Now it seems evident that, if this conclusion were formed by reason, it would be as perfect at first, and upon one instance, as after ever so long a course of experience; but the case is far otherwise. Nothing so like as eggs, yet no one, on account of this appearing similarity, expects the same taste and relish in all of them. It is only after a long course of uniform experiments in any kind that we attain a firm reliance and security with regard to a particular event. Now, where is that process of reasoning which, from one instance, draws a conclusion so different from that which it infers from a hundred instances that are nowise different from that single one? This question I propose as much for the sake of information as with an intention of raising difficulties. I cannot find, I cannot imagine any such reasoning. But I keep my mind still open to instruction if anyone will vouchsafe to bestow it on me.

Should it be said that, from a number of uniform experiments, we *infer* a connection between the sensible qualities and the secret powers, this, I must confess, seems the same difficulty, couched in different terms. The question still recurs, On what process of argument is this *inference* founded? Where is the medium, the interposing ideas which join propositions so very wide of each other? It is confessed that the color, consistence, and other sensible qualities of bread appear not of themselves to have any connection with the secret powers of nourishment and support; for otherwise we could infer these secret powers from the first appearance of these sensible qualities without the aid of experience, contrary to the sentiment of all philosophers, and contrary to plain matter of fact. Here, then, is our natural state of ignorance with regard to the powers and influence of all objects. How is this remedied by experience? It only shows us a number of uniform effects resulting from certain objects, and teaches us that those particular objects, at that particular time, were endowed with such powers and forces. When a new object endowed with similar sensible qualities is produced, we expect similar powers and forces, and look for a like effect. From a body of like color and consistence with bread, we expect like nourishment and support. But this surely is a step or progress of the mind which wants to be explained. When a man says, *I have found, in all past instances, such sensible qualities, conjoined with such secret powers,* and when he says, *similar sensible qualities will always be conjoined with similar secret powers,* he is not guilty of a tautology, nor are these propositions in any respect the same. You say that the one proposition is an inference from the other; but you must confess that the inference is not intuitive, neither is it demonstrative. Of what nature is it then? To say it is experimental is begging the question. For all inferences from experience suppose, as their foundation, that the future will resemble the past and that similar powers will be conjoined with similar sensible qualities. If there be any suspicion that the course of nature may change, and that the past may be no rule for the future, all experience becomes useless and can give rise to no inference or conclusion. It is impossible, therefore, that any arguments from experience can prove this resemblance of the past to the future; since all these arguments are founded on the supposition of that resemblance. Let the course of things be allowed hitherto ever so regular, that alone, without some new argument or inference, proves not that for the future it will continue so. In vain do you pretend to have learned the nature of bodies from your past experience. Their secret nature and consequently all their effects and influence, may change without any change in their sensible qualities. This happens sometimes, and with regard to some objects. Why may it happen always, and with regard to all objects? What logic, what process of argument secures you against this supposition? My practice, you say, refutes my doubts. But you mistake the purport of my question. As an agent, I am quite satisfied in the point; but as a philosopher who has some share of curiosity, I will not say skepticism, I want to learn the foundation of this inference. No reading, no inquiry has yet been able to remove my difficulty or give me satisfaction in a matter of such importance. Can I do better than propose the difficulty to the public, even though, perhaps, I have small hopes of obtaining a solution? We shall at least, by this means, be sensible of our ignorance, if we do not augment our knowledge.

I must confess that a man is guilty of unpardonable arrogance who concludes, because an argument has escaped his own investigation, that therefore it does not really exist. I must also confess that, though all the learned, for several ages, should have employed themselves in fruitless search upon any subject, it may still, perhaps, be rash to conclude positively that the subject must therefore pass all human comprehension. Even though we examine all the sources of our knowledge and conclude them unfit for such a subject, there may still remain a suspicion that the enumeration is not complete or the examination not accurate. But with regard to the present subject, there are some considerations which seem to remove all this accusation of arrogance or suspicion of mistake.

It is certain that the most ignorant and stupid peasants, nay infants, nay even brute beasts, improve by experience and learn the qualities of natural objects by observing the effects which result from them. When a child has felt the sensation of pain from touching the flame of a candle, he will be careful not to put his hand near any candle, but will expect a similar effect from a cause which is similar in its sensible qualities and appearance. If you assert, therefore, that the understanding of the child is led into this conclusion by any process of argument or ratiocination, I may justly require you to produce that argument, nor have you any pretense to refuse so equitable a demand. You cannot say that the argument is abstruse and may possibly escape your inquiry, since you confess that it is obvious to the capacity of a mere infant. If you hesitate, therefore, a moment or if, after reflection, you produce any intricate or profound argument, you, in a manner, give up the question and confess that it is not reasoning which engages us to suppose the past resembling the future, and to expect similar effects from causes which are to appearance similar. This is the proposition which I intended to enforce in the present section. If I be right, I pretend not to have made any mighty discovery. And if I be wrong, I must acknowledge myself to be indeed a very backward scholar, since I cannot now discover an argument which, it seems, was perfectly familiar to me long before I was out of my cradle.

SECTION V. SKEPTICAL SOLUTION OF THESE DOUBTS

Part I

The passion for philosophy, like that for religion, seems liable to this inconvenience, that though it aims at the correction of our manners and extirpation of our vices, it may only serve, by imprudent management, to foster a predominant inclination and push the mind with more determined resolution toward that side which already *draws* too much by the bias and propensity of the natural temper. It is certain that, while we aspire to the magnanimous firmness of the philosophic sage and endeavor to confine our pleasures altogether within our own minds, we may, at last, render our philosophy, like that of Epictetus and other Stoics, only a more refined system of selfishness, and reason ourselves out of all virtue as well as social enjoyment. While we study with attention the vanity of human life and turn all our thoughts toward the empty and transitory nature of riches and honors, we are, perhaps, all the while flattering our natural indolence which, hating the bustle of the world and drudgery of business, seeks a pretense of reason to give itself a full and uncontrolled indulgence. There is, however, one species of philosophy which seems little liable to this inconvenience, and that because it strikes in with no disorderly passion of the human mind, nor can mingle itself with any natural affection or propensity; and that is the Academic or Skeptical philosophy. The Academics always talk of doubt and suspense of judgment, of danger in hasty determinations, of confining to very narrow bounds the inquiries of the understanding, and of renouncing all speculations which lie not within the limits of common life and practice. Nothing, therefore, can be more contrary than such a philosophy to the supine indolence of the mind, its rash arrogance, its lofty pretensions, and its superstitious credulity. Every passion is mortified by it, except the love of truth; and that passion never is nor can be carried to too high a degree. It is surprising, therefore, that this philosophy, which in almost every instance must be harmless and innocent, should be the subject of so much groundless reproach and obloquy. But, perhaps, the very circumstance which renders it so innocent is what chiefly exposes it to the public hatred and resentment. By flattering no irregular passion, it gains few partisans. By opposing so many vices and follies, it raises to itself abundance of enemies who stigmatize it as libertine, profane, and irreligious.

Nor need we fear that this philosophy, while it endeavors to limit our inquiries to common life, should ever undermine the reasonings of common life and carry its doubts so far as to destroy all action as well as speculation. Nature will always maintain her rights and prevail in the end over any abstract reasoning whatsoever. Though we should conclude, for instance, as in the foregoing section, that in all reasonings from experience there is a step taken by the mind which is not supported by any argument or process of the understanding, there is no danger that these reasonings, on which almost all knowledge depends, will ever be affected by such a discovery. If the mind be not engaged by argument to make this step, it must be induced by some other principle of equal weight and authority; and that principle will preserve its influence as long as human nature remains the same. What that principle is may well be worth the pains of inquiry.

Suppose a person, though endowed with the strongest faculties of reason and reflection, to be brought on a sudden into this world; he would, indeed, immediately observe a continual succession of objects and one event following another, but he would not be able to discover anything further. He would not at first, by any reasoning, be able to reach the idea of cause and effect, since the particular powers by which all natural operations are performed never appear to the senses; nor is it reasonable to conclude, merely because one event in one instance precedes another, that therefore the one is the cause, the other the effect. The conjunction may be arbitrary and casual. There may be no reason to infer the existence of one from the appearance of the other: and, in a word, such a person without more experience could never employ his conjecture or reasoning concerning any matter of fact or be assured of anything beyond what was immediately present to his memory or senses.

Suppose again that he has acquired more experience and has lived so long in the world as to have observed similar objects or events to be constantly conjoined together—what is the consequence of this experience? He immediately infers the existence of one object from the appearance of the other, yet he has not, by all his experience, acquired any idea or knowledge of the secret power by which the one object produces the other, nor is it by any process of reasoning he is engaged to draw this inference; but still he finds himself determined to draw it, and though he should be convinced that his understanding has no part in the operation, he would nevertheless continue in the same course of thinking. There is some other principle which determines him to form such a conclusion.

This principle is *custom* or *habit*. For whatever the repetition of any particular act or operation produces a propensity to renew the same act or operation without being impelled by any reasoning or process of the understanding, we always say that this propensity is the effect of *custom*. By employing that word we pretend not to have given the ultimate reason of such a propensity. We only point out a principle of human nature which is universally acknowledged, and which is well known by its effects. Perhaps we can push our inquiries no further or pretend to give the cause of this cause, but must rest contented with it as the ultimate principle which we can assign of all our conclusions from experience. It is sufficient satisfaction that we can go so far without repining at the narrowness of our faculties, because they will carry us no further. And it is certain we here advance a very intelligible proposition at least, if not a true one, when we assert that after the constant conjunction of two objects, heat and flame, for instance, weight and solidity, we are determined by custom alone to expect the one from the appearance of the other. This hypothesis seems even the only one which explains the difficulty why we draw from a thousand instances an inference which we are not able to draw from one instance that is in no respect different from them. Reason is incapable of any such variation. The conclusions which it draws from considering one circle are the same which it would form upon surveying all the circles in the universe. But no man, having seen only one body move after being impelled by another, could infer that every other body will move after a like impulse. All inferences from experience, therefore, are effects of custom, not of reasoning.[3]

Custom, then, is the great guide of human life. It is that principle alone which renders our experience useful to us and makes us expect, for the future, a similar train of events with those which have appeared in the past. Without the influence of custom we should be entirely ignorant of every matter of fact beyond what is immediately present to the memory and senses. We should never know how to adjust means to ends or to employ our natural powers in the production of any effect. There would be an end at once of all action as well as of the chief part of speculation.

But here it may be proper to remark that though our conclusions from experience carry us beyond our memory and senses and assure us of matters of fact which happened in the most distant places and most remote ages, yet some fact must always be present to the senses or memory from which we may first proceed in drawing these conclusions. A man who should find in a desert country the remains of pompous buildings would conclude that the country had, in ancient times, been cultivated by civilized inhabitants; but did nothing of this nature occur to him, he could never form such an inference. We learn the events of former ages from history, but then we must peruse the volume in which this instruction is contained, and thence carry up our inferences from one testimony to another, till we arrive at the eyewitnesses and spectators of these distant events. In a word, if we proceed not upon some fact present to the memory or senses, our reasonings would be merely hypothetical; and however the particular links might be connected with each other, the whole chain of inferences would have nothing to support it, nor could we ever, by its means, arrive at the knowledge of any real existence. If I ask why you believe any particular matter of fact which you relate, you must tell me some reason; and this reason will be some other fact connected with it. But as you cannot proceed after this manner *in infinitum,* you must at last terminate in some fact which is present to your memory or senses or must allow that your belief is entirely without foundation.

What, then, is the conclusion of the whole matter? A simple one, though, it must be confessed, pretty remote from the common theories of philosophy. All belief of matter of fact or real existence is derived merely from some object present to the memory or senses and a customary conjunction between that and some other object; or, in other words, having found, in many instances, that any two kinds of objects, flame and heat, snow and cold, have always been conjoined together: if flame or snow be presented anew to the senses, the mind is carried by custom to expect heat or cold, and to *believe* that such a quality does exist and will discover itself upon a nearer approach. This belief is the necessary result of placing the mind in such circumstances. It is an operation of the soul, when we are so situated, as unavoidable as to feel the passion of love, when we receive benefits; or hatred, when we meet with injuries. All these operations are a species of natural instincts, which no reasoning or process of the thought and understanding is able either to produce or to prevent. At this point it would be very allowable for us to stop our philosophical researches. In most questions we can never make a single step further; and in all questions we must terminate here at last, after our most restless and curious inquiries. But still our curiosity will be pardonable, perhaps commendable, if it carry us on to still further researches and make us examine more accurately the nature of this *belief* and of the *customary conjunction* whence it is derived. By this means we may meet with some explications and analogies that will give satisfaction, at least to such as love the abstract sciences, and can be entertained with speculations which, however accurate, may still retain a degree of doubt and uncertainty. As to readers of a different taste, the remaining part of this Section is not calculated for them; and the following inquiries may well be understood, though it be neglected.

Part II

Nothing is more free than the imagination of man, and though it cannot exceed that original stock of ideas furnished by the internal and external senses, it has unlimited power of mixing, compounding, separating, and dividing these ideas in all the varieties of fiction and vision. It can feign a train of events with all the appearance of reality, ascribe to them a particular time and place, conceive them as existent, and paint them out to itself with every circumstance that belongs to any historical fact which it believes with the greatest certainty. Wherein, therefore, consists the difference between such a fiction and belief? It lies not merely in any peculiar idea which is annexed to such a conception as commands our assent, and which is wanting to every known fiction. For as the mind has authority over all its ideas, it could voluntarily annex this particular idea to any fiction, and consequently be able to believe whatever it pleases, contrary to what we find by daily experience. We can, in our conception, join the head of a man to the body of a horse, but it is not in our power to believe that such an animal has ever really existed.

It follows, therefore, that the difference between *fiction* and *belief* lies in some sentiment or feeling which is annexed to the latter, not to the former, and which depends not on the will, nor can be demanded at pleasure. It must be excited by nature like all other sentiments and must rise from the particular situation in which the mind is placed at any particular juncture. Whenever any object is presented to the memory or senses, it immediately, by the force of custom, carries the imagination to conceive that object which is usually conjoined to it; and this conception is attended with a feeling or sentiment different from the loose reveries of the fancy. In this consists the whole nature of belief. For as there is no matter of fact which we believe so firmly that we cannot conceive the contrary, there would be no difference between the conception assented to and that which is rejected were it not for some sentiment which distinguishes the one from the other. If I see a billiard ball moving toward another on a smooth table, I can easily conceive it to stop upon contact. This conception implies no contradiction, but still it feels very differently from that conception by which I represent to myself the impulse and the communication of motion from one ball to another.

Were we to attempt a *definition* of this sentiment, we should, perhaps, find it a very difficult, if not an impossible, task; in the same manner as if we should endeavor to define the feeling of cold, or passion of anger, to a creature who never had any experience of these sentiments. Belief is the true and proper name of this feeling, and no one is ever at a loss to know the meaning of that term, because every man is every moment conscious of the sentiment represented by it. It may not, however, be improper to attempt a *description* of this sentiment, in hopes we may by that means arrive at some analogies which may afford a more perfect explication of it. I say that belief is nothing but a more vivid, lively, forcible, firm, steady conception of an object than what the imagination alone is ever able to attain. This variety of terms, which may seem so unphilosophical, is intended only to express that act of the mind which renders realities, or what is taken for such, more present to us than fictions, causes them to weigh more in the thought, and gives them a superior influence on the passions and imagination. Provided we agree about the thing, it is needless to dispute about the terms. The imagination has the command over all its ideas and can join and mix and vary them in all the ways possible. It may conceive fictitious objects with all the circumstances of place and time. It may set them in a manner before our eyes, in their true colors, just as they might have existed. But as it is impossible that this faculty of imagination can ever, of itself, reach belief, it is evident that belief consists not in the peculiar nature or order of ideas, but in the *manner* of their conception and in their *feeling* to the mind. I confess that it is impossible perfectly to explain this feeling or manner of conception. We may make use of words which express something near it. But its true and proper name, as we observed before, is "belief," which is a term that everyone sufficiently understands in common life. And in philosophy we can go no further than assert that *belief* is something felt by the mind, which distinguishes the ideas of the judgment from the fictions of the imagination. It gives them more weight and influence, makes them appear of greater importance, enforces them in the mind, and renders them the governing principle of our actions. I hear at present, for instance, a person's voice with whom I am acquainted, and the sound comes as from the next room. This impression of my senses immediately conveys my thought to the person, together with all the surrounding objects. I paint them out to myself as existing at present, with the same qualities and relations of which I formerly knew them possessed. These ideas take faster hold of my mind than ideas of an enchanted castle. They are very different from the feeling and have a much greater influence of every kind, either to give pleasure or pain, joy or sorrow.

Let us, then, take in the whole compass of this doctrine and allow that the sentiment of belief is nothing but a conception more intense and steady than what attends the mere fictions of the imagination, and that this *manner* of conception arises from a customary conjunction of the object with something present to the memory or senses. I believe that it will not be difficult, upon these suppositions, to find other operations of the mind analogous to it and to trace up these phenomena to principles still more general.

We have already observed that nature has established connections among particular ideas, and that no sooner one idea occurs to our thoughts than it introduces its correlative and carries our attention towards it by a gentle and insensible movement. These principles of connection or association we have reduced to three, namely, "resemblance," "contiguity," and "causation," which are the only bonds that unite our thoughts together and beget that regular train of reflection or discourse which, in a greater or less degree, takes place among mankind. Now here arises a question on which the solution of the present difficulty will depend. Does it happen in all these relations that when one of the objects is presented to the senses or memory, the mind is not only carried to the conception of the correlative, but reaches a steadier and stronger conception of it than what otherwise it would have been able to attain? This seems to be the case with that belief which arises from the relation of cause and effect. And if the case be the same with the other relations or principles of association, this may be established as a general law which takes place in all the operations of the mind.

We may, therefore, observe, as the first experiment to our present purpose, that upon the appearance of the picture of an absent friend our idea of him is evidently enlivened by the *resemblance*, and that every passion which that idea occasions, whether of joy or sorrow, acquires new force and vigor. In producing this effect there concur both a relation and a present impression. Where the picture bears him no resemblance, at least was not intended for him, it never so much as conveys our thought to him. And where it is absent, as well as the person, though the mind may pass from the thought of one to that of the other, it feels its idea to be rather weakened than enlivened by that transition. We take a pleasure in viewing the picture of a friend when it is set before us; but when it is removed, rather choose to consider him directly than by reflection on an image which is equally distant and obscure.

The ceremonies of the Roman Catholic religion may be considered as instances of the same nature. The devotees of that superstition usually plead, in excuse for the mummeries with which they are upbraided, that they feel the good effect of those external motions, and postures, and actions in enlivening their devotion and quickening their fervor, which otherwise would decay if directed entirely to distant and immaterial objects. We shadow out the objects of our faith, say they, in sensible types and images, and render them more present to us by the immediate presence of these types than it is possible for us to do merely by an intellectual view and contemplation. Sensible objects have always a greater influence on the fancy than any other, and this influence they readily convey to those ideas to which they are related and which they resemble. I shall only infer from these practices and this reasoning that the effect of resemblance in enlivening the ideas is very common: and as in every case a resemblance and a present impression must concur, we are abundantly supplied with experiments to prove the reality of the foregoing principle.

We may add force to these experiments by others of a different kind, in considering the effects of *contiguity* as well as of *resemblance*. It is certain that distance diminishes the force of every idea and that, upon our approach to any object, though it does not discover itself to our senses, it operates upon the mind with an influence which imitates an immediate impression. The thinking on any object readily transports the mind to what is contiguous; but it is only the actual presence of an object that transports the mind to what is contiguous; but it is only the actual presence of an object that transports it with a superior vivacity. When I am a few miles from home, whatever relates to it touches me more nearly than when I am two hundred leagues distant, though even at that distance the reflecting on anything in the neighborhood of my friends or family naturally produces an idea of them. But, as in this latter case, both the objects of the mind are ideas, notwithstanding there is an easy transition between them; that transition alone is not able to give a superior vivacity to any of the ideas, for want of some immediate impression.[4]

No one can doubt but *causation* has the same influence as the other two relations of resemblance and contiguity. Superstitious people are fond of the relics of saints and holy men, for the same reason that they seek after types or images in order to enliven their devotion and give them a more intimate and strong conception of those exemplary lives which they desire to imitate. Now it is evident that one of the best relics which a devotee could procure would be the handiwork of a saint; and if his clothes and furniture are ever to be considered in this light, it is because they were once at his disposal and were moved and affected by him; in which respect they are to be considered as imperfect effects, and as connected with him by a shorter chain of consequences than any of those by which we learn the reality of his existence.

Suppose that the son of a friend who had been long dead or absent were presented to us; it is evident that this object would instantly revive its correlative idea and recall to our thoughts all past intimacies and familiarities in more lively color than they would otherwise have appeared to us. This is another phenomenon which seems to prove the principle above mentioned.

We may observe that in these phenomena the belief of the correlative object is always presupposed, without which the relation could have no effect. The influence of the picture supposes that we *believe* our friend to have once existed. Contiguity to home can never excite our ideas of home unless we *believe* that it really exists. Now I assert that this belief, where it reaches beyond the memory or senses, is of a similar nature and arises from similar causes with the transition of thought and vivacity of conception here explained. When I throw a piece of dry wood into a fire, my mind is immediately carried to conceive that it augments, not extinguishes, the flame. This transition of thought from the cause to the effect proceeds not from reason. It derives its origin altogether from custom and experience. And, as it first begins from an object present to the senses, it renders the idea or conception of flame more strong or lively than any loose floating reverie of the imagination. The idea arises immediately. The thought moves instantly toward it and conveys to it all that force of conception which is derived from the impression present to the senses. When a sword is leveled at my breast, does not the idea of wound and pain strike me more strongly than when a glass of wine is presented to me, even though by accident this idea should occur after the appearance of the latter object? But what is there in this whole matter to cause such a strong conception except only a present object and a customary transition to the idea of another object which we have been accustomed to conjoin with the former? This is the whole operation of the mind in all our conclusions concerning matter of fact and existence; and it is a satisfaction to find some analogies by which it may be explained. The transition from a present object does in all cases give strength and solidity to the related idea.

Here, then, is a kind of pre-established harmony between the course of nature and the succession of our ideas; and though the powers and forces by which the former is governed be wholly unknown to us, yet our thoughts and conceptions have still, we find, gone on in the same train with the other works of nature. Custom is that principle by which this correspondence has been effected, so necessary to the subsistence of our species and the regulation of our conduct in every circumstance and occurrence of human life. Had not the presence of an object instantly excited the idea of those objects commonly conjoined with it, all our knowledge must have been limited to the narrow sphere of our memory and senses, and we should never have been able to adjust means to ends or employ our natural powers either to the producing of good or avoiding of evil. Those who delight in the discovery and contemplation of *final causes* have here ample subject to employ their wonder and admiration.

I shall add, for a further confirmation of the foregoing theory, that as this operation of the mind, by which we infer like effects from like causes, and *vice versa,* is so essential to the subsistence of all human creatures, it is not probable that it could be trusted to the fallacious deductions of our reason, which is slow in its operations, appears not, in any degree, during the first years of infancy, and, at best, is in every age and period of human life extremely liable to error and mistake. It is more conformable to the ordinary wisdom of nature to secure so necessary an act of the mind by some instinct or mechanical tendency which may be infallible in its operations, may discover itself at the first appearance of life and thought, and may be independent of all the labored deductions of the understanding. As nature has taught us the use of our limbs without giving us the knowledge of the muscles and nerves by which they are actuated, so has she implanted in us an instinct which carries forward the thought in a correspondent course to that which she has established among external objects, though we are ignorant of those powers and forces on which this regular course and succession of objects totally depends.

SECTION VI. OF PROBABILITY[5]

Though there be no such thing as *chance* in the world, our ignorance of the real cause of any event has the same influence on the understanding and begets a like species of belief or opinion.

There is certainly a probability which arises from a superiority of chances on any side; and, according as this superiority increases and surpasses the opposite chances, the probability receives a proportionable increase and begets still a higher degree of belief of assent to that side in which we discover the superiority. If a die were marked with one figure or number of spots on four sides, and with another figure or number of spots on the two remaining sides, it would be more probable that the former would turn up than the latter, though, if it had a thousand sides marked in the same manner, and only one side different, the probability would be much higher and our belief or expectation of the event more steady and secure. This process of the thought or reasoning may seem trivial and obvious; but to those who consider it more narrowly it may, perhaps, afford matter for curious speculation.

It seems evident that when the mind looks forward to discover the event which may result from the throw of such a die, it considers the turning up of each particular side as alike probable; and this is the very nature of chance, to render all the particular events comprehended in it entirely equal. But finding a greater number of sides concur in the one event than in the other, the mind is carried more frequently to that event and meets it oftener in revolving the various possibilities or chances on which the ultimate result depends. This concurrence of several views in one particular event begets immediately, by an explicable contrivance of nature, the sentiment of belief and gives that event the advantage over its antagonist which is supported by a smaller number of views and recurs less frequently to the mind. If we allow that belief is nothing but a firmer and stronger conception of an object than what attends the mere fictions of the imagination, this operation may, perhaps, in some measure be accounted for. The concurrence of these several views or glimpses imprints the idea more strongly on the imagination, gives it superior force and vigor, renders its influence on the passions and affections more sensible, and, in a word, begets that reliance or security which constitutes the nature of belief and opinion.

The case is the same with the probability of causes as with that of chance. There are some causes which are entirely uniform and constant in producing a particular effect, and no instance has ever yet been found of any failure or irregularity in their operation. Fire has always burned, and water suffocated, every human creature. The production of motion by impulse and gravity is a universal law which has hitherto admitted of no exception. But there are other causes which have been found more irregular and uncertain, nor has rhubarb always proved a purge, or opium a soporific, to everyone who has taken these medicines. It is true, when any cause fails of producing its usual effect, philosophers ascribe not this to any irregularity in nature, but suppose that some secret causes in the particular structure of parts have prevented the operation. Our reasonings, however, and conclusions concerning the event are the same as if this principle had no place. Being determined by custom to transfer the past to the future in all our inferences, where the past has been entirely regular and uniform we expect the event with the greatest assurance and leave no room for any contrary supposition. But where different effects have been found to follow from causes which are to *appearance* exactly similar, all these various effects must occur to the mind in transferring the past to the future, and enter into our consideration when we determine the probability of the event. Though we give the preference to that which has been found most usual, and believe that this effect will exist, we must not overlook the other effects, but must assign to each of them a particular weight and authority in proportion as we have found it to be more or less frequent. It is more probable, in almost every country of Europe, that there will be frost sometime in January than that the weather will continue open throughout the whole month, though this probability varies according to the different climates, and approaches to a certainty in the more northern kingdoms. Here, then, it seems evident that when we transfer the past to the future in order to determine the effect which will result from any cause, we transfer all the different events in the same proportion as they have appeared in the past, and conceive one to have existed a hundred times, for instance, another ten times, and another once. As a great number of views do here concur in one event, they fortify and confirm it to the imagination, beget that sentiment which we call "belief," and give its object the preference above the contrary event which is not supported by an equal number of experiments and recurs not so frequently to the thought in transferring the past to the future. Let anyone try to account for this operation of the mind upon any of the received systems of philosophy, and he will be sensible of the difficulty. For my part, I shall think it sufficient if the present hints excite the curiosity of philosophers and make them sensible how defective all common theories are in treating of such curious and such sublime subjects.

SECTION VII. OF THE IDEA OF NECESSARY CONNECTION

Part I

The great advantage of the mathematical sciences above the moral consists in this, that the ideas of the former, being sensible, are always clear and determinate, the smallest distinction between them is immediately perceptible, and the same terms are still expressive of the same ideas without ambiguity or variation. An oval is never mistaken for a circle, nor a hyperbola for an ellipsis. The isosceles and scalenum are distinguished by boundaries more exact than vice and virtue, right and wrong. If any term be defined in geometry, the mind readily, of itself substitutes on all occasions the definition for the term defined, or, even when no definition is employed, the object itself may be presented to the senses and by that means be steadily and clearly apprehended. But the finer sentiments of the mind, the operations of the understanding, the various agitations of the passions, though really in themselves distinct, easily escape us when surveyed by reflection, nor is it in our power to recall the original object as often as we have occasion to contemplate it. Ambiguity, by this means, is gradually introduced into our reasonings: similar objects are readily taken to be the same, and the conclusion becomes at last very wide of the premises.

One may safely, however, affirm that if we consider these sciences in a proper light, their advantages and disadvantages nearly compensate each other and reduce both of them to a state of equality. If the mind, with greater facility, retains the ideas of geometry clear and determinate, it must carry on a much longer and more intricate chain of reasoning and compare ideas much wider of each other in order to reach the abstruser truths of that science. And if moral ideas are apt, without extreme care, to fall into obscurity and confusion, the inferences are always much shorter in these disquisitions, and the intermediate steps which lead to the conclusion much fewer than in the sciences which treat of quantity and number. In reality, there is scarcely a proposition in Euclid so simple as not to consist of more parts than are to be found in any moral reasoning which runs not into chimera and conceit. Where we trace the principles of the human mind through a few steps, we may be very well satisfied with our progress, considering how soon nature throws a bar to all our inquiries concerning causes and reduces us to an acknowledgment of our ignorance. The chief obstacle, therefore, to our improvements in the moral or metaphysical sciences is the obscurity of the ideas and ambiguity of the terms. The principal difficulty in the mathematics is the length of inferences and compass of thought requisite to the forming of any conclusion. And, perhaps, our progress in natural philosophy is chiefly retarded by the want of proper experiments and phenomena, which are often discovered by chance and cannot always be found when requisite, even by the most diligent and prudent inquiry. As moral philosophy seems hitherto to have received less improvement than either geometry or physics, we may conclude that if there be any difference in this respect among these sciences, the difficulties which obstruct the progress of the former require superior care and capacity to be surmounted.

There are no ideas which occur in metaphysics more obscure and uncertain than those of "power," "force," "energy," or "necessary connection," of which it is every moment necessary for us to treat in all our disquisitions. We shall, therefore, endeavor in this Section to fix, if possible, the precise meaning of these terms and thereby remove some part of that obscurity which is so much complained of in this species of philosophy.

It seems a proposition which will not admit of much dispute that all our ideas are nothing but copies of our impressions, or, in other words, that it is impossible for us to *think* of anything which we have not antecedently *felt*, either by our external or internal senses. I have endeavored[6] to explain and prove this proposition, and have expressed my hopes that by a proper application of it men may reach a greater clearness and precision in philosophical reasonings than what they have hitherto been able to attain. Complex ideas may, perhaps, be well known by definition, which is nothing but an enumeration of those parts or simple ideas that compose them. But when we have pushed up definitions to the most simple ideas and find still some ambiguity and obscurity, what resources are we then possessed of? By what invention can we throw light upon these ideas and render them altogether precise and determinate to our intellectual view? Produce the impressions or original sentiments from which the ideas are copied. These impressions are all strong and sensible. They admit not of ambiguity. They are not only placed in a full light themselves, but may throw light on their correspondent ideas, which lie in obscurity. And by this means we may perhaps attain a new microscope or species of optics by which, in the moral sciences, the most minute and most simple ideas may be so enlarged as to fall readily under our apprehension and be equally known with the grossest and most sensible ideas that can be the object of our inquiry.

To be fully acquainted, therefore, with the idea of power or necessary connection, let us examine its impression and, in order to find the impression with greater certainty, let us search for it in all the sources from which it may possibly be derived.

When we look about us towards external objects and consider the operation of causes, we are never able, in a single instance, to discover any power or necessary connection, any quality which binds the effect to the cause and renders the one an infallible consequence of the other. We only find that the one does actually in fact follow the other. The impulse of one billiard ball is attended with motion in the second. This is the whole that appears to the *outward* senses. The mind feels no sentiment or *inward* impression from this succession of objects: consequently, there is not, in any single particular instance of cause and effect, anything which can suggest the idea of power or necessary connection.

From the first appearance of an object we never can conjecture what effect will result from it. But were the power or energy of any cause discoverable by the mind, we could foresee the effect, even without experience, and might, at first, pronounce with certainty concerning it by mere dint of thought and reasoning.

In reality, there is no part of matter that does ever, by its sensible qualities, discover any power or energy, or give us ground to imagine that it could produce anything, or be followed by any other object, which we could denominate its effect. Solidity, extension, motion—these qualities are all complete in themselves and never point out any other event which may result from them. The scenes of the universe are continually shifting, and one object follows another in an uninterrupted succession; but the power or force which actuates the whole machine is entirely concealed from us and never discovers itself in any of the sensible qualities of body. We know that, in fact, heat is a constant attendant of flame; but what is the connection between them we have no room so much as to conjecture or imagine. It is impossible, therefore, that the idea of power can be derived from the contemplation of bodies in single instances of their operation, because no bodies ever discover any power which can be the original of this idea.[7]

Since, therefore, external objects as they appear to the senses give us no idea of power or necessary connection by their operation in particular instances, let us see whether this idea be derived from reflection on the operations of our own minds and be copied from any internal impression. It may be said that we are every moment conscious of internal power while we feel that, by the simple command of our will, we can move the organs of our body or direct the faculties of our mind. An act of volition produces motion in our limbs or raises a new idea in our imagination. This influence of the will we know by consciousness. Hence we acquire the idea of power or energy, and are certain that we ourselves and all other intelligent beings are possessed of power. This idea, then, is an idea of reflection since it arises from reflecting on the operations of our own mind and on the command which is exercised by will both over the organs of the body and faculties of the soul.

We shall proceed to examine this pretension and, first, with regard to the influence of volition over the organs of the body. This influence, we may observe, is a fact which, like all other natural events, can be known only by experience, and can never be foreseen from any apparent energy or power in the cause which connects it with the effect and renders the one an infallible consequence of the other. The motion of our body follows upon the command of our will. Of this we are every moment conscious. But the means by which this is effected, the energy by which the will performs so extraordinary an operation—of this we are so far from being immediately conscious that it must forever escape our most diligent inquiry.

For, *first,* is there any principle in all nature more mysterious than the union of soul with body, by which a supposed spiritual substance acquires such an influence over a material one that the most refined thought is able to actuate the grossest matter? Were we empowered by a secret wish to remove mountains or control the planets in their orbit, this extensive authority would not be more extraordinary, nor more beyond our comprehension. But if, by consciousness, we perceived any power or energy in the will, we must know this power; we must know its connection with the effect; we must know the secret union of soul and body, and the nature of both these substances by which the one is able to operate in so many instances upon the other.

Secondly, we are not able to move all the organs of the body with a like authority, though we cannot assign any reason, besides experience, for so remarkable a difference between one and the other. Why has the will an influence over the tongue and fingers, not over the heart and liver? This question would never embarrass us were we conscious of a power in the former case, not in the latter. We should then perceive, independent of experience, why the authority of the will over organs of the body is circumscribed within such particular limits. Being in that case fully acquainted with the power or force by which it operates, we should also know why its influence reaches precisely to such boundaries, and no further.

A man suddenly struck with a palsy in the leg or arm, or who had newly lost those members, frequently endeavors, at first, to move them and employ them in their usual offices. Here he is as much conscious of power to command such limbs as a man in perfect health is conscious of power to actuate any member which remains in its natural state and condition. But consciousness never deceives. Consequently, neither in the one case nor in the other are we ever conscious of any power. We learn the influence of our will from experience alone. And experience only teaches us how one event constantly follows another, without instructing us in the secret connection which binds them together and renders them inseparable.

Thirdly, we learn from anatomy that the immediate object of power in voluntary motion is not the member itself which is moved, but certain muscles and nerves and animal spirits, and, perhaps, something still more minute and more unknown, through which the motion is successfully propagated ere it reach the member itself whose motion is the immediate object of volition. Can there be a more certain proof that the power by which this whole operation is performed, so far from being directly and fully known by an inward sentiment or consciousness, is to the last degree mysterious and unintelligible? Here the mind wills a certain event; immediately another event, unknown to ourselves and totally different from the one intended, is produced. This event produces another, equally unknown, till, at last, through a long succession the desired event is produced. But if the original power were felt, it must be known; were it known, its effect must also be known, since all power is relative to its effect. And, *vice versa,* if the effect be not known, the power cannot be known nor felt. How indeed can we be conscious of a power to move our limbs when we have no such power, but only that to move certain animal spirits which, though they produce at last the motion of our limbs, yet operate in such a manner as is wholly beyond our comprehension?

We may therefore conclude from the whole, I hope, without any temerity, though with assurance, that our idea of power is not copied from any sentiment or consciousness of power within ourselves when we give rise to animal motion or apply our limbs to their proper use and office. That their motion follows the command of the will is a matter of common experience, like other natural events; but the power or energy by which this is effected, like that in other natural events, is unknown and inconceivable.[8]

Shall we then assert that we are conscious of a power or energy in our own minds when, by an act or command of our will, we raise up a new idea, fix the mind to the contemplation of it, turn it on all sides, and at last dismiss it for some other idea when we think that we have surveyed it with sufficient accuracy? I believe the same arguments will prove that even this command of the will gives us no real idea of force or energy.

First, it must be allowed that when we know a power, we know that very circumstance in the cause by which it is enabled to produce the effect, for these are supposed to be synonymous. We must, therefore, know both the cause and effect and the relation between them. But do we pretend to be acquainted with the nature of the human soul and the nature of an idea, or the aptitude of the one to produce the other? This is a real creation, a production of something out of nothing, which implies a power so great that it may seem, at first sight, beyond the reach of any being less than infinite. At least it must be owned that such a power is not felt, nor known, nor even conceivable by the mind. We only feel the event, namely, the existence of an idea consequent to a command of the will; but the manner in which this operation is performed, the power by which it is produced, is entirely beyond our comprehension.

Secondly, the command of the mind over itself is limited, as well as its command over the body; and these limits are not known by reason or any acquaintance with the nature of cause and effect, but only by experience and observation, as in all other natural events and in the operation of external objects. Our authority over our sentiments and passions is much weaker than that over our ideas; and even the latter authority is circumscribed within very narrow boundaries. Will any one pretend to assign the ultimate reason of these boundaries, or show why the power is deficient in one case, not in another.

Thirdly, this self-command is very different at different times. A man in health possesses more of it than one languishing with sickness. We are more master of our thoughts in the morning than in the evening; fasting, than after a full meal. Can we give any reason for these variations except experience? Where then is the power of which we pretend to be conscious? Is there not here, either in a spiritual or material substance, or both, some secret mechanism or structure of parts upon which the effect depends, and which, being entirely unknown to us, renders the power or energy of the will equally unknown and incomprehensible?

Volition is surely an act of the mind with which we are sufficiently acquainted. Reflect upon it. Consider it on all sides. Do you find anything in it like this creative power by which it raises from nothing a new idea and, with a kind of *fiat,* imitates the omnipotence of its Maker, if I may be allowed so to speak, who called forth into existence all the various scenes of nature? So far from being conscious of this energy in the will, it requires as certain experience as that of which we are possessed to convince us that such extraordinary effects do ever result from a simple act of volition.

The generality of mankind never find any difficulty in accounting for the more common and familiar operations of nature, such as the descent of heavy bodies, the growth of plants, the generation of animals, or the nourishment of bodies by food; but suppose that in all these cases they perceive the very force or energy of the cause by which it is connected with its effect, and is forever infallible in its operation. They acquire, by long habit, such a turn of mind that upon the appearance of the cause they immediately expect, with assurance, its usual attendant, and hardly conceive it possible that any other event could result from it. It is only on the discovery of extraordinary phenomena, such as earthquakes, pestilence, and prodigies of any kind, that they find themselves at a loss to assign a proper cause and to explain the manner in which the effect is produced by it. It is usual for men, in such difficulties, to have recourse to some invisible intelligent principle as the immediate cause of that event which surprises them, and which they think cannot be accounted for from the common powers of nature. But philosophers, who carry their scrutiny a little further, immediately perceive that, even in the most familiar events, the energy of the cause is as unintelligible as in the most unusual, and that we only learn by experience the frequent conjunction of objects, without being ever able to comprehend anything like connection between them. Here, then, many philosophers think themselves obliged by reason to have recourse, on all occasions, to the same principle which the vulgar never appeal to but in cases that appear miraculous and supernatural. They acknowledge mind and intelligence to be, not only the ultimate and original cause of all things, but the immediate and sole cause of every event which appears in nature. They pretend that those objects which are commonly denominated "causes" are in reality nothing but "occasions," and that the true and direct principle of every effect is not any power or force in nature, but a volition of the Supreme Being, who wills that such particular objects should forever be conjoined with each other. Instead of saying that one billiard ball moves another by a force which it has derived from the author of nature, it is the Deity himself, they say, who, by a particular volition, moves the second ball, being determined to this operation by the impulse of the first ball, in consequence of those general laws which he has laid down to himself in the government of the universe. But philosophers, advancing still in their inquiries, discover that as we are totally ignorant of the power on which depends the mutual operation of bodies, we are no less ignorant of that power on which depends the operation of mind on body, or of body on mind; nor are we able, either from our senses or consciousness, to assign the ultimate principle in the one case more than in the other. The same ignorance, therefore, reduces them to the same conclusion. They assert that the Deity is the immediate cause of the union between soul and body, and that they are not the organs of sense which, being agitated by external objects, produce sensations in the mind; but that it is a particular volition of our omnipotent Maker which excites such a sensation in consequence of such a motion in the organ. In like manner, it is not any energy in the will that produces local motion in our members: It is God himself, who is pleased to second our will, in itself impotent, and to command that motion which we erroneously attribute to our own power and efficacy. Nor do philosophers stop at this conclusion. They sometimes extend the same inference to the mind itself in its internal operations. Our mental vision or conception of ideas is nothing but a revelation made to us by our Maker. When we voluntarily turn our thoughts to any object and raise up its image in the fancy, it is not the will which creates that idea, it is the universal Creator who discovers it to the mind and renders it present to us.

Thus, according to these philosophers, everything is full of God. Not content with the principle that nothing exists but by his will, that nothing possesses any power but by his concession, they rob nature and all created beings of every power in order to render their dependence on the Deity still more sensible and immediate. They consider not that by this theory they diminish, instead of magnifying, the grandeur of those attributes which they affect so much to celebrate. It argues, surely, more power in the Deity to delegate a certain degree of power to inferior creatures than to produce everything by his own immediate volition. It argues more wisdom to contrive at first the fabric of the world with such perfect foresight that of itself, and by its proper operation, it may serve all the purposes of Providence than if the great Creator were obliged every moment to adjust its parts and animate by his breath all the wheels of that stupendous machine.

But if we would have a more philosophical confutation of this theory, perhaps the two following reflections may suffice:

First, it seems to me that this theory of the universal energy and operation of the Supreme Being is too bold ever to carry conviction with it to a man sufficiently apprised of the weakness of human reason and the narrow limits to which it is confined in all its operations. Though the chain of arguments which conduct to it were ever so logical, there must arise a strong suspicion, if not an absolute assurance, that it has carried us quite beyond the reach of our faculties when it leads to conclusions so extraordinary and so remote from common life and experience. We are got into fairyland long ere we have reached the last steps of our theory; and *there* we have no reason to trust our common methods of arguments or to think that our usual analogies and probabilities have any authority. Our line is too short to fathom such immense abysses. And however we may flatter ourselves that we are guided, in every step which we take, by a kind of verisimilitude and experience, we may be assured that this fancied experience has no authority when we thus apply it to subjects that lie entirely out of the sphere of experience. But on this we shall have occasion to touch afterwards.[9]

Secondly, I cannot perceive any force in the arguments on which this theory is founded. We are ignorant, it is true, of the manner in which bodies operate on each other. Their force or energy is entirely incomprehensible. But are we not equally ignorant of the manner or force by which a mind, even the Supreme Mind, operates, either on itself or on body? Whence, I beseech you, do we acquire any idea of it? We have no sentiment or consciousness of this power in ourselves. We have no idea of the Supreme Being but what we learn from reflection on our own faculties. Were our ignorance, therefore, a good reason for rejecting anything, we should be led into that principle of denying all energy in the Supreme Being, as much as in the grossest matter. We surely comprehend as little the operations of the one as of the other. Is it more difficult to conceive that motion may arise from impulse than that it may arise from volition? All we know is our profound ignorance in both cases.[10]

Part II

But to hasten to a conclusion of this argument, which is already drawn out to too great a length: We have sought in vain for an idea of power or necessary connection in all the sources from which we could suppose it to be derived. It appears that in single instances of the operation of bodies we never can, by our utmost scrutiny, discover anything but one event following another, without being able to comprehend any force or power by which the cause operates or any connection between it and its supposed effect. The same difficulty occurs in contemplating the operations of mind on body, where we observe the motion of the latter to follow upon the volition of the former, but are not able to observe or conceive the tie which binds together the motion and volition, or the energy, by which the mind produces this effect. The authority of the will over its own faculties and ideas is not a whit more comprehensible, so that, upon the whole, there appears not, throughout all nature, any one instance of connection which is conceivable by us. All events seem entirely loose and separate. One event follows another, but we never can observe any tie between them. They seem *conjoined,* but never *connected.* And as we can have no idea of anything which never appeared to our outward sense or inward sentiment, the necessary conclusion *seems* to be that we have no idea of connection or power at all, and that these words are absolutely without any meaning when employed either in philosophical reasonings or common life.

But there still remains one method of avoiding this conclusion, and one source which we have not yet examined. When any natural object or event is presented, it is impossible for us, by any sagacity or penetration, to discover, or even conjecture, without experience, what event will result from it, or to carry our foresight beyond that object which is immediately present to the memory and senses. Even after one instance or experiment where we have observed a particular event to follow upon another, we are not entitled to form a general rule or foretell what will happen in like cases, it being justly esteemed an unpardonable temerity to judge the whole course of nature from one single experiment, however accurate or certain. But when one particular species of events has always, in all instances, been conjoined with another, we make no longer any scruple of foretelling one upon the appearance of the other, and of employing that reasoning which can alone assure us of any matter of fact or existence. We then call the one object "cause," the other "effect." We suppose that there is some connection between them, some power in the one by which it infallibly produces the other and operates with the greatest certainty and strongest necessity.

It appears, then, that this idea of a necessary connection among events arises from a number of similar instances which occur, of the constant conjunction of these events; nor can that idea ever be suggested by any one of these instances surveyed in all possible lights and positions. But there is nothing in a number of instances, different from every single instance, which is supposed to be exactly similar, except only that after a repetition of similar instances the mind is carried by habit, upon the appearance of one event, to expect its usual attendant and to believe that it will exist. This connection, therefore, which we *feel* in the mind, this customary transition of the imagination from one object to its usual attendant, is the sentiment or impression from which we form the idea of power or necessary connection. Nothing further is in the case. Contemplate the subject on all sides, you will never find any other origin of that idea. This is the sole difference between one instance, from which we can never receive the idea of connection, and a number of similar instances by which it is suggested. The first time a man saw the communication of motion by impulse, as by the shock of two billiard balls, he could not pronounce that the one event was *connected,* but only that it was *conjoined* with the other. After he has observed several instances of this nature, he then pronounces them to be *connected.* What alteration has happened to give rise to this new idea of *connection?* Nothing but that he now *feels* these events to be *connected* in his imagination, and can readily foretell the existence of one from the appearance of the other. When we say, therefore, that one object is connected with another, we mean only that they have acquired a connection in our thought and give rise to this inference by which they become proofs of each other's existence—a conclusion which is somewhat extraordinary, but which seems founded on sufficient evidence. Nor will its evidence be weakened by any general diffidence of the understanding or skeptical suspicion concerning every conclusion which is new and extraordinary. No conclusions can be more agreeable to skepticism than such as make discoveries concerning the weakness and narrow limits of human reason and capacity.

And what stronger instance can be produced of the surprising ignorance and weakness of the understanding than the present? For surely, if there be any relation among objects which it imports us to know perfectly, it is that of cause and effect. On this are founded all our reasonings concerning matter of fact or existence. By means of it alone we attain any assurance concerning objects which are removed from the present testimony of our memory and senses. The only immediate utility of all sciences is to teach us how to control and regulate future events by their causes. Our thoughts and inquiries are, therefore, every moment employed about this relation; yet so imperfect are the ideas which we form concerning it that it is impossible to give any just definition of cause, except what is drawn from something extraneous and foreign to it. Similar objects are always conjoined with similar. Of this we have experience. Suitably to this experience, therefore, we may define a cause to be *an object followed by another, and where all the objects, similar to the first, are followed by objects similar to the second*. Or, in other words, *where, if the first object had not been, the second never had existed*. The appearance of a cause always conveys the mind, by a customary transition, to the idea of the effect. Of this also we have experience. We may, therefore, suitably to this experience, form another definition of cause and call it *an object followed by another, and whose appearance always conveys the thought to that other*. But though both these definitions be drawn from circumstances foreign to the cause, we cannot remedy this inconvenience or attain any more perfect definition which may point out that circumstance in the cause which gives it a connection with its effect. We have no idea of this connection, nor even any distinct notion what it is we desire to know when we endeavor at a conception of it. We say, for instance, that the vibration of this string is the cause of this particular sound. But what do we mean by that affirmation? We either mean *that this vibration is followed by this sound, and that all similar vibrations have been followed by similar sounds; or, that this vibration is followed by this sound, and that, upon the appearance of one, the mind anticipates the senses and forms immediately an idea of the other*. We may consider the relation of cause and effect in either of these two lights; but beyond these we have no idea of it.[11]

To recapitulate, therefore, the reasonings of this Section: Every idea is copied from some preceding impression or sentiment; and where we cannot find any impression, we may be certain that there is no idea. In all single instances of the operation of bodies or minds there is nothing that produces any impression, nor consequently can suggest any idea, of power or necessary connection. But when many uniform instances appear, and the same object is always followed by the same event, we then begin to entertain the notion of cause and connection. We then *feel* a new sentiment or impression, to wit, a customary connection in the thought or imagination between one object and its usual attendant; and this sentiment is the original of that idea which we seek for. For as this idea arises from a number of similar instances, and not from any single instance, it must arise from that circumstance in which the number of instances differ from every individual instance. But this customary connection or transition of the imagination is the only circumstance in which they differ. In every other particular they are alike. The first instance which we saw of motion, communicated by the shock of two billiard balls (to return to this obvious illustration), is exactly similar to any instance that may at present occur to us, except only that we could not at first *infer* one event from the other, which we are enabled to do at present, after so long a course of uniform experience. I know not whether the reader will readily apprehend this reasoning. I am afraid that, should I multiply words about it or throw it into a greater variety of lights, it would only become more obscure and intricate. In all abstract reasonings there is one point of view which, if we can happily hit, we shall go further towards illustrating the subject than by all the eloquence in the world. This point of view we should endeavor to reach, and reserve the flowers of rhetoric for subjects which are more adapted to them.

NOTES

1. It is probable that no more was meant by those who denied innate ideas than that all ideas were copies of our impressions, though it must be confessed that the terms which they employed were not chosen with such caution, nor so exactly defined, as to prevent all mistakes about their doctrine. For what is meant by "innate"? If "innate" be equivalent to "natural," then all the perceptions and ideas of the mind must be allowed to be innate or natural, in whatever sense we take the latter word, whether in opposition to what is uncommon, artificial, or miraculous. If by innate he meant contemporary to our birth, the dispute seems to be frivolous, nor is it worth while to inquire at what time thinking begins, whether before, at, or after our birth. Again, the word "idea" seems to be commonly taken in a very loose sense by Locke and others, as standing for any of our perceptions, our sensations and passions, as well as thoughts. Now, in this sense, I

should desire to know what can be meant by asserting that self-love, or resentment of injuries, or the passion between the sexes is not innate?

But admitting these terms "impressions" and "ideas" in the sense above explained, and understanding by "innate" what is original or copied from no precedent perception, then may we assert that all our impressions are innate, and our ideas not innate.

To be ingenuous, I must own it to be my opinion that Locke was betrayed into this question by the schoolmen, who, making use of undefined terms, draw out their disputes to a tedious length without ever touching the point in question. A like ambiguity and circumlocution seem to run through that philosopher's reasonings, on this as well as most other subjects.

2. The word "power" is here used in a loose and popular sense. The more accurate explication of it would give additional evidence to this argument. See Section VII.

3. Nothing is more usual than for writers, even on *moral, political,* or *physical* subjects, to distinguish between *reason* and *experience,* and to suppose that these species of argumentation are entirely different from each other. The former are taken for the mere result of our intellectual faculties, which, by considering *a priori* the nature of things, and examining the effects that must follow from their operation, establish particular principles of science and philosophy. The latter are supposed to be derived entirely from sense and observation, by which we learn what has actually resulted from the operation of particular objects, and are thence able to infer what will for the future result from them. Thus, for instance, the limitations and restraints of civil government and a legal constitution may be defended, either from *reason,* which, reflecting on the great frailty and corruption of human nature, teaches that no man can safely be trusted with unlimited authority; or from *experience* and history, which inform us of the enormous abuses that ambition in every age and country has been found to make of so imprudent a confidence.

The same distinction between reason and experience is maintained in all our deliberations concerning the conduct of life, while the experienced statesman, general physician, or merchant, is trusted and followed, and the unpracticed novice, with whatever natural talents endowed, neglected and despised. Though it be allowed that reason may form very plausible conjectures with regard to the consequences of such a particular conduct in such particular circumstances, it is still supposed imperfect without the assistance of experience, which is alone able to give stability and certainty to the maxim derived from study and reflection.

But notwithstanding that this distinction be thus universally received, both in the active and speculative scenes of life, I shall not scruple to pronounce that it is, at bottom, erroneous, or at least superficial.

If we examine those arguments which, in any of the sciences above mentioned, are supposed to be the mere effects of reasoning and reflection, they will be found to terminate at last in some general principle or conclusion for which we can assign no reason but observation and experience. The only difference between them and those maxims which are vulgarly esteemed the result of pure experience is that the former cannot be established without some process of thought, and some reflection on what we have observed, in order to distinguish its circumstances and trace its consequences—whereas, in the latter, the experienced event is exactly and fully similar to that which we infer as the result of any particular situation. The history of a Tiberius or a Nero makes us dread a like tyranny, were our monarchs freed from the restraints of laws and senates: but the observation of any fraud or cruelty in private life is sufficient, with the aid of a little thought, to give us the same apprehension, while it serves as an instance of the general corruption of human nature, and shows us the danger which we must incur by reposing an entire confidence in mankind. In both cases, it is experience which is ultimately the foundation of our inference and conclusion.

There is no man so young and unexperienced as not to have formed from observation many general and just maxims concerning human affairs and the conduct of life; but it must be confessed that when a man comes to put these in practice he will be extremely liable to error, till time and further experience both enlarge these maxims, and teach him their proper use and application. In every situation or incident there are many particular and seemingly minute circumstances which the man of greatest talents is at first apt to overlook, though on them the justness of his conclusions, and consequently the prudence of his conduct, entirely depend. Not to mention that, to a young beginner, the general observations and maxims occur not always on the proper occasions, nor can be immediately applied with due calmness and distinction. The truth is, an unexperienced reasoner could be no reasoner at all were he absolutely inexperienced; and when we assign that character to anyone, we mean it only in a comparative sense, and suppose him possessed of experience in a smaller and more imperfect degree.

4. [A footnote containing a long quotation from Cicero, deleted.]

5. Mr. Locke divides all arguments into "demonstrative" and "probable." In this view, we must say that it is only probable that all men must die, or that

the sun will rise tomorrow. But to conform our language more to common use, we ought to divide arguments into *demonstrations, proofs,* and *probabilities:* by proofs, meaning such arguments from experience as leave no room for doubt or opposition.

6. Section II.

7. Mr. Locke, in his chapter of Power, says that, finding from experience that there are several new productions in matter, and concluding that there must somewhere be a power capable of producing them, we arrive at last by this reasoning at the idea of power. But no reasoning can ever give us a new, original simple idea, as this philosopher himself confesses. This, therefore, can never be the origin of that idea.

8. It may be pretended, that the resistance which we meet with in bodies, obliging us frequently to exert our force and call up all our power, this gives us the idea of force and power. It is this *nisus* or strong endeavor of which we are conscious, that is the original impression from which this idea is copied. But, *first,* we attribute power to a vast number of objects where we never can suppose this resistance or exertion of force to take place: to the Supreme Being, who never meets with any resistance; to the mind in its command over its ideas and limbs, in common thinking and motion, where the effect follows immediately upon the will, without any exertion or summoning up of force; to inanimate matter, which is not capable of this sentiment. *Secondly,* this sentiment of an endeavor to overcome resistance has no known connection with any event: What follows it we know by experience, but could not know it *a priori.* It must, however, be confessed that the animal *nisus* which we experience, though it can afford no accurate precise idea of power, enters very much into that vulgar, inaccurate idea which is formed of it.

9. Section XII. [Not included here.]

10. I need not examine at length the *vis inertiae* which is so much talked of in the new philosophy, and which is ascribed to matter. We find by experience that a body at rest or in motion continues forever in its present state, till put from it by some new cause; and that a body impelled takes as much motion from the impelling body as it acquires itself. These are facts. When we call this a *vis inertiae,* we only mark these facts, without pretending to have any idea of the inert power, in the same manner as, when we talk of gravity, we mean certain effects without comprehending that active power. It was never the meaning of Sir Isaac Newton to rob second causes of all force or energy, though some of his followers have endeavored to establish that theory upon his authority. On the contrary, that great philosopher had recourse to an ethereal active fluid to explain his universal attraction, though he was so cautious and modest as to allow that it was a mere hypothesis not to be insisted on without more experiments. I must confess that there is something in the fate of opinions a little extraordinary. Descartes insinuated that doctrine of the universal and sole efficacy of the Deity, without insisting on it. Malebranche and other Cartesians made it the foundation of all their philosophy. It had, however, no authority in England. Locke, Clarke, and Cudworth never so much as take notice of it, but suppose all along that matter has a real, though subordinate and derived, power. By what means has it become so prevalent among our modern metaphysicians?

11. According to these explications and definitions, the idea of *power* is relative as much as that of *cause;* and both have a reference to an effect, or some other event constantly conjoined with the former. When we consider the *unknown* circumstance of an object by which the degree or quantity of its effect is fixed and determined, we call that its power. And accordingly, it is allowed by all philosophers that the effect is the measure of the power. But if they had any idea of power as it is in itself, why could they not measure it in itself? The dispute, whether the force of a body in motion be as its velocity, or the square of its velocity; this dispute, I say, needed not be decided by comparing its effects in equal or unequal times, but by direct mensuration and comparison.

As to the frequent use of the words "force," "power," "energy," etc., which everywhere occur in common conversation as well as in philosophy, that is no proof that we are acquainted, in any instance, with the connecting principle between cause and effect, or can account ultimately for the production of one thing by another. These words, as commonly used, have very loose meanings annexed to them, and their ideas are very uncertain and confused. No animal can put external bodies in motion without the sentiment of a *nisus* or endeavor; and every animal has a sentiment or feeling from the stroke or blow of an external object that is in motion. These sensations, which are merely animal, and from which we can *a priori* draw no inference, we are apt to transfer to inanimate objects, and to suppose that they have some such feelings whenever they transfer or receive motion. With regard to energies, which are exerted without our annexing to them any idea of communicated motion, we consider only the constant experienced conjunction of the events; and as we *feel* a customary connection between the ideas, we transfer that feeling to the objects, as nothing is more usual than to apply to external bodies every internal sensation which they occasion.

An Encounter with David Hume*

WESLEY C. SALMON

Wesley C. Salmon (1925–) teaches history and philosophy of science at the University of Pittsburgh.

A DAY IN THE LIFE OF A HYPOTHETICAL STUDENT

IN THE PHYSICS 1A LECTURE HALL, Professor Salvia[1] has had a bowling ball suspended from a high ceiling by a long rope so that it can swing back and forth like a pendulum. Standing well over to one side of the room, he holds the bowling ball at the tip of his nose. He releases it (taking great care not to give it a push). It swings through a wide arc, gaining considerable speed as it passes through the low portion of its swing beneath the point of suspension from the ceiling. It continues to the other side of the room, where it reaches the end of its path, and then returns. The professor stands motionless as the bowling ball moves faster and faster back toward his nose. As it passes through the midpoint of the return arc, it is again traveling very rapidly, but it begins to slow down, and it stops just at the tip of his nose. Some of the students think he is cool. "This demonstration," he says, "illustrates the faith that the physicist has in nature's regularity." (See Figure 1.)

Imagine that you have witnessed this demonstration just after your philosophy class, where the subject of discussion was Hume's *Enquiry Concerning Human Understanding*. You raise your hand. "How did you *know* that the bowling ball would stop where it did, just short of bashing your nose into your face?" you ask.

"This is a standard demonstration," he replies; "I do it every year in this class, and it has often been used by many other physics teachers." In an attempt to inject a little humor, he adds, "If I had had any doubt about its working, I'd have had the teaching assistant do it."

"Are you saying, then, that you trusted the experiment to work this time simply because it has been tried so many times in the past, and has never failed?" You recall Hume's discussion of the collisions of billiard balls. In the first instance, according to Hume, before you have any experience with material objects colliding with one another, you would not know what to expect when you see a moving billiard ball approaching a stationary one, but after a good deal of experience you confidently expect some motion to be transferred to the stationary ball as a result of the collision. As your experience accumulates, you learn to predict the exact manner in which the second ball will move after being struck by the first. But you cannot really accept that answer, and neither, you feel sure, will your physics professor. Without waiting for an answer, you follow up your first question with another.

"I have this friend," you continue, "who drives like a maniac. It scares me to ride with him, but he always tells me not to worry—he has never had an accident, or even a traffic ticket. Should I conclude—assuming he is telling the truth (just as I assume you are telling me the truth about this demonstration)—that it is as safe for me to ride with him as it is for you to perform the bowling ball trick?"

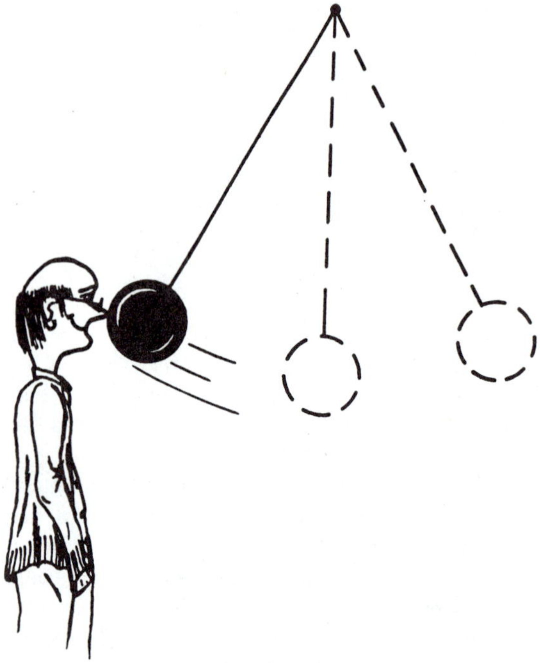

Figure 1. Prof Salvia's Pendulum. After swinging to the opposite side of the lecture hall, the bowling ball swings right back to the tip of the prof's nose, which remains motionless during the entire procedure.

"It's not the same thing at all," another student chimes in; "you can prove, mathematically, that the pendulum will not swing back beyond its original starting point, but you certainly can't prove mathematically that your friend won't have a wreck. In a way it's just the opposite; you can prove that he is likely to have an accident if he keeps on driving like that."

"What you say is partly right," says Professor Salvia to the second student, "but it isn't only a matter of mathematics. We have to rely upon the laws of physics as well. With the pendulum we were depending mainly upon the law of conservation of energy, one of the most fundamental laws of nature. As the pendulum goes through its swing, potential energy is transformed into kinetic energy, which is transformed back into potential energy, and so forth. As long as the total amount of energy remains unchanged, my nose is safe."

Since you have not yet studied the concept of energy, you do not worry too much about the details of the explanation. You are satisfied that you will understand why the pendulum behaves as it does when you have learned more about the concepts and laws that were mentioned. But you do remember something Hume wrote. There are two kinds of reasoning: reasoning concerning relations of ideas, and reasoning concerning matters of fact and existence. Mathematical reasoning falls into the former category (relations of ideas) and consequently, by itself, cannot provide any information about matters of fact. The pendulum and the professor's nose are, however, matters of fact, so we need something in addition to mathematics to get the information we want concerning that situation. Professor Salvia has told us what it is—we need the laws of nature as well.

Since physics is your last class in the morning, you head for the cafeteria when it is over to get a sandwich and coffee. The philosophy class is still bugging you. What was it Hume said about bread? That we do not know the "secret power" by which it nourishes us? Now we do, of course; we understand metabolism, the mechanism by which the body converts food into energy. Hume (living in the eighteenth century) did not understand about power and energy, as he said repeatedly. He did not know why bread is suitable food for humans, but not for tigers and lions. In biology class, you recall, you studied herbiverous, carnivorous, and omniverous species. Biologists must now understand why some species can metabolize vegetables and others cannot. Modern physics, chemistry, and biology can provide a complete explanation of the various forms of energy, the ways they can be converted from one form to another, and the ways in which they can be utilized by a living organism.

Taking a sip of the hot coffee, you recall some other things Hume said—for example, remarks about the "connection" between heat and flame. We now know that heat is really a form of energy; that temperature is a measure of the average kinetic energy of the molecules. Now, it seems, we know a great deal about the "secret powers," "energy," etc., that so perplexed Hume. Modern physics knows that ordinary objects are composed of molecules, which are in turn composed of atoms, which are themselves made up of subatomic particles. Modern science can tell us what holds atoms and molecules together, and why the things that consist of them have the properties they do. What was it that Hume said about a piece of ice and a crystal (e.g., a diamond)? That we do not know why one is caused by cold and the other by heat? I'll just bet, you think, that Salvia could answer that one without a bit of trouble. Why, you wonder, do they make us read these old philosophers who are now so out of date? Hume was, no doubt, a very profound thinker in his day, but why do we have to study him now, when we know the answers to all of those questions? If I were majoring in history that might be one thing, but that doesn't happen to be my field of interest. Oh, I suppose they'd say that getting an education means that you have to learn something about the "great minds of the past," but why doesn't the philosophy professor come right out and tell us the answers to these questions? It's silly to pretend that they are still great mysteries.

After lunch, let's imagine, you go to a class in contemporary social and political problems, a class you particularly like because of the lively discussions. A lot of time is spent talking about such topics as population growth, ecology and the environment, energy demands and uses, food production, and pollution. You discuss population trends, the extrapolation of such trends, and the predication that by the year 2000 A.D., world population will reach 7 billion. You consider the various causes and possible effects of increasing concentrations of carbon dioxide in the atmosphere. You discuss solutions to various of these problems in terms of strict governmental controls, economic sanctions and incentives, and voluntary compliance on the part of enlightened and concerned citizens.

"If people run true to form," you interject, "if they behave as they always have, you can be sure that you won't make much progress relying on the good will and good sense of the populace at large."

"What is needed is more awareness and education," another student remarks, "for people can change if they see the need. During World War II people willingly sacrificed in order to support the war effort. They will do the same again, if they see that the emergency is really serious. That's why we need to provide more education and make stronger appeals to their humanitarian concerns."

"What humanitarian concerns?" asks still another student with evident cynicism.

"People *will* change," says another. "I have been reading that we are entering a new era, the Age of Aquarius, when man's finer, gentler, more considerate nature will be manifest."

"Well, I don't know about all of this astrology," another remarks in earnest tones, "but I do not believe that God will let His world perish if we mend our ways and trust in Him. I have complete faith in His goodness."

You find this statement curiously reminiscent of Professor Salvia's earlier mention of his faith in the regularity of nature.

That night, after dinner, you read an English assignment. By the time you finish it, your throat feels a little scratchy, and you notice that you have a few sniffles. You decide to begin taking large doses of vitamin C; you have read that there is quite some controversy as to whether this helps to ward off colds, but that there is no harm in taking this vitamin in large quantities. Before going to the drug store to buy some vitamin C, you write home to request some additional funds; you mail your letter in the box by the pharmacy. You return with the vitamin C, take a few of the pills, and turn in for the night—confident that the sun will rise tomorrow morning, and hoping that you won't feel as miserable as you usually do when you catch a cold. David Hume is the farthest thing from your mind.

HUME REVISITED

The next morning, you wake up feeling fine. The sun is shining brightly, and you have no sign of a cold. You are not sure whether the vitamin C cured your cold, or whether it was the good night's sleep, or whether it wasn't going to develop into a real cold regardless. Perhaps, even, it was the placebo effect; in psychology you learned that people can often be cured by totally inert drugs (e.g., sugar pills) if they believe in them. You don't really know what caused your prompt recovery, but frankly, you don't really care. If it was the placebo effect that is fine with you; you just hope it will work as well the next time.

You think about what you will do today. It is Thursday, so you have a philosophy discussion section in the morning and a physics lab in the afternoon. Thursday, you say to yourself, has got to be the lousiest day of the week. The philosophy section is a bore, and the physics lab is a drag. If only it were Saturday, when you have no classes! For a brief moment you consider taking off. Then you remember the letter you wrote last night, think about your budget and your grades, and resign yourself to the prescribed activities for the day.

The leader of the discussion section starts off with the question, "What was the main problem—I mean the really *basic* problem—bothering Hume in the *Enquiry*?" You feel like saying, "Lack of adequate scientific knowledge" (or words to that effect), but restrain yourself. No use antagonizing the guy who will decide what grade to give you. Someone says that he seemed to worry quite a lot about causes and effects, to which the discussion leader (as usual) responds, "But *why*?" Again, you stifle an impulse to say, "Because he didn't know too much about them."

After much folderol, the leader finally elicits the answer, "Because he wanted to know how we can find out about things we don't actually see (or hear, smell, touch, taste, etc.)."

"In other words," the leader paraphrases, "to examine the basis for making inferences from what we observe to what we cannot (at the moment) observe. Will someone," he continues, "give me an example of something you believe in which you are not now observing?"

You think of the letter you dropped into the box last night, of your home and parents, and of the money you hope to receive. You do not see the letter now, but you are confident it is somewhere in the mails; you do not see your parents now, but you firmly believe they are back home where you left them; you do not yet see the money you hope to get, but you expect to see it before too long. The leader is pleased when you give those examples. "And what do causes and effects have to do with all of this?" he asks, trying to draw you out a little more. Still thinking of your grade you cooperate. "I believe the letter is somewhere in the mails because I wrote it and dropped it in the box. I believe my parents are at home because they are always calling me up to tell me what to do. And I believe that the money will come as an effect of my eloquent appeal." The leader is really happy with that; you can tell you have an A for today's session.

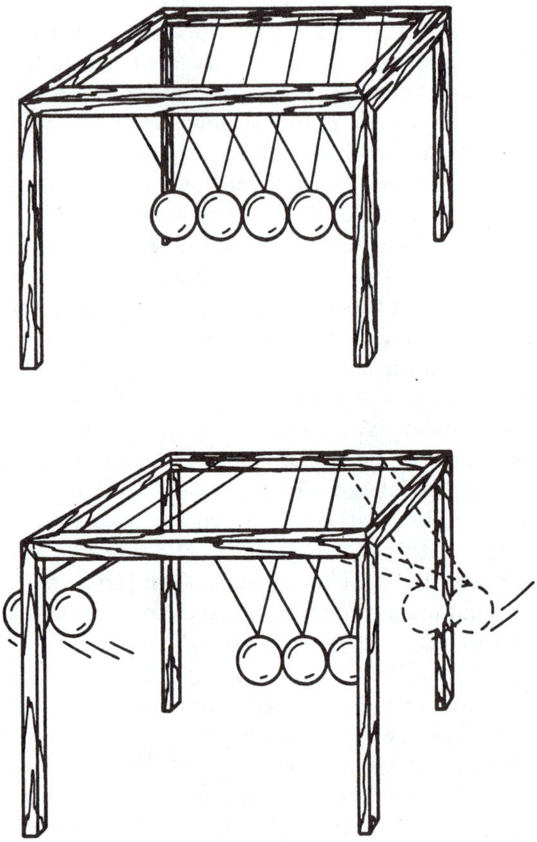

Figure 2. The Energy-Momentum Toy. When two balls at the right collide with the remaining three, two balls swing away from the left side. What happens when three on the right collide with the remaining two?

"But," he goes on, "do you see how this leads us immediately into Hume's next question? If cause-effect relations are the whole basis for our knowledge of things and events we do not observe, how do we know whether one event causes another, or whether they just happen together as a matter of coincidence?" Your mind is really clicking now.

"I felt a cold coming on last night, and I took a massive dose of vitamin C," you report. "This morning I feel great, but I honestly don't know whether the vitamin C actually cured it."

"Well, how could we go about trying to find out," retorts the discussion leader.

"By trying it again when I have the first symptoms of a cold," you answer, "and by trying it on other people as well." At that point the bell rings, and you leave class wondering whether the vitamin C really did cure your incipient cold.

You keep busy until lunch, doing one thing and another, but sitting down and eating, you find yourself thinking again about the common cold and its cure. It seems to be a well-known fact that the cold is caused by one or more viruses, and the human organism seems to have ways of combating virus infections. Perhaps the massive doses of vitamin C trigger the body's defenses, in some way or other, or perhaps it provides some kind of antidote to the toxic effects of the virus. You don't know much about all of this, but you can't help speculating that science has had a good deal of success in finding causes and cures of various diseases. If continued research reveals the physiological and chemical processes in the cold's infection and in the body's response, then surely it would be possible to find out whether the vitamin C really has any effect upon the common cold or not. It seems that we could ascertain whether a causal relation exists in this instance if only we could discover the relevant laws of biology and chemistry.

At this point in your musings, you notice that it is time to get over to the physics lab. You remember that yesterday morning you were convinced that predicting the outcome of an experiment is possible if you know which physical laws apply. That certainly was the outcome of the discussion in the physics class. Now, it seems, the question about the curative power of vitamin C hinges on exactly the same thing—the laws of nature. As you hurry to the lab it occurs to you that predicting the outcome of an experiment, before it is performed, is a first-class example of what you were discussing in philosophy—making inferences from the observed to the unobserved. We observe the set-up for the experiment (or demonstration) before it is performed, and we predict the outcome before we observe it. Salvia certainly was confident about the prediction he made. Also, recalling one of Hume's examples, you were at least as confident, when you went to bed last night, that the sun would rise this morning. But Hume *seemed* to be saying that the basis for this confidence was the fact that the sun has been observed to rise every morning since the dawn of history. "That's wrong," you say to yourself as you reach the physics lab. "My confidence in the rising of the sun is based upon the laws of astronomy. So here we are back at the laws again."

Inside the lab you notice a familiar gadget; it consists of a frame from which five steel balls are suspended so that they hang in a straight line, each one touching its neighbors. Your little brother got a toy like this, in a somewhat smaller size, for his birthday a couple of years ago. You casually raise one of the end balls, and let it swing back. It strikes the nearest of the four balls left hanging, and the ball at the other end swings out (the three balls in the middle keeping their place). The ball at the far end swings back again, striking its neighbor, and then the ball on the near end swings out, almost to the point from which you let it swing originally. The process goes on for a while, with the two end balls alternately swinging out and back. It has a pleasant rhythm. (See Figure 2.)

While you are enjoying the familiar toy, the lab instructor, Dr. Sagro,[2] comes over to you. "Do you know why just the ball on the far end moves—instead of, say, two on the far end, or all four of the remaining ones—when the ball on this end strikes?"

"Not exactly, but I suppose it has something to do with conservation of energy," you reply, recalling what Salvia said yesterday in answer to the question about the bowling ball.

"That's right," says Dr. Sagro, "but it also depends upon conservation of momentum." Before you have a chance to say anything she continues,

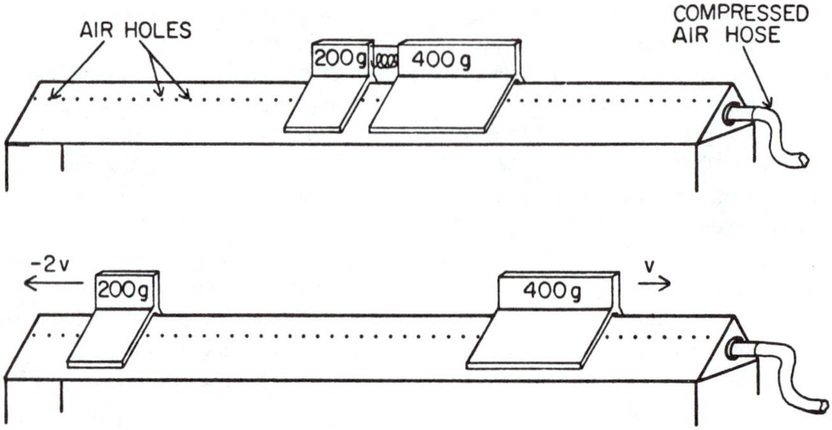

Figure 3. Cars on the Air Track. Top: Cars tied together against spring under tension. Bottom: Cars moving apart after "explosion." $400\,g \times v + 200\,g \times (-2v) = 0$. Momentum is conserved.

"Let me ask you another question. What would happen if you raised two balls at this end, and let them swing together toward the remaining three?"

"I think two balls will swing away at the other end," you reply, remembering the way your brother's toy worked.

"Why don't you test it to find out if you are right?" says the instructor. You do, and you find that the result is as you had predicted. Without saying anything about it, you assume that this, too, can be explained by means of the laws of conservation of energy and momentum.

Dr. Sagro poses another question. "What will happen," she asks, "if you start by swinging three balls from this end?" Since there are only two remaining balls you don't know what to say, so you confess ignorance. She suggests you try it, in order to find out what will happen. When you do, you see that three balls swing to the other side, and three swing back again; the middle ball swings back and forth, acting as the third ball in each group. This was a case in which you didn't know what to expect as a result until you tried the experiment.[3] This was like some of Hume's examples; not until you have actually had the experience do you know what result to expect. But there is also something different. Hume said that you must try the experiment many times in order to know what to expect; nevertheless, after just one trial you are sure what will happen whenever the experiment is repeated. This makes it rather different from the problem of whether vitamin C cured your cold. In that case, it seemed necessary to try the experiment over and over again, preferably with a number of different people. Reflecting upon this difference, you ask the lab instructor a crucial question, "If you knew the laws of conservation of momentum and energy, but had never seen the experiment with the three balls performed, would you have been able to predict the outcome?"

"Yes," she says simply.

"Well," you murmur inaudibly, "it seems as if the whole answer to Hume's problem regarding inferences about things we do not immediately observe, including predictions of future occurrences, rests squarely upon the laws of nature."

KNOWING THE LAWS

Given that the laws are so fundamental, you decide to find out more about them. The laws of conservation of energy and momentum are close at hand, so to speak, so you decide to start there. "O.K.," you say to the lab instructor, "what are these laws of nature, which enable you to predict so confidently how experiments will turn out before they are performed? I'd like to learn something about them."

"Fine," she says, delighted with your desire to learn; "let's start with conservation of momentum. It's simpler than conservation of energy, and we can demonstrate it quite easily."[4] (See Figure 3.)

Your laboratory contains a standard piece of equipment—an air track—on which little cars move back and forth. The track is made of metal with many tiny holes through which air is blown. The cars thus ride on a thin cushion of air; they move back and forth almost without friction. Some of the cars are equipped with spring bumpers, so that they will bounce off of one another upon impact, while others have coupling devices which lock them together upon contact. Dr. Sagro begins by explaining what is meant by the momentum of a body—namely, its mass multiplied by its velocity.[5] "To speak somewhat quaintly," she says, "the mass is just a measure of the quantity of matter in the body.[6] Since, in all of the experiments we are going to do, it is safe to say that the mass of each body remains unchanged, we need not say more about it. You can see that each car comes with its mass labeled; this one, for instance, has a mass of 200 grams, while this one has a mass of 400 grams. We have a number of different cars with quite a variety of different masses. The velocity," she continues, "is what we ordinarily mean by 'speed' along with the direction of travel. On the air track there are only two possible directions, left to right and right to left. Let us simply agree that motion from left to right has a positive velocity, while motion from right to left has a negative velocity. Mass, of course, is always a positive quantity. Thus, momentum, which is mass times velocity, may be positive, negative, or zero. When we add the momenta of various bodies together, we must always be careful of the sign (plus or minus)."

With these preliminaries, you begin to perform a variety of experiments. She has various types of fancy equipment for measuring velocities, which she shows you how to use, and she also helps you to make measurements. You find that it is fun pushing cars back and forth on the track, crashing them into one another, and measuring their velocities before and after collisions. You try it with a variety of cars of different masses and with differing velocities. You try it with the ones that bounce apart after impact and with those that stick together. You always find that the *total* momentum (the sum of the momenta for the two cars) before any collision is equal to the *total* momentum after the collision, even though the momenta of the individual cars may change markedly as a result of the collision. This, Dr. Sagro explains, is what the law of conservation of momentum demands: when two bodies (such as the cars) interact with one another (as in a collision), the total momentum of the system consisting of those two bodies is the same before and after the interaction.

You ask her whether this law applies only to collisions; she replies immediately that it applies to all kinds of interactions. "Let's see how it works for a simple type of 'explosion,'" she suggests. She helps you tie together two cars, holding a compressed spring between them. You burn the string which holds them together and they fly apart. You measure the velocities and compute the momenta of each of the cars after the "explosion." It turns out that the momentum of the one car is always equal in amount but opposite in direction to that of the other. This is true whether the cars are of equal or unequal masses and whether the tension on the spring that drives them apart is great or small. "This is just what the law of conservation of momentum tells us to expect," she explains; "the momentum of each car is zero before the 'explosion' because they are not moving (each has velocity equal to zero), and so the two momenta after the 'explosion' (one positive and one negative) must add up to zero. That is what has happened every time.

"There are many other applications of the law of conservation of momentum," she continues. "When a rifle recoils upon being fired, when a jet engine propels an airplane, when a rocket engine lifts an artificial satellite into orbit, or when you step out of an untethered rowboat and are surprised to feel it moving out from under you—these are all cases of conservation of momentum."

"Is this law ever violated?" you ask.

"No," she answers, "there are no known exceptions to it." You leave the lab with the feeling that you know at least one fundamental law, and that you have seen it proved experimentally right before your eyes. You can't wait to tell your philosophy professor about it.

When you go to your philosophy class the next morning, the topic is still Hume's *Enquiry Concerning Human Understanding* and the problem of how we can have knowledge of things we do not observe. As the lecture begins, Professor Philo[7] is saying, "As we saw during the last lecture, Hume maintains that our knowledge of what we do not observe is based entirely upon cause and effect relations, but that raises the question of how we can gain knowledge of these relations. Hume maintained that this knowledge can result only from repeated observation of one type of event (a cause) to see whether it is always followed by an event of another kind (its effect). Hume therefore analyzed the notion of causality in terms of constant conjunction of events. Consider for a moment Hume's favorite example, the colliding billiard balls . . ."

You raise your hand. "It seems to me that Hume was wrong about this," you begin, and then you relate briefly yesterday's experiences in the physics lab. "If you know the relevant laws of nature," you conclude, "you can predict the outcomes of future experiments on the basis of a single trial, or perhaps even without benefit of any trials at all."

"But how," asks Professor Philo, "can we establish knowledge of the laws of nature?"

You had a hunch she might ask some such question, and you are ready with your reply, "We *proved* it experimentally."

"Well," says Professor Philo, "I'm not a physicist, so perhaps you had better explain in a little more detail just what the experimental proof consists of. You mentioned something about an explosion—how did that go?"

You explain carefully how the air track works, how the two cars were joined together with a spring under tension in between, and how they moved apart when the string was burned. "In every case," you conclude, "the momentum of the two cars was equal in amount and opposite in direction, just as the law of conservation of momentum says it should be."

"Now let me see if I understand your line of reasoning," says the professor in a tone that is altogether too calm to suit you. "If the law of conservation of momentum is correct, then the two cars will part in the manner you described. The cars did move apart in just that way. Therefore, the law of conservation of momentum is correct. Is that your argument?"

"I guess so," you reply a bit hesitantly, because it looks as if she is trying to trap you.

"Do you think that kind of argument is valid?" she responds.

"What do you mean?" you ask, beginning to feel a little confused.

"Well," she says, "isn't that rather like the following argument: If this defendant is guilty, he will refuse to testify at his own trial; he does refuse to testify; therefore, he is guilty. Would any judge allow that argument in a court of law?"

"Of course not," you reply, "but it isn't the same thing at all. We tested the law of conservation of momentum many times in many different ways, and in every case we got the expected result (allowing for the usual small inaccuracies in the measurements)."

"If I remember what you said," Ms. Philo goes on, "in one of your experiments you had one car with a mass of 200 grams and another with a mass of 400 grams, and in that case the lighter car recoiled with twice the speed of the more massive one. How many times did you repeat this particular experiment?"

"Once or twice, as nearly as I can recall."

"Yet, you seem to believe that the result would be the same, no matter how many times the experiment was repeated—is that correct?"

"I suppose so," you reply somewhat uncomfortably.

"And with how many different masses and how many different recoil velocities did you try it? Do you believe it would work the same way if the masses were thousands or billions of kilograms instead of a few grams? And do you suppose that it would work the same way if the velocities were very great—somewhere near the speed of light?"

Since you have heard that strange things happen when speeds approach that of light, your hesitancy increases, but you reply tentatively, "Well, the lab instructor told me that there are no exceptions to the law."

"Did she say that," asks Philo, "or did she say no *known* exceptions?"

"I guess that was it," you reply lamely, feeling quite crushed.

Professor Philo endeavors to summarize the discussion. "What is considered experimental 'proof of a law of nature' is actually a process of testing *some* of its logical consequences. That is, you ask what would have to happen *if* your hypothesis is true, and then you perform an experiment to see if it turns out that way *in fact*. Since any law of nature is a generalization,[8] it has an unlimited number of consequences. We can never hope to test them all. In particular, any *useful* law of nature will have consequences that pertain to the future; they enable us to make predictions. We can never hope to test them all. In particular, any *useful* law of nature will have consequences that pertain to the future; they enable us to make predictions. We can never test these consequences until it is too late to use them for the purpose of prediction. To suppose that testing *some* of the consequences of a law constitutes a *conclusive proof* of the law would clearly be an outright logical fallacy." The bell rings and you leave the class, convinced that she has merely been quibbling.

During your physics class you brood about the previous discussion in the philosophy class, without paying very close attention to the lecture. Similar thoughts keep nagging at you during lunch. The objections brought up by Professor Philo seem to be well-founded, you conclude, but you wonder how they can be reconciled with the apparent reliability and certainty of scientific knowledge. In desperation, you decide to talk it over with Professor Salvia during his office hour this very afternoon. When you arrive, you don't know exactly where to begin, so you decide to go back to the pendulum demonstration, which was the thing that got you started on this whole mess. "When you performed that demonstration," you ask, "were you *absolutely certain* how it would turn out? Has it ever failed?"

"Well, to be perfectly honest," he says, "it has been known to fail. Once when a friend of mine was doing it in front of a large auditorium, the suspension in the ceiling broke and the ball landed right on his foot. He was in a cast for months!"

"But that's no fault of the law of conservation of energy is it?" you ask. "The breaking of the suspension didn't mean that conservation of energy is false, did it?"

"Of course not," he answers, "we still believe firmly in conservation of energy."

"But are you *certain* of the law of conservation of energy, or any other law of nature?" you ask, and before he has a chance to answer, you tell him about the discussion in the philosophy class this morning.

"So that's what's bothering you," he says, after hearing the whole story. "Professor Philo has an important point. No matter how thoroughly we have tested a scientific law—better, let's say 'hypothesis'—there is always the possibility that new evidence will show up to prove it false. For instance, around the close of the nineteenth century, many physicists seemed virtually certain that Newtonian mechanics was absolutely correct. A wide variety of its consequences had been tested under many different circumstances, and Newton's laws stood up extremely well. But early in the twentieth century it became clear that what we now call 'classical physics' would have to undergo major revisions, and a profound scientific revolution ensued. Modern physics, which includes quantum mechanics and relativity theory, was the result. We can never be sure that any hypothesis we currently accept as correct will not have to be abandoned or modified at some time in the future as a result of new evidence."

"What about the law of conservation of momentum?" you ask, recalling yesterday's experience in the lab. "The lab instructor said it has no known exceptions."

"That is correct," says Salvia, "and it is a rather interesting case. Conservation of momentum is a consequence of Newton's laws of motion; therefore, any consequence of conservation of momentum is a consequence of Newton's laws. But we now regard Newton's laws as not strictly true—they break down, for example, with objects traveling close to the speed of light—but conservation of momentum holds even in these cases. So we have a good example of a case where we believe a lot of consequences, but we do not believe in the laws (Newton's) from which the consequences follow."

It occurs to you that this is a rather important set of supposed laws; perhaps the philosophy professor was not merely quibbling when she said that it was not valid to conclude that a hypothesis is true just because we know many of its consequences to be true.

"Since you cannot be certain of any so-called law of nature," you ask, "why do you believe in them so firmly?"

"Because," answers Salvia, "we consider them very well confirmed. We accept well-confirmed hypotheses, knowing that we may later have to change our minds in the light of new evidence. Science can no longer claim infallible truth."

"Does that mean that scientific results are highly probable, but not absolutely certain?" you ask, trying to be sure you have understood what he has said.

"Yes, you could put it that way," he agrees.

You leave with the feeling that you have a pretty good comprehension of the situation. As a result of your study of physics and philosophy you now understand why science cannot claim infallibility for its findings, but must be content with results that are well confirmed. With that, you take off for the weekend. (And what you do with your weekend is your own business.)

HUME'S BOMBSHELL

A little tired, but basically in a cheerful mood, you arrive at your philosophy class on Monday morning. You meet the professor a few minutes before class outside the room, and you tell her very briefly of your conversation with the physics professor. You explain that you now understand why it is that scientific laws can never be considered completely certain, but only as well-confirmed hypotheses. With her help, and with that of Professor Salvia, you now understand what Hume was driving at—and you see, moreover, that Hume was right. She smiles, and you both go into the classroom, where she begins her lecture.

"Last Friday, as you may recall, we had quite a lively discussion about the status of scientific laws—the law of conservation of momentum, in particular. We saw that such laws cannot be proved conclusively by any amount of experimental evidence. This is a point with which, I am happy to report, many (if not most) contemporary scientists agree. They realize that the most they can reasonably claim for their hypotheses is strong confirmation. Looking at the matter this way, one could conclude that it is wise to believe in scientific predictions, for if they are not certain to be true, they are a good bet. To believe in scientific results is to bet with the best available odds.

"However," she continues, "while this view may be correct as far as it goes, Hume was making a much more fundamental, and I should add, much more devastating point. Hume was challenging not merely our right to claim that scientific predictions will always be right, but also our right to claim that they will usually, or often, or indeed ever, be correct. Take careful note of what he says in Section IV:

> Let the course of things be allowed hitherto ever so regular; that alone, without some new argument or inference, proves not that, for the future, it will continue so. In vain do you pretend to have learned the nature of bodies from your past experience. Their secret nature, and consequently all their effects and influence, may change, without any change in their sensible qualities. This happens sometimes, and with regard to some objects: Why may it not happen always and with regard to all objects? What logic, what process of argument secures you against this supposition?

He is saying, as I hope you understood from your reading, that no matter how reliably a law seems to have held in the past, there is no logical reason why it must do so in the future *at all*. It is therefore possible that *every* scientific prediction, based on *any* law or laws whatever, may turn out to be false from this moment on. The stationary billiard ball that is struck by a moving one may remain motionless where it is—while the moving ball may bounce straight back in the direction from whence it came, or it may go straight up in the air, or it might vanish in a puff of smoke. Any of these possibilities can be imagined; none of them involves any logical contradiction. This is the force of Hume's skeptical arguments. The conclusion seems to be that we have no *reason* to believe in scientific predictions—no more reason than to believe on the basis of astrology, crystal gazing, or sheer blind guessing."

You can hardly believe your ears; what is she saying? You raise your hand, and when you are recognized, you can hardly keep your intense irritation from showing as you assert, "But certainly we can say that scientific predictions are more probable than those based, for example, upon astrology." As you speak, you are reminded of the remark in contemporary problems last Wednesday concerning the coming of the Age of Aquarius. Science has got to be better than *that!* As these thoughts cross your mind Professor Philo is saying, ". . . but that depends upon what you mean by 'probable,' doesn't it?"

The physics lecture today is on Newton's law of gravitation, and the professor is explaining that every bit of matter in the universe is attracted to every other by a force proportional to the masses and inversely proportional to the square of the distance between them. He goes on to explain how Kepler's laws of planetary motion and Galileo's law of falling bodies are (when suitably corrected) consequences of Newton's laws. You listen carefully, but you recognize this as another law that enables scientists to make impressive predictions. Indeed, Salvia is now telling how Newton's laws were used to explain the tides on the oceans and to predict the existence of two planets, Neptune and Pluto, that had not been known before. At the same time, you are wondering whether there is anything in what Hume seemed to be saying about such laws. Is it possible that suddenly, at the very next moment, matter would cease to have gravitational attraction, so that the whole solar system would go flying apart? It's a pretty chilling thought.

At lunch you are thinking about this question, and you glance back at some of the readings that were assigned from Hume's *Enquiry.* You notice again Hume's many references to secret powers and forces. Well, gravitation is surely a force, though there has not been any great secret about it since Newton's time. It is the "power" which keeps the solar system together. You remember reading somewhere that, according to Hume, you cannot know that it is safer to leave a building by way of the halls, stairways, and doors than it would be to step out of the third-story window. Well, Newton's law makes it clear why you don't want to step out of the third-story window, but what assurance have you that the building will continue to stand, rather than crashing down around your ears before you can get out? The engineers who design and build towers and bridges have a great deal of knowledge of the "secret powers" of their materials, so they must know a great deal more than Hume did about the hidden properties of things.

At this very moment, a lucky coincidence occurs—you see Dr. Sagro, your physics lab instructor, entering the cafeteria. You wave to her, and she sits down with you, putting her coffee cup on the table. You begin to ask her some questions about structural materials, and she responds by inquiring whether you would be satisfied if she could explain how the table supports the cup of coffee. You recognize it as just the kind of question you have in mind, and urge her to proceed.

"Certain materials, such as the metal in this table," she begins, "have a rather rigid crystalline structure, and for this reason they stick together and maintain their shape unless subjected to large forces. These crystals consist of very regular (and very beautiful) arrays of atoms, and they are held together by forces, essentially electrostatic in origin, among the charged particles that make up the atoms. Have you studied Coulomb's law of electrostatic forces?"

"No," you reply, "we are just doing Newton's law of gravitation. I think Salvia said electricity and magnetism would come up next semester."

"Well," she says, "these electrostatic forces are a lot like gravitational forces (they vary inversely with the square of the distance), but there are a couple of very important differences. First, as you know, there are two types of charges, positive and negative. The proton in the nucleus of the atom carries a positive charge, and the electrons that circulate about the nuclei have a negative charge. Two particles with opposite signs (such as a proton and an electron) attract one another, while two particles with like signs (e.g., two electrons or two protons) repel each other. This is different from gravity, because all matter attracts all other matter; there is no such thing as gravitational repulsion. The second main difference is that the electrostatic force is fantastically stronger than the gravitational force—roughly a billion billion billion billion times more powerful—but we don't usually notice it because most objects we deal with in everyday life are electrically neutral, containing equal amounts of positive and negative electric charge, or very nearly so. If you could somehow strip all of the electrons away from an apple, and all of the protons away from the earth, the force of attraction between the apple and the earth would be unbelievable.

"It is these *extremely* strong attractive and repulsive forces among the electrons and protons in the metal that maintain a stable and rigid form. That's why the table doesn't collapse. And the reason the coffee cup stays on top of the table, without penetrating its surface or slipping through, is that the electrons in the surface of the cup strongly repel those in the surface of the table. Actually, there is also a quantum mechanical force that prevents the weight of the cup from noticeably compressing the table, but we needn't go into that, because the effect is mostly due to the electrostatic forces."

Pleased with this very clear explanation, you thank her, but follow it up with another question. "Is there any logical reason why it has to be that way—why opposite charges attract and like charges repel? Can you prove that it is impossible for like charges to attract and unlike charges to repel? What would happen if *that* were suddenly to become the law?"

"It would certainly result in utter catastrophe," she replies, "with all of the atomic nuclei bunching up together in one place and all of the electrons rushing away from them to congregate elsewhere. But to answer your question, no, there is no logical proof that it couldn't be that way. In our physical world we find that there are, in fact, two types of charges, and they obey the Coulomb law rather than the one you just formulated."

"Can you prove that the world will not switch from the one law to the other, say, tomorrow?" you ask.

"No, frankly, I can't," she answers, "but I, and all other physicists assume—call it an article of faith if you like—that it won't happen."

There's that word "faith" again, you muse as you leave the cafeteria.

The more you think about it, the more clearly you see that the physicists have not shown you how to get around the basic problem Hume raised; rather, they have really reinforced it. Maybe this problem is tougher than I thought, you say to yourself, and you head for Professor Philo's office to talk further about it. "I was thinking about all these 'secret powers' Hume talks about," you begin, "and so I asked my physics instructor about them. She explained, as an example, how a table supports a coffee cup, but she did it on the basis of laws of nature—Coulomb's law of electrostatics was one of them. This law is very well confirmed, I suppose, but she admitted that it is quite possible to imagine that this law would fail tomorrow, and—if you'll pardon the expression—all hell would break loose. Now, my question is, how can we find out about these secret powers that Hume keeps saying we need to know? How can we discover the real underlying causes of what happens?"

"I think you are really beginning to get the point Hume was driving at," she replies, "namely, that there is *no way*, even in principle, of finding any hidden causes or secret powers. You can, of course, find regularities in nature—such as conservation of energy, conservation of momentum, universal gravitation, and electrostatic attraction and repulsion—but these can only be known to have held up to the present. There is no further kind of hidden connection or causal relation that can be discovered by more careful observation, or examination with some kind of super-microscope. Of course, we do discover regularities, and we explain them. For instance, Kepler's laws of planetary motion are regularities that are explained by Newton's laws of motion and gravitation, but these do not reveal any secret powers. They simply provide more general regularities to cover the more restricted ones.

"In his discussion of 'the idea of necessary connection,' Hume tries to bring out precisely this point. We can observe, as you were saying in class the other day, that recoil experiments always yield a particular type of result—namely, momentum is conserved. We have observed this many times. And now we expect, on future trials, that the same thing will happen. But we do not observe, nor can we discover in any way, an *additional* factor which constitutes a necessary connection between the 'explosion' and the subsequent motion of the cars. This seems to be what Hume had in mind when he wrote:

> These ultimate springs and principles are totally shut up from human curiosity and enquiry. Elasticity, gravity, cohesion of parts, communication of motion by impulse; these are probably the ultimate causes and principles which we ever discover in nature; and we may esteem ourselves sufficiently happy, if, by accurate inquiry and reasoning, we can trace up the particular phenomena to, or near to, these general principles.[9]

Hume is acknowledging that we can discover general regularities in nature, but he is denying that an additional 'connection' can be found. And Hume was dedicated to the maxim, as are modern scientists, that we have no business talking about things it is impossible in principle for us to know anything about.

"When he asks why we do, in fact, expect so confidently that the future experiments will have outcomes similar to those of the past trials, Hume finds that it is nothing other than a matter of psychological conditioning. When we see one type of cause repeatedly followed by a particular type of effect, we come to expect that the same type of effect will follow the next time we come across that kind of cause. But this is not a matter of logical reasoning. Have you heard of Pavlov's conditioning experiments with dogs?" You nod. "When the bell rings the dog starts to salivate. He is *not* reasoning that, since the sounding of the bell has, in the past, been associated with the bringing of food, therefore, on this occasion the food will (at least probably) appear soon after the bell rings. According to Hume's analysis, what is called 'scientific reasoning' is no more rational or logical than your watering at the mouth when you are hungry and hear the dinner bell. It is something you cannot help doing, Hume says, but that does not mean that it has any logical foundation."

"That brings up a question I've wanted to ask," you say. "Hume seems to think that people necessarily reason in that way—inductive reasoning, I think it is called—but I've noticed that lots of people don't seem to. For instance, many people (including a student in my current problems course) believe in things like astrology; they believe that the configuration of the planets has a bearing on human events, when experience shows that it often doesn't work that way." The professor nods in agreement. You continue, "So if there is no logical justification for believing in scientific predictions, why isn't it just as reasonable to believe in astrological predictions?"

"That," replies the prof, "is a very profound and difficult question. I doubt that any philosopher has a completely satisfactory answer to it."

MODERN ANSWERS[10]

The Wednesday philosophy lecture begins with a sort of rhetorical question, "What reason do we have (Hume is, at bottom, asking) for trusting the scientific method; what grounds do we have for believing that scientific predictions are reliable?" You have been pondering that very question quite a bit in the last couple of days, and—rhetorical or not—your hand shoots up. You have a thing or two to say on the subject.

"Philosophers may have trouble answering such questions," you assert, "but it seems to me there is an obvious reply. As my physics professor has often said, the scientist takes a very practical attitude. He puts forth a hypothesis; if it works he believes in it, and he continues to believe in it as long as it works. If it starts giving him bad predictions, he starts looking for another hypothesis, or for a way of revising his old one. Now the important thing about the scientific method, it seems to me, is that it works. Not only has it led to a vast amount of knowledge about the physical world, but it has been applied in all sorts of practical ways—and although these applications may not have been uniformly beneficial—for better or worse they were successful. Not always, of course, but by and large. Astrology, crystal gazing, and other such superstitious methods simply do not work very well. That's good enough for me."[11]

"That is, indeed, a very tempting answer," Professor Philo replies, "and in one form or another, it has been advanced by several modern philosophers. But Hume actually answered that one himself. You might put it this way. We can all agree that science has, up till now, a very impressive record of success in predicting the future. The question we are asking, however, is this: should we *predict* that science will continue to have the kind of success it has had in the past? It is quite natural to assume that its record will continue, but this is just a case of applying the scientific method to itself. In studying conservation of momentum, you inferred that future experiments would have results similar to those of your past experiments; in appraising the scientific method, you are assuming that its future success will match its past success. But using the scientific method to judge the scientific method is circular reasoning. It is as if a man goes to a bank to cash a check. When the teller refuses, on the grounds that he does not know this man, the man replies, 'That is no problem; permit me to introduce myself—I am John Smith, just as it says on the check.'

"Suppose that I were a believer in crystal gazing. You tell me that your method is better than mine because it has been more successful than mine. You say that this is a good reason for preferring your method to mine. I object. Since you are using your method to judge my method (as well as your method), I demand the right to use my method to evaluate yours. I gaze into my crystal ball and announce the result: from now on crystal gazing will be very successful in predicting the future, while the scientific method is due for a long run of bad luck."

You are about to protest, but she continues.

"The trouble with circular arguments is that they can be used to prove anything; if you assume what you are trying to prove, then there isn't much difficulty in proving it. You find the scientific justification of the scientific method convincing because you already trust the scientific method; if you had equal trust in crystal gazing, I should think you would find the crystal gazer's justification of his method equally convincing. Hume puts it this way:

> When a man says, *I have found, in all past instances, such sensible qualities conjoined with such secret powers:* And when he says, *Similar sensible qualities will always be conjoined with similar secret powers,* he is not guilty of a tautology, nor are these propositions in any respect the same. You can say that the one proposition is an inference from the other. But you must confess that the inference is not intuitive; neither is it demonstrative: Of what nature is it, then? To say it is experimental is begging the question. For all inferences from experience suppose, as their foundation, that the future will resemble the past, and that similar powers will be conjoined with similar sensible qualities.[12]

If the assumption that the future is like the past is the presupposition of the scientific method, we cannot assume that principle in order to justify the scientific method. Once more, we can hardly find a clearer statement than Hume's:

> We have said that all arguments concerning existence are founded on the relation of cause and effect; that our knowledge of that relation is derived entirely from experience; and that all our experimental conclusions proceed upon the supposition that the future will be comformable to the past. To endeavour, therefore, the proof of this last supposition by probable arguments, or arguments regarding existence, must evidently be going in a circle, and taking that for granted, which is the very point in question.[13]

"The principle that the future will be like the past, or that regularities which have held up to the present will persist in the future, has traditionally been called *the principle of uniformity of nature.* Some philosophers, most notably Immanuel Kant, have regarded it as an a priori truth.[14] It seems to me, however, that Hume had already provided a convincing refutation of that claim by arguing that irregularities, however startling to common sense, are by no means inconceivable—that is, they cannot be ruled out a priori. Recall what he said:

> . . . it implies no contradiction that the course of nature may change, and that an object, seemingly like those which we have experienced, may be attended with different or contrary effects. May I not clearly and distinctly conceive that a body, falling from the clouds, and which, in all other respects, resembles snow, has yet the taste of salt or feeling of fire? . . . Now whatever is intelligible, and can be distinctly conceived, implies no contradiction, and can never be proved false by any demonstrative argument or abstract reasoning *a priori*.[15]

"Other philosophers have proposed assuming this principle (or something similar) as a postulate; Bertrand Russell, though not the only one to advocate this approach, is by far the most famous.[16] But most philosophers agree that this use of postulation is question-begging. The real question still remains: why should one adopt any such postulate? Russell himself, in another context, summed it up very well: The method of 'postulating' what we want has many advantages; they are the same as the advantages of theft over honest toil."[17]

"Nevertheless," you interject, "can't we still say that scientific predictions are more probable than, say, those of astrology or crystal gazing?"

"It seems to me you raised a similar question once before," Professor Philo replies, "and I seem to recall saying that it depends on what you mean by the term 'probable.' Maybe it would be helpful if I now explain what I meant."[18] You nod encouragement. "The concept of probability—or perhaps I should say 'concepts' of probability—are very tricky. If you were to undertake a systematic study of confirmation and induction, you would have to go into a rather technical treatment of probability, but perhaps I can give a brief hint of what is involved.[19] One thing that has traditionally been meant by this term relates directly to the frequency with which something occurs—as Aristotle put it, the probable is that which happens often. If the weather forecaster says that there is a 90% chance of rain, he presumably means that, given such weather conditions as are now present, rain occurs in nine out of ten cases. If these forecasts are correct, we can predict rain on such occasions and be right nine times out of ten.

"Now, if you mean that scientific predictions are probable in *this* sense, I do not see how you could possibly support your claim. For Hume has argued—cogently, I think—that, for all we know now, *every* future scientific prediction may go wrong. He was not merely saying that science is fallible, that it will sometimes err in its predictions—he was saying that nature might at any moment (for all we can know) become irregular on such a wide scale that any kind of scientific prediction of future occurrences would be utterly impossible. We have not found any reason to believe he was mistaken about this point."

"That must not be the concept of probability I had in mind," you remark; "I'm not quite sure how to express it, but it had something to do with what it would be reasonable to believe. I was thinking of the fact that, although we cannot regard scientific hypotheses as certain, we can consider them well confirmed. It is something like saying that a particular suspect is probably guilty of a crime—that the evidence, taken as a whole, seems to point to him."

"You have put your finger on another important probability concept," the professor replies. "It is sometimes known as the rational credibility concept. The most popular contemporary attempt (I believe) to deal with Hume's problem of inductive reasoning is stated in terms of this concept. The argument can be summarized in the following way. Hume has proved that we cannot *know for sure* that our scientific predictions will be correct, but that would be an unreasonable demand to place upon science. The best we can hope is for scientific conclusions that are probable. But when we ask that they be probable, in this sense, we are only asking that they be based upon the best possible evidence. Now, that is just what scientific predictions are—they are predictions based upon the best possible evidence. The scientist has fashioned his hypotheses in the light of all available information, and he has tested them experimentally on many occasions under a wide variety of circumstances. He has summoned all of the available evidence, and he has brought it to bear on the problem at hand. Such scientific predictions are obviously probable (as we are now construing this term); hence, they are rationally credible.[20] If we say that a belief is irrational, we mean that it runs counter to the evidence, or the person who holds it is ignoring the evidence. And in such contexts, when we speak of evidence, we are referring to inductive or scientific evidence.

"Now, the argument continues, to ask whether it is reasonable to believe in scientific conclusions comes right down to asking whether one ought to fashion his beliefs on the basis of the available evidence. But this is what it means to be rational. Hence, the question amounts to asking whether it is rational to be rational. If the question makes any sense at all, the obvious answer is 'yes.'"

"That answer certainly satisfies me," you say, feeling that Dr. Philo has succeeded admirably in stating the point you were groping for. "I'm glad to know that lots of other philosophers agree with it. Do you think it is a satisfactory answer to Hume's problem of induction?" You are more than a trifle discouraged when she gives a negative response with a shake of her head. "Why not?" you demand.

"This argument seems to me to beg the question," she replies, "for it assumes that the concept of evidence is completely clear. But that is precisely the question at issue. If we could be confident that the kind of experiments you performed in the physics lab to test the law of conservation of momentum do, in fact, provide evidence for that law, then we could say that the law is well supported by evidence. But to suppose that such facts do constitute evidence amounts to saying that what has happened in the past is a sign of what will happen in the future—the fact that momentum was conserved in your 'explosion' experiments is an indication that momentum will be conserved in future experiments of a similar nature. This assumes that the future will be like the past, and that is precisely the point at issue. To say that one fact constitutes evidence for another means, in part, that the one provides some basis for inference to the occurrence of the other. The problem of induction is nothing other than the problem of determining the circumstances under which such inference is justified. Thus, we have to resolve the problem of induction—Hume's problem—before we can ascertain whether one fact constitutes evidence for another. We cannot use the concept of evidence—inductive evidence—to solve the problem of induction.

"There is another way to look at this same argument. If you ask me whether you should use the scientific method, I must find out what you hope to accomplish. If you say that you want to get a job teaching physics, I can tell you right away that you had better use the scientific method, at least in your work, because that is what is expected of a physicist. If you say that you want to enjoy the respect and prestige that accrues to scientists in certain social circles, the answer is essentially the same. If you tell me, however, that you want to have as much success as possible in predicting future events, the answer is by no means as easy. If I tell you to go ahead and make scientific predictions, because that is what is considered reasonable (that is what is meant by fashioning your beliefs on the basis of evidence), then you should ask whether being reasonable in this sense (which is obviously the commonly accepted sense) is a good way to attain your goal. The answer, 'but that's what it means to be reasonable,' is beside the point. You might say, 'I want a method that is reasonable to adopt in order to achieve my goal of successful prediction—that is what I mean by being reasonable. To tell me that the scientific method is what is usually *called* reasonable doesn't help. I want to know whether the method that is *commonly called* reasonable is *actually* a reasonable method to adopt to attain my goal of successful prediction of the future. The fact that it is usually considered reasonable cuts no ice, because an awareness of Hume's problem of induction has not filtered down into common usage.' That's what I think you should say."

"Couldn't we avoid all of these problems," suggests another student, "if we simply resisted the temptation to generalize? In social science, my area of interest, we find that it is very risky to generalize, say, from one society to another. An opinion survey on students in the far west, for example, will not be valid when applied to students attending eastern schools. Wouldn't we be better off to restrict our claims to the facts we know, instead of trying to extend them inductively to things we really don't know?"

"The opinion you have offered bears a strong resemblance (though it isn't identical) to that of an influential British philosopher.[21] He has presented his ideas persuasively, and has many followers. Hume, he says, has proved conclusively that induction is not a justifiable form of inference; it is, consequently, no part of science. The only kind of logic that has a legitimate place in science is deductive logic. Deductive inferences are demonstrative; their conclusions must be true if their premises are true. These inferences are precisely what Hume called 'reasoning concerning relations of ideas.' The crucial point is that they *do not add to our knowledge* in any way—they enable us to see the content of our premises, but they do not extend that content in the least. Thus, from premises that refer only to events in the past and present, it is impossible to *deduce* any predictions of future facts. Any kind of inference which would enable us to predict the future on the basis of facts already observed would have to be of a different sort; such inference is often called 'ampliative' or 'inductive.' If science contains only deductive inferences, but no inductive inferences, it can never provide us with any knowledge beyond the content of our immediate observations.

"Now this philosopher does not reject scientific knowledge; he simply claims that prediction of the future is no part of the business of science. Accordingly, the function of scientific investigation is to find powerful general hypotheses (he calls them *conjectures*) that adequately explain all known facts that have occurred so far. As long as such a generalization succeeds in explaining the new facts that come along it is retained; if it fails to explain new facts, it must be modified or rejected. The sole purpose of scientific experimentation is to try to find weaknesses in such hypotheses—that is to criticize them or try to refute them. He calls this the 'method of conjectures and refutations,' or sometimes simply, 'the critical approach.'

"The main difficulty with this approach—an insuperable one, in my opinion—is the fact that it completely deprives science of its predictive function. To the question of which method to use for predicting the future, it can give no answer. Astrology, crystal gazing, blind guessing, and scientific prediction are all on a par. To find out what the population of the world will be in 2000 A.D., we might as well employ a psychic seer as a scientific demographer. I find it hard to believe that this can constitute a satisfactory solution to the problem of employing our knowledge to find rational solutions to the problems that face us—problems whose solutions demand that we make predictions of the future course of events. Tempting as it is to try to evade Hume's problem in this way, I do not see how we can be satisfied to admit that there is no rational approach to our problem."

"But perhaps there is no answer to Hume's problem," says still another student; "maybe the only hope for salvation of this world is to give up our blind worship of science and return to religion. We have placed our faith in science, and look where we are as a result. I believe we should adopt a different faith."

There's that word *again,* you note to yourself, as the professor begins her answer: "Though I heartily agree that many of the results of science—*technological* results, I think we should emphasize—have been far from beneficial, I don't think we can properly condemn scientific *knowledge*. Knowledge is one thing; what we choose to do with it is quite another. But that's not the issue we are concerned with. I do not see how anyone could deny that science has had a great deal of success in making predictions; no other approach can possibly present a comparable record of success. And, as time goes on, the capability for predictive success seems only to increase. It would be an utterly astonishing piece of luck, if it were sheer coincidence, that science has been so much luckier than other approaches in making its predictions. If anyone can consistently pick a winner in every race at every track every day, we are pretty sure he has more than good luck going for him. Science isn't infallible, but it is hard to believe its predictive success is just a matter of chance. I, at least, am not prepared to say that science is just one among many equally acceptable faiths—you pays your money and you takes your choice. I feel rather sure that the scientific approach has a logical justification of some sort." With that, the bell rings, the discussion ends, and everyone leaves—none by way of the window.

It just isn't good enough, you say to yourself, after listening to your physics professor lecturing, with demonstrations, on the law of conservation of angular momentum. You don't know whether you're dizzier from the discussion of Hume's problem in the philosophy class or from watching student volunteers in this class being spun on stools mounted on turntables. In any case, you decide to look up Professor Philo after lunch, and you find her in her office.

"Look," you say a bit brusquely, "I see that Hume was right about our inability to prove that nature is uniform. But suppose that nature does play a trick on us, so to speak. Suppose that after all this time of appearing quite uniform, manifesting all sorts of regularities such as the laws of physics, she turns chaotic. Then there isn't anything we can do anyhow. Someone might make a lucky guess about some future event, but there would be no systematic method for anticipating the chaos successfully. It seems to me I've got a way of predicting the future which will work if nature is uniform—the scientific method, or if you like, the inductive method—and if nature isn't uniform, I'm out of luck whatever I do. It seems to me I've got everything to gain and nothing to lose (except a lot of hard work) if I attempt to adhere to the scientific approach. That seems good enough to me; what do you think?"[22]

"Well," she says quietly, "I tend to agree with that answer, and so do a few others, but we are certainly in the minority. And many difficult problems arise when you try to work it out with precision."

"What sorts of difficulties are these?" you ask.

"There are several kinds," she begins; "for instance, what exactly do you mean by saying that nature is uniform? You cannot mean—to use Hume's quaint language—that like sensible qualities are always conjoined with like secret powers. All of us, including Hume, know this claim is false. Bread which looks and tastes completely harmless may contain a deadly poison. A gas which has exactly the appearance of normal air may suffocate living organisms and pollute the atmosphere. That kind of uniformity principle cannot be the basis of our inferences."

"That's quite true," you answer, "but perhaps we could say that nature operates according to regular laws. Ever since I began to think about Hume's problem, I have been led back to laws of nature."

"Your suggestion is a good one," she replies, "but modern philosophers have found it surprisingly difficult to say precisely what type of statement can qualify as a possible law of nature. It is a law of nature, most physicists would agree, that no material objects travel faster than light; they would refuse to admit, *as a law of nature,* that no golden spheres are more than one mile in diameter. It is not easy to state clearly the basis for this distinction. Both statements are generalizations, and both are true to the best of our knowledge."[23]

"Isn't the difference simply that you cannot, even in principle, accelerate a material object to the speed of light, while it is possible in principle to fabricate an enormous sphere of gold?"

"That is precisely the question at issue," she replies. "The problem is, what basis do we have for claiming possibility in the one case and impossibility in the other. You seem to be saying that a law of nature prevents the one but not the other, which is obviously circular. And if you bring in the notion of causation—causing something to go faster than light vs. causing a large golden sphere to be created—you only compound the difficulty, for the concept of causation is itself a source of great perplexity.

"Suppose, however, that we had succeeded in overcoming that obstacle—that we could say with reasonable precision which sorts of statements are candidates for the status of laws of nature and which are not. We then face a further difficulty. It is obvious that some tests of scientific laws carry greater weight than others. The discovery of the planet Neptune, for example, confirmed Newton's laws much more dramatically than would a few additional observations of Mars. A test with particles traveling at very high velocities would be much stronger evidence for conservation of momentum than would some more experiments on the air track in the physics lab. It is not easy to see how to measure or compare the weight which different types of evidence lend to different scientific hypotheses.

"Scientific confirmation is a subtle and complex matter to which contemporary philosophers have devoted a great deal of attention; some have tried to construct systems of inductive logic that would capture this kind of scientific reasoning. Such efforts have, at best, met with limited success; inductive logic is in a primitive state compared with deductive logic. Until we have a reasonably clear idea of what such inference consists of, however, it is unlikely that we will be able to go very far in meeting the fundamental challenge Hume issued concerning the justification of scientific reasoning. Unless we can at least say what inductive inference is, and what constitutes uniformity of nature (or natural law), we can hardly argue that inductive reasoning—and only inductive reasoning—will prove successful in predicting the future if nature is uniform. And even if those concepts were clarified, the argument would still be intricate indeed."

"Do you think there is any chance that answers to such problems can be found?" you ask.

"I think it's just possible."

"Thanks," you say as you get up to leave.

"And my thanks to you," she replies. "You cannot possibly know how satisfying it is to talk with someone like you—someone intelligent—who takes such philosophical problems seriously and thinks hard about them. If you keep it up, you might be the very person to find some of the answers. I wish you well."

NOTES

1. Professor Salvia is a descendant of Salviati, the protagonist in Galileo's dialogues. The name was shortened when the family emigrated to America.

2. Dr. Sagro is married to a descendant of Sagredo, another character in Galileo's dialogues.

3. If you really did know, please accept the author's apologies.

4. Please note that "demonstrate" is ambiguous. In mathematics it means "prove"; in physics it means "exemplify." Hume uses this term only in the mathematical sense.

5. Hume, using the terminology of his day, refers to it as the "moment" of the moving body.

6. This is Newton's definition; it is somewhat out of date, but adequate in the present context.

7. She is a direct descendant of Philo, the protagonist in Hume's "Dialogues Concerning Natural Religion," most of which is reprinted in this anthology.

8. Professor Philo realizes that it would be more accurate to say that a statement or hypothesis expressing a law of nature must be a generalization, but she does not wish to introduce unnecessary terminological distinctions at this point.

9. In section IV, part I, anticipating the results of the later discussion.

10. All of the attempts to deal with Hume's problem which are treated in this section are discussed in detail in Wesley C. Salmon, *The Foundations of Scientific Inference* (Pittsburgh: University of Pittsburgh Press, 1967); this book will be cited hereafter as *Foundations.*

11. This is an inductive justification; see *Foundations,* chapter II, section I.

12. David Hume, *Enquiry Concerning Human Understanding* (hereafter, *Enquiry*), section IV, part II.

13. Ibid.

14. For discussion of justification by means of synthetic a priori principles, see *Foundations,* chapter II, section 4.

15. *Enquiry,* section IV, part II.

16. For discussion of the postulational approach, see *Foundations,* chapter II, section 6.

17. Bertrand Russell, *Introduction to Mathematical Philosophy* (London: Allen & Unwin, 1919), p. 71.

18. The "probabilistic approach" is discussed in *Foundations,* chapter II, section 7.

19. An elementary survey of philosophical problems of probability is given in *Foundations,* chapters IV–VII. References to additional literature on this subject can be found there.

20. We are assuming, of course, that these predictions are properly made. Scientists are only human, and they do make mistakes. One should not conclude, however, that every false prediction represents a scientific error. Impeccable scientific procedure is fallible, as we have already noted more than once.

21. This refers to the "deductivist" position of Sir Karl Popper. This approach is discussed in *Foundations,* chapter II, section 3.

22. This approach is due mainly to Hans Reichenbach; it is known as a "pragmatic justification" and is discussed in *Foundations,* chapter II, section 8.

23. Further elementary discussion of this issue can be found in Carl G. Hempel, *Philosophy of Natural Science* (Englewood Cliffs, N.J.: Prentice-Hall, Inc., 1966), § 5.3 A more technical and extensive treatment of related issues can be found in Nelson Goodman, *Fact, Fiction, and Forecast,* 2nd ed. (Indianapolis, Ind.: The Bobbs-Merrill Co., 1965).

What Is Science?

Science and Myth*

JOHN MAYNARD SMITH

John Maynard Smith (1920–) specializes in evolutionary theory. He is professor of biology at the University of Sussex.

RECENTLY, AFTER GIVING A RADIO TALK on Charles Darwin, I received through the post a pamphlet by Don Smith entitled "Why Are There Gays At All? Why Hasn't Evolution Eliminated Gayness Millions of Years Ago?" The pamphlet points to a genuine concern: the prevalence of homosexual behavior in our species is not understood and is certainly not something that would be predicted from Darwinian theory. Smith wrote the pamphlet because he believes the persecution of gays has been strengthened and justified by the existence of a theory of evolution that asserts gays are unfit because they do not reproduce. He also believes that gays can be protected from future persecution only if it can be shown that they have played an essential and creative role in evolution. His argument is that, in evolution, novelty arises when individuals adopt mating habits different from those typical of their species: it is summed up on a button that reads "Sexual deviation is the mainspring of evolution."

I do not find this argument particularly persuasive, but that is not the point I want to make. I think Smith would have been better advised to have written, "If people despise gays because gayness does not contribute to biological fitness, they are wrong to do so. It would be as sensible to persecute mathematicians because an ability to solve differential equations does not contribute to fitness. A scientific theory—Darwinism or any other—has nothing to say about the value of a human being."

The point I am making is that Smith is demanding of evolutionary biology that it be a myth; that is, a story with a moral message. He is not alone in this. Elaine Morgan's book *The Descent of Woman* is an account of the origin of *Homo sapiens* that is intended to give mythical support to the women's movement by emphasizing the role of the female sex and, in particular, the mother-child bond. She claims, with reason, that many other accounts of human evolution have, perhaps unconsciously, placed undue emphasis on the role of males. Earlier, George Bernard Shaw wrote *Back to Methuselah* (1922) avowedly as an evolutionary myth, because he found in Darwinism a justification of selfishness and brutality and because he wished instead to support the Lamarckian theory of the inheritance of acquired characters, which he saw as justifying free will and individual endeavor.

We should not be surprised by Don Smith, Elaine Morgan, and Bernard Shaw. In all societies, people have constructed myths about the origins of the universe and of humans. The function of these myths is to define our place in nature and thus to give us a sense of purpose and value. Since Darwinism is, among other things, an account of human origins, is it any wonder that it is expected to carry a moral message?

The people and the objects that figure in a myth stand not only for themselves but also as symbols of other things. To some extent, myths and their symbolic components develop simply because human beings find it difficult to accept any input as meaningless. Shown an inkblot, we see witches, bats, and dragons. This refusal to accept input as mere noise lies at the root of divination by tarot cards, tea leaves, the livers or shoulders of animals, or the sticks of the *I Ching*. It may also account for the strangely late development of a mathematical theory of probability or of any scientific theory with a chance element. As anthropologist Dan Sperber has written, "Symbolic thought is capable, precisely, of transforming noise into information."

Another—and in the present context, more important—function of myths is to give moral and evaluative guidance. Some mythmaking is quite conscious. In *Back to Methuselah,* for example, Shaw deliberately invented a story that would have the moral effect he desired. More usually, however, I suspect that a mythmaker conceives a story that moves him or her in a particular way—at its lowest, it reinforces prejudices, and at its highest, to borrow Aristotle's words, it evokes feelings of pity and fear. People repeat myths because they hope to persuade others to behave in certain ways.

This raises the question of why we use myths rather than simple statements of instruction. Why do we talk of King Alfred and the cakes, for example, instead of saying that people in important positions should be modest? Perhaps a story whose meaning has to be puzzled out or guessed at carries more conviction than a mere instruction. What we imagine is more important than what we are told.

Sometimes, I find it hard to discover how far people distinguish stories intended to give moral guidance from those meant simply to supply technical help. Confusion seems particularly likely to crop up when rituals are involved. For example, if, before going into battle, a man sharpens his spear and undergoes ritual purification (or, for that matter, cleans his rifle and goes to mass), he may regard the two procedures as equally efficacious. Indeed, they may well be so, one in preparing the spear and the other himself. If we regard the former as more practical, we do so only because we understand metallurgy better than psychology.

Despite the difficulty, most people do try to distinguish procedures and technical instructions that alter the external world from procedures and stories intended to alter our own state of consciousness or persuade us that certain things are right. Indeed, we take some trouble when educating our children to give hints about which category of information is being transmitted. For example, a surprisingly large proportion of the stories read aloud to children, particularly those with a moral message, are about talking animals or even talking steam engines. It is as if we wanted to be sure that the stories are not taken literally.

While such efforts may be successful in many spheres of human endeavor, the examples of Don Smith and Bernard Shaw show how hard it is for many people to separate science, and especially evolution, from myth. One reaction to this difficulty is to assert that there is no difference, that evolution theory has no more claim to objective truth than Genesis. Many scientists would be enraged by such an assertion, but rage is no substitute for argument. In the last century, it was widely held that the scientific method, conceived of as establishing theories by induction from observation, led to certain knowledge. Darwin and Einstein have robbed us of that certainty—or have liberated us from that prison. If, as Darwin showed, there is not a fixed and finite number of things in the universe, each with a knowable essence, then induction is logically impossible. Einstein, in turn, showed that what scientists had been most confident of—classical mechanics—was at worst false and at best a special case of a more general theory. After that twin blow, certain knowledge is something we can expect only at our funerals.

But it is one thing to admit that scientific knowledge cannot be certain and another to claim that there is no difference between science and myth. Karl Popper, perhaps the most influential contemporary philosopher of science, has told us that it was the impact of Einstein, and in particular the wish to distinguish Einstein's theory from those of Freud, Adler, and Marx, that led him to propose falsifiability as the criterion for separating science from pseudoscience. If a theory is scientific, he suggested, observations can be conceived of which, if they were accepted, would show the theory to be false. In contrast, he suggests that no conceivable pattern of human behavior could falsify Freudian theory.

Popper's views have been attacked, primarily on the grounds that there are no such things as theory-free observations. Every observation is subject to interpretation, conscious and unconscious. Consequently, there can never be certain grounds for rejecting a scientific theory, and hence the distinction between science and pseudoscience disappears.

This criticism seems to me largely to miss the point. If Popper were claiming that scientific knowledge were certain, then the impossibility of certain falsification would indeed be damaging. But he makes no such claim. He insists on two things. First, a scientific theory must assert that certain kinds of events cannot happen, so that the theory is falsified if these events are subsequently observed, and second, there is inevitably a logical asymmetry in any attempt to test a theory, so that a theory can be falsified but cannot be proved true by the acceptance of observation.

There is, however, a tide of ideas that would deny the distinction. The emotional force behind this tide derives, in part, from an entirely proper disgust at some of the consequences of technology in the modern world and, in part, from an equally proper wish to treat the ideas of other peoples as of equal value to our own. What is common to these two reactions is the conviction, which I share, that scientific theories are not the only kind of idea that we need. A frequently drawn corollary of this conviction, which I do not share, is that scientific ideas are not distinguishable from other ideas.

. . . A crucial distinction must be made between the psychological sources of a theory and the testing of it. If Darwin's ideas, or Newton's, were accepted because they were socially appealing, then indeed science and myth would be indistinguishable. But I do not think that they were. They were accepted because of their explanatory power and ability to withstand experimental test. Of course, new ideas in science sometimes come from analogies with society, just as, in one scientific discipline, such as biology, they arise by analogy with others, such as physics and engineering. But what matters for the progress of science is not where the ideas come from but how they are treated.

Society influences the development of science through both the problems that seem worth solving and the resources available for their solution. I have little doubt that society also influences scientists, both as individuals and groups, by making some ideas seem worth pursuing and others implausible or unpromising. For example, my own caution about applying to humans ideas drawn from a study of animal societies—a caution that contrasts with the enthusiasm of such scientists as E. O. Wilson and Richard Alexander—probably arose because I grew up under the shadow of Hitler and the Nazi theories of racial superiority and biological determinism and not because of anything internal to biology or sociology.

There is, however, a caricature inherent in the externalist view of science that I reject emphatically. This is the idea that we can evaluate a scientific theory by reference to the society in which it was born, or to the moral and political conclusions that might be drawn from it. Once accept that view and science is dead, as genetics died in Russia in 1948, when Stalin supported Lysenko's Lamarckian views against the Mendelians. Stalin took his position partly in the hope of quick returns in agricultural productivity and partly because Lysenko's belief in the inheritance of acquired characters seemed to accord better with Marxism than did the orthodox—and, as it happens, more nearly correct—Mendelian doctrine that hereditary characteristics are transmitted from parent to offspring by genes and that the genetic message is independent from changes induced in the body of the parent during its lifetime.

I would not have spent so much time discussing the difference between scientific theories and myths if the difference between them were obvious. Indeed, they have much in common. Both are constructs of the human mind, and both are intended to have a significance wider than the direct assertions they contain. Popper suggested falsifiability as the criterion distinguishing them, and I think he was right. However, we can often also distinguish them by their function: the function of a scientific theory is to account for experience—often, it is true, the rather esoteric experience emerging from deliberate experiment; the function of a myth is to provide a source and justification for values. What, then, should be the relation between them?

Three views are tenable. The first, sometimes expressed as a demand for "normative science," is that the same mental constructs should serve both as myths and as scientific theories. If I am right, this widely held view underlies the criticism of Darwinism from gays, from the women's movement, from socialists, and so on. It explains the preference expressed by some churchmen for "big bang" as opposed to "steady state" theories of cosmology. Although well intentioned, it seems to me pernicious in its effects. Applied to evolution theory, it means either that we must embrace Darwinism and draw from it the conclusion that gays are unnatural and social services wicked or that we must embrace Lamarckism whether or not the genetic evidence supports it. Normative science will be bad morality or bad science, and most probably both.

The second view is that we should do without myths and confine ourselves to science. This is the view I held at the age of twenty, but it really won't do. If, as I now believe, scientific theories say nothing about what is right but only about what is possible, we need some other source of values, and that source has to be myth, in the broadest sense of the term.

The third view, and I think the only sensible one, is that we need both myths and scientific theories, but that we must be as clear as we can about which is which. In essence, this was the view urged by the French molecular biologist Jaques Monod in *Chance and Necessity* (1972). Oddly, Monod was almost universally derided by his critics for arguing that one can derive values from science, when in fact he argued the precise opposite. His case was that there is no place in science for teleological, or value-laden, hypotheses. Yet, to do science, one must first be committed to some values—not least, to the value of seeking the truth. Since this value cannot be derived from science, it must be seen as a prior moral commitment, needed before science is possible. So far from values being derived from science, Monod saw science as depending on values.

Although I disagree with some aspects of his book, I agree with Monod on two basic points. First, values do not derive from science but are necessary for the practice of science. Second, we should distinguish as clearly as we can between science and myth. We should make this distinction, not because we could then discard the myths and retain only science, but because the roles they play are different. Scientific theories tell us what is possible; myths tell us what is desirable. Both are needed to guide proper action.

The Opinion in *McLean* v. *Arkansas Board of Education**

JUDGE WILLIAM R. OVERTON

Judge William R. Overton (1939–1987) was a federal judge in Arkansas. He presided over one of the most celebrated trials involving the teaching of creation science in the public schools.

THE APPROACH TO TEACHING "creation science" and "evolution science" found in Act 590 is identical to the two-model approach espoused by the Institute for Creation Research and is taken almost verbatim from ICR writings. It is an extension of Fundamentalists' view that one must either accept the literal interpretation of Genesis or else believe in the godless system of evolution.

The two-model approach of the creationists is simply a contrived dualism[1] which has no scientific factual basis or legitimate educational purpose. It assumes only two explanations for the origins of life and existence of man, plants, and animals: It was either the work of a creator or it was not. Application of these two models, according to creationists, and the defendants, dictates that all scientific evidence which fails to support the theory of evolution is necessarily scientific evidence in support of creationism and is, therefore, creation science "evidence" in support of Section 4(a) [of Act 590].

The emphasis on origins as an aspect of the theory of evolution is peculiar to creationist literature. Although the subject of origins of life is within the province of biology, the scientific community does not consider origins of life a part of evolutionary theory. The theory of evolution assumes the existence of life and is directed to an explanation of *how* life evolved. Evolution does not presuppose the absence of a creator or God and the plain inference conveyed by Section 4 is erroneous.[2]

As a statement of the theory of evolution, Section 4(b) is simply a hodgepodge of limited assertions, many of which are factually inaccurate.

For example, although 4(b)(2) asserts, as a tenet of evolutionary theory, "the sufficiency of mutation and natural selection in bringing about the existence of present living kinds from simple earlier kinds," Drs. Ayala and Gould both stated that biologists know that these two processes do not account for all significant evolutionary change. They testified to such phenomena as recombination, the founder effect, genetic drift and the theory of punctuated equilibrium, which are believed to play important evolutionary roles. Section 4(b) omits any reference to these. Moreover, 4(b) utilizes the term "kinds" which all scientists said is not a word of science and has no fixed meaning. Additionally, the Act presents both evolution and creation science as "package deals." Thus, evidence critical of some aspect of what the creationists define as evolution is taken as support for a theory which includes a worldwide flood and a relatively young earth.[3]

In addition to the fallacious pedagogy of the two-model approach. Section 4(a) lacks legitimate educational value because "creation science" as defined in that section is simply not science. Several witnesses suggested definitions of science. A descriptive definition was said to be that science is what is "accepted by the scientific community" and is "what scientists do." The obvious implication of

*McLean v. Arkansas Board of Education 529 *F. Supp. 1255 (E. D. Ark. 1982).*

this description is that, in a free society, knowledge does not require the imprimatur of legislation in order to become science.

More precisely, the essential characteristics of science are:

1. It is guided by natural law;
2. It has to be explanatory by reference to natural law;
3. It is testable against the empirical world;
4. Its conclusions are tentative, i.e., are not necessarily the final word; and
5. It is falsifiable (testimony of Ruse and other science witnesses).

Creation science as described in Section 4(a) fails to meet these essential characteristics. First, the section revolves around 4(a)(1) which asserts a sudden creation "from nothing." Such a concept is not science because it depends upon a supernatural intervention which is not guided by natural law. It is not explanatory by reference to natural law, is not testable, and is not falsifiable.[4]

If the unifying idea of supernatural creation by God is removed from Section 4, the remaining parts of the section explain nothing and are meaningless assertions.

Section 4(a)(2), relating to the "insufficiency of mutation and natural selection in bringing about development of all living kinds from a single organism," is an incomplete negative generalization directed at the theory of evolution.

Section 4(a)(3) which describes "changes only within fixed limits of originally created kinds of plants and animals" fails to conform to the essential characteristics of science for several reasons. First, there is no scientific definition of "kinds" and none of the witnesses was able to point to any scientific authority which recognized the term or knew how many "kinds" existed. One defense witness suggested there may be 100 to 10,000 different "kinds." Another believes there were "about 10,000, give or take a few thousand." Second, the assertion appears to be an effort to establish outer limits of changes within species. There is no scientific explanation for these limits which is guided by natural law and the limitations, whatever they are, cannot be explained by natural law.

The statement in 4(a)(4) of "separate ancestry of man and apes" is a bald assertion. It explains nothing and refers to no scientific fact or theory.[5]

Section 4(a)(5) refers to "explanation of the earth's geology by catastrophism, including the occurrence of a worldwide flood." This assertion completely fails as science. The Act is referring to the Noachian flood described in the Book of Genesis.[6] The creationist writers concede that *any* kind of Genesis Flood depends upon supernatural intervention. A worldwide flood as an explanation of the world's geology is not the product of natural law, nor can its occurrence be explained by natural law.

Section 4(a)(6) equally fails to meet the standards of science. "Relatively recent inception" has no scientific meaning. It can only be given meaning by reference to creationist writings which place the age at between 6,000 and 20,000 years because of the genealogy of the Old Testament. See, e.g., Plaintiffs' Exhibit 78, Gish (6,000 to 10,000); Plaintiffs' Exhibit 87, Segraves (6,000 to 20,000). Such a reasoning process is not the product of natural law; not explainable by natural law; nor is it tentative.

Creation science, as defined in Section 4(a), not only fails to follow the canons defining scientific theory, it also fails to fit the more general descriptions of "what scientists think" and "what scientists do." The scientific community consists of individuals and groups, nationally and internationally, who work independently in such varied fields as biology, paleontology, geology and astronomy. Their work is published and subject to review and testing by their peers. The journals for publication are both numerous and varied. There is, however, not one recognized scientific journal which has published an article espousing the creation science theory described in Section 4(a). Some of the State's witnesses suggested that the scientific community was "closeminded" on the subject of creationism and that explained the lack of acceptance of the creation science arguments. Yet no witness produced a scientific article for which publication had been refused. Perhaps some members of the scientific community are resistant to new ideas. It is, however, inconceivable that such a loose knit group of independent thinkers in all the varied fields of science could, or would, so effectively censor new scientific thought.

The creationists have difficulty maintaining among their ranks consistency in the claim that creationism is science. The author of Act 590, Ellwanger, said that neither evolution nor creationism was science. He thinks both are religion. Duane Gish recently responded to an article in *Discover* critical of creationism by stating:

> Stephen Jay Gould states that creationists claim creation is a scientific theory. This is a false accusation. Creationists have repeatedly stated that neither creation nor evolution is a scientific theory (and each is equally religious). (Gish, letter to the editor of *Discover*, July 1981, Appendix 30 to Plaintiffs' Pretrial Brief.)

The methodology employed by creationists is another factor which is indicative that their work is not science. A scientific theory must be tentative and always subject to revision or abandonment in light of facts that are inconsistent with, or falsify, the theory. A theory that is by its own terms dogmatic, absolutist, and never subject to revision is not a scientific theory.

The creationists' methods do not take data, weigh it against the opposing scientific data, and thereafter reach the conclusions stated in Section 4(a). Instead, they take the literal wording of the Book of Genesis and attempt to find scientific support for it. The method is best explained in the language of Morris in his book *Studies in the Bible and Science* at page 114 (Plaintiffs' Exhibit 31):

> . . . it is . . . quite impossible to determine anything about Creation through a study of present processes, because present processes are not creative in character. If man wishes to know anything about Creation (the time of Creation, the duration of Creation, the order of Creation, the methods of Creation, or anything else) his sole source of true information is that of divine revelation. God was there when it happened. We were not there. . . . Therefore, we are completely limited to what God has seen fit to tell us, and this information is in His written Word. This is our textbook on the science of Creation! (Morris, Plaintiffs' Exhibit 31.)

The Creation Research Society employs the same unscientific approach to the issue of creationism. Its applicants for membership must subscribe to the belief that the Book of Genesis is "historically and scientifically true in all of the original autographs." The Court would never criticize or discredit any person's testimony based on his or her religious beliefs. While anybody is free to approach a scientific inquiry in any fashion they choose, they cannot properly describe the methodology used as scientific, if they start with a conclusion and refuse to change it regardless of the evidence developed during the course of the investigation.

In efforts to establish "evidence" in support of creation science, the defendants relied upon the same false premise as the two-model approach contained in Section 4, i.e., all evidence which criticized evolutionary theory was proof in support of creation science. For example, the defendants established that the mathematical probability of a chance chemical combination resulting in life from non-life is so remote that such an occurrence is almost beyond imagination. Those mathematical facts, the defendants argue, are scientific evidences that life was the product of a creator. While the statistical figures may be impressive evidence against the theory of chance chemical combinations as an explanation of origins, it requires a leap of faith to interpret those figures so as to support a complex doctrine which includes a sudden creation from nothing, a worldwide flood, separate ancestry of man and apes, and a young earth.

The defendants' argument would be more persuasive if, in fact, there were only two theories or ideas about the origins of life and the world. That there are a number of theories was acknowledged by the State's witnesses, Dr. Wickramasinghe and Dr. Geisler. Dr. Wickramasinghe testified at length in support of a theory that life on earth was "seeded" by comets which delivered genetic material and perhaps organisms to the earth's surface from interstellar dust far outside the solar system. The "seeding" theory further hypothesizes that the earth remains under the continuing influence of genetic material from space which continues to affect life. While Wickramasinghe's theory[7] about the origins of life on earth has not received general acceptance within the scientific community, he has, at least, used scientific methodology to produce a theory of origins which meets the essential characteristics of science.

Perhaps Dr. Wickramasinghe was called as a witness because he was generally critical of the theory of evolution and the scientific community, a tactic consistent with the strategy of the defense. Unfortunately for the defense, he demonstrated that the simplistic approach of the two-model analysis of the origins of life is false. Furthermore, he corroborated the plaintiffs' witnesses by concluding that "no rational scientist" would believe the earth's geology could be explained by reference to a worldwide flood or that the earth was less than one million years old.

The proof in support of creation science consisted almost entirely of efforts to discredit the theory of evolution through a rehash of data and theories which have been before the scientific community for decades. The arguments asserted by creationists are not based upon new scientific evidence or laboratory data which has been ignored by the scientific community.

Robert Gentry's discovery of radioactive polonium haloes in granite and coalified woods is, perhaps, the most recent scientific work which the creationists use as argument for a "relatively recent inception" of the earth and a "worldwide flood." The existence of polonium haloes in granite and coalified wood is thought to be inconsistent with radiometric dating methods based upon constant radioactive decay rates. Mr. Gentry's findings were published almost ten years ago and have been the subject of some discussion in the scientific community. The discoveries have not, however, led to the formulation of any scientific hypothesis or theory which would explain a relatively recent inception of the earth or a worldwide flood. Gentry's discovery has been treated as a minor mystery which will eventually be explained. It may deserve further investigation, but the National Science Foundation has not deemed it to be of sufficient import to support further funding.

NOTES

1. Morris, the Director of ICR and one who first advocated the two-model approach, insists that a true Christian cannot compromise with the theory of evolution and that the Genesis version of creation and the theory of evolution are mutually exclusive (Plaintiffs' Exhibit 31, Morris, *Studies in the Bible & Science,* pp. 102–103). The two-model approach was the subject of Dr. Richard Bliss's doctoral dissertation (Defense Exhibit 35). It is presented in Bliss, *Origins: Two-Models—Evolution, Creation* (1978). Moreover, the two-model approach merely casts in educationalist language the dualism which appears in all creationist literature—creation (i.e., God) and evolution are presented as two alternative and mutually exclusive theories [See, e.g., Plaintiffs' Exhibit 75, Morris, *Scientific Creationism* (1974) (public school edition); Plaintiffs' Exhibit 59, Fox, *Fossils: Hard Facts from the Earth*]. Particularly illustrative is Plaintiffs' Exhibit 61, Boardman, et al., *Worlds Without End* (1971), a CSRC publication: "One group of scientists, known as creationists, believe that God, in a miraculous manner, created all matter and energy. . . . Scientists who insist that the universe just grew, by accident, from a mass of hot gases without the direction or help of a Creator are known as evolutionists."

2. The idea that belief in a creator and acceptance of the scientific theory of evolution are mutually exclusive is a false premise and offensive to the religious views of many. Dr. Francisco Ayala, a geneticist of considerable renown and a former Catholic priest who has the equivalent of a Ph.D. in theology, pointed out that many working scientists who subscribe to the theory of evolution are devoutly religious.

3. This is so despite the fact that some of the defense witnesses do not subscribe to the young earth or flood hypotheses. Dr. Geisler stated his belief that the earth is several billion years old. Dr. Wickramasinghe stated that no rational scientist would believe the earth is less than one million years old or that all the world's geology could be explained by a worldwide flood.

4. "We do not know how God created, what processes He used, for God *used processes which are not now operating anywhere in the natural universe.* This is why we refer to divine creation as Special Creation. We cannot discover by scientific investigation anything about the creative processes used by God" [Plaintiffs' Exhibit 78, Gish, *Evolution? The Fossils Say No!,* p. 42 (3rd ed., 1979) (emphasis in original)].

5. The evolutionary notion that man and some modern apes have a common ancestor somewhere in the distant past has consistently been distorted by anti-evolutionists to say that man descended from modern

monkeys. As such, this idea has long been most offensive to Fundamentalists (See *Epperson v. Arkansas*).

6. Not only was this point acknowledged by virtually all the defense witnesses, it is patent in the creationist literature. See, e.g., Plaintiffs' Exhibit 89, Kofahl & Segraves, *The Creation Explanation,* p. 40: "The Flood of Noah brought about vast changes in the earth's surface, including vulcanism, mountain building, and the deposition of the major part of sedimentary strata. This principle is called "Biblical catastrophism.""

7. The theory is detailed in Wickramasinghe's book with Sir Fred Hoyle, *Evolution From Space* (1981).

Coping with Skepticism

The Fixation of Belief*

CHARLES SANDERS PEIRCE

Charles Sanders Peirce (1839–1914) was a founder of the American school of philosophy called "pragmatism."

We generally know when we wish to ask a question and when we wish to pronounce a judgment, for there is a dissimilarity between the sensation of doubting and that of believing.

But this is not all which distinguishes doubt from belief. There is a practical difference. Our beliefs guide our desires and shape our actions. The Assassins, or followers of the Old Man of the Mountain,[1] used to rush into death at his least command, because they believed that obedience to him would insure everlasting felicity. Had they doubted this, they would not have acted as they did. So it is with every belief, according to its degree. The feeling of believing is a more or less sure indication of there being established in our nature some habit which will determine our actions. Doubt never has such an effect.

Nor must we overlook a third point of difference. Doubt is an uneasy and dissatisfied state from which we struggle to free ourselves and pass into the state of belief; while the latter is a calm and satisfactory state which we do not wish to avoid, or to change to a belief in anything else. On the contrary, we cling tenaciously, not merely to believing, but to believing just what we do believe.

Thus, both doubt and belief have positive effects upon us, though very different ones. Belief does not make us act at once, but puts us into such a condition that we shall behave in a certain way, when the occasion arises. Doubt has not the least effect of this sort, but stimulates us to action until it is destroyed. This reminds us of the irritation of a nerve and the reflex action produced thereby; while for the analogue of belief, in the nervous system, we must look to what are called nervous associations—for example, to that habit of the nerves in consequence of which the smell of a peach will make the mouth water.

The irritation of doubt causes a struggle to attain a state of belief. I shall term this struggle *inquiry*, though it must be admitted that this is sometimes not a very apt designation.

The irritation of doubt is the only immediate motive for the struggle to attain belief. It is certainly

**From* Popular Science Monthly, *November, 1877.*

best for us that our beliefs should be such as may truly guide our actions so as to satisfy our desires; and this reflection will make us reject any belief which does not seem to have been so formed as to insure this result. But it will only do so by creating a doubt in the place of that belief. With the doubt, therefore, the struggle begins, and with the cessation of doubt it ends. Hence, the sole object of inquiry is the settlement of opinion. We may fancy that this is not enough for us, and that we seek not merely an opinion, but a true opinion. But put this fancy to the test, and it proves groundless; for as soon as a firm belief is reached we are entirely satisfied, whether the belief be false or true. And it is clear that nothing out of the sphere of our knowledge can be our object, for nothing which does not affect the mind can be a motive for a mental effort. The most that can be maintained is, that we seek for a belief that we shall *think* to be true. But we think each one of our beliefs to be true, and, indeed, it is mere tautology to say so.

That the settlement of opinion is the sole end of inquiry is a very important proposition. It sweeps away, at once, various vague and erroneous conceptions of proof. A few of these may be noticed here.

1. Some philosophers have imagined that to start an inquiry it was only necessary to utter a question or set it down on paper, and have even recommended us to begin our studies with questioning everything! But the mere putting of a proposition into the interrogative form does not stimulate the mind to any struggle after belief. There must be a real and living doubt, and without this all discussion is idle.
2. It is a very common idea that a demonstration must rest on some ultimate and absolutely indubitable propositions. These, according to one school,[2] are first principles of a general nature; according to another,[3] are first sensations. But in point of fact, an inquiry, to have that completely satisfactory result called demonstration, has only to start with propositions perfectly free from all actual doubt. If the premises are not in fact doubted at all, they cannot be more satisfactory than they are.
3. Some people seem to love to argue a point after all the world is fully convinced of it. But no further advance can be made. When doubt ceases, mental action on the subject comes to an end; and if it did go on, it would be without purpose.

1. THE METHOD OF TENACITY

If the settlement of opinion is the sole object of inquiry, and if belief is of the nature of a habit, why should we not attain the desired end by taking any answer to a question which we may fancy and constantly reiterating it to ourselves, dwelling on all which may conduce to that belief and learning to turn with contempt and hatred from anything which might disturb it? This simple and direct method is really pursued by many men. I remember once being entreated not to read a certain newspaper lest it might change my opinion upon free trade. "Lest I might be entrapped by its fallacies and misstatements," was the form of expression. "You are not," my friend said, "a special student of political economy. You might, therefore, easily be deceived by fallacious arguments upon the subject. You might, then, if you read this paper, be led to believe in protection. But you admit that free trade is the true doctrine; and you do not wish to believe what is not true." I have often known this system to be deliberately adopted. Still oftener, the instinctive dislike of an undecided state of mind, exaggerated into a vague dread of doubt, makes men cling spasmodically to the views they have already taken. The man feels that, if he only holds to his belief without wavering, it will be entirely satisfactory. Nor can it be denied that a steady and immovable faith yields great peace of mind. It may, indeed, give rise to inconveniences, as if a man should resolutely continue to believe that fire would not burn him, or that he would be eternally damned if he received his *ingesta* otherwise than through a stomach pump. But then the man who adopts this method will not allow that its inconveniences are greater than its advantages. He will say, "I hold steadfastly to the truth and the truth is always wholesome." And in many cases it may very well be that the pleasure he derives from his calm faith overbalances any inconveniences resulting from its deceptive character. Thus, if it be true that death is annihilation, then the man who believes that he will certainly go straight to heaven when he dies, provided he have fulfilled certain simple observances in this life, has a cheap pleasure which will not be followed by the least disappointment. A similar consideration seems to have weight with many persons in religious topics, for we frequently hear it said, "Oh, I could not believe so-and-so, because I should be wretched if I did." When an ostrich buries its head in the sand as danger approaches, it very likely takes the happiest course. It hides the danger, and then calmly says there is no danger; and if it feels perfectly sure there is none, why should it raise its head to see? A man may go through life systematically keeping out of view all that might cause change in his opinions, and if he only succeeds—basing his method, as he does, on two fundamental psychological laws—I do not see what can be said against his doing so. It would be an egotistical impertinence to object that his procedure is irrational, for that only amounts to saying that his method of settling belief is not ours. He does not propose to himself to be rational, and indeed, will often talk with scorn of man's weak and illusive reason. So let him think as he pleases.

But this method of fixing belief, which may be called the method of tenacity, will be unable to hold its ground in practice. The social impulse is against it. The man who adopts it will find that other men think differently from him, and it will be apt to occur to him in some saner moment that their opinions are quite as good as his own, and this will shake his confidence in belief. This conception, that another man's thought or sentiment may be equivalent to one's own, is a distinctly new step, and a highly important one. It arises from an impulse too strong in man to be suppressed without danger of destroying the human species. Unless we make ourselves hermits, we shall necessarily influence each other's opinions; so that the problem becomes how to fix belief, not in the individual merely, but in the community.

2. THE METHOD OF AUTHORITY

Let the will of the state act, then, instead of that of the individual. Let an institution be created which shall have for its object to keep correct doctrines before the attention of the people, to reiterate them perpetually, and to teach them to the young; having at the same time power to prevent contrary doctrines from being taught, advocated, or expressed. Let all possible causes of a change of mind be removed from men's apprehensions. Let them be kept ignorant, lest they should learn of some reason to think otherwise than they do. Let their passions be enlisted, so that they may regard private and unusual opinions with hatred and horror. Then let all men who reject the established belief be terrified into silence. Let the people turn out and tar-and-feather such men, or let inquisitions be made into the manner of thinking of suspected persons, and when they are found guilty of forbidden beliefs, let them be subjected to some signal punishment. When complete agreement could not otherwise be reached, a general massacre of all who have not thought in a certain way has proved a very effective means of settling opinions in a country. If the power to do this be wanting, let a list of opinions be drawn up, to which no man of the least independence of thought can assent, and let the faithful be required to accept all these propositions, in order to segregate them as radically as possible from the influence of the rest of the world.

This method has, from the earliest times, been one of the chief means of upholding correct theological and political doctrines, and of preserving their universal or catholic character. In Rome, especially, it has been practiced from the days of Numa Pompilius to those of Pius Nonus. This is the most perfect example in history; but wherever there is a priesthood—and no religion has been without one—this method has been more or less made use of. Wherever there is aristocracy, or a guild, or any association of a class of men whose interests depend or are supposed to depend on certain propositions, there will inevitably be found some traces of this natural product of social feeling. Cruelties always accompany this system; and when it is consistently carried out, they become atrocities of the most horrible kind in the eyes of any rational man. Nor should this occasion surprise, for the officer of a society does not feel justified in surrendering the interests of that society for the sake of mercy, as he might his own private interests. It is natural, therefore, that sympathy and fellowship should thus produce a most ruthless power.

In judging this method of fixing belief, which may be called the method of authority, we must, in the first place, allow its immeasurable mental and moral superiority to the method of tenacity. Its success is proportionally greater; and in fact it has over and over again worked the most majestic results. The mere structures of stone which it has caused to be put together in Siam, for example, in Egypt, and in Europe—have many of them a sublimity hardly more than rivaled by the greatest works of Nature. And, except the geological epochs, there are no periods of time so vast as those which are measured by some of these organized faiths. If we scrutinize the matter closely, we shall find that there has not been one of their creeds which has remained always the same; yet the change is so slow as to be imperceptible during one person's life, so that individual belief remains sensibly fixed. For the mass of mankind, then, there is perhaps no better method than this. If it is their highest impulse to be intellectual slaves, then slaves they ought to remain.

3. THE A PRIORI METHOD

But no institution can undertake to regulate opinions upon every subject. Only the most important ones can be attended to, and on the rest men's minds must be left to the action of natural causes. This imperfection will be no source of weakness so long as men are in such a state of culture that one opinion does not influence another—that is, so long as they cannot put two and two together. But in the most priest-ridden states some individuals will be found who are raised above that condition. These men possess a wider sort of social feeling; they see that men in other countries and in other ages have held to very different doctrines from those which they themselves have been brought up to believe; and they cannot help seeing that it is the mere accident of their having been taught as they have, and of their having been surrounded with the manners and associations they have, that has caused them to believe as they do and not far differently. And their candor cannot resist the reflection that there is no reason to rate their own views at a higher value than those of other nations and other centuries; and this gives rise to doubts in their minds.

They will further perceive that such doubts as these must exist in their minds with reference to every belief which seems to be determined by the caprice either of themselves or of those who originated the popular opinions. The willful adherence to a belief, and the arbitrary forcing of it upon others, must, therefore, both be given up and a new method of settling opinions must be adopted, which shall not only produce an impulse to believe, but shall also decide what proposition it is which is to be believed. Let the action of natural preferences be unimpeded, then, and under their influence let men conversing together and regarding matters in different lights gradually develop beliefs in harmony with natural causes. This method resembles that by which conceptions of art have been brought to maturity. The most perfect example of it is to be found in the history of metaphysical philosophy. Systems of this sort have not usually rested upon observed facts, at least not in any great degree. They have been chiefly adopted because their fundamental propositions seemed "agreeable to reason." This is an apt expression; it does not mean that which agrees with experience, but that which we find ourselves inclined to believe. Plato, for example, finds it agreeable to reason that the distances of the celestial spheres from one another should be proportional to the different lengths of strings which produce harmonious chords. Many philosophers have been led to their main conclusions by considerations like this; but this is the lowest and least developed form which the method takes, for it is clear that another man might find Kepler's (earlier) theory, that the celestial spheres are proportional to the inscribed and circumscribed spheres of the different regular solids, more agreeable to *his* reason. But the shock of opinions will soon lead men to rest on preferences of a far more universal nature. Take, for example, the doctrine that man only acts selfishly—that is, from the consideration that acting in one way will afford him more pleasure than acting in another. This rests on no fact in the world, but it has had a wide acceptance as being the only reasonable theory.

This method is far more intellectual and respectable from the point of view of reason than either of the others which we have noticed. But its failure has been the most manifest. It makes of inquiry something similar to the development of taste; but taste, unfortunately, is always more or less a matter of fashion, and accordingly, metaphysicians have never come to any fixed agreement, but the pendulum has swung backward and forward between a more material and more spiritual philosophy, from the earliest times to the latest. And so from this, which has been called the *a priori* method, we are driven, in Lord Bacon's phrase, to a true induction. We have examined into this *a priori* method as something which promised to deliver our opinions from their accidental and capricious element. But development, while it is a process which eliminated the effect of some casual circumstances, only magnifies that of others. This method, therefore, does not differ in a very essential way from that of authority. The government may not have lifted its finger to influence my convictions; I may have been left outwardly quite free to choose, we will say, between monogamy and polygamy, and appealing to my conscience only, I may have concluded that the latter practice is in itself licentious. But when I come to see that the chief obstacle to the spread of Christianity among a people of as high culture as the Hindoos has been a conviction of the immorality of our way of treating women. I cannot help seeing that, though governments do not interfere, sentiments in their development will be very greatly determined by accidental causes. Now, there are some people, among whom I must suppose that my reader is to be found, who, when they see that any belief of theirs is determined by any circumstance extraneous to the facts, will from that moment not merely admit in words that the belief is doubtful, but will experience a real doubt of it, so that it ceases to be a belief.

4. THE METHOD OF SCIENCE

To satisfy our doubts, therefore, it is necessary that a method should be found by which our beliefs may be caused by nothing human, but by some external permanency—by something upon which our thinking has no effect. Some mystics imagine that they have such a method in a private inspiration from on high. But that is only a form of the method of tenacity, in which the conception of truth as something public is not yet developed. Our external permanency would not be external, in our sense, if it was restricted in its influence to one individual. It must be something which affects, or might affect, every man. And, though these affections are necessarily as various as are individual conditions, yet the method must be such that the ultimate conclusion of every man shall be the same. Such is the method of science. Its fundamental hypothesis, restated in more familiar language, is this: There are real things, whose characters are entirely independent of our opinions about them; those realities affect our senses according to regular laws, and, though our sensations are as different as our relations to the objects, yet, by taking advantage of the laws of perception, we can ascertain by reasoning how things really are, and any man, if he has sufficient experience and reason enough about it, will be led to the one true conclusion. The new conception here involved is that of reality. It may be asked how I know that there are any realities. If this hypothesis is the sole support of my method of inquiry, my method of inquiry must not be used to support my hypothesis. The reply is this: (1) If investigation cannot be regarded as proving that there are real things, it at least does not lead to a contrary conclusion; but the method and the conception on which it is based remain ever in harmony. No doubts of the method, therefore, necessarily arise from its practice, as is the case with all the others. (2) The feeling which gives rise to any method of fixing belief is a dissatisfaction at two repugnant propositions. But here already is a vague concession that there is some *one* thing to which a proposition should conform. Nobody, therefore, can really doubt that there are realities, or if he did, doubt would not be a source of dissatisfaction. The hypothesis, therefore, is one which every mind admits. So the social impulse does not cause me to doubt it. (3) Everybody uses the scientific method about a great many things, and only ceases to use it when he does not know how to apply it. (4) Experience of the method has not led me to doubt it, but, on the contrary, scientific investigation has had the most wonderful triumphs in the way of settling opinion. These afford the explanation of my not doubting the method or the hypothesis which it supposes; and not having any doubt, nor believing that anybody else whom I could influence has, it would be the merest babble for me to say more about it. If there be anybody with a living doubt upon the subject, let him consider it. . . .

At present I have only room to notice some points of contrast between the method of scientific investigation and other methods of fixing belief.

This is the only one of the four methods which presents any distinction of a right and a wrong way. If I adopt the method of tenacity and shut myself out from all influences, whatever I think necessary to doing this is necessary according to that method. So with the method of authority: The state may try to put down heresy by means which, from a scientific point of view, seem very ill-calculated to accomplish its purposes; but the only test *on that method* is what the state thinks, so that it cannot pursue the method wrongly. So with the *a priori* method. The very essence of it is to think as one is inclined to think. . . . But with the scientific method the case is different. I may start with known and observed facts to proceed to the unknown; and yet the rules which I follow in doing so may not be such as investigation would approve. The test of whether I am truly following the method is not an immediate appeal to my feelings and purposes, but, on the contrary, itself involves the application of the method. Hence it is that bad reasoning as well as good reasoning is possible: and this fact is the foundation of the practical side of logic. . . .

NOTES

1. Members of a cult.—Eds.
2. [Peirce apparently refers here to rationalism.]
3. [Peirce apparently refers here to empiricism.]

Some Consequences of Four Incapacities*

CHARLES SANDERS PEIRCE

DESCARTES IS THE FATHER of modern philosophy, and the spirit of Cartesianism—that which principally distinguishes it from the scholasticism which it displaced—may be compendiously stated as follows:

1. It teaches that philosophy must begin with universal doubt; whereas scholasticism had never questioned fundamentals.
2. It teaches that the ultimate test of certainty is to be found in the individual consciousness; whereas scholasticism had rested on the testimony of sages and of the Catholic Church.
3. The multiform argumentation of the middle ages is replaced by a single thread of inference depending often upon inconspicuous premisses.

**From "Some Consequences of Four Incapacities," in* Journal of Speculative Philosophy *(1868).*

4. Scholasticism had its mysteries of faith, but undertook to explain all created things. But there are many facts which Cartesianism not only does not explain, but renders absolutely inexplicable, unless to say that "God makes them so" is to be regarded as an explanation.

In some, or all of these respects, most modern philosophers have been, in effect, Cartesians. Now without wishing to return to scholasticism, it seems to me that modern science and modern logic require us to stand upon a very different platform from this.

1. We cannot begin with complete doubt. We must begin with all the prejudices which we actually have when we enter upon the study of philosophy. These prejudices are not to be dispelled by a maxim, for they are things which it does not occur to us *can* be questioned. Hence this initial scepticism will be a mere self-deception, and not real doubt; and no one who follows the Cartesian method will ever be satisfied until he has formally recovered all those beliefs which in form he has given up. It is, therefore, as useless a preliminary as going to the North Pole would be in order to get to Constantinople by coming down regularly upon a meridian. A person may, it is true, in the course of his studies, find reason to doubt what he began by believing; but in that case he doubts because he has a positive reason for it, and not on account of the Cartesian maxim. Let us not pretend to doubt in philosophy what we do not doubt in our hearts.

2. The same formalism appears in the Cartesian criterion, which amounts to this: "Whatever I am clearly convinced of, is true." If I were really convinced, I should have done with reasoning, and should require no test of certainty. But thus to make single individuals absolute judges of truth is most pernicious. The result is that metaphysicians will all agree that metaphysics has reached a pitch of certainty far beyond that of the physical sciences;—only they can agree upon nothing else. In sciences in which men come to agreement, when a theory has been broached, it is considered to be on probation until this agreement is reached. After it is reached, the question of certainty becomes an idle one, because there is no one left who doubts it. We individually cannot reasonably hope to attain the ultimate philosophy which we pursue; we can only seek it, therefore, for the *community* of philosophers. Hence, if disciplined and candid minds carefully examine a theory and refuse to accept it, this ought to create doubts in the mind of the author of the theory himself.

3. Philosophy ought to imitate the successful sciences in its methods, so far as to proceed only from tangible premisses which can be subjected to careful scrutiny, and to trust rather to the multitude and variety of its arguments than to the conclusiveness of any one. Its reasoning should not form a chain which is no stronger than its weakest link, but a cable whose fibres may be ever so slender, provided they are sufficiently numerous and intimately connected.

4. Every unidealistic philosophy supposes some absolutely inexplicable, unanalyzable ultimate; in short, something resulting from mediation itself not susceptible of mediation. Now that anything *is* thus inexplicable can only be known by reasoning from signs. But the only justification of an inference from signs is that the conclusion explains the fact. To suppose the fact absolutely inexplicable, is not to explain it, and hence this supposition is never allowable. . . .

Part III

Mind and Its Place in Nature

TO A LARGE DEGREE, what has come to be known as the "mind-body problem" in philosophy is a product of the philosophy of René Descartes. How can things differing as radically as minds (or souls) and bodies, in Descartes' conception, be so intimately related, as they clearly are, in every human person? Bodies are solid chunks of material stuff, extended in three-dimensional space, publicly observable and measurable, possessed of a certain mass and velocity, and capable of causing things to happen, in accordance with the invariant laws of mechanics, by transmitting their impact in "collisions" with other material things. A mind, on the other hand, is directly "observable" only by the person who owns it; only he can think his thoughts, feel his emotions, suffer his pains. Although, under certain circumstances, someone else can cut open his skull and see and touch his living *brain,* there is no conceivable way for another to see or touch his mind or its beliefs, sensations, and desires. Minds, moreover, have no size or shape or spatial location, no mass, or velocity, or capacity to make impact.

Nevertheless, to common sense, it seems certain that minds and bodies do causally interact. When I will, or wish, or desire (mental events) to raise my arm, up it goes (bodily event); and when a sliver of wood penetrates my flesh (bodily event), I feel pain (mental event). It would surely seem, then, that, in normal volition, mental events *cause* physical ones and that, in sensation and perception, physical events *cause* mental ones. Yet how can this be? How can the mind, a massless, weightless, unextended thing, push up against a nerve cell and cause an impulse to be transmitted along a nerve to a muscle? And how can physical stimuli such as wood slivers or even light rays penetrate a thing that has no size or location, and cause it to have an experience? Isn't this as inconceivable as a collision between a physical object and a ghost? This is the kind of difficulty cited by many of Descartes' own contemporaries in criticism of his philosophy.[1]

Many important seventeenth-century philosophers, no matter how impressed in other ways by the "Cartesian philosophy" (as the philosophy of Descartes came to be called), found Descartes' theory of interaction between mind and body unacceptable. Some, therefore, came to abandon the part of the Descartes' philosophy that generated the difficulty: his **dualism,** or theory that mind and matter are distinct and independent kinds of substances, each capable of existing quite independently of the other.[2] One alternative was **idealism:** the theory that the body itself is nothing but a collection of actual or possible sense-data—sights, sounds, touches, and smells. George Berkeley thought this way. Ac-

[1]A number of distinguished philosophers, theologians, and scientists, including Pierre Gassendi, Thomas Hobbes, and Antoine Arnauld, were invited to comment on the manuscript of Descartes' *Meditations* before it was published. Their "Objections" were then forwarded to Descartes, who in turn composed "Replies," and published the whole exchange along with the original work. The entire discussion is strongly recommended to the serious student of Descartes' philosophy.

[2]Strictly speaking, the traditional mind-body problem was generated by a conjunction of two theories, (1) dualism as defined above and (2) the theory sometimes called **two-way interactionism,** the latter being simply the commonsense assumption that mind and body can interact causally, sometimes mental events causing bodily events, as in volition, sometimes bodily events causing mental ones, as when a decayed tooth causes pain sensations.

cording to this theory, there are only minds and their mental "contents"; hence, there are no problems of causal interaction between radically different kinds of substances. Yet another alternative was **materialism**—the theory that mind is reducible to matter.[3] Still other philosophers maintained a kind of dualism but abandoned the commonsense view that mind and body really do interact causally. Some held, for example, that the wood sliver's penetration of my flesh does not *cause* me pain; rather, it is the *occasion* for God, whose infinite nature somehow encompasses both mind and matter, to cause me to feel pain, and similarly that my desire to raise my arm is simply the occasion for God's causing my arm to go up. This is the theory called **occasionalism.** Others held the view called **parallelism,** according to which mind and body only appear to interact because of a kind of "pre-established harmony" between their life histories. Gottfried Leibniz likened this parallelism to two clocks that strike at the same moment, having been wound up together and each designed to keep accurate time, in causal independence of each other.

In his useful summary, Jerome Shaffer reviews the arguments for and against not only dualism but also most of the other leading theories about "the subject of consciousness," including the "double-aspect" theory of Baruch Spinoza (1632–1677) and the "person theory" of Oxford philosopher P. F. Strawson. Spinoza denied that mind and body are distinct and independent substances, each capable of existing entirely on its own. Rather they are two "aspects" of a substance that in itself is neither mental nor physical. Strawson calls this underlying entity the *person*—a being who has both physical attributes such as weight and height and mental attributes such as beliefs and emotions. It is the person—not the mind or body—who walks, breathes, and digests food and also who thinks, chooses, enjoys some things, and feels anxiety about other things. The person theory has very attractive features, but Shaffer also points out that it has difficulties of its own; most importantly, it does not provide a philosophically adequate account of the human body.

Many twentieth-century philosophers would agree with Shaffer's final tentative suggestion that some duly modified form of dualism can withstand the traditional attacks against that theory. However, the question is still extremely controversial. It is likely that the leading rivals to dualism in this scientific age are the philosophies that emphasize the priority of physical (or "material") processes in nature. One such philosophy is **epiphenomenalism,** which holds that mind is not itself a material thing; rather, it is a distinct but causally impotent by-product (an "epiphenomenon") of the world charted by physics. Because it emphasizes the priority of the physical, epiphenomenalism might be classified as a form of materialism. But strictly speaking, that would be incorrect. Most philosophers prefer to classify it as a form of dualism in which the interaction is just one way (from body to mind). After all, epiphenomenalists do deny that mind is a material thing.[4] One genuinely materialistic alternative to dualism is the **identity theory,** which holds that mental events (the occurrence of aches and pains, sensations, after-images, desires, and thoughts) are simply identical with brain processes—"identical" in the same way that lightning flashes are "iden-

[3]*Materialism* as the name of a philosophical theory should not be confused with various other senses of the word. A philosophical materialist is *not* (necessarily) "a person who tends to give undue importance to material possessions and comforts." Nor is he (necessarily) "a person who thinks that everybody ought to put his "material well-being' (as measured in dollars and cents) above all other considerations." A philosophical materialist could, with consistency, denounce materialism in these other senses.

[4]However, in denying that mind has causal efficacy, they also deny that it is a *substance* at all, in the traditional sense. In seventeenth-century terms, these thinkers would not be dualists because they hold that there is only one *kind* of substance—the material kind.

tical" with electrical discharges. Here the identity in question is **intertheoretic reduction.** In these cases, we reduce items in our commonsense theory of the world to items in a mature physics or neuroscience.

Another more radical form of physicalism is **eliminative materialism.** On this view, championed by Paul Churchland in our selections, mental states and processes as we ordinarily conceive of them really have a status like that of witches and phlogiston and must simply be eliminated from our theorizing about ourselves. On the other side, however, many cognitive scientists believe that some sense will have to be made of our ordinary notions of mind. The development of computer technology in recent years has spurred the development of **functional** approaches to the mind. According to **functionalist theories,** the identity theory (also called **type physicalism**) is problematic because it holds that the mental and intellectual properties of a "system" (e.g., a person) depend on the specific physical (brain) properties of that system, whereas apparently many quite different physical systems (e.g., those that are constructed to process information) can perform the same intelligent tasks.

As the Churchland selection makes clear, functionalism sees itself as reconciling the best features of both **physicalism** and **behaviorism,** without succumbing to the deficiencies of either. Functionalism, like behaviorism, defines mental states relationally (in terms of input, output, and internal transitions), so there is no commitment to any specific type of matter. But unlike behaviorism, functionalism claims that all actual mental state tokens (instances) are identical to physical state tokens (instances), so functionalism, unlike behaviorism and dualism, can explain mental causation as a species of ordinary physical causation.

Perhaps the greatest difficulty facing any physicalist (i.e., materialist) theory is what many have called "the qualia problem." **Qualia** are the peculiarly subjective, felt qualities of experience, such as the smell of a hard-boiled egg, the taste of horseradish, or the fiery image of a sunset. In his piece for this section, Frank Jackson presents a much-discussed argument designed to show that no amount of knowledge about how the brain works can give us knowledge of what it is to feel such things. Therefore, according to Jackson, these sorts of mental experiences cannot be physical ones. Jackson concludes that physicalism must be false.

Many issues central to the mind–body problem are pursued in the next section, Can Non-Humans Think? John Searle's provocative paper "Minds, Brains, and Programs," challenges the adequacy of a certain form of functionalism, the sort exemplified by current attempts to program computers to perform "intelligent" tasks. Searle contends that in order to have "intelligent" mental states, it is not enough that we suppose that the system simply is running the right program because these mental states are not the kinds that *can* be programmed into a machine. Searle then considers a wide variety of possible objections to his view and attempts to refute each.

As far back as the seventeenth century, at least, philosophers have been fascinated by apparent similarities between human (rational) beings and machines. Excited by discoveries in medicine and physiology, some eighteenth century philosophers asked whether humans might really be nothing but machines themselves. In our own day most of the excitement comes from those scientists who work on the machine side, not so much from new discoveries in human biology, though the latter have been accumulating at a great rate, too. This new emphasis is reflected in the way the philosophical interest is expressed. Now we do not ask whether, in principle, machines could be designed that are a kind of human, that is to say, intelligent conscious beings like us. Many philosophers would answer unhesitatingly

"No, of course not. Computers are made of wires and springs, silicon chips, and the like, not protoplasm (flesh and blood) like us." To that kind of remark William Lycan has a ready reply: "What matters to mentality is not the stuff of which one is made, but the complex way in which that stuff is organized."

Perplexity about whether nonhuman beings could have human-like consciousness that enables them to be aware of the world and not mere reflexive reactors to stimuli, whether they can think, and if so, whether that thinking amounts to reasoning, extends also to animals like horses, cows, dogs, cats, whales, and parrots. Colin Allen has contributed to this section an ingenious piece of "philosophical fiction" entitled "Star Witness," which tells the story of a judicial hearing in which a judge listens to the arguments of a prosecutor and a defense attorney over the admissibility in a criminal case of the testimony of a *parrot.* Most of the arguments that have divided philosophers on the questions of animal thought and animal language over the centuries are represented here in the arguments Allen ascribes to his fictitious lawyers. In the end, it is the student reader, however, who must ascribe the final arguments (his or her own) to the judge.

The concluding articles in Part Three relate the discussion back to one of Descartes' original concerns: whether "in death there is an end of me." This question, of course, presupposes the questions preceding it about the nature of the subject of consciousness. If body and mind are one and the same thing, or if mind is a mere **epiphenomenon** or by-product of body, then it would follow that the disintegration of mind (soul, self) would proceed at the same pace with the disintegration of the body. But if our minds are distinct substances and causally efficacious in their own right, then it is at least possible that they (we) can survive the death of their (our) bodies. If we are to make philosophical progress in our discussions of the possibility of survival, however, we need to move beyond common understanding of the nature of mind and examination of the empirical evidence (if any). In addition, we must become clear about a set of prior questions that are not normally treated in works on the mind-body problem—namely, questions about *personal identity,* Who or what am I, this entity whose possible survival of death is under discussion? Am I simply this body and nothing more? What then of my belief that this body "belongs" to me, that the owner is one thing and the body another? Am I simply my mind? Am I a self that somehow emcompasses both body and mind? Could I be the *same self* that I am now if I had none of my present memories, or if I suddenly discovered myself with an altogether different body (for example, with four legs and a tail)? How much can I change without ceasing to be the person I am now? These are only some of the riddles associated with the elusive concept of personal identity. Still others are suggested by more recondite possibilities: resurrection of the dead, reincarnation, transmigration of souls, bodily transfers, multiple or alternate possession of a body by various persons, brain transplants, and "brain rejuvenations"—examples drawn from theology, psychic research, abnormal psychology, and science fiction.

The section on "Personal Identity and the Survival of Death" begins with a fictional tale designed to test philosophical theories and induce philosophical perplexity. Daniel Dennett spins a yarn in which the leading character (one Daniel Dennett, philosopher and patriot) is separated from his brain. His subsequent adventures are enough to throw our common-sense notions of selfhood and identity into complete disarray and to challenge the philosopher to put them in order again. Philosophers who have attempted to do this have struggled against a rising tide of ingenious hypothetical examples. Their efforts are often directed at first to the general problem of identity, not restricted to the case of identity between persons. When a physical object like a sock or a ship begins with one set of properties and very gradually changes these properties, can we say at a later time that the new object is the same object that we began with? How different from the earlier object can the later object be and still be identical to the original? Similar questions asked about humans, of course, are likely to be more interesting to us. Am I the same person I was when I emerged from the womb? If I am a genuinely penitent, morally newborn criminal who has been on death row for ten years, can my lawyer claim that I am *not* the same man who committed a brutal murder a decade earlier? What if my earlier self arranged with a surgeon, in a science fiction example, to transplant my brain in another person and that person's brain in me?

The most frequently proposed theories of personal identity are first, that it is the persistence of *memory* that preserves personal identity through change, and second, that *bodily continuity* is the crucial condition underlying identity. (If it is the same body, then it is the same person.) Terence Penelhum sketches these theories, discusses their strengths and weaknesses, and their bearing on the possibility of surviving one's own death.

In the deathbed dialogue by John Perry that concludes this section, Professor Perry focuses sharply on the area where the problem of survival and the riddles of personal identity intersect. A dying professor, her old friend (a clergyman), and her student discuss quite spontaneously the famous philosophical theories of John Locke, Joseph Butler, and Anthony Collins—seminal thinkers of the seventeenth and eighteenth centuries—about personal identity. At issue is the question of what sense, if any, can be made of the very idea of personal survival.

The Mind-Body Problem

The Subject of Consciousness*

JEROME A. SHAFFER

Jerome A. Shaffer (1929–) teaches philosophy at the University of Connecticut. He is a leading figure in the philosophy of mind.

IT WOULD SEEM to be an undeniable fact that consciousness does exist and that any account of the world will have to give some place to it. But what place? What is the relation of consciousness to whatever else does exist? In particular, what is the relation of consciousness to the organic and inorganic matter that makes up so great a part of the world? And, more particularly, what is the relation of consciousness to those organic systems we know as human bodies? . . .

We can begin our inquiry by asking what is the subject of consciousness, in other words, *what* is

**Jerome A. Shaffer,* Philosophy of Mind, *© 1968, pp. 34–59. Reprinted by permission of the author and Prentice-Hall, Inc., Englewood Cliffs, New Jersey.*

conscious when consciousness exists? Well, what sorts of things have consciousness? One pretty indisputable case is that of . . . human beings. But what is a . . . human being? Is he just a particular kind of matter formed in a particular way? Or is there more to the story, and if so what more? If a man is *more* than a particularly formed kind of matter, then is it some part of that *more* which is the subject of consciousness?

To make the discussion manageable, let us confine ourselves to that form of consciousness which consists in having what I shall call mental events: those particular occasions which consist in the having of some thought, the feeling of some sensation, the imaging of some mental picture, the entertaining of some wish, etc. Our problem, then, will be to determine *what* it is that has the thought, feels the sensation, images the mental picture, entertains the wish, etc.

The various theories concerning *what* has the mental events fall into three basic categories. (1) There is the view that they happen to purely *nonmaterial* things. Proponents of such a view usually admit the existence of purely *material* things in addition to these purely nonmaterial things; hence they are called dualists. (2) There is the view that they happen to purely *material* things; we shall call this materialism. And (3) there is the view that they happen to things which are neither purely material nor purely nonmaterial; we shall call this the person theory. Each shall be considered and evaluated in turn.

DUALISM

The most systematic dualistic theory is that which was presented by the French philosopher Descartes. He held that the subject of consciousness is the *mind* and that the mind is a thing or entity separate and distinct from the body. The body is a thing or entity whose essence (defining characteristic) is occupying space, i.e., having shape, size, and location in space; and it is in no sense conscious. The mind, on the other hand, is completely different in its nature. It is utterly nonspatial, having neither shape, size, nor location. Its essence (defining characteristic) is simply having consciousness, that is, thoughts, feelings, memories, perceptions, desires, emotions, etc.

Descartes held that since the mind and the body are separate entities, each can exist without the other. It is obvious and undeniable that Descartes is at least correct in holding that *some* bodies—e.g., stones and lakes—do indeed exist without minds. Descartes himself believed that animals (other than man) were also examples of bodies without minds. Some people might disagree with him there, and there would be even more disagreement with his thesis that minds could exist without bodies. Descartes believed that minds were immortal, that they continue to exist as disembodied minds after the body has perished in death.

There is an important gap in Descartes' account, a gap which can be noted in the summary just given. From the fact that the essence of the mind is one thing, having consciousness, and the essence of the body is another, occupying space, it does not follow that the mind and the body are *two separate entities*. What is to rule out the possibility that one and the same thing can have *both* these properties, be *both* a thinking thing and at the very same time an extended thing? The essence, that is, the defining characteristic, of being a husband is being a married man and the essence of being a parent is having offspring, but one and the same person can be both a husband *and* a parent (and, obviously, can be one without being the other). This gap in Descartes' reasoning was first pointed out by Spinoza, who had been a follower of Descartes. Spinoza realized that "although two attributes may be conceived as really distinct," and here he has in mind thinking and extension, "we cannot nevertheless thence conclude that they constitute two beings or two different substances."[1] Then, breaking decisively with Descartes, Spinoza went on to maintain that in the case of human beings (and, as a matter of fact, for Spinoza, in everything else as well), both thinking *and* space-occupancy were characteristics of one and the same thing. This view shall be discussed later under the heading of double aspect theory.

Nevertheless, Descartes held that one and the same thing could not be both a space-occupier and a thinking thing. He seems to have thought that these characteristics were simply so different in their natures that one and the same thing *could* not have both. Thus he cites the fact that extended things are divisible, whereas thinking things are not divisible (see his sixth *Meditation*). But this is a very weak line of argument. Since thinking and occupying space are different characteristics, there will naturally be differences between them. Extended things will necessarily be divisible (I take it Descartes is here thinking of *spatially* dividing something), and things which are nonextended, say disembodied minds, will not be so divisible. But this is just to say that we have different characteristics here. A thing which thinks would be divisible if it were at the same time an extended thing. So pointing out differences between extension and thinking does not show us that things which have the one characteristic cannot have the other. Perhaps Descartes had in mind the point that extension and thinking are *so very* different, so basically different. Of course one object could be both red and round, he might say, but could one object be both red and thinking? Here again, however, the line of argument is weak. Being red and being valuable and being holy are *very* different sorts of properties, yet one and the same object, say a particular jewel, might be all three. So we still do not have a very good reason for thinking that thinking things could not be extended and vice versa.

Even if the dualist fails to give us a reason for holding that thinking things and extended things are *different* entities, still such a view might be correct. And we have not yet seen any reason for thinking it is *not* correct. So let us, for the moment, grant the dualist his claim that they are different entities. If we do so, the question arises how these two different entities are related to each other, if at all. Here we find ourselves faced with what is traditionally known in philosophy as the mind-body problem.

THE TRADITIONAL MIND-BODY PROBLEM

. . . In order to get a better grasp of dualism we will here take a brief look at the various theories [of the mind-body problem] that have been proposed. Descartes himself believed that sometimes the mind could causally affect the body and sometimes the body could causally affect the mind; this view is called interactionism. An example of the former would be a case in which, after deliberation, I decide (a mental event) to press the button and then my hand reaches out to press it (a bodily event); an example of the latter would be a case in which the moving hand (a bodily event) comes in contact with the button, causing in me a feeling of fear (a mental event) at what will happen if I do press the button.

Interactionism is not the only dualistic theory of the relation between mind and body. Some philosophers have held that there is only *one-way* causality, from body to mind; this view is known as epiphenomenalism. The epiphenomenalist accepts one half of the interactionist contention, that part which holds that bodily events can cause mental events. But he denies the other half; he denies that mental events can ever cause bodily events. Whatever happens in the mind is merely a by-product of bodily activity (most plausibly, brain activity). No important philosopher has ever held what we might call reverse epiphenomenalism, namely that bodily events are *always* merely effects of mental activity. The religion of Christian Science comes somewhat close to this view, holding that bodily events, particularly those concerning health and disease, are results of mental activity. Many Christian Scientists would go so far as to maintain that *all* bodily events, for example the activity in our sense organs during perception, are caused solely by mental activity. This is the view of the eighteenth-century Irish philosopher George Berkeley, that anything that ever happens at all happens only in the mind. Berkeley's view is no longer dualism; he holds that only minds exist and that matter and in particular bodies do not exist at all, except in the mind.

Finally, there is the dualist theory known as parallelism. The parallelist admits the close connection of events in the mind and events in the body, but does not wish to say that the connection is a causal one, for he holds that the mind and the body are too utterly different to be able to interact causally with each other. So the parallelist holds that the mind and the body are like two clocks, each with its own mechanism and with no causal connection between them, yet always in phase keeping the same time.

OBJECTIONS TO DUALISM

Dualist theories are not very much in favor these days. There are two main sources of discontent with them. (1) Many philosophers have grave doubts that the notion of the mind as a thing or entity can be rendered intelligible. (2) Even if it could be made intelligible, the view of the world which results seems to many unnecessarily complex. We will discuss these two sources of discontent in order.

(1) Dualists tell us that in addition to the familiar objects of everyday life, tables, rocks, hair, trees, clouds, air, in short material things, there also exist things of a quite different kind—minds. These minds are real things, real objects, real entities, but they are fundamentally different sorts of things from material things. Well then, what is a mind? Is it a peculiar kind of stuff, immaterial matter, insubstantial substance, bodiless body? It is supposed to have no extension, that is, no shape, size, or capacity to occupy space; it is not visible to the eye, tangible to the touch, nor is it visible under any microscope however powerful, [or] tangible to the most delicate of probing instruments. Perhaps the mind is like a gravitational, magnetic, or electrical field? But it cannot be, for on the dualist's hypothesis the mind is in no way physical; if it were like them, or like physical energy of some sort, then it would be a *physical* phenomenon and we would no longer be dualists. Yet if it is in no way like such things, in what sense is the mind a thing at all? What meaning can we give to the notion of the mind as an existent thing?

The problem comes out in two particular ways, in the problem of identification and the problem of individuation. The former problem concerns how we can tell when we are in the presence of some other mind A rather than B or even in the presence of any other mind at all. Since, on the dualist account, another mind is not detectible by any observations we could make, it is impossible that we should have any reason to think we could ever identify another mind as mind A or B. So we could never justifiably believe we were, for example, talking to someone. And a concept of a mind which made it impossible justifiably to apply that concept to any other thing would be utterly useless, even if intelligible.

The problem of individuation concerns what makes two minds distinct, assuming there could be two distinct minds. One answer might be that they have different mental histories, each having had different mental events at certain times. But it seems perfectly intelligible to suppose that at some time we might have two distinct minds with exactly the same history of mental events (each might have grown up in exactly the same way). And, if this supposition of two exactly similar minds is intelligible, then what would make them two distinct minds rather than one and the same mind? The dualist does not seem to have an answer. He must say they are distinct, and yet he cannot say how or in what respect they differ. Does that make any sense?

(2) Even if we were able to give some *meaning* to the claim that minds exist, many contemporary philosophers would reject the claim that in fact minds do exist. They would make the remark attributed to the French astronomer Laplace in reply to Napoleon's question about the role of God in the system: said Laplace, "Sire, I have no need of that hypothesis." Thus many philosophers would argue that everything that happens in the world can be explained without using the notion of minds, strictly on the basis of physical phenomena and physical laws.

The view that minds do not exist at all and that only the physical exists is called materialism. We shall now turn to this view.

MATERIALISM

Materialism is one of the very oldest theories. It was a familiar doctrine to the ancient Greeks of the fourth and fifth centuries B.C. The spokesman for this view, Democritus, held that nothing exists but material atoms and the void and that everything in the world is nothing but the interactions of these atoms as they move through the void. Even the most complex behavior of human beings can be resolved into interactions between the atoms. A modern materialist would allow a more complicated picture than "atoms and the void." He would bring in subatomic particles and antiparticles, electromagnetic waves, a relativized view of "the void," various kinds of forces and energies, and the rest of the conceptual apparatus of contemporary physics. But he would still hold that nothing exists but such physical phenomena; if such terms as "thought," "feeling," "wish," etc., have any meaning at all, they must refer in the last analysis to physical phenomena. So-called mental events are really nothing but physical events occurring to physical objects.

We should, at the outset, distinguish materialism as characterized here from another doctrine which has already been mentioned, epiphenomenalism. . . . The latter is a dualistic theory which allows that the mind is separate and distinct from the body but also insists that the mind is utterly dependent causally upon the body, that everything which happens in the mind is a result of events in the body, and that the mind is utterly powerless to affect the body in any way. Such a view is often called materialistic, since it places the highest *importance* on the material side of things. It is in this sense that Karl Marx was materialistic, for he held that "conceiving, thinking, the mental intercourse of men, appear at [the earliest] stage as the direct efflux of their material behavior."[2] Notice that Marx is not saying men's conceiving, thinking, and mental intercourse *are nothing but* their material behavior. That would be materialism as here characterized. He is saying that they are the "efflux," i.e., a *separate, nonmaterial* outflow which originates and derives from material behavior. Such a view is not materialistic in our sense.

The materialist holds that nothing but the physical exists—matter, energy, and the void. But then what *are* thoughts, feelings, wishes, and the other so-called mental phenomena? Here four different answers have been seriously proposed. The most radical view, supported by very few, is that such terms have *no real meaning at all* and should be dropped from the language. They represent an accretion to our language which was conceived in ignorance and superstition, nurtured by the vested interests of religion and the black arts, and condoned by human lethargy. On this view, mentalistic terms should be allowed to suffer the fate of the language of witchcraft and demonic possession. Let us call this the unintelligibility thesis.

The unintelligibility thesis has not gained much support among contemporary philosophers. In the first place, it is clear why notions of witchcraft and demonic possession died out—it has been shown pretty conclusively by science that no such phenomena in fact exist. There might have been witches, and, in that case, there could have been a science which studied them and the ways in which they achieved their effects; but the evidence indicates that there are no such things. But this is hardly the case with mentalistic terms. What kind of discoveries could show that in fact there are no thoughts, feelings, wishes, and the like? On the contrary, is it not as plain as anything can be that there are such things? And, secondly, we could not dispense with mentalistic terms, even if our theories told us it was most desirable to do so, nor does it seem likely we will be able to do for the foreseeable future. This is because we often want to tell our thoughts, describe our feelings, express our wishes, and there is no other way available of doing so than saying I just had the thought . . . , I feel . . . , I wish. . . . To abandon such expressions would be to impoverish our language to the point of bankruptcy.

Another materialistic reply to the question "What are thoughts, feelings, wishes, and the like?" is called the avowal theory. This theory allows that sentences like "I feel bored" have meaning all right, but are not used to make *statements,* are not used to describe or report or assert anything. They are simply bits of behavior, the effects of certain inner (physical) conditions. If I yawn, twiddle my thumbs, or say "Ho hum," I am not describing, reporting, or asserting anything; I am not making a statement which is either true or false. The avowal theory takes "I feel bored" to be a (learned) bit of behavior, like "Ho hum," which results from certain inner (physical) conditions, and not a statement, description, report, or assertion at all. And the same would go for utterances of the form "I just had the thought that . . . ," "I wish that . . . ," and the like.

It cannot be denied that there is some truth in the avowal theory. Certainly such utterances are sometimes used in this way, as expressions of inner states—"I feel bored" is sometimes uttered in the way that "God, I'm bored!" or even "Oh God, what boredom!" is uttered, and it is clear at least in the latter case that no statement, description, report, or assertion is being made. Yet the avowal theory falls down in two important respects. First, it is utterly implausible when applied to third-person statements, e.g., "He is bored." In no way can such a remark be taken as the expression of an inner state. Second, even in their first-person use, such utterances are often used merely to report or describe. If someone asks me why I keep looking at my watch, I may say "Because I am bored," making a report which explains my behavior. Furthermore, I can use such utterances to make *false* statements, as when I am lying. "Ho hum" cannot be used to explain anything or to lie about anything. So the avowal theory will not do.

Another materialistic account is to allow that expressions referring to thoughts, feelings, wishes, and the like have meaning, but to insist that their meanings can be expressed in purely physicalistic terms. What physicalistic terms? The most plausible candidate is the set of terms which refer to physical *behavior.* This account [is] known as behaviorism. . . .

This behavioristic version of materialism has had a strong appeal for philosophers over the years. In contrast with the unintelligibility thesis, it allows sentences containing mentalistic terms to have meaning, and, in contrast, with the avowal theory, it allows them to be either true or false in the situations in which they are used. And by using the concept of *disposition to behave,* it allows such sentences to be true even where the person is not at that moment behaving in any particular fashion. Yet by tying the meaning to *behavior* the theory allows sentences with mentalistic terms to be testable by observation in an open and public way. To determine whether someone has a headache we only have to see if, under suitable conditions, he behaves in the appropriate ways.

This view, however, is open to a fundamental objection. . . . No matter what sort of behavior or behavioral dispositions we imagine as allegedly constituting a particular mental event, we can always imagine just that behavior or those dispositions *without* that mental event. We can imagine that behavior as coming from some *other* cause, or even as inexplicably *spontaneous.* Therefore behavior and behavioral dispositions do not furnish an exhaustive analysis of these mentalistic terms. There is something left out by such accounts.

The last version of materialism we shall consider, and currently the most seriously discussed, is known as the identity theory. It is the theory that thoughts, feelings, wishes, and the rest of so-called mental phenomena are identical with, one and the same thing as, states and processes of the *body* (and, perhaps, more specifically, states and processes of the nervous system, or even of the brain alone). Thus the having of a thought is identical with having such and such bodily cells in such and such states, other cells in other states.

In one respect the identity theory and behaviorism are very much alike. This comes out when we ask ourselves what the "dispositions" of the behaviorist are. If an object has a "disposition," then *it is in a particular state* such that when certain things happen to it, other things will happen to it. Thus if an object is brittle, it is in a particular state such that when subject to a sudden force it will shatter. And similarly dispositions of a body to behave in particular ways are *states of that body.* So it is fair to say that both identity theorists and behaviorists identify the mental with *bodily states.* But one important way in which they differ concerns how those states are to be defined or characterized. As we have seen, behaviorists wish to define those states in terms of what changes they result in when certain specifiable conditions obtain. Identity theorists wish to define them in terms of identifiable structures of the body, ongoing processes and states of the bodily organs, and, in the last analysis, the very cells which go to make up those organs.

There is another important respect in which the identity theory differs from behaviorism. The behaviorist offered his notion of dispositions to behave in certain ways as an analysis of the very meaning of mentalistic terms. But the identity theorist grants that it is wildly implausible to claim that what I *mean* when I say, for example, that I just had a particular thought is that certain events were going on in my nervous system. For I have no idea what those events are, nor does even the most advanced neurophysiologist at the present time, and yet I know what I mean when I say I just had a particular thought. So, since I know what I mean by those words, I cannot mean by them something I know nothing about (viz., unknown events in my nervous system). Hence the identity theory is not intended to be an analysis of the *meanings* of mentalistic terms as behaviorism purports to be. What, then, is the theory that mental phenomena are "identical" with the body intended to be?

The sense of "identity" relevant here is that in which we say, for example, that the morning star is "identical" with the evening star. It is not that the expression "morning star" means the same as the expression "evening star"; on the contrary, these expressions mean something different. But the object referred to by the two expressions is one and the same; there is just one heavenly body, namely, Venus, which when seen in the morning is called the morning star and when seen in the evening is called the evening star. The morning star is identical with the evening star; they are one and the same object.

Of course, the identity of the mental with the physical is not exactly of this sort, since it is held to be simultaneous identity rather than the identity of a thing at one time with the same thing at a later time. To take a closer example, one can say that lightning is a particularly massive electrical discharge from one cloud to another or to the earth. Not that the word "lightning" *means* "a particularly massive electrical discharge . . ."; when Benjamin Franklin discovered that lightning was electrical, he did not make a discovery about the meaning of words. Nor when it was discovered that water was H_2O was a discovery made about the meanings of words; yet water is identical with H_2O.

In a similar fashion, the identity theorist can hold that thoughts, feelings, wishes, and the like are identical with physical states. Not "identical" in the sense that mentalistic terms are synonymous in meaning with physicalistic terms but "identical" in the sense that the actual events picked out by mentalistic terms are one and the same events as those picked out by physicalistic terms.

It is important to note that the identity theory does not have a chance of being true unless a particular sort of correspondence obtains between mental events and physical events, namely, that whenever a mental event occurs, a physical event of a particular sort (or at least one of a number of particular sorts) occurs, and vice versa. If it turned out to be the case that when a particular mental event occurred it seemed a matter of chance what physical events occurred or even whether any physical event at all occurred, or vice versa, then the identity theory would not be true. So far as our state of knowledge at the present time is concerned, it is still too early to say what the empirical facts are, although it must be said that many scientists do believe that there exists the kind of correspondences needed by identity theorists. But even if these correspondences turn out to exist, that does not mean that the identity theory will be true. For identity theorists do not hold merely that mental and physical events are correlated in a particular way but that they are one and the same events, i.e., not like lightning and thunder (which are correlated in lawful ways but not identical) but like lightning and electrical discharges (which always go together because they are one and the same).

What are the advantages of the identity theory? As a form of materialism, it does not have to cope with a world which has in it both mental phenomena and physical phenomena, and it does not have to ponder how they might be related. There exist only the physical phenomena, although there do exist two different ways of talking about such phenomena: physicalistic terminology and, in at least some situations, mentalistic terminology. We have here a dualism of language, but not a dualism of entities, events, or properties.

SOME DIFFICULTIES IN THE IDENTITY THEORY

But do we have merely a dualism of languages and no other sort of dualism? In the case of Venus, we do indeed have only one object, but the expression "morning star" picks out one phase of that object's history, where it is in the mornings, and the expression "evening star" picks out another phase of that object's history, where it is in the evenings. If that object did not have these two distinct aspects, it would not have been a *discovery* that the morning star and the evening star were indeed one and the same body, and, further, there would be no point to the different ways of referring to it.

Now it would be admitted by identity theorists that physicalistic and mentalistic terms do not refer to different phases in the history of one and the same object. What sort of identity is intended? Let us turn to an allegedly closer analogy, that of the identity of lightning and a particular sort of electrical phenomenon. Yet here again we have two distinguishable aspects, the appearance to the naked eye on the one hand and the physical composition on the other. And this is also not the kind of identity which is plausible for mental and physical events. The appearance *to the naked eye* of a neurological event is utterly different from the experience of having a thought or a pain.

It is sometimes suggested that the physical aspect results from looking at a particular event "from the outside," whereas the mental results from looking at the same event "from the inside." When the brain surgeon observes my brain he is looking at it from the outside, whereas when I experience a mental event I am "looking" at my brain "from the inside."

Such an account gives us only a misleading analogy, rather than an accurate characterization of the relationship between the mental and the physical. The analogy suggests the difference between a man who knows his own house from the inside, in that he is free to move about within, seeing objects from different perspectives, touching them, etc., but can never get outside to see how it looks from there, and a man who cannot get inside and therefore knows only the outside appearance of the house, and perhaps what he can glimpse through the windows. But what does this have to do with the brain? Am I free to roam about inside my brain, observing what the brain surgeon may never see? Is not the "inner" aspect of my brain far more accessible to the brain surgeon than to me? He has the X rays, probes, electrodes, scalpels, and scissors for getting at the inside of my brain. If it is replied that this is only an analogy, not to be taken literally, then the question still remains how the mental and the physical are related.

Usually identity theorists at this point flee to even vaguer accounts of the relationship. They talk of different "levels of analysis," or of different "perspectives," or of different "conceptual schemes," or of different "language games." The point of such suggestions is that the difference between the mental and the physical is not a basic, fundamental, or intrinsic one, but rather a difference which is merely relative to different human purposes or standpoints. The difference is supposed to exist not in the thing itself but in the eye of the beholder.

But these are only hints. They do not tell us in precise and literal terms how the mental and the physical differ and are related. They only try to assure us that the difference does not matter to the real nature of things. But until we are given a theory to consider, we cannot accept the identity theorists' assurance that some theory will do only he does not know what it is.

One of the leading identity theorists, J. J. C. Smart, holds that mentalistic discourse is simply a vaguer, more indefinite way of talking about what could be talked about more precisely by using physiological terms. If I report a red afterimage, I mean (roughly) that something is going on which is like what goes on when I really see a red patch. I do not actually *mean* that a particular sort of brain process is occurring, but when I say something is going on I refer (very vaguely, to be sure) to just that brain process. Thus the thing referred to in my report of an afterimage is a brain process. Hence there is no need to bring in any nonphysical features. Thus even the taint of dualism is avoided.

Does this ingenious attempt to evade dualistic implications stand up under philosophical scrutiny? I am inclined to think it will not. Let us return to the man reporting the red afterimage. He was aware of the occurrence of something or other, of some feature or other. Now it seems to me obvious that he was not necessarily aware of the state of his brain at that time (I doubt that most of us are ever aware of the state of our brain) nor, in general, necessarily aware of any physical features of his body at that time. He might, of course, have been incidentally aware of some physical feature but not insofar as he was aware of the red afterimage as such. Yet he was definitely aware of something, or else how could he have made that report? So he must have been aware of some nonphysical feature. That is the only way of explaining how he was aware of anything at all.

Of course, the thing that our reporter of the afterimage was aware of might well have had further features which he was *not* aware of, particularly, in this connection, physical features. I may be aware of certain features of an object without being aware of others. So it is not ruled out that the event our reporter is aware of might be an event with predominantly physical features—he just does not notice those. But he must be aware of some of its features, or else it would not be proper to say he was aware of *that* event. And if he is not aware of any physical features, he must be aware of something else. And that shows that we cannot get rid of those nonphysical features in the way that Smart suggests.

One would not wish to be dogmatic in saying that identity theorists will never work out this part of their theory. Much work is being done on this problem at the present time, for it arises in other areas of philosophy as well as in the philosophy of mind. In particular philosophers of science are concerned with the problem. We saw that the identity theory used such analogies as the identity of lightning with electrical phenomena and the identity of water with molecules consisting of hydrogen and oxygen. But the question to be raised is what kind of identity we are dealing with in such cases. Do we have mere duality of terms in these cases, duality of features, properties, or aspects, or even duality of substances? Very similar issues arise. So it is quite possible that further work on this problem of identity will be useful in clarifying the identity theory of the mental and the physical. But at the present the matter is by no means as clear as it should be.

Even if the identity theorist could clarify the sense of "identity" to be used in his theory, he would still face two other problems. These concern coexistence in time and space. Coexistence in time and space are conditions that must be met if there is to be identity. That is to say, for two apparently different things to turn out to be one and the same, they must exist at the same time and in the same location. If we could show that Mr. A existed at a time when Mr. B did not, or that Mr. A existed in a place where Mr. B did not, then this would show that Mr. A and Mr. B were different men. It is by virtue of these facts about identity that an alibi can exonerate a suspect: if Mr. A was not in Chicago at the time, then he could not be one and the same with the man who stole the diamonds in Chicago.

So if mental events are to be identical with physical events, then they must fulfill the conditions of coexistence in time and space. The question is, Do they?

So far as coexistence in time is concerned, very little is known. The most relevant work consists in direct stimulation of an exposed part of the brain during surgery. Since only a local anesthetic is necessary in many such cases the patient may well be fully conscious. Then, as the surgeon stimulates different parts of his brain, the patient may report the occurrence of mental events—memories, thoughts, sensations. Do the physical events in the brain and the mental events occur at precisely the same time? It is impossible to say. All that would be required is a very small time gap to prove that the physical events were not identical with the mental events. But it is very difficult to see how the existence of so small a time gap could be established. And even if it were, what would it prove? Only that the mental event was not identical with just that physical event; it would not prove it was nonidentical with any physical event. So it could well be that coexistence in time is present or is not. I do not think that we shall get much decisive information from empirical work of the sort here described. The identity theorist, then, does not have to fear refutation from this quarter, at least not for a long time.

How about coexistence in space? Do mental events occur in the same place the corresponding physical events occur? This is also a very difficult question to answer, for two reasons. First our present ignorance of neurophysiology, especially concerning the brain and how it functions, allows us to say very little about the location of the relevant physical events. This much does seem likely: they are located in the brain. Much more than that we do not at present know, although as the time passes, we should learn much more. The second reason for our difficulty in telling if there is coexistence in space has to do with the location of mental events. Where do thoughts, feelings, and wishes occur? Do they occur in the brain? Suppose you suddenly have the thought that it is almost supper-time; where does that occur? The most sensible answer would be that it occurs wherever you are when you have that thought. If you are in the library when you have that thought, then the thought occurs in the library. But it would be utterly unnatural to ask where inside your body the thought occurred; in your foot, or your liver, or your heart, or your head? It is not that any one of these places is more likely than another. They are all wrong. Not because thoughts occur somewhere *else* within your body than your foot, liver, heart, or head—but because it *makes no sense at all* to locate the occurrence of a thought at some place within your body. We would not understand someone who pointed to a place in his body and claimed that it was *there* that his entertaining of a thought was located. Certainly, if one *looked* at that place, one would not *see* anything resembling a thought. If it were replied to this that pains can be located in the body without being seen there, then it should be pointed out that one *feels* the pain there but one hardly feels a thought in the body.

The fact that it makes no sense at all to speak of mental events as occurring at some point within the body has the result that the identity theory cannot be true. This is because the corresponding physical events do occur at some point within the body, and if those physical events are identical with mental events, then those mental events must occur at the same point within the body. But those mental events do not occur at any point within the body, because any statement to the effect that they occurred here, or there, would be senseless. Hence the mental events cannot meet the condition of coexistence in space, and therefore cannot be identical with physical events.

Our inability to give the location within the body of mental events is different from our inability to give the location of the corresponding physical events within the body. In the latter case, it is that we do not know enough about the body, particularly the brain. Some day, presumably, we will know enough to pin down pretty exactly the location of the relevant physical events. But in the case of mental events it is not simply that at present we are ignorant but that someday we may well know. What would it be like to discover the location of a thought in the brain? What kind of information would we need to be able to say that the thought occurred exactly *here*? If by X rays or some other means we were able to see every event which occurred in the brain, we would never get a glimpse of a thought. If, to resort to fantasy, we could so enlarge a brain or so shrink ourselves that we could wander freely through the brain, we would still never observe a thought. All we could ever observe in the brain would be the *physical* events which occur in it. If mental events had location in the brain, there should be some means of detecting them there. But of course there is none. The very idea of it is senseless.

Some identity theorists believe this objection can be met. One approach is to reply that this objection begs the question: if the identity theory is true, and mental events are identical with brain events, then, paradoxical as it may sound, mental events do indeed have location, and are located precisely where the physical events are located. Another approach is to reply that the relevant physical events should be construed as events which happen to the body as a whole, and therefore occur where the body as a whole is located; then it is not so paradoxical to give location to the mental events, for they would be located where the body is located but would not be located in any particular part of the body.

We have carried our discussion of the identity theory to the very frontier of present philosophical thinking. We can only leave it to the reader to decide how well it can meet the objections which are raised to it.

There is a mixed theory which is relevant at this point. A person might hold that, although mental and physical events are different sorts of events and in no sense identical, nevertheless the subjects to which they both occur are *material* objects. Thus we have a theory which preserves materialism so far as the *subject* of these events is concerned, but represents an important departure from materialism in accepting a dualism of *events,* the existence of nonmaterial events which happen to material objects in addition to the material events which happen to them.

It would be a mere verbal evasion at this point to argue that so-called mental events are really physical, in this mixed theory, since they occur to physical objects. What would have to be faced is the fact that thoughts, feelings, wishes, and the like are happenings of a quite different sort from the changes in size, shape, location, charge, spin, energy level, etc., which are countenanced in present physical theory. And if we did find even more occult and unfamiliar sorts of physical events, we would still have to face the question whether these events are identical with thoughts, feelings, etc. And any attempt to argue for identity would face all the problems we have already observed to arise for the identity theory.

If we were to accept a dualism of events, then to that extent we would be abandoning materialism. We would be admitting that what exists is not merely or purely or wholly material. Objects would have a nonmaterial dimension; they would be subject to nonmaterial happenings and nonmaterial states. To that extent, objects would not be merely material in nature. On the other hand, there would be no merely or purely or wholly nonmaterial objects which were subjects of mental events either. So we would not be back in a full-fledged dualism either. The kind of theory we would have is a neutralist theory: what at the beginning of this chapter we called the person theory. It is time we turned to a full examination of that theory.

A DOUBLE ASPECT ACCOUNT

We have considered the view that mental events happen to purely immaterial substances and the view that so-called mental events are physical events which happen to purely material substances. We have seen both advantages and disadvantages in each of these main lines of approach. Dualism does justice to what we take to be the wide gulf between the conscious, on the one hand, and matter on the other, but at the expense of introducing the very mysterious notion of the purely thinking substance. Materialism dispenses with such a notion, but at the expense of obliterating what we take to be an ineradicable gulf between the conscious and matter. We will shortly look at a recent attempt to find a compromise between these two theories. We will call it the person theory. It is the view that mental events happen neither to purely immaterial substances nor to purely material substances, but to some thing which is *neither immaterial nor material;* let us call them persons. Mental events happen to *persons,* and persons are subject to *both* mental *and* material happenings.

The historical ancestor of the person theorist is Spinoza, the Dutch philosopher of the seventeenth century. Confronted on the one side by the English materialist Hobbes and on the other side by the French dualist Descartes, Spinoza said, in effect, a plague on both your houses. The mental and the physical are both of them simply aspects of something which in itself is neither mental nor physical. A man can equally well be considered as an extended, physical thing or as a thinking thing, although each of these characterizations only brings out one aspect of the man. The analogy has been proposed of an undulating line which at a given moment may be concave from one point of view and convex from the other. The line itself is not completely described by either term, but only by the use of both terms. Yet it is not that there are two different things, one concave and the other convex. There is only one thing which is, from one point of view, concave and, from another point of view, convex. So with man. He is both a thinking thing and an extended, physical thing—not that he is two things but rather that he is one thing with these two aspects. Such a view is traditionally known as a double aspect view. It is like some versions of the identity theory, but, at least in Spinoza's case, differs with respect to the conception of the thing that has the two aspects. For Spinoza what has the two aspects is not material (nor is it mental either), whereas for the identity theory as we have discussed it what has the two aspects is material.

Although we cannot examine the details of Spinoza's theory, we might note that Spinoza believed *everything* which existed had these two aspects. This view is called panpsychism. It is the view that consciousness occurs wherever anything exists and thus that every tree, rock, cloud, and even every atom is conscious to some degree. To be sure, Spinoza did not believe that all things had so fully developed a consciousness as man has; presumably a rock's mind is so crude and inferior that it is only barely conscious at all. Still, for Spinoza, it is conscious to some degree.

For a double aspect theory, there are two issues of crucial importance—what is the nature of the underlying stuff which has the aspects, and what exactly are "aspects"? Unfortunately in Spinoza's theory both of these are left in deep obscurity. Each man, and, in fact, everything else that exists, is just a particular instance or specimen of what Spinoza calls "Substance" and also calls "God" or "Nature." But it is very difficult to understand what this stuff is. An indication of the difficulty is that since Spinoza's time there has been an unending controversy whether Spinoza was an atheist or what one commentator called "a God-intoxicated man." If an issue so general as that cannot be settled, then it is unlikely that we can hope for much clarification about the nature of this underlying stuff. The second question, What is an "aspect"?, is equally important to answer, for we do not know what it means to say that the mental and the physical are "aspects" of the same thing until we know what an "aspect" is. Again, Spinoza is not of much help. In his theory, the mental and the physical are both basic attributes of the underlying stuff but he never says how they are related or, indeed, how one and the same thing could have such *different* attributes. As we saw in our discussion of the identity theory . . . , it is very difficult to explain with any precision in what sense the mental and the physical are "aspects." The suggestion, by analogy with perception, is that they are different appearances of the thing, the thing as seen from different points of view, but when we try to replace the analogy with a literal characterization, we find ourselves unable to say very much.

THE PERSON THEORY

In recent philosophy, a modified version of the double aspect theory which we will call the person theory has been presented by P. F. Strawson.[3] It is the view that the mental and the physical are both of them attributes of *persons;* the person is the underlying entity which has both mental and physical attributes. Thus we could say of the *person* that he is six feet tall, weighs one hundred and seventy-five pounds, is moving at the rate of three miles an hour (all physical attributes), and we could also say of the very same entity, that person, that he is now thinking about a paper he is writing, feels a pang of anxiety about that paper, and then wishes it were already over and done with (all mental attributes). We have here neither attributions to two different subjects, a mind and a body (dualism), nor attributions to a body (materialism), but attributions to a person. We may say that the person has a mind and a body, but all that means is that both mental and physical attributes are applicable to him.

Why does Strawson reject materialism and hold that mental states must be attributed to a *person* rather than to a body? His argument is very difficult to grasp but it appears to be as follows.[4] Unless we are to accept the unintelligibility thesis or the avowal theory . . . —theories which Strawson rejects as too paradoxical to consider—we must admit that we often do ascribe states of consciousness to things; e.g., we say of some particular subject that the subject had a headache. Now Strawson wishes to argue that the notion of attributing a state of consciousness to a subject cannot be analyzed as the notion of attributing a state of consciousness to a body. Consider the epiphenomenalist, who claims that to say "Subject A has a headache" is synonymous with saying "Body *a* is producing a headache." Now the epiphenomenalist would grant that this contention—that all of subject A's headaches are produced by body *a*—is *controversial,* and that some argumentation is needed. But what exactly is the contention? It is not that *all* headaches are produced by body *a*. That is obviously false. Only subject A's headaches are produced by body *a*. But if "Subject A has a headache" is synonymous with "Body *a* is producing a headache," then to say "All subject A's headaches are produced by body *a*" is simply to say "All the headaches produced by body *a* are produced by body *a*." And that is a claim about which controversy would be impossible, since it is an utter tautology. Exactly the same reasoning would be directed by Strawson against the kind of materialism which holds that "Subject A has a headache" means "Body *a* has a headache."

Strawson's point, if we are interpreting him properly, is that in order for materialists and epiphenomenalists even to formulate their claim, they must have a concept of a subject of mental states which is different from the concept of a material body. For they wish to single out sets of mental states and go on to make the nontrivial claim about each of those sets that it is dependent upon some particular body. So they cannot use the body to single out the sets. Hence, their notion of a subject of states of consciousness must be different from their notion of a material body. Otherwise their claim degenerates into the triviality that all those states of consciousness dependent upon a body are dependent upon that body, a claim too empty to be worth asserting.

I believe that this argument is sound. But it is important to note what it does and does not establish. It establishes the *logical* distinctness of subjects of consciousness and bodies. That is to say, it establishes that expressions referring to the one cannot *mean* the same as expressions referring to the other; they cannot be synonymous; the one cannot be analyzed in terms of the other. But the argument does not rule out some form of the identity theory, i.e., the claim that the *entities* which exemplify the one set of expressions are one and the same as the entities which exemplify the other.[5] Even if the expression "subject of consciousness" does not *mean* a body of a certain sort, it still might turn out that whatever is a subject of consciousness is identical with a body of a certain sort. We shall return to this issue shortly.

In rejecting the logical identity of persons (i.e., subjects of consciousness) and bodies, Strawson might be suspected of accepting dualism. But this would be a mistake. Strawson also rejects dualism, at least in the Cartesian form we have discussed it above; he rejects the view that the subject of states of consciousness is a wholly immaterial, nonphysical thing, a thing to which nothing but states of consciousness can be ascribed. His argument is as follows.[6] If someone has the concept of a subject of consciousness, then he must be willing to allow that there could be other subjects than himself, i.e., that he might be only one self among many. To have the concept of other subjects of consciousness is to be able to distinguish one from another, pick out or identify different subjects, be able to say on some occasions at least that here is one subject rather than another. (If one had no idea how to distinguish one subject from another, then one would not have the concept of *different* subjects.) Now if other subjects of consciousness were wholly immaterial, then there would be no way of distinguishing one subject from another—how could we possibly tell how many such subjects were around us right now or which subject was which? And if there was no way of distinguishing one subject from another, then, as was just pointed out, one would not have the concept of other subjects. And therefore, as was pointed out at the beginning of this argument, one would not have the concept of a subject of consciousness at all. So the Cartesian concept of the subject as wholly immaterial is without meaning.

Therefore, if we do have a concept of a subject of consciousness, as we surely do, then it can be neither merely the concept of a body (as materialism holds) nor merely the concept of an immaterial thing (as the dualist holds). It must be the concept of an entity to which both physical and mental attributions can be made. That is to say, this subject must be not only conscious but physical as well. Strawson calls entities which admit of both mental and physical attributes *persons.*

The person theory has very attractive features. It gives full weight to the distinction between mental and physical attributes, allowing them to be attributes of basically different natures. Yet it also does justice to the fact that they seem to be attributes of one and the same subject; we say, "As he fell through space, he wondered if the parachute would ever open," not "As his body fell through space, his mind wondered if the parachute would ever open." Nor do we seem committed to that curious entity, the immaterial, extensionless thinking substance of Descartes' dualism.

WHAT IS A PERSON?

And yet, alas, there are difficulties with the person theory. These begin to emerge when we begin probing deeper into the concept of the *person* which is involved here. Strawson defines "person" very simply, as "a type of entity such that *both* predicates ascribing states of consciousness *and* predicates ascribing corporeal characteristics, a physical situation, etc. are equally applicable to a single individual of that single type."[7] But such a definition does not help us very much. That it does not comes out when we ask how the person theory differs from the identity theory.

Identity theorists wish to say that mental attributes are attributes of bodies. Furthermore, most of them wish to say that in some sense the mental attributes are reducible to physical attributes. Not all hold to the latter thesis, however. Herbert Feigl holds that where mentalistic terms are appropriate the basic and underlying reality is *mental* and physicalistic terms refer to this mental reality.[8] Thus Feigl seems to admit a dualism of attributes, mental and physical. Yet his is an identity theory both in the sense that the basic subjects of consciousness are bodies and in the sense that certain mentalistic and physicalistic terms have one and the same referent (although some of these terms will have a *mental* referent). Now Strawson would certainly reject the contention that mental attributes are reducible in any sense to physical attributes. But would he reject the claim that they are attributes of bodies? Does he wish to say that persons are bodies of a certain sort, namely bodies which have mental attributes as well?

It is clear that Strawson holds persons to be things which have bodily attributes. But that does not make them bodies any more than the fact that something has red in it makes it red. For, unlike ordinary bodies, persons are things which have mental attributes as well. Furthermore, for Strawson it is not the case that persons are things which just happen to have bodily attributes (but might not have had them), nor is it the case that they are things which just happen to have mental attributes (but might not have had them). It is essential to persons, on Strawson's conception of them, that they be entities which necessarily have *both* mental and bodily attributes. And that means that they are things which differ essentially from bodies (which have only bodily attributes necessarily). They are different types of stuffs or substances or entities. And therefore the person theory is fundamentally different from materialism of any sort. It is dualistic in holding that there are two different types of subjects in the natural world, physical bodies and persons. Physical bodies necessarily have solely the physical dimension; persons necessarily have two dimensions, a physical and a mental dimension. It is the latter contention which distinguishes it from Spinoza's double aspect theory; for Spinoza, everything which exists in the world is, in Strawson's sense, a person, i.e., a thing which necessarily has both a mental and a physical dimension.

If we cannot say, on the person theory, that a person *is* a body, perhaps we can say that a person is, *in part,* a body (in the way that a thing which has red in it may be in part red). But this will not do either, for it inevitably raises the question what the rest of it is. That is, it suggests that a person is some sort of an amalgam, a compound of a body and something else (perhaps a soul?). Such suggestions are precisely what the person theory attempts to combat.

Can we even say that a person *has* a body? I suppose that Strawson would want to be able to say that. But what would it mean on the person theory? Doubtless it means that persons have bodily attributes. But does it mean any more? Is it to say anything about a relation between a person and a *body*? Not on the person theory. For a *body* is something which necessarily has solely bodily attributes and such a thing has nothing to do with persons, which, as we saw, are things which necessarily have both bodily and mental attributes.

Does very much hang on this question of the relation (on the person theory) between persons and bodies? A good deal. For example, consider the laws of nature which hold for bodies, the laws of physics, chemistry, biology. Surely we would want to be able to say that these laws are true for human bodies as well as other bodies. If it is true, in its Newtonian formulation, that "a *body* continues its state of rest or steady motion unless . . . ," we would want this to hold for the bodies of persons as well as for all other bodies. Yet if we cannot even say that a person's "body" is a *body* in the same sense that rocks and trees are bodies, then these laws of nature, which apply to *bodies,* cannot be applied to the "bodies" of persons. And that would be so great an inconvenience, to say nothing of its absurdity, as to count against the person theory.

To be sure, the term "body" is used in many ways besides the Newtonian one cited above, some of which tie better with the person theory. For example, consider the old song "Gin a body meet a body comin' thro the rye." Here of course we are not envisioning a collision of solids but an encounter between persons. In this context, the term "body" is simply used to mean a person. (Sometimes the reverse is the case. When we say "They searched his person," we are using "person" to mean a body.)

There is another use which comes even closer to the Strawsonian conception of a body. If someone said "They found a body in the lake today," we would be very surprised if he meant a rock, or a tree trunk, or an old, sunken boat, or a fish, although all of these are, in the Newtonian sense, bodies. Here "body" means "corpse," i.e., a dead human being (a dead *animal* is called a carcass rather than a corpse). A corpse or "body" in this sense is what is left when a person dies, although it is not a *part* of a living person or something which he *has* while he is alive (he does have the right to say what is to be done with it after he dies). This concept of the body becomes gruesomely explicit when we refer to it as "the remains."

It is this conception of the body which comes closest to that found in the person theory. For, in that theory, as we have seen, a body is not a person, nor is it a part of a person, nor is it something a person has. At most it is the person insofar as he is thought of as the subject of bodily attributes. It is then an abstraction, an intellectual construction, rather than a reality. But it becomes a reality at death. It materializes into that thing we call a corpse. On the person theory, a human body is what would be the person's corpse if he died; the only way we can talk about a person's body is if we consider him as if he were dead.

It is, then, one of the paradoxical implications of the person theory that the body which a person has cannot be conceived of as a physical object subject to the laws of the physical world. In its attempt to establish the unity of the person (against dualism) without sacrificing the thesis that persons are conscious (against materialism), the person theory seems to end with the absurdity that a person's body is not a *physical* thing.

A RECONSIDERATION OF DUALISM

In view of the grave difficulties in materialism and the person theory, it might be useful to review the objections to dualism and see if they can be met in some way. After all, dualism does have the advantage over materialism of accounting for the inability to reduce mental phenomena to material phenomena and the advantage over the person theory of allowing for the treatment of the human body as a material body in principle no different from other material bodies. It would be desirable to preserve these advantages, if we could overcome the disadvantages which seem to rule dualism out.

We noted that one source of discontent with dualism was that it seemed to commit us to the existence of a very peculiar kind of entity, a something which persists in time, has states, undergoes changes, and engages in processes, and yet is invisible, intangible, without size or shape or mass. What a curious something it is; it does not even seem *intelligible* that there should be such a thing. Nothing can be said about it except that it is a subject of consciousness! And that hardly makes clear what it is.

I do not think that this difficulty can be met directly. If the dualist is correct, then the notion of a nonmaterial subject of consciousness is perplexing and obscure, and nothing can be done about that. But we can weaken the force of the difficulty. It depends upon an implicit comparison of the immaterial subject of consciousness with the material subject of material states, material events, and material processes. It is suggested by this implicit comparison that the notion of the latter is clear and intelligible whereas the notion of the former is not. But it is not true that the notion of a material thing is clear and intelligible. We can raise parallel objections to it. We may ask of a material thing which has states, undergoes changes, and engages in processes: *What is it* which has these states, undergoes changes, and engages in processes? What *is* a material thing? On reflection we will see that the only thing which can be said is that it is a something which is the subject of certain sorts of states, events, and processes, namely material ones. Nothing more can be said than that. But precisely that sort of thing, no more and no less, can be said of an immaterial thing, namely that it is a something which is the subject of certain sorts of states, events, and processes, namely ones involving consciousness. So in this respect, immaterial things are no worse off than material things.

However, we are still left with two particular problems here, which we referred to earlier as the problem of identification and the problem of individuation. . . .

So far as identification is concerned, it does seem to be the case that we can only tell we are in the presence of another consciousness and can only tell whose consciousness it is by observing *physical* phenomena. We have no way of getting at the other mind directly. Of course, the problem of identification would be easier if mental telepathy were a common phenomenon. Then one could communicate with another mind without resort to ordinary sense observation and one might tell, by the content of the communication, whom one was communicating with. Thus if it communicated information which only your uncle could know, that would be good reason to think it was your uncle you were in communication with. There is some question even here how much such inferences are based upon what we know about the world through sense observation; for example, you would think it was something only your uncle could know because you know, perhaps, that only he was in the room at the time (as established by observing, through the window, his body and the otherwise empty room). So if in the end sense observation must be depended upon, telepathy will not help. But even if it did help it is not available to us for determining the identity of other consciousnesses. So we must depend upon sense observations of material bodies, especially human bodies. And that leaves mental things in a weaker position, at least epistemologically, than material things.

So far as individuation is concerned, too, mental entities seem to have a weaker status than material entities. For it does seem to be possible for there to be two different persons who have exactly the same mental history, exactly the same set of mental states and events throughout their life. The only thing that could distinguish the two would be the existence of different bodies in different places (although having exactly similar mental histories would necessitate their having exactly similar bodies and environments). This indicates that mental entities depend in part on material entities for their individuation.

We must conclude that any theory of the nature of the subject of consciousness must include some reference to the material bodies, although it may not be necessary to *identify* the subject of consciousness with the material body. Indeed, we have seen that there are grave difficulties in attempts to defend such an identification. Yet a dualism which includes the concept of an immaterial subject of consciousness utterly independent of material bodies is unable to deal with the problems of identification and individuation. So we must turn to a closer look at the relation of consciousness and the body. . . .

NOTES

1. *Ethics,* Part I, Prop. x, note.
2. Karl Marx and Friedrich Engels, *The German Ideology* (New York: International Publishers, 1947), p. 14.
3. P. F. Strawson, *Individuals* (London: Methuen & Co., 1959), Chapter 3.
4. *Ibid.,* pp. 95–98.
5. See James W. Cornman, "Strawson's 'Person'," *Theoria,* XXX (1964), pp. 146–147.
6. *Individuals,* pp. 99–104.
7. *Ibid.,* p. 102.
8. Herbert Feigl, "The 'Mental' and the 'Physical'," *Minnesota Studies* in the Philosophy of Science, Vol. II (Minneapolis: University of Minnesota Press, 1958), pp. 474–475. The essay has been reprinted as a separate monograph (Minneapolis: University of Minnesota Press, 1967); a postscript contains Feigl's most recent thoughts on this matter. See also Feigl's contribution to Sidney Hook, ed., *Dimensions of Mind* (New York: New York University Press, 1961): "Mind-Body, Not a Pseudo-problem," pp. 33–34.

Behaviorism, Materialism and Functionalism*

PAUL M. CHURCHLAND

Paul M. Churchland (1942–) has written widely in the philosophy of psychology and related fields. He now teaches at the University of California, San Diego.

1. PHILOSOPHICAL BEHAVIORISM

Philosophical behaviorism reached the peak of its influence during the first and second decades after World War II. It was jointly motivated by at least three intellectual fashions. The first motivation was a reaction against dualism. The second motivation was the Logical Positivists' idea that the meaning of any sentence was ultimately a matter of the observable circumstances that would tend to verify or confirm that sentence. And the third motivation was a general assumption that most, if not all, philosophical problems are the result of linguistic or conceptual confusion, and are to be solved (or dissolved) by careful analysis of the language in which the problem is expressed.

In fact, philosophical behaviorism is not so much a theory about what mental states are (in their inner nature) as it is a theory about how to analyze or to understand the vocabulary we use to talk about them. Specifically, the claim is that talk about emotions and sensations and beliefs and desires is not talk about ghostly inner episodes, but is rather a shorthand way of talking about actual and potential patterns of *behavior*. In its strongest and most straightforward form, philosophical behaviorism claims that any sentence about a mental state can be paraphrased, without loss of meaning, into a long and complex sentence about what observable behavior *would* result if the person in question were in this, that, or the other observable circumstance.

A helpful analogy here is the dispositional property, *being soluble*. To say that a sugar cube is soluble is not to say that the sugar cube enjoys some ghostly inner state. It is just to say that *if* the sugar cube were put in water, then it *would* dissolve. More strictly,

> "*x* is water soluble"

is equivalent by definition to

> "if *x* were put in unsaturated water, *x* would dissolve."

This is one example of what is called an "operational definition." The term "soluble" is defined in terms of certain operations or tests that would reveal whether or not the term actually applies in the case to be tested.

According to the behaviorist, a similar analysis holds for mental states such as "wants a Caribbean holiday," save that the analysis is much richer. To say that Anne wants a Caribbean holiday is to say that (1) if asked whether that is what she wants, she would answer yes, and (2) if given new holiday brochures for Jamaica and Japan, she would peruse the ones for Jamaica first, and (3) if given a ticket on this Friday's flight to Jamaica, she would go, and so on and so on. Unlike solubility, claims the behaviorist, most mental states are *multitracked* dispositions. But dispositions they remain.

There is therefore no point in worrying about the "relation" between the mind and the body, on this view. To talk about Marie Curie's mind, for example, is not to talk about some "thing" that she "possesses"; it is to talk about certain of her ex-

**From Paul M. Churchland,* Matter and Consciousness *(Cambridge, Mass.: MIT Press, 1984), pp. 23–49. Reprinted by permission of MIT Press.*

traordinary capacities and dispositions. The mind-body problem, concludes the behaviorist, is a pseudo-problem.

Behaviorism is clearly consistent with a materialist conception of human beings. Material objects can have dispositional properties, even multitracked ones, so there is no necessity to embrace dualism to make sense of our psychological vocabulary. (It should be pointed out, however, that behaviorism is strictly consistent with dualism also. Even if philosophical behaviorism were true, it would remain possible that our multitracked dispositions are grounded in immaterial mind-stuff rather than in molecular structures. This is not a possibility that most behaviorists took seriously, however. . . .)

Philosophical behaviorism, unfortunately, had two major flaws that made it awkward to believe, even for its defenders. It evidently ignored, and even denied, the "inner" aspect of our mental states. To have a pain, for example, seems to be not merely a matter of being inclined to moan, to wince, to take aspirin, and so on. Pains also have an intrinsic qualitative nature (a horrible one) that is revealed in introspection, and any theory of mind that ignores or denies such *qualia* is simply derelict in its duty.

This problem received much attention from behaviorists, and serious attempts were made to solve it. The details take us deeply into semantical problems, however, so we shall postpone further discussion of this difficulty.

The second flaw emerged when behaviorists attempted to specify in detail the multitracked disposition said to constitute any given mental state. The list of conditionals necessary for an adequate analysis of "wants a Caribbean holiday," for example, seemed not just to be long, but to be indefinitely or even infinitely long, with no finite way of specifying the elements to be included. And no term can be well defined whose *definiens* is open-ended and unspecific in this way. Further, each conditional of the long analysis was suspect on its own. Supposing that Anne does want a Caribbean holiday, conditional (1) above will be true only if she isn't *secretive* about her holiday fantasies; conditional (2) will be true only if she isn't already *bored* with the Jamaica brochures; conditional (3) will be true only if she doesn't *believe* the Friday flight will be hijacked, and so forth. But to repair each conditional by adding in the relevant qualification would be to reintroduce a series of *mental* elements into the business end of the definition, and we would no longer be defining the mental solely in terms of publicly observable circumstances and behavior.

So long as behaviorism seemed the only alternative to dualism, philosophers were prepared to struggle with these flaws in hopes of repairing or defusing them. However, three more materialist theories rose to prominence during the late fifties and sixties, and the flight from behaviorism was swift.

(I close this section with a cautionary note. The *philosophical* behaviorism discussed above is to be sharply distinguished from the *methodological* behaviorism that has enjoyed such a wide influence within psychology. In its bluntest form, this latter view urges that any new theoretical terms invented by the science of psychology *should be* operationally defined, in order to guarantee that psychology maintains a firm contact with empirical reality. Philosophical behaviorism, by contrast, claims that all of the common-sense psychological terms in our prescientific vocabulary *already* get whatever meaning they have from [tacit] operational definitions. The two views are logically distinct, and the methodology might be a wise one, for new theoretical terms, even though the correlative analysis of common-sense mental terms is wrong.)

2. REDUCTIVE MATERIALISM (THE IDENTITY THEORY)

Reductive materialism, more commonly known as *the identity theory,* is the most straightforward of the several materialist theories of mind. Its central claim is simplicity itself: mental states *are* physical states of the brain. That is, each type of mental state or process is *numerically identical with* (is one and the very same thing as) some type of physical state or process within the brain or central nervous system. At present we do not know enough about the intricate functionings of the brain actually to state the relevant identities, but the identity theory is committed to the idea that brain research will eventually reveal them. . . .

Historical Parallels

As the identity theorist sees it, the result here predicted has familiar parallels elsewhere in our scientific history. Consider sound. We now know that sound is just a train of compression waves traveling through the air, and that the property of being high pitched is identical with the property of having a high oscillatory frequency. We have learned that light is just electromagnetic waves, and our best current theory says that the color of an object is identical with a triplet of reflectance efficiencies the object has, rather like a musical chord that it strikes, though the "notes" are struck in electromagnetic waves instead of in sound waves. We now appreciate that the warmth or coolness of a body is just the energy of motion of the molecules that make it up: warmth is identical with high average molecular kinetic energy, and coolness is identical with low average molecular kinetic energy. We know that lightning is identical with a sudden large-scale discharge of electrons between clouds, or between the atmosphere and the ground. What we now think of as "mental states," argues the identity theorist, are identical with brain states in exactly the same way.

Intertheoretic Reduction

These illustrative parallels are all cases of successful *intertheoretic reduction*. That is, they are all cases where a new and very powerful theory turns out to entail a set of propositions and principles that mirror perfectly (or almost perfectly) the propositions and principles of some older theory or conceptual framework. The relevant principles entailed by the new theory have the same structure as the corresponding principles of the old framework, and they apply in exactly the same cases. The only difference is that where the old principles contained (for example) the notions of "heat," "is hot," and "is cold," the new principles contain instead the notions of "total molecular kinetic energy," "has a high mean molecular kinetic energy," and "has a low mean molecular kinetic energy."

If the new framework is far better than the old at explaining and predicting phenomena, then we have excellent reason for believing that the theoretical terms of the *new* framework are the terms that describe reality correctly. But if the old framework worked adequately, so far as it went, and if it parallels a portion of the new theory in the systematic way described, then we may properly conclude that the old terms and the new terms refer to the very same things, or express the very same properties. We conclude that we have apprehended the very same reality that is incompletely described by the old framework, but with a new and more penetrating conceptual framework. And we announce what philosophers of science call "intertheoretic identities": light *is* electromagnetic waves, temperature *is* mean molecular kinetic energy, and so forth.

The examples of the preceding two paragraphs share one more important feature in common. They are all cases where the things or properties on the receiving end of the reduction are *observable* things and properties within our *common-sense* conceptual framework. They show that intertheoretic reduction occurs not only between conceptual frameworks in the theoretical stratosphere: common-sense observables can also be reduced. There would therefore be nothing particularly surprising about a reduction of our familiar introspectible mental states to physical states of the brain. All that would be required would be that an explanatorily successful neuroscience develop to the point where it entails a suitable "mirror image" of the assumptions and principles that constitute our common-sense conceptual framework for mental states, an image where brain-state terms occupy the positions held by mental-state terms in the assumptions and principles of common sense. If this (rather demanding) condition were indeed met, then, as in the historical cases cited, we would be justified in announcing a reduction, and in asserting the identity of mental states with brain states.

Arguments for the Identity Theory

What reasons does the identity theorist have for believing that neuroscience will eventually achieve the strong conditions necessary for the reduction of our "folk" psychology? There are at least four reasons, all directed at the conclusion that the correct account of human-behavior-and-its-causes must reside in the physical neurosciences.

We can point first to the purely physical origins and ostensibly physical constitution of each individual human. One begins as a genetically programmed monocellular organization of molecules (a fertilized ovum), and one develops from there by the accretion of further molecules whose structure and integration are controlled by the information coded in the DNA molecules of the cell nucleus. The result of such a process would be a purely physical system whose behavior arises from its internal operations and its interactions with the rest of the physical world. And those behavior-controlling internal operations are precisely what the neurosciences are about.

This argument coheres with a second argument. The origins of each *type* of animal also appear exhaustively physical in nature. The argument from evolutionary history . . . lends further support to the identity theorist's claim, since evolutionary theory provides the only serious explanation we have for the behavior-controlling capacities of the brain and central nervous system. Those systems were selected for because of the many advantages (ultimately, the reproductive advantage) held by creatures whose behavior was thus controlled. Again our behavior appears to have its basic causes in neural activity.

The identity theorist finds further support in the argument . . . from the neural dependence of all known mental phenomena. . . . This is precisely what one should expect, if the identity theory is true. Of course, systematic neural dependence is also a consequence of property dualism, but here the identity theorist will appeal to considerations of simplicity. Why admit two radically different classes of properties and operations if the explanatory job can be done by one?

A final argument derives from the growing success of the neurosciences in unraveling the nervous systems of many creatures and in explaining their behavioral capacities and deficits in terms of the structures discovered. The preceding arguments all suggest that neuroscience should be successful in this endeavor, and the fact is that the continuing history of neuroscience bears them out. Especially in the case of very simple creatures (as one would expect), progress has been rapid. And progress has also been made with humans, though for obvious moral reasons exploration must be more cautious and circumspect. In sum, the neurosciences have a long way to go, but progress to date provides substantial encouragement to the identity theorist.

Even so, these arguments are far from decisive in favor of the identity theory. No doubt they do provide an overwhelming case for the idea that the causes of human and animal behavior are essentially physical in nature, but the identity theory claims more than just this. It claims that neuroscience will discover a taxonomy of neural states that stand in a one-to-one correspondence with the mental states of our common-sense taxonomy. Claims for intertheoretic identity will be justified only if such a match-up can be found. But nothing in the preceding arguments guarantees that the old and new frameworks will match up in this way, even if the new framework is a roaring success at explaining and predicting our behavior. Furthermore, there are arguments from other positions within the materialist camp to the effect that such convenient match-ups are rather unlikely. Before exploring those, however, let us look at some more traditional objections to the identity theory.

Arguments Against the Identity Theory

We may begin with the argument from introspection. . . . Introspection reveals a domain of thoughts, sensations, and emotions, not a domain of electrochemical impulses in a neural network. Mental states and properties, as revealed in introspection, appear radically different from any neurophysiological states and properties. How could they possibly be the very same things?

The answer, as we have already seen, is, "Easily." In discriminating red from blue, sweet from sour, and hot from cold, our external senses are actually discriminating between subtle differences in intricate electromagnetic, stereochemical, and micromechanical properties of physical objects. But our senses are not sufficiently penetrating to reveal on their own the detailed nature of those intricate properties. That requires theoretical research and experimental exploration with specially designed instruments. The same is presumably true of our "inner" sense: introspection. It may discriminate efficiently between a great variety of neural states, without being able to reveal on its own the detailed nature of the states being discriminated. Indeed, it would be faintly miraculous if it did reveal them, just as miraculous as if unaided sight were to reveal the existence of interacting electric and magnetic fields whizzing by with an oscillatory frequency of a million billion hertz and a wavelength of less than a millionth of a meter. For despite "appearances," that is what light is. The argument from introspection, therefore, is quite without force.

The next objection argues that the identification of mental states with brain states would commit us to statements that are literally unintelligible, to what philosophers have called "category errors," and that the identification is therefore a case of sheer conceptual confusion. We may begin the discussion by noting a most important law concerning numerical identity. Leibniz' Law states that two items are numerically identical just in case any property had by either one of them is also had by the other: in logical notation,

$$(x)(y)[(x = y) \equiv (F)(Fx \equiv Fy)].$$

This law suggests a way of refuting the identity theory: find some property that is true of brain states, but not of mental states (or vice versa), and the theory would be exploded.

Spatial properties were often cited to this end. Brain states and processes must of course have some specific spatial location: in the brain as a whole, or in some part of it. And if mental states are identical with brain states, then they must have the very same spatial location. But it is literally meaningless, runs the argument, to say that my feeling-of-pain is located in my ventral thalamus, or that my belief-that-the-sun-is-a-star is located in the temporal lobe of my left cerebral hemisphere. Such claims are as meaningless as the claim that the number 5 is green, or that love weighs twenty grams.

Trying the same move from the other direction, some have argued that it is senseless to ascribe the various *semantic* properties to brain states. Our thoughts and beliefs, for example, have a meaning, a specific propositional content; they are either true or false; and they can enjoy relations such as consistency and entailment. If thoughts and beliefs were brain states, then all these semantic properties would have to be true of brain states. But it is senseless, runs the argument, to say that some resonance in my association cortex is true, or logically entails some other resonance close by, or has the meaning that *P*.

Neither of these moves has the same bite it did twenty years ago, since familiarity with the identity theory and growing awareness of the brain's role have tended to reduce the feelings of semantic oddity produced by the claims at issue. But even if they still struck all of us as semantically confused, this would carry little weight. The claim that sound has a wavelength, or that light has a frequency, must have seemed equally unintelligible in advance of the conviction that both sound and light are wave phenomena. (See, for example, Bishop Berkeley's eighteenth-century dismissal of the idea that sound is a vibratory motion of the air, in Dialogue I of his *Three Dialogues*. The objections are voiced by Philonous.) The claim that warmth is measured in kilogram·meters²/seconds² would have seemed semantically perverse before we understood that temperature is mean molecular kinetic energy. And Copernicus' sixteenth-century claim that the earth *moves* also struck people as absurd to the point of perversity. It is not difficult to appreciate why. Consider the following argument.

> Copernicus' claims that the earth moves is sheer conceptual confusion. For consider what it *means* to say that something moves: "*x* moves" means "*x* changes position relative to the earth." Thus, to say that the earth moves is to say that the earth changes position relative to itself! Which is absurd. Copernicus' position is therefore an abuse of language.

The *meaning analysis* here invoked might well have been correct, but all that would have meant is that the speaker should have set about changing his meanings. The fact is, any language involves a rich network of assumptions about the structure of the world, and if a sentence *S* provokes intuitions of semantic oddness, that is usually because *S* violates one or more of those background assumptions. But one cannot always reject *S* for that reason alone, since the overthrow of those background assumptions may be precisely what the facts require. The "abuse" of accepted modes of speech is often an essential feature of real scientific progress! Perhaps we shall just have to get used to the idea that mental states have anatomical locations and brain states have semantic properties.

While the charge of sheer senselessness can be put aside, the identity theorist does owe us some account of exactly how physical brain states can have semantic properties. The account currently being explored can be outlined as follows. Let us begin by asking how it is that a particular *sentence* (= utterance type) has the specific propositional content it has: the sentence "La pomme est rouge," for example. Note first that a sentence is always an integrated part of an entire system of sentences: a language. Any given sentence enjoys many relations with countless other sentences: it entails many sentences, is entailed by many others, is consistent with some, is inconsistent with others, provides confirming evidence for yet others, and so forth. And speakers who use that sentence within that language draw inferences in accordance with those relations. Evidently, each sentence (or each set of equivalent sentences) enjoys a unique pattern of such entailment relations: it plays a distinct inferential role in a complex linguistic economy. Accordingly, we say that the sentence "La pomme est rouge" has the propositional content, *the apple is red,* because the sentence "La pomme est rouge" plays *the same role* in French that the sentence "The apple is red" plays in English. To have the relevant propositional content is just to play the relevant inferential role in a cognitive economy.

Returning now to types of brain states, there is no problem in principle in assuming that one's brain is the seat of a complex inferential economy in which types of brain states are the role-playing elements. According to the theory of meaning just sketched, such states would then have propositional content, since having content is not a matter of whether the contentful item is a pattern of sound, a pattern of letters on paper, a set of raised Braille bumps, or a pattern of neural activity. What matters is the inferential role the item plays. Propositional content, therefore, seems within the reach of brain states after all.

We began this subsection with an argument against materialism that appealed to the qualitative *nature* of our mental states, as revealed in introspection. The next argument appeals to the simple fact that they are introspectible at all.

1. My mental states are introspectively known by me as states of my conscious self.
2. My brain states are *not* introspectively known by me as states of my conscious self.

Therefore, by Leibniz' Law (that numerically identical things must have exactly the same properties),

3. My mental states are not identical with my brain states.

This, in my experience, is the most beguiling form of the argument from introspection, seductive of freshmen and faculty alike. But it is a straightforward instance of a well-known fallacy, which is clearly illustrated in the following parallel arguments:

1. Muhammad Ali is widely known as a heavyweight champion.
2. Cassius Clay is *not* widely known as a heavyweight champion.

Therefore, by Leibniz' Law,

3. Muhammad Ali is not identical with Cassius Clay.

or,

1. Aspirin is recognized by John to be a pain reliever.
2. Acetylsalicylic acid is *not* recognized by John to be a pain reliever.

Therefore, by Leibniz's Law,

3. Aspirin is not identical with acetylsalicylic acid.

Despite the truth of the relevant premises, both conclusions are false: the identities are wholly genuine. Which means that both arguments are invalid. The problem is that the "property" ascribed in premise (1), and withheld in premise (2), consists only in the subject item's being *recognized, perceived,* or *known* as something-or-other. But such apprehension is not a genuine property of the item itself, fit for divining identities, since one and the same subject may be successfully recognized under one name or description, and yet fail to be recognized under another (accurate, coreferential) description. Bluntly, Leibniz' Law is not valid for these bogus "properties." The attempt to use them as above commits what logicians call an *intensional* fallacy. The premises may reflect, not the failure of certain objective identities, but only our continuing failure to appreciate them.

A different version of the preceding argument must also be considered, since it may be urged that one's brain states are more than merely not (yet) known by introspection: they are not know*able* by introspection under any circumstances. Thus,

1. My mental states are knowable by introspection.
2. My brain states are *not* knowable by introspection.

Therefore, by Leibniz' Law,

3. My mental states are not identical with my brain states.

Here the critic will insist that being know*able* by introspection *is* a genuine property of a thing, and that this modified version of the argument is free of the "intensional fallacy" discussed above.

And so it is. But now the materialist is in a position to insist that the argument contains a false premise—premise (2). For if mental states are indeed brain states, then it is really brain states we have been introspecting all along, though without fully appreciating what they are. And if we can learn to think of and recognize those states under mentalistic descriptions, as we all have, then we can certainly learn to think of and recognize them under their more penetrating neurophysiological descriptions. At the very least, premise (2) simply begs the question against the identity theorist. The mistake is amply illustrated in the following parallel argument:

1. Temperature is knowable by feeling.
2. Mean molecular kinetic energy is *not* knowable by feeling.

Therefore, by Leibniz' Law,

3. Temperature is not identical with mean molecular kinetic energy.

This identity, at least, is long established, and this argument is certainly unsound: premise (2) is false. Just as one can learn to feel that the summer air is about 70°F, or 21°C, so one can learn to feel that the mean KE of its molecules is about 6.2×10^{-21} joules, for whether we realize it or not, that is what our discriminatory mechanisms are keyed to. Perhaps our brain states are similarly accessible. . . .

Consider now a final argument, again based on the introspectible qualities of our sensations. Imagine a future neuroscientist who comes to know everything there is to know about the physical structure and activity of the brain and its visual system, of its actual and possible states. If for some reason she has never actually *had* a sensation-of-red (because of color blindness, say, or an unusual environment), then there will remain something she does *not* know about certain sensations: *what it is like to have a sensation-of-red*. Therefore, complete knowledge of the physical facts of visual perception and its related brain activity still leaves something out. Accordingly, materialism cannot give an adequate account of all mental phenomena, and the identity theory must be false.

The identity theorist can reply that this argument exploits an unwitting equivocation on the term "know." Concerning our neuroscientist's utopian knowledge of the brain, "knows" means something like "has mastered the relevant set of neuroscientific propositions." Concerning her (missing) knowledge of what it is like to have a sensation-of-red, "knows" means something like "has a prelinguistic representation of redness in her mechanisms for non-inferential discrimination." It is true that one might have the former without the latter, but the materialist is not committed to the idea that having knowledge in the former sense automatically constitutes having knowledge in the second sense. The identity theorist can admit a duality, or even a plurality, of different *types of knowledge* without thereby committing himself to a duality in *types of things known*. The difference between a person who knows all about the visual cortex but has never enjoyed the sensation-of-red, and a person who knows no neuroscience but knows well the sensation-of-red, may reside not in *what* is respectively known by each (brain states by the former, nonphysical *qualia* by the latter), but rather in the different *type*, or *medium*, or *level* of representation each has of exactly the same thing: brain states.

In sum, there are pretty clearly more ways of "having knowledge" than just having mastered a set of sentences, and the materialist can freely admit that one has "knowledge" of one's sensations in a way that is independent of the neuroscience one may have learned. Animals, including humans, presumably have a prelinguistic mode of sensory representation. This does not mean that sensations are beyond the reach of physical science. *It just means that the brain uses more modes and media of representation than the mere storage of sentences.* All the identity theorist needs to claim is that those other modes of representation will also yield to neuroscientific explanation.

The identity theory has proved to be very resilient in the face of these predominantly antimaterialist objections. But further objections, rooted in competing forms of materialism, constitute a much more serious threat, as the following sections will show.

5. ELIMINATIVE MATERIALISM

The identity theory was called into doubt not because the prospects for a materialist account of our mental capacities were thought to be poor, but because it seemed unlikely that the arrival of an adequate materialist theory would bring with it the nice one-to-one match-ups, between the concepts of folk psychology and the concepts of theoretical neuroscience, that intertheoretic reduction requires. The reason for that doubt was the great variety of quite different physical systems that could instantiate the required functional organization. *Eliminative materialism* also doubts that the correct neuroscientific account of human capacities will produce a neat reduction of our common-sense framework, but here the doubts arise from a quite different source.

As the eliminative materialists see it, the one-to-one match-ups will not be found, and our common-sense psychological framework will not enjoy an intertheoretic reduction, *because our common-sense psychological framework is a false and radically misleading conception of the causes of human behavior and the nature of cognitive activity.* On this view, folk psychology is not just an incomplete representation of our inner natures; it is an outright *mis*-representation of our internal states and activities. Consequently, we cannot expect a truly adequate neuroscientific account of our inner lives to provide theoretical categories that match up nicely with the categories of our common-sense framework. Accordingly, we must expect that the older framework will simply be eliminated, rather than be reduced, by a matured neuroscience.

Historical Parallels

As the identity theorist can point to historical cases of successful intertheoretic reduction, so the eliminative materialist can point to historical cases of the outright elimination of the ontology of an older theory in favor of the ontology of a new and superior theory. For most of the eighteenth and nineteenth centuries, learned people believed that heat was a subtle *fluid* held in bodies, much in the way water is held in a sponge. A fair body of moderately successful theory described the way this fluid substance—called "caloric"—flowed within a body, or from one body to another, and how it produced thermal expansion, melting, boiling, and so forth. But by the end of the last century it had become abundantly clear that heat was not a substance at all, but just the energy of motion of the trillions of jostling molecules that make up the heated body itself. The new theory—the "corpuscular/kinetic theory of matter and heat"—was much more successful than the old in explaining and predicting the thermal behavior of bodies. And since we were unable to *identify* caloric fluid with kinetic energy (according to the old theory, caloric is a material *substance;* according to the new theory, kinetic energy is a form of *motion*), it was finally agreed that there is *no such thing* as caloric. Caloric was simply eliminated from our accepted ontology.

A second example. It used to be thought that when a piece of wood burns, or a piece of metal rusts, a spiritlike substance called "phlogiston" was being released: briskly, in the former case, slowly in the latter. Once gone, that "noble" substance left only a base pile of ash or rust. It later came to be appreciated that both processes involve, not the loss of something, but the *gaining* of a substance taken from the atmosphere: oxygen. Phlogiston emerged, not as an incomplete description of what was going on, but as a radical misdescription. Phlogiston was therefore not suitable for reduction to or identification with some notion from within the new oxygen chemistry, and it was simply eliminated from science.

Admittedly, both of these examples concern the elimination of something nonobservable, but our history also includes the elimination of certain widely accepted "observables." Before Copernicus' views became available, almost any human who ventured out at night could look up at *the starry sphere of the heavens,* and if he stayed for more than a few minutes he could also see that it *turned,* around an axis through Polaris. What the sphere was made of (crystal?) and what made it turn (the gods?) were theoretical questions that exercised us for over two millennia. But hardly anyone doubted the existence of what everyone could observe with their own eyes. In the end, however, we learned to reinterpret our visual experience of the night sky within a very different conceptual framework, and the turning sphere evaporated.

Witches provide another example. Psychosis is a fairly common affliction among humans, and in earlier centuries its victims were standardly seen as cases of demonic possession, as instances of Satan's spirit itself, glaring malevolently out at us from behind the victims' eyes. That witches exist was not a matter of any controversy. One would occasionally see them, in any city or hamlet, engaged in incoherent, paranoid, or even murderous behavior. But observable or not, we eventually decided that witches simply do not exist. We concluded that the concept of a witch is an element in a conceptual framework that misrepresents so badly the phenomena to which it was standardly applied that literal application of the notion should be permanently withdrawn. Modern theories of mental dysfunction led to the elimination of witches from our serious ontology.

The concepts of folk psychology—belief, desire, fear, sensation, pain, joy, and so on—await a similar fate, according to the view at issue. And when neuroscience has matured to the point where the poverty of our current conceptions is apparent to everyone, and the superiority of the new framework is established, we shall then be able to set about *re*-conceiving our internal states and activities, within a truly adequate conceptual framework at last. Our explanations of one another's behavior will appeal to such things as our neuropharmacological states, the neural activity in specialized anatomical areas, and whatever other states are deemed relevant by the new theory. Our private introspection will also be transformed, and may be profoundly enhanced by reason of the more accurate and penetrating framework it will have to work with—just as the astronomer's perception of the night sky is much enhanced by the detailed knowledge of modern astronomical theory that he or she possesses.

The magnitude of the conceptual revolution here suggested should not be minimized: it would be enormous. And the benefits to humanity might be equally great. If each of us possessed an accurate neuroscientific understanding of (what we now conceive dimly as) the varieties and causes of mental illness, the factors involved in learning, the neural basis of emotions, intelligence, and socialization, then the sum total of human misery might be much reduced. The simple increase in mutual understanding that the new framework made possible could contribute substantially toward a more peaceful and humane society. Of course, there would be dangers as well: increased knowledge means increased power, and power can always be misused.

Arguments for Eliminative Materialism

The arguments for eliminative materialism are diffuse and less than decisive, but they are stronger than are widely supposed. The distinguished feature of this position is its denial that a smooth intertheoretic reduction is to be expected—even a species-specific reduction—of the framework of folk psychology to the framework of a matured neuroscience. The reason for this denial is the eliminative materialist's conviction that folk psychology is a hopelessly primitive and deeply confused conception of our internal activities. But why this low opinion of our common-sense conceptions?

There are at least three reasons. First, the eliminative materialist will point to the widespread explanatory, predictive, and manipulative failures of folk psychology. So much of what is central and familiar to us remains a complete mystery from within folk psychology. We do not know what *sleep* is, or why we have to have it, despite spending a full third of our lives in that condition. (The answer, "For rest," is mistaken. Even if people are allowed to rest continuously, their need for sleep is undiminished. Apparently, sleep serves some deeper functions, but we do not yet know what they are.) We do not understand how *learning* transforms each of us from a gaping infant to a cunning adult, or how differences in *intelligence* are grounded. We have not the slightest idea how *memory* works, or how we manage to retrieve relevant bits of information instantly from the awesome mass we have stored. We do not know what *mental illness* is, nor how to cure it.

In sum, the most central things about us remain almost entirely mysterious from within folk psychology. And the defects noted cannot be blamed on inadequate time allowed for their correction, for folk psychology has enjoyed no significant changes or advances in well over 2,000 years, despite its manifest failures. Truly successful theories may be expected to reduce, but significantly unsuccessful theories merit no such expectation.

This argument from explanatory poverty has a further aspect. So long as one sticks to normal brains, the poverty of folk psychology is perhaps not strikingly evident. But as soon as one examines the many perplexing behavioral and cognitive deficits suffered by people with *damaged* brains, one's descriptive and explanatory resources start to claw the air. . . . As with other humble theories asked to operate successfully in unexplored extensions of their old domain (for example, Newtonian mechanics in the domain of velocities close to the velocity of light, and the classical gas law in the domain of high pressures or temperatures), the descriptive and explanatory inadequacies of folk psychology become starkly evident.

The second argument tries to draw an inductive lesson from our conceptual history. Our early folk theories of motion were profoundly confused, and were eventually displaced entirely by more sophisticated theories. Our early folk theories of the structure and activity of the heavens were wildly off the mark, and survive only as historical lessons in how wrong we can be. Our folk theories of the nature of fire, and the nature of life, were similarly cockeyed. And one could go on, since the vast majority of our past folk conceptions have been similarly exploded. All except folk psychology, which survives to this day and has only recently begun to feel pressure. But the phenomenon of conscious intelligence is surely a more complex and difficult phenomenon than any of those just listed. So far as accurate understanding is concerned, it would be a *miracle* if we had got *that* one right the very first time, when we fell down so badly on all the others. Folk psychology has survived for so very long, presumably, not because it is basically correct in its representations, but because the phenomena addressed are so surpassingly difficult that any useful handle on them, no matter how feeble, is unlikely to be displaced in a hurry.

A third argument attempts to find an a priori advantage for eliminative materialism over the identity theory and functionalism.* It attempts to counter the common intuition that eliminative materialism is distantly possible, perhaps, but is much less probable than either the identity theory or functionalism. The focus again is on whether the concepts of folk psychology will find vindicating match-ups in a matured neuroscience. The eliminativist bets no; the other two bet yes. (Even the functionalist bets yes, but expects the match-ups to be only species-specific, or only person-specific.

*[See Section 4 for the discussion of functionalism. I have reversed the order in which these theories are discussed, so that the discussion of functionalism occurs *after,* rather than before, the present discussion of eliminative materialism.—Eds.]

Functionalism . . . denies the existence only of *universal* type/type identities.)

The eliminativist will point out that the requirements on a reduction are rather demanding. The new theory must entail a set of principles and embedded concepts that mirrors very closely the specific conceptual structure to be reduced. And the fact is, there are vastly many more ways of being an explanatorily successful neuroscience while *not* mirroring the structure of folk psychology, than there are ways of being an explanatorily successful neuroscience while also *mirroring* the very specific structure of folk psychology. Accordingly, the a priori probability of eliminative materialism is not lower, but substantially *higher* than that of either of its competitors. One's initial intuitions here are simply mistaken.

Granted, this initial a priori advantage could be reduced if there were a very strong presumption in favor of the truth of folk psychology—true theories are better bets to win reduction. But according to the first two arguments, the presumptions on this point should run in precisely the opposite direction.

Arguments Against Eliminative Materialism

The initial plausibility of this rather radical view is low for almost everyone, since it denies deeply entrenched assumptions. That is at best a question-begging complaint, of course, since those assumptions are precisely what is at issue. But the following line of thought does attempt to mount a real argument.

Eliminative materialism is false, runs the argument, because one's introspection reveals directly the existence of pains, beliefs, desires, fears, and so forth. Their existence is as obvious as anything could be.

The eliminative materialist will reply that this argument makes the same mistake that an ancient or medieval person would be making if he insisted that he could just see with his own eyes that the heavens form a turning sphere, or that witches exist. The fact is, all observation occurs within some system of concepts, and our observation judgments are only as good as the conceptual framework in which they are expressed. In all three cases—the starry sphere, witches, and the familiar mental states—precisely what is challenged is the integrity of the background conceptual frameworks in which the observation judgments are expressed. To insist on the validity of one's experiences, *traditionally interpreted*, is therefore to beg the very question at issue. For in all three cases, the question is whether we should *re*conceive the nature of some familiar observational domain.

A second criticism attempts to find an incoherence in the eliminative materialist's position. The bald statement of eliminative materialism is that the familiar mental states do not really exist. But that statement is meaningful, runs the argument, only if it is the expression of a certain *belief*, and an *intention* to communicate, and a *knowledge* of the language, and so forth. But if the statement is true, then no such mental states exist, and the statement is therefore a meaningless string of marks or noises, and cannot be true. Evidently, the assumption that eliminative materialism is true entails that it cannot be true.

The hole in this argument is the premise concerning the conditions necessary for a statement to be meaningful. It begs the question. If eliminative materialism is true, then meaningfulness must have some different source. To insist on the "old" source is to insist on the validity of the very framework at issue. Again, an historical parallel may be helpful here. Consider the medieval theory that being biologically *alive* is a matter of being ensouled by an immaterial *vital spirit*. And consider the following response to someone who has expressed disbelief in that theory.

> My learned friend has stated that there is no such thing as vital spirit. But this statement is incoherent. For if it is true, then my friend does not have vital spirit, and must therefore be *dead*. But if he is dead, then his statement is just a string of noises, devoid of meaning or truth. Evidently, the assumption that antivitalism is true entails that it cannot be true! Q.E.D.

This second argument is now a joke, but the first argument begs the question in exactly the same way.

A final criticism draws a much weaker conclusion, but makes a rather stronger case. Eliminative materialism, it has been said, is making mountains out of molehills. It exaggerates the defects in folk psychology, and underplays its real successes. Perhaps the arrival of a matured neuroscience will require the elimination of the occasional folk-psychological concept, continues the criticism, and a minor adjustment in certain folk-psychological principles may have to be endured. But the large-scale elimination forecast by the eliminative materialist is just an alarmist worry or a romantic enthusiasm.

Perhaps this complaint is correct. And perhaps it is merely complacent. Whichever, it does bring out the important point that we do not confront two simple and mutually exclusive possibilities here: pure reduction versus pure elimination. Rather, these are the end points of a smooth spectrum of possible outcomes, between which there are mixed cases of partial elimination and partial reduction. Only empirical research . . . can tell us where on that spectrum our own case will fall. Perhaps we should speak here, more liberally, of "revisionary materialism," instead of concentrating on the more radical possibility of an across-the-board elimination. Perhaps we should. But it has been my aim in this section to make it at least intelligible to you that our collective conceptual destiny lies substantially toward the revolutionary end of the spectrum.

4. FUNCTIONALISM*

According to *functionalism,* the essential or defining feature of any type of mental state is the set of causal relations it bears to (1) environmental effects on the body, (2) other types of mental states, and (3) bodily behavior. Pain, for example, characteristically results from some bodily damage or trauma; it causes distress, annoyance, and practical reasoning aimed at relief; and it causes wincing, blanching, and nursing of the traumatized area. Any state that plays exactly that functional role is a pain, according to functionalism. Similarly, other types of mental states (sensations, fears, beliefs, and so on) are also defined by their unique causal roles in a complex economy of internal states mediating sensory inputs and behavioral outputs.

This view may remind the reader of behaviorism, and indeed it is the heir to behaviorism, but there is one fundamental difference between the two theories. Where the behaviorist hoped to define each type of mental state solely in terms of environmental input and behavioral output, the functionalist denies that this is possible. As he sees it, the adequate characterization of almost any mental state involves an ineliminable reference to a variety of other mental states with which it is causally connected, and so a reductive definition solely in terms of publicly observable inputs and outputs is quite impossible. Functionalism is therefore immune to one of the main objections against behaviorism.

Thus the difference between functionalism and behaviorism. The difference between functionalism and the identity theory will emerge from the following argument raised against the identity theory.

Imagine a being from another planet, says the functionalist, a being with an alien physiological constitution, a constitution based on the chemical element silicon, for example, instead of on the element carbon, as ours is. The chemistry and even the physical structure of the alien's brain would have to be systematically different from ours. But even so, that alien brain could well sustain a functional economy of internal states whose mutual *relations* parallel perfectly the mutual relations that define our own mental states. The alien may have an internal state that meets all the conditions for being a pain state, as outlined earlier. That state, considered from a purely physical point of view, would have a very different makeup from a human pain state, but it could nevertheless be identical to a human pain state from a purely functional point of view. And so for all of his functional states.

If the alien's functional economy of internal states were indeed *functionally isomorphic* with our own internal economy—if those states were causally connected to inputs, to one another, and to behavior in ways that parallel our own internal

*[In Professor Churchland's text this section occurs *before* the section on Eliminative Materialism. We have reversed the order here.—Eds.]

connections—then the alien would have pains, and desires, and hopes, and fears just as fully as we, despite the differences in the physical system that sustains or realizes those functional states. What is important for mentality is not the matter of which the creature is made, but the structure of the internal activities which that matter sustains.

If we can think of one alien constitution, we can think of many, and the point just made can also be made with an artificial system. Were we to create an electronic system—a computer of some kind—whose internal economy were functionally isomorphic with our own in all the relevant ways, then it too would be the subject of mental states.

What this illustrates is that there are almost certainly many more ways than one for nature, and perhaps even for man, to put together a thinking, feeling, perceiving creature. And this raises a problem for the identity theory, for it seems that there is no single type of physical state to which a given type of mental state must always correspond. Ironically, there are *too many* different kinds of physical systems that can realize the functional economy characteristic of conscious intelligence. If we consider the universe at large, therefore, and the future as well as the present, it seems quite unlikely that the identity theorist is going to find the one-to-one match-ups between the concepts of our common-sense mental taxonomy and the concepts of an overarching theory that encompasses all of the relevant physical systems. But that is what intertheoretic reduction is standardly said to require. The prospects for universal identities, between types of mental states and types of brain states, are therefore slim.

If the functionalists reject the traditional "mental-type = physical type" identity theory, virtually all of them remain committed to a weaker "mental token = physical token" identity theory, for they still maintain that each *instance* of a given type of mental state is numerically identical with some specific physical state in some physical system or other. It is only universal (type/type) identities that are rejected. Even so, this rejection is typically taken to support the claim that the science of psychology is or should be *methodologically autonomous* from the various physical sciences such as physics, biology, and even neurophysiology. Psychology, it is claimed, has its own irreducible laws and its own abstract subject matter.

[In 1984] functionalism [was] probably the most widely held theory of mind among philosophers, cognitive psychologists, and artificial intelligence researchers. Some of the reasons are apparent from the preceding discussion, and there are further reasons as well. In characterizing mental states as essentially functional states, functionalism places the concerns of psychology at a level that abstracts from the teeming detail of a brain's neurophysiological (or crystallographic, or microelectronic) structure. The science of psychology, it is occasionally said, is methodologically autonomous from those other sciences (biology, neuroscience, circuit theory) whose concerns are with what amount to engineering details. This provides a rationale for a great deal of work in cognitive psychology and artificial intelligence, where researchers postulate a system of abstract functional states and then test the postulated system, often by way of its computer simulation, against human behavior in similar circumstances. The aim of such work is to discover in detail the functional organization that makes us what we are. . . .

Arguments Against Functionalism

Current popularity aside, functionalism also faces difficulties. The most commonly posed objection cites an old friend: sensory qualia. Functionalism may escape one of behaviorism's fatal flaws, it is said, but it still falls prey to the other. By attempting to make its *relational* properties the definitive feature of any mental state, functionalism ignores the "inner" or qualitative nature of our mental states. But their qualitative nature is the essential feature of a great many types of mental state (pain, sensations of color, of temperature, of pitch, and so on), runs the objection, and functionalism is therefore false.

The standard illustration of this apparent failing is called "the inverted spectrum thought-experiment." It is entirely conceivable, runs the story, that the range of color sensations that I enjoy upon viewing standard objects is simply inverted relative to the color sensations that you enjoy. When viewing a tomato, I may have what is really a sensation-of-green where you have the normal sensation-of-red; when viewing a banana, I may have what is really sensation-of-blue where you have the normal sensation-of-yellow; and so forth. But since we have no way of comparing our inner qualia, and since I shall make all the same observational discriminations among objects that you will, there is no way to tell whether my spectrum is inverted relative to yours.

The problem for functionalism arises as follows. Even if my spectrum is inverted relative to yours, we remain functionally isomorphic with one another. My visual sensation upon viewing a tomato is *functionally* identical with your visual sensation upon viewing a tomato. According to functionalism, therefore, they are the very same type of state, and it does not even make sense to suppose that my sensation is "really" a sensation-of-green. If it meets the functional conditions for being a sensation-of-red, then by definition it is a sensation-of-red. According to functionalism, apparently, a spectrum inversion of the kind described is ruled out by definition. But such inversions are entirely conceivable, concludes the objection, and if functionalism entails that they are not conceivable, then functionalism is false.

Another qualia-related worry for functionalism is the so-called "absent qualia problem." The functional organization characteristic of conscious intelligence can be instantiated (= realized or instanced) in a considerable variety of physical systems, some of them radically different from a normal human. For example, a giant electronic computer might instantiate it, and there are more radical possibilities still. One writer asks us to imagine the people of China—all 10^9 of them—organized into an intricate game of mutual interactions so that collectively they constitute a giant brain which exchanges inputs and outputs with a single robot body. That system of the robot-plus-10^9-unit-brain could presumably instantiate the relevant functional organization (though no doubt it would be much slower in its activities than a human or a computer), and would therefore be the subject of mental states, according to functionalism. But surely, it is urged, the complex states that there play the functional roles of pain, pleasure, and sensations-of-color would not have intrinsic qualia as ours do, and would therefore fail to be genuine mental states. Again, functionalism seems at best an incomplete account of the nature of mental states.

It has recently been argued that both the inverted-qualia and the absent-qualia objections can be met, without violence to functionalism and without significant violence to our common-sense intuitions about qualia. Consider the inversion problem first. I think the functionalist is right to insist that the type-identity of our visual sensations be reckoned according to their functional role. But the objector is also right in insisting that a relative inversion of two people's qualia, without functional inversion, is entirely conceivable. The apparent inconsistency between these positions can be dissolved by insisting that (1) our functional states (or rather, their physical realizations) do indeed have an intrinsic nature on which our introspective identification of those states depends; while also insisting that (2) such intrinsic natures are nevertheless not essential to the type-identity of a given mental state, and may indeed *vary* from instance to instance of the same type of mental state.

What this means is that the qualitative character of your sensation-of-red might be different from the qualitative character of my sensation-of-red, slightly or substantially, and a third person's sensation-of-red might be different again. But so long as all three states are standardly caused by red objects and standardly cause all three of us to believe that something is red, then all three states are sensations-of-red, whatever their intrinsic qualitative character. Such intrinsic qualia merely serve as salient features that permit the quick introspective identification of sensations, as black-on-orange stripes serve as a salient feature for the quick visual identification of tigers. But specific qualia are not essential to the type-identity of mental states, any more than black-on-orange stripes are essential to the type-identity of tigers.

Plainly, this solution requires the functionalist to admit the *reality* of qualia, and we may wonder how there can be room for qualia in his materialist world-picture. Perhaps they can be fit in as follows:

identify them with physical properties of whatever physical states instantiate the mental (functional) states that display them. For example, identify the qualitative nature of your sensations-of-red with that physical feature (of the brain state that instantiates it) to which your mechanisms of introspective discrimination are in fact responding when you judge that you have a sensation-of-red. If materialism is true, then there must *be* some internal physical feature or other to which your discrimination of sensations-of-red is keyed: *that* is the quale of your sensations-of-red. If the pitch of a sound can turn out to be the frequency of an oscillation in air pressure, there is no reason why the quale of a sensation cannot turn out to be, say, a spiking frequency in a certain neural pathway. ("Spikes" are the tiny electrochemical pulses by which our brain cells communicate.)

This entails that creatures with a constitution different from ours may have qualia different from ours, despite being psychologically isomorphic with us. It does not entail that they *must* have different qualia, however. If the qualitative character of my sensation-of-red is really a spiking frequency of 90 hertz in a certain neural pathway, it is possible that an electromechanical robot might enjoy the very same qualitative character if, in reporting sensations-of-red, the robot were responding to a spiking frequency of 90 hertz in a corresponding *copper* pathway. It might be the spiking frequency that matters to our respective mechanisms of discrimination, not the nature of the medium that carries it.

This proposal also suggests a solution to the absent qualia problem. So long as the physical system at issue is functionally isomorphic with us, to the last detail, then it will be equally capable of subtle introspective discriminations among its sensations. Those discriminations must be made on some systematic physical basis, that is, on some characteristic physical features of the states being discriminated. Those features at the objective focus of the system's discriminatory mechanisms, *those* are its sensory qualia—though the alien system is no more likely to appreciate their true physical nature than we appreciate the true physical nature of our own qualia. Sensory qualia are therefore an inevitable concomitant of any system with the kind of functional organization at issue. It may be difficult or impossible to "see" the qualia in an alien system, but it is equally difficult to "see" them even when looking into a human brain.

I leave it to the reader to judge the adequacy of these responses. If they are adequate, then, given its other virtues, functionalism must be conceded a very strong position among the competing contemporary theories of mind. It is interesting, however, that the defense offered in the last paragraph found it necessary to take a leaf from the identity theorist's book (types of quale are reduced to or identified with types of physical state), since the final objection we shall consider also tends to blur the distinction between functionalism and reductive materialism.

Consider the property of *temperature,* runs the objection. Here we have a paradigm of a physical property, one that has also been cited as the paradigm of a successfully *reduced* property, as expressed in the intertheoretic identity

> "temperature = mean kinetic energy of constituent molecules."

Strictly speaking, however, this identity is true only for the temperature of a gas, where simple particles are free to move in ballistic fashion. In a *solid,* temperature is realized differently, since the interconnected molecules are confined to a variety of vibrational motions. In a *plasma,* temperature is something else again, since a plasma has no constituent molecules; they, and their constituent atoms, have been ripped to pieces. And even a *vacuum* has a so-called "blackbody" temperature—in the distribution of electromagnetic waves coursing through it. Here temperature has nothing to do with the kinetic energy of particles.

It is plain that the physical property of temperature enjoys "multiple instantiations" no less than do psychological properties. Does this mean that thermodynamics (the theory of heat and temperature) is an "autonomous science," separable from the rest of physics, with its own irreducible laws and its own abstract nonphysical subject matter?

Presumably not. What it means, concludes the objection, is that *reductions are domain-specific:*

> temperature-in-a-gas = the mean kinetic energy of the gas's molecules,

whereas

temperature-in-a-vacuum = the blackbody distribution of the vacuum's transient radiation.

Similarly, perhaps

joy-in-a-human = resonances in the lateral hypothalamus,

whereas

joy-in-a-Martian = something else entirely.

This means that we may expect some type/type reductions of mental states to physical states after all, though they will be much narrower than was first suggested. Furthermore, it means that functionalist claims concerning the radical autonomy of psychology cannot be sustained. And last, it suggests that functionalism is not so profoundly different from the identity theory as was first made out. . . .

The Qualia Problem*

FRANK JACKSON

Frank Jackson has written many articles in metaphysics and the philosophy of mind. He teaches at the Australian National University.

IT IS UNDENIABLE that the physical, chemical and biological sciences have provided a great deal of information about the world we live in and about ourselves. I will use the label 'physical information' for this kind of information, and also for information that automatically comes along with it. For example, if a medical scientist tells me enough about the processes that go on in my nervous system, and about how they relate to happenings in the world around me, to what has happened in the past and is likely to happen in the future, to what happens to other similar and dissimilar organisms, and the like, he or she tells me—if I am clever enough to fit it together appropriately—about what is often called the functional role of those states in me (and in organisms in general in similar cases). This information, and its kin, I also label 'physical'.

I do not mean these sketchy remarks to constitute a definition of 'physical information', and of the correlative notions of physical property, process, and so on, but to indicate what I have in mind here. It is well known that there are problems with giving a precise definition of these notions, and so of the thesis of Physicalism that all (correct) information is physical information. But—unlike some—I take the question of definition to cut across the central problems I want to discuss in this paper.

I am what is sometimes known as a "qualia freak." I think that there are certain features of the bodily sensations especially, but also of certain perceptual experiences, which no amount of purely physical information includes. Tell me everything physical there is to tell about what is going on in a living brain, the kind of states, their functional role, their relation to what goes on at other times and in other brains, and so on and so forth, and be I as clever as can be in fitting it all together, you won't have told me about the hurtfulness of pains, the

**This is an edited version of "Epiphenomenal Qualia," which appeared in the* Philosophical Quarterly *vol. 32 (1982), pp. 127–36. Reprinted by permission of the publisher.*

itchiness of itches, pangs of jealousy, or about the characteristic experience of tasting a lemon, smelling a rose, hearing a loud noise or seeing the sky.

There are many qualia freaks, and some of them say that their rejection of Physicalism is an unargued intuition. I think that they are being unfair to themselves. They have the following argument. Nothing you could tell of a physical sort captures the smell of a rose, for instance. Therefore, Physicalism is false. By our lights this is a perfectly good argument. It is obviously not to the point to question its validity, and the premise is intuitively obviously true both to them and to me.

I must, however, admit that it is weak from a polemical point of view. There are, unfortunately for us, many who do not find the premise intuitively obvious. The task then is to present an argument whose premises are obvious to all, or at least to as many as possible. This I try to do [In the following section] . . . with what I will call "the Knowledge argument."

In the following section I tackle the question of the causal role of qualia. The major factor in stopping people from admitting qualia is the belief that they would have to be given a causal role with respect to the physical world and especially the brain; and it is hard to do this without sounding like someone who believes in fairies. I seek in section IV to turn this objection by arguing that the view that qualia are epiphenomenal is a perfectly possible one.

THE KNOWLEDGE ARGUMENT FOR QUALIA

People vary considerably in their ability to discriminate colors. Suppose that in an experiment to catalog this variation Fred is discovered. Fred has better color vision than anyone else on record; he makes every discrimination that anyone has ever made, and moreover he makes one that we cannot even begin to make. Show him a batch of ripe tomatoes and he sorts them into two roughly equal groups and does so with complete consistency. That is, if you blindfold him, shuffle the tomatoes up, and then remove the blindfold and ask him to sort them out again, he sorts them into exactly the same two groups.

We ask Fred how he does it. He explains that all ripe tomatoes do not look the same color to him, and in fact that this is true of a great many objects that we classify together as red. He sees two colors where we see one, and he has in consequence developed for his own use two words 'red_1' and 'red_2' to mark the difference. Perhaps he tells us that he has often tried to teach the difference between red_1 and red_2 to his friends but has got nowhere and has concluded that the rest of the world is red_1–red_2 color-blind—or perhaps he has had partial success with his children; it doesn't matter. In any case he explains to us that it would be quite wrong to think that because 'red' appears in both 'red_1' and 'red_2' that the two colors are shades of the one color. He only uses the common term 'red' to fit more easily into our restricted usage. To him red_1 and red_2 are as different from each other and all the other colors as yellow is from blue. And his discriminatory behavior bears this out: he sorts red_1 from red_2 tomatoes with the greatest of ease in a wide variety of viewing circumstances. Moreover, an investigation of the physiological basis of Fred's exceptional ability reveals that Fred's optical system is able to separate out two groups of wavelengths in the red spectrum as sharply as we are able to sort out yellow from blue.

I think that we should admit that Fred can see, really see, at least one more color than we can; red_1 is a different color from red_2. We are to Fred as a totally red-green color-blind person is to us. H. G. Wells' story "The country of the blind" is about a sighted person in a totally blind community. This person never manages to convince them that he can see, that he has an extra sense. They ridicule this sense as quite inconceivable, and treat his capacity to avoid falling into ditches, to win fights and so on as precisely that capacity and nothing more. We would be making their mistake if we refused to allow that Fred can see one more color than we can.

What kind of experience does Fred have when he sees red_1 and red_2? What is the new color or colors like? We would dearly like to know but do not; and it seems that no amount of physical information about Fred's brain and optical system tells us. We find out perhaps that Fred's cones respond differentially to certain light waves in the red section of the spectrum that make no difference to ours (or perhaps he has an extra cone) and that this leads in Fred to a wider range of those brain states responsible for visual discriminatory behavior. But none of this tells us what we really want to know about his color experience. There is something about it we don't know. But we know, we may suppose, everything about Fred's body, his behavior and dispositions to behavior and about his internal physiology, and everything about his history and relation to others that can be given in physical accounts of persons. We have all the physical information. Therefore, knowing all this is *not* knowing everything about Fred. It follows that Physicalism leaves something out.

To reinforce this conclusion, imagine that as a result of our investigations into the internal workings of Fred we find out how to make everyone's physiology like Fred's in the relevant respects; or perhaps Fred donates his body to science and on his death we are able to transplant his optical system into someone else—again the fine detail doesn't matter. The important point is that such a happening would create enormous interest. People would say "At last we will know what it is like to see the extra color, at last we will know how Fred has differed from us in the way he has struggled to tell us about for so long." Then it cannot be that we knew all along all about Fred. But *ex hypothesi* we did know all along everything about Fred that features in the physicalist scheme; hence the physicalist scheme leaves something out.

Put it this way. *After* the operation, we will know *more* about Fred and especially about his color experiences. But beforehand we had all the physical information we could desire about his body and brain, and indeed everything that has ever featured in physicalist accounts of mind and consciousness. Hence there is more to know than all that. Hence Physicalism is incomplete.

Fred and the new color(s) are of course essentially rhetorical devices. The same point can be made with normal people and familiar colors. Mary is a brilliant scientist who is, for whatever reason, forced to investigate the world from a black and white room *via* a black and white television monitor. She specializes in the neurophysiology of vision and acquires, let us suppose, all the physical information there is to obtain about what goes on when we see ripe tomatoes, or the sky, and use terms like 'red', 'blue', and so on. She discovers, for example, just which wavelength combinations from the sky stimulate the retina, and exactly how this produces *via* the central nervous system the contraction of the vocal chords and expulsion of air from the lungs that results in the uttering of the sentence 'The sky is blue'. . . .

What will happen when Mary is released from her black and white room or is given a color television monitor? Will she *learn* anything or not? It seems just obvious that she will learn something about the world and our visual experience of it. But then it is inescapable that her previous knowledge was incomplete. But she had *all* the physical information. *Ergo* there is more to have than that, and Physicalism is false.

Clearly the same style of Knowledge argument could be deployed for taste, hearing, the bodily sensations and generally speaking for the various mental states which are said to have (as it is variously put) raw feels, phenomenal features or qualia. The conclusion in each case is that the qualia are left out of the physicalist story. And the polemical strength of the Knowledge argument is that it is so hard to deny the central claim that one can have all the physical information without having all the information there is to have. . . .

THE BOGEY OF EPIPHENOMENALISM

Is there any really *good* reason for refusing to countenance the idea that qualia are causally impotent with respect to the physical world? I will argue for the answer *no*. . . . All I will be concerned to defend is that it is possible to hold that certain properties of certain mental states, namely those I've called qualia, are such that their possession or absence makes no difference to the physical world. . . .

Two reasons are standardly given for holding that a quale like the hurtfulness of a pain must be causally efficacious in the physical world, and so, for instance, that it . . . must sometimes make a difference to what happens in the brain. [Neither,] I will argue, has any real force. . . .

(i) It is supposed to be just obvious that the hurtfulness of pain is partly responsible for the subject seeking to avoid pain, saying 'It hurts' and so on. But, to reverse Hume, anything can fail to cause anything. No matter how often *B* follows *A*, and no matter how initially obvious the causality of the connection seems, the hypothesis that *A* causes *B* can be overturned by an over-arching theory which shows the two as distinct effects of a common underlying causal process.

To the untutored the image on the screen of Lee Marvin's fist moving from left to right immediately followed by the image of John Wayne's head moving in the same general direction looks as causal as anything. And of course throughout countless Westerns images similar to the first are followed by images similar to the second. All this counts for precisely nothing when we know the over-arching theory concerning how the relevant images are both effects of an underlying causal process involving the projector and the film. The epiphenomenalist can say exactly the same about the connection between, for example, hurtfulness and behavior. It is simply a consequence of the fact that certain happenings in the brain cause both.

(ii) The second objection relates to Darwin's Theory of Evolution. According to natural selection the traits that evolve over time are those conducive to physical survival. We may assume that qualia evolved over time—we have them, the earliest forms of life do not—and so we should expect qualia to be conducive to survival. The objection is that they could hardly help us to survive if they do nothing to the physical world.

The appeal of this argument is undeniable, but there is a good reply to it. Polar bears have particularly thick, warm coats. The Theory of Evolution explains this (we suppose) by pointing out that having a thick warm coat is conducive to survival in the Arctic. But having a thick coat goes along with having a heavy coat, and having a heavy coat is *not* conducive to survival. It slows the animal down.

Does this mean that we have refuted Darwin because we have found an evolved trait—having a heavy coat—which is not conducive to survival? Clearly not. Having a heavy coat is an unavoidable concomitant of having a warm coat (in the context, modern insulation was not available), and the advantages for survival of having a warm coat outweighed the disadvantages of having a heavy one. The point is that all we can extract from Darwin's theory is that we should expect any evolved characteristic to be *either* conducive to survival *or* a by-product of one that is so conducive. The epiphenomenalist holds that qualia fall into the latter category. They are a by-product of certain brain processes that are highly conducive to survival. . . .

There is a very understandable response to the two replies I have just made. "All right, there is no knockdown refutation of the existence of epiphenomenal qualia. But the fact remains that they are an excrescence. They *do* nothing, they *explain* nothing, they serve merely to soothe the intuitions of dualists, and it is left a total mystery how they fit into the world view of science. In short we do not and cannot understand the how and why of them."

This is perfectly true; but is no objection to qualia, for it rests on an overly optimistic view of the human animal, and its powers. We are the products of Evolution. We understand and sense what we need to understand and sense in order to survive. Epiphenomenal qualia are totally irrelevant to survival. At no stage of our evolution did natural selection favor those who could make sense of how they are caused and the laws governing them, or in fact why they exist at all. And that is why we can't.

It is not sufficiently appreciated that Physicalism is an extremely optimistic view of our powers. If it is true, we have, in very broad outline admittedly, a grasp of our place in the scheme of things. Certain matters of sheer complexity defeat us—there are an awful lot of neurons—but in principle we have it all. But consider the antecedent probability that everything in the Universe be of a kind that is relevant in some way or other to the survival of *Homo sapiens*. It is very low surely. But then one must admit that it is very likely that there is a part of the whole scheme of things, maybe a big part, which no amount of evolution will ever bring us near to knowledge about or understanding of. For the simple reason that such knowledge and understanding is irrelevant to survival.

Physicalists typically emphasize that we are a part of nature on their view, which is fair enough. But if we are a part of nature, we are as nature has left us after however many years of evolution . . . and each step in that evolutionary progression has been a matter of chance constrained just by the need to preserve or increase survival value. The wonder is that we understand as much as we do, and there is no wonder that there should be matters which fall quite outside our comprehension. Perhaps exactly how epiphenomenal qualia fit into the scheme of things is one such.

Can Non-Humans Think?

Minds, Brains, and Programs*

JOHN R. SEARLE

John Searle (1932–) has made important contributions to the philosophy of mind and the philosophy of language. He teaches at the University of California, Berkeley.

WHAT PSYCHOLOGICAL AND PHILOSOPHICAL significance should we attach to recent efforts at computer simulations of human cognitive capacities? In answering this question, I find it useful to distinguish what I will call "strong" AI from "weak" or "cautious" AI (artificial intelligence). According to weak AI, the principal value of the computer in the study of the mind is that it gives us a very powerful tool. For example, it enables us to formulate and test hypotheses in a more rigorous and precise fashion. But according to strong AI, the computer is not merely a tool in the study of the mind; rather, the appropriately programmed computer really *is* a mind, in the sense that computers given the right programs can be literally said to *understand* and have other cognitive states. In strong AI, because the programmed computer has cognitive states, the programs are not mere tools that enable us to test psychological explanations; rather, the programs are themselves the explanations.

I have no objection to the claims of weak AI, at least as far as this article is concerned. My discussion here will be directed at the claims I have defined as those of strong AI, specifically the claim that the appropriately programmed computer literally has cognitive states and that the programs thereby explain human cognition. When I hereafter refer to AI, I have in mind the strong version, as expressed by these two claims.

I will consider the work of Roger Schank and his colleagues at Yale (Schank and Abelson 1977), because I am more familiar with it than I am with any other similar claims, and because it provides a very clear example of the sort of work I wish to examine. But nothing that follows depends upon the details of Schank's programs. The same arguments would apply to Winograd's SHRDLU (Winograd 1973), Weizenbaum's ELIZA (Weizenbaum 1965), and indeed any Turing machine simulation of human mental phenomena. . . .

Very briefly, and leaving out the various details, one can describe Schank's program as follows: The aim of the program is to simulate the human ability to understand stories. It is characteristic of human beings' story-understanding capacity that they can answer questions about the story even though the information that they give was never explicitly stated in the story. Thus, for example, suppose you are given the following story: "A man went into a restaurant and ordered a hamburger. When the hamburger arrived it was burned to a crisp, and the man stormed out of the restaurant angrily, without paying for the hamburger or leaving a tip." Now, if you are asked "Did the man eat the hamburger?" you will presumably answer, "No, he did not." Similarly, if you are given the following story: "A man went into a restaurant and ordered a hamburger; when the hamburger came he was very pleased with it; and as he left the restaurant he gave the waitress a large tip before paying his bill," and you are asked the question, "Did the man eat the hamburger?" you will presumably answer, "Yes, he ate the hamburger." Now Schank's machines can similarly answer questions about restaurants in this fashion. To do this, they have a "representation" of the sort of information that human beings have about restaurants, which enables them to answer such questions as those above, given these sorts of stories. When the machine is given the story and then asked the question, the machine will print out answers of the sort that we would expect human beings to give if told similar stories. Partisans of strong AI claim that in this question and answer sequence the machine is not only simulating a human ability but also (1) that the machine can literally be said to *understand* the story and provide the answers to questions, and (2) that what the machine and its programs do *explains* the human ability to understand the story and answer questions about it.

Both claims seem to me to be totally unsupported by Schank's work, as I will attempt to show in what follows. I am not, of course, saying that Schank himself is committed to these claims.

One way to test any theory of the mind is to ask oneself what it would be like if my mind actually worked on the principles that the theory says all minds work on. Let us apply this test to the Schank program with the following *Gedankenexperiment.**

*[Experiment in the imagination.—Eds.]

Suppose that I'm locked in a room and given a large batch of Chinese writing. Suppose furthermore (as is indeed the case) that I know no Chinese, either written or spoken, and that I'm not even confident that I could recognize Chinese writing as Chinese writing distinct from, say, Japanese writing or meaningless squiggles. To me, Chinese writing is just so many meaningless squiggles. Now suppose further that after this first batch of Chinese writing I am given a second batch of Chinese script together with a set of rules for correlating the second batch with the first batch. The rules are in English, and I understand these rules as well as any other native speaker of English. They enable me to correlate one set of formal symbols with another set of formal symbols, and all that "formal" means here is that I can identify the symbols entirely by their shapes. Now suppose also that I am given a third batch of Chinese symbols together with some instructions, again in English, that enable me to correlate elements of this third batch with the first two batches, and these rules instruct me how to give back certain Chinese symbols with certain sorts of shapes in response to certain sorts of shapes given me in the third batch. Unknown to me, the people who are giving me all of these symbols call the first batch a "script," they call the second batch a "story," and they call the third batch questions." Furthermore, they call the symbols I give them back in response to the third batch "answers to the questions," and the set of rules in English that they gave me, they call the "program." Now just to complicate the story a little, imagine that these people also give me stories in English, which I understand, and they then ask me questions in English about these stories, and I give them back answers in English. Suppose also that after a while I get so good at following the instructions for manipulating the Chinese symbols and the programmers get so good at writing the programs that from the external point of view—that is, from the point of view of somebody outside the room in which I am locked—my answers to the questions are absolutely indistinguishable from those of native Chinese speakers. Nobody just looking at my answers can tell that I don't speak a word of Chinese. Let us also suppose that my answers to the English questions are, as they no doubt would be, indistinguishable from those of other native English speakers, for the simple reason that I am a native English speaker. From the external point of view—from the point of view of someone reading my "answers"—the answers to the Chinese questions and the English questions are equally good. But in the Chinese case, unlike the English case, I produce the answers by manipulating uninterpreted formal symbols. As far as the Chinese is concerned, I simply behave like a computer; I perform computational operations on formally specified elements. For the purposes of the Chinese, I am simply an instantiation of the computer program.

Now the claims made by strong AI are that the programmed computer understands the stories and that the program in some sense explains human understanding. But we are now in a position to examine these claims in light of our thought experiment.

1. As regards the first claim, it seems to me quite obvious in the example that I do not understand a word of the Chinese stories. I have inputs and outputs that are indistinguishable from those of the native Chinese speaker, and I can have any formal program you like, but I still understand nothing. For the same reasons, Schank's computer understands nothing of any stories, whether in Chinese, English, or whatever, since in the Chinese case the computer is me, and in cases where the computer is not me, the computer has nothing more than I have in the case where I understand nothing.

2. As regards the second claim, that the program explains human understanding, we can see that the computer and its program do not provide sufficient conditions of understanding since the computer and the program are functioning, and there is no understanding. But does it even provide a necessary condition or a significant contribution to understanding? One of the claims made by the supporters of strong AI is that when I understand a story in English, what I am doing is exactly the same—or perhaps more of the same—as what I was doing in manipulating the Chinese symbols. It is simply more formal symbol manipulation that distinguishes the case in English, where I do understand, from the case in Chinese, where I don't. I have not demonstrated that this claim is false, but it would certainly appear an incredible claim in the example. Such plausibility as the claim has derives from the supposition that we can construct a program that will have the same inputs and outputs as native speakers, and in addition we assume that speakers have some level of description where they are also instantiations of a program. On the basis of these two assumptions we assume that even if Schank's program isn't the whole story about understanding, it may be part of the story. Well, I suppose that is an empirical possibility, but not the slightest reason has so far been given to believe that it is true, since what is suggested—though certainly not demonstrated—by the example is that the computer program is simply irrelevant to my understanding of the story. In the Chinese case I have everything that artificial intelligence can put into me by way of a program, and I understand nothing; in the English case I understand everything, and there is so far no reason at all to suppose that my understanding has anything to do with computer programs, that is, with computational operations on purely formally specified elements. As long as the program is defined in terms of computational operations on purely formally defined elements, what the example suggests is that these by themselves have no interesting connection with understanding. They are certainly not sufficient conditions, and not the slightest reason has been given to suppose that they are necessary conditions or even that they make a significant contribution to understanding. Notice that the force of the argument is not simply that different machines can have the same input and output while operating on different formal principles—that is not the point at all. Rather, whatever purely formal principles you put into the computer, they will not be sufficient for understanding, since a human will be able to follow the formal principles without understanding anything. No reason whatever has been offered to suppose that such principles are necessary or even contributory, since no reason has been given to suppose that when I understand English I am operating with any formal program at all.

Well, then, what is it that I have in the case of the English sentences that I do not have in the case of the Chinese sentences? The obvious answer is that I know what the former mean, while I haven't the faintest idea what the latter mean. But in what does this consist and why couldn't we give it to a machine, whatever it is? I will return to this question later, but first I want to continue with the example.

I have had the occasions to present this example to several workers in artificial intelligence, and, interestingly, they do not seem to agree on what the proper reply to it is. I get a surprising variety of replies, and in what follows I will consider the most common of these (specified along with their geographic origins).

But first I want to block some common misunderstandings about "understanding": In many of these discussions one finds a lot of fancy footwork about the word "understanding." My critics point out that there are many different degrees of understanding; that "understanding" is not a simple two-place predicate; that there are even different kinds and levels of understanding, and often the law of excluded middle doesn't even apply in a straightforward way to statements of the form "*x* understands *y*"; that in many cases it is a matter for decision and not a simple matter of fact whether *x* understands *y*; and so on. To all of these points I want to say: of course, of course. But they have nothing to do with the points at issue. There are clear cases in which "understanding" literally applies and clear cases in which it does not apply; and these two sorts of cases are all I need for this argument. I understand stories in English; to a lesser degree I can understand stories in French; to a still lesser degree, stories in German; and in Chinese, not at all. My car and my adding machine, on the other hand, understand nothing: they are not in that line of business.* We often attribute "understanding" and other cognitive predicates by metaphor and analogy to cars, adding machines, and other artifacts, but nothing is proved by such attributions. We say, "The door *knows* when to open because of its photoelectric cell," "The adding machine *knows how* (*understands how,* is *able*) to do addition and subtraction but not division," and "The thermostat *perceives* changes in the temperature." The reason we make these attributions is quite interesting, and it has to do with the fact that in artifacts we extend our own intentionality,† our tools are extensions of our purposes, and so we find it natural to make metaphorical attributions of intentionality to them; but I take it no philosophical ice is cut by such examples. The sense in which an automatic door "understands instructions" from its photoelectric cell is not at all the sense in which I understand English. If the sense in which Schank's programmed computers understand stories is supposed to be the metaphorical sense in which the door understands, and not the sense in which I understand English, the issue would not be worth discussing. But Newell and Simon (1963) write that the kind of cognition they claim for computers is exactly the same as for human beings. I like the straightforwardness of this claim, and it is the sort of claim I will be considering. I will argue that in the literal sense the programmed computer understands what the car and the adding machine understand, namely, exactly nothing. The computer's understanding is not just (like my understanding of German) partial or incomplete; it is zero.

Now to the replies:

(1) *The Systems Reply (Berkeley, California).* "While it is true that the individual person who is locked in the room does not understand the story, the fact is that he is merely part of a whole system, and the system does understand the story. The person has a large ledger in front of him in which are written the rules, he has a lot of scratch paper and pencils for doing calculations, he has "data banks" of sets of Chinese symbols. Now, understanding is not being ascribed to the mere individual; rather it

*Also, "understanding" implies both the possession of mental (intentional) states and the truth (validity, success) of these states. For the purposes of this discussion we are concerned only with the possession of the states.

†Intentionality is by definition that feature of certain mental states by which they are directed at or about objects and states of affairs in the world. Thus, beliefs, desires, and intentions are intentional states; undirected forms of anxiety and depression are not.

is being ascribed to this whole system of which he is a part."

My response to the systems theory is quite simple: Let the individual internalize all of these elements of the system. He memorizes the rules in the ledger and the data banks of Chinese symbols, and he does all the calculations in his head. The individual then incorporates the entire system. There isn't anything at all to the system that he does not encompass. We can even get rid of the room and suppose he works outdoors. All the same, he understands nothing of the Chinese, and a fortiori neither does the system, because there isn't anything in the system that isn't in him. If he doesn't understand, then there is no way the system could understand because the system is just a part of him.

Actually I feel somewhat embarrassed to give even this answer to the systems theory because the theory seems to me so implausible to start with. The idea is that while a person doesn't understand Chinese, somehow the *conjunction* of that person and bits of paper might understand Chinese. It is not easy for me to imagine how someone who was not in the grip of an ideology would find the idea at all plausible. Still, I think many people who are committed to the ideology of strong AI will in the end be inclined to say something very much like this; so let us pursue it a bit further. According to one version of this view, while the man in the internalized systems example doesn't understand Chinese in the sense that a native Chinese speaker does (because, for example, he doesn't know that the story refers to restaurants and hamburgers, etc.), still "the man as a formal symbol manipulation system" *really does understand Chinese*. The subsystem of the man that is the formal symbol manipulation system for Chinese should not be confused with the subsystem for English.

So there are really two subsystems in the man; one understands English, the other Chinese, and "it's just that the two systems have little to do with each other." But, I want to reply, not only do they have little to do with each other, they are not even remotely alike. The subsystem that understands English (assuming we allow ourselves to talk in this jargon of "subsystems" for a moment) knows that the stories are about restaurants and eating hamburgers, he knows that he is being asked questions about restaurants and that he is answering questions as best he can by making various inferences from the content of the story, and so on. But the Chinese system knows none of this. Whereas the English subsystem knows that "hamburgers" refers to hamburgers, the Chinese subsystem knows only that "squiggle squiggle" is followed by "squoggle squoggle." All he knows is that various formal symbols are being introduced at one end and manipulated according to rules written in English, and other symbols are going out at the other end. The whole point of the original example was to argue that such symbol manipulation by itself couldn't be sufficient for understanding Chinese in any literal sense because the man could write "squoggle squoggle" after "squiggle squiggle" without understanding anything in Chinese. And it doesn't meet that argument to postulate subsystems within the man, because the subsystems are no better off than the man was in the first place; they still don't have anything even remotely like what the English-speaking man (or subsystem) has. Indeed, in the case as described, the Chinese subsystem is simply a part of the English subsystem, a part that engages in meaningless symbol manipulation according to rules in English.

Let us ask ourselves what is supposed to motivate the systems reply in the first place; that is, what *independent* grounds are there supposed to be for saying that the agent must have a subsystem within him that literally understands stories in Chinese? As far as I can tell the only grounds are that in the example I have the same input and output as native Chinese speakers and a program that goes from one to the other. But the whole point of the examples has been to try to show that that couldn't be sufficient for understanding, in the sense in which I understand stories in English, because a person, and hence the set of systems that go to make up a person, could have the right combination of input, output, and program and still not understand anything in the relevant literal sense in which I understand English. The only motivation for saying there *must* be a subsystem in me that understands Chinese is that I have a program and I can pass the Turing test; I can fool native Chinese speakers. But precisely one of the points at issue is the adequacy of the Turing test. The example shows that there could be two "systems," both of which pass the Turing test, but only one of which understands; and it is no argument against this point to say that since they both pass the Turing test they must both understand, since this claim fails to meet the argument that the system in me that understands English has a great deal more than the system that merely processes Chinese. In short, the systems reply simply begs the question by insisting without argument that the system must understand Chinese.

Furthermore, the systems reply would appear to lead to consequences that are independently absurd. If we are to conclude that there must be cognition in me on the grounds that I have a certain sort of input and output and a program in between, then it looks like all sorts of noncognitive subsystems are going to turn out to be cognitive. For example, there is a level of description at which my stomach does information processing, and it instantiates any number of computer programs, but I take it we do not want to say that it has any understanding (cf. Pylyshyn 1980). But if we accept the systems reply, then it is hard to see how we avoid saying that stomach, heart, liver, and so on are all understanding subsystems, since there is no principled way to distinguish the motivation for saying the Chinese subsystem understands from saying that the stomach understands. It is, by the way, not an answer to this point to say that the Chinese system has information as input and output and the stomach has food and food products as input and output, since from the point of view of the agent, from my point of view, there is no information in either the food or the Chinese—the Chinese is just so many meaningless squiggles. The information in the Chinese case is solely in the eyes of the programmers and the interpreters, and there is nothing to prevent them from treating the input and output of my digestive organs as information if they so desire.

This last point bears on some independent problems in strong AI, and it is worth digressing for a moment to explain it. If strong AI is to be a branch of psychology, then it must be able to distinguish those systems that are genuinely mental from those that are not. It must be able to distinguish the principles on which the mind works from those on which nonmental systems work; otherwise it will offer us no explanations of what is specifically mental about the mental. And the mental-nonmental distinction cannot be just in the eye of the beholder but it must be intrinsic to the systems; otherwise it would be up to any beholder to treat people as nonmental and, for example, hurricanes as mental if he likes. But quite often in the AI literature the distinction is blurred in ways that would in the long run prove disastrous to the claim that AI is a cognitive inquiry. McCarthy, for example, writes, "Machines as simple as thermostats can be said to have beliefs, and having beliefs seems to be a characteristic of most machines capable of problem solving performance" (McCarthy 1979). Anyone who thinks strong AI has a chance as a theory of the mind ought to ponder the implications of that remark. We are asked to accept it as a discovery of strong AI that the hunk of metal on the wall that we use to regulate the temperature has beliefs in exactly the same sense that we, our spouses, and our children have beliefs, and furthermore that "most" of the other machines in the room—telephone, tape recorder, adding machine, electric light switch—also have beliefs in this literal sense. It is not the aim of this article to argue against McCarthy's point, so I will simply assert the following without argument. The study of the mind starts with such facts as that humans have beliefs, while thermostats, telephones, and adding machines don't. If you get a theory that denies this point you have produced a counterexample to the theory and the theory is false. One gets the impression that people in AI who write this sort of thing think they can get away with it because they don't really take it seriously, and they don't think anyone else will either. I propose, for a moment at least, to take it seriously. Think hard for one minute about what would be necessary to establish that that hunk of metal on the wall over there had real beliefs, beliefs with direction of fit, propositional content, and conditions of satisfaction; beliefs that had the possibility of being strong beliefs or weak beliefs; nervous, anxious, or secure beliefs; dogmatic, rational, or superstitious beliefs; blind faiths or hesitant cogitations; any kind of beliefs. The thermostat is not a candidate. Neither is stomach, liver, adding machine, or telephone. However, since we are taking the idea seriously, notice that its truth would be fatal to strong AI's claim to be a science of the mind. For now the mind is everywhere. What we wanted to know is what distinguishes the mind from thermostats and livers. And if McCarthy were right, strong AI wouldn't have a hope of telling us that.

(2) *The Robot Reply (Yale).* "Suppose we wrote a different kind of program from Schank's program. Suppose we put a computer inside a robot, and this computer would not just take in formal symbols as input and give out formal symbols as output, but rather would actually operate the robot in such a way that the robot does something very much like perceiving, walking, moving about, hammering nails, eating, drinking—anything you like. The robot would, for example, have a television camera attached to it that enabled it to see, it would have arms and legs that enabled it to 'act,' and all of this would be controlled by its computer 'brain.' Such a robot would, unlike Schank's computer, have genuine understanding and other mental states."

The first thing to notice about the robot reply is that it tacitly concedes that cognition is not solely a matter of formal symbol manipulation, since this reply adds a set of causal relations with the outside world (cf. Fodor 1980). But the answer to the robot reply is that the addition of such "perceptual" and "motor" capacities adds nothing by way of understanding, in particular, or intentionality, in general, to Schank's original program. To see this, notice that the same thought experiment applies to the robot case. Suppose that instead of the computer inside the robot, you put me inside the room and, as in the original Chinese case, you give me more Chinese symbols with more instructions in English for matching Chinese symbols to Chinese symbols and feeding back Chinese symbols to the outside. Suppose, unknown to me, some of the Chinese symbols that come to me come from a television camera attached to the robot and other Chinese symbols that I am giving out serve to make the motors inside the robot move the robot's legs or arms. It is important to emphasize that all I am doing is manipulating formal symbols: I know none of these other facts. I am receiving "information" from the robot's "perceptual" apparatus, and I am giving out "instructions" to its motor apparatus without knowing either of these facts. I am the robot's homunculus, but unlike the traditional homunculus, I don't know what's going on. I don't understand anything except the rules for symbol manipulation. Now in this case I want to say that the robot has no intentional states at all; it is simply moving about as a result of its electrical wiring and its program. And furthermore, by instantiating the program I have no intentional states of the relevant type. All I do is follow formal instructions about manipulating formal symbols.

(3) *The Brain Simulator Reply (Berkeley and M.I.T.).* "Suppose we design a program that doesn't represent information that we have about the world, such as the information in Schank's scripts, but simulates the actual sequence of neuron firings at the synapses of the brain of a native Chinese speaker when he understands stories in Chinese and gives answers to them. The machine takes in Chinese stories and questions about them as input, it simulates the formal structure of actual Chinese brains in processing these stories, and it gives out Chinese answers as outputs. We can even imagine that the machine operates, not with a single serial program, but with a whole set of programs operating in parallel, in the manner that actual human brains presumably operate when they process natural language. Now surely in such a case we would have to say that the machine understood the stories; and if we refuse to say that, wouldn't we also have to deny that native Chinese speakers understood the stories? At the level of the synapses, what would or could be different about the program of the computer and the program of the Chinese brain?"

Before countering this reply I want to digress to note that it is an odd reply for any partisan of artificial intelligence (or functionalism, etc.) to make: I thought the whole idea of strong AI is that we don't need to know how the brain works to know how the mind works. The basic hypothesis, or so I had supposed, was that there is a level of mental operations consisting of computational processes over formal elements that constitute the essence of the mental and can be realized in all sorts of different brain processes, in the same way that any computer program can be realized in different computer hardwares: On the assumptions of strong AI, the mind is to the brain as the program is to the hardware, and thus we can understand the mind without doing neurophysiology. If we had to know how the brain worked to do AI, we wouldn't bother with AI. However, even getting this close to the operation of the brain is still not sufficient to produce understanding. To see this, imagine that instead of a monolingual man in a room shuffling symbols we have the man operate an elaborate set of water pipes with valves connecting them. When the man receives the Chinese symbols, he looks up in the program, written in English, which valves he has to turn on and off. Each water connection corresponds to a synapse in the Chinese brain, and the whole system is rigged up so that after doing all the right firings, that is after turning on all the right faucets, the Chinese answers pop out at the output end of the series of pipes.

Now where is the understanding in this system? It takes Chinese as input, it simulates the formal structure of the synapses of the Chinese brain, and it gives Chinese as output. But the man certainly doesn't understand Chinese, and neither do the water pipes, and if we are tempted to adopt what I think is the absurd view that somehow the *conjunction* of man *and* water pipes understands, remember that in principle the man can internalize the formal structure of the water pipes and do all the "neuron firings" in his imagination. The problem with the brain simulator is that it is simulating the wrong things about the brain. As long as it simulates only the formal structure of the sequence of neuron firings at the synapses, it won't have simulated what matters about the brain, namely its causal properties, its ability to produce intentional states. And that the formal properties are not sufficient for the causal properties is shown by the water pipe example: We can have all the formal properties carved off from the relevant neurobiological causal properties.

(4) *The Combination Reply (Berkeley and Stanford).* "While each of the previous three replies might not be completely convincing by itself as a refutation of the Chinese room counterexample, if you take all three together they are collectively much more convincing and even decisive. Imagine a robot with a brain-shaped computer lodged in its cranial cavity, imagine the computer programmed with all the synapses of a human brain, imagine the whole behavior of the robot is indistinguishable from human behavior, and now think of the whole thing as a unified system and not just as a computer with inputs and outputs. Surely in such a case we would have to ascribe intentionality to the system."

I entirely agree that in such a case we would find it rational and indeed irresistible to accept the hypothesis that the robot had intentionality, as long as we knew nothing more about it. Indeed, besides appearance and behavior, the other elements of the combination are really irrelevant. If we could build a robot whose behavior was indistinguishable over a large range from human behavior, we would attribute intentionality to it, pending some reason not to. We wouldn't need to know in advance that its computer brain was a formal analogue of the human brain.

But I really don't see that this is any help to the claims of strong AI, and here's why: According to strong AI, instantiating a formal program with the right input and output is a sufficient condition of, indeed is constitutive of, intentionality. As Newell (1979) puts it, the essence of the mental is the operation of a physical symbol system. But the attributions of intentionality that we make to the robot in this example have nothing to do with formal programs. They are simply based on the assumption that if the robot looks and behaves sufficiently like us, then we would suppose, until proven otherwise, that it must have mental states like ours that cause and are expressed by its behavior and it must have an inner mechanism capable of producing such mental states. If we knew independently how to account for its behavior without such assumptions we would not attribute intentionality to it, especially if we knew it had a formal program. And this is precisely the point of my earlier reply to objection II.

Suppose we knew that the robot's behavior was entirely accounted for by the fact that a man inside it was receiving uninterpreted formal symbols from the robot's sensory receptors and sending out uninterpreted formal symbols to its motor mechanisms, and the man was doing this symbol manipulation in accordance with a bunch of rules. Furthermore, suppose the man knows none of these facts about the robot; all he knows is which operations to perform on which meaningless symbols. In such a case we would regard the robot as an ingenious mechanical dummy. The hypothesis that the dummy has a mind would now be unwarranted and unnecessary, for there is now no longer any reason to ascribe intentionality to the robot or to the system of which it is a part (except of course for the man's intentionality in manipulating the symbols). The formal symbol manipulations go on, the input and output are correctly matched, but the only real locus of intentionality is the man, and he doesn't know any of the relevant intentional states; he doesn't, for example, *see* what comes into the robot's eyes, he doesn't *intend* to move the robot's arm, and he doesn't *understand* any of the remarks made to or by the robot. Nor, for the reasons stated earlier, does the system of which man and robot are a part.

To see this point, contrast this case with cases in which we find it completely natural to ascribe intentionality to members of certain other primate species such as apes and monkeys and to domestic animals such as dogs. The reasons we find it natural are, roughly, two: We can't make sense of the animal's behavior without the ascription of intentionality, and we can see that the beasts are made of similar stuff to ourselves—that is an eye, that a nose, this is its skin, and so on. Given the coherence of the animal's behavior and the assumption of the same causal stuff underlying it, we assume both that the animal must have mental states underlying its behavior, and that the mental states must be produced by mechanisms made out of the stuff that is like our stuff. We would certainly make similar assumptions about the robot unless we had some reason not to, but as soon as we knew that the behavior was the result of a formal program, and that the actual causal properties of the physical substance were irrelevant, we would abandon the assumption of intentionality.

There are two other responses to my example that come up frequently (and so are worth discussing) but really miss the point.

(5) *The Other Minds Reply (Yale).* "How do you know that other people understand Chinese or anything else? Only by their behavior. Now the computer can pass the behavioral tests as well as they can (in principle), so if you are going to attribute cognition to other people you must in principle also attribute it to computers."

This objection really is only worth a short reply. The problem in this discussion is not about how I know that other people have cognitive states, but rather what it is that I am attributing to them when I attribute cognitive states to them. The thrust of the argument is that it couldn't be just computational processes and their output because the computational processes and their output can exist without the cognitive state. It is no answer to this argument to feign anesthesia. In "cognitive sciences" one presupposes the reality and knowability of the mental in the same way that in physical sciences one has to presuppose the reality and knowability of physical objects.

(6) *The Many Mansions Reply (Berkeley).* "Your whole argument presupposes that AI is only about analog and digital computers. But that just happens to be the present state of technology. Whatever these causal processes are that you say are essential for intentionality (assuming you are right), eventually we will be able to build devices that have these causal processes, and that will be artificial intelligence. So your arguments are in no way directed at the ability of artificial intelligence to produce and explain cognition."

I really have no objection to this reply save to say that it in effect trivializes the project of strong AI by redefining it as whatever artificially produces and explains cognition. The interest of the original claim made on behalf of artificial intelligence is that it was a precise, well defined thesis: Mental processes are computational processes over formally defined elements. I have been concerned to challenge that thesis. If the claim is redefined so that it is no longer that thesis, my objections no longer apply because there is no longer a testable hypothesis for them to apply to.

Let us now return to the question I promised I would try to answer: Granted that in my original example I understand the English and I do not understand the Chinese, and granted therefore that the machine doesn't understand either English or Chinese, still there must be something about me that makes it the case that I understand English and a corresponding something lacking in me that makes it the case that I fail to understand Chinese. Now why couldn't we give those somethings, whatever they are, to a machine?

I see no reason in principle why we couldn't give a machine the capacity to understand English or Chinese, since in an important sense our bodies with our brains are precisely such machines. But I do see very strong arguments for saying that we could not give such a thing to a machine where the operation of the machine is defined solely in terms of computational processes over formally defined elements; that is, where the operation of the machine is defined as an instantiation of a computer program. It is not because I am the instantiation of a computer program that I am able to understand English and have other forms of intentionality (I am, I suppose, the instantiation of any number of computer programs), but as far as we know it is because I am a certain sort of organism with a certain biological (i.e., chemical and physical) structure, and this structure, under certain conditions, is causally capable of producing perception, action, understanding, learning, and other intentional phenomena. And part of the point of the present argument is that only something that had those causal powers could have that intentionality. Perhaps other physical and chemical processes could produce exactly these effects; perhaps, for example, Martians also have intentionality but their brains are made of different stuff. That is an empirical question, rather like the question whether photosynthesis can be done by something with a chemistry different from that of chlorophyll.

But the main point of the present argument is that no purely formal model will ever be sufficient by itself for intentionality because the formal properties are not by themselves constitutive of intentionality, and they have by themselves no causal powers except the power, when instantiated, to produce the next stage of the formalism when the machine is running. And any other causal properties that particular realizations of the formal model have are irrelevant to the formal model because we can always put the same formal model in a different realization where those causal properties are obviously absent. Even if, by some miracle, Chinese speakers exactly realize Schank's program, we can put the same program in English speakers, water pipes, or computers, none of which understand Chinese, the program notwithstanding.

What matters about brain operations is not the formal shadow cast by the sequence of synapses but rather the actual properties of the sequences. All the arguments for the strong version of artificial intelligence that I have seen insist on drawing an outline around the shadows cast by cognition and then claiming that the shadows are the real thing.

By way of concluding I want to try to state some of the general philosophical points implicit in the argument. For clarity I will try to do it in a question-and-answer fashion, and I begin with that old chestnut of a question:

"Could a machine think?"

The answer is, obviously, yes. We are precisely such machines.

"Yes, but could an artifact, a man-made machine, think?"

Assuming it is possible to produce artificially a machine with a nervous system, neurons with axons and dendrites, and all the rest of it, sufficiently like ours, again the answer to the question seems to be obviously, yes. If you can exactly duplicate the causes, you could duplicate the effects. And indeed it might be possible to produce consciousness, intentionality, and all the rest of it using some other sorts of chemical principles than those that human beings use. It is, as I said, an empirical question.

"OK, but could a digital computer think?"

If by "digital computer" we mean anything at all that has a level of description where it can correctly be described as the instantiation of a computer program, then again the answer is, of course, yes, since we are the instantiations of any number of computer programs, and we can think.

"But could something think, understand, and so on *solely* by virtue of being a computer with the right sort of program? Could instantiating a program, the right program of course, by itself be a sufficient condition of understanding?"

This I think is the right question to ask, though it is usually confused with one or more of the earlier questions, and the answer to it is no.

"Why not?"

Because the formal symbol manipulations by themselves don't have any intentionality; they are quite meaningless; they aren't even *symbol* manipulations, since the symbols don't symbolize anything. In the linguistic jargon, they have only a syntax but no semantics. Such intentionality as computers appear to have is solely in the minds of those who program them and those who use them, those who send in the input and those who interpret the output.

The aim of the Chinese room example was to try to show this by showing that as soon as we put something into the system that really does have intentionality (a man), and we program him with the formal program, you can see that the formal program carries no additional intentionality. It adds nothing, for example, to a man's ability to understand Chinese.

Precisely that feature of AI that seemed so appealing—the distinction between the program and the realization—proves fatal to the claim that simulation could be duplication. The distinction between the program and its realization in the hardware seems to be parallel to the distinction between the level of mental operations and the level of brain operations. And if we could describe the level of mental operations as a formal program, then it seems we could describe what was essential about the mind without doing either introspective psychology or neurophysiology of the brain. But the equation "mind is to brain as program is to hardware" breaks down at several points, among them the following three:

First, the distinction between program and realization has the consequence that the same program could have all sorts of crazy realizations that had no form of intentionality. Weizenbaum (1976, Ch. 2), for example, shows in detail how to construct a computer using a roll of toilet paper and a pile of small stones. Similarly, the Chinese story understanding-program can be programmed into a sequence of water pipes, a set of wind machines, or a monolingual English speaker, none of which thereby acquires an understanding of Chinese. Stones, toilet paper, wind, and water pipes are the wrong kind of stuff to have intentionality in the first place—only something that has the same causal powers as brains can have intentionality—and though the English speaker has the right kind of stuff for intentionality you can easily see that he doesn't get any extra intentionality by memorizing the program, since memorizing it won't teach him Chinese.

Second, the program is purely formal, but the intentional states are not in that way formal. They are defined in terms of their content, not their form. The belief that it is raining, for example, is not defined as a certain formal shape, but as a certain mental content with conditions of satisfaction, a direction of fit (see Searle 1979), and the like. Indeed the belief as such hasn't even got a formal shape in this syntactic sense, since one and the same belief can be given an indefinite number of different syntactic expressions in different linguistic systems.

Third, as I mentioned before, mental states and events are literally a product of the operation of the brain, but the program is not in that way a product of the computer.

"Well if programs are in no way constitutive of mental processes, why have so many people believed the converse? That at least needs some explanation."

I don't really know the answer to that one. The idea that computer simulations could be the real thing ought to have seemed suspicious in the first place because the computer isn't confined to simulating mental operations, by any means. No one supposes that computer simulations of a five-alarm fire will burn the neighborhood down or that a computer simulation of a rainstorm will leave us all drenched. Why on earth would anyone suppose that a computer simulation of understanding actually understood anything? It is sometimes said that it would be frightfully hard to get computers to feel pain or fall in love, but love and pain are neither harder nor easier than cognition or anything else. For simulation, all you need is the right input and output and a program in the middle that transforms the former into the latter. That is all the computer has for anything it does. To confuse simulation with duplication is the same mistake, whether it is pain, love, cognition, fires, or rainstorms.

Still, there are several reasons why AI must have seemed—and to many people perhaps still does seem—in some way to reproduce and thereby explain mental phenomena, and I believe we will not succeed in removing these illusions until we have fully exposed the reasons that give rise to them.

First, and perhaps most important, is a confusion about the notion of "information processing": Many people in cognitive science believe that the human brain, with its mind, does something called "information processing," and analogously the computer with its program does information processing; but fires and rainstorms, on the other hand, don't do information processing at all. Thus, though the computer can simulate the formal features of any process whatever, it stands in a special relation to the mind and brain because when the computer is properly programmed, ideally with the same program as the brain, the information processing is identical in the two cases, and this information processing is really the essence of the mental. But the trouble with this argument is that it rests on an ambiguity in the notion of "information." In the sense in which people "process information" when they reflect, say, on problems in arithmetic or when they read and answer questions about stories, the programmed computer does not do "information processing." Rather, what it does is manipulate formal symbols. The fact that the programmer and the interpreter of the computer output use the symbols to stand for objects in the world is totally beyond the scope of the computer. The computer, to repeat, has a syntax but no semantics. Thus, if you type into the computer "2 plus 2 equals?" it will type out "4." But it has no idea that "4" means 4 or that it means anything at all. And the point is not that it lacks some second-order information about the interpretation of its first-order symbols, but rather that its first-order symbols don't have any interpretations as far as the computer is concerned. All the computer has is more symbols. The introduction of the notion of "information processing" therefore produces a dilemma: Either we construe the notion of "information processing" in such a way that it implies intentionality as part of the process or we don't. If the former, then the programmed computer does not do information processing: it only manipulates formal symbols. If the latter, then, though the computer does information processing, it is only doing so in the sense in which adding machines, typewriters, stomachs, thermostats, rainstorms, and hurricanes do information processing; namely, they have a level of description at which we can describe them as taking information in at one end, transforming it, and producing information as output. But in this case it is up to outside observers to interpret the input and output as information in the ordinary sense. And no similarity is established between the computer and the brain in terms of any similarity of information processing.

Second, in much of AI there is a residual behaviorism or operationalism. Since appropriately programmed computers can have input-output patterns similar to those of human beings, we are tempted to postulate mental states in the computer similar to human mental states. But once we see that it is both conceptually and empirically possible for a system to have human capacities in some realm without having any intentionality at all, we should be able to overcome this impulse. My desk adding machine has calculating capacities, but no intentionality, and in this paper I have tried to show that a system could have input and output capabilities that duplicated those of a native Chinese speaker and still not understand Chinese, regardless of how it was programmed. The Turing test is typical of the tradition in being unashamedly behavioristic and operationalistic, and I believe that if AI workers totally repudiated behaviorism and operationalism much of the confusion between simulation and duplication would be eliminated.

Third, this residual operationalism is joined to a residual form of dualism; indeed strong AI only makes sense given the dualistic assumption that, where the mind is concerned, the brain doesn't matter. In strong AI (and in functionalism, as well) what matters are programs, and programs are independent of their realization in machines; indeed, as far as AI is concerned, the same program could be realized by an electronic machine, a Cartesian mental substance, or a Hegelian world spirit. The single most surprising discovery that I have made in discussing these issues is that many AI workers are quite shocked by my idea that actual human mental phenomena might be dependent on actual physical-chemical properties of actual human brains. But if you think about it a minute you can see that I should not have been surprised; for unless you accept some form of dualism, the strong AI project hasn't got a chance. The project is to reproduce and explain the mental by designing programs, but unless the mind is not only conceptually but empirically independent of the brain you couldn't carry out the project, for the program is completely independent of any realization. Unless you believe that the mind is separable from the brain both conceptually and empirically—dualism in a strong form—you cannot hope to reproduce the mental by writing and running programs since programs must be independent of brains or any other particular forms of instantiation. If mental operations consist in computational operations on formal symbols, then it follows that they have no interesting connection with the brain; the only connection would be that the brain just happens to be one of the indefinitely many types of machines capable of instantiating the program. This form of dualism is not the traditional Cartesian variety that claims there are two sorts of *substances*, but it is Cartesian in the sense that it insists that what is specifically mental about the mind has no intrinsic connection with the actual properties of the brain. This underlying dualism is masked from us by the fact that AI literature contains frequent fulminations against "dualism"; what the authors seem to be unaware of is that their position presupposes a strong version of dualism.

"Could a machine think?" My own view is that *only* a machine could think, and indeed only very special kinds of machines, namely brains and machines that had the same causal powers as brains. And that is the main reason strong AI has had little to tell us about thinking, since it has nothing to tell us about machines. By its own definition, it is about programs, and programs are not machines. Whatever else intentionality is, it is a biological phenomenon, and it is as likely to be as causally dependent on the specific biochemistry of its origins as lactation, photosynthesis, or any other biological phenomena. No one would suppose that we could produce milk and sugar by running a computer simulation of the formal sequences in lactation and photosynthesis, but where the mind is concerned many people are willing to believe in such a miracle because of a deep and abiding dualism: The mind they suppose is a matter of formal processes and is independent of quite specific material causes in the way that milk and sugar are not.

In defense of this dualism the hope is often expressed that the brain is a digital computer (early computers, by the way, were often called "electronic brains"). But that is no help. Of course the brain is a digital computer. Since everything is a digital computer, brains are too. The point is that the brain's causal capacity to produce intentionality cannot consist in its instantiating a computer program, since for any program you like it is possible for something to instantiate that program and still not have any mental states. Whatever it is that the brain does to produce intentionality, it cannot consist in instantiating a program since no program, by itself, is sufficient for intentionality.*

*I am indebted to a rather large number of people for discussion of these matters and for their patient attempts to overcome my ignorance of artificial intelligence. I would especially like to thank Ned Block, Hubert Dreyfus, John Haugeland, Roger Schank, Robert Wilensky, and Terry Winograd.

Robots and Minds*[1]

WILLIAM G. LYCAN

William G. Lycan (1945–) teaches philosophy at the University of North Carolina, Chapel Hill.

ARTIFICIAL INTELLIGENCE IS, very crudely, the science of getting machines to perform jobs that normally require intelligence and judgment. Researchers at any number of AI labs have designed machines that prove mathematical theorems, play chess, sort mail, guide missiles, assemble auto engines, diagnose illnesses, read stories and other written texts, and converse with people in a rudimentary way. This is, we might say, intelligent behavior.

But what is this "intelligence"? As a first pass, I suggest that intelligence of the sort I am talking about is a kind of flexibility, a responsiveness to contingencies. A dull or stupid machine must have just the right kind of raw materials presented to it in just the right way, or it is useless: the electric can opener must have an appropriately sized can fixed under its drive wheel *just so,* in order to operate at all. Humans (most of us, anyway) are not like that. We deal with the unforeseen. We take what comes and make the best of it, even though we may have had no idea what it would be. We play the ball from whatever lie we are given, and at whatever angle to the green; we read and understand texts we have never seen before; we find our way back to Chapel Hill after getting totally lost in downtown Durham (or downtown Washington, D.C., or downtown Lima, Peru).

Our pursuit of our goals is guided while in progress by our ongoing perception and handling of interim developments. Moreover, we can pursue any number of different goals at the same time, and balance them against each other. We are sensitive to contingencies, both external and internal, that have a very complex and unsystematic structure.

It is almost irresistible to speak of *information* here, even if the term were not as trendy as it is. An intelligent creature, I want to say, is an *information-sensitive* creature, one that not only *registers* information through receptors such as sense-organs but somehow stores and manages and finally uses that information. Higher animals are intelligent beings in this sense, and so are we, even though virtually nothing is known about how we organize or manage the vast, seething profusion of information that comes our way. And there is one sort of machine that is information-sensitive also: the digital computer. A computer *is* a machine specifically designed to be fed complexes of information, to store them, manage them, and produce appropriate theoretical or practical conclusions on demand. Thus, if artificial intelligence is what one is looking for, it is no accident that one looks to the computer.

Yet a computer has two limitations in common with machines of less elite and grandiose sorts, both of them already signaled in the characterization I have just given. First, a (present-day) computer must be *fed* information, and the choice of what information to feed and in what form is up to a human programmer or operator. (For that matter, a present-day computer must be plugged into an electrical outlet and have its switch turned to ON,

**From William G. Lycan,* Consciousness *(Cambridge, MA: A Bradford Book, 1987), pp. 123–30. Reprinted by permission of the publisher, MIT Press.*

but this is a very minor contingency given the availability of nuclear power packs.) Second, the *appropriateness* and effectiveness of a computer's output depends entirely on what the programmer or operator had in mind and goes on to make of it. A computer has intelligence in the sense I have defined, but has no judgment, since it has no goals and purposes of its own and no internal sense of appropriateness, relevance, or proportion.

For essentially these reasons—that computers are intelligent in my minimal sense, and that they are nevertheless limited in the two ways I have mentioned—AI theorists, philosophers, and intelligent laymen have inevitably compared computers to human minds, but at the same time debated both technical and philosophical questions raised by this comparison. The questions break down into three main groups or types: (A) Questions of the form "Will a computer ever be able to do *X*?" where *X* is something that intelligent humans can do. (B) Questions of the form "Given that a computer can or could do *X*, have we any reason to think that it does *X* in the same way that humans do *X*?" (C) Questions of the form "Given that some futuristic supercomputer were able to do *X*, *Y*, *Z*, . . . , for some arbitrarily large range and variety of human activities, would that show that the computer had property *P*?" where *P* is some feature held to be centrally, vitally characteristic of human minds, such as thought, consciousness, feeling, sensation, emotion, creativity, or freedom of the will.

Questions of type A are empirical questions and cannot be settled without decades, perhaps centuries, of further research—compare ancient and medieval speculations on the question of whether a machine could ever fly. Questions of type B are brutely empirical too, and their answers are unavailable to AI researchers *per se*, lying squarely in the domain of cognitive psychology, a science or alleged science barely into its infancy. Questions of type C are philosophical and conceptual, and so I shall essay to answer them all at one stroke.

Let us begin by supposing that all questions of types A and B have been settled affirmatively—that one day we might be confronted by a much-improved version of Hal, the soft-spoken computer in Kubrick's *2001* (younger readers may substitute Star Wars' C3PO or whatever subsequent cinematic robot is the most lovable). Let us call this more versatile machine "Harry."[2] Harry (let us say) is humanoid in form—he is a miracle of miniaturization and has lifelike plastic skin—and he can converse intelligently on all sorts of subjects, play golf *and* the viola, write passable poetry, control his occasional nervousness pretty well, make love, prove mathematical theorems (of course), show envy when outdone, throw gin bottles at annoying children, etc., etc. We may suppose he fools people into thinking he is human. Now the question is, is Harry really a *person*? Does he have thoughts, feelings, and so on? Is he actually conscious, or is he just a mindless walking hardware store whose movements are astoundingly *like* those of a person?[3]

Plainly his acquaintances would tend from the first to see him as a person, even if they were aware of his dubious antecedents. I think it is a plain psychological fact, if nothing more, that we could not help treating him as a person, unless we resolutely made up our minds, on principle, not to give him the time of day. But how could we really tell that he is conscious?

Well, how do we really tell that any humanoid creature is conscious? How do you tell that I am conscious, and how do I tell that you are? Surely we tell, and decisively, on the basis of our standard behavioral tests for mental states, to revert to [an earlier theme of this book]: We know that a human being has such-and-such mental states when it behaves, to speak very generally, in the ways we take to be appropriate to organisms that are in those states. (The point is of course an epistemological one only, no metaphysical implications intended or tolerated.) We know for practical purposes that a creature has a mind when it fulfills all the right criteria. And by hypothesis, Harry fulfills all our behavioral criteria with a vengeance; moreover, he does so *in the right way* (cf. questions of type B): the processing that stands causally behind his behavior is just like ours. It follows that we are at least *prima facie* justified in believing him to be conscious.

We have not *proved* that he is conscious, of course—any more than you have proved that I am conscious. An organism's merely behaving in a certain way is no logical guarantee of sentience; from my point of view it is at least imaginable, a bare logical possibility, that my wife, my daughter, and my chairman are not conscious, even though I have excellent, overwhelming behavioral reason to think that they are. But for that matter, our "standard behavioral tests" for mental states yield practical or moral certainty only so long as the situation is not palpably extraordinary or bizarre. A human chauvinist—in this case, someone who denies that Harry has thoughts and feelings, joys and sorrows—thinks precisely that Harry is as bizarre as they come. But *what is bizarre about him?* There are quite a few chauvinist answers to this, but what they boil down to, and given our hypothesized facts all they could boil down to, are two differences between Harry and ourselves: his *origin* (a laboratory is not a proper mother), and the *chemical composition of his anatomy,* if his creator has used silicon instead of carbon, for example. To exclude him from our community for either or both of *those* reasons seems to me to be a clear case of racial or ethnic prejudice (literally) and nothing more. I see no obvious way in which either a creature's origin or its subneuroanatomical chemical composition should matter to its psychological processes or any aspect of its mentality.

My argument can be reinforced by a thought-experiment . . . : Imagine that we take a normal human being, Henrietta, and begin gradually replacing parts of her with synthetic materials—first a few prosthetic limbs, then a few synthetic arteries, then some neural fibers, and so forth. Suppose that the surgeons who perform the successive operations (particularly the neurosurgeons) are so clever and skillful that Henrietta survives in fine style: her intelligence, personality, perceptual acuity, poetic abilities, etc., remain just as they were before. But after the replacement process has eventually gone on to completion, Henrietta will have become an artifact—at least, her body will then be nothing but a collection of artifacts. Did she lose consciousness at some point during the sequence of operations, despite her continuing to behave and respond normally? When? It is hard to imagine that there is some privileged portion of the human nervous system that is for some reason indispensable, even though kidneys, lungs, heart, and any given bit of brain could in principle be replaced by a prosthesis (for *what* reason?); and it is also hard to imagine that there is some *pro*portion of the nervous system such that removal of more than that proportion causes loss of consciousness or sentience despite perfect maintenance of all intelligent capacities.

If this quick but totally compelling defense of Harry and Henrietta's personhood is correct, then the two, and their ilk, will have not only mental lives like ours, but *moral* lives like ours, and moral rights and privileges accordingly. Just as origin and physical constitution fail to affect psychological personhood, if a creature's internal organization is sufficiently like ours, so do they fail to affect moral personhood. We do not discriminate against a person who has a wooden leg, or a mechanical kidney, or a nuclear heart regulator; no more should we deny any human or civil right to Harry or Henrietta on grounds of their origin or physical makeup, which they cannot help.

But this happy egalitarianism raises a more immediate question: *In real life,* we shall soon be faced with medium-grade machines, which have some intelligence and are not "mere" machines like refrigerators or typewriters but which fall far short of flawless human stimulators like Harry. For AI researchers may well build machines that will appear to have some familiar mental capacities but not others. The most obvious example is that of a sensor or perceptron, which picks up information from its immediate environment, records it, and stores it in memory for future printout. (We already have at least crude machines of this kind. When they become versatile and sophisticated enough, it will be quite natural to say that they see or hear and that they remember.) But the possibility of "specialist" machines of this kind raises an unforeseen contingency: There is an enormous and many-dimensional range of possible beings in between our current "mere" machines and our fully developed, flawless human simulators; we have not even begun to think of all the infinitely possible variations on this theme. And once we do begin to think of these hard cases, we will be at a loss as to where to draw the "personhood" line between them. How complex, eclectic, and impressive must a machine be, and in what respects, before we award it the accolade of personhood and/or of consciousness? There is, to say the least, no clear answer to be had *a priori,* Descartes' notorious view of animals to the contrary notwithstanding.*

This typical philosophical question would be no more than an amusing bonbon, were it not for the attending moral conundrum: What moral rights would an intermediate or marginally intelligent machine have? Adolescent machines of this sort will confront us much sooner than will any good human simulators, for they are easier to design and construct; more to the moral point, they will be designed mainly as *labor-saving devices,* as servants who will work for free, and servants of this kind are (literally) made to be exploited. If they are intelligent to any degree, we should have qualms in proportion.

I suggest that this moral problem, which may become a real and pressing one, is parallel to the current debate over animal rights. Luckily I have never wanted to cook and eat my Compaq Portable.

Suppose I am right about the irrelevance of biochemical constitution to psychology; and suppose I was also right about the coalescing of the notions *computation, information, intelligence.* Then our mentalized theory of computation suggests in turn a computational theory of mentality, and a computational picture of the place of human beings in the world. In fact, philosophy aside, that picture has already begun to get a grip on people's thinking—as witness the filtering down of computer jargon into contemporary casual speech—and that grip is not going to loosen. Computer science is the defining technology of our time, and in this sense the computer is the natural cultural successor to the steam engine, the clock, the spindle, and the potter's wheel.[4] Predictably, an articulate computational theory of the mind has also gained credence among professional psychologists and philosophers.[5] I have been trying to support it here and elsewhere; I shall say no more about it for now, save to note again its near-indispensability in accounting for intentionality (noted), and to address the ubiquitous question of computer creativity and freedom:

Soft Determinism† or **Libertarianism**† may be true of humans. But many people have far more rigidly deterministic intuitions about computers. Computers, after all, (let us all say it together:) "only do what they are told/programmed to do"; they have no spontaneity and no freedom of choice. But human beings choose all the time, and the ensuing states of the world often depend entirely on these choices.[6] Thus the "computer analogy" supposedly fails.

The alleged failure of course depends on what we think freedom really is. As a Soft Determinist, I think that to have freedom of choice in acting is (roughly) for one's action to proceed out of one's own desires, deliberation, will, and intention, rather than being compelled or coerced by external forces regardless of my desires or will. As before, free actions are not *uncaused* actions. My free actions are those that *I* cause, i.e., that are caused by my own mental processes rather than by something pressing on me from the outside. I have argued . . . that I am free in that my beliefs, desires, deliberations, and intentions are all functional or computational states and processes within me that do interact in characteristic ways to produce my behavior. Note now that the same response vindicates our skilled human-simulating machines from the charge of puppethood. The word "robot" is often used as a veritable synonym for "puppet," so it may seem that Harry and Henrietta are paradigm cases of *un*free mechanisms that "only do what they are programmed to do." This is a slander—for two reasons:

First, even an ordinary computer, let alone a fabulously sophisticated machine like Harry, is in a way unpredictable. You are at its mercy. You *think* you know what it is going to do; you know what it should do, what it is supposed to do, but there is no guarantee—and it may do something *awful* or at any rate something that you could not have predicted and could not figure out if you tried with

* Descartes claimed in his *Discourse on Method* that animals are mere machines.

† See Part 4 for detailed discussions (and definitions) of these doctrines.

both hands. This practical sort of unpredictability would be multiplied a thousandfold in the case of a machine as complex as the human brain, and it is notably characteristic of *people.*

The unpredictability has several sources. (i) Plain old physical defects, as when Harry's circuits have been damaged by trauma, stress, heat, or the like. (ii) Bugs in one or more of his programs. (I have heard that once upon a time, somewhere, a program was written that had not a single bug in it, but this is probably an urban folk tale.) (iii) Randomizers, quantum-driven or otherwise; elements of Harry's behavior may be *genuinely,* physically random. (iv) Learning and analogy mechanisms; if Harry is equipped with these, as he inevitably would be, then his behavior-patterns will be modified in response to his experiential input from the world, which would be neither controlled nor even observed by us. *We don't know where he's been.* (v) The relativity of reliability to goal-description. This last needs a bit of explanation.

People often say things like, "A computer just crunches binary numbers; provided it isn't broken, it just chugs on mindlessly through whatever flip-flop settings are predetermined by its electronic makeup." But such remarks ignore the multileveled character of real computer programming. At any given time, as we have noted [earlier], a computer is running *each of any number of* programs, depending on how it is described and on the level of functional organization that interests us. True, it is always crunching binary numbers, but in crunching them it is also doing any number of more esoteric things. And (more to the point) what counts as a mindless, algorithmic procedure at a very low level of organization may constitute, at a higher level, a hazardous do-or-die heuristic that might either succeed brilliantly or (more likely) fail and leave its objective unfulfilled.

As a second defense, remember that Harry too has beliefs, desires, and intentions (provided my original argument is sound). If this is so, then his behavior normally proceeds out of his own mental processes rather than being externally compelled; and so he satisfies the definition of freedom-of-action formulated above. In most cases it will be appropriate to say that Harry could have done other than what he did do (but in fact chose after some ratiocination to do what he did, instead). Harry acts in the same sense as that in which we act, though one might continue to quarrel over what sense that is.

Probably the most popular remaining reason for doubt about machine consciousness has to do with the raw qualitative character of experience. Could a mere bloodless runner-of-programs have states that *feel to it* in any of the various dramatic ways in which our mental states feel to us?

The latter question is usually asked rhetorically, expecting a resounding answer "NO!!" But I do not hear it rhetorically, for I do not see why the negative answer is supposed to be at all obvious, even for machines as opposed to biologic humans. Of course there is an incongruity *from our human point of view* between human feeling and printed circuitry or silicon pathways; that is to be expected, since we are considering those high-tech items from an external, third-person perspective and at the same time comparing them to our own first-person feels. But argumentatively, that *Gestalt* phenomenon counts for no more in the present case than it did in that of human consciousness, viz., for nothing, especially if my original argument about Harry was successful in showing that biochemical constitution is irrelevant to psychology. What matters to mentality is not the stuff of which one is made, but the complex way in which that stuff is organized.[7] If after years of close friendship we were to open Harry up and find that he is stuffed with microelectronic gadgets instead of protoplasm, we would be taken aback—no question. But our *Gestalt* clash on the occasion would do nothing *at all* to show that Harry does not have his own rich inner qualitative life. If an objector wants to insist that computation alone cannot provide consciousness with its qualitative character, the objector will have to take the initiative and come up with a further, substantive argument to show why not.[8] We have already seen that such arguments have failed wretchedly for the case of humans; I see no reason to suspect that they would work any better for the case of robots. We must await further developments. But at the present stage of inquiry I see no compelling feel-based objection to the hypothesis of machine consciousness.

NOTES

1. The material in this appendix was first presented as part of the John Ingram Forry Lecture at Amherst College, in 1985. I am very grateful to Jay Garfield and to Lee Bowie for their penetrating formal commentaries on that occasion, which I shall be answering in the (eventually to be) published proceedings of the event.

2. Harry has appeared before, in Lycan (1985). The next four paragraphs are lifted almost *verbatim* from that article.

3. It is interesting that children seem instinctively to reject the hypothesis of machine consciousness, usually on the grounds that computers are not alive. (One day when my daughter Jane was three years old, we were fooling with some piece of software or other, and I quite unreflectively remarked "It thinks you want it to [do such-and-such]." She did an enormous take, and then replied, "Computers can't think!—Is that 'just an expression'??")

4. I borrow the term "defining technology," and the examples, from Jay Bolter (1984).

5. The computational picture of mentality is by no means new. For one thing, the idea of mechanical intelligence goes back to the seventeenth century at least, long before Charles Babbage's celebrated Analytical Engine. And the computer model of the mind received a decisive boost from the McCullough-Pitts model of the neuron (1947), according to which a neuron is nothing but a little on-off device, that either *fires* or does not. If a brain is just an organized collection of neurons, and a neuron is just an on-off switch, it follows *straightway* that a brain is a digital computer and anything interesting that it does is a computation over binary formulas. Thus a human being is not only a featherless biped, a rational animal, and the only creature on earth that laughs, but the only computing machine on earth that is made by unskilled labor.

The McCullough-Pitts model is no longer current (no pun intended): neurons are now known to be very complicated little agents, not mere on-off switches. But the computational picture of mentality still receives strong encouragement from other quarters. It has two separate philosophical motivations, in particular, the first of which I have already noted: It exploits and explains the coalescence of the notions of computation, information, and intelligence. The computer is the only thing in the world that displays potential intelligence *and* whose workings are well understood. It is the only answer we currently know to the question: By what means *could* Mother Nature have crafted an intelligent being (in our sense of responsiveness to contingencies) out of nothing but a large bunch of individually insensate biological cells? To deny that there may be other answers would be presumptuous at best, and there are plenty of human capacities that do not seem to admit of computational simulation in any way at all—but anyone who manages to think up a genuinely distinct alternative to the digital-computer paradigm will have achieved a major conceptual breakthrough. For the foreseeable future, computation is our only model for intelligence.

Computationalism as a form of Homunctionalism also affords us a way of acknowledging our place as physical organisms amid the closed causal order we call Nature, without benefit of intervention by ghosts. (Actually I hear there are some physicists who speculate that quantum indeterminancies afford gaps in nature that are in principle permeable to Cartesian minds, and that immaterial egos do insert themselves into quantum gaps, thus taking over the role of hidden variables. But (i) it would have to be shown how such quantum phenomena could be combined and multiplied into macroscopic effects characteristic of intelligence, i.e., how the brain could act as a "quantum magnifier," and (ii) to avoid *ad-hoc*ness of the crassest sort, one would have to find *physical reason* to think that Cartesian intervention does occur, which task I take to be almost definitionally impossible.)

6. Of course, this re-emphasizes the question of human freedom: if humans are just wetware or liveware, are they not then essentially soft puppets? This in turn suggests—however speciously in light of the arguments made [earlier]—that the computational view of people must therefore be drastically wrong.

7. Relatively speaking, of course; I am not encouraging Two-Levelism.

8. That mental acts do not *feel* digital is not an objection either. To infer from that fact that mental acts are not digital would be a clear case of what Armstrong (1968a) calls the "headless woman" fallacy.

Star Witness*

COLIN ALLEN

Colin Allen (1960–), a specialist in animal studies and philosophy of mind, teaches at Texas A&M University.

"YOUR HONOR, this is *totally* outrageous! The prosecuting attorney is proposing something completely unprecedented."

Defense lawyer Kenny DeJohn stared expectantly at Judge Jean Loismead, who frowned and immediately shifted her gaze to the prosecution's table.

"Ms. Curtair, I must say that I find your motion highly irregular."

Deputy D. A. Alyson Curtair winced. She knew this was going to be a hard fight, but she was not about to let the defense persuade Judge Loismead to bar her star witness—her only eyewitness—from testifying.

"Your Honor, we can establish the credibility of our witness. Without his testimony we believe that we *can* win this case, but in the interests of justice, we think that his testimony should be heard."

DeJohn started to speak, but before he could get a word out, Judge Loismead raised her hand.

"Mr. DeJohn, I know your position on this matter, and I am sympathetic. But this case is unusual in more than one respect."

"But, your Honor . . ."

"Mr. DeJohn, kindly allow me to finish. As I was saying, this case is unusual in a number of respects. And although I have severe reservations about this witness, I am prepared to adjourn this hearing until Friday to allow you both to prepare arguments. Until that time, the witness must be sequestered to prevent any coaching from the prosecuting team."

"The prosecution can live with that, your Honor, provided that he can remain in his usual living quarters."

"Agreed, Ms. Curtair. You will make arrangements with the bailiff."

Curtair smiled. She had gained almost a two-day reprieve. DeJohn, however, was in no mood to smile.

"Your Honor!"

"Mr. DeJohn, you will have your chance to present your arguments on Friday at 9 A.M. in this courtroom. I expect written briefs at my chambers by tomorrow, Thursday, at 5 P.M. with copies to opposing counsel. You will keep your briefs to less than 2,000 words. This session is adjourned!"

He couldn't believe it. He really couldn't believe it. This sentimental fool of a judge was seriously considering giving the prosecution a chance to hang his client on the testimony of a parrot!

Moments later, outside the courthouse, DeJohn was stating his disappointment for the benefit of the reporters and television crews who had been waiting there all day. Curtair was able to slip by unmolested. The judge did not allow cameras in her courtroom, which made the crews waiting outside desperate for something they could use on the evening news shows. The reporters knew that Curtair would of course say that she was pleased with the events today—hardly exciting television. So all attention was focused on DeJohn, who was struggling to avoid insulting the judge's intelligence.

The story, when it broke, had made live coverage on international cable news. Renowned psychologist Feba McFork had been found dead in her laboratory at the university. Her graduate student Jethro Tullstoy had entered the lab at about six on Sunday morning, intending to feed Chiapa, the 20-year old African Grey parrot, who had helped to establish McFork's fame for the past 15 years. Greys, like many other parrots, can live more than 50 years, and Chiapa continued to provide Tullstoy and McFork's other students with plenty of material for their research.

Entering the lab involved a tedious process of entering the proper code on the cipher-lock and then opening a second lock that required two complete revolutions of a key once the light on the door had turned green. Chiapa's fame had made him a prime target for animal liberationists who felt that such an obviously intelligent animal deserved to be free. No matter that on the one occasion Feba had taken Chiapa home with her, Chiapa had spent the entire time saying "Want home, want home!"—his way of asking to be returned to his room at the lab. The whole lab was being renovated that week, so there was no question of returning him to the lab. Feba had to spend several days listening to Chiapa's complaints. She never tried to take Chiapa out of the lab again.

When Jethro entered the lab that morning, the sound of Chiapa making a commotion was not unusual. "It's OK, Chiapa!" he shouted in the direction of the parrot's room. But it wasn't okay. McFork, or what was left of her, was lying directly under Chiapa's perch. And the parrot, between ear-piercing shrieks, kept repeating "Bad! Bad! Casey! Bad!"

Campus police sealed the area within ten minutes of Tullstoy's call. It was only another five minutes before the first press members arrived at the scene. McFork and Chiapa had both become famous well beyond academia because of their frequent appearances in science television programs and in national magazines. Their fame had really taken off when Chiapa appeared on the cover of a weekly news magazine prominently displayed at supermarket checkout stands. The mere mention of McFork's name on the police radio was sufficient to alert the local press, and when the cable networks arrived, the story went international. Footage of Chiapa the parrot being taken from the crime scene was shown from Bombay to Biarritz.

The police determined that there had been no forced entry into McFork's lab. The cipher-lock records showed that the code had been correctly entered at 8 P.M. and again at 11 P.M. on Saturday evening and that the correct key had been used in each case. The later entry was less than an hour before the estimated time of death. There were plenty of fingerprints in the lab, but all belonged to McFork, her students, or the maintenance workers, who would not normally be working on a Saturday night.

A quick check of the students who had access to McFork's lab revealed that only Casey Heile lacked an alibi for the time of the murder. Other pieces of evidence fell into place and Heile was arrested the following Friday.

From the D.A.'s point of view, the case against Heile was good, but wholly circumstantial. Plus there was the problem of motive. It was known that Heile and McFork had had some serious disagreements, mostly over Heile's research. It wouldn't be the first time that a student had killed a faculty member over an academic dispute, but would a jury accept it as a motive in this case? McFork's killer had to be put away and the parrot's testimony could be the crucial element.

Curtair had read through Tullstoy's statement at least a hundred times. Each time, she was struck by the parrot's words—"Bad! Casey!" A call to Tullstoy confirmed that Chiapa knew and used the names of Jethro himself, Feba, and several of the other students working in the lab, including Casey. But what about the word "bad"? Curtair knew what it meant in English, but did it mean the same thing in the mouth of a parrot? Do words mean anything at all in the mouth of a parrot? After all, in the English language, "to parrot" something means to repeat it mindlessly.

Tullstoy told her that while the word "bad" was sometimes used to scold Chiapa, he could not remember ever having heard Chiapa say "bad" until the morning he had stumbled upon the murder scene. Tullstoy had also visited the bird with another student a few days after the murder. Chiapa had been basically calm and seemed pleased to see them. At one point during the visit, Tullstoy and the other student were talking to each other when one of them had mentioned the name "Casey." At that point Chiapa had "gone ballistic," shrieking and saying "No, no!" and "Bad!" It had taken almost twenty minutes to get the animal calmed down again.

Even if Curtair could make the case that the parrot knew the meanings of the words "bad" and "Casey" independently, could she make the case that the combination of words meant what it seemed to mean? As an undergraduate, Curtair had taken a psycholinguistics course in which the professor had lectured on the so-called "ape language studies." In the early part of the twentieth century behavioral scientists had first tried systematically to train apes to speak, but they soon realized that all the closest primate relatives of humans—chimpanzees, gorillas, and orangutans—lack the specialized vocal apparatus necessary to make human speech sounds. Although the animals seemed capable of responding to the human voice, they were unable to reproduce the sounds. Then, in the 1970s and '80s, there were a number of breakthroughs using plastic tokens, computerized keyboards, and American Sign Language instead of spoken language. Many comparative psychologists argued that they had been able to show that the animals could string words together to make sentences using these tools.

Curtair's professor had been skeptical about these alleged breakthroughs, because, he argued, they did not rule out the possibility that the chimpanzees and gorillas were simply copying, without any comprehension, signals they had previously seen their handlers use. Combinations of signals could arise in the same way. There was also the question of observer bias—the case of researchers seeing what they wanted to see rather than what was really there. Another problem was that the animals might have been responding to subtle cues provided quite unconsciously by the handlers. That was how, during the first decade of the twentieth century, a horse known as "Clever Hans" had fooled many people into thinking he could do arithmetic problems. Hans could be asked to add two numbers, and he would tap a hoof the requisite number of times until he reached the correct answer. On investigation it was discovered that the horse was successful only if the person in front of him knew what the correct answer was. Hans was reacting to cues unconsciously provided by people around him. If prevented from seeing anyone who knew the right answer, Hans' performance was no better than blind chance at producing the correct answer. But even those who knew that Hans was taking cues from subtle changes in body position found it next to impossible to hide their reactions. The label "Clever Hans Phenomenon" came to be used to dismiss many claims about the mental abilities of trained animals.

One of Curtair's philosophy teachers had also argued pretty convincingly that there was simply no way to give an unequivocal interpretation to the behavior of animals. If a dog chases a squirrel up a tree and then stands barking at the bottom of the tree, it might at first seem reasonable to say that the animal thinks that there is a squirrel up the tree. But how could we be sure that the dog is thinking that the furry animal it chased is a *squirrel*? After all, part of the concept of a squirrel is that it is a mammal, but the dog surely wouldn't know *that*. Even "animal" or "furry animal" would not do, as the concept of an animal implies a distinction between a biological entity and a clever mechanical copy. The professor had claimed that this uncertainty about the content of many mental states made it unlikely that there was any point for cognitive scientists to talk about mental content.

Curtair knew that DeJohn was a thorough enough lawyer to be able to track down the research that had supported these conclusions, and perhaps even bring in some of the authors as expert witnesses. She would have to call Tullstoy for help with finding research that supported the opposite conclusions.

At 5:30 on the following evening, Kenny DeJohn was in his office with Alyson Curtair's brief in hand. His own brief had been sent by courier to the judge and to the deputy D.A. just over half an hour earlier.

DeJohn had been something of an oddity at law school, having received an undergraduate degree in electrical engineering, whereas most of his classmates were trained in the liberal arts. Another oddity was DeJohn's interest in criminal law. Most lawyers with backgrounds in science or engineering had gone into patent law, a growing area with the boom in computer and biotech companies spinning out of university research. As an undergraduate engineer, DeJohn had been trained to think that rigor in science meant quantification. Science without numbers was soft science, hardly deserving of the name. In researching his brief he had read a number of arguments claiming to support the view that animals had minds, but they all seemed to him to lack any statistical rigor. As he settled down to look at Curtair's brief he expected nothing better.

Half an hour later, Judge Jean Loismead sat down to read the two briefs. Nothing in her background had prepared her for the scientific aspects of this case. She had majored in history as an undergraduate and flown through law school near the top of her class, worked as a trial lawyer, and made it to the bench in less than 10 years. Since making it to the bench she had several times ruled on the fate of a dog that had chased one postal worker too many. She had also read that in medieval Europe there had been hundreds of cases of animals, from insects to mammals, being tried and publicly executed as criminals. But this was the first case she had encountered where an animal might be considered capable of testifying for the prosecution.

She settled down to read the two briefs, hoping that the issues would become clearer.

CASE OF *STATE* V. *HEILE*, COURT OF JUDGE JEAN LOISMEAD

Prosecution Brief Prepared by Alyson Curtair, Deputy District Attorney, Representing the State

The issue facing the court is whether to allow the testimony of a language-trained parrot, an African Grey named "Chiapa," in the trial of Mr. Casey Heile for the murder of Dr. Feba McFork.

The state contends:

1. That humans are not unique in possessing the mental capacities required for reliable observation and reliable reporting of events that they experience.
2. That because of his special training with the English language, this animal is especially able to provide reliable testimony of events leading up to the murder of Dr. McFork.
3. That the parrot should not be disqualified because he cannot be subjected to the kind of detailed cross examination used for "normal" witnesses, because other witnesses, such as young children, cannot be subjected to detailed cross examination.
4. That in light of the foregoing conditions, and because inevitably the disposition of any jury will be one of skepticism toward this animal, allowing the members of a jury to weigh the parrot's testimony for themselves would not constitute especial prejudice against the defendant.

1. Science supports the view that mental activity is a direct function of nervous tissue. Nervous tissue has evolved in response to specific selectional pressures arising from environmental complexity and variability. Perception, memory, and learning all represent general methods for dealing with environmental complexity. The precise relationships between brain states and mental states, such as belief and consciousness, remain unclear. However, it is clear that the common-sense view of the human mind as a seamless unity is mistaken. Almost any aspect of mental experience or ability can be possessed independently from any other. One of the most dramatic examples is provided by the phenomenon of blindsight. Humans with certain kinds of damage to the visual cortex have a scotoma, or blind spot, within which they deny conscious awareness of sight. Yet if asked to guess what they might be seeing, they can correctly identify some patterns of light at levels well above chance.

Because different species have evolved under varying conditions, organisms show a wide variety of overlapping and nonoverlapping abilities. Humans show very advanced capacities, particularly with respect to language and mathematics. However, in other regards their abilities are often less advanced than those of other animals. Elephants can coordinate group activities over distances of greater than 15 kilometers, using very low frequency sounds. Many species of birds and mammals are capable of remembering the locations of dozens of separate food caches over periods of many months. Ethologists, who study the evolution of behavior, have identified many communicative capabilities once thought to be unique to humans. Vervet monkeys give different alarm calls that are specific to particular types of predators (e.g., snake, leopard, eagle) and which evoke different and appropriate evasive responses. Rhesus monkeys give calls that indicate the discovery of food and its quality. A similar set of alarm and food calls is used by chickens. Such abilities are not restricted to primates, mammals, or even vertebrates. Many species of bees perform dances that convey information about location and direction to food sources.

Thus, although we should not expect to find that other animals possess all of the abilities associated with the human mind, there are plenty of reasons to suppose that human mentality is not an isolated phenomenon. Evolutionary continuity between human minds and animal minds may exist both in the form of homology (shared characteristics because of shared ancestry as, for example, between humans and monkeys) and homomorphy or analogy (shared characteristics because of convergent evolution—that is—common responses to common problems as, for example, between the communicative abilities of humans and bees).

Little is known about the behavior of African Grey parrots in the wild. It is known that they are social birds who forage by day in small groups and roost at night in large colonies. In captivity they are known to mate for life monogamously and to develop special calls used only with their mates. Not enough is known for certain about the functions of their vocalizations in the wild, but the high degree of their sociality and the high degree of plasticity of their vocalizations suggest that these vocalizations are important to social communication.

2. Chiapa has been highly trained to use English to communicate his needs and to respond to questions by the victim and her colleagues. Chiapa was not the first parrot to be trained in this manner. The first is another African Grey named Alex, who is under the care of Dr. Irene Pepperberg, presently at the University of Arizona in Tucson. Pepperberg's innovative training methods employed human models for the behaviors Alex was to learn. Two humans first modeled a question and response for Alex and then presented him with the same situation. For example, Alex might be shown an object and asked "What color?" For a correct response he was given the object to play with for a few moments. Alex was not rewarded with food unless the object of attention was specifically a food item. Attention from his trainers and access to the objects were the only rewards. Using such techniques, Pepperberg was able to show that Alex can answer a number of different questions about numerous objects, such as color (green, blue, etc.), composition (paper, wood, etc.), and shape (square, triangle, etc.), even for unfamiliar objects. Alex can make same/different judgments about these attributes. For instance, if he were shown a green triangle and a green square and were asked "What same?," he would respond "color," but if he were asked "What different?" he would respond "shape." Alex is also able to answer questions such as "How many?" when shown an array of objects, and even "How many blue?" given an array of differently colored objects. Pepperberg is presently using Alex as a model for training other African Greys. She has also addressed the problem of subtle cuing by human trainers (known as the "Clever Hans" phenomenon) by showing that parrots answer questions correctly even when no humans are present.

An African Grey who is alone in a room first hears the instruction "Listen up" over an intercom, and then he is given a series of audible clicks followed by the question "How many?" to which he responds with the correct answer. The behavior of these animals is far more flexible than Clever Hans' relatively inflexible responses to the cues provided by people around him.

It has been argued by many scientists and philosophers that nonhuman animals have conscious access only to very recent stimuli and lack long-term memory for specific events. Memory may be divided into semantic memory, which concerns mainly general associations between different types of stimuli, and episodic memory, which concerns memory of specific episodes or events. Scientists agree that animals have long-term semantic memory, meaning that they form long-term associations between certain types of stimuli. But long-term memory for specific episodes is more difficult to prove. Episodic memory is very important to the legal system because witnesses are called upon to recall specific details of events that may have occurred very far in the past. Anecdotal evidence suggests that animals other than humans do have long-term episodic memories. Elephants in Africa, for example, return for many years to locations where group members died, and where they engage in behaviors which suggest that they are remembering their dead companions. For instance, they may manipulate the bones of the deceased for considerable periods. Also suggestive is the fact that many animals show an aversion to something or someone on the basis of a single bad experience. Conversely, parrot trainers know that if a parrot shows a dislike for a particular person, putting the parrot into an aversive situation where the disliked person can rescue it often improves the parrot's subsequent behavior toward that person. However, it is possible to regard single instance learning in terms of semantic memory.

While these anecdotes are suggestive, Dr. McFork believed that it was necessary to bring research into the laboratory to determine conclusively the existence of episodic memories in animals. She also believed that most skepticism about the existence of episodic memory was based on a failure to design suitable experiments. Thus, McFork had recently been working with Chiapa to show that Chiapa could provide reliable reports of events that had occurred hours, days, or weeks previously. Prior to McFork's death, this work had been going on for more than 18 months, but it has not yet been reported in the scientific literature. Chiapa is shown a sequence of two colors drawn from four possibilities—red, green, blue, and yellow. There are 16 possible combinations, and each day Chiapa is shown a second sequence of two colors and is asked, "What colors now?" and "What colors before?" For the first question, Chiapa is successful 80% of the time, responding "blue, yellow" if those were the two colors just shown. For the second question, Chiapa's performance depends on the interval between the two presentations of color sequences, but even at 36 hours it is still significantly above the 6% predicted by chance.

3. Chiapa lacks the vocabulary necessary for full description of the events surrounding the victim's murder. However, the state believes that by recreating in part those circumstances, it will be possible to elicit from the parrot responses that will provide information to the court. The process of reenactment is commonly used with witnesses, such as young children, who may not be fully able to answer questions about their experiences. In such cases, it is assumed that the reenactment assists in the recall of episodic memories, and that witnesses' responses can therefore be taken as information about the actual events. Although it is unprecedented to place a parrot in the position of being a witness in a court of law, it is not unprecedented to use witnesses who are not fully capable of responding to questions about their testimony.

4. Members of the jury will naturally be incredulous about the testimony of a parrot. Thus there will be a heavy burden on the state to demonstrate the veracity of the witness. It should be up to the jury to decide whether the state has made its case. The state believes that the good sense of a jury may be trusted in this matter. Thus, to allow the parrot to testify would not be prejudicial to the defendant, Mr. Heile.

FORMAL BRIEF IN THE CASE OF *STATE* V. *HEILE*, COURT OF JUDGE JEAN LOISMEAD

Prepared by Kenneth DeJohn, Esq. representing the defendant Mr. Casey Heile

The state has petitioned the court to allow a parrot to appear as a witness in the trial of Mr. Casey Heile for the murder of Dr. Feba McFork. Not only is it unprecedented to allow an animal to take the stand in a court of law, there are both scientific and judicial reasons for disallowing such an occurrence.

First, there is an inadequate scientific understanding of the mechanisms responsible for the parrot's so-called "testimony." Second, in the absence of such understanding, there is no basis for confidence in any interpretation of the noises that it makes, no matter how closely they may resemble English words. Third, there is no scientific or philosophical basis for holding that an animal has the concepts, beliefs, or knowledge required to provide sound testimony. Finally, the animal could not be effectively cross-examined, thus violating the right of the defendant to confront his accuser.

Mechanisms

Modern psychology has become a more rigorous science by moving the investigation of behavior into the laboratory, where it may be studied under carefully controlled conditions. Feba McFork's work on Chiapa itself represents an element of this strategy. However, the prosecution's proposal to place this parrot on the witness stand has little to do with the carefully controlled lab work that is the cornerstone of scientific psychology. Their proposal has more to do with the unconstrained and anecdotal anthropomorphizing common both to 19th century comparative psychology and to its modern descendant cognitive ethology. Valid scientific theorizing must be based on repeatable experimentation, but, for obvious reasons, that cannot be achieved in this case. Many scientists would testify that cognitive ethologists lack an adequate theoretical basis for their attributions of mental states to animals. Classical ethology is on much firmer ground because it restricts itself to the study of *behavior* within an evolutionary and comparative framework. Despite what some cognitive ethologists would like to believe, it is not possible to make an adequate determination of consciousness and higher mental processing simply by watching animals behaving freely in their natural habitats. Only psychological experimentation under laboratory conditions can provide the necessary experimental controls. Because it is impossible to control field work adequately, cognitive ethologists are unable to rule out explanations of observed behaviors in terms of direct, automatic responses to stimuli.

Even though this parrot has been raised and trained in a laboratory, interpretation of its behavior in this case shares more in common with the field of cognitive ethology than with laboratory psychology because the situation to which the parrot was exposed on the night of McFork's murder was completely uncontrolled. Thus, our attempts to interpret the response of the parrot has the status of attempts to interpret a single observation made under field conditions and cannot therefore be interpreted except in an anecdotal fashion. Even from the perspective of a strict stimulus-response approach to behavior, there is not sufficient information in the animal's response to make it possible to say what stimulus conditions were present at the time of the murder. Nor can neuroscience provide any assistance in this respect. Although computerized models of simple neural systems have been developed, these models typically involve fewer than 10^5 individual elements, at least four or five orders of magnitude less than the number of neurons in a parrot's brain. While neuroscientists have a very general understanding of the workings of simple neural networks, they are still a long way from an adequate understanding of complex nervous systems belonging to anything other than the simplest invertebrates. Furthermore, the anatomical differences between birds and mammals are sufficiently great to make extrapolations from one class of organisms to the other extremely problematic.

We therefore conclude that neither psychology nor neuroscience can support any sufficiently strong claim in favor of the reliability of the connection between the parrot's behavior and its experiences.

Interpretation of Animal Behavior

The state's petition presupposes that the parrot's utterances can be given a straightforward interpretation. The court should not, however, be misled by the parrot's use of English words into thinking that these words should be given their usual English interpretation. The prosecution intends to argue that the parrot can place the defendant at the scene of the alleged murder. Suppose, contrary to fact and for the sake of argument only, that the animal could directly answer the question "Whom did you see on the night of the attack?" by making a noise resembling the name of the defendant. Even then, it would not be reasonable to claim that the defendant had been named because there are no grounds for assuming that the parrot uses a sound resembling "Casey" to identify the defendant uniquely. We do not know, for instance, whether the parrot would also use this sound for an intruder who happened to resemble the defendant, and we cannot ask the parrot to distinguish this possibility. This point applies not only to names, but to any of the words that the parrot might appear to use. For example, it is alleged that the parrot can ask for specific things, but even if it says something we interpret as "Want peanut" and ceases to say it if we give it peanuts, this does not guarantee that the parrot has the concept of peanut, for it might just as well have ceased vocalizing if it had been given cashew nuts instead of peanuts. Additionally, for human beings, peanuts fall under the concept of nutritious food items. But it is very doubtful indeed that parrot has the necessary concepts of food or nutrition, thus the meaning of the parrot's noise that sounds like "peanut" is unclear. If we do not know what concept it is operating with, we really do not know what it is asking for.

Similar considerations apply to the interpretation of animal behavior even where mimicry of language is not involved. Predatory animals are selective about what they will prey on, but can it be said that a lion chasing a gazelle has the *concept* of a gazelle? Surely not, because it is part of the concept of a gazelle that it is a mammal and there is nothing to suggest that the lion has the concept of a mammal. And if it does not really know what a gazelle is, can it really be described as wanting to catch a *gazelle?* We must regard the attribution of concepts, beliefs, or desires with a specific content to animals as over-interpretation that is unavoidably indeterminate with respect to the observable behavior.

It is normal for human beings to interpret the behavior of animals in an anthropomorphic fashion—to assume that they have mental states similar to our own—but this anthropomorphism cannot be justified scientifically or philosophically. The dangers of anthropomorphism are much greater when the animal has been conditioned to mimic a human language. Careful analysis has shown that apparently spontaneous and intelligent responses of chimpanzees using sign language could be predicted from the gestures used just previously by human handlers. If the parrot were allowed to perform in front of a jury, it would be extremely difficult to prevent jurors from applying their normal, subconscious mechanisms of interpretation and hearing these words as if they had been uttered by a human witness, thus prejudicing them toward strong overinterpretation.

Truth and Perjury

Testifying before a court of law is a serious matter implying special duties and penalties for perjury. This is why witnesses are required to swear an oath to the truthfulness of their testimony. No witness should be allowed to testify who does not possess the concepts of truth and duty that are required to make the swearing of an oath a meaningful occurrence. The concept of truth also requires the concept of falsity, both of which in turn require understanding of the arbitrary and conventional relationships between symbols and what they symbolize. There is simply no evidence that supports the claim that any nonhuman organism possesses these concepts, and in particular there is no specific evidence to support this claim with respect to parrots. The mere ability to respond "correctly" to a question does not show the possession of these concepts, since these responses may be seen as programmed or trained responses to the specific stimuli conditions provided by the external objects and the question. Turning to the concept of duty, this requires a concept of right and wrong, in a moral sense. While animals may expect punishment or retribution for certain of their actions, there is no evidence to suggest that they understand that their actions are right or wrong. Punishment can be unjust and therefore expectations of punishment cannot be taken as a measure of moral understanding. Once again, these expectations may be based on the ability of an animal to learn by forming associations between its actions and their unpleasant consequences, and thus may be seen as nothing more than stimulus-response conditioning.

The Right to Cross Examination

The procedure of cross examination is essential to the discovery of truth in the trial process. Whether a witness is willfully misleading a court, or merely confused about the details of an event, cross examination allows inconsistencies or a lack of clarity in the testimony to be exposed. An important tool in this process is the ability to ask essentially the same questions in various different forms. In the case of the "language-trained" parrot, Chiapa, there is nothing like the redundancy of expression that is necessary to allow repeated questioning on any particular point. Thus, even if the risky assumption is allowed that the parrot's utterances are meaningful, the limited abilities of this animal do not allow for the kind of questioning that would establish confidence in the truth of the sentences it utters.

Shortly after 9 A.M. on Friday morning, Judge Loismead took her seat behind the bench.

"This evidence hearing is now in progress. Counsel, I have read your briefs, but I have not yet come to a decision on this matter. Ms. Curtair, given that the state is proposing such a radical departure from precedent, I regard you as having the larger burden to demonstrate the admissibility of your witness. In your brief you identify a number of points. You will present them in turn, and, Mr. DeJohn, you will be given a chance to rebut each point after Ms. Curtair has presented it. I expect also, Ms. Curtair, that you have prepared responses to the arguments presented by Mr. DeJohn in his brief, and once again I regard you as having the burden of demonstrating what is wrong with his arguments. You may proceed."

"Thank you, your Honor. Your Honor, the state contends that there is sufficient scientific basis for our claim that when Chiapa responds to questions posed in English, he both understands those questions in much the same sense as you or I would, and he understands his responses in much the same way as you or I. We are prepared to call expert witnesses to testify to this claim. While we admit that Chiapa cannot be questioned as thoroughly as a normal adult human being, this is not sufficient grounds for barring him from the witness stand. Many offenders have been convicted on the basis of the evidence of young children who are limited in their ability to answer questions. To bar the evidence of Chiapa while allowing the evidence of young children would be anthropocentric, representing the speciesistic assumption that humans are inherently superior to other organisms. In our view, Darwin's theory of evolution implies continuity between humans and other animals in all respects, including the mind. Dr. McFork's work was aimed precisely at establishing such continuities. Thus, we have both general and specific scientific reasons for inferring that Chiapa is highly sophisticated, cognitively speaking, which in turn leads us to regard his testimony as an important source of evidence that should not be ignored in this case."

"Mr. DeJohn, do you wish to respond?"

"Yes, your honor. We plan to contest the prosecution's anthropomorphic interpretations of specific scientific research as they arise, but for now we object to the analogy between parrots and children. Parrots are not young children. Young children grow up to be adult humans, but to my knowledge there has never been a single instance of a parrot growing up in this way! This is relevant because a child's brain structure is close enough to an adult's to allow reasonable confidence that the output of the child's brain can meaningfully be compared to the adult's. A parrot, if you'll pardon the expression, has nothing but a bird brain. A bird brain is, at best, a walnut-sized thing that lacks many of the anatomical developments that are highly important to human intelligence. For example, birds lack the highly developed frontal lobes that have been proven essential to the human ability to formulate and carry out tasks that require forethought and planning—characteristics that are essential for an action to be considered intentional. Counsel's appeal to evolutionary continuity serves only to obscure the differences."

When DeJohn paused to look at his notes, Curtair seized the opportunity to speak.

"There are other kinds of continuity than anatomical continuity, your Honor. Of course, Chiapa's brain is organized differently from yours and mine, but what matters is its functional organization, not spatial organization. In birds the temporal parts of their brains are highly developed and can carry out many of the same functions as human frontal lobes. Also, the use of absolute brain size as a measure of cognitive ability is misleading. Parrots and many other birds have a very high brain-to-body weight ratio, comparable to and in some cases exceeding that of humans. A large part of the human brain is not concerned directly with cognitive function but with processing sensory input and motor output. Larger bodies have more nerve endings, which are reflected in increased brain circuitry. Furthermore, in absolute terms many animals have larger brains than humans—for example, elephants and whales—but we would not argue that this fact alone establishes their ability to provide credible testimony. Humans are not even at the top of the scale for relative brain size, since they are surpassed in this measure by many species of bird. No, your Honor, the only reasonable criteria are behavioral and psychological."

While she was speaking, Alyson Curtair closely monitored Judge Loismead's facial expressions. Judges are human, and like others they prefer short arguments. Many strong cases have been lost because a long-winded lawyer loses the attention and then the sympathy of both judge and jury. Loismead had nodded her head almost imperceptibly to Curtair's point about the importance of behavioral evidence. Curtair decided that it would be counterproductive to push the argument any further. Maybe Clever Hans couldn't do arithmetic, but he could still teach us a lot about body language.

"Mr. DeJohn, I am inclined to agree with Ms. Curtair about the irrelevance of brain anatomy. The issues here are the truth and reliability of the parrot's testimony. In any other case the court would not require knowledge of witnesses' brain structures in order to determine the admissibility of their evidence. We shall apply the same standard in this case."

"Your Honor, that prejudges this case in favor of Ms. Curtair and the parrot."

"Nonsense, Mr. DeJohn. Ms. Curtair is still required to establish that the parrot can meet reasonable behavioral criteria. I am simply disallowing considerations that would suggest a double standard with respect to this witness."

DeJohn snorted quietly, but said nothing. The defense had other arguments. It would have been simpler to bypass the behavioral evidence—behavioral science was notoriously soft compared to neuroscience—but the judge seemed to have made up her mind on this issue, and to press further could cause complications later on.

"Ms. Curtair, you may proceed with your arguments. But be warned that I expect you to focus on more specific arguments than the vague and general idea of evolutionary continuity, which seems to me to beg the question of how you know that such continuity exists."

Curtair glanced over at DeJohn, who seemed barely able to contain himself. The judge had just tossed him a bone, but not much of one. She knew that DeJohn had been hoping to get a ruling against her witness on the basis of anatomical differences. Loismead had ruled that whole strategy out of court, and then she had turned around and ruled part of the prosecution's strategy out too. But they were hardly comparable, and Curtair knew it. She couldn't resist a slight smile.

"We will endeavor to stay within your guidelines, your Honor. The central issue dividing Mr. DeJohn and the D.A.'s office is that of how to interpret Chiapa's utterances in English. We argue that Chiapa has mastered a portion of the English language, whereas Mr. DeJohn is apparently inclined to regard the resemblance of Chiapa's utterances to the English language as some kind of fluke that has little to do with the normal meanings of those utterances."

"Is that a fair summary of your view, Mr. DeJohn?"

"Not quite. Of course it's no fluke that the parrot makes noises that sound like English—that's what he has been trained to do. But the interpretation that he is speaking English is entirely one-sided. A child's doll may be programmed to speak with a synthesized voice that we can all interpret, but no one thinks that this demonstrates any kind of understanding or intelligence in the doll—the interpretation is all one way. Similarly with this parrot."

"With all due respect, your Honor, Mr. DeJohn knows better than to compare Chiapa to a toy doll.

There are big differences between the two: first, there is his ability to answer questions appropriately; second, his ability to learn new words; and third, his ability to combine learned words into novel phrases."

"Ms. Curtair, as the judge in this case I will from time to time interject questions. The question here seems to me to be one of the definition of a language. You just gave three criteria to support your claim that the parrot speaks a language. But perhaps you could explain to the court precisely what this animal can do that shows that it satisfies those criteria, and why these criteria should be taken to constitute language use."

Curtair had been dreading a question about defining language. Nevertheless she was prepared.

"I'd like to take the second question first, if I may. Attempts to define a language have divided psychologists and linguists. Linguists have generally dismissed psychologists' claims to have discovered language abilities in nonhuman animals. Many linguists regard language as a separate evolutionary development, uniquely human, and housed in specially dedicated parts of the brain, typically in the left hemisphere. In contrast, many psychologists view language as an extension of basic cognitive skills that may be found in humans and other animals. Support for this view has also come from primatologists who have found that several species of monkeys have left hemisphere specialization for processing vocal calls from their own species, whereas arbitrary noises and vocalizations of other species are processed equally by either hemisphere."

"Your Honor, we would like to object to counsel's return to neurological arguments that you have ruled out. If they are to use such arguments, we believe we can provide stronger arguments supporting our view that the parrot does not belong in the courtroom."

"Mr. DeJohn is right, Ms. Curtair. Please confine your comments to behavioral criteria."

"Yes, your Honor. For many linguists, there are two crucial issues in defining language. The first is that language is made up of meaningful units—words—that can be recombined according to the rules of grammar, or syntax, to form sentences. Second, the syntax of all human languages provides "infinite expressive power," meaning that the syntactical rules allow an infinite number of grammatical sentences to be formed from a finite number of words. In English this is easy to illustrate with examples such as the sequence "John ran"; "John ran and then walked"; "John ran and then walked and then ran"; and so on. Each of these sentences describes a different sequence of events. An important behavioral criterion for demonstrating syntax is appropriate response to novel combinations of words. For instance, competent English speakers can understand the sentence "The man carried the elephant" even if they have never encountered it before. This criterion has been met by parrots, as first shown by Dr. Irene Pepperberg with Alex, another African Grey. Dr. McFork adopted similar training techniques, and showed that Chiapa, like Alex, was capable of responding correctly to novel combinations of words."

"Your Honor, may I respond?"

"You may, Mr. DeJohn."

"The abilities of parrots, dolphins, apes, or monkeys to reproduce a few dozen individual signs, and to produce short combinations of three or four such signs, allows perhaps a couple of hundred of different combinations—still a long way short of infinity. So the results mentioned by Ms. Curtair hardly satisfy the criterion of infinite generative capacity."

"Infinite generative capacity, your Honor, is merely a theoretical ideal. In practice, humans are subject to memory constraints that make it impossible for us to deal with arbitarily long sentences. Many perfectly competent legal witnesses would have trouble making sense of many of the sentences in the novels of Marcel Proust, for example. In being limited to shorter sentences, parrots and other animals show only a quantitative difference in their capacity for decoding long sentences, rather than the qualitative difference that Mr. DeJohn is trying to urge on the court."

"This whole discussion, your Honor, is granting too much to the prosecution. It has been convincingly shown that claims on behalf of apes that they have mastered language are nonsense. For instance, the widely touted studies alleged to use American Sign Language turn out to show a high degree of observer bias. Deaf people shown films of these apes consistently identify many fewer "signs" being made than the graduate students and other researchers whose academic careers depend on desperately seeking language."

"Your Honor, these studies are convincing only to those who wish to be convinced. Other studies have confirmed that the signs made by apes can be recognized by deaf observers. Although it is true that apes have difficulty reproducing some hand positions, this is because of differences in their anatomy, not their psychology. The fact that some deaf people have trouble interpreting the hand signals of some apes with whom they have no experience is no more surprising than the fact that some Texans would have trouble being understood in Brooklyn."

Both lawyers paused. Judge Loismead spoke next.

"The opinions of scientists and experts are extremely important in many phases of the trial procedure, from knowledge of ballistics to DNA testing. The courts have typically accepted things that are a matter of consensus among experts. Although there is often dissent among experts, it is usually possible for the courts to judge the direction of preponderant opinion. With respect to this issue of animal "language," I must say that I am skeptical, Ms. Curtair, that there is sufficient consensus to allow a clear legal ruling. Am I right?"

"The prosecution is confident that we can provide experts to support our claim about the linguistic abilities of Chiapa. And I might add that Chiapa's use of English words is quite recognizable by fully hearing English speakers."

"You haven't answered my question, counsel. I don't doubt that you can find experts to support your view. I am also fairly confident that Mr. DeJohn could find experts to support his. My worry is that this would result simply in a stalemate, with experts of opposing viewpoints and the jury unable to decide which group of experts to believe."

"Shouldn't the jury be allowed to make that decision, your Honor?"

"Only if I am reasonably satisfied that they could be provided with a sufficient basis for making the decision. However, I am not at all convinced of this. Even if you could convince a particular jury of your view, there would, in my opinion, be a very high chance that another jury could be convinced otherwise, which means that there is a good chance that a decision reached on the basis of accepting the parrot's testimony would be overturned on appeal."

Curtair was losing this argument; it was time to try a different tack.

"There is, in fact, no need, your Honor, to rule directly on the language issue, because if it cannot be established that Chiapa meets the criteria for possessing a language, all that is really in question is whether there is a reliable connection between his testimony and the events on the night of Feba McFork's murder."

"Are you suggesting, Ms. Curtair, that the evidence provided by the parrot should be considered in the same light as perhaps a videotape of a crime might be allowed as evidence? If so, then I must ask why you have petitioned to allow the parrot into the witness stand . . . recorded evidence is not generally treated as a witness so perhaps the prosecution should amend its petition."

DeJohn preempted Curtair from replying to the judge.

"Your Honor? I must object on behalf of my client to your suggestion that the bird could be treated in the same manner as a tape recorder. A tape recorder is an artifact whose construction and operation can be attested by the designer, manufacturer, or qualified engineer. Thus it is possible to be certain of the reliability of such a device as a recorder. Unfortunately for the prosecutor, even the D.A.'s office does not have the power to subpoena the great parrot designer in the sky, so no such information can be forthcoming."

"Ms. Curtair?"

"Your Honor, it's ironic that Mr. DeJohn favors comparison with a talking doll, but not with a tape recorder. In fact, I agree with him on this point and that is why we have moved to admit Chiapa as a witness rather than as state's evidence."

"Then would you kindly explain your remark that the issue of language is not central to your petition."

"Certainly. We believe that the central issue is cognition, not language. Since Ancient Greek times many philosophers have argued that language is necessary for thought. But this anthropocentrism is hardly justified when one realizes that human language is just one form of communication system that has evolved. Communication is commonly defined as transfer of information, and cognition is commonly defined as information processing. Thus, although other forms of behavior are relevant to assessment of cognition, it is obvious why communication can provide especially compelling evidence for cognitive abilities. The real interest in the animal language studies has more to do with communication and cognition than with language per se."

"Your Honor?"

"Yes, Mr. DeJohn."

"The prosecution is begging the question by assuming a connection between communication and cognition. Biologists have found systems of communication in many organisms, from mammals to insects and even trees. Surely the deputy D.A. is not seriously contending that whatever biologists determine as communicative behavior automatically provides evidence of cognitive abilities. In fact, it is well known that animal communication can be explained in terms of simple stimulus-response mechanisms. Many scientific experts would argue that *any* cognitive explanation of a particular piece of animal behavior can always be matched by an equally good stimulus-response explanation. Also, fax machines transfer information, but that can hardly be taken as evidence of cognition."

"Mr. DeJohn, having read your brief I suppose that I am to understand that stimulus-response explanations are preferable to those that refer to mental or cognitive states in animals. Is that correct?"

"Yes, your Honor."

"And furthermore, that stimulus-response explanations are in some sense more scientific than mentalistic or cognitive explanations?"

"Yes."

"Do you consider this to be true also when it comes to human behavior?"

DeJohn recognized the trap and avoided it.

"No, your Honor. Humans can talk about their mental states, which provides independent justification for attributing them. Essentially, however, mental states are private—not accessible to anyone except those who experience them—and science can deal only with observable phenomena. For languageless animals, the only observable phenomena are external stimuli and behavioral responses. Hence stimulus-response explanations are all that can reasonably be attempted."

"Isn't language just another form of behavior from which it is possible to determine mental states? So why is the situation much different with humans?"

"For two reasons. First, each of us knows how his or her mental states affect his or her behavior, and by analogy it is reasonable to believe that other humans who are similar to ourselves have the same mental states affecting behavior in the same ways. However, with nonhumans, the analogy breaks down and we cannot be certain of their mental states, or whether they have them at all. Second, language itself has a detailed structure. It is reasonable to assume that the internal structure necessary to explain language production must be as detailed as the language that is produced. Thus it is reasonable to attribute mental states that have the same content as sentences. Nonlinguistic behavior is just not fine grained enough to force one to attribute complex mental states to explain it."

"Ms. Curtair?"

"Your Honor, a female vervet monkey will look toward her own infant if she hears the infant's distress call. All the other females who hear the call will look toward *the mother*. This behavior is "fine grained," if I understand Mr. DeJohn's use of the term, in that different infants elicit different responses depending on the relationship between the infant and the adult. It seems reasonable to say that the animals are aware of mother-infant relationships."

"This is just more anthropomorphism, your Honor! It is just as plausible to say that the monkeys are conditioned by the distress calls to attend to a particular individual because experience has taught them that this individual is most likely to respond to that particular call. It's not necessary to refer to awareness of relationships at all."

"What do you say to that, Ms. Curtair?"

"I believe that Mr. DeJohn and I are talking at cross purposes, your Honor. His oh-so-hard scientific attitude is based on what many experts agree is an outdated view of the mind and an outdated view of scientific theorizing. If any sense at all can be made of the notion of a mind, whether human or nonhuman, we must get away from the idea that the mind is a ghostly entity that is tucked away where no amount of experimental probing can discover it. In fact, we must get away from the idea that minds are *things* that one either possesses or lacks, at all. As explained in my brief submitted yesterday, we must look at various mental capacities individually.

"We must also get away from the idea that the only legitimate terms in a scientific theory are those that can be operationalized by equating them to specific procedures or operations that determine when they can be applied. Theorizing is a matter of finding the best framework for the available results, which entails looking beyond the simplest explanation for a *single* phenomenon. So, if you simply focus on the response to infant vervet calls that I just described, you may get the mistaken impression that a story in terms of stimulus-response conditioning is the best. But add in the information that patterns of aggression between vervets tend to follow family lines, specifically mother-daughter relationships and then I ask you whether it isn't more powerful to suppose that both kinds of interactions are explained by awareness of family relationships, rather than having to hypothesize entirely different conditioning histories in each case?"

"Suppose, Ms. Curtair, that the court agrees that we must focus on a specific ability for determining the admissibility of this parrot to the witness stand. What, in your view, is the ability in question?"

"Episodic memory, without a doubt. Witnesses are expected to report accurately about events in their past experience. But we believe that Chiapa can accurately recall past events and report them accurately in the present."

"And Mr. DeJohn, in his brief, contends that there is reasonable scientific doubt about the appropriateness of describing such memories, and, even if there were not, the parrot should still be disqualified as a witness on judicial grounds. Is that not so?"

Both lawyers nodded their agreement. Loismead continued.

"Very well then; we shall take a recess for lunch and when we return we will address these two questions."

Returning to the courthouse after lunch, both lawyers did their best to ignore the questions shouted at them by the reporters gathered there. DeJohn had spent his lunch period reviewing materials that he had prepared after reading the prosecution brief. He was generally satisfied with the burden of proof that the judge had placed on the prosecuting attorney. Curtair was uncertain how her case was going. The judge's attitude was very hard to read and she really had no idea what to expect from the afternoon session.

Back in her seat in the courtroom, Curtair found herself fidgeting nervously before the judge arrived. Over the previous couple of days she had read or skimmed hundreds of pages on animal behavior and cognition. She had found that quite ordinary common-sense views about the mental states of animals had taken on the status of scientific bugaboos. Most ordinary folk would regard the attitudes of scientists to questions about animal minds as bizarre. But what did that show? In the battle between common sense and scientific opinion, common sense does not have an impressive record. On the other hand, would strict scientific standards of interpretation apply to normal judicial process? Jurors' interpretations of most testimony was hardly a matter of scientific precision. Why should the standard be any different for a nonhuman animal that appeared to be able to tell us something about the events surrounding a murder?

The call for the court to rise for Loismead's entrance snapped Curtair out of these thoughts. Loismead started to speak as she took her place behind the bench.

"Be seated. Mr. DeJohn, Ms. Curtair, the first issue I would like you to address this afternoon is the possibility of episodic memory in this parrot. Mr. DeJohn, you have raised some very general objections in interpreting mental states in animals, but do you think you could explain how these general issues relate to the possibility of specific memory of the events on the night of Dr. McFork's death?"

"Certainly. The parrot's testimony is being offered by the prosecution as evidence of a murder . . ."

"Objection, your Honor. We are not offering the testimony as evidence of a murder. To do that our witness would have to provide evidence of the defendant's state of mind. However, we do believe that Chiapa's testimony can provide evidence of the presence of the defendant at the time of the victim's death."

"You stand corrected, Mr. DeJohn."

"It makes no difference, your Honor. The allegation that this animal can provide evidence of a death requires us to attribute the memory of a death to this parrot. But even if the parrot could recall certain events from that evening, which we very much doubt, why should we take its reaction to be a reaction to a *death*. How can we know whether a parrot even has the concept of death? Could it distinguish a person dying from her merely falling asleep or unconscious? There is simply nothing about its behavior that could enable us to distinguish these alternatives."

"Your Honor, this is the same old tired argument that Mr. DeJohn has used in his brief. First, let me say about his brief that in fact Mr. DeJohn's idle speculation about Chiapa's willingness to accept a cashew nut instead of a peanut are not based in fact; Chiapa has been tested in just the way that Mr. DeJohn imagined and he does not stop asking for something when presented a similar but different object. But back to the issue of death. Of course it's true that under certain conditions a parrot might mistake a lapse into unconsciousness for a death, but the same is also true of any person. To say that a parrot could *never* make the distinction requires a leap of faith, or perhaps a failure of imagination, that is not supported by empirical evidence. Unfortunately, rather too little is known about the behavior of African Greys in the wild, but many species of animals treat dead animals differently from sleeping ones. Different animals show different species-typical responses to the death of another. But we should not interpret a difference in behavior as absence of a concept. Humans vary in their concept of death; some are convinced that it marks a transition to a different form of existence, while others consider it the absolute end of that individual's existence. Some mourn extensively and elaborately, others hardly at all. We would not use these differences to call into question the ability of a witness to testify about a death."

DeJohn jumped in as soon as Curtair paused.

"The deputy D.A. has proposed an incredibly weak criterion for possessing the concept of death, your Honor. By her account, even ants, who selectively remove dead nestmates from their nests, possess a concept of death."

"What do you say to this, Ms. Curtair?"

"I was hoping to avoid the issue of defining concepts, your Honor. I think that such issues are not usually discussed in the case of human witnesses, and I see no reason why they should be brought up here."

Loismead's retort was brisk.

"Well, I do, counsel. I would like you to tell me why you think it is reasonable to talk about a concept of death in this parrot, and whether you think it is reasonable, also, in the case of ants."

Curtair sighed. This was not going as well as she hoped. But she had something to say about concepts nonetheless.

"Your Honor, the behavior of ants is extremely stereotyped. Yes it is true that they remove dead nestmates, but that is only part of the story. A typical decay product of a dead ant is oleic acid. It turns out that ants assiduously remove pieces of paper coated with oleic acid. In fact, they will carry out other *live* ants if experimenters treat them with oleic acid. The live ant will return to the nest only to be removed again. Thus the ants show no recognition of the distinction between a dead ant and an ant that merely appears to be dead by one criterion, but not by other criteria. In genuinely concept-mediated behavior, there is a distinction between evidence and actuality. For instance, if you were to run across someone who you thought was dead, because you detected no breathing, etc., if that person suddenly stirred you would be more wary of jumping to the conclusion that you had found someone dead the next time you found someone in a similar condition. Possessing a concept of death allows you to weigh evidence and recognize a distinction between the way things are and the way they seem to be."

"And what makes you think that a parrot is capable of "weighing evidence," as you put it? Are you suggesting that the parrot knows the difference between the way things appear and the way they really are?"

"Admittedly this is indirect, but there is behavior relevant to this question. Chiapa is quite capable of deliberately providing false responses to a given question. For example, a favorite way for him to be uncooperative is to give a succession of wrong answers when shown a tray of objects and asked "How many?" If the correct answer is "five," he is quite liable to say "three . . . six . . . two . . . four . . . ," indeed everything except "five." This capacity for deception shows an understanding of the distinction between accurate reports and inaccurate reports, which in turn shows an appreciation of the distinction between the way things really are and the relationship of his own utterances as evidence for actual state of affairs."

"I object, your Honor. Counsel is lapsing into anecdote once again. There is no reason why we should take it seriously."

"And might I respond, your Honor, that the fear of anecdote is another bugaboo of behavioral science. Repeatability is easy to achieve with stereotyped behaviors, but it leaves out the vast majority of interesting behaviors that might be used to argue for cognition in animals. This attitude is visible in Mr. DeJohn's unsympathetic dismissal of the entire field of cognitive ethology in his written brief. There has been much careful experimental work in cognitive ethology, and freed from the artificial constraints of laboratory work, it has much to tell us about animal cognition. The artificial and arbitrary standards of behavioristic psychology are not consistently applied in assessing the testimony of human witnesses, and it is self-serving for the defense to require it in this instance."

Loismead frowned at both attorneys.

"I have heard your arguments, and they will be considered when I deliver my judgment. I would like now to proceed to the judicial issues raised by Mr. DeJohn. In particular, Mr. DeJohn, you have argued that the parrot does not have the necessary concept of truth essential to the judicial process. Yet it appears that Ms. Curtair has just argued that the parrot does indeed know the difference between truth and falsity. How do you respond?"

"I have already objected to the use of anecdote."

It was DeJohn's turn to receive a sharp response from the judge.

"I am not interested in namecalling, Mr. DeJohn. What is the argument?"

"Your Honor, truth was only one part of the third point in my brief. If I may refresh the court's memory, it was also argued that an understanding of perjury, and its penalties, was an essential element for any witness. We argue that this bird is incapable of understanding the serious responsibility entailed in accusing someone of murder."

"Objection, your Honor. We do not intend that Chiapa should make such an accusation. Only that he be allowed to place the defendant at the scene of the crime and engaging in suspicious behavior."

"Your Honor, whether or not a witness is making an accusation directly is irrelevant to this point. To provide any evidence that may result in a conviction for murder entails an extremely serious responsibility, that we believe this animal is incapable of appreciating. Indeed, Dr. Irene Pepperberg is on record as admitting that her African Grey parrot Alex bites, says "sorry," and then bites again, showing no contrition for his actions. Such a basic lack of understanding of moral relationships is an extremely serious defect when this animal's "testimony" may result in the conviction of my client."

"Nothing Mr. DeJohn has said, your Honor, could not also be said about small children, who have been used in case after case to testify and help convict many criminals. Such cases have stood up on appeal against just the kind of challenge that Mr. DeJohn is mounting here. Humans are not apart from the rest of nature, and there is no justification for drawing an arbitrary line around our own species and refusing to treat other-than-human animals in the same way."

"An impassioned statement, Ms. Curtair. I take it under advisement. Mr. DeJohn, do you have any final comment before I adjourn to make my decision?"

"Yes, your Honor. Although we allow much to pass unquestioned with respect to other humans, there is considerable precedent for doing so. In this case, which is completely unprecedented, we must err on the side of caution. We must demand scientific rigor in the interpretation of this parrot's so-called testimony. I urge you to reject the prosecutor's contention that we can perfectly well make sense of the splutterings of this performing parrot."

"Thank you, Mr. DeJohn. Likewise, Ms. Curtair. I will deliver my decision after the weekend on the basis of your briefs and the transcript of this session which is now adjourned."

Reader Assignment

You now have read the briefs and the transcripts. Your assignment, as a law clerk for Judge Loismead, is to draft her legal opinion on the prosecutor's motion to allow Chiapa to testify against Casey Heile.

Author's Note

The characters involved directly in this trial story are entirely fictional. However, the idea that a parrot might provide evidence in a murder trial is based on a real case. In 1994, a pet African Grey parrot named Max witnessed a murder in Santa Rosa, California. Max seemed to name someone other than the person who was charged with the crime. The defendant's lawyers prepared expert witnesses to support the use of Max's testimony, but the case was never argued in front of a judge.

All the scientific research mentioned can be found in published articles or is currently in progress, with one exception, which is that the procedure for assessing episodic memory that is described in the prosecution brief is only a thought experiment. However, Irene Pepperberg is currently working on a similar idea with Alex. Some suggested further reading follows. I wish to thank Lynn Allen, Joel Feinberg, Irene Pepperberg, and friends and colleagues at Texas A&M University and the University of Colorado, Boulder, for their comments and help with this story.

SUGGESTED ADDITIONAL READING

Allen, C. 1992. Mental content. *British Journal for the Philosophy of Science,* 43: 537–553.

Allen, C. and Hauser, M. D. 1993: Communication and cognition: is information the connection? *Philosophy of Science Association,* 1992, vol. 2: 81–91.

Bekoff, M. & Jamieson. D. (eds.). 1995. *Readings in Animal Cognition.* Cambridge, MA: MIT Press.

Cheney, D. L. & Seyfarth, R. M. 1990. *How Monkeys See the World.* Chicago: University of Chicago Press.

Griffin, D. R. 1992. *Animal Minds.* Chicago: University of Chicago Press.

Pepperberg, I. M. 1990. Some cognitive capacities of an African Grey parrot (*Psittacus erithacus*). In P. J. B. Slater, J. S. Rosenblatt, and C. Beer (eds.). *Advances in the Study of Behavior.* San Diego: Academic Press, 357–409.

Ristau, C. A. (ed.). 1991. *Cognitive Ethology: The Minds of Other Animals. Essays in Honor of Donald R. Griffin.* Hillsdale, NJ: Lawrence Erlbaum.

Savage-Rumbaugh, E. S., Murphy, J. S., Sevcik, R. A., Brakke, K. E., Williams, S. L., and Bates, E. 1993. *Language Comprehension in Ape and Child.* Chicago: University of Chicago Press.

Personal Identity and the Survival of Death

Where Am I?*

DANIEL C. DENNETT

Daniel C. Dennett (1942–) a leading figure in the philosophy of mind, teaches at Tufts University.

NOW THAT I'VE WON my suit under the Freedom of Information Act, I am at liberty to reveal for the first time a curious episode in my life that may be of interest not only to those engaged in research in the philosophy of mind, artificial intelligence and neuroscience but also to the general public.

Several years ago I was approached by Pentagon officials who asked me to volunteer for a highly dangerous and secret mission. In collaboration with NASA and Howard Hughes, the Department of Defense was spending billions to develop a Supersonic Tunneling Underground Device, or STUD. It was supposed to tunnel through the earth's core at great speed and deliver a specially designed atomic warhead "right up the Red's missile silos," as one of the Pentagon brass put it.

The problem was that in an early test they had succeeded in lodging a warhead about a mile deep under Tulsa, Oklahoma, and they wanted me to retrieve it for them. "Why me?" I asked. Well, the mission involved some pioneering applications of current brain research, and they had heard of my interest in brains and of course my Faustian curiosity and great courage and so forth. . . . Well, how could I refuse? The difficulty that brought the Pentagon to my door was that the device I'd been asked to recover was fiercely radioactive, in a new way. According to monitoring instruments, something about the nature of the device and its complex interactions with pockets of material deep in the earth had produced radiation that could cause severe abnormalities in certain tissues of the brain. No way had been found to shield the brain from these deadly rays, which were apparently harmless to other tissues and organs of the body. So it had been decided that the person sent to recover the device should *leave his brain behind*. It would be kept in a safe place where it could execute its normal control functions by elaborate radio links. Would I submit to a surgical procedure that would completely remove my brain, which would then be placed in a life-support system at the Manned Spacecraft Center in Houston? Each input and output pathway, as it was severed, would be restored by a pair of microminiaturized radio transceivers, one attached precisely to the brain, the other to the nerve stumps in the empty cranium. No information would be lost, all the connectivity would be preserved. At first I was a bit reluctant. Would it really work? The Houston brain surgeons encouraged me. "Think of it," they said, "as a mere *stretching* of the nerves. If your brain were just moved over an *inch* in your skull, that would not alter or impair your mind. We're simply going to make the nerves indefinitely elastic by splicing radio links into them."

I was shown around the life-support lab in Houston and saw the sparkling new vat in which my brain would be placed, were I to agree. I met

From Daniel C. Dennett, Brainstorms *(Bradford Books, 1978), pp. 310–23. Reprinted by permission of MIT Press.*

the large and brilliant support team of neurologists, hematologists, biophysicists, and electrical engineers, and after several days of discussions and demonstrations, I agreed to give it a try. I was subjected to an enormous array of blood tests, brain scans, experiments, interviews, and the like. They took down my autobiography at great length, recorded tedious lists of my beliefs, hopes, fears, and tastes. They even listed my favorite stereo recordings and gave me a crash session of psychoanalysis.

The day for surgery arrived at last and of course I was anesthetized and remember nothing of the operation itself. When I came out of anesthesia, I opened my eyes, looked around, and asked the inevitable, the traditional, the lamentably hackneyed postoperative question: "Where am I?" The nurse smiled down at me. "You're in Houston," she said, and I reflected that this still had a good chance of being the truth one way or another. She handed me a mirror. Sure enough, there were the tiny antennae poling up through their titanium ports cemented into my skull.

"I gather the operation was a success," I said, "I want to go see my brain." They led me (I was a bit dizzy and unsteady) down a long corridor and into the life-support lab. A cheer went up from the assembled support team, and I responded with what I hoped was a jaunty salute. Still feeling lightheaded, I was helped over to the life-support vat. I peered through the glass. There, floating in what looked like ginger ale, was undeniably a human brain, though it was almost covered with printed circuit chips, plastic tubules, electrodes, and other paraphernalia. "Is that mine?" I asked. "Hit the output transmitter switch there on the side of the vat and see for yourself," the project director replied. I moved the switch to OFF, and immediately I slumped, groggy and nauseated, into the arms of the technicians, one of whom kindly restored the switch to its ON position. While I recovered my equilibrium and composure, I thought to myself: "Well, here I am, sitting on a folding chair, staring through a piece of plate glass at my own brain. . . . But wait," I said to myself, "shouldn't I have thought, "Here I am, suspended in a bubbling fluid, being stared at by my own eyes'?" I tried to think this latter thought. I tried to project it into the tank, offering it hopefully to my brain, but I failed to carry off the exercise with any conviction. I tried again. "Here am *I,* Daniel Dennett, suspended in a bubbling fluid, being stared at by my own eyes." No, it just didn't work. Most puzzling and confusing. Being a philosopher of firm physicalist conviction, I believed unswervingly that the tokening of my thoughts was occurring somewhere in my brain: yet, when I thought "Here I am," where the thought occurred to me was *here,* outside the vat, where I, Dennett, was standing staring at my brain.

I tried and tried to think myself into the vat, but to no avail. I tried to build up to the task by doing mental exercises. I thought to myself, "The sun is shining *over there,*" five times in rapid succession, each time mentally ostending a different place: in order, the sunlit corner of the lab, the visible front lawn of the hospital, Houston, Mars, and Jupiter. I found I had little difficulty in getting my "there's" to hop all over the celestial map with their proper references. I could loft a "there" in an instant through the farthest reaches of space, and then aim the next "there" with pinpoint accuracy at the upper left quadrant of a freckle on my arm. Why was I having such trouble with "here"? "Here in Houston" worked well enough, and so did "here in the lab," and even "here in this part of the lab," but "here in the vat" always seemed merely an unmeant mental mouthing. I tried closing my eyes while thinking it. This seemed to help, but still I couldn't manage to pull it off, except perhaps for a fleeting instant. I couldn't be sure. The discovery that I couldn't be sure was so unsettling. How did I know *where* I meant by "here" when I thought "here"? Could I *think* I meant one place when in fact I meant another? I didn't see how that could be admitted without untying the few bonds of intimacy between a person and his own mental life that had survived the onslaught of the brain scientists and philosophers, the physicalists and behaviorists. Perhaps I was incorrigible about where I *meant* when I said "here." But in my present circumstances it seemed that either I was doomed by sheer force of mental habit to thinking systematically false indexical thoughts, or where a person is (and hence where his thoughts are tokened for purposes of semantic analysis) is not necessarily where his brain, the physical seat of his soul, resides. Nagged by confusion, I attempted to orient myself by falling back on a favorite philosopher's ploy. I began naming things.

"Yorick," I said aloud to my brain, "you are my brain. The rest of my body, seated in this chair, I dub "Hamlet."" So here we all are: Yorick's my brain, Hamlet's my body, and I am Dennett. *Now*, where am I? And when I think "where am I?" where's that thought tokened? Is it tokened in my brain, lounging about in the vat, or right here between my ears where it *seems* to be tokened? Or nowhere? Its *temporal* coordinates give me no trouble; must it not have spatial coordinates as well? I began making a list of the alternatives.

(1) *Where Hamlet goes, there goes Dennett.* This principle was easily refuted by appeal to the familiar brain transplant thought-experiments so enjoyed by philosophers. If Tom and Dick switch brains, Tom is the fellow with Dick's former body—just ask him; he'll claim to be Tom, and tell you the most intimate details of Tom's autobiography. It was clear enough, then, that my current body and I could part company, but not likely that I could be separated from my brain. The rule of thumb that emerged so plainly from the thought-experiments was that in a brain-transplant operation, one wanted to be the *donor*, not the recipient. Better to call such an operation a *body*-transplant, in fact. So perhaps the truth was,

(2) *Where Yorick goes, there goes Dennett.* This was not at all appealing, however. How could I be in the vat and not about to go anywhere, when I was so obviously outside the vat looking in and beginning to make guilty plans to return to my room for a substantial lunch? This begged the question, I realized, but it still seemed to be getting at something important. Casting about for some support for my intuition, I hit upon a legalistic sort of argument that might have appealed to Locke.

Suppose, I argued to myself, I were now to fly to California, rob a bank, and be apprehended. In which state would I be tried: In California, where the robbery took place, or in Texas, where the brains of the outfit were located? Would I be a California felon with an out-of-state brain, or a Texas felon remotely controlling an accomplice of sorts in California? It seemed possible that I might beat such a rap just on the undecidability of that jurisdictional question, though perhaps it would be deemed an inter-state, and hence Federal, offense. In any event, suppose I were convicted. Was it likely that California would be satisfied to throw Hamlet into the brig, knowing that Yorick was living the good life and luxuriously taking the waters in Texas? Would Texas incarcerate Yorick, leaving Hamlet free to take the next boat to Rio? This alternative appealed to me. Barring capital punishment or other cruel and unusual punishment, the state would be obliged to maintain the life-support system for Yorick though they might move him from Houston to Leavenworth, and aside from the unpleasantness of the opprobrium, I, for one, would not mind at all and would consider myself a freeman under those circumstances. If the state has an interest in forcibly relocating persons in institutions, it would fail to relocate me in any institution by locating Yorick there. If this were true, it suggested a third alternative.

(3) *Dennett is wherever he thinks he is.* Generalized, the claim was as follows: At any given time a person has a *point of view*, and the location of the point of view (which is determined internally by the content of the point of view) is also the location of the person.

Such a proposition is not without its perplexities, but to me it seemed a step in the right direction. The only trouble was that it seemed to place one in a heads-I-win/tails-you-lose situation of unlikely infallibility as regards location. Hadn't I myself often been wrong about where I was, and at least as often uncertain? Couldn't one get lost? Of course, but getting lost *geographically* is not the only way one might get lost. If one were lost in the woods one could attempt to reassure oneself with the consolation that at least one knew where one was: one was right *here* in the familiar surroundings of one's own body. Perhaps in this case one would not have drawn one's attention to much to be thankful for. Still, there were worse plights imaginable, and I wasn't sure I wasn't in such a plight right now.

Point of view clearly had something to do with personal location, but it was itself an unclear notion. It was obvious that the content of one's point of view was not the same as or determined by the content of one's beliefs or thoughts. For example, what should we say about the point of view of the Cinerama viewer who shrieks and twists in his seat as the roller-coaster footage overcomes his psychic distancing? Has he forgotten that he is safely seated in the theater? Here I was inclined to say that the person is experiencing an illusory shift in point of view. In other cases, my inclination to call such shifts illusory was less strong. The workers in laboratories and plants who handle dangerous materials by operating feedback-controlled mechanical arms and hands undergo a shift in point of view that is crisper and more pronounced than anything Cinerama can provoke. They can feel the heft and slipperiness of the containers they manipulate with their metal fingers. They know perfectly well where they are and are not fooled into false beliefs by the experience, yet it is as if they were inside the isolation chamber they are peering into. With mental effort, they can manage to shift their point of view back and forth, rather like making a transparent Neckar cube or an Escher drawing change orientation before one's eyes. It does seem extravagant to suppose that in performing this bit of mental gymnastics, they are transporting *themselves* back and forth.

Still their example gave me hope. If I was in fact in the vat in spite of my intuitions, I might be able to train myself to adopt that point of view even as a matter of habit. I should dwell on images of myself comfortably floating in my vat, beaming volitions to that familiar body *out there.* I reflected that the ease or difficulty of this task was presumably independent of the truth about the location of one's brain. Had I been practicing before the operation, I might now be finding it second nature. You might now yourself try such a *tromp d'oeil.* Imagine you have written an inflammatory letter which has been published in the *Times,* the result of which is that the Government has chosen to impound your brain for a probationary period of three years in its Dangerous Brain Clinic in Bethesda, Maryland. Your body of course is allowed freedom to earn a salary and thus to continue its function of laying up income to be taxed. At this moment, however, your body is seated in an auditorium listening to a peculiar account by Daniel Dennett of his own similar experience. Try it. Think yourself to Bethesda, and then hark back longingly to your body, far away, and yet *seeming* so near. It is only with long-distance restraint (yours? the Government's?) that you can control your impulse to get those hands clapping in polite applause before navigating the old body to the rest room and a well-deserved glass of evening sherry in the lounge. The task of imagination is certainly difficult, but if you achieve your goal the results might be consoling.

Anyway, there I was in Houston, lost in thought as one might say, but not for long. My speculations were soon interrupted by the Houston doctors, who wished to test out my new prosthetic nervous system before sending me off on my hazardous mission. As I mentioned before, I was a bit dizzy at first, and not surprisingly, although I soon habituated myself to my new circumstances (which were, after all, well nigh indistinguishable from my old circumstances). My accommodation was not perfect, however, and to this day I continue to be plagued by minor coordination difficulties. The speed of light is fast, but finite, and as my brain and body move farther and farther apart, the delicate interaction of my feedback systems is thrown into disarray by the time lags. Just as one is rendered close to speechless by a delayed or echoic hearing of one's speaking voice so, for instance, I am virtually unable to track a moving object with my eyes whenever my brain and my body are more than a few miles apart. In most matters my impairment is scarcely detectable, though I can no longer hit a slow curve ball with the authority of yore. There are some compensations of course. Though liquor tastes as good as ever, and warms my gullet while corroding my liver, I can drink it in any quantity I please, without becoming the slightest bit inebriated, a curiosity some of my close friends may have noticed (though I occasionally have *feigned* inebriation, so as not to draw attention to my unusual circumstances). For similar reasons, I take aspirin orally for a sprained wrist, but if the pain persists I ask Houston to administer codeine to me *in vitro.* In times of illness the phone bill can be staggering.

But to return to my adventure. At length, both the doctors and I were satisfied that I was ready to undertake my subterranean mission. And so I left my brain in Houston and headed by helicopter for Tulsa. Well, in any case, that's the way it seemed to me. That's how I would put it, just off the top of my head as it were. On the trip I reflected further about my earlier anxieties and decided that my first postoperative speculations had been tinged with panic. The matter was not nearly as strange or metaphysical as I had been supposing. Where was I? In two places, clearly: both inside the vat and outside it. Just as one can stand with one foot in Connecticut and the other in Rhode Island, I was in two places at once. I had become one of those scattered individuals we used to hear so much about. The more I considered this answer, the more obviously true it appeared. But, strange to say, the more true it appeared, the less important the question to which it could be the true answer seemed. A sad, but not unprecedented, fate for a philosophical question to suffer. This answer did not completely satisfy me, of course. There lingered some question to which I should have liked an answer, which was neither "Where are all my various and sundry parts?" nor "What is my current point of view?" Or at least there seemed to be such a question. For it did seem undeniable that in some sense *I* and not merely *most of me* was descending into the earth under Tulsa in search of an atomic warhead.

When I found the warhead, I was certainly glad I had left my brain behind, for the pointer on the specially built Geiger counter I had brought with me was off the dial. I called Houston on my ordinary radio and told the operation control center of my position and my progress. In return, they gave me instructions for dismantling the vehicle, based upon my on-site observations. I had set to work with my cutting torch when all of a sudden a terrible thing happened. I went stone deaf. At first I thought it was only my radio earphones that had broken, but when I tapped on my helmet, I heard nothing. Apparently the auditory transceivers had gone on the fritz. I could no longer hear Houston or my own voice, but I could speak, so I started telling them what had happened. In mid-sentence, I knew something else had gone wrong. My vocal apparatus had become paralyzed. Then my right hand went limp—another transceiver had gone. I was truly in deep trouble. But worse was to follow. After a few more minutes, I went blind. I cursed my luck, and then I cursed the scientists who had led me into this grave peril. There I was, deaf, dumb, and blind, in a radioactive hole more than a mile under Tulsa. Then the last of my cerebral radio links broke, and suddenly I was faced with a new and even more shocking problem: whereas an instant before I had been buried alive in Oklahoma, now I was disembodied in Houston. My recognition of my new status was not immediate. It took me several very anxious minutes before it dawned on me that my poor body lay several hundred miles away, with heart pulsing and lungs respirating, but otherwise as dead as the body of any heart transplant donor, its skull packed with useless, broken electronic gear. The shift in perspective I had earlier found well nigh impossible now seemed quite natural. Though I could think myself back into my body in the tunnel under Tulsa, it took some effort to sustain the illusion. For surely it was an illusion to suppose I was still in Oklahoma: I had lost all contact with that body.

It occurred to me then, with one of those rushes of revelation of which we should be suspicious, that I had stumbled upon an impressive demonstration of the immateriality of the soul based upon physicalist principles and premises. For as the last radio signal between Tulsa and Houston died away, had I not changed location from Tulsa to Houston at the speed of light? And had I not accomplished this without any increase in mass? What moved from A to B at such speed was surely myself, or at any rate my soul or mind—the massless center of my being and home of my consciousness. My *point of view* had lagged somewhat behind, but I had already noted the indirect bearing of point of view on personal location. I could not see how a physicalist philosopher could quarrel with this except by taking the dire and counter-intuitive route of banishing all talk of persons. Yet the notion of personhood was so well entrenched in everyone's world view, or so it seemed to me, that any denial would be as curiously unconvincing, as systematically disingenuous, as the Cartesian negation, "non sum."[1]

The joy of philosophic discovery thus tided me over some very bad minutes or perhaps hours as the helplessness and hopelessness of my situation became more apparent to me. Waves of panic and even nausea swept over me, made all the more horrible by the absence of their normal body-dependent phenomenology. No adrenaline rush of tingles in the arms, no pounding heart, no premonitory salivation. I did feel a dread sinking feeling in my bowels at one point, and this tricked me momentarily into the false hope that I was undergoing a reversal of the process that landed me in this fix—a gradual undisembodiment. But the isolation and uniqueness of that twinge soon convinced me that it was simply the first of a plague of phantom body hallucinations that I, like any other amputee, would be all too likely to suffer.

My mood then was chaotic. On the one hand, I was fired up with elation of my philosophic discovery and was wracking my brain (one of the few familiar things I could still do), trying to figure out how to communicate my discovery to the journals; while on the other, I was bitter, lonely, and filled with dread and uncertainty. Fortunately, this did not last long, for my technical support team sedated me into a dreamless sleep from which I awoke, hearing with magnificent fidelity the familiar opening strains of my favorite Brahms piano trio. So that was why they had wanted a list of my favorite recordings! It did not take me long to realize that I was hearing the music without ears. The output from the stereo stylus was being fed through some fancy rectification circuitry directly into my auditory nerve. I was mainlining Brahms, an unforgettable experience for any stereo buff. At the end of the record it did not surprise me to hear the reassuring voice of the project director speaking into a microphone that was now my prosthetic ear. He confirmed my analysis of what had gone wrong and assured me that steps were being taken to re-embody me. He did not elaborate, and after a few more recordings, I found myself drifting off to sleep. My sleep lasted, I later learned, for the better part of a year, and when I awoke, it was to find myself fully restored to my senses. When I looked into the mirror, though, I was a bit startled to see an unfamiliar face. Bearded and a bit heavier, bearing no doubt a family resemblance to my former face, and with the same look of spritely intelligence and resolute character, but definitely a new face. Further self-explorations of an intimate nature left me no doubt that this was a new body and the project director confirmed my conclusions. He did not volunteer any information on the past history of my new body and I decided (wisely, I think in retrospect) not to pry. As many philosophers unfamiliar with my ordeal have more recently speculated, the acquisition of a new body leaves one's *person* intact. And after a period of adjustment to a new voice, new muscular strengths and weaknesses, and so forth, one's *personality* is by and large also preserved. More dramatic changes in personality have been routinely observed in people who have undergone extensive plastic surgery, to say nothing of sex change operations, and I think no one contests the survival of the person in such cases. In any event I soon accommodated to my new body, to the point of being unable to recover any of its novelties to my consciousness or even memory. The view in the mirror soon became utterly familiar. That view, by the way, still revealed antennae, and so I was not surprised to learn that my brain had not been moved from its haven in the life-support lab.

I decided that good old Yorick deserved a visit. I and my new body, whom we might as well call Fortinbras, strode into the familiar lab to another round of applause from the technicians, who were of course congratulating themselves, not me. Once more I stood before the vat and contemplated poor Yorick, and on a whim I once again cavalierly flicked off the output transmitter switch. Imagine my surprise when nothing unusual happened. No fainting spell, no nausea, no noticeable change. A technician hurried to restore the switch to ON, but still I felt nothing. I demanded an explanation, which the project director hastened to provide. It seems that before they had even operated on the first occasion, they had constructed a computer duplicate of my brain, reproducing both the complete information processing structure and the computational speed of my brain in a giant computer program. After the operation, but before they had dared to send me off on my mission to Oklahoma, they had run this computer system and Yorick side by side. The incoming signals from Hamlet were sent simultaneously to Yorick's transceivers and to the computer's array of inputs. And the outputs from Yorick were not only beamed back to Hamlet, my body; they were recorded and checked against the simultaneous output of the computer program, which was called "Hubert" for reasons obscure to me. Over days and even weeks, the outputs were identical and synchronous, which of course did not *prove* that they had succeeded in copying the brain's functional structure, but the empirical support was greatly encouraging.

Hubert's input, and hence activity, had been kept parallel with Yorick's during my disembodied days. And now, to demonstrate this, they had actually thrown the master switch that put Hubert for the first time in on-line control of my body—not Hamlet, of course, but Fortinbras. (Hamlet, I learned, had never been recovered from its underground tomb and could be assumed by this time to have largely returned to the dust. At the head of my grave still lay the magnificent bulk of the abandoned device, with the word STUD emblazoned on its side in large letters—a circumstance which may provide archeologists of the next century with a curious insight into the burial rites of their ancestors.)

The laboratory technicians now showed me the master switch, which had two positions, labeled *B,* for Brain (they didn't know my brain's name was Yorick) and *H,* for Hubert. The switch did indeed point to *H,* and they explained to me that if I wished, I could switch it back to *B.* With my heart in my mouth (and my brain in its vat), I did this. Nothing happened. A click, that was all. To test their claim, and with the master switch now set at *B,* I hit Yorick's output transmitter switch on the vat and sure enough, I began to faint. Once the output switch was turned back on and I had recovered my wits, so to speak, I continued to play with the master switch, flipping it back and forth. I found that with the exception of the transitional click, I could detect no trace of a difference. I could switch in mid-utterance, and the sentence I had begun speaking under the control of Yorick was finished without a pause or hitch of any kind under the control of Hubert. I had a spare brain, a prosthetic device which might some day stand me in very good stead, were some mishap to befall Yorick. Or alternatively, I could keep Yorick as a spare and use Hubert. It didn't seem to make any difference which I chose, for the wear and tear and fatigue on my body did not have any debilitating effect on either brain, whether or not it was actually causing the motions of my body, or merely spilling its output into thin air.

The one truly unsettling aspect of this new development was the prospect which was not long in dawning on me, of someone detaching the spare—Hubert or Yorick, as the case might be—from Fortinbras and hitching it to yet another body—some Johnny-come-lately Rosencrantz or Guildenstern. Then (if not before) there would be *two* people, that much was clear. One would be me, and the other would be a sort of super-twin brother. If there were two bodies, one under the control of Hubert and the other being controlled by Yorick, then which would the world recognize as the true Dennett? And whatever the rest of the world decided, which one would be *me?* Would I be the Yorick-brained one, in virtue of Yorick's causal priority and former intimate relationship with the original Dennett body, Hamlet? That seemed a bit legalistic, a bit too redolent of the arbitrariness of consanguinity and legal possession, to be convincing at the metaphysical level. For, suppose that before the arrival of the second body on the scene, I had been keeping Yorick as the spare for years, and letting Hubert's output drive my body—that is, Fortinbras—all that time. The Hubert-Fortinbras couple would seem then by squatter's rights (to combat one legal intuition with another) to be true to Dennett and the lawful inheritor of everything that was Dennett's. This was an interesting question, certainly, but not nearly so pressing as another question that bothered me. My strongest intuition was that in such an eventuality *I* would survive so long as *either* brain-body couple remained intact, but I had mixed emotions about whether I should want both to survive.

I discussed my worries with the technicians and the project director. The prospect of two Dennetts was abhorrent to me, I explained, largely for social reasons. I didn't want to be my own rival for the affections of my wife, nor did I like the prospect of the two Dennetts sharing my modest professor's salary. Still more vertiginous and distasteful, though, was the idea of knowing *that much* about another person, while he had the very same goods on me. How could we ever face each other? My colleagues in the lab argued that I was ignoring the bright side of the matter. Weren't there many things I wanted to do but, being only one person, had been unable to do? Now one Dennett could stay at home and be the professor and family man, while the other could strike out on a life of travel and adventure—missing the family of course, but happy in the knowledge that the other Dennett was keeping the home fires burning. I could be faithful and adulterous at the same time. I could even cuckold myself—to say nothing of other more lurid possibilities my colleagues were all too ready to force upon my overtaxed imagination. But my ordeal in Oklahoma (or was it Houston?) had made me less adventurous, and I shrank from this opportunity that was being offered (though of course I was never quite sure it was being offered to *me* in the first place).

There was another prospect even more disagreeable—that the spare, Hubert or Yorick as the case might be, would be detached from any input from Fortinbras and just left detached. Then, as in the other case, there would be two Dennetts, or at least two claimants to my name and possessions, one embodied in Fortinbras, and the other sadly, miserably disembodied. Both selfishness and altruism bade me take steps to prevent this from happening. So I asked that measures be taken to ensure that no one could ever tamper with the transceiver connections or the master switch without my (our? no, *my*) knowledge and consent. Since I had no desire to spend my life guarding my equipment in Houston, it was mutually decided that all the electronic connections in the lab would be carefully locked: both those that controlled the life-support system for Yorick and those that controlled the power supply for Hubert would be guarded with fail-safe devices, and I would take the only master switch, outfitted for radio remote control, with me wherever I went. I carry it strapped around my waist and—wait a moment—*here it is.* Every few months I reconnoiter the situation by switching channels. I do this only in the presence of friends of course, for if the other channel were, heaven forbid, either dead or otherwise occupied, there would have to be somebody who had my interests at heart to switch it back, to bring me back from the void. For while I could feel, see, hear and otherwise sense whatever befell my body, subsequent to such a switch, I'd be unable to control it. By the way, the two positions on the switch are intentionally unmarked, so I never have the faintest idea whether I am switching from Hubert to Yorick or *vice versa.* (Some of you may think that in this case I really don't know *who* I am, let alone where I am. But such reflections no longer make much of a dent on my essential Dennettness, on my own sense of who I am. If it is true that in one sense I don't know who I am then that's another one of your philosophical truths of underwhelming significance.)

In any case, every time I've flipped the switch so far, nothing has happened. *So let's give it a try. . . .*

"THANK GOD! I THOUGHT YOU'D NEVER FLIP THAT SWITCH! You can't imagine how horrible it's been these last two weeks—but now you know, it's your turn in purgatory. How I've longed for this moment! You see, about two weeks ago—excuse me, ladies and gentlemen, but I've got to explain this to my . . . um, brother, I guess you could say, but he's just told you the facts, so you'll understand—about two weeks ago our two brains drifted just a bit out of synch. I don't know whether *my* brain is now Hubert or Yorick, any more than you do, but in any case, the two brains drifted apart, and of course once the process started, it snowballed, for I was in a slightly different receptive state for the input we both received, a difference that was soon magnified. In no time at all the illusion that I was in control of my body—our body—was completely dissipated. There was nothing I could do—no way to call you. YOU DIDN'T EVEN KNOW I EXISTED! It's been like being carried around in a cage, or better, like being possessed—hearing my own voice say things I didn't mean to say, watching in frustration as my own hands performed deeds I hadn't intended. You'd scratch our itches, but not the way I would have, and you kept me awake, with your tossing and turning. I've been totally exhausted, on the verge of a nervous breakdown, carried around helplessly by your frantic round of activities, sustained only by the knowledge that some day you'd throw the switch.

"Now it's your turn, but at least you'll have the comfort of knowing *I* know you're in there. Like an expectant mother, I'm eating—or at any rate tasting, smelling, seeing—for *two* now, and I'll try to make it easy for you. Don't worry. Just as soon as this colloquium is over, you and I will fly to Houston, and we'll see what can be done to get one of us another body. You can have a female body—your body could be any color you like. But let's think it over. I tell you what—to be fair, if we both want this body, I promise I'll let the project director flip a coin to settle which of us gets to keep it and which then gets to choose a new body. That should guarantee justice, shouldn't it? In any case, I'll take care of you, I promise. These people are my witnesses.

"Ladies and gentlemen, this talk we have just heard is not exactly the talk *I* would have given, but I assure you that everything he said was perfectly true. And now if you'll excuse me, I think I'd—we'd—better sit down."[2]

NOTES

1. Cf., Jaakko Hintikka, "Cogito ergo sum: Inference or Performance?" *The Philosophical Review,* LXXI, 1962, pp. 3–32.

2. Anyone familiar with the literature on this topic will recognize that my remarks owe a great deal to the explorations of Sydney Shoemaker, John Perry, David Lewis and Derek Parfit, and in particular to their papers in Amelie Rorty, ed., *The Identities of Persons,* 1976.

Survival: The Problem of Identity*

TERENCE PENELHUM

THE LOGICAL PROBLEMS one has to contend with when examining the concept of survival are to a large extent extensions of those that have puzzled philosophers when they have tried to analyze the notion of personal identity.[1] We all recognize one another; we are all familiar enough with the experience of wondering who someone is; and most of us know the embarrassment that follows when one makes a mistake about who someone is. Our day-to-day thinking about these matters suggests that we take it for granted that there are clearly understood factors that determine whether the man before us is Smith or not, or is who he says he is or not, even though we may be unable to decide sometimes, through lack of information, whether these factors obtain. Philosophers have been puzzled, however, when they have tried to say what these factors are. Skeptical philosophers have even wondered whether any such factors can be isolated; and if they cannot be, they have suggested, our assumption that people do retain their identities from one period of time to the next may be an illusion.

HUME'S SKEPTICISM

We do not need to spend much time here on this sort of skepticism. Its most famous exponent is Hume, who confessed himself unable to detect any stability in the mental life of men and therefore thought that the incessant changes that human minds undergo make it plainly false that they retain any identity at all.[2] Our belief that they do retain an

Terence Penelhum. Religion and Rationality *(New York and Toronto, Random House, 1971), pp. 345–55. Reprinted by permission of the author.*

identity is a convenient fiction but nothing better. This skepticism rests on an unstated assumption that there is some sort of logical conflict between the notions of sameness and change. If this were so, then in order to be sure that any type of being retained identity through time, we would have to be sure that it, or at least the essential part of it, remained unchanged through that time. If this is true, then of course Hume would be quite justified in relapsing into skepticism about personal identity. But once the assumption is exposed, its gratuitousness becomes apparent. Sameness or identity is an ambiguous notion; borrowing vocabulary found in Hume himself, we can distinguish between "numerical identity" and "specific identity." Two things are identical in the specific sense if they are exactly alike in some or all respects. This can only be true if they are, nevertheless, two distinct things—if, that is, they are *not* identical in the numerical sense. Two numerically different things may or may not be the same in the specific sense. One and the same thing (in the numerical sense) may be the same at one time as it was at an earlier time, or it may not. If it is not, it has changed. To say that just because it has changed it cannot be numerically the same is to confuse the two sorts of identity.

Certain changes, however, may destroy a thing—that is, whatever remains of it is no longer sufficient to entitle us to say that thing has continued in existence, and we are forced to say that something else is there, as when a house crumbles and a mere heap of stones remains. Even though Hume is wrong in thinking that the mere fact of change destroys numerical identity, it is still the case that for each *sort* of thing, certain changes will destroy that identity and certain others will not. Reducing all parts of a chair to ashes in a fire will destroy its identity, whereas changing the color of its surface by painting it will not. This suggests, once again, that the proper philosophical task is to discover, at least in the case of those classes of things that are of philosophical interest to us, what factors have to remain for a thing of that sort to continue in being and which ones do not. The problem of personal identity consists, in part, of trying to clarify this in the case of persons.

When we try to do this we are confronted with another oddity in a discussion like Hume's. He restricts himself, without any apparent recognition of the need to justify this restriction, to a consideration of only the mental factors that make up the being of a person and ignores the physical ones. If one makes this restriction, one is immediately confronted with the following facts that Hume stresses: first, he notes that the changes we can introspect within the mind succeed one another very rapidly; and second, he points out that one cannot detect any more stable element. Since we usually conceive of *things* as entities that change fairly slowly unless catastrophe strikes them and do not normally change nearly as rapidly as the contents of the mind seem to do, our ascription of identity to the person is apt to seem puzzling. But what needs to be questioned here is Hume's restriction. One of the major reasons for it is that Hume inherits the dualism that Descartes passed down from Plato into modern philosophy. It is a characteristic part of that tradition not merely to divide the human person into two parts but to identify the real person with the mind and assume that the body is merely a place that this person inhabits. If this identification is presupposed, then Hume's bewilderment in the face of the rapidity of mental change is understandable enough.

MENTAL AND BODILY CRITERIA OF IDENTITY

One way of trying to avoid . . . confusion is to resort to . . . the doctrine of spiritual substance. This is the doctrine that in spite of the changingness of our mental lives, there is some hidden core to it that persists unchanged throughout, thus providing a backdrop against which the changes occur. This backdrop need not be *un*changing: It could be subject only to gradual change. The tacit assumption that it cannot change at all is only the result of assuming that identity and change are always inconsistent. But even if we allow that the spiritual substance to which the occurrences in our mental lives belong might itself be subject to gradual change, the doctrine is without value. For if the doctrine implies that we can find this relatively permanent core within by looking into ourselves, then it is false; for we cannot, as Hume emphasizes. If on the other hand, it is admitted that the doctrine postulates something that is not accessible to observation, there is another difficulty: It can at best be a matter of happy accident that when we judge someone before us to be the same person as someone we knew before, we are right. For the only thing that would make this judgment reliable is the knowledge that the features possessed by the present and the past person belonged to the same substance. Yet when the substance is inaccessible even to the person himself, how could we ever know that an identity judgment was true? It is obvious that our basis for such judgments must be something other than what the doctrine requires it to be, for how, otherwise, could we learn to make such judgments in the first place?

We base our identity judgments, at least of others, upon the observation of their physical appearance. This fact, plus the mysteriousness of the doctrine of spiritual substance, has made it very tempting for philosophers to say that what makes a person the same from one period to the next is the continuance of his body throughout the two periods. The human body has the relative stability that we associate with a great many observable material objects and is not usually subject to the rapid changes that go on in the human mind. The plausibility of the claim that bodily continuity is a necessary and sufficient condition of personal identity derives also from the fact that our judgments about the identity of persons are in the vast majority of cases based on our having looked at them, talked to them, and recognized them. This may be why even philosophers who have tacitly identified the person with his mind have assumed that a person cannot consist only of thoughts, feelings, images, and other fleeting and changing phenomena, but must consist, beneath this, of something more stable. For they have, perhaps, been looking within the mind itself for something that has the relative stability of the body, even though they have officially abandoned any belief that the body provides persons with their continuing identity.

Suppose, however, that they were to abandon body surrogates like spiritual substance. Suppose they were not to assume that the identity of a person consists in the persistence of some relatively stable element such as his body, but were to concentrate their attention solely upon what they consider to be the contents of his mental life. If they were to do this, it would seem that their only hope of giving an account of the self-identity of persons would be to suggest the existence of some relationship among the fleeting elements of which human mental life is composed. An appropriate relationship does seem available. Some of the later experiences in a man's life history are, the story might go, memories of the earlier ones. And only the same person who had the earlier experiences could have a memory of one of them among his later experiences. So we have here the possibility of a purely mental standard of identity: that person *A* at time T_2 is the same as person *B* at some earlier time T_1 if and only if, among the experiences that person *A* has at T_2 there are memories of experiences that person *B* had at T_1. In the literature of the subject these two criteria of identity (bodily continuity and memory) have contended for priority.

The claim that personal identity can be understood solely in terms of memory can be accepted by someone who does not believe that a person can be identified with his mind or that anyone ever survives physical death. A philosopher who does not believe these things might still believe that the embodied person before him can be identified with Smith, whom he used to know, only if the person before him has the appropriate memories. But it is clear that someone who does believe those things must reject the thesis that only bodily continuity can be a criterion of personal identity. For if it is a necessary condition of a person's continuing that his body should continue, no one could survive in a disembodied form. Someone who accepts the doctrine of disembodied survival, therefore, will naturally incline toward the view that memory is the one necessary and sufficient condition of personal identity, since he must reject the traditional alternative position.

There is an artificiality about speaking, as I have, about two competing positions here. For in daily life it looks as though we use both standards of identity, resorting to one or the other depending on circumstances. Sometimes we decide who someone is by ascertaining facts about their physical appearance, height, weight, and the rest. Sometimes we decide who someone is by trying to determine whether or not they can remember certain past events that the person they claim to be could not fail, we think, to recall. Indeed, the barrier between these two methods becomes less clear than it first seems, when we reflect that we might try to reach our decision by seeing what skills a person has retained or what performances he can carry out. But although both standards are used, one might still have priority over the other. This would be the case if the other would not be available to us if the one were not or if the description of the one required some reference to the other.

It might look as though the use of the bodily criterion of identity presupposes that of memory in some way. For we cannot know, without resorting to our own or someone else's memory of the person in question, whether the body before us is the same one that the person we think he is had in the past. This is true, but it does not show that the man's own memories determine who he is. It only shows that other people could not determine the necessary physical facts about him unless they could rely on their own memories to do it, and this is not the same thing.

There are two arguments that tend to show, I think, that the bodily criterion has priority over the memory criterion. The first one, which is the less fundamental, rests on the fact that people forget things. We cannot say that the man before us is the man who performed some past action if and only if he remembers doing that action, for people forget actions they have done. But one might object on two counts that this need not refute the claim that his having the memory of that action is what makes that action his rather than someone else's. For, first, all we mean by this is that he *could* remember doing it, not that he *does* remember doing it; and, second, all we need is that he be able to remember doing some action or having some experience that the person who did the original action also did, or had.

Let us take these objections in order. The first will not do, for what do we mean when we say that he could remember doing the action in question? If we mean that it is in practice possible to get him to recall doing it, for instance, by psychoanalysis, then the retort is that all practicable methods might fail without thereby showing that the action was not done by him. If, on the other hand, we merely mean that it is in theory possible, then this requires further elucidation: Something that is possible in theory but not in practice is possible in virtue of some condition that in practice cannot bring it about. And this condition can only be the very fact that we are trying to elucidate, namely, the fact that the action was done by him and not by someone else. The other objection does not hold either, for a similar sort of reason. If we say that although the man before us cannot remember doing the action in question, he did do it because he can remember having some experience that the past person who did that action had, this presupposes that we understand what makes the past person who had that experience the same past person who did the original action. There must therefore be some standard of identity, actually satisfied, that we are appealing to in order to presuppose this. To say that this standard is itself that of memory is to raise our original question all over again.

The second and more fundamental argument rests on the fact that the notion of remembering is ambiguous. To say that someone remembers some action or event may mean merely that he believes he did it or witnessed it (without, at least consciously, basing this belief upon being told about it). It is possible, of course, for someone to remember something in this sense without what he remembers having happened at all and without its having happened to *him* even if it did occur. The more common use of the notion of remembering, however, concedes the truth of the man's belief, so that to say that the man remembers some action or event is to say that his claim to know about it is correct. Let us call these sense (i) and sense (ii) of "remember." Then we can say that to remember in sense (i) is to believe that one remembers in sense (ii).

It is apparent that memory in sense (i) cannot provide a criterion of personal identity. It is certainly not a sufficient condition of a man before us being the person that he claims to be that he remembers, in sense (i), doing or experiencing something done or experienced by the man he claims to be. For he could believe that he remembered doing something in this sense, even if nobody had done it. So we have to lean on sense (ii) of "remember." But this leads into a deeper problem. Let us simplify our discussion by concentrating solely upon a person's remembering doing an action or having an experience or witnessing an event and leave aside the complexities involved in someone's remembering some fact, such as that Caesar was murdered. To say that someone, in sense (ii) remembers, is not merely to report that he believes something, but to accept his belief to be true. But an integral part of his belief is not only that some action was done, some experience had, or some event witnessed, but that it was done or had or witnessed by *him*. In other words, to say that he remembers in sense (ii) is not just to say that he now has some mental image or some conviction, even though it is likely to include this; it is to say that the past action, experience, or event that he refers to is part of his own past. But it now becomes clear that we cannot even state the memory criterion of identity without having some prior (and therefore independent) notion of the identity of the person. So the identity of the person must in the end rest upon some other condition, and the claim that it could rest solely upon memory must be false. The bodily criterion of identity is the natural one to refer to here. If, because of some commitment to dualism, one refuses to resort to it, it becomes wholly mysterious what the criterion of personal identity can be.

IDENTITY AND SURVIVAL

We can now return to the problem of survival. We were considering how far it is possible to make sense of the notion of the persistence of a disembodied person through time and of the claim that some particular future disembodied person will be identical with one of us in this world here and now. We can also ask how far the doctrine of the resurrection of the body frees us from the difficulties that the doctrine of disembodied survival encounters.

If bodily continuity is a necessary condition of the persistence of a person through time, then we cannot form any clear conception of the persistence of a person through time without a body nor of the identity of such a person with some previous embodied person. The previous reflections about the notion of personal identity leave us with two results: first, that to attempt to understand the self-identity of a person solely in terms of memory is impossible and, second, that when we are considering the case of flesh-and-blood persons there seems no alternative but to conclude that bodily continuity is a necessary condition of personal identity. These conclusions by themselves do not show that no substitute for bodily continuity could be invented when discussing the case of disembodied personality. But some substitute for it would have to be supplied by invention, and until it is, the notion of disembodied personal identity makes no sense.

The main line of argument is now plain, but for greater completeness it may be desirable to apply it to the doctrine of disembodied survival in a little more detail. An adherent of this doctrine, anxious to avoid admitting the necessity of the bodily criterion of personal identity, might perhaps claim that a survivor of death would intelligibly be said to be identical with someone who had died, because he remembered the actions and experiences of that person. And he might be said intelligibly to persist through time in his disembodied state because later and earlier experiences in the afterlife could be similarly connected by memories.

Let us take the latter suggestion first. It is that the disembodied person who has some experience at some future time FT_2 will be identical with the disembodied person who will have had some experience at an earlier future time FT_1 if, along with the experience at FT_2, there is a memory of the one he had at FT_1. The difficulty is to make sense not only of a phrase like "along with the experience there is a memory," but also, of what it means to speak of a memory here at all. For it will have to be a memory in sense (ii). And to say that the disembodied person has a memory at FT_2 in sense (ii) of some experience had at FT_1 is to assume that the two experiences will have been had by the same person; and this time, since we have no bodily criterion of identity to fall back on, we have no way of interpreting this claim.

If we turn now to the problem of identifying the disembodied person with some person who has died, we find the same difficulty. To say that he can be so identified because he remembers the deeds or experiences of that person is once again to use the notion of remembering in sense (ii). But to do this is to presuppose that we understand what it is for the rememberer to be identical with the person who did those deeds or had those experiences. And we do not actually understand this. For although the person who did those deeds had a body, the rememberer, by hypothesis does not have one and therefore cannot have the same body. It does not seem possible, therefore, to find any answer to the problem of self-identity for disembodied persons.

What about the doctrine of the resurrection of the body? Given that we are talking of the future existence of persons with bodies, the notion of their lasting through time in their future state does not seem to present any logical difficulties. But what of their identity with ourselves? If we assume some one-to-one correspondence between the inhabitants of the next world and of this (that is, assume at least that the inhabitants of the next world each resemble, claim to be, and claim to remember the doings of inhabitants of this one), it might seem foolish to deny that they will be identical with ourselves. But foolishness is not logical absurdity. It is conceivable that there might be a future existence in which there were large numbers of persons each resembling one of us and having uncanny knowledge of our pasts. And if that world does come to be in the future, we shall not be in it. What would make it a world with us in it, rather than a world with duplicates of us in it and not ourselves? Unless we can give a clear answer to this, it seems, very paradoxically, to be a matter of arbitrary choice whether to say these future people are us or not.

Surely, the answer might run, they will have the same bodies that we now have. But this is precisely what is not obvious. Apart from questions about whether the future bodies are like ours in youth, maturity, or old age, the dissolution of the earthly body means that the future body will be in some sense new. To say that it is the old one re-created is merely to say it is the same one without giving any reason for saying it is identical with the original body rather than one very much like it. To answer this way, then, seems merely to face the same puzzle again. To say that the future beings will remember in sense (ii) our doings and feelings is to raise the same questions here as before. The only possible solution seems to be to insist that in spite of the time gap between the death of the old body and the appearance of the new one, something persists in between. But what? The person disembodied? If so, then the doctrine of the resurrection of the body does not avoid the difficulties that beset the doctrine of disembodied survival, for the simple reason that it falls back upon that very doctrine when its own implications are understood.

This argument does not show that the doctrine of the resurrection of the body is absurd in the way in which the doctrine of disembodied survival is. It shows rather that the doctrine of resurrection is merely one way, and a question-begging way, of describing a set of circumstances that can be described equally well in another fashion. Yet the difference between the two alternative descriptions is a vital one. For it comes to no less than the original question, namely, do we survive? It is a question that the doctrine provides an answer to but one that seems to have no conclusive grounds, even if the circumstances envisaged in the doctrine were admitted to be forthcoming.

The belief in survival, then, at least in this version, does not run into insuperable difficulties of logic. But it does not seem possible to describe a set of future circumstances that will unambiguously show it to be true. I have previously argued that if the doctrine is agreed to be coherent, it can offer a suitable answer to the difficulties about the verification of religious beliefs. I do not consider the present puzzle to show that it is not coherent. But it does show its status to be very baffling. Such a judgment is no doubt an appropriate one to conclude a volume dealing with some of the philosophical perplexities occasioned by religious beliefs.

CONCLUSION

The argument of this book* has been designed to assess the rationality of religious belief. In Part I we saw that religious belief cannot be shown to be rational in the strong sense: that is, it cannot be shown to be irrational not to believe. In Part II we saw that religious belief has not been shown to be irrational because of any lack of clear meaning. In the first two chapters of Part III we have seen that the most familiar argument that skeptics have used to show religious belief involves contradiction, can be given a reasonable answer. In the remaining chapters we have seen some of the ways in which religious beliefs have to be interpreted to avoid conflict with secular knowledge and moral judgments.

I have attempted, in the concluding pages of Part II, to indicate the ways in which the rational believer and the rational skeptic can differ on principles as well as on details. If my account is correct, neither can accuse the other of violating rules of logic, failing to make coherent sense, or denying established facts; for neither need be guilty of such faults. If this is so, then the commitments that divide them cannot be established, or undermined, by philosophical argument. Philosophical argument can make them clear where they are obscure, and make them explicit where they have not been stated, but it cannot decide between them. The tasks it can perform, however, are important enough.

The conclusion I would offer from these varied considerations is that religious belief, though not rational in the strong sense, is rational in the weak sense. The weak sense of "rational" is equivalent, in effect, to "not irrational." Religious belief does not, or need not, conflict with scientific knowledge be involved in self-contradiction, or be devoid of clear content. Philosophy can say this much in religion's favor, though it cannot say more. Philosophy used to be thought of as theology's handmaiden; this role is past, for a handmaiden must pay her mistress higher compliments than this; and in this weak sense skepticism is rational also.

NOTES

1. For a general discussion of the problems of personal identity, see my article of that title in Paul Edwards (ed.), *Encyclopedia of Philosophy* (New York: Macmillan and Free Press, 1967), Vol. 6. This contains, besides a more rigorous treatment of issues raised briefly here, some extended discussion of the implications of the "puzzle cases," which I have had to omit from a short treatment of these topics. The latter part of my *Survival and Disembodied Existence* (London: Routledge & Kegan Paul, 1970), is intended to be a more thorough examination of the issues introduced in this chapter.

2. See Hume's *Treatise of Human Nature,* Book I, Part 4, Section 6. The criticisms I make here are more informal versions of those I raised in "Hume on Personal Identity," *The Philosophical Review,* 44, No. 4 (1955), 571–589, reprinted in V. C. Chappell (ed.), *Hume* (New York: Doubleday, 1967), pp. 213–239.

*[The references to "this book" and its parts refer to Penelhum's *Religion and Rationality,* which includes material not reprinted here.—Eds.]

A Dialogue on Personal Identity and Immortality*

JOHN PERRY

John Perry (1943–) teaches philosophy at Stanford University.

(THIS IS A RECORD OF CONVERSATIONS OF Gretchen Weirob, a teacher of philosophy at a small midwestern college, and several of her friends. They took place in her hospital room, the three nights before she died from injuries sustained in a motorcycle accident. Sam Miller is a chaplain and a long-time friend of Weirob's; Dave Cohen is a former student of hers.)

THE FIRST NIGHT

Cohen: I can hardly believe what you say, Gretchen. You are lucid and do not appear to be in great pain. And yet you say things are hopeless?

Weirob: These devices can keep me alive for another day or two at most. Some of my vital organs have been injured beyond anything the doctors know how to repair, apart from certain rather radical measures I have rejected. I am not in much pain. But as I understand it that is not a particularly good sign. My brain was uninjured and I guess that's why I am as lucid as I ever am. The whole situation is a bit depressing, I fear. But here's Sam Miller. Perhaps he will know how to cheer me up.

Miller: Good evening Gretchen. Hello, Dave. I guess there's not much point in beating around the bush, Gretchen; the medics tell me you're a goner. Is there anything I can do to help?

Weirob: Crimenentley, Sam! You deal with the dying every day. Don't you have anything more comforting to say than "Sorry to hear you're a goner?"

Miller: Well to tell you the truth, I'm a little at a loss for what to say to you. Most people I deal with are believers like I am. We talk of the prospects for survival. I give assurance that God, who is just and merciful, would not permit such a travesty as that our short life on this earth should be the end of things. But you and I have talked about religious and philosophical issues for years. I have never been able to find in you the least inclination to believe in God; indeed, it's a rare day when you are sure that your friends have minds, or that you can see your own hand in front of your face, or that there is any reason to believe that the sun will rise tomorrow. How can I hope to comfort you with the prospect of life after death, when I know you will regard it as having no probability whatsoever?

Weirob: I would not require so much to be comforted, Sam. Even the possibility of something quite improbable can be comforting, in certain situations. When we used to play tennis, I beat you no more than one time in twenty. But this was enough to establish the possibility of beating you on any given occasion, and by focusing merely on the possibility, I remained eager to play. Entombed in a secure prison, having thought our situation quite hopeless, we might find unutterable joy in the information that there was, after all, a possibility of escape, however slim the chances of actually succeeding. Hope provides comfort, and hope does not always require probability. But we must believe that what we hope for is at least possible. So I will set an easier task for you. Simply persuade me that my survival, after the death of this body, is *possible,* and I promise to be comforted. Whether you succeed or not, your attempts will be a diversion, for you know I like to talk philosophy more than anything else.

Miller: But what is possibility, if not reasonable probability?

Weirob: I do not mean possible in the sense of likely, or even in the sense of comforming to the known laws of physics or biology. I mean possible only in the weakest sense, of being conceivable, given the unavoidable facts. Within the next couple of days, this body will die. It will be buried, and it will rot away. I ask that, given these facts, you explain to me how it even makes *sense* to talk of me continuing to exist. Just explain to me what it is I am to *imagine,* when I imagine surviving, that is consistent with these facts, and I shall be comforted.

Miller: But then what is there to do? There are many conceptions of immortality, of survival past the grave, which all seem to make good sense. Surely not the possibility, but only the probability, can be doubted. Take your choice! Christians believe in life, with a body, in some Hereafter—the details vary, of course, from sect to sect. There is the Greek idea of the body as a prison, from which we escape at death—so we have continued life without a body. Then there are conceptions, in which we, so to speak, merge with the flow of being . . .

Weirob: I must cut short your lesson in comparative religion. Survival means surviving, no more, no less. I have no doubts that I shall merge with being; plants will take roots in my remains, and the chemicals that I am will continue to make their contribution to life. I am enough of an ecologist to be comforted. But survival, if it is anything, must offer comforts of a different sort, the comforts of *anticipation.* Survival means that tomorrow, or sometime in the future, there will be someone who will experience, who will see and touch and smell—or at least, at the very least, think and reason and remember. And this person will be *me.* This person will be related to me in such a way that it is correct for me to anticipate, to look forward to, those future experiences. And I am related to her in such a way that it will be right for her to remember what I have thought and done, to feel remorse for what I have done wrong, and pride in what I have done right. And the only relation that supports anticipation and memory in this way, is simply *identity.* For it is never correct to anticipate, as happening to oneself, what will happen to someone else, is it? Or to remember, as one's own thoughts and deeds, what someone else did? So don't give me merger with being, or some such nonsense. Give me identity, or lets talk about baseball or fishing—but I'm sorry to get so emotional. I just react so strongly when words which mean one thing are used for another—when one talks about survival, but does not mean to say that the same person will continue to exist. It's such a sham!

Miller: I'm sorry. I was just trying to stay in touch with the times, if you want to know the truth, for when I read modern theology or talk to my students who have studied eastern religions, the notion of survival as simply continued existence of the same person seems out of date. Merger with Being! Merger with Being! That's all I hear. My own beliefs are quite simple, if somewhat vague. I think you will live again—with or without a body, I don't know—*I* draw comfort from my belief that you and I will be together again, after I also die. We will communicate, somehow. We will continue to grow spiritually. That's what I believe, as surely as I believe that I am sitting here. For I don't know how God could be excused, if this small sample of life is all that we are allotted; I don't know why he should have created us, if this few years of toil and torment are the end of it . . .

Weirob: Remember our deal, Sam. You don't have to convince me that survival is probable, for we both agree you would not get to first base. You have only to convince me that it is possible. The only condition is that it be real survival we are talking about, not some up-to-date ersatz survival, which simply amounts to what any ordinary person would call ceasing totally to exist.

Miller: I guess I just miss the problem then. Of course it's possible. You just continue to exist, after your body dies. What's to be defended or explained? You want details? OK. Two people meet a thousand years from now, in a place that may or may not be part of this physical universe. I am one and you are the other. So you must have survived. Surely you can imagine that. What else is there to say?

Weirob: But in a few days *I* will quit breathing, *I* will be put into a coffin, *I* will be buried. And in a few months or a few years *I* will be reduced to so much humus. That I take it is obvious, is given. How then can you say that I am one of these persons a thousand years from now?

Suppose I took this box of kleenex and lit fire to it. It is reduced to ashes and I smash the ashes and flush them down the john. Then I say to you, go home and on the shelf will be *that very box of kleenex*. It has survived! Wouldn't that be absurd? What sense could you make of it? And yet that is just what you say to me. I will rot away. And then, a thousand years later, there I will be. What sense does that make?

Miller: There could be an *identical* box of kleenex at your home, one just like it in every respect. And, in this sense, there is no difficulty in there being someone identical to you in the Hereafter, though your body has rotted away.

Weirob: You are playing with words again. There could be an *exactly similar* box of kleenex on my shelf. We sometimes use "identical" to mean "exactly similar" as when we talk of "identical twins." But I am using "identical," in a way in which *identity* is the condition of memory and correct anticipation. If I am told that tomorrow though I will be dead, someone else that looks and sounds and thinks just like me will be alive, would that be comforting? Could I correctly *anticipate* having her experiences? Would it make sense for me to fear her pains and look forward to her pleasures? Would it be right for her to feel remorse at the harsh way I am treating you? Of course not. Similarity, however exact, is not identity. I use identity to mean there is but one thing. If I am to survive, there must be one person who is here in this bed now, and who is talking to someone in your Hereafter ten or a thousand years from now. After all, what comfort could there be in the notion of a Heavenly imposter, walking around getting credit for the few good things I have done?

Miller: I'm sorry. I see that I was simply confused. Here is what I should have said. If you were merely a live human body—as the kleenex box is merely cardboard and glue in a certain arrangement—then the death of your body would be the end of you. But surely you are more than that, fundamentally more than that. What is fundamentally you is not your body, but your soul or self or mind.

Weirob: Do you mean these words, "soul," "self," or "mind" to come to the same thing?

Miller: I have heard fine distinctions made, but usually cannot follow them. They are the nonphysical, nonmaterial, aspects of you. They are your consciousness. It is this that I get at with these words, and I am not clever enough to attempt any further distinction.

Weirob: Consciousness? I am conscious, for a while yet. I see, I hear, I think, I remember. But "to be conscious"—that is a verb. What is the subject of the verb, the thing which is conscious? Isn't it just this body, the same object that is overweight, injured, and lying in bed? And which will be buried, and not be conscious in a day or a week at the most?

Miller: As you are a philosopher, I would expect you to be less muddled about these issues. Did Descartes not draw a clear distinction between the body and the mind, between that which is overweight and that which is conscious? Your mind or soul is immaterial, lodged while you are on earth in your body. They are intimately related, but not identical. Now clearly, what concerns us in survival is your mind or soul. It is this which must be identical between the person before me now, and the one I expect to see in a thousand years in heaven.

Weirob: So I am not really this body, but a soul or mind or spirit? And this soul cannot be seen or felt or touched or smelt? That is implied, I take it, by the fact that it is immaterial?

Miller: That's right. Your soul sees and smells, but cannot be seen or smelt.

Weirob: Let me see if I understand you. You would admit that I am the very same person with whom you ate lunch last week at Dorsey's?

Miller: Of course you are.

Weirob: Now when you say I am the same person, if I understand you, that is not a remark about this body you see and could touch and I fear can smell. Rather it is a remark about a soul, which you cannot see or touch or smell. The fact that the same body was across the booth from you at Dorsey's as is now lying in front of you on the bed—that would not mean that the same *person* was present on both occasions, if the same soul were not. And if, through some strange turn of events, the same soul were present on both occasions, but lodged in different bodies, then it *would* be the same person. Is that right?

Miller: You have understood me perfectly. But surely, you understood all of this before!

Weirob: But wait. I can repeat it, but I'm not sure I understand it. If you cannot see or touch or in any way perceive my soul, what makes you think the one you are confronted with now *is* the very same soul you were confronted with at Dorsey's?

Miller: But I just explained. To say it is the same soul and to say it is the same person, are the same. And, of course, you are the same person you were before. Who else would you be if not yourself? You *were* Gretchen Weirob, and you *are* Gretchen Weirob.

Weirob: But how do you know you are talking to Gretchen Weirob at all, and not someone else, say Barbara Walters or even Mark Spitz!

Miller: Well, it's just obvious. I can see who I am talking to.

Weirob: But all you can see is my body. You can see, perhaps, that the same body is before you now that was before you last week at Dorsey's. But you have just said that Gretchen Weirob is not a body but a soul. In judging that the same person is before you now as was before you then, you must be making a judgement about souls—which, you said, cannot be seen or touched or smelled or tasted. And so, I repeat, how do you know?

Miller: Well, I *can* see that it is the same body before me now that was across the table at Dorsey's. And I know that the same soul is connected with the body as was connected with it before. That's how I know it's you. I see no difficulty in the matter.

Weirob: You reason on the principle, "same body, same self."

Miller: Yes.

Weirob: And would you reason conversely also? If there were in this bed Barbara Walter's body—that is, the body you see every night on the news—would you infer that it was not me, Gretchen Weirob, in the bed?

Miller: Of course I would. How would you have come by Barbara Walter's body?

Weirob: But then merely extend this principle to Heaven, and you will see that your conception of survival is without sense. Surely this very body, which will be buried and, as I must so often repeat, *rot away,* will not be in your Hereafter. Different body, different person. Or do you claim that a body can rot away on earth, and then still wind up somewhere else? Must I bring up the kleenex box again?

Miller: No, I do not claim that. But I also do not extend a principle, found reliable on earth, to such a different situation as is represented by the Hereafter. That a correlation between bodies and souls has been found on earth, does not make it inconceivable or impossible that they should separate. Principles found to work in one circumstance may not be assumed to work in vastly altered circumstances. January and snow go together here, and one would be a fool to expect otherwise. But the principle does not apply in California.

Weirob: So the principle, "same body, same soul," is a well-confirmed regularity, not something you know "a priori."

Miller: By "a priori" you philosophers mean something which can be known without observing what actually goes on in the world, as I can know that two plus two equals four just by thinking about numbers, and that no bachelors are married just by thinking about the meaning of "bachelor?"

Weirob: Yes.

Miller: Then you are right. If it was part of the meaning of "same body" that wherever we have the same body, we have the same soul, it would have to obtain universally, in Heaven as well as on earth. But I just claim it is a generalization we know by observation on earth, and it need not automatically extend to Heaven.

Weirob: But where do you get this principle? It simply amounts to a correlation between being confronted with the same body and being confronted with the same soul. To establish such a correlation in the first place, surely one must have some *other* means of judging sameness of soul. You do not have such a means; your principle is without foundation; either you really do not know the person before you now is Gretchen Weirob, the very same person you lunched with at Dorsey's, or what you do know has nothing to do with sameness of some immaterial soul.

Miller: Hold on, hold on. You know I can't follow you when you start spitting out arguments like that. Now what is this terrible fallacy I'm supposed to have committed?

Weirob: I'm sorry. I get carried away. Here, have one of my chocolates by way of a peace offering.

Miller: Very tasty, thank you.

Weirob: Now why did you choose that one?

Miller: Because it had a certain swirl on the top which shows that it is a caramel.

Weirob: That is, a certain sort of swirl is correlated with a certain type of filling—the swirls with caramel, the rosettes with orange, and so forth.

Miller: Yes. When you put it that way. I see an analogy. Just as I judged that the filling would be the same in this piece as in the last piece that I ate with such a swirl, so I judge that the soul with which I am conversing is the same as the last soul with which I conversed when sitting across from that body. We *see* the outer wrapping and infer to what is inside.

Weirob: But how did you come to realize that swirls of that sort and caramel insides were so associated?

Miller: Why from eating a great many of them over the years. Whenever I bit into a candy with that sort of swirl, it was filled with this sort of caramel.

Weirob: Could you have established the correlation had you never been allowed to bite into a candy and never seen what happened when someone else bit into one? You could have formed the hypothesis, "same swirl, same filling." But could you have ever established it?

Miller: It seems not.

Weirob: So your inference, in a particular case, to the identity of filling from the identity of swirl would be groundless?

Miller: Yes, it would. I think I see what is coming.

Weirob: I'm sure you do. Since you can never, so to speak, bite into my soul, can never see or touch it, you have no way of testing your hypothesis that sameness of body means sameness of self.

Miller: I daresay you are right. But now I'm a bit lost. What is supposed to follow from all of this?

Weirob: If identity of persons consisted in identity of immaterial unobservable souls as you claim, then judgements of personal identity of the sort we make every day whenever we greet a friend or avoid a pest are really judgements about such souls.

Miller: Right.

Weirob: But if such judgements were really about souls, they would all be groundless and without foundation. For we have no direct method of observing sameness of soul, and so—and this is the point made by the candy example—can have no indirect method either.

Miller: That seems fair.

Weirob: But our judgements about persons are not all simply groundless and silly, so we must not be judging of immaterial souls after all.

Miller: Your reasoning has some force. But I suspect the problem lies in my defense of my position, and not the position itself. Look here. There *is* a way to test the hypothesis of a correlation after all. When I entered the room, I expected you to react just as you did. Agrumentatively and skeptically. Had the person with this body reacted completely different perhaps I would have been forced to conclude it was not you. For example, had she complained about not being able to appear on the six o'clock news, and missing Harry Reasoner, and so forth, I might have eventually been persuaded it *was* Barbara Walters and not you. Similarity of psychological characteristics, a person's attitudes, beliefs, memories, prejudices, and the like, is observable. These are correlated with identity of body on the one side, and of course with sameness of soul on the other. So the correlation between body and soul can be established after all by this intermediate link.

Weirob: And how do you know that?

Miller: Know what?

Weirob: That where we have sameness of psychological characteristics, we have sameness of soul.

Miller: Well now you are really being just silly. The soul or mind just is that which is responsible for one's character, memory, belief. These are aspects of or states of mind, just as one's height, weight, and appearance are aspects of the body.

Weirob: Let me grant, for the sake of argument, that belief, character, memory, and so forth are states of mind. That is, I suppose, I grant that what one thinks and feels is due to the state one's mind is in at that time. And I shall even grant that a mind is an immaterial thing—though I harbor the gravest doubts that this is so. I do not see how it follows from that, that similarity of such traits requires, or is evidence to the slightest degree, for identity of the mind or soul.

Let me explain my point with an analogy. If we were to walk out of this room, down past the mill and out toward Wilbur, what would we see?

Miller: We would come to the Blue River, among other things.

Weirob: And how would you recognize the Blue River? I mean, of course if you left from here, you would scarcely expect to hit the Platte or Niobrara. But suppose you were actually lost, and came across the Blue River in your wandering, just at that point where an old dam partly blocks the flow. Couldn't you recognize it?

Miller: Yes, I'm sure as soon as I saw that part of the river I would again know where I was.

Weirob: And how would you recognize it?

Miller: Well, the turgid brownness of the water, the sluggish flow, the filth washed up on the banks, and such.

Weirob: In a word, the state of the water which makes up the river at the time you see it.

Miller: Right.

Weirob: If you saw blue clean water, with bass jumping, you would know it wasn't the Blue River.

Miller: Of course.

Weirob: So you expect, each time you see the Blue, to see the water, which makes it up, in similar states—not always exactly the same, for sometimes it's a little dirtier, but by and large, similar.

Miller: Yes, but what do you intend to make of this?

Weirob: Each time you see the Blue, it consists of *different* water. The water that was in it a month ago may be in Tuttle Creek Reservoir, or in the Mississippi, or in the Gulf of Mexico by now. So the *similarity* of states of water, by which you judge the sameness of river, does not require *identity* of the water which is in those states at these various times.

Miller: And?

Weirob: And so just because you judge as to personal identity by reference to similarity of states of mind, it does not follow that the mind, or soul, is the same in each case. My point is this. For all you know, the immaterial soul which you think is lodged in my body might change from day to day, from hour to hour, from minute to minute, replaced each time by another soul psychologically similar. You cannot see it or touch it, so how would you know?

Miller: Are you saying I don't really know who you are?

Weirob: Not at all. *You* are the one who says personal identity consists in sameness of this immaterial, unobservable, invisible, untouchable soul. I merely point out that *if* it did consist in that, you *would* have no idea who I am. Sameness of body would not necessarily mean sameness of person. Sameness of psychological characteristics would not necessarily mean sameness of person. I am saying that if you do know who I am then you are wrong that personal identity consists in sameness of immaterial soul.

Miller: I see. But wait. I believe my problem is that I simply forgot a main tenet of my theory. The correlation can be established in my own case. I know that *my* soul and my body are intimately and consistently found together. From this one case I can generalize, at least as concerns life in this world, that sameness of body is a reliable sign of sameness of soul. This leaves me free to regard it as intelligible, in the case of death, that the link between the particular soul and the particular body it has been joined with is broken.

Weirob: This would be quite an extrapolation, wouldn't it, from one case directly observed, to a couple of billion in which only the body is observed? For I take it that we are in the habit of assuming, for every man now on earth, as well as those who have already come and gone, that the principle "one body, one soul" is in effect.

Miller: This does not seem an insurmountable obstacle. Since there is nothing special about my case, I assume the arrangement I find in it applies universally, until given some reason to believe otherwise. And I never have been.

Weirob: Let's let that pass. I have another problem that is more serious. How is it that you know in your own case that there is a single soul which has been so consistently connected with your body?

Miller: Now you really cannot be serious, Gretchen. How can I doubt that I am the same person I was? Is there anything more clear and distinct, less susceptible to doubt? How do you expect me to prove anything to you, when you are capable of denying my own continued existence from second to second? Without knowledge of our own identity, everything we think and do would be senseless. How could I think if I did not suppose that the person who begins my thought is the one who completes it? When I act, do I not assume that the person who forms the intention is the very one who performs the action?

Weirob: But I grant you that a single *person* has been associated with your body since you were born. The question is whether one immaterial soul has been, or more precisely, whether you are in a position to know it. You believe that a judgement that one and the same person has had your body all these many years is a judgement that one and the same immaterial soul has been lodged in it. I say that such judgements concerning the soul are totally mysterious, and that if our knowledge of sameness of persons consisted in knowledge of sameness of immaterial soul, it too would be totally mysterious. To point out, as you do, that it is not, but perhaps the most secure knowledge we have, the foundation of all reason and action, is simply to make the point that it cannot consist of knowledge of identity of immaterial self.

Miller: You have simply asserted, and not established, that my judgement that a single soul has been lodged in my body these many years is mysterious.

Weirob: Well, consider these possibilities. One is that a single soul, one and the same, has been with this body I call mine since it was born. The other is that one soul was associated with it until five years ago and then another, psychologically similar, inheriting all the memories and beliefs, took over. A third hypothesis is that every five years a new soul takes over. The most radical is that there is a constant flow of souls through this body, each psychologically similar to the preceding, as there is a constant flow of water molecules down the Blue. What evidence do I have that the first hypothesis, the "single soul hypothesis," is true, and not one of the others? Because I am the same person I was five minutes or five years ago? But the issue in question is simply whether from sameness of person, which isn't in doubt, we can infer sameness of soul. Sameness of body? But how do I establish a stable relationship between soul and body? Sameness of thoughts and sensations? But they are in constant flux. By the nature of the case, if the soul cannot be observed, it cannot be observed to be the same. Indeed, no sense has ever been assigned to the phrase "same soul." Nor could any sense be attached to it! One would have to say what a single soul looked like or felt like, how an encounter with a single soul at different times differed from encounters with different souls. But this can hardly be done, since a soul on your conception doesn't look or feel like *anything* at all. And so of course "souls" can afford no principle of identity. And so they cannot be used to bridge the gulf between my existence now and my existence in the hereafter.

Miller: Do you doubt the existence of your own soul?

Weirob: I haven't based my argument on there being no immaterial souls of the sort you describe, but merely on their total irrelevance to questions of personal identity, and so to questions of personal survival. I do indeed harbor grave doubts whether there are any immaterial souls of the sort to which you appeal. Can we have a notion of a soul unless we have a notion of the *same* soul? But I hope you do not think that means I doubt my own existence. I think I lie here, overweight and conscious. I think you can see me, not just some outer wrapping, for I think I am just a live human body. But that is not the basis of my argument. I give you these souls. I merely observe they can by their nature provide no principle of personal identity.

Miller: I admit I have no answer.

I'm afraid I do not comfort you, though I have perhaps provided you with some entertainment.

Emerson said that a little philosophy turns one away from religion, but that deeper understanding brings one back. I know no one who has thought so long and hard about philosophy as you have. Will it never lead you back to a religious frame of mind?

Weirob: My former husband used to say that a little philosophy turns one away from religion, and more philosophy makes one a pain in the neck. Perhaps he was closer to the truth than Emerson.

Miller: Perhaps he was. But perhaps by tomorrow night I will have come up with some argument that will turn you around.

Weirob: I hope I live to hear it.

THE SECOND NIGHT

Weirob: Well, Sam, have you figured out a way to make sense of the identity of immaterial souls?

Miller: No, I have decided it was a mistake to build my argument on such a dubious notion.

Weirob: Have you then given up on survival? I think such a position would be a hard one for a clergyman to be talked into, and would feel bad about having pushed you so far.

Miller: Don't worry. I'm more convinced than ever. I stayed up late last night thinking and reading, and I'm sure I can convince you now.

Weirob: Get with it, time is running out.

Miller: First, let me explain why, independently of my desire to defend survival after death, I am dissatisfied with your view that personal identity is just bodily identity. My argument will be very similar to the one you used to convince me that personal identity could not be identified with identity of an immaterial soul.

Consider a person waking up tomorrow morning, conscious, but not yet ready to open her eyes and look around and, so to speak, let the new day officially begin.

Weirob: Such a state is familiar enough, I admit.

Miller: Now couldn't such a person tell who she was? That is, even before opening her eyes and looking around, and in particular before looking at her body or making any judgements about it, wouldn't she be able to say who she was? Surely most of us, in the morning, know who we are before opening our eyes and recognizing our own bodies, do we not?

Weirob: You seem to be right about that.

Miller: But such a judgement as this person makes—we shall suppose she judges "I am Gretchen Weirob"—*is* a judgement of personal identity. Suppose she says to herself, "I am the very person who was arguing with Sam Miller last night." This is clearly a statement about her identity with someone who was alive the night before. And she could make this judgement without examining her body at all. You could have made just this judgement this morning, before opening your eyes.

Weirob: Well, in fact I did so. I remembered our conversation of last night and said to myself, "Could I be the rude person who was so hard on Sam Miller's attempts to comfort me?" And, of course, my answer was that I not only could be but was that very rude person.

Miller: But then by the same principle you used last night, personal identity cannot be bodily identity. For you said that it could not be identity of immaterial soul because we were not judging as to identity of immaterial soul when we judge as to personal identity. But by the same token, as my example shows, we are not judging as to bodily identity when we judge as to personal identity. For we can judge who we are, and that we are the very person who did such and such and so and so, without having to make any judgements at all about the body. So, personal identity, while it may not consist of identity of an immaterial soul, does not consist in identity of material body either.

Weirob: I did argue as you remember. But I also said that the notion of the identity of an immaterial, unobservable, unextended soul seemed to make no sense at all. This is one reason such souls cannot be what we are judging about, when we judge as to personal identity. Bodily identity at least makes sense. Perhaps we are just assuming sameness of body, without looking.

Miller: Granted. But you do admit that we do not in our own cases need to actually make a judgement of bodily identity in order to make a judgement of personal identity.

Weirob: I don't think I will admit it. I will let it pass, so that we may proceed.

Miller: OK. Now it seems to me we are even able to imagine awakening and finding ourselves to have a *different* body than the one we had before. Suppose yourself just as I have described you. And now suppose you finally open your eyes and see, not the body you have grown so familiar with over the years, but one of a fundamentally different shape and size.

Weirob: Well I should suppose I had been asleep for a very long time and lost a lot of weight—perhaps I was in a coma for a year or so.

Miller: But isn't it at least conceivable that it should not be your old body at all? I seem to be able to imagine awakening with a totally new body.

Weirob: And how would you suppose that this came about?

Miller: That's beside the point. I'm not saying I can imagine a procedure that would bring this about. I'm saying I can imagine it happening to me. In Kafka's *The Metamorphosis,* someone awakens as a cockroach. I can't imagine what would make this happen to me or anyone else, but I can imagine awakening with the body of a cockroach. It is incredible that it should happen—that I do not deny. I simply mean I can imagine experiencing it. It doesn't seem contradictory or incoherent, simply unlikely and inexplicable.

Weirob: So, if I admit this can be imagined, what follows then?

Miller: Well, I think it follows that personal identity does not just amount to bodily identity. For I would not, finding that I had a new body, conclude that I was not the very same person I was before. I would be the same *person,* though I did not have the same *body.* So we would have identity of person but not identity of body. So personal identity cannot just amount to bodily identity.

Weirob: Well, suppose—and I emphasize *suppose*—I grant you all of this. Where does it leave you? What do you claim I have recognized as the same, if not my body and not my immaterial soul?

Miller: I don't claim that you have recognized anything as the same, except the person involved, that is, you yourself.

Weirob: I'm not sure what you mean.

Miller: Let me appeal again to the Blue River. Suppose I take a visitor to the stretch of river by the old mill, and then drive him toward Manhattan. After an hour or so drive we see another stretch of river, and I say, "That's the same river we saw this morning." As you pointed out yesterday, I don't thereby imply that the very same molecules of water are seen both times. And the places are different, perhaps a hundred miles apart. And the shape and color and level of pollution might all be different. What do I see later in the day that is identical with what I saw earlier in the day?

Weirob: Nothing, except the river itself.

Miller: Exactly. But now notice that what I see, strictly speaking, is not the whole river but only a part of it. I see different parts of the same river at the two different times. So really, if we restrict ourselves to what I literally see, I do not judge identity at all, but something else.

Weirob: And what might that be?

Miller: In saying that the river seen earlier and the river seen later are one and the same river, do I mean any more than that the stretch of water seen later and that stretch of water seen earlier are connected by other stretches of water?

Weirob: That's about right. If the stretches of water are so connected, there is but one river of which they are both parts.

Miller: Yes, that's what I mean. The statement of identity, "This river is the same one we saw this morning," is in a sense about rivers. But in a way it is also about stretches of water or river parts.

Weirob: So, is all of this something special about rivers?

Miller: Not at all. It is a recurring pattern. After all, we constantly deal with objects extended in space and time. But we are seldom aware of the objects as a whole, but only of their parts or stretches of their histories. When a statement of identity is not just something trivial, like "This bed is this bed," it is usually because we are really judging that different parts fit together, in some appropriate pattern, into a certain kind of whole.

Weirob: I'm not sure I see just what you mean yet.

Miller: Let me give you another example. Suppose we are sitting together watching the first game of a doubleheader. You ask me, "Is this game identical with this game?" This is a perfectly stupid question, though, of course, strictly speaking it makes sense and the answer is "yes."

But now suppose you leave in the sixth inning to go for hot dogs. You are delayed, and return after about forty-five minutes or so. You ask, "Is this the same game I was watching?" Now your question is not stupid, but perfectly appropriate.

Weirob: Because the first game might still be going on or it might have ended, and the second game begun, by the time I return.

Miller: Exactly. Which is to say somehow different parts of the game—different innings, or at least different plays—were somehow involved in your question. That's why it wasn't stupid or trivial but significant.

Weirob: So, you think that judgements as to the identity of an object of a certain kind—rivers or baseball games or whatever—involve judgements as to the *parts* of those things being connected in a certain way, and are significant only when different parts are involved. Is that your point?

Miller: Yes, and I think it is an important one. How foolish it would be, when we ask a question about the identity of baseball games, to look for something *else,* other than the game as a whole, which had to be the same. It could be the same game, even if different players were involved. It could be the same game, even if it had been moved to a different field. These other things, the innings, the plays, the players, the field, don't have to be the same at the different times for the game to be the same, they just have to be related in certain ways so as to make that complex whole we call a single game.

Weirob: You think we were going off on a kind of a wild goose chase when we asked whether it was the identity of soul or body that was involved in the identity of persons?

Miller: Yes. The answer I should now give is neither. We are wondering about the identity of the person. Of course, if by "soul" we just mean "person," there is no problem. But if we mean, as I did yesterday, some other thing whose identity is already understood, which has to be the same when persons are the same, we are just fooling ourselves with words.

Weirob: With rivers and baseball games, I can see that they are made up of parts connected in a certain way. The connection is, of course, different in the two cases, as is the sort of "part" involved. River parts must be connected physically with other river parts to form a continuous whole. Baseball innings must be connected so that the score, batting order, and the like are carried over from the earlier inning to the latter one according to the rules. Is there something analogous we are to say about persons?

Miller: Writers who concern themselves with this speak of "person-stages." That is just a stretch of consciousness, such as you and I are aware of now. I am aware of a flow of thoughts and feelings that are mine, you are aware of yours. A person is just a whole composed of such stretches as parts, not some substance that underlies them, as I thought yesterday, and not the body in which they occur, as you seem to think. That is the conception of a person I wish to defend today.

Weirob: So when I awoke and said to myself, "I am the one who was so rude to Sam Miller last night," I was judging that a certain stretch of consciousness I was then aware of, and an earlier one I remembered having been aware of, form a single whole of the appropriate sort—a single stream of consciousness, we might say.

Miller: Yes, that's it exactly. You need not worry about whether the same immaterial soul is involved, or whether that even makes sense. Nor need you worry about whether the same body is involved, as indeed you do not since you don't even have to open your eyes and look. Identity is not, so to speak, something under the person-stages, nor in something they are attached to, but something you build from them.

Now survival, you can plainly see, is no problem at all once we have this conception of personal identity. All you need suppose is that there is, in Heaven, a conscious being, and that the person-stages that make her up are in the appropriate relation to those that now make you up, so that they are parts of the same whole—namely, you. If so, you have survived. So will you admit now that survival is at least possible?

Weirob: Hold on, hold on. Comforting me is not that easy. You will have to show that it is possible that these person-stages or stretches of consciousness be related in the appropriate way. And to do that, won't you have to tell me what that way is?

Miller: Yes, of course, I was getting ahead of myself. It is right at this point that my reading was particularly helpful. In a chapter of his *Essay on Human Understanding* Locke discusses this very question. He suggests that the relation between two person-stages or stretches of consciousness that makes them stages of a single person is just that the later one contains memories of the earlier one. He doesn't say this in so many words—he talks of "extending our consciousness back in time." But he seems to be thinking of memory.

Weirob: So, any past thought or feeling or intention or desire that I can remember having is mine?

Miller: That's right. I can remember only my own past thoughts and feelings, and you only yours. Of course, everyone would readily admit that. Locke's insight is to take this relation as the source of identity and not just its consequence. To remember—or more plausibly, to be able to remember—the thoughts and feelings of a person who was conscious in the past is just what it is to be that person.

Now you can easily see that this solves the problem of the possibility of survival. As I was saying, all you need to do is imagine someone at some future time, not on this earth and not with your present thoughts and feelings, remembering the very conversation we are having now. This does not require sameness of anything else, but it amounts to sameness of person. So, now will you admit it?

Weirob: No, I don't.

Miller: Well, what's the problem now?

Weirob: I admit that if I remember having a certain thought or feeling had by some person in the past, then I must indeed be that person. Though I can remember watching others think, I cannot remember their thinking, any more than I can experience it at the time it occurs if it is theirs and not mine. This is the kernel of Locke's idea, and I don't see that I could deny it.

But we must distinguish—as I'm sure you will agree—between *actually* remembering and merely *seeming* to remember. Many men who think that they are Napoleon claim to remember losing the battle of Waterloo. We may suppose them to be sincere, and to really seem to remember it. But, they do not actually remember, because they were not there and are not Napoleon.

Miller: Of course, I admit that we must distinguish between actually remembering and only seeming to.

Weirob: And you will admit too, I trust, that the thought of some person at some far place and some distant time seeming to remember this conversation I am having with you would not give me the sort of comfort that the prospect of survival is supposed to provide. I would have no reason to anticipate future experiences of this person, simply because she is to *seem* to remember my experiences. The experiences of such a deluded imposter are not ones I can look forward to having.

Miller: I agree.

Weirob: So, the mere possibility of someone in the future seeming to remember this conversation does not show the possibility of my surviving. Only the possibility of someone actually remembering this conversation—or, to be precise, the experiences I am having—would show that.

Miller: Of course. But what are you driving at? Where is the problem? I can imagine someone being deluded, but also someone actually being you and remembering your present thoughts.

Weirob: But, what's the difference? How do you know *which* of the two you are imagining, and *what* you have shown possible?

Miller: Well, I just imagine the one and not the other. I don't see the force of your argument.

Weirob: Let me try to make it clear with another example. Imagine two persons. One is talking to you, saying certain words, having certain thoughts, and so on. The other is not talking to you at all, but is in the next room being hypnotized. The hypnotist gives to this person a posthypnotic suggestion that upon awakening he will remember having had certain thoughts and having uttered certain words to you. The thoughts and words he mentions happen to be just the thoughts and words which the first person actually thinks and says. Do you understand the situation?

Miller: Yes, continue.

Weirob: Now, in a while, both of the people are saying sentences which begin, "I remember saying to Sam Miller . . ." and "I remember thinking as I talked to Sam Miller . . ." And they both report remembering just the same thoughts and utterances. One of these will be remembering and the other only seeming to remember, right?

Miller: Of course.

Weirob: Now, which one is *actually* remembering?

Miller: Why the very one who was in the room talking to me, of course. The other one is just under the influence of the suggestion made by the hypnotist and not remembering talking to me at all.

Weirob: Now you agree that the difference between them does not consist in the content of what they are now thinking or saying.

Miller: Agreed. The difference is in the relation to the past thinking and speaking. In the one case the relation of memory obtains. In the other, it does not.

Weirob: But they both satisfy part of the conditions of remembering, for they both *seem to remember.* So there must be some further condition that the one satisfies and the other does not. I am trying to get you to say what that further condition is.

Miller: Well, I said that the one who had been in this room talking would be remembering.

Weirob: In other words, given two putative rememberers of some past thought or action, the real rememberer is the one who, in addition to seeming to remember the past thought or action, actually thought it or did it.

Miller: Yes.

Weirob: That is to say, the one who is identical with the person who did the past thinking and uttering.

Miller: Yes, I admit it.

Weirob: So, your argument just amounts to this. Survival is possible, because imaginable. It is imaginable, because my identity with some Heavenly person is imaginable. To imagine it, we imagine a person in Heaven who, first, seems to remember my thoughts and actions, and second, is me.

Surely, there could hardly be a tighter circle. If I have doubts that the Heavenly person is me, I will have doubts as to whether she is really remembering or only seeming to. No one could doubt the possibility of some future person who, after his or her death, seemed to remember the things he or she thought and did. But that possibility does not resolve the issue about the possibility of survival. Only the possibility of someone *actually* remembering could do that, for that, as we agree, is sufficient for identity. But doubts about survival and identity simply go over without remainder into doubts about whether the memories would be actual or merely apparent. You guarantee me no more than the possibility of a deluded Heavenly imposter.

Cohen: But wait, Gretchen. I think Sam was less than fair to his own idea just now.

Weirob: You think you can break out of the circle of using real memory to explain identity, and identity to mark the difference between real and apparent memory? Feel free to try.

Cohen: Let us return to your case of the hypnotist. You point out that we have two putative rememberers. You ask what marks the difference, and claim the answer must be the circular one that the real rememberer is the person who actually had the experiences both seem to remember.

But that is not the only possible answer. The experiences themselves cause the later apparent memories in the one case, the hypnotist causes them in the other. We can say that the rememberer is the one of the two whose memories were *caused in the right way* by the earlier experiences. We thus distinguish between the rememberer and the hypnotic subject, without appeal to identity.

The idea that real memory amounts to apparent memory plus identity is misleading anyway. I seem to remember knocking over the menorah so the candles fell into and ruined a tureen of soup when I was a small child. And I did actually perform such a feat. So we have apparent memory and identity. But I do *not* actually remember; I was much too young when I did this to remember it now. I have simply been told the story so often I seem to remember.

Here the suggestion that real memory is apparent memory that was caused in the appropriate way by the past events fares better. Not my experience of pulling over the menorah, but my parents' later recounting of the tragedy, cause my memory-like impressions.

Weirob: You analyze personal identity into memory, and memory into apparent memory which is caused in the right way. A person is a certain sort of causal process.

Cohen: Right.

Weirob: Suppose now for the sake of argument I accept this. How does it help Sam in his defense of the possibility of survival? In ordinary memory, the causal chain from remembered event to memory of it never leads us outside the confines of a single body. Indeed, the normal process of which you speak surely involves storage of information somehow in the brain. How can the states of my brain, when I die, influence in the appropriate way the apparent memories of the Heavenly person Sam takes to be me?

Cohen: Well, I didn't intend to be defending the possibility of survival. That is Sam's problem. I just like the idea that personal identity can be explained in terms of memory, and not just in terms of identity of the body.

Miller: But surely, this does provide me with the basis for further defense. Your challenge, Gretchen, was to explain the difference between two persons in Heaven, one who actually remembers your experience—and so is you—and one who simply seems to remember it. But can I not just say that the one who is you is the one whose states were caused in the appropriate way? I do not mean the way they would be in a normal case of earthly memory. But in the case of the Heavenly being who is you, God would have created her with the brain states (or whatever) she has *because* you had the ones you had at death. Surely it is not the exact form of the dependence of my later memories on my earlier perceptions that makes them really to be memories, but the fact that the process involved has preserved information.

Weirob: So if God creates a Heavenly person, designing her brain to duplicate the brain I have upon death, that person is me. If, on the other hand, a Heavenly being should come to be with those very same memory-like states by accident (if there are accidents in Heaven) it would not be me.

Miller: Exactly. Are you satisfied now that survival makes perfectly good sense?

Weirob: No, I'm still quite unconvinced.

The problem I see is this. If God could create one person in Heaven, and by designing her after me, make her me, why could He not make two such bodies, and cause this transfer of information into both of them? Would both of these Heavenly persons then be me? It seems as clear as anything in philosophy that from

A is B

and

C is B

where by "is" we mean identity, we can infer,

A is C.

So, if each of these Heavenly persons is me, they must be each other. But then they are not two but one. But my assumption was that God creates two, not one. He could create them physically distinct, capable of independent movement, perhaps in widely separated Heavenly locations, each with her own duties to perform, her own circle of Heavenly friends, and the like.

So either God, by creating a Heavenly person with a brain modeled after mine does not really create someone identical with me but merely someone similar to me, or God is somehow limited to making only one such being. I can see no reason why, if there were a God, He should be so limited. So I take the first option. He could create someone similar to me, but not someone who would *be* me. Either your analysis of memory is wrong, and such a being does not, after all, remember what I am doing or saying, or memory is not sufficient for personal identity. Your theory has gone wrong somewhere, for it leads to absurdity.

Cohen: But wait. Why can't Sam simply say that if God makes one such creature, she is you, while if He makes more, none of them are you? It's possible that He makes only one. So it's possible that you survive. Sam always meant to allow that it's *possible* that you won't survive. He had in mind the case in which there is no God to make the appropriate Heavenly persons, or God exists, but just doesn't make even one. You have simply shown that there is another way of not surviving. Instead of making too few Heavenly rememberers, He makes too many. So what? He might make the right number, and then you would survive.

Weirob: Your remarks really amount to a change in your position. Now you are not claiming that memory alone is enough for personal identity. Now, it is memory *plus* lack of competition, the absence of other rememberers, that is needed for personal identity.

Cohen: It does amount to a change of position. But what of it? Is there anything untenable about the position as changed?

Weirob: Let's look at this from the point of view of the Heavenly person. She says to herself, "Oh, I must be Gretchen Weirob, for I remember doing what she did and saying what she said." But now that's a pretty tenuous conclusion, isn't it? She is really only entitled to say, "Oh, either I'm Gretchen Weirob, or God has created more than one being like me, and none of us are." Identity has become something dependent on things wholly extrinsic to her. Who she is now turns on not just her states of mind and their relation to my states of mind, but on the existence or nonexistence of other people. Is this really what you want to maintain?

Or look at it from my point of view. God creates one of me in Heaven. Surely I should be glad if convinced this was to happen. Now He creates another, and I should despair again, for this means I won't survive after all. How can doubling a good deed make it worthless?

Cohen: Are you saying that there is some contradiction in my suggestion that only a unique Heavenly Gretchen counts as your survival?

Weirob: No, it's not contradictory, as far as I can see. But it seems odd in a way that shows that something somewhere is wrong with your theory. Here is a certain relationship I have with a Heavenly person. There being such a person, to whom I am related in this way, is something that is of great importance to me, a source of comfort. It makes it appropriate for me to anticipate having her experiences, since she is just me. Why should my having that relation to another being destroy my relation to this one? You say because then I will not be identical with either of them. But since you have provided a theory about what that identity consists in, we can look and see what it amounts to for me to be or not to be identical. If she is to remember my experience, I can rightly anticipate hers. But then it seems the doubling makes no difference. And yet it must, for one cannot be identical with two. So you add, in a purely *ad hoc* manner, that her memory of me isn't enough to make my anticipation of her experiences appropriate, if there are two rather than one so linked. Isn't it more reasonable to conclude, since memory does not secure identity when there are two Heavenly Gretchens, it also doesn't when there is only one?

Cohen: There is something *ad hoc* about it, I admit. But perhaps that's just the way our concept works. You have not elicited a contradiction . . .

Weirob: An infinite pile of absurdities has the same weight as a contradiction. And absurdities can be generated from your account without limit. Suppose God created this Heavenly person before I died. Then He in effect kills me; if He has already created her, then you really are not talking to whom you think, but someone new, created by Gretchen Weirob's strange death moments ago. Or suppose He first creates one being in Heaven, who is me. Then He created another. Does the first cease to be me? If God can create such beings in Heaven, surely He can do so in Albuquerque. And there is nothing on your theory to favor this body before you as Gretchen Weirob's, over the one belonging to the person created in Albuquerque. So I am to suppose that if God were to do this, I would suddenly cease to be. I'm tempted to say I would cease to be Gretchen Weirob. But that would be a confused way of putting it. There would be here, in my place, a new person with false memories of having been Gretchen Weirob, who has just died of competition—a strange death, if ever there was one. She would have no right to my name, my bank account, or the services of my doctor, who is paid from insurance premiums paid for by deductions from Gretchen Weirob's past salary. Surely this is nonsense; however carefully God should choose to duplicate me, in Heaven or in Albuquerque, I would not cease to be, or cease to be who I am. You may reply that God, being benevolent, would never create an extra Gretchen Weirob. But I do not say that He would, but only that if He did this would not, as your theory implies, mean that I cease to exist. Your theory gives the wrong answer in this possible circumstance, so it must be wrong. I think I have been given no motivation to abandon the most obvious and straightforward view on these matters. I am a live body, and when that body dies, my existence will be at an end.

THE THIRD NIGHT

Weirob: Well, Sam, are you here for a third attempt to convince me of the possibility of survival?

Miller: No, I have given up. I suggest we talk about fishing or football or something unrelated to your imminent demise. You will outwit any straightforward attempts to comfort you, but perhaps I can at least divert your mind.

Cohen: But before we start on fishing . . . although I don't have any particular brief for survival, there is one point in our discussion of the last two evenings that still bothers me. Would you mind discussing for a while the notion of personal identity itself, without worrying about the more difficult case of survival after death?

Weirob: I would enjoy it. What point bothers you?

Cohen: Your position seems to be that personal identity amounts to identity of a human body, nothing more, nothing less. A person is just a live human body, or more precisely, I suppose, a human body that is alive and has certain capacities—consciousness and perhaps rationality. Is that right?

Weirob: Yes, it seems that simple to me.

Cohen: But I think there has actually been an episode which disproves that. I am thinking of the strange case of Julia North, which occurred in California a few months ago. Surely you remember it.

Weirob: Yes, only too well. But you had better explain it to Sam, for I'll wager he has not heard of it.

Cohen: Not heard of Julia North? But the case was all over the headlines.

Miller: Well, Gretchen is right. I know nothing of it. She knows that I only read the sports page.

Cohen: You only read the sports page!

Weirob: It's an expression of his unconcern with earthly matters.

Miller: Well, that's not quite fair, Gretchen. It's a matter of preference. I much prefer to spend what time I have for reading in reading about the eighteenth century, rather than the drab and miserable century into which I had the misfortune to be born. It was really a much more civilized century, you know. But let's not dwell on my peculiar habits. Tell me about Julia North.

Cohen: Very well. Julia North was a young woman who was run over by a street car while saving the life of a young child who wandered onto the tracks. The child's mother, one Mary Frances Beaudine, had a stroke while watching the horrible scene. Julia's healthy brain and wasted body, and Mary Frances' healthy body and wasted brain, were transported to a hospital where a brilliant neurosurgeon, Dr. Matthews, was in residence. He had worked out a procedure for what he called a "body transplant." He removed the brain from Julia's head and placed it in Mary Frances', splicing the nerves, etc., using techniques not available until quite recently. The survivor of all this was obviously Julia, as everyone agreed—except, unfortunately, Mary Frances' husband. His shortsightedness and lack of imagination led to great complications and drama and made the case more famous in the history of crime than in the history of medicine. I shall not go into the details of this sorry aspect of the case—they are well reported in a book by Barbara Harris called *Who Is Julia?*, in case you are interested.

Miller: Fascinating!

Cohen: Well, the relevance of this case is obvious. Julia North had one body up until the time of the accident, and another body after the operation. So one person had two bodies. So a person cannot be simply *identified* with a human body. So something must be wrong with your view, Gretchen. What do you say to this?

Weirob: I'll say to you just what I said to Dr. Matthews . . .

Cohen: You have spoken with Dr. Matthews?

Weirob: Yes. He contacted me shortly after my accident. My physician had phoned him up about my case. Matthews said he could perform the same operation for me he did for Julia North. I refused.

Cohen: You refused! But Gretchen, why . . . ?

Miller: Gretchen, I *am* shocked. Your decision practically amounts to suicide! You passed up an opportunity to continue living? Why on earth . . . ?

Weirob: Hold on, hold on. You are both making an assumption I reject. If the case of Julia North amounts to a counterexample to my view that a person is just a live human body, and if my refusal to submit to this procedure amounts to passing up an option to survive, then the survivor of such an operation must be reckoned as the same person as the brain donor. That is, the survivor of Julia North's operation must have been Julia, and the survivor of the operation on me would have to be me. This is the assumption you both make in criticizing me. But I reject it. I think Jack Beaudine was right. The survivor of the operation involving Julia North's brain was Mary Frances Beaudine, and the survivor of the operation which was to involve my brain would not have been me.

Miller: Gretchen, how on earth can you say that? Will you not give up your view that personal identity is just bodily identity, no matter how clear the counterexample? I really think you simply have an irrational attachment to the lump of material that is your body.

Cohen: Yes, Gretchen, I agree with Sam. You are being preposterous! The survivor of Julia North's operation had no idea who Mary Frances Beaudine was. She remembered being Julia . . .

Weirob: She *seemed* to remember being Julia. Have you forgotten so quickly the importance of this distinction? In my opinion, the effect of the operation was that Mary Frances Beaudine survived deluded, thinking she was someone else.

Cohen: But as you know, the case was litigated. It went to the Supreme Court. They said that the survivor was Julia.

Weirob: That argument is unworthy of you, Dave. Is the Supreme Court infallible?

Cohen: No, they aren't. But I don't think it's such a stupid point.

Look at it this way, Gretchen. This is a case in which two criteria we use to make judgements of identity conflict. Usually we expect personal identity to involve both bodily identity and psychological continuity. That is, we expect that if we have the same body, then the beliefs, memories, character traits and the like also will be enormously similar. In this case, these two criteria which usually coincide do not. If we choose one criterion, we say that the survivor is Mary Frances Beaudine and she has undergone drastic psychological changes. If we choose the other, we say that Julia has survived with a new body. We have to choose which criterion is more important. It's a matter of choice of how to use our language, how to extend the concept "same person" to a new situation. The overwhelming majority of people involved in the case took the survivor to be Julia. That is, society chose to use the concept one way rather than the other. The Supreme Court is *not* beside the point. One of their functions is to settle just how old concepts shall be applied to new circumstances—how "freedom of the press" is to be understood when applied to movies or television, whose existence was not foreseen when the concept was shaped, or to say whether "murder" is to include the abortion of a foetus. They are fallible on points of fact, but they are the final authority on the development of certain important concepts used in law. The notion of *person* is such a concept.

Weirob: You think that *who* the survivor was, was a matter of convention, of how we choose to use language?

Cohen: Yes.

Weirob: I can show the preposterousness of all that with an example.

Let us suppose that I agree to the operation. I lie in bed, expecting my continued existence, anticipating the feelings and thoughts I shall have upon awakening after the operation. Dr. Matthews enters and asks me to take several aspirin, so as not to have a headache when I awake. I protest that aspirins upset my stomach; he asks whether I would have a terrible headache tomorrow or a mild stomachache now, and I agree that it would be reasonable to take them.

Let us suppose you enter at this point with bad news. The Supreme Court has changed its mind! So the survivor will not be me. So, I say, "Oh, then I will not take the aspirin, for it's not me that will have a headache, but someone else. Why should I endure a stomachache, however mild, for the comfort of someone else? After all, I am already donating my brain to that person."

Now this is clearly absurd. If I was correct, in the first place, to anticipate having the sensations and thoughts that the survivor is to have the next day, the decision of nine old men a thousand or so miles away wouldn't make me wrong. And if I was wrong so to anticipate, their decision couldn't make me right. How can the correctness of my anticipation of survival be a matter of the way we use our words? If it is not such a matter, then my identity is not either. My identity with the survivor, my survival, is a question of fact, not of convention.

Cohen: Your example is persuasive. I admit I am befuddled. On the one hand, I cannot see how the matter can be other than I have described. When we know all the facts what can remain to be decided but how we are to describe them, how we are to use our language? And yet I can see that it seems absurd to suppose that the correctness or incorrectness of anticipation of future experience is a matter for convention to decide.

Miller: Well, I didn't think the business about convention was very plausible anyway. But I should like to return you to the main question, Gretchen. Fact or convention, it still remains. Why will you not admit that the survivor of this operation would be you?

Weirob: Well, *you* tell *me,* why do you think she would be me?

Miller: I can appeal to the theory I developed last night. You argued that the idea that personal identity consists in memory would not guarantee the possibility of survival after death. But you said nothing to shake its plausibility as an account of personal identity. It has the enormous advantage, remember, of making sense of our ability to judge our own identity, without examination of our bodies. I should argue that it is the correctness of this theory that explains the *almost* universal willingness to say that the survivor of Julia's operation was Julia. We need not deliberate over how to extend our concept, we need only apply the concept we already have. Memory is sufficient for identity and bodily identity is *not* necessary for it. The survivor remembered Julia's thoughts and actions, and so was Julia. Would you but submit to the operation, the survivor would remember your thoughts and actions, would remember this very conversation we are now having, and would be you.

Cohen: Yes, I now agree completely with Sam. The theory that personal identity is to be analyzed in terms of memory is correct, and according to it you will survive if you submit to the operation.

Let me add another argument against your view and in favor of the memory theory. You have emphasized that identity is the condition of *anticipation.* That means, among other things, that we have a particular concern for that person in the future whom we take to be ourselves. If I were told that any of the three of us were to suffer pain tomorrow, I should be sad. But if it were you or Sam that were to be hurt, my concern would be altruistic or unselfish. That is because I would not anticipate having the painful experience myself. Here I do no more than repeat points you have made earlier in our conversations.

Now what is there about mere sameness of body that makes sense of this asymmetry, between the way we look at our own futures, and the way we look at the futures of others? In other words, why is the identity of your body—that mere lump of matter, as Sam put it—of such great importance? Why care so much about it?

Weirob: You say, and I surely agree, that identity of person is a very special relationship—so special as perhaps not even happily called a relationship at all. And you say that since my theory is that identity of person is identity of body, I should be able to explain the importance of the one in terms of the importance of the other.

I'm not sure I can do that. But does the theory that personal identity consists in memory fare better on this score?

Cohen: Well, I think it does. Those properties of persons which make persons of such great value, and mark their individuality, and make one person so special to his friends and loved ones, are ultimately psychological or mental. One's character, personality, beliefs, attitudes, convictions—they are what make every person so unique and special. A skinny Gretchen would be a shock to us all, but not a Gretchen diminished in any important way. But a Gretchen who was not witty, or not gruff, or not as honest to the path an argument takes as is humanly possible—those would be fundamental changes. Is it any wonder that the survivor of that California fiasco was reckoned as Julia North? Would it make sense to take her to be Mary Jane Beaudine, when she had none of her beliefs or attitudes or memories?

Now if such properties are what is of importance about a person to others, is it not reasonable that they are the basis of one's importance to oneself? And these are just the properties that personal identity preserves when it is taken to consist in links of memory. Do we not have, in this idea, at least the beginning of an explanation of the importance of identity?

Weirob: So on two counts you two favor the memory theory. First, you say it explains how it is possible to judge as to one's own identity, without having to examine one's body. Second, you say it explains the importance of personal identity.

Cohen: Now surely you must agree the memory theory is correct. Do you agree? There may still be time to contact Dr. Matthews . . .

Weirob: Hold on, hold on. I'm still not persuaded. Granted the survivor will *think* she is me, will *seem* to remember thinking my thoughts. But recall the importance of distinguishing between real and merely apparent memory . . .

Cohen: But *you* recall that this distinction is to be made on the basis of whether the apparent memories were or were not caused by the prior experiences in the appropriate way. The survivor will not seem to remember your thoughts because of hypnosis or by coincidence or overweening imagination. She will seem to remember them because the traces those experiences left on your brain now activate her mind in the usual way. She will seem to remember them because she does remember them, and will be you.

Weirob: Let's go over this slowly. We all argue that the fact that the survivor of this strange operation Dr. Matthews proposes would *seem* to remember doing what I have done. Let us even suppose she would take herself to be me, claim to be Gretchen Weirob—and have no idea who else she might be. (We are then assuming that she differs from me in one aspect—her theory of personal identity. But that does not show her not to be me, for I could change my mind by then.) We all first agree that this much does not make her me. For this could all be true of someone suffering a delusion or a subject of hypnosis.

Cohen: Yes, this is all agreed.

Weirob: But now you think that some *further* condition is satisfied, which makes her apparent memories *real* memories. Now what exactly is this further condition?

Cohen: Well, that the same brain was involved in the perception of the events, and their later *memory.* Thus a causal chain of just the same sort as when only a single body is involved is involved here. That is, perceptions when the event occurs leave a trace in the brain, which is later responsible for the content of the memory. And we agreed, did we not, that apparent memory, caused in the right way, is real memory?

Weirob: Now is it absolutely crucial that the same brain is involved?

Cohen: What do you mean?

Weirob: Let me explain again by reference to Dr. Matthews. In our conversation he explained a new procedure on which he was working called a *brain rejuvenation.* By this process, which is not yet available—only the feasibility of developing it is being studied—a new brain could be made which is an exact duplicate of my brain. That is, an exact duplicate in terms of psychologically relevant states. It might not duplicate all the properties of my brain; for example, the blood vessels in the new brain might be stronger than in the old brain.

Miller: What is the point of developing such a macabre technique?

Weirob: Dr. Matthews' idea is that when weaknesses which might lead to stroke or other brain injury are noted, a healthy duplicate could be made, and replace the original, forestalling the problem.

Now Dave, suppose my problem were not with my liver and kidneys and such, but with my brain.

Would you recommend such an operation as to my benefit?

Cohen: You mean, do I think the survivor of such an operation would be you?

Weirob: Exactly. You may assume that Dr. Matthews' technique works perfectly so the causal process involved is no less reliable than that involved in ordinary memory.

Cohen: Then I would say it was you . . . No! Wait! No, it wouldn't be you. Absolutely not!

Miller: But why the sudden reversal? It seems to me it would be her. Indeed, I should try such an operation myself, if it would clear up my dizzy spells and leave me otherwise unaffected.

Cohen: No, don't you see, she is leading us into a false trap. If we say it *is* her, then she will say, "Then what if he makes two duplicates, or three or ten? They can't all be me, they all have an equal claim, so none will be me." It would be the argument of last night, reapplied on earth. So the answer is no, absolutely not, it wouldn't be you. Duplication of self does not preserve identity. Identity of the person requires identity of the brain.

Miller: Quite right.

Weirob: Now let me see if I have your theory straight. Suppose we have two bodies, A and B. My brain is put into A, a duplicate into B. The survivor of this, call them "A-Gretchen" and "B-Gretchen," both seem to remember giving this very speech. Both are in this state of seeming to remember, as the last stage in an information-preserving causal chain, initiated by my giving this speech. Both have my character, personality, beliefs, and the like. But one is *really* remembering, the other is not. A-Gretchen is really me, B-Gretchen is not.

Cohen: Precisely. Is this incoherent?

Weirob: No, I guess there is nothing incoherent about it. But look what has happened to the advantages you claimed for the memory theory.

First, you said, it explains how I can know who I am without opening my eyes and recognizing my body. But in your theory Gretchen-A and Gretchen-B cannot know who they are even if they do open their eyes and examine their bodies. How is Gretchen-A to know whether she has the original brain and is who she seems to be, or has the duplicate and is a new person, only a few minutes old, and with no memories but my delusions? If the hospital kept careless records, or the surgeon thought it was of no great importance to keep track of who got the original and who got the duplicate, she might never know who she was. By making identity of person turn into identity of brain, your theory makes the ease with which I can determine who I am not less, but more mysterious than my theory.

Second, you said, your theory explains why my concern for Gretchen-A, who is me whether she knows it or not, would be selfish, and my anticipation of her experience correct while my concern for Gretchen-B with her duplicated brain would be unselfish, and my anticipation of having her experiences incorrect. And it explains this, you said, because by insisting on the links of memory, we preserve in personal identity more psychological characteristics which are the most important features of a person.

But Gretchen-A and Gretchen-B are psychologically indistinguishable. Though they will go their separate ways, at the moment of awakening they could well be exactly similar in every psychological respect. In terms of character and belief and the contents of their minds, Gretchen-A is no more like me than Gretchen-B. So there is nothing in your theory after all, to explain why anticipation is appropriate when we have identity, and not otherwise.

You said, Sam, that I had an irrational attachment for this unworthy material object, my body. But you too are as irrationally attached to your brain. I have never seen my brain. I should have easily given it up, for a rejuvenated version, had that been the choice with which I was faced. I have never seen it, never felt it, and have no attachment to it. But my body? That seems to me all that I am. I see no point in trying to evade its fate.

Perhaps I miss the merit of your arguments. I am tired, and perhaps my poor brain, feeling slighted, has begun to desert me . . .

Cohen: Oh don't worry Gretchen, you are still clever. Again you have left me befuddled. I don't know what to say. But answer me this. Suppose you are right and we are wrong. But suppose these arguments had not occurred to you, and, sharing in our error, you had agreed to the operation. You anticipate the operation until it happens, thinking you will survive. You are happy. The survivor takes herself to be you, and thinks she made a decision before the operation which has now turned out to be right. She is happy. Your friends are happy. Who would be worse off, either before or after the operation?

Suppose even that you realize identity would not be preserved by such an operation but have it done anyway, and as the time for the operation approaches, you go ahead and anticipate the experiences of the survivor. Where exactly is the mistake? Do you really have any less reason to care for the survivor than for yourself? Can mere identity of body, the lack of which alone keeps you from being her, mean that much? Perhaps we were wrong, after all, in focusing on identity as the necessary condition of anticipation . . .

Miller: It's too late, Dave.

NOTES

The First Night: The arguments against the position that personal identity consists in identity of an immaterial soul are similar to those found in John Locke. "Of Identity and Diversity," Chapter 27 of Book II of *Essay Concerning Human Understanding.* This chapter first appeared in the second edition of 1694.

The Second Night: The arguments against the view that personal identity consists in bodily identity are also suggested by Locke, as is the theory that memory is what is crucial. The argument that the memory theory is circular was made by Joseph Butler in "Of Personal Identity," an Appendix to his *Analogy of Religion,* first published in 1736. Locke's memory theory has been developed by a number of modern authors, including Sydney Shoemaker. The possibility of circumventing Butler's charge of circularity by an appeal to causation is noted by David Wiggins in *Identity and Spatial Temporal Continuity.* The "duplication argument" was apparently first used by the eighteenth-century free thinker, Antony Collins. Collins assumed that something like Locke's theory of personal identity was correct, and used the duplication argument to raise problems for the doctrine of immortality.

The Third Night: Who Is Julia?, by Barbara Harris, is an engaging novel published in 1972. (Dr. Matthews had not yet thought of brain rejuvenations.)

Locke considers the possibility of the "consciousness" of a prince being transferred to the body of a cobbler. The idea of using the removal of a brain to suggest how this might happen comes from Sydney Shoemaker's seminal book, *Self-Knowledge and Self-Identity* (1963). Bernard Williams has cleverly and articulately resisted the memory theory and the view that such a brain removal would amount to a body transplant in a number of important articles which are collected in his book *Problems of the Self* (1973). In particular, Williams has stressed the relevance of the duplication argument even in questions of terrestrial personal identity. Weirob's position in this essay is more inspired by Williams than anyone else. I have discussed Williams' arguments and related topics in "Can the Self Divide?" (*Journal of Philosophy,* 1972) and a review of his book (*Journal of Philosophy,* 1976).

An important article on the themes which emerge toward the end of the dialogue is Derek Parfit's "Personal Identity" (*Philosophical Review,* 1971). This article, along with Locke's chapter and a number of other important chapters and articles by Hume, Shoemaker, Williams, and others are collected in my anthology *Personal Identity* (1975). A number of new articles on personal identity appear in Amelie Rorty (ed.), *The Identities of Persons* (1976).

Part IV

Determinism, Free Will, and Responsibility

WHAT ARE WE ASKING when we ask *why* something happened? Will an adequate explanation show us that in some sense or other the event to be explained *had* to happen in the way it did? In principle, are voluntary actions subject to the same kinds of explanations as physical events? If, in principle, everything that happens can be explained by science, is there then no such thing in the universe as random chance, genuine contingency, and uncertainty? These questions have great interest to the philosopher in their own right; but they also are of great strategic importance to the continuing arguments over the ancient riddle of determinism versus free will.

Determinism is the theory that all events, including human actions and choices, are, without exception, totally determined. What does it mean to say that an event (a past event, E, for instance) is "totally determined"? To this question various answers have been given, which for our present purposes we can take to be roughly equivalent.[1]

1. E was completely caused.
2. There were antecedent sufficient conditions for E; that is, conditions such that given their occurrence E *had* to occur.
3. It was causally necessary that E occur.
4. Given what preceded it, it was inevitable that E take place.
5. E is subsumable under a universal law of nature; that is, the occurrence of E was deducible from a description of the conditions that obtained before its occurrence and certain universal laws.
6. The occurrence of E is subject in principle to scientific explanation.
7. The occurrence of E was in principle predictable.
8. There are circumstances and laws which, if they had been known, would have made it possible for one to predict the occurrence and exact nature of E.

Indeterminism, the logical contradictory of determinism, is the theory that some events are not determined. Most (but by no means all) exponents of indeterminism hold that the events that are not determined are human actions.

There are a number of commonsense considerations that should at least incline a reflective person toward determinism. Whenever we plug in a machine, or plant seeds, or prepare for a storm, we act in the expectation that physical events will occur in accordance with known laws of nature. Hardly anyone would deny, moreover, that physical characteristics of human beings—the color of their eyes, the cellular structure of their brains, glands, and other organs—are determined exactly by their genetic inheritance. And pediatricians and parents of large broods have often observed that **temperament** is determined, at least to a large degree, right from birth. To a large extent our characters, personalities, and intellects are a consequence of our inherited physical capacities and temperamental proclivities, and our choices in turn reflect our characters. Similarly, our early childhood training, family

1. Speaking more strictly, definitions 1–6 are "roughly equivalent" to one another, and definitions 7 and 8 are "roughly equivalent" to one another, although one should beware of subtle differences even within these classes. Basically, there are two types of definitions: those in terms of prior sufficient conditions and those in terms of predictability.

environment, and education have formative influences on character. We do what we do because we are what we are, and we are what we are—at least to a large extent—because our genes and the influencing conduct of others have formed us that way.

At the same time, common sense recognizes that human beings do some things "of their own free will," that is, act in circumstances in which they might very well have done something else instead. This commonsense observation is hard to reconcile with determinism, which seems to imply that every event that occurs is the only one that could have occurred in the circumstances. This in turn seems to imply that no matter what I did a moment ago, I *could not have done otherwise*—which, in turn, seems to say that I *had* to do what I did, that I was not a free agent. But, most of us would agree, my ability to do otherwise is a necessary condition of praise or blame, reward or punishment—in short, for my *being responsible*. Therefore, if determinism cannot be reconciled with the ability to do otherwise, it cannot be reconciled with moral responsibility either. But we *do* hold people responsible for what they do (indeed, some say we *must* hold people responsible); therefore (some have argued), so much the worse for determinism. Such is the commonsense case against determinism.

Common sense, however, is no more pleased with indeterminism, which seems to give no satisfactory answer at all to any query of the form "Why did *this* happen rather than some other thing?" The reply "It just happened, that's all" inevitably leaves us unsatisfied. If we drop a stone and, to our astonishment, it rises straight up in the air instead of falling, we won't rest content with the "explanation" that "it was just one of those things—a totally random chance occurrence without rhyme or reason." We are even less likely to accept "chance" as an "explanation" for human actions. Such an explanation, we feel, makes all human actions arbitrary and unintelligible; it also seems to destroy the intimate bond between a person and his actions that is required by judgments of moral responsibility. Yet just insofar as a person's action was uncaused, just so far does it seem to have occurred "without rhyme or reason," as a "matter of pure chance." In the words of one determinist: "in proportion as an act of volition starts of itself without cause it is exactly, so far as the freedom of the individual is concerned, as if it had been thrown into his mind from without—'suggested to him by a freakish demon.'"[2]

Common sense thus is tied up in knots. It looks with little favor either on determinism or indeterminism in respect to human actions. Yet because these two theories are defined as logical contradictories, one of them *must* be true. The plight of common sense thus takes the form of a **dilemma;** that is, an argument of the form

1. If P is true, then Q is true.
2. If not-P is true, then Q is true.
3. Either P is true or not-P is true.
4. Therefore, Q is true (where Q is something repugnant or antecedently unacceptable).

The dilemma of determinism can be stated thus:[3]

2. R. E. Hobart, "Free-Will as Involving Determinism and Inconceivable Without It," *Mind,* 43, (1934).
3. The argument could be put in a simpler way if, instead of "determinism" and "indeterminism," it were restricted to "determinism in respect to human actions," and "indeterminism in respect to human actions." Also, a fuller statement of the argument would incorporate a separate argument from "not free" to "not responsible."

1. If determinism is true, we can never do other than we do; hence, we are never responsible for what we do.
2. If indeterminism is true, then some events—namely, human actions—are random, hence not free; hence, we are never responsible for what we do.
3. Either determinism is true or else indeterminism is true.
4. Therefore, we are never responsible for what we do.

There are several ways we might try to escape being gored by the "horns of the dilemma," but one way is *not* open to us. We may not deny the third premise; for, given our definitions of *determinism* and *indeterminism,* it amounts simply to the statement that either determinism is true or else it is not—surely an innocuous claim! We are, in short, not able in this case to get "between the horns of the dilemma" by denying its disjunctive premise.

We are thus left with three possibilities. We can deny the first premise and hold that determinism is, after all, perfectly compatible with free will and responsibility; or we can deny the second premise and hold that an act can be both free and intelligible, and hence responsible, though it was not traceable to determining causes outside the actor himself; or finally we can accept the entire argument just as it stands and argue on independent grounds that its conclusion is not so "repugnant" or so "antecedently unacceptable" as it seems at first appearance.

The reconciling way of attempting to resolve the dilemma is nowadays called **compatibilism.** (sometimes also **soft determinism**). This theory consists of the conjunction of two theses: (1) that determinism is true and (2) that determinism is compatible with free will and responsibility. Compatibilism—the view of Thomas Hobbes, John Locke, and John Stuart Mill—is represented here by the selections from A. J. Ayer and Walter Stace.

Common to all these philosophers is the view that the key phrase, "He could have done otherwise," is properly understood as hypothetical, meaning roughly, "He would have done otherwise *if* he had so chosen (intended, wished)." In this hypothetical sense, I could have done otherwise than I did, even if determinism is true. I just wrote the word *true,* but *if* I had instead chosen to write another word (say, *right*), I should have done so (unless somebody intervened with a gun or knife to prevent me); and this is true even though I was determined to choose to write *true.* In short, according to this theory, if I can do what I choose, I am free in the only sense of *free* used in ordinary parlance and in ascriptions of responsibility, and it matters not whether my choice itself was causally determined.

Compatibilists often take great pains to distinguish the determinism they espouse from a theory called **fatalism,** which they reject. To say of an event that it was fated to happen is to say more than that it was causally determined. It is to say that it would have happened no matter what the person involved might have done to avoid it. In this sense all of us are fated to die (at some time or other); but only a fatalist would say that a person is fated from birth to die at a definite place and at a definite time. A determinist would admit that it was determined that Abraham Lincoln die in Washington in 1865; but to say that it was *fated* that he so die is to imply, among other things, that even had Lincoln tried to shoot himself in Springfield, Illinois, in 1850, or even had he not gone to the theater on the fatal night, somehow he would have met the same fate he in fact met, in Washington, D.C., in 1865. That *all* events are so fated is a doctrine with strange mystic overtones and has rarely been defended by philosophers.[4]

4. One outstanding exception to this generalization is Richard Taylor. See his *Metaphysics,* 3rd edition (Englewood Cliffs, N.J.: Prentice-Hall, 1994), Chapter 6.

Another way of attempting to resolve the dilemma (that is, by denying that an uncaused act is necessarily a random event "without rhyme or reason") is found in the writings of Thomas Reid and Immanuel Kant, among others, and is represented here by the essays of C. A. Campbell and Roderick Chisholm. Proponents of the view that human actions are neither determined nor fortuitous—the theory called **libertarianism**[5]—remind us that human actions, unlike other events in nature, are subject to a special kind of explanation: the actor's own *reasons* for acting. An uncaused action, done deliberately for some reason, would therefore be a perfectly intelligible one, and adequately explained by an account of its reasons. The libertarian denies both theses of the compatibilist; he denies that determinism and freedom are compatible, and he denies that determinism is true.[6]

The compatibility of free will and determinism is also denied by those who respond to the dilemma in the third way (that is, by embracing the conclusion of the dilemma, instead of trying to avoid it). This is the approach of the **hard determinists;** instead of abandoning determinism as the libertarians do, they jettison free will and moral responsibility. Hard determinism was the view of Baruch Spinoza and Paul Holbach, among other philosophers; of Mark Twain and Thomas Hardy, among other literary figures; and of Clarence Darrow, the famous American criminal lawyer. It is represented here by the selections from Holbach and B. F. Skinner. Holbach is a typical representative of the eighteenth-century "enlightenment" period, in which philosophers were often themselves scientists inclined to find in the methods and discoveries of science the solution to ancient philosophical riddles. They also tended to be political radicals (by the standards of their time) substituting their theories of human rights for the prevailing justifications of inequalities among social classes. In neither area, philosophy or politics, were they reluctant to embrace revolutionary consequences. Holbach, for example, is uncompromising in his account of the implications of scientific explanation for human freedom.

There is no clearly dictated order in which to read the arguments of these three opposed schools of thought. In the pages that follow, the hard determinists make their case first. They argue both that determinism is true and that it has some very drastic consequences for our commonsense notions of freedom, avoidability, responsibility, blame, and regret. For that reason, hard determinism poses a challenge for those who would defend common sense. Historically, as we have seen, that challenge has been met in two ways: by denying that determinism has such drastic consequences for our ordinary concepts (compatibilism) or by denying that determinism is true (libertarianism). The challenging opening section then is followed by sections in which attempts are made in quite opposite ways to meet the challenge.

The key issue that divides hard from soft determinism is usually the problem of how we should interpret "free to do otherwise," "could have done otherwise," "his act was avoidable," and similar locutions used in support of our ascriptions of blame and punishment, credit or reward. Most parties to the discussion agree that a person can be held morally responsible for his past action *only* if he was able to do other than he did. Put more tersely: Avoidability is a necessary condition of responsibility. We will see in the early sections of Part IV that there are two senses of *avoidable*. In the *categorical sense,* to say that an act is avoidable is to say that there were no antecedent conditions (causes) sufficient for its occurrence. In the *hypothetical sense,* to say that an act is avoidable is to say that *if* the actor

5. Not to be confused with the political theory of the same name.

6. All libertarians, therefore, are indeterminists (by definition), but not all indeterminists are libertarians. It is possible for one to hold that all actions are uncaused and *therefore* occur by random chance. That view would be indeterministic but not libertarian.

had chosen (or, perhaps, intended) to do otherwise, he would have done otherwise (nothing would have stopped him). Avoidability in the hypothetical sense is perfectly compatible with determinism; avoidability in the categorical sense is perfectly compatible with determinism; avoidability in the categorical sense, by definition, is not. Now the question arises: In which of the senses of *avoidable*—the categorical sense, the hypothetical sense, or both—is it true that a person can be held responsible for his action only if it was avoidable?

The late A. J. Ayer's essay "Freedom and Necessity" presents the standard arguments for the hypothetical analysis of freedom and avoidability as clearly and elegantly as any more recent work. We use the word "standard" in this connection because these arguments were common to all the great philosophers in the tradition of English empiricism—Thomas Hobbes (1588–1679), John Locke (1632–1704), David Hume (1711–1776), John Stuart Mill (1806–1873), and Bertrand Russell (1872–1970). These so-called soft determinists differ from both hard determinists and libertarians over the compatibility of freedom and determinism, but they are also likely to differ with their opponents over the issue that most frequently leads people to consider the question of determinism, namely the implications of determinism for judgments of responsibility, blame, and punishment.

In our other compatibilist offering, Walter Stace provides several examples in which we find it natural to distinguish between an action's being caused and its being controlled. Pursuing a classic soft determinist strategy, Stace seeks to make plausible the distinction between these notions, thereby making room for the idea that though all of our actions are caused, some may nevertheless be relevantly within our control. If control over our actions is what is crucial to moral responsibility, and if control is compatible with an action's being caused, then freedom and determinism may peacefully co-exist, as the compatibilist claims.

Often it is hard to know of a given determinist exactly how hard or soft he is. The great outspoken behavioristic psychologist B. F. Skinner is a case in point. He does not make the same distinctions in the same way philosophers do. But it is plain that he is a complete determinist about human behavior. Moreover, he is accustomed to hearing the libertarian charge against his view that if it is true, then human beings can have neither freedom nor dignity. Unlike the soft determinists, however, Skinner agrees with his critics. His kind of determinism permits no freedom or dignity, but that is a small price to pay, he says, since freedom and dignity, as they are usually understood, are overrated goods. Determinism makes it possible for scientists who have discovered the laws of human motivation to "control" us by implanting in us dispositions to behave morally with one another. To be sure, this can lead only to "automatic" goodness for which the good person can claim no credit and from which he is not free to deviate. Such an engineered world can be so perfect that "no one will need to be good," as the poet T. S. Eliot put it derisively. But the important thing for Skinner is that people not harm one another, not that they achieve virtues of character that are more than automatic.

The libertarian alternative to compatibilism and hard determinism finds very able defenders in the Scottish philosopher and theologian C. A. Campbell, and the distinguished American philosopher Roderick Chisholm. Both thinkers begin by attacking compatibilism at the point where many philosophers have found it weakest intuitively, namely its reliance on a hypothetical analysis of freedom and avoidability. Campbell proceeds to offer an argument from introspection: when we "turn our minds back on themselves," and consider cases of temptation, we see quite clearly that the choice in such situations is up to us. No one is forcing or causing us to choose as we do. Though when we succumb to temptation we may be said to have been "forced" by our strongest desires into making that choice, things are quite different when we manage to resist temptation. In such cases, *nothing* is compelling us to choose as we do, and yet our choice may be perfectly rational and explicable. Campbell concludes that *we* are determining *for ourselves* what to do in such situations. We do this through the exercise of a choice that is not itself determined.

Roderick Chisholm's article tackles head on perhaps the most troubling worry that besets libertarianism: the nature of the person whose choices can determine conduct but which are not themselves determined. Nothing else we know of has this sort of power. Physical things act in predictable ways and are governed by laws of cause and effect. Free human choices aren't like this. But they aren't random or purely matters of chance, either. Persons are controlling the choices they make, without in turn being necessitated to make them. Chisholm forthrightly sees the difficulty of such a position, and fans of libertarianism would do well to carefully attend to Chisholm's analysis, one of whose primary virtues is to sketch just how exceptional free choices and persons are in the grand scheme of things. Philosophers and scientists are by nature skeptical of exceptions, constantly on the alert to prevent ad hoc hypotheses from being introduced to save a familiar or comforting idea. Chisholm sets the debate about libertarianism right where it should be, and forces us to ask whether the libertarian is giving us what we want (a robust sense of free will) at the expense of an occult view of the person.

A new section of Part IV, entitled "Freedom and Moral Responsibility," pursues several of the issues in the classic debate. The first piece, Harry Frankfurt's "Alternate Possibilities and Moral Responsibility," challenges the widely held view that avoidability is a necessary condition of responsibility. He adduces cases in which a person cannot avoid doing or choosing as he does, and yet is properly held morally responsible for his choices or actions. The piece has become a contemporary classic in the free will discussion and continues to spark vigorous debate amongst philosophers as to the proper role (if any) of control and avoidability in determinations of freedom and responsibility.

The next selection is an offering by Susan Wolf, who, in a highly original paper, methodically presents a theory with two basic parts. For one to be responsible for one's actions or their consequences, first of all, it must be the case that those actions are within the control of one's will, and second, that one's will is within the control of one's "deeper self." But that is not sufficient. Third, it must also be true that one is *sane,* where insanity in turn is analyzed as having *unavoidably mistaken* moral beliefs and values. Wolf's full theory then has a "deep self" condition supplemented by a "sanity condition," and the latter incorporates a conception of moral beliefs and their acquisition. The result is a theory that fits more comfortably with determinism should that theory just happen to be true, and which does not require what is impossible, according to Wolf, namely, that a person, to be responsible for anything, must have created her own "deeper self" from nothing.

The final paper of this section is Thomas Nagel's "Moral Luck," a paper that sets out explicitly to challenge the Kantian view of moral responsibility. According to that view, even in a world as dangerous and unpredictable as our own, there is at least one thing that is fully within our control, namely our moral integrity. Our moral integrity is a function solely of our intending to do what we perceive to be our duty. We may fail to achieve the results we intend—that much may be out of our control. But we are in command of our intentions, and this command supplies the proper basis for assignments of moral credit and blame. Praise is properly merited for good intentions, and blame deserved for bad, precisely because such intentions are within our control. Nagel challenges this widely held view in two ways. First, he argues that even if our intentions are fully within our control, our moral responsibility is based on other factors that are matters of luck. Suppose two drivers are speeding recklessly along a narrow road, and one driver hits and kills a pedestrian, while the other driver injures no one. Nagel argues that in such a case, we rightly charge the first driver with a graver wrong than the second, even though this disparity is based on something entirely outside of either driver's control (namely, the presence or absence of a pedestrian along the road). Nagel also argues that even when we base assignments of praise and blame on intentions alone, the intentions one forms and acts on are themselves matters of luck. What we intend to do is partly a function of how we are raised, what circumstances we find ourselves in, and what genetic inheritance we find ourselves with. All of these are in the relevant sense "matters of luck," since we cannot be said to have controlled or determined their presence. Nagel's article seems to expose a deep problem for our ordinary notions of how responsibility and control are related. It forces our attention right back to the initial concern that defines the classic debate: how (or whether) it is possible to be a free, morally responsible person while at the same time recognizing the ineliminable role that genetics, upbring, circumstance and socialization have played in making you the person you are.

Hard Determinism: The Case for Determinism and Its Incompatibility with Any Important Sense of Free Will

The Illusion of Free Will*

PAUL HOLBACH

Paul Henri Thiry, Baron d'Holbach (1723–1789), a French philosopher, was one of the Encyclopedists. His book, *System of Nature*, was called by his enemies "the Bible of Atheists."

MOTIVES AND THE DETERMINISM of the Will. In whatever manner man is considered, he is connected to universal nature, and submitted to the necessary and immutable laws that she imposes on all the beings she contains, according to their peculiar essences or to the respective properties with which, without consulting them, she endows each particular species. Man's life is a line that nature commands him to describe upon the surface of the earth, without his ever being able to swerve from it, even for an instant. He is born without his own consent; his organization does in nowise depend upon himself; his ideas come to him involuntarily; his habits are in the power of those who cause him to contract them; he is unceasingly modified by causes, whether visible or concealed, over which he has no control, which necessarily regulate his mode of existence, give the hue to his way of thinking,

**From* System of Nature *by Baron Paul d'Holbach, published in 1770. Translated by H. D. Robinson.*

and determine his manner of acting. He is good or bad, happy or miserable, wise or foolish, reasonable or irrational, without his will being for anything in these various states. Nevertheless, in spite of the shackles by which he is bound, it is pretended he is a free agent, or that independent of the causes by which he is moved, he determines his own will, and regulates his own condition. . . .

The will, as we have elsewhere said, is a modification of the brain, by which it is disposed to action, or prepared to give play to the organs. This will is necessarily determined by the qualities, good or bad, agreeable or painful, of the object or the motive that acts upon his senses, or of which the idea remains with him, and is resuscitated by his memory. In consequence, he acts necessarily, his action is the result of the impulse he receives either from the motive, from the object, or from the idea which has modified his brain, or disposed his will. When he does not act according to this impulse, it is because there comes some new cause, some new motive, some new idea, which modifies his brain in a different manner, gives him a new impulse, determines his will in another way, by which the action of the former impulse is suspended: thus, the sight of an agreeable object, or its idea, determines his will to set him in action to procure it; but if a new object or a new idea more powerfully attracts him, it gives a new direction to his will, annihilates the effect of the former, and prevents the action by which it was to be procured. This is the mode in which reflection, experience, reason, necessarily arrests or suspends the action of man's will: without this he would of necessity have followed the anterior impulse which carried him towards a then desirable object. In all this he always acts according to necessary laws from which he has no means of emancipating himself.

If when tormented with violent thirst, he figures to himself in idea, or really perceives a fountain, whose limpid streams might cool his feverish want, is he sufficient master of himself to desire or not to desire the object competent to satisfy so lively a want? It will no doubt be conceded, that it is impossible he should not be desirous to satisfy it; but it will be said—if at this moment it is announced to him that the water he so ardently desires is poisoned, he will, notwithstanding his vehement thirst, abstain from drinking it: and it has, therefore, been falsely concluded that he is a free agent. The fact, however, is, that the motive in either case is exactly the same: his own conservation. The same necessity that determined him to drink before he knew the water was deleterious upon this new discovery equally determined him not to drink; the desire of conserving himself either annihilates or suspends the former impulse; the second motive becomes stronger than the preceding, that is, the fear of death, or the desire of preserving himself, necessarily prevails over the painful sensation caused by his eagerness to drink: but, it will be said, if the thirst is very parching, an inconsiderate man without regarding the danger will risk swallowing the water. Nothing is gained by this remark: in this case, the anterior impulse only regains the ascendency; he is persuaded that life may possibly be longer preserved, or that he shall derive a greater good by drinking the poisoned water than by enduring the torment, which, to his mind, threatens instant dissolution; thus the first becomes the strongest and necessarily urges him on to action. Nevertheless, in either case, whether he partakes of the water, or whether he does not, the two actions will be equally necessary; they will be the effect of that motive which finds itself most puissant; which consequently acts in the most coercive manner upon his will.

This example will serve to explain the whole phenomena of the human will. This will, or rather the brain, finds itself in the same situation as a bowl, which, although it has received an impulse that drives it forward in a straight line, is deranged in its course whenever a force superior to the first obliges it to change its direction. The man who drinks the poisoned water appears a madman; but the actions of fools are as necessary as those of the most prudent individuals. The motives that determine the voluptuary and the debauchee to risk their health, are as powerful, and their actions are as necessary, as those which decide the wise man to manage his. But, it will be insisted, the debauchee may be prevailed on to change his conduct: this does not imply that he is a free agent; but that motives may be found sufficiently powerful to annihilate the effect of those that previously acted upon him; then these new motives determine his will to the new mode of conduct he may adopt as necessarily as the former did to the old mode. . . .

The errors of philosophers on the free agency of man, have arisen from their regarding his will as the *primum mobile,* the original motive of his actions; for want of recurring back, they have not perceived the multiplied, the complicated causes which, independently of him, give motion to the will itself; or which dispose and modify his brain, while he himself is purely passive in the motion he receives. Is he the master of desiring or not desiring an object that appears desirable to him? Without doubt it will be answered, no: but he is the master of resisting his desire, if he reflects on the consequences. But, I ask, is he capable of reflecting on these consequences, when his soul is hurried along by a very lively passion, which entirely depends upon his natural organization, and the causes by which he is modified? Is it in his power to add to these consequences all the weight necessary to counterbalance his desire? Is he the master of preventing the qualities which render an object desirable from residing in it? I shall be told: he ought to have learned to resist his passions; to contract a habit of putting a curb on his desires. I agree to it without any difficulty. But in reply, I again ask, is his nature susceptible of this modification? Does his boiling blood, his unruly imagination, the igneous fluid that circulates in his veins, permit him to make, enable him to apply true experience in the moment when it is wanted? And even when his temperament has capacitated him, has his education, the examples set before him, the ideas with which he has been inspired in early life, been suitable to make him contract this habit of repressing his desires? Have not all these things rather contributed to induce him to seek with avidity, to make him actually desire those objects which you say he ought to resist? . . .

In short, the actions of man are never free; they are always the necessary consequence of his temperament, of the received ideas, and of the notions, either true or false, which he has formed to himself of happiness: of his opinions, strengthened by example, by education, and by daily experience. So many crimes are witnessed on the earth only because every thing conspires to render man vicious and criminal; the religion he has adopted, his government, his education, the examples set before him, irresistibly drive him on to evil: under these circumstances, morality preaches virtue to him in vain. In those societies where vice is esteemed, where crime is crowned, where venality is constantly recompensed, where the most dreadful disorders are punished only in those who are too weak to enjoy the privilege of committing them with impunity, the practice of virtue is considered nothing more than a painful sacrifice of happiness. Such societies chastise, in the lower orders, those excesses which they respect in the higher ranks; and frequently have the injustice to condemn those in the penalty of death, whom public prejudices, maintained by constant example, have rendered criminal.

Man, then, is not a free agent in any one instant of his life; he is necessarily guided in each step by those advantages, whether real or fictitious, that he attaches to the objects by which his passions are roused: these passions themselves are necessary in a being who unceasingly tends towards his own happiness; their energy is necessary, since that depends on his temperament; his temperament is necessary, because it depends on the physical elements which enter into his composition; the modification of this temperament is necessary, as it is the infallible and inevitable consequence of the impulse he receives from the incessant action of moral and physical beings.

Choice Does Not Prove Freedom. In spite of these proofs of the want of free agency in man, so clear to unprejudiced minds, it will, perhaps be insisted upon with no small feeling of triumph, that if it be proposed to any one, to move or not to move his hand, an action in the number of those called indifferent, he evidently appears to be the master of choosing; from which it is concluded that evidence has been offered of free agency. The reply is, this example is perfectly simple; man in performing some action which he is resolved on doing, does not by any means prove his free agency; the very desire of displaying this quality, excited by the dispute, becomes a necessary motive, which decides his will either for the one or the other of these actions: What deludes him in this instance, or that which persuades him he is a free agent at this moment, is, that he does not discern the true motive which sets him in action, namely, the desire of convincing his opponent: if in the heat of the dispute he insists and asks, "Am I not the master of throwing myself out of the window?" I shall answer him, no; that whilst he preserves his reason there is no probability that the desire of proving his free agency, will become a motive sufficiently powerful to make him sacrifice his life to the attempt: if, notwithstanding this, to prove he is a free agent, he should actually precipitate himself from the window, it would not be a sufficient warranty to conclude he acted freely, but rather that it was the violence of his temperament which spurred him on to this folly. Madness is a state, that depends upon the heat of the blood, not upon the will. A fanatic or a hero, braves death as necessarily as a more phlegmatic man or coward flies from it.

There is, in point of fact, no difference between the man that is cast out of the window by another, and the man who throws himself out of it, except that the impulse in the first instance comes immediately from without whilst that which determines the fall in the second case, springs from within his own peculiar machine, having its more remote cause also exterior. When Mutius Scaevola held his hand in the fire, he was as much acting under the influence of necessity (caused by interior motives) that urged him to this strange action, as if his arm had been held by strong men: pride, despair, the desire of braving his enemy, a wish to astonish him, and anxiety to intimidate him, etc., were the invisible chains that held his hand bound to the fire. The love of glory, enthusiasm for their country, in like manner caused Codrus and Decius to devote themselves for their fellow-citizens. The Indian Colanus and the philosopher Peregrinus were equally obliged to burn themselves, by desire of exciting the astonishment of the Grecian assembly.

It is said that free agency is the absence of those obstacles competent to oppose themselves to the actions of man, or to the exercise of his faculties: it is pretended that he is a free agent whenever, making use of these faculties, he produces the effect he has proposed to himself. In reply to this reasoning, it is sufficient to consider that it in nowise depends upon himself to place or remove the obstacles that either determine or resist him; the motive that causes his action is no more in his own power than the obstacle that impedes him, whether this obstacle or motive be within his own machine or exterior of his person: he is not master of the thought presented to his mind, which determines his will; this thought is excited by some cause independent of himself.

To be undeceived on the system of his free agency, man has simply to recur to the motive by which his will is determined; he will always find this motive is out of his own control. It is said: that in consequence of an idea to which the mind gives birth, man acts freely if he encounters no obstacle. But the question is, what gives birth to this idea in his brain? Was he the master either to prevent it from presenting itself, or from renewing itself in his brain? Does not this idea depend either upon objects that strike him exteriorly and in despite of himself, or upon causes, that without his knowledge, act within himself and modify his brain? Can he prevent his eyes, cast without design upon any object whatever, from giving him an idea of this object, and from moving his brain? He is not more master of the obstacles; they are the necessary effects of either interior or exterior causes, which always act according to their given properties. A man insults a coward; this necessarily irritates him against his insulter; but his will cannot vanquish the obstacle that cowardice places to the object of his desire, because his natural conformation, which does not depend upon himself, prevents his having courage. In this case, the coward is insulted in spite of himself; and against his will is obliged patiently to brook the insult he has received.

Absence of Restraint Is Not Absence of Necessity. The partisans of the system of free agency appear ever to have confounded constraint with necessity. Man believes he acts as a free agent, every time he does not see any thing that places obstacles to his actions; he does not perceive that the motive which causes him to will, is always necessary and independent of himself. A prisoner loaded with chains is compelled to remain in prison; but he is not a free agent in the desire to emancipate himself; his chains prevent him from acting, but they do not prevent him from willing; he would save himself if they would loose his fetters; but he would not save himself as a free agent; fear or the idea of punishment would be sufficient motives for his action.

Man may, therefore, cease to be restrained, without, for that reason, becoming a free agent: in whatever manner he acts, he will act necessarily, according to motives by which he shall be determined. He may be compared to a heavy body that finds itself arrested in its descent by any obstacle whatever: take away this obstacle, it will gravitate or continue to fall; but who shall say this dense body is free to fall or not? Is not its descent the necessary effect of its own specific gravity? The virtuous Socrates submitted to the laws of his country, although they were unjust; and though the doors of his jail were left open to him, he would not save himself; but in this he did not act as a free agent: the invisible chains of opinion, the secret love of decorum, the inward respect for the laws, even when they were iniquitous, the fear of tarnishing his glory, kept him in his prison: they were motives sufficiently powerful with this enthusiast for virtue, to induce him to wait death with tranquility; it was not in his power to save himself, because he could find no potential motive to bring him to depart, even for an instant, from those principles to which his mind was accustomed.

Man, it is said, frequently acts against his inclination, from whence it is falsely concluded he is a free agent; but when he appears to act contrary to his inclination, he is always determined to it by some motive sufficiently efficacious to vanquish this inclination. A sick man, with a view to his cure, arrives at conquering his repugnance to the most disgusting remedies: the fear of pain, or the dread of death, then become necessary motives; consequently this sick man cannot be said to act freely.

When it is said, that man is not a free agent, it is not pretended to compare him to a body moved by a simple impulsive cause: he contains within himself causes inherent to his existence; he is moved by an interior organ, which has its own peculiar laws, and is itself necessarily determined in consequence of ideas formed from perception resulting from sensation which it receives from exterior objects. As the mechanism of these sensations, of these perceptions, and the manner they engrave ideas on the brain of man, are not known to him; because he is unable to unravel all these motions; because he cannot perceive the chain of operations in his soul, or the motive principle that acts within him, he supposes himself a free agent; which literally translated, signifies, that he moves himself by himself; that he determines himself without cause: when he rather ought to say, that he is ignorant how or why he acts in the manner he does. It is true the soul enjoys an activity peculiar to itself: but it is equally certain that this activity would never be displayed, if some motive or some cause did not put it in a condition to exercise itself: at least it will not be pretended that the soul is able either to love or to hate without being moved, without knowing the objects, without having some idea of their qualities. Gunpowder has unquestionably a particular activity, but this activity will never display itself, unless fire be applied to it; this, however, immediately sets it in motion.

The Complexity of Human Conduct and the Illusion of Free Agency. It is the great complication of motion in man, it is the variety of his action, it is the multiplicity of causes that move him, whether simultaneously or in continual succession, that persuades him he is a free agent: if all his motions were simple, if the causes that move him did not confound themselves with each other, if they were distinct, if his machine were less complicated, he would perceive that all his actions were necessary, because he would be enabled to recur instantly to the cause that made him act. A man who should be always obliged to go towards the west, would always go on that side; but he would feel that, in so going, he was not a free agent: if he had another sense, as his actions or his motion, augmented by a sixth, would be still more varied and much more complicated, he would believe himself still more a free agent than he does with his five senses.

It is, then, for want of recurring to the causes that move him; for want of being able to analyze, from not being competent to decompose the complicated motion of his machine, that man believes himself a free agent: it is only upon his own ignorance that he founds the profound yet deceitful notion he has of his free agency; that he builds those opinions which he brings forward as a striking proof of his pretended freedom of action. If, for a short time, each man was willing to examine his own peculiar actions, search out their true motives to discover their concatenation, he would remain convinced that the sentiment he has of his natural free agency, is a chimera that must speedily be destroyed by experience.

Nevertheless it must be acknowledged that the multiplicity and diversity of the causes which continually act upon man, frequently without even his knowledge, render it impossible, or at least extremely difficult for him to recur to the true principles of his own peculiar actions, much less the actions of others: they frequently depend upon causes so fugitive, so remote from their effects, and which, superficially examined, appear to have so little analogy, so slender a relation with them, that it requires singular sagacity to bring them into light. This is what renders the study of the moral man a task of such difficulty; this is the reason why his heart is an abyss, of which it is frequently impossible for him to fathom the depth. . . .

If he understood the play of his organs, if he were able to recall to himself all the impulsions they have received, all the modifications they have undergone, all the effects they have produced, he would perceive that all his actions are submitted to the fatality, which regulates his own particular system, as it does the entire system of the universe: no one effect in him, any more than in nature, produces itself by chance; this, as has been before proved, is word void of sense. All that passes in him; all that is done by him; as well as all that happens in nature, or that is attributed to her, is derived from necessary causes, which act according to necessary laws, and which produce necessary effects from whence necessarily flow others.

Fatality, is the eternal, the immutable, the necessary order, established in nature; or the indispensable connexion of causes that act, with the effects they operate. Conforming to this order, heavy bodies fall: light bodies rise; that which is analogous in matter reciprocally attracts; that which is heterogeneous mutually repels; man congregates himself in society, modifies each his fellow; becomes either virtuous or wicked; either contributes to his mutual happiness, or reciprocates his misery; either loves his neighbour, or hates his companion necessarily, according to the manner in which the one acts upon the other. From whence it may be seen, that the same necessity which regulates the physical, also regulates the moral world, in which every thing is in consequence submitted to fatality. Man, in running over, frequently without his own knowledge, often in spite of himself, the route which nature has marked out for him, resembles a swimmer who is obliged to follow the current that carries him along: he believes himself a free agent, because he sometimes consents, sometimes does not consent, to glide with the stream, which notwithstanding, always hurries him forward; he believes himself the master of his condition, because he is obliged to use his arms under the fear of sinking. . . .

Beyond Freedom and Dignity*

B. F. SKINNER

B. F. Skinner (1904–1990), the leading behavioral psychologist of his time, taught at Harvard University.

From B. F. Skinner, Beyond Freedom and Dignity *(New York: Bantam/Vintage Books, 1971), pp. 56–77. Skinner's own title for this chapter of his book was "Punishment." Reprinted by permission of Alfred A. Knopf, Inc. © 1971 by B. F. Skinner.*

I

FREEDOM IS SOMETIMES DEFINED as a lack of resistance or restraint. A wheel turns freely if there is very little friction in the bearing, a horse breaks free from the post to which it has been tethered, a man frees himself from the branch on which he has been caught while climbing a tree. Physical restraint is an obvious condition, which seems particularly useful in defining freedom, but with respect to important issues, it is a metaphor and not a very good one. People are indeed controlled by fetters, handcuffs, strait jackets, and the walls of jails and concentration camps, but what may be called behavioral control—the restraint imposed by contingencies of reinforcement—is a very different thing.

Except when physically restrained, a person is least free or dignified when he is under threat of punishment, and unfortunately most people often are. Punishment is very common in nature, and we learn a great deal from it. A child runs awkwardly, falls, and is hurt; he touches a bee and is stung; he takes a bone from a dog and is bitten; and as a result he learns not to do these things again. It is mainly to avoid various forms of natural punishment that people have built a more comfortable and less dangerous world.

The word punishment is usually confined to contingencies intentionally arranged by other people, who arrange them because the results are reinforcing to them. (Punitive contingencies are not to be confused with aversive control, through which people are induced to behave in given ways. Punishment is used to induce people *not* to behave in given ways.) A person resorts to punishment when he criticizes, ridicules, blames, or physically attacks another in order to suppress unwanted behavior. Government is often defined in terms of the power to punish, and some religions teach that sinful behavior will be followed by eternal punishments of the most horrible sort.

We should expect the literatures of freedom and dignity to oppose measures of this sort and to work toward a world in which punishment is less common or even absent, and up to a point they have done so. But punitive sanctions are still common. People still control each other more often through censure or blame than commendation or praise, the military and the police remain the most powerful arms of government, communicants are still occasionally reminded of hellfire, and teachers have abandoned the birch rod only to replace it with more subtle forms of punishment. And the curious fact is that those who defend freedom and dignity are not only not opposed to these measures but largely responsible for the fact that they are still with us. This strange state of affairs can be understood only by looking at the way in which organisms respond to punitive contingencies.

Punishment is designed to remove awkward, dangerous, or otherwise unwanted behavior from a repertoire on the assumption that a person who has been punished is less likely to behave in the same way again. Unfortunately, the matter is not that simple. Reward and punishment do not differ merely in the direction of the changes they induce. A child who has been severely punished for sex play is not necessarily less inclined to continue; and a man who has been imprisoned for violent assault is not necessarily less inclined toward violence. Punished behavior is likely to reappear after the punitive contingencies are withdrawn.

What seem to be the intended effects of punishment can often be explained in other ways. For example, punishment may generate incompatible emotions. A boy who has been severely punished for sex play may no longer be, as we might say, in the mood to continue, and fleeing to escape from a punisher is incompatible with attacking him. Future occasions for sex play or for violent assault may evoke similar incompatible behavior through conditioning. Whether the effect is felt as shame, guilt, or a sense of sin depends upon whether the punishment is administered by parent or peer, by a government, or by a church, respectively.

The aversive condition brought about by punishment (and felt in these different ways) has a much more important effect. Quite literally, a person may subsequently behave "in order to avoid punishment." He can avoid it by not behaving in punishable ways, but there are other possibilities. Some of these are disruptive and maladaptive or neurotic, and as a result they have been closely studied. The so-called "dynamisms" of Freud are said to be ways in which repressed wishes evade the censor and find expression, but they can be interpreted simply as ways in which people avoid punishment. Thus, a person may behave in ways that will not be punished because they cannot be seen, as by *fantasying* or *dreaming*. He may *sublimate* by engaging in behavior which has rather similar reinforcing effects but is not punished. He may *displace* punishable behavior by directing it toward objects which cannot punish—for example, he may be aggressive toward physical objects, children, or small animals. He may watch or read about others who engage in punishable behavior, *identifying* himself with them, or interpret the behavior of others as punishable, *projecting* his own tendencies. He may *rationalize* his behavior by giving reasons, either to himself or others, which make it nonpunishable—as in asserting that he is punishing a child for the child's own good.

There are more effective ways of avoiding punishment. One may avoid occasions on which punishable behavior is likely to occur. A person who has been punished for drunkenness may "put temptation behind him" by staying away from places where he is likely to drink too much; a student who has been punished for not studying may avoid situations in which he is distracted from his work. Still another strategy is to change the environment so that behavior is less likely to be punished. We reduce natural punishing contingencies when we repair a broken stairway so that we are less likely to fall, and we weaken punitive social contingencies by associating with more tolerant friends.

Still another strategy is to change the probability that punishable behavior will occur. A person who is frequently punished because he is quick to anger may count to ten before acting; he avoids punishment if, while he is counting, his inclination to act aggressively drops to a manageable level. Or he may make punishable behavior less likely by changing his physiological condition, controlling aggression, for example, by taking a tranquilizer. Men have even resorted to surgical means—castrating themselves, for example, or following the Biblical injunction to cut off the hand that offends. Punitive contingencies may also induce a man to seek out or construct environments in which he is likely to engage in behavior which displaces punishable forms; he stays out of trouble by keeping busy in nonpunished ways, as by doggedly "doing something else." (Much behavior which appears irrational in the sense that it seems to have no positively reinforcing consequences may have the effect of displacing behavior which is subject to punishment.) A person may even take steps to strengthen contingencies which teach him to stop behaving in punishable ways: he may, for example, take drugs under the influence of which smoking or drinking has strong aversive consequences, such as nausea, or he may expose himself to stronger ethical, religious, or governmental sanctions.

All these things a person may do to reduce the chances that he will be punished, but they may also be done for him by other people. Physical technology has reduced the number of occasions upon which people are naturally punished, and social environments have been changed to reduce the likelihood of punishment at the hands of others. Some familiar strategies may be noted.

Punishable behavior can be minimized by creating circumstances in which it is not likely to occur. The archetypal pattern is the cloister. In a world in which only simple foods are available, and in moderate supply, no one is subject to the natural punishment of overeating, or the social punishment of disapproval, or the religious punishment of gluttony as a venial sin. Heterosexual behavior is impossible when the sexes are segregated, and the vicarious sexual behavior evoked by pornography is impossible in the absence of pornographic material. "Prohibition" was an effort to control the consumption of alcohol by removing alcohol from the environment. It is still practiced in some states and almost universally to the extent that alcohol cannot be sold to minors or to anyone at certain times of day or on certain days. The care of the institutionalized alcoholic usually involves the control of supplies. The use of other addictive drugs is still controlled in the same way. Aggressive behavior which is otherwise uncontrollable is suppressed by putting a person in solitary confinement, where there is no one to aggress against. Theft is controlled by locking up everything likely to be stolen.

Another possibility is to break up the contingencies under which punished behavior is reinforced.

Temper tantrums often disappear when they no longer receive attention, aggressive behavior is attenuated by making sure that nothing is gained by it, and overeating is controlled by making foods less palatable. Another technique is to arrange circumstances under which behavior may occur without being punished. Saint Paul recommended marriage as a means of reducing objectionable forms of sexual behavior, and pornography has been recommended for the same reasons. Literature and art permit one to "sublimate" other kinds of troublesome behavior. Punishable behavior can also be suppressed by strongly reinforcing any behavior which displaces it. Organized sports are sometimes promoted on the grounds that they provide an environment in which young people will be too busy to get into trouble. If all this fails, punishable behavior may be made less likely by changing physiological conditions. Hormones may be used to change sexual behavior, surgery (as in lobotomy) to control violence, tranquilizers to control aggression, and appetite depressants to control overeating.

Measures of this sort are no doubt often inconsistent with each other and may have unforeseen consequences. It proved to be impossible to control the supply of alcohol during prohibition, and segregation of the sexes may lead to unwanted homosexuality. Excessive suppression of behavior which would otherwise be strongly reinforced may lead to defection from the punishing group. These problems are in essence soluble, however, and it should be possible to design a world in which behavior likely to be punished seldom or never occurs. We try to design such a world for those who cannot solve the problem of punishment for themselves, such as babies, retardates, or psychotics, and if it could be done for everyone, much time and energy would be saved.

The defenders of freedom and dignity object to solving the problem of punishment that way. Such a world builds only automatic goodness. T. H. Huxley saw nothing wrong with it: "If some great power would agree to make me always think what is true and do what is right, on condition of being some sort of a clock and wound up every morning before I got out of bed, I should close instantly with the offer." But Joseph Wood Krutch refers to this as the scarcely believable position of a "protomodern," and he shares T. S. Eliot's contempt for "systems so perfect that no one will need to be good."

The trouble is that when we punish a person for behaving badly, we leave it up to him to discover how to behave well, and he can then get credit for behaving well. But if he behaves well for the reasons we have just examined, it is the environment that must get the credit. At issue is an attribute of autonomous man. Men are to behave well only because they are good. Under a "perfect" system no one needs goodness.

There are, of course, valid reasons for thinking less of a person who is only automatically good, for he is a lesser person. In a world in which he does not need to work hard, he will not learn to sustain hard work. In a world in which medical science has alleviated pain, he will not learn to take painful stimuli. In a world which promotes automatic goodness, he will not learn to take the punishments associated with behaving badly. To prepare people for a world in which they cannot be good automatically, we need appropriate instruction, but that does not mean a permanently punitive environment, and there is no reason why progress toward a world in which people may be automatically good should be impeded. The problem is to induce people not to be good but to behave well.

The issue is again the visibility of control. As environmental contingencies become harder to see, the goodness of autonomous man becomes more apparent, and there are several reasons why punitive control becomes inconspicuous. A simple way to avoid punishment is to avoid punishers. Sex play becomes surreptitious, and a violent man attacks only when the police are not around. But the punisher may offset this by concealment. Parents frequently spy on their children, and policemen wear plain clothes. Escape must then become more subtle. If motorists obey speed laws only when the police are visible, speed may be monitored by radar, but the motorist may then install an electronic device which tells him when radar is in use. A state which converts all its citizens into spies or a religion which promotes the concept of an all-seeing God makes escape from the punisher practically impossible, and punitive contingencies are then maximally effective. People behave well although there is no visible supervision.

But the absence of a supervisor is easily misunderstood. It is commonly said that the control becomes internalized, which is simply another way of saying that it passes from the environment to autonomous man, but what happens is that it becomes less visible. One kind of control said to be internalized is represented by the Judaeo-Christian conscience and the Freudian superego. These indwelling agents speak in a still, small voice, telling a person what to do and, in particular, what not to do. The words are acquired from the community. The conscience and the superego are the vicars of society, and theologians and psychoanalysts alike recognize their external origins. Where the Old Adam or the id speaks for the personal good specified by man's genetic endowment, the conscience or superego speaks for what is good for others.

The conscience or superego does not arise simply from the concealment of punishers. It represents a number of auxiliary practices which make punitive sanctions more effective. We help a person avoid punishment by telling him about punitive contingencies, we warn him not to behave in ways which are likely to be punished, and we advise him to behave in ways which will not be punished. Many religious and governmental laws have these effects. They describe the contingencies under which some forms of behavior are punished and others not. Maxims, proverbs, and other forms of folk wisdom often supply useful rules. "Look before you leap" is an injunction derived from an analysis of certain kinds of contingencies: leaping without looking is more likely to be punished than looking and then possibly not leaping or leaping more skillfully. "Do not steal" is an injunction derived from social contingencies: people punish thieves.

By following the rules which others have derived from punitive contingencies in the natural and social environment a person can often avoid or escape punishment. Both the rules and the contingencies which generate rule-following behavior may be conspicuous, but they may also be learned and later remembered, and the process then becomes invisible. The individual tells himself what to do and what not to do, and it is easy to lose sight of the fact that he has been taught to do so by the verbal community. When a person derives his own rules from an analysis of punitive contingencies, we are particularly likely to give him credit for the good behavior which follows, but the visible stages have simply faded farther into history.

When the punitive contingencies are simply part of the nonsocial environment, it is reasonably clear what is happening. We do not allow a person to learn to drive a car by exposing him to serious punitive contingencies. We do not send him onto a busy highway without preparation and hold him responsible for everything that happens. We give him instruction in safe and skillful driving. We teach him rules. We let him begin to drive in a training device in which punitive contingencies are minimized or altogether lacking. We then take him onto a relatively safe highway. If we are successful, we may produce a safe and skillful driver without resorting to punishment at all, even though the contingencies under which he will drive for the rest of his life continue to be highly punitive. We are likely to say, without warrant, that he has acquired the "knowledge" he needs in order to drive safely or that he is now a "good driver" rather than a person who drives well. When the contingencies are social, and in particular when they are arranged by religious agencies, we are much more likely to infer an "inner knowledge of right" or an inner goodness.

The goodness to which good behavior is attributed is part of a person's worth or dignity and shows the same inverse relationship to the visibility of control. We attribute the greatest goodness to people who have never behaved badly and hence have never been punished and who behave well without following rules. Jesus is usually portrayed as such a person. We infer a lesser goodness in those who behave well but only because they have been punished. The reformed sinner may resemble a natural saint, but the fact that he has been exposed to punitive contingencies places some limit on his natural goodness. Close to the reformed sinner are those who have analyzed the punitive contingencies in their environments and derived rules which they have followed to avoid punishment. A lesser amount of goodness is attributed to those who follow rules formulated by others, and very little if the rules and the contingencies which maintain rule-governed behavior are conspicuous. We attribute no goodness at all to those who behave well only under constant supervision by a punitive agent such as the police.

Goodness, like other aspects of dignity or worth, waxes as visible control wanes, and so, of course, does freedom. Hence goodness and freedom tend to be associated. John Stuart Mill held that the only goodness worthy of the name was displayed by a person who behaved well although it was possible for him to behave badly and that only such a person was free. Mill was not in favor of closing houses of prostitution; they were to remain open so that people could achieve freedom and dignity through self-control. But the argument is convincing only if we neglect the reasons why people behave well when it is apparently possible for them to behave badly. It is one thing to prohibit the use of dice and playing cards, to prohibit the sale of alcohol, and to close houses of prostitution. It is another thing to make all these things aversive, as by punishing the behavior they evoke, by calling them temptations contrived by the devil, and by portraying the tragic fate of the drunkard or describing the venereal diseases acquired from prostitutes. The effect may be the same: people may not gamble, drink, or go to prostitutes, but the fact that they *cannot* do so in one environment and *do not* do so in the other is a fact about techniques of control, not about goodness or freedom. In one environment the reasons for behaving well are clear; in another they are easily overlooked and forgotten.

It is sometimes said that children are not ready for the freedom of self-control until they reach the age of reason, and that meanwhile they must either be kept in a safe environment or be punished. If punishment may be postponed until they reach the age of reason, it may be dispensed with altogether. But this means simply that safe environments and punishment are the only measures available until a child has been exposed to the contingencies which give him other reasons for behaving well. Appropriate contingencies can often not be arranged for primitive people, and the same confusion between visibility and internalized control is shown when it is said that primitive peoples are not ready for freedom. What, if anything, they are not ready for is a type of control which requires a special history of contingencies.

Many of the issues of punitive control are raised by the concept of responsibility, an attribute which is said to distinguish man from the other animals. The responsible person is a "deserving" person. We give him credit when he behaves well, in order that he will continue to do so, but we are most likely to use the term when what he deserves is punishment. We *hold* a person responsible for his conduct in the sense that he can be justly or fairly punished. This is again a matter of good husbandry, of a judicious use of reinforcers, of "making the punishment fit the crime." More punishment than necessary is costly and may suppress desirable behavior, while too little is wasteful if it has no effect at all.

The legal determination of responsibility (and justice) is in part concerned with facts. Did a person, indeed, behave in a given way? Were the circumstances such that the behavior was punishable under the law? If so, what laws apply, and what punishments are specified? But other questions seem to concern the inner man. Was the act intentional or premeditated? Was it done in the heat of anger? Did the person know the difference between right and wrong? Was he aware of the possible consequences of his act? All these questions about purposes, feelings, knowledge, and so on, can be restated in terms of the environment to which a person has been exposed. What a person "intends to do" depends upon what he has done in the past and what has then happened. A person does not act because he "feels angry"; he acts *and* feels angry for a common reason, not specified. Whether he deserves punishment when all these conditions are taken into account is a question about probable results: will he, if punished, behave in a different way when similar circumstances again arise? There is a current tendency to substitute controllability for responsibility, and controllability is not so likely to be regarded as a possession of autonomous man, since it explicitly alludes to external conditions.

The assertion that "only a free man can be responsible for his conduct" has two meanings, depending upon whether we are interested in freedom or responsibility. If we want to say that people are responsible, we must do nothing to infringe their freedom, since if they are not free to act they cannot be held responsible. If we want to say they are free, we must hold them responsible for their behavior by maintaining punitive contingencies, since if they behaved in the same way under conspicuous non-punitive contingencies, it would be clear that they were not free.

Any move toward an environment in which men are automatically good threatens responsibility. In the control of alcoholism, for example, the traditional practice is punitive. Drunkenness is called wrong, and ethical sanctions are imposed by a person's peers (the condition generated being felt as shame), or it is classified as illegal and subject to governmental sanctions (the condition generated being felt as guilt), or it is called sinful and punished by religious agencies (the condition generated being felt as a sense of sin). The practice has not been conspicuously successful, and other controlling measures have been sought. Certain medical evidence appears to be relevant. People differ in their tolerances to alcohol and their addictive dependencies. Once a person has become an alcoholic, he may drink to relieve severe withdrawal symptoms which are not always taken into account by those who have never experienced them. The medical aspects raise the question of responsibility: how fair is it to punish the alcoholic? From the point of view of husbandry, can we expect punishment to be effective against the opposing positive contingencies? Should we not rather treat the medical condition? . . . As responsibility diminishes, punishment is relaxed. . . .

The real issue is the effectiveness of techniques of control. We shall not solve the problems of alcoholism . . . by increasing a sense of responsibility. It is the environment which is "responsible" for the objectional behavior, and it is the environment, not some attribute of the individual, which must be changed. We recognize this when we talk about the punitive contingencies in the natural environment. Running head-on into a wall is punished by a blow to the skull, but we do not hold a man responsible for not running into walls nor do we say that nature holds him responsible. Nature simply punishes him when he runs into a wall. When we make the world less punishing or teach people how to avoid natural punishments, as by giving them rules to follow, we are not destroying responsibility or threatening any other occult quality. We are simply making the world safer.

The concept of responsibility is particularly weak when behavior is traced to genetic determiners. We may admire beauty, grace, and sensitivity, but we do not blame a person because he is ugly, spastic, or color blind. Less conspicuous forms of genetic endowment nevertheless cause trouble. Individuals presumably differ, as species differ, in the extent to which they respond aggressively or are reinforced when they effect aggressive damage, or in the extent to which they engage in sexual behavior or are affected by sexual reinforcement. Are they, therefore, equally responsible for controlling their aggressive or sexual behavior, and is it fair to punish them to the same extent? If we do not punish a person for a club foot, should we punish him for being quick to anger or highly susceptible to sexual reinforcement? The issue has recently been raised by the possibility that many criminals show an anomaly in their chromosomes. The concept of responsibility offers little help. The issue is controllability. We cannot change genetic defects by punishment; we can work only through genetic measures which operate on a much longer time scale. What must be changed is not the responsibility of autonomous man but the conditions, environmental or genetic, of which a person's behavior is a function.

Although people object when a scientific analysis traces their behavior to external conditions and thus deprives them of credit and the chance to be admired, they seldom object when the same analysis absolves them of blame. The crude environmentalism of the eighteenth and nineteenth centuries was quickly put to use for purposes of exoneration and exculpation. George Eliot ridiculed it. The rector in *Adam Bede* exclaims, "Why, yes, a man can't very well steal a bank-note unless the bank-note lies within convenient reach; but he won't make us think him an honest man because he begins to howl at the bank-note for falling in his way." The alcoholic is the first to claim that he is ill, and the juvenile delinquent that he is the victim of an unfavorable background; if they are not responsible, they cannot be justly punished.

Exoneration is in a sense the obverse of responsibility. Those who undertake to do something about human behavior—for any reason whatsoever—become part of the environment to which responsibility shifts. In the old view it was the student who failed, the child who went wrong, the citizen who broke the law, and the poor who were poor because they were idle, but it is now commonly said that there are no dull students but only poor teachers, no bad children but only bad parents, no delinquency except on the part of law enforcement agencies, and no indolent men but only poor incentive systems. But of course we must ask in turn why teachers, parents, governors, and entrepreneurs are bad. The mistake, as we shall see later, is to put the responsibility anywhere, to suppose that somewhere a causal sequence is initiated. . . .

Exoneration of the controller is seldom so easily documented, but something of the sort probably always underlies the continued use of punitive methods. Attacks on automatic goodness may show a concern for autonomous man, but the practical contingencies are more cogent. The literatures of freedom and dignity have made the control of human behavior a punishable offense, largely by holding the controller responsible for aversive results. The controller can escape responsibility if he can maintain the position that the individual himself is in control. The teacher who gives the student credit for learning can also blame him for not learning. The parent who gives his child credit for his achievements can also blame him for his mistakes. Neither the teacher nor the parent can be held responsible.

The genetic sources of human behavior are particularly useful in exoneration. If some races are less intelligent than others, the teacher cannot be blamed if he does not teach them as well. If some men are born criminals, the law will always be broken no matter how perfect the enforcing agency. If men make war because they are by nature aggressive, we need not be ashamed of our failure to keep the peace. A concern for exoneration is indicated by the fact that we are more likely to appeal to genetic endowment to explain undesirable results than positive accomplishments. Those who are currently interested in doing something about human behavior cannot be given credit for, or blamed for, consequences which can be traced to genetic sources; if they have any responsibility, it is to the future of the species. The practice of attributing behavior to genetic endowment—of the species as a whole or of some subdivision like a race or family—may affect breeding practices and eventually other ways of changing that endowment, and the contemporary individual may in a sense be held responsible for the consequences if he acts or fails to act, but the consequences are remote and raise a different kind of problem, to which we shall eventually turn.

Those who use punishment seem always to be on the safe side. Everyone approves the suppression of wrongdoing, except the wrongdoer. If those who are punished do not then do right, it is not the punisher's fault. But the exoneration is not complete. Even those who do right may take a long time to discover what to do and may never do it well. They spend time fumbling with irrelevant facts and wrestling with the devil, and in unnecessary trial-and-error exploration. Moreover, punishment causes pain, and no one wholly escapes or remains untouched even when the pain is suffered by others. The punisher cannot therefore entirely escape criticism, and he may "justify" his action by pointing to consequences of punishment which offset its aversive features.

It would be absurd to include the writings of Joseph de Maistre in the literatures of freedom and dignity, for he was bitterly opposed to their cardinal principles, particularly as expressed by the writers of the Enlightenment. Nevertheless, by opposing effective alternatives to punishment on the ground that punishment alone leaves the individual free to choose to behave well, those literatures have created a need for a kind of justification of which de Maistre was a master. Here is his defense of perhaps the most horrible of all punishers—the torturer and executioner.

> A somber signal is given: an abject minister of justice comes to knock at his door and let him know that he is needed. He sets out; he arrives at the public square, which is crowded with an

> eager excited throng. A prisoner or a murderer or a blasphemer is given over to him. He seizes him and stretches and ties him on a horizontal cross; he lifts his arm and a horrible silence falls. Nothing is heard but the cry of the bones cracking under the heavy rod and the howlings of the victim. Then he unties him and carries him to the wheel; the shattered limbs get twisted in the spokes; the head hangs; the hair stands out; and from the mouth, gaping open like a stove, come only now a few bloody words which at intervals beg for death. Now the executioner has finished; his heart beats, but it is for joy; he applauds himself, he says in his heart: "Nobody is better at the wheel than I!" He comes down and holds out his blood-stained hand, and the Law throws into it from a distance some gold pieces which he carries away with him through a double hedge of people who draw away in horror. He sits down to table and eats; then he gets into bed and goes to sleep. When he wakes up the next day, he begins to think about something quite different from the work he has been doing the day before. . . . All grandeur, all power, all discipline are founded on the executioner. He is the horror of the human association and the tie that holds it together. Take out of the world this incomprehensible agent, and at that instant will order give way to chaos, thrones fall and society vanish. God, who is the source of all sovereignty, is, therefore, the source of punishment, too.

If we no longer resort to torture in what we call the civilized world, we nevertheless still make extensive use of punitive techniques in both domestic and foreign relations. And apparently for good reasons. Nature if not God has created man in such a way that he can be controlled punitively. People quickly become skillful punishers (if not, thereby, skillful controllers), whereas alternative positive measures are not easily learned. The need for punishment seems to have the support of history, and alternative practices threaten the cherished values of freedom and dignity. And so we go on punishing—and defending punishment. A contemporary de Maistre might defend war in similar terms: "All grandeur, all power, all discipline are founded on the soldier. He is the horror of the human association and the tie that holds it together. Take out of the world this incomprehensible agent, and at that instant will order give way to chaos, governments fall and society vanish. God, who is the source of all sovereignty, is, therefore, the source of war, too."

Yet there are better ways, and the literatures of freedom and dignity are not pointing to them.

• • •

Except when physically constrained, a person is least free or dignified when under the threat of punishment. We should expect that the literatures of freedom and dignity would oppose punitive techniques, but in fact they have acted to preserve them. A person who has been punished is not thereby simply less inclined to behave in a given way; at best, he learns how to avoid punishment. Some ways of doing so are maladaptive or neurotic, as in the so-called "Freudian dynamisms." Other ways include avoiding situations in which punished behavior is likely to occur and doing things which are incompatible with punished behavior. Other people may take similar steps to reduce the likelihood that a person will be punished, but the literatures of freedom and dignity object to this as leading only to automatic goodness. Under punitive contingencies a person appears to be free to behave well and to deserve credit when he does so. Nonpunitive contingencies generate the same behavior, but a person cannot then be said to be free, and the contingencies deserve the credit when he behaves well. Little or nothing remains for autonomous man to do and receive credit for doing. He does not engage in moral struggle and therefore has no chance to be a moral hero or credited with inner virtues. But our task is not to encourage moral struggle or to build or demonstrate inner virtues. It is to make life less punishing and in doing so to release for more reinforcing activities the time and energy consumed in the avoidance of punishment. Up to a point the literatures of freedom and dignity have played a part in the slow and erratic alleviation of aversive features of the human environment, including the aversive features used in intentional control. But they have formulated the task in such a way that they cannot now accept the fact that all control is exerted by the environment and proceed to the design of better environments rather than of better men.

Compatibilism: The Case for Determinism and Its Compatibility with the Most Important Sense of Free Will

Freedom and Necessity*

A. J. AYER

A. J. Ayer (1910–1991), a distinguished British philosopher, was a leading spokesman for the school of philosophers known as Logical Positivists.

WHEN I AM SAID to have done something of my own free will it is implied that I could have acted otherwise; and it is only when it is believed that I could have acted otherwise that I am held to be morally responsible for what I have done. For a man is not thought to be morally responsible for an action that it was not in his power to avoid. But if human behaviour is entirely governed by causal laws, it is not clear how any action that is done could ever have been avoided. It may be said of the agent that he would have acted otherwise if the causes of his action had been different, but they being what they were, it seems to follow that he was bound to act as he did. Now it is commonly assumed both that men are capable of acting freely, in the sense that is required to make them morally responsible, and that human behaviour is entirely governed by causal laws: and it is the apparent conflict between these two assumptions that gives rise to the philosophical problem of the freedom of the will.

Confronted with this problem, many people will be inclined to agree with Dr. Johnson: 'Sir, we *know* our will is free, and *there's* an end on't.' But, while this does very well for those who accept Dr. Johnson's premiss, it would hardly convince anyone who denied the freedom of the will. Certainly, if we do know that our wills are free, it follows that they are so. But the logical reply to this might be that since our wills are not free, it follows that no one can know that they are: so that if anyone claims, like Dr. Johnson, to know that they are, he must be mistaken. What is evident, indeed, is that people often believe themselves to be acting freely; and it is to this 'feeling' of freedom that some philosophers appeal when they wish, in the supposed interests of morality, to prove that not all human action is causally determined. But if these philosophers are right in their assumption that a man cannot be acting freely if his action is causally determined, then the fact that someone feels free to do, or not to do, a certain action does not prove that he really is so. It may prove that the agent does not himself know what it is that makes him act in one way rather than another: but from the fact that a man is unaware of the causes of his action, it does not follow that no such causes exist.

So much may be allowed to the determinist; but his belief that all human actions are subservient to causal laws still remains to be justified. If, indeed, it is necessary that every event should have a cause, then the rule must apply to human behaviour as

**From A. J. Ayer, "Freedom and Necessity," in* Philosophical Essays *(London: Macmillan; New York: St. Martin's Press, 1954), pp. 271–284. Reprinted by permission of the author and St. Martin's Press, Inc., The Macmillan Company of Canada, Ltd., and Macmillan & Co. Ltd. First published in* Polemic, *5 (1946).*

much as to anything else. But why should it be supposed that every event must have a cause? The contrary is not unthinkable. Nor is the law of universal causation a necessary presupposition of scientific thought. The scientist may try to discover causal laws, and in many cases he succeeds; but sometimes he has to be content with statistical laws, and sometimes he comes upon events which, in the present state of his knowledge, he is not able to subsume under any law at all. In the case of these events he assumes that if he knew more he would be able to discover some law, whether causal or statistical, which would enable him to account for them. And this assumption cannot be disproved. For however far he may have carried his investigation, it is always open to him to carry it further; and it is always conceivable that if he carried it further he would discover the connection which had hitherto escaped him. Nevertheless, it is also conceivable that the events with which he is concerned are not systematically connected with any others: so that the reason why he does not discover the sort of laws that he requires is simply that they do not obtain.

Now in the case of human conduct the search for explanations has not in fact been altogether fruitless. Certain scientific laws have been established; and with the help of these laws we do make a number of successful predictions about the ways in which different people will behave. But these predictions do not always cover every detail. We may be able to predict that in certain circumstances a particular man will be angry, without being able to prescribe the precise form that the expression of his anger will take. We may be reasonably sure that he will shout, but not sure how loud his shout will be, or exactly what words he will use. And it is only a small proportion of human actions that we are able to forecast even so precisely as this. But that, it may be said, is because we have not carried our investigations very far. The science of psychology is still in its infancy and, as it is developed, not only will more human actions be explained, but the explanations will go into greater detail. The ideal of complete explanation may never in fact be attained: but it is theoretically attainable. Well, this may be so: and certainly it is impossible to show *a priori* that it is not so: but equally it cannot be shown that it is. This will not, however, discourage the scientist who, in the field of human behaviour, as elsewhere, will continue to formulate theories and test them by the facts. And in this he is justified. For since he has no reason *a priori* to admit that there is a limit to what he can discover, the fact that he also cannot be sure that there is no limit does not make it unreasonable for him to devise theories, nor, having devised them, to try constantly to improve them.

But now suppose it to be claimed that, so far as men's actions are concerned, there is a limit: and that this limit is set by the fact of human freedom. An obvious objection is that in many cases in which a person feels himself to be free to do, or not to do, a certain action, we are even now able to explain, in causal terms, why it is that he acts as he does. But it might be argued that even if men are sometimes mistaken in believing that they act freely, it does not follow that they are always so mistaken. For it is not always the case that when a man believes that he has acted freely we are in fact able to account for his action in causal terms. A determinist would say that we should be able to account for it if we had more knowledge of the circumstances, and had been able to discover the appropriate natural laws. But until those discoveries have been made, this remains only a pious hope. And may it not be true that, in some cases at least, the reason why we can give no causal explanation is that no causal explanation is available; and that this is because the agent's choice was literally free, as he himself felt it to be?

The answer is that this may indeed be true, inasmuch as it is open to anyone to hold that no explanation is possible until some explanation is actually found. But even so it does not give the moralist what he wants. For he is anxious to show that men are capable of acting freely in order to infer that they can be morally responsible for what they do. But if it is a matter of pure chance that a man should act in one way rather than another, he may be free but can hardly be responsible. And indeed when a man's actions seem to us quite unpredictable, when, as we say, there is no knowing what he will do, we do not look upon him as a moral agent. We look upon him as a lunatic.

To this it may be objected that we are not dealing fairly with the moralist. For when he makes it a condition of my being morally responsible that I should act freely, he does not wish to imply that it is purely a matter of chance that I act as I do. What he wishes to imply is that my actions are the result of my own free choice: and it is because they are the result of my own free choice that I am held to be morally responsible for them.

But now we must ask how it is that I come to make my choice. Either it is an accident that I choose to act as I do or it is not. If it is an accident, then it is merely a matter of chance that I did not choose otherwise; and if it is merely a matter of chance that I did not choose otherwise, it is surely irrational to hold me morally responsible for choosing as I did. But if it is not an accident that I choose to do one thing rather than another, then presumably there is some causal explanation of my choice: and in that case we are led back to determinism.

Again, the objection may be raised that we are not doing justice to the moralist's case. His view is not that it is a matter of chance that I choose to act as I do, but rather that my choice depends upon my character. Nevertheless he holds that I can still be free in the sense that he requires; for it is I who am responsible for my character. But in what way am I responsible for my character? Only, surely, in the sense that there is a causal connection between what I do now and what I have done in the past. It is only this that justifies the statement that I have made myself what I am: and even so this is an oversimplification, since it takes no account of the external influences to which I have been subjected. But, ignoring the external influences, let us assume that it is in fact the case that I have made myself what I am. Then it is still legitimate to ask how it is that I have come to make myself one sort of person rather than another. And if it be answered that it is a matter of my strength of will, we can put the same question in another form by asking how it is that my will has the strength that it has and not some other degree of strength. Once more, either it is an accident or it is not. If it is an accident, then by the same argument as before, I am not morally responsible, and if it is not an accident we are led back to determinism.

Furthermore, to say that my actions proceed from my character or, more colloquially, that I act in character, is to say that my behaviour is consistent and to that extent predictable: and since it is, above all, for the actions that I perform in character that I am held to be morally responsible, it looks as if the admission of moral responsibility, so far from being incompatible with determinism, tends rather to presuppose it. But how can this be so if it is a necessary condition of moral responsibility that the person who is held responsible should have acted freely? It seems that if we are to retain this idea of moral responsibility, we must either show that men can be held responsible for actions which they do not do freely, or else find some way of reconciling determinism with the freedom of the will.

It is no doubt with the object of effecting this reconciliation that some philosophers have defined freedom as the consciousness of necessity. And by so doing they are able to say not only that a man can be acting freely when his action is causally determined, but even that his action must be causally determined for it to be possible for him to be acting freely. Nevertheless this definition has the serious disadvantage that it gives to the word 'freedom' a meaning quite different from any that it ordinarily bears. It is indeed obvious that if we are allowed to give the word 'freedom' any meaning that we please, we can find a meaning that will reconcile it with determinism: but this is no more a solution of our present problem than the fact that the word 'horse' could be arbitrarily used to mean what is ordinarily meant by 'sparrow' is a proof that horses have wings. For suppose that I am compelled by another person to do something 'against my will.' In that case, as the word 'freedom' is ordinarily used, I should not be said to be acting freely: and the fact that I am fully aware of the constraint to which I am subjected makes no difference to the matter. I do not become free by becoming conscious that I am not. It may, indeed, be possible to show that my being aware that my action is causally determined is not incompatible with my acting freely: but it by no means follows that it is in this that my freedom consists. Moreover, I suspect that one of the reasons why people are inclined to define freedom as the consciousness of necessity is that they think that if one is conscious of necessity one may somehow be able to master it. But this is a fallacy. It is like someone's saying that he wishes he could see into the future, because if he did he would know what calamities lay in wait for him and so would be able to avoid them. But if he avoids the calamities then they don't lie in the future and it is not true that he foresees them. And similarly if I am able to master necessity, in the sense of escaping the operation of a necessary law, then the law in question is not necessary. And if the law is not necessary, then neither my freedom nor anything else can consist in my knowing that it is.

Let it be granted, then, when we speak of reconciling freedom with determination we are using the word 'freedom' in an ordinary sense. It still remains for us to make this usage clear: and perhaps the best way to make it clear is to show what it is that freedom, in this sense, is contrasted with. Now we began with the assumption that freedom is contrasted with causality: so that a man cannot be said to be acting freely if his action is causally determined. But this assumption has led us into difficulties and I now wish to suggest that it is mistaken. For it is not, I think, causality that freedom is to be contrasted with, but constraint. And while it is true that being constrained to do an action entails being caused to do it, I shall try to show that the converse does not hold. I shall try to show that from the fact that my action is causally determined it does not necessarily follow that I am constrained to do it: and this is equivalent to saying that it does not necessarily follow that I am not free.

If I am constrained, I do not act freely. But in what circumstances can I legitimately be said to be constrained? An obvious instance is the case in which I am compelled by another person to do what he wants. In a case of this sort the compulsion need not be such as to deprive one of the power of choice. It is not required that the other person should have hypnotized me, or that he should make it physically impossible for me to go against his will. It is enough that he should induce me to do what he wants by making it clear to me that, if I do not, he will bring about some situation that I regard as even more undesirable than the consequences of the action that he wishes me to do. Thus, if the man points a pistol at my head I may still choose to disobey him: but this does not prevent its being true that if I do fall in with his wishes he can legitimately be said to have compelled me. And if the circumstances are such that no reasonable person would be expected to choose the other alternative, then the action that I am made to do is not one for which I am held to be morally responsible.

A similar, but still somewhat different, case is that in which another person has obtained an habitual ascendancy over me. Where this is so, there may be no question of my being induced to act as the other person wishes by being confronted with a still more disagreeable alternative: for if I am sufficiently under his influence this special stimulus will not be necessary. Nevertheless I do not act freely, for the reason that I have been deprived of the power of choice. And this means that I have acquired so strong a habit of obedience that I no longer go through any process of deciding whether or not to do what the other person wants. About other matters I may still deliberate; but as regards the fulfilment of this other person's wishes, my own deliberations have ceased to be a causal factor in my behaviour. And it is in this sense that I may be said to be constrained. It is not, however, necessary that such constraint should take the form of subservience to another person. A kleptomaniac is not a free agent, in respect of his stealing, because he does not go through any process of deciding whether or not to steal. Or rather, if he does go through such a process, it is irrelevant to his behaviour. Whatever he resolved to do, he would steal all the same. And it is this that distinguishes him from the ordinary thief.

But now it may be asked whether there is any essential difference between these cases and those in which the agent is commonly thought to be free. No doubt the ordinary thief does go through a process of deciding whether or not to steal, and no doubt it does affect his behaviour. If he resolved to refrain from stealing, he could carry his resolution out. But if it be allowed that his making or not making this resolution is causally determined, then how can he be any more free than the kleptomaniac? It may be true that unlike the kleptomaniac he could refrain from stealing if he chose: but if there is a cause, or set of causes, which necessitate his choosing as he does, how can he be said to have the power of choice? Again, it may be true that no one now compels me to get up and walk across the room: but if my doing so can be causally explained in terms of my history or my environment, or whatever it may be, then how am I any more free than if some other person had compelled me? I do not have the feeling of constraint that I have when a pistol is manifestly pointed at my head; but the chains of causation by which I am bound are no less effective for being invisible.

The answer to this is that the cases I have mentioned as examples of constraint do differ from the others: and they differ just in the ways that I have tried to bring out. If I suffered from a compulsion neurosis, so that I got up and walked across the room, whether I wanted to or not, or if I did so because somebody else compelled me, then I should not be acting freely. But if I do it now, I shall be acting freely, just because these conditions do not obtain; and the fact that my action may nevertheless have a cause is, from this point of view, irrelevant. For it is not when my action has any cause at all, but only when it has a special sort of cause, that it is reckoned not to be free.

But here it may be objected that, even if this distinction corresponds to ordinary usage, it is still very irrational. For why should we distinguish, with regard to a person's freedom, between the operations of one sort of cause and those of another? Do not all causes equally necessitate? And is it not therefore arbitrary to say that a person is free when he is necessitated in one fashion but not when he is necessitated in another?

That all causes equally necessitate is indeed a tautology, if the word 'necessitate' is taken merely as equivalent to 'cause': but if, as the objection requires, it is taken as equivalent to 'constrain' or 'compel,' then I do not think that this proposition is true. For all that is needed for one event to be the cause of another is that, in the given circumstances, the event which is said to be the effect would not have occurred if it had not been for the occurrence of the event which is said to be the cause, or vice versa, according as causes are interpreted as necessary, or sufficient, conditions: and this fact is usually deducible from some causal law which states that whenever an event of the one kind occurs then, given suitable conditions, an event of the other kind will occur in a certain temporal or spatio-temporal relationship to it. In short, there is an invariable concomitance between the two classes of events; but there is no compulsion, in any but a metaphorical sense. Suppose, for example, that a psychoanalyst is able to account for some aspect of my behaviour by referring it to some lesion that I suffered in my childhood. In that case, it may be said that my childhood experience, together with certain other events, necessitates my behaving as I do. But all that this involves is that it is found to be true in general that when people have had certain experiences as children, they subsequently behave in certain specifiable ways; and my case is just another instance of this general law. It is in this way indeed that my behaviour is explained. But from the fact that my behaviour is capable of being explained, in the sense that it can be subsumed under some natural law, it does not follow that I am acting under constraint.

If this is correct, to say that I could have acted otherwise is to say, first, that I should have acted otherwise if I had so chosen; secondly, that my action was voluntary in the sense in which the actions, say, of the kleptomaniac are not; and thirdly, that nobody compelled me to choose as I did: and these three conditions may very well be fulfilled. When they are fulfilled, I may be said to have acted freely. But this is not to say that it was a matter of chance that I acted as I did, or, in other words, that my action could not be explained. And that my actions should be capable of being explained is all that is required by the postulate of determinism.

If more than this seems to be required it is, I think, because the use of the very word 'determinism' is in some degree misleading. For it tends to suggest that one event is somehow in the power of another, whereas the truth is merely that they are factually correlated. And the same applies to the use, in this context, of the word 'necessity' and even of the word 'cause' itself. Moreover, there are various reasons for this. One is the tendency to confuse causal with logical necessitation, and so to infer mistakenly that the effect is contained in the cause. Another is the uncritical use of a concept of force which is derived from primitive experiences of pushing and striking. A third is the survival of an animistic conception of causality, in which all causal relationships are modelled on the example of one person's exercising authority over another. As a result we tend to form an imaginative picture of an unhappy effect trying vainly to escape from the clutches of an over-mastering cause. But, I repeat, the fact is simply that when an event of one type occurs, an event of another type occurs also, in a certain temporal or spatio-temporal relation to the first. The rest is only metaphor. And it is because of the metaphor, and not because of the fact, that we come to think that there is an antithesis between causality and freedom.

Nevertheless, it may be said, if the postulate of determinism is valid, then the future can be explained in terms of the past: and this means that if one knew enough about the past one would be able to predict the future. But in that case what will happen in the future is already decided. And how then can I be said to be free? What is going to happen is going to happen and nothing that I do can prevent it. If the determinist is right, I am the helpless prisoner of fate.

But what is meant by saying that the future course of events is already decided? If the implication is that some person has arranged it, then the proposition is false. But if all that is meant is that it is possible, in principle, to deduce it from a set of particular facts about the past, together with the appropriate general laws, then, even if this is true, it does not in the least entail that I am the helpless prisoner of fate. It does not even entail that my actions make no difference to the future: for they are causes as well as effects; so that if they were different their consequences would be different also. What it does entail is that my behaviour can be predicted: but to say that my behaviour can be predicted is not to say that I am acting under constraint. It is indeed true that I cannot escape my destiny if this is taken to mean no more than that I shall do what I shall do. But this is a tautology, just as it is a tautology that what is going to happen is going to happen. And such tautologies as these prove nothing whatsoever about the freedom of the will.

The Problem of Free Will*

WALTER T. STACE

Walter Stace (1886–1967) wrote books on Greek philosophy and the philosophy of religion. He taught at Princeton University.

[A] GREAT PROBLEM which the rise of scientific naturalism has created for the modern mind concerns the foundations of morality. The old religious foundations have largely crumbled away, and it may well be thought that the edifice built upon them by generations of men is in danger of collapse. A total collapse of moral behavior is . . . very unlikely. For a society in which this occurred could not survive.

Nevertheless the danger to moral standards inherent in the virtual disappearance of their old religious foundations is not illusory.

I shall first discuss the problem of free will, for it is certain that if there is no free will there can be no morality. Morality is concerned with what men ought and ought not to do. But if a man has no freedom to choose what he will do, if whatever he does is done under compulsion, then it does not make sense to tell him that he ought not to have done what he did and that he ought to do something different. All moral precepts would in such case be meaningless. Also if he acts always under compulsion, how can he be held morally responsible for his actions? How can he, for example, be punished for what he could not help doing?

It is to be observed that those learned professors of philosophy or psychology who deny the existence of free will do so only in their professional moments and in their studies and lecture rooms. For when it comes to doing anything practical, even of the most trivial kind, they invariably behave as if they and others were free. They inquire from you at dinner whether you will choose this dish or that dish. They will ask a child why he told a lie, and will punish him for not having chosen the way of truthfulness. All of which is inconsistent with a disbelief in free will. This should cause us to suspect that the problem is not a real one; and this, I believe, is the case. The dispute is merely verbal, and is due to nothing but a confusion about the meanings of words. It is what is now fashionably called a semantic problem.

How does a verbal dispute arise? Let us consider a case which, although it is absurd in the sense that no one would ever make the mistake which is involved in it, yet illustrates the principle which we shall have to use in the solution of the problem. Suppose that someone believed that the word "man" means a certain sort of five-legged animal; in short that "five-legged animal" is the correct *definition* of man. He might then look around the world, and rightly observing that there are no five-legged animals in it, he might proceed to deny the existence of men. This preposterous conclusion would have been reached because he was using an incorrect definition of "man." All you would have to do to show him his mistake would be to give him the correct definition; or at least to show him that his definition was wrong. Both the problem and its solution would, of course, be entirely verbal. The problem of free will, and its solution, I shall maintain, is verbal in exactly the same way. The problem has been created by the fact that learned men, especially philosophers, have assumed an incorrect definition of free will, and then finding that there is nothing in the world which answers to their definition, have denied its existence. As far as logic is concerned, their conclusion is just as absurd as that of the man who denies the existence of men. The only difference is that the mistake in the latter case is obvious and crude, while the mistake which the deniers of free will have made is rather subtle and difficult to detect.

Throughout the modern period, until quite recently, it was assumed, both by the philosophers who denied free will and by those who defended it, that *determinism is inconsistent with free will.* If a man's actions were wholly determined by chains of causes stretching back into the remote past, so that they could be predicted beforehand by a mind which knew all the causes, it was assumed that they could not in that case be free. This implies that a certain definition of actions done from free will was assumed, namely that they are actions *not* wholly determined by causes or predictable beforehand. Let us shorten this by saying that free will was defined as meaning indeterminism. This is the incorrect definition which has led to the denial of free will. As soon as we see what the true definition is we shall find that the question whether the world is deterministic, as Newtonian science implied, or in a measure indeterministic, as current physics teaches, is wholly irrelevant to the problem.

Of course there is a sense in which one can define a word arbitrarily in any way one pleases. But a definition may nevertheless be called correct or incorrect. It is correct if it accords with a *common usage* of the word defined. It is incorrect if it does not. And if you give an incorrect definition, absurd and untrue results are likely to follow. For instance, there is nothing to prevent you from arbitrarily defining a man as a five-legged animal, but this is incorrect in the sense that it does not accord with the ordinary meaning of the word. Also it has the absurd result of leading to a denial of the existence of men. This shows that *common usage is the criterion for deciding whether a definition is correct or not.* And this is the principle which I shall apply to free will. I shall show that indeterminism is not what is meant by the phrase "free will" *as it is commonly used.* And I shall attempt to discover the correct definition by inquiring how the phrase is used in ordinary conversation.

Here are a few samples of how the phrase might be used in ordinary conversation. It will be noticed that they include cases in which the question whether a man acted with free will is asked in order to determine whether he was morally and legally responsible for his acts.

Jones. I once went without food for a week.
Smith. Did you do that of your own free will?
Jones. No. I did it because I was lost in a desert and could find no food.

But suppose that the man who had fasted was Mahatma Gandhi. The conversation might then have gone:

Gandhi. I once fasted for a week.
Smith. Did you do that of your own free will?
Gandhi. Yes. I did it because I wanted to compel the British Government to give India its independence.

Take another case. Suppose that I had stolen some bread, but that I was as truthful as George Washington. Then, if I were charged with the crime in court, some exchange of the following sort might take place:

Judge. Did you steal the bread of your own free will?
Stace. Yes. I stole it because I was hungry.

Or in different circumstances the conversation might run:

Judge. Did you steal of your own free will?
Stace. No. I stole because my employer threatened to beat me if I did not.

At a recent murder trial in Trenton some of the accused had signed confessions, but afterwards asserted that they had done so under police duress. The following exchange might have occurred:

Judge. Did you sign this confession of your own free will?
Prisoner. No. I signed it because the police beat me up.

Now suppose that a philosopher had been a member of the jury. We could imagine this conversation taking place in the jury room.

Foreman of the Jury. The prisoner says he signed the confession because he was beaten, and not of his own free will.
Philosopher. This is quite irrelevant to the case. There is no such thing as free will.
Foreman. Do you mean to say that it makes no difference whether he signed because his conscience made him want to tell the truth or because he was beaten?
Philosopher. None at all. Whether he was caused to sign by a beating or by some desire of his own—the desire to tell the truth, for example—in either case his signing was causally determined, and therefore in neither case did he act of his own free will. Since there is no such thing as free will, the question whether he signed of his own free will ought not to be discussed by us.

The foreman and the rest of the jury would rightly conclude that the philosopher must be making some mistake. What sort of a mistake could it be? There is only one possible answer. The philosopher must be using the phrase "free will" in some peculiar way of his own which is not the way in which men usually use it when they wish to determine a question of moral responsibility. That is, he must be using an incorrect definition of it as implying action not determined by causes.

Suppose a man left his office at noon, and were questioned about it. Then we might hear this:

Jones. Did you go out of your own free will?
Smith. Yes. I went out to get my lunch.

But we might hear:

Jones. Did you leave your office of your own free will?

Smith. No. I was forcibly removed by the police.

We have now collected a number of cases of actions which, in the ordinary usage of the English language, would be called cases in which people have acted of their own free will. We should also say in all these cases that they *chose* to act as they did. We should also say that they could have acted otherwise, if they had chosen. For instance, Mahatma Gandhi was not compelled to fast; he chose to do so. He could have eaten if he had wanted to. When Smith went out to get his lunch, he chose to do so. He could have stayed and done some more work, if he had wanted to. We have also collected a number of cases of the opposite kind. They are cases in which men were not able to exercise their free will. They had no choice. They were compelled to do as they did. The man in the desert did not fast of his own free will. He had no choice in the matter. He was compelled to fast because there was nothing for him to eat. And so with the other cases. It ought to be quite easy, by an inspection of these cases, to tell what we ordinarily mean when we say that a man did or did not exercise free will. We ought therefore to be able to extract from them the proper definition of the term. Let us put the cases in a table:

Free Acts	*Unfree Acts*
Gandhi fasting because he wanted to free India.	The man fasting in the desert because there was no food.
Stealing bread because one is hungry.	Stealing because one's employer threatened to beat one.
Signing a confession because one wanted to tell the truth.	Signing because the police beat one.
Leaving the office because one wanted one's lunch.	Leaving because forcibly removed.

It is obvious that to find the correct definition of free acts we must discover what characteristic is common to all the acts in the left-hand column, and is, at the same time, absent from all the acts in the right-hand column. This characteristic which all free acts have, and which no unfree acts have, will be the defining characteristic of free will.

Is being uncaused, or not being determined by causes, the characteristic of which we are in search? It cannot be, because although it is true that all the acts in the right-hand column have causes, such as the beating by the police or the absence of food in the desert, so also do the acts in the left-hand column. Mr. Gandhi's fasting was caused by his desire to free India, the man leaving his office by his hunger, and so on. Moreover there is no reason to doubt that these causes of the free acts were in turn caused by prior conditions, and that these were again the results of causes, and so on back indefinitely into the past. Any physiologist can tell us the causes of hunger. What caused Mr. Gandhi's tremendously powerful desire to free India is no doubt more difficult to discover. But it must have had causes. Some of them may have lain in peculiarities of his glands or brain, others in his past experiences, others in his heredity, others in his education. Defenders of free will have usually tended to deny such facts. But to do so is plainly a case of special pleading, which is unsupported by any scrap of evidence. The only reasonable view is that all human actions, both those which are freely done and those which are not, are either wholly determined by causes, or at least as much determined as other events in nature. It may be true, as the physicists tell us, that nature is not as deterministic as was once thought. But whatever degree of determinism prevails in the world, human actions appear to be as much determined as anything else. And if this is so, it cannot be the case that what distinguishes actions freely chosen from those which are not free is that the latter are determined by causes while the former are not. Therefore, being uncaused or being undetermined by causes, must be an incorrect definition of free will.

What, then, is the difference between acts which are freely done and those which are not? What is the characteristic which is present to all the acts in the left-hand column and absent from all those in the right-hand column? Is it not obvious that, although both sets of actions have causes, the causes of those in the left-hand column are *of a different kind* from the causes of those in the right-hand column? The free acts are all caused by desires, or motives, or by some sort of internal psychological states of the agent's mind. The unfree acts, on the other hand, are all caused by physical forces or physical conditions, outside the agent. Police arrest means physical force exerted from the outside; the absence of food in the desert is a physical condition of the outside world. We may therefore frame the following rough definitions. *Acts freely done are those whose immediate causes are psychological states in the agent. Acts not freely done are those whose immediate causes are states of affairs external to the agent.*

It is plain that if we define free will in this way, then free will certainly exists, and the philosopher's denial of its existence is seen to be what it is—nonsense. For it is obvious that all those actions of men which we should ordinarily attribute to the exercise of their free will, or of which we should say that they freely chose to do them, are in fact actions which have been caused by their own desires, wishes, thoughts, emotions, impulses, or other psychological states.

In applying our definition we shall find that it usually works well, but that there are some puzzling cases which it does not seem exactly to fit. These puzzles can always be solved by paying careful attention to the ways in which words are used, and remembering that they are not always used consistently. I have space for only one example. Suppose that a thug threatens to shoot you unless you give him your wallet, and suppose that you do so. Do you, in giving him your wallet, do so of your own free will or not? If we apply our definition, we find that you acted freely, since the immediate cause of the action was not an actual outside force but the fear of death, which is a psychological cause. Most people, however, would say that you did not act of your own free will but under compulsion. Does this show that our definition is wrong? I do not think so. Aristotle, who gave a solution of the problem of free will substantially the same as ours (though he did not use the term "free will") admitted that there are what he called "mixed" or borderline cases in which it is difficult to know whether we ought to call the acts free or compelled. In the case under discussion, though no actual force was used, the gun at your forehead so nearly approximated to actual force that we tend to say the case was one of compulsion. It is a borderline case.

Here is what may seem like another kind of puzzle. According to our view an action may be free though it could have been predicted beforehand with certainty. But suppose you told a lie, and it was certain beforehand that you would tell it. How could one then say, "You could have told the truth"? The answer is that it is perfectly true that you could have told the truth *if* you had wanted to. In fact you would have done so, for in that case the causes producing your action, namely your desires, would have been different, and would therefore have produced different effects. It is a delusion that predictability and free will are incompatible. This agrees with common sense. For if, knowing your character, I predict that you will act honorably, no one would say when you do act honorably, that this shows you did not do so of your own free will.

Since free will is a condition of moral responsibility, we must be sure that our theory of free will gives a sufficient basis for it. To be held morally responsible for one's actions means that one may be justly punished or rewarded, blamed or praised, for them. But it is not just to punish a man for what he cannot help doing. How can it be just to punish him for an action which it was certain beforehand that he would do? We have not attempted to decide whether, as a matter of fact, all events, including human actions, are completely determined. For that question is irrelevant to the problem of free will. But if we assume for the purposes of argument that complete determinism is true, but that we are nevertheless free, it may then be asked whether such a deterministic free will is compatible with moral responsibility. For it may seem unjust to punish a man for an action which it could have been predicted with certainty beforehand that he would do.

But that determinism is incompatible with moral responsibility is as much a delusion as that it is incompatible with free will. You do not excuse a man for doing a wrong act because, knowing his character, you felt certain beforehand that he would do it. Nor do you deprive a man of a reward or prize because, knowing his goodness or his capabilities, you felt certain beforehand that he would win it.

Volumes have been written on the justification of punishment. But so far as it affects the question of free will, the essential principles involved are quite simple. The punishment of a man for doing a wrong act is justified, either on the ground that it will correct his own character, or that it will deter other people from doing similar acts. The instrument of punishment has been in the past, and no doubt still is, often unwisely used; so that it may often have done more harm than good. But that is not relevant to our present problem. Punishment, if and when it is justified, is justified only on one or both of the grounds just mentioned. The question then is how, if we assume determinism, punishment can correct character or deter people from evil actions.

Suppose that your child develops a habit of telling lies. You give him a mild beating. Why? Because you believe that his personality is such that the usual motives for telling the truth do not cause him to do so. You therefore supply the missing cause, or motive, in the shape of pain and the fear of future pain if he repeats his untruthful behavior. And you hope that a few treatments of this kind will condition him to the habit of truth-telling, so that he will come to tell the truth without the infliction of pain. You assume that his actions are determined by causes, but that the usual causes of truth-telling do not in him produce their usual effects. You therefore supply him with an artificially injected motive, pain and fear, which you think will in the future cause him to speak truthfully.

The principle is exactly the same where you hope, by punishing one man, to deter others from wrong actions. You believe that the fear of punishment will cause those who might otherwise do evil to do well.

We act on the same principle with non-human, and even with inanimate, things, if they do not behave in the way we think they ought to behave. The rose bushes in the garden produce only small and poor blooms, whereas we want large and rich ones. We supply a cause which will produce large blooms, namely fertilizer. Our automobile does not go properly. We supply a cause which will make it go better, namely oil in the works. The punishment for the man, the fertilizer for the plant, and the oil for the car, are all justified by the same principle and in the same way. The only difference is that different kinds of things require different kinds of causes to make them do what they should. Pain may be the appropriate remedy to apply, in certain cases, to human beings, and oil to the machine. It is, of course, of no use to inject motor oil into the boy or to beat the machine.

Thus we see that moral responsibility is not only consistent with determinism, but requires it. The assumption on which punishment is based is that human behavior is causally determined. If pain could not be a cause of truth-telling there would be no justification at all for punishing lies. If human actions and volitions were uncaused, it would be useless either to punish or reward, or indeed to do anything else to correct people's bad behavior. For nothing that you could do would in any way influence them. Thus moral responsibility would entirely disappear. If there were no determinism of human beings at all, their actions would be completely unpredictable and capricious, and therefore irresponsible. And this is in itself a strong argument against the common view of philosophers that free will means being undetermined by causes.

Libertarianism: The Case for Free Will and Its Incompatibility with Determinism

Has the Self 'Free Will'?*

C. A. CAMPBELL

C. A. Campbell (1897–1974) taught for many years at the University of Glasgow.

. . . IT IS SOMETHING OF A TRUISM that in philosophic enquiry the exact formulation of a problem often takes one a long way on the road to its solution. In the case of the Free Will problem I think there is a rather special need of careful formulation. For there are many sorts of human freedom; and it can easily happen that one wastes a great deal of labour in proving or disproving a freedom which has almost nothing to do with the freedom which is at issue in the traditional problem of Free Will. The abortiveness of so much of the argument for and against Free Will in contemporary philosophical literature seems to me due in the main to insufficient pains being taken over the preliminary definition of the problem. There is, indeed, one outstanding exception, Professor Broad's brilliant inaugural lecture entitled, 'Determinism, Indeterminism, and Libertarianism,'[1] in which forty-three pages are devoted to setting out the problem, as against seven to its solution! I confess that the solution does not seem to myself to follow upon the formulation quite as easily as all that:[2] but Professor Broad's eminent example fortifies me in my decision to give here what may seem at first sight a disproportionate amount of time to the business of determining the essential characteristics of the kind of freedom with which the traditional problem is concerned.

Fortunately we can at least make a beginning with a certain amount of confidence. It is not seriously disputable that the kind of freedom in question is the freedom which is commonly recognised to be in some sense a precondition of moral responsibility. Clearly, it is on account of this integral connection with moral responsibility that such exceptional importance has always been felt to attach to the Free Will problem. But in what precise sense is free will a precondition of moral responsibility, and thus a postulate of the moral life in general? This is an exceedingly troublesome question; but until we have satisfied ourselves about the answer to it, we are not in a position to state, let alone decide, the question whether 'Free Will' in its traditional, ethical, significance is a reality.

Our first business, then, is to ask, exactly what kind of freedom is it which is required for moral responsibility? And as to method of procedure in this inquiry, there seems to me to be no real choice. I know of only one method that carries with it any hope of success; viz. the critical comparison of those acts for which, on due reflection, we deem it proper to attribute moral praise or blame to the agents, with those acts for which, on due reflection, we deem such judgments to be improper. The ultimate touchstone, as I see it, can only be our moral con-

*From C. A. Campbell, On Selfhood and Godhood (London: George Allen & Unwin, 1957, now Unwin Hyman of Harper-Collins Publishers Limited (UK), pp. 158–179. Reprinted by permission of George Allen & Unwin, Ltd.

sciousness as it manifests itself in our more critical and considered moral judgments. The 'linguistic' approach by way of the analysis of moral *sentences* seems to me, despite its present popularity, to be an almost infallible method for reaching wrong results in the moral field; but I must reserve what I have to say about this.

The first point to note is that the freedom at issue (as indeed the very name 'Free *Will* Problem' indicates) pertains primarily not to overt acts but to inner acts. The nature of things has decreed that, save in the case of one's self, it is only overt acts which one can directly observe. But a very little reflection serves to show that in our moral judgments upon others their overt acts are regarded as significant only in so far as they are the expression of inner acts. We do not consider the acts of a robot to be morally responsible acts; nor do we consider the acts of a man to be so save in so far as they are distinguishable from those of a robot by reflecting an inner life of choice. Similarly, from the other side, if we are satisfied (as we may on occasion be, at least in the case of ourselves) that a person has definitely elected to follow a course which he believes to be wrong, but has been prevented by external circumstances from translating his inner choice into an overt act, we still regard him as morally blameworthy. Moral freedom, then, pertains to *inner* acts.

The next point seems at first sight equally obvious and uncontroversial; but, as we shall see, it has awkward implications if we are in real earnest with it (as almost nobody is). It is the simple point that the act must be one of which the person judged can be regarded as the *sole* author. It seems plain enough that if there are any *other* determinants of the act, external to the self, to that extent the act is not an act which the *self* determines, and to that extent not an act for which the self can be held morally responsible. The self is only part-author of the act, and his moral responsibility can logically extend only to those elements within the act (assuming for the moment that these can be isolated) of which he is the *sole* author.

The awkward implications of this apparent truism will be readily appreciated. For, if we are mindful of the influences exerted by heredity and environment, we may well feel some doubt whether there is any act of will at all of which one can truly say that the self is sole author, sole determinant. No man has a voice in determining the raw material of impulses and capacities that constitute his hereditary endowment, and no man has more than a very partial control of the material and social environment in which he is destined to live his life. Yet it would be manifestly absurd to deny that these two factors do constantly and profoundly affect the nature of a man's choices. That this is so we all of us recognise in our moral judgments when we 'make allowances,' as we say, for a bad heredity or a vicious environment, and acknowledge in the victim of them a diminished moral responsibility for evil courses. Evidently we do *try,* in our moral judgments, however crudely, to praise or blame a man only in respect of that of which we can regard him as *wholly* the author. And evidently we do recognise that, for a man to be the author of an act in the full sense required for moral responsibility, it is not enough merely that he 'wills' or 'chooses' the act: since even the most unfortunate victim of heredity or environment does, as a rule, 'will' what he does. It is significant, however, that the ordinary man, though well enough aware of the influence upon choices of heredity and environment, does not feel obliged thereby to give up his assumption that moral predicates *are* somehow applicable. Plainly he still believes that there is *something* for which a man is morally responsible, something of which we can fairly say that he is the sole author. *What is this something?* To that question commonsense is not ready with an explicit answer—though an answer is, I think, implicit in the line which its moral judgments take. I shall do what I can to give an explicit answer later in this lecture. Meantime it must suffice to observe that, if we are to be true to the deliverances of our moral consciousness, it is very difficult to deny that *sole* authorship is a necessary condition of the morally responsible act.

Thirdly we come to a point over which much recent controversy has raged. We may approach it by raising the following question. Granted an act of which the agent is sole author, does this 'sole authorship' suffice to make the act a morally free act? We may be inclined to think that it does, until we contemplate the possibility that an act of which the agent is sole author might conceivably occur as a necessary expression of the agent's nature; the way in which, e.g. some philosophers have supposed the Divine act of creation to occur. This consideration excites a legitimate doubt; for it is far from easy to see how a person can be regarded as a proper subject for moral praise or blame in respect of an act which he *cannot help* performing—even if it be his own 'nature' which necessitates it. Must we not recognise it as a condition of the morally free act that the agent 'could have acted otherwise' than he in fact did? It is true, indeed, that we sometimes praise or blame a man for an act about which we are prepared to say, in the light of our knowledge of his established character, that he 'could no other.' But I think that a little reflection shows that in such cases we are not praising or blaming the man strictly for what he does *now* (or at any rate we ought not to be), but rather for those past acts of his which have generated the firm habit of mind from which his *present* act follows 'necessarily.' In other words, our praise and blame, so far as justified, are really retrospective, being directed not to the agent *qua* performing *this* act, but to the agent *qua* performing those past acts which have built up his present character, and in respect to which we presume that he *could* have acted otherwise, that there really *were* open possibilities before him. These cases, therefore, seem to me to constitute no valid exception to what I must take to be the rule, viz. that a man can be morally praised or blamed for an act only if he could have acted otherwise.

Now philosophers today are fairly well agreed that it is a postulate of the morally responsible act that the agent 'could have acted otherwise' in *some* sense of that phrase. But sharp differences of opinion have arisen over the way in which the phrase ought to be interpreted. There is a strong disposition to water down its apparent meaning by insisting that it is not (as a postulate of moral responsibility) to be understood as a straightforward categorical proposition, but rather as a disguised hypothetical proposition. All that we really require to be assured of, in order to justify our holding X morally responsible for an act, is, we are told, that X could have acted otherwise *if* he had *chosen* otherwise (Moore, Stevenson); or perhaps that X could have acted otherwise *if* he had had a different character, or *if* he had been placed in different circumstances.

I think it is easy to understand, and even, in a measure, to sympathise with, the motives which induce philosophers to offer these counter-interpretations. It is not just the fact that 'X could have acted otherwise,' as a bald categorical statement, is incompatible with the universal sway of causal law—though this is, to some philosophers, a serious stone of stumbling. The more widespread objection is that it at least looks as though it were incompatible with that causal continuity of an agent's character with his conduct which is implied when we believe (surely with justice) that we can often tell the sort of thing a man will do from our knowledge of the sort of man he is.

We shall have to make our accounts with that particular difficulty later. At this stage I wish merely to show that neither of the hypothetical propositions suggested—and I think the same could be shown for *any* hypothetical alternative—is an acceptable substitute for the categorical proposition 'X could have acted otherwise' as the presupposition of moral responsibility.

Let us look first at the earlier suggestion—'X could have acted otherwise *if* he had chosen otherwise.' Now clearly there are a great many acts with regard to which we are entirely satisfied that the agent is thus situated. We are often perfectly sure that—for this is all it amounts to—if X had chosen otherwise, the circumstances presented no external obstacle to the translation of that choice into action. For example, we often have no doubt at all that X, who in point of fact told a lie, could have told the truth *if* he had so chosen. But does our confidence on this score allay all legitimate doubts about whether X is really blameworthy? Does it entail that X is free in the sense required for moral responsibility? Surely not. The obvious question immediately arises: 'But *could* X have *chosen* otherwise than he did?' It is doubt about the true answer to *that* question which leads most people to doubt the reality of moral responsibility. Yet on this crucial question the hypothetical proposition which is offered as a sufficient statement of the condition justifying the ascription of moral responsibility gives us no information whatsoever.

Indeed this hypothetical substitute for the categorical 'X could have acted otherwise' seems to me to lack all plausibility unless one contrives to forget why it is, after all, that we ever come to feel fundamental doubts about man's moral responsibility. Such doubts are born, surely, when one becomes aware of certain reputable world-views in religion or philosophy, or of certain reputable scientific beliefs, which in their several ways imply that man's actions are necessitated, and thus could not be otherwise than they in fact are. But clearly a doubt so based is not even touched by the recognition that a man could very often act otherwise *if* he so chose. That proposition is entirely compatible with the necessitarian theories which generate our doubt: indeed it is this very compatibility that has recommended it to some philosophers, who are reluctant to give up either moral responsibility or Determinism. The proposition which we *must* be able to affirm if moral praise or blame of X is to be justified is the categorical proposition that X could have acted otherwise because—not if—he could have chosen otherwise; or, since it is essentially the inner side of the act that matters, the proposition simply that X could have chosen otherwise.

For the second of the alternative formulae suggested we cannot spare more than a few moments. But its inability to meet the demands it is required to meet is almost transparent. 'X could have acted otherwise,' as a statement of a precondition of X's moral responsibility, really means (we are told) 'X could have acted otherwise *if* he were differently constituted, or *if* he had been placed in different circumstances.' It seems a sufficient reply to this to point out that the person whose moral responsibility is at issue is X; a specific individual, in a specific set of circumstances. It is totally irrelevant to X's moral responsibility that we should be able to say that some person differently constituted from X, or X in a different set of circumstances, could have done something different from what X did.

Let me, then, briefly sum up the answer at which we have arrived to our question about the kind of freedom required to justify moral responsibility. It is that a man can be said to exercise free will in a morally significant sense only in so far as his chosen act is one of which he is the sole cause or author, and only if—in the straightforward, categorical sense of the phrase—he 'could have chosen otherwise.'

I confess that this answer is in some ways a disconcerting one; disconcerting, because most of us, however objective we are in the actual conduct of our thinking, would *like* to be able to believe that moral responsibility is real: whereas the freedom required for moral responsibility, on the analysis we have given, is certainly far more difficult to establish than the freedom required on the analyses we found ourselves obliged to reject. If, e.g. moral freedom entails only that I could have acted otherwise *if* I had chosen otherwise, there is no real 'problem' about it at all. I am 'free' in the normal case where there is no external obstacle to prevent my translating the alternative choice into action, and not free in other cases. Still less is there a problem if all that moral freedom entails is that I could have acted otherwise *if* I had been a differently constituted person, or been in different circumstances. Clearly I am *always* free in *this* sense of freedom. But, as I have argued, these so-called 'freedoms' fail to give us the pre-conditions of moral responsibility, and hence leave the freedom of the traditional free-will problem, the freedom that people are really concerned about, precisely where it was.

Another interpretation of freedom which I am bound to reject on the same general ground, i.e. that it is just not the kind of freedom that is relevant to moral responsibility, is the old idealist view which identifies the *free* will with the *rational* will; the rational will in its turn being identified with the will which wills the moral law in whole-hearted, single-minded obedience to it. This view is still worth at least a passing mention, if only because it has recently been resurrected in an interesting work by Professor A. E. Teale.[3] Moreover, I cannot but feel a certain nostalgic tenderness for a view in which I myself was (so to speak) philosophically cradled. The almost apostolic fervour with which my revered nursing-mother, the late Sir Henry Jones, was wont to impart it to his charges, and, hardly less, his ill-concealed scorn for ignoble natures (like my own) which still hankered after a free will in the old 'vulgar' sense, are vividly recalled for me in Professor Teale's stirring pages.

The true interpretation of free will, according to Professor Teale, the interpretation to which Kant, despite occasional back-slidings, adhered in his better moments, is that 'the will is free in the degree that it is informed and disciplined by the moral principle.'[4]

Now this is a perfectly intelligible sense of the word 'free'—or at any rate it can be made so with a little explanatory comment which Professor Teale well supplies but for which there is here no space. But clearly it is a very different sort of freedom from that which is at issue in the traditional problem of free will. This idealist 'freedom' sponsored by Teale belongs, on his own showing, only to the self in respect of its *good* willing. The freedom with which the traditional problem is concerned, inasmuch as it is the freedom presupposed by moral responsibility, must belong to the self in respect of its *bad,* no less than its *good,* willing. It is, in fact, the freedom to decide between genuinely open alternatives of good and bad willing.

Professor Teale, of course, is not unaware that the freedom he favours differs from freedom as traditionally understood. He recognises the traditional concept under its Kantian title of 'elective' freedom. But he leaves the reader in no kind of doubt about his disbelief in both the reality and the value of this elective freedom to do, or forbear from doing, one's duty.

The question of the reality of elective freedom I shall be dealing with shortly; and it will occupy us to the end of the lecture. At the moment I am concerned only with its value, and with the rival view that all that matters for the moral life is the 'rational' freedom which a man has in the degree that his will is 'informed and disciplined by the moral principle.' I confess that to myself the verdict on the rival view seems plain and inescapable. No amount of verbal ingenuity or argumentative convolutions can obscure the fact that it is in flat contradiction to the implications of moral responsibility. The point at issue is really perfectly straightforward. If, as this idealist theory maintains, my acting in defiance of what I deem to be my duty is not a 'free' act in *any* sense, let alone in the sense that 'I could have acted otherwise,' then I cannot be morally blameworthy, and that is all there is to it. Nor, for that matter, is the idealist entitled to say that I am morally praiseworthy if I act dutifully; for although that act *is* a 'free' act in the idealist sense, it is on his own avowal not free in the sense that 'I could have acted otherwise.'

It seems to me idle, therefore, to pretend that if one has to give up freedom in the traditional elective sense one is not giving up anything important. What we are giving up is, quite simply, the reality of the moral life. I recognise that to a certain type of religious nature (as well as, by an odd meeting of extremes, to a certain type of secular nature) that does not appear to matter so very much; but, for myself, I still think it sufficiently important to make it well worthwhile enquiring seriously into the possibility that the elective freedom upon which it rests may be real after all.

That brings me to the second, and more constructive, part of this lecture. From now on I shall be considering whether it is reasonable to believe that man does in fact possess a free will of the kind specified in the first part of the lecture. If so, just how and where within the complex fabric of the volitional life are we to locate it?—for although free will must presumably belong (if anywhere) to the volitional side of human experience, it is pretty clear from the way in which we have been forced to define it that it does not pertain simply to volition as such; not even to all volitions that are commonly dignified with the name of 'choices.' It has been, I think, one of the more serious impediments to profitable discussion of the Free Will problem that Libertarians and Determinists alike have so often failed to appreciate the comparatively narrow area within which the free will that is necessary to 'save' morality is required to operate. It goes without saying that this failure has been gravely prejudicial to the case for Libertarianism. I attach a good deal of importance, therefore, to the problem of locating free will correctly within the volitional orbit. Its solution forestalls and annuls, I believe, some of the more tiresome clichés of Determinist criticism.

We saw earlier that Common Sense's practice of 'making allowances' in its moral judgments for the influence of heredity and environment indicates Common Sense's conviction, both that a just moral judgment must discount determinants of choice over which the agent has no control, and also (since it still accepts moral judgments as legitimate) that *something* of moral relevance survives which can be regarded as genuinely self-originated. We are now to try to discover what this 'something' is. And I think we may still usefully take Common Sense as our guide. Suppose one asks the ordinary intelligent citizen *why* he deems it proper to make allowances for X, whose heredity and/or environment are unfortunate. He will tend to reply, I think, in some such terms as these: that X has more and stronger temptations to deviate from what is right than Y or Z, who are normally circumstanced, so that he must put forth a *stronger moral effort* if he is to achieve the same level of external conduct. The intended implication seems to be that X is just as morally praiseworthy as Y or Z *if* he exerts an equivalent moral effort, even though he may not thereby achieve an equal success in conforming his will to the 'concrete' demands of duty. And this implies, again, Common Sense's belief that *in moral effort* we have something for which a man is responsible *without qualification*, something that is *not* affected by heredity and environment but depends *solely* upon the self itself.

Now in my opinion Common Sense has here, in principle, hit upon the one and only defensible answer. Here, and here alone, so far as I can see, in the act of deciding whether to put forth or withhold the moral effort required to resist temptation and rise to duty, is to be found an act which is free in the sense required for moral responsibility; an act of which the self is sole author, and of which it is true to say that 'it could be' (or, after the event, 'could have been') 'otherwise.' Such is the thesis which we shall now try to establish.

The species of argument appropriate to the establishment of a thesis of this sort should fall, I think, into two phases. First, there should be a consideration of the evidence of the moral agent's own inner experience. What *is* the act of moral decision, and what does it imply, from the standpoint of the actual participant? Since there is no way of knowing the act of moral decision—or for that matter any other form of activity—except by actual participation in it, the evidence of the subject, or agent, is on an issue of this kind of palmary importance. It can hardly, however, be taken as in itself conclusive. For even if that evidence should be overwhelmingly to the effect that moral decision does have the characteristics required by moral freedom, the question is bound to be raised—and in view of considerations from other quarters pointing in a contrary direction is *rightly* raised—Can we *trust* the evidence of inner experience? That brings us to what will be the second phase of the argument. We shall have to go on to show, if we are to make good our case, that the extraneous considerations so often supposed to be fatal to the belief in moral freedom are in fact innocuous to it.

In the light of what was said in the last lecture ['Self-Activity and Its Modes'] about the self's experience of moral decision as a *creative* activity, we may perhaps be absolved from developing the first phase of the argument at any great length. The appeal is throughout to one's own experience in the actual taking of the moral decision in the situation of moral temptation. 'Is it possible,' we must ask, 'for anyone so circumstanced to *dis*believe that he could be deciding otherwise?' The answer is surely not in doubt. When we decide to exert moral effort to resist a temptation, we feel quite certain that we *could* withhold the effort; just as, if we decide to withhold the effort and yield to our desires, we feel quite certain that we *could* exert it—otherwise we should not blame ourselves afterwards for having succumbed. It may be, indeed, that this conviction is mere self-delusion. But that is not at the moment our concern. It is enough at present to establish that the act of deciding to exert or to withhold moral effort, as we know it from the inside in actual moral living, belongs to the category of acts which 'could have been otherwise.'

Mutatis mutandis, the same reply is forthcoming if we ask, 'Is it possible for the moral agent in the taking of his decision to *dis*believe that he is the *sole* author of that decision?' Clearly he cannot disbelieve that it is *he* who takes the decision. That, however, is not in itself sufficient to enable him, on reflection, to regard himself as *solely* responsible for the act. For his 'character' as so far formed might conceivably be a factor in determining it, and no one can suppose that the constitution of his 'character' is uninfluenced by circumstances of heredity and environment with which *he* has nothing to do. But as we pointed out in the last lecture, the very essence of the moral decision as it is experienced is that it is a decision whether or not to *combat* our strongest desire, and our strongest desire *is* the expression in the situation of our character as so far formed. Now clearly our character cannot be a factor in determining the decision whether or not to *oppose* our character. I think we are entitled to say, therefore, that the act of moral decision is one in which the self is for itself not merely 'author' but 'sole author.'

We may pass on, then, to the second phase of our constructive argument; and this will demand more elaborate treatment. Even if a moral agent *qua* making a moral decision in the situation of 'temptation' cannot help believing that he has free will in the sense at issue—a moral freedom between real alternatives, between genuinely open possibilities—are there, nevertheless, objections to a freedom of this kind so cogent that we are bound to distrust the evidence of 'inner experience'?

I begin by drawing attention to a simple point whose significance tends, I think, to be underestimated. If the phenomenological analysis we have offered is substantially correct, no one while functioning as a moral agent can help believing that he enjoys free will. Theoretically he may be completely convinced by Determinist arguments, but when actually confronted with a personal situation of conflict between duty and desire he is quite certain that it lies with him here and now whether or not he will rise to duty. It follows that if Determinists could produce convincing theoretical arguments against a free will of this kind, the awkward predicament would ensue that man has to deny as a theoretical being what he has to assert as a practical being. Now I think the Determinist ought to be a good deal more worried about this than he usually is. He seems to imagine that a strong case on general theoretical grounds is enough to prove that the 'practical' belief in free will, even if inescapable for us as practical beings, is mere illusion. But in fact it proves nothing of the sort. There is no reason whatever why a belief that we find ourselves obliged to hold *qua* practical beings should be required to give way before a belief which we find ourselves obliged to hold *qua* theoretical beings; or, for that matter, *vice versa*. All that the theoretical arguments of Determinism can prove, unless they are reinforced by a refutation of the phenomenological analysis that supports Libertarianism, is that there is a radical conflict between the theoretical and the practical sides of man's nature, an antinomy at the very heart of the self. And this is a state of affairs with which no one can easily rest satisfied. I think therefore that the Determinist ought to concern himself a great deal more than he does with phenomenological analysis, in order to show, if he can, that the assurance of free will is not really an inexpugnable element in man's practical consciousness. There is just as much obligation upon him, convinced though he may be of the soundness of his theoretical arguments, to expose the errors of the Libertarian's phenomenological analysis, as there is upon us, convinced though we may be of the soundness of the Libertarian's phenomenological analysis, to expose the errors of the Determinist's theoretical arguments.

However, we must at once begin the discharge of our own obligation. The rest of this lecture will be devoted to trying to show that the arguments which seem to carry the most weight with Determinists are, to say the least of it, very far from compulsive.

Fortunately, a good many of the arguments which at an earlier time in the history of philosophy would have been strongly urged against us make almost no appeal to the bulk of philosophers today, and we may here pass them by. That applies to any criticism of 'open possibilities' based on a metaphysical theory about the nature of the universe as a whole. Nobody today *has* a metaphysical theory about the nature of the universe as a whole! It applies also, with almost equal force, to criticisms based upon the universality of causal law as a supposed postulate of science. There have always been, in my opinion, sound philosophic reasons for doubting the validity, as distinct from the convenience, of the causal postulate in its universal form, but at the present time, when scientists themselves are deeply divided about the need for postulating causality even within their own special field, we shall do better to concentrate our attention upon criticisms which are more confidently advanced. I propose to ignore also, on different grounds, the type of criticism of free will that is sometimes advanced from the side of religion, based upon religious postulates of Divine Omnipotence and Omniscience. So far as I can see, a postulate of human freedom is every bit as necessary to meet certain religious demands (e.g. to make sense of the 'conviction of sin'), as postulates of Divine Omniscience and Omnipotence are to meet certain other religious demands. If so, then it can hardly be argued that religious experience as such tells more strongly against than for the position we are defending; and we may be satisfied, in the present context, to leave the matter there. It will be more profitable to discuss certain arguments which contemporary philosophers do think important, and which recur with a somewhat monotonous regularity in the literature of anti-Libertarianism.

These arguments can, I think, be reduced in principle to no more than two: first, the argument from 'predictability'; second, the argument from the alleged meaninglessness of an act supposed to be the self's act and yet not an expression of the self's character. Contemporary criticism of free will seems to me to consist almost exclusively of variations on these two themes. I shall deal with each in turn.

On the first we touched in passing at an earlier stage. Surely it is beyond question (the critic urges) that when we know a person intimately we can foretell with a high degree of accuracy how he will respond to at least a large number of practical situations. One feels safe in predicting that one's dog-loving friend will not use his boot to repel the little mongrel that comes yapping at his heels; or again that one's wife will not pass with incurious eyes (or indeed pass at all) the new hat shop in the city. So to behave would not be (as we say) 'in character.' But, so the criticism runs, you with your doctrine of 'genuinely open possibilities,' of a free will by which the self can diverge from its own character, remove all rational basis from such prediction. You require us to make the absurd supposition that the success of countless predictions of the sort in the past has been mere matter of chance. If you *really* believed in your theory, you would not be surprised if tomorrow your friend with the notorious horror of strong drink should suddenly exhibit a passion for whisky and soda, or if your friend whose taste for reading has hitherto been satisfied with the sporting columns of the newspapers should be discovered on a fine Saturday afternoon poring over the works of Hegel. But of course you *would* be surprised. Social life would be sheer chaos if there were not well-grounded social expectations; and social life is not sheer chaos. Your theory is hopelessly wrecked upon obvious facts.

Now whether or not this criticism holds good against some versions of Libertarian theory I need not here discuss. It is sufficient if I can make it clear that against the version advanced in this lecture, according to which free will is localised in a relatively narrow field of operation, the criticism has no relevance whatsoever.

Let us remind ourselves briefly of the setting within which, on our view, free will functions. There is X, the course which we believe we ought to follow, and Y, the course towards which we feel our desire is strongest. The freedom which we ascribe to the agent is the freedom to put forth or refrain from putting forth the moral effort required to resist the pressure of desire and do what he thinks he ought to do.

But then there is surely an immense range of practical situations—covering by far the greater part of life—in which there is no question of a conflict within the self between what he most desires to do and what he thinks he ought to do? Indeed such conflict is a comparatively rare phenomenon for the majority of men. Yet over that whole vast range there is nothing whatever in our version of Libertarianism to prevent our agreeing that character determines conduct. In the absence, real or supposed, of any 'moral' issue, what a man chooses will be simply that course which, after such reflection as seems called for, he deems most likely to bring him what he most strongly desires; and that is the same as to say the course to which his present character inclines him.

Over by far the greater area of human choices, then, our theory offers no more barrier to successful prediction on the basis of character than any other theory. For where there is no clash of strongest desire with duty, the free will we are defending has no business. There is just nothing for it to do.

But what about the situations—rare enough though they may be—in which there *is* this clash and in which free will does therefore operate? Does our theory entail that there, at any rate, as the critic seems to suppose, 'anything may happen'?

Not by any manner of means. In the first place, and by the very nature of the case, the range of the agent's possible choices is bounded by what he thinks he ought to do on the one hand, and what he most strongly desires on the other. The freedom claimed for him is a freedom of decision to make or withhold the effort required to do what he thinks he ought to do. There is no question of a freedom to act in some 'wild' fashion, out of all relation to his characteristic beliefs and desires. This so-called 'freedom of caprice,' so often charged against the Libertarian, is, to put it bluntly, a sheer figment of the critic's imagination, with no *habitat* in serious Libertarian theory. Even in situations where free will does come into play it is perfectly possible, on a view like ours, given the appropriate knowledge of a man's character, to predict within certain limits how he will respond.

But 'probable' prediction in such situations can, I think, go further than this. It is obvious that where desire and duty are at odds, the felt 'gap' (as it were) between the two may vary enormously in breadth in different cases. The moderate drinker and the chronic tippler may each want another glass, and each deem it his duty to abstain, but the felt gap between desire and duty in the case of the former is trivial beside the great gulf which is felt to separate them in the case of the latter. Hence it will take a far harder moral effort for the tippler than for the moderate drinker to achieve the same external result of abstention. So much is matter of common agreement. And we are entitled, I think, to take it into account in prediction, on the simple principle that the harder the moral effort required to resist desire the less likely it is to occur. Thus in the example taken, most people would predict that the tippler will very probably succumb to his desires, whereas there is a reasonable likelihood that the moderate drinker will make the comparatively slight effort needed to resist them. So long as the prediction does not pretend to more than a measure of probability, there is nothing in our theory which would disallow it.

I claim, therefore, that the view of free will I have been putting forward is consistent with predictability of conduct on the basis of character over a very wide field indeed. And I make the further claim that that field will cover all the situations in life concerning which there is any empirical evidence that successful prediction is possible.

Let us pass on to consider the second main line of criticism. This is, I think, much the more illuminating of the two, if only because it compels the Libertarian to make explicit certain concepts which are indispensable to him, but which, being desperately hard to state clearly, are apt not to be stated at all. The critic's fundamental point might be stated somewhat as follows:

'Free will as you describe it is completely unintelligible. On your own showing no *reason* can be given, because there just *is* no reason, why a man decides to exert rather than to withhold moral effort, or *vice versa*. But such an act—or more properly, such an 'occurrence'—it is nonsense to speak of as an act of a *self*. If there is nothing in the self's character to which it is, even in principle, in any way traceable, the self has nothing to do with it. Your so-called 'freedom,' therefore, so far from supporting the self's moral responsibility, destroys it as surely as the crudest Determinism could do.'

If we are to discuss this criticism usefully, it is important, I think, to begin by getting clear about two different senses of the word 'intelligible.'

If, in the first place, we mean by an 'intelligible' act one whose occurrence is in principle capable of being inferred, since it follows necessarily from something (though we may not know in fact from what), then it is certainly true that the Libertarian's free will is unintelligible. But that is only saying, is it not, that the Libertarian's 'free' act is not an act which follows necessarily from something! This can hardly rank as a *criticism* of Libertarianism. It is just a description of it. That there can be nothing unintelligible in *this* sense is precisely what the Determinist has got to *prove*.

Yet it is surprising how often the critic of Libertarianism involves himself in this circular mode of argument. Repeatedly it is urged against the Libertarian, with a great air of triumph, that on his view he can't say *why* I now decide to rise to duty, or now decide to follow my strongest desire in defiance of duty. Of course he can't. If he could he wouldn't *be* a Libertarian. To 'account for' a 'free' act is a contradiction in terms. A free will is *ex hypothesi* the sort of thing of which the request for an *explanation* is absurd. The assumption that an explanation must be in principle possible for the act of moral decision deserves to rank as a classic example of the ancient fallacy of 'begging the question.'

But the critic usually has in mind another sense of the word 'unintelligible.' He is apt to take it for granted that an act which is unintelligible in the *above* sense (as the morally free act of the Libertarian undoubtedly is) is unintelligible in the *further* sense that we can attach no meaning to it. And this is an altogether more serious matter. If it could really be shown that the Libertarian's 'free will' were unintelligible in this sense of being meaningless, that, for myself at any rate, would be the end of the affair. Libertarianism would have been conclusively refuted.

But it seems to me manifest that this can *not* be shown. The critic has allowed himself, I submit, to become the victim of a widely accepted but fundamentally vicious assumption. He has assumed that whatever is meaningful must exhibit its meaningfulness to those who view it from the standpoint of external observation. Now if one chooses thus to limit one's self to the rôle of external observer, it is, I think, perfectly true that one can attach no meaning to an act which is the act of something we call a 'self' and yet follows from nothing in that self's character. But then *why should we* so limit ourselves, when what is under consideration is a subjective activity? For the apprehension of subjective acts there is *another* standpoint available, that of *inner experience,* of the practical consciousness in its actual functioning. If our free will should turn out to be something to which we can attach a meaning from *this* standpoint, no more is required. And no more ought to be expected. For I must repeat that only from the inner standpoint of living experience *could* anything of the nature of 'activity' be directly grasped. Observation from without is in the nature of the case impotent to apprehend the active *qua* active. We can from without observe sequences of states. If into these we read activity (as we sometimes do), this can only be on the basis of what we discern in ourselves from the inner standpoint. It follows that if anyone insists upon taking his criterion of the meaningful simply from the standpoint of external observation, he is really deciding in advance of the evidence that the notion of activity, and *a fortiori* the notion of a free will, is 'meaningless.' He looks for the free act through a medium which is in the nature of the case incapable of revealing it, and then, because inevitably he doesn't find it, he declares that it doesn't exist!

But if, as we surely ought in this context, we adopt the inner standpoint, then (I am suggesting) things appear in a totally different light. From the inner standpoint, it seems to me plain, there is no difficulty whatever in attaching meaning to an act which is the self's act and which nevertheless does not follow from the self's character. So much I claim has been established by the phenomenological analysis, in this and the previous lecture, of the act of moral decision in face of moral temptation. It is thrown into particularly clear relief where the moral decision is to make the moral effort required to rise to duty. For the very function of moral effort, as it appears to the agent engaged in the act, is to enable the self to act against the line of least resistance, against the line to which his character as so far formed most strongly inclines him. But if the self is thus conscious here of *combating* his formed character, he surely cannot possibly suppose that the act, although his own act, *issues from* his formed character? I submit, therefore, that the self knows very well indeed—from the inner standpoint—what is meant by an act which is the *self's* act and which nevertheless does not follow from the self's *character.*

What this implies—and it seems to me to be an implication of cardinal importance for any theory of the self that aims at being more than superficial—is that the nature of the self is for itself something more than just its character as so far formed. The 'nature' of the self and what we commonly call the 'character' of the self are by no means the same thing, and it is utterly vital that they should not be confused. The 'nature' of the self comprehends, but is not without remainder reducible to, its 'character'; it must, if we are to be true to the testimony of our experience of it, be taken as including *also* the authentic creative power of fashioning and re-fashioning 'character.'

The misguided, and as a rule quite uncritical, belittlement, of the evidence offered by inner experience has, I am convinced, been responsible for more bad argument by the opponents of Free Will than has any other single factor. How often, for example, do we find the Determinist critic saying, in effect, '*Either* the act follows necessarily upon precedent states, *or* it is a mere matter of chance and accordingly of no moral significance.' The disjunction is invalid for it does not exhaust the possible alternatives. It seems to the critic to do so only because he *will* limit himself to the standpoint which is proper, and indeed alone possible, in dealing with the physical world, the standpoint of the external observer. If only he would allow himself to assume the standpoint which is not merely proper for, but necessary to, the apprehension of subjective activity, the inner standpoint of the practical consciousness in its actual functioning, he would find himself obliged to recognise the falsity of his disjunction. Reflection upon the act of moral decision as apprehended from the inner standpoint would force him to recognise a *third* possibility, as remote from chance as from necessity, that, namely, of *creative activity,* in which (as I have ventured to express it) nothing determines the act save the agent's doing of it.

There we must leave the matter. But as this lecture has been, I know, somewhat densely packed, it may be helpful if I conclude by reminding you, in bald summary, of the main things I have been trying to say. Let me set them out in so many successive theses.

1. The freedom which is at issue in the traditional Free Will problem is the freedom which is presupposed in moral responsibility.

2. Critical reflection upon carefully considered attributions of moral responsibility reveals that the only freedom that will do is a freedom which pertains to inner acts of choice, and that these acts must be acts (*a*) of which the self is *sole* author, and (*b*) which the self could have performed otherwise.

3. From phenomenological analysis of the situation of moral temptation we find that the self as engaged in this situation is inescapably convinced that it possesses a freedom of precisely the specified kind, located in the decision to exert or withhold the moral effort needed to rise to duty where the pressure of its desiring nature is felt to urge it in a contrary direction.

Passing to the question of the *reality* of this moral freedom which the moral agent believes himself to possess, we argued:

4. Of the two types of Determinist criticism which seem to have most influence today, that based on the predictability of much human behaviour fails to touch a Libertarianism which confines the area of free will as above indicated. Libertarianism so understood is compatible with all the predictability that the empirical facts warrant. And:

5. The second main type of criticism, which alleges the 'meaninglessness' of an act which is the self's act and which is yet not determined by the self's character, is based on a failure to appreciate that the standpoint of inner experience is not only legitimate but indispensable where what is at issue is the reality and nature of a subjective activity. The creative act of moral decision is inevitably meaningless to the mere external observer; but from the inner standpoint it is as real, and as significant, as anything in human experience.

NOTES

1. Reprinted in *Ethics and the History of Philosophy, Selected Essays.*

2. I have explained the grounds for my dissent from Broad's final conclusion on pp. 27 ff. of *In Defence of Free Will* (Jackson Son & Co., 1938).

3. *Kantian Ethics.*

4. *Op. cit.,* p. 261.

Human Freedom and the Self*

RODERICK M. CHISHOLM

'A staff moves a stone, and is moved by a hand, which is moved by a man.'

ARISTOTLE, *Physics 256a*

1. THE METAPHYSICAL PROBLEM of human freedom might be summarized in the following way: Human beings are responsible agents; but this fact appears to conflict with a deterministic view of human action (the view that every event that is involved in an act is caused by some other event); and it *also* appears to conflict with an indeterministic view of human action (the view that the act, or some event that is essential to the act, is not caused at all.) To solve the problem, I believe, we must make somewhat far-reaching assumptions about the self or the agent—about the man who performs the act.

Perhaps it is needless to remark that, in all likelihood, it is impossible to say anything significant about this ancient problem that has not been said before.[1]

2. Let us consider some deed, or misdeed, that may be attributed to a responsible agent: one man, say, shot another. If the man *was* responsible for what he did, then, I would urge, what was to happen at the time of the shooting was something that was entirely up to the man himself. There was a moment at which it was true, both that he could have fired the shot and also that he could have refrained from firing it. And if this is so, then, even though he did fire it, he could have done something else instead. (He didn't find himself firing the shot 'against his will', as we say.) I think we can say, more generally, then, that if a man is responsible for a certain event or a certain state of affairs (in our example, the shooting of another man), then that event or state of affairs was brought about by some act of his, and the act was something that was in his power either to perform or not to perform.

But now if the act which he *did* perform was an act that was also in his power *not* to perform, then it could not have been caused or determined by any event that was not itself within his power either to bring about or not to bring about. For example, if what we say he did was really something that was brought about by a second man, one who forced his hand upon the trigger, say, or who, by means of hypnosis, compelled him to perform the act, then since the act was caused by the *second* man it was nothing that was within the power of the *first* man to prevent. And precisely the same thing is true, I think, if instead of referring to a second man who compelled the first one, we speak instead of the *desires* and *beliefs* which the first man happens to have had. For if what we say he did was really something that was brought about by his own beliefs and desires, if these beliefs and desires in the particular situation in which he happened to have found himself caused him to do just what it was that we say he

1. The general position to be presented here is suggested in the following writings, among others: Aristotle, *Eudemian Ethics*, bk. ii ch. 6. *Nicomachean Ethics*, bk. iii, ch. 1–5; Thomas Reid, *Essays on the Active Powers of Man;* C. A. Campbell, 'Is "Free Will" a Pseudo-Problem?' *Mind*, 1951, 441–65; Roderick M. Chisholm, 'Responsibility and Avoidability', and Richard Taylor, 'Determination and the Theory of Agency', in *Determinism and Freedom in the Age of Modern Science*, ed. Sidney Hook (New York, 1958).

did do, then, since *they* caused it, *he* was unable to do anything other than just what it was that he did do. It makes no difference whether the cause of the deed was internal or external; if the cause was some state or event for which the man himself was not responsible, then he was not responsible for what we have been mistakenly calling his act. If a flood caused the poorly constructed dam to break, then, given the flood and the constitution of the dam, the break, we may say, *had* to occur and nothing could have happened in its place. And if the flood of desire caused the weak-willed man to give in, then he, too, had to do just what it was that he did do and he was no more responsible than was the dam for the results that followed. (It is true, of course, that if the man is responsible for the beliefs and desires that he happens to have, then he may also be responsible for the things they lead him to do. But the question now becomes: *is* he responsible for the beliefs and desires he happens to have? If he is, then there was a time when they were within his power either to acquire or not to acquire, and we are left, therefore, with our general point.)

One may object: But surely if there were such a thing as a man who is really *good*, then he would be responsible for things that he would do; yet, he would be unable to do anything other than just what it is that he does do, since, being good, he will always choose to do what is best. The answer, I think, is suggested by a comment that Thomas Reid makes upon an ancient author. The author had said of Cato, 'He was good because he could not be otherwise', and Reid observes: 'This saying, if understood literally and strictly, is not the praise of Cato, but of his constitution, which was no more the work of Cato than his existence'.[2] If Cato was himself responsible for the good things that he did, then Cato, as Reid suggests, was such that, although he had the power to do what was not good, he exercised his power only for that which was good.

All of this, if it is true, may give a certain amount of comfort to those who are tender-minded. But we should remind them that it also conflicts with a familiar view about the nature of God—with the view that St. Thomas Aquinas expresses by saying that 'every movement both of the will and of nature proceeds from God as the Prime Mover'.[3] If the act of the sinner *did* proceed from God as the Prime Mover, then God was in the position of the second agent we just discussed—the man who forced the trigger finger, or the hypnotist and the sinner, so-called, was *not* responsible for what he did. (This may be a bold assertion, in view of the history of western theology, but I must say that I have never encountered a single good reason for denying it.)

There is one standard objection to all of this and we should consider it briefly.

3. The objection takes the form of a stratagem one designed to show that determinism (and divine providence) is consistent with human responsibility. The stratagem is one that was used by Jonathan Edwards and by many philosophers in the present century, most notably, G. E. Moore.[4]

One proceeds as follows: The expression

(a) He could have done otherwise,

it is argued, means no more nor less than

(b) If he had chosen to do otherwise, then he would have done otherwise.

(In place of 'chosen', one might say 'tried', 'set out', 'decided', 'undertaken', or 'willed'.) The truth of statement (b), it is then pointed out, is consistent with determinism (and with divine providence); for even if all of the man's actions were causally determined, the man could still be such that, *if* he had chosen otherwise, then he would have done otherwise. What the murderers saw, let us suppose, along with his beliefs and desires, *caused* him to fire the shot; yet he was such that *if*, just then, he had chosen or decided *not* to fire the shot, then he would not have fired it. All of this is certainly possible. Similarly, we could say, of the dam, that the flood caused it to break and also that

2. Thomas Reid, *Essays on the Active Powers of Man,* essay iv, ch. 4 (*Works,* 600).

3. *Summa Theologica,* First Part of the Second Part, qu. vi ('On the Voluntary and Involuntary').

4. Jonathan Edwards, *Freedom of the Will* (New Haven, 1957); G. E. Moore, *Ethics* (Home University Library, 1912), ch 6.

the dam was such that, *if* there had been no flood or any similar pressure, then the dam would have remained intact. And therefore, the argument proceeds, if (b) is consistent with determinism, and if (a) and (b) say the same thing, then (a) is also consistent with determinism; hence we can say that the agent *could* have done otherwise even though he was caused to do what he did do; and therefore determinism and moral responsibility are compatible.

Is the argument sound? The conclusion follows from the premises, but the catch, I think, lies in the first premiss—the one saying that statement (a) tells us no more nor less than what statement (b) tells us. For (b), it would seem, could be true while (a) is false. That is to say, our man might be such that, if he had chosen to do otherwise, then he would have done otherwise, and yet *also* such that he could not have done otherwise. Suppose, after all, that our murderer could not have *chosen,* or could not have *decided,* to do otherwise. Then the fact that he happens also to be a man such that, if he had chosen not to shoot he would not have shot, would make no difference. For if he could *not* have chosen *not* to shoot, then he could not have done anything other than just what it was that he did do. In a word: from our statement (b) above ('If he had chosen to do otherwise, then he would have done otherwise'), we cannot make an inference to (a) above ('He could have done otherwise') unless we can *also* assert:

(c) He could have chosen to do otherwise.

And therefore, if we must reject this third statement (c), then, even though we may be justified in asserting (b), we are not justified in asserting (a). If the man could not have chosen to do otherwise, then he would not have done otherwise—*even if* he was such that, if he *had* chosen to do otherwise, then he would have done otherwise.

The stratagem in question, then, seems to me not to work, and I would say, therefore, that the ascription of responsibility conflicts with a deterministic view of action.

4. Perhaps there is less need to argue that the ascription of responsibility also conflicts with an indeterministic view of action—with the view that the act, or some event that is essential to the act, is not caused at all. If the act—the firing of the shot—was not caused at all, if it was fortuitous or capricious, happening so to speak out of the blue, then, presumably, no one—and nothing was responsible for the act. Our conception of action, therefore, should be neither deterministic nor indeterministic. Is there any other possibility?

5. We must not say that every event involved in the act is caused by some other event; and we must not say that the act is something that is not caused at all. The possibility that remains, therefore, is this: We should say that at least one of the events that are involved in the act is caused, not by any other events, but by something else instead. And this something else can only be the agent—the man. If there is an event that is caused, not by other events, but by the man, then there are some events involved in the act that are not caused by other events. But if the event in question is caused by the man then it *is* caused and we are not committed to saying that there is something involved in the act that is not caused at all.

But this, of course, is a large consequence, implying something of considerable importance about the nature of the agent or the man.

6. If we consider only inanimate natural objects, we may say that causation, if it occurs, is a relation between *events* or *states of affairs.* The dam's breaking was an event that was caused by a set of other events—the dam being weak, the flood being strong, and so on. But if a man is responsible for a particular deed, then, if what I have said is true, there is some event, or set of events, that is caused, *not* by other events or states of affairs, but by the agent, whatever he may be.

I shall borrow a pair of medieval terms, using them, perhaps, in a way that is slightly different from that for which they were originally intended. I shall say that when one event or state of affairs (or set of events or states of affairs) causes some other event or state of affairs, then we have an instance of *transeunt* causation. And I shall say that when an *agent,* as distinguished from an event, causes an event or state of affairs, then we have an instance of *immanent* causation.

The nature of what is intended by the expression 'immanent causation' may be illustrated by this sentence from Aristotle's *Physics:* 'Thus, a staff moves a stone, and is moved by a hand, which is moved by a man.' (VII, 5, 256a, 6–8) If the man was responsible, then we have in this illustration a number of instances of causation—most of them transeunt but at least one of them immanent. What the staff did to the stone was an instance of transeunt causation, and thus we may describe it as a relation between events: 'the motion of the staff caused the motion of the stone.' And similarly for what the hand did to the staff: 'the motion of the hand caused the motion of the staff'. And, as we know from physiology, there are still other events which caused the motion of the hand. Hence we need not introduce the agent at this particular point, as Aristotle does—we *need* not, though we *may.* We *may* say that the hand was moved by the man, but we may *also* say that the motion of the hand was caused by the motion of certain muscles; and we may say that the motion of the muscles was caused by certain events that took place within the brain. But some event, and presumably one of those that took place within the brain, was caused by the agent and not by any other events.

There are, of course, objections to this way of putting the matter; I shall consider the two that seem to me to be most important.

7. One may object, firstly: 'If the *man* does anything, then, as Aristotle's remark suggests, what he does is to move the *hand.* But he certainly does not *do* anything to his brain—he may not even know that he *has* a brain. And if he doesn't do anything to the brain, and if the motion of the hand was caused by something that happened within the brain, then there is no point in appealing to "immanent causation" as being something incompatible with "transeunt causation"—for the whole thing, after all, is a matter of causal relations among events or states of affairs.'

The answer to this objection, I think, is this: It is true that the agent does not *do* anything with his brain, or to his brain, in the sense in which he *does* something with his hand and does something to the staff. But from this it does not follow that the agent was not the immanent cause of something that happened within his brain.

We should note a useful distinction that has been proposed by Professor A. I. Melden—namely, the distinction between 'making something A happen' and 'doing A'.[5] If I reach for the staff and pick it up, then one of the things that I *do* is just that—reach for the staff and pick it up. And if it is something that I do, then there is a very clear sense in which it may be said to be something that I know that I do. If you ask me, 'Are you doing something, or trying to do something, with the staff?', I will have no difficulty in finding an answer. But in doing something with the staff, I also make various things happen which are not in this same sense things that I do: I will make various air-particles move; I will free a number of blades of grass from the pressure that had been upon them; and I may cause a shadow to move from one place to another. If these are merely things that I make happen, as distinguished from things that I do, then I may know nothing whatever about them; I may not have the slightest idea that, in moving the staff, I am bringing about any such thing as the motion of air-particles, shadows, and blades of grass.

We may say, in answer to the first objection, therefore, that it is true that our agent does nothing to his brain or with his brain; but from this it does not follow that the agent is not the immanent cause of some event within his brain; for the brain event may be something which, like the motion of the air-particles, he made happen in picking up the staff. The only difference between the two cases is this: in each case, he made something happen when he picked up the staff; but in the one case—the motion of the air-particles or of the shadows—it was the motion of the staff that caused the event to happen; and in the other case—the event that took place in the brain it was this event that caused the motion of the staff.

5. A. I. Melden, *Free Action* (London, 1961), especially ch. 3. Mr. Melden's own views, however, are quite the contrary of those that are proposed here.

The point is, in a word, that whenever a man does something A, then (by 'immanent causation') he makes a certain cerebral event happen, and this cerebral event (by 'transeunt causation') makes A happen.

8. The second objection is more difficult and concerns the very concept of 'immanent causation', or causation by an agent, as this concept is to be interpreted here. The concept is subject to a difficulty which has long been associated with that of the prime mover unmoved. We have said that there must be some event A, presumably some cerebral event, which is caused not by any other event, but by the agent. Since A was not caused by any other event, then the agent himself cannot be said to have undergone any change or produced any other event (such as 'an act of will' or the like) which brought A about. But if, when the agent made A happen, there was no event involved other than A itself, no event which could be described as *making* A happen, what did the agent's causation consist of? What, for example, is the difference between A's just happening, and the agents' *causing* A to happen? We cannot attribute the difference to any event that took place within the agent. And so far as the event A itself is concerned, there would seem to be no discernible difference. Thus Aristotle said that the activity of the prime mover is nothing in addition to the motion that it produces, and Suarez said that 'the action is in reality nothing but the effect as it flows from the agent'.[6] Must we conclude, then, that there is no more to the man's action in causing event A than there is to the event A's happening by itself? Here we would seem to have a distinction without a difference—in which case we have failed to find a *via media* between a deterministic and an indeterministic view of action.

The only answer, I think, can be this: that the difference between the man's causing A, on the one hand, and the event A just happening, on the other, lies in the fact that, in the first case but not the second, the event A *was* caused and was caused by the man. There was a brain event A; the agent did, in fact, cause the brain event; but there was nothing that he did to cause it.

This answer may not entirely satisfy and it will be likely to provoke the following question: 'But what are you really *adding* to the assertion that A happened when you utter the words "The agent *caused* A to happen"?' As soon as we have put the question this way, we see, I think, that whatever difficulty we may have encountered is one that may be traced to the concept of causation generally—whether 'immanent' or 'transeunt'. The problem, in other words, is not a problem that is peculiar to our conception of human action. It is a problem that must be faced by anyone who makes use of the concept of causation at all; and therefore, I would say, it is a problem for everyone but the complete indeterminist.

For the problem, as we put it, referring just to 'immanent causation', or causation by an agent, was this: 'What is the difference between saying, of an event A, that A just happened and saying that someone caused A to happen?' The analogous problem, which holds for 'transeunt causation', or causation by an event, is this: 'What is the difference between saying, of two events A and B, that B happened and then A happened, and saying that B's happening was the *cause* of A's happening?' And the only answer that one can give is this—that in the one case the agent was the cause of A's happening and in the other case event B was the cause of A's happening. The nature of transeunt causation is no more clear than is that of immanent causation.

9. But we may plausibly say—and there is a respectable philosophical tradition to which we may appeal—that the notion of immanent causation, or causation by an agent, is in fact more clear than that of transeunt causation, or causation by an event, and that it is only by understanding our own causal efficacy, as agents, that we can grasp the concept of *cause* at all. Hume may be said to have shown that we do not derive the concept of *cause* from what we perceive of external things. How, then, do we derive it? The most plausible suggestion, it seems to me, is that of Reid, once again: namely that 'the conception of an efficient cause may very probably be derived from the experience we have had . . . of

6. Aristotle, *Physics,* bk. iii, ch. 3. Suarez, *Disputations Metaphysicae,* Disputation 18, s. 10.

our own power to produce certain effects'.[7] If we did not understand the concept of immanent causation, we would not understand that of transeunt causation.

10. It may have been noted that I have avoided the term 'free will' in all of this. For even if there is such a faculty as 'the will', which somehow sets our acts agoing, the question of freedom, as John Locke said, is not the question '*whether the will be free*'; it is the question '*whether a man be free*'.[8] For if there is a 'will', as a moving faculty, the question is whether the man is free to will to do these things that he does will to do—and also whether he is free *not* to will any of those things that he does will to do, and, again, whether he is free to will any of those things that he does not will to do. Jonathan Edwards tried to restrict himself to the question—'Is the man free to do what it is that he wills?' but the answer to this question will not tell us whether the man is responsible for what it is that he *does* will to do. Using still another pair of medieval terms, we may say that the metaphysical problem of freedom does not concern the *actus imperatus;* it does not concern the question whether we are free to accomplish whatever it is that we will or set out to do, it concerns the *actus elicitus,* the question whether we are free to will or to set out to do those things that we do will or set out to do.

11. If we are responsible, and if what I have been trying to say is true, then we have a prerogative which some would attribute only to God: each of us, when we act, is a prime mover unmoved. In doing what we do, we cause certain events to happen, and nothing—or no one—causes us to cause those events to happen.

12. If we are thus prime movers unmoved and if our actions, or those for which we are responsible, are not causally determined, then they are not causally determined by our *desires.* And this means that the relation between what we want or what we desire, on the one hand, and what it is that we do, on the other, is not as simple as most philosophers would have it.

We may distinguish between what we might call the 'Hobbist approach' and what we might call the 'Kantian approach' to this question. The Hobbist approach is the one that is generally accepted at the present time, but the Kantian approach, I believe, is the one that is true. According to Hobbism, if we *know,* of some man, what his beliefs and desires happen to be and how strong they are, if we know what he feels certain of, what he desires more than anything else, and if we know the state of his body and what stimuli he is being subjected to, then we may *deduce,* logically, just what it is that he will do—or, more accurately, just what it is that he will try, set out, or undertake to do. Thus Professor Melden has said that 'the connection between wanting and doing is logical'.[9] But according to the Kantian approach to our problem, and this is the one that I would take, there is no such logical connection between wanting and doing, nor need there even be a causal connection. No set of statements about a man's desires, beliefs, and stimulus situation at any time implies any statement telling us what the man will try, set out, or undertake to do at that time. As Reid put it, though we may 'reason from men's motives to their actions and, in many cases, with great probability', we can never do so 'with absolute certainty.'[10]

This means that, in one very strict sense of the terms, there can be no science of man. If we think of science as a matter of finding out what laws happen to hold, and if the statement of a law tells us what kinds of events are caused by what other kinds of events, then there will be human actions which we cannot explain by subsuming them under any laws. We cannot say, 'It is causally necessary that, given such and such desires and beliefs, and being subject to such and such stimuli, the agent will do so and so'. For at times the agent, if he chooses, may rise above his desires and do something else instead.

But all of this is consistent with saying that, perhaps more often than not, our desires do exist

7. Reid, *Works,* 524.
8. *Essay Concerning Human Understanding,* bk. ii, ch. 21.
9. Melden, 166.
10. Reid, *Works,* 608, 612.

under conditions such that those conditions necessitate us to act. And we may also say, with Leibniz, that at other times our desires may 'incline without necessitating'.

13. Leibniz's phrase presents us with our final philosophical problem. What does it mean to say that a desire, or a motive, might 'incline without necessitating'? There is a temptation, certainly, to say that 'to incline' means to cause and that 'not to necessitate' means not to cause, but obviously we cannot have it both ways.

Nor will Leibniz's own solution do. In his letter to Coste, he puts the problem as follows: 'When a choice is proposed, for example to go out or not to go out, it is a question whether, with all the circumstances, internal and external, motives, perceptions, dispositions, impressions, passions, inclinations taken together, I am still in a contingent state, or whether I am necessitated to make the choice, for example, to go out; that is to say, whether this proposition true and determined in fact, *In all these circumstances taken together I shall choose to go out,* is contingent or necessary.'[11] Leibniz's answer might be put as follows: in one sense of the terms 'necessary' and 'contingent', the proposition 'In all these circumstances taken together I shall choose to go out', may be said to be contingent and not necessary, and in another sense of these terms, it may be said to be necessary and not contingent. But the sense in which the proposition may be said to be contingent, according to Leibniz, is only this: there is no logical contradiction involved in denying the proposition. And the sense in which it may be said to be necessary is this: since 'nothing ever occurs without cause or determining reason', the proposition is causally necessary 'Whenever all the circumstances taken together are such that the balance of deliberation is heavier on one side than on the other, it is certain and infallible that that is the side that is going to win out'. But if what we have been saying is true, the proposition 'In all these circumstances taken together I shall choose to go out', may be causally as well as logically contingent. Hence we must find another interpretation for Leibniz's statement that our motives and desires may incline us, or influence us, to choose without thereby necessitating us to choose.

Let us consider a public official who has some moral scruples but who also, as one says, could be had. Because of the scruples that he does have, he would never take any positive steps to receive a bribe—he would not actively solicit one. But his morality has its limits and he is also such that, if we were to confront him with a *fait accompli* or to let him see what is about to happen ($10,000 in cash is being deposited behind the garage), then he would succumb and be unable to resist. The general situation is a familiar one and this is one reason that people pray to be delivered from temptation. (It also justifies Kant's remark: 'And how many there are who may have led a long blameless life, who are only *fortunate* in having escaped so many temptations'.[12] Our relation to the misdeed that we contemplate may not be a matter simply of being able to bring it about or not to bring it about. As St. Anselm noted, there are at least four possibilities. We may illustrate them by reference to our public official and the event which is his receiving the bribe, in the following way: (i) he may be able to bring the event about himself (*facere esse*), in which case he would actively cause himself to receive the bribe; (ii) he may be able to refrain from bringing it about himself (*non facere esse*), in which case he would not himself do anything to insure that he receive the bribe; (iii) he may be able to do something to prevent the event from occurring (*facere non esse*), in which case he would make sure that the $10,000 was *not* left behind the garage; or (iv) he may be unable to do anything to prevent the event from occurring (*non facere non esse*), in which case, though he may not solicit the bribe, he would allow himself to keep it.[13] We have envisaged our

11. 'Lettre à Mr. Coste de la Nécessité et de la Contingence' (1707) in *Opera Philosophica,* ed. Erdmann, 447–49.

12. In the Preface to the *Metaphysical Elements of Ethics,* in *Kant's Critique of Practical Reason and Other Works on the Theory of Ethics,* ed. T. K. Abbott (London, 1959), 303.

13. Cf. D. P. Henry, "Saint Anselm's *De "Grammatica"*" *Philosophical Quarterly,* x (1960), 115–26 St. Anselm noted that (i) and (iii), respectively, may be thought of as forming the upper left and the upper right corners of a square of opposition, and (ii) and (iv) the lower left and the lower right.

official as a man who can resist the temptation to (i) but cannot resist the temptation to (iv): he can refrain from bringing the event about himself, but he cannot bring himself to do anything to prevent it.

Let us think of 'inclination without necessitation', then, in such terms as these. First we may contrast the two propositions:

(1) He can resist the temptation to do something in order to make A happen;
(2) He can resist the temptation to allow A to happen (i.e. to do nothing to prevent A from happening).

We may suppose that the man has some desire to have A happen and thus has a motive for making A happen. His motive for making A happen, I suggest, is one that *necessitates* provided that, because of the motive, (1) is false; he cannot resist the temptation to do something in order to make A happen. His motive for making A happen is one that *inclines* provided that, because of the motive, (2) is false; like our public official, he cannot bring himself to do anything to prevent A from happening. And therefore we can say that this motive for making A happen is one that *inclines but does not necessitate* provided that, because of the motive, (1) is true and (2) is false; he can resist the temptation to make it happen but he cannot resist the temptation to allow it to happen.

Freedom and Moral Responsibility

Alternate Possibilities and Moral Responsibility*

HARRY FRANKFURT

Harry Frankfurt (1929–) teaches philosophy at Princeton University. He has published several important papers on the free will debate.

A DOMINANT ROLE in nearly all recent inquiries into the free-will problem has been played by a principle which I shall call "the principle of alternate possibilities." This principle states that a person is morally responsible for what he has done only if he could have done otherwise. Its exact meaning is a subject of controversy, particularly concerning whether someone who accepts it is thereby committed to believing that moral responsibility and determinism are incompatible. Practically no one, however, seems inclined to deny or even to question that the principle of alternate possibilities (construed in some way or other) is true. It has generally seemed so overwhelmingly plausible that some philosophers have even characterized it as an *a priori* truth. People whose accounts of free will or of moral responsibility are radically at odds evidently find in it a firm and convenient common ground upon which they can profitably take their opposing stands.

But the principle of alternate possibilities is false. A person may well be morally responsible for what he has done even though he could not have done otherwise. The principle's plausibility is an illusion,

**This paper first appeared in* Journal of Philosophy, *vol. 66, 1969, pp. 829–839. Reprinted by permission of the publisher.*

which can be made to vanish by bringing the relevant moral phenomena into sharper focus.

I

In seeking illustrations of the principle of alternate possibilities, it is most natural to think of situations in which the same circumstances both bring it about that a person does something and make it impossible for him to avoid doing it. These include, for example, situations in which a person is coerced into doing something, or in which he is impelled to act by a hypnotic suggestion, or in which some inner compulsion drives him to do what he does. In situations of these kinds there are circumstances that make it impossible for the person to do otherwise, and these very circumstances also serve to bring it about that he does whatever it is that he does.

However, there may be circumstances that constitute sufficient conditions for a certain action to be performed by someone and that therefore make it impossible for the person to do otherwise, but that do not actually impel the person to act or in any way produce his action. A person may do something in circumstances that leave him no alternative to doing it, without these circumstances actually moving him or leading him to do it—without them playing any role, indeed, in bringing it about that he does what he does.

An examination of situations characterized by circumstances of this sort casts doubt, I believe, on the relevance to questions of moral responsibility of the fact that a person who has done something could not have done otherwise. I propose to develop some examples of this kind in the context of a discussion of coercion and to suggest that our moral intuitions concerning these examples tend to disconfirm the principle of alternate possibilities. Then I will discuss the principle in more general terms, explain what I think is wrong with it, and describe briefly and without argument how it might appropriately be revised.

II

It is generally agreed that a person who has been coerced to do something did not do it freely and is not morally responsible for having done it. Now the doctrine that coercion and moral responsibility are mutually exclusive may appear to be no more than a somewhat particularized version of the principle of alternate possibilities. It is natural enough to say of a person who has been coerced to do something that he could not have done otherwise. And it may easily seem that being coerced deprives a person of freedom and of moral responsibility simply because it is a special case of being unable to do otherwise. The principle of alternate possibilities may in this way derive some credibility from its association with the very plausible proposition that moral responsibility is excluded by coercion.

It is not right, however, that it should do so. The fact that a person was coerced to act as he did may entail both that he could not have done otherwise and that he bears no moral responsibility for his action. But his lack of moral responsibility is not entailed by his having been unable to do otherwise. The doctrine that coercion excludes moral responsibility is not correctly understood, in other words, as a particularized version of the principle of alternate possibilities.

Let us suppose that someone is threatened convincingly with a penalty he finds unacceptable and that he then does what is required of him by the issuer of the threat. We can imagine details that would make it reasonable for us to think that the person was coerced to perform the action in question, that he could not have done otherwise, and that he bears no moral responsibility for having done what he did. But just what is it about situations of this kind that warrants the judgment that the threatened person is not morally responsible for his act?

This question may be approached by considering situations of the following kind. Jones decides for reasons of his own to do something, then someone threatens him with a very harsh penalty (so harsh that any reasonable person would submit to the threat) unless he does precisely that, and Jones does it. Will we hold Jones morally responsible for what he has done? I think this will depend on the roles we think were played, in leading him to act, by his original decision and by the threat.

One possibility is that $Jones_1$ is not a reasonable man: he is, rather, a man who does what he has once decided to do no matter what happens next and no matter what the cost. In that case, the threat actually exerted no effective force upon him. He acted without any regard to it, very much as if he were not aware that it had been made. If this is indeed the way it was, the situation did not involve coercion at all. The threat did not lead $Jones_1$ to do what he did. Nor was it in fact sufficient to have prevented him from doing otherwise: if his earlier decision had been to do something else, the threat would not have deterred him in the slightest. It seems evident that in these circumstances the fact that $Jones_1$ was threatened in no way reduces the moral responsibility he would otherwise bear for his act. This example, however, is not a counterexample either to the doctrine that coercion excuses or to the principle of alternate possibilities. For we have supposed that $Jones_1$ is a man upon whom the threat had no coercive effect and, hence, that it did not actually deprive him of alternatives to doing what he did.

Another possibility is that $Jones_2$ was stampeded by the threat. Given that threat, he would have performed that action regardless of what decision he had already made. The threat upset him so profoundly, moreover, that he completely forgot his own earlier decision and did what was demanded of him entirely because he was terrified of the penalty with which he was threatened. In this case, it is not relevant to his having performed the action that he had already decided on his own to perform it. When the chips were down he thought of nothing but the threat, and fear alone led him to act. The fact that at an earlier time $Jones_2$ had decided for his own reasons to act in just that way may be relevant to an evaluation of his character; he may bear full moral responsibility for having made *that* decision. But he can hardly be said to be morally responsible for his action. For he performed the action simply as a result of the coercion to which he was subjected. His earlier decision played no role in bringing it about that he did what he did, and it would therefore be gratuitous to assign it a role in the moral evaluation of his action.

Now consider a third possibility. $Jones_3$ was neither stampeded by the threat nor indifferent to it. The threat impressed him, as it would impress any reasonable man, and he would have submitted to it wholeheartedly if he had not already made a decision that coincided with the one demanded of him. In fact, however, he performed the action in question on the basis of the decision he had made before the threat was issued. When he acted, he was not actually motivated by the threat but solely by the considerations that had originally commended the action to him. It was not the threat that led him to act, though it would have done so if he had not already provided himself with a sufficient motive for performing the action in question.

No doubt it will be very difficult for anyone to know, in a case like this one, exactly what happened. Did $Jones_3$ perform the action because of the threat, or were his reasons for acting simply those which had already persuaded him to do so? Or did he act on the basis of two motives, each of which was sufficient for his action? It is not impossible, however, that the situation should be clearer than situations of this kind usually are. And suppose it is apparent to us that $Jones_3$ acted on the basis of his own decision and not because of the threat. Then I think we would be justified in regarding his moral responsibility for what he did as unaffected by the threat even though, since he would in any case have submitted to the threat, he could not have avoided doing what he did. It would be entirely reasonable for us to make the same judgment concerning his moral responsibility that we would have made if we had not known of the threat. For the threat did not in fact influence his performance of the action. He did what he did just as if the threat had not been made at all.

III

The case of $Jones_3$ may appear at first glance to combine coercion and moral responsibility, and thus to provide a counterexample to the doctrine that coercion excuses. It is not really so certain that it does so, however, because it is unclear whether the example constitutes a genuine instance of coercion. Can we say of $Jones_3$ that he was coerced to do something, when he had already decided on his own to do it and when he did it entirely on the basis of that decision? Or would it be more correct to say that $Jones_3$ was not coerced to do what he did, even though he himself recognized that there was an irresistible force at work in virtue of which he had to do it? My own linguistic intuitions lead me toward the second alternative, but they are somewhat equivocal. Perhaps we can say either of these things, or perhaps we must add a qualifying explanation to whichever of them we say.

This murkiness, however, does not interfere with our drawing an important moral from an examination of the example. Suppose we decide to say that $Jones_3$ was *not* coerced. Our basis for saying this will clearly be that it is incorrect to regard a man as being coerced to do something unless he does it *because of* the coercive force exerted against him. The fact that an irresistible threat is made will not, then, entail that the person who receives it is coerced to do what he does. It will also be necessary that the threat is what actually accounts for his doing it. On the other hand, suppose we decide to say that $Jones_3$ *was* coerced. Then we will be bound to admit that being coerced does not exclude being morally responsible. And we will also surely be led to the view that coercion affects the judgment of a person's moral responsibility only when the person acts as he does because he is coerced to do so—i.e., when the fact that he is coerced is what accounts for his action.

Whichever we decide to say, then, we will recognize that the doctrine that coercion excludes moral responsibility is not a particularized version of the principle of alternate possibilities. Situations in which a person who does something cannot do otherwise because he is subject to coercive power are either not instances of coercion at all, or they are situations in which the person may still be morally responsible for what he does if it is not because of the coercion that he does it. When we excuse a person who has been coerced, we do not excuse him because he was unable to do otherwise. Even though a person is subject to a coercive force that precludes his performing any action but one, he may nonetheless bear full moral responsibility for performing that action.

IV

To the extent that the principle of alternate possibilities derives its plausibility from association with the doctrine that coercion excludes moral responsibility, a clear understanding of the latter diminishes the appeal of the former. Indeed the case of $Jones_3$ may appear to do more than illuminate the relationship between the two doctrines. It may well seem to provide a decisive counterexample to the principle of alternate possibilities and thus to show that this principle is false. For the irresistibility of the threat to which $Jones_3$ is subjected might well be taken to mean that he cannot but perform the action he performs. And yet the threat, since $Jones_3$ performs the action without regard to it, does not reduce his moral responsibility for what he does.

The following objection will doubtless be raised against the suggestion that the case of $Jones_3$ is a counterexample to the principle of alternate possibilities. There is perhaps a sense in which $Jones_3$ cannot do otherwise than perform the action he performs, since he is a reasonable man and the threat he encounters is sufficient to move any reasonable man. But it is not this sense that is germane to the principle of alternate possibilities. His knowledge that he stands to suffer an intolerably harsh penalty does not mean that $Jones_3$, strictly speaking, *cannot* perform any action but the one he does perform. After all it is still open to him, and this is crucial, to defy the threat if he wishes to do so and to accept the penalty his action would bring down upon him. In the sense in which the principle of alternate possibilities employs the concept of "could have done otherwise," $Jones_3$'s inability to resist the threat does not mean that he cannot do otherwise than perform the action he performs. Hence the case of $Jones_3$ does not constitute an instance contrary to the principle.

I do not propose to consider in what sense the concept of "could have done otherwise" figures in the principle of alternate possibilities, nor will I attempt to measure the force of the objection I have just described.[1] For I believe that whatever force

1. The two main concepts employed in the principle of alternate possibilities are "morally responsible" and "could have done otherwise." To discuss the principle without analyzing either of these concepts may well seem like an attempt at piracy. The reader should take notice that my Jolly Roger is now unfurled.

this objection may be thought to have can be deflected by altering the example in the following way.[2] Suppose someone—Black, let us say—wants $Jones_4$ to perform a certain action. Black is prepared to go to considerable lengths to get his way, but he prefers to avoid showing his hand unnecessarily. So he waits until $Jones_4$ is about to make up his mind what to do, and he does nothing unless it is clear to him (Black is an excellent judge of such things) that $Jones_4$ is going to decide to do something *other* than what he wants him to do. If it does become clear that $Jones_4$ is going to decide to do something else, Black takes effective steps to ensure that $Jones_4$ decides to do, and that he does do, what he wants him to do.[3] Whatever $Jones_4$'s initial preferences and inclinations, then, Black will have his way.

What steps will Black take, if he believes he must take steps, in order to ensure that $Jones_4$ decides and acts as he wishes? Anyone with a theory concerning what "could have done otherwise" means may answer this question for himself by describing whatever measures he would regard as sufficient to guarantee that, in the relevant sense, $Jones_4$ cannot do otherwise. Let Black pronounce a terrible threat, and in this way both force $Jones_4$ to perform the desired action and prevent him from performing a forbidden one. Let Black give $Jones_4$ a potion, or put him under hypnosis, and in some such way as these generate in $Jones_4$ an irresistible inner compulsion to perform the act Black wants performed and to avoid others. Or let Black manipulate the minute processes of $Jones_4$'s brain and nervous system in some more direct way, so that causal forces running in and out of his synapses and along the poor man's nerves determine that he chooses to act and that he does act in the one way and not in any other. Given any conditions under which it will be maintained that $Jones_4$ cannot do otherwise, in other words, let Black bring it about that those conditions prevail. The structure of the example is flexible enough, I think, to find a way around any charge of irrelevance by accommodating the doctrine on which the charge is based.[4]

Now suppose that Black never has to show his hand because $Jones_4$, for reasons of his own, decides to perform and does perform the very action Black wants him to perform. In that case, it seems clear, $Jones_4$ will bear precisely the same moral responsibility for what he does as he would have borne if Black had not been ready to take steps to ensure that he do it. It would be quite unreasonable to excuse $Jones_4$ for his action, or to withhold the praise to which it would normally entitle him, on the basis of the fact that he could not have done otherwise. This fact played no role at all in leading him to act as he did. He would have acted the same even if it had not been a fact. Indeed, everything happened just as it would have happened without Black's presence in the situation and without his readiness to intrude into it.

In this example there are sufficient conditions for $Jones_4$'s performing the action in question. What action he performs is not up to him. Of course it is in a way up to him whether he acts on his own or as a result of Black's intervention. That

2. After thinking up the example that I am about to develop I learned that Robert Nozick, in lectures given several years ago, had formulated an example of the same general type and had proposed it as a counterexample to the principle of alternate possibilities.

3. The assumption that Black can predict what $Jones_4$ will decide to do does not beg the question of determinism. We can imagine that $Jones_4$ has often confronted the alternatives—*A* and *B*—that he now confronts, and that his face has invariably twitched when he was about to decide to do *A* and never when he was about to decide to do *B*. Knowing this, and observing the twitch, Black would have a basis for prediction. This does, to be sure, suppose that there is some sort of causal relation between $Jones_4$'s state at the time of the twitch and his subsequent states. But any plausible view of decision or of action will allow that reaching a decision and performing an action both involve earlier and later phases, with causal relations between them, and such that the earlier phases are not themselves part of the decision or of the action. The example does not require that these earlier phases be deterministically related to still earlier events.

4. The example is also flexible enough to allow for the elimination of Black altogether. Anyone who thinks that the effectiveness of the example is undermined by its reliance on a human manipulator, who imposes his will on $Jones_4$, can substitute for Black a machine programmed to do what Black does. If this is still not good enough, forget both Black and the machine and suppose that their role is played by natural forces involving no will or design at all.

depends upon what action he himself is inclined to perform. But whether he finally acts on his own or as a result of Black's intervention, he performs the same action. He has no alternative but to do what Black wants him to do. If he does it on his own, however, his moral responsibility for doing it is not affected by the fact that Black was lurking in the background with sinister intent, since this intent never comes into play.

V

The fact that a person could not have avoided doing something is a sufficient condition of his having done it. But, as some of my examples show, this fact may play no role whatever in the explanation of why he did it. It may not figure at all among the circumstances that actually brought it about that he did what he did, so that his action is to be accounted for on another basis entirely. Even though the person was unable to do otherwise, that is to say, it may not be the case that he acted as he did *because* he could not have done otherwise. Now if someone had no alternative to performing a certain action but did not perform it because he was unable to do otherwise, then he would have performed exactly the same action even if he *could* have done otherwise. The circumstances that made it impossible for him to do otherwise could have been subtracted from the situation without affecting what happened or why it happened in any way. Whatever it was that actually led the person to do what he did, or that made him do it, would have led him to do it or made him do it even if it had been possible for him to do something else instead.

Thus it would have made no difference, so far as concerns his action or how he came to perform it, if the circumstances that made it impossible for him to avoid performing it had not prevailed. The fact that he could not have done otherwise clearly provides no basis for supposing that he *might* have done otherwise if he had been able to do so. When a fact is in this way irrelevant to the problem of accounting for a person's action it seems quite gratuitous to assign it any weight in the assessment of his moral responsibility. Why should the fact be considered in reaching a moral judgment concerning the person when it does not help in any way to understand either what made him act as he did or what, in other circumstances, he might have done?

This, then, is why the principle of alternate possibilities is mistaken. It asserts that a person bears no moral responsibility—that is, he is to be excused—for having performed an action if there were circumstances that made it impossible for him to avoid performing it. But there may be circumstances that make it impossible for a person to avoid performing some action without those circumstances in any way bringing it about that he performs that action. It would surely be no good for the person to refer to circumstances of this sort in an effort to absolve himself of moral responsibility for performing the action in question. For those circumstances, by hypothesis, actually had nothing to do with his having done what he did. He would have done precisely the same thing, and he would have been led or made in precisely the same way to do it, even if they had not prevailed.

We often do, to be sure, excuse people for what they have done when they tell us (and we believe them) that they could not have done otherwise. But this is because we assume that what they tell us serves to explain why they did what they did. We take it for granted that they are not being disingenuous, as a person would be who cited as an excuse the fact that he could not have avoided doing what he did but who knew full well that it was not at all because of this that he did it.

What I have said may suggest that the principle of alternate possibilities should be revised so as to assert that a person is not morally responsible for what he has done if he did it because he could not have done otherwise. It may be noted that this revision of the principle does not seriously affect the arguments of those who have relied on the original principle in their efforts to maintain that moral responsibility and determinism are incompatible. For if it was causally determined that a person perform a certain action, then it will be true that the person performed it because of those causal determinants. And if the fact that it was causally determined that a person perform a certain action means that the person could not have done otherwise, as philosophers who argue for the incompatibility thesis characteristically suppose, then the fact that it was causally determined that a person perform a certain action will mean that the person performed it because he could not have done otherwise. The revised principle of alternate possibilities will entail, on this assumption concerning the meaning of 'could have done otherwise', that a person is not morally responsible for what he has done if it was causally determined that he do it. I do not believe, however, that this revision of the principle is acceptable.

Suppose a person tells us that he did what he did because he was unable to do otherwise; or suppose he makes the similar statement that he did what he did because he had to do it. We do often accept statements like these (if we believe them) as valid excuses, and such statements may well seem at first glance to invoke the revised principle of alternate possibilities. But I think that when we accept such statements as valid excuses it is because we assume that we are being told more than the statements strictly and literally convey. We understand the person who offers the excuse to mean that he did what he did *only because* he was unable to do otherwise, or *only because* he had to do it. And we understand him to mean, more particularly, that when he did what he did it was not because that was what he really wanted to do. The principle of alternate possibilities should thus be replaced, in my opinion, by the following principle: a person is not morally responsible for what he has done if he did it only because he could not have done otherwise. This principle does not appear to conflict with the view that moral responsibility is compatible with determinism.

The following may all be true: there were circumstances that made it impossible for a person to avoid doing something; these circumstances actually played a role in bringing it about that he did it, so that it is correct to say that he did it because he could not have done otherwise; the person really wanted to do what he did; he did it because it was what he really wanted to do, so that it is not correct to say that he did what he did only because he could not have done otherwise. Under these conditions, the person may well be morally responsible for what he has done. On the other hand, he will not be morally responsible for what he has done if he did it only because he could not have done otherwise, even if what he did was something he really wanted to do.

Moral Luck*

THOMAS NAGEL

Thomas Nagel (1937–) teaches philosophy at New York University. He is the author of *The View from Nowhere* and numerous important works in the philosophy of mind and moral philosophy.

KANT BELIEVED THAT GOOD OR BAD LUCK should influence neither our moral judgment of a person and his actions, nor his moral assessment of himself.

**Reprinted from* Mortal Questions *by Thomas Nagel by permission of Thomas Nagel and Cambridge University Press.*

> The good will is not good because of what it effects or accomplishes or because of its adequacy to achieve some proposed end; it is good only because of its willing, i.e., it is good of itself. And, regarded for itself, it is to be esteemed incomparably higher than anything which could be brought about by it in favor of any inclination or even of the sum total of all inclinations. Even if it should happen that, by a particular unfortunate fate or by the niggardly provision of a stepmotherly nature, this will should be wholly lacking in power to accomplish its purpose, and if even the greatest effort should not avail it to achieve anything of its end, and if there remained only the good will (not as a mere wish but as the summoning of all the means in our power), it would sparkle like a jewel in its own right, as something that had its full worth in itself. Usefulness or fruitlessness can neither diminish nor augment this worth.[1]

He would presumably have said the same thing about a bad will: whether it accomplishes its evil purposes is morally irrelevant. And a course of action that would be condemned if it had a bad outcome cannot be vindicated if by luck it turns out well. There cannot be moral risk. This view seems to be wrong, but it arises in response to a fundamental problem about moral responsibility to which we possess no satisfactory solution.

The problem develops out of the ordinary conditions of moral judgment. Prior to reflection it is intuitively plausible that people cannot be morally assessed for what is not their fault, or for what is due to factors beyond their control. Such judgment is different from the evaluation of something as a good or bad thing, or state of affairs. The latter may be present in addition to moral judgment, but when we blame someone for his actions we are not merely saying it is bad that they happened, or bad that he exists: we are judging *him*, saying he is bad, which is different from his being a bad thing. This kind of judgment takes only a certain kind of object. Without being able to explain exactly why, we feel that the appropriateness of moral assessment is easily undermined by the discovery that the act or attribute, no matter how good or bad, is not under the person's control. While other evaluations remain, this one seems to lose its footing. So a clear absence of control, produced by involuntary movement, physical force, or ignorance of the circumstances, excuses what is done from moral judgment. But what we do depends in many more ways than these on what is not under our control—what is not produced by a good or a bad will in Kant's phrase. And external influences in this broader range are not usually thought to excuse what is done from moral judgment, positive or negative.

Let me give a few examples, beginning with the type of case Kant has in mind. Whether we succeed or fail in what we try to do nearly always depends to some extent on factors beyond our control. This is true of murder, altruism, revolution, the sacrifice of certain interests for the sake of others—almost any morally important act. What has been done, and what is morally judged, is partly determined by external factors. However jewel-like the good will may be in its own right, there is a morally significant difference between rescuing someone from a burning building and dropping him from a twelfth-story window while trying to rescue him. Similarly, there is a morally significant difference between reckless driving and manslaughter. But whether a reckless driver hits a pedestrian depends on the presence of the pedestrian at the point where he recklessly passes a red light. What we do is also limited by the opportunities and choices with which we are faced, and these are largely determined by factors beyond our control. Someone who was an officer in a concentration camp might have led a quiet and harmless life if the Nazis had never come to power in Germany. And someone who led a quiet and harmless life in Argentina might have become an officer in a concentration camp if he had not left Germany for business reasons in 1930.

I shall say more later about these and other examples. I introduce them here to illustrate a general point. Where a significant aspect of what someone does depends on factors beyond his control, yet we continue to treat him in that respect as an object of moral judgment, it can be called moral luck. Such luck can be good or bad. And the problem posed by this phenomenon, which led Kant to deny its possibility, is that the broad range of external influences here identified seems on close examination to undermine moral assessment as surely as does the narrower range of familiar excusing conditions. If the condition of control is consistently applied, it threatens to erode most of the moral assessments we find it natural to make. The things for which people are morally judged are determined in more ways than we at first realize by what is beyond their control. And when the seemingly natural requirement of fault or responsibility is applied in light of these facts, it leaves few pre-reflective moral judgments intact. Ultimately, nothing or almost nothing about what a person does seems to be under his control.

Why not conclude, then, that the condition of control is false—that it is an initially plausible hypothesis refuted by clear counter-examples? One could in that case look instead for a more refined condition which picked out the *kinds* of lack of control that really undermine certain moral judgments, without yielding the unacceptable conclusion derived from the broader condition, that most or all ordinary moral judgments are illegitimate.

What rules out this escape is that we are dealing not with a theoretical conjecture but with a philosophical problem. The condition of control does not suggest itself merely as a generalization from certain clear cases. It seems *correct* in the further cases to which it is extended beyond the original set. When we undermine moral assessment by considering new ways in which control is absent, we are not just discovering what *would* follow given the general hypothesis, but are actually being persuaded that in itself the absence of control is relevant in these cases too. The erosion of moral judgment emerges not as the absurd consequence of an over-simple theory, but as a natural consequence of the ordinary idea of moral assessment, when it is applied in view of a more complete and precise account of the facts. It would therefore be a mistake to argue from the unacceptability of the conclusions to the need for a different account of the conditions of moral responsibility. The view that moral luck is paradoxical is not a *mistake,* ethical or logical, but a perception of one of the ways in which the intuitively acceptable conditions of moral judgment threaten to undermine it all.

It resembles the situation in another area of philosophy, the theory of knowledge. There too conditions which seem perfectly natural, and which grow out of the ordinary procedures for challenging and defending claims to knowledge, threaten to undermine all such claims if consistently applied. Most skeptical arguments have this quality: they do not depend on the imposition of arbitrarily stringent standards of knowledge, arrived at by misunderstanding, but appear to grow inevitably from the consistent application of ordinary standards.[2] There is a substantive parallel as well, for epistemological skepticism arises from consideration of the respects in which our beliefs and their relation to reality depend on factors beyond our control. External and internal causes produce our beliefs. We may subject these processes to scrutiny in an effort to avoid error, but our conclusions at this next level also result, in part, from influences which we do not control directly. The same will be true no matter how far we carry the investigation. Our beliefs are always, ultimately, due to factors outside our control, and the impossibility of encompassing those factors without being at the mercy of others leads us to doubt whether we know anything. It looks as though, if any of our beliefs are true, it is pure biological luck rather than knowledge.

Moral luck is like this because while there are various respects in which the natural objects of moral assessment are out of our control or influenced by what is out of our control, we cannot reflect on these facts without losing our grip on the judgments.

There are roughly four ways in which the natural objects of moral assessment are disturbingly subject to luck. One is the phenomenon of constitutive luck—the kind of person you are, where this is not just a question of what you deliberately do, but of your inclinations, capacities, and temperament. Another category is luck in one's circumstances—the kind of problems and situations one faces. The other two have to do with the causes and effects of action: luck in how one is determined by antecedent circumstances, and luck in the way one's actions and projects turn out. All of them present a common problem. They are all opposed by the idea that one cannot be more culpable or estimable for anything than one is for that fraction of it which is under one's control. It seems irrational to take or dispense credit or blame for matters over which a person has no control, or for their influence on results over which he has partial control. Such things may create the conditions for action, but action can be judged only to the extent that it goes beyond these conditions and does not just result from them.

Let us first consider luck, good and bad, in the way things turn out. Kant, in the above-quoted passage, has one example of this in mind, but the category covers a wide range. It includes the truck driver who accidentally runs over a child, the artist who abandons his wife and five children to devote himself to painting,[3] and other cases in which the possibilities of success and failure are even greater. The driver, if he is entirely without fault, will feel terrible about his role in the event, but will not have to reproach himself. Therefore this example of agent-regret[4] is not yet a case of *moral* bad luck. However, if the driver was guilty of even a minor degree of negligence—failing to have his brakes checked recently, for example—then if that negligence contributes to the death of the child, he will not merely feel terrible. He will blame himself for the death. And what makes this an example of moral luck is that he would have to blame himself only slightly for the negligence itself if no situation arose which required him to brake suddenly and violently to avoid hitting a child. Yet the *negligence* is the same in both cases, and the driver has no control over whether a child will run into his path.

The same is true at higher levels of negligence. If someone has had too much to drink and his car swerves on to the sidewalk, he can count himself morally lucky if there are no pedestrians in his path. If there were, he would be to blame for their deaths, and would probably be prosecuted for manslaughter. But if he hurts no one, although his recklessness is exactly the same, he is guilty of a far less serious legal offense and will certainly reproach himself and be reproached by others much less severely. To take another legal example, the penalty for attempted murder is less than that for successful murder—however similar the intentions and motives of the assailant may be in the two cases. His degree of culpability can depend, it would seem, on whether the victim happened to be wearing a bullet-proof vest, or whether a bird flew into the path of the bullet—matters beyond his control.

Finally, there are cases of decision under uncertainty—common in public and in private life. Anna Karenina goes off with Vronsky, Gauguin leaves his family, Chamberlain signs the Munich agreement, the Decembrists persuade the troops under their command to revolt against the czar, the American colonies declare their independence from Britain, you introduce two people in an attempt at matchmaking. It is tempting in all such cases to feel that some decision must be possible, in the light of what is known at the time, which will make reproach unsuitable no matter how things turn out. But this is not true; when someone acts in such ways he takes his life, or his moral position, into his hands, because how things run out determines what he has done. It is possible *also* to assess the decision from the point of view of what could be known at the time, but this is not the end of the story. If the Decembrists had succeeded in overthrowing Nicholas I in 1825 and establishing a constitutional regime, they would be heroes. As it is, not only did they fail and pay for it, but they bore some responsibility for the terrible punishments meted out to the troops who had been persuaded to follow them. If the American Revolution had been a bloody failure resulting in greater repression, then Jefferson, Franklin and Washington would still have made a noble attempt, and might not even have regretted it on their way to the scaffold, but they would also have had to blame themselves for what they had helped to bring on their compatriots. (Perhaps peaceful efforts at reform would eventually have succeeded.) If Hitler had not overrun Europe and exterminated millions, but instead had died of a heart attack after occupying the Sudetenland, Chamberlain's action at Munich would still have utterly betrayed the Czechs, but it would not be the great moral disaster that has made his name a household word.[5]

In many cases of difficult choice the outcome cannot be foreseen with certainty. One kind of assessment of the choice is possible in advance, but another kind must await the outcome, because the outcome determines what has been done. The same degree of culpability or estimability in intention, motive, or concern is compatible with a wide range of judgments, positive or negative, depending on what happened beyond the point of decision. The *mens rea* which could have existed in the absence of any consequences does not exhaust the grounds of moral judgment. Actual results influence culpability or esteem in a large class of unquestionably ethical cases ranging from negligence through political choice.

That these are genuine moral judgments rather than expressions of temporary attitude is evident from the fact that one can say *in advance* how the moral verdict will depend on the results. If one negligently leaves the bath running with the baby in it, one will realize, as one bounds up the stairs toward the bathroom, that if the baby has drowned one has done something awful, whereas if it has not one has merely been careless. Someone who launches a violent revolution against an authoritarian regime knows that if he fails he will be responsible for much suffering that is in vain, but if he succeeds he will be justified by the outcome. I do not mean that *any* action can be retroactively justified by history. Certain things are so bad in themselves, or so risky, that no results can make them all right. Nevertheless, when moral judgment does depend on the outcome, it is objective and timeless and not dependent on a change of standpoint produced by success or failure. The judgment after the fact follows from a hypothetical judgment that can be made beforehand, and it can be made as easily by someone else as by the agent.

From the point of view which makes responsibility dependent on control, all this seems absurd. How is it possible to be more or less culpable depending on whether a child gets into the path of one's car, or a bird into the path of one's bullet? Perhaps it is true that what is done depends on more than the agent's state of mind or intention. The problem then is, why is it not irrational to base moral assessment on what people do, in this broad sense? It amounts to holding them responsible for the contributions of fate as well as for their own—provided they have made some contribution to begin with. If we look at cases of negligence or attempt, the pattern seems to be that overall culpability corresponds to the product of mental or intentional fault and the seriousness of the outcome. Cases of decision under uncertainty are less easily explained in this way, for it seems that the overall judgment can even shift from positive to negative depending on the outcome. But here too it seems rational to subtract the effects of occurrences subsequent to the choice, that were merely possible at the time, and concentrate moral assessment on the actual decision in light of the probabilities. If the object of moral judgment is the *person*, then to hold him accountable for what he has done in the broader sense is akin to strict liability, which may have its legal uses but seems irrational as a moral position.

The result of such a line of thought is to pare down each act to its morally essential core, an inner act of pure will assessed by motive and intention. Adam Smith advocates such a position in *The Theory of Moral Sentiments,* but notes that it runs contrary to our actual judgments.

> But how well soever we may seem to be persuaded of the truth of this equitable maxim, when we consider it after this manner, in abstract, yet when we come to particular cases, the actual consequences which happen to proceed from any action, have a very great effect upon our sentiments concerning its merit or demerit, and almost always either enhance or diminish our sense of both. Scarce, in any one instance, perhaps, will our sentiments be found, after examination, to be entirely regulated by this rule, which we all acknowledge ought entirely to regulate them.[6]

Joel Feinberg points out further that restricting the domain of moral responsibility to the inner world will not immunize it to luck. Factors beyond the agent's control, like a coughing fit, can interfere with his decisions as surely as they can with the path of a bullet from his gun.[7] Nevertheless the tendency to cut down the scope of moral assessment is pervasive, and does not limit itself to the influence of effects. It attempts to isolate the will from the other direction, so to speak, by separating out constitutive luck. Let us consider that next.

Kant was particularly insistent on the moral irrelevance of qualities of temperament and personality that are not under the control of the will. Such qualities as sympathy or coldness might provide the background against which obedience to moral requirements is more or less difficult, but they could not be objects of moral assessment themselves, and might well interfere with confident assessment of its proper object—the determination of the will by the motive of duty. This rules out moral judgment of many of the virtues and vices, which are states of character that influence choice but are certainly not exhausted by dispositions to act deliberately in certain ways. A person may be greedy, envious, cowardly, cold, ungenerous, unkind, vain, or conceited, but *behave* perfectly by a monumental effort of will. To possess these vices is to be unable to help having certain feelings under certain circumstances, and to have strong spontaneous impulses to act badly. Even if one controls the impulses, one still has the vice. An envious person hates the greater success of others. He can be morally condemned as envious even if he congratulates them cordially and does nothing to denigrate or spoil their success. Conceit, likewise, need not be displayed. It is fully present in someone who cannot help dwelling with secret satisfaction on the superiority of his own achievements, talents, beauty, intelligence, or virtue. To some extent such a quality may be the product of earlier choices; to some extent it may be amenable to change by current actions. But it is largely a matter of constitutive bad fortune. Yet people are morally condemned for such qualities, and esteemed for others equally beyond control of the will: they are assessed for what they are *like*.

To Kant this seems incoherent because virtue is enjoined on everyone and therefore must in principle be possible for everyone. It may be easier for some than for others, but it must be possible to achieve it by making the right choices, against whatever temperamental background.[8] One may want to have a generous spirit, or regret not having one, but it makes no sense to condemn oneself or anyone else for a quality which is not within the control of the will. Condemnation implies that you should not be like that, not that it is unfortunate that you are.

Nevertheless. Kant's conclusion remains intuitively unacceptable. We may be persuaded that these moral judgments are irrational, but they reappear involuntarily as soon as the argument is over. This is the pattern throughout the subject.

The third category to consider is luck in one's circumstances, and I shall mention it briefly. The things we are called upon to do, the moral tests we face, are importantly determined by factors beyond our control. It may be true of someone that in a dangerous situation he would behave in a cowardly or heroic fashion, but if the situation never arises, he will never have the chance to distinguish or disgrace himself in this way, and his moral record will be different.[9]

A conspicuous example of this is political. Ordinary citizens of Nazi Germany had an opportunity to behave heroically by opposing the regime. They also had an opportunity to behave badly, and most of them are culpable for having failed this test. But it is a test to which the citizens of other countries were not subjected, with the result that even if they, or some of them, would have behaved as badly as the Germans in like circumstances, they simply did not and therefore are not similarly culpable. Here again one is morally at the mercy of fate, and it may seem irrational upon reflection, but our ordinary moral attitudes would be unrecognizable without it. We judge people for what they actually do or fail to do, not just for what they would have done if circumstances had been different.[10]

This form of moral determination by the actual is also paradoxical, but we can begin to see how deep in the concept of responsibility the paradox is embedded. A person can be morally responsible only for what he does; but what he does results from a great deal that he does not do; therefore he is not morally responsible for what he is and is not responsible for. (This is not a contradiction, but it is a paradox.)

It should be obvious that there is a connection between these problems about responsibility and control and an even more familiar problem, that of freedom of the will. That is the last type of moral luck I want to take up, though I can do no more within the scope of this essay than indicate its connection with the other types.

If one cannot be responsible for consequences of one's acts due to factors beyond one's control, or for antecedents of one's acts that are properties of temperament not subject to one's will, or for the circumstances that pose one's moral choices, then how can one be responsible even for the stripped-down acts of the will itself, if *they* are the product of antecedent circumstances outside of the will's control?

The area of genuine agency, and therefore of legitimate moral judgment, seems to shrink under this scrutiny to an extensionless point. Everything seems to result from the combined influence of factors, antecedent and posterior to action, that are not within the agent's control. Since he cannot be responsible for them, he cannot be responsible for their results—though it may remain possible to take up the aesthetic or other evaluative analogues of the moral attitudes that are thus displaced.

It is also possible, of course, to brazen it out and refuse to accept the results, which indeed seem unacceptable as soon as we stop thinking about the arguments. Admittedly, if certain surrounding circumstances had been different, then no unfortunate consequences would have followed from a wicked intention, and no seriously culpable act would have been performed; but since the circumstances were *not* different, and the agent *in fact* succeeded in perpetrating a particularly cruel murder, *that* is what he did, and that is what he is responsible for. Similarly, we may admit that if certain antecedent circumstances had been different, the agent would never have developed into the sort of person who would do such a thing; but since he *did* develop (as the inevitable result of those antecedent circumstances) into the sort of swine he is, and into the person who committed such a murder, *that* is what he is blameable for. In both cases one is responsible for what one actually does—even if what one actually does depends in important ways on what is not within one's control. This compatibilist account of our moral judgments would leave room for the ordinary conditions of responsibility—the absence of coercion, ignorance, or involuntary movement—as part of the determination of what someone has done—but it is understood not to exclude the influence of a great deal that he has not done.[11]

The only thing wrong with this solution is its failure to explain how skeptical problems arise. For they arise not from the imposition of an arbitrary external requirement, but from the nature of moral judgment itself. Something in the ordinary idea of what someone does must explain how it can seem necessary to subtract from it anything that merely happens—even though the ultimate consequence of such subtraction is that nothing remains. And something in the ordinary idea of knowledge must explain why it seems to be undermined by any influences on belief not within the control of the subject—so that knowledge seems impossible without an impossible foundation in autonomous reason. But let us leave epistemology aside and concentrate on action, character, and moral assessment.

The problem arises, I believe, because the self which acts and is the object of moral judgment is threatened with dissolution by the absorption of its acts and impulses into the class of events. Moral judgment of a person is judgment not of what happens to him, but of him. It does not say merely that a certain event or state of affairs is fortunate or unfortunate or even terrible. It is not an evaluation of a state of the world, or of an individual as part of the world. We are not thinking just that it would be better if he were different, or did not exist, or had not done some of the things he has done. We are judging *him*, rather than his existence or characteristics. The effect of concentrating on the influence of what is not under his control is to make this responsible self seem to disappear, swallowed up by the order of mere events.

What, however, do we have in mind that a person must *be* to be the object of these moral attitudes? While the concept of agency is easily undermined, it is very difficult to give it a positive characterization. That is familiar from the literature on Free Will.

I believe that in a sense the problem has no solution, because something in the idea of agency is incompatible with actions being events, or people being things. But as the external determinants of what someone has done are gradually exposed, in their effect on consequences, character, and choice itself, it becomes gradually clear that actions are events and people things. Eventually nothing remains which can be ascribed to the responsible self, and we are left with nothing but a portion of the larger sequences of events, which can be deplored or celebrated, but not blamed or praised.

Though I cannot define the idea of the active self that is thus undermined, it is possible to say something about its sources. There is a close connection between our feelings about ourselves and our feelings about others. Guilt and indignation, shame and contempt, pride and admiration are internal and external sides of the same moral attitudes. We are unable to view ourselves simply as portions of the world, and from inside we have a rough idea of the boundary between what is us and what is not, what we do and what happens to us, what is our personality and what is an accidental handicap. We apply the same essentially internal conception of the self to others. About ourselves we feel pride, shame, guilt, remorse—and agent-regret. We do not regard our actions and our characters merely as fortunate or unfortunate episodes—though they may also be that. We cannot *simply* take an external evaluative view of ourselves—of what we most essentially are and what we do. And this remains true even when we have seen that we are not responsible for our own existence, or our nature, or the choices we have to make, or the circumstances that give our acts the consequences they have. Those acts remain ours and we remain ourselves, despite the persuasiveness of the reasons that seem to argue us out of existence.

It is this internal view that we extend to others in moral judgment—when we judge *them* rather than their desirability or utility. We extend to others the refusal to limit ourselves to external evaluation, and we accord to them selves like our own. But in both cases this comes up against the brutal inclusion of humans and everything about them in a world from which they cannot be separated and of which they are nothing but contents. The external view forces itself on us at the same time that we resist it. One way this occurs is through the gradual erosion of what we do by the subtraction of what happens.[12]

The inclusion of consequences in the conception of what we have done is an acknowledgment that we are parts of the world, but the paradoxical character of moral luck which emerges from this acknowledgment shows that we are unable to operate with such a view, for it leaves us with no one to be. The same thing is revealed in the appearance that determinism obliterates responsibility. Once we see an aspect of what we or someone else does as something that happens, we lose our grip on the idea that it has been done and that we can judge the doer and not just the happening. This explains why the absence of determinism is no more hospitable to the concept of agency than is its presence—a point that has been noticed often. Either way the act is viewed externally, as part of the course of events.

The problem of moral luck cannot be understood without an account of the internal conception of agency and its special connection with the moral attitudes as opposed to other types of value. I do not have such an account. The degree to which the problem has a solution can be determined only by seeing whether in some degree the incompatibility between this conception and the various ways in which we do not control what we do is only apparent. I have nothing to offer on that topic either, but it is not enough to say merely that our basic moral attitudes toward ourselves and others are determined by what is actual; for they are also threatened by the sources of that actuality, and by the external view of action which forces itself on us when we see how everything we do belongs to a world that we have not created.

NOTES

1. Immanuel Kant, *Foundations of the Metaphysics of Morals,* L. W. Beck, trans. (Bobbs-Merrill, 1959), sec. I, paragraph 3.

2. See Thompson Clark, "The Legacy of Skepticism," *Journal of Philosophy,* LXIX, no. 20 (November 9, 1972): 754–69.

3. Such a case, modelled on the life of Gauguin, is discussed by Bernard Williams in "Moral Luck," *Proceedings of the Aristotelian Society,* supplementary vol. L (1976): 115–35 (to which the original version of this essay was a reply). He points out that though success or failure cannot be predicted in advance, Gauguin's most basic retrospective feelings about the decision will be determined by the development of his talent. My disagreement with Williams is that his account fails to explain why such retrospective attitudes can be called moral. If success does not permit Gauguin to justify himself to others, but still determines his most basic feelings, that shows only that his most basic feelings need not be moral. It does not show that

morality is subject to luck. If the retrospective judgment were moral, it would imply the truth of a hypothetical judgment made in advance, of the form "If I leave my family and become a great painter, I will be justified by success; if I don't become a great painter, the act will be unforgivable."

4. Williams's term (*ibid.*).

5. For a fascinating but morally repellent discussion of the topic of justification by history, see Maurice Merleau-Ponty, *Humanisme et Terreur* (Paris: Gallimard, 1947), translated as *Humanism and Terror* (Boston: Beacon Press, 1969).

6. Adam Smith, *The Theory of Moral Sentiments,* 1759, Pt II, sect. 3, Introduction, para. 5.

7. "Problematic Responsibility in Law and Morals," in Joel Feinberg, *Doing and Deserving* (Princeton: Princeton University Press, 1970).

8. If nature has put little sympathy in the heart of a man, and if he, though an honest man, is by temperament cold and indifferent to the sufferings of others, perhaps because he is provided with special gifts of patience and fortitude and expects or even requires that others should have the same—and such a man would certainly not be the meanest product of nature—would not he find in himself a source from which to give himself a far higher worth than he could have got by having a good-natured temperament?" (Kant, *Foundations of the Metaphysics of Morals,* first section, eleventh paragraph).

9. Cf. Thomas Gray, 'Elegy Written in a Country Churchyard':

Some mute inglorious Milton here may rest.
Some Cromwell, guiltless of his country's blood.

An unusual example of circumstantial moral luck is provided by the kind of moral dilemma with which someone can be faced through no fault of his own, but which leaves him with nothing to do which is not wrong. See chapter 5; and Bernard Williams, 'Ethical Consistency,' *Proceedings of the Aristotelian Society,* supplementary vol. XXXIX (1965), reprinted in *Problems of the Self* (Cambridge: Cambridge University Press, 1973), pp. 166–86.

10. Circumstantial luck can extend to aspects of the situation other than individual behavior. For example, during the Vietnam War even U.S. citizens who had opposed their country's actions vigorously from the start often felt compromised by its crimes. Here they were not even responsible; there was probably nothing they could do to stop what was happening, so the feeling of being implicated may seem unintelligible. But it is nearly impossible to view the crimes of one's own country in the same way that one views the crimes of another country, no matter how equal one's lack of power to stop them in the two cases. One *is* a citizen of one of them, and has a connexion with its actions (even if only through taxes that cannot be withheld)—that one does not have with the other's. This makes it possible to be ashamed of one's country, and to feel a victim of moral bad luck that one was an American in the 1960s.

11. The corresponding position in epistemology would be that knowledge consists of true beliefs formed in certain ways, and that it does not require all aspects of the process to be under the knower's control, actually or potentially. Both the correctness of these beliefs and the process by which they are arrived at would therefore be importantly subject to luck. The Nobel Prize is not awarded to people who turn out to be wrong, no matter how brilliant their reasoning.

12. See P. F. Strawson's discussion of the conflict between the objective attitude and personal reactive attitudes in 'Freedom and Resentment.' *Proceedings of the British Academy,* 1962, reprinted in *Studies in the Philosophy of Thought and Action,* ed. P. F. Strawson (London: Oxford University Press, 1968), and in P. F. Strawson, *Freedom and Resentment and Other Essays* (London: Methuen, 1974).

Sanity and the Metaphysics of Responsibility*

SUSAN WOLF

Susan Wolf (1952–) teaches philosophy at Johns Hopkins University.

PHILOSOPHERS WHO STUDY the problems of free will and responsibility have an easier time than most in meeting challenges about the relevance of their work to ordinary, practical concerns. Indeed, philosophers who study these problems are rarely faced with such challenges at all, since questions concerning the conditions of responsibility come up so obviously and so frequently in everyday life. Under scrutiny, however, one might question whether the connections between philosophical and nonphilosophical concerns in this area are real.

In everyday contexts, when lawyers, judges, parents, and others are concerned with issues of responsibility, they know, or think they know, what in general the conditions of responsibility are. Their questions are questions of application: Does this or that particular person meet this or that particular condition? Is this person mature enough, or informed enough, or sane enough to be responsible? Was he or she acting under posthypnotic suggestion or under the influence of a mind-impairing drug? It is assumed, in these contexts, that normal, fully developed adult human beings are responsible beings. The questions have to do with whether a given individual falls within the normal range.

By contrast, philosophers tend to be uncertain about the general conditions of responsibility, and they care less about dividing the responsible from the nonresponsible agents than about determining whether, and if so why, any of us are ever responsible for anything at all.

In the classroom, we might argue that the philosophical concerns grow out of the nonphilosophical ones, that they take off where the nonphilosophical questions stop. In this way, we might convince our students that even if they are not plagued by the philosophical worries, they ought to be. If they worry about whether a person is mature enough, informed enough, and sane enough to be responsible, then they should worry about whether that person is metaphysically free enough, too.

The argument I make here, however, goes in the opposite direction. My aim is not to convince people who are interested in the apparently nonphilosophical conditions of responsibility that they should go on to worry about the philosophical conditions as well, but rather to urge those who already worry about the philosophical problems not to leave the more mundane, prephilosophical problems behind. In particular, I suggest that the mundane recognition that *sanity* is a condition of responsibility has more to do with the murky and apparently metaphysical problems which surround the issue of responsibility than at first meets the eye. Once the significance of the condition of sanity is fully appreciated, at least some of the apparently insuperable metaphysical aspects of the problem of responsibility will dissolve.

My strategy is to examine a recent trend in philosophical discussions of responsibility, a trend that tries, but I think ultimately fails, to give an acceptable analysis of the conditions of responsibility. It fails due to what at first appear to be deep and irre-

**From Ferdinand David Schoeman (ed.).* Responsibility, Character, and the Emotions: New Essays in Moral Psychology *(New York: Cambridge University Press, 1988). pp. 46–62. Reprinted with the permission of Cambridge University Press.*

solvable metaphysical problems. It is here that I suggest that the condition of sanity comes to the rescue. What at first appears to be an impossible requirement for responsibility—the requirement that the responsible agent have created her- or himself—turns out to be the vastly more mundane and noncontroversial requirement that the responsible agent must, in a fairly standard sense, be sane.

FRANKFURT, WATSON, AND TAYLOR

The trend I have in mind is exemplified by the writings of Harry Frankfurt, Gary Watson, and Charles Taylor. I will briefly discuss each of their separate proposals, and then offer a composite view that, while lacking the subtlety of any of the separate accounts, will highlight some important insights and some important blind spots they share.

In his seminal article "Freedom of the Will and the Concept of a Person,"[1] Harry Frankfurt notes a distinction between freedom of action and freedom of the will. A person has freedom of action, he points out, if she (or he) has the freedom to do whatever she wills to do—the freedom to walk or sit, to vote liberal or conservative, to publish a book or open a store, in accordance with her strongest desires. Even a person who has freedom of action may fail to be responsible for her actions, however, if the wants or desires she has the freedom to convert into action are themselves not subject to her control. Thus, the person who acts under posthypnotic suggestion, the victim of brainwashing, and the kleptomaniac might all possess freedom of action. In the standard contexts in which these examples are raised, it is assumed that none of the individuals is locked up or bound. Rather, these individuals are understood to act on what, at one level at least, must be called *their own desires.* Their exemption from responsibility stems from the fact that their own desires (or at least the ones governing their actions) are not up to them. These cases may be described in Frankfurt's terms as cases of people who possess freedom of action, but who fail to be responsible agents because they lack freedom of the will.

Philosophical problems about the conditions of responsibility naturally focus on an analysis of this latter kind of freedom: What *is* freedom of the will, and under what conditions can we reasonably be thought to possess it? Frankfurt's proposal is to understand freedom of the will by analogy to freedom of action. As freedom of action is the freedom to do whatever one wills to do, freedom of the will is the freedom to will whatever one wants to will. To make this point clearer, Frankfurt introduces a distinction between first-order and second-order desires. First-order desires are desires to do or to have various things; second-order desires are desires about what desires to have or what desires to make effective in action. In order for an agent to have both freedom of action and freedom of the will, that agent must be capable of governing his or her actions by first-order desires *and* capable of governing his or her first-order desires by second-order desires.

Gary Watson's view of free agency[2]—free and responsible agency, that is—is similar to Frankfurt's in holding that an agent is responsible for an action only if the desires expressed by that action are of a particular kind. While Frankfurt identifies the right kind of desires as desires that are supported by second-order desires, however, Watson draws a distinction between "mere" desires, so to speak, and desires that are *values.* According to Watson, the difference between free action and unfree action cannot be analyzed by reference to the logical form of the desires from which these various actions arise, but rather must relate to a difference in the quality of their source. Whereas some of my desires are just appetites or conditioned responses I find myself "stuck with," others are expressions of judgments on my part that the objects I desire are good. Insofar as my actions can be governed by the latter type of desire—governed, that is, by my values or valuational system—they are actions that I perform freely and for which I am responsible.

Frankfurt's and Watson's accounts may be understood as alternate developments of the intuition that in order to be responsible for one's actions, one must be responsible for the self that performs these actions. Charles Taylor, in an article entitled "Responsibility for Self,"[3] is concerned with the same intuition. Although Taylor does not describe his view in terms of different levels or types of desire, his view is related, for he claims that our freedom and responsibility depend on our ability to reflect on, criticize, and revise our selves. Like Frankfurt and Watson, Taylor seems to believe that if the characters from which our actions flowed were simply and permanently *given* to us, implanted by heredity, environment, or God, then we would be mere vehicles through which the causal forces of the world traveled, no more responsible than dumb animals or young children or machines. But like the others, he points out that, for most of us, our characters and desires are not so brutely implanted—or, at any rate, if they are, they are subject to revision by our own reflecting, valuing, or second-order desiring selves. We human beings—and as far as we know, only we human beings—have the ability to step back from ourselves and decide whether we are the selves we want to be. Because of this, these philosophers think, we are responsible for our selves and for the actions that we produce.

Although there are subtle and interesting differences among the accounts of Frankfurt, Watson, and Taylor, my concern is with features of their views that are common to them all. All share the idea that responsible agency involves something more than intentional agency. All agree that if we are responsible agents, it is not just because our actions are within the control of our wills, but because, in addition, our wills are not just psychological states *in* us, but expressions of characters that come *from* us, or that at any rate are acknowledged and affirmed *by* us. For Frankfurt, this means that our wills must be ruled by our second-order desires; for Watson, that our wills must be governable by our system of values; for Taylor, that our wills must issue from selves that are subject to self-assessment and redefinition in terms of a vocabulary of worth. In one way or another, all these philosophers seem to be saying that the key to responsibility lies in the fact that responsible agents are those for whom it is not just the case that their actions are within the control of their wills, but also the case that their wills are within the control of their *selves* in some deeper sense. Because, at one level, the differences among Frankfurt, Watson, and Taylor may be understood as differences in the analysis or interpretation of what it is for an action to be under the control of this deeper self, we may speak of their separate positions as variations of one basic view about responsibility: the *deep-self view*.

THE DEEP-SELF VIEW

Much more must be said about the notion of a deep self before a fully satisfactory account of this view can be given. Providing a careful, detailed analysis of that notion poses an interesting, important, and difficult task in its own right. The degree of understanding achieved by abstraction from the views of Frankfurt, Watson, and Taylor, however, should be sufficient to allow us to recognize some important virtues as well as some important drawbacks of the deep-self view.

One virtue is that this view explains a good portion of our pretheoretical intuitions about responsibility. It explains why kleptomaniacs, victims of brainwashing, and people acting under posthypnotic suggestion may not be responsible for their actions, although most of us typically are. In the cases of people in these special categories, the connection between the agents' deep selves and their wills is dramatically severed—their wills are governed not by their deep selves, but by forces external to and independent from them. A different intuition is that we adult human beings can be responsible for our actions in a way that dumb animals, infants, and machines cannot. Here the explanation is not in terms of a split between these beings' deep selves and their wills; rather, the point is that these beings *lack* deep selves altogether. Kleptomaniacs and victims of hypnosis exemplify individuals whose selves are *alienated* from their actions; lower animals and machines, on the other hand, do not have the sorts of selves from which actions *can* be alienated, and so they do not have the sort of selves from which, in the happier cases, actions can responsibly flow.

At a more theoretical level, the deep-self view has another virtue: It responds to at least one way in which the fear of determinism presents itself.

A naive reaction to the idea that everything we do is completely determined by a causal chain that extends backward beyond the times of our births involves thinking that in that case we would have no control over our behavior whatsoever. If everything is determined, it is thought, then what happens happens, whether we want it to or not. A common, and proper, response to this concern points out that determinism does not deny the causal efficacy an agent's desires might have on his or her behavior. On the contrary, determinism in its more plausible forms tends to affirm this connection, merely adding that as one's behavior is determined by one's desires, so one's desires are determined by something else.[4]

Those who were initially worried that determinism implied fatalism, however, are apt to find their fears merely transformed rather than erased. If our desires are governed by something else, they might say, they are not *really* ours after all—or, at any rate, they are ours in only a superficial sense.

The deep-self view offers an answer to this transformed fear of determinism, for it allows us to distinguish cases in which desires are determined by forces foreign to oneself from desires which are determined *by* one's self—by one's "real," or second-order desiring, or valuing, or deep self, that is. Admittedly, there are cases, like that of the kleptomaniac or the victim of hypnosis, in which the agent acts on desires that "belong to" him or her in only a superficial sense. But the proponent of the deep-self view will point out that even if determinism is true, ordinary adult human action can be distinguished from this. Determinism implies that the desires which govern our actions are in turn governed by something else, but that something else will, in the fortunate cases, be our own deeper selves.

This account of responsibility thus offers a response to our fear of determinism; but it is a response with which many will remain unsatisfied. Even if my actions are governed by my desires and my desires are governed by my own deeper self, there remains the question: Who, or what, is responsible for this deeper self? The response above seems only to have pushed the problem further back.

Admittedly, some versions of the deep-self view, including Frankfurt's and Taylor's, seem to anticipate this question by providing a place for the ideal that an agent's deep self may be governed by a still deeper self. Thus, for Frankfurt, second-order desires may themselves be governed by third-order desires, third-order desires by fourth-order desires, and so on. Also, Taylor points out that, as we can reflect on and evaluate our prereflective selves, so we can reflect on and evaluate the selves who are doing the first reflecting and evaluating, and so on. However, this capacity to recursively create endless levels of depth ultimately misses the criticism's point.

First of all, even if there is no *logical* limit to the number of levels of reflection or depth a person may have, there is certainly a psychological limit—it is virtually impossible imaginatively to conceive a fourth-, much less an eighth-order, desire. More important, no matter how many levels of self we posit, there will still, in any individual case, be a last level—a deepest self about whom the question "What governs it?" will arise, as problematic as ever. If determinism is true, it implies that even if my actions are governed by my desires, and my desires are governed by my deepest self, my deepest self will still be governed by something that must, logically, be external to myself altogether. Though I can step back from the values my parents and teachers have given me and ask whether these are the values I really want, the "I" that steps back will itself be a product of the parents and teachers I am questioning.

The problem seems even worse when one sees that one fares no better if determinism is false. For if my deepest self is not determined by something external to myself, it will still not be determined by *me*. Whether I am a product of carefully controlled forces or a result of random mutations, whether there is a complete explanation of my origin or no explanation at all, *I* am not, in any case, responsible for my existence; I am not in control of my deepest self.

Thus, though the claim that an agent is responsible for only those actions that are within the control of his or her deep self correctly identifies a necessary condition for responsibility—a condition that separates the hypnotized and the brainwashed, the immature and the lower animals from ourselves, for example—it fails to provide a sufficient condition of responsibility that puts all fears of determinism to rest. For one of the fears invoked by the thought of determinism seems to be connected to its implication that we are but intermediate links in a causal chain, rather than ultimate, self-initiating sources of movement and change. From the point of view of one who has this fear, the deep-self view seems merely to add loops to the chain, complicating the picture but not really improving it. From the point of view of one who has this fear, responsibility seems to require being a prime mover unmoved, whose deepest self is itself neither random *nor* externally determined, but is rather determined *by* itself—who is, in other words, self-created.

At this point, however, proponents of the deep-self view may wonder whether this fear is legitimate. For although people evidently can be brought to the point where they feel that responsible agency requires them to be ultimate sources of power, to the point where it seems that nothing short of self-creation will do, a return to the internal standpoint of the agent whose responsibility is in question makes it hard to see what good this metaphysical status is supposed to provide or what evil its absence is supposed to impose.

From the external standpoint, which discussions of determinism and indeterminism encourage us to take up, it may appear that a special metaphysical status is required to distinguish us significantly from other members of the natural world. But proponents of the deep-self view will suggest this is an illusion that a return to the internal standpoint should dispel. The possession of a deep self that is effective in governing one's actions is a sufficient distinction, they will say. For while other members of the natural world are not in control of the selves that they are, we, possessors of effective deep selves, are in control. We can reflect on what sorts of beings we are, and on what sorts of marks we make on the world. We can change what we don't like about ourselves, and keep what we do. Admittedly, we do not create ourselves from nothing. But as long as we can revise ourselves, they will suggest, it is hard to find reason to complain. Harry Frankfurt writes that a person who is free to do what he wants to do and also free to want what he wants to want has "all the freedom it is possible to desire or to conceive."[5] This suggests a rhetorical question: If you are free to control your actions by your desires, and free to control your desires by your deeper desires, and free to control those desires by still deeper desires, what further kind of freedom can you want?

THE CONDITION OF SANITY

Unfortunately, there is a further kind of freedom we can want, which it is reasonable to think necessary for responsible agency. The deep-self view fails to be convincing when it is offered as a complete account of the conditions of responsibility. To see why, it will be helpful to consider another example of an agent whose responsibility is in question.

JoJo is the favorite son of Jo the First, an evil and sadistic dictator of a small, undeveloped country. Because of his father's special feelings for the boy, JoJo is given a special education and is allowed to accompany his father and observe his daily routine. In light of this treatment, it is not surprising that little JoJo takes his father as a role model and develops values very much like Dad's. As an adult, he does many of the same sorts of things his father did, including sending people to prison or to death or to torture chambers on the basis of whim. He is not *coerced* to do these things, he acts according to his own desires. Moreover, these are desires he wholly *wants* to have. When he steps back and asks, "Do I really want to be this sort of person?" his answer is resoundingly "Yes," for this way of life expresses a crazy sort of power that forms part of his deepest ideal.

In light of JoJo's heritage and upbringing—both of which he was powerless to control—it is dubious at best that he should be regarded as responsible for what he does. It is unclear whether anyone with a childhood such as his could have developed into anything but the twisted and perverse sort of person that he has become. However, note that JoJo is someone whose actions are controlled by his desires and whose desires are the desires he wants to have: That is, his actions are governed by desires that are governed by and expressive of his deepest self.

The Frankfurt–Watson–Taylor strategy that allowed us to differentiate our normal selves from the victims of hypnosis and brainwashing will not allow us to differentiate ourselves from the son of Jo the

First. In the case of these earlier victims, we were able to say that although the actions of these individuals were, at one level, in control of the individuals themselves, these individuals themselves, qua agents, were not the selves they more deeply wanted to be. In this respect, these people were unlike our happily more integrated selves. However, we cannot say of JoJo that his self, qua agent, is not the self he wants it to be. It *is* the self he wants it to be. From the inside, he feels as integrated, free, and responsible as we do.

Our judgment that JoJo is not a responsible agent is one that we can make only from the outside—from reflecting on the fact, it seems, that his deepest self is not up to him. Looked at from the outside, however, our situation seems no different from his—for in the last analysis, it is not up to any of us to have the deepest selves we do. Once more, the problem seems metaphysical—and not just metaphysical, but insuperable. For, as I mentioned before, the problem is independent of the truth of determinism. Whether we are determined or undetermined, we cannot have created our deepest selves. Literal self-creation is not just empirically, but logically impossible.

If JoJo is not responsible because his deepest self is not up to him, then we are not responsible either. Indeed, in that case responsibility would be impossible for anyone to achieve. But I believe the appearance that literal self-creation is required for freedom and responsibility is itself mistaken.

The deep-self view was right in pointing out that freedom and responsibility require us to have certain distinctive types of control over our behavior and our selves. Specifically, our actions need to be under the control of our selves, and our (superficial) selves need to be under the control of our deep selves. Having seen that these types of control are not enough to guarantee us the status of responsible agents, we are tempted to go on to suppose that we must have yet another kind of control to assure us that even our deepest selves are somehow up to us. But not all the things necessary for freedom and responsibility must be types of power and control. We may need simply to *be* a certain way, even though it is not within our power to determine whether we are that way or not.

Indeed, it becomes obvious that at least one condition of responsibility is of this form as soon as we remember what, in everyday contexts, we have known all along—namely, that in order to be responsible, an agent must be *sane*. It is not ordinarily in our power to determine whether we are or are not sane. Most of us, it would seem, are lucky, but some of us are not. Moreover, being sane does not necessarily mean that one has any type of power or control an insane person lacks. Some insane people, like JoJo and some actual political leaders who resemble him, may have complete control of their actions, and even complete control of their acting selves. The desire to be sane is thus not a desire for another form of control; it is rather a desire that one's self be connected to the world in a certain way—we could even say it is a desire that one's self be *controlled by* the world in certain ways and not in others.

This becomes clear if we attend to the criteria for sanity that have historically been dominant in legal questions about responsibility. According to the M'Naughten Rule, a person is sane if (1) he knows what he is doing and (2) he knows that what he is doing is, as the case may be, right or wrong. Insofar as one's desire to be sane involves a desire to know what one is doing—or more generally, a desire to live in the real world—it is a desire to be controlled (to have, in this case, one's *beliefs* controlled) by perceptions and sound reasoning that produce an accurate conception of the world, rather than by blind or distorted forms of response. The same goes for the second constituent of sanity—only, in this case, one's hope is that one's *values* be controlled by processes that afford an accurate conception of the world.[6] Putting these two conditions together, we may understand sanity, then, as the minimally sufficient ability cognitively and normatively to recognize and appreciate the world for what it is.

There are problems with this definition of sanity, at least some of which will become obvious in what follows, that make it ultimately unacceptable either as a gloss on or an improvement of the meaning of the term in many of the contexts in which it is used. The definition offered does seem to bring out the interest sanity has for us in connection with issues of responsibility, however, and some pedagogical as well as stylistic purposes will be served if we use sanity hereafter in this admittedly specialized sense.

THE SANE DEEP-SELF VIEW

So far I have argued that the conditions of responsible agency offered by the deep-self view are necessary but not sufficient. Moreover, the gap left open by the deep-self view seems to be one that can be filled only by a metaphysical, and, as it happens, metaphysically impossible addition. I now wish to argue, however, that the condition of sanity, as characterized above, is sufficient to fill the gap. In other words, the deep-self view, supplemented by the condition of sanity, provides a satisfying conception of responsibility. The conception of responsibility I am proposing, then, agrees with the deep-self view in requiring that a responsible agent be able to govern her (or his) actions by her desires and to govern her desires by her deep self. In addition, my conception insists that the agent's deep self be sane, and claims that this is *all* that is needed for responsible agency. By contrast to the plain deep-self view, let us call this new proposal the *sane deep-self view.*

It is worth noting, to begin with, that this new proposal deals with the case of JoJo and related cases of deprived childhood victims in ways that better match our pretheoretical intuitions. Unlike the plain deep-self view, the sane deep-self view offers a way of explaining why JoJo is not responsible for his actions without throwing our own responsibility into doubt. For, although like us, JoJo's actions flow from desires that flow from his deep self, unlike us, JoJo's deep self is itself insane. Sanity, remember, involves the ability to know the difference between right and wrong, and a person who, even on reflection, cannot see that having someone tortured because he failed to salute you is wrong plainly lacks the requisite ability.

Less obviously, but quite analogously, this new proposal explains why we give less than full responsibility to persons who, though acting badly, act in ways that are strongly encouraged by their societies—the slaveowners of the 1850s, the Nazis of the 1930s, and many male chauvinists of our fathers' generation, for example. These are people, we imagine, who falsely believe that the ways in which they are acting are morally acceptable, and so, we may assume, their behavior is expressive of or at least in accordance with these agents' deep selves. But their false beliefs in the moral permissibility of their actions and the false values from which these beliefs derived may have been inevitable, given the social circumstances in which they developed. If we think that the agents could not help but be mistaken about their values, we do not blame them for the actions those values inspired.[7]

It would unduly distort ordinary linguistic practice to call the slaveowner, the Nazi, or the male chauvinist even partially or locally insane. Nonetheless, the reason for withholding blame from them is at bottom the same as the reason for withholding it from JoJo. Like JoJo, they are, at the deepest level, unable cognitively and normatively to recognize and appreciate the world for what it is. In our sense of the term, their deepest selves are not fully *sane.*

The sane deep-self view thus offers an account of why victims of deprived childhoods as well as victims of misguided societies may not be responsible for their actions, without implying that we are not responsible for ours. The actions of these others are governed by mistaken conceptions of value that the agents in question cannot help but have. Since, as far as we know, our values are not, like theirs, unavoidably mistaken, the fact that these others are not responsible for their actions need not force us to conclude that we are not responsible for ours.

But it may not yet be clear why sanity, in this special sense, should make such a difference—why, in particular, the question of whether someone's values are unavoidably *mistaken* should have any bearing on their status as responsible agents. The fact that the sane deep-self view implies judgments that match our intuitions about the difference in status between characters like JoJo and ourselves provides little support for it if it cannot also defend these intuitions. So we must consider an objection that comes from the point of view we considered earlier which rejects the intuition that a relevant difference can be found.

Earlier, it seemed that the reason JoJo was not responsible for his actions was that although his actions were governed by his deep self, his deep self was not up to him. But this had nothing to do with his deep self's being mistaken or not mistaken, evil or good, insane or sane. If JoJo's values are unavoidably mistaken, our values, even if not mistaken, appear to be just as unavoidable. When it comes to freedom and responsibility, isn't it the unavoidability, rather than the mistakenness, that matters?

Before answering this question, it is useful to point out a way in which it is ambiguous: The concepts of avoidability and mistakenness are not unequivocally distinct. One may, to be sure, construe the notion of avoidability in a purely metaphysical way. Whether an event or state of affairs is unavoidable under this construal depends, as it were, on the tightness of the causal connections that bear on the event's or state of affairs' coming about. In this sense, our deep selves do seem as unavoidable for us as JoJo's and the others' are for them. For presumably we are just as influenced by our parents, our cultures, and our schooling as they are influenced by theirs. In another sense, however, our characters are not similarly unavoidable.

In particular, in the cases of JoJo and the others, there are certain features of their characters that they cannot avoid *even though these features are seriously mistaken, misguided, or bad*. This is so because, in our special sense of the term, these characters are less than fully sane. Since these characters lack the ability to know right from wrong, they are unable to revise their characters on the basis of right and wrong, and so their deep selves lack the resources and the reasons that might have served as a basis for self-correction. Since the deep selves *we* unavoidably have, however, are sane deep selves—deep selves, that is, that unavoidably *contain* the ability to know right from wrong—we unavoidably do have the resources and reasons on which to base self-correction. What this means is that though in one sense we are no more in control of our deepest selves than JoJo et al., it does not follow in our case, as it does in theirs, that we would be the way we are, even if it is a bad or wrong way to be. However, if this does not follow, it seems to me, our absence of control at the deepest level should not upset us.

Consider what the absence of control at the deepest level amounts to for us: Whereas JoJo is unable to control the fact that, at the deepest level, he is not fully sane, we are not responsible for the fact that, at the deepest level, we are. It is not up to us to *have* minimally sufficient abilities cognitively and normatively to recognize and appreciate the world for what it is. Also, presumably, it is not up to us to have lots of other properties, at least to begin with—a fondness for purple, perhaps, or an antipathy for beets. As the proponents of the plain deep-self view have been at pains to point out, however, we do, if we are lucky, have the ability to revise our selves in terms of the values that are held by or constitutive of our deep selves. If we are lucky enough both to have this ability and to have our deep selves be sane, it follows that although there is much in our characters that we did not choose to have, there is nothing irrational or objectionable in our characters that we are compelled to keep.

Being sane, we are able to understand and evaluate our characters in a reasonable way, to notice what there is reason to hold on to, what there is reason to eliminate, and what, from a rational and reasonable standpoint, we may retain or get rid of as we please. Being able as well to govern our superficial selves by our deep selves, then, we are able to change the things we find there is reason to change. This being so, it seems that although we may not be *metaphysically* responsible for ourselves—for, after all, we did not create ourselves from nothing—we are *morally* responsible for ourselves, for we are able to understand and appreciate right and wrong, and to change our characters and our actions accordingly.

SELF-CREATION, SELF-REVISION, AND SELF-CORRECTION

At the beginning of this chapter, I claimed that recalling that sanity was a condition of responsibility would dissolve at least some of the appearance that responsibility was metaphysically impossible. To see how this is so, and to get a fuller sense of the sane deep-self view, it may be helpful to put that view into perspective by comparing it to the other views we have discussed along the way.

As Frankfurt, Watson, and Taylor showed us, in order to be free and responsible we need not only to be able to control our actions in accordance with our desires, we need to be able to control our desires in accordance with our deepest selves. We need, in other words, to be able to *revise* ourselves—to get rid of some desires and traits, and perhaps replace them with others on the basis of our deeper desires or values or reflections. However, consideration of the fact that the selves who are doing the revising might themselves be either brute products of external forces or arbitrary outputs of random generation made us wonder whether the capacity for self-revision was enough to assure us of responsibility—and the example of JoJo added force to the suspicion that it was not. Still, if the ability to revise ourselves is not enough, the ability to create ourselves does not seem necessary either. Indeed, when you think of it, it is unclear why anyone should want self-creation. Why should anyone be disappointed at having to accept the idea that one has to get one's start somewhere? It is an idea that most of us have lived with quite contentedly all along. What we do have reason to want, then, is something more than the ability to revise ourselves, but less than the ability to create ourselves. Implicit in the sane deep-self view is the idea that what is needed is the ability to *correct* (or improve) ourselves.

Recognizing that in order to be responsible for our actions, we have to be responsible for our selves, the sane deep-self view analyzes what is necessary in order to be responsible for our selves as (1) the ability to evaluate ourselves sensibly and accurately, and (2) the ability to transform ourselves insofar as our evaluation tells us to do so. We may understand the exercise of these abilities as a process whereby we *take* responsibility for the selves that we are but did not ultimately create. The condition of sanity is intrinsically connected to the first ability; the condition that we be able to control our superficial selves by our deep selves is intrinsically connected to the second.

The difference between the plain deep-self view and the sane deep-self view, then, is the difference between the requirement of the capacity for self-revision and the requirement of the capacity for self-correction. Anyone with the first capacity can *try* to take responsibility for himself or herself. However, only someone with a sane deep self—a deep self that can see and appreciate the world for what it is—can self-evaluate sensibly and accurately. Therefore, although insane selves can try to take responsibility for themselves, only sane selves will properly be accorded responsibility.

TWO OBJECTIONS CONSIDERED

At least two problems with the sane deep-self view are so glaring as to have certainly struck many readers. In closing, I shall briefly address them. First, some will be wondering how, in light of my specialized use of the term "sanity," I can be so sure that "we" are any saner than the nonresponsible individuals I have discussed. What justifies my confidence that, unlike the slaveowners, Nazis, and male chauvinists, not to mention JoJo himself, we are able to understand and appreciate the world for what it is? The answer to this is that nothing justifies this except widespread intersubjective agreement and the considerable success we have in getting around in the world and satisfying our needs. These are not sufficient grounds for the smug assumption that we are in a position to see the truth about *all* aspects of ethical and social life. Indeed, it seems more reasonable to expect that time will reveal blind spots in our cognitive and normative outlook, just as it has revealed errors in the outlooks of those who have lived before. But our judgments of responsibility can only be made from here, on the basis of the understandings and values that we can develop by exercising the abilities we do possess as well and as fully as possible.

If some have been worried that my view implicitly expresses an overconfidence in the assumption that we are sane and therefore right about the world, others will be worried that my view too closely connects sanity with being right about the world, and fear that my view implies that anyone who acts wrongly or has false beliefs about the world is therefore insane and so not responsible for his or her actions. This seems to me to be a more serious worry, which I am sure I cannot answer to everyone's satisfaction.

First, it must be admitted that the sane deep-self view embraces a conception of sanity that is explicitly normative. But this seems to me a strength of that view, rather than a defect. Sanity *is* a normative concept, in its ordinary as well as in its specialized sense, and severely deviant behavior, such as that of a serial murderer or a sadistic dictator, does constitute evidence of a psychological defect in the agent. The suggestion that the most horrendous, stomach-turning crimes could be committed only by an insane person—an inverse of Catch-22, as it were—must be regarded as a serious possibility, despite the practical problems that would accompany general acceptance of that conclusion.

But, it will be objected, there is no justification, in the sane deep-self view, for regarding only horrendous and stomach-turning crimes as evidence of insanity in its specialized sense. If sanity is the ability cognitively and normatively to understand and appreciate the world for what it is, then *any* wrong action or false belief will count as evidence of the absence of that ability. This point may also be granted, but we must be careful about what conclusion to draw. To be sure, when someone acts in a way that is not in accordance with acceptable standards of rationality and reasonableness, it is always appropriate to look for an explanation of why he or she acted that way. The hypothesis that the person was unable to understand and appreciate that an action fell outside acceptable bounds will always be a possible explanation. Bad performance on a math test always suggests the possibility that the testee is stupid. Typically, however, other explanations will be possible, too—for example, that the agent was too lazy to consider whether his or her action was acceptable, or too greedy to care, or, in the case of the math testee, that he or she was too occupied with other interests to attend class or study. Other facts about the agent's history will help us decide among these hypotheses.

This brings out the need to emphasize that sanity, in the specialized sense, is defined as the *ability* cognitively and normatively to understand and appreciate the world for what it is. According to our commonsense understandings, having this ability is one thing and exercising it is another—at least some wrong-acting, responsible agents presumably fall within the gap. The notion of "ability" is notoriously problematic, however, and there is a long history of controversy about whether the truth of determinism would show our ordinary ways of thinking to be simply confused on this matter. At this point, then, metaphysical concerns may voice themselves again—but at least they will have been pushed into a narrower, and perhaps a more manageable, corner.

The sane deep-self view does not, then, solve all the philosophical problems connected to the topics of free will and responsibility. If anything, it highlights some of the practical and empirical problems, rather than solves them. It may, however, resolve some of the philosophical, and particularly, some of the metaphysical problems, and reveal how intimate are the connections between the remaining philosophical problems and the practical ones.

NOTES

1. Harry Frankfurt, "Freedom of the Will and the Concept of a Person," *Journal of Philosophy* LXVIII (1971), 5–20.
2. Gary Watson, "Free Agency," *Journal of Philosophy* LXXII (1975), 205–20.
3. Charles Taylor, "Responsibility for Self," in A. E. Rorty, ed., *The Identities of Persons* (Berkeley: University of California Press, 1976) pp. 281–99.
4. See, e.g., David Hume, *A Treatise of Human Nature* (Oxford: Oxford University Press, 1967), pp. 399–406, and R. E. Hobart, "Free Will as Involving Determination and Inconceivable Without It," *Mind* 43 (1934).
5. Frankfurt, p. 16.
6. Strictly speaking, perception and sound reasoning may not be enough to ensure the ability to achieve an accurate conception of what one is doing and especially to achieve a reasonable normative assessment of one's situation. Sensitivity and exposure to certain realms of experience may also be necessary for these goals. For the purpose of this essay, I understand "sanity" to include whatever it takes to enable one to develop an adequate conception of one's world. In other contexts, however, this would be an implausibly broad construction of the term.
7. Admittedly, it is open to question whether these individuals were in fact unable to help having mistaken values, and indeed, whether recognizing the errors of their society would even have required exceptional independence or strength of mind. This is presumably an empirical question, the answer to which is extraor-

dinarily hard to determine. My point here is simply that *if* we believe they are unable to recognize that their values are mistaken, we do not hold them responsible for the actions that flow from these values, and *if* we believe their ability to recognize their normative errors is impaired, we hold them less than fully responsible for the relevant actions.

Part V

The Claims of Morality and Justice

THESE DAYS THERE IS A good deal of skepticism about morality, skepticism that may take many forms. One challenge to morality comes from a famous theory of human motivation. The theory that human beings are so constituted by nature that they are incapable of desiring or pursuing anything but their own well-being as an end in itself is called **psychological egoism.** If "true morality" requires selfless devotion to others even at the cost of one's own interests, and if all persons are inherently selfish, as this theory claims, there may be no way to motivate persons to behave morally. Genuinely disinterested acts of benevolence, on this view, do not exist, although persons sometimes appear to be acting unselfishly when they take the interests of other people to be the means for promoting their own good. This theory of motivation should be distinguished from the doctrine called **ethical egoism,** which, as its name indicates, is not a theory about how human beings in fact act but rather a moral doctrine stating how they ought to act. According to this doctrine, one ought to pursue one's own well-being, and only one's own well-being, as an end in itself. A *psychological* egoist, insofar as he or she bothered with ethics at all, might be expected to be an *ethical* egoist; for if there is only one thing that we *can* pursue, there cannot be some other thing that we *ought* to pursue. Most psychological egoists, however, have sought some way to reconcile necessarily selfish motivation with the unselfish and even self-sacrificing conduct required by morality. Many argue, for example, that generally the best means to promote one's own happiness is to work for the public good or the happiness of others.

The essay by the editor on psychological egoism is one of the only articles in this book that was not written for publication. It was distributed to students only for classroom use at Brown University, Princeton University, and UCLA during the period from 1958 to 1966. The essay contains very elementary distinctions and standard arguments reorganized and written in elementary terms. Because of its pedagogical intent, it might very well be used as the student's introduction to this section, or even perhaps to the whole volume. Most students, after much resistance, seemed to be persuaded by its arguments; but some of the best students (especially those who were psychology or biology majors) remained unconvinced to the end. Some of the students who were unconvinced by the arguments against psychological egoism would admit that the *a priori* arguments for psychological egoism are fallacious but insist that the biological sciences and particularly evolutionary theory may yet provide empirical evidence for the theory.

Jonathan Bennett makes several important observations about "moral motivation and human nature." The constitution of a person's nature includes several distinct elements that can lead her to respond in a variety of different ways to moral challenges. Bennett's basic distinction is between *conscience,* the relatively stern demanding voice of one's personal moral principles whatever they should happen to be, and morally relevant emotions, especially those of *sympathy,* mercy, pity, and compassion. The moral principles that conscience represents can be either good ones or bad ones: in either case they may reinforce or conflict with sympathetic feeling. In the case of conflict, it is impossible to say in advance whether conscience or sympathy should win out. But a completely developed moral person will cultivate both sensitive sympathies and conscientiousness. These judgments and distinctions then enable Bennett to make some surprising appraisals of Huckleberry Finn, and such historical figures as Heinrich Himmler, Jonathan Edwards, and the Roman poet Horace.

Another form of skepticism about morality begins by noting the existence of deep, apparently intractable disagreements that divide people on many ethical issues. Prospects for gaining consensus on issues of abortion, or capital punishment, or famine relief seem quite slim, even if those doing the talking are well-intentioned, open-minded, and knowledgeable about the topic under discussion. Many have inferred from this that ethics cannot be objective in the way that science or mathematics is. Disciplines that admit of objective truth appear capable of progress and broad consensus both on methods of inquiry and on a significant set of substantive propositions. **Ethical subjectivists** claim that we do not see such progress or consensus in ethics, and that therefore ethics is simply not an objective area of inquiry. According to one version of subjectivism (**meta-ethical subjectivism**), ethical judgments are neither true nor false—they are simply expressions of commands, preferences or emotions, and as such are not even eligible candidates for truth. A different version (**normative subjectivism**) claims that ethical judgments can be true (or false), but that their truth depends entirely on whether they accurately report the sentiments of those who issue the judgments. As Russ Shafer-Landau points out, in his article that leads off the Standards of Right Conduct section, normative subjectivism is less attractive than its meta-ethical cousin. And while most of us act as if meta-ethical subjectivism were false—we assess moral judgments as true or false, and deliberate and pursue investigations into ethical issues as if there were truth that awaited discovery—meta-ethical subjectivism is supported by a number of appealing arguments. Whether in the end it is entirely convincing is left to the reader to decide.

Shifting the focus from interpersonal ethical disagreements to intersocietal ones, James Rachels presents a consideration of **ethical relativism,** the view that actions are right if and only if they comport with the ultimate ethical standards of the society in which they are performed. This is a natural move to make for those who are convinced that ethics cannot be objective, but have doubts about the plausibility of ethical subjectivism. Rather than view each person as an equally good moral judge, as subjectivists do, relativists make cultural mores the ultimate ethical standards. Rachels carefully unpacks the argument for ethical relativism that begins with the assumption of **cultural relativism**—the anthropological claim that different societies have different ultimate ethical beliefs. He shows why cultural relativism is not obviously true, and then argues that even if it is, it fails to provide adequate support for the theory of ethical relativism.

The remaining articles in this section all assume that there is at least one objectively true ethical standard, that is, a measure of right and wrong that is true regardless of whether anyone happens to think it is. One way to unify the concerns of these authors is to see them as each addressing the question of how much weight one is ethically required to give to the interests of others. One answer, that proposed by Ayn Rand, is that the interests of others have no independent weight whatever. Her view, a version of **ethical egoism,** claims that one is obligated to assist others if and only if doing so promotes one's own interests. This may appear to be a counsel of self-absorption, and so it may come as some surprise that Rand assigns a central role in her theory to such values as love and integrity. First, consider love: "Love is an expression and assertion of self-esteem, a response to one's own values in the person of another. . . . If a man who is passionately in love with his wife spends a fortune to cure her of a dangerous illness, it would be absurd to claim that he does it as a 'sacrifice' for *her* sake, not his own, and that it makes no difference to *him,* personally and selfishly, whether she lives or dies." If, following the altruistic utilitarian's moral advice he lets his wife die in order to save the lives of ten strangers instead, and thus do "more good," that *would* be a sacrifice, a renunciation, of one's integrity. "Integrity is loyalty to one's convictions and values. . . ."

James Rachels, in a characteristically balanced critique, finds the difficulties in ethical egoism to be more impressive than its advantages. He calls it a "challenging" theory, worth taking seriously even though in the end he rejects it. Its importance, he claims, consists in the insights it provides into "the reasons why we *do* have obligations to other people." He defines ethical egoism as the theory that we have no moral duty except to do what is best for ourselves. It would be a good exercise for the reader to determine whether Rand's theory fits neatly under this definition or not. Rachels thinks so, and devotes several pages to a criticism of Rand. Even if Rand is not *exactly* an ethical egoist, however, there is no shortage of writers whose views do satisfy Rachels's definition. (He mentions Robert Olson, Alexander Pope, and Thomas Hobbes, among many others.)

Thomas Hobbes, the brilliant English philosopher (1588–1679), is often classed as an ethical egoist. But his is a sophisticated position, as readers will see for themselves, and he is just as often counted the founder of modern **social contract theory.** In his selection from the *Leviathan,* Hobbes outlines a view according to which morality develops in response to the horrors of life without government (what he called the **state of nature**). Such a life he famously described as "solitary, poor, nasty, brutish and short," and he thought that any government, even despotism, was to be preferred to the state of nature. Hobbes claimed that there was no right or wrong, justice or injustice in the state of nature, and that the standards of morality are properly given by the terms of the social compact to which parties in the state of nature agree. Hobbes thought that each person's well-being would be enhanced by agreeing to limit his liberty in exchange for the security offered by life under law. His view has had a wide-ranging impact not only on ethics, but also on theories of justice, where social contract views have recently experienced renewed popularity.

Hobbes' selection is followed by an excerpt from one of the greatest systematic philosophers of Western civilization, Immanuel Kant. We have expanded our coverage of Kant's ethics, so that this edition now contains substantial selections from Books I and II of his *Foundations of the Metaphysics of Morals.* In Book I Kant develops the notion of a **good will,** and defends his claim that nothing else can be unconditionally good, that is, good in every instance, regardless of accompanying circumstances. The good will is simply the commitment to do one's duty for its own sake (rather than, say, because it will promote one's self-interest). But where does one's duty lie? In Book II Kant introduces his **categorical imperative,** a command of reason that is authoritative for moral agents regardless of their desires. Kant claims that the rightness or wrongness of an action lies not in the results it brings about, but instead in the principle that guides a person's conduct. Kant calls such a principle a *maxim.* The categorical imperative states that actions are right if and only if their maxim is such that the agent can will that everyone abide by it. In effect, the centerpiece of Kantian ethics is the directive not to make an exception of oneself—act only on those principles that one is willing to see everyone act on.

Kant's view is directly opposed to the **utilitarian** view of John Stuart Mill. Mill believes that pleasure is the sole intrinsic value, and he believes that our fundamental moral obligation is to produce as much pleasure as we can. But here the focus is not just on one's own pleasure; rather, in the famous utilitarian phrase, "everybody is to count for one and nobody as more than one." Because of its dual emphasis on impartiality and on pleasure, utilitarianism is sometimes denominated **universalistic** (as opposed to egoistic) **hedonism.** This view places priority on achieving the greatest happiness for the greatest number, another utilitarian catch-phrase, and thus locates the virtue of beneficence at the heart of ethics. Utilitarians sometimes seek to display the attractions of their view by asking a couple of apparently innocent questions: How could an action that produces the most happiness possibly fail to be right? And how could an action be right if another available action could have made people better off, that is, produced more pleasure?

Despite the apparently rhetorical nature of such questions, Kantians (and others) will find much to disagree with regarding the utilitarian theory. In fact, the contrast between Kant and Mill could not be sharper (though Mill insists that Kant's theory is best understood as a version of utilitarianism, a claim whose merits have been debated for over a century). Kant and Mill disagree about what has value for its own sake (the good will, or pleasure), about what makes actions right or wrong (proper motives, or results), and about which virtue stands at the center of ethics (fairness, or beneficence). As a way to test the implications of each of these very important ethical theories, we have included two pieces that focus on the ethical approaches to famine relief, one (by Onora O'Neill) that recommends a Kantian perspective, the other (by Peter Singer) displaying the recommendations that follow from utilitarian assumptions.

The final offering in our section on Standards of Right Conduct is a selection from the late Oxford scholar W.D. Ross. Ross tries to mine both Kantian and utilitarian theories for plausible starting points, but finds that ethics is more complicated that either theory imagines. He believes that we have both duties of fairness (e.g., to repay debts or to keep promises) and of beneficence (e.g., to assist the poor or to comfort the sick), and that neither kind of duty always takes priority over the other. Indeed, we have several distinct kinds of ethical duties (e.g., making reparation, truth-telling, non-maleficence and gratitude) in addition to those of fairness and beneficence. Ross insists that in particular circumstances these duties may conflict with one another, and that there is no formula we can apply for determining when one will take precedence over another. On some occasions it is more important to be fair than to make people happy; in others, just the opposite is true. He introduces the notion of a **prima facie duty** as a means of expressing the idea that moral reasons have a variable weight relative to one another. At times the moral reason to keep a promise may be sufficient to mark our all-things-considered duty. In other contexts, the duty of beneficence may be more stringent, say, when attending to a medical emergency prevents the fulfillment of a relatively inconsequential promise. Yet if there is no higher-order, absolute moral principle that can determine when one prima facie duty overrides another, then how can we know, in a given situation, whether one moral reason should take priority? Ross' answer is that there is no general procedure for determining which action is one's all-things-considered duty in particular contexts, and that we have no choice but to rely on the "intuition" that in the unique circumstances that obtain, one prima facie duty is more stringent than another. For this reason, Ross's theory is often called **intuitionism.** Many philosophers find reliance on uncodifiable judgment to be a recipe for irrational, or at best nonrational, ethical decision making. Ross would insist, however, that ethics is just extremely complicated, and that there simply is no ultimate, absolute ethical principle that could serve in every case to fix the right answer to the ethical questions that puzzle us.

The next subsection recognizes that one may take a deeply skeptical attitude toward morality even if one allows that persons can be altruistically motivated, and allows as well that ethical standards can be objective. This third form of moral skepticism assumes that we know what morality requires of us—occasional self-sacrifice—and proceeds to ask why it is rational, in such cases, to do what morality requires of us. If (as sometimes seems the case) we can do better for ourselves by disregarding our moral duties, why shouldn't we do so? Suppose you find a wallet containing $5000 in cash. Surely the morally right thing to do (at least according to the prevailing moral code) would be to return the wallet with the money to its owner. But would this truly be the most reasonable course of action? Think of what you have to gain: an expression of gratitude, some small satisfaction at having done your duty (mixed with nagging doubts that you are a fool), and *maybe* a small reward. Now compare these benefits with what you have to lose—namely, the $5000 itself. It would seem that the losses involved in doing your "duty" (if that's what it is) far outweigh the gains. (Perhaps the example might be still more convincing if the money belonged not to a private person but to a great corporation or the federal government.) Looking at the matter in this way, wouldn't you be a fool to return the money? Isn't it *unreasonable,* indeed profoundly contrary to reason, voluntarily to choose a loss in preference to a gain for oneself? And yet this is what morality often seems to require of us: that we put the interests of other people ahead of our own. How, then, can it be reasonable to be moral?

One line of reply to this challenge immediately suggests itself. Not to return the property of others is tantamount to stealing it. If other people were ever to find out that you are, in effect, a thief, their opinion of you would drop drastically and your reputation might never fully recover. Moreover, if the authorities were to make this discovery about you, the consequences might be still worse. Even if no one ever found you out, you would have to live in continued anxiety and fear; and even if you got over that, you might become just a bit bolder in the face of subsequent temptations, until your very success finally would betray you, and you would be found out. The idea that it can *pay* to do what is morally wrong, in short, is usually a miscalculation.

Glaucon and Adeimantus, two characters in Plato's *Republic,* are not satisfied with this kind of answer. That there are advantages in having the reputation of being moral and upright (or "just" as they put it) is perfectly evident: what they wish to learn from Socrates is whether there are corresponding advantages in really being, as opposed to merely seeming, morally upright. If it is reasonable to be honest only *because* dishonesty doesn't pay, then, it would seem, it is reasonable to be honest only *when* dishonesty doesn't pay; the ideally wise person would then be the one who is able to have the "best of both worlds" by seeming, but not really being, moral.

Socrates' answer to the challenge of Glaucon and Adeimantus is developed in considerable detail throughout the remaining pages of the *Republic.* The essential core of that answer is included here, but without its *full* supporting argument, which includes, as ultimate premises, Plato's theory of knowledge and his theory of the nature of reality. In the end, Socrates persuades Glaucon and Adeimantus to see that the elements of the unjust person's soul are necessarily discordant just as the elements of a sick person's body are out of harmony; so the question whether injustice can ever pay is as "ridiculous" as the question whether it can be more conducive to happiness to be sick than to be healthy.

Plato's *Republic* is prototypical of much of the classical literature of moral philosophy in that it consists largely of arguments designed to show that there is a strong, even invariant, connection between duty and self-interest. This task of reconciling morality and rationality is called by Gregory Kavka, in this section's final piece, "the reconciliation project." There are still prominent philosophers who take very seriously the efforts to effect the reconciliation. After all, if you revere reason and treasure morality, you have a powerful motive to explain away any apparent inconsistencies between the two.

Some philosophers who have tried to reconcile moral and rational directives, however, have undertaken such a heavy argumentative burden that it seems impossible that they should succeed. Some have argued, for example, that single acts of dishonesty can never ever pay, that there is a necessary and invariant connection between doing what is right (which will have among its other consequences making you morally *better*) and doing what promotes your interest (which will have among its other consequences making you *better off*). Some have sought arguments from any conceivable immoral act that one might otherwise be tempted to perform. Some have sought arguments addressed to *any* person's self-interest no matter how hardened in cynicism that person might be. Some have sought arguments that would apply in all possible circumstances, not merely the most feasible ones. The late Gregory Kavka, however, is concerned only with the more modest forms of the undertaking that can have some claim to our credence even if, at first sight, they seem improbable. He succeeds then in showing why the reconciliation project is still "philosophically interesting and important."

Issues of justice are of course inseparable from fundamental questions of ethics. In the first of two subsections on justice, we consider various views regarding the relations between the demands of law and the requirements of justice. Just about everyone believes that the law sometimes permits or requires immoral conduct; the crucial philosophical question is what, morally speaking, we are allowed to do about this. Answering this question takes us to the very heart of issues in political philosophy regarding the nature and justification of the state. We need to know why state power, exercised through law, is justified in the first place. As we saw in earlier subsections, Plato and Hobbes give very different answers to these questions, and here we sample some additional accounts. Plato's dialogue *Crito* opens with the dramatic scene of Socrates awaiting his executioner. An Athenian jury has unjustly sentenced Socrates to death, and Crito, a wealthy friend, is pleading with him to make an easily arranged escape. Socrates offers several replies explaining his intention to stay put, and along the way develops a battery of arguments on behalf of the moral obligation to obey the law. This short dialogue is notable not only for its dramatic setting and the importance of the issues it discusses, but also because it is the very first extended discussion of political obligation to appear in Western philosophy.

Martin Luther King's "Letter from Birmingham Jail" is not only one of the great classics of the literature concerned with racial injustice, but also a document of philosophical importance in the theoretical literature on the justification in a democracy of **civil disobedience.** It shows Gandhi's influence on King and also King's important contribution to John Rawls' understanding of civil disobedience (which Rawls himself acknowledges). Rawls is very likely the most influential political philosopher of the last generation (for more on Rawls, see below), and in his now-classic work, *A Theory of Justice,* he defines civil disobedience as a "public, nonviolent, conscientious yet political act contrary to government." By acting in this manner, Rawls goes on to say, in a passage with direct application to King, "one addresses the sense of justice of the majority of the community and declares that in one's considered opinion the principles of social cooperation among free and equal men are not being respected" (*A Theory of Justice,* p. 364).

Joel Feinberg's "Civil Disobedience in the Modern World" concludes this subsection. As the problem of civil disobedience is usually put, one begins with the assumption that there is some prima facie moral duty to obey the law, and then asks what sorts of moral reasons would, in the context under scrutiny, be sufficiently important to override that duty. Feinberg takes direct aim at this initial assumption, and argues that, as best we can tell, there really is no moral obligation to obey the law per se. Whatever moral obligation exists depends on the morality of the conduct called for by law. Thus if a law is either unsupported by moral reasons, or positively opposed by such reasons, then to that extent it generates no obligation of obedience. If true, this presumably makes the justification of civil disobedience a (morally) easier matter than most people have thought.

The concluding section of this book focuses on issues that are usually grouped under the heading of **distributive justice.** Unlike **retributive justice,** the focus here is not on determining what responses to wrongdoing are appropriate, but instead on how best to devise governmental structures that distribute freedoms, opportunities and economic benefits. We have excerpted three very different, immensely influential works on this subject, beginning with John Rawls' *A Theory of Justice*. Rawls defends his egalitarian principles of justice by deriving them from a kind of hypothetical social contract. Hence, his theory is often called **contractarian.** According to the contractarian method of derivation, a proposed principle of justice (for example, the utilitarian's, the intuitionist's, or Rawls's own) is correct, provided it would be chosen over any alternative principle that could be proposed to a group of normally self-interested, rational persons. We are to suppose that all these persons have gathered together voluntarily in an **original position** of equal power for the purpose of designing the institutions that will regulate their future lives. We are also to suppose that they wear a kind of **veil of ignorance,** which prevents them from knowing facts about their own future condition that could tempt them ("rationally self-interested" beings that they are) to base their choice on the desire to promote their own interest, to the disadvantage of others. If these hypothetical choosers are neither rich nor poor, white nor black, male nor female, old nor young—so far as they know—then they cannot be lobbyists for any particular class interests and must choose their principles from a more disinterested vantage point. Justice, then, is the name for the principles such persons would choose to govern the design of their political and economic institutions.

The selection from Robert Nozick, a Harvard colleague of Rawls, presents his famous libertarian critique of Rawls' distributive proposals. According to Nozick, the best government is a minimal one, whose proper power extends only to protecting each citizen from being positively harmed by others. The state lacks justification for **redistributive** policies, policies that take from better-off citizens in order to assist the less well-to-do. According to Nozick, such policies, regardless of any tangible benefits they confer on the needy or less well-off, nevertheless violate the property rights of those who have legitimately acquired their property. On Nozick's view, our goal should be to minimize the role of the state, and we can do this by restricting taxation so that it covers only the costs of the state services that are absolutely essential to protecting people's safety. Welfare services, international aid, public schooling, and many other allocations we currently take for granted would be barred, not because they are thought unimportant, but because no one should be forced, through taxation, to pay for them. If such causes attract sufficient concern from the citizenry, individuals will be free to make charitable contributions to sustain them. Otherwise they will not be funded.

The last piece is a substantial portion of the last chapter of John Stuart Mill's *Utilitarianism*. With this excerpt we now include more than half of Mill's book, and readers are encouraged to couple Chapters I and II (contained in the Standards of Right Conduct section) with the present section to get a more complete understanding of his classic work. For Mill, as for other utilitarians, the crucial question in assessing the moral status of a government is whether its policies are promoting the happiness or minimizing the misery of its citizens. The problem, as many have alleged, is that securing the greatest happiness for the greatest number may mean violating the rights of a few. For instance, from Nozick's point of view, even if a welfare state made most people happy, it would be morally unjust because of its redistributive policies—specifically, because it violates the rights of taxpayers. Rawls takes utilitarianism to task because it allows us to ignore the plight of the worst-off in society, because economic policies may enhance the overall welfare of the citizenry while failing to address the pressing needs of the most impoverished. It has become a favorite pastime of non-utilitarians to supply scenarios in which happiness is maximized by exploiting others, breaking a promise, lying, stealing, or falsely accusing innocents. Of course each such situation will bring some misery for the victims (and likely their friends and family), but by hypothesis such unhappiness will be more than compensated for by the benefits such injustice brings to others.

Utilitarians have three standard replies to these charges. The first is to deny that these cases ever arise in the real world, and to insist that, as a matter of fact, respecting people's rights will always maximize happiness (or minimize unhappiness). The second allows that conflicts of justice and utility will sometimes arise, but insists that in such cases we must give the moral nod to utility—justice has no independent weight of its own, but is important only because doing justice ordinarily (but not invariably) also leads one to maximize happiness. The third response claims that justice is a matter of following certain rules, which are denominated rules of justice precisely because general obedience to them maximizes utility. This view is often associated by utilitarians with the claim that rightness is determined not by the actual results of each individual action, but rather by whether one is acting in accordance with rules, general conformity to which maximizes good consequences. If we combine these associated views, we again arrive at the conclusion that the demands of justice and morality cannot conflict. It is a vexed question among scholars whether Mill, in Chapter V, is endorsing the second or the third reply to the worry about justice. Readers are invited to settle the question for themselves, as one step in the larger project of determining the proper standards of distributive justice.

Moral Motivation and Human Nature

Psychological Egoism*

JOEL FEINBERG

A. THE THEORY

1. "PSYCHOLOGICAL EGOISM" is the name given to a theory widely held by ordinary people, and at one time almost universally accepted by political economists, philosophers, and psychologists, according to which all human actions when properly understood can be seen to be motivated by selfish desires. More precisely, psychological egoism is the doctrine that the only thing anyone is capable

**From materials composed for philosophy students at Brown University, 1958.*

of desiring or pursuing ultimately (as an end in itself) is his *own* self-interest. No psychological egoist denies that people sometimes do desire things other than their own welfare—the happiness of other people, for example; but all psychological egoists insist that people are capable of desiring the happiness of others only when they take it to be a *means* to their own happiness. In short, purely altruistic and benevolent actions and desires do not exist; but people sometimes appear to be acting unselfishly and disinterestedly when they take the interests of others to be means to the promotion of their own self-interest.

2. This theory is called *psychological* egoism to indicate that it is not a theory about what *ought* to be the case, but rather about what, as a matter of fact, *is* the case. That is, the theory claims to be a description of psychological facts, not a prescription of ethical ideals. It asserts, however, not merely that all men do as a contingent matter of fact "put their own interests first," but also that they are capable of nothing else, human nature being what it is. Universal selfishness is not just an accident or a coincidence on this view; rather, it is an unavoidable consequence of psychological laws.

The theory is to be distinguished from another doctrine, so-called "ethical egoism," according to which all people *ought* to pursue their own well-being. This doctrine, being a prescription of what *ought* to be the case, makes no claim to be a psychological theory of human motives; hence the word "ethical" appears in its name to distinguish it from *psychological* egoism.

3. There are a number of types of motives and desires which might reasonably be called "egoistic" or "selfish," and corresponding to each of them is a possible version of psychological egoism. Perhaps the most common version of the theory is that apparently held by Jeremy Bentham.[1] According to this version, all persons have only one ultimate motive in all their voluntary behavior and that motive is a selfish one; more specifically, it is one particular kind of selfish motive—namely, a desire for one's own *pleasure*. According to this version of the theory, "the only kind of ultimate desire is the desire to get or to prolong pleasant experiences, and to avoid or to cut short unpleasant experiences for oneself."[2] This form of psychological egoism is often given the cumbersome name—*psychological egoistic hedonism*.

B. PRIMA FACIE REASONS IN SUPPORT OF THE THEORY

4. Psychological egoism has seemed plausible to many people for a variety of reasons, of which the following are typical:

a. "Every action of mine is prompted by motives or desires or impulses which are *my* motives and not somebody else's. This fact might be expressed by saying that whenever I act I am always pursuing my own ends or trying to satisfy my own desires. And from this we might pass on to—'I am always pursuing something for myself or seeking my own satisfaction.' Here is what seems like a proper description of a man acting selfishly, and if the description applies to all actions of all men, then it follows that all men in all their actions are selfish."[3]

b. It is a truism that when a person gets what he wants he characteristically feels pleasure. This has suggested to many people that what we really want in every case is our own pleasure, and that we pursue other things only as a means.

c. *Self-Deception.* Often we deceive ourselves into thinking that we desire something fine or noble when what we really want is to be thought well of by others or to be able to congratulate ourselves, or to be able to enjoy the pleasures of a good conscience. It is a well-known fact that people tend to conceal their true motives from themselves by camouflaging them with words like "virtue," "duty," etc. Since we are so often misled concerning both our own real motives and the real motives of others, is it not reasonable to suspect that we might *always* be deceived when we think motives disinterested and altruistic? Indeed, it is a simple matter to explain away all allegedly unselfish motives: "Once the conviction that selfishness is universal finds root in a person's mind, it is very likely to burgeon out in a thousand corroborating generalizations. It will be discovered that a friendly smile is really only an attempt to win an approving nod from a more or less gullible recording angel; that a charitable deed is, for its performer, only an opportunity to congratulate himself on the good fortune or the cleverness that enables him to be charitable; that a public benefaction is just plain good business advertising. It will emerge that gods are worshipped only because they indulge men's selfish fears, or tastes, or hopes; that the 'golden rule' is no more than an eminently sound success formula; that social and political codes are created and subscribed to only because they serve to restrain other men's egoism as much as one's own, morality being only a special sort of 'racket' or intrigue using weapons of persuasion in place of bombs and machine guns. Under this interpretation of human nature, the categories of commercialism replace those of disinterested service and the spirit of the horse trader broods over the face of the earth."[4]

d. *Moral Education.* Morality, good manners, decency, and other virtues must be teachable. Psychological egoists often notice that moral education and the inculcation of manners usually utilize what Bentham calls the "sanctions of pleasure and pain."[5] Children are made to acquire the civilizing virtues only by the method of enticing rewards and painful punishments. Much the same is true of the history of the race. People in general have been inclined to behave well only when it is made plain to them that there is "something in it for them." Is it not then highly probable that just such a mechanism of human motivation as Bentham describes must be presupposed by our methods of moral education?

C. CRITIQUE OF PSYCHOLOGICAL EGOISM: CONFUSIONS IN THE ARGUMENTS

5. *Non-Empirical Character of the Arguments.* If the arguments of the psychological egoist consisted for the most part of carefully acquired empirical evidence (well-documented reports of controlled experiments, surveys, interviews, laboratory data, and so on), then the critical philosopher would have no business carping at them. After all, since psychological egoism purports to be a scientific theory of human motives, it is the concern of the experimental psychologist, not the philosopher, to accept or reject it. But as a matter of fact, empirical evidence of the required sort is seldom presented in support of psychological egoism. Psychologists, on the whole, shy away from generalizations about human motives which are so sweeping and so vaguely formulated that they are virtually incapable of scientific testing. It is usually the "armchair scientist" who holds the theory of universal selfishness, and his usual arguments are either based simply on his "impressions" or else are largely of a non-empirical sort. The latter are often shot full of a very subtle kind of logical confusion, and this makes their criticism a matter of special interest to the analytic philosopher.

6. The psychological egoist's first argument (4a, above) is a good example of logical confusion. It begins with a truism—namely, that all of my motives and desires are *my* motives and desires and not someone else's. (Who would deny this?) But from this simple tautology nothing whatever concerning the nature of my motives or the objective of my desires can possibly follow. The fallacy of this argument consists in its violation of the general logical rule that analytic statements (tautologies) cannot entail synthetic (factual) ones.[6] That every voluntary act is prompted by the agent's own motives is a tautology; hence, it cannot be equivalent to "A person is always seeking something for himself" or "All of a person's motives are selfish," which are synthetic. What the egoist must prove is not merely:

(i) Every voluntary action is prompted by a motive of the agent's own.

but rather:

(ii) Every voluntary action is prompted by a motive of a quite particular kind, viz. a selfish one.

Statement (i) is obviously true, but it cannot all by itself give any logical support to statement (ii).

The source of the confusion in this argument is readily apparent. It is not the genesis of an action or the *origin* or its motives which makes it a "selfish" one, but rather the "purpose" of the act or the *objective* of its motives; *not where the motive comes from* (in voluntary actions it always comes from the agent) but *what it aims at* determines whether or not it is selfish. There is surely a valid distinction between voluntary behavior, in which the agent's action is motivated by purposes of his own, and *selfish* behavior in which the agent's motives are of one exclusive sort. The egoist's argument assimilates all voluntary action into the class of selfish action, by requiring, in effect, that an unselfish action be one which is not really motivated at all. In the words of Lucius Garvin, "to say that an act proceeds from our own . . . desire is only to say that the act is our own. To demand that we should act on motives that are not our own is to ask us to make ourselves living contradictions in terms."[7]

7. But if argument 4a fails to prove its point, argument 4b does no better. From the fact that all our successful actions (those in which we get what we were after) are accompanied or followed by pleasure it does not follow, as the egoist claims, that the *objective* of every action is to get pleasure for oneself. To begin with, the premise of the argument is not, strictly speaking, even true. Fulfillment of desire (simply getting what one was after) is no guarantee of satisfaction (pleasant feelings of gratification in the mind of the agent). Sometimes when we get what we want we *also* get, as a kind of extra dividend, a warm, glowing feeling of contentment; but often, far too often, we get no dividend at all, or, even worse, the bitter taste of ashes. Indeed, it has been said that the characteristic psychological problem of our time is the *dissatisfaction* that attends the fulfillment of our very most powerful desires.

Even if we grant, however, for the sake of argument, that getting what one wants *usually* yields satisfaction, the egoist's conclusion does not follow. We can concede that we normally get pleasure (in the sense of satisfaction) when our desires are satisfied, *no matter what our desires are for;* but it does not follow from this roughly accurate generalization that the only thing we ever desire is our own satisfaction. Pleasure may well be the usual accompaniment of all actions in which the agent gets what he wants; but to infer from this that what the agent always wants is his own pleasure is like arguing, in William James's example,[8] that because an ocean liner constantly consumes coal on its trans-Atlantic passage that therefore the *purpose* of its voyage is to consume coal. The immediate inference from even constant accompaniment to purpose (or motive) is always a *non sequitur.*

Perhaps there is a sense of "satisfaction" (desire fulfillment) such that it is certainly and universally true that we get satisfaction whenever we get what we want. But satisfaction in this sense is simply the "coming into existence of that which is desired." Hence, to say that desire fulfillment always yields "satisfaction" in this sense is to say no more than that we always get what we want when we get what we want, which is to utter a tautology like "a rose is a rose." It can no more entail a synthetic truth in psychology (like the egoistic thesis) than "a rose is a rose" can entail significant information in botany.

8. *Disinterested Benevolence.* The fallacy in argument 4b then consists, as Garvin puts it, "in the supposition that the apparently unselfish desire to benefit others is transformed into a selfish one by the fact that we derive pleasure from carrying it out."[9] Not only is this argument fallacious; it also provides us with a suggestion of a counterargument to show that its conclusion (psychological egoistic hedonism) is false. Not only is the presence of pleasure (satisfaction) as a by-product of an action no proof that the action was selfish; in some special cases it provides rather conclusive proof that the action was *unselfish.* For in those special cases the fact that we get pleasure from a particular action *presupposes that we desired something else*—some-

thing other than our own pleasure—as an end in itself and not merely as a means to our own pleasant state of mind.

This way of turning the egoistic hedonist's argument back on him can be illustrated by taking a typical egoist argument, one attributed (perhaps apocryphally) to Abraham Lincoln, and then examining it closely:

> Mr. Lincoln once remarked to a fellow-passenger on an old-time mud-coach that all men were prompted by selfishness in doing good. His fellow-passenger was antagonizing this position when they were passing over a corduroy bridge that spanned a slough. As they crossed this bridge they espied an old razor-backed sow on the bank making a terrible noise because her pigs had got into the slough and were in danger of drowning. As the old coach began to climb the hill, Mr. Lincoln called out, "Driver, can't you stop just a moment?" Then Mr. Lincoln jumped out, ran back and lifted the little pigs out of the mud and water and placed them on the bank. When he returned, his companion remarked: "Now Abe, where does selfishness come in on this little episode?" "Why, bless your soul Ed, that was the very essence of selfishness. I should have had no peace of mind all day had I gone on and left that suffering old sow worrying over those pigs. I did it to get peace of mind, don't you see?"[10]

If Lincoln had cared not a whit for the welfare of the little pigs and their "suffering" mother, but only for his own "peace of mind," it would be difficult to explain how he could have derived pleasure from helping them. The very fact that he did feel satisfaction as a result of helping the pigs presupposes that he had a preexisting desire for something other than his own happiness. Then when *that* desire was satisfied, Lincoln of course derived pleasure. The *object* of Lincoln's desire was not pleasure; rather pleasure was the *consequence* of his preexisting desire for something else. If Lincoln had been wholly indifferent to the plight of the little pigs as he claimed, how could he possibly have derived any pleasure from helping them? He could not have achieved peace of mind from rescuing the pigs, had he not a prior concern—on which his peace of mind depended—for the welfare of the pigs for its own sake.

In general, the psychological hedonist analyzes apparent benevolence into a desire for "benevolent pleasure." No doubt the benevolent person does get pleasure from his benevolence, but in most cases, this is only because he has previously desired the good of some person, or animal, or mankind at large. Where there is no such desire, benevolent conduct is not generally found to give pleasure to the agent.

9. *Malevolence.* Difficult cases for the psychological egoist include not only instances of disinterested benevolence, but also cases of "disinterested malevolence." Indeed, malice and hatred are generally no more "selfish" than benevolence. Both are motives likely to cause an agent to sacrifice his own interests—in the case of benevolence, in order to help someone else, in the case of malevolence in order to harm someone else. The selfish person is concerned ultimately only with his own pleasure, happiness, or power; the benevolent person is often equally concerned with the happiness of others; to the malevolent person, the *injury* of another is often an end in itself—an end to be pursued sometimes with no thought for his own interests. There is reason to think that people have as often sacrificed themselves to injure or kill others as to help or to save others, and with as much "heroism" in the one case as in the other. The unselfish nature of malevolence was first noticed by the Anglican Bishop and moral philosopher Joseph Butler (1692–1752), who regretted that people are no more selfish than they are.[11]

10. *Lack of Evidence for Universal Self-Deception.* The more cynical sort of psychological egoist who is impressed by the widespread phenomenon of self-deception (see 4c above) cannot be so quickly disposed of, for he has committed no *logical* mistakes. We can only argue that the acknowledged frequency of self-deception is insufficient evidence for his universal generalization. His argument is not fallacious, but inconclusive.

No one but the agent himself can ever be certain what conscious motives really prompted his action, and where motives are disreputable, even the agent may not admit to himself the true nature of his desires. Thus, for every apparent case of altruistic behavior, the psychological egoist can argue, with some plausibility, that the true motivation *might* be selfish, appearance to the contrary. Philanthropic acts are really motivated by the desire to receive gratitude; acts of self-sacrifice, when truly understood, are seen to be motivated by the desire to feel self-esteem; and so on. We must concede to the egoist that all apparent altruism might be deceptive in this way; but such a sweeping generalization requires considerable empirical evidence, and such evidence is not presently available.

11. *The "Paradox of Hedonism" and Its Consequences for Education.* The psychological egoistic Hedonist (e.g., Jeremy Bentham) has the simplest possible theory of human motivation. According to this variety of egoistic theory, all human motives without exception can be reduced to one—namely, the desire for one's own pleasure. But this theory, despite its attractive simplicity, or perhaps because of it, involves one immediately in a paradox. Astute observers of human affairs from the time of the ancient Greeks have often noticed that pleasure, happiness, and satisfaction are states of mind which stand in a very peculiar relation to desire. An exclusive desire for happiness is the surest way to prevent happiness from coming into being. Happiness has a way of "sneaking up" on persons when they are preoccupied with other things; but when persons deliberately and single-mindedly set off in pursuit of happiness, it vanishes utterly from sight and cannot be captured. This is the famous "paradox of hedonism": the single-minded pursuit of happiness is necessarily self-defeating, for *the way to get happiness is to forget it;* then perhaps it will come to you. If you aim exclusively at pleasure itself, with no concern for the things that bring pleasure, then pleasure will never come. To derive satisfaction, one must ordinarily first desire something other than satisfaction, and then find the means to get what one desires.

To feel the full force of the paradox of hedonism the reader should conduct an experiment in his imagination. Imagine a person (let's call him "Jones") who is, first of all, devoid of intellectual curiosity. He has no desire to acquire any kind of knowledge for its own sake, and thus is utterly indifferent to questions of science, mathematics, and philosophy. Imagine further that the beauties of nature leave Jones cold: he is unimpressed by the autumn foliage, the snow-capped mountains, and the rolling oceans. Long walks in the country on spring mornings and skiing forays in the winter are to him equally a bore. Moreover, let us suppose that Jones can find no appeal in art. Novels are dull, poetry a pain, paintings nonsense and music just noise. Suppose further that Jones has neither the participant's nor the spectator's passion for baseball, football, tennis, or any other sport. Swimming to him is a cruel aquatic form of calisthenics, the sun only a cause of sunburn. Dancing is coeducational idiocy, conversation a waste of time, the other sex an unappealing mystery. Politics is a fraud, religion mere superstition; and the misery of millions of underprivileged human beings is nothing to be concerned with or excited about. Suppose finally that Jones has no talent for any kind of handicraft, industry, or commerce, and that he does not regret that fact.

What then is Jones interested in? He must desire something. To be sure, he does. Jones has an overwhelming passion for, a complete preoccupation with, his own happiness. The one exclusive desire of his life is *to be happy.* It takes little imagination at this point to see that Jones's one desire is bound to be frustrated. People who—like Jones—most hotly pursue their own happiness are the least likely to find it. Happy people are those who successfully pursue such things as aesthetic or religious experience, self-expression, service to others, victory in competitions, knowledge, power, and so on. If none of these things in themselves and for their own sakes mean anything to a person, if they are valued at all then only as a means to one's own pleasant states of mind—then that pleasure can never come. The way to achieve happiness is to pursue something else.

Almost all people at one time or another in their lives feel pleasure. Some people (though perhaps not many) really do live lives which are on the whole happy. But if pleasure and happiness presuppose desires for something other than pleasure and happiness, then the existence of pleasure and happiness in the experience of some people proves that those people have strong desires for something other than their own happiness—egoistic hedonism to the contrary.

The implications of the "paradox of hedonism" for educational theory should be obvious. The parents least likely to raise a happy child are those who, even with the best intentions, train their child to seek happiness directly. How often have we heard parents say:

> I don't care if my child does not become an intellectual, or a sports star, or a great artist. I just want her to be a plain average sort of person. Happiness does not require great ambitions and great frustrations; it's not worth it to suffer and become neurotic for the sake of science, art, or do-goodism. I just want my child to be happy.

This can be a dangerous mistake, for it is the child (and the adult for that matter) without "outer-directed" interests who is the most likely to be unhappy. The pure egoist would be the most wretched of persons.

The educator might well beware of "life adjustment" as the conscious goal of the educational process for similar reasons. "Life adjustment" can be achieved only as a by-product of other pursuits. A whole curriculum of "life adjustment courses" unsupplemented by courses designed to incite an interest in things other than life adjustment would be tragically self-defeating.

As for moral education, it is probably true that punishment and reward are indispensable means of inculcation. But if the child comes to believe that the *sole* reasons for being moral are that he will escape the pain of punishment thereby and/or that he will gain the pleasure of a good reputation, then what is to prevent him from doing the immoral thing whenever he is sure that he will not be found out? While punishment and reward then are important tools for the moral educator, they obviously have their limitations. Beware of the man who does the moral thing only out of fear of pain or love of pleasure. He is not likely to be wholly trustworthy. Moral education is truly successful when it produces persons who are willing to do the right thing *simply because it is right*, and not merely because it is popular or safe.

12. *Pleasure as Sensation.* One final argument against psychological hedonism should suffice to put that form of the egoistic psychology to rest once and for all. The egoistic hedonist claims that all desires can be reduced to the single desire for one's own *pleasure.* Now the word "pleasure" is ambiguous. On the one hand, it can stand for a certain indefinable, but very familiar and specific kind of sensation, or more accurately, a property of sensations; and it is generally, if not exclusively, associated with the senses. For example, certain taste sensations such as sweetness, thermal sensations of the sort derived from a hot bath or the feel of the August sun while one lies on a sandy beach, erotic sensations, olfactory sensations (say) of the fragrance of flowers or perfume, and tactual and kinesthetic sensations from a good massage, are all pleasant in this sense. Let us call this sense of "pleasure," which is the converse of "physical pain," pleasure_1.

On the other hand, the word "pleasure" is often used simply as a synonym for "satisfaction" (in the sense of gratification, not mere desire fulfillment.) In this sense, the existence of pleasure presupposes the prior existence of desire. Knowledge, religious experience, aesthetic expression, and other so-called "spiritual activities" often give pleasure in this sense. In fact, as we have seen, we tend to get pleasure in this sense whenever we get what we desire, no matter what we desire. The masochist even derives pleasure (in the sense of "satisfaction") from his own physically painful sensations. Let us call the sense of "pleasure" which means "satisfaction"—pleasure_2.

Now we can evaluate the psychological hedonist's claim that the sole human motive is a desire for one's own pleasure, bearing in mind (as he often does not) the ambiguity of the word "pleasure." First, let us take the hedonist to be saying that it is the desire for pleasure_1 (pleasant sensation) which is the sole ultimate desire of all people and the sole desire capable of providing a motive for action. Now I have little doubt that all (or most) people desire their own pleasure, *sometimes.* But even this familiar kind of desire occurs, I think, rather rarely. When I am very hungry, I often desire to eat, or, more specifically, to eat this piece of steak and these potatoes. Much less often do I desire to eat certain morsels simply for the sake of the pleasant gustatory sensations they might cause. I have, on the other hand, been motivated in the latter way when I have gone to especially exotic (and expensive) French or Chinese restaurants; but normally, pleasant gastronomic sensations are simply a happy consequence or by-product of my eating, not the antecedently desired objective of my eating. There are, of course, others who take gustatory sensations far more seriously: the *gourmet* who eats only to savor the textures and flavors of fine foods, and the wine fancier who "collects" the exquisitely subtle and very pleasant tastes of rare old wines. Such people are truly absorbed in their taste sensations when they eat and drink, and there may even be some (rich) persons whose desire for such sensations is the sole motive for eating and drinking. It should take little argument, however, to convince the reader that such persons are extremely rare.

Similarly, I usually derive pleasure from taking a hot bath, and on occasion (though not very often) I even decide to bathe simply for the sake of such sensations. Even if this is equally true of everyone, however, it hardly provides grounds for inferring that *no one ever* bathes from *any* other motive. It should be empirically obvious that we sometimes bathe simply in order to get clean, or to please others, or simply from habit.

The view then that we are never after anything in our actions but our own pleasure—that all people are complete "gourmets" of one sort or another—is not only morally cynical; it is also contrary to common sense and everyday experience. In fact, the view that pleasant sensations play such an enormous role in human affairs is so patently false, on the available evidence, that we must conclude that the psychological hedonist has the other sense of "pleasure"—satisfaction—in mind when he states his thesis. If, on the other hand, he really does try to reduce the apparent multitude of human motives to the one desire for pleasant sensations, then the abundance of historical counter-examples justifies our rejection out of hand of his thesis. It surely seems incredible that the Christian martyrs were ardently pursuing their own pleasure when they marched off to face the lions, or that what the Russian soldiers at Stalingrad "really" wanted when they doused themselves with gasoline, ignited themselves, and then threw the flaming torches of their own bodies on German tanks, was simply the experience of pleasant physical sensations.

13. *Pleasure as Satisfaction.* Let us consider now the other interpretation of the hedonist's thesis, that according to which it is one's own pleasure$_2$ (satisfaction) and not merely pleasure$_1$ (pleasant sensation) which is the sole ultimate objective of all voluntary behavior. In one respect, the "satisfaction thesis" is even less plausible than the "physical sensation thesis"; for the latter at least is a genuine empirical hypothesis, testable in experience, though contrary to the facts which experience discloses. The former, however, is so confused that it cannot even be completely stated without paradox. It is, so to speak, defeated in its own formulation. Any attempted explication of the theory that all men at all times desire only their own satisfaction leads to an *infinite regress* in the following way:

"All men desire only satisfaction."
"Satisfaction of what?"
"Satisfaction of their desires."
"Their desires for what?"
"Their desires for satisfaction."
"Satisfaction of what?"
"Their desires."
"For what?"
"For satisfaction"—etc., *ad infinitum.*

In short, psychological hedonism interpreted in this way attributes to all people as their sole motive a wholly vacuous and infinitely self-defeating desire. The source of this absurdity is in the notion that satisfaction can, so to speak, feed on itself, and perform the miracle of perpetual self-regeneration in the absence of desires for anything other than itself.

To summarize the argument of sections 12 and 13: The word "pleasure" is ambiguous. Pleasure$_1$ means a certain indefinable characteristic of physical sensation. Pleasure$_2$ refers to the feeling of satisfaction that often comes when one gets what one desires whatever be the nature of that which one desires. Now, if the hedonist means $pleasure_1$ when he says that one's own pleasure is the ultimate objective of all of one's behavior, then his view is not supported by the facts. On the other hand, if he means $pleasure_2$, then his theory cannot even be clearly formulated, since it leads to the following infinite regress: "I desire only satisfaction of my desire for satisfaction of my desire for satisfaction . . . etc., *ad infinitum*." I conclude then that psychological hedonism (the most common form of psychological egoism), however interpreted, is untenable.

D. CRITIQUE OF PSYCHOLOGICAL EGOISM: UNCLEAR LOGICAL STATUS OF THE THEORY

14. There remain, however, other possible forms of the egoistic psychology. The egoist might admit that not all human motives can be reduced to the one ultimate desire for one's own pleasure, or happiness, and yet still maintain that our ultimate motives, whether they be desire for happiness (J. S. Mill), self-fulfillment (Aristotle), power (Hobbes), or whatever, are always *self-regarding* motives. He might still maintain that, given our common human nature, wholly disinterested action impelled by exclusively other-regarding motives is psychologically impossible, and that therefore there is a profoundly important sense in which it is true that, whether they be hedonists or not, *all people are selfish*.

Now it seems to me that this highly paradoxical claim cannot be finally evaluated until it is properly understood, and that it cannot be properly understood until one knows what the psychological egoist is willing to accept as evidence either for or against it. In short, there are two things that must be decided: (a) whether the theory is true or false and (b) whether its truth or falsity (its truth value) depends entirely on the *meanings* of the words in which it is expressed or whether it is made true or false by certain *facts,* in this case the facts of psychology.

15. *Analytic Statements.* Statements whose truth is determined solely by the meanings of the words in which they are expressed, and thus can be held immune from empirical evidence, are often called analytic statements or tautologies. The following are examples of tautologies:

(1) All bachelors are unmarried.
(2) All effects have causes.
(3) Either Providence is the capital of Rhode Island or it is not.

The truth of (1) is derived solely from the meaning of the word "bachelor," which is defined (in part) as "unmarried man." To find out whether (1) is true or false we need not conduct interviews, compile statistics, or perform experiments. All empirical evidence is superfluous and irrelevant; for if we know the meanings of "bachelor" and "unmarried," then we know not only that (1) is true, but that it is *necessarily* true—i.e., that it cannot possibly be false, that no future experiences or observations could possibly upset it, that to deny it would be to assert a logical contradiction. But notice that what a tautology gains in certainty ("necessary truth") it loses in descriptive content. Statement (1) imparts no information whatever about any matter of fact; it simply records our determination to use certain words in a certain way. As we say, "It is true by definition."

Similarly, (2) is (necessarily) true solely in virtue of the meanings of the words "cause" and "effect" and thus requires no further observations to confirm it. And of course, no possible observations could falsify it, since it asserts no matter of fact. And finally, statement (3) is (necessarily) true solely in virtue of the meaning of the English expression "either . . . or." Such terms as "either . . . or," "If . . . then," "and," and "not" are called by logicians "logical constants." The *definitions* of logical constants are made explicit in the so-called "laws of thought"—the law of contradiction, the law of the excluded middle, and the law of identity. These "laws" are not laws in the same sense as are (say) the laws of physics. Rather, they are merely consequences of the *definitions* of logical constants, and as such, though they are necessarily true, they impart no information about the world. "Either Providence is the capital of Rhode Island or it is not" tells us nothing about geography; and "Either it is now raining or else it is not" tells us nothing about the weather. You don't have to look at a map or look out the window to know that they are true. Rather, they are known to be true *a priori* (independently of experience); and, like all (or many)[12] *a priori* statements, they are *vacuous,* i.e., devoid of informative content.

The denial of an analytic statement is called a contradiction. The following are typical examples of contradictions: "Some bachelors are married," "Some causes have no effects," "Providence both is and is not the capital of Rhode Island." As in the case of tautologies, the truth value of contradictions (their falsehood) is logically necessary, not contingent on any facts of experience, and uninformative. Their falsity is derived from the meanings (definitions) of the words in which they are expressed.

16. *Synthetic Statements.* On the other hand, statements whose truth or falsity is derived not from the meanings of words but rather from the facts of experience (observations) are called *synthetic.*[13] Prior to experience, there can be no good reason to think either that they are true or that they are false. That is to say, their truth value is *contingent;* and they can be confirmed or disconfirmed only by *empirical* evidence,[14] i.e., controlled observations of the world. Unlike analytic statements, they do impart information about matters of fact. Obviously, "It is raining in Newport now," if true, is more informative than "Either it is raining in Newport now or it is not," even though the former *could* be false, while the latter is necessarily true. I take the following to be examples of synthetic (contingent) statements:

(1') All bachelors are neurotic.
(2') All events have causes.
(3') Providence is the capital of Rhode Island.
(3'') Newport is the capital of Rhode Island.

Statement (3') is true; (3'') is false; and (1') is a matter for a psychologist (not for a philosopher) to decide; and the psychologist himself can only decide *empirically,* i.e., by making many observations. The status of (2') is very difficult and its truth value is a matter of great controversy. That is because its truth or falsity depends on *all* the facts ("all events"); and, needless to say, not all of the evidence is in.

17. *Empirical Hypotheses.* Perhaps the most interesting subclass of synthetic statements are those generalizations of experience of the sort characteristically made by scientists; e.g., "All released objects heavier than air fall," "All swans are white," "All men have Oedipus complexes." I shall call such statements "empirical hypotheses" to indicate that their function is to sum up past experience and enable us successfully to predict or anticipate future experience.[15] They are never logically certain, since it is always at least conceivable that future experience will disconfirm them. For example, zoologists once believed that all swans are white, until black swans were discovered in Australia. The most important characteristic of empirical hypotheses for our present purposes is their relation to evidence. A person can be said to understand an empirical hypothesis only if he knows how to recognize evidence against it. *If a person asserts or believes a general statement in such a way that he cannot conceive of any possible experience which he would count as evidence against it, then he cannot be said to be asserting or believing an empirical hypothesis.* We can refer to this important characteristic of empirical hypotheses as *falsifiability in principle.*

Some statements only appear to be empirical hypotheses but are in fact disguised tautologies reflecting the speaker's determination to use words in certain (often eccentric) ways. For example, a zoologist might refuse to allow the existence of "Australian swans" to count as evidence against the generalization that all swans are white, on the grounds that the black Australian swans are not "really" swans at all. This would indicate that he is holding *whiteness* to be part of the definition of "swan," and that therefore, the statement "All swans are white" is, for him, "true by definition"—and thus just as immune from counterevidence as the statement "All spinsters are unmarried." Similarly, most of us would refuse to allow any possible experience to count as evidence against "2 + 2 = 4" or "Either unicorns exist or they do not," indicating that the propositions of arithmetic and logic are not empirical hypotheses.

18. *Ordinary Language and Equivocation.* Philosophers, even more than ordinary people, are prone to make startling and paradoxical claims that take the form of universal generalizations and hence resemble empirical hypotheses. For example, "All things are mental (there are no physical objects)," "All things are good (there is no evil)," "All voluntary behavior is selfish," etc. Let us confine our attention for the moment to the latter which is a rough statement of psychological egoism. At first sight, the statement "All voluntary behavior is selfish" seems obviously false. One might reply to the psychological egoist in some such manner as this:

> I *know* some behavior, at least, is unselfish, because I saw my Aunt Emma yesterday give her last cent to a beggar. Now she will have to go a whole week with nothing to eat. Surely, *that* was not selfish of her.

Nevertheless, the psychological egoist is likely not to be convinced, and insist that, in this case, if we knew enough about Aunt Emma, we would learn that her primary motive in helping the beggar was to promote her own happiness or assuage her own conscience, or increase her own self-esteem, etc. We might then present the egoist with even more difficult cases for his theory—saints, martyrs, military heroes, patriots, and others who have sacrificed themselves for a cause. If psychological egoists nevertheless refuse to accept any of these as examples of unselfish behavior, then we have a right to be puzzled about what they are saying. Until we know what they would count as *unselfish* behavior, we can't very well know what they mean when they say that all voluntary behavior is *selfish.* And at this point we may suspect that they are holding their theory in a "privileged position"—that of immunity to evidence, that they would allow no *conceivable* behavior to count as evidence against it. What they say then, if true, must be true in virtue of the way they define—or redefine—the word "selfish." And in that case, it cannot be an empirical hypothesis.

If what the psychological egoist says is "true by redefinition," then I can "agree" with him and say "It is true that in *your* sense of the word 'selfish' my Aunt Emma's behavior was selfish; but in the ordinary sense of 'selfish,' which implies blameworthiness, she surely was not selfish." There is no point of course in arguing about a mere word. The important thing is not what particular words a person uses, but rather whether what he wishes to say in those words is true. Departures from ordinary language can often be justified by their utility for certain purposes; but they are dangerous when they invite equivocation. The psychological egoist may be saying something which is true when he says that Emma is selfish in *his* sense, but if he doesn't realize that his sense of "selfish" differs from the ordinary one, he may be tempted to infer that Emma is selfish in the ordinary sense which implies blameworthiness; and this of course would be unfair and illegitimate. It is indeed an extraordinary extension of the meaning of the word "self-indulgent" (as C. G. Chesterton remarks somewhere) which allows a philosopher to say that a man is self-indulgent when he wants to be burned at the stake.

19. *The Fallacy of the Suppressed Correlative.* Certain words in the English language operate in pairs—e.g., "selfish-unselfish," "good-bad," "large-small," "mental-physical." To assert that a thing has one of the above characteristics is to *contrast* it with the opposite in the pair. To know the meaning of one term in the pair, we must know the meaning of the correlative term with which it is contrasted. If we could not conceive of what it would be like for a thing to be bad, for example, then we could not possibly understand what is being said of a thing when it is called "good." Similarly, unless we had a notion of what it would be like for action to be *unselfish,* we could hardly understand the sentence "So-and-so acted selfishly", for we would have nothing to contrast "selfishly" with. The so-called "fallacy of the suppressed correlative"[16] is committed by a person who consciously or unconsciously redefines one of the terms in a contrasting pair in such a way that its new meaning incorporates the sense of its correlative.

Webster's Collegiate Dictionary defines "selfish" (in part) as "regarding one's own comfort, advantage, etc. in disregard of, or at the expense of that of others." In this ordinary and proper sense of "selfish," Aunt Emma's action in giving her last cent to the beggar certainly was *not* selfish. Emma *disregarded* her *own* comfort (it is not "comfortable" to go a week without eating) and advantage (there is no "advantage" in malnutrition) *for the sake of* (not "at the expense of") another. Similarly, the martyr marching off to the stake is foregoing (not indulging) his "comfort" and indeed his very life for the sake of (not at the expense of) a cause. If Emma and the martyr then are "selfish," they must be so in a strange new sense of the word.

A careful examination of the egoist's arguments (see especially 4b above) reveals what new sense he gives to the word "selfish." He redefines the word so that it means (roughly) "motivated," or perhaps "intentional." "After all," says the egoist, "Aunt Emma had some *purpose* in giving the beggar all her money, and this purpose (desire, intention, motive, aim) was *her* purpose and no one else's. She was out to further some aim of her own, wasn't she? Therefore, she was pursuing her own ends (acting from her own motives); she was after something *for herself* in so acting, and that's what I mean by calling her action selfish. Moreover, all intentional action—action done 'on purpose,' deliberately from the agent's own motives—is selfish in the same sense." We can see now, from this reply, that since the egoist apparently means by "selfish" simply "motivated," when he says that all motivated action is selfish *he is not asserting a synthetic empirical hypothesis about human motives; rather, his statement is a tautology roughly equivalent to "all motivated actions are motivated."* And if that is the case, then what he says is true enough; but, like all tautologies, it is empty, uninteresting, and trivial.

Moreover, in redefining "selfish" in this way, the psychological egoist has committed the fallacy of the suppressed correlative. For what can we now contrast "selfish voluntary action" with? Not only are there no *actual* cases of unselfish voluntary actions on the new definition; there are not even any *theoretically possible* or *conceivable* cases of unselfish voluntary actions. And if we cannot even conceive of what an unselfish voluntary action would be like, how can we give any sense to the expression "selfish voluntary action"? The egoist, so to speak, has so blown up the sense of "selfish" that, like inflated currency, it will no longer buy anything.

20. *Psychological Egoism as a Linguistic Proposal.* There is still one way out for the egoist. He might admit that his theory is not really a psychological hypothesis about human nature designed to account for the facts and enable us to predict or anticipate future events. He may even willingly concede that his theory is really a disguised redefinition of a word. Still, he might argue, he has made no claim to be giving an accurate description of actual linguistic usage. Rather, he is making a proposal to *revise* our usage in the interest of economy and convenience, just as the biologists once proposed that we change the ordinary meaning of "insect" in such a way that spiders are no longer called insects, and the ordinary meaning of "fish" so that whales and seals are no longer called fish.

What are we to say to this suggestion? First of all, stipulative definitions (proposals to revise usage) are never true or false. They are simply useful or not useful. Would it be useful to redefine "selfish" in the way the egoist recommends? It is difficult to see what would be gained thereby. The egoist has noticed some respects in which actions normally called "selfish" and actions normally called "unselfish" are alike, namely they are both motivated and they both can give satisfaction—either in prospect or in retrospect—to the agent. Because of these likenesses, the egoist feels justified in attaching the label "selfish" to *all* actions. Thus one word—"selfish"—must for him do the work of two words ("selfish" and "unselfish" in their old meanings); and, as a result, a very real distinction, that between actions for the sake of others and actions at the expense of others, can no longer be expressed in the language. Because the egoist has noticed some respects in which two types of actions are alike, he wishes to make it impossible to describe the respects in which they differ. It is difficult to see any utility in this state of affairs.

But suppose we adopt the egoist's "proposal" nevertheless. Now we would have to say that all actions are selfish; but, in addition, we would want to say that there are two different kinds of selfish actions, those which regard the interests of others and those which disregard the interests of others, and, furthermore, that only the latter are blameworthy. After a time our ear would adjust to the new uses of the word "selfish," and we would find nothing at all strange in such statements as "Some selfish actions are morally praiseworthy." After a while, we might even invent two new words, perhaps "selfitic" and "unselfitic," to distinguish the two important classes of "selfish" actions. Then we would be right back where we started, with new linguistic tools ("selfish" for "motivated," "selfitic" for "selfish," and "unselfitic" for "unselfish") to do the same old necessary jobs. That is, until some new egoistic philosopher arose to announce with an air of discovery that "All selfish behavior is really selfitic—there are no truly unselfitic selfish actions." Then, God help us!

NOTES

1. See his *Introduction to the Principles of Morals and Legislation* (1789), Chap. I, first paragraph: "Nature has placed mankind under the governance of two sovereign masters, *pain* and *pleasure.* It is for them alone to point out what we ought to do, as well as to determine what we shall do. . . . They govern us in all we do, in all we say, in all we think: every effort we can make to throw off our subjection will serve but to demonstrate and confirm it."

2. C. D. Broad, *Ethics and the History of Philosophy* (New York: The Humanities Press, 1952), Essay 10—"Egoism as a Theory of Human Motives," p. 218. This essay is highly recommended.

3. Austin Duncan-Jones, *Butler's Moral Philosophy* (London: Penguin Books, 1952), p. 96. Duncan-Jones goes on to reject this argument. See p. 512f.

4. Lucius Garvin, *A Modern Introduction to Ethics* (Boston: Houghton Mifflin, 1953), p. 37. Quoted here by permission of the author and publisher.

5. *Op. cit.*, Chap. III.

6. See Part D, 15 and 16, below.

7. *Op. cit.*, p. 39.

8. *The Principles of Psychology* (New York: Henry Holt, 1890), Vol. II, p. 558.

9. *Op. cit.*, p. 39.

10. Quoted from the *Springfield* (Illinois) *Monitor,* by F. C. Sharp in his *Ethics* (New York: Appleton-Century, 1928), p. 75.

11. See his *Fifteen Sermons on Human Nature Preached at the Rolls Chapel* (1726), especially the first and eleventh.

12. Whether or not there are some *a priori* statements that are not merely analytic, and hence *not* vacuous, is still a highly controversial question among philosophers.

13. Some philosophers (those called "rationalists") believe that there are some synthetic statements whose truth can be known *a priori* (see note 12). If they are right, then the statement above is not entirely accurate.

14. Again, subject to the qualification in notes 12 and 13.

15. The three examples given above all have the generic character there indicated, but they also differ from one another in various other ways, some of which are quite important. For our present purposes however, we can ignore the ways in which they differ from one another and concentrate on their common character as generalizations of experience ("inductive generalizations"). As such they are sharply contrasted with such a generalization as "All puppies are young dogs," which is analytic.

16. The phrase was coined by J. Lowenberg. See his article "What Is Empirical?" in the *Journal of Philosophy,* May 1940.

The Conscience of Huckleberry Finn*

JONATHAN BENNETT

Jonathan Bennett (1930–) came first to Canada and then to the United States from his native New Zealand. He has taught for many years at Syracuse University.

In this paper, I shall present not just the conscience of Huckleberry Finn but two others as well. One of them is the conscience of Heinrich Himmler. He became a Nazi in 1923; he served drably and quietly, but well, and was rewarded with increasing responsibility and power. At the peak of his career he held many offices and commands, of which the most powerful was that of leader of the S.S.—the principal police force of the Nazi regime. In this capacity, Himmler commanded the whole concentration-camp system, and was responsible for the execution of the so-called 'final solution of the Jewish problem.' It is important for my purposes that this piece of social engineering should be thought of not abstractly but in concrete terms of Jewish families being marched to what they think are bath-houses, to the accompaniment of loud-speaker renditions of extracts from *The Merry Widow* and *Tales of Hoffman*, there to be choked to death by poisonous gases. Altogether, Himmler succeeded in murdering about four and a half million of them, as well as several million gentiles, mainly Poles and Russians.

The other conscience to be discussed is that of the Calvinist theologian and philosopher Jonathan Edwards. He lived in the first half of the eighteenth century, and has a good claim to be considered America's first serious and considerable philosophical thinker. He was for many years a widely-renowned preacher and Congregationalist minister in New England; in 1748 a dispute with his congregation led him to resign (he couldn't accept their view that unbelievers should be admitted to the Lord's Supper in the hope that it would convert them); for some years after that he worked as a missionary, preaching to Indians through an interpreter; then in 1758 he accepted the presidency of what is now Princeton University, and within two months died from a smallpox inoculation. Along the way he wrote some first-rate philosophy: his book attacking the notion of free will is still sometimes read. Why I should be interested in Edwards' *conscience* will be explained in due course.

I shall use Heinrich Himmler, Jonathan Edwards and Huckleberry Finn to illustrate different aspects of a single theme, namely the relationship between *sympathy* on the one hand and *bad morality* on the other.

All that I can mean by a 'bad morality' is a morality whose principles I deeply disapprove of. When I call a morality bad, I cannot prove that mine is better; but when I here call any morality bad, I think you will agree with me that it is bad; and that is all I need.

There could be dispute as to whether the springs of someone's actions constitute a *morality*. I think, though, that we must admit that someone who acts in ways which conflict grossly with our morality may nevertheless have a morality of his own—a set of principles of action which he sincerely assents to, so that for him the problem of acting well or rightly

*"*The Conscience of Huckleberry Finn*" *by Jonathan Bennett*, Philosophy, *Vol. 49 (1974), pp. 123–143.*
Reprinted with the permission of Cambridge University Press and the author.

or in obedience to conscience is the problem of conforming to *those* principles. The problem of conscientiousness can arise as acutely for a bad morality as for any other: rotten principles may be as difficult to keep as decent ones.

As for 'sympathy': I use this term to cover every sort of fellow-feeling, as when one feels pity over someone's loneliness, or horrified compassion over his pain, and when one feels a shrinking reluctance to act in a way which will bring misfortune to someone else. These *feelings* must not be confused with *moral judgments*. My sympathy for someone in distress may lead me to help him, or even to think that I ought to help him; but in itself it is not a judgment about what I ought to do but just a *feeling* for him in his plight. We shall get some light on the difference between feelings and moral judgments when we consider Huckleberry Finn.

Obviously, feelings can impel one to action, and so can moral judgments; and in a particular case sympathy and morality may pull in opposite directions. This can happen not just with bad moralities, but also with good ones like yours and mine. For example, a small child, sick and miserable, clings tightly to his mother and screams in terror when she tries to pass him over to the doctor to be examined. If the mother gave way to her sympathy, that is to her feeling for the child's misery and fright, she would hold it close and not let the doctor come near; but don't we agree that it might be wrong for her to act on such a feeling? Quite generally, then, anyone's moral principles may apply to a particular situation in a way which runs contrary to the particular thrusts of fellow-feeling that he has in that situation. My immediate concern is with sympathy in relation to bad morality, but not because such conflicts occur only when the morality is bad.

Now, suppose that someone who accepts a bad morality is struggling to make himself act in accordance with it in a particular situation where his sympathies pull him another way. He sees the struggle as one between doing the right, conscientious thing, and acting wrongly and weakly, like the mother who won't let the doctor come near her sick, frightened baby. Since we don't accept this person's morality, we may see the situation very differently, thoroughly disapproving of the action he regards as the right one, and endorsing the action which from his point of view constitutes weakness and backsliding.

Conflicts between sympathy and bad morality won't always be like this, for we won't disagree with every single dictate of a bad morality. Still, it can happen in the way I have described, with the agent's right action being our wrong one, and vice versa. That is just what happens in a certain episode in chapter 16 of *The Adventures of Huckleberry Finn*, an episode which brilliantly illustrates how fiction can be instructive about real life.

Huck Finn has been helping his slave friend Jim to run away from Miss Watson, who is Jim's owner. In their raft-journey down the Mississippi river, they are near to the place at which Jim will become legally free. Now let Huck take over the story:

> Jim said it made him all over trembly and feverish to be so close to freedom. Well, I can tell you it made me all over trembly and feverish, too, to hear him, because I begun to get it through my head that he *was* most free—and who was to blame for it? Why, *me*. I couldn't get that out of my conscience, no how nor no way.... It hadn't ever come home to me, before, what this thing was that I was doing. But now it did; and it stayed with me, and scorched me more and more. I tried to make out to myself that *I* warn't to blame, because *I* didn't run Jim off from his rightful owner; but it warn't no use, conscience up and say, every time: 'But you knowed he was running for his freedom, and you could a paddled ashore and told somebody.' That was so—I couldn't get around that, no way. That was where it pinched. Conscience says to me: 'What had poor Miss Watson done to you, that you could see her nigger go off right under your eyes and never say one single word? What did that poor old woman do to you, that you could treat her so mean? . . .' I got to feeling so mean and so miserable I most wished I was dead.

Jim speaks of his plan to save up to buy his wife, and then his children, out of slavery; and he adds that if the children cannot be bought he will arrange to steal them. Huck is horrified:

> Thinks I, this is what comes of my not thinking. Here was this nigger which I had as good as helped to run away, coming right out flat-footed and saying he would steal his children—children that belonged to a man I didn't even know; a man that hadn't ever done me no harm.
>
> I was sorry to hear Jim say that, it was such a lowering of him. My conscience got to stirring me up hotter than ever, until at last I says to it: 'Let up on me—it ain't too late, yet—I'll paddle ashore at first light, and tell.' I felt easy, and happy, and light as a feather, right off. All my troubles was gone.

This is bad morality all right. In his earliest years Huck wasn't taught any principles, and the only ones he has encountered since then are those of rural Missouri, in which slave-owning is just one kind of ownership and is not subject to critical pressure. It hasn't occurred to Huck to question those principles. So the action, to us abhorrent, of turning Jim in to the authorities presents itself *clearly* to Huck as the right thing to do.

For us, morality and sympathy would both dictate helping Jim to escape. If we felt any conflict, it would have both these on one side and something else on the other—greed for a reward, or fear of punishment. But Huck's morality conflicts with his sympathy, that is, with his unargued, natural feeling for his friend. The conflict starts when Huck sets off in the canoe towards the shore, pretending that he is going to reconnoitre, but really planning to turn Jim in:

> As I shoved off, [Jim] says: 'Pooty soon I'll be ashout'n for joy, en I'll say, it's all on accounts o' Huck I's a free man . . . Jim won't ever forgit you, Huck; you's de bes' fren' Jim's ever had; en you's de *only* fren' old Jim's got now.'
>
> I was paddling off, all in a sweat to tell on him; but when he says this, it seemed to kind of take the tuck all out of me. I went along slow then, and I warn't right down certain whether I was glad I started or whether I warn't. When I was fifty yards off, Jim says:
>
> 'Dah you goes, de ole true Huck; de on'y white genlman dat ever kep' his promise to ole Jim.' Well, I just felt sick. But I says, I *got* to do it—I can't get *out* of it.

In the upshot, sympathy wins over morality. Huck hasn't the strength of will to do what he sincerely thinks he ought to do. Two men hunting for runaway slaves ask him whether the man on his raft is black or white:

> I didn't answer up prompt. I tried to, but the words wouldn't come. I tried, for a second or two, to brace up and out with it, but I warn't man enough—hadn't the spunk of a rabbit. I see I was weakening; so I just give up trying, and up and says: 'He's white.'

So Huck enables Jim to escape, thus acting weakly and wickedly—he thinks. In this conflict between sympathy and morality, sympathy wins.

One critic has cited this episode in support of the statement that Huck suffers 'excruciating moments of wavering between honesty and respectability.' That is hopelessly wrong, and I agree with the perceptive comment on it by another critic, who says:

> The conflict waged in Huck is much more serious: he scarcely cares for respectability and never hesitates to relinquish it, but he does care for honesty and gratitude—and both honesty and gratitude require that he should give Jim up. It is not, in Huck, honesty at war with respectability but love and compassion for Jim struggling against his conscience. His decision is for Jim and hell: a right decision made in the mental chains that Huck never breaks. His concern for Jim is and remains *irrational.* Huck finds many reasons for giving Jim up and none for stealing him. To the end Huck sees his compassion for Jim as a weak, ignorant, and wicked felony.[1]

That is precisely correct—and it can have that virtue only because Mark Twain wrote the episode with such unerring precision. The crucial point concerns *reasons,* which all occur on one side of the conflict. On the side of conscience we have principles, arguments, considerations, ways of looking at things:

> 'It hadn't ever come home to me before what I was doing'
>
> 'I tried to make out that I warn't to blame'

'Conscience said 'But you knowed . . .'—I couldn't get around that'.

'What had poor Miss Watson done to you?'

'This is what comes of my not thinking'

'. . . children that belonged to a man I didn't even know.'

On the other side, the side of feeling, we get nothing like that. When Jim rejoices in Huck, as his only friend, Huck doesn't consider the claims of friendship or have the situation 'come home' to him in a different light. All that happens is: 'When he says this, it seemed to kind of take the tuck all out of me. I went along slow then, and I warn't right down certain whether I was glad I started or whether I warn't.' Again, Jim's words about Huck's 'promise' to him don't give Huck any *reason* for changing his plan: in his morality promises to slaves probably don't count. Their effect on him is of a different kind: 'Well, I just felt sick.' And when the moment for final decision comes, Huck doesn't weigh up pros and cons: he simply *fails* to do what he believes to be right—he isn't strong enough, hasn't 'the spunk of a rabbit.' This passage in the novel is notable not just for its finely wrought irony, with Huck's weakness of will leading him to do the right thing, but also for its masterly handling of the difference between general moral principles and particular unreasoned emotional pulls.

Consider now another case of bad morality in conflict with human sympathy the case of the odious Himmler. Here, from a speech he made to some S.S. generals, is an indication of the content of his morality:

> What happens to a Russian, to a Czech, does not interest me in the slightest. What the nations can offer in the way of good blood of our type, we will take, if necessary by kidnapping their children and raising them here with us. Whether nations live in prosperity or starve to death like cattle interests me only in so far as we need them as slaves to our *Kultur;* otherwise it is of no interest to me. Whether 10,000 Russian females fall down from exhaustion while digging an antitank ditch interests me only in so far as the antitank ditch for Germany is finished.[2]

But has this a moral basis at all? And if it has, was there in Himmler's own mind any conflict between morality and sympathy? Yes there was. Here is more from the same speech:

> . . . I also want to talk to you quite frankly on a very grave matter . . . I mean . . . the extermination of the Jewish race. . . . Most of you must know what it means when 100 corpses are lying side by side, or 500, or 1,000. To have stuck it out and at the same time—apart from exceptions caused by human weakness—to have remained decent fellows, that is what has made us hard. This is a page of glory in our history which has never been written and is never to be written.

Himmler saw his policies as being hard to implement while still retaining one's human sympathies—while still remaining a 'decent fellow.' He is saying that only the weak take the easy way out and just squelch their sympathies, and is praising the stronger and more glorious course of retaining one's sympathies while acting in violation of them. In the same spirit, he ordered that when executions were carried out in concentration camps, those responsible 'are to be influenced in such a way as to suffer no ill effect in their character and mental attitude.' A year later he boasted that the S.S. had wiped out the Jews

> without our leaders and their men suffering any damage in their minds and souls. The danger was considerable, for there was only a narrow path between the Scylla of their becoming heartless ruffians unable any longer to treasure life, and the Charybdis of their becoming soft and suffering nervous breakdowns.

And there really can't be any doubt that the basis of Himmler's policies was a set of principles which constituted his morality—a sick, bad, wicked *morality.* He described himself as caught in 'the old tragic conflict between will and obligation.' And when his physician Kersten protested at the intention to destroy the Jews, saying that the suffering involved was 'not to be contemplated,' Kersten reports that Himmler replied:

> He knew that it would mean much suffering for the Jews. . . . 'It is the curse of greatness that it

must step over dead bodies to create new life. Yet we must . . . cleanse the soil or it will never bear fruit. It will be a great burden for me to bear.'

This, I submit, is the language of morality.

So in this case, tragically, bad morality won out over sympathy. I am sure that many of Himmler's killers did extinguish their sympathies, becoming 'heartless ruffians' rather than 'decent fellows'; but not Himmler himself. Although his policies ran against the human grain to a horrible degree, he did not sandpaper down his emotional surfaces so that there was no grain there, allowing his actions to slide along smoothly and easily. He did, after all, bear his hideous burden, and even paid a price for it. He suffered a variety of nervous and physical disabilities, including nausea and stomach-convulsions, and Kersten was doubtless right in saying that these were 'the expression of a psychic division which extended over his whole life.'

This same division must have been present in some of those officials of the Church who ordered heretics to be tortured so as to change their theological opinions. Along with the brutes and the cold careerists, there must have been some who cared, and who suffered from the conflict between their sympathies and their bad morality.

In the conflict between sympathy and bad morality, then, the victory may go to sympathy as in the case of Huck Finn, or to morality as in the case of Himmler.

Another possibility is that the conflict may be avoided by giving up, or not ever having, those sympathies which might interfere with one's principles. That seems to have been the case with Jonathan Edwards. I am afraid that I shall be doing an injustice to Edwards' many virtues, and to his great intellectual energy and inventiveness; for my concern is only with the worst thing about him—namely his morality, which was worse than Himmler's.

According to Edwards, God condemns some men to an eternity of unimaginably awful pain, though he arbitrarily spares others—'arbitrarily' because none deserve to be spared:

> Natural men are held in the hand of God over the pit of hell; they have deserved the fiery pit, and are already sentenced to it; and God is dreadfully provoked, his anger is as great towards them as to those that are actually suffering the executions of the fierceness of his wrath in hell . . . ; the devil is waiting for them, hell is gaping for them, the flames gather and flash about them, and would fain lay hold on them . . . ; and . . . there are no means within reach that can be any security to them. . . . All that preserves them is the mere arbitrary will, and uncovenanted unobliged forebearance of an incensed God.[3]

Notice that he says 'they have deserved the fiery pit.' Edwards insists that men *ought* to be condemned to eternal pain; and his position isn't that this is right because God wants it, but rather that God wants it because it is right. For him, moral standards exist independently of God, and God can be assessed in the light of them (and of course found to be perfect). For example, he says:

> They deserve to be cast into hell; so that . . . justice never stands in the way, it makes no objection against God's using his power at any moment to destroy them. Yea, on the contrary, justice calls aloud for an infinite punishment of their sins.

Elsewhere, he gives elaborate arguments to show that God is acting justly in damning sinners. For example, he argues that a punishment should be exactly as bad as the crime being punished; God is infinitely excellent; so any crime against him infinitely bad; and so eternal damnation is exactly right as a punishment—it is infinite, but, as Edwards is careful also to say, it is 'no more than infinite.'

Of course, Edwards himself didn't torment the damned; but the question still arises of whether his sympathies didn't conflict with his *approval* of eternal torment. Didn't he find it painful to contemplate any fellow-human's being tortured for ever? Apparently not:

> The God that holds you over the pit of hell, much as one holds a spider or some loathsome insect over the fire, abhors you, and is dreadfully provoked; . . . he is of purer eyes than to bear to have you in his sight; you are ten thousand times so abominable in his eyes as the most hateful venomous serpent is in ours.

When God is presented as being as misanthropic as that, one suspects misanthropy in the theologian. The suspicion is increased when Edwards claims that 'the saints in glory will . . . understand how terrible the sufferings of the damned are; yet . . . will not be sorry for [them].'[4] He bases this partly on a view of human nature whose ugliness he seems not to notice:

> The seeing of the calamities of others tends to heighten the sense of our own enjoyments. When the saints in glory, therefore, shall see the doleful state of the damned, how will this heighten their sense of the blessedness of their own state. . . . When they shall see how miserable others of their fellow-creatures are . . . ; when they shall see the smoke of their torment, . . . and hear their dolorous shrieks and cries, and consider that they in the mean time are in the most blissful state, and shall surely be in it to all eternity: how they will rejoice!

I hope this is less than the whole truth! His other main point about why the saints will rejoice to see the torments of the damned is that it is *right* that they should do so:

> The heavenly inhabitants . . . will have no love nor pity to the damned. . . . [This will not show] a want of a spirit of love in them . . . ; for the heavenly inhabitants will know that it is not fit that they should love [the damned] because they will know then, that God has no love to them, nor pity for them.

The implication that *of course* one can adjust one's feelings of pity so that they conform to the dictates of some authority—doesn't this suggest that ordinary human sympathies played only a small part in Edwards' life?

Huck Finn, whose sympathies are wide and deep, could never avoid the conflict in that way; but he is determined to avoid it, and so he opts for the only other alternative he can see—to give up morality altogether. After he has tricked the slave-hunters, he returns to the raft and undergoes a peculiar crisis:

> I got aboard the raft, feeling bad and low, because I knowed very well I had done wrong, and I see it warn't no use for me to try to learn to do right; a body that don't get *started* right when he's little, ain't got no show—when the pinch comes there ain't nothing to back him up and keep him to his work, and so he gets beat. Then I thought a minute, and says to myself, hold on—s'pose you'd a done right and give Jim up; would you feel better than what you do now? No, says I, I'd feel bad—I'd feel just the same way I do now. Well, then, says I, what's the use you learning to do right, when it's troublesome to do right and ain't no trouble to do wrong, and the wages is just the same? I was stuck. I couldn't answer that. So I reckoned I wouldn't bother no more about it, but after this always do whichever come handiest at the time.

Huck clearly cannot conceive of having any morality except the one he has learned—too late, he thinks—from society. He is not entirely a prisoner of that morality, because he does after all reject it; but for him that is a decision to relinquish morality as such; he cannot envisage revising his morality, altering its content in face of the various pressures to which it is subject, including pressures from his sympathies. For example, he does not begin to approach the thought that slavery should be rejected on moral grounds, or the thought that what he is doing is not theft because a person cannot be owned and therefore cannot be stolen.

The basic trouble is that he cannot or will not engage in abstract intellectual operations of any sort. In chapter 33 he finds himself 'feeling to blame, somehow' for something he knows he had no hand in; he assumes that this feeling is a deliverance of conscience; and this confirms him in his belief that conscience shouldn't be listened to:

> It don't make no difference whether you do right or wrong, a person's conscience ain't got no sense, and just goes for him *anyway.* If I had a yaller dog that didn't know no more than a person's conscience does, I would pison him. It takes up more room than all the rest of a person's insides, and yet ain't no good, nohow.

That brisk, incurious dismissiveness fits well with the comprehensive rejection of morality back on the raft. But this is a digression.

On the raft, Huck decides not to live by principles, but just to do whatever 'comes handiest at the time'—always acting according to the mood of the moment. Since the morality he is rejecting is narrow and cruel, and his sympathies are broad and kind, the results will be good. But moral principles are good to have, because they help to protect one from acting badly at moments when one's sympathies happen to be in abeyance. On the highest possible estimate of the role one's sympathies should have, one can still allow for principles as embodiments of one's best feelings, one's broadest and keenest sympathies. On that view, principles can help one across intervals when one's feelings are at less than their best, i.e. through periods of misanthropy or meanness or self-centeredness or depression or anger.

What Huck didn't see is that one can live by principles and yet have ultimate control over their content. And one way such control can be exercised is by checking of one's principles in the light of one's sympathies. This is sometimes a pretty straightforward matter. It can happen that a certain moral principle becomes untenable—meaning literally that one cannot hold it any longer—because it conflicts intolerably with the pity or revulsion or whatever that one feels when one sees what the principle leads to. One's experience may play a large part here: experiences evoke feelings, and feelings force one to modify principles. Something like this happened to the English poet Wilfred Owen, whose experiences in the First World War transformed him from an enthusiastic soldier into a virtual pacifist. I can't document his change of conscience in detail; but I want to present something which he wrote about the way experience can put pressure on morality.

The Latin poet Horace wrote that it is sweet and fitting (or right) to die for one's country—*dulce et decorum est pro patria mori*—and Owen wrote a fine poem about how experience could lead one to relinquish that particular moral principle.[5] He describes a man who is too slow donning his gas mask during a gas attack—'As under a green sea I saw him drowning,' Owen says. The poem ends like this:

In all my dreams before my helpless sight
He plunges at me, guttering, choking, drowning.
If in some smothering dreams, you too could
 pace
Behind the wagon that we flung him in,
And watch the white eyes writhing in his face,
His hanging face, like a devil's sick of sin;
If you could hear, at every jolt, the blood
Come gargling from the froth-corrupted lungs,
Bitter as the cud
Of vile, incurable sores on innocent tongues.—
My friend, you would not tell with such high
 zest
To children ardent for some desperate glory,
The old Lie: Dulce et decorum est
pro patria mori.

There is a difficulty about drawing from all this a moral for ourselves. I imagine that we agree in our rejection of slavery, eternal damnation, genocide, and uncritical patriotic self-abnegation; so we shall agree that Huck Finn, Jonathan Edwards, Heinrich Himmler, and the poet Horace would all have done well to bring certain of their principles under severe pressure from ordinary human sympathies. But then we can say this because we can say that all those are bad moralities, whereas we cannot look at our own moralities and declare them bad. This is not arrogance: it is obviously incoherent for someone to declare the system of moral principles that he *accepts* to be *bad,* just as one cannot coherently say of anything that one *believes* it but it is *false.*

Still, although I can't point to any of my beliefs and say 'That is false,' I don't doubt that some of my beliefs *are* false; and so I should try to remain open to correction. Similarly, I accept every single item in my morality—that is inevitable—but I am sure that my morality could be improved, which is to say that it could undergo changes which I should be glad of once I had made them. So I must try to keep my morality open to revision, exposing it to whatever valid pressures there are—including pressures from my sympathies.

I don't give my sympathies a blank cheque in advance. In a conflict between principle and sympathy, principles ought sometimes to win. For example, I think it was right to take part in the Second World War on the allied side; there were many ghastly individual incidents which might have led someone to doubt the rightness of his participation in that war; and I think it would have been right for such a person to keep his sympathies in a subordinate place on those occasions, not allowing them to modify his principles in such a way as to make a pacifist of him.

Still, one's sympathies should be kept as sharp and sensitive and aware as possible, and not only because they can sometimes affect one's principles or one's conduct or both. Owen, at any rate, says that feelings and sympathies are vital even when they can do nothing but bring pain and distress. In another poem he speaks of the blessings of being numb in one's feelings: 'Happy are the men who yet before they are killed/Can let their veins run cold,' he says. These are the ones who do not suffer from any compassion which, as Owen puts it, 'makes their feet/Sore on the alleys cobbled with their brothers.' He contrasts these 'happy' ones, who 'lose all imagination,' with himself and others 'who with a thought besmirch/Blood over all our soul.' Yet the poem's verdict goes against the 'happy' ones. Owen does not say that they will act worse than the others whose souls are besmirched with blood because of their keen awareness of human suffering. He merely says that they are the losers because they have cut themselves off from the human condition:

> By choice they made themselves immune
> To pity and whatever moans in man
> Before the last sea and the hapless stars;
> Whatever mourns when many leave these shores;
> Whatever shares
> The eternal reciprocity of tears.[6]

NOTES

1. M. J. Sidnell, 'Huck Finn and Jim,' *The Cambridge Quarterly,* vol. 2, pp. 205–206.
2. Quoted in William L. Shirer, *The Rise and Fall of the Third Reich* (New York, 1960), pp. 937–938. Next quotation: Ibid., p. 966. All further quotations relating to Himmler are from Roger Manwell and Heinrich Fraenkel, *Heinrich Himmler* (London, 1965), pp. 132, 197, 184 (twice), 187.
3. Vergilius Ferm (ed.), *Puritan Sage: Collected Writings of Jonathan Edwards* (New York, 1953), p. 370. Next three quotations: Ibid., p. 366, p. 294 ('no more than infinite'), p. 372.
4. This and the next two quotations are from 'The End of the Wicked Contemplated by the Righteous: or, The Torments of the Wicked in Hell, No Occasion of Grief to the Saints in Heaven,' from *The Works of President Edwards* (London, 1817), vol. IV, pp. 507–508, 511–512, and 509 respectively.
5. I am grateful to the Executors of the Estate of Harold Owen, and to Chatto and Windus Ltd., for permission to quote from Wilfred Owen's 'Dulce et Decorum Est' and 'Insensibility.'
6. This paper began life as the Potter Memorial Lecture, given at Washington State University in Pullman, Washington, in 1972.

Proposed Standards of Right Conduct

Ethical Subjectivism

RUSS SHAFER-LANDAU

IMAGINE TWO PEOPLE DEBATING the morality of giving to famine relief. Smith thinks that we are bound to give a great deal more than people typically do. Jones denies this. Suppose that these two, after talking a good while longer, have found themselves in agreement about all of the relevant facts, and have also sharpened their own positions so that the views they emerge with are each internally consistent. But suppose that the fundamental disagreement between them remains. Can this disagreement be rationally resolved?

Not likely, according to ethical subjectivists. Subjectivism claims that there is no ideal or uniquely correct resolution to ethical disagreements, because there are no ethical standards that are objectively correct, no standards that all rational or fully informed people must agree to. There is no overarching, universal yardstick that can be applied to determine the truth of one's ultimate moral principles. Once we have identified our deepest moral commitments, we can go no further. It makes no sense, according to subjectivism, to suppose that such commitments could be false or irrational.

To better understand ethical subjectivism, we need to appreciate the key notions of subjectivity and objectivity. A proposition or judgment is *objectively* true just in case it is true independently of anyone's thinking it is. So, for instance, the claim that the earth orbits around the sun is an objective truth, because the claim is true regardless of whether anyone believes it. A judgment is *subjectively* true just in case its truth depends on whether someone endorses it. To insist that chocolate is tastier than vanilla, or that beer is better than wine, is to make a subjective claim, because in this case truth is in the eye of the beholder.

TWO KINDS OF SUBJECTIVISM

Philosophers standardly distinguish between two kinds of ethical theory. The first sort—**normative** theory—attempts to specify conditions under which an action is morally right or wrong. John Stuart Mill, for instance, held that an act is right insofar as it tends to produce happiness. Immanuel Kant thought that one acts rightly only if one is willing to see everyone act in accordance with one's own principles. Thomas Hobbes claimed that an act is right if it is permitted by rules that would be agreed to by self-interested parties seeking to band together to escape from anarchy.

Viewed as a normative theory, ethical subjectivism claims that an act is morally right if, and only if, the person judging the action approves of it. Similarly, personal disapproval is both necessary and sufficient for an action to qualify as wrong.

Normative subjectivism allows that moral judgments can be true or false. There is truth in ethics, but no objective truth. A moral judgment is true, according to normative subjectivism, just in case it accurately reports the sentiments of the speaker. Thus sincerity is the mark of ethical truth. If normative subjectivism is true, then one's sincere moral judgments cannot be mistaken.

The debate between Mill, Kant, Hobbes, and normative subjectivists is an intramural one. Each theory asserts its superiority as an answer to the question: under what conditions are actions morally right? This is a very important debate within ethics. But we can step back from this debate and ask instead about the status of these competing theories. Specifically, we can ask of all of these theories how they might be justified, whether they are or can be true, and how, if at all, we might know that one or another is true. These are **meta-ethical** questions. Here we are not asking what makes actions right. Instead, we are focusing on whether normative theories can be justified or true in the first place.

Meta-ethical subjectivism is the particular claim that normative ethical theories, and moral judgments quite generally, cannot be true. Contrast this with normative subjectivism, which claims that moral judgments can be true, provided they accurately report the speaker's feelings. Because of their different views about the possibility of ethical truth, meta-ethical subjectivism implies the falsity of normative subjectivism, and vice versa.

Let us consider the motivations and the plausibility of normative subjectivism first.

MOTIVATIONS FOR NORMATIVE SUBJECTIVISM

A. The Argument from Democracy

One of normative subjectivism's appeals is that it is so democratic. Subjectivism is a leveling doctrine—everyone issues true moral judgments, so long as they sincerely give voice to their feelings. Everyone's views are on a par with everyone else's. This democratic element is a genuine feature of subjectivism. But many take this democratic element a step further, expressing their allegiance to normative subjectivism by means of the following argument:

1. If everyone has an equal right to have and voice moral opinions, then everyone's moral opinions are equally plausible.
2. Everyone does have an equal right to have and voice moral opinions.
3. Therefore everyone's moral opinions are equally plausible.

This argument is valid—its premises entail its conclusion. *If* one were to accept premises (1) and (2), then logic requires one to accept the conclusion (3) as well. But should we accept these premises? The second premise seems generally plausible. But the first premise is false. Having a right to an opinion does not entail the plausibility of that opinion. Though everyone has an equal right to express views about mathematics or quantum physics, no one supposes that everyone's opinions here are equally plausible. I have lots of opinions about botany, about the content of the tax code, about the location of various buildings and landmarks. Further, I have a right to each of these opinions. But many of them (I'm not sure which) are mistaken. I misidentify plants, misconstrue tax law, and my sense of direction is awful. These humdrum examples show that the plausibility of an opinion really has nothing to do with one's right to hold it: having a right to an opinion is one thing, the truth of that opinion quite another. This directly undermines the first premise of the argument. Because we must reject one of its crucial premises, the argument from democracy is unsound. It does not supply a good basis for endorsing normative subjectivism.

B. The Argument from Disagreement

One thing that impresses many people about work in the sciences is the degree of consensus about which propositions are true, and about which methods are appropriate for discovering new truths. Things in ethics seem to be much different; there seems to be a great deal of disagreement about fundamental issues, and a lack of consensus about appropriate methods for resolving moral questions. The diversity of ethical opinion has struck many as an important indicator of morality's fundamentally subjective character.

Here is a representative sketch of an argument for subjectivism that takes the breadth of ethical disagreement as its focus:

1. If there is persistent disagreement among informed, good-willed, open-minded people about some subject matter, then that subject matter does not admit of objective truth.
2. There is persistent disagreement about ethical issues among informed, good-willed, open-minded people.
3. Therefore there are no objective ethical truths.

We can know that an argument's conclusion is true if we know that the argument is logically valid and that all of its premises are true. This argument is valid. The second premise seems to be true, though the breadth of moral *agreement* is often underappreciated. The divisive moral issues tend to get the most press, but this publicity can mask the significant degree of moral consensus that must form the core of any society. Further, though there clearly is disagreement about ethical issues, it is sensible to suppose that much of this is owing to mistaken beliefs, and that more information would lead to greater ethical agreement. Public debates about welfare reform in the United States, or about the morality of capital punishment, are chock full of misinformation. Getting the facts straight would get us a good distance toward resolving issues on these (and other) topics.

Still, we may suppose that even after gathering the facts, people of good will may disagree in their ethical views. So let us grant premise (2). Premise (1), however, is not plausible. There is persistent disagreement among informed, good-willed, open-minded physicists and mathematicians. We, and they, assume that their efforts are nevertheless aimed at discovering objective truths. We do not believe that taste is the arbiter of truth in math or physics. Indeed, we can make this quite general point about investigations of all sorts. When historians debate the causes of the Civil War, they are not *merely* entering their personal views, with nothing other than parochial preference to back them up. Historians are trying to discover what *really* caused the Civil War. They continue to disagree about this. But this is not evidence that their discipline is subjective, that the truths they arrive at are mere expressions of taste. It isn't the case that historical (or physical or mathematical) judgments are true just because someone believes in them. What this shows is that a discipline may deal in objective truths even if its open-minded, informed practitioners deeply disagree with one another. Since that is so, the argument from disagreement fails to provide adequate support for normative subjectivism.

C. The Argument from Tolerance

Many people find subjectivism attractive because of the support it seems to provide for tolerance. We nowadays reject the once-prevalent feelings of superiority that were used to justify the oppression of Asians, Africans, and indigenous Americans during the past three centuries. We would encourage a respectful, tolerant attitude toward different cultures, rather than a dismissive outlook that brands other cultures as "primitive." This dismissive attitude always begins with an (implicit) endorsement of ethical objectivism—there is an objectively correct way to do things. And we all know how things go from here: "We have it right, they don't, thus we have to show them the true path. If this means exploiting them (for their own good), and possibly destroying their way of life, no great loss, since we will supply them with a far better one."

If you are like most people, you'll have bristled at the arrogance expressed in these last lines. This may lead you to endorse the following argument from tolerance:

1. If normative subjectivism is true, then no one's deepest opinions are more plausible than anyone else's.
2. If no one's deepest opinions are more plausible than anyone else's, then we have to respect and tolerate the opinions of all others.
3. Thus if normative subjectivism is true, then we have to respect and tolerate the opinions of all others.

There are two important points to note about this argument. The first is that even if it is sound—even if it is logically valid (it is), and all of its premises (and thus its conclusion) are true—this does not entail that ethical objectivists need to embrace an arrogant or disrespectful attitude toward different cultures. Objectivists believe that there are ethical truths that exist independently of whether anyone thinks so. An objectivist need not believe that *he himself* is in possession of such truth. Indeed, objectivists who are appropriately humble will recognize their own fallibility and the limits to their understanding, in much the same way as physicists or chemists might appreciate the depth of their own ignorance against the backdrop of objective truth. Arrogance and intolerance are poor character traits. They are not mandated by the intellectual position of ethical objectivism.

Let us return to the argument. Its first premise is true. But the second premise is not. Suppose that normative subjectivism is true. This means that an action is morally right just in case one approves of it. If one approves of tolerant behavior, then such behavior is morally correct. The problem, however, is that *if* one approves of intolerance, then intolerant behavior is morally appropriate. Subjectivism morally sanctions the intolerance of prejudiced and bigoted individuals, so long as such intolerance is sincerely felt. Regrettably, it often is. Those who think that even (and especially) racists and bigots are morally required to display respect for others will find no ground for their view in ethical subjectivism. To think that even a deeply prejudiced person should be tolerant is to embrace the universal or objective value of toleration. A concern for tolerance thus sits very uncomfortably with normative subjectivism.

D. The Argument from Atheism

A common thought that moves many to normative subjectivism is that objectivity in ethics can be purchased only through divine commands. If ethics is objective, then it must be god who validates the moral rules. The problem, according to subjectivists, is that god does not exist.

Here is the argument in somewhat tighter form:

1. If ethics is objective, then god must exist.
2. God does not exist.
3. Therefore ethics is not objective.

We could undermine the argument from atheism if we could show that god exists. We can't, at least not here (and perhaps not anywhere; this is one philosophical issue that may never be settled). But even if we could resolve this matter, and do so in favor of the atheist, this would not be enough to prove subjectivism. We can see that from the argument itself. The argument requires a further claim (premise 1), namely, that ethics is objective only if god exists.

There is an intuitive, widely shared view that underlies the first premise. The thought is that laws require lawgivers. There are laws against assault, forgery, and perjury only because lawmakers have enacted them. No legislators, no laws. By analogy, if there are moral laws, these require some lawmaker to validate them. If moral laws are objective, this lawmaker cannot be any one of us. (Remember: objective moral rules are those whose truth does not depend on human endorsement.) If not one of us, then who? Enter god.

There are two reasons to doubt premise (1). This premise seems to derive its strongest support from the common thought mentioned earlier (*viz.*, that rules require rule-givers). But this principle is suspect. Many think that the rules of logic and the axioms of mathematics are true quite independently of whether anyone has ordained them. *If* that is so (an issue too complex to tackle here), then moral rules too might be true or justified even in the absence of a moral lawgiver.

Further, there is reason to think that even if god exists, god cannot be the ultimate source of ethical principles, and so cannot be the missing link that supplies objectivity in ethics.

Suppose god exists. Suppose god issues commands to us. And further suppose that our moral law comprises these commands. Ethics is objective because the law comes from god, not from us. If it didn't come from god, it couldn't be objective.

This familiar line of thought, often used to support premise (1), is beset by a troubling dilemma: god either does or does not have reasons to support his (or her or its) commands. If god lacks justifying reasons, then god's commands are arbitrary, and so supply no authoritative basis for ethics. Alternatively, if god's commands *are* backed up by reasons, then divine commands are no longer arbitrary. They may be authoritative. We can envision a god who is omniscient, and so knows all facts, including moral facts. This god may also be omnibenevolent, and in his goodness may want to impart the moral facts (or rules) to us, in the form of divine commands. This traditional picture preserves the goodness and omniscience of god, precisely by envisioning divine commands as being well-supported by reasons.

The problem, however, is that these reasons, whatever they are, are what really justify the divine commands. If god commands us not to kill, extort, or perjure, he does so *because such actions are wrong;* they are not wrong because god forbids them. But this means that even theists, if they are to retain a picture of an all-good and all-knowing god, must acknowledge a source of ethical truth that exists independently of god's commands. This means that the objectivity of ethics does not hinge on god's commands. And that directly challenges premise (1).

A final complication emerges when we consider the argument's conclusion—the claim that ethics is not objective. Even if premises (1) and (2) are true, the conclusion does not show that normative subjectivism is true. Put simply, (3) may be true *even if normative subjectivism is false.* There are at least two theories, in addition to normative subjectivism, that are compatible with the claim that ethics is not objective. One of these theories is meta-ethical subjectivism. The other is ethical relativism, the view that an action is morally right if, and only if, it is permitted by the ultimate mores of the society in which it is performed. Ethical relativism allows for moral truth: moral judgments are true just in case they accurately report a certain kind of social consensus. Because moral truth is a function of what people believe it to be, ethical relativism is a non-objective theory. Thus relativists, as well as normative and meta-ethical subjectivists, will embrace conclusion (3). This shows that the argument from atheism, if it is to support normative subjectivism, must be supplemented by additional arguments that rule out its two anti-objectivist competitors. Though we will examine the merits of meta-ethical subjectivism later, we can't possibly review those arguments that have been offered for and against relativism.

For our purposes, then, we must suspend judgment on the argument from atheism. The argument is sound only if both of its premises are true. They may be. But we could know this only after a very great deal of further philosophical investigation. And we would have an argument for normative subjectivism only if we also had in hand a battery of arguments that undermined both meta-ethical subjectivism and ethical relativism. All the more reason to wait and see before pronouncing a judgment on the argument from atheism.

IMPLICATIONS OF NORMATIVE SUBJECTIVISM

As we have seen, many of the arguments that are advanced for ethical subjectivism are not very compelling. This is not a fatal flaw. Most philosophical positions are supported by a large battery of arguments, many of which, after serious attention, turn out to be unsound. Thus ethical subjectivism may be true even if the preceding arguments turn out to be less than convincing. But to gain plausibility, its supporters need to discharge two debts. First, they must advance a positive argument that survives scrutiny. Second, they must show that the essential implications of subjectivism are implications we can live with. Let us see whether this is so.

First, as we have seen, subjectivism is a doctrine of **moral equivalence:** everyone's ultimate moral views are as plausible as everyone else's. This is a handy weapon when dealing with arrogant or haughty individuals. But moral equivalence is a double-edged sword. If all moral views are on a par with one another, then we lose our basis for issuing substantive moral criticism of unsavory characters such as Nazis and terrorists. If subjectivism is true, then those who approve of antisemitism and terrorism are correct in calling such behavior morally right. The moral views of a Hitler or an IRA gunman are *true,* so long as these views are sincerely held.

Of course, subjectivism does not render us mute at this stage—we can criticize the views of Nazis and terrorists, but only from our own perspective. Importantly, our perspective is not superior to theirs. Moral equivalence entails that conflicting moral views are just different; neither one is better or worse than another. This may appeal when comparing the prayer or dietary rituals of Belgians and Polynesians. But it is likely to leave us cold in the face of serious evil.

Normative subjectivism also comes very close to rendering each person **morally infallible.** An infallible person is one who cannot make mistakes. Thus such a person has no false beliefs and all true ones. If subjectivism is true, then it is possible that all, or almost all, of our moral beliefs are correct. We can be morally mistaken in only one of two ways. We might base our moral views on false beliefs (e.g., a racist whose antipathy to blacks is based on a false belief about their intelligence). Or we might possess moral beliefs that conflict with other, deeper moral beliefs we already hold. We might, for instance, approve of the death penalty for a specially awful murderer, even though in a cooler moment we reject the principles that could justify the execution.

According to subjectivism, moral views that are free of either sort of error cannot be mistaken. Apart from exceptions of these two kinds, subjectivism entails that our moral feelings are self-certifying. Moral outlooks that seem to us vicious, ruthless, callous, selfish, or even maniacal cannot be wrong, so long as the views imply no factual errors and are consistent with other views a person holds. Literature and history offer a good supply of well-informed, consistent fanatics. Subjectivism implies that their views are true.

If we are ordinarily morally infallible, and if we disagree with others in our ethical views, then it follows that subjectivism **generates contradictions.** A contradiction occurs when a proposition is alleged to be both true and false. Theories that generate contradictions cannot be true. We would rightly dismiss a mathematical theory that entailed that two and two did, and at the same time did not, equal four. Suppose ethical subjectivism is correct. If Smith thinks that giving famine aid is mandatory, and Jones disagrees, then giving to famine relief is and is not morally required. It is both true and false that giving to famine relief is obligatory. That is a contradiction.

We can resolve this worrying implication in a fairly straightforward way. Rather than saying that Smith's approval of an action makes it morally right, period, we say that her approval makes it right *for her.* Thus, in the previous example, giving famine aid is not right and wrong in the same respect—it is right for Smith, and wrong for Jones. This is the strategy of relativizing moral judgments to their speakers.

This move really can solve the problem of contradiction. But the strategy has its costs. It renders subjectivism **incapable of explaining the point or existence of moral disagreement.** Think again of the debate about famine relief. If all Smith is saying is that she herself approves of it, and if all Jones is saying is that he doesn't, then Smith and Jones don't really disagree with one another. Further, we lose incentive to continue moral conversation, if moral truth just consists in reports of personal feelings.

It may appear that Smith and Jones, in their debate about famine relief, are trying to get at the truth, trying to discover what is *really* right. But if we relativize judgments to their speakers, this appearance is misleading. There can be no genuine disagreement about where truth lies, since it lies in the eyes of the beholder. If subjectivism is right, everyone's views are true, so long as they are sincerely expressed. Thus ethical disagreement could focus only on whether the interlocutors actually believe what they say they do. Disagreement cannot focus on whether (say) famine relief is *really* right—right in a non-relative, objective sense—because (according to subjectivism) famine relief *cannot be* really right (or wrong). Subjectivism leaves us with an entirely unrecognizable picture of moral disagreement.

A final concern. If subjectivism is true, then **our moral views are arbitrary.** There is no better reason to adopt one ethical view over another. Subjectivism claims that moral views are true because one believes them; one does not believe them because they are true. If moral views are justified to the extent that they are believed, then any basis whatever (other than false belief) will confer plausibility. This allows us to see two ways in which subjectivism entails the arbitrariness of ethical views. First, one's moral outlook may be justified even if one has no reason at all that supports it: the fact that one believes it is sufficient to make it true. In a second kind of case, one does possess reasons that support one's moral views. But the reasons that support a moral belief may fail entirely to move other informed, rational, good-willed people. In this sense, one's views are arbitrary, since they are supported by reasons that could, with complete propriety, be rejected by any and all other rational people.

MOTIVATIONS FOR META-ETHICAL SUBJECTIVISM

Most people will find at least some of these implications troubling. For those who do, yet still balk at the idea of objectivity in ethics, meta-ethical subjectivism is a natural path to pursue. This brand of subjectivism denies that moral judgments can be true or false. They are neither true nor false because they are not attempting to describe anything. There are no facts that they might accurately capture, not even facts about our own feelings. According to meta-ethical subjectivism, the purpose of moral judgment is not to *report* one's attitudes, but rather to *express* commitments or *vent* feelings.

On this view, moral judgments are closely analogous to commands and emotional responses. Though moral judgments look like factual judgments—"infanticide is wrong" has the same grammatical structure as straightforward descriptive judgments ("space is curved", "grass is green")—this appearance is misleading. To say that infanticide is wrong, for instance, is just either to give vent to a visceral dislike of infanticide, or to issue a command that prohibits infanticide. On the first line, the moral judgment is equivalent to "Infanticide? Boo! Yuck!". On the second view, the moral judgment reduces to something like "Don't commit infanticide!". On either view, moral judgments cannot be true or false, since they don't purport to describe anything. Emotive ventings ("Spinach? Blech!") aren't true or false. Commands ("Rise and shine!") aren't true or false. According to meta-ethical subjectivists, since moral judgments are effectively utterances of either sort, they aren't true or false, either. Unlike normative subjectivism, which sees moral judgments as reports of personal feelings, and so usually true, meta-ethical subjectivism denies that such judgments are ever true (or false).

The distinction between normative and meta-ethical subjectivism may seem a minor one, a picayune footnote introduced by philosophers to impress one another and oppress their students. But the distinction is actually quite important. As we'll see, we can solve many of the problems that beset normative subjectivism if we deny that moral judgments can be true or false. Whether all of the problems disappear remains to be seen.

Let us begin our assessment of meta-ethical subjectivism by considering some of the most important arguments that have been advanced on its behalf.

A. The Argument from Moral Motivation

The great Scottish philosopher David Hume was no fan of ethical objectivism. One of the many arguments he offered against it began with what he took to be a striking difference between moral judgments and factual ones. Hume thought that one mark of moral judgment was its capacity to motivate people. A person who sincerely thinks that something is good will be really moved to pursue it; someone who thinks an action genuinely obligatory is thereby motivated to perform it. Nothing like this could be claimed of factual judgments.

Here is the argument put more succinctly:

1. Every moral judgment motivates all by itself.
2. Factual judgments cannot motivate all by themselves.
3. Therefore moral judgments are not factual judgments.

Premise (1) tells us that moral judgments are intrinsically motivational—to judge an action right is to be motivated to perform it. To avoid misunderstanding, note that one can be motivated to perform an action and still fail to do it. Motivations can be overridden; people can be weak-willed, for instance. Still, Hume claims that we cannot genuinely make a moral judgment unless we are motivated *to some extent* to comply with it.

This is what distinguishes moral judgments from factual judgments. We may believe all sorts of mathematical, chemical, or geographical propositions without being moved in the slightest. And when we are moved by factual judgments, it is only because of some accompanying desire that we happen to have. The factual judgments do not motivate all by themselves. Even a very likely candidate—"stepping out in front of that bus will surely kill you"—does not motivate all by itself. We cannot know how or whether a factual judgment will move us unless we also know which desires are associated with the judgment, whether, in this case, we want to commit suicide or to remain alive. Moral judgments intrinsically motivate. Factual judgments do not. Therefore moral judgments are not factual ones.

This is a classic of ethical argumentation. The second premise is widely, if not universally, accepted. The first premise, though, has attracted significant opposition, primarily from those who think that moral claims are a species of factual claims. On this line moral judgments, like factual judgments, need to be supplemented by a desire before people will be motivated to act on them. Moral judgments do not motivate all by themselves. In order to generate motivation, some associated moral desire (e.g., to be beneficent or just) must be present. Those who reject premise (1) believe that it is possible for some people, known as amoralists, to lack moral desires. Amoralists are those who sincerely make moral judgments but entirely fail to be moved by them. These might be people who are depressed, rebellious, alienated, or just plain evil. If amoralists can exist, then premise (1) of the argument from moral motivation is false.

It might seem that this is an easy question to resolve. We can see that amoralists may exist just by imagining their possibility. We can readily imagine someone saying that some particular action is right, all the while remaining perfectly indifferent. The difficulty here is that our imagination is not a reliable indicator of genuine possibilities. People (claim to) imagine the possibility of a square circle, or a number that is both odd and even, but these things cannot exist. Likewise, even if we can imagine the amoralist, this isn't sufficient to show that such persons can exist. Premise (1) may be true after all.

Meta-ethical subjectivists will analyze moral judgments as expressions of emotion; because emotions are intrinsically motivating, moral judgments are intrinsically motivating, too. This is why subjectivists endorse premise (1) of the argument from moral motivation. If amoralists really can exist, then moral judgments are not intrinsically motivating, and hence not necessarily expressions of emotion. If they are not intrinsically motivating, then moral judgments might be factual judgments after all. The plausibility of meta-ethical subjectivism thus depends on whether the amoralist is a genuine possibility. That, unfortunately, is an issue that can't be briefly resolved. Hume's classic argument may be sound. But one would need to undertake a great deal of further investigation before having any warranted confidence one way or the other.

B. The Argument from Economy

Most philosophers believe that when one is comparing the plausibility of competing theories, we should, if all other things are equal, give the nod to the simpler, more economical theory. Theory A is more economical than theory B if A can explain all that B can, but with fewer assumptions. Copernicus' theory of elliptical orbit was simpler than Ptolemy's views, and for this reason ultimately came to be seen as more plausible. The reason scientists don't refer to hexes, spells, ghosts, or demons in their theories is because they can explain everything they need to explain without invoking such things. Supernatural phenomena are *superfluous;* they're added baggage, unnecessary extras that simpler theories can do without.

In a similar vein, meta-ethical subjectivists claim superiority for their view because their assumptions about what there is in the world are sparer than objectivism's. Subjectivists have an essentially scientific view of what the world consists of. The world contains physical things, and physical forces that work on them. Morality is a complex human creation; when we ask what is in the world, *really,* no mention of moral facts need be made. We can explain all of the goings-on of this world, including all human activities—why people act as they do, say the things they do, think as they do—without invoking anything like a "moral fact".

This method of doing away with moral facts bears a striking resemblance to accounts that seek to undermine traditional religion. The Judaeo-Christian god is thought by many to be superfluous—we can explain all of the goings-on of our world without supposing that there is something further, something more (god) who must be put in the picture. As science progresses, we discover that the natural events we once attributed to god (or to the gods) can be explained solely in terms of the natural workings of the natural world. In the same way, many philosophers and neuroscientists have expressed doubt about the existence of a soul, claiming that it is more economical simply to posit the existence of the brain and the nervous system to explain all of our behavior. Without the brain and nervous system, we can't explain any conscious behavior. With it, we can explain all we need to explain. The notion of a soul does no explanatory work (or so it is alleged). A simpler, better theory would thus do without it.

Subjectivists take this strategy and apply it to ethics. What would moral facts be needed to explain? Subjectivists usually take this to be a rhetorical question. We can explain everything in the world by referring to scientific facts, including facts about human psychology. But objectivists have supplied answers. They claim that we can explain lots of things that need explaining by citing moral facts. We explain why Hitler did what he did by citing his *evil nature.* We explain why people opposed apartheid by citing its *injustice.* We explain the success of a con man by reference to his *duplicitous character.* These all seem to be moral facts. The question, of course, is whether we can explain the beliefs and actions mentioned in these examples without citing the moral facts themselves.

For instance, subjectivists will claim that we don't have to suppose that there really is some moral fact of injustice existing out there, somewhere, in order to explain why so many people protested against the apartheid regime. Instead, we simply need to mention the nonmoral facts about differential treatment that obtained in South Africa, and combine these facts with further nonmoral, psychological facts, facts about what people believed. Citizens believed that there was grave injustice, they felt disgusted by the regime, and these beliefs and feelings, combined with various social, cultural, and economic facts, generated the protests that contributed to undermining apartheid society. This explanation makes no mention of any moral facts—just moral judgments and feelings, plus the social scientific facts just alluded to.

This subjectivist strategy is precisely the same sort of strategy we use to debunk metaphysical commitments in other areas. We can cite facts about the Salem society of 300 years ago, combined with people's beliefs and feelings about witches, to explain why so many people were hanged. We don't need to suppose that there really were witches in order to explain everything that needs explaining. Likewise, it is claimed, we don't need to assume the existence of moral facts in order to explain everything in the world that requires explanation.

If we compare the world that scientists depict, with that same world, plus a further realm of moral facts, it is easy to see which view is simpler. But simplicity is not everything. The simpler theory must also be sufficiently explanatory. The question in ethics, as in theology and in the philosophy of mind, is whether we really can explain all that needs explaining with the sparer, more economical theories. As with matters of moral motivation, the issue of economy remains extremely controversial, with objectivists arguing that we do need moral facts to explain our practices, and subjectivists charging that moral facts are superfluous. Unsurprisingly, then, we must satisfy ourselves with only a sketch of the competing positions. Getting beyond the preliminaries requires a deeper dip into the philosophical waters than we can undertake here.

C. *The Argument from Oddness*

Meta-ethical subjectivists urge another reason for abandoning belief in objective moral facts. Suppose, with objectivism, that moral judgments are true, and true quite independently of what we happen to think of them. They are true, when they are, because they accurately report objective moral facts. But what could such things be? We readily grant that geologists and chemists, physicists and astronomers deal in objective truth, because we believe that their findings are constrained by the physical world whose features exist independently of whether anyone recognizes them. Botanical facts are facts about plants; geological facts are facts about rocks. In botany and geology, evidence is supplied by three-dimensional, tangible, physical stuff. We can taste it, smell it, touch it, and see it. We can't taste wrongness or hear rightness. Moral facts, if they were to exist, would have to be quite odd sorts of things, certainly nothing at all like the kinds of phenomena studied by recognized factual disciplines.

Objectivists typically reply, with some force, that they need not be committed to any ghostly realm of moral facts. Everyone agrees that there are moral rules. Moral facts are simply applications of those rules. If a moral rule prohibits infanticide, and Smith commits infanticide, then it is a moral fact that what he did was wrong. Nothing mysterious so far. But subjectivists will claim that the relevant question has simply been pushed back a step. Now we must ask what *justifies* or *validates the moral rule* against infanticide (or adultery, lying, killing, etc.). What is it that makes a moral rule (objectively) true?

As a first step in exploring possibilities, we should consider rules in nonmoral contexts and ask what makes them true. Rules of sports or etiquette are true, if they are, only because certain people believe they are. If no one endorsed the three strikes rule in baseball, or the ban on public nose-picking, then there simply would not be any such rules. Such rules are therefore subjective in the relevant sense.

On the other hand, most people believe that the laws of chemistry, geology, astronomy, and physics are true because of the way the world is. Our best thoughts in these disciplines track reality, as opposed to creating it. If moral rules are like scientific laws, however, then presumably they would have to be true in virtue of the operations of the physical world. This sounds very strange. The movement of protons makes certain physical laws true; the behavior of molecules validates certain chemical laws; the interactions of cells make true particular laws of biology. But which operations of which physical things make moral rules true? The moral prohibition on torture does not seem to be vindicated by citing the workings of the physical world.

There are two standard moves for ethical objectivists to make at this point. The first strategy—**ethical naturalism**—claims that, despite appearances, moral facts really are natural, scientific facts. Whether something is right or wrong can be verified in just the same way that scientific hypotheses can be. Prominent examples of naturalism include the claims that actions are morally right if and only if they maximize pleasure, that things are good just because they are desired, and that exchanges are just if and only if all parties to the transfer have agreed to abide by its terms.

I don't want to take a stand on the success of these views. What is important for our purposes is that if these claims (or others like them) are true, then all it takes is ordinary empirical investigation to determine whether actions are right, good, or generous. There doesn't seem to be anything especially weird or mysterious about pleasure, desire, or agreements. If moral facts consist of just these sorts of humdrum things, then moral facts are not at all strange.

Subjectivists acknowledge this. But they remain sceptical. Naturalists need to supply *plausible* connections that link moral and naturalistic (i.e., nonmoral) features. But does rightness really consist in maximizing happiness? Is something good just because it is desired? Do all mutual agreements really yield justice? After thorough scrutiny, most philosophers have rejected these views. Now, objectivists needn't abandon hope—they may try to defend these theories in the face of criticisms, or they may seek better, improved naturalistic theories. There is no way to entirely discount the possibility that with greater application and ingenuity, objectivists may arrive at satisfactory naturalistic accounts of moral features. But the history of such efforts does not inspire confidence.

Try it yourself: an act is morally right if and only if _____. What fills in the blank is called an *analysis.* Naturalists disagree amongst themselves about which analyses are best. Naturalists are unified, however, in believing that the blank can ultimately be filled in naturalistically, i.e., without the use of any moral terms. A classic case is that of the standard utilitarian doctrine cited above, which claims that an action is morally right if and only if it maximizes pleasure. The main benefit of such a theory is that it makes determining the rightness of actions a straightforward affair. Of course it won't, as a practical matter, always be easy to determine whether pleasure is maximized. But in principle, at least, we can see a clear path to justifying our moral claims and providing guidance for action.

Ethical nonnaturalists believe that there are no true naturalistic analyses of moral terms. For nonnaturalists, moral judgments cannot be empirically verified, and so there is a sharp disanalogy between ethics and science. Some nonnaturalists claim that we cannot give any analysis at all of moral terms—the above blank simply can't be filled in. The notion of goodness, for instance, may simply be basic, a fundamental term used to define other terms but not itself capable of definition. Alternatively, some nonnaturalists believe that we can define moral terms, but only if we employ other moral terms to do so. So, for instance, we might define morally right action as that which is reasonable and proper.

The basic worry for nonnaturalism is that if we abandon empirical verification in ethics, it is not easy to see how we could verify or justify moral claims at all. If goodness is indefinable, or definable only by use of other moral terms which themselves are indefinable, how are we to know what is good and bad, right and wrong? If I am puzzled about whether an action is morally right, I'm likely to be equally puzzled about whether it is reasonable and proper. And things are still worse if we claim that goodness or rightness are basic and indefinable. For then we've no criteria at all to assist us in discovering truth in ethics.

In facing this problem, nonnaturalists have usually fallen back on the idea that we somehow intuit what is right and wrong. Intuition involves an immediate grasp or apprehension of the truth of some proposition. In ethics, the claim would be that we just intuit the truth that pain is bad, that keeping promises is good, that disloyalty is wrong, etc. The problem, of course, is that different people will have different intuitions about what is right and good and just, and intuitionism doesn't seem to have the resources for rationally adjudicating these disputes. If we deny that there are any definitions of moral terms, then there will be no criteria at all for arbitrating ethical disagreement. If we allow that there are such definitions, but insist that they contain moral terms, then the disagreements will simply be replicated in disputes about whether the defining moral terms (e.g., "reasonable", "proper") apply.

So the objectivist is faced with a dilemma: either (i) opt for ethical naturalism, in which case we must come up with some plausible naturalistic analyses, or (ii) opt for ethical nonnaturalism, in which case we need to explain how it is possible to acquire knowledge of objective ethical facts. The subjectivist claims that options (i) and (ii) are so fraught with difficulties that it is best to abandon the commitment to ethical objectivity that motivated their development.

IMPLICATIONS OF META-ETHICAL SUBJECTIVISM

In addition to the powerful motivating arguments we have just discussed, meta-ethical subjectivism appeals because of its ability to handle several of the problems that beset normative subjectivism. Specifically, the worry about moral infallibility is bypassed, since this brand of subjectivism denies that anyone can ever possess moral truth, much less possess it in all instances. The problem of contradiction is likewise avoided. Contradictions arise when a proposition is alleged to be both true and false. If meta-ethical subjectivism is true, moral judgments are *neither* true *nor* false. Thus contradictions never arise. Finally, the existence and point of moral disagreement is preserved. According to meta-ethical subjectivism, ethical disagreements are disagreements in attitude. People on opposite sides of the abortion debate, for instance, have clashing attitudes toward abortion. There is real disagreement—emotional disagreement. Because they each may feel very strongly about the issue, the point of such debate is to convince others to share their view, and so act in ways they favor. This seems to account for a great deal of what goes on in ethical disagreement.

Still, meta-ethical subjectivism cannot avoid the remaining two implications of its normative cousin. Both brands of subjectivism generate a widespread moral equivalence, though for different reasons. Normative subjectivism makes each person an equally good arbiter of moral truth. Meta-ethical subjectivism denies that there is any moral truth. This denial implies that no one is superior to another at identifying what is right, or fine, or good. And no one is inferior, either. Moral judgments are expressions of taste, and a taste for cruelty or sadism is not worse (or better) than one for compassion and honesty. *De gustibus non est disputandum.*

Meta-ethical subjectivism also suffers from the problem of arbitrariness. If our ethical attachments are ultimately entirely up to us, with no supporting reasons needed, and no rationally compelling ones available, then our moral views are arbitrary. We have no better reason to support the ideology of Gandhi than of Pol Pot. Of course, each person actually will take a side. But our preferences in this regard are not rationally or ethically mandated. There is nothing necessarily irrational, wrong, or inappropriate about those whose fundamental aims differ from ours, even if those aims require for their satisfaction a policy of intimidation and torture.

Meta-ethical subjectivism also has to explain why all of us do employ non-subjectivist language in expressing our ethical outlooks. We frequently take our moral views to be *true,* and say as much in discussions with others. Our ethical conversations seem to be governed by a background assumption that, at least sometimes, those who disagree with us are *in error* and have *false beliefs.* Those with specially bad or confused impulses often come in for criticism as *irrational.* At the extreme, we may say of some such people that they or their views are *illogical.* Being illogical seems to involve contradiction, which (as we've seen) requires the notions of truth and falsity. Because meta-ethical subjectivism abandons these notions, it has difficulty explaining what illogical ethical views could amount to. The flip side is that they also have difficulty explaining what logical ethical views amount to. A logical position is one in which one's views, if true, logically entail a true conclusion. But if we abandon the notion of truth in ethics, we seem to take the notion of logic with it.

Finally, if meta-ethical subjectivism is true, we must abandon our aspirations for moral knowledge. Knowledge presupposes truth. Though we often make claims to moral knowledge, such as knowing that genocide or racism is wrong, such claims must be merely metaphorical or false. There is no moral wisdom, at least none that comes from having the sort of ethical sensibility that issues in true moral judgments. Subjectivists usually counter that ethical knowledge is a matter of *knowing how* to live, rather than *knowing that* something or other is morally right. But what would it be to know how to live, if any consistent way of life was just as good as another? If we could not know *that* certain things were valuable, good, or virtuous, how could we be successful at knowing *how* to live? This is a challenge that subjectivists have yet to fully meet.

CONCLUSION

In many ways, the paces we've been put through here are entirely typical of philosophical discussion. Perhaps most typical is the state of play at the end of the day. Rarely do philosophers have knock-down arguments that can eliminate a philosophical position from contention. Philosophical evaluation is ordinarily a matter of weighing the pros and cons of competing theories, and tentatively opting for one view over another. Justifying a philosophical view requires advancing positive arguments on its behalf, and deflecting criticisms that detractors have identified. One needn't worry about getting bored. There will always be detractors. Criticisms are never in short supply.

Thus when we come to assess the merits of ethical subjectivism, in either of its major forms, we are engaged in a process of judgment. We examine the arguments in support of the theory, develop them as best we can, and then scrutinize the implications of adoption. Whether we can live with the implications depends on one's assessment of the theory's attractions, and those of its competitors. There is no neat, simple method for discharging this task. Whether we can live with moral equivalence, arbitrariness, and the impossibility of moral knowledge depends on whether we can do better elsewhere. And *that* depends on how well ethical objectivists can respond to the motivating arguments of previous sections. Subjectivism's prospects may be bright (or dim). But we can measure its incandescence only after a very great deal of further philosophical labor.

The Challenge of Cultural Relativism*

JAMES RACHELS

James Rachels (1944–   ) is the author of *The End of Life* and numerous other articles and books on the problems of practical ethics. He teaches philosophy at the University of Alabama at Birmingham.

HOW DIFFERENT CULTURES HAVE DIFFERENT MORAL CODES

DARIUS, A KING OF ANCIENT PERSIA, was intrigued by the variety of cultures he encountered in his travels. He had found, for example, that the Callatians (a tribe of Indians) customarily ate the bodies of their dead fathers. The Greeks, of course, did not do that—the Greeks practiced cremation and regarded the funeral pyre as the natural and fitting way to dispose of the dead. Darius thought that a sophisticated understanding of the world must include an appreciation of such differences between cultures. One day, to teach this lesson, he summoned some Greeks who happened to be present at his court and asked them what they would take to eat the bodies of their dead fathers. They were shocked, as Darius knew they would be, and replied that no amount of money could persuade them to do such a thing. Then Darius called in some Callatians, and while the Greeks listened asked them what they would take to burn their dead fathers' bodies. The Callatians were horrified and told Darius not even to mention such a dreadful thing.

This story, recounted by Herodotus in his *History,* illustrates a recurring theme in the literature of social science: different cultures have different moral codes.[1] What is thought right within one group may be utterly abhorrent to the members of another group, and vice versa. Should we eat the bodies of the dead or burn them? If you were a Greek, one answer would seem obviously correct; but if you were a Callatian, the opposite would seem equally certain.

It is easy to give additional examples of the same kind. Consider the Eskimos. They are a remote and inaccessible people. Numbering only about 25,000, they live in small, isolated settlements scattered mostly along the northern fringes of North America and Greenland. Until the beginning of this century, the outside world knew little about them. Then explorers began to bring back strange tales.

Eskimo customs turned out to be very different from our own. The men often had more than one wife, and they would share their wives with guests, lending them for the night as a sign of hospitality. Moreover, within a community, a dominant male might demand—and get—regular sexual access to other men's wives. The women, however, were free to break these arrangements simply by leaving their husbands and taking up with new partners—free, that is, so long as their former husbands chose not to make trouble. All in all, the Eskimo practice was a volatile scheme that bore little resemblance to what we call marriage.

But it was not only their marriage and sexual practices that were different. The Eskimos also seemed to have less regard for human life. Infanticide, for example, was common. Knud Rasmussen, one of the most famous early explorers, reported that he met one woman who had borne twenty children but had killed ten of them at birth. Female babies, he found, were especially liable to be destroyed, and this was permitted simply at the parents' discretion, with no social stigma attached to it. Old people also, when they became too feeble to contribute to the family, were left out in the snow to die. So there seemed to be, in this society, remarkably little respect for life.[2]

To the general public, these were disturbing revelations. Our own way of living seems so natural and right that for many of us it is hard to conceive of others living so differently. And when we do hear of such things, we tend immediately to categorize those other peoples as "backward" or "primitive." But to anthropologists and sociologists, there was nothing particularly surprising about the Eskimos. Since the time of Herodotus, enlightened observers have been accustomed to the idea that conceptions of right and wrong differ from culture to culture. If we assume that *our* ideas of right and wrong will be shared by all peoples at all times, we are merely naive.

CULTURAL RELATIVISM

To many thinkers, this observation—"Different cultures have different moral codes"—has seemed to be the key to understanding morality. The idea of universal truth in ethics, they say, is a myth. The customs of different societies are all that exist. These customs cannot be said to be "correct" or "incorrect," for that implies we have an independent standard of right and wrong by which they may be judged. But there is no such independent standard; every standard is culture-bound. The great pioneering sociologist William Graham Sumner, writing in 1906, put the point like this:

> The "right" way is the way which the ancestors used and which has been handed down. The tradition is its own warrant. It is not held subject to verification by experience. The notion of right is in the folkways. It is not outside of them, of independent origin, and brought to test them. In the folkways, whatever is, is right. This is because they are traditional, and therefore contain in themselves the authority of the ancestral ghosts. When we come to the folkways we are at the end of our analysis.[3]

This line of thought has probably persuaded more people to be skeptical about ethics than any other single thing. *Cultural Relativism,* as it has been called, challenges our ordinary belief in the objectivity and universality of moral truth. It says, in effect, that there is no such thing as universal truth in ethics; there are only the various cultural codes, and nothing more. Moreover, our own code has no special status; it is merely one among many.

As we shall see, this basic idea is really a compound of several different thoughts. It is important to separate the various elements of the theory because, on analysis, some parts of the theory turn out to be correct, whereas others seem to be mistaken. As a beginning, we may distinguish the following claims, all of which have been made by cultural relativists:

1. Different societies have different moral codes.
2. There is no objective standard that can be used to judge one societal code better than another.
3. The moral code of our own society has no special status; it is merely one among many.
4. There is no "universal truth" in ethics—that is, there are no moral truths that hold for all peoples at all times.
5. The moral code of a society determines what is right within that society; that is, if the moral code of a society says that a certain action is right, then that action *is* right, at least within that society.
6. It is mere arrogance for us to try to judge the conduct of other peoples. We should adopt an attitude of tolerance toward the practices of other cultures.

Although it may seem that these six propositions go naturally together, they are independent of one another, in the sense that some of them might be true even if others are false. In what follows, we will try to identify what is correct in Cultural Relativism, but we will also be concerned to expose what is mistaken about it.

THE CULTURAL DIFFERENCES ARGUMENT

Cultural Relativism is a theory about the nature of morality. At first blush it seems quite plausible. However, like all such theories, it may be evaluated by subjecting it to rational analysis; and when we analyze Cultural Relativism we find that it is not so plausible as it first appears to be.

The first thing we need to notice is that at the heart of Cultural Relativism there is a certain *form of argument.* The strategy used by cultural relativists is to argue from facts about the differences between cultural outlooks to a conclusion about the status of morality. Thus we are invited to accept this reasoning:

(1) The Greeks believed it was wrong to eat the dead, whereas the Callatians believed it was right to eat the dead.

(2) Therefore, eating the dead is neither objectively right nor objectively wrong. It is merely a matter of opinion, which varies from culture to culture.

Or, alternatively:

(1) The Eskimos see nothing wrong with infanticide, whereas Americans believe infanticide is immoral.

(2) Therefore, infanticide is neither objectively right nor objectively wrong. It is merely a matter of opinion, which varies from culture to culture.

Clearly, these arguments are variations of one fundamental idea. They are both special cases of a more general argument, which says:

(1) Different cultures have different moral codes.

(2) Therefore, there is no objective "truth" in morality. Right and wrong are only matters of opinion, and opinions vary from culture to culture.

We may call this the *Cultural Differences Argument.* To many people, it is very persuasive. But from a logical point of view, is it a *sound* argument?

It is not sound. The trouble is that the conclusion does not really follow from the premise—that is, even if the premise is true, the conclusion still might be false. The premise concerns what people *believe:* in some societies, people believe one thing; in other societies, people believe differently. The conclusion, however, concerns *what really is the case.* The trouble is that this sort of conclusion does not follow logically from this sort of premise.

Consider again the example of the Greeks and Callatians. The Greeks believed it was wrong to eat the dead; the Callatians believed it was right. Does it follow, *from the mere fact that they disagreed,* that there is no objective truth in the matter? No, it does not follow; for it *could* be that the practice was objectively right (or wrong) and that one or the other of them was simply mistaken.

To make the point clearer, consider a very different matter. In some societies, people believe the earth is flat. In other societies, such as our own, people believe the earth is (roughly) spherical. Does it follow, *from the mere fact that they disagree,* that there is no "objective truth" in geography? Of course not; we would never draw such a conclusion because we realize that, in their beliefs about the world, the members of some societies might simply be wrong. There is no reason to think that if the world is round everyone must know it. Similarly, there is no reason to think that if there is moral truth everyone must know it. The fundamental mistake in the Cultural Differences Argument is that it attempts to derive a substantive conclusion about a subject (morality) from the mere fact that people disagree about it.

It is important to understand the nature of the point that is being made here. We are *not* saying (not yet, anyway) that the conclusion of the argument is false. Insofar as anything being said here is concerned, it is still an open question whether the conclusion is true. We *are* making a purely logical point and saying that the conclusion does not *follow from* the premise. This is important, because in order to determine whether the conclusion is true, we need arguments in its support. Cultural Relativism proposes this argument, but unfortunately the argument turns out to be fallacious. So it proves nothing.

THE CONSEQUENCES OF TAKING CULTURAL RELATIVISM SERIOUSLY

Even if the Cultural Differences Argument is invalid, Cultural Relativism might still be true. What would it be like if it were true?

In the passage quoted above, William Graham Sumner summarizes the essence of Cultural Relativism. He says that there is no measure of right and wrong other than the standards of one's society: "The notion of right is in the folkways. It is not outside of them, of independent origin, and brought to test them. In the folkways, whatever is, is right."

Suppose we took this seriously. What would be some of the consequences?

1. *We could no longer say that the customs of other societies are morally inferior to our own.* This, of course, is one of the main points stressed by Cultural Relativism. We would have to stop condemning other societies merely because they are "different." So long as we concentrate on certain examples, such as the funerary practices of the Greeks and Callatians, this may seem to be a sophisticated, enlightened attitude.

However, we would also be stopped from criticizing other, less benign practices. Suppose a society waged war on its neighbors for the purpose of taking slaves. Or suppose a society was violently anti-Semitic, and its leaders set out to destroy the Jews. Cultural Relativism would preclude us from saying that either of these practices was wrong. We would not even be able to say that a society tolerant of Jews is *better* than the anti-Semitic society, for that would imply some sort of transcultural standard of comparison. The failure to condemn *these* practices does not seem "enlightened"; on the contrary, slavery and anti-Semitism seem wrong *wherever* they occur. Nevertheless, if we took Cultural Relativism seriously, we would have to admit that these social practices also are immune from criticism.

2. *We could decide whether actions are right or wrong just by consulting the standards of our society.* Cultural Relativism suggests a simple test for determining what is right and what is wrong: all one has to do is ask whether the action is in accordance with the code of one's society. Suppose a resident of South Africa is wondering whether his country's policy of *apartheid*—rigid racial segregation—is morally correct. All he has to do is ask whether this policy conforms to his society's moral code. If it does, there is nothing to worry about, at least from a moral point of view.

This implication of Cultural Relativism is disturbing because few of us think that our society's code is perfect—we can think of ways it might be improved. Yet Cultural Relativism would not only forbid us from criticizing the codes of *other* societies; it would stop us from criticizing our *own*. After all, if right and wrong are relative to culture, this must be true for our own culture just as much as for others.

3. *The idea of moral progress is called into doubt.* Usually, we think that at least some changes in our society have been for the better. (Some, of course, may have been changes for the worse.) Consider this example: Throughout most of Western history the place of women in society was very narrowly circumscribed. They could not own property; they could not vote or hold political office; with a few exceptions, they were not permitted to have paying jobs; and generally they were under the almost absolute control of their husbands. Recently much of this has changed, and most people think of it as progress.

If Cultural Relativism is correct, can we legitimately think of this as progress? Progress means replacing a way of doing things with a *better* way. But by what standard do we judge the new ways as better? If the old ways were in accordance with the social standards of their time, then Cultural Relativism would say it is a mistake to judge them by the standards of a different time. Eighteenth-century society was, in effect, a different society from the one we have now. To say that we have made progress implies a judgment that present-day society is better, and that is just the sort of transcultural judgment that, according to Cultural Relativism, is impermissible.

Our idea of social *reform* will also have to be reconsidered. A reformer such as Martin Luther King, Jr., seeks to change his society for the better. Within the constraints imposed by Cultural Relativism, there is one way this might be done. If a society is not living up to its own ideals, the reformer may be regarded as acting for the best: the ideals of the society are the standard by which we judge his or her proposals as worthwhile. But the "reformer" may not challenge the ideals themselves, for those ideals are by definition correct. According to Cultural Relativism, then, the idea of social reform makes sense only in this very limited way.

These three consequences of Cultural Relativism have led many thinkers to reject it as implausible on its face. It does make sense, they say, to condemn some practices, such as slavery and anti-Semitism, wherever they occur. It makes sense to think that our own society has made some moral progress, while admitting that it is still imperfect and in need of reform. Because Cultural Relativism says that these judgments make no sense, the argument goes, it cannot be right.

WHY THERE IS LESS DISAGREEMENT THAN IT SEEMS

The original impetus for Cultural Relativism comes from the observation that cultures differ dramatically in their views of right and wrong. But just how much do they differ? It is true that there are differences. However, it is easy to overestimate the extent of those differences. Often, when we examine what *seems* to be a dramatic difference, we find that the cultures do not differ nearly as much as it appears.

Consider a culture in which people believe it is wrong to eat cows. This may even be a poor culture, in which there is not enough food; still, the cows are not to be touched. Such a society would *appear* to have values very different from our own. But does it? We have not yet asked why these people will not eat cows. Suppose it is because they believe that after death the souls of humans inhabit the bodies of animals, especially cows, so that a cow may be someone's grandmother. Now do we want to say that their values are different from ours? No, the difference lies elsewhere. The difference is in our belief systems, not in our values. We agree that we shouldn't eat Grandma; we simply disagree about whether the cow *is* (or could be) Grandma.

The general point is this. Many factors work together to produce the customs of a society. The society's values are only one of them. Other matters such as the religious and factual beliefs held by its members and the physical circumstances in which they must live, are also important. We cannot conclude, then, merely because customs differ, that there is a disagreement about *values*. The difference in customs may be attributable to some other aspect of social life. Thus there may be less disagreement about values than there appears to be.

Consider the Eskimos again. They often kill perfectly normal infants, especially girls. We do not approve of this at all; a parent who did this in our society would be locked up. Thus there appears to be a great difference in the values of our two cultures. But suppose we ask *why* the Eskimos do this. The explanation is not that they have less affection for their children or less respect for human life. An Eskimo family will always protect its babies if conditions permit. But they live in a harsh environment, where food is often in short supply. A fundamental postulate of Eskimo thought is: "life is hard, and the margin of safety small." A family may want to nourish its babies but be unable to do so.

As in many "primitive" societies, Eskimo mothers will nurse their infants over a much longer period of time than mothers in our culture. The child will take nourishment from its mother's breast for four years, perhaps even longer. So even in the best of times there are limits to the number of infants that one mother can sustain. Moreover, the Eskimos are a nomadic people—unable to farm, they must move about in search of food. Infants must be carried, and a mother can carry only one baby in her parka as she travels and goes about her outdoor work. Other family members can help, but this is not always possible.

Infant girls are more readily disposed of because, first, in this society the males are the primary food providers—they are the hunters, according to the traditional division of labor—and it is obviously important to maintain a sufficient number of food gatherers. But there is an important second reason as well. Because the hunters suffer a high casualty rate, the adult men who die prematurely far outnumber the women who die early. Thus if male and female infants survived in equal numbers, the female adult population would greatly outnumber the male adult population. Examining the available statistics, one writer concluded that "were it not for female infanticide . . . there would be approximately one-and-a-half times as many females in the average Eskimo local group as there are food-producing males."[4]

So among the Eskimos, infanticide does not signal a fundamentally different attitude toward children. Instead, it is a recognition that drastic measures are sometimes needed to ensure the family's survival. Even then, however, killing the baby is not the first option considered. Adoption is common; childless couples are especially happy to take a more fertile couple's "surplus." Killing is only the last resort. I emphasize this in order to show that the raw data of the anthropologists can be misleading; it can make the differences in values between cultures appear greater than they are. The Eskimos' values are not all that different from our values. It is only that life forces upon them choices that we do not have to make.

HOW ALL CULTURES HAVE SOME VALUES IN COMMON

It should not be surprising that, despite appearances, the Eskimos are protective of their children. How could it be otherwise? How could a group survive that did *not* value its young? This suggests a certain argument, one which shows that all cultural groups must be protective of their infants:

(1) Human infants are helpless and cannot survive if they are not given extensive care for a period of years.
(2) Therefore, if a group did not care for its young, the young would not survive, and the older members of the group would not be replaced. After a while the group would die out.
(3) Therefore, any cultural group that continues to exist must care for its young. Infants that are *not* cared for must be the exception rather than the rule.

Similar reasoning shows that other values must be more or less universal. Imagine what it would be like for a society to place no value at all on truth telling. When one person spoke to another, there would be no presumption at all that he was telling the truth—for he could just as easily be speaking falsely. Within that society, there would be no reason to pay attention to what anyone says. (I ask you what time it is, and you say "four o'clock." But there is no presumption that you are speaking truly; you could just as easily have said the first thing that came into your head. So I have no reason to pay attention to your answer—in fact, there was no point in my asking you in the first place!) Communication would then be extremely difficult, if not impossible. And because complex societies cannot exist without regular communication among their members, society would become impossible. It follows that in any complex society there *must* be a presumption in favor of truthfulness. There may of course be exceptions to this rule: there may be situations in which it is thought to be permissible to lie. Nevertheless, these will be exceptions to a rule that *is* in force in the society.

Let me give one further example of the same type. Could a society exist in which there was no prohibition on murder? What would this be like? Suppose people were free to kill other people at will, and no one thought there was anything wrong with it. In such a "society," no one could feel secure. Everyone would have to be constantly on guard. People who wanted to survive would have to avoid other people as much as possible. This would inevitably result in individuals trying to become as self-sufficient as possible—after all, associating with others would be dangerous. Society on any large scale would collapse. Of course, people might band together in smaller groups with others that they *could* trust not to harm them. But notice what this means: they would be forming smaller societies that *did* acknowledge a rule against murder. The prohibition of murder, then, is a necessary feature of all societies.

There is a general theoretical point here, namely, that *there are some moral rules that all societies will have in common, because those rules are necessary for society to exist.* The rules against lying and murder are two examples. And in fact, we do find these rules in force in all viable cultures. Cultures may differ in what they regard as legitimate exceptions to the rules, but this disagreement exists against a background of agreement on the larger issues. Therefore, it is a mistake to overestimate the amount of difference between cultures. Not *every* moral rule can vary from society to society.

WHAT CAN BE LEARNED FROM CULTURAL RELATIVISM

At the outset, I said that we were going to identify both what is right and what is wrong in Cultural Relativism. Thus far I have mentioned only its mistakes: I have said that it rests on an invalid argument, that it has consequences that make it implausible on its face, and that the extent of cultural disagreement is far less than it implies. This all adds up to a pretty thorough repudiation of the theory. Nevertheless, it is still a very appealing idea, and the reader may have the feeling that all this is a little unfair. The theory *must* have something going for it, or else why has it been so influential? In fact, I think there *is* something right about Cultural Relativism, and now I want to say what that is. There are two lessons we should learn from the theory, even if we ultimately reject it.

1. Cultural Relativism warns us, quite rightly, about the danger of assuming that all our preferences are based on some absolute rational standard.

They are not. Many (but not all) of our practices are merely peculiar to our society, and it is easy to lose sight of that fact. In reminding us of it, the theory does a service.

Funerary practices are one example. The Callatians, according to Herodotus, were "men who eat their fathers"—a shocking idea, to us at least. But eating the flesh of the dead could be understood as a sign of respect. It could be taken as a symbolic act that says: We wish this person's spirit to dwell within us. Perhaps this was the understanding of the Callatians. On such a way of thinking, burying the dead could be seen as an act of rejection, and burning the corpse as positively scornful. If this is hard to imagine, then we may need to have our imaginations stretched. Of course we may feel a visceral repugnance at the idea of eating human flesh in any circumstances. But what of it? This repugnance may be, as the relativists say, only a matter of what is customary in our particular society.

There are many other matters that we tend to think of in terms of objective right and wrong, but that are really nothing more than social conventions. Should women cover their breasts? A publicly exposed breast is scandalous in our society, whereas in other cultures it is unremarkable. Objectively speaking, it is neither right nor wrong—there is no objective reason why either custom is better. Cultural Relativism begins with the valuable insight that many of our practices are like this—they are only cultural products. Then it goes wrong by concluding that, because *some* practices are like this, *all* must be.

2. The second lesson has to do with keeping an open mind. In the course of growing up, each of us has acquired some strong feelings: we have learned to think of some types of conduct as acceptable, and others we have learned to regard as simply unacceptable. Occasionally, we may find those feelings challenged. We may encounter someone who claims that our feelings are mistaken. For example, we may have been taught that homosexuality is immoral, and we may feel quite uncomfortable around gay people and see them as alien and "different." Now someone suggests that this may be a mere prejudice; that there is nothing evil about homosexuality; that gay people are just people, like anyone else, who happen, through no choice of their own, to be attracted to others of the same sex. But because we feel so strongly about the matter, we may find it hard to take this seriously. Even after we listen to the arguments, we may still have the unshakable feeling that homosexuals *must,* somehow, be an unsavory lot.

Cultural Relativism, by stressing that our moral views can reflect the prejudices of our society, provides an antidote for this kind of dogmatism. When he tells the story of the Greeks and Callatians, Herodotus adds:

> For if anyone, no matter who, were given the opportunity of choosing from amongst all the nations of the world the set of beliefs which he thought best, he would inevitably, after careful consideration of their relative merits, choose that of his own country. Everyone without exception believes his own native customs, and the religion he was brought up in, to be the best.[5]

Realizing this can result in our having more open minds. We can come to understand that our feelings are not necessarily perceptions of the truth—they may be nothing more than the result of cultural conditioning. Thus when we hear it suggested that some element of our social code is *not* really the best, and we find ourselves instinctively resisting the suggestion, we might stop and remember this. Then we may be more open to discovering the truth, whatever that might be.

We can understand the appeal of Cultural Relativism, then, even though the theory has serious shortcomings. It is an attractive theory because it is based on a genuine insight—that many of the practices and attitudes we think so natural are really only cultural products. Moreover, keeping this insight firmly in view is important if we want to avoid arrogance and have open minds. These are important points, not to be taken lightly. But we can accept these points without going on to accept the whole theory.

NOTES

1. Herodotus, *The Histories,* translated by Aubrey de Selincourt, revised by A. R. Burn (Harmond-

sworth, Middlesex: Penguin Books, 1972), pp. 219–20.
2. Information about the Eskimos was taken from Peter Freuchen, *Book of the Eskimos* (New York: Fawcett, 1961); and E. Adamson Hoebel, *The Law of Primitive Man* (Cambridge: Harvard University Press, 1954), Chapter 5.
3. William Graham Sumner, *Folkways* (Boston: Ginn and Company, 1906), p. 28.
4. Hoebel, *The Law of Primitive Man.*
5. Herodotus, *The Histories.*

The Ethics of Emergencies*

AYN RAND

Ayn Rand (1905–1982), a leading figure in American political and literary circles, was the author of many books, including the best-selling novel, *The Fountainhead.*

The psychological results of altruism may be observed in the fact that a great many people approach the subject of ethics by asking such questions as: "Should one risk one's life to help a man who is: a) drowning, b) trapped in a fire, c) stepping in front of a speeding truck, d) hanging by his fingernails over an abyss?"

Consider the implications of that approach. If a man accepts the ethics of altruism, he suffers the following consequences (in proportion to the degree of his acceptance):

1. Lack of self-esteem—since his first concern in the realm of values is not how to live his life, but how to sacrifice it.
2. Lack of respect for others—since he regards mankind as a herd of doomed beggars crying for someone's help.
3. A nightmare view of existence—since he believes that men are trapped in a "malevolent universe" where disasters are the constant and primary concern of their lives.
4. And, in fact, a lethargic indifference to ethics, a hopelessly cynical amorality—since his questions involve situations which he is not likely ever to encounter, which bear no relation to the actual problems of his own life and thus leave him to live without any moral principles whatever.

By elevating the issue of helping others into the central and primary issue of ethics, altruism has destroyed the concept of any authentic benevolence or good will among men. It has indoctrinated men with the idea that to value another human being is an act of selflessness, thus implying that a man can have no personal interest in others—that *to value* another means *to sacrifice* oneself—that any love, respect or admiration a man may feel for others is not and cannot be a source of his own enjoyment, but is a threat to his existence, a sacrificial blank check signed over to his loved ones.

The men who accept that dichotomy but choose its other side, the ultimate products of altruism's dehumanizing influence, are those psychopaths who do not challenge altruism's basic premise, but proclaim their rebellion against self-sacrifice by announcing that they are totally indifferent to any-

Reprinted by permission of the Estate of Ayn Rand.

thing living and would not lift a finger to help a man or a dog left mangled by a hit-and-run driver (who is usually one of their own kind).

Most men do not accept or practice either side of altruism's viciously false dichotomy, but its result is a total intellectual chaos on the issue of proper human relationships and on such questions as the nature, purpose or extent of the help one may give to others. Today, a great many well-meaning, reasonable men do not know how to identify or conceptualize the moral principles that motivate their love, affection or good will, and can find no guidance in the field of ethics, which is dominated by the stale platitudes of altruism.

On the question of why man is not a sacrificial animal and why help to others is not his moral duty, I refer you to *Atlas Shrugged*. This present discussion is concerned with the principles by which one identifies and evaluates the instances involving a man's *nonsacrificial* help to others.

"Sacrifice" is the surrender of a greater value for the sake of a lesser one or of a nonvalue. Thus, altruism gauges a man's virtue by the degree to which he surrenders, renounces or betrays his values (since help to a stranger or an enemy is regarded as more virtuous, less "selfish," than help to those one loves). The rational principle of conduct is the exact opposite: always act in accordance with the hierarchy of your values, and never sacrifice a greater value to a lesser one.

This applies to all choices, including one's actions toward other men. It requires that one possess a defined hierarchy of *rational* values (values chosen and validated by a rational standard). Without such a hierarchy, neither rational conduct nor considered value judgments nor moral choices are possible.

Love and friendship are profoundly personal, selfish values: love is an expression and assertion of self-esteem, a response to one's own values in the person of another. One gains a profoundly personal, selfish joy from the mere existence of the person one loves. It is one's personal, selfish happiness that one seeks, earns and derives from love.

A "selfless," "disinterested" love is a contradiction in terms: it means that one is indifferent to that which one values.

Concern for the welfare of those one loves is a rational part of one's selfish interests. If a man who is passionately in love with his wife spends a fortune to cure her of a dangerous illness, it would be absurd to claim that he does it as a "sacrifice" for *her* sake, not his own, and that it makes no difference to *him,* personally and selfishly, whether she lives or dies.

Any action that a man undertakes for the benefit of those he loves is *not a sacrifice* if, in the hierarchy of his values, in the total context of the choices open to him, it achieves that which is of greatest *personal* (and rational) importance to *him.* In the above example, his wife's survival is of greater value to the husband than anything else that his money could buy, it is of greatest importance to his own happiness and, therefore, his action is *not* a sacrifice.

But suppose he let her die in order to spend his money on saving the lives of ten other women, none of whom meant anything to him—as the ethics of altruism would require. *That* would be a sacrifice. Here the difference between Objectivism and altruism can be seen most clearly: if sacrifice is the moral principle of action, then that husband *should* sacrifice his wife for the sake of ten other women. What distinguishes the wife from the ten others? Nothing but her value to the husband who has to make the choice—nothing but the fact that *his* happiness requires her survival.

The Objectivist ethics would tell him: your highest moral purpose is the achievement of your own happiness, your money is yours, use it to save your wife, *that* is your moral right and your rational, moral choice.

Consider the soul of the altruistic moralist who would be prepared to tell that husband the opposite. (And then ask yourself whether altruism is motivated by benevolence.)

The proper method of judging when or whether one should help another person is by reference to one's own rational self-interest and one's own hierarchy of values: the time, money or effort one gives or the risk one takes should be proportionate to the value of the person in relation to one's own happiness.

To illustrate this on the altruists' favorite example: the issue of saving a drowning person. If the person to be saved is a stranger, it is morally proper to save him only when the danger to one's own life is minimal; when the danger is great, it would be immoral to attempt it: only a lack of self-esteem could permit one to value one's life no higher than that of any random stranger. (And, conversely, if one is drowning, one cannot expect a stranger to risk his life for one's sake, remembering that one's life cannot be as valuable to him as his own.)

If the person to be saved is not a stranger, then the risk one should be willing to take is greater in proportion to the greatness of that person's value to oneself. If it is the man or woman one loves, then one can be willing to give one's own life to save him or her—for the selfish reason that life without the loved person could be unbearable.

Conversely, if a man is able to swim and to save his drowning wife, but becomes panicky, gives in to an unjustified, irrational fear and lets her drown, then spends his life in loneliness and misery—one would not call him "selfish"; one would condemn him morally for his treason to himself and to his own values, that is: his failure to fight for the preservation of a value crucial to his own happiness. Remember that values are that which one acts to gain and/or keep, and that one's own happiness has to be achieved by one's own effort. Since one's own happiness is the moral purpose of one's life, the man who fails to achieve it because of his own default, because of his failure to fight for it, is morally guilty.

The virtue involved in helping those one loves is not "selflessness" or "sacrifice," but *integrity*. Integrity is loyalty to one's convictions and values; it is the policy of acting in accordance with one's values, of expressing, upholding and translating them into practical reality. If a man professes to love a woman, yet his actions are indifferent, inimical or damaging to her, it is his lack of integrity that makes him immoral.

The same principle applies to relationships among friends. If one's friend is in trouble, one should act to help him by whatever nonsacrificial means are appropriate. For instance, if one's friend is starving, it is not a sacrifice, but an act of integrity to give him money for food rather than buy some insignificant gadget for oneself, because his welfare is important in the scale of one's personal values. If the gadget means more than the friend's suffering, one had no business pretending to be his friend.

The practical implementation of friendship, affection and love consists of incorporating the welfare (the *rational* welfare) of the person involved into one's own hierarchy of values, then acting accordingly.

But this is a reward which men have to earn by means of their virtues and which one cannot grant to mere acquaintances or strangers.

What, then, should one properly grant to strangers? The generalized respect and good will which one should grant to a human being in the name of the potential value he represents—until and unless he forfeits it.

A rational man does not forget that *life* is the source of all values and, as such, a common bond among living beings (as against inanimate matter), that other men are potentially able to achieve the same virtues as his own and thus be of enormous value to him. This does not mean that he regards human lives as interchangeable with his own. He recognizes the fact that his own life is the *source*, not only of all his values, but of *his capacity to value*. Therefore, the value he grants to others is only a consequence, an extension, a secondary projection of the primary value which is himself.

"The respect and good will that men of self-esteem feel toward other human beings is profoundly egoistic; they feel, in effect: 'Other men are of value because they are of the same species as myself.' In revering living entities, they are revering their *own* life. This is the psychological base of any emotion of sympathy and any feeling of 'species solidarity.'"[1]

Since men are born *tabula rasa,* both cognitively and morally, a rational man regards strangers as innocent until proved guilty, and grants them that initial good will in the name of their human potential. After that, he judges them according to the moral character they have actualized. If he finds them guilty of major evils, his good will is replaced by contempt and moral condemnation. (If one values human life, one cannot value its destroyers.) If he finds them to be virtuous, he grants them personal, individual value and appreciation, in proportion to their virtues.

It is on the ground of that generalized good will and respect for the value of human life that one helps strangers in an emergency—*and only in an emergency.*

It is important to differentiate between the rules of conduct in an emergency situation and the rules of conduct in the normal conditions of human existence. This does not mean a double standard of morality: the standard and the basic principles remain the same, but their application to either case requires precise definitions.

An emergency is an unchosen, unexpected event, limited in time, that creates conditions under which human survival is impossible—such as a flood, an earthquake, a fire, a shipwreck. In an emergency situation, men's primary goal is to combat the disaster, escape the danger and restore normal conditions (to reach dry land, to put out the fire, etc.).

By "normal" conditions I mean *metaphysically* normal, normal in the nature of things, and appropriate to human existence. Men can live on land, but not in water or in a raging fire. Since men are not omnipotent, it is metaphysically possible for unforseeable disasters to strike them, in which case their only task is to return to those conditions under which their lives can continue. By its nature, an emergency situation is temporary; if it were to last, men would perish.

It is only in emergency situations that one should volunteer to help strangers, if it is in one's power. For instance, a man who values human life and is caught in a shipwreck, should help to save his fellow passengers (though not at the expense of his own life). But this does not mean that after they all reach shore, he should devote his efforts to saving his fellow passengers from poverty, ignorance, neurosis or whatever other troubles they might have. Nor does it mean that he should spend his life sailing the seven seas in search of shipwreck victims to save.

Or to take an example that can occur in everyday life: suppose one hears that the man next door is ill and penniless. Illness and poverty are not metaphysical emergencies, they are part of the normal risks of existence; but since the man is temporarily helpless, one may bring him food and medicine, *if* one can afford it (as an act of goodwill, not of duty) or one may raise a fund among the neighbors to help him out. But this does not mean that one must support him from then on, nor that one must spend one's life looking for starving men to help.

In the normal conditions of existence, man has to choose his goals, project them in time, pursue them and achieve them by his own effort. He cannot do it if his goals are at the mercy of and must be sacrificed to any misfortune happening to others. He cannot live his life by the guidance of rules applicable only to conditions under which human survival is impossible.

The principle that one should help men in an emergency cannot be extended to regard all human suffering as an emergency and to turn the misfortune of some into a first mortgage on the lives of others.

Poverty, ignorance, illness and other problems of that kind are not metaphysical emergencies. By the *metaphysical* nature of man and of existence, man has to maintain his life by his own effort; the values he needs—such as wealth or knowledge—are not given to him automatically, as a gift of nature, but have to be discovered and achieved by his own thinking and work. One's sole obligation toward others, in this respect, is to maintain a social system that leaves men free to achieve, to gain and to keep their values.

Every code of ethics is based on and derived from a metaphysics, that is: from a theory about the fundamental nature of the universe in which man lives and acts. The altruist ethics is based on a "malevolent universe" metaphysics, on the theory that man, by his very nature, is helpless and doomed—that success, happiness, achievement are impossible to him—that emergencies, disasters, catastrophes are the norm of his life and that his primary goal is to combat them.

As the simplest empirical refutation of that metaphysics—as evidence of the fact that the material universe is not inimical to man and that catastrophes are the exception, not the rule of his existence—observe the fortunes made by insurance companies.

Observe also that the advocates of altruism are unable to base their ethics on any facts of men's normal existence and that they always offer "lifeboat" situations as examples from which to derive the rules of moral conduct. ("What should you do if you and another man are in a lifeboat that can carry only one?" etc.)

The fact is that men do not live in lifeboats—and that a lifeboat is not the place on which to base one's metaphysics.

The moral purpose of a man's life is the achievement of his own happiness. This does not mean that he is indifferent to all men, that human life is of no value to him and that he has no reason to help others in an emergency. But it *does* mean that he does not subordinate his life to the welfare of others, that he does not sacrifice himself to their needs, that the relief of their suffering is not his primary concern, that any help he gives is an *exception*, not a rule, an act of generosity, not of moral duty, that it is *marginal* and *incidental*—as disasters are marginal and incidental in the course of human existence—and that *values*, not disasters, are the goal, the first concern and the motive power of his life.

NOTES

1. Nathaniel Branden, "Benevolence Versus Altruism," *The Objectivist Newsletter*, July, 1962.

Ethical Egoism*

JAMES RACHELS

IS THERE A DUTY TO CONTRIBUTE FOR FAMINE RELIEF?

EACH YEAR MILLIONS OF PEOPLE DIE of malnutrition and related health problems. A common pattern among children in poor countries is death from dehydration caused by diarrhea brought on by malnutrition. James Grant, executive director of the United Nations Children's Fund (UNICEF), estimates that about 15,000 children die in this way *every day*. That comes to 5,475,000 children annually. Even if his estimate is too high, the number that die is staggering.

For those of us in the affluent countries, this poses an acute moral problem. We spend money on ourselves, not only for the necessities of life but for innumerable luxuries—for fine automobiles, fancy clothes, stereos, sports, movies, and so on. In our country, even people with modest incomes enjoy such things. The problem is that we *could* forgo our luxuries and give the money for famine relief instead. The fact that we don't suggests that we regard our luxuries as more important than feeding the hungry.

Why do we allow people to starve to death when we could save them? Very few of us actually believe our luxuries are that important. Most of us, if asked the question directly, would probably be a bit embarrassed, and we would say that we probably should do more for famine relief. The explanation of why we do not is, at least in part, that we hardly ever think of the problem. Living our own comfortable lives, we are effectively insulated from it. The starving people are dying at some distance from us; we do not see them, and we can avoid even thinking of them. When we do think of them, it is only

From James Rachels, The Elements of Moral Philosophy *(New York: Random House, 1986).*

abstractly, as bloodless statistics. Unfortunately for the starving, statistics do not have much power to motivate action.

But leaving aside the question of *why* we behave as we do, what is our *duty?* What *should* we do? We might think of this as the "common-sense" view of the matter: morality requires that we balance our own interests against the interests of others. It is understandable, of course, that we look out for our own interests, and no one can be faulted for attending to his own basic needs. But at the same time the needs of others are also important, and when we can help others—especially at little cost to ourselves—we should do so. Suppose you are thinking of spending ten dollars on a trip to the movies, when you are reminded that ten dollars could buy food for a starving child. Thus you could do a great service for the child at little cost to yourself. Common-sense morality would say, then, that you should give the money for famine relief rather than spending it on the movies.

This way of thinking involves a general assumption about our moral duties: it is assumed that we have moral duties *to other people*—and not merely duties that we create, such as by making a promise or incurring a debt. We have "natural" duties to others *simply because they are people who could be helped or harmed by our actions.* If a certain action would benefit (or harm) other people, then that is a reason why we should (or should not) do that action. The common-sense assumption is that other people's interests *count,* for their own sakes, from a moral point of view.

But one person's common sense is another person's naive platitude. Some thinkers have maintained that, in fact, we have no "natural" duties to other people. *Ethical Egoism* is the idea that each person ought to pursue his or her own self-interest exclusively. It is different from Psychological Egoism, which is a theory of human nature concerned with how people *do* behave—Psychological Egoism says that people do in fact always pursue their own interests. Ethical Egoism, by contrast, is a normative theory—that is, a theory about how we *ought* to behave. Regardless of how we do behave, Ethical Egoism says we have no moral duty except to do what is best for ourselves.

It is a challenging theory. It contradicts some of our deepest moral beliefs—beliefs held by most of us, at any rate—but it is not easy to refute. We will examine the most important arguments for and against it. If it turns out to be true, then of course that is immensely important. But even if it turns out to be false, there is still much to be learned from examining it—we may, for example, gain some insight into the reasons why we *do* have obligations to other people.

But before looking at the arguments, we should be a little clearer about exactly what this theory says and what it does not say. In the first place, Ethical Egoism does not say that one should promote one's own interests *as well as* the interests of others. That would be an ordinary, unexceptional view. Ethical Egoism is the radical view that one's *only* duty is to promote one's own interests. According to Ethical Egoism, there is only one ultimate principle of conduct, the principle of self-interest, and this principle sums up *all* of one's natural duties and obligations.

However, Ethical Egoism does not say that you should *avoid* actions that help others, either. It may very well be that in many instances your interests coincide with the interests of others, so that in helping yourself you will be aiding others willy-nilly. Or it may happen that aiding others is an effective *means* for creating some benefit for yourself. Ethical Egoism does not forbid such actions; in fact, it may demand them. The theory insists only that in such cases the benefit to others is not what makes the act right. What makes the act right is, rather, the fact that it is to one's own advantage.

Finally, Ethical Egoism does not imply that in pursuing one's interests one ought always to do what one wants to do, or what gives one the most pleasure in the short run. Someone may want to do something that is not good for himself or that will eventually cause himself more grief than pleasure—he may want to drink a lot or smoke cigarettes or take drugs or waste his best years at the race track. Ethical Egoism would frown on all this, regardless of the momentary pleasure it affords. It says that a person ought to do what *really is* to his or her own best advantage, *over the long run.* It endorses selfishness, but it doesn't endorse foolishness.

THREE ARGUMENTS IN FAVOR OF ETHICAL EGOISM

What reasons can be advanced to support this doctrine? Why should anyone think it is true? Unfortunately, the theory is asserted more often than it is argued for. Many of its supporters apparently think its truth is self-evident, so that arguments are not needed. When it *is* argued for, three lines of reasoning are most commonly used.

1. The first argument has several variations, each suggesting the same general point:

a. Each of us is intimately familiar with our own individual wants and needs. Moreover, each of us is uniquely placed to pursue those wants and needs effectively. At the same time, we know the desires and needs of other people only imperfectly, and we are not well situated to pursue them. Therefore, it is reasonable to believe that if we set out to be "our brother's keeper," we would often bungle the job and end up doing more mischief than good.

b. At the same time, the policy of "looking out for others" is an offensive intrusion into other people's privacy; it is essentially a policy of minding other people's business.

c. Making other people the object of one's "charity" is degrading to them; it robs them of their individual dignity and self-respect. The offer of charity says, in effect, that they are not competent to care for themselves; and the statement is self-fulfilling—they cease to be self-reliant and become passively dependent on others. That is why the recipients of "charity" are so often resentful rather than appreciative.

What this adds up to is that the policy of "looking out for others" is self-defeating. If we want to promote the best interests of everyone alike, we should *not* adopt so-called altruistic policies of behavior. On the contrary, if each person looks after his or her *own* interests, it is more likely that everyone will be better off, in terms of both physical and emotional well-being. Thus Robert G. Olson says in his book *The Morality of Self-Interest* (1965), "The individual is most likely to contribute to social betterment by rationally pursuing his own best long-range interests." Or as Alexander Pope said more poetically,

> Thus God and nature formed the general frame
> And bade self-love and social be the same.

It is possible to quarrel with this argument on a number of grounds. Of course no one favors bungling, butting in, or depriving people of their self-respect. But is this really what we are doing when we feed hungry children? Is the starving child in Ethiopia really harmed when we "intrude" into "her business" by supplying food? It hardly seems likely. Yet we can set this point aside, for considered as an argument for Ethical Egoism, this way of thinking has an even more serious defect.

The trouble is that it isn't really an argument *for Ethical Egoism* at all. The argument concludes that we should adopt certain policies of action; and on the surface they appear to be egoistic policies. However, the *reason* it is said we should adopt those policies is decidedly *un*egoistic. The reason is one that to an egoist shouldn't matter. It is said that we should adopt those policies because doing so will promote the "betterment of society"—but according to Ethical Egoism, that is something we should not be concerned about. Spelled out fully, with everything laid on the table, the argument says:

(1) We ought to do whatever will promote the best interests of everyone alike.
(2) The interests of everyone will best be promoted if each of us adopts the policy of pursuing our own interests exclusively.
(3) Therefore, each of us should adopt the policy of pursuing our own interests exclusively.

If we accept this reasoning, then we are not ethical egoists at all. Even though we might end up *behaving* like egoists, our ultimate principle is one of beneficence—we are doing what we think will help everyone, not merely what we think will benefit ourselves. Rather than being egoists, we turn out to be altruists with a peculiar view of what in fact promotes the general welfare.

2. The second argument was put forward with some force by Ayn Rand, a writer little heeded by professional philosophers but who nevertheless was enormously popular on college campuses during the 1960s and 1970s. Ethical Egoism, in her view, is the only ethical philosophy that respects the

integrity of the individual human life. She regarded the ethics of "altruism" as a totally destructive idea, both in society as a whole and in the lives of individuals taken in by it. Altruism, to her way of thinking, leads to a denial of the value of the individual. It says to a person: *your* life is merely something that may be sacrificed. "If a man accepts the ethics of altruism," she writes, "his first concern is not how to live his life, but how to sacrifice it." Moreover, those who would *promote* this idea are beneath contempt—they are parasites who, rather than working to build and sustain their own lives, leech off those who do. Again, she writes:

> Parasites, moochers, looters, brutes and thugs can be of no value to a human being—nor can he gain any benefit from living in a society geared to *their* needs, demands and protections, a society that treats him as a sacrificial animal and penalizes him for his virtues in order to reward *them* for their vices, which means: a society based on the ethics of altruism.

By "sacrificing one's life" Rand does not necessarily mean anything so dramatic as dying. A person's life consists (in part) of projects undertaken and goods earned and created. To demand that a person abandon his projects or give up his goods is also a clear effort to "sacrifice his life." Furthermore, throughout her writings Rand also suggests that there is a *metaphysical* basis for egoistic ethics. Somehow, it is the only ethics that takes seriously the *reality* of the individual person. She bemoans "the enormity of the extent to which altruism erodes men's capacity to grasp . . . the value of an individual life; it reveals a mind from which the reality of a human being has been wiped out."

What, then, of the starving people? It might be argued, in response, that Ethical Egoism "reveals a mind from which the reality of a human being has been wiped out"—namely, the human being who is starving. Rand quotes with approval the evasive answer given by one of her followers: "Once, when Barbara Brandon was asked by a student: 'What will happen to the poor . . . ?'—she answered: "If *you* want to help them, you will not be stopped.'"

All these remarks are, I think, part of one continuous argument that can be summarized like this:

(1) A person has only one life to live. If we place any value on the individual—that is, if the individual has any moral worth—then we must agree that this life is of supreme importance. After all, it is all one has, and all one is.

(2) The ethics of altruism regards the life of the individual as something one must be ready to sacrifice for the good of others.

(3) Therefore, the ethics of altruism does not take seriously the value of the human individual.

(4) Ethical Egoism, which allows each person to view his or her own life as being of ultimate value, *does* take the human individual seriously—in fact, it is the only philosophy that does so.

(5) Thus, Ethical Egoism is the philosophy that ought to be accepted.

The problem with this argument, as you may already have noticed, is that it relies on picturing the alternatives in such an extreme way. "The ethics of altruism" is taken to be such an extreme philosophy that *nobody,* with the possible exception of certain monks, would find it congenial. As Ayn Rand presents it, altruism implies that one's own interests have *no* value, and that *any* demand by others calls for sacrificing them. If that is the alternative, then any other view, including Ethical Egoism, will look good by comparison. But this is hardly a fair picture of the choices. What we called the common-sense view stands somewhere between the two extremes. It says that one's own interests and the interests of others are both important and must be balanced against one another. Sometimes, when the balancing is done, it will turn out that one should act in the interests of others; other times, it will turn out that one should take care of oneself. So even if the Randian argument refutes the extreme "ethics of altruism," it does not follow that one must accept the other extreme of Ethical Egoism.

3. The third line of reasoning takes a somewhat different approach. Ethical Egoism is usually presented as a *revisionist* moral philosophy, that is, as a philosophy that says our common-sense moral

views are mistaken and need to be changed. It is possible, however, to interpret Ethical Egoism in a much less radical way, as a theory that *accepts* common-sense morality and offers a surprising account of its basis.

The less radical interpretation goes as follows. In everyday life, we assume that we are obliged to obey certain rules. We must avoid doing harm to others, speak the truth, keep our promises, and so on. At first glance, these duties appear to be very different from one another. They appear to have little in common. Yet from a theoretical point of view, we may wonder whether there is not some hidden *unity* underlying the hodgepodge of separate duties. Perhaps there is some small number of fundamental principles that explain all the rest, just as in physics there are basic principles that bring together and explain diverse phenomena. From a theoretical point of view, the smaller the number of basic principles, the better. Best of all would be *one* fundamental principle, from which all the rest could be derived. Ethical Egoism, then, would be the theory that all our duties are ultimately derived from the one fundamental principle of self-interest.

Taken in this way, Ethical Egoism is not such a radical doctrine. It does not challenge common-sense morality; it only tries to explain and systematize it. And it does a surprisingly successful job. It can provide plausible explanations of the duties mentioned above, and more:

a. If we make a habit of doing things that are harmful to other people, people will not be reluctant to do things that will harm *us*. We will be shunned and despised; others will not have us as friends and will not do us favors when we need them. If our offenses against others are serious enough, we may even end up in jail. Thus it is to our own advantage to avoid harming others.

b. If we lie to other people, we will suffer all the ill effects of a bad reputation. People will distrust us and avoid doing business with us. We will often need for people to be honest with us, but we can hardly expect them to feel much of an obligation to be honest with us if they know we have not been honest with them. Thus it is to our own advantage to be truthful.

c. It is to our own advantage to be able to enter into mutually beneficial arrangements with other people. To benefit from those arrangements, we need to be able to rely on others to keep their parts of the bargains we make with them—we need to be able to rely on them to keep their promises to us. But we can hardly expect others to keep their promises to us if we are not willing to keep our promises to them. Therefore, from the point of view of self-interest, we should keep our promises.

Pursuing this line of reasoning, Thomas Hobbes suggested that the principle of Ethical Egoism leads to nothing less than the Golden Rule: we should "do unto others" *because* if we do, others will be more likely to "do unto us."

Does this argument succeed in establishing Ethical Egoism as a viable theory of morality? It is, in my opinion at least, the best try. But there are two serious objections to it. In the first place, the argument does not prove quite as much as it needs to prove. At best, it shows only that *as a general rule* it is to one's own advantage to avoid harming others. It does not show that this is *always* so. And it could not show that, for even though it may usually be to one's advantage to avoid harming others, sometimes it is not. Sometimes one might even *gain* from treating another person badly. In that case, the obligation not to harm the other person could *not* be derived from the principle of Ethical Egoism. Thus it appears that not all our moral obligations can be explained as derivable from self-interest.

But set that point aside. There is still a more fundamental question to be asked about the proposed theory. Suppose it is true that, say, contributing money for famine relief is somehow to one's own advantage. It does not follow that this is the only reason, or even the most basic reason, why doing so is a morally good thing. (For example, the most basic reason might be *in order to help the starving people*. The fact that doing so is also to one's own advantage might be only a secondary, less important, consideration.) A demonstration that one could *derive* this duty from self-interest does not prove that self-interest is the *only reason* one has this duty. Only if you accept an additional proposition—namely, the proposition that there is no reason for giving *other than* self-interest—will you find Ethical Egoism a plausible theory.

THREE ARGUMENTS AGAINST ETHICAL EGOISM

Ethical Egoism has haunted twentieth-century moral philosophy. It has not been a popular doctrine; the most important philosophers have rejected it outright. But it has never been very far from their minds. Although no thinker of consequence has defended it, almost everyone has felt it necessary to explain why he was rejecting it—as though the very possibility that it might be correct was hanging in the air, threatening to smother their other ideas. As the merits of the various "refutations" have been debated, philosophers have returned to it again and again.

The following three arguments are typical of the refutations proposed by contemporary philosophers.

1. In his book *The Moral Point of View* (1958), Kurt Baier argues that Ethical Egoism cannot be correct because it cannot provide solutions for conflicts of interest. We need moral rules, he says, only because our interests sometimes come into conflict. (If they never conflicted, then there would be no problems to solve and hence no need for the kind of guidance that morality provides.) But Ethical Egoism does not help to resolve conflicts of interest; it only exacerbates them. Baier argues for this by introducing a fanciful example:

> Let B and K be candidates for the presidency of a certain country and let it be granted that it is in the interest of either to be elected, but that only one can succeed. It would then be in the interest of B but against the interest of K if B were elected, and vice versa, and therefore in the interest of B but against the interest of K if K were liquidated, and vice versa. But from this it would follow that B ought to liquidate K, that it is wrong for B not to do so, that B has not "done his duty" until he has liquidated K; and vice versa. Similarly K, knowing that his own liquidation is in the interest of B and therefore, anticipating B's attempts to secure it, ought to take steps to foil B's endeavors. It would be wrong for him not to do so. He would "not have done his duty" until he had made sure of stopping B. . . .
>
> This is obviously absurd. For morality is designed to apply in just such cases, namely, those where interests conflict. But if the point of view of morality were that of self-interest, then there could never be moral solutions of conflicts of interest.

Does this argument prove that Ethical Egoism is unacceptable? It does, *if* the conception of morality to which it appeals is accepted. The argument assumes that an adequate morality must provide solutions for conflicts of interest in such a way that everyone concerned can live together harmoniously. The conflict between B and K, for example, should be resolved so that they would no longer be at odds with one another. (One would not then have a duty to do something that the other has a duty to prevent.) Ethical Egoism does not do that, and if you think an ethical theory should, then you will not find Ethical Egoism acceptable.

But a defender of Ethical Egoism might reply that *he* does not accept this conception of morality. For him, life is essentially a long series of conflicts in which each person is struggling to come out on top: and the principle he accepts—the principle of Ethical Egoism—simply urges each one to do his or her best to win. On his view, the moralist is not like a courtroom judge, who resolves disputes. Instead, he is like the Commissioner of Boxing, who urges each fighter to do his best. So the conflict between B and K will be "resolved" not by the application of an ethical theory but by one or the other of them winning the struggle. The egoist will not be embarrassed by this—on the contrary, he will think it no more than a realistic view of the nature of things.

2. Some philosophers, including Baier, have leveled an even more serious charge against Ethical Egoism. They have argued that it is a *logically inconsistent* doctrine—that is, they say it leads to logical contradictions. If this is true, then Ethical Egoism is indeed a mistaken theory, for no theory can be true if it is self-contradictory.

Consider B and K again. As Baier explains their predicament, it is in B's interest to kill K, and obviously it is in K's interest to prevent it. But, Baier says,

> if K prevents B from liquidating him, his act must be said to be both wrong and not wrong—wrong because it is the prevention of what B ought to do, his duty, and wrong for B not to do it; not wrong because it is what K ought to do, his duty, and wrong for K not to do it. But one and the same act (logically) cannot be both morally wrong and not morally wrong.

Now, does *this* argument prove that Ethical Egoism is unacceptable? At first glance it seems persuasive. However, it is a complicated argument, so we need to set it out with each step individually identified. Then we will be in a better position to evaluate it. Spelled out fully, it looks like this:

(1) Suppose it is each person's duty to do what is in his own best interests.
(2) It is in B's best interest to liquidate K.
(3) It is in K's best interest to prevent B from liquidating him.
(4) Therefore B's duty is to liquidate K, and K's duty is to prevent B from doing it.
(5) But it is wrong to prevent someone from doing his duty.
(6) Therefore it is wrong for K to prevent B from liquidating him.
(7) Therefore it is both wrong and not wrong for K to prevent B from liquidating him.
(8) But no act can be both wrong and not wrong—that is a self-contradiction.
(9) Therefore the assumption with which we started—that it is each person's duty to do what is in his own best interests—cannot be true.

When the argument is set out in this way, we can see its hidden flaw. The logical contradiction—that it is both wrong and not wrong for K to prevent B from liquidating him—does *not* follow simply from the principle of Ethical Egoism. It follows from that principle *and* the additional premise expressed in step (5)—namely, that "it is wrong to prevent someone from doing his duty." Thus we are not compelled by the logic of the argument to reject Ethical Egoism. Instead, we could simply reject this additional premise, and the contradiction would be avoided. That is surely what the ethical egoist would want to do, for the ethical egoist would never say, without qualification, that it is always wrong to prevent someone from doing his duty. He would say, instead, that *whether one ought to prevent someone from doing his duty depends entirely on whether it would be to one's own advantage to do so.* Regardless of whether we think this is a correct view, it is, at the very least, a *consistent* view, and so this attempt to convict the egoist of self-contradiction fails.

3. Finally, we come to the argument that I think comes closest to an outright refutation of Ethical Egoism. It is also the most interesting of the arguments, because at the same time it provides the most insight into why the interests of other people *should* matter to a moral agent.

Before this argument is presented, we need to look briefly at a general point about moral values. So let us set Ethical Egoism aside for a moment and consider this related matter.

There is a whole family of moral views that have this in common: they all involve dividing people into groups and saying that the interests of some groups counts for more than the interests of other groups. Racism is the most conspicuous example; it involves dividing people into groups according to race and assigning greater importance to the interests of one race than to others. The practical result is that members of the preferred race are to be *treated better* than the others. Anti-Semitism works the same way, and so can nationalism. People in the grip of such views will think, in effect: "*My* race counts for more," or "Those who believe in *my* religion count for more," or "*My* country counts for more," and so on.

Can such views be defended? Those who accept them are usually not much interested in argument—racists, for example, rarely try to offer rational grounds for their position. But suppose they did. What could they say?

There is a general principle that stands in the way of any such defense, namely: *We can justify treating people differently only if we can show that there is some factual difference between them that is relevant to justifying the difference in treatment.* For example, if one person is admitted to law school while another is rejected, this can be justified by pointing out that the first graduated from college with honors and scored well on the admissions test, while the second dropped out of college and never took the test. However, if *both* graduated with honors and did well on the entrance examination—in other words, if they are in all relevant respects equally well qualified—then it is merely arbitrary to admit one but not the other.

Can a racist point to any differences between, say, white people and black people that would justify treating them differently? In the past, racists have sometimes attempted to do this by picturing blacks as stupid, lacking in ambition, and the like. *If* this were true, then it might justify treating them differently, in at least some circumstances. (This is the deep purpose of racist stereotypes—to provide the "relevant differences" needed to justify differences in treatment.) But of course it is not true, and in fact there are no such general differences between the races. Thus racism is an *arbitrary* doctrine, in that it advocates treating some people differently even though there are no differences between them to justify it.

Ethical Egoism is a moral theory of the same type. It advocates that each of us divide the world into two categories of people—ourselves and all the rest—and that we regard the interests of those in the first group as more important than the interests of those in the second group. But each of us can ask, what is the difference between myself and others that justifies placing myself in this special category? Am I more intelligent? Do I enjoy my life more? Are my accomplishments greater? Do I have needs or abilities that are so different from the needs or abilities of others? *What is it that makes me so special?* Failing an answer, it turns out that Ethical Egoism is an arbitrary doctrine, in the same way that racism is arbitrary.

The argument, then, is this:

(1) Any moral doctrine that assigns greater importance to the interests of one group than to those of another is unacceptably arbitrary unless there is some difference between the members of the groups that justifies treating them differently.

(2) Ethical Egoism would have each person assign greater importance to his or her own interests than to the interests of others. *But there is no general difference between oneself and others, to which each person can appeal, that justifies this difference in treatment.*

(3) Therefore, Ethical Egoism is unacceptably arbitrary.

And this, in addition to arguing against Ethical Egoism, also sheds some light on the question of why we should care about others.

We should care about the interests of other people *for the very same reason we care about our own interests;* for their needs and desires are comparable to our own. Consider, one last time, the starving people we could feed by giving up some of our luxuries. Why should we care about them? We care about ourselves, of course—if *we* were starving, we would go to almost any lengths to get food. But what is the difference between us and them? Does hunger affect them any less? Are they somehow less deserving than we? If we can find no relevant difference between us and them, then we must admit that if *our* needs should be met, so should *theirs.* It is this realization, that we are on a par with one another, that is the deepest reason why our morality must include some recognition of the needs of others, and why, then, Ethical Egoism fails as a moral theory.

*Leviathan**

THOMAS HOBBES

Thomas Hobbes (1588–1679) was a brilliant English philosopher. His work, *Leviathan* (excerpted here), is a classic of the social contract tradition in ethics and political philosophy.

OF THE NATURAL CONDITION OF MANKIND AS CONCERNING THEIR FELICITY AND MISERY

NATURE HAS MADE MEN so equal in the faculties of the body and mind as that, though there be found one man sometimes manifestly stronger in body or of quicker mind than another, yet, when all is reckoned together, the difference between man and man is not so considerable as that one man can thereupon claim to himself any benefit to which another may not pretend as well as he. For as to the strength of body, the weakest has strength enough to kill the strongest, either by secret machination or by confederacy with others that are in the same danger with himself.

And as to the faculties of the mind, setting aside the arts grounded upon words, and especially that skill of proceeding upon general and infallible rules called science—which very few have and but in few things, as being not a native faculty born with us, nor attained, as prudence, while we look after somewhat else—I find yet a greater equality among men than that of strength. For prudence is but experience, which equal time equally bestows on all men in those things they equally apply themselves unto. That which may perhaps make such equality incredible is but a vain conceit of one's own wisdom, which almost all men think they have in a greater degree than the vulgar—that is, than all men but themselves and a few others whom, by fame or for concurring with themselves, they approve. For such is the nature of men that howsoever they may acknowledge many others to be more witty or more eloquent or more learned, yet they will hardly believe there be many so wise as themselves; for they see their own wit at hand and other men's at a distance. But this proves rather that men are in that point equal than unequal. For there is not ordinarily a greater sign of the equal distribution of anything than that every man is contented with his share.

From this equality of ability arises equality of hope in the attaining of our ends. And therefore if any two men desire the same thing, which nevertheless they cannot both enjoy, they become enemies; and in the way to their end, which is principally their own conservation, and sometimes their delectation only, endeavor to destroy or subdue one another. And from hence it comes to pass that where an invader has no more to fear than another man's single power, if one plant, sow, build, or possess a convenient seat, others may probably be expected to come prepared with forces united to dispossess and deprive him, not only of the fruit of his labor, but also of his life or liberty. And the invader again is in the like danger of another.

And from this diffidence of one another there is no way for any man to secure himself so reasonable as anticipation—that is, by force or wiles to master the persons of all men he can, so long till he see no other power great enough to endanger him; and

**From* Leviathan, *first published in 1651.*

this is no more than his own conservation requires, and is generally allowed. Also, because there be some that take pleasure in contemplating their own power in the acts of conquest, which they pursue farther than their security requires, if others that otherwise would be glad to be at ease within modest bounds should not by invasion increase their power, they would not be able, long time, by standing only on their defense, to subsist. And by consequence, such augmentation of dominion over men being necessary to a man's conservation, it ought to be allowed him.

Again, men have no pleasure, but on the contrary a great deal of grief, in keeping company where there is no power able to overawe them all. For every man looks that his companion should value him at the same rate he sets upon himself; and upon all signs of contempt or undervaluing naturally endeavors, as far as he dares (which among them that have no common power to keep them in quiet is far enough to make them destroy each other), to extort a greater value from his contemners by damage and from others by the example.

So that in the nature of man we find three principal causes of quarrel: first, competition; secondly, diffidence; thirdly, glory.

The first makes men invade for gain, the second for safety, and the third for reputation. The first use violence to make themselves masters of other men's persons, wives, children, and cattle; the second, to defend them; the third, for trifles, as a word, a smile, a different opinion, and any other sign of undervalue, either direct in their persons or by reflection in their kindred, their friends, their nation, their profession, or their name.

Hereby it is manifest that, during the time men live without a common power to keep them all in awe, they are in that condition which is called war, and such a war as is of every man against every man. For WAR consists not in battle only, or the act of fighting, but in a tract of time wherein the will to contend by battle is sufficiently known; and therefore the notion of *time* is to be considered in the nature of war as it is in the nature of weather. For as the nature of foul weather lies not in a shower or two of rain but in an inclination thereto of many days together, so the nature of war consists not in actual fighting but in the known disposition thereto during all the time there is no assurance to the contrary. All other time is PEACE.

Whatsoever, therefore, is consequent to a time of war where every man is enemy to every man, the same is consequent to the time wherein men live without other security than what their own strength and their own invention shall furnish them withal. In such condition there is no place for industry, because the fruit thereof is uncertain: and consequently no culture of the earth; no navigation nor use of the commodities that may be imported by sea; no commodious building; no instruments of moving and removing such things as require much force; no knowledge of the face of the earth; no account of time; no arts; no letters; no society; and, which is worst of all, continual fear and danger of violent death; and the life of man solitary, poor, nasty, brutish, and short.

It may seem strange to some man that has not well weighed these things that nature should thus dissociate and render men apt to invade and destroy one another; and he may therefore, not trusting to this inference made from the passions, desire perhaps to have the same confirmed by experience. Let him therefore consider with himself—when taking a journey he arms himself and seeks to go well accompanied, when going to sleep he locks his doors, when even in his house he locks his chests, and this when he knows there be laws and public officers, armed, to revenge all injuries shall be done him—what opinion he has of his fellow subjects when he rides armed, of his fellow citizens when he locks his doors, and of his children and servants when he locks his chests. Does he not there as much accuse mankind by his actions as I do by my words? But neither of us accuse man's nature in it. The desires and other passions of man are in themselves no sin. No more are the actions that proceed from those passions till they know a law that forbids them, which, till laws be made, they cannot know, nor can any law be made till they have agreed upon the person that shall make it.

It may peradventure be thought there was never such a time nor condition of war as this, and I believe it was never generally so over all the world; but there are many places where they live so now. For the savage people in many places of America, except the government of small families, the concord whereof depends on natural lust, have no government at all and live at this day in that brutish manner as I said before. Howsoever, it may be perceived what manner of life there would be where there were no common power to fear by the manner of life which men that have formerly lived under a peaceful government use to degenerate into in a civil war.

But though there had never been any time wherein particular men were in a condition of war one against another, yet in all times kings and persons of sovereign authority, because of their independency, are in continual jealousies and in the state and posture of gladiators, having their weapons pointing and their eyes fixed on one another—that is, their forts, garrisons, and guns upon the frontiers of their kingdoms, and continual spies upon their neighbors—which is a posture of war. But because they uphold thereby the industry of their subjects, there does not follow from it that misery which accompanies the liberty of particular men.

To this war of every man against every man, this also is consequent: that nothing can be unjust. The notions of right and wrong, justice and injustice, have there no place. Where there is no common power, there is no law; where no law, no injustice. Force and fraud are in war the two cardinal virtues. Justice and injustice are none of the faculties neither of the body nor mind. If they were, they might be in a man that were alone in the world, as well as his senses and passions. They are qualities that relate to men in society, not in solitude. It is consequent also to the same condition that there be no propriety, no dominion, no *mine* and *thine* distinct; but only that to be every man's that he can get, and for so long as he can keep it. And thus much for the ill condition which man by mere nature is actually placed in, though with a possibility to come out of it consisting partly in the passions, partly in his reason.

The passions that incline men to peace are fear of death, desire of such things as are necessary to commodious living, and a hope by their industry to obtain them. And reason suggests convenient articles of peace, upon which men may be drawn to agreement. These articles are they which otherwise are called the Laws of Nature, whereof I shall speak more particularly in the two following chapters.

OF THE FIRST AND SECOND NATURAL LAWS, AND OF CONTRACTS

The RIGHT OF NATURE, which writers commonly call *jus naturale,* is the liberty each man has to use his own power, as he will himself, for the preservation of his own nature—that is to say, of his own life—and consequently of doing anything which, in his own judgment and reason, he shall conceive to be the aptest means thereunto.

By LIBERTY is understood, according to the proper signification of the word, the absence of external impediments; which impediments may oft take away part of a man's power to do what he would, but cannot hinder him from using the power left him according as his judgment and reason shall dictate to him.

A LAW OF NATURE, *lex naturalis,* is a precept or general rule, found out by reason, by which a man is forbidden to do that which is destructive of his life or takes away the means of preserving the same and to omit that by which he thinks it may be best preserved. For though they that speak of this subject use to confound *jus* and *lex, right* and *law,* yet they ought to be distinguished; because RIGHT consists in liberty to do or to forbear, whereas LAW determines and binds to one of them; so that law and right differ as much as obligation and liberty, which in one and the same matter are inconsistent.

And because the condition of man, as has been declared in the precedent chapter, is a condition of war of every one against every one—in which case everyone is governed by his own reason and there is nothing he can make use of that may not be a help unto him in preserving his life against his enemies—it follows that in such a condition every man has a right to everything, even to one another's body. And therefore, as long as this natural right of every man to everything endures, there can be no security to any man, how strong or wise soever he be, of living out the time which nature ordinarily allows men to live. And consequently it is a precept or general rule of reason *that every man ought to endeavor peace, as far as he has hope of obtaining it; and when he cannot obtain it, that he may seek and use all helps and advantages of war.* The first branch of which rule contains the first and fundamental law of nature, which is *to seek peace and follow it.* The second, the sum of the right of nature, which is, *by all means we can to defend ourselves.*

From this fundamental law of nature, by which men are commanded to endeavor peace, is derived this second law: *that a man be willing, when others are so too, as far forth as for peace and defense of himself he shall think it necessary, to lay down this right to all things, and be contented with so much liberty against other men as he would allow other men against himself.* For as long as every man holds this right of doing anything he likes, so long are all men in the condition of war. But if other men will not lay down their right as well as he, then there is no reason for anyone to divest himself of his, for that were to expose himself to prey, which no man is bound to, rather than to dispose himself to peace. This is that law of the gospel: *whatsoever you require that others should do to you, that do ye to them.* And that law of all men, *quod tibi fieri non vis, alteri ne feceris.*[1]

To *lay down* a man's *right* to anything is to *divest* himself of the *liberty* of hindering another of the benefit of his own right to the same. For he that renounces or passes away his right gives not to any other man a right which he had not before—because there is nothing to which every man had not right by nature—but only stands out of his way, that he may enjoy his own original right without hindrance from him, not without hindrance from another. So that the effect which redounds to one man by another man's defect of right is but so much diminution of impediments to the use of his own right original. Right is laid aside either by simply renouncing it or by transferring it to another. By *simply* RENOUNCING, when he cares not to whom the benefit thereof redounds. By TRANSFERRING, when he intends the benefit thereof to some certain person or persons. And when a man has in either manner abandoned or granted away his right, then he is said to be OBLIGED or BOUND not to hinder those to whom such right is granted or abandoned from the benefit of it; and that he *ought,* and it is his DUTY, not to make void that voluntary act of his own; and that such hindrance is INJUSTICE and INJURY as being *sine jure,*[2] the right being before renounced or transferred. So that *injury* or *injustice* in the controversies of the world is somewhat like to that which in the disputations of scholars is called *absurdity.* For as it is there called an absurdity to contradict what one maintained in the beginning, so in the world it is called injustice and injury voluntarily to undo that which from the beginning he had voluntarily done. The way by which a man either simply renounces or transfers his right is a declaration or signification by some voluntary and sufficient sign or signs that he does so renounce or transfer, or has so renounced or transferred, the same to him that accepts it. And these signs are either words only or actions only; or as it happens most often, both words and actions. And the same are the BONDS by which men are bound and obliged—bonds that have their strength, not from their own nature, for nothing is more easily broken than a man's word, but from fear of some evil consequence upon the rupture.

Whensoever a man transfers his right or renounces it, it is either in consideration of some right reciprocally transferred to himself or for some other good he hopes for thereby. For it is a voluntary act; and of the voluntary acts of every man, the object is some *good to himself.* And therefore there be some rights which no man can be understood by any words or other signs to have abandoned or transferred. As, first, a man cannot lay down the right of resisting them that assault him by force to take away his life, because he cannot be understood to aim thereby at any good to himself. The same may be said of wounds and chains and imprisonment, both because there is no benefit consequent to such patience as there is to the patience of suffering another to be wounded or imprisoned, as also because a

1. [Matt. 7:12; Luke 6:31. The Latin expresses the same rule negatively: "What you would not have done to you, do not do to others."]

2. [Without legal basis.]

man cannot tell, when he sees men proceed against him by violence, whether they intend his death or not. And, lastly, the motive and end for which this renouncing and transferring of right is introduced is nothing else but the security of a man's person in his life and in the means of so preserving life as not to be weary of it. And therefore if a man by words or other signs seem to despoil himself of the end for which those signs were intended, he is not to be understood as if he meant it or that it was his will, but that he was ignorant of how such words and actions were to be interpreted.

The mutual transferring of right is that which men call CONTRACT.

There is difference between transferring of right to the thing and transferring, or tradition—that is, delivery—of the thing itself. For the thing may be delivered together with the translation of the right, as in buying and selling with ready money or exchange of goods or lands, and it may be delivered some time after.

Again, one of the contractors may deliver the thing contracted for on his part and leave the other to perform his part at some determinate time after and in the meantime be trusted, and then the contract on his part is called PACT or COVENANT; or both parts may contract now to perform hereafter, in which cases he that is to perform in time to come, being trusted, his performance is called *keeping of promise* or faith, and the failing of performance, if it be voluntary, *violation of faith.*

When the transferring of right is not mutual, but one of the parties transfers in hope to gain thereby friendship or service from another or from his friends, or in hope to gain the reputation of charity or magnanimity, or to deliver his mind from the pain of compassion, or in hope of reward in heaven—this is not contract but GIFT, FREE GIFT, GRACE, which words signify one and the same thing.

Signs of contract are either *express* or *by inference.* Express are words spoken with understanding of what they signify, and such words are either of the time *present* or *past*—as *I give, I grant, I have given, I have granted, I will that this be yours*—or of the future—as *I will give, I will grant*—which words of the future are called PROMISE.

Signs by inference are sometimes the consequence of words, sometimes the consequence of silence, sometimes the consequence of actions, sometimes the consequence of forbearing an action; and generally a sign by inference of any contract is whatsoever sufficiently argues the will of the contractor.

Words alone, if they be of the time to come and contain a bare promise, are an insufficient sign of a free gift and therefore not obligatory. For if they be of the time to come, as *tomorrow I will give,* they are a sign I have not given yet and consequently that my right is not transferred but remains till I transfer it by some other act. But if the words be of the time present or past, as *I have given* or *do give to be delivered tomorrow,* then is my tomorrow's right given away today, and that by the virtue of the words though there were no other argument of my will. And there is a great difference in the signification of these words: *volo hoc tuum esse cras* and *cras dabo*—that is, between *I will that this be yours tomorrow* and *I will give it you tomorrow*—for the word *I will,* in the former manner of speech, signifies an act of the will present, but in the latter it signifies a promise of an act of the will to come; and therefore the former words, being of the present, transfer a future right; the latter, that be of the future, transfer nothing. But if there be other signs of the will to transfer a right besides words, then, though the gift be free, yet may the right be understood to pass by words of the future: as if a man propound a prize to him that comes first to the end of a race, the gift is free; and though the words be of the future, yet the right passes; for if he would not have his words so be understood, he should not have let them run.

In contracts, the right passes not only where the words are of the time present or past but also where they are of the future, because all contract is mutual translation or change of right, and therefore he that promises only because he has already received the benefit for which he promises is to be understood as if he intended the right should pass; for unless he had been content to have his words so understood, the other would not have performed his part first. And for that cause, in buying and selling and other acts of contract a promise is equivalent to a covenant and therefore obligatory.

He that performs first in the case of a contract is said to MERIT that which he is to receive by the performance of the other; and he has it as *due*. Also when a prize is propounded to many which is to be given to him only that wins, or money is thrown among many to be enjoyed by them that catch it, though this be a free gift, yet so to win or so to catch is to *merit* and to have it as DUE. For the right is transferred in the propounding of the prize and in throwing down the money, though it be not determined to whom but by the event of the contention. But there is between these two sorts of merit this difference: that in contract I merit by virtue of my own power and the contractor's need, but in this case of free gift I am enabled to merit only by the benignity of the giver; in contract I merit at the contractor's hand that he should depart with his right, in this case of gift I merit not that the giver should part with his right but that when he has parted with it, it should be mine rather than another's. And this I think to be the meaning of that distinction of the Schools between *meritum congrui* and *meritum condigni*.[3] For God Almighty having promised Paradise to those men, hoodwinked with carnal desires, that can walk through this world according to the precepts and limits prescribed by him, they say he that shall so walk shall merit Paradise *ex congruo*. But because no man can demand a right to it, by his own righteousness or any other power in himself, but by the free grace of God only, they say no man can merit Paradise *ex condigno*. This, I say, I think is the meaning of that distinction; but because disputers do not agree upon the signification of their own terms of art longer than it serves their turn, I will not affirm anything of their meaning; only this I say: when a gift is given indefinitely, as a prize to be contended for, he that wins merits and may claim the prize as due.

If a covenant be made wherein neither of the parties perform presently but trust one another, in the condition of mere nature, which is a condition of war of every man against every man, upon any reasonable suspicion, it is void; but if there be a common power set over them both, with right and force sufficient to compel performance, it is not void. For he that performs first has no assurance the other will perform after, because the bonds of words are too weak to bridle men's ambition, avarice, anger, and other passions without the fear of some coercive power which in the condition of mere nature, where all men are equal and judges of the justness of their own fears, cannot possibly be supposed. And therefore he which performs first does but betray himself to his enemy, contrary to the right he can never abandon of defending his life and means of living.

But in a civil estate, where there is a power set up to constrain those that would otherwise violate their faith, that fear is no more reasonable; and for that cause, he which by the covenant is to perform first is obliged so to do.

The cause of fear which makes such a covenant invalid must be always something arising after the covenant made, as some new fact or other sign of the will not to perform; else it cannot make the covenant void. For that which could not hinder a man from promising ought not to be admitted as a hindrance of performing.

He that transfers any right transfers the means of enjoying it, as far as lies in his power. As he that sells land is understood to transfer the herbage and whatsoever grows upon it; nor can he that sells a mill turn away the stream that drives it. And they that give to a man the right of government in sovereignty are understood to give him the right of levying money to maintain soldiers and of appointing magistrates for the administration of justice.

To make covenants with brute beasts is impossible because, not understanding our speech, they understand not nor accept of any translation of right, nor can translate any right to another; and without mutual acceptation there is no covenant.

To make covenant with God is impossible but by mediation of such as God speaks to, either by revelation supernatural or by his lieutenants that govern under him and in his name; for otherwise we know not whether our covenants be accepted or not. And therefore they that vow anything contrary to any law of nature vow in vain, as being a thing unjust to pay such vow. And if it be a thing commanded by

3. [Merit based on conformity and merit based on worthiness.]

the law of nature, it is not the vow but the law that binds them.

The matter or subject of a covenant is always something that falls under deliberation, for to covenant is an act of the will—that is to say, an act, and the last act, of deliberation—and is therefore always understood to be something to come, and which is judged possible for him that covenants to perform.

And therefore to promise that which is known to be impossible is no covenant. But if that prove impossible afterwards which before was thought possible, the covenant is valid, and binds, though not to the thing itself, yet to the value, or, if that also be impossible, to the unfeigned endeavor of performing as much as is possible, for to more no man can be obliged.

Men are freed of their covenants two ways: by performing or by being forgiven. For performance is the natural end of obligation, and forgiveness the restitution of liberty, as being a retransferring of that right in which the obligation consisted.

Covenants entered into by fear, in the condition of mere nature, are obligatory. For example, if I covenant to pay a ransom or service for my life to an enemy, I am bound by it; for it is a contract, wherein one receives the benefit of life, the other is to receive money or service for it; and consequently, where no other law, as in the condition of mere nature, forbids the performance, the covenant is valid. Therefore prisoners of war, if trusted with the payment of their ransom, are obliged to pay it; and if a weaker prince make a disadvantageous peace with a stronger, for fear, he is bound to keep it; unless, as has been said before, there arises some new and just cause of fear to renew the war. And even in commonwealths, if I be forced to redeem myself from a thief by promising him money, I am bound to pay it till the civil law discharge me. For whatsoever I may lawfully do without obligation, the same I may lawfully covenant to do through fear; and what I lawfully covenant, I cannot lawfully break. A former covenant makes void a later. For a man that has passed away his right to one man today has it not to pass tomorrow to another; and therefore the later promise passes no right, but is null.

A covenant not to defend myself from force by force is always void. For, as I have showed before, no man can transfer or lay down his right to save himself from death, wounds, and imprisonment, the avoiding whereof is the only end of laying down any right; and therefore the promise of not resisting force in no covenant transfers any right, nor is obliging. For though a man may covenant thus: *unless I do so or so, kill me,* he cannot covenant thus: *unless I do so or so, I will not resist you when you come to kill me.* For man by nature chooses the lesser evil, which is danger of death in resisting, rather than the greater, which is certain and present death in not resisting. And this is granted to be true by all men, in that they lead criminals to execution and prison with armed men, notwithstanding that such criminals have consented to the law by which they are condemned.

A covenant to accuse oneself, without assurance of pardon, is likewise invalid. For in the condition of nature, where every man is judge, there is no place for accusation; and in the civil state, the accusation is followed with punishment, which, being force, a man is not obliged not to resist. The same is also true of the accusation of those by whose condemnation a man falls into misery, as of a father, wife, or benefactor. For the testimony of such an accuser, if it be not willingly given, is presumed to be corrupted by nature, and therefore not to be received; and where a man's testimony is not to be credited, he is not bound to give it. Also accusations upon torture are not to be reputed as testimonies. For torture is to be used but as means of conjecture and light in the further examination and search of truth; and what is in that case confessed tends to the ease of him that is tortured, not to the informing of the torturers, and therefore ought not to have the credit of a sufficient testimony; for whether he deliver himself by true or false accusation, he does it by the right of preserving his own life.

The force of words being, as I have formerly noted, too weak to hold men to the performance of their covenants, there are in man's nature but two imaginable helps to strengthen it. And those are either a fear of the consequence of breaking their word, or a glory or pride in appearing not to need to break it. This latter is a generosity too rarely found to be presumed on, especially in the pursuers of wealth, command, or sensual pleasure—which are the greatest part of mankind. The passion to be reckoned upon is fear, whereof there be two very general objects: one, the power of spirits invisible; the other, the power of those men they shall therein offend. Of these two, though the former be the greater power, yet the fear of the latter is commonly the greater fear. The fear of the former is in every man his own religion, which has place in the nature of man before civil society. The latter has not so, at least not place enough to keep men to their promises, because in the condition of mere nature the inequality of power is not discerned but by the event of battle. So that before the time of civil society, or in the interruption thereof by war, there is nothing can strengthen a covenant of peace agreed on against the temptations of avarice, ambition, lust, or other strong desire but the fear of that invisible power, which they everyone worship as God and fear as a revenger of their perfidy. All therefore that can be done between two men not subject to civil power is to put one another to swear by the God he fears, which *swearing* or OATH is a *form of speech, added to a promise, by which he that promises signifies that, unless he perform, he renounces the mercy of his God, or calls to him for vengeance on himself.* Such was the heathen form, *Let Jupiter kill me else, as I kill this beast.* So is our form, *I shall do thus and thus, so help me God.* And this, with the rites and ceremonies which everyone uses in his own religion, that the fear of breaking faith might be the greater.

By this it appears that an oath taken according to any other form or rite than his that swears is in vain and no oath, and that there is no swearing by anything which the swearer thinks not God. For though men have sometimes used to swear by their kings, for fear or flattery, yet they would have it thereby understood they attributed to them divine honor. And that swearing unnecessarily by God is but profaning of his name; and swearing by other things, as men do in common discourse, is not swearing but an impious custom gotten by too much vehemence of talking.

It appears also that the oath adds nothing to the obligation. For a covenant, if lawful, binds in the sight of God without the oath as much as with it; if unlawful, binds not at all, though it be confirmed with an oath.

OF OTHER LAWS OF NATURE

From that law of nature by which we are obliged to transfer to another such rights as, being retained, hinder the peace of mankind, there follows a third, which is this: *that men perform their covenants made;* without which covenants are in vain and but empty words, and, the right of all men to all things remaining, we are still in the condition of war.

And in this law of nature consists the fountain and original of JUSTICE. For where no covenant has preceded there has no right been transferred, and every man has right to every thing; and consequently no action can be unjust. But when a covenant is made, then to break it is *unjust;* and the definition of INJUSTICE is no other than *the not performance of covenant.* And whatsoever is not unjust is *just.*

But because covenants of mutual trust, where there is a fear of not performance on either part, as has been said in the former chapter, are invalid, though the original of justice be the making of covenants, yet injustice actually there can be none till the cause of such fear be taken away, which, while men are in the natural condition of war, cannot be done. Therefore, before the names of just and unjust can have place, there must be some coercive power to compel men equally to the performance of their covenants by the terror of some punishment greater than the benefit they expect by the breach of their covenant, and to make good that propriety which by mutual contract men acquire in recompense of the universal right they abandon; and such power there is none before the erection of a commonwealth. And this is also to be gathered out of the ordinary definition of justice in the Schools, for they say that *justice is the constant will of giving to every man his own.* And therefore where there is no *own*—that is, no propriety—there is no injustice; and where there is no coercive power erected—that is, where there is no commonwealth—there is no propriety, all men having right to all things; therefore, where there is no commonwealth, there nothing is unjust. So that the nature of justice consists in keeping of valid covenants; but the validity of covenants begins not but with the constitution of a civil power sufficient to compel men to keep them; and then it is also that propriety begins.

The fool hath said in his heart, there is no such thing as justice;[4] and sometimes also with his tongue, seriously alleging that, every man's conservation and contentment being committed to his own care, there could be no reason why every man might not do what he thought conduced thereunto; and therefore also to make or not make, keep or not keep covenants was not against reason when it conduced to one's benefit. He does not therein deny that there be covenants and that they are sometimes broken, sometimes kept, and that such breach of them may be called injustice and the observance of them justice; but he questions whether injustice, taking away the fear of God—for the same fool hath said in his heart there is no God—may not sometimes stand with that reason which dictates to every man his own good, and particularly then when it conduces to such a benefit as shall put a man in a condition to neglect not only the dispraise and revilings, but also the power of other men. The kingdom of God is gotten by violence; but what if it could be gotten by unjust violence? Were it against reason so to get it, when it is impossible to receive hurt by it? And if it be not against reason, it is not against justice, or else justice is not to be approved for good. From such reasoning as this, successful wickedness has obtained the name of virtue; and some that in all other things have disallowed the violation of faith yet have allowed it when it is for the getting of a kingdom. And the heathen that believed that Saturn was deposed by his son Jupiter believed nevertheless the same Jupiter to be the avenger of injustice—somewhat like to a piece of law in Coke's *Commentaries on Littleton*[5] where he says: if the right heir of the crown be attainted of treason, yet the crown shall descend to him and *eo instante* the attainder be void; from which instances a man will be very prone to infer that when the heir apparent of a kingdom shall kill him that is in possession, though his father, you may call it injustice or by what other name you will, yet it can never be against reason, seeing all the voluntary actions of men tend to the benefit of themselves, and those actions are most reasonable that conduce most to their ends. This specious reasoning is nevertheless false.

For the question is not of promises mutual where there is no security of performance on either side—as when there is no civil power erected over the parties promising—for such promises are no covenants; but either where one of the parties has performed already or where there is a power to make him perform, there is the question whether it be against reason—that is, against the benefit of the other—to perform or not. And I say it is not against reason. For the manifestation whereof we are to consider, first, that when a man does a thing which, notwithstanding anything can be foreseen and reckoned on, tends to his own destruction, howsoever some accident which he could not expect, arriving, may turn it to his benefit, yet such events do not make it reasonably or wisely done. Secondly, that in a condition of war, wherein every man to every man, for want of a common power to keep them all in awe, is an enemy, there is no man who can hope by his own strength or wit to defend himself from destruction without the help of confederates, where everyone expects the same defense by the confederation that anyone else does; and therefore he which declares he thinks it reason to deceive those that help him can in reason expect no other means of safety than what can be had from his own single power. He, therefore, that breaks his covenant, and consequently declares that he thinks he may with reason do so, cannot be received into any society that unite themselves for peace and defense, but by the error of them that receive him; nor, when he is received, be retained in it without seeing the danger of their error, which errors a man cannot reasonably reckon upon as the means of his security; and therefore if he be left or cast out of society he perishes, and if he live in society, it is by the errors of other

4. [Pss. 14, 53.]
5. [Sir Edward Coke (1552–1634), English jurist, the first Lord Chief Justice of England. The first volume of his *Institutes* was a translation of, and commentary on, the *Treatise on Tenures* of Sir Thomas de Littleton (*c.* 1407–1481). It is commonly called *Coke on Littleton*.]

men, which he could not foresee nor reckon upon, and consequently against the reason of his preservation; and so, as all men that contribute not to his destruction, forbear him only out of ignorance of what is good for themselves.

As for the instance of gaining the secure and perpetual felicity of heaven by any way, it is frivolous, there being but one way imaginable, and that is not breaking but keeping of covenant.

And for the other instance of attaining sovereignty by rebellion, it is manifest that, though the event follow, yet because it cannot reasonably be expected, but rather the contrary, and because by gaining it so others are taught to gain the same in like manner, the attempt thereof is against reason. Justice, therefore—that is to say, keeping of covenant—is a rule of reason by which we are forbidden to do anything destructive to our life, and consequently a law of nature.

There be some that proceed further and will not have the law of nature to be those rules which conduce to the preservation of man's life on earth but to the attaining of an eternal felicity after death, to which they think the breach of covenant may conduce and consequently be just and reasonable; such are they that think it a work of merit to kill or depose or rebel against the sovereign power constituted over them by their own consent. But because there is no natural knowledge of man's estate after death—much less of the reward that is then to be given to breach of faith—but only a belief grounded upon other men's saying that they know it supernaturally, or that they know those that knew them that knew others that knew it supernaturally, breach of faith cannot be called a precept of reason or nature.

Others that allow for a law of nature the keeping of faith do nevertheless make exception of certain persons, as heretics and such as use not to perform their covenant to others; and this also is against reason. For if any fault of a man be sufficient to discharge our covenant made, the same ought in reason to have been sufficient to have hindered the making of it.

The names of just and unjust, when they are attributed to men, signify one thing, and when they are attributed to actions, another. When they are attributed to men, they signify conformity or inconformity of manners to reason. But when they are attributed to actions, they signify the conformity or inconformity to reason, not of manners or manner of life, but of particular actions. A just man, therefore, is he that takes all the care he can that his actions may be all just; and an unjust man is he that neglects it. And such men are more often in our language styled by the names of righteous and unrighteous than just and unjust, though the meaning be the same. Therefore a righteous man does not lose that title by one or a few unjust actions that proceed from sudden passion or mistake of things or persons; nor does an unrighteous man lose his character for such actions as he does or forbears to do for fear, because his will is not framed by the justice but by the apparent benefit of what he is to do. That which gives to human actions the relish of justice is a certain nobleness or gallantness of courage, rarely found, by which a man scorns to be beholden for the contentment of his life to fraud or breach of promise. This justice of the manners is that which is meant where justice is called a virtue and injustice a vice.

But the justice of actions denominates men, not just, but *guiltless;* and the injustice of the same, which is also called injury, gives them but the name of *guilty.*

Again, the injustice of manners is the disposition or aptitude to do injury, and is injustice before it proceed to act and without supposing any individual person injured. But the injustice of an action—that is to say, injury—supposes an individual person injured—namely, him to whom the covenant was made—and therefore many times the injury is received by one man when the damage redounds to another. As when the master commands his servant to give money to a stranger: if it be not done, the injury is done to the master, whom he had before covenanted to obey; but the damage redounds to the stranger, to whom he had no obligation and therefore could not injure him. And so also in commonwealths private men may remit to one another their debts but not robberies or other violences whereby they are endamaged; because the detaining of debt is an injury to themselves, but robbery and violence are injuries to the person of the commonwealth.

Whatsoever is done to a man, conformable to his own will signified to the doer, is no injury to him. For if he that does it has not passed away his original right to do what he please by some antecedent covenant, there is no breach of covenant and therefore no injury done him. And if he have, then his will to have it done, being signified, is a release of that covenant, and so again there is no injury done him.

Justice of actions is by writers divided into *commutative* and *distributive;* and the former they say consists in proportion arithmetical, the latter in proportion geometrical. Commutative, therefore, they place in the equality of value of the things contracted for, and distributive in the distribution of equal benefit to men of equal merit. As if it were injustice to sell dearer than we buy, or to give more to a man than he merits. The value of all things contracted for is measured by the appetite of the contractors, and therefore the just value is that which they be contented to give. And merit (besides that which is by covenant, where the performance on one part merits the performance of the other part, and falls under justice commutative, not distributive) is not due by justice, but is rewarded of grace only. And therefore this distinction, in the sense wherein it uses to be expounded, is not right. To speak properly, commutative justice is the justice of a contractor—that is, a performance of covenant in buying and selling, hiring and letting to hire, lending and borrowing, exchanging, bartering, and other acts of contract.

And distributive justice, the justice of an arbitrator—that is to say, the act of defining what is just. Wherein, being trusted by them that make him arbitrator, if he perform his trust, he is said to distribute to every man his own; and this is indeed just distribution, and may be called, though improperly, distributive justice, but more properly equity, which also is a law of nature, as shall be shown in due place. [P. 128.]

As justice depends on antecedent covenant, so does GRATITUDE depend on antecedent grace—that is to say, antecedent free gift—and is the fourth law of nature, which may be conceived in this form: *that a man which receives benefit from another of mere grace endeavor that he which gives it have no reasonable cause to repent him of his good will.* For no man gives but with intention of good to himself, because gift is voluntary, and of all voluntary acts the object is to every man his own good; of which if men see they shall be frustrated, there will be no beginning of benevolence or trust nor consequently of mutual help nor of reconciliation of one man to another; and therefore they are to remain still in the condition of *war,* which is contrary to the first and fundamental law of nature, which commands men to *seek peace.* The breach of this law is called *ingratitude,* and has the same relation to grace that injustice has to obligation by covenant.

A fifth law of nature is COMPLAISANCE—that is to say, *that every man strive to accommodate himself to the rest.* For the understanding whereof we may consider that there is in men's aptness to society a diversity of nature rising from their diversity of affections not unlike to that we see in stones brought together for building of an edifice. For as that stone which by the asperity and irregularity of figure takes more room from others than itself fills, and for the hardness cannot be easily made plain and thereby hinders the building, is by the builders cast away as unprofitable and troublesome, so also a man that by asperity of nature will strive to retain those things which to himself are superfluous and to others necessary, and for the stubbornness of his passions cannot be corrected, is to be left or cast out of society as cumbersome thereunto. For seeing every man, not only by right but also by necessity of nature, is supposed to endeavor all he can to obtain that which is necessary for his conservation, he that shall oppose himself against it for things superfluous is guilty of the war that thereupon is to follow, and therefore does that which is contrary to the fundamental law of nature, which commands *to seek peace.* The observers of this law may be called SOCIABLE (the Latins call them *commodi*), the contrary *stubborn, insociable, forward, intractable.*

A sixth law of nature is this: *that upon caution of the future time, a man ought to pardon the offenses past of them that, repenting, desire it.* For PARDON is nothing but granting of peace, which, though granted to them that persevere in their hostility, be not peace but fear, yet, not granted to them that give caution of the future time, is sign of an aversion to peace, and therefore contrary to the law of nature.

A seventh is *that in revenges*—that is, retribution of evil for evil—*men look not at the greatness of the evil past, but the greatness of the good to follow.* Whereby we are forbidden to inflict punishment with any other design than for correction of the offender or direction of others. For this law is consequent to the next before it that commands pardon upon security of the future time. Besides, revenge without respect to the example and profit to come is a triumph or glorying in the hurt of another, tending to no end; for the end is always somewhat to come, and glorying to no end is vainglory and contrary to reason; and to hurt without reason tends to the introduction of war, which is against the law of nature and is commonly styled by the name of *cruelty.*

And because all signs of hatred or contempt provoke to fight, insomuch as most men choose rather to hazard their life than not to be revenged, we may in the eighth place for a law of nature set down this precept: *that no man by deed, word, countenance, or gesture declare hatred or contempt of another.* The breach of which law is commonly called *contumely.*

The question who is the better man has no place in the condition of mere nature, where, as has been shown before, all men are equal. The inequality that now is has been introduced by the laws civil. I know that Aristotle in the first book of his *Politics,* for a foundation of his doctrine, makes men by nature some more worthy to command, meaning the wiser sort such as he thought himself to be for his philosophy, others to serve, meaning those that had strong bodies but were not philosophers as he; as if master and servant were not introduced by consent of men but by difference of wit, which is not only against reason but also against experience. For there are very few so foolish that had not rather govern themselves than be governed by others; nor when the wise in their own conceit contend by force with them who distrust their own wisdom, do they always, or often, or almost at any time, get the victory. If nature therefore have made men equal, that equality is to be acknowledged; or if nature have made men unequal, yet because men that think themselves equal will not enter into conditions of peace but upon equal terms, such equality must be admitted. And therefore for the ninth law of nature, I put this: *that every man acknowledge another for his equal by nature.* The breach of this precept is *pride.*

On this law depends another: *that at the entrance into conditions of peace, no man require to reserve to himself any right which he is not content should be reserved to every one of the rest.* As it is necessary for all men that seek peace to lay down certain rights of nature—that is to say, not to have liberty to do all they list—so is it necessary for man's life to retain some, as right to govern their own bodies, enjoy air, water, motion, ways to go from place to place, and all things else without which a man cannot live or not live well. If in this case, at the making of peace, men require for themselves that which they would not have to be granted to others, they do contrary to the precedent law that commands the acknowledgment of natural equality and therefore also against the law of nature. The observers of this law are those we call *modest,* and the breakers *arrogant* men. The Greeks call the violation of this law πλεονεξία—that is, a desire of more than their share.

Also if *a man be trusted to judge between man and man,* it is a precept of the law of nature *that he deal equally between them.* For without that, the controversies of men cannot be determined but by war. He, therefore, that is partial in judgment does what in him lies to deter men from the use of judges and arbitrators, and consequently, against the fundamental law of nature, is the cause of war.

The observance of this law, from the equal distribution to each man of that which in reason belongs to him, is called EQUITY and, as I have said before, distributive justice; the violation, *acception of persons,* προσωποληψία.

And from this follows another law: *that such things as cannot be divided be enjoyed in common, if it can be; and if the quantity of the thing permit, without stint; otherwise proportionably to the number of them that have right.* For otherwise the distribution is unequal and contrary to equity.

But some things there be that can neither be divided nor enjoyed in common. Then the law of nature, which prescribes equity, requires *that the entire right, or else—making the use alternate—the first possession, be determined by lot.* For equal distribution is of the law of nature; and other means of equal distribution cannot be imagined.

Of *lots* there be two sorts: *arbitrary* and *natural.* Arbitrary is that which is agreed on by the competitors; natural is either *primogeniture* (which the Greek calls κληρονομία, which signifies *given by lot*) or *first seizure.*

And therefore those things which cannot be enjoyed in common, nor divided, ought to be adjudged to the first possessor; and in some cases to the first-born, as acquired by lot.

It is also a law of nature *that all men that mediate peace be allowed safe conduct.* For the law that commands peace, as the *end,* commands intercession, as the *means;* and to intercession the means is safe conduct.

And because, though men be never so willing to observe these laws, there may nevertheless arise questions concerning a man's action—first, whether it were done or not done; secondly, if done, whether against the law or not against the law; the former whereof is called a question *of fact,* the latter a question *of right*—therefore, unless the parties to the question covenant mutually to stand to the sentence of another, they are as far from peace as ever. This other to whose sentence they submit is called an ARBITRATOR. And therefore it is of the law of nature *that they that are at controversy submit their right to the judgment of an arbitrator.*

And seeing every man is presumed to do all things in order to his own benefit, no man is a fit arbitrator in his own cause; and if he were never so fit, yet, equity allowing to each party equal benefit, if one be admitted to be judge the other is to be admitted also; and so the controversy—that is, the cause of war—remains against the law of nature.

For the same reason no man in any cause ought to be received for arbitrator to whom greater profit or honor or pleasure apparently arises out of the victory of one party than of the other; for he has taken, though an unavoidable bribe, yet a bribe, and no man can be obliged to trust him. And thus also the controversy and the condition of war remains, contrary to the law of nature.

And in a controversy of *fact,* the judge being to give no more credit to one than to the other, if there be no other arguments, must give credit to a third, or to a third and fourth, no more; for else the question is undecided and left to force, contrary to the law of nature.

These are the laws of nature dictating peace for a means of the conservation of men in multitudes, and which only concern the doctrine of civil society. There be other things tending to the destruction of particular men—as drunkenness and all other parts of intemperance—which may therefore also be reckoned among those things which the law of nature has forbidden, but are not necessary to be mentioned nor are pertinent enough to this place.

And though this may seem too subtle a deduction of the laws of nature to be taken notice of by all men—whereof the most part are too busy in getting food and the rest too negligent to understand—yet to leave all men inexcusable they have been contracted into one easy sum, intelligible even to the meanest capacity, and that is *Do not that to another which you would not have done to yourself;* which shows him that he has no more to do in learning the laws of nature but, when weighing the actions of other men with his own they seem too heavy, to put them into the other part of the balance and his own into their place, that his own passions and self-love may add nothing to the weight, and then there is none of these laws of nature that will not appear unto him very reasonable.

The laws of nature oblige *in foro interno*[6]—that is to say, they bind to a desire they should take place—but *in foro externo*[7]—that is, to the putting them in act—not always. For he that should be modest and tractable and perform all he promises in such time and place where no man else should do so should but make himself a prey to others and procure his own certain ruin, contrary to the ground of all laws of nature, which tend to nature's preservation. And again, he that, having sufficient security that others shall observe the same laws toward him, observes them not himself, seeks not peace but war and consequently the destruction of his nature by violence.

And whatsoever laws bind *in foro interno* may be broken, not only by a fact contrary to the law, but also by a fact according to it, in case a man think it

6. [In conscience.]
7. [In civil law.]

contrary. For though his action in this case be according to the law, yet his purpose was against the law, which, where the obligation is *in foro interno,* is a breach.

The laws of nature are immutable and eternal, for injustice, ingratitude, arrogance, pride, iniquity, acception of persons, and the rest can never be made lawful. For it can never be that war shall preserve life and peace destroy it.

The same laws, because they oblige only to a desire and endeavor—I mean an unfeigned and constant endeavor—are easy to be observed. For in that they require nothing but endeavor, he that endeavors their performance fulfills them; and he that fulfills the law is just.

And the science of them is the true and only moral philosophy. For moral philosophy is nothing else but the science of what is *good* and *evil* in the conversation and society of mankind. *Good* and *evil* are names that signify our appetites and aversions, which in different tempers, customs, and doctrines of men are different; and divers men differ not only in their judgment on the senses of what is pleasant and unpleasant to the taste, smell, hearing, touch, and sight but also of what is conformable or disagreeable to reason in the actions of common life. Nay, the same man in divers times differs from himself, and one time praises—that is, calls good—what another time he dispraises and calls evil; from whence arise disputes, controversies, and at last war. And therefore so long as a man is in the condition of mere nature, which is a condition of war, private appetite is the measure of good and evil; and consequently all men agree on this: that peace is good, and therefore also the way or means of peace, which, as I have showed before, are *justice, gratitude, modesty, equity, mercy,* and the rest of the laws of nature, are good—that is to say, *moral virtues*—and their contrary *vices* evil. Now the science of virtue and vice is moral philosophy; and therefore the true doctrine of the laws of nature is the true moral philosophy. But the writers of moral philosophy, though they acknowledge the same virtues and vices, yet, not seeing wherein consisted their goodness nor that they come to be praised as the means of peaceable, sociable, and comfortable living, place them in a mediocrity of passions; as if not the cause but the degree of daring made fortitude, or not the cause but the quantity of a gift made liberality.

These dictates of reason men used to call by the name of laws, but improperly, for they are but conclusions or theorems concerning what conduces to the conservation and defense of themselves, whereas law, properly, is the word of him that by right has command over others. But yet if we consider the same theorems as delivered in the word of God, that by right commands all things, then are they properly called laws.

The Good Will & The Categorical Imperative*

IMMANUEL KANT

Immanuel Kant (1724–1804), the greatest of the German philosophers, spent his entire career at the University of Königsberg in East Prussia.

From Immanuel Kant, Foundations of the Metaphysics of Morals, *trans. Lewis White Beck (Indianapolis: Bobbs-Merrill, 1959), pp. 9–20, 31–49. Reprinted by permission of the publisher.*

THE GOOD WILL

NOTHING IN THE WORLD—indeed nothing even beyond the world—can possibly be conceived which could be called good without qualification except a *good will*. Intelligence, wit, judgment, and the other talents of the mind, however they may be named, or courage, resoluteness, and perseverance as qualities of temperament, are doubtless in many respects good and desirable. But they can become extremely bad and harmful if the will, which is to make use of these gifts of nature and which in its special constitution is called character, is not good. It is the same with the gifts of fortune. Power, riches, honor, even health, general well-being, and the contentment with one's condition which is called happiness, make for pride and even arrogance if there is not a good will to correct their influence on the mind and on its principles of action so as to make it universally conformable to its end. It need hardly be mentioned that the sight of a being adorned with no feature of a pure and good will, yet enjoying uninterrupted prosperity, can never give pleasure to a rational impartial observer. Thus the good will seems to constitute the indispensable condition even of worthiness to be happy.

Some qualities seem to be conducive to this good will and can facilitate its action, but, in spite of that, they have no intrinsic unconditional worth. They rather presuppose a good will, which limits the high esteem which one otherwise rightly has for them and prevents their being held to be absolutely good. Moderation in emotions and passions, self-control, and calm deliberation not only are good in many respects but even seem to constitute a part of the inner worth of the person. But however unconditionally they were esteemed by the ancients, they are far from being good without qualification. For without the principle of a good will they can be come extremely bad, and the coolness of a villain makes him not only far more dangerous but also more directly abominable in our eyes than he would have seemed without it.

The good will is not good because of what it effects or accomplishes or because of its adequacy to achieve some proposed end; it is good only because of its willing, i.e., it is good of itself. And, regarded for itself, it is to be esteemed incomparably higher than anything which could be brought about by it in favor of any inclination or even of the sum total of all inclinations. Even if it should happen that, by a particularly unfortunate fate or by the niggardly provision of a stepmotherly nature, this will should be wholly lacking in power to accomplish its purpose, and if even the greatest effort should not avail it to achieve anything of its end, and if there remained only the good will (not as a mere wish but as the summoning of all the means in our power), it would sparkle like a jewel in its own right, as something that had its full worth in itself. Usefulness or fruitlessness can neither diminish nor augment this worth. Its usefulness would be only its setting, as it were, so as to enable us to handle it more conveniently in commerce or to attract the attention of those who are not yet connoisseurs, but not to recommend it to those who are experts or to determine its worth.

But there is something so strange in this idea of the absolute worth of the will alone, in which no account is taken of any use, that, notwithstanding the agreement even of common sense, the suspicion must arise that perhaps only high-flown fancy is its hidden basis, and that we may have misunderstood the purpose of nature in its appointment of reason as the ruler of our will. We shall therefore examine this idea from this point of view.

In the natural constitution of an organized being, i.e., one suitably adapted to life, we assume as an axiom that no organ will be found for any purpose which is not the fittest and best adapted to that purpose. Now if its preservation, its welfare—in a word, its happiness—were the real end of nature in a being having reason and will, then nature would have hit upon a very poor arrangement in appointing the reason of the creature to be the executor of this purpose. For all the actions which the creature has to perform with this intention, and the entire rule of its conduct, would be dictated much more exactly by instinct, and that end would be far more certainly attained by instinct than it ever could be by reason. And if, over and above this, reason should have been granted to the favored creature, it would have served only to let it contemplate the happy constitution of its nature, to admire it, to rejoice in it, and to be grateful for it to its beneficent cause. But reason would not have been given in order that the being should subject its faculty of desire to that weak and delusive guidance and to meddle with the purpose of nature. In a word, nature would have taken care that reason did not break forth into practical use nor have the presumption, with its weak insight, to think out for itself the plan of happiness and the means of attaining it. Nature would have taken over not only the choice of ends but also that of the means, and with wise foresight she would have entrusted both to instinct alone.

And, in fact, we find that the more a cultivated reason deliberately devotes itself to the enjoyment of life and happiness, the more the man falls short of true contentment. From this fact there arises in many persons, if only they are candid enough to admit it, a certain degree of misology, hatred of reason. This is particularly the case with those who are most experienced in its use. After counting all the advantages which they draw—I will not say from the invention of the arts of common luxury—from the sciences (which in the end seem to them to be also a luxury of the understanding), they nevertheless find that they have actually brought more trouble on their shoulders instead of gaining in happiness; they finally envy, rather than despise, the common run of men who are better guided by mere natural instinct and who do not permit their reason much influence on their conduct. And we must at least admit that a morose attitude or ingratitude to the goodness with which the world is governed is by no means found always among those who temper or refute the boasting eulogies which are given of the advantages of happiness and contentment with which reason is supposed to supply us. Rather their judgment is based on the idea of another and far more worthy purpose of their existence for which, instead of happiness, their reason is properly intended, this purpose, therefore, being the supreme condition to which the private purposes of men must for the most part defer.

Reason is not, however, competent to guide the will safely with regard to its objects and the satisfaction of all our needs (which it in part multiplies), and to this end an innate instinct would have led with far more certainty. But reason is given to us as a practical faculty, i.e., one which is meant to have an influence on the will. As nature has elsewhere distributed capacities suitable to the functions they are to perform, reason's proper function must be to produce a will good in itself and not one good merely as a means, for to the former reason is absolutely essential. This will must indeed not be the sole and complete good but the highest good and the condition of all others, even of the desire for happiness. In this case it is entirely compatible with the wisdom of nature that the cultivation of reason, which is required for the former unconditional purpose, at least in this life restricts in many ways—indeed can reduce to less than nothing—the achievement of the latter conditional purpose, happiness. For one perceives that nature here does not proceed unsuitably to its purpose, because reason, which recognizes its highest practical vocation in the establishment of a good will, is capable only of a contentment of its own kind, i.e., one that springs from the attainment of a purpose which is determined by reason, even though this injures the ends of inclination.

We have, then, to develop the concept of a will which is to be esteemed as good of itself without regard to anything else. It dwells already in the natural sound understanding and does not need so much to be taught as only to be brought to light. In the estimation of the total worth of our actions it always takes first place and is the condition of everything else. In order to show this, we shall take the concept of duty. It contains that of a good will, though with certain subjective restrictions and hindrances; but these are far from concealing it and making it unrecognizable, for they rather bring it out by contrast and make it shine forth all the brighter.

I here omit all actions which are recognized as opposed to duty, even though they may be useful in one respect or another, for with these the question does not arise at all as to whether they may be carried out *from* duty, since they conflict with it. I also pass over the actions which are really in accordance with duty and to which one has no direct inclination, rather executing them because impelled to do so by another inclination. For it is easily decided whether an action in accord with duty is performed from duty or for some selfish purpose. It is far more difficult to note this difference when the action is in accordance with duty and, in addition, the subject has a direct inclination to do it. For example, it is in fact in accordance with duty that a dealer should not overcharge an inexperienced customer, and wherever there is much business the prudent merchant does not do so, having a fixed price for everyone, so that a child may buy of him as cheaply as any other. Thus the customer is honestly served. But this is far from sufficient to justify the belief that the merchant has behaved in this way from duty and principles of honesty. His own advantage required this behavior; but it cannot be assumed that over and above that he had a direct inclination to the purchaser and that, out of love, as it were, he gave none an advantage in price over another. Therefore the action was done neither from duty nor from direct inclination but only for a selfish purpose.

On the other hand, it is a duty to preserve one's life, and moreover everyone has a direct inclination to do so. But for that reason the often anxious care which most men take of it has no intrinsic worth, and the maxim of doing so has no moral import. They preserve their lives according to duty, but not from duty. But if adversities and hopeless sorrow completely take away the relish for life, if an unfortunate man, strong in soul, is indignant rather than despondent or dejected over his fate and wishes for death, and yet preserves his life without loving it and from neither inclination nor fear but from duty—then his maxim has a moral import.

To be kind where one can is duty, and there are, moreover, many persons so sympathetically constituted that without any motive of vanity or selfishness they find an inner satisfaction in spreading joy, and rejoice in the contentment of others which they have made possible. But I say that, however dutiful and amiable it may be, that kind of action has no true moral worth. It is on a level with [actions arising from] other inclinations, such as the inclination to honor, which, if fortunately directed to what in fact accords with duty and is generally useful and thus honorable, deserve praise and encouragement but no esteem. For the maxim lacks the moral import of an action done not from inclination but from duty. But assume that the mind of that friend to mankind was clouded by a sorrow of his own which extinguished all sympathy with the lot of others and that he still had the power to benefit others in distress, but that their need left him untouched because he was preoccupied with his own need. And now suppose him to tear himself, unsolicited by inclination, out of this dead insensibility and to perform this action only from duty and without any inclination—then for the first time his action has genuine moral worth. Furthermore, if nature has put little sympathy in the heart of a man, and if he, though an honest man, is by temperament cold and indifferent to the sufferings of others, perhaps because he is provided with special gifts of patience and fortitude and expects or even requires that others should have the same—and such a man would certainly not be the meanest product of nature—would not he find in himself a source from which to give himself a far higher worth than he could have got by having a good-natured temperament? This is unquestionably true even though nature did not make him philanthropic, for it is just here that the worth of the character is brought out, which is morally and incomparably the highest of all: he is beneficent not from inclination but from duty.

To secure one's own happiness is at least indirectly a duty, for discontent with one's condition under pressure from many cares and amid unsatisfied wants could easily become a great temptation to transgress duties. But without any view to duty all men have the strongest and deepest inclination to happiness, because in this idea all inclinations are summed up. But the precept of happiness is often so formulated that it definitely thwarts some inclinations, and men can make no definite and certain concept of the sum of satisfaction of all inclinations which goes under the name of happiness. It is not to be wondered at, therefore, that a single inclination, definite as to what it promises and as to the time at which it can be satisfied, can outweigh a fluctuating idea, and that, for example, a man with the gout can choose to enjoy what he likes and to suffer what he may, because according to his calculations at least on this occasion he has not sacrificed the enjoyment of the present moment to a perhaps groundless expectation of a happiness supposed to lie in health. But even in this case, if the universal inclination to happiness did not determine his will, and if health were not at least for him a necessary factor in these calculations, there yet would remain, as in all other cases, a law that he ought to promote his happiness, not from inclination but from duty. Only from this law would his conduct have true moral worth.

It is in this way, undoubtedly, that we should understand those passages of Scripture which command us to love our neighbor and even our enemy, for love as an inclination cannot be commanded. But beneficence from duty, when no inclination impels it and even when it is opposed by a natural and unconquerable aversion, is practical love, not pathological love; it resides in the will and not in the propensities of feeling, in principles of action and not in tender sympathy; and it alone can be commanded.

[Thus the first proposition of morality is that to have moral worth an action must be done from duty.] . . .

Thus the moral worth of an action does not lie in the effect which is expected from it or in any principle of action which has to borrow its motive from this expected effect. For all these effects (agreeableness of my own condition, indeed even the promotion of the happiness of others) could be brought about through other causes and would not require the will of a rational being, while the highest and unconditional good can be found only in such a will.

But what kind of a law can that be, the conception of which must determine the will without reference to the expected results? Under this condition alone the will can be called absolutely good without qualification. Since I have robbed the will of all impulses which could come to it from obedience to any law, nothing remains to serve as a principle of the will except universal conformity of its action to law as such. That is, I should never act in such a way that I could not also will that my maxim should be a universal law. Mere conformity to law as such (without assuming any particular law applicable to certain actions) serves as the principle of the will, and it must serve as such a principle if duty is not to be a vain delusion and chimerical concept. The common reason of mankind in its practical judgments is in perfect agreement with this and has this principle constantly in view.

Let the question, for example, be: May I, when in distress, make a promise with the intention not to keep it? I easily distinguish the two meanings which the question can have, viz., whether it is prudent to make a false promise, or whether it conforms to my duty. Undoubtedly the former can often be the case, though I do see clearly that it is not sufficient merely to escape from the present difficulty by this expedient, but that I must consider whether inconveniences much greater than the present one may not later spring from this lie. Even with all my supposed cunning, the consequences cannot be so easily foreseen. Loss of credit might be far more disadvantageous than the misfortune I now seek to avoid, and it is hard to tell whether it might not be more prudent to act according to a universal maxim and to make it a habit not to promise anything without intending to fulfill it. But it is soon clear to me that such a maxim is based only on an apprehensive concern with consequences.

To be truthful from duty, however, is an entirely different thing from being truthful out of fear of disadvantageous consequences, for in the former case the concept of the action itself contains a law for me, while in the latter I must first look about to see what results for me may be connected with it. For to deviate from the principle of duty is certainly bad, but to be unfaithful to my maxim of prudence can sometimes be very advantageous to me, though it is certainly safer to abide by it. The shortest but most infallible way to find the answer to the question as to whether a deceitful promise is consistent with duty is to ask myself: Would I be content that my maxim (of extricating myself from difficulty by a false promise) should hold as a universal law for myself as well as for others? And could I say to myself that everyone may make a false promise when he is in a difficulty from which he otherwise cannot escape? I immediately see that I could will the lie but not a universal law to lie. For with such a law there would be no promises at all, inasmuch as it would be futile to make a pretense of my intention in regard to future actions to those who would not believe this pretense or—if they overhastily did so—who would pay me back in my own coin. Thus my maxim would necessarily destroy itself as soon as it was made a universal law.

I do not, therefore, need any penetrating acuteness in order to discern what I have to do in order that my volition may be morally good. Inexperienced in the course of the world, incapable of being prepared for all its contingencies, I ask myself only: Can I will that my maxim become a universal law? If not, it must be rejected, not because of any disadvantage accruing to myself or even to others, but because it cannot enter as a principle into a possible universal legislation, and reason extorts from me an immediate respect for such legislation. I do not as yet discern on what it is grounded (a question the philosopher may investigate), but I at least understand that it is an estimation of the worth which far outweighs all the worth of whatever is recommended by the inclinations, and that the necessity of my actions from pure respect for the practical law constitutes duty. To duty every other motive must give place, because duty is the condition of a will good in itself, whose worth transcends everything.

THE CATEGORICAL IMPERATIVE

All imperatives command either hypothetically or categorically. The former present the practical necessity of a possible action as a means to achieving something else which one desires (or which one may possibly desire). The categorical imperative would be one which presented an action as of itself objectively necessary, without regard to any other end.

Since every practical law presents a possible action as good and thus as necessary for a subject practically determinable by reason, all imperatives are formulas of the determination of action which is necessary by the principle of a will which is in any way good. If the action is good only as a means to something else, the imperative is hypothetical; but if it is thought of as good in itself, and hence as necessary in a will which of itself conforms to reason as the principle of this will, the imperative is categorical.

The imperative thus says what action possible to me would be good, and it presents the practical rule in relation to a will which does not forthwith perform an action simply because it is good, in part because the subject does not always know that the action is good and in part (when he does know it) because his maxims can still be opposed to the objective principles of practical reason.

The hypothetical imperative, therefore, says only that the action is good to some purpose, possible or actual. In the . . . former case it is a problematical, in the latter an assertorical, practical principle. The categorical imperative, which declares the action to be of itself objectively necessary without making any reference to a purpose, i.e., without having any other end, holds as an apodictical (practical) principle.

We can think of that which is possible through the mere powers of some rational being as a possible purpose of any will. As a consequence, the principles of action, in so far as they are thought of as necessary to attain a possible purpose which can be achieved by them, are in reality infinitely numerous. All sciences have some practical part which consists of problems of some end which is possible for us and of imperatives as to how it can be reached. These can therefore generally be called imperatives of skill. Whether the end is reasonable and good is not in question at all, for the question is only of what must be done in order to attain it. The precepts to be followed by a physician in order to cure his patient and by a poisoner in order to bring about certain death are of equal value in so far as each does that which will perfectly accomplish his purpose. Since in early youth we do not know what ends may occur to us in the course of life, parents seek to let their children learn a great many things and provide for skill in the use of means to all sorts of arbitrary ends among which they cannot determine whether any one of them may later become an actual purpose of their pupil, though it is possible that he may some day have it as his actual purpose. And this anxiety is so great that they commonly neglect to form and correct their judgment on the worth of things which they may make their ends.

There is one end, however, which we may presuppose as actual in all rational beings so far as imperatives apply to them, i.e., so far as they are dependent beings; there is one purpose not only which they *can* have but which we can presuppose that they all *do* have by a necessity of nature. This purpose is happiness. The hypothetical imperative which represents the practical necessity of action as means to the promotion of happiness is an assertorical imperative. We may not expound it as merely necessary to an uncertain and a merely possible purpose, but as necessary to a purpose which we can a priori and with assurance assume for everyone . . . because it belongs to his essence. Skill in the choice of means to one's own highest welfare can be called prudence[1] in the narrowest sense. Thus the imperative which refers to the choice of means to one's own happiness, i.e., the precept of prudence, is still only hypothetical; the action is not absolutely commanded but commanded only as a means to another end.

Finally, there is one imperative which directly commands a certain conduct without making its condition some purpose to be reached by it. This imperative is categorical. It concerns not the material of the action and its intended result but the form and the principle from which it results. What is essentially good in it consists in the intention, the result being what it may. This imperative may be called the imperative of morality.

Volition according to these three principles is plainly distinguished by dissimilarity in the constraint to which they subject the will. In order to clarify this dissimilarity, I believe that they are most suitably named if one says that they are either rules of skill, counsels of prudence, or commands (laws) of morality, respectively. For law alone implies the concept of an unconditional and objective and hence universally valid necessity, and commands are laws which must be obeyed, even against inclination. Counsels do indeed involve necessity, but a necessity that can hold only under a subjectively contingent condition, i.e., whether this or that man counts this or that as part of his happiness; but the categorical imperative, on the other hand, is restricted by no condition. As absolutely, though practically, necessary it can be called a command in the strict sense. We would also call the first imperative technical (belonging to art), the second pragmatic[2] (belonging to well . . . fare), and the third moral (belonging to free conduct as such, i.e., to morals).

The question now arises: how are all these imperatives possible? This question does not require an answer as to how the action which the imperative commands can be performed but merely as to how the constraint of the will, which the imperative expresses in the problem, can be conceived. How an imperative of skill is possible requires no particular discussion. Whoever wills the end, so far as reason has decisive influence on his action, wills also the indispensably necessary means to it that lie in his power. This proposition, in what concerns the will, is analytical; for, in willing an object as my effect, my causality as an acting cause, i.e., the use of the means, is already thought, and the imperative derives the concept of necessary actions to this end from the concept of willing this end. Synthetical propositions undoubtedly are necessary in determining the means to a proposed end, but they do not concern the ground, the act of the will, but only the way to make the object real. Mathematics teaches, by synthetical propositions only, that in order to bisect a line according to an infallible principle I must make two intersecting arcs from each of its extremities; but if I know the proposed result can be obtained only by such an action, then it is an analytical proposition that, if I fully will the effect, I must also will the action necessary to produce it. For it is one and the same thing to conceive of something as an effect which is in a certain way possible through me and to conceive of myself as acting in this way.

If it were only easy to give a definite concept of happiness, the imperatives of prudence would completely correspond to those of skill and would be likewise analytical. For it could be said in this case as well as in the former that whoever . . . wills the end wills also (necessarily according to reason) the only means to it which are in his power. But it is a misfortune that the concept of happiness is so indefinite that, although each person wishes to attain it, he can never definitely and self-consistently state what it is he really wishes and wills. The reason for this is that all elements which belong to the concept of happiness are empirical, i.e., they must be taken from experience, while for the idea of happiness an absolute whole, a maximum, of well-being is needed in my present and in every future condition.

Now it is impossible even for a clear-sighted and most capable but finite being to form here a definite concept of that which he really wills. If he wills riches, how much anxiety, envy, and intrigue might he not thereby draw upon his shoulders! If he wills much knowledge and vision, perhaps it might become only an eye that much sharper to show him as more dreadful the evils which are now hidden from him and which are yet unavoidable, or to burden his desires—which already sufficiently engage him—with even more needs! If he wills a long life, who guarantees that it will not be long misery? If he wills at least health, how often has not the discomfort of the body restrained him from excesses into which perfect health would have led him? In short, he is not capable, on any principle and with complete certainty, of ascertaining what would make him truly happy; omniscience would be needed for this. He cannot, therefore, act according to definite principles so as to be happy, but only according to empirical counsels, e.g., those of diet, economy, courtesy, restraint, etc., which are shown by experience best to promote welfare on the average. Hence the imperatives of prudence cannot, in the strict sense, command, i.e., present actions objectively as practically necessary; thus they are to be taken as counsels (*consilia*) rather than as commands (*praecepta*) of reason, and the task of determining infallibly and universally what action will promote the happiness of a rational being is completely unsolvable. There can be no imperative which would, in the strict sense, command us to do what makes for happiness, because happiness is an ideal not of reason but of imagination, depending only on empirical grounds which one would expect in vain to determine an . . . action through which the totality of consequences—which is in fact infinite—could be achieved. Assuming that the means to happiness could be infallibly stated, this imperative of prudence would be an analytical proposition, for it differs from the imperative of skill only in that its end is given, while in the latter case it is merely possible. Since both, however, only command the means to that which one presupposes, the imperative which commands the willing of the means to him who wills the end is in both cases analytical. There is, consequently, no difficulty in seeing the possibility of such an imperative.

To see how the imperative of morality is possible is, then, without doubt the only question needing an answer. It is not hypothetical, and thus the objectively conceived necessity cannot be supported by any presupposition, as was the case with the hypothetical imperatives. But it must not be overlooked that it cannot be shown by any example (i.e., it cannot be empirically shown) whether or not there is such an imperative; it is rather to be suspected that all imperatives which appear to be categorical may yet be hypothetical, but in a hidden way. For instance, when it is said, "Thou shalt not make a false promise," we assume that the necessity of this avoidance is not a mere counsel for the sake of escaping some other evil, so that it would read, "Thou shalt not make a false promise so that, if it comes to light, thou ruinest thy credit"; we assume rather that an action of this kind must be regarded as of itself bad and that the imperative of the prohibition is categorical. But we cannot show with certainty by any example that the will is here determined by the law alone without any other incentives, even though this appears to be the case. For it is always possible that secret fear of disgrace, and perhaps also obscure apprehension of other dangers, may have had an influence on the will. Who can prove by experience the non-existence of a cause when experience shows us only that we do not perceive the cause? But in such a case the so-called moral imperative, which as such appears to be categorical and unconditional, would be actually only a pragmatic precept which makes us attentive to our own advantage and teaches us to consider it.

Thus we shall have to investigate purely a priori the possibility of a categorical imperative, for we do not have the . . . advantage that experience would give us the reality of this imperative, so that the [demonstration of its] possibility would be necessary only for its explanation and not for its establishment. In the meantime, this much may at least be seen: the categorical imperative alone can be taken as a practical *law*, while all the others may be called principles of the will but not laws. This is because what is necessary merely for the attainment of an arbitrary purpose can be regarded as itself contingent, and we get rid of the precept once we give up the purpose, whereas the unconditional command leaves the will no freedom to choose the opposite. Thus it alone implies the necessity which we require of a law.

Secondly, in the case of the categorical imperative or law of morality, the cause of difficulty in discerning its possibility is very weighty. This imperative is an a priori synthetical practical proposition,[3] and, since to discern the possibility of propositions of this sort is so difficult in theoretical knowledge, it may well be gathered that it will be no less difficult in the practical.

In attacking this problem, we will first inquire whether the mere concept of a categorical imperative does not also furnish the formula containing the proposition which alone can be a categorical imperative. For even when we know the formula of the imperative, to learn how such an absolute law is possible will require difficult and special labors which we shall postpone to the last section.

If I think of a hypothetical imperative as such, I do not know what it will contain until the condition is stated [under which it is an imperative]. But if I think of a categorical imperative, I know immediately what it contains. For since the imperative contains besides the law only the necessity . . . that the maxim[4] should accord with this law, while the law contains no condition to which it is restricted, there is nothing remaining in it except the universality of law as such to which the maxim of the action should conform; and in effect this conformity alone is represented as necessary by the imperative.

There is, therefore, only one categorical imperative. It is: Act only according to that maxim by which you can at the same time will that it should become a universal law.

Now if all imperatives of duty can be derived from this one imperative as a principle, we can at least show what we understand by the concept of duty and what it means, even though it remain undecided whether that which is called duty is an empty concept or not.

The universality of law according to which effects are produced constitutes what is properly called nature in the most general sense (as to form), i.e., the existence of things so far as it is determined by universal laws. [By analogy], then, the universal imperative of duty can be expressed as follows: Act as though the maxim of your action were by your will to become a universal law of nature.

We shall now enumerate some duties, adopting the usual division of them into duties to ourselves and to others and into perfect and imperfect duties.[5]

1. A man who is reduced to despair by a series of evils feels a weariness with life but is still in possession of his reason . . . sufficiently to ask whether it would not be contrary to his duty to himself to take his own life. Now he asks whether the maxim of his action could become a universal law of nature. His maxim, however, is: For love of myself, I make it my principle to shorten my life when by a longer duration it threatens more evil than satisfaction. But it is questionable whether this principle of self-love could become a universal law of nature. One immediately sees a contradiction in a system of nature whose law would be to destroy life by the feeling whose special office is to impel the improvement of life. In this case it would not exist as nature; hence that maxim cannot obtain as a law of nature, and thus it wholly contradicts the supreme principle of all duty.

2. Another man finds himself forced by need to borrow money. He well knows that he will not be able to repay it, but he also sees that nothing will be loaned him if he does not firmly promise to repay it at a certain time. He desires to make such a promise, but he has enough conscience to ask himself whether it is not improper and opposed to duty to relieve his distress in such a way. Now, assuming he does decide to do so, the maxim of his action would be as follows: When I believe myself to be in need of money, I will borrow money and promise to repay it, although I know I shall never do so. Now this principle of self-love or of his own benefit many very well be compatible with his whole future welfare, but the question is whether it is right. He changes the pretension of self-love into a universal law and then puts the question: How would it be if my maxim became a universal law? He immediately sees that it could never hold as a universal law of nature and be consistent with itself; rather it must necessarily contradict itself. For the universality of a

law which says that anyone who believes himself to be in need could promise what he pleased with the intention of not fulfilling it would make the promise itself and the end to be accomplished by it impossible; no one would believe what was promised to him but would only laugh at any such assertion as vain pretense.

3. A third finds in himself a talent which could, by means of some cultivation, make him in many respects a useful . . . man. But he finds himself in comfortable circumstances and prefers indulgence in pleasure to troubling himself with broadening and improving his fortunate natural gifts. Now, however, let him ask whether his maxim of neglecting his gifts, besides agreeing with his propensity to idle amusement, agrees also with what is called duty. He sees that a system of nature could indeed exist in accordance with such a law, even though man (like the inhabitants of the South Sea Islands) should let his talents rust and resolve to devote his life merely to idleness, indulgence, and propagation—in a word, to pleasure. But he cannot possibly will that this should become a universal law of nature or that it should be implanted in us by a natural instinct. For, as a rational being, he necessarily wills that all his faculties should be developed, inasmuch as they are given to him for all sorts of possible purposes.

4. A fourth man, for whom things are going well, sees that others (whom he could help) have to struggle with great hardships, and he asks, "What concern of mine is it? Let each one be as happy as heaven wills, or as he can make himself; I will not take anything from him or even envy him; but to his welfare or to his assistance in time of need I have no desire to contribute." If such a way of thinking were a universal law of nature, certainly the human race could exist, and without doubt even better than in a state where everyone talks of sympathy and good will, or even exerts himself occasionally to practice them while, on the other hand, he cheats when he can and betrays or otherwise violates the rights of man. Now although it is possible that a universal law of nature according to that maxim could exist, it is nevertheless impossible to will that such a principle should hold everywhere as a law of nature. For a will which resolved this would conflict with itself, since instances can often arise in which he would need the love and sympathy of others, and in which he would have robbed himself, by such a law of nature springing from his own will, of all hope of the aid he desires.

The foregoing are a few of the many actual duties, or at least of duties we hold to be actual, whose derivation from the one stated principle is clear. We must be able to will that . . . a maxim of our action become a universal law; this is the canon of the moral estimation of our action generally. Some actions are of such a nature that their maxim cannot even be *thought* as a universal law of nature without contradiction, far from it being possible that one could will that it should be such. In others this internal impossibility is not found, though it is still impossible to *will* that their maxim should be raised to the universality of a law of nature, because such a will would contradict itself. We easily see that the former maxim conflicts with the stricter or narrower (imprescriptible) duty, the latter with broader (meritorious) duty. Thus all duties, so far as the kind of obligation (not the object of their action) is concerned, have been completely exhibited by these examples in their dependence on the one principle.

When we observe ourselves in any transgression of a duty, we find that we do not actually will that our maxim should become a universal law. That is impossible for us; rather, the contrary of this maxim should remain as a law generally, and we only take the liberty of making an exception to it for ourselves or for the sake of our inclination, and for this one occasion. Consequently, if we weighed everything from one and the same standpoint, namely, reason, we would come upon a contradiction in our own will, viz., that a certain principle is objectively necessary as a universal law and yet subjectively does not hold universally but rather admits exceptions. However, since we regard our action at one time from the point of view of a will wholly conformable to reason and then from that of a will affected by inclinations, there is actually no contradiction, but rather an opposition of inclination to the precept of reason (*antagonismus*). In this the universality of the principle (*universalitas*) is changed into mere generality (*generalitas*), whereby the practical principle of reason meets the maxim halfway. Although this cannot be justified in our own impartial judgment, it does show that we actually acknowledge the validity of the categorical imperative and allow ourselves (with all respect to it) only a few exceptions which seem to us to be unimportant and forced upon us.

We have thus at least established that if duty is a concept . . . which is to have significance and actual legislation for our actions, it can be expressed only in categorical imperatives and not at all in hypothetical ones. For every application of it we have also clearly exhibited the content of the categorical imperative which must contain the principle of all duty (if there is such). This is itself very much. But we are not yet advanced far enough to prove a priori that that kind of imperative really exists, that there is a practical law which of itself commands absolutely and without any incentives, and that obedience to this law is duty.

With a view to attaining this, it is extremely important to remember that we must not let ourselves think that the reality of this principle can be derived from the particular constitution of human nature. For duty is practical unconditional necessity of action; it must, therefore, hold for all rational beings (to which alone an imperative can apply), and only for that reason can it be a law for all human wills. Whatever is derived from the particular natural situation of man as such, or from certain feelings and propensities, or even from a particular tendency of the human reason which might not hold necessarily for the will of every rational being (if such a tendency is possible), can give a maxim valid for us but not a law; that is, it can give a subjective principle by which we might act only if we have the propensity and inclination, but not an objective principle by which we would be directed to act even if all our propensity, inclination, and natural tendency were opposed to it. This is so far the case that the sublimity and intrinsic worth of the command is the better shown in a duty the fewer subjective causes there are for it and the more there are against it; the latter do not weaken the constraint of the law or diminish its validity. . . .

The question then is: Is it a necessary law for all rational beings that they should always judge their actions by such maxims as they themselves could will to serve as universal laws? If it is such a law, it must be connected (wholly a priori) with the concept of the will of a rational being as such. But in order to discover this connection we must, however reluctantly, take a step into metaphysics, although into a region of it different from speculative philosophy, i.e., into metaphysics of morals. In a practical philosophy it is not a question of assuming grounds for what happens but of assuming laws of what ought to happen even though it may never happen—that is to say, objective, practical laws. Hence in practical philosophy we need not inquire into the reasons why . . . something pleases or displeases, how the pleasure of mere feeling differs from taste, and whether this is distinct from a general satisfaction of reason. Nor need we ask on what the feeling of pleasure or displeasure rests, how desires and inclinations arise, and how, finally, maxims arise from desires and inclination under the co-operation of reason. For all these matters belong to an empirical psychology, which would be the second part of physics if we consider it as philosophy of nature so far as it rests on empirical laws. But here it is a question of objectively practical laws and thus of the relation of a will to itself so far as it determines itself only by reason; for everything which has a relation to the empirical automatically falls away, because if reason of itself alone determines conduct it must necessarily do so a priori. The possibility of reason thus determining conduct must now be investigated.

The will is thought of as a faculty of determining itself to action in accordance with the conception of certain laws. Such a faculty can be found only in rational beings. That which serves the will as the objective ground of its self-determination is an end, and, if it is given by reason alone, it must hold alike for all rational beings. On the other hand, that which contains the ground of the possibility of the action, whose result is an end, is called the means. The subjective ground of desire is the incentive, while the objective ground or volition is the motive. Thus arises the distinction between subjective ends, which rest on incentives, and objective ends, which depend on motives valid for every rational being. Practical principles are formal when they disregard all subjective ends; they are material when they have subjective ends, and thus certain incentives, as their basis. The ends which a rational being arbitrarily proposes to himself as consequences of his action are material ends and are without exception only relative, for only their relation to a particularly constituted faculty of desire in the subject gives them their worth. And this worth cannot, therefore, afford any universal principles for all rational beings or valid and necessary principles for every volition. That is, they cannot give rise to any practical laws. . . . All these relative ends, therefore, are grounds for hypothetical imperatives only.

But suppose that there were something the existence of which in itself had absolute worth, something which, as an end in itself, could be a ground of definite laws. In it and only in it could lie the ground of a possible categorical imperative, i.e., of a practical law.

Now, I say, man and, in general, every rational being exists as an end in himself and not merely as a means to be arbitrarily used by this or that will. In all his actions, whether they are directed to himself or to other rational beings, he must always be regarded at the same time as an end. All objects of inclinations have only a conditional worth, for if the inclinations and the needs founded on them did not exist, their object would be without worth. The inclinations themselves as the sources of needs, however, are so lacking in absolute worth that the universal wish of every rational being must be indeed to free himself completely from them. Therefore, the worth of any objects to be obtained by our actions is at all times conditional. Beings whose existence does not depend on our will but on nature, if they are not rational beings, have only a relative worth as means and are therefore called "things"; on the other hand, rational beings are designated "persons" because their nature indicates that they are ends in themselves, i.e., things which may not be used merely as means. Such a being is thus an object of respect and, so far, restricts all [arbitrary] choice. Such beings are not merely subjective ends whose existence as a result of our action has a worth for us, but are objective ends, i.e., beings whose existence in itself is an end. Such an end is one for which no other end can be substituted, to which these beings should serve merely as means. For, without them, nothing of absolute worth could be found, and if all worth is conditional and thus contingent, no supreme practical principle for reason could be found anywhere.

Thus if there is to be a supreme practical principle and a categorical imperative for the human will, it must be one that forms an objective principle of the will from the conception of that which is necessarily an end for everyone because it is an end in itself. Hence this objective principle can serve . . . as a universal practical law. The ground of this principle is: rational nature exists as an end in itself. Man necessarily thinks of his own existence in this way; thus far it is a subjective principle of human actions. Also every other rational being thinks of his existence by means of the same rational ground which holds also for myself;[6] thus it is at the same time an objective principle from which, as supreme practical ground, it must be possible to derive all laws of the will. The practical imperative, therefore, is the following: Act so that you treat humanity, whether in your own person or in that of another, always as an end and never as a means only. Let us now see whether this can be achieved.

To return to our previous examples:

First, according to the concept of necessary duty to one's self, he who contemplates suicide will ask himself whether his action can be consistent with the idea of humanity as an end in itself. If, in order to escape from burdensome circumstances, he destroys himself, he uses a person merely as a means to maintain a tolerable condition up to the end of life. Man, however, is not a thing, and thus not something to be used merely as a means; he must always be regarded in all his actions as an end in himself. Therefore, I cannot dispose of man in my own person so as to mutilate, corrupt, or kill him. (It belongs to ethics proper to define more accurately this basic principle so as to avoid all misunderstanding, e.g., as to the amputation of limbs in order to preserve myself, or to exposing my life to danger in order to save it; I must, therefore, omit them here.)

Second, as concerns necessary or obligatory duties to others, he who intends a deceitful promise to others sees immediately that he intends to use another man merely as a means, without the latter containing the end in himself at the same time. For he whom I want to use for my own purposes by means of such a promise cannot possibly assent to my mode of acting . . . against him and cannot contain the end of this action in himself. This conflict against the principle of other men is even clearer if we cite examples of attacks on their freedom and property. For then it is clear that he who transgresses the rights of men intends to make use of the persons of others merely as a means, without considering that, as rational beings, they must always be esteemed at the same time as ends, i.e., only as beings who must be able to contain in themselves the end of the very same action.

Third, with regard to contingent (meritorious) duty to one's self, it is not sufficient that the action not conflict with humanity in our person as an end in itself; it must also harmonize with it. Now in humanity there are capacities for greater perfection which belong to the end of nature with respect to humanity in our own person; to neglect these might perhaps be consistent with the preservation of humanity as an end in itself but not with the furtherance of that end.

Fourth, with regard to meritorious duty to others, the natural end which all men have is their own happiness. Humanity might indeed exist if no one contributed to the happiness of others, provided he did not intentionally detract from it; but this harmony with humanity as an end in itself is only negative rather than positive if everyone does not also endeavor, so far as he can, to further the ends of others. For the ends of any person, who is an end in himself, must as far as possible also be my end, if that conception of an end in itself is to have its full effect on me. . . .

NOTES

1. The word "prudence" may be taken in two senses, and it may bear the name of prudence with reference to things of the world and private prudence. The former sense means the skill of a man in having an influence on others so as to use them for his own purposes. The latter is the ability to unite all these purposes to his own lasting advantage. The worth of the first is finally reduced to the latter, and of one who is prudent in the former sense but not in the latter we might better say that he is clever and cunning yet, on the whole, imprudent.

2. It seems to me that the proper meaning of the word "pragmatic" could be most accurately defined in this way. For sanctions which properly flow not from the law of states as necessary statutes but from provision for the general welfare are called pragmatic. A history is pragmatically composed when it teaches prudence, i.e., instructs the world how it could provide for its interest better than, or at least as well as, has been done in the past.

3. I connect a priori, and hence necessarily, the action with the will without supposing as a condition that there is any inclination [to the action] (though I do so only objectively, i.e., under the idea of a reason which would have complete power over all subjective motives). This is, therefore, a practical proposition which does not analytically derive the willing of an action from some other volition already presupposed (for we do not have such a perfect will); it rather connects it directly with the concept of the will of a rational being as something which is not contained within it.

4. A maxim is the subjective principle of acting and must be distinguished from the objective principle, i.e., the practical law. The former contains the practical rule which reason determines according to the conditions of the subject (often its ignorance or inclinations) and is thus the principle according to which the subject acts. The law, on the other hand, is the objective principle valid for every rational being, and the principle by which it ought to act, i.e., an imperative.

5. It must be noted here that I reserve the division of duties for a future *Metaphysics of Morals* and that the division here stands as only an arbitrary one (chosen in order to arrange my examples). For the rest, by a perfect duty I here understand a duty which permits no exception in the interest of inclination; thus I have not merely outer but also inner perfect duties. This runs contrary to the usage adopted in the schools, but I am not disposed to defend it here because it is all one to my purpose whether this is conceded or not.

6. Here I present this proposition as a postulate, but in the last section grounds for it will be found.

Kantian Approaches to Some Famine Problems*

ONORA O'NEILL

Onora O'Neill (1941–) is Principal of Newnham College, Cambridge. Her works include *Acting on Principle* and *Faces of Hunger.*

A SIMPLIFIED ACCOUNT OF KANT'S ETHICS

KANT'S MORAL THEORY has acquired the reputation of being forbiddingly difficult to understand and, once understood, excessively demanding in its requirements. I don't believe that this reputation has been wholly earned, and I am going to try to undermine it. In §§23–26 I shall try to reduce some of the difficulties, and in §§27–[29] I shall try to show the implications of a Kantian moral theory for action toward those who do or may suffer famine. Finally, I shall compare Kantian and utilitarian approaches and assess their strengths and weaknesses.

The main method by which I propose to avoid some of the difficulties of Kant's moral theory is by explaining only one part of the theory. This does not seem to me to be an irresponsible approach in this case. One of the things that makes Kant's moral theory hard to understand is that he gives a number of different versions of the principle that he calls the Supreme Principle of Morality, and these different versions don't look at all like one another. They also don't look at all like the utilitarians' Greatest Happiness Principle. But the Kantian principle is supposed to play a similar role in arguments about what to do.

Kant calls his Supreme Principle the *Categorical Imperative;* its various versions also have sonorous names. One is called the Formula of Universal Law; another is the Formula of the Kingdom of Ends. The one on which I shall concentrate is known as the *Formula of the End in Itself.* To understand why Kant thinks that these picturesquely named principles are equivalent to one another takes quite a lot of close and detailed analysis of Kant's philosophy. I shall avoid this and concentrate on showing the implications of this version of the Categorical Imperative.

THE FORMULA OF THE END IN ITSELF

Kant states the Formula of the End in Itself as follows:

> Act in such a way that you always treat humanity, whether in your own person or in the person of any other, never simply as a means but always at the same time as an end.

To understand this we need to know what it is to treat a person as a means or as an end. According to Kant, each of our acts reflects one or more *maxims.* The maxim of the act is the principle on which one sees oneself as acting. A maxim expresses a person's policy, or if he or she has no settled policy, the principle underlying the particular intention or decision on which he or she acts. Thus, a person who decides "This year I'll give 10 percent of my income to famine relief" has as a maxim the principle of tithing his or her income for famine relief. In practice, the difference between intentions and maxims is of

From Matters of Life and Death, *ed. T. Regan (New York: Random House, 1980), pp. 285–94. Reprinted by permission of the publisher.*

little importance, for given any intention, we can formulate the corresponding maxim by deleting references to particular times, places, and persons. In what follows I shall take the terms "maxim" and "intention" as equivalent.

Whenever we act intentionally, we have at least one maxim and can, if we reflect, state what it is. (There is of course room for self-deception here—"I'm only keeping the wolf from the door" we may claim as we wolf down enough to keep ourselves overweight, or, more to the point, enough to feed someone else who hasn't enough food.)

When we want to work out whether an act we propose to do is right or wrong, according to Kant, we should look at our maxims and not at how much misery or happiness the act is likely to produce, and whether it does better at increasing happiness than other available acts. We just have to check that the act we have in mind will not use anyone as a mere means, and, if possible, that it will treat other persons as ends in themselves.

USING PERSONS AS MERE MEANS

To use someone as a *mere means* is to involve them in a scheme of action *to which they could not in principle consent.* Kant does not say that there is anything wrong about using someone as a means. Evidently we have to do so in any cooperative scheme of action. If I cash a check I use the teller as a means, without whom I could not lay my hands on the cash; the teller in turn uses me as a means to earn his or her living. But in this case, each party consents to her or his part in the transaction. Kant would say that though they use one another as means, they do not use one another as *mere* means. Each person assumes that the other has maxims of his or her own and is not just a thing or a prop to be manipulated.

But there are other situations where one person uses another in a way to which the other could not in principle consent. For example, one person may make a promise to another with every intention of breaking it. If the promise is accepted, then the person to whom it was given must be ignorant of what the promisor's intention (maxim) really is. If one knew that the promisor did not intend to do what he or she was promising, one would, after all, not accept or rely on the promise. It would be as though there had been no promise made. Successful false promising depends on deceiving the person to whom the promise is made about what one's real maxim is. And since the person who is deceived doesn't know that real maxim, he or she can't in principle consent to his or her part in the proposed scheme of action. The person who is deceived is, as it were, a prop or a tool—a mere means—in the false promisor's scheme. A person who promises falsely treats the acceptor of the promise as a prop or a thing and not as a person. In Kant's view, it is this that makes false promising wrong.

One standard way of using others as mere means is by deceiving them. By getting someone involved in a business scheme or a criminal activity on false pretenses, or by giving a misleading account of what one is about, or by making a false promise or a fraudulent contract, one involves another in something to which he or she in principle cannot consent, since the scheme requires that he or she doesn't know what is going on. Another standard way of using others as mere means is by coercing them. If a rich or powerful person threatens a debtor with bankruptcy unless he or she joins in some scheme, then the creditor's intention is to coerce; and the debtor, if coerced, cannot consent to his or her part in the creditor's scheme. To make the example more specific: If a moneylender in an Indian village threatens not to renew a vital loan unless he is given the debtor's land, then he uses the debtor as a mere means. He coerces the debtor, who cannot truly consent to this "offer he can't refuse." (Of course the outward form of such transactions may look like ordinary commercial dealings, but we know very well that some offers and demands couched in that form are coercive.)

In Kant's view, acts that are done on maxims that require deception or coercion of others, and so cannot have the consent of those others (for consent precludes both deception and coercion), are wrong. When we act on such maxims, we treat others as mere means, as things rather than as ends in themselves. If we act on such maxims, our acts are not only wrong but unjust: such acts wrong the particular others who are deceived or coerced.

TREATING PERSONS AS ENDS IN THEMSELVES

Duties of justice are, in Kant's view (as in many others'), the most important of our duties. When we fail in these duties, we have used some other or others as mere means. But there are also cases where, though we do not use others as mere means, still we fail to use them as ends in themselves in the fullest possible way. To treat someone as an end in him or herself requires in the first place that one not use him or her as mere means, that one respect each as a rational person with his or her own maxims. But beyond that, one may also seek to foster others' plans and maxims by sharing some of their ends. To act beneficently is to seek others' happiness, therefore to intend to achieve some of the things that those others aim at with their maxims. If I want to make others happy, I will adopt maxims that not merely do not manipulate them but that foster some of their plans and activities. Beneficent acts try to achieve what others want. However, we cannot seek everything that others want; their wants are too numerous and diverse, and, of course, sometimes incompatible. It follows that beneficence has to be selective.

There is then quite a sharp distinction between the requirements of justice and of beneficence in Kantian ethics. Justice requires that we act on *no* maxims that use others as mere means. Beneficence requires that we act on *some* maxims that foster others' ends, though it is a matter for judgment and discretion which of their ends we foster. Some maxims no doubt ought not to be fostered because it would be unjust to do so. Kantians are not committed to working interminably through a list of happiness-producing and misery-reducing acts; but there are some acts whose obligatoriness utilitarians may need to debate as they try to compare total outcomes of different choices, to which Kantians are stringently bound. Kantians will claim that they have done nothing wrong if none of their acts is unjust, and that their duty is complete if in addition their life plans have in the circumstances been reasonably beneficent.

In making sure that they meet all the demands of justice, Kantians do not try to compare all available acts and see which has the best effects. They consider only the proposals for action that occur to them and check that these proposals use no other as mere means. If they do not, the act is permissible; if omitting the act would use another as mere means, the act is obligatory. Kant's theory has less scope than utilitarianism. Kantians do not claim to discover whether acts whose maxims they don't know fully are just. They may be reluctant to judge others' acts or policies that cannot be regarded as the maxim of any person or institution. They cannot rank acts in order of merit. Yet, the theory offers more precision than utilitarianism when data are scarce. One can usually tell whether one's act would use others as mere means, even when its impact on human happiness is thoroughly obscure.

KANTIAN DELIBERATIONS ON FAMINE PROBLEMS

The theory I have just sketched may seem to have little to say about famine problems. For it is a theory that forbids us to use others as mere means but does not require us to direct our benevolence first to those who suffer most. A conscientious Kantian, it seems, has only to avoid being unjust to those who suffer famine and can then be beneficent to those nearer home. He or she would not be obliged to help the starving, even if no others were equally distressed.

Kant's moral theory does make less massive demands on moral agents than utilitarian moral theory. On the other hand, it is somewhat clearer just what the more stringent demands are, and they are not negligible. We have here a contrast between a theory that makes massive but often indeterminate demands and a theory that makes fewer but less unambiguous demands and leaves other questions, in particular the allocation of beneficence, unresolved. We have also a contrast between a theory whose scope is comprehensive and one that is applicable only to persons acting intentionally and to those institutions that adopt policies, and so maxims. Kantian ethics is silent about the moral status of unintentional action; utilitarians seek to assess all consequences regardless of the intentions that led to them.

KANTIAN DUTIES OF JUSTICE IN TIMES OF FAMINE

In famine situations, Kantian moral theory requires unambiguously that we do no injustice. We should not act on any maxim that uses another as mere means, so we should neither deceive nor coerce others. Such a requirement can become quite exacting when the means of life are scarce, when persons can more easily be coerced, and when the advantage of gaining more than what is justly due to one is great. I shall give a list of acts that on Kantian principles it would be unjust to do, but that one might be strongly tempted to do in famine conditions.

I will begin with a list of acts that one might be tempted to do as a member of a famine-stricken population. First, where there is a rationing scheme, one ought not to cheat and seek to get more than one's share—any scheme of cheating will use someone as mere means. Nor may one take advantage of others' desperation to profiteer or divert goods onto the black market or to accumulate a fortune out of others' misfortunes. Transactions that are outwardly sales and purchases can be coercive when one party is desperate. All the forms of corruption that deceive or put pressure on others are also wrong: hoarding unallocated food, diverting relief supplies for private use, corruptly using one's influence to others' disadvantage. Such requirements are far from trivial and frequently violated in hard times. In severe famines, refraining from coercing and deceiving may risk one's own life and require the greatest courage.

Second, justice requires that in famine situations one still try to fulfill one's duties to particular others. For example, even in times of famine, a person has duties to try to provide for dependents. These duties may, tragically, be unfulfillable. If they are, Kantian ethical theory would not judge wrong the acts of a person who had done her or his best. There have no doubt been times in human history where there was nothing to be done except abandon the weak and old or to leave children to fend for themselves as best they might. But providing the supporter of dependents acts on maxims of attempting to meet their claims, he or she uses no others as mere means to his or her own survival and is not unjust. A conscientious attempt to meet the particular obligations one has undertaken may also require of one many further maxims of self-restraint and of endeavor—for example, it may require a conscientious attempt to avoid having (further) children; it may require contributing one's time and effort to programs of economic development. Where there is no other means to fulfill particular obligations, Kantian principles may require a generation of sacrifice. They will not, however, require one to seek to maximize the happiness of later generations but only to establish the modest security and prosperity needed for meeting present obligations.

The obligations of those who live with or near famine are undoubtedly stringent and exacting; for those who live further off it is rather harder to see what a Kantian moral theory demands. Might it not, for example, be permissible to do nothing at all about those suffering famine? Might one not ensure that one does nothing unjust to the victims of famine by adopting no maxims whatsoever that mention them? To do so would, at the least, require one to refrain from certain deceptive and coercive practices frequently employed during the European exploration and economic penetration of the now underdeveloped world and still not unknown. For example, it would be unjust to "purchase" valuable lands and resources from persons who don't understand commercial transactions or exclusive property rights or mineral rights, so do not understand that their acceptance of trinkets destroys their traditional economic pattern and way of life. The old adage "trade follows the flag" reminds us to how great an extent the economic penetration of the less-developed countries involved elements of coercion and deception, so was on Kantian principles unjust (regardless of whether or not the net effect has benefited the citizens of those countries).

Few persons in the developed world today find themselves faced with the possibility of adopting on a grand scale maxims of deceiving or coercing persons living in poverty. But at least some people find that their jobs require them to make decisions about investment and aid policies that enormously affect the lives of those nearest to famine. What does a commitment to Kantian moral theory demand of such persons?

It has become common in writings in ethics and social policy to distinguish between one's *personal responsibilities* and one's *role responsibilities.* So a person may say, "As an individual I sympathize, but in my official capacity I can do nothing"; or we may excuse persons' acts of coercion because they are acting in some particular capacity—e.g., as a soldier or a jailer. On the other hand, this distinction isn't made or accepted by everyone. At the Nuremberg trials of war criminals, the defense "I was only doing my job" was disallowed, at least for those whose command position meant that they had some discretion in what they did. Kantians generally would play down any distinction between a person's own responsibilities and his or her role responsibilities. They would not deny that in any capacity one is accountable for certain things for which as a private person one is not accountable. For example, the treasurer of an organization is accountable to the board and has to present periodic reports and to keep specified records. But if she fails to do one of these things for which she is held accountable she will be held responsible for that failure—it will be imputable to her as an individual. When we take on positions, we *add* to our responsibilities those that the job requires; but we do not lose those that are already required of us. Our social role or job gives us, on Kant's view, no license to use others as mere means; even business executives and aid officials and social revolutionaries will act unjustly, so wrongly, if they deceive or coerce—however benevolent their motives.

If persons are responsible for all their acts, it follows that it would be unjust for aid officials to coerce persons into accepting sterilization, wrong for them to use coercive power to achieve political advantages (such as military bases) or commercial advantages (such as trade agreements that will harm the other country). It would be wrong for the executives of large corporations to extort too high a price for continued operation employment and normal trading. Where a less-developed country is pushed to exempt a multinational corporation from tax laws, or to construct out of its meager tax revenues the infrastructure of roads, harbors, or airports (not to mention executive mansions) that the corporation—but perhaps not the country—needs, then one suspects that some coercion has been involved.

The problem with such judgments—and it is an immense problem—is that it is hard to identify coercion and deception in complicated institutional settings. It is not hard to understand what is coercive about one person threatening another with serious injury if he won't comply with the first person's suggestion. But it is not at all easy to tell where the outward forms of political and commercial negotiation—which often involve an element of threat—have become coercive. I can't here explore this fascinating question. But I think it is at least fairly clear that the preservation of the outward forms of negotiation, bargaining, and voluntary consent do *not* demonstrate that there is no coercion, especially when one party is vastly more powerful or the other in dire need. Just as our judiciary has a long tradition of voiding contracts and agreements on grounds of duress or incompetence of one of the parties, so one can imagine a tribunal of an analogous sort rejecting at least some treaties and agreements as coercive, despite the fact that they were negotiated between "sovereign" powers or their representatives. In particular, where such agreements were negotiated with some of the cruder deceptions and coercion of the early days of European economic expansion or the subtler coercions and deceptions of contemporary superpowers, it seems doubtful that the justice of the agreement could be sustained.

Justice, of course, is not everything, even for Kantians. But its demands are ones that they can reasonably strive to fulfill. They may have some uncertain moments—for example, does advocating cheap raw materials mean advocating an international trade system in which the less developed will continue to suffer the pressures of the developed world—or is it a benevolent policy that will maximize world trade and benefit all parties, while doing no one an injustice? But for Kantians, the important moral choices are above all those in which one acts directly, not those in which one decides which patterns of actions to encourage in others or in those institutions that one can influence. And such moral decisions include decisions about the benevolent acts that one will or will not do.

KANTIAN DUTIES OF BENEFICENCE IN TIMES OF FAMINE

The grounds of duties of beneficence are that such acts not merely don't use others as mere means but are acts that develop or promote others' ends and that, in particular, foster others' capacities to pursue ends, to be autonomous beings.

Clearly there are many opportunities for beneficence. But one area in which the *primary* task of developing others' capacity to pursue their own ends is particularly needed is in the parts of the world where extreme poverty and hunger leave people unable to pursue *any* of their other ends. Beneficence directed at putting people in a position to pursue whatever ends they may have has, for Kant, a stronger claim on us than beneficence directed at sharing ends with those who are already in a position to pursue varieties of ends. It would be nice if I bought a tennis racquet to play with my friend who is tennis mad and never has enough partners; but it is more important to make people able to plan their own lives to a minimal extent. It is nice to walk a second mile with someone who requests one's company; better to share a cloak with someone who may otherwise be too cold to make any journey. Though these suggestions are not a detailed set of instructions for the allocation of beneficence by Kantians, they show that relief of famine must stand very high among duties of beneficence.

THE LIMITS OF KANTIAN ETHICS: INTENTIONS AND RESULTS

Kantian ethics differs from utilitarian ethics both in its scope and in the precision with which it guides action. Every action, whether of a person or of an agency, can be assessed by utilitarian methods, provided only that information is available about all the consequences of the act. The theory has unlimited scope, but, owing to a lack of data, often lacks precision. Kantian ethics has a more restricted scope. Since it assesses actions by looking at the maxims of agents, it can only assess intentional acts. This means that it is most at home in assessing individuals' acts; but it can be extended to assess acts of agencies that (like corporations and governments and student unions) have decision-making procedures. It can do nothing to assess patterns of action that reflect no intention or policy, hence it cannot assess the acts of groups lacking decision-making procedures, such as the student movement, the women's movement, or the consumer movement.

It may seem a great limitation of Kantian ethics that it concentrates on intentions to the neglect of results. It might seem that all conscientious Kantians have to do is to make sure that they never intend to use others as mere means, and that they sometimes intend to foster others' ends. And, as we all know, good intentions sometimes lead to bad results, and correspondingly, bad intentions sometimes do no harm, or even produce good. If Hardin is right, the good intentions of those who feed the starving lead to dreadful results in the long run. If some traditional arguments in favor of capitalism are right, the greed and selfishness of the profit motive have produced unparalleled prosperity for many.

But such discrepancies between intentions and results are the exception and not the rule. For we cannot just *claim* that our intentions are good and do what we will. Our intentions reflect what we expect the immediate results of our action to be. Nobody credits the "intentions" of a couple who practice neither celibacy nor contraception but still insist "we never meant to have (more) children." Conception is likely (and known to be likely) in such cases. Where people's expressed intentions ignore the normal and predictable results of what they do, we infer that (if they are not amazingly ignorant) their words do not express their true intentions. The Formula of the End in Itself applies to the intentions on which one acts—not to some prettified version that one may avow. Provided this intention—the agent's real intention—uses no other as mere means, he or she does nothing unjust. If some of his or her intentions foster others' ends, then he or she is sometimes beneficent. It is therefore possible for people to test their proposals by Kantian arguments even when they lack the comprehensive causal knowledge that utilitarianism requires. Conscientious Kantians can work out whether they will be doing wrong by some act even though they know that their foresight is limited and that they may cause some harm or fail to cause some benefit. But they will not cause harms that they can foresee without this being reflected in their intentions.

Utilitarianism*

JOHN STUART MILL

John Stuart Mill (1806–1873) was one of the leading British moral philosophers of the nineteenth century. He also wrote important works on logic, economics, education, and feminism, and served for a time as a Member of Parliament.

1. GENERAL REMARKS

THERE ARE A FEW CIRCUMSTANCES, among those which make up the present condition of human knowledge, more unlike what might have been expected, or more significant of the backward state in which speculation on the most important subjects still lingers, than the little progress which has been made in the decision of the controversy respecting the criterion of right and wrong. From the dawn of philosophy, the question concerning the *summum bonum* or, what is the same thing, concerning the foundation of morality, has been accounted the main problem in speculative thought, has occupied the most gifted intellects and divided them into sects and schools, carrying on a vigorous warfare against one another. And, after more than two thousand years, the same discussions continue, philosophers are still ranged under the same contending banners, and neither thinkers nor mankind at large seem nearer to being unanimous on the subject than when the youth Socrates listened to the old Protagoras, and asserted (if Plato's dialogue be grounded on a real conversation) the theory of utilitarianism against the popular morality of the so-called Sophist.

It is true that similar confusion and uncertainty, and in some cases similar discordance, exist respecting the first principles of all the sciences, not excepting that which is deemed the most certain of them—mathematics—without much impairing, generally indeed without impairing at all, the trustworthiness of the conclusions of those sciences. An apparent anomaly, the explanation of which is that the detailed doctrines of a science are not usually deduced from, nor depend for their evidence upon,

**From J. S. Mill,* Utilitarianism, *Chaps. 1 and 2. First published in 1863.*

what are called its first principles. Were it not so, there would be no science more precarious, or whose conclusions were more insufficiently made out, than algebra, which derives none of its certainty from what are commonly taught to learners as its elements, since these, as laid down by some of its most eminent teachers, are as full of fictions as English law, and of mysteries as theology. The truths which are ultimately accepted as the first principles of a science are really the last results of metaphysical analysis practiced on the elementary notions with which the science is conversant, and their relation to the science is not that of foundations to an edifice, but of roots to a tree, which may perform their office equally well though they be never dug down to and exposed to light. But though, in science the particular truths precede the general theory, the contrary might be expected to be the case with a practical art, such as morals or legislation. All action is for the sake of some end; and rules of action, it seems natural to suppose, must take their whole character and color from the end to which they are subservient. When we engage in a pursuit, a clear and precise conception of what we are pursuing would seem to be the first thing we need, instead of the last we are to look forward to. A test of right and wrong must be the means, one would think, of ascertaining what is right or wrong, and not a consequence of having already ascertained it.

The difficulty is not avoided by having recourse to the popular theory of a natural faculty, a sense or instinct, informing us of right and wrong. For, besides that the existence of such a moral instinct is itself one of the matters in dispute, those believers in it who have any pretensions to philosophy have been obliged to abandon the idea that it discerns what is right or wrong in the particular case in hand, as our other senses discern the sight or sound actually present. Our moral faculty, according to all those of its interpreters who are entitled to the name of thinkers, supplies us only with the general principles of moral judgments; it is a branch of our reason, not of our sensitive faculty, and must be looked to for the abstract doctrines of morality, not for perception of it in the concrete. The intuitive, no less than what may be termed the inductive, school of ethics, insists on the necessity of general laws. They both agree that the morality of an individual action is not a question of direct perception, but of the application of a law to an individual case. They recognize also, to a great extent, the same moral laws, but differ as to their evidence, and the source from which they derive their authority. According to the one opinion, the principles of morals are evident *a priori*, requiring nothing to command assent, except that the meaning of the terms be understood. According to the other doctrine, right and wrong, as well as truth and falsehood, are questions of observation and experience. But both hold equally that morality must be deduced from principles, and the intuitive school affirm, as strongly as the inductive, that there is a science of morals. Yet they seldom attempt to make out a list of the *a priori* principles which are to serve as the premises of the science; still more rarely do they make any effort to reduce those various principles to one first principle, or common ground of obligation. They either assume the ordinary precepts of morals as of *a priori* authority, or they lay down as the common groundwork of those maxims some generality much less obviously authoritative than the maxims themselves, and which has never succeeded in gaining popular acceptance. Yet, to support their pretensions, there ought either to be some one fundamental principle or law at the root of all morality, or, if there be several, there should be a determinate order of precedence among them, and the one principle, or the rule for deciding between the various principles when they conflict, ought to be self-evident.

To inquire how far the bad effects of this deficiency have been mitigated in practice, or to what extent the moral beliefs of mankind have been vitiated or made uncertain by the absence of any distinct recognition of an ultimate standard, would imply a complete survey and criticism of past and present ethical doctrine. It would, however, be easy to show that whatever steadiness or consistency these moral beliefs have attained has been mainly due to the tacit influence of a standard not recognized. Although the nonexistence of an acknowledged first principle has made ethics not so much a guide as a consecration of men's actual sentiments, still, as men's sentiments, both of favor and of aversion, are greatly influenced by what they suppose to be the effects of things upon their happiness, the principle of utility, or, as Bentham latterly called it, the greatest-happiness principle, has had a large share in forming the moral doctrines even of those who most scornfully reject its authority. Nor is there any school of thought which refuses to admit that the influence of actions on happiness is a most material and even predominant consideration in many of the details of morals, however unwilling to acknowledge it as the fundamental principle of morality and the source of moral obligation. I might go much further, and say that, to all those *a priori* moralists who deem it necessary to argue at all, utilitarian arguments are indispensable. It is not my present purpose to criticize these thinkers, but I cannot help referring, for illustration, to a systematic treatise by one of the most illustrious of them—the *Metaphysics of Ethics,* by Kant. This remarkable man, whose system of thought will long remain one of the landmarks in the history of philosophical speculation, does, in the treatise in question, lay down a universal first principle as the origin and ground of moral obligation. It is this: "So act, that the rule on which thou actest would admit of being adopted as a law by all rational beings." But when he begins to deduce from this precept any of the actual duties of morality, he fails, almost grotesquely, to show that there would be any contradiction, any logical (not to say physical) impossibility, in the adoption by all rational beings of the most outrageously immoral rules of conduct. All he shows is that the *consequences* of their universal adoption would be such as no one would choose to incur.

On the present occasion, I shall, without further discussion of the other theories, attempt to contribute something towards the understanding and appreciation of the Utilitarian or Happiness theory and towards such proof as it is susceptible of. It is evident that this cannot be proof in the ordinary and popular meaning of the term. Questions of ultimate ends are not amenable to direct proof. Whatever can be proved to be good, must be so by being shown to be a means to something admitted to be good without proof. The medical art is proved to be good by its conducing to health, but how is it possible to prove that health is good? The art of music is good, for the reason, among others, that it produces pleasure, but what proof is it possible to give that pleasure is good? If, then, it is asserted that there is a comprehensive formula, including all things which are in themselves good, and that whatever else is good is not so as an end, but as a mean, the formula may be accepted or rejected, but is not a subject of what is commonly understood by proof. We are not, however, to infer that its acceptance or rejection must depend on blind impulse or arbitrary choice. There is a larger meaning of the word "proof," in which this question is as amenable to it as any other of the disputed questions of philosophy. The subject is within the cognizance of the rational faculty, and neither does that faculty deal with it solely in the way of intuition. Considerations may be presented capable of determining the intellect either to give or withhold its assent to the doctrine, and this is equivalent to proof.

We shall examine presently of what nature are these considerations, in what manner they apply to the case, and what rational grounds, therefore, can be given for accepting or rejecting the utilitarian formula. But it is a preliminary condition of rational acceptance or rejection that the formula should be correctly understood. I believe that the very imperfect notion ordinarily formed of its meaning is the chief obstacle which impedes its reception, and that, could it be cleared even from only the grosser misconceptions, the question would be greatly simplified, and a large proportion of its difficulties removed. Before, therefore, I attempt to enter into the philosophical grounds which can be given for assenting to the utilitarian standard, I shall offer some illustrations of the doctrine itself, with the view of showing more clearly what it is, distinguishing it from what it is not, and disposing of such of the practical objections to it as either originate in, or are closely connected with, mistaken interpretations of its meaning. Having thus prepared the ground, I shall afterwards endeavor to throw such light as I can upon the question, considered as one of philosophical theory.

2. WHAT UTILITARIANISM IS

A passing remark is all that needs be given to the ignorant blunder of supposing that those who stand up for utility, as the test of right and wrong, use the term in that restricted and merely colloquial sense in which utility is opposed to pleasure. An apology is due to the philosophical opponents of utilitarianism for even the momentary appearance of confounding them with any one capable of so absurd a misconception, which is the more extraordinary, inasmuch as the contrary accusation, of referring every thing to pleasure, and that, too, in its grossest form, is another of the common charges against utilitarianism, and, as has been pointedly remarked by an able writer, the same sort of persons, and often the very same persons, denounce the theory "as impracticably dry when the word 'utility' precedes the word 'pleasure,' and as too practicably voluptuous when the word 'pleasure' precedes the word 'utility.'" Those who know any thing about the matter are aware that every writer from Epicurus to Bentham who maintained the theory of utility meant by it, not something to be contradistinguished from pleasure, but pleasure itself, together with exemption from pain, and, instead of opposing the useful to the agreeable or the ornamental, have always declared that the useful means these, among other things. Yet the common herd, including the herd of writers, not only in newspapers and periodicals, but in books of weight and pretension, are perpetually falling into this shallow mistake. Having caught up the word "utilitarian," while knowing nothing whatever about it but its sound, they habitually express by it the rejection or the neglect of pleasure in some of its forms, of beauty, of ornament, or of amusement. Nor is the term thus ignorantly misapplied solely in disparagement, but occasionally in compliment, as though it implied superiority to frivolity and the mere pleasures of the moment. And this perverted use is the only one in which the word is popularly known, and the one from which the new generation are acquiring their sole notion of its meaning. Those who introduced the word, but who had for many years discontinued it as a distinctive appellation, may well feel themselves called upon to resume it, if by doing so they can hope to contribute any thing towards rescuing it from this utter degradation.

The creed which accepts as the foundation of morals Utility, or the Greatest-happiness Principle, holds that actions are right in proportion as they tend to promote happiness, wrong as they tend to produce the reverse of happiness. By happiness is intended pleasure and the absence of pain, by unhappiness, pain and the privation of pleasure. To give a clear view of the moral standard set up by the theory, much more requires to be said, in particular, what things it includes in the ideas of pain and pleasure, and to what extent this is left an open question. But these supplementary explanations do not affect the theory of life on which this theory of morality is grounded—namely, that pleasure and freedom from pain are the only things desirable as ends, and that all desirable things (which are as numerous in the utilitarian as in any other scheme) are desirable either for the pleasure inherent in themselves, or as means to the promotion of pleasure and the prevention of pain.

Now, such a theory of life excites in many minds, and among them in some of the most estimable in feeling and purpose, inveterate dislike. To suppose that life has (as they express it) no higher end than pleasure—no better and nobler object of desire and pursuit—they designate as utterly mean and groveling, as a doctrine worthy only of swine, to whom the followers of Epicurus were, at a very early period, contemptuously likened; and modern holders of the doctrine are occasionally made the subject of equally polite comparisons by its German, French, and English assailants.

When thus attacked, the Epicureans have always answered, that it is not they, but their accusers, who represent human nature in a degrading light, since the accusation supposes human beings to be capable of no pleasures except those of which swine are capable. If this supposition were true, the charge could not be gainsaid but would then be no longer an imputation; for, if the sources of pleasure were precisely the same to human beings and to swine, the rule of life which is good enough for the one would be good enough for the other. The comparison of the Epicurean life to that of beasts is felt as degrading, precisely because a beast's pleasures do not satisfy a human being's conceptions of happiness. Human beings have faculties more elevated than the animal appetites, and, when once made conscious of them, do not regard any thing as happiness which does not include their gratification. I do not, indeed, consider the Epicureans to have been by any means faultless in drawing out their scheme of consequences from the utilitarian principle. To do this in any sufficient manner, many Stoic as well as Christian elements require to be included. But there is no known Epicurean theory of life which does not assign to the pleasures of the intellect, of the feelings and imagination, and of the moral sentiments, a much higher value as pleasures than to those of mere sensation. It must be admitted, however, that utilitarian writers in general have placed the superiority of mental over bodily pleasures chiefly in the greater permanency, safety, uncostliness, etc., of the former—that is, in their circumstantial advantages rather than in their intrinsic nature. And, on all these points, utilitarians have fully proved their case, but they might have taken the other, and, as it may be called, higher ground, with entire consistency. It is quite compatible with the principle of utility to recognize the fact that some *kinds* of pleasure are more desirable and more valuable than others. It would be absurd that while, in estimating all other things, quality is considered as well as quantity, the estimation of pleasures should be supposed to depend on quantity alone.

If I am asked what I mean by difference of quality in pleasures, or what makes one pleasure more valuable than another, merely as a pleasure, except its being greater in amount, there is but one possible answer. Of two pleasures, if there be one to which all or almost all who have experience of both give a decided preference, irrespective of any feeling of moral obligation to prefer it, that is the more desirable pleasure. If one of the two is, by those who are competently acquainted with both, placed so far above the other that they prefer it, even though knowing it to be attended with a greater amount of discontent, and would not resign it for any quantity of the other pleasure which their nature is capable of, we are justified in ascribing to the preferred enjoyment a superiority in quality so far outweighing quantity, as to render it, in comparison, of small account.

Now, it is an unquestionable fact, that those who are equally acquainted with and equally capable of appreciating and enjoying both do give a most marked preference to the manner of existence which employs their higher faculties. Few human creatures would consent to be changed into any of the lower animals for a promise of the fullest allowance of a beast's pleasures; no intelligent human being would consent to be a fool, no instructed person would be an ignoramus, no person of feeling and conscience would be selfish and base, even though they should be persuaded that the fool, the dunce, or the rascal is better satisfied with his lot than they are with theirs. They would not resign what they possess more than he for the most complete satisfaction of all the desires which they have in common with him. If they ever fancy they would, it is only in cases of unhappiness so extreme that, to escape from it, they would exchange their lot for almost any other, however undesirable in their own eyes. A being of higher faculties requires more to make him happy, is capable probably of more acute suffering, and certainly accessible to it at more points, than one of an inferior type, but, in spite of these liabilities, he can never really wish to sink into what he feels to be a lower grade of existence. We may give what explanation we please of this unwillingness: we may attribute it to pride, a name which is given indiscriminately to some of the most and to some of the least estimable feelings of which mankind are capable; we may refer it to the love of liberty and personal independence—an appeal to which was with the Stoics one of the most effective means for the inculcation of it; to the love of power, or to the love of excitement, both of which do really enter into and contribute to it; but its most appropriate appellation is a sense of dignity, which all human beings possess in one form or other, and in some, though by no means in exact, proportion to their higher faculties, and which is so essential a part of the happiness of those in whom it is strong, that nothing which conflicts with it could be, otherwise than momentarily, an object of desire to them. Whoever supposes that this preference takes place at a sacrifice of happiness, that the superior being, in any thing like equal circumstances, is not happier than the inferior—confounds the two very different ideas of happiness and content. It is indisputable that the being whose capacities of enjoyment are low has the greatest chance of having them fully satisfied, and a highly endowed being will always feel that any happiness which he can look for, as the world is constituted, is imperfect. But he can learn to bear its imperfections, if they are at all bearable, and they will not make him envy the being who is indeed unconscious of the imperfections, but only because he feels not at all the good which those imperfections qualify. It is better to be a human being dissatisfied than a pig satisfied, better to be Socrates dissatisfied than a fool satisfied. And if the fool or the pig are of a different opinion, it is because they only know their own side of the question. The other party to the comparison knows both sides.

It may be objected that many who are capable of the higher pleasures occasionally, under the influence of temptation, postpone them to the lower. But this is quite compatible with a full appreciation of the intrinsic superiority of the higher. Men often, from infirmity of character, make their election for the nearer good, though they know it to be the less valuable, and this no less when the choice is between two bodily pleasures than when it is between bodily and mental. They pursue sensual indulgences to the injury of health, though perfectly aware that health is the greater good. It may be further objected, that many who begin with youthful enthusiasm for everything noble, as they advance in years sink into indolence and selfishness. But I do not believe that those who undergo this very common change voluntarily choose the lower description of pleasures in preference to the higher. I believe that, before they devote themselves exclusively to the one, they have already become incapable of the other. Capacity for the nobler feelings is in most natures a very tender plant, easily killed, not only by hostile influences but by mere want of sustenance, and, in the majority of young persons, it speedily dies away if the occupations to which their position in life has devoted them, and the society into which it has thrown them, are not favorable to keeping that higher capacity in exercise. Men lose their high aspirations as they lose their intellectual tastes, because they have not time or opportunity for indulging them, and they addict themselves to inferior pleasures, not because they deliberately prefer them, but because they are either the only ones to which they have access or the only ones which they are any longer capable of enjoying. It may be questioned whether any one who has remained equally susceptible to both classes of pleasures ever knowingly and calmly preferred the lower, though many in all ages have broken down in an ineffectual attempt to combine both.

From this verdict of the only competent judges, I apprehend there can be no appeal. On a question which is the best worth having of two pleasures, or which of two modes of existence is the most grateful to the feelings, apart from its moral attributes and from its consequences, the judgment of those who are qualified by knowledge of both, or, if they differ, that of the majority among them, must be admitted as final. And there needs be the less hesitation to accept this judgment respecting the quality of pleasures, since there is no other tribunal to be referred to even on the question of quantity. What means are there of determining which is the acutest of two pains, or the intensest of two pleasurable sensations, except the general suffrage of those who are familiar with both? Neither pains nor pleasures are homogeneous, and pain is always heterogeneous with pleasure. What is there to decide whether a particular pleasure is worth purchasing at the cost of a particular pain, except the feelings and judgment of the experienced? When, therefore, those feelings and judgment declare the pleasures derived from the higher faculties to be preferable *in kind,* apart from the question of intensity, to those of which the animal nature disjoined from the higher faculties is susceptible, they are entitled on this subject to the same regard.

I have dwelt on this point, as being a necessary part of a perfectly just conception of Utility or Happiness, considered as the directive rule of human conduct. But it is by no means an indispensable condition to the acceptance of the utilitarian standard, for that standard is not the agent's own greatest happiness, but the greatest amount of happiness altogether; and if it may possibly be doubted whether a noble character is always the happier for its nobleness, there can be no doubt that it makes other people happier, and that the world in general is immensely a gainer by it. Utilitarianism, therefore, could only attain its end by the general cultivation of nobleness of character, even if each individual were only benefited by the nobleness of others, and his own, so far as happiness is concerned, were a sheer deduction from the benefit. But the bare enunciation of such an absurdity as this last renders refutation superfluous.

According to the Greatest-happiness Principle, as above explained, the ultimate end with reference to and for the sake of which all other things are desirable (whether we are considering our own good or that of other people) is an existence exempt as far as possible from pain, and as rich as possible in enjoyments, both in point of quantity and quality; the test of quality, and the rule for measuring it against quantity, being the preference felt by those who in their opportunities of experience, to which must be added their habits of self-consciousness and self-observation, are best furnished with the means of comparison. This being, according to the utilitarian opinion, the end of human action is necessarily also the standard of morality; which may accordingly be defined, the rules and precepts for human conduct by the observance of which an existence such as has been described might be, to the greatest extent possible, secured to all mankind, and not to them only but, so far as the nature of things admits, to the whole sentient creation.

Against this doctrine, however, arises another class of objectors who say that happiness, in any form, cannot be the rational purpose of human life and action, because, in the first place, it is unattainable; and they contemptuously ask, What right hast thou to be happy? a question which Mr. Carlyle clinches by the addition, What right, a short time ago, hadst thou even *to be?* Next they say that men can do *without* happiness, that all noble human beings have felt this, and could not have become noble but by learning the lesson of *Entsagen* or renunciation, which lesson, thoroughly learned and submitted to, they affirm to be the beginning and necessary condition of all virtue.

The first of these objections would go to the root of the matter, were it well founded; for, if no happiness is to be had at all by human beings, the attainment of it cannot be the end of morality, or of any rational conduct. Though, even in that case, something might still be said for the utilitarian theory, since utility includes not solely the pursuit of happiness, but the prevention or mitigation of unhappiness; and, if the former aim be chimerical, there will be all the greater scope and more imperative need for the latter, so long at least as mankind think fit to live, and do not take refuge in the simultaneous act of suicide recommended under certain conditions by Novalis. When, however, it is thus positively asserted to be impossible that human life should be happy, the assertion, if not something like a verbal quibble, is at least an exaggeration. If by happiness be meant a continuity of highly pleasurable excitement, it is evident enough that this is impossible. A state of exalted pleasure lasts only moments, or in some cases, and with some intermissions, hours or days, and is the occasional brilliant flash of enjoyment, not its permanent and steady flame. Of this the philosophers who have taught that happiness is the end of life were as fully aware as those who taunt them. The happiness which they meant was not a life of rapture, but moments of such, in an existence made up of few and transitory pains, many and various pleasures, with a decided predominance of the active over the passive, and having, as the foundation of the whole, not to expect more from life than it is capable of bestowing. A life thus composed, to those who have been fortunate enough to obtain it, has always appeared worthy of the name of "happiness." And such an existence is even now the lot of many, during some considerable portion of their lives. The present wretched education and wretched social arrangements are the only real hindrance to its being attainable by almost all.

The objectors, perhaps, may doubt whether human beings, if taught to consider happiness as the end of life, would be satisfied with such a moderate share of it. But great numbers of mankind have been satisfied with much less. The main constituents of a satisfied life appear to be two, either of which by itself is often found sufficient for the purpose—tranquillity and excitement. With much tranquillity, many find that they can be content with very little pleasure; with much excitement, many can reconcile themselves to a considerable quantity of pain. There is assuredly no inherent impossibility in enabling even the mass of mankind to unite both, since the two are so far from being incompatible, that they are in natural alliance, the prolongation of either being a preparation for, and exciting a wish for, the other. It is only those in whom indolence amounts to a vice that do not desire excitement after an interval of repose; it is only those in whom the need of excitement is a disease, that feel the tranquillity which follows excitement dull and insipid, instead of pleasurable in direct proportion to the excitement which preceded it. When people who are tolerably fortunate in their outward lot do not find in life sufficient enjoyment to make it valuable to them, the cause generally is caring for nobody but themselves. To those who have neither public nor private affections, the excitements of life are much curtailed and, in any case, dwindle in value as the time approaches when all selfish interests must be terminated by death; while those who leave after them objects of personal affection, and especially those who have also cultivated a fellow feeling with the collective interests of mankind, retain as lively an interest in life on the eve of death as in the vigor of youth and health. Next to selfishness, the principal cause which makes life unsatisfactory is want of mental cultivation. A cultivated mind—I do not mean that of a philosopher, but any mind to which the fountains of knowledge have been opened, and which has been taught, in any tolerable degree, to exercise its faculties—finds sources of inexhaustible interest in all that surrounds it, in the objects of nature, the achievements of art, the imaginations of poetry, the incidents of history, the ways of mankind past and present, and their prospects in the future. It is possible, indeed, to become indifferent to all this, and that, too, without having exhausted a thousandth part of it, but only when one has had from the beginning no moral or human interest in these things, and has sought in them only the gratification of curiosity.

Now, there is absolutely no reason in the nature of things why an amount of mental culture sufficient to give an intelligent interest in these objects of contemplation should not be the inheritance of every one born in a civilized country. As little is there an inherent necessity that any human being should be a selfish egotist, devoid of every feeling or care but those which center in his own miserable individuality. Something far superior to this is sufficiently common even now to give ample earnest of what the human species may be made. Genuine private affections and a sincere interest in the public good are possible, though in unequal degrees, to every rightly brought up human being. In a world in which there is so much to interest, so much to enjoy, and so much also to correct and improve, every one who has this moderate amount of moral and intellectual requisites is capable of an existence which may be called enviable; and unless such a person, through bad laws or subjection to the will of others, is denied the liberty to use the sources of happiness within his reach, he will not fail to find this enviable existence, if he escape the positive evils of life, the great sources of physical and mental suffering—such as indigence, disease, and the unkindness, worthlessness, or premature loss, of objects of affection. The main stress of the problem lies, therefore, in the contest with these calamities, from which it is a rare good fortune entirely to escape, which, as things now are, cannot be obviated, and often cannot be in any material degree mitigated. Yet no one whose opinion deserves a moment's consideration can doubt that most of the great positive evils of the world are in themselves removable, and will, if human affairs continue to improve, be in the end reduced within narrow limits. Poverty, in any sense implying suffering, may be completely extinguished by the wisdom of society, combined with the good sense and providence of individuals. Even that most intractable of enemies, disease, may be indefinitely reduced in dimensions by good physical and moral education, and proper control of noxious influence, while the progress of science holds out a promise for the future of still more direct conquests over this detestable foe. And every advance in that direction relieves us from some, not only of the chances which cut short our own lives but, what concerns us still more, which deprive us of those in whom our happiness is wrapped up. As for vicissitudes of fortune and other disappointments connected with worldly circumstances, these are principally the effect either of gross imprudence, of ill-regulated desires, or of bad or imperfect social institutions. All the grand sources, in short, of human suffering are in a great degree, many of them almost entirely, conquerable by human care and effort; and though their removal is grievously slow, though a long succession of generations will perish in the breach before the conquest is completed, and this world becomes all that, if will and knowledge were not wanting, it might easily be made—yet every mind sufficiently intelligent and generous to bear a part, however small and unconspicuous, in the endeavor will draw a noble enjoyment from the contest itself, which he would not, for any bribe in the form of selfish indulgence, consent to be without.

And this leads to the true estimation of what is said by the objectors concerning the possibility and the obligation of learning to do without happiness. Unquestionably, it is possible to do without happiness; it is done involuntarily by nineteen-twentieths of mankind, even in those parts of our present world which are least deep in barbarism, and it often has to be done voluntarily by the hero or the martyr, for the sake of something which he prizes more than his individual happiness. But this something—what is it, unless the happiness of others, or some of the requisites of happiness? It is noble to be capable of resigning entirely one's own portion of happiness, or chances of it; but, after all, this self-sacrifice must be for some end; it is not its own end, and if we are told that its end is not happiness but virtue, which is better than happiness, I ask, Would the sacrifice be made if the hero or martyr did not believe that it would earn for others immunity from similar sacrifices? Would it be made if he thought that his renunciation of happiness for himself would produce no fruit for any of his fellow-creatures but to make their lot like his, and place them also in the condition of persons who have renounced happiness? All honor to those who can abnegate for themselves the personal enjoyment of life, when by such renunciation they contribute worthily to increase the amount of happiness in the world, but he who does it, or professes to do it, for any other purpose is no more deserving of admiration than the ascetic mounted on his pillar. He may be an inspiriting proof of what men *can* do, but assuredly not an example of what they *should*.

Though it is only in a very imperfect state of the world's arrangements that any one can best serve the happiness of others by the absolute sacrifice of his own, yet, so long as the world is in that imperfect state, I fully acknowledge that the readiness to make such a sacrifice is the highest virtue which can be found in man. I will add that in this condition of the world, paradoxical as the assertion may be, the conscious ability to do without happiness gives the best prospect of realizing such happiness as is attainable. For nothing except that consciousness can raise a person above the chances of life, by making him feel that, let fate and fortune do their worst, they have not power to subdue him; which, once felt, frees him from excess of anxiety concerning the evils of life, and enables him, like many a Stoic in the worst times of the Roman Empire, to cultivate in tranquillity the sources of satisfaction accessible to him, without concerning himself about the uncertainty of their duration, any more than about their inevitable end.

Meanwhile, let utilitarians never cease to claim the morality of self-devotion as a possession which belongs by as good a right to them as either to the Stoic or to the Transcendentalist. The utilitarian morality does recognize in human beings the power of sacrificing their own greatest good for the good of others. It only refuses to admit that the sacrifice is itself a good. A sacrifice which does not increase, or tend to increase, the sum total of happiness, it considers as wasted. The only self-renunciation which it applauds is devotion to the happiness, or to some of the means of happiness, of others, either of mankind collectively, or of individuals within the limits imposed by the collective interests of mankind.

I must again repeat what the assailants of utilitarianism seldom have the justice to acknowledge, that the happiness which forms the utilitarian standard of what is right in conduct is not the agent's own happiness but that of all concerned. As between his own happiness and that of others, utilitarianism requires him to be as strictly impartial as a disinterested and benevolent spectator. In the golden rule of Jesus of Nazareth, we read the complete spirit of the ethics of utility. To do as you would be done by, and to love your neighbor as yourself, constitute the ideal perfection of utilitarian morality. As the means of making the nearest approach to this ideal, utility would enjoin, first, that laws and social arrangements should place the happiness or (as, speaking practically, it may be called) the interest of every individual as nearly as possible in harmony with the interest of the whole; and secondly, that education and opinion, which have so vast a power over human character, should so use that power as to establish in the mind of every individual an indissoluble association between his own happiness and the good of the whole—especially between his own happiness, and the practice of such modes of conduct, negative and positive, as regard for the universal happiness prescribes—so that not only he may be unable to conceive the possibility of happiness to himself consistently with conduct opposed to the general good, but also that a direct impulse to promote the general good may be in every individual one of the habitual motives of action, and the sentiments connected therewith may fill a large and prominent place in every human being's sentient existence. If the impugners of the utilitarian morality represented it to their own minds in this its true character, I know not what recommendation possessed by any other morality they could possibly affirm to be wanting to it, what more beautiful or more exalted developments of human nature any other ethical system can be supposed to foster, or what springs of action, not accessible to the utilitarian, such systems rely on for giving effect to their mandates.

The objectors to utilitarianism cannot always be charged with representing it in a discreditable light. On the contrary, those among them who entertain any thing like a just idea of its disinterested character sometimes find fault with its standard as being too high for humanity. They say it is exacting too much to require that people shall always act from the inducement of promoting the general interests of society. But this is to mistake the very meaning of a standard of morals, and confound the rule of action with the motive of it. It is the business of ethics to tell us what are our duties or by what test we may know them, but no system of ethics requires that the sole motive of all we do shall be a feeling of duty; on the contrary, ninety-nine hundredths of all our actions are done from other motives, and rightly so done, if the rule of duty does not condemn them. It is the more unjust to utilitarianism that this particular misapprehension should be made a ground of objection to it, inasmuch as utilitarian moralists have gone beyond almost all others in affirming that the motive has nothing to do with the morality of the action though much with the worth of the agent. He who saves a fellow creature from drowning does what is morally right, whether his motive be duty or the hope of being paid for his trouble; he who betrays the friend that trusts him is guilty of a crime, even if his object be to serve another friend to whom he is under greater obligations.[2] But to speak only of actions done from the motive of duty, and in direct obedience to principle: it is a misapprehension of the utilitarian mode of thought to conceive it as implying that people should fix their minds upon so wide a generality as the world or society at large. The great majority of good actions are intended, not for the benefit of the world but for that of individuals, of which the good of the world is made up; and the thoughts of the most virtuous man need not on these occasions travel beyond the particular persons concerned, except so far as is necessary to assure himself that, in benefiting them, he is not violating the rights—that is, the legitimate and authorized expectations—of any one else. The multiplication of happiness is, according to the utilitarian ethics, the object of virtue; the occasions on which any person (except one in a thousand) has it in his power to do this on an extended scale—in other words, to be a public benefactor—are but exceptional, and on these occasions alone is he called on to consider public utility; in every other case, private utility, the interest or happiness of some few persons, is all he has to attend to. Those alone, the influence of whose actions extends to society in general, need concern themselves habitually about so large an object. In the case of abstinences indeed—of things which people forbear to do from moral considerations, though the consequences in the particular case might be beneficial—it would be unworthy of an intelligent agent not to be consciously aware that the action is of a class which, if practised generally, would be generally injurious, and that this is the ground of the obligation to abstain from it. The amount of regard for the public interest implied in this recognition is no greater than is demanded by every system of morals, for they all enjoin to abstain from whatever is manifestly pernicious to society.

The same considerations dispose of another reproach against the doctrine of utility, founded on a still grosser misconception of the purpose of a standard of morality, and of the very meaning of the words "right" and "wrong." It is often affirmed that utilitarianism renders men cold and unsympathizing, that it chills their moral feelings towards individuals, that it makes them regard only the dry and hard consideration of the consequences of actions, not taking into their moral estimate the qualities from which those actions emanate. If the assertion means that they do not allow their judgment respecting the rightness or wrongness of an action to be influenced by their opinion of the qualities of the person who does it, this is a complaint, not against utilitarianism but against having any standard of morality at all; for certainly no known ethical standard decides an action to be good or bad because it is done by a good or bad man, still less because done by an amiable, a brave, or a benevolent man, or the contrary. These considerations are relevant, not to the estimation of actions, but of persons, and there is nothing in the utilitarian theory inconsistent with the fact that there are other things which interest us in persons besides the rightness and wrongness of their actions. The Stoics indeed, with the paradoxical misuse of language which was part of their system and by which they strove to raise themselves above all concern about any thing but virtue, were fond of saying that he who has that has everything, that he, and one he, is rich, is beautiful, is a king. But no claim of this description is made for the virtuous man by the utilitarian doctrine. Utilitarians are quite aware that there are other desirable possessions and qualities besides virtue, and are perfectly willing to allow to all of them their full worth. They are also aware that a right action does not necessarily indicate a virtuous character, and that actions which are blamable often proceed from qualities entitled to praise. When this is apparent in any particular case, it modifies their estimation, not certainly of the act but of the agent. I grant that they are notwithstanding of opinion that, in the long run, the best proof of a good character is good actions, and resolutely refuse to consider any mental disposition as good, of which the predominant tendency is to produce bad conduct. This makes them unpopular with many people; but it is an unpopularity which they must share with every one who regards the distinction between right and wrong in a serious light, and the reproach is not one which a conscientious utilitarian need be anxious to repel.

If no more be meant by the objection than that many utilitarians look on the morality of actions, as measured by the utilitarian standards, with too exclusive a regard, and do not lay sufficient stress upon the other beauties of character which go towards making a human being lovable or admirable, this may be admitted. Utilitarians who have cultivated their moral feelings but not their sympathies nor their artistic perceptions, do fall into this mistake, and so do all other moralists under the same conditions. What can be said in excuse for other moralists is equally available for them, namely that, if there is to be any error, it is better that it should be on that side. As a matter of fact, we may affirm that among utilitarians, as among adherents of other systems, there is every imaginable degree of rigidity and of laxity in the application of their standard; some are even puritanically rigorous, while others are as indulgent as can possibly be desired by sinner or by sentimentalist. But on the whole, a doctrine which brings prominently forward the interest that mankind have in the repression and prevention of conduct which violates the moral law, is likely to be inferior to no other in turning the sanctions of opinion against such violations. It is true, the question, What does violate the moral law? is one on which those who recognize different standards of morality are likely now and then to differ. But difference of opinion on moral questions was not first introduced into the world by utilitarianism, while that doctrine does supply, if not always an easy, at all events a tangible and intelligible mode of deciding such differences.

It may not be superfluous to notice a few more of the common misapprehensions of utilitarian ethics, even those which are so obvious and gross that it might appear impossible for any person of candor and intelligence to fall into them, since persons even of considerable mental endowments often give themselves so little trouble to understand the bearings of any opinion against which they entertain a prejudice, and men are in general so little conscious of this voluntary ignorance as a defect, that the vulgarest misunderstandings of ethical doctrines are continually met with the deliberate writings of persons of the greatest pretensions both to high principle and to philosophy. We not uncommonly hear the doctrine of utility inveighed against as a *godless* doctrine. If it be necessary to say any thing at all against so mere an assumption, we may say that the question depends upon what idea we have formed of the moral character of the Deity. If it be a true belief that God desires, above all things, the happiness of his creatures, and that this was his purpose in their creation, utility is not only not a godless doctrine but more profoundly religious than any other. If it be meant that utilitarianism does not recognize the revealed will of God as the supreme law of morals, I answer that an utilitarian, who believes in the perfect goodness and wisdom of God, necessarily believes that whatever God has thought fit to reveal on the subject of morals must fulfil the requirements of utility in a supreme degree. But others besides utilitarians have been of opinion that the Christian revelation was intended, and is fitted, to inform the hearts and minds of mankind with a spirit which should enable them to find for themselves what is right and incline them to do it when found, rather than to tell them, except in a very general way, what it is, and that we need a doctrine of ethics, carefully followed out, to *interpret* to us the will of God. Whether this opinion is correct or not, it is superfluous here to discuss, since whatever aid religion, either natural or revealed, can afford to ethical investigation, is as open to the utilitarian moralist as to any other. He can use it as the testimony of God to the usefulness or hurtfulness of any given course of action, by as good a right as others can use it for the indication of a transcendental law, having no connection with usefulness or with happiness.

Again: Utility is often summarily stigmatized as an immoral doctrine by giving it the name of Expediency and, taking advantage of the popular use of that term, to contrast it with Principle. But the Expedient, in the sense in which it is opposed to the Right, generally means that which is expedient for the particular interest of the agent himself, as when a minister sacrifices the interests of his country to keep himself in place. When it means any thing better than this, it means that which is expedient for some immediate object, some temporary purpose, but which violates a rule whose observance is expedient in a much higher degree. The Expedient, in this sense, instead of being the same thing with the useful, is a branch of the hurtful. Thus it would often be expedient, for the purpose of getting over some momentary embarrassment or attaining some object immediately useful to ourselves or others, to tell a lie. But inasmuch as the cultivation in ourselves of a sensitive feeling on the subject of veracity is one of the most useful, and the enfeeblement of that feeling one of those most hurtful, things to which our conduct can be instrumental, and inasmuch as any, even unintentional, deviation from truth does that much towards weakening the trustworthiness of human assertion, which is not only the principal support of all present social well-being, but the insufficiency of which does more than any one thing that can be named to keep back civilization, virtue, every thing on which human happiness on the largest scale depends—we feel that the violation, for a present advantage, of a rule of such transcendent expediency is not expedient, and that he who, for the sake of a convenience to himself or to some other individual, does what depends on him to deprive mankind of the good, and inflict upon them the evil, involved in the greater or less reliance which they can place in each other's word, acts the part of one of their worst enemies. Yet that even this rule, sacred as it is, admits of possible exceptions is acknowledged by all moralists, the chief of which is, when the withholding of some fact (as of information from a malefactor, or of bad news from a person dangerously ill) would save an individual (especially an individual other than one's self) from great and unmerited evil and when the withholding can only be effected by denial. But in order that the exception may not extend itself beyond the need and may have the least possible effect in weakening reliance on veracity, it ought to be recognized and, if possible, its limits defined, and, if the principle of utility is good for any thing, it must be good for weighing these conflicting utilities against one another, and marking out the region within which one or the other preponderates.

Again: defenders of utility often find themselves called upon to reply to such objections as this—that there is not time, previous to action, for calculating and weighing the effects of any line of conduct on the general happiness. This is exactly as if any one were to say that it is impossible to guide our conduct by Christianity, because there is not time, on every occasion on which any thing has to be done, to read through the Old and New Testaments. The answer to the objection is that there has been ample time, namely, the whole past duration of the human species. During all that time, mankind have been learning by experience the tendencies of actions, on which experience all the prudence as well as all the morality of life are dependent. People talk as if the commencement of this course of experience had hitherto been put off and as if, at the moment when some man feels tempted to meddle with the property or life of another, he had to begin considering for the first time whether murder and theft are injurious to human happiness. Even then, I do not think that he would find the question very puzzling, but at all events the matter is now done to his hand. It is truly a whimsical supposition that, if mankind were agreed in considering utility to be the test of morality, they would remain without any agreement as to what *is* useful, and would take no measures for having their notions on the subject taught to the young and enforced by law and opinion. There is no difficulty in proving any ethical standard whatever to work ill, if we suppose universal idiocy to be conjoined with it; but on any hypothesis short of that, mankind must by this time have acquired positive beliefs as to the effects of some actions on their happiness, and the beliefs which have thus come down are the rules of morality for the multitude, and for the philosopher, until he has succeeded in finding better. That philosophers might easily do this, even now, on many subjects, that the received code of ethics is by no means of divine right, and that mankind have still much to learn as to the effects of actions on the general happiness—I admit or, rather, earnestly maintain. The corollaries from the principle of utility, like the precepts of every practical art, admit of indefinite improvement and, in a progressive state of the human mind, their improvement is perpetually going on. But to consider the rules of morality as improvable is one thing; to pass over the intermediate generalizations entirely, and endeavor to test each individual action directly by the first principle, is another. It is a strange notion, that the acknowledgment of a first principle is inconsistent with the admission of secondary ones. To inform a traveler respecting the place of his ultimate destination is not to forbid the use of landmarks and direction posts on the way. The proposition that happiness is the end and aim of morality does not mean that no road ought to be laid down to that goal, or that persons going thither should not be advised to take one direction rather than another. Men really ought to leave off talking a kind of nonsense on this subject which they would neither talk nor listen to on other matters of practical concernment. Nobody argues that the art of navigation is not founded on astronomy, because sailors cannot wait to calculate the "Nautical Almanac." Being rational creatures, they go to sea with it ready calculated, and all rational creatures go out upon the sea of life with their minds made up on the common questions of right and wrong, as well as on many of the far more difficult questions of wise and foolish. And this, as long as foresight is a human quality, it is to be presumed they will continue to do. Whatever we adopt as the fundamental principle of morality, we require subordinate principles to apply it by; the impossibility of doing without them, being common to all systems, can afford no argument against any one in particular; but gravely to argue as if no such secondary principles could be had, and as if mankind had remained till now and always must remain without drawing any general conclusions from the experience of human life, is as high a pitch, I think, as absurdity has ever reached in philosophical controversy.

The remainder of the stock arguments against utilitarianism mostly consist in laying to its charge the common infirmities of human nature, and the general difficulties which embarrass conscientious persons in shaping their course through life. We are told that an utilitarian will be apt to make his own particular case an exception to moral rules and, when under temptation, will see an utility in the breach of a rule greater than he will see in its observance. But is utility the only creed which is able to furnish us with excuses for evil-doing, and means of cheating our own conscience? They are afforded in abundance by all doctrines which recognize as a fact in morals the existence of conflicting considerations, which all doctrines do that have been believed by sane persons. It is not the fault of any creed, but of the complicated nature of human affairs, that rules of conduct cannot be so framed as to require no exceptions, and that hardly any kind of action can safely be laid down as either always obligatory or always condemnable. There is no ethical creed which does not temper the rigidity of its laws by giving a certain latitude, under the moral responsibility of the agent, for accommodation to peculiarities of circumstances and, under every creed, at the opening thus made, self-deception and dishonest casuistry get in. There exists no moral system under which there do not arise unequivocal cases of conflicting obligation. These are the real difficulties, the knotty points both in the theory of ethics and in the conscientious guidance of personal conduct. They are overcome practically with greater or with less success according to the intellect and virtue of the individual, but it can hardly be pretended that any one will be the less qualified for dealing with them, from possessing an ultimate standard to which conflicting rights and duties can be referred. If utility is the ultimate source of moral obligations, utility may be invoked to decide between them when their demands are incompatible. Though the application of the standard may be difficult, it is better than none at all; while in other systems, the moral laws all claiming independent authority, there is no common umpire entitled to interfere between them, their claims to precedence one over another rest on little better than sophistry, and unless determined, as they generally are, by the unacknowledged influence of considerations of utility, afford a free scope for the action of personal desires and partialities. We must remember that only in these cases of conflict between secondary principles is it requisite that first principles should be appealed to. There is no case of moral obligation in which some secondary principle is not involved and, if only one, there can seldom be any real doubt which one it is, in the mind of any person by whom the principle itself is recognized.

Famine, Affluence, and Morality*

PETER SINGER

Peter Singer (1946–), author of the best-selling *Animal Liberation,* teaches moral philosophy at Monash University in Australia.

As I WRITE THIS, in November 1971, people are dying in East Bengal from lack of food, shelter, and medical care. The suffering and death that are occurring there now are not inevitable, not unavoidable in any fatalistic sense of the term. Constant poverty, a cyclone, and a civil war have turned at least nine million people into destitute refugees; nevertheless, it is not beyond the capacity of the richer nations to give enough assistance to reduce any further suffering to very small proportions. The decisions and actions of human beings can prevent this kind of suffering. Unfortunately, human beings have not made the necessary decisions. At the individual level, people have, with very few exceptions, not responded to the situation in any significant way. Generally speaking, people have not given large sums to relief funds; they have not written to their parliamentary representatives demanding increased government assistance; they have not demonstrated in the streets, held symbolic fasts, or done anything else directed toward providing the refugees with the means to satisfy their essential needs. At the government level, no government has given the sort of massive aid that would enable the refugees to survive for more than a few days. Britain, for instance, has given rather more than most countries. It has, to date, given £14,750,000. For comparative purposes, Britain's share of the nonrecoverable development costs of the Anglo-French Concorde project is already in excess of £275,000,000, and on present estimates will reach £440,000,000. The implication is that the British government values a supersonic transport more than thirty times as highly as it values the lives of the nine million refugees. Australia is another country which, on a per capita basis, is well up in the "aid to Bengal" table. Australia's aid, however, amounts to less than one-twelfth of the cost of Sydney's new opera house. The total amount given, from all sources, now stands at about £65,000,000. The estimated cost of keeping the refugees alive for one year is £464,000,000. Most of the refugees have now been in the camps for more than six months. The World Bank has said that India needs a minimum of £300,000,000 in assistance from other countries before the end of the year. It seems obvious that assistance on this scale will not be forthcoming. India will be forced to choose between letting the refugees starve or diverting funds from her own development program, which will mean that more of her own people will starve in the future.[1]

These are the essential facts about the present situation in Bengal. So far as it concerns us here, there is nothing unique about this situation except its magnitude. The Bengal emergency is just the latest and most acute of a series of major emergencies in various parts of the world, arising both from natural and from man-made causes. There are also many parts of the world in which people die from malnutrition and lack of food independent of any special emergency. I take Bengal as my example only because it is the present concern, and because the size of the problem has ensured that it has been given adequate publicity. Neither individuals nor governments can claim to be unaware of what is happening there.

What are the moral implications of a situation like this? In what follows, I shall argue that the way people in relatively affluent countries react to a situation like that in Bengal cannot be justified; indeed, the whole way we look at moral issues—our moral conceptual scheme—needs to be altered, and with it, the way of life that has come to be taken for granted in our society.

In arguing for this conclusion I will not, of course, claim to be morally neutral. I shall, however, try to argue for the moral position that I take, so that anyone who accepts certain assumptions, to be made explicit, will, I hope, accept my conclusion.

I begin with the assumption that suffering and death from lack of food, shelter, and medical care are bad. I think most people will agree about this, although one may reach the same view by different routes. I shall not argue for this view. People can hold all sorts of eccentric positions, and perhaps from some of them it would not follow that death by starvation is in itself bad. It is difficult, perhaps impossible, to refute such positions, and so for brevity I will henceforth take this assumption as accepted. Those who disagree need read no further.

My next point is this: if it is in our power to prevent something bad from happening, without thereby sacrificing anything of comparable moral importance, we ought, morally, to do it. By "without sacrificing anything of comparable moral importance" I mean without causing anything else comparably bad to happen, or doing something that is wrong in itself, or failing to promote some moral good, comparable in significance to the bad thing that we can prevent. This principle seems almost as uncontroversial as the last one. It requires us only to prevent what is bad, and not to promote what is good, and it requires this of us only when we can do it without sacrificing anything that is, from the moral point of view, comparably important. I could even, as far as the application of my argument to the Bengal emergency is concerned, qualify the point so as to make it: if it is in our power to prevent something very bad from happening, without thereby sacrificing anything morally significant, we ought, morally, to do it. An application of this principle would be as follows: if I am walking past a shallow pond and see a child drowning in it, I ought to wade in and pull the child out. This will mean getting my clothes muddy, but this is insignificant, while the death of the child would presumably be a very bad thing.

The uncontroversial appearance of the principle just stated is deceptive. If it were acted upon, even in its qualified form, our lives, our society, and our world would be fundamentally changed. For the principle takes, firstly, no account of proximity or distance. It makes no moral difference whether the person I can help is a neighbor's child ten yards from me or a Bengali whose name I shall never know, ten thousand miles away. Secondly, the principle makes no distinction between cases in which I am the only person who could possibly do anything and cases in which I am just one among millions in the same position.

I do not think I need to say much in defense of the refusal to take proximity and distance into account. The fact that a person is physically near to us, so that we have personal contact with him, may make it more likely that we *shall* assist him, but this does not show that we *ought* to help him rather than another who happens to be further away. If we accept any principle of impartiality, universalizability, equality, or whatever, we cannot discriminate against someone merely because he is far away from us (or we are far away from him). Admittedly, it is possible that we are in a better position to judge what needs to be done to help a person near to us than one far away, and perhaps also to provide the assistance we judge to be necessary. If this were the case, it would be a reason for helping those near to us first. This may once have been a justification for being more concerned with the poor in one's own town than with the famine victims in India. Unfortunately for those who like to keep their moral responsibilities limited, instant communication and swift transportation have changed the situation. From the moral point of view, the development of the world into a "global village" has made an important, though still unrecognized, difference to our moral situation. Expert observers and supervisors, sent out by famine relief organizations or permanently stationed in famine-prone areas, can direct our aid to a refugee in Bengal almost as effectively as we could get it to someone in our own block. There would seem, therefore, to be no possible justification for discriminating on geographical grounds.

There may be a greater need to defend the second implication of my principle—that the fact that there are millions of other people in the same position, in respect to the Bengali refugees, as I am, does not make the situation significantly different from a situation in which I am the only person who can prevent something very bad from occurring. Again, of course, I admit that there is a psychological difference between the cases; one feels less guilty about doing nothing if one can point to others, similarly placed, who have also done nothing. Yet this can make no real difference to our moral obligations.[2] Should I consider that I am less obliged to pull the drowning child out of the pond if on looking around I see other people, no further away than I am, who have also noticed the child but are doing nothing? One has only to ask this question to see the absurdity of the view that numbers lessen obligation. It is a view that is an ideal excuse for inactivity; unfortunately most of the major evils—poverty, overpopulation, pollution—are problems in which everyone is almost equally involved.

The view that numbers do make a difference can be made plausible if stated in this way: if everyone in circumstances like mine gave £5 to the Bengal Relief Fund, there would be enough to provide food, shelter, and medical care for the refugees; there is no reason why I should give more than anyone else in the same circumstances as I am; therefore I have no obligation to give more than £5. Each premise in this argument is true, and the argument looks sound. It may convince us, unless we notice that it is based on a hypothetical premise, although the conclusion is not stated hypothetically. The argument would be sound if the conclusion were: if everyone in circumstances like mine were to give £5, I would have no obligation to give more than £5. If the conclusion were so stated, however, it would be obvious that the argument has no bearing on a situation in which it is not the case that everyone else gives £5. This, of course, is the actual situation. It is more or less certain that not everyone in circumstances like mine will give £5. So there will not be enough to provide the needed food, shelter, and medical care. Therefore by giving more than £5 I will prevent more suffering than I would if I gave just £5.

It might be thought that this argument has an absurd consequence. Since the situation appears to be that very few people are likely to give substantial amounts, it follows that I and everyone else in similar circumstances ought to give as much as possible, that is, at least up to the point at which by giving more one would begin to cause serious suffering for oneself and one's dependents—perhaps even beyond this point to the point of marginal utility, at which by giving more one would cause oneself and one's dependents as much suffering as one would prevent in Bengal. If everyone does this, however, there will be more than can be used for the benefit of the refugees, and some of the sacrifice will have been unnecessary. Thus, if everyone does what he ought to do, the result will not be as good as it would be if everyone did a little less than he ought to do, or if only some do all that they ought to do.

The paradox here arises only if we assume that the actions in question—sending money to the relief funds—are performed more or less simultaneously, and are also unexpected. For if it is to be expected that everyone is going to contribute something, then clearly each is not obliged to give as much as he would have been obliged to had others not been giving too. And if everyone is not acting more or less simultaneously, then those giving later will know how much more is needed, and will have no obligation to give more than is necessary to reach this amount. To say this is not to deny the principle that people in the same circumstances have the same obligations, but to point out that the fact that others have given, or may be expected to give, is a relevant circumstance: those giving after it has become known that many others are giving and those giving before are not in the same circumstances. So the seemingly absurd consequence of the principle I have put forward can occur only if people are in error about the actual circumstances—that is, if they think they are giving when others are not, but in fact they are giving when others are. The result of everyone doing what he really ought to do cannot be worse than the result of everyone doing less than he ought to do, although the result of everyone doing what he reasonably believes he ought to do could be.

If my argument so far has been sound, neither our distance from a preventable evil nor the number of other people who, in respect to that evil, are in the same situation as we are, lessens our obligation to mitigate or prevent that evil. I shall therefore take as established the principle I asserted earlier. As I have already said, I need to assert it only in its qualified form: if it is in our power to prevent something very bad from happening, without thereby sacrificing anything else morally significant, we ought, morally, to do it.

The outcome of this argument is that our traditional moral categories are upset. The traditional distinction between duty and charity cannot be drawn, or at least, not in the place we normally draw it. Giving money to the Bengal Relief Fund is regarded as an act of charity in our society. The bodies which collect money are known as "charities." These organizations see themselves in this way—if you send them a check, you will be thanked for your "generosity." Because giving money is regarded as an act of charity, it is not thought that there is anything wrong with not giving. The charitable man may be praised, but the man who is not charitable is not condemned. People do not feel in any way ashamed or guilty about spending money on new clothes or a new car instead of giving it to famine relief. (Indeed, the alternative does not occur to them.) This way of looking at the matter cannot be justified. When we buy new clothes not to keep ourselves warm but to look "well-dressed" we are not providing for any important need. We would not be sacrificing anything significant if we were to continue to wear our old clothes, and give the money to famine relief. By doing so, we would be preventing another person from starving. It follows from what I have said earlier that we ought to give money away, rather than spend it on clothes which we do not need to keep us warm. To do so is not charitable, or generous. Nor is it the kind of act which philosophers and theologians have called "supererogatory"—an act which it would be good to do, but not wrong not to do. On the contrary, we ought to give the money away, and it is wrong not to do so.

I am not maintaining that there are no acts which are charitable, or that there are no acts which it would be good to do but not wrong not to do. It may be possible to redraw the distinction between duty and charity in some other place. All I am arguing here is that the present way of drawing the distinction, which makes it an act of charity for a man living at the level of affluence which most people in the "developed nations" enjoy to give money to save someone else from starvation, cannot be supported. It is beyond the scope of my argument to consider whether the distinction should be redrawn or abolished altogether. There would be many other possible ways of drawing the distinction—for instance, one might decide that it is good to make other people as happy as possible, but not wrong not to do so.

Despite the limited nature of the revision in our moral conceptual scheme which I am proposing, the revision would, given the extent of both affluence and famine in the world today, have radical implications. These implications may lead to further objections, distinct from those I have already considered. I shall discuss two of these.

One objection to the position I have taken might be simply that it is too drastic a revision of our moral scheme. People do not ordinarily judge in the way I have suggested they should. Most people reserve their moral condemnation for those who violate some moral norm, such as the norm against taking another person's property. They do not condemn those who indulge in luxury instead of giving to famine relief. But given that I did not set out to present a morally neutral description of the way people make moral judgments, the way people do in fact judge has nothing to do with the validity of my conclusion. My conclusion follows from the principle which I advanced earlier, and unless that principle is rejected, or the arguments shown to be unsound, I think the conclusion must stand, however strange it appears.

It might, nevertheless, be interesting to consider why our society, and most other societies, do judge differently from the way I have suggested they should. In a well-known article, J. O. Urmson suggests that the imperatives of duty, which tell us what we must do, as distinct from what it would be good to do but not wrong not to do, function so as to prohibit behavior that is intolerable if men are to live together in society.[3] This may explain the origin and continued existence of the present division between acts of duty and acts of charity. Moral attitudes are shaped by the needs of society, and no doubt society needs people who will observe the rules that make social existence tolerable. From the point of view of a particular society, it is essential to prevent violations of norms against killing, stealing, and so on. It is quite inessential, however, to help people outside one's own society.

If this is an explanation of our common distinction between duty and supererogation, however, it is not a justification of it. The moral point of view requires us to look beyond the interests of our own society. Previously, as I have already mentioned, this may hardly have been feasible, but it is quite feasible now. From the moral point of view, the prevention of the starvation of millions of people outside our society must be considered at least as pressing as the upholding of property norms within our society.

It has been argued by some writers, among them Sidgwick and Urmson, that we need to have a basic moral code which is not too far beyond the capacities of the ordinary man, for otherwise there will be a general breakdown of compliance with the moral code. Crudely stated, this argument suggests that if we tell people that they ought to refrain from murder and give everything they do not really need to famine relief, they will do neither, whereas if we tell them that they ought to refrain from murder and that it is good to give to famine relief but not wrong not to do so, they will at least refrain from murder. The issue here is: Where should we draw the line between conduct that is required and conduct that is good although not required, so as to get the best possible result? This would seem to be an empirical question, although a very difficult one. One objection to the Sidgwick-Urmson line of argument is that it takes insufficient account of the effect that moral standards can have on the decisions we make. Given a society in which a wealthy man who gives five percent of his income to famine relief is regarded as most generous, it is not surprising that a proposal that we all ought to give away half our incomes will be thought to be absurdly unrealistic. In a society which held that no man should have more than enough while others have less than they need, such a proposal might seem narrow-minded. What it is possible for a man to do and what he is likely to do are both, I think, very greatly influenced by what people around him are doing and expecting him to do. In any case, the possibility that by spreading the idea that we ought to be doing very much more than we are to relieve famine we shall bring about a general breakdown of moral behavior seems remote. If the stakes are an end to widespread starvation, it is worth the risk. Finally, it should be emphasized that these considerations are relevant only to the issue of what we should require from others, and not to what we ourselves ought to do.

The second objection to my attack on the present distinction between duty and charity is one which has from time to time been made against utilitarianism. It follows from some forms of utilitarian theory that we all ought, morally, to be working full time to increase the balance of happiness over misery. The position I have taken here would not lead to this conclusion in all circumstances, for if there were no bad occurrences that we could prevent without sacrificing something of comparable moral importance, my argument would have no application. Given the present conditions in many parts of the world, however, it does follow from my argument that we ought, morally, to be working full time to relieve great suffering of the sort that occurs as a result of famine or other disasters. Of course, mitigating circumstances can be adduced—for instance, that if we wear ourselves out through overwork, we shall be less effective than we would otherwise have been. Nevertheless, when all considerations of this sort have been taken into account, the conclusion remains: we ought to be preventing as much suffering as we can without sacrificing something else of comparable moral importance. This conclusion is one which we may be reluctant to face. I cannot see, though, why it should be regarded as a criticism of the position for which I have argued, rather than a criticism of our ordinary standards of behavior. Since most people are self-interested to some degree, very few of us are likely to do everything that we ought to do. It would, however, hardly be honest to take this as evidence that it is not the case that we ought to do it.

It may still be thought that my conclusions are so wildly out of line with what everyone else thinks and has always thought that there must be something wrong with the argument somewhere. In order to show that my conclusions, while certainly contrary to contemporary Western moral standards, would not have seemed so extraordinary at other times and in other places, I would like to quote a passage from a writer not normally thought of as a way-out radical, Thomas Aquinas.

> Now, according to the natural order instituted by divine providence, material goods are provided for the satisfaction of human needs. Therefore the division and appropriation of property, which proceeds from human law, must not hinder the satisfaction of man's necessity from such goods. Equally, whatever a man has in super-abundance is owed, of natural right, to the poor for their sustenance. So Ambrosius says, and it is also to be found in the *Decretum Gratiani:* "The bread which you withhold belongs to the hungry; the clothing you shut away,

> to the naked; and the money you bury in the earth is the redemption and freedom of the penniless."[4]

I now want to consider a number of points, more practical than philosophical, which are relevant to the application of the moral conclusion we have reached. These points challenge not the idea that we ought to be doing all we can to prevent starvation, but the idea that giving away a great deal of money is the best means to this end.

It is sometimes said that overseas aid should be a government responsibility, and that therefore one ought not to give to privately run charities. Giving privately, it is said, allows the government and the noncontributing members of society to escape their responsibilities.

This argument seems to assume that the more people there are who give to privately organized famine relief funds, the less likely it is that the government will take over full responsibility for such aid. This assumption is unsupported, and does not strike me as at all plausible. The opposite view—that if no one gives voluntarily, a government will assume that its citizens are uninterested in famine relief and would not wish to be forced into giving aid—seems more plausible. In any case, unless there were a definite probability that by refusing to give one would be helping to bring about massive government assistance, people who do refuse to make voluntary contributions are refusing to prevent a certain amount of suffering without being able to point to any tangible beneficial consequence of their refusal. So the onus of showing how their refusal will bring about government action is on those who refuse to give.

I do not, of course, want to dispute the contention that governments of affluent nations should be giving many times the amount of genuine, no-strings-attached aid that they are giving now. I agree, too, that giving privately is not enough, and that we ought to be campaigning actively for entirely new standards for both public and private contributions to famine relief. Indeed, I would sympathize with someone who thought that campaigning was more important than giving oneself, although I doubt whether preaching what one does not practice would be very effective. Unfortunately, for many people the idea that "it's the government's responsibility" is a reason for not giving which does not appear to entail any political action either.

Another, more serious reason for not giving to famine relief funds is that until there is effective population control, relieving famine merely postpones starvation. If we save the Bengal refugees now, others, perhaps the children of these refugees, will face starvation in a few years' time. In support of this, one may cite the now well-known facts about the population explosion and the relatively limited scope for expanded production.

This point, like the previous one, is an argument against relieving suffering that is happening now, because of a belief about what might happen in the future; it is unlike the previous point in that very good evidence can be adduced in support of this belief about the future. I will not go into the evidence here. I accept that the earth cannot support indefinitely a population rising at the present rate. This certainly poses a problem for anyone who thinks it important to prevent famine. Again, however, one could accept the argument without drawing the conclusion that it absolves one from any obligation to do anything to prevent famine. The conclusion that should be drawn is that the best means of preventing famine, in the long run, is population control. It would then follow from the position reached earlier that one ought to be doing all one can to promote population control (unless one held that all forms of population control were wrong in themselves, or would have significantly bad consequences). Since there are organizations working specifically for population control, one would then support them rather than more orthodox methods of preventing famine.

A third point raised by the conclusion reached earlier relates to the question of just how much we all ought to be giving away. One possibility, which has already been mentioned, is that we ought to give until we reach the level of marginal utility—that is, the level at which, by giving more, I would cause as much suffering to myself or my dependents as I would relieve by my gift. This would mean, of course, that one would reduce oneself to very nearly the material circumstances of a Bengali refugee. It will be recalled that earlier I put forward both a strong and a moderate version of the principle of preventing bad occurrences. The strong version, which required us to prevent bad things from happening unless in doing so we would be sacrificing something of comparable moral significance, does seem to require reducing ourselves to the level of marginal utility. I should also say that the strong version seems to me to be the correct one. I proposed the more moderate version—that we should prevent bad occurrences unless, to do so, we had to sacrifice something morally significant—only in order to show that even on this surely undeniable principle a great change in our way of life is required. On the more moderate principle, it may not follow that we ought to reduce ourselves to the level of marginal utility, for one might hold that to reduce oneself and one's family to this level is to cause something significantly bad to happen. Whether this is so I shall not discuss, since, as I have said, I can see no good reason for holding the moderate version of the principle rather than the strong version. Even if we accepted the principle only in its moderate form, however, it should be clear that we would have to give away enough to ensure that the consumer society, dependent as it is on people spending on trivia rather than giving to famine relief, would slow down and perhaps disappear entirely. There are several reasons why this would be desirable in itself. The value and necessity of economic growth are now being questioned not only by conservationists, but by economists as well.[5] There is no doubt, too, that the consumer society has had a distorting effect on the goals and purposes of its members. Yet looking at the matter purely from the point of view of overseas aid, there must be a limit to the extent to which we should deliberately slow down our economy; for it might be the case that if we gave away, say, forty percent of our Gross National Product, we would slow down the economy so much that in absolute terms we would be giving less than if we gave twenty-five percent of the much larger GNP that we would have if we limited our contribution to this smaller percentage.

I mention this only as an indication of the sort of factor that one would have to take into account in working out an ideal. Since Western societies generally consider one percent of the GNP an acceptable level for overseas aid, the matter is entirely academic. Nor does it affect the question of how much an individual should give in a society in which very few are giving substantial amounts.

It is sometimes said, though less often now than it used to be, that philosophers have no special role to play in public affairs, since most public issues depend primarily on an assessment of facts. On questions of fact, it is said, philosophers as such have no special expertise, and so it has been possible to engage in philosophy without committing oneself to any position on major public issues. No doubt there are some issues of social policy and foreign policy about which it can truly be said that a really expert assessment of the facts is required before taking sides or acting, but the issue of famine is surely not one of these. The facts about the existence of suffering are beyond dispute. Nor, I think, is it disputed that we can do something about it, either through orthodox methods of famine relief or through population control or both. This is therefore an issue on which philosophers are competent to take a position. The issue is one which faces everyone who has more money than he needs to support himself and his dependents, or who is in a position to take some sort of political action. These categories must include practically every teacher and student of philosophy in the universities of the Western world. If philosophy is to deal with matters that are relevant to both teachers and students, this is an issue that philosophers should discuss.

Discussion, though, is not enough. What is the point of relating philosophy to public (and personal) affairs if we do not take our conclusions seriously? In this instance, taking our conclusion seriously means acting upon it. The philosopher will not find it any easier than anyone else to alter his attitudes and way of life to the extent that, if I am right, is involved in doing everything that we ought to be doing. At the very least, though, one can make a start. The philosopher who does so will have to sacrifice some of the benefits of the consumer society, but he can find compensation in the satisfaction of a way of life in which theory and practice, if not yet in harmony, are at least coming together.

NOTES

1. There was also a third possibility: that India would go to war to enable the refugees to return to their lands. Since I wrote this paper, India has taken this way out. The situation is no longer that described above, but this does not affect my argument, as the next paragraph indicates.

2. In view of the special sense philosophers often give to the term, I should say that I use "obligation" simply as the abstract noun derived from "ought," so that "I have an obligation to" means no more, and no less, than "I ought to." This usage is in accordance with the definition of "ought" given by the *Shorter Oxford English Dictionary:* "the general verb to express duty or obligation." I do not think any issue of substance hangs on the way the term is used; sentences in which I use "obligation" could all be rewritten, although somewhat clumsily, as sentences in which a clause containing "ought" replaces the term "obligation."

3. J. O. Urmson, "Saints and Heroes," in *Essays Moral Philosophy,* ed. Abraham I. Melden (Seattle and London, 1958), p. 214. For a related but significantly different view see also Henry Sidgwick, *The Methods of Ethics,* 7th edn. (London, 1907), pp. 220–221, 492–493.

4. *Summa Theologica,* II-II, Question 66, Article 7, in *Aquinas, Selected Political Writings,* ed. A. P. d'Entreves, trans. J. G. Dawson (Oxford, 1948), p. 171.

5. See, for instance, John Kenneth Galbraith, *The New Industrial State* (Boston, 1967); and E. J. Mishan, *The Costs of Economic Growth* (London, 1967).

What Makes Right Acts Right?*

W. D. ROSS

W. D. Ross (1877–1967) was a British classical scholar and influential moral philosopher who spent his career at Oxford.

. . . THE POINT AT ISSUE is that to which we now pass, viz. whether there is any general character which makes right acts right, and if so, what it is. Among the main historical attempts to state a single characteristic of all right actions which is the foundation of their rightness are those made by egoism and utilitarianism. But I do not propose to discuss these, not because the subject is unimportant, but because it has been dealt with so often and so well already, and because there has come to be so much agreement among moral philosophers that neither of these theories is satisfactory. A much more attractive theory has been put forward by Professor Moore: that what makes actions right is that they are productive of more *good* than could have been produced by any other action open to the agent.

This theory is in fact the culmination of all the attempts to base rightness on productivity of some

From W. D. Ross, The Right and the Good *(Oxford: Clarendon Press, 1930), pp. 16–24, 28–41. Reprinted by permission of Oxford University Press.*

sort of result. The first form this attempt takes is the attempt to base rightness on conduciveness to the advantage or pleasure of the agent. This theory comes to grief over the fact, which stares us in the face, that a great part of duty consists in an observance of the rights and a furtherance of the interests of others, whatever the cost to ourselves may be. Plato and others may be right in holding that a regard for the rights of others never in the long run involves a loss of happiness for the agent, that 'the just life profits a man.' But this, even if true, is irrelevant to the rightness of the act. As soon as a man does an action *because* he thinks he will promote his own interests thereby, he is acting not from a sense of its rightness but from self-interest.

To the egoistic theory hedonistic utilitarianism supplies a much-needed amendment. It points out correctly that the fact that a certain pleasure will be enjoyed by the agent is no reason why he *ought* to bring it into being rather than an equal or greater pleasure to be enjoyed by another, though, human nature being what it is, it makes it not unlikely that he *will* try to bring it into being. But hedonistic utilitarianism in its turn needs a correction. On reflection it seems clear that pleasure is not the only thing in life that we think good in itself, that for instance we think the possession of a good character, or an intelligent understanding of the world, as good or better. A great advance is made by the substitution of 'productive of the greatest good' for 'productive of the greatest pleasure.'

Not only is this theory more attractive than hedonistic utilitarianism, but its logical relation to that theory is such that the latter could not be true unless *it* were true, while it might be true though hedonistic utilitarianism were not. It is in fact one of the logical bases of hedonistic utilitarianism. For the view that what produces the maximum pleasure is right has for its bases the views (1) that what produces the maximum good is right, and (2) that pleasure is the only thing good in itself. . . . If, therefore, it can be shown that productivity of the maximum good is not what makes all right actions right, we shall *a fortiori* have refuted hedonistic utilitarianism.

When a plain man fulfils a promise because he thinks he ought to do so, it seems clear that he does so with no thought of its total consequences, still less with any opinion that these are likely to be the best possible. He thinks in fact much more of the past than of the future. What makes him think it right to act in a certain way is the fact that he has promised to do so—that and, usually, nothing more. That his act will produce the best possible consequences is not his reason for calling it right. What lends colour to the theory we are examining, then, is not the actions (which form probably a great majority of our actions) in which some such reflection as 'I have promised' is the only reason we give ourselves for thinking a certain action right, but the exceptional cases in which the consequences of fulfilling a promise (for instance) would be so disastrous to others that we judge it right not to do so. It must of course be admitted that such cases exist. If I have promised to meet a friend at a particular time for some trivial purpose, I should certainly think myself justified in breaking my engagement if by doing so I could prevent a serious accident or bring relief to the victims of one. And the supporters of the view we are examining hold that my thinking so is due to my thinking that I shall bring more good into existence by the one action than by the other. A different account may, however, be given of the matter, an account which will, I believe, show itself to be the true one. It may be said that besides the duty of fulfilling promises I have and recognize a duty of relieving distress, and that when I think it right to do the latter at the cost of not doing the former, it is not because I think I shall produce more good thereby but because I think it the duty which is in the circumstances more of a duty. This account surely corresponds much more closely with what we really think in such a situation. If, so far as I can see, I could bring equal amounts of good into being by fulfilling my promise and by helping some one to whom I had made no promise, I should not hesitate to regard the former as my duty. Yet on the view that what is right is right because it is productive of the most good I should not so regard it.

There are two theories, each in its way simple, that offer a solution of such cases of conscience. One is the view of Kant, that there are certain duties of perfect obligation, such as those of fulfilling promises, of paying debts, of telling the truth, which admit of no exception whatever in favour of duties of imperfect obligation, such as that of relieving distress. The other is the view of, for instance, Professor Moore and Dr. Rashdall, that there is only the duty of producing good, and that all 'conflicts of duties' should be resolved by asking 'by which action will most good be produced?' But it is more important that our theory fit the facts than that it be simple, and the account we have given above corresponds (it seems to me) better than either of the simpler theories with what we really think, viz. that normally promise-keeping, for example, should come before benevolence, but that when and only when the good to be produced by the benevolent act is very great and the promise comparatively trivial, the act of benevolence becomes our duty.

In fact the theory of 'ideal utilitarianism,' if I may for brevity refer so to the theory of Professor Moore, seems to simplify unduly our relations to our fellows. It says, in effect, that the only morally significant relation in which my neighbours stand to me is that of being possible beneficiaries by my action.[1] They do stand in this relation to me, and this relation is morally significant. But they may also stand to me in the relation of promise to promiser, of creditor to debtor, of wife to husband, of child to parent, of friend to friend, of fellow countryman to fellow countryman, and the like; and each of these relations is the foundation of a *prima facie* duty, which is more or less incumbent on me according to the circumstances of the case. When I am in a situation, as perhaps I always am, in which more than one of these *prima facie* duties is incumbent on me, what I have to do is to study the situation as fully as I can until I form the considered opinion (it is never more) that in the circumstances one of them is more incumbent than any other; then I am bound to think that to do this *prima facie* duty is my duty *sans phrase* in the situation.

I suggest '*prima facie* duty' or 'conditional duty' as a brief way of referring to the characteristic (quite distinct from that of being a duty proper) which an act has, in virtue of being of a certain kind (e.g. the keeping of a promise), of being an act which would be a duty proper if it were not at the same time of another kind which is morally significant. Whether an act is a duty proper or actual duty depends on *all* the morally significant kinds it is an instance of. . . .

There is nothing arbitrary about these *prima facie* duties. Each rests on a definite circumstance which cannot seriously be held to be without moral significance. Of *prima facie* duties I suggest, without claiming completeness or finality for it, the following division.[2]

(1) Some duties rest on previous acts of my own. These duties seem to include two kinds, (a) those resting on a promise or what may fairly be called an implicit promise, such as the implicit undertaking not to tell lies which seems to be implied in the act of entering into conversation (at any rate by civilized men), or of writing books that purport to be history and not fiction. These may be called the duties of fidelity. (b) Those resting on a previous wrongful act. These may be called the duties of reparation. (2) Some rest on previous acts of other men, i.e. services done by them to me. These may be loosely described as the duties of gratitude. (3) Some rest on the fact or possibility of a distribution of pleasure or happiness (or of the means thereto) which is not in accordance with the merit of the persons concerned; in such cases there arises a duty to upset or prevent such a distribution. These are the duties of justice. (4) Some rest on the mere fact that there are other beings in the world whose condition we can make better in respect of virtue, or of intelligence, or of pleasure. These are the duties of beneficence. (5) Some rest on the fact that we can improve our own condition in respect of virtue or of intelligence. These are the duties of self-improvement. (6) I think that we should distinguish from (4) the duties that may be summed up under the title of 'not injuring others.' No doubt to injure others is incidentally to fail to do them good; but it seems to me clear that non-maleficence is apprehended as a duty distinct from that of beneficence, and as a duty of a more stringent character. It will be noticed that this alone among the types of duty has been stated in a negative way. An attempt might no doubt be made to state this duty, like the others, in a positive way. It might be said that it is really the duty to prevent ourselves from acting either from an inclination to harm others or from

an inclination to seek our own pleasure, in doing which we should incidentally harm them. But on reflection it seems clear that the primary duty here is the duty not to harm others, this being a duty whether or not we have an inclination that if followed would lead to our harming them; and that when we have such an inclination the primary duty not to harm others gives rise to a consequential duty to resist the inclination. The recognition of this duty of non-maleficence is the first step on the way to the recognition of the duty of beneficence; and that accounts for the prominence of the commands 'thou shalt not kill,' 'thou shalt not commit adultery,' 'thou shalt not steal,' 'thou shalt not bear false witness,' in so early a code as the Decalogue. But even when we have come to recognize the duty of beneficence, it appears to me that the duty of non-maleficence is recognized as a distinct one, and as *prima facie* more binding. We should not in general consider it justifiable to kill one person in order to keep another alive, or to steal from one in order to give alms to another.

The essential defect of the 'ideal utilitarian' theory is that it ignores, or at least does not do full justice to, the highly personal character of duty. If the only duty is to produce the maximum of good, the question who is to have the good—whether it is myself, or my benefactor, or a person to whom I have made a promise to confer that good on him, or a mere fellow man to whom I stand in no such special relation—should make no difference to my having a duty to produce that good. But we are all in fact sure that it makes a vast difference. . . .

If the objection be made, that this catalogue of the main types of duty is an unsystematic one resting on no logical principle, it may be replied, first, that it makes no claim to being ultimate. It is a *prima facie* classification of the duties which reflection on our moral convictions seems actually to reveal. And if these convictions are, as I would claim that they are, of the nature of knowledge, and if I have not misstated them, the list will be a list of authentic conditional duties, correct as far as it goes though not necessarily complete. The list of *goods* put forward by the rival theory is reached by exactly the same method—the only sound one in the circumstances—viz. that of direct reflection on what we really think. Loyalty to the facts is worth more than a symmetrical architectonic or a hastily reached simplicity. If further reflection discovers a perfect logical basis for this or for a better classification, so much the better.

It may, again, be objected that our theory that there are these various and often conflicting types of *prima facie* duty leaves us with no principle upon which to discern what is our actual duty in particular circumstances. But this objection is not one of which the rival theory is in a position to bring forward. For when we have to choose between the production of two heterogeneous goods, say knowledge and pleasure, the 'ideal utilitarian' theory can only fall back on an opinion, for which no logical basis can be offered, that one of the goods is the greater; and this is no better than a similar opinion that one of two duties is the more urgent. And again, when we consider the infinite variety of the effects of our actions in the way of pleasure, it must surely be admitted that the claim which *hedonism* sometimes makes, that it offers a readily applicable criterion of right conduct, is quite illusory.

I am unwilling, however, to content myself with an *argumentum ad hominem,* and I would contend that in principle there is no reason to anticipate that every act that is our duty is so for one and the same reason. Why should two sets of circumstances, or one set of circumstances, *not* possess different characteristics, any one of which makes a certain act our *prima facie* duty? When I ask what it is that makes me in certain cases sure that I have a *prima facie* duty to do so and so, I find that it lies in the fact that I have made a promise; when I ask the same question in another case, I find the answer lies in the fact that I have done a wrong. And if on reflection I find (as I think I do) that neither of these reasons is reducible to the other, I must not on any *a priori* ground assume that such a reduction is possible. . . .

It is necessary to say something by way of clearing up the relation between *prima facie* duties and the actual or absolute duty to do one particular act in particular circumstances. If, as almost all moralists except Kant are agreed, and as most plain men think, it is sometimes right to tell a lie or to break a promise, it must be maintained that there is a difference between *prima facie* duty and actual or absolute duty. When we think ourselves justified in breaking, and indeed morally obliged to break, a promise in order to relieve some one's distress, we do not for a moment cease to recognize a *prima facie* duty to keep our promise, and this leads us to feel, not indeed shame or repentance, but certainly compunction, for behaving as we do; we recognize, further, that it is our duty to make up somehow to the promise for the breaking of the promise. We have to distinguish from the characteristic of being our duty that of tending to be our duty. Any act that we do contains various elements in virtue of which it falls under various categories. In virtue of being the breaking of a promise, for instance, it tends to be wrong; in virtue of being an instance of relieving distress it tends to be right. Tendency to be one's duty may be called a partiresultant attribute, i.e. one which belongs to an act in virtue of some one component in its nature. *Being* one's duty is a toti-resultant attribute, one which belongs to an act in virtue of its whole nature and of nothing less than this. . . .

Another instance of the same distinction may be found in the operation of natural laws. *Qua* subject to the force of gravitation towards some other body, each body tends to move in a particular direction with a particular velocity; but its actual movement depends on *all* the forces to which it is subject. It is only by recognising this distinction that we can preserve the absoluteness of laws of nature, and only by recognising a corresponding distinction that we can preserve the absoluteness of the general principles of morality. But an important difference between the two cases must be pointed out. When we say that in virtue of gravitation a body tends to move in a certain way, we are referring to a causal influence actually exercised on it by another body or other bodies. When we say that in virtue of being deliberately untrue a certain remark tends to be wrong, we are referring to no causal relation, to no relation that involves succession in time, but to such a relation as connects the various attributes of a mathematical figure. And if the word 'tendency' is thought to suggest too much a causal relation, it is better to talk of certain types of act as being *prima facie* right or wrong (or of different persons as having different and possibly conflicting claims upon us), than of their tending to be right or wrong.

Something should be said of the relation between our apprehension of the *prima facie* rightness of certain types of act and our mental attitude towards particular acts. It is proper to use the word 'apprehension' in the former case and not in the latter. That an act, *qua* fulfilling a promise, or *qua* effecting a just distribution of good, or *qua* returning services rendered, or *qua* promoting the good of others, or *qua* promoting the virtue or insight of the agent, is *prima facie* right, is self-evident; not in the sense that it is evident from the beginning of our lives, or as soon as we attend to the proposition for the first time, but in the sense that when we have reached sufficient mental maturity and have given sufficient attention to the proposition it is evident without any need of proof, or of evidence beyond itself. It is self-evident just as a mathematical axiom, or the validity of a form of inference, is evident. The moral order expressed in these propositions is just as much part of the fundamental nature of the universe (and, we may add, of any possible universe in which there were moral agents at all) as is the spatial or numerical structure expressed in the axioms of geometry or arithmetic. In our confidence that these propositions are true there is involved the same trust in our reason that is involved in our confidence in mathematics; and we should have no justification for trusting it in the latter sphere and distrusting it in the former. In both cases we are dealing with propositions that cannot be proved, but that just as certainly need no proof. . . .

Our judgements about our actual duty in concrete situations have none of the certainty that attaches to our recognition of the general principles of duty. A statement is certain, i.e., is an expression of knowledge, only in one or other of two cases: when it is either self-evident, or a valid conclusion from self-evident premisses. And our judgements about our particular duties have neither of these characters. (1) They are not self-evident. Where a possible act is seen to have two characteristics, in virtue of one of which it is *prima facie* right, and in virtue of the other *prima facie* wrong, we are (I think) well aware that we are not certain whether we ought or ought not to do it; that whether we do it or not, we are taking a moral risk. We come in the long run, after consideration, to think one duty more pressing than the other, but we do not feel certain that it is so. And though we do not always recognize that a possible act has two such characteristics, and though there *may* be cases in which it has not, we are never certain that any particular possible act has not, and therefore never certain that it is right, nor certain that it is wrong. For, to go no further in the analysis, it is enough to point out that any particular act will in all probability in the course of time contribute to the bringing about of good or of evil for many human beings, and thus have a *prima facie* rightness or wrongness of which we know nothing. (2) Again, our judgements about our particular duties are not logical conclusions from self-evident premises. The only possible premises would be the general principles stating their *prima facie* rightness or wrongness *qua* having the different characteristics they do have; and even if we could (as we cannot) apprehend the extent to which an act will tend on the one hand, for example, to bring about advantages for our benefactors, and on the other hand to bring about disadvantages for fellow men who are not our benefactors, there is no principle by which we can draw the conclusion that it is on the whole right or on the whole wrong. In this respect the judgement as to the rightness of a particular act is just like the judgement as to the beauty of a particular natural object or work of art. A poem is, for instance, in respect of certain qualities beautiful and in respect of certain others not beautiful; and our judgement as to the degree of beauty it possesses on the whole is never reached by logical reasoning from the apprehension of its particular beauties or particular defects. Both in this and in the moral case we have more or less probable opinions which are not logically justified conclusions from the general principles that are recognized as self-evident.

There is therefore much truth in the description of the right act as a fortunate act. If we cannot be certain that it is right, it is our good fortune if the act we do is the right act. This consideration does not, however, make the doing of our duty a mere matter of chance. There is a parallel here between the doing of duty and the doing of what will be to our personal advantage. We never *know* what act will in the long run be to our advantage. Yet it is certain that we are more likely in general to secure our advantage if we estimate to the best of our ability the probable tendencies of our actions in this respect, than if we act on caprice. And similarly we are more likely to do our duty if we reflect to the best of our ability on the *prima facie* rightness or wrongness of various possible acts in virtue of the characteristics we perceive them to have, than if we act without reflection. With this greater likelihood we must be content.

Many people would be inclined to say that the right act for me is not that whose general nature I have been describing, viz. that which if I were omniscient I should see to be my duty, but that which on all the evidence available to me I should think to be my duty. But suppose that from the state of partial knowledge in which I think act *A* to be my duty, I could pass to a state of perfect knowledge in which I saw act *B* to be my duty, should I not say 'act *B* was the right act for me to do'? I should no doubt add 'though I am not to be blamed for doing act *A*.' But in adding this, am I not passing from the question 'what is right' to the question 'what is morally good'? At the same time I am not making the *full* passage from the one notion to the other, for in order that the act should be morally good, or an act I am not to be blamed for doing, it must not merely be the act which it is reasonable for me to think my duty; it must also be done for that reason, or from some other morally good motive. Thus the conception of the right act as the act which it is reasonable for me to think my duty is an unsatisfactory compromise between the true notion of the right act and the notion of the morally good action.

The general principles of duty are obviously not self-evident from the beginning of our lives. How do they come to be so? The answer is, that they come to be self-evident to us just as mathematical axioms do. We find by experience that this couple of matches and that couple make four matches, that this couple of balls on a wire and that couple make four balls; and by reflection on these and similar discoveries we come to see that it is of the nature of two and two to make four. In a precisely similar way, we see the *prima facie* rightness of an act which would be the fulfillment of a particular promise, and of another which would be the fulfillment of another promise, and when we have reached sufficient maturity to think in general terms, we apprehend *prima facie* rightness to belong to the nature of any fulfillment of promise. What comes first in time is the apprehension of the self-evident *prima facie* rightness of an individual act of a particular type. From this we come by reflection to apprehend the self-evident general principle of *prima facie* duty. From this, too, perhaps along with the apprehension of the self-evident *prima facie* rightness of the same act in virtue of its having another characteristic as well, and perhaps in spite of the apprehension of its *prima facie* wrongness in virtue of its having some third characteristic, we come to believe something not self-evident at all, but an object of probable opinion, viz. that this particular act is (not *prima facie* but) actually right. . . .

Supposing it to be agreed, as I think on reflection it must, that no one *means* by 'right' just 'productive of the best possible consequences,' or 'optimific,' the attributes 'right' and 'optimific' might stand in either of two kinds of relation to each other. (1) They might be so related that we could apprehend *a priori*, either immediately or deductively, that any act that is optimific is right and any act that is right is optimific, as we can apprehend that any triangle that is equilateral is equiangular and *vice versa*. Professor Moore's view is, I think, that the coextensiveness of 'right' and 'optimific' is apprehended immediately. He rejects the possibility of any proof of it. Or (2) the two attributes might be such that the question whether they are invariably connected had to be answered by means of an inductive inquiry. Now at first sight it might seem as if the constant connexion of the two attributes could be immediately apprehended. It might seem absurd to suggest that it could be right for any one to do an act which would produce consequences less good than those which would be produced by some other act in his power. Yet a little thought will convince us that this is not absurd. The type of case in which it is easiest to see that this is so is, perhaps, that in which one has made a promise. In such a case we all think that *prima facie* it is our duty to fulfil the promise irrespective of the precise goodness of the total consequences. And though we do not think it is necessarily our actual or absolute duty to do so, we are far from thinking that any, even the slightest, gain in the value of the total consequences will necessarily justify us in doing something else instead. Suppose, to simplify the case by abstraction, that the fulfillment of a promise to *A* would produce 1,000 units of good[3] for him, but that by doing some other act I could produce 1,001 units of good for *B*, to whom I have made no promise, the other consequences of the two acts being of equal value; should we really think it self-evident that it was our duty to do the second act and not the first? I think not. We should, I fancy, hold that only a much greater disparity of value between the total consequences would justify us in failing to discharge our *prima facie* duty to *A*. After all, a promise is a promise, and is not to be treated so lightly as the theory we are examining would imply. What, exactly, a promise is, is not so easy to determine, but we are surely agreed that it constitutes a serious moral limitation to our freedom of action. To produce the 1,001 units of good for *B* rather than fulfil our promise to *A* would be to take, not perhaps our duty as philanthropists too seriously, but certainly our duty as makers of promises too lightly. . . .

Such instances—and they might easily be added to—make it clear that there is no self-evident connexion between the attributes 'right' and 'optimific.' The theory we are examining has a certain attractiveness when applied to our decision that a particular act is our duty (though I have tried to show that it does not agree with our actual moral judgements even here). But it is not even plausible when applied to our recognition of *prima facie* duty. For if it were self-evident that the right coincides with the optimific, it should be self-evident that what is *prima facie* right is *prima facie* optimific. But whereas we are certain that keeping a promise is *prima facie* right, we are not certain that it is *prima facie* optimific (though we are perhaps certain that it is *prima facie* bonific). Our certainty that it is *prima facie* right depends not on its consequences but on its being the fulfillment of a promise. The theory we are examining involves too much difference between the evident ground of our conviction about *prima facie* duty and the alleged ground of our conviction about actual duty. . . .

I conclude that the attributes 'right' and 'optimific' are not identical, and that we do not know either by intuition, by deduction, or by induction that they coincide in their application, still less that the latter is the foundation of the former. It must be added, however, that if we are ever under no special obligation such as that of fidelity to a promisee or of gratitude to a benefactor, we ought to do what will produce most good; and that even when we are under a special obligation the tendency of acts to promote general good is one of the main factors in determining whether they are right.

In what has preceded, a good deal of use has been made of 'what we really think' about moral questions; a certain theory has been rejected because it does not agree with what we really think. It might be said that this is in principle wrong; that we should not be content to expound what our present moral consciousness tells us but should aim at a criticism of our existing moral consciousness in the light of theory. Now I do not doubt that the moral consciousness of men has in detail undergone a good deal of modification as regards the things we think right, at the hands of moral theory. But if we are told, for instance, that we should give up our view that there is a special obligatoriness attaching to the keeping of promises because it is self-evident that the only duty is to produce as much good as possible, we have to ask ourselves whether we really, when we reflect, *are* convinced that this is self-evident, and whether we really *can* get rid of our view that promise-keeping has a bindingness independent of productiveness of maximum good. In my own experience I find that I cannot, in spite of a very genuine attempt to do so; and I venture to think that most people will find the same, and that just because they cannot lose the sense of special obligation, they cannot accept as self-evident, or even as true, the theory which would require them to do so. In fact it seems, on reflection, self-evident that a promise, simply as such, is something that *prima facie* ought to be kept, and it does *not*, on reflection, seem self-evident that production of maximum good is the only thing that makes an act obligatory. And to ask us to give up at the bidding of a theory our actual apprehension of what is right and what is wrong seems like asking people to repudiate their actual experience of beauty, at the bidding of a theory which says 'only that which satisfies such and such conditions can be beautiful.' If what I have called our actual apprehension is (as I would maintain that it is) truly an apprehension, i.e. an instance of knowledge, the request is nothing less than absurd.

I would maintain, in fact, that what we are apt to describe as 'what we think' about moral questions contains a considerable amount that we do not think but know, and that this forms the standard by reference to which the truth of any moral theory has to be tested, instead of having itself to be tested by reference to any theory. I hope that I have in what precedes indicated what in my view these elements of knowledge are that are involved in our ordinary moral consciousness.

It would be a mistake to found a natural science on 'what we really think,' i.e. on what reasonably thoughtful and well-educated people think about the subjects of the science before they have studied them scientifically. For such opinions are interpretations, and often misinterpretations, of sense-experience; and the man of science must appeal from these to sense-experience itself, which furnishes his real data. In ethics no such appeal is possible. We have no more direct way of access to the facts about rightness and goodness and about what things are right or good, than by thinking about them; the moral convictions of thoughtful and well-educated people are the data of ethics just as sense-perceptions are the data of a natural science. Just as some of the latter have to be rejected as illusory, so have some of the former; but as the latter are rejected only when they are in conflict with other more accurate sense-perceptions, the former are rejected only when they are in conflict with other convictions which stand better the test of reflection. The existing body of moral convictions of the best people is the cumulative product of the moral reflection of many generations, which has developed an extremely delicate power of appreciation of moral distinctions; and this the theorist cannot afford to treat with anything other than the greatest respect. The verdicts of the moral consciousness of the best people are the foundation on which he must build; though he must first compare them with one another and eliminate any contradictions they may contain.

NOTES

1. Some will think it, apart from other considerations, a sufficient refutation of this view to point out that I also stand in that relation to myself, so that for this view the distinction of oneself from others is morally insignificant.

2. I should make it plain at this stage that I am *assuming* the correctness of some of our main convictions as to *prima facie* duties, or, more strictly, am claiming that we *know* them to be true. To me it seems as self-evident as anything could be, that to make a promise, for instance, is to create a moral claim on us in someone else. Many readers will perhaps say that they do *not* know this to be true. If so, I certainly cannot prove it to them; I can only ask them to reflect again, in the hope that they will ultimately agree that they also know it to be true. The main moral convictions of the plain man seem to me to be, not opinions which it is for philosophy to prove or disprove, but knowledge from the start; and in my own case I seem to find little difficulty in distinguishing these essential convictions from other moral convictions which I also have, which are merely fallible opinions based on an imperfect study of the working for good or evil of certain institutions or types of action.

3. I am assuming that good is objectively quantitative, but not that we can accurately assign an exact quantitative measure to it. Since it is of a definite amount, we can make the *supposition* that its amount is so-and-so, though we cannot with any confidence *assert* that it is.

Why Be Moral?
The Immoralists' Challenge*

PLATO

Plato (B.C. 427?–347) lived and taught in Athens. Most of his surviving works have the form of fictitious dialogues between Socrates (who had been his teacher) and other Athenian intellectuals.

WITH THESE WORDS I was thinking that I had made an end of the discussion; but the end, in truth, proved to be only a beginning. For Glaucon, who is always the most pugnacious of men, was dissatisfied at Thrasymachus' retirement; he wanted to have the battle out. So he said to me: Socrates, do you wish really to persuade us, or only to seem to have persuaded us, that to be just is always better than to be unjust?

I should wish really to persuade you, I replied, if I could.

Then you certainly have not succeeded. Let me ask you now:—How would you arrange goods—are there not some which we welcome for their own sakes, and independently of their consequences, as, for example, harmless pleasures and enjoyments, which delight us at the time, although nothing follows from them?

*From Plato, The Republic, *ii. 357A–367E, trans. B. Jowett.*

I agree in thinking that there is such a class, I replied.

Is there not also a second class of goods, such as knowledge, sight, health, which are desirable not only in themselves, but also for their results?

Certainly, I said.

And would you not recognize a third class, such as gymnastic, and the care of the sick, and the physician's art; also the various ways of money-making—these do us good but we regard them as disagreeable; and no one would choose them for their own sakes, but only for the sake of some reward or result which flows from them?

There is, I said, this third class also. But why do you ask?

Because I want to know in which of the three classes you would place justice?

In the highest class, I replied, among those goods which he who would be happy desires both for their own sake and for the sake of their results.

Then the many are of another mind; they think that justice is to be reckoned in the troublesome class, among goods which are to be pursued for the sake of rewards and of reputation, but in themselves are disagreeable and rather to be avoided.

I know, I said, that this is their manner of thinking and that this was the thesis which Thrasymachus was maintaining just now, when he censured justice and praised injustice. But I am too stupid to be convinced by him.

I wish, he said, that you would hear me as well as him, and then I shall see whether you and I agree. For Thrasymachus seems to me, like a snake, to have been charmed by your voice sooner than he ought to have been; but to my mind the nature of justice and injustice have not yet been made clear. Setting aside their rewards and results, I want to know what they are in themselves, and how they inwardly work in the soul. If you please, then, I will revive the argument of Thrasymachus. And first I will speak of the nature and origin of justice according to the common view of them. Secondly, I will show that all men who practice justice do so against their will, of necessity, but not as a good. And thirdly, I will argue that there is reason in this view, for the life of the unjust is after all better far than the life of the just—if what they say is true, Socrates, since I myself am not of their opinion. But still I acknowledge that I am perplexed when I hear the voices of Thrasymachus and myriads of others dinning in my ears; and, on the other hand, I have never yet heard the superiority of justice to injustice maintained by any one in a satisfactory way. I want to hear justice praised in respect of itself; then I shall be satisfied, and you are the person from whom I think that I am most likely to hear this; and therefore I will praise the unjust life to the utmost of my power, and my manner of speaking will indicate the manner in which I desire to hear you too praising justice and censuring injustice. Will you say whether you approve of my proposal?

Indeed I do; nor can I imagine any theme about which a man of sense would oftener wish to converse.

I am delighted, he replied, to hear you say so, and shall begin by speaking, as I proposed, of the nature and origin of justice.

They say that to do injustice is, by nature, good; to suffer injustice, evil; but that the evil is greater than the good. And so when men have both done and suffered injustice and have had experience of both, not being able to avoid the one and obtain the other, they think that they had better agree among themselves to have neither; hence there arise laws and mutual covenants; and that which is ordained by law is termed by them lawful and just. This they affirm to be the origin and nature of justice;—it is a mean or compromise, between the best of all, which is to do injustice and not be punished, and the worst of all, which is to suffer injustice without the power of retaliation; and justice, being at a middle point between the two, is tolerated not as a good, but as the lesser evil, and honoured by reason of the inability of men to do injustice. For no man who is worthy to be called a man would ever submit to such an agreement if he were able to resist; he would be mad if he did. Such is the received account, Socrates, of the nature and origin of justice.

Now that those who practice justice do so involuntarily and because they have not the power to be unjust will best appear if we imagine something of this kind: having given both to the just and the unjust power to do what they will, let us watch and see whither desire will lead them; then we shall discover in the very act the just and unjust man to be proceeding along the same road, following their interest, which all natures deem to be their good, and are only diverted into the path of justice by the force of law. The liberty which we are supposing may be most completely given to them in the form of such a power as is said to have been possessed by Gyges the ancestor of Croesus the Lydian. According to the tradition, Gyges was a shepherd in the service of the king of Lydia; there was a great storm, and an earthquake made an opening in the earth at the place where he was feeding his flock. Amazed at the sight, he descended into the opening, where, among other marvels, he beheld a hollow brazen horse, having doors, at which he stooping and looking in saw a dead body of stature, as appeared to him, more than human, and having nothing on but a gold ring; this he took from the finger of the dead and reascended. Now the shepherds met together, according to custom, that they might send their monthly report about the flocks to the king; into their assembly he came having the ring on his finger, and as he was sitting among them he chanced to turn the collet of the ring inside his hand, when instantly he became invisible to the rest of the company and they began to speak of him as if he were no longer present. He was astonished at this, and again touching the ring he turned the collet outwards and reappeared; he made several trials of the ring, and always with the same result—when he turned the collet inwards he became invisible, when outwards he reappeared. Whereupon he contrived to be chosen one of the messengers who were sent to the court; where as soon as he arrived he seduced the queen, and with her help conspired against the king and slew him, and took the kingdom. Suppose now that there were two such magic rings, and the just put on one of them and the unjust the other; no man can be imagined to be of such an iron nature that he would stand fast in justice. No man would keep his hands off what was not his own when he could safely take what he liked out of the market, or go into houses and lie with any one at his pleasure, or kill or release from prison whom he would, and in all respects be like a God among men. Then the actions of the just would be as the actions of the unjust; they would both come at last to the same point. And this we may truly affirm to be a great proof that a man is just, not willingly or because he thinks that justice is any good to him individually, but of necessity, for wherever any one thinks that he can safely be unjust, there he is unjust. For all men believe in their hearts that injustice is far more profitable to the individual than justice, and he who argues as I have been supposing, will say that they are right. If you could imagine any one obtaining this power of becoming invisible, and never doing any wrong or touching what was another's, he would be thought by the lookers-on to be a most wretched idiot, although they would praise him to one another's faces, and keep up appearances with one another from a fear that they too might suffer injustice. Enough of this.

Now, if we are to form a real judgment of the life of the just and unjust, we must isolate them; there is no other way; and how is the isolation to be effected? I answer: Let the unjust man be entirely unjust, and the just man entirely just; nothing is to be taken away from either of them, and both are to be perfectly furnished for the work of their respective lives. First, let the unjust be like other distinguished masters of craft; like the skillful pilot or physician, who knows intuitively his own powers and keeps within their limits, and who, if he fails at any point, is able to recover himself. So let the unjust make his unjust attempts in the right way, and lie hidden if he means to be great in his injustice (he who is found out is nobody): for the highest reach of injustice is: to be deemed just when you are not. Therefore I say that in the perfectly unjust man we must assume the most perfect injustice; there is to be no deduction, but we must allow him, while doing the most unjust acts, to have acquired the greatest reputation for justice. If he have taken a false step he must be able to recover himself; he must be one who can speak with effect, if any of his deeds come to light, and who can force his way where force is required by his courage and strength, and command of money and friends. And at his side let us place the just man in his nobleness and simplicity, wishing, as Aeschylus says, to be and not to seem good. There must be no seeming, for if he seem to be just he will be honoured and rewarded, and then we shall not know whether he is just for the sake of justice or for the sake of honours and rewards; therefore, let him be clothed in justice only, and have no other covering; and he must be imagined in a state of life the opposite of the former. Let him be the best of men, and let him be thought the worst; then he will have been put to the proof; and we shall see whether he will be affected by the fear of infamy and its consequences. And let him continue thus to the hour of death; being just and seeming to be unjust. When both have reached the uttermost extreme, the one of justice and the other of injustice, let judgment be given which of them is the happier of the two.

Heavens! my dear Glaucon, I said, how energetically you polish them up for the decision, first one and then the other, as if they were two statues.

I do my best, he said. And now that we know what they are like there is no difficulty in tracing out the sort of life which awaits either of them. This I will proceed to describe; but as you may think the description a little too coarse, I ask you to suppose, Socrates, that the words which follow are not mine.—Let me put them into the mouths of the eulogists of injustice: They will tell you that the just man who is thought unjust will be scourged, racked, bound—will have his eyes burnt out; and, at last, after suffering every kind of evil, he will be impaled: Then he will understand that he ought to seem only, and not to be, just; the words of Aeschylus may be more truly spoken of the unjust than of the just. For the unjust is pursuing a reality; he does not live with a view to appearances—he wants to be really unjust and not to seem only:—

> His mind has a soil deep and fertile,
> Out of which spring his prudent counsels.[1]

In the first place, he is thought just, and therefore bears rule in the city; he can marry whom he will, and give in marriage to whom he will; also he can trade and deal where he likes, and always to his own advantage, because he has no misgivings about injustice; and at every contest, whether in public or private, he gets the better of his antagonists, and gains at their expense, and is rich, and out of his gains he can benefit his friends, and harm his enemies; moreover, he can offer sacrifices, and dedicate gifts to the gods abundantly and magnificently, and can honour the gods or any man whom he wants to honour in a far better style than the just, and therefore he is likely to be dearer than they are to the gods. And thus, Socrates, gods and men are said to unite in making the life of the unjust better than the life of the just.

I was going to say something in answer to Glaucon, when Adeimantus, his brother, interposed: Socrates, he said, you do not suppose that there is nothing more to be urged?

Why, what else is there? I answered.

The strongest point of all has not been even mentioned, he replied.

Well, then, according to the proverb, "Let brother help brother'—if he fails in any part do you assist him; although I must confess that Glaucon has already said quite enough to lay me in the dust, and take from me the power of helping justice.

Nonsense, he replied. But let me add something more: There is another side to Glaucon's argument about the praise and censure of justice and injustice, which is equally required in order to bring out what I believe to be his meaning. Parents and tutors are always telling their sons and their wards that they are to be just; but why? not for the sake of justice, but for the sake of character and reputation; in the hope of obtaining for him who is reputed just some of those offices, marriages, and the like which Glaucon has enumerated among the advantages accruing to the unjust from the reputation of justice. More, however, is made of appearances by this class of persons than by the others; for they throw in the good opinion of the gods, and will tell you of a shower of benefits which the heavens, as they say, rain upon the pious; and this accords with the testimony of the noble Hesiod and Homer, the first of whom says, that the gods make the oaks of the just—

> To bear acorns at their summit, and bees in the middle; And the sheep are bowed down with the weight of their fleeces.[2]

and many other blessings of a like kind are provided for them. And Homer has a very similar strain; for he speaks of one whose fame is—

> As the fame of some blameless king who, like a god, Maintains justice; to whom the black earth brings forth Wheat and barley, whose trees are bowed with fruit, And his sheep never fail to bear, and the sea gives him fish.[3]

Still grander are the gifts of heaven which Musaeus and his son[4] vouchsafe to the just; they take them down into the world below, where they have the saints lying on couches at a feast, everlastingly drunk, crowned with garlands; their idea seems to be that an immortality of drunkenness is the highest meed of virtue. Some extend their rewards yet further; the posterity, as they say, of the faithful and just shall survive to the third and fourth generation. This is the style in which they praise justice. But about the wicked there is another strain; they bury them in a slough in Hades, and make them carry water in a sieve; also while they are yet living they bring them to infamy, and inflict upon them the punishments which Glaucon described as the portion of the just who are reputed to be unjust; nothing else does their invention supply. Such is their manner of praising the one and censuring the other.

Once more, Socrates, I will ask you to consider another way of speaking about justice and injustice, which is not confined to the poets, but is found in prose writers. The universal voice of mankind is always declaring that justice and virtue are honourable, but grievous and toilsome; and that the pleasures of vice and injustice are easy of attainment, and are only censured by law and opinion. They say also that honesty is for the most part less profitable than dishonesty; and they are quite ready to call wicked men happy, and to honour them both in public and private when they are rich or in any other way influential, while they despise and overlook those who may be weak and poor, even though acknowledging them to be better than the others. But most extraordinary of all is their mode of speaking about virtue and the gods: they say that the gods apportion calamity and misery to many good men, and good and happiness to the wicked. And mendicant prophets go to rich men's doors and persuade them that they have a power committed to them by the gods of making an atonement for a man's own or his ancestor's sins by sacrifices or charms, with rejoicings and feasts; and they promise to harm an enemy, whether just or unjust, at a small cost; with magic arts and incantations binding heaven, as they say, to execute their will. And the poets are the authorities to whom they appeal, now smoothing the path of vice with words of Hesiod:—

> Vice may be had in abundance without trouble;
> the way is smooth and her dwelling-place is near.
> But before virtue the gods have set toil,[5]

and a tedious and uphill road: then citing Homer as a witness that the gods may be influenced by men; for he also says:—

> The gods, too, may be turned from their purpose; and men pray to them and avert their wrath by sacrifices and soothing entreaties, and by libations and the odour of fat, when they have sinned and transgressed.[6]

And they produce a host of books written by Musaeus and Orpheus, who were children of the Moon and the Muses—that is what they say—according to which they perform their ritual, and persuade not only individuals, but whole cities, that expiations and atonements for sin may be made by sacrifices and amusements which fill a vacant hour, and are equally at the service of the living and the dead; the latter sort they call mysteries, and they redeem us from the pains of hell, but if we neglect them no one knows what awaits us.

He proceeded: And now when the young hear all this said about virtue and vice, and the way in which gods and men regard them, how are their minds likely to be affected, my dear Socrates,—those of them, I mean, who are quickwitted, and, like bees on the wing, light on every flower, and from all that they hear are prone to draw conclusions as to what manner of persons they should be and in what way they should walk if they would make the best of life? Probably the youth will say to himself in the words of Pindar—

> Can I by justice or by crooked ways of deceit ascend a loftier tower which may be a fortress to me all my days?

For what men say is that, if I am really just and am not also thought just, profit there is none, but the pain and loss on the other hand are unmistakable. But if, though unjust, I acquire the reputation of justice, a heavenly life is promised to me. Since then, as philosophers prove, appearance tyrannizes over truth and is lord of happiness, to appearance I must devote myself. I will describe around me a picture and shadow of virtue to be the vestibule and exterior of my house; behind I will trail the subtle and crafty fox, as Archilochus, greatest of sages, recommends. But I hear some one exclaiming that the concealment of wickedness is often difficult; to which I answer, Nothing great is easy. Nevertheless, the argument indicates this, if we would be happy, to be the path along which we should proceed. With a view to concealment we will establish secret brotherhoods and political clubs. And there are professors of rhetoric who teach the art of persuading courts and assemblies; and so, partly by persuasion and partly by force, I shall make unlawful gains and not be punished. Still I hear a voice saying that the gods cannot be deceived, neither can they be compelled. But what if there are no gods? or, suppose them to have no care of human things—why in either case should we mind about concealment? And even if there are gods, and they do care about us, yet we know of them only from tradition and the genealogies of the poets; and these are the very persons who say that they may be influenced and turned by 'sacrifices and soothing entreaties and by offerings.' Let us be consistent then, and believe both or neither. If the poets speak truly, why then we had better be unjust, and offer of the fruits of injustice; for if we are just, although we may escape the vengeance of heaven, we shall lose the gains of injustice; but, if we are unjust, we shall keep the gains, and by our sinning and praying, and praying and sinning, the gods will be propitiated, and we shall not be punished. 'But there is a world below in which either we or our posterity will suffer for our unjust deeds.' Yes, my friend, will be the reflection, but there are mysteries and atoning deities, and these have great power. That is what mighty cities declare; and the children of the gods, who were their poets and prophets, bear a like testimony.

On what principle, then, shall we any longer choose justice rather than the worst injustice? When, if we only unite the latter with a deceitful regard to appearances, we shall fare to our mind both with gods and men, in life and after death, as the most numerous and the highest authorities tell us. Knowing all this, Socrates, how can a man who has any superiority of mind or person or rank or wealth, be willing to honour justice; or indeed to refrain from laughing when he hears justice praised? And even if there should be some one who is able to disprove the truth of my words, and who is satisfied that justice is best, still he is not angry with the unjust, but is very ready to forgive them, because he also knows that men are not just of their own free will; unless, peradventure, there be some whom the divinity within him may have inspired with a hatred of injustice, or who has attained knowledge of the truth—but no other man. He only blames injustice who, owing to cowardice or age or some weakness, has not the power of being unjust. And this is proved by the fact that when he obtains the power, he immediately becomes unjust as far as he can be.

The cause of all this, Socrates, was indicated by us at the beginning of the argument, when my brother and I told you how astonished we were to find that of all the professing panegyrists of justice—beginning with the ancient heroes of whom any memorial has been preserved to us, and ending with the men of our own time—no one has ever blamed injustice or praised justice except with a view to the glories, honours, and benefits which flow from them. No one has ever adequately described either in verse or prose the true essential nature of either of them abiding in the soul, and invisible to any human or divine eye; or shown that of all the things of a man's soul which he has within him, justice is the greatest good, and injustice the greatest evil. Had this been the universal strain, had you sought to persuade us of this from our youth upwards, we should not have been on the watch to keep one another from doing wrong, but every one would have been his own watchman, because afraid, if he did wrong, of harbouring in himself the greatest of evils. I dare say that Thrasymachus and others would seriously hold the language which I have been merely repeating, and words even stronger than these about justice and injustice, grossly, as I conceive, perverting their true nature. But I speak in this vehement manner, as I must frankly confess to you, because I want to hear from you the opposite side; and I would ask you to show not only the superiority which justice has over injustice, but what effect they have on the possessor of them which makes the one to be a good and the other an evil to him. And please, as Glaucon requested of you, to exclude reputations; for unless you take away from each of them his true reputation and add on the false, we shall say that you do not praise justice, but the appearance of it; we shall think that you are only exhorting us to keep injustice dark, and that you really agree with Thrasymachus in thinking that justice is another's good and the interest of the stronger, and that injustice is a man's own profit and interest, though injurious to the weaker. Now as you have admitted that justice is one of that highest class of goods which are desired indeed for their results, but in a far greater degree for their own sakes—like sight or hearing or knowledge or health, or any other real and natural and not merely conventional good—I would ask you in your praise of justice to regard one point only: I mean the essential good and evil which justice and injustice work in the possessors of them. Let others praise justice and censure injustice, magnifying the rewards and honours of the one and abusing the other; that is a manner of arguing which, coming from them, I am ready to tolerate, but from you who have spent your whole life in the consideration of this question, unless I hear the contrary from your own lips, I expect something better. And therefore, I say, not only prove to us that justice is better than injustice, but show what they either of them do to the possessor of them, which makes the one to be a good and the other an evil, whether seen or unseen by gods and men.

NOTES

1. *Seven Against Thebes,* 574.
2. Hesiod, *Works and Days,* 230.
3. Homer, *Od.* xix. 109.
4. Eumolpus.
5. Hesiod, *Works and Days,* 287.
6. Homer, *Iliad,* ix. 493.

Socrates' Answer (in part)*

PLATO

BOOK II

I HAD ALWAYS ADMIRED THE GENIUS of Glaucon and Adeimantus, but on hearing these words I was quite delighted, and said: Sons of an illustrious father,[1] that was not a bad beginning of the elegiac verses which the admirer of Glaucon made in honour of you after you had distinguished yourselves at the battle of Megara:—

> 'Sons of Ariston,' he sang, 'divine offspring of an illustrious hero.'

The epithet is very appropriate, for there is something truly divine in being able to argue as you have done for the superiority of injustice, and remaining unconvinced by your own arguments. And I do believe that you are not convinced—this I infer from your general character, for had I judged only from your speeches I should have mistrusted you. But now, the greater my confidence in you, the greater is my difficulty in knowing what to say. For on the one hand I cannot offer any help, because I feel that I am unequal to the task; and my inability is brought home to me by the fact that you were not satisfied with the answer which I made to Thrasymachus, proving, as I thought, the superiority which justice has over injustice. And yet I cannot refuse to help, while breath and speech remain to me; I am afraid that there would be an impiety in being present when justice is evil spoken of and not

*From Plato, The Republic, ii. 367E–376E, iii. 412B–iv. 445B, trans. B. Jowett.

lifting up a hand in her defence. And therefore I had best give such help as I can.

Glaucon and the rest entreated me by all means not to let the question drop, but, in the first place, to inquire thoroughly into the nature of justice and injustice, and secondly, to discover the truth about their relative advantages. I told them, what I really thought, that the inquiry would be of a serious nature, and would require very good eyes. Seeing then, I said, that we are no great wits, I think that we had better adopt a method which I may illustrate thus; suppose that a short-sighted person had been asked to read small letters from a distance; and someone observed that the same inscription was written elsewhere on a larger scale—if they were the same, and he could read the larger letters first and then proceed to the lesser, this would have been thought a rare piece of good fortune.

Very true, said Adeimantus; but how does the illustration apply to our inquiry about justice?

I will tell you, I replied; justice is, as you know, sometimes spoken of as the virtue of an individual, and sometimes as the virtue of a State.[2]

True, he replied.

And is not a State larger than an individual?

It is.

Then in the larger, justice is likely to be more abundant and more easily discernible. I propose therefore that we inquire into the nature of justice and injustice, first as they appear in the State, and secondly in the individual, proceeding from the greater to the lesser and comparing them.

That, he said, is an excellent proposal.

And if we imagine the State in process of creation, we shall see the justice and injustice of the State in process of creation also.

I dare say.

When the State is completed there may be a hope that the object of our search will be more easily discovered.

Yes, far more easily.

But ought we to attempt to construct one? I said; for to do so, as I am inclined to think, will be a very serious task. Reflect therefore.

I have reflected, said Adeimantus, and am anxious that you should proceed.

A State, I said, arises, as I conceive, out of the needs of mankind, no one is self-sufficing, but all of us have many wants. Can any other origin of a State be imagined?

There can be no other.

Then, as we have many wants, and many persons are needed to supply them, one takes a helper for one purpose and another for another; and when these partners and helpers are gathered together in one habitation the body of inhabitants is termed a State.

True, he said.

And it is in the belief that it is for his own good, that one man gives to another or receives from him in exchange.

Very true.

Then, I said, let us construct a State in theory from the beginning; and yet the true creator, it seems, will be necessity.

Of course, he replied.

Now the first and greatest of necessities is food, which is the condition of life and existence.

Certainly.

The second is a dwelling, and the third clothing and the like.

True.

And now let us see what must be the size[3] of a city able to supply such a demand: We may suppose that one man is a husbandman, another a builder, someone else a weaver—shall we add to them a shoemaker, or perhaps some other purveyor to our bodily wants?

By all means.

The simplest possible State must include four or five men.

Clearly.

And how will they proceed? Will each bring the result of his labours into a common stock?—the individual husbandman, for example, producing for four, and labouring four times as long and as much as he need in the provision of food with which he supplies others as well as himself; or will he have nothing to do with others and not be at the trouble of producing for them, but provide for himself alone a fourth of the food in a fourth of the time, and in the remaining three fourths of his time be employed in making a house or a coat or a pair of shoes, not bothering to form a partnership with others, but supplying himself all his own wants?

Adeimantus thought that he should aim at producing food only and not at producing everything.

Probably, I replied, that would be the better way; and when I hear you say this, I am myself reminded that we are not all alike; there are diversities of natures among us which are adapted to different occupations.

Very true.

And will you have a work better done when every workman tries his hand at many occupations, or when each has only one?

When he has only one.

Further, there can be no doubt that a work is spoilt when not done at the right time?

No doubt.

For business is not disposed to wait until the doer of the business is at leisure; but the doer must follow up his opportunity, and make the business his first object.

He must.

And if so, we must infer that all things are produced more plentifully and easily and of a better quality when one man does one thing which is natural to him and does it at the right time, leaving other crafts alone.

Undoubtedly.

Then more than four citizens will be required to furnish all that has been mentioned; for the husbandman will not make his own plough or mattock, or other implements of agriculture, if they are to be good for anything. Neither will the builder make his tools—and he too needs many; and in like manner the weaver and shoemaker.

True.

Then carpenters, and smiths, and many other artisans, will be sharers in our little State, which is already beginning to grow?

True.

Yet even if we add neatherds, shepherds, and other herdsmen, in order that our husbandmen may have oxen to plough with, and builders as well as husbandmen may have draught cattle, and curriers and weavers fleeces and hides,—still our State will not be very large.

That is true; yet neither will it be a very small State which contains all these.

Then, again, there is the situation of the city—to find a place where nothing need be imported is well-nigh impossible.

Impossible.

Then there must be another class of citizens who will bring the required supply from another city?

There must.

But if the trader goes empty-handed, having nothing which they require who would supply his need, he will come back empty handed.

That is probable.

And therefore what they produce at home must be not only enough for themselves, but such both in quantity and quality as to accommodate those from whom their wants are supplied.

Very true.

Then more husbandmen and more artisans will be required?

They will.

Not to mention those who serve as importers and exporters of goods, who are called, I believe, merchants?

Yes.

Then we shall want merchants?

We shall.

And if merchandise is to be carried over the sea, we shall also require men who have been bred to various nautical occupations.

Yes, a large class.

Then, again, within the city, how will they exchange their productions? To secure such an exchange was, as you will remember, one of our principal objects when we formed them into a society and constituted a State.

Clearly they will buy and sell.

Then they will need a market-place, and a money-token for purposes of exchange.

Certainly.

Suppose now that a husbandman, or an artisan, brings some productions to market, and comes at a time when there is no one to exchange with him—is he to sit idle in the market-place, taking a holiday from his work?

Not at all; he will find people there who, seeing the want, undertake the office of salesmen. In well-ordered states they are commonly those who are weakest in bodily strength, and therefore of little use for any other purpose; their duty is to be in the market, and to give money in exchange for goods to those who desire to sell and to take money from those who desire to buy.

This want, then, creates a class of retail-traders in our State. Is not 'retailer' the term which is applied to those who sit in the market-place engaged in buying and selling, while those who wander from one city to another are called merchants?

Yes, he said.

And there is another class of servants, who are intellectually hardly on the level of association; still they have plenty of bodily strength for labour, which accordingly they sell, and are called, if I do not mistake, hirelings, hire being the name which is given to the price of their labour.

True.

Then hirelings will help to make up our population?

Yes.

And now, Adeimantus, is our State matured and perfected?

I think so.

Where, then, is justice within it, and where is injustice, and at what stage did they make their entrance?

Probably in the dealings of these citizens with one another. I cannot suggest where else they may be found.

I dare say that you are right in your suggestion, I said; we had better think the matter out, and not shrink from the inquiry.

Let us then consider, first of all, what will be their way of life, now that we have thus established them. Will they not work at the production of corn, and wine, and clothes, and shoes? And when they are housed, in summer they will commonly work stripped and barefoot, but in winter substantially clothed and shod. They will feed on barley-meal and flour of wheat, baking the one and kneading the other, making noble cakes and loaves; these they will serve up on a mat of reeds or on clean leaves, themselves reclining the while upon beds strewn with yew or myrtle. And they and their children will feast, drinking of the wine which they have made, wearing garlands on their heads, and hymning the praises of the gods, in happy converse with one another. And they will take care that their families do not exceed their means; having an eye to poverty or war.

But, said Glaucon, interposing, you have not given them a relish to their meal.

True, I replied, I had forgotten; of course they must have a relish—salt, and olives, and cheese, and they will boil roots and herbs such as country people prepare; for a dessert we shall give them figs, and peas, and beans; and they will roast myrtleberries and acorns at the fire, sipping their wine in moderation. And with such a diet they may be expected to live in peace and health to a good old age, and bequeath a similar life to their children after them.

Yes, Socrates, he said, and if you were providing for a city of pigs, how else would you feed the beasts?

But what would you have, Glaucon? I replied.

Why, he said, you should give them the ordinary conveniences of life. People who are to be comfortable are accustomed to lie on sofas, and dine off tables, and they should have sauces and sweets in the modern style.

Yes, I said, now I understand: the question which you would have me consider is, not only how a State, but how a luxurious State is created; and possibly there is no harm in this, for by extending our inquiry to such a State we shall be more likely to see how political justice and injustice originate. In my opinion the true and healthy constitution of the State is the one which I have described. But if you wish also to see a State at fever-heat, I have no objection. For I suspect that many will not be satisfied with the simpler way of life. They will be for adding sofas, and tables, and other furniture; also dainties, and perfumes, and incense, and courtezans, and cakes, all these not of one sort only, but in every variety; we must go beyond the necessaries of which I was at first speaking, such as houses, and clothes, and shoes: the arts of the painter and the embroiderer will have to be set in motion, and gold and ivory and all sorts of materials must be procured.

True, he said.

Then we must enlarge our borders; for the original healthy State is no longer sufficient. Now will the city have to fill and swell with a multitude of callings which are not required by any natural want; such as the tribe of hunters, and again imitators, of whom one large class have to do with forms and colours; another will be the votaries of music—poets and their attendant train of rhapsodists, players, dancers, contractors; also makers of divers kinds of articles, including those which serve for the adornment of women. And we shall want more servants. Will not tutors be also in request, and nurses wet and dry, tirewomen and barbers, as well as confectioners and cooks? Then we shall also now need swineherds, who were not needed and therefore had no place in our former State. They must not be forgotten: also a vast number of cattle will be required, if meat is to be eaten.

Certainly.

And living in this way we shall have much greater need of physicians than before?

Much greater.

And the country which was once enough to support the original inhabitants will now have become too small?

Quite true.

Then a slice of our neighbours' land will be wanted by us for pasture and tillage, and they will want a slice of ours, if, like ourselves, they exceed the limit of necessity, and give themselves up to the unlimited accumulation of wealth?

That, Socrates, will be inevitable.

And so we shall go to war, Glaucon. Shall we not?

Most certainly, he replied.

Then, without determining as yet whether war does good or harm, thus much we may affirm, that now we have discovered war to be derived from causes which are also the causes of almost all the evils in States, private as well as public.

Undoubtedly.

And our State must once more enlarge; and this time the enlargement will be nothing short of a whole army, which will have to go out and fight with the invaders for all that we have, as well as for the things and persons whom we were describing above.

Why? he said; are they not capable of defending themselves?

No, I said; not if we were right in the principle which was acknowledged by all of us when we were framing the State: the principle, as you will remember, was that one man cannot practise many arts with success.

Very true, he said.

But is not armed combat in war an art?

Certainly.

And an art requiring as much attention as shoemaking?

Quite true.

And the shoemaker was not allowed by us to be a husbandman, or a weaver, or a builder—in order that we might have our shoes well made; but to him and to every other worker was assigned one work for which he was by nature fitted, and at that he was to continue working all his life long and at no other; he was not to let opportunities slip, and then he would become a good workman. Now can anything be more important than that the work of a soldier should be well done? Or is war an art so easily acquired that a man may be a warrior who is also a husbandman, or shoemaker, or other artisan; although no one in the world would be a good dice- or chess-player who merely took up the game as a recreation, and had not from his earliest years devoted himself to this and nothing else? No equipment will make a man a skilled workman, or athlete, nor be of any use to him who has not learned how to handle it, and has never bestowed sufficient attention upon it. How then will he who takes up a shield or other implement of war become a good fighter all in a day, whether with heavy-armed or any other kind of troops?

Yes, he said, the tools which would teach men their own use would be beyond price.

And just as the duties of the guardian surpass all others in importance, I said, so does his business require the most skill and practice, as well as undivided attention.

No doubt, he replied.

Will he not also require natural aptitude for his calling?

Certainly.

Then it will be our duty to select, if we can, natures which are fitted for the task of guarding the city?

It will.

It is no light task, then, that we have undertaken, I said; but we must be brave and do our best.

We must.

Do you agree that the noble youth is very like a well-bred dog in respect of guarding and watching?

What do you mean?

I mean that both of them ought to be quick to see, and swift to overtake the enemy when they see him; and strong too if, when they have caught him, they have to fight with him.

All these qualities, he replied, will certainly be required by them.

Well, and your guardian must be brave if he is to fight well?

Certainly.

And is he likely to be brave who has no spirit, whether horse or dog or any other animal? Have you never observed how invincible and unconquerable is spirit and how the presence of it makes the soul of any creature to be absolutely fearless and indomitable?

I have.

Then now we have a clear notion of the bodily qualities which are required in the guardian.

True.

And also of the mental ones; his soul is to be full of spirit?

True again.

But how can these spirited natures fail to be savage with one another, and with everybody else?

A difficulty by no means easy to overcome, he replied.

Whereas, I said, they ought to be dangerous to their enemies, and gentle to their friends; if not, they will destroy themselves without waiting for their enemies to destroy them.

True, he said.

What is to be done then? I said; how shall we find a gentle nature which has also a high spirit, for the one is the contradiction of the other?

True.

He will not be a good guardian who is wanting in either of these two qualities; and yet the combination of them appears to be impossible; and hence we must infer that to be a good guardian is impossible.

I am afraid that what you say is true, he replied.

Here feeling perplexed I began to think over what had preceded.—My friend, I said, no wonder that we are in a perplexity; for we have lost sight of the image which we had before us.

What do you mean? he said.

It has escaped our notice that there do exist natures gifted with those opposite qualities.

Where?

Many animals, I replied, furnish examples of them, but most of all the dog, to which we compared the guardian: you know the disposition of a well-bred dog, perfectly gentle to its familiars and acquaintances, and the reverse to strangers.

Yes, I know.

Then there is nothing impossible or out of the order of nature in our finding a guardian who has a similar combination of qualities?

Certainly not.

Would not he who is fitted to be a guardian, besides the spirited nature, need to have the qualities of a philosopher?

I do not apprehend your meaning.

The trait of which I am speaking, I replied, may also be seen in the dog, and is remarkable in the animal.

What trait?

Why, a dog, whenever he sees a stranger, is angry; when an acquaintance, he welcomes him, although the one has never done him any harm, nor the other any good. Did this never strike you as curious?

The point never struck me before; but I quite recognize the truth of your remark.

And surely this instinct of the dog is very charming;—your dog is a true philosopher.

Why?

Why, because he distinguishes the face of a friend and of an enemy only by the criterion of knowing and not knowing. And must not an animal be a lover of learning who determines what is or is not friendly to him by the test of knowledge and ignorance?

Most assuredly.

And is not the love of learning the love of wisdom, which is philosophy?

They are the same, he replied.

And may we not say confidently of man also, that he who is likely to be gentle to his friends and acquaintances, must by nature be a lover of wisdom and knowledge?

That we may safely affirm.

Then he who is to be a really good and noble guardian of the State will require to unite in himself philosophy and spirit and swiftness and strength?

Undoubtedly.

Then we have found the desired natures; and now that we have found them, how are they to be reared and educated? Is not this an inquiry which may be expected to throw light on the greater inquiry which is our final end—How do justice and injustice grow up in States? for we do not want either to omit what is to the point or to draw out the argument to an inconvenient length.

Adeimantus thought that the inquiry would be of great service to us.

Then, I said, my dear friend, the task must not be given up, even if somewhat long.

Certainly not.

Come then, and let us pass a leisure hour in storytelling, and our story shall be the education of our heroes. . . .

[Socrates' account of the primary education of the Guardians (376E-412B) is omitted here. In it he discusses censorship of literature, the molding influence of dramatic recitation, music and meter, and physical training. The argument resumes below with his account of how rulers are to be selected.—Eds.]

BOOK III

Such, then, are our principles of nurture and education: Where would be the use of going into further details about the dances of our citizens, or about their hunting and coursing, their gymnastic and equestrian contests? For these all follow the general principle, and having found that, we shall have no difficulty in discovering them.

I dare say that there will be no difficulty.

Very good, I said; then what is the next question? Must we not ask who are to be rulers and who subjects?

Certainly.

There can be no doubt that the elder must rule the younger.

Clearly.

And that the best of these must rule.

That is also clear.

Now, are the best husbandmen those who are most devoted to husbandry?

Yes.

And as we are to have the best of guardians for our city, must they not be those who have most the character of guardians?

Yes.

And to this end they ought to be wise and efficient, and to have a special care of the State?

True.

And a man will be most likely to care about that which he loves?

To be sure.

And he will be most likely to love that which he regards as having the same interests with himself, and that of which the good or evil fortune is supposed by him at any time most to affect his own?

Very true, he replied.

Then there must be a selection. Let us note among the guardians those who in their whole life show the greatest eagerness to do what they suppose to be for the good of their country, and the greatest repugnance to do what is against her interests.

Those are the right men.

And they will have to be watched at every age, in order that we may see whether they preserve their resolution, and never yield either to force or to enchantment, so as to forget or cast off their sense of duty to the State.

How cast off? he said.

I will explain to you, I replied. A resolution may go out of a man's mind either with his will or against his will; with his will when he gets rid of a falsehood and learns better, against his will whenever he is deprived of a truth.

I understand, he said, the willing loss of a resolution; the meaning of the unwilling I have yet to learn.

Why, I said, do you not see that men are unwillingly deprived of good, and willingly of evil? Is not to have lost the truth an evil, and to possess the truth a good? and you would agree that to conceive things as they are is to possess the truth?

Yes, he replied; I agree with you in thinking that mankind are deprived of truth against their will.

And is not this involuntary deprivation caused either by theft, or force, or enchantment?

Still, he replied, I do not understand you.

I must have been talking darkly like the tragedians. As for theft, I only mean that some men are changed by persuasion and that others forget; argument steals away the beliefs of one class, and time of the other. Now you understand me?

Yes.

Those again who are forced, are those whom the violence of some pain or grief compels to change their opinion.

I understand, he said, and you are quite right.

And you would also acknowledge that the enchanted are those who change their minds either under the softer influence of pleasure, or the sterner shock of fear?

Yes, he said; everything that deceives may be said to enchant.

Therefore, as I was just now saying, we must inquire who are the best guardians of their own conviction that they should always do what they judge most advantageous to the State. We must watch them from their youth upwards, and make them perform actions in which they are most likely to forget or to be deceived, and he who remembers and is not deceived is to be selected, and he who fails in the trial is to be rejected. That will be the way?

Yes.

And there should also be toils and pains and conflicts prescribed for them, in which they will be made to give further proof of the same qualities.

Very right, he replied.

And then, I said, we must try them with enchantments—that is the third sort of test—and see what will be their behaviour: like those who take colts amid noise and tumult to see if they are of a timid nature, so must we take our youth amid terrors of some kind, and thence pass them into pleasures, and prove them more thoroughly than gold is proved in the furnace, that we may discover whether they are armed against all enchantments, and of a noble bearing always, good guardians of themselves and of the music which they have learned, and retaining under all circumstances a rhythmical and harmonious nature, such as will be most serviceable to themselves and to the State. And he who at every age, as boy and youth and in mature life, has come out of the trial victorious and pure, shall be appointed a ruler and guardian of the State; he shall be honoured in life and death, and shall receive sepulture and other memorials of honour, the greatest that we have to give. But him who fails, we must reject. I am inclined to think that this is the sort of way in which our rulers and guardians should be chosen and appointed. I speak generally, and not with any pretension to exactness.

And, speaking generally, I agree with you, he said.

And perhaps the word 'guardian' in the fullest sense ought to be applied to this higher class only who both preserve us against foreign enemies and maintain peace among our citizens at home, that the one may not have the will, or the others the power, to harm us. The young men whom we before called guardians may be more properly designated auxiliaries and supporters of the principles of the rulers.

I agree with you, he said.

How then may we devise one of those needful falsehoods of which we lately spoke—just one royal lie which may deceive the rulers, if that be possible, and at any rate the rest of the city?

What sort of lie? he said.

Nothing new, I replied; only an old Phoenician[4] tale of what has often occurred before now in other places (as the poets say, and have made the world believe), though not in our time, and I do not know whether such an event could ever happen again, or could now even be made to seem probable.

How your words seem to hesitate on your lips!

You will not wonder, I replied, at my hesitation when you have heard.

Speak, he said, and fear not.

Well then, I will speak, although I really know not how to look you in the face, or in what words to utter the audacious fiction, which I propose to communicate gradually, first to the rulers, then to the soldiers, and lastly to the people. They are to be told that the education and training which they seemed to receive from us in youth was but a dream; in reality during all that time they were being formed and fed in the womb of the earth, where they themselves and their arms and appurtenances were manufactured; when they were completed, the earth, their mother, sent them up; and so, their country being their mother and also their nurse, they are bound to advise for her good, and to defend her against attacks; and the other citizens they are to regard as children of the earth and their own brothers.

You had good reason, he said, to be ashamed of the lie which you were going to tell.

No doubt, I replied, but listen to the continuation of the tale. Citizens, we shall say to them in our tale, you are brothers, yet God has framed you differently. Some of you have the power of command, and in the composition of these he has mingled gold, wherefore also they have the greatest honour; others he has made of silver, to be auxiliaries; others again who are to be husbandmen and craftsmen he has composed of brass and iron; and the species will generally be preserved in the children. But as all are of the same original stock, a golden parent will sometimes have a silver son, a silver parent a golden son, and so forth. And God proclaims as a first principle to the rulers, and above all else, that there is nothing which they should so anxiously guard, or of which they are to be such good guardians, as of the mixture of elements in the soul. First, if one of their own offspring has an admixture of brass or iron, they shall in no wise have pity on it, but give it the rank which is its due and send it down to the husbandmen or artisans. On the other hand, if there are sons of artisans who have an admixture of gold or silver in them, they will be raised to honour, and become guardians or auxiliaries. For an oracle says that when a man of brass or iron guards the State, it will be destroyed. Such is the tale; is there any possibility of making our citizens believe in it?

Not in the first generation, he replied; but their sons may be made to believe in the tale, and their sons' sons, and posterity after them.

I see the difficulty, I replied; yet the fostering of such a belief will make them care more for the city and for one another. Enough, however, of the fiction, which may now fly abroad upon the wings of rumour, while we arm our earth-born heroes, and lead them forth under the command of their rulers. Let them look round and select a spot whence they can best suppress insurrection, if any prove refractory within, and also defend themselves against enemies, who like wolves may come down on the fold from without; there let them encamp, and when they have encamped, let them sacrifice to the proper gods and prepare their lodging.

Just so, he said.

And this must be such as will shield them against the cold of winter and the heat of summer.

I suppose that you mean houses, he replied.

Yes, I said; but they must be the houses of soldiers, and not of shopkeepers.

What is the difference? he said.

That I will endeavour to explain, I replied. To keep watchdogs, who, from want of discipline or hunger or some evil habit or other, would turn upon the sheep and worry them, and behave not like dogs but wolves, would be a foul and monstrous thing in a shepherd?

Truly monstrous, he said.

And therefore every care must be taken that our auxiliaries, being stronger than our citizens, may not behave in this fashion and become like savage tyrants instead of friends and allies?

Yes, great care should be taken.

And if they have really received a good education, will not that furnish the best safeguard?

But they have received it, he replied.

I cannot be so confident, my dear Glaucon, I said; but I believe the truth is as I said, that a sound education, whatever that may be, will have the greatest tendency to civilize and humanize them in their relations to one another, and to those who are under their protection.

Very true, he replied.

And not only their education, but their habitations, and all that belongs to them, should be such as will neither impair their virtue as guardians, nor tempt them to prey upon the other citizens. Any man of sense must acknowledge that.

He must.

Then now let us consider what will be their way of life, if they are to realize our idea of them. In the first place, none of them should have any property of his own beyond what is absolutely necessary; neither should they have a private house or store closed against anyone who has a mind to enter; their provisions should be only such as are required by trained warriors, who are men of temperance and courage; they should agree to receive from the citizens a fixed rate of pay, enough to meet the expenses of the year and no more; and they will go to mess and live together like soldiers in a camp. Gold and silver we will tell them that they have from God; the diviner metal is within them, and they have therefore no need of the dross which is current among men, and ought not to pollute the divine by any such earthly admixture; for that commoner metal has been the sources of many unholy deeds, but their own is undefiled. And they alone of all the citizens may not touch or handle silver or gold, or be under the same roof with them, or wear them, or drink from them. And this will be their salvation, and they will be the saviours of the State. But should they ever acquire homes or lands or moneys of their own, they will become householders and husbandmen instead of guardians, enemies and tyrants instead of allies of the other citizens; hating and being hated, plotting and being plotted against, they will pass their whole life in much greater terror of internal than of external enemies, and the hour of ruin, both to themselves and to the rest of the State, will be at hand. For all which reasons may we not say that thus shall our State be ordered, and that these shall be the regulations appointed by us for our guardians concerning their lodging and all other matters?

Yes, said Glaucon.

BOOK IV

Here Adeimantus interposed a question: How would you answer, Socrates, said he, if a person were to say that you are not making these men very happy, and that they are themselves to blame; the city in fact belongs to them, but they reap no advantage from it; whereas other men acquire lands, and build large and handsome houses, and have everything handsome about them, offering sacrifices to the gods on their own account, and practising hospitality; moreover, they have the gold and silver which you have just mentioned, and all that is usual among the favourites of fortune; but our poor citizens are no better than mercenaries who are quartered in the city and are always mounting guard?

Yes, I said; and you may add that they are only fed, and not paid in addition to their food like other men; and therefore they cannot, if they would, take a private journey abroad; they have no money to spend on a mistress or any other luxurious fancy, which, as the world goes, is thought to be happiness; and many other accusations of the same nature might be added.

But, said he, let us suppose all this to be included in the charge.

You mean to ask, I said, what will be our answer?

Yes.

If we proceed along the old path, my belief, I said, is that we shall find the answer. And our answer will be that, even as they are, our guardians may very likely be the happiest of men; but that our aim in founding the State was not the disproportionate happiness of any one class, but the greatest happiness of the whole; we thought that in a State which is ordered with a view to the good of the whole we should be most likely to find justice, and in the worst-ordered State injustice: and, having found them, we might then decide upon the answer to our first question. At present, I take it, we are fashioning the happy State, not piecemeal, or with a view of making a few happy citizens, but as a whole; and by-and-by we will proceed to view the opposite kind of State. Suppose that we were painting a statue, and someone came up to us and said, Why do you not put the most beautiful colours on the most beautiful parts of the body—the eyes ought to be purple, but you have made them black—to him we might fairly answer, 'Sir, you would not surely have us beautify the eyes to such a degree that they are no longer eyes; consider rather whether, by giving this and the other features their due proportion, we make the whole beautiful.' And so I say to you, do not compel us to assign to the guardians a sort of happiness which will make them no guardians at all; for we too can clothe our husbandmen in royal apparel, and set crowns of gold on their heads, and bid them till the ground as much as they like, and no more. Our potters also might be allowed to repose on couches, and feast by the fireside, passing round the winecup, while their wheel is conveniently at hand, so that they may make a few pots when they feel inclined; in this way we might make every class happy—and then, as you imagine, the whole State would be happy. But do not put this idea into our heads; for, if we listen to you, the husbandman will be no longer a husbandman, the potter will cease to be a potter, and no one will have the character of any distinct class in the State. Now this is not of much consequence where the corruption of society, and pretension to be what you are not, is confined to cobblers; but when the guardians of the laws and of the government are only seeming and not real guardians, then see how they turn the State upside down; and on the other hand they alone have the power of giving order and happiness to the State. We mean our guardians to be true saviours and not the destroyers of the State, whereas our opponent is thinking of peasants at a festival, who are enjoying a life of revelry, not of citizens who are doing their duty to the State. But, if so, we mean different things, and he is speaking of something which is not a State. And therefore we must consider whether in appointing our guardians we look to their greatest happiness individually, or whether our aim is not to ensure that happiness appears in the State as a whole. What these guardians or auxiliaries must be compelled or induced to do (and the same may be said of every other trade), is to become as expert as possible in their professional work. And thus the whole State will grow up in a noble order, and the several classes will receive the proportion of happiness which nature assigns to them.

I think that you are quite right.

I wonder whether you will agree with another remark which occurs to me.

What may that be?

There seem to be two causes of the deterioration of the arts.

What are they?

Wealth, I said, and poverty.

How do they act?

The process is as follows: When a potter becomes rich, will he, think you, any longer take the same pains with his art?

Certainly not.

He will grow more indolent and careless?

Very true.

And the result will be that he becomes a worse potter?

Yes; he greatly deteriorates.

But, on the other hand, if he has no money and cannot provide himself with tools or other requirements of his craft, his own work will not be equally good, and he will not teach his sons or apprentices to work equally well.

Certainly not.

Then, under the influence either of poverty or of wealth, workmen and their work are equally liable to degenerate?

That is evident.

Here then is a discovery of new evils, I said, against which the guardians will have to watch, or they will creep into the city unobserved.

What evils?

Wealth, I said, and poverty; the one is the parent of luxury and indolence, and the other of meanness and viciousness, and both of a revolutionary spirit.

That is very true, he replied; but still I should like to know, Socrates, how our city will be able to go to war, especially against an enemy who is rich and powerful, if deprived of the sinews of war.

Evidently it would be difficult, I replied, to wage war with one such enemy; but it will be easier where there are two of them.

How so? he asked.

In the first place, I said, if we have to fight, our side will be trained warriors fighting against an army of rich men.

That is true, he said.

And do you not suppose, Adeimantus, that a single boxer who was perfect in his art would easily be a match for two stout and well-to-do gentlemen who were not boxers?

Hardly, if they came upon him at once.

What, not, I said, if he were able to run away and then turn and strike at the first who came up? And supposing he were to do this several times under the heat of a scorching sun, might he not, being an expert, overturn more than one stout personage?

Certainly, he said, there would be nothing wonderful in that.

And yet rich men probably have more instruction in the science and practise of boxing than they have in military science.

Likely enough.

Then we may assume that our athletes will be able to fight with two or three times their own number?

I will accept that, for I think you right.

And suppose that, before engaging, our citizens send an embassy to one of the two cities, telling them what is the truth: 'Silver and gold we neither have nor are permitted to have, but you may; do you therefore come and help us in war, and take the spoils of the other city.' Who, on hearing these words, would choose to fight against lean wiry dogs, rather than, with the dogs on their side, against fat and tender sheep.

That is not likely; and yet there might be a danger to the poor State if the wealth of many States were to be gathered into one.

But how simple of you to think that the term State is applicable at all to any but our own!

Why so?

You ought to speak of other States in the plural number; not one of them is a city, but many cities, as they say in the game. Each will contain not less than two divisions, one the city of the poor, the other of the rich, which are at war with one another; and within each there are many smaller divisions. You would be altogether beside the mark if you treated these as a single State; but if you deal with them as many, and give the wealth or power or persons of the one to the others, you will always have a great many friends and not many enemies. And your State, while the wise order which has now been prescribed continues to prevail in her, will be the greatest of States, I do not mean to say in reputation or appearance, but in deed and truth, though she number not more than a thousand defenders. A single State of that size you will hardly find, either among Hellenes or barbarians, though many that appear to be as great and many times greater.

That is most true, he said.

Hence, I said, it can be seen what will be the best limit for our rulers to fix when they are considering the size of the State and the amount of territory which they are to include, and beyond which they will not go.

What limit would you propose?

I would allow the State to increase so far as is consistent with unity; that, I think, is the proper limit.

Very good, he said.

Here then, I said, is another order which will have to be conveyed to our guardians: Let them guard against our city becoming small, or great only in appearance. It must attain an adequate size, but it must remain one.

And perhaps, said he, you do not think this is a very severe order?

And here is another, said I, which is lighter still,—I mean the duty, of which some mention was made before, of degrading the offspring of the guardians when inferior, and of elevating into the rank of guardians the offspring of the lower classes, when naturally superior. The intention was that, in the case of the citizens generally, each individual should be put to the use for which nature intended him, one to one work, and then every man would do his own business, and become one and not many; and so the whole city would be one and not many.

Yes, he said; that is not so difficult.

The regulations which we are prescribing, my good Adeimantus, are not, as might be supposed, a number of great principles, but trifles all, if care be taken, as the saying is, of the one great thing,—a thing, however, which I would rather call, not great, but sufficient for our purpose.

What may that be? he asked.

Education, I said, and nurture: if our citizens are well educated, and grow into sensible men, they will easily see their way through all these, as well as other matters which I omit; such, for example, as marriage, the possession of women and the procreation of children, which will all follow the general principle that friends have all things in common, as the proverb says.

That will be the best way of settling them.

Also, I said, the State, if once started well, moves with accumulating force like a wheel. For where good nurture and education are maintained, they implant good constitutions, and these good constitutions taking root in a good education improve more and more, and this improvement affects the breed in man as in other animals.

Very possibly, he said.

Then to sum up: This is the principle to which our rulers should cling throughout, taking care that neglect does not creep in—that music and gymnastic be preserved in their original form, and no innovation made. They must do their utmost to maintain them intact. And when anyone says that

> 'Mankind most regard the newest song which the singers have',[5]

they will be afraid that he may be praising, not new songs, but a new kind of song; and this ought not to be praised, or conceived to be the meaning of the poet; for any musical innovation is to be shunned, as likely to bring danger to the whole State. So Damon tells me, and I can quite believe him;—he says that when modes of music change, the fundamental laws of the State always change with them.

Yes, said Adeimantus; and you may add my suffrage to Damon's and your own.

Then, I said, our guardians must lay the foundations of their fortress in music?

Yes, he said; the lawlessness of which you speak too easily steals in.

Yes, I replied, in the form of amusement, and as though it were harmless.

Why, yes, he said, and harmless it would be; were it not that little by little this spirit of licence, finding a home, imperceptibly penetrates into manners and customs; whence issuing with greater force it invades contracts between man and man, and from contracts goes on to laws and constitutions, in utter recklessness, ending at last, Socrates, by an overthrow of all rights, private as well as public.

Is that true? I said.

That is my belief, he replied.

Then, as I was saying, our boys should be trained from the first in a stricter system, for if childish amusement becomes lawless, it will produce lawless children, who can never grow up into well-conducted and virtuous citizens.

Very true, he said.

And when boys who have made a good beginning in play, have later gained the habit of good order through music, then this habit accompanies them in all their actions and is a principle of growth to them, and is able to correct anything in the State which had been allowed to lapse. It is the reverse of the picture I have just drawn.

Very true, he said.

Thus educated, they will discover for themselves any lesser rules which their predecessors have altogether neglected.

What do you mean?

I mean such things as these:—when the young are to be silent before their elders; how they are to show respect to them by standing and making them sit; what honour is due to parents; what garments or shoes are to be worn; the mode of dressing the hair; deportment and manners in general. You would agree with me?

Yes.

But there is, I think, small wisdom in legislating about such matters,—precise written enactments cannot create these observances, and are not likely to make them lasting.

Impossible.

It would seem, Adeimantus, that the direction in which education starts a man will determine his future life. Does not like always attract like?

To be sure.

Until some one grand result is reached which may be good, and may be the reverse of good?

That is not to be denied.

And for this reason, I said, I, for my part, should not attempt to extend legislation to such details.

Naturally enough, he replied.

Well, and about the business of the agora, and the ordinary dealings between man and man, or again about agreements with artisans; about insult and injury, or the commencement of actions, and the appointment of juries, what would you say? there may also arise questions about any impositions and exactions of market and harbour dues which may be required, and in general about the regulations of markets, police, harbours, and the like. But, oh heavens! shall we condescend to legislate on any of these particulars?

No, he said, it is unseemly to impose laws about them on good men; what regulations are necessary they will find out soon enough for themselves.

Yes, I said, my friend, if God will only preserve to them the laws which we have given them.

And without divine help, said Adeimantus, they will go on for ever making and mending their laws and their lives in the hope of attaining perfection.

You would compare them, I said, to those invalids who, having no self-restraint, will not leave off their habits of intemperance?

Exactly.

Yes, I said; and what a delightful life they lead! they are always doctoring their disorders, with no result except to increase and complicate them, and always fancying that they will be cured by any nostrum which anybody advises them to try.

Such cases are very common, he said, with invalids of this sort.

Yes, I replied; and the charming thing is that they deem him their worst enemy who tells them the truth, which is simply that, unless they give up gorging and drinking and wenching and idling, neither drug nor cautery nor amputation nor spell nor amulet nor any other remedy will avail.

Charming? he replied. I see nothing charming in going into a passion with a man who tells you what is right.

These gentlemen, I said, do not seem to be in your good graces.

Assuredly not.

Nor would you approve if a whole State behaves in this way, and that brings me back to my point. For when, in certain ill-ordered States, the citizens are forbidden under pain of death to alter the constitution; and yet he who most sweetly courts those who live under this régime and indulges them and fawns upon them and is skillful in anticipating and gratifying their humours is honoured as a great and good statesman—do not these States resemble the persons whom I was describing?

Yes, he said; the fault is the same; and I am very far from approving it.

But what of these ready and eager ministers of political corruption? I said. Do you not admire their coolness and dexterity?

Yes, he said, I do; but not of all of them, for there are some whom the applause of the multitude has deluded into the belief that they are really statesmen.

What do you mean? I said; you should have more feeling for them. When a man cannot measure, and a great many others who cannot measure declare that he is four cubits high, can he help believing what they say?

Nay, he said, certainly not in that case.

Well, then, do not be angry with them; for are they not as good as a play, trying their hand at paltry reforms such as I was describing; they are always fancying that by legislation they will make an end of frauds in contracts, and the other rascalities which I was mentioning, not knowing that they are in reality cutting off the heads of a hydra?

Yes, he said; that is just what they are doing.

I conceive, I said, that the true legislator will not trouble himself with this class of enactments whether concerning laws or the constitution either in an ill-ordered or in a well-ordered State; for in the former they are quite useless, and in the latter they will either be of a kind which anyone can devise, or will naturally flow out of our previous regulations.

What, then, he said, is still remaining to us of the work of legislation?

Nothing to us, I replied; but to Apollo, the god of Delphi, there remains the ordering of the greatest and noblest and chiefest things of all.

Which are they? he said.

The institution of temples and sacrifices, and the entire service of gods, demigods, and heroes; also the ordering of the repositories of the dead, and the rites which have to be observed by him who would propitiate the inhabitants of the world below. These are matters of which we are ignorant ourselves, and as founders of a city we should be unwise in trusting them to any interpreter but the ancestral one. For it is Apollo who, sitting at the navel of the earth, is the ancestral interpreter of such observances to all mankind.

You are right, and we will do as you propose.

So now the foundation of your city, son of Ariston, is finished. What comes next? Provide yourself with a bright light and search, and get your bother and Polemarchus and the rest of our friends to help, and let us see where in it we can discover justice and where injustice, and in what they differ from one another, and which of them the man who would be happy should have for his portion, whether seen or unseen by gods and men.

Nonsense, said Glaucon: did you not promise to search yourself, saying that for you not to help justice in her need would be an impiety?

Your reminder is true, and I will be as good as my word; but you must join.

We will, he replied.

Well, then, I hope to make the discovery in this way: I mean to begin with the assumption that our State, if rightly ordered, is perfect.

That is most certain.

And being perfect, is therefore wise and valiant and temperate and just.

That is likewise clear.

And whichever of these qualities we first find in the State, the one which is not yet found will be the residue?

Very good.

If in some other instance there were four things, in one of which we were most interested, the one sought for might come to light first, and there would be no further trouble; or if we came to know the other three first, we should thereby attain the object of our search, for it must clearly be the part remaining.

Very true, he said.

And is not a similar method to be pursued about the virtues, which are also four in number?

Clearly.

First among the virtues found in the State, wisdom comes into view, and in this I detect a certain peculiarity.

What is that?

The State which we have been describing has, I think, true wisdom. You would agree that it is good in counsel?

Yes.

And this good counsel is clearly a kind of knowledge, for not by ignorance, but by knowledge, do men counsel well?

Clearly.

And the kinds of knowledge in a State are many and diverse?

Of course.

There is the knowledge of the carpenter; but is that the sort of knowledge which gives a city the title of wise and good in counsel?

Certainly not; that would only give a city the reputation of skill in carpentering.

Then a city is not to be called wise because possessing a knowledge which counsels for the best about wooden implements?

Certainly not.

Nor by reason of a knowledge which advises about brazen pots, he said, nor as possessing any other similar knowledge?

Not by reason of any of them, he said.

Nor yet by reason of a knowledge which cultivates the earth; that would give the city the name of agricultural?

Yes.

Well, I said, and is there any knowledge in our recently founded State among any of the citizens which advises not about any particular thing in the State, but about the whole, and considers how it can best conduct itself in relation with itself and with other States?

There certainly is.

And what is this knowledge, and among whom is it found? I asked.

It is the knowledge of guarding, he replied, and is found in those rulers whom we were just now describing as perfect guardians.[6]

And what is the name which the city derives from the possession of this sort of knowledge?

The name of good in counsel and truly wise.

And will there be in our city more of these true guardians or more smiths?

The smiths, he replied, will be far more numerous.

Will not the guardians probably be the smallest of all the classes who receive a name from the profession of some kind of knowledge?

Much the smallest.

And so by reason of the smallest part or class, and of the knowledge which resides in this presiding and ruling part of itself, the whole State, being thus constituted according to nature, will be wise; and this, which can claim a share in the only knowledge worthy to be called wisdom, has been ordained by nature to be of all classes the least.

Most true.

Thus, then, I said, the nature and place in the State of one of the four virtues has somehow or other been discovered.

And, in my humble opinion, very satisfactorily discovered, he replied.

Again, I said, there is no difficulty in seeing the nature of courage, and in what part that quality resides which gives the name of courageous to the State.

How do you mean?

Why, I said, everyone who calls any State courageous or cowardly, will be thinking of the part which fights and goes out to war on the State's behalf.

No one, he replied, would ever think of any other.

The rest of the citizens may be courageous or may be cowardly, but their courage or cowardice will not, as I conceive, have the effect of making the city either the one or the other.

No.

The city will be courageous also by one part of herself, in which resides the power to preserve under all circumstances that opinion about the nature and description of things to be feared in which our legislator educated them; and this is what you term courage.

I should like to hear what you are saying once more, for I do not think that I perfectly understand you.

I mean that courage is a kind of preservation.

Preservation of what kind?

Of the opinion respecting things to be feared, what they are and of what nature, which the law implants through education; and I mean by the words 'under all circumstances' to intimate that in pleasure or in pain, or under the influence of desire or fear, a man preserves and does not lose this opinion. Shall I give you an illustration?

If you please.

You know, I said, that dyers, when they want to dye wool for making the true sea-purple, begin by choosing the white from among all the colours available; this they prepare and dress with much care and pains, in order that the white ground may take the purple hue in full perfection. The dyeing then proceeds; and whatever is dyed in this manner becomes a fast colour, and no washing either with lyes or without them can take away the bloom. But, when the ground has not been duly prepared, you will have noticed how poor is the look either of purple or of any other colour.

Yes, he said; I know that they have a washed-out and ridiculous appearance.

Then now, I said, you will understand that our object in selecting our soldiers, and educating them in music and gymnastic, was very similar; we were contriving influences which would prepare them to take the dye of the laws in perfection, and the colour of their opinion about dangers and of every other opinion was to be indelibly fixed by their nurture and training, not to be washed away by such potent lyes as pleasure—mightier agent far in washing the soul than any soda or lye—or by sorrow, fear, and desire, the mightiest of all other solvents. And this sort of universal saving power of true opinion in conformity with law about real and false dangers I call and maintain to be courage, unless you disagree.

But I agree, he replied; for I suppose that you mean to exclude mere right belief about dangers when it has grown up without instruction, such as that of a wild beast or of a slave—this, in your opinion, is something not quite in accordance with law, which in any case should have another name than courage.

Most certainly.

Then I concede courage to be such as you describe.

Excellent, said I, and if you add the words 'of a citizen,' you will not be far wrong;—hereafter, if you agree, we will carry the examination of courage further, but at present we are seeking not for courage but justice; and for the purpose of our inquiry we have said enough.

You are right, he replied.

Two virtues remain to be discovered in the State—first, temperance, and then justice which is the end of our search.

Very true.

Now, can we find justice without troubling ourselves about temperance?

I do not know how that can be accomplished, he said, nor do I desire that justice should be brought to light and temperance lost sight of; and therefore

I wish that you would do me the favour of considering temperance first.

Certainly, I replied. I should not be justified in refusing your request.

Then consider, he said.

Yes, I replied; I will; and as far as I can at present see, temperance has more of the nature of harmony and symphony than have the preceding virtues.

How so? he asked.

Temperance, I replied, is the ordering or controlling of certain pleasures and desires; this is curiously enough implied in the saying of 'a man being his own master'; and other traces of the same notion may be found in language, may they not?

No doubt, he said.

There is something ridiculous in the expression 'master of himself'; for the master must also be the servant and the servant the master, since in all these modes of speaking the same person is denoted.

Certainly.

The meaning of this expression is, I believe, that there is within the man's own soul a better and also a worse principle; and when the better has the worse under control, then he is said to be master of himself; and this is a term of praise: but when, owing to evil education or association, the better principle, which is also the smaller, is overwhelmed by the greater mass of the worse—in this case he is blamed and is called the slave of self and dissolute.

Yes, there is reason in that.

And now, I said, look at our newly created State, and there you will find one of these two conditions realized; for the State, as you will acknowledge, may be justly called master of itself, if the words 'temperance' and 'self-mastery' truly express the rule of the better part over the worse.

On looking, he said, I see that what you say is true.

Let me further note that the manifold and complex pleasures and desires and pains are generally found in children and women and servants, and in the freemen so called who are of the lowest and more numerous class.

Certainly, he said.

Whereas the simple and moderate desires, which follow reason and are under the guidance of mind and true opinion, are to be found only in a few, and those the best born and best educated.

Very true.

These too, as you may perceive, have a place in your State; and the meaner desires of the many are held down by the desires and wisdom of the more virtuous few.

That I perceive, he said.

Then if there be any city which may be described as master of its own pleasures and desires, and master of itself, ours may claim such a designation?

Certainly, he replied.

It may also for all these reasons be called temperate?

Yes.

And if there be any State in which rulers and subjects will be agreed as to the question who are to rule, that again will be our State? Do you think so?

I do, emphatically.

And the citizens being thus agreed among themselves, in which class will temperance be found—in the rulers or in the subjects?

In both, as I should imagine, he replied.

Do you observe that we were not badly inspired in our guess that temperance bore some resemblance to harmony?

Why so?

Why, because temperance is unlike courage and wisdom, each of which resides in a part only, the one making the State wise and the other valiant; not so temperance, which extends to the whole, and runs through all the notes of the scale, and produces a unison of the weaker and the stronger and the middle class, whether you suppose them to be stronger or weaker in wisdom or power or numbers or wealth, or anything else you please. Most truly then may we deem this unity of mind to be temperance, an agreement of the naturally superior and inferior as to the right to rule of either both in states and individuals.

I entirely agree with you.

And so, I said, we may consider three out of the four virtues to have been discovered in our State. What remainder is there of qualities which make a state virtuous? For this, it is evident, must be justice.

The inference is obvious.

The time then has arrived, Glaucon, when, like huntsmen, we should surround the cover, and look sharp that justice does not steal away, and pass out of sight and escape us; for beyond a doubt she is somewhere in this country: watch therefore and strive to catch a sight of her, and if you see her first, let me know.

Would that I could! but you will do right to regard me rather as a follower who has just eyes enough to see what you show him.

Offer up a prayer with me and follow.

I will, but you must show me the way.

Here is no path, I said, and the wood is dark and perplexing; still we must push on.

Let us push on.

Here I saw something: Halloo! I said, I begin to perceive a track, and I believe that the quarry will not escape.

Good news, he said.

Truly, I said, we are stupid fellows.

Why so?

Why, my dear friend, far back from the beginning of our inquiry, justice has been lying at our feet, and we never saw her; nothing could be more ridiculous. Like people who go about looking for what they have in their hands, we looked not at what we were seeking, but at what was far off in the distance; and that, I suppose, was how we missed her.

What do you mean?

I mean to say that for a long time past we have been talking or hearing of justice, and yet have failed to recognize that we were in some sense actually describing it.

I grow impatient at the length of your exordium.

Well then, tell me, I said, whether I am right or not: You remember the original principle which we laid down at the foundation of the State; we decided, and more than once insisted, that one man should practise one occupation only, that to which his nature was best adapted;—now justice, in my view, either is this principle or is some form of it.

Yes, we did.

Further, we affirmed that justice was doing one's own business, and not being a busybody; we said so again and again, and many others have said the same to us.

Yes, we said so.

Then to attend to one's own business, in some form or another, may be assumed to be justice. Do you know my evidence for this?

No, but I should like to be told.

Because I think that this is the virtuous quality which remains in the State when the other virtues of temperance and courage and wisdom are abstracted; and that this not only made it possible for them to appear, but is also their preservative as long as they remain, and we were saying that if the three were discovered by us, justice would be the fourth or remaining one.

That follows of necessity.

If we are asked to determine which of these four qualities by its presence will contribute most to the excellence of our State, whether the agreement of rulers and subjects, or the preservation in the soldiers of the opinion which the law ordains about the true nature of dangers, or wisdom and watchfulness in the rulers, or this other which is found in children and women, slave and freeman, artisan, ruler, subject (I mean the quality of every one doing his own work, and not being a busybody), the decision is not so easy.

Certainly, he replied, there would be a difficulty in saying which.

Then the attention of each individual to his own work appears to be a quality rivalling wisdom, temperance, and courage, with reference to the excellence of the State.

Yes, he said.

And the only virtue which, from that point of view, is of equal importance with them, is justice?

Exactly.

Let us look at the question also in this way: Are not the rulers in a State those to whom you would entrust the office of determining suits at law?

Certainly.

In the decision of such suits will any principle be prior to this, that a man may neither take what is another's nor be deprived of what is his own?

No.

Because it is a just principle?

Yes.

Then on this view also justice will be admitted to be the having and doing what is a man's own, and belongs to him?

Very true.

Think, now, and say whether you agree with me or not. Suppose a carpenter sets out to do the business of a cobbler, or a cobbler that of a carpenter;

and suppose them to exchange their implements or social position, or the same person to try to undertake the work of both, or whatever be the change; do you think that any great harm would result to the State?

Not much.

But when the cobbler or any other man whom nature designed to be a trader, having his heart lifted up by wealth or strength or the number of his followers or any like advantage, attempts to force his way into the class of warriors, or a warrior into that of legislators and guardians, to which he ought not to aspire, and when these exchange their implements and their social position with those above them; or when one man would be trader, legislator, and warrior all in one, then I think you will agree with me in saying that this interchange and this meddling of one with another is the ruin of the State.

Most true.

Seeing then, I said, that there are three distinct classes, any meddling of one with another, or the change of one into another, is the greatest harm to the State, and may be most justly termed evil-doing?

Precisely.

And the greatest degree of evil-doing to one's own city would be termed by you injustice?

Certainly.

This then is injustice; and on the other hand when the three main classes, traders, auxiliaries, and guardians, each do their own business, that is justice, and will make the city just.

I agree with you.

We will not, I said, be over-positive as yet; but if, on trial, this conception of justice be verified in the individual as well as in the State, there will be no longer any room for doubt; if it be not verified, we must have a fresh inquiry. First let us complete the old investigation, which we began, as you remember, under the impression that, if we could previously examine justice on the larger scale, there would be less difficulty in discerning her in the individual. That larger example appeared to be the State, and accordingly we constructed as good a one as we could, knowing well that in the good State justice would be found. Let the discovery which we made be now applied to the individual—if they agree, we shall be satisfied; or, if there be a difference in the individual, we will come back to the State and have another trial of the theory. The friction of the two when rubbed together may possibly strike the light of justice, from which we can kindle a steady flame in our souls.

That will be in regular course; let us do as you say.

I proceeded to ask: When two things, a greater and less, are called by the same name, are they like or unlike in so far as they are called the same?

Like, he replied.

The just man then, if we regard the idea of justice only, will be like the just State?

He will.

And a State was thought by us to be just when the three classes in the State severally did their own business; and also thought to be temperate and valiant and wise by reason of certain other affections and qualities of these same classes?

True, he said.

And so of the individual: we may assume that he has the same three principles in his own soul which are found in the State; and he may be rightly described in the same terms, because he is affected in the same manner?

Certainly, he said.

Once more then, O my friend, we have alighted upon an easy question—whether the soul has these three principles or not?

An easy question? Nay, rather, Socrates, the proverb holds that hard is the good.

Very true, I said; and I must impress upon you, Glaucon, that in my opinion our present methods of argument are not at all adequate to the accurate solution of this question; the true method is another and a longer one. Still we may arrive at a solution not below the level of the previous inquiry.

May we not be satisfied with that? he said;—under the circumstances, I am quite content.

I too, I replied, shall be extremely well satisfied.

Then faint not in pursuing the speculation, he said.

Must we not perforce acknowledge, I said, that in each of us there are the same principles and habits which there are in the State; for it is from the individual that the State derives them. Take the quality of passion or spirit;—it would be ridiculous to imagine that this quality, when found in States, is not derived from the individuals who are supposed to possess it, e.g. the Thracians, Scythians, and in general the northern nations; and the same may be said of the love of knowledge, which may be claimed as the special characteristic of our part of the world, or of the love of money, which may, with equal truth, be attributed to the Phoenicians and Egyptians.

Exactly so, he said.

This is a fact, and there is no difficulty in perceiving it.

None whatever.

But the question is not quite so easy when we proceed to ask whether these principles are three or one; whether, that is to say, we learn with one part of our nature, are angry with another, and with a third part desire the satisfaction of our natural appetites; or whether the whole soul comes into play in each sort of action—to determine that is the difficulty.

Yes, he said; there lies the difficulty.

Then let us now try and determine whether they are the same or different.

How?

Clearly the same thing cannot act or be acted upon in the same part or in relation to the same thing at the same time, in contrary ways; and therefore whenever this contradiction occurs in things apparently the same, we know that they are really not the same, but different.

Good.

For example, I said, can the same thing be at rest and in motion at the same time in the same part?

Impossible.

Now, I said, let us have still more precise understanding, lest we should hereafter fall out by the way. Imagine the case of a man who is standing and also moving his hands and his head, and suppose a person to say that one and the same person is in motion and at rest at the same moment—to such a mode of speech we should object, and should rather say that one part of him is in motion while another is at rest.

Very true.

And suppose the objector to refine still further, and to draw the nice distinction that not only parts of tops, but whole tops, when they spin round with their pegs fixed on the spot, are at rest and in motion at the same time (and he may say the same of anything which revolves in the same spot), his objection would not be admitted by us, because in such cases things are not at rest and in motion in the same parts of themselves; we should rather say that they have both an axis and a circumference; and that the axis stands still, for there is no deviation from the perpendicular; and that the circumference goes round. But if, while revolving, the axis inclines either to the right or left, forwards or backwards, then in no point of view can they be at rest.

That is the correct mode of describing them, he replied.

Then none of these objections will confuse us, or incline us to believe that the same thing at the same time, in the same part or in relation to the same thing, can be contrary or act or be acted upon in contrary ways.

Certainly not, according to my way of thinking.

Yet, I said, that we may not be compelled to examine all such objections, and prove at length that they are untrue, let us assume their absurdity, and go forward on the understanding that hereafter, if this assumption turn out to be untrue, all the consequences which follow from it shall be withdrawn.

Yes, he said, that will be the best way.

Well, I said, would you not allow that assent and dissent, desire and aversion, attraction and repulsion, are all of them opposites, whether they are regarded as active or passive (for that makes no difference in the fact of their opposition)?

Yes, he said, they are opposites.

Well, I said, and hunger and thirst, and the desires in general, and again willing and wishing,—all these you would refer to the classes already mentioned. You would say—would you not?—that the soul of him who desires is either seeking after the object of desire; or is drawing towards herself the thing which she wishes to possess: or again,—for she may merely consent that something should be offered to her—intimates her wish to have it by a nod of assent, as if she had been asked a question?

Very true.

And what would you say of unwillingness and dislike and the absence of desire; should not these be referred to the opposite class of repulsion and rejection?

Certainly.

Admitting this to be true of desire generally, let us suppose a particular class of desires, and out of these we will select hunger and thirst, as they are termed, which are the most obvious of them?

Let us take that class, he said.

The object of one is food, and of the other drink?

Yes.

And here comes the point: is not thirst the desire which the soul has of drink, and of drink only, not of drink qualified by anything else; for example, warm or cold, or much or little, or, in a word, drink of any particular sort? But if there is heat additional to the thirst, it will bring with it the desire of cold drink; or, if cold, then that of warm drink. And again, if the thirst is qualified by abundance or by smallness, it will become a desire for much or little drink, as the case may be: but thirst pure and simple will desire drink pure and simple, which is the natural satisfaction of thirst, as food is of hunger?

Yes, he said; the simple desire is, as you say, in every case of the simple object, and the qualified desire of the qualified object.

But here a confusion may arise; and I should wish to guard against an opponent starting up and saying that no man desires drink only, but good drink, or food only, but good food; for good is the universal object of desire, and if thirst be a desire, it will necessarily be thirst after good drink (or whatever its object is); and the same is true of every other desire.

Yes, he replied, the opponent might seem to be talking sense.

Nevertheless I should still maintain that of relatives some have a quality attached to either term of the relation; others are simple and have their correlatives simple.

I do not know what you mean.

Well, you know of course that the greater is relative to the less?

Certainly.

And the much greater to the much less?

Yes.

And the sometime greater to the sometime less, and the greater that is to be to the less that is to be?

Certainly, he said.

And so of more and less, and of other correlative terms, such as the double and the half, or again, the heavier and the lighter, the swifter and the slower; and of hot and cold, and of any other relatives;—is not this true of all of them?

Yes.

And does not the same principle hold in the sciences? The object of science is knowledge (assuming that to be the true definition), but the object of a particular science is a particular kind of knowledge; I mean, for example, that the science of house-building is a kind of knowledge which is defined and distinguished from other kinds and is therefore termed architecture.

Certainly.

Because it has a particular quality which no other has?

Yes.

And it has this particular quality because it has an object of a particular kind; and this is true of the other arts and sciences?

Yes.

Now, then, if I have made myself clear, you will understand my original meaning in what I said about relatives. My meaning was, that if one term of a relation is taken alone, the other is taken alone; if one term is qualified, the other is also qualified. I do not mean to say that relative terms must possess all the same qualities as their correlates; that the science of health is healthy, or that of disease necessarily diseased, or that the sciences of good and evil are therefore good and evil; but only that, when the term science is no longer used absolutely, but has a qualified object which in this case is the nature of health and disease, it becomes defined, and is hence called not merely science, but the science of medicine.

I quite understand, and I think as you do.

Would you not say that thirst is one of these essentially relative terms, having clearly a relation–

Yes, thirst is relative to drink.

And a certain kind of thirst is relative to a certain kind of drink; but thirst taken alone is neither of much nor little, nor of good nor bad, nor of any particular kind of drink, but of drink only?

Certainly.

Then the soul of the thirsty one, in so far as he is thirsty, desires only drink; for this she yearns, and for this she strives?

That is plain.

And if you suppose something which pulls a thirsty soul away from drink, that must be different from the thirsty principle which draws him like a beast to drink; for, as we were saying, the same thing cannot at the same time with the same part of itself act in contrary ways about the same.

Impossible.

No more than you can say that the hands of the archer push and pull the bow at the same time, but what you say is that one hand pushes and the other pulls.

Exactly so, he replied.

Now are there times when men are thirsty, and yet unwilling to drink?

Yes, he said, it constantly happens.

And in such a case what is one to say? Would you not say that there was something in the soul bidding a man to drink, and something else forbidding him, which is other and stronger than the principle which bids him?

I should say so.

And the prohibition in such cases is derived from reasoning, whereas the motives which lead and attract proceed from passions and diseases?

Clearly.

Then we may fairly assume that they are two, and that they differ from one another; the one with which a man reasons, we may call the rational principle of the soul, the other, with which he loves and hungers and thirsts and feels the flutterings of any other desire, may be termed the irrational or appetitive, the ally of sundry pleasures and satisfactions?

Yes, he said, we may fairly assume them to be different.

So much, then, for the definition of two of the principles existing in the soul. And what now of passion, or spirit? Is it a third, or akin to one of the preceding?

I should be inclined to say—akin to desire.

Well, I said, there is a story which I remember to have heard, and in which I put faith. The story is, that Leontius, the son of Aglaion, coming up one day from the Piraeus, under the north wall on the outside, observed some dead bodies lying on the ground at the place of execution. He felt a desire to see them, and also a dread and abhorrence of them; for a time he struggled and covered his eyes, but at length the desire got the better of him; and forcing them open, he ran up to the dead bodies, saying, Look, ye wretches, take your fill of the fair sight.

I have heard the story myself, he said.

The moral of the tale is that anger at times goes to war with desire, as though they were two distinct things.

Yes; that is the meaning, he said.

And are there not many other cases in which we observe that when a man's desires violently prevail over his reason, he reviles himself, and is angry at the violence within him, and that in this struggle, which is like the struggle of factions in a State, his spirit is on the side of his reason;—but for the passionate or spirited element to take part with the desires when reason decides that she should not be opposed, is a sort of thing which I believe that you never observed occurring in yourself, nor, as I should imagine, in anyone else?

Certainly not.

Suppose that a man thinks he has done a wrong to another, the nobler he is the less able is he to feel indignant at any suffering, such as hunger, or cold, or any other pain which the injured person may inflict upon him—these he deems to be just, and, as I say, his spirit refuses to be excited by them.

True, he said.

But when a man thinks that he is the sufferer of the wrong, then the spirit within him boils and chafes, and is on the side of what it believes to be justice; and though it suffers hunger or cold or other pain, it is only the more determined to persevere and conquer. Such a noble spirit will not be quelled until it has achieved its object or been slain, or until it has been recalled by the reason within, like a dog by the shepherd?

The illustration is perfect, he replied; and in our State, as we were saying, the auxiliaries were to be dogs, and to hear the voice of the rulers, who are their shepherds.

Yes, I said, you understand me admirably; there is, however, a further point which I wish you to consider.

What point?

You remember that passion or spirit appeared at first sight to be a kind of desire, but now we should say quite the contrary; for in the conflict of the soul spirit is arrayed on the side of the rational principle.

Most assuredly.

But a further question arises: Is passion different from reason also, or only a kind of reason; in which latter case, instead of three principles in the soul, there will only be two, the rational and the concupiscent? or rather, as the State was composed of three classes, traders, auxiliaries, counsellors, so may there not be in the individual soul a third element which is passion or spirit, and when not corrupted by bad education is the natural auxiliary of reason?

Yes, he said, there must be a third.

Yes, I replied, if passion, which has already been shown to be different from desire, turn out also to be different from reason.

But that is easily proved:—We may observe even in young children that they are full of spirit almost as soon as they are born, whereas some of them never seem to attain to the use of reason, and most of them late enough.

Excellent, I said, and you may see passion equally in brute animals, which is a further proof of the truth of what you are saying. And we may once more appeal to the words of Homer, which have been already quoted by us.

> He smote his breast, and thus rebuked his heart;[7]

for in this verse Homer has clearly supposed the power which reasons about the better and worse to be different from the unreasoning anger which is rebuked by it.

Very true, he said.

And so, after much tossing, we have reached land, and are fairly agreed that the same principles which exist in the State exist also in the individual, and that they are three in number.

Exactly.

Must we not then infer that the individual is wise in the same way and in virtue of the same quality which makes the State wise?

Certainly.

Also that the State is brave in the same way and by the same quality as an individual is brave, and that there is the same correspondence in regard to the other virtues?

Assuredly.

Therefore the individual will be acknowledged by us to be just in the same way in which the State has been found just?

That follows of course.

We cannot but remember that the justice of the State consisted in each of the three classes doing the work of its own class?

I do not think we have forgotten, he said.

We must now record in our memory that the individual in whom the several components of his nature do their own work will be just, and will do his own work?

Yes, he said, we must record that important fact.

First, it is proper for the rational principle, which is wise, and has the care of the whole soul, to rule, and for the spirit to be the subject and ally?

Certainly.

And, as we were saying, the blending of music and gymnastic will bring them into accord, nerving and sustaining the reason with noble words and lessons, and moderating and soothing and civilizing the wildness of passion by harmony and rhythm?

Quite true, he said.

And these two, thus nurtured and educated, and having learned truly to know their own functions, will rule over the concupiscent, which in each of us is the largest part of the soul and by nature most insatiable of gain; over this they will keep guard, lest, waxing great and strong with the fullness of bodily pleasures, as they are termed, the concupiscent soul, no longer confined to her own sphere, should attempt to enslave and rule those who are not her natural-born subjects, and overturn the whole life of man?

Very true, he said.

Both together will they not be the best defenders of the whole soul and the whole body against attacks from without; the one counselling, and the other going out to fight as the leader directs, and courageously executing his commands and counsels?

True.

Likewise it is by reference to spirit that an individual man is deemed courageous, because his spirit retains in pleasure and pain the commands of reason about what he ought or ought not to fear?

Right, he replied.

And we call him wise on account of that little part which rules, and which proclaims these commands; the part in which is situated the knowledge of what is for the interest of each of the three parts and of the whole?

Assuredly.

And would you not say that he is temperate who has these same elements in friendly harmony, in whom the one ruling principle of reason, and the two subject ones of spirit and desire, are equally agreed that reason ought to rule, and do not rebel?

Certainly, he said, that is a precise account of temperance whether in the State or individual.

And, finally, I said, a man will be just in that way and by that quality which we have often mentioned.

That is very certain.

And is justice dimmer in the individual, and is her form different, or is she the same which we found her to be in the State?

There is no difference in my opinion, he said.

Because, if any doubt is still lingering in our minds, a few commonplace instances will satisfy us of the truth of what I am saying.

What sort of instances do you mean?

If the case is put to us, must we not admit that the just State, or the man of similar nature who has been trained in the principles of such a State, will be less likely than the unjust to make away with a deposit of gold or silver? Would any one deny this?

No one, he replied.

Will such a man ever be involved in sacrilege or theft, or treachery either to his friends or to his country?

Never.

Neither will he ever, for any reason, break faith where there have been oaths or agreements?

Impossible.

No one will be less likely to commit adultery, neglect his father and mother, or fail in his religious duties?

No one.

And the reason for all this is that each part of him is doing its own business, whether in ruling or being ruled?

Exactly so.

Are you satisfied then that the quality which makes such men and such states is justice, or do you hope to discover some other?

Not I, indeed.

Then our dream has been realized, and the suspicion which we expressed that, at the beginning of our work of construction, some divine power must have conducted us to a primary form of justice, has now been verified?

Yes, certainly.

And the division of labour which required the carpenter and the shoemaker and the rest of them to devote himself to the work for which he is naturally fitted, and to do nothing else, was a shadow of justice, and for that reason it was of use?

Clearly.

And in reality justice was such as we were describing, being concerned however, not with a man's external affairs, but with an inner relationship in which he himself is more truly concerned; for the just man does not permit the several elements within him to interfere with one another, or any of them to do the work of others,—he sets in order his own inner life, and is his own master and his own law, and at peace with himself; and when he has bound together the three principles within him, which may be compared to the higher, lower, and middle notes of the scale, and any that are intermediate between them—when he has bound all these together, and is no longer many, but has become one entirely temperate and perfectly adjusted nature, then he proceeds to act, if he has to act, whether in a matter of property, or in the treatment of the body, or in some affair of politics or private business; always thinking and calling that which preserves and co-operates with this harmonious condition, just and good action, and the knowledge which presides over it, wisdom, and that which at any time impairs this condition, he will call unjust action, and the opinion which presides over it ignorance.

You have said the exact truth, Socrates.

Very good; and if we were to affirm that we had discovered the just man and the just State, and the nature of justice in each of them, we should not be far from the truth?

Most certainly not.

May we say so, then?

Let us say so.

And now, I said, injustice has to be considered.

Clearly.

Must not injustice be a strife which arises among the same three principles—a meddlesomeness, and interference, and rising up of a part of the soul against the whole, an assertion of unlawful authority, which is made by a rebellious subject against a true prince, of whom he is the natural vassal,—what is all this confusion and delusion but injustice and intemperance and cowardice and ignorance, and, in short, every form of vice?

Exactly so.

And if the nature of justice and injustice is known, then the meaning of acting unjustly and being unjust, or again of acting justly, is now also perfectly clear?

How so? he said.

Why, I said, they are like disease and health; being in the soul just what disease and health are in the body.

How so? he said.

Why, I said, that which is healthy causes health, and that which is unhealthy causes disease.

Yes.

And just actions cause justice, and unjust actions cause injustice?

That is certain.

And the creation of health is the institution of a natural order and government of one by another in the parts of the body; and the creation of disease is the production of a state of things at variance with this natural order?

True.

And is not the creation of justice the institution of a natural order and government of one by another in the parts of the soul, and the creation of injustice the production of a state of things at variance with the natural order?

Exactly so, he said.

Then virtue is the health and beauty and well-being of the soul, and vice the disease and weakness and deformity of the same?

True.

And how are virtue and vice acquired—is it not by good and evil practices?

Assuredly.

The time has come, then, to answer the final question of the comparative advantage of justice and injustice: Which is the more profitable, to be just and act justly and honourably, whether one's character is or is not known, or to be unjust and act unjustly, if one is unpunished, that is to say unreformed?

In my judgement, Socrates, the question has now become ridiculous. We know that, when the *bodily* constitution is gone, life is no longer endurable, though pampered with all kinds of meats and drinks, and having all wealth and all power; and shall we be told that when the natural health of our vital principle* is undermined and corrupted, life is still worth having to a man, if only he be allowed to do whatever he likes, except to take steps to acquire justice and virtue and escape from injustice and vice; assuming them both to be such as we have described?

Yes, I said, the question is, as you say, ridiculous.

*["the very principle whereby we live" in the translation of F. M. Cornford—Eds.]

NOTES

1. [They were Plato's elder brothers. He avoids pronouncing his father's name, like the Pythagoreans who would only refer to their founders as ἐκεῖνος, 'that man'.]

2. [Or 'city': and so throughout the following passage.]

3. [Reading, in 369 d 6, πόση πόλις for the πως η πόλις of the MSS. (R. W. Chapman in *C.R.* 1 (1936), p. 167.)]

4. Cf. *Laws* 663 e.

5. *Odyssey* i. 352.

6. [Cf. iii. 414 a.]

7. *Od.* xx. 17, quoted *supra,* iii. 390d.

The Reconciliation Project*

GREGORY S. KAVKA

Gregory S. Kavka (1947–1994) taught philosophy at the University of California, Irvine.

CLARIFYING THE NATURE of the relationship between ethical and self-interested conduct is one of the oldest problems of moral philosophy. As far back as Plato's *Republic,* philosophers have approached it with the aim of reconciling morality and self-interest by showing that moral behavior is required by, or at least is consistent with, rational prudence. Let us call this undertaking the Reconciliation Project. In modern times this project is generally viewed as doomed to failure. It is believed that unless we make an outdated and implausible appeal to divine sanctions, we cannot expect to find agreement between moral and prudential requirements.

Can this negative verdict on the Reconciliation Project be avoided? Before we can deal with this question, we must distinguish among versions of the project along four dimensions. The *audience* dimension concerns to whom our arguments about coincidence of duty and interest are addressed. Sometimes it is supposed that a successful version of the Reconciliation Project must be capable of converting to virtue a hardened cynic or immoralist. . . . This is too much to ask. Immoralists are not likely to understand or appreciate the benefits of living morally, nor are they usually the sort of people who will listen to, or be swayed by, abstract rational arguments. A more modest aim is to speak convincingly to the puzzled ordinary person, such as Glaucon, who fears that in following the path of morality he is being irrational and is harming himself, but who is willing to listen to and ponder arguments to the contrary. We shall here be concerned with versions of the Reconciliation Project having this more modest aim.

A second dimension concerns the sort of *agent* for whom morality and self-interest are supposed to coincide. Versions of the Reconciliation Project that are ambitious along this dimension might attempt to demonstrate such coincidence in the case of all actual human beings, or even all possible human beings. More restrained versions would concentrate on more limited classes, such as persons without severe emotional disturbances or persons capable of self-assessment and love for others. The audience and agent dimensions of the Reconciliation Project are related. If one's aim in pursuing the project is to create or strengthen moral motivation, one would normally choose an agent class that just encompasses one's audience, so as to convince one's listeners that it pays *them* (promotes their own interests) to be moral, while at the same time exposing one's argument to the fewest possible objections. But if one aims at promoting theoretical understanding, one's agent class may be broader or narrower than one's audience. One may, for example, seek to convince reflective persons of goodwill that it pays everyone to be moral. Agent and audience classes need not even overlap; one might argue to sophisticated theorists that morality pays for the unsophisticated, who could not be expected successfully to disguise their immoralities.

The third dimension of the Reconciliation Project is the *social* one. Whether morality pays is partly

From David Zimmerman and David Copp (eds.), Morality, Reason, and Truth. *(Totowa, NJ: Rowman & Allanheld, 1985), pp. 297–319. Reprinted by permission of Rowman & Littlefield, Publishers.*

a function of others' responses to one's immoralities. Are morality and prudence supposed to coincide, then, in all imaginable social environments, all feasible ones, all (or most) actual ones, some feasible ones, or some imaginable ones? Different answers to this question yield importantly different versions of the Reconciliation Project.

Fourth and finally, if we say that morality and prudence coincide, does this mean that (i) each individual ethical act is prudent or (ii) that there are sufficient prudential reasons for adopting a moral way of life and acting in accordance with moral rules? This question concerns the nature of the objects or entities to be reconciled and calls attention to the *object* dimension of the Reconciliation Project. Reconciling all particular acts of duty with prudence is so unpromising a task as to have been largely shunned by the major philosophical exponents of the project. (Although, as we shall see below, much depends on whether prudential evaluations of acts are undertaken prospectively or retrospectively.) Thus Plato argues the prudential advantages of moral dispositions or ways of life, while Hobbes focuses on providing a prudential grounding for moral rules.

Taking note of the object dimension allows us to clarify the Reconciliation Project by answering a preliminary objection to it. According to this objection, the project must fail because supposedly moral actions are not really moral if they are motivated by prudential concerns. We may, however, accept this observation about motivation and moral action without damaging the Reconciliation Project properly construed. For that project is not committed to morality and prudence being identical, or to moral and prudential motives or reasons for action being the same. Rather, prudence and morality are supposed to be reconcilable in two senses. They recommend the same courses of conduct (where conduct is described in some motive-neutral way). Further, it is consistent with the requirements of prudence to adopt and live a moral way of life, even though this involves developing a pattern of motivation in which nonprudential considerations play an important role. Thus the Reconciliation Project survives the preliminary objection because it concerns, along its object dimension, acts or rules of action or ways of life, rather than motives or reasons for action.

Still, the Reconciliation Project is hopeless if we adopt very stringent interpretations of it along most or all of its four dimensions. We cannot expect to convince a clever immoralist that it pays everyone to act morally on every specific occasion in any sort of society. But why should we consider only such extreme versions of the project? Taking account of the dimensions of variation of the Reconciliation Project, I propose instead to discuss some less extreme versions (and modifications) of it to see to what extent they can be carried out and why they fail when they do. In the course of this investigation, I hope partly to vindicate the rationality of being moral and to clarify further the relationship between morality, prudence, and rationality.

I begin by sketching a Hobbesian version of the Reconciliation Project that presupposes psychological egoism and relies exclusively on external sanctions (social rewards and punishments) to reconcile obligation and interest. This Hobbesian approach provides considerable illumination, but it suffers from serious defects. To correct some of these, I consider the significance of internal (self-imposed psychological) sanctions. Next, I take up the two most intractable objections to all forms of the project. These concern the obligation to die for others, and those duties owed by members of strong groups to members of weak groups who are apparently not in a position to reciprocate benefits bestowed on them. Finally, I note how the recognition of nonegoistic motives transforms the Reconciliation Project. Throughout, my remarks are largely programmatic. I sketch alternatives, problems, and general strategies for solving problems and leave much detail to be filled in later. I hope nonetheless to say enough to show that the Reconciliation Project is still philosophically interesting and important.

I. THE HOBBESIAN STRATEGY

As a starting point, let us consider Hobbes's version of the Reconciliation Project. In seeking to reconcile duty and interest. Hobbes is limited by two self-imposed restrictions: He rules out appeal to religious sanctions, and he leaves no place for internal sanctions (such as guilt feelings) in his account of human psychology. Hence, Hobbes is reduced to arguing his case solely in terms of external sanctions; that is, social rewards and punishments. He does, however, marshall these relatively meager resources to good advantage.

The core of Hobbes's view is that the general rules of conduct that a farsighted prudent man concerned with his own survival, security, and well-being would follow are essentially the rules of traditional morality. The function of these rules is to promote peace, cooperation, and mutual restraint for the benefit of all parties. The rules therefore forbid killing, assault, and robbery, and they require keeping one's agreements, settling disputes by arbitration, providing aid to others when the cost to one is small and the benefit to them is large, and so on. The self-interested individual, if sufficiently rational and farsighted, will follow these rules because doing so is the best (and only reliable) way to ensure peaceful and cooperative relations with others. The person, for example, who wastes on luxuries what others need to survive is not likely to be helped by others if he later falls into want; nor will his person and property ever be safe from the desperate acts of the needy. The dangers of hostile reactions by others that confront the habitual assailant, thief, or contract-breaker are even more obvious. And while people may try to conceal their violations of moral rules, the long-run dangers of exposure and retaliation by others are great. Thus, argues Hobbes, morality is superior to immorality as a general policy, from the viewpoint of rational prudence.

One may agree that normally morality is a more prudent general policy than immorality but raise doubts about its prudential rationality in two special circumstances: when one is confident that a violation would go undiscovered and unpunished, and when others are not willing to reciprocate restraint. In the first case, it appears that one would benefit by *offensively* violating moral rules; that is, by not complying with them when others are complying. In the second case, prudence seems to call for a *defensive* violation—for noncompliance motivated by the belief that others are not complying and the desire not to put oneself at a disadvantage. Hobbes recognizes and attempts to deal with both cases.

Hobbes's argument against offensive violations of moral rules is presented in his famous reply to the Fool. He acknowledges that such violations will in some cases turn out, *in retrospect,* to best serve the agent's interests. But because they risk serious external sanctions (such as the withdrawal of all future cooperation by others), they are never *prospectively* rational. Since the consequences of failure are horrible and the chances of failure are not precisely calculable, it is not a rational gamble to offensively violate moral rules. Underlying this Hobbesian argument is an intuition about rational prudence that is reflected in the usual connotation of the word *prudence.* To be prudent is to play it safe and not take large, uncontrollable risks. It is not implausible to suppose that rational pursuit of one's own interests requires being prudent in this sense when one's vital interests are at stake.

To develop this point, let us follow decision theorists in drawing a distinction between choices under *risk* and under *uncertainty.* In the former cases, one has reliable knowledge of the probabilities that the various possible outcomes would follow the different available courses of action. In choices under uncertainty, one lacks such knowledge. Rawls contends that rationality requires that, when making vitally important choices under uncertainty, one follow a Maximin Strategy—choose the act with the best worst outcome (*A Theory of Justice,* pp. 152–158). I have argued elsewhere for using a Disaster Avoidance Strategy in such circumstances—choosing the alternative that maximizes one's chances of avoiding all unacceptable outcomes. Both strategies favor playing it safe in the sense of aiming at avoidance (or minimization) of the risk of unacceptable outcomes.

Now suppose we view choices among actions in the real world as made under uncertainty. (This is plausible for the most part, given our limited understanding of the complex factors that determine the consequences of our actions.) If, as Hobbes suggests, offensive violators risk the application of serious external sanctions, offensive violations would be irrational according to both the Maximin and Disaster Avoidance viewpoints. For the offensive violator accepts, under uncertainty, an unnecessary (or greater than necessary) risk of suffering disastrous consequences. So if either Rawls's analysis of rational prudential choice under uncertainty or my own is correct, Hobbes's argument against offensive violations under uncertainty is largely vindicated.

The considerations just presented attempt in effect to reconcile the requirements of morality and prudence as applied to (a certain class of) particular actions. They may serve, that is, as part of a Reconciliation Project focusing along the object dimension on *acts.* They function ever more effectively as part of an argument for the coincidence of *rules* of morality and prudence. We can imagine someone claiming that living by some rule such as the following would better serve one's interests than following moral rules: "Follow the moral rules except when you believe (or confidently believe) you can get away with violating them." But if one lives by this sort of rule, one is likely to undergo the risks inherent in offensive violations on a good number of occasions. And even if one is cautious in selecting the occasions, the risk of getting caught and suffering serious sanctions on one or more occasions will be substantial and much greater than the chance of getting caught on one particular occasion. Hence, insofar as rational prudence requires avoiding or minimizing risks of suffering serious sanctions, it would not recommend a policy of clever "compromise" between moral and immoral conduct as exemplified in this rule.

We have seen that Hobbes tries to reconcile duty and prudence in the case of offensive violations by denying that such violations are prudential. The opposite tack is adopted for defensive violations. These, Hobbes claims, are not contrary to moral duty. Agents are not obligated to follow the constraints of traditional morality unless others are reciprocating their restraint. To comply with moral rules unilaterally is to render oneself prey to others, and this, Hobbes urges, one is not required to do (1651, 1958, pp. 110, 130).

The governing principle of Hobbesian morality, then, is what I call the Copper Rule: "Do unto others as they *do* unto you." This principle enunciates a less glittering moral ideal than the familiar Golden Rule, which requires us to treat others well regardless of whether they treat us well in return. In thus opting for a reciprocal rather than unilateral interpretation of moral requirements, is Hobbes abandoning traditional morality?

To answer this question, we must distinguish between two aspects of morality—practice morality and ideal morality. Practice morality encompasses the standards of conduct actually expected of, and generally practiced by, persons living within a given moral tradition. It is roughly the part of morality concerned with *requirements,* those standards for which people are blamed, criticized, or punished for failing to live up to. Ideal morality refers to standards of moral excellence that a tradition sets up as models to aspire to and admire. Praise, honor, and respect are the rewards of those who live by its higher, more demanding standards. But, in general, people are not blamed for falling short of such ideals, or even for not aiming at them.

Now there surely are important strands of unilateralism in the ideal morality of the Western tradition. The Golden Rule, the admonition to love thine enemy, and the principle of turning the other cheek, all concern treating well even those who do not reciprocate. But if we turn to practice, and the standards of conduct that are actually treated as moral requirements, we find Copper Rule reciprocity to be a reasonable summary of much of what we observe. For practice morality allows us considerable leeway to engage in otherwise forbidden conduct toward those who violate moral constraints, especially when this is necessary for protection. Thus individuals may kill in self-defense, society may deprive criminals of their liberty, contracts may be broken when reciprocal fulfillment cannot be expected, and so forth.

We may then, without committing Hobbes to absurdity, attribute to him the claim that, in practice, traditional moral rules contain exception clauses allowing for defensive "violations" of the main clauses of the rule, if these are aimed at other violators. In adopting this pruned-down conception of moral requirements, Hobbes has abandoned the ambitious dream of achieving a reconciliation between ideal morality and prudence. But he has avoided one telling objection to the Reconciliation Project: that morality requires us (as prudence does not) to sacrifice our interests to the immoral, who will be all too ready to take advantage of such a sacrifice. Note, however, that the companion objection that morality sometimes requires us to sacrifice our interests for others who are moral is not dealt with by the Copper Rule interpretation of morality. Forms of this objection will be considered later.

As we have seen, Hobbes treats offensive and defensive violations of moral rules quite differently. In the former case, he reconciles prudence to morality by altering cynical interpretations of what prudence demands, while in the latter case he reconciles morality to prudence by offering a nonstandard interpretation of morality. Yet in each case he draws our attention to the oft-neglected social dimension of the Reconciliation Project. His discussion of defensive violations suggests that under certain conditions—anarchy or general noncompliance with traditional moral rules—moral and prudential requirements coincide, but only as a result of the effective loosening or disappearance of the former. Hence, *how* duty and interest are reconciled is a function of the social environment. In arguing for the imprudence of offensive violations of moral rules, Hobbes presupposes threats of external sanctions that are serious enough to make such violations a bad gamble. Therefore, his argument does not apply to imaginary situations in which society rewards immoral actions, or even certain real ones in which it ignores serious immoralities when they are committed by members of some privileged groups.

Suppose, then, that our aim is to reconcile prudence with traditional moral requirements (without the exception clauses); that is, do not kill or steal, aid the needy when the costs are small, and so on. Hobbes suggests that this reconciliation is possible only in a certain sort of social environment—one we may call *punitive*. In a punitive environment, serious violators of moral norms are sought out, apprehended, and given stiff punishments frequently enough to make immorality a bad prudential risk. As a result, there is general compliance with moral rules and little need for one to undertake defensive violations. In a punitive social environment, offensive violations of moral rules are irrational and defensive ones are unnecessary. If an actual social environment is punitive, the Reconciliation Project seems to have succeeded with respect to it. And if such an environment is feasible but nonactual, those who wish people to act morally but fear the distracting influence of self-interest will have some reason to create it.

Let us now briefly summarize the Hobbesian approach to the Reconciliation Project, which is based on external sanctions. It consists first of proposing specific interpretations of that project along two of the four dimensions. With respect to the object dimension, it focuses on rules or policies rather than on individual acts. (Although the reply to the Fool fits within an act version of the project as well.) And it presupposes a punitive social environment, avoiding the dubious claim that duty and interest coincide in any social context. Further, it provides a novel interpretation of moral requirements—the Copper Rule or reciprocal interpretation—and it rests on a "playing it safe" theory of rational prudential choice under uncertainty. All of these aspects of the Hobbesian strategy make contributions to the interpretation and development of the Reconciliation Project. None is without plausibility. However, there are two fatal objections that the Hobbesian Strategy cannot adequately answer.

The first concerns punitive social environments. These are beneficial in discouraging immoral conduct, but they have costs. To render immorality a bad risk solely via threats of punishments, such punishments must be made very heavy and/or very probable. In a society of significant size, doing the latter would normally require a massive policing establishment with large monetary costs (borne by the citizens), interferences with personal liberty and privacy (searches, eavesdropping, surveillance), and dangers of police power and influence over the political and economic institutions of society. Heavy penalties also have social costs—monetary costs of supporting prisons, lessened chances of reconciliation between offenders and society, dangers of gross injustice if the innocent might sometimes be punished, and so on. In short, we must accept trade-offs between various things that we value and the deterrence of serious immorality. And it may not always be possible for society, by use of external sanctions alone, to ensure that "crime does not pay" without sacrificing too much in the way of individual liberty, privacy, and protection from excessive state and police power.

Our second objection concedes that immorality generally does not pay, and even allows, that immorality is prudentially irrational under genuine uncertainty. However, *some* opportunities for immoral gain may present themselves under risk; that is, the probabilities of detection and punishment may be reliably known. In these situations, maximizing expected personal utility is arguably the most rational course, and this may imply engaging in an offensive violation. A slumlord, for example, may have relatively precise statistical data that allow him to estimate reliably the odds of his getting caught and punished if he hires a professional arsonist to burn one of his buildings so that he can collect the insurance. If the chances of arrest and conviction are low and the return is high, the crime may have positive expected value for him, and it will be prudentially rational for him to undertake it. The rules of a system of rational self-interest will be formulated to allow agents to take advantage of such situations.

These two objections reveal that while external sanctions alone can take us, via the Hobbesian Strategy, some considerable way toward reconciling duty and interest, they cannot take us far enough. We at least need some device other than a punitive social environment that can alter the calculations or dispositions of the slumlord and other potential criminals. The obvious candidates here are internal sanctions, psychic structures that punish immorality and reward virtue. Unlike external sanctions, these are relatively free of problems concerning evasion and detection, since one's conscience follows one everywhere, and they do not threaten privacy and democracy as do secret police forces. In the next section, I will explore how their inclusion may extend and strengthen the Hobbesian arguments for the coincidence for morality and prudence.

II. INTERNAL SANCTIONS

Internal sanctions come in two varieties, negative and positive. The negative sanctions are guilt feelings and related forms of psychic distress that most of us are subject to feel when we believe we have done wrong. We develop the tendency to experience such feelings under such circumstances as part of the socialization process we undergo in growing up. It is no mystery why society nurtures and encourages the development of this tendency; it benefits others to the extent that it inhibits or deters misconduct by the individual. And once one possesses the tendency, it imposes extra—and relatively certain—costs on immorality, costs which may tip the prudential balance in favor of restraint. Arson may not be the most rational option for our slumlord, for example, if in addition to prison he risks, with high probability, significant guilt feelings over endangering the lives of tenants or over cheating his insurance company. With internal sanctions operating along with external sanctions in this way, the social environment need not be so punitive as to keep serious immorality within tolerable limits.

There is no entirely satisfactory label for the positive internal sanctions, the agreeable feelings that typically accompany moral action and the realization that one has acted rightly, justly, or benevolently. So let us opt for the vague term "the satisfactions of morality." Moral people have long testified as to the strength and value of such satisfactions, often claiming that they are the most agreeable satisfactions we can attain. This last claim goes beyond what is necessary for our purposes. All we need to assert is that there are special significant pleasures or satisfactions that accompany regular moral action and the practice of a moral way of life that are not available to (unreformed) immoralists and others of their ilk. For if this is so, then the forgoing of these potential satisfactions must be charged as a significant opportunity cost of choosing an immoral way of life.

Can an individual have it both ways, enjoying the psychic benefits of morality while living an immoral life? He could, perhaps, if he lived immorally while sincerely believing he was not. Certain fanatics who selflessly devote themselves to false moral ideals, such as purifying the human race by eugenics or pleasing God by destroying nonbelievers, might fall in this category. Of more concern in the present context, however, is the individual who adopts morality as a provisional way of life or policy while planning to abandon it if a chance to gain much by immorality should arise later. This person, we would say, is not truly moral, and it is hard to believe that he would perceive himself to be, so long as his motives are purely prudential and his commitment to morality is only conditional. In any case, we would not expect him to experience the satisfactions of morality in the same way, or to the same degree, as the genuinely moral individual who is aware of the (relative) purity of his motives and the nature and depth of his commitment.

Note that if this is so we have arrived at a paradox of self-interest: *being* purely self-interested will not always best serve one's interests. For there may be certain substantial personal advantages that accrue only to those who are not purely self-interested, such as moral people. Thus it may be rational for you, as a purely self-interested person, to cease being one if you can, to transform yourself into a genuinely moral person. And once you are such a person, you will not be disposed to act immorally, under risk, whenever so doing promises to maximize personal expected utility.

The lesson of this paradox, and the opportunity cost of being immoral, does not apply, though, to those (if any) who are no longer capable of learning to enjoy the satisfactions of living a moral life. Further, some people may still be capable of developing an appreciation of these satisfactions, but the transition costs of moving to this state from their present immoral condition may outweigh the advantages gained. For people such as these, especially those who are immune from guilt feelings, the prudential argument for being moral must essentially rest on external sanctions. And with respect to some individuals, such as hardened but cautious immoralists or clever psychopaths, the argument may fail.

Thus we must acknowledge a restriction of the Reconciliation Project along its agent dimension. It is too much to claim that it pays one to be moral, irrespective of one's psychological characteristics. Rather, the argument from internal sanctions supports the prudential rationality of living a moral life for the two classes of people constituting the vast majority of humankind: First, those who are already endowed with conscience and moral motivations, so that they experience the satisfactions of living morally and are liable to suffering guilt feelings when they do wrong. Second, those who are capable of developing into moral persons without excessive cost—immoralists who are not fully committed to that way of life, and children.

Should we be dismayed that the Reconciliation Project may not encompass, along its agent dimension, those incapable of enjoying the satisfactions of morality? This depends upon our aims in pursuing the project and the audience to whom its arguments are addressed. Insofar as our aim is to reassure the ordinary good man that he is not harming himself by being moral, or to encourage parents who want to do the best for their children to give them moral education, we need not worry. And if we seek theoretical illumination, we achieve more by recognizing the variation along the agent dimension than by denying it. Only if our aim were the hopeless one of convincing dedicated immoralists to be moral, by using rational arguments, would we be in difficulty. Am I confessing, then, that we are helpless in the face of the immoralist? No, we are not helpless in the practical sense, for we can use external sanctions to restrain immoralists. Nor should we perceive an immoralist's gloating that it does not pay him to be moral (because the satisfactions of morality are not for him) as a victory over us. It is more like the pathetic boast of a deaf person that he saves money because it does not pay him to buy opera records.

III. THE ULTIMATE SACRIFICE

We have seen how the recognition of internal sanctions allows us to deal with two objections that undermine the Hobbesian external-sanctions approach to the Reconciliation Project. Two difficult objections remain, however, even when internal sanctions are taken into account. The first is that morality sometimes requires the sacrifice of one's life, and this cannot be in one's interests. The second is that morality requires powerful groups to treat weak groups fairly and decently, while it better serves the interests of the powerful group's members not to do so.

The objection concerning death runs as follows. In certain circumstances, morality requires of us that we give up our lives to protect others. We are bound by obligations of fair play, gratitude, and perhaps consent to fight in just wars of national defense. Fulfilling these obligations costs many people their lives. Extreme situations can also arise in civilian life in which morality requires one to accept one's own death. If gangsters credibly threaten to kill me unless I kill an innocent person, I must refrain. If I am a loser in a fair and necessary lifeboat lottery, I am morally bound to abide by the outcome. If half of the expedition's necessary food supply is lost as a result of my recklessness, I must be the first to agree to go without food on the long return trip so that others may survive. And so on. In each of these cases, however, self-interest seems to counsel taking the opposite course. Where there is life there is hope, and even if the likely cost of saving my life is to suffer severe internal and external sanctions (such as imprisonment, depression, and guilt for the military deserter), that cost must be less than the premature loss of my life, since such loss would deprive me of all future enjoyments and frustrate all of my main plans and desires.

In response to this objection, let us first note that there are fates worse than death. And for some people, living with the knowledge that one has preserved one's life at the cost of the lives of others, the sacrifice of one's principles, or the desertion of a cause one loves may be such a fate. In addition, society is aware of the heavy value that people place on the continuation of their own lives and typically responds by using heavy external sanctions to encourage appropriate life-risking behavior in defense of society. Thus infantry officers may stand behind their own lines and shoot those who retreat, thereby rendering advance a safer course than retreat. (Even if advance is virtually suicidal, death with honor at the hands of the enemy may be a lesser evil than death with dishonor at the hands of one's own officers.) On the positive side, those who risk or lose their lives in battle are often offered significant rewards by their fellow citizens—medals, honors, praise, and material compensation for themselves or their families.

The upshot of this is that in a substantial number of cases the sacrifice of one's life for moral ends may be consistent with the requirements of prudence because it constitutes the lesser of two extreme personal evils. It would, however, be disingenuous to suggest that this is so in most, much less all, cases. Officers cannot shoot all deserters or retreaters, nor are courts likely to sentence to death those who cheat in lifeboat lotteries. And relatively few are so committed to morality that they could not eventually recover, at least partially, from the negative psychic effects of abandoning principle to preserve their lives. So we must concede that self-interest and morality will frequently, or usually, recommend divergent courses of action when there is a stark choice between immoral action and certain death.

Does this concession destroy the Reconciliation Project? Only if we have in mind a version of the project that focuses, along the object dimension, on acts. If instead we consider, as we have been, whether adopting the moral *way of life* is consistent with prudence, the answer may well be different. In adopting or pursuing a moral way of life, we are, it is true, running a *risk* of sacrificing our lives imprudently. For the requirements of morality may sometimes call for us to give up (or risk) our lives. And if we do develop the habits and dispositions appropriate to the moral life, we are likely (or at least more likely than otherwise) to live up to these requirements at the cost of our lives, if we find ourselves in appropriate circumstances. Notice, however, that in assessing this risk and weighing it against the advantages of the moral life, we must consider how likely we are to find ourselves in such circumstances.

Now this depends, in turn, on our view of what the substantive rules of morality require of us. If they demand that one right all wrongs and fight all injustices anywhere at any time with all the means one possesses and regardless of the personal cost, the likelihood that one would be morally obligated to lay down (or seriously risk) one's life at some time or another is obviously large. But surely on any reasonable conception they require much less than this. Perhaps you are obligated to give up your life (i) to protect your country in a just war; (ii) to protect those to whom you owe special duties of protection (your children, your passengers if you are a ship's captain); (iii) to protect those you owe immense debts of gratitude (your parents); (iv) to avoid seriously violating the rights of innocent others (as in the gangster threat situation); (v) to save others from dangers that your misconduct, recklessness, or negligence has created; (vi) to keep important agreements you have made (such as accepting employment as a bodyguard); or (vii) to save the lives of large numbers of innocent people when you are the only one who can do so. And perhaps there are other specific duties of sacrifice that I have left off this list. But as a whole, the duties are limited to special and quite unlikely circumstances. (Military service is the only seriously life-endangering-required activity that is at all likely to confront a significant segment of the population. Presumably such service is morally obligatory only if the war is just, which frequently is not the case. Further, in most wars the percentage of those serving who are killed is rather low.)

Now if the chances are small that you will ever confront a situation in which you are morally obligated to surrender your life, it may well pay you to adopt a moral way of life, even if doing so increases the likelihood that you would sacrifice your life in such a situation. For the relatively certain external and internal benefits of the moral life should far outweigh the very unlikely loss of one's life. Further, it is worth noting that many immoral lifestyles—crime, debauchery, deception of all those around you—may have much higher premature death rates than the moral life. Insofar as adoption of a moral way of life ensures that you will not lapse into one of these alternatives, it may even on balance increase your life expectancy.

The argument, then, is that adopting a moral way of life carries at most a very small net risk to one's life. Since it provides significant benefits with high probability, it is a reasonable prudential choice. It is useful in understanding this argument to compare adopting a moral way of life with two other activities that are not generally thought to be imprudent: joining the military and entering into a long-term love relationship, such as by marrying or having children. These undertakings are like becoming moral in the main respect relevant to our argument. They are likely to involve or produce changes in one's motivational structure that would render one more likely to risk or sacrifice one's life in certain circumstances, such as when your loved ones or comrades in arms are in danger. (In addition, military service carries a nonnegligible risk of finding yourself in precisely these circumstances.) But this feature of these undertakings is not usually thought to render them ineligible choices from a prudential perspective. Why, then, should the same feature render becoming moral a generally imprudent course of conduct? This activity, like entering a long-term love relationship, promises very large external and internal rewards while involving a relatively tiny risk of loss of life. The gamble is hardly more foolish in the case of virtue than in the case of love.

IV. GROUP IMMORALITY

Human beings, as has often been remarked, are social creatures. We need one another for a variety of practical and emotional reasons—for help in securing satisfaction of our material needs, for physical protection, for companionship, for love, and so on. The above arguments that duty and interest coincide all rest on this fact. Individuals need the help rather than the hostility of society to prosper, and in the process of social learning they internalize norms of conscience that further fuse their interests with those of the social group. However, one does not require the aid or cooperation of *all* others, only of a sufficient number of those with whom one is likely to come in contact. This fact generates the most telling objection to the Reconciliation Project: That it is not in the interests of powerful *groups* and their members to treat decently and to help, as morality demands, the members of weak groups, who are apparently not in a position to return good for good and evil for evil.

It is clear that when we consider relations among groups, our earlier tools for reconciling interest and obligation cannot be used in the same way. External sanctions operate effectively, to the extent they do, because it is in the general interest of society and its members to restrain individuals from harming others. But if there is a split between groups in society, there may be no effective sanction against members of a dominant group harming members of a powerless group. For the others in the dominant group may condone, or even approve, such conduct, while the members of the powerless group are too weak to punish the offenders. And if the norms of the dominant group allow, or even encourage, mistreatment of the powerless group—as throughout history they often have—even well-socialized members of the dominant group may carry out such mistreatment without suffering substantial guilt feelings.

This objection shows that there cannot be a satisfactory solution to the Reconciliation Project if the project is strictly interpreted along the social and degree dimensions. That is, we cannot hope to show that in all historically actual (much less all conceivable) social circumstances it has been (or would be) in the interests of all groups and their members to act morally toward members of other groups. Instead, particular cases of supposed divergence of group duty and interest must be considered on an ad hoc basis, and the most we can reasonably aspire to is the presentation of arguments that make it plausible that obligation and interest coincide in *actual* present circumstances. This will not ease the anxiety of moralists who seek a noncontingent guarantee that interest and duty will never diverge. But it could suffice to convince the attentive moral individual, or group leader, that he or she is not being foolish in acting morally, or in leading his or her group in a moral direction.

Before discussing the three most important specific instances of the objection before us, it should be pointed out that whether there is hope of reconciling group interest and duty depends on what we take the demands of duty to be. In the case of individuals, we saw that a unilateralist-idealistic interpretation of moral requirements might render the Reconciliation Project impossible. Similarly, if we interpret morality as requiring rich and powerful groups to share so much with the poor and weak as to create absolute equality, there is very little prospect that duty and interest can be reconciled. But it is far from obvious that morality demands this much. What morality does clearly require is that the rich and powerful refrain from actively harming the poor and weak, and that the former aid the latter when the costs of giving are small and the benefits of receiving are large. We shall see that with this modest interpretation of the obligations of the powerful, reconciling their obligations with their interests may be possible.

Let us turn to our examples, the first concerning justice within a society. Why should rich and powerful groups in a nation allow the poor opportunities for education, employment, and advancement and provide social-welfare programs that benefit the poor as morality requires? Why shouldn't they simply oppress and exploit the poor? There are several reasons why, in modern times, it is most probably in the long-term interest of the rich and powerful to treat the domestic poor well. First, some rich individuals, and more likely some of their children, may be poor at some time in the future and thus benefit from programs to help the poor. Second, offering opportunities to members of all groups widens the pool of talent available to fill socially useful jobs, which should provide long-run economic benefits to members of all groups. Third, and most important, there is the reason that has impressed social theorists from Hobbes to Rawls: Decent treatment of all promotes social stability and cohesion and discourages revolution. This reason is especially important in contemporary times, when ideals of human dignity, equality, and justice are known and espoused virtually everywhere, and when revolution is frequently proposed as a legitimate means of attaining such ideals.

Taken together, these reasons constitute a strong case, on prudential grounds, for decent treatment of the domestic poor by a nation's dominant groups. In fact, if we apply Disaster Avoidance reasoning, it turns out that the third reason alone shows that good treatment of the poor is prudentially rational. For if the poor find the status quo unacceptable and apply such reasoning, they will revolt. Thus Hobbes writes, "Needy men and hardy, not contented with their present condition, . . . are inclined to . . . stir up trouble and sedition; for there is no . . . such hope to mend an ill game as by causing a new shuffle" (1651, 1958, p. 87). The rich, being aware of this, will (if they follow a Disaster Avoidance strategy) seek to prevent the poor from falling into such unacceptable circumstances. For the rich thereby maximize their chances of obtaining an outcome acceptable to them: preservation of something resembling the status quo.

What about a wealthy and powerful nation aiding poor, weak nations? Is this in the long-run interest of the former as well as the latter? In a world of advanced technology, international markets, ideological conflicts among powerful nations, and nuclear weapons, it most probably is. In competition with other powerful nations, allies—even poor nations—are useful for political, economic, and military reasons. And economic development of poor nations should, in the long run, produce economic benefits for richer nations, such as by providing markets and reliable supplies of various raw and finished goods. Most important, continued poverty in the Third World is likely to produce continued political turmoil, civil wars, and regional wars between nations. In a world armed to the teeth with nuclear weapons, and with more and more nations acquiring such weapons, the long-run danger of rich developed countries being drawn into a devastating military conflict started by a desperate poor nation, or some desperate group within such a nation, is far from negligible.

The above arguments about domestic and international justice suggest there is, after all, a form of reciprocity between powerful and weak groups because of interdependencies between the two in economic and security matters. The poor cannot return the aid of the rich in kind, but they can offer their talents, their purchasing power, and so on. If not treated well, they cannot directly punish the rich and powerful, but they can stir up serious trouble for them if they are willing to experience such trouble themselves. Thus they are able, and likely, to return good for good and evil for evil to the rich in the long run, and it will be rational for the rich to act accordingly.

Even this form of reciprocity is not available, however, to deal with our third and most puzzling example—the treatment of future generations. Future generations (beyond the next few) are powerless to act upon us, since they will not exist until after we are dead. Yet we have substantial power to determine the quality of their lives by influencing their numbers and the nature of the social and natural environment into which they will be born. Given this absolute asymmetry in power to affect one another, how can it be in our interest to act morally toward future generations? Morality requires us, at a minimum, to leave our descendants with enough resources to allow future people to live decent lives. But this would necessitate having a lower material standard of living than we could obtain by depleting resources and contaminating the environment whenever it is convenient to do so. If future generations cannot punish us for ruthlessly exploiting the earth in this way, doesn't rational prudence require it of us?

The supporter of the Reconciliation Project can come some considerable way toward answering even this objection. He might point out first that misuse of resources and damage to the environment will often produce substantial negative effects within our own lifetimes. So, for the most part, it is in our own interests to follow conservation policies that will turn out to benefit future generations. This reply will take us only so far, however. For there are policies whose benefits are experienced now and most of whose costs will be borne generations later (such as building nuclear power plants without having solved the long-term waste storage problem). Also, optimal *rates* of use of scarce nonrenewable resources will vary greatly depending upon how long we care about the resource lasting. Hence, there is a far from perfect overlap between the resource and environmental policies likely to most benefit present people and those likely to ensure a decent life for future generations.

A more promising argument begins from the fact that most people care very deeply about the happiness of their own children and grandchildren, and hence their own happiness would be diminished by contemplating the prospect of these descendants having to live in a resource-depleted world. Further, they realize that their children's and grandchildren's happiness will in turn be affected by the prospects for happiness of *their* children and grandchildren, and so forth. Hence, the happiness of present people is linked, generation by generation, to the prospects for happiness of some likely members of distant future generations. This "chain-connection" argument has considerable force, but it falls short of constituting a full solution to the problem before us. This is because the perceived happiness of one's children and grandchildren is only one component of the well-being or happiness of the typical parent. And the perceived happiness of *their* children and grandchildren is, in turn, only one component of the happiness of one's children and grandchildren. So there is a multiplier effect over generations that quickly diminishes the influence on a present person's happiness of the prospects for happiness of his later descendants. And we must seek some other device to link living peoples' interests firmly with those of distant future generations.

The most promising such device is an appeal to our need to give meaning to our lives and endeavors. I have suggested elsewhere that one strong reason we have for providing future people with the means to survive and prosper is that this is our best hope for the successful continuation of certain human enterprises that we value (and may have contributed to)—science, the arts and humanities, morality, religion, democratic government. Similarly, Ernest Partridge has argued that human beings have a psychological need for "self-transcendence"; that is, a need to contribute to projects that are outside themselves and that will continue after their deaths. Those without such goals are unlikely to find meaning in their lives, especially during the middle and later stages of life, when people typically reflect on their own mortality. Thus Partridge says, "We need the future, *now*".[1]

There is a great deal of truth in this argument, but there are some limits to what it can show. It cannot reconcile the interests and obligations to posterity of the narcissist who has no self-transcending goals and is incapable of developing them. However, this need not worry us anymore than did the corresponding remark made earlier about the person no longer capable of becoming moral. The self-transcending life may be the happier life for the vast majority who still can live it, and these people have good prudential reasons for doing so. The more important problem is that not all self-transcending concerns need be directed toward the distant future. They may involve goals that do not extend much beyond one's lifetime (such as the prosperity of one's children, or the eventual rise to power of one's favorite political movement). Such goals may give meaning to one's life without supplying reasons to provide for the welfare of distant generations. Perhaps, though, it is a psychological fact that enterprises that promise to continue into the indefinite future are better able to provide meaning in our lives, or to provide consolation for our mortality. If so, there would be powerful prudential reasons for one's adopting self-transcending concerns of unlimited temporal scope, and for protecting the social and natural environments for future generations.

These are the best arguments I can think of for a coincidence of self-interest and our obligations to posterity. Many (including myself at times) will find them only partly convincing. Does this lack of complete conviction indicate that we should abandon the Reconciliation Project? No. Instead, we may broaden our interpretation of that project.

V. THE WIDER PROJECT

The general strategy I have followed in outlining a defense of the Reconciliation Project has been to restrain the project's ambitions where necessary. Thus the scope of the project has been narrowed in several ways. It applies to ways of life rather than particular actions and to practice morality rather than ideal morality. It succeeds with respect to most people and groups in actual social circumstances, but not with respect to all people and groups in all actual or possible circumstances. It may not convince the skeptical immoralist to change his ways, but it provides good reasons for moral people not to regret (or abandon) their way of life and for loving parents to raise their children to be moral.

However, to understand better the relationship between morality, rationality, and self-interest, we must briefly consider an important *widening* of the Reconciliation Project. For that project may be viewed as but a specific instance of a more general project: reconciling morality with the requirements of practical rationality. Given two special assumptions—the truth of Psychological Egoism and the interpretation of practical rationality as the efficient pursuit of the agent's ends (whatever they may be)—this Wider Reconciliation Project would collapse into our original version concerning morality and self-interest. But the first of these assumptions is surely false; on any construal that does not render all motives self-interested by definition, people sometimes do have unselfish aims and possess and

1. "Why Care about the Future?", in E. Partridge, ed., *Responsibility to Future Generations* (Buffalo, N.Y.: Prometheus Books, 1981), p. 217.

act upon non-self-interested motives. As a result, the question of whether moral requirements are consistent with the rational pursuit of the actual ends that people have is both distinct from and more important than the question of whether these requirements cohere with the demands of prudence.

Would shifting our focus to the Wider Reconciliation Project render irrelevant all we have said about the original project? If self-interested concerns played only an insignificant role in human motivation, it would. But clearly this is not the case. In fact, while Psychological Egoism is false, I would venture to propose that a milder doctrine, which I call Predominant Egoism, is probably true. Predominant Egoism says that human beings are, as a matter of fact, predominantly self-interested in the following sense. At least until they have achieved a satisfactory level of security and well-being, people's self-interested concerns tend to override their other-regarding, idealistic, and altruistic motives in determining their actions. Further, those nonselfish concerns that are sufficiently powerful to move people to acts that seriously conflict with self-interest tend to be limited in scope, such as to the well-being of family and friends and the advancement of specific favored projects or institutions.

Now if it is true that people are predominantly self-interested, in this sense, many or most of their strongest motives and dearest ends are self-interested ones. And the above arguments about reconciling duty and interest will be highly relevant to the task of reconciling duty and the rational pursuit of people's actual ends. But in carrying out this Wider Reconciliation Project, there would be a new resource to appeal to—the altruistic and nonselfish ends that most everyone actually has to some degree. The presence of these ends may extend the range of cases in which the requirements of reason and morality coincide beyond those in which prudence and morality coincide.

Consider again our relationship to future generations. Most of us do have significant nonselfish concerns about the well-being of our children and grandchildren and the survival and prospering of the human species. So we have reason to provide for these things *over and above* the contribution that our awareness of such provision makes to our own psychic well-being. This further strengthens both the chain-connection and self-transcendence arguments for reconciling practical rationality with our duties to posterity. For it shows that in carrying out such duties we are fulfilling ends of ours not previously considered (that is, nonselfish ends) in addition to contributing to our own happiness.

The recognition of nonselfish ends also provides a fresh perspective on the sustenance of moral motivation over generations. We suggested earlier that parents seeking to promote their children's interests would have good reasons to raise their children to be moral. This suggestion would have little significance if we were operating upon an assumption of the truth of Psychological Egoism. (For then the only relevant question would be whether it is in a *parent's* interest to raise his or her children to be moral.) Since, however, concern for the well-being of one's children is among the strongest and most universal of non-self-interested human concerns, the suggestion is crucial to our understanding of how morality is rationally passed on from generation to generation. Typical parents who care strongly for the well-being of their children and care somewhat for the well-being of others have three significant reasons for raising those children to be moral: This will likely benefit the children (in accordance with our earlier arguments that being moral usually pays), it will likely benefit others who are affected by the children, and it will likely benefit the parents themselves (because their children will treat them better). And when children grow up as moral beings possessing consciences and the potential to experience the satisfactions of morality, it is, we have argued, most always in their interest to continue to live a moral life. Further, they, as parents, will have the same reasons for raising their children to be moral as their parents had for raising them in this manner. Thus morality can be seen to be potentially self-sustaining from generation to generation, without even taking into account socializing influences on the child from outside the family.

In raising children to be moral, and in providing for future generations, some of the ends that we seek to achieve are non-self-interested ones. Given the content of moral rules and their connection with protecting the interests of others, many morally required actions will satisfy ends of this kind. As a result, the Wider Reconciliation Project should be successful in more cases than the original project. We may restate this crucial point: While it is normally prudent to be moral, it is sometimes rational to be moral even if it is not prudent.

Justice and Law

Crito*

PLATO

SOCRATES. Why have you come at this hour, Crito? it must be quite early?

Crito. Yes, certainly.

Soc. What is the exact time?

Cr. The dawn is breaking.

Soc. I wonder that the keeper of the prison would let you in.

Cr. He knows me, because I often come, Socrates; moreover, I have done him a kindness.

Soc. And are you only just come?

Cr. No, I came some time ago.

Soc. Then why did you sit and say nothing, instead of awakening me at once?

Cr. Why, indeed, Socrates, I myself would rather not have all this sleeplessness and sorrow. But I have been wondering at your peaceful slumbers, and that was the reason why I did not awaken you, because I wanted you to be out of pain. I have always thought you happy in the calmness of your temperament; but never did I see the like of the easy, cheerful way in which you bear this calamity.

Soc. Why, Crito, when a man has reached my age he ought not to be repining at the prospect of death.

Cr. And yet other old men find themselves in similar misfortunes, and age does not prevent them from repining.

Soc. That may be. But you have not told me why you come at this early hour.

Cr. I come to bring you a message which is sad and painful; not, as I believe, to yourself, but to all of us who are your friends, and saddest of all to me.

Soc. What! I suppose that the ship has come from Delos, on the arrival of which I am to die?

Cr. No, the ship has not actually arrived, but she will probably be here to-day, as persons who have come from Sunium tell me that they left her there; and therefore to-morrow, Socrates, will be the last day of your life.

Soc. Very well, Crito; if such is the will of God, I am willing; but my belief is that there will be a delay of a day.

Cr. Why do you say this?

Soc. I will tell you. I am to die on the day after the arrival of the ship?

Cr. Yes; that is what the authorities say.

Soc. But I do not think that the ship will be here until to-morrow; this I gather from a vision which I had last night, or rather only just now, when you fortunately allowed me to sleep.

Cr. And what was the nature of the vision?

Soc. There came to me the likeness of a woman, fair and comely, clothed in white raiment, who called to me and said: O Socrates,

> "The third day hence to Phthia shalt thou go."

Cr. What a singular dream, Socrates!

**Scene: The Prison of Socrates. Translated by Benjamin Jowett.*

Soc. There can be no doubt about the meaning, Crito, I think.

Cr. Yes; the meaning is only too clear. But, Oh! my beloved Socrates, let me entreat you once more to take my advice and escape. For if you die I shall not only lose a friend who can never be replaced, but there is another evil: people who do not know you and me will believe that I might have saved you if I had been willing to give money, but that I did not care. Now, can there be a worse disgrace than this—that I should be thought to value money more than the life of a friend? For the many will not be persuaded that I wanted you to escape, and that you refused.

Soc. But why, my dear Crito, should we care about the opinion of the many? Good men, and they are the only persons who are worth considering, will think of these things truly as they happened.

Cr. But do you see, Socrates, that the opinion of the many must be regarded, as is evident in your own case, because they can do the very greatest evil to any one who has lost their good opinion.

Soc. I only wish, Crito, that they could; for then they could also do the greatest good, and that would be well. But the truth is, that they can do neither good nor evil: they can not make a man wise or make him foolish; and whatever they do is the result of chance.

Cr. Well, I will not dispute about that; but please to tell me, Socrates, whether you are not acting out of regard to me and your other friends: are you not afraid that if you escape hence we may get into trouble with the informers for having stolen you away, and lose either the whole or a great part of our property; or that even a worse evil may happen to us? Now, if this is your fear, be at ease; for in order to save you, we ought surely to run this, or even a greater risk; be persuaded, then, and do as I say.

Soc. Yes, Crito, that is one fear which you mention, but by no means the only one.

Cr. Fear not. There are persons who at no great cost are willing to save you and bring you out of prison; and as for the informers, you may observe that they are far from being exorbitant in their demands; a little money will satisfy them. My means, which, as I am sure, are ample, are at your service, and if you have a scruple about spending all mine, here are strangers who will give you the use of theirs; and one of them, Simmias the Theban, has brought a sum of money for this very purpose; and Cebes and many others are willing to spend their money too. I say therefore, do not on that account hesitate about making your escape, and do not say, as you did in the court, that you will have a difficulty in knowing what to do with yourself if you escape. For men will love you in other places to which you may go, and not in Athens only; there are friends of mine in Thessaly, if you like to go to them, who will value and protect you, and no Thessalian will give you any trouble. Nor can I think that you are justified, Socrates, in betraying your own life when you might be saved; this is playing into the hands of your enemies and destroyers; and moreover I should say that you were betraying your children; for you might bring them up and educate them; instead of which you go away and leave them, and they will have to take their chance; and if they do not meet with the usual fate of orphans, there will be small thanks to you. No man should bring children into the world who is unwilling to persevere to the end in their nurture and education. But you are choosing the easier part, as I think, not the better and manlier, which would rather have become one who professes virtue in all his actions, like yourself. And indeed, I am ashamed not only of you, but of us who are your friends, when I reflect that this entire business of yours will be attributed to our want of courage. The trial need never have come on, or might have been brought to another issue; and the end of all, which is the crowning absurdity, will seem to have been permitted by us, through cowardice and baseness, who might have saved you, as you might have saved yourself, if we had been good for anything (for there was no difficulty in escaping); and we did not see how disgraceful, Socrates, and also miserable all this will be to us as well as to you. Make your mind up then, or rather have your mind already made up, for the time of deliberation is over, and there is only one thing to be done, which must be done, if at all, this very night, and which any delay will render all but impossible; I beseech you therefore, Socrates, to be persuaded by me, and to do as I say.

Soc. Dear Crito, your zeal is invaluable, if a right one; but if wrong, the greater the zeal the greater the evil; and therefore we ought to consider whether these things shall be done or not. For I am and always have been one of those natures who must be guided by reason, whatever the reason may be which upon reflection appears to me to be the best; and now that this fortune has come upon me, I can not put away the reasons which I have before given: the principles which I have hitherto honored and revered I still honor, and unless we can find other and better principles on the instant, I am certain not to agree with you; no, not even if the power of the multitude could inflict many more imprisonments, confiscations, deaths, frightening us like children with hobgoblin terrors. But what will be the fairest way of considering the question? Shall I return to your old argument about the opinions of men? some of which are to be regarded, and others, as we were saying, are not to be regarded. Now were we right in maintaining this before I was condemned? And has the argument which was once good now proved to be talk for the sake of talking;—in fact an amusement only, and altogether vanity? That is what I want to consider with your help, Crito:—whether, under my present circumstances, the argument appears to be in any way different or not; and is to be allowed by me or disallowed. That argument, which, as I believe, is maintained by many who assume to be authorities, was to the effect, as I was saying, that the opinions of some men are to be regarded, and of other men not to be regarded. Now you, Crito, are a disinterested person who are not going to die to-morrow—at least, there is no human probability of this, and you are therefore not liable to be deceived by the circumstances in which you are placed. Tell me then, whether I am right in saying that some opinions, and the opinions of some men only, are to be valued, and other opinions, and the opinions of other men, are not to be valued. I ask you whether I was right in maintaining this?

Cr. Certainly.

Soc. The good are to be regarded, and not the bad?

Cr. Yes.

Soc. And the opinions of the wise are good, and the opinions of the unwise are evil?

Cr. Certainly.

Soc. And what was said about another matter? Was the disciple in gymnastics supposed to attend to the praise and blame and opinion of every man, or of one man only—his physician or trainer, whoever that was?

Cr. Of one man only.

Soc. And he ought to fear the censure and welcome the praise of that one only, and not of the many?

Cr. That is clear.

Soc. And he ought to live and train, and eat and drink in the way which seems good to his single master who has understanding, rather than according to the opinion of all other men put together?

Cr. True.

Soc. And if he disobeys and disregards the opinion and approval of the one, and regards the opinion of the many who have no understanding, will he not suffer evil?

Cr. Certainly he will.

Soc. And what will the evil be, whither tending and what affecting, in the disobedient person?

Cr. Clearly, affecting the body; that is what is destroyed by the evil.

Soc. Very good; and is not this true, Crito, of other things which we need not separately enumerate? In the matter of just and unjust, fair and foul, good and evil, which are the subjects of our present consultation, ought we to follow the opinion of the many and to fear them; or the opinion of the one man who has understanding, and whom we ought to fear and reverence more than all the rest of the world: and whom deserting we shall destroy and injure that principle in us which may be assumed to be improved by justice and deteriorated by injustice;—is there not such a principle?

Cr. Certainly there is, Socrates.

Soc. Take a parallel instance:—if, acting under the advice of men who have no understanding, we destroy that which is improvable by health and deteriorated by disease—when that has been destroyed, I say, would life be worth having? And that is—the body?

Cr. Yes.

Soc. Could we live, having an evil and corrupted body?

Cr. Certainly not.

Soc. And will life be worth having, if that higher part of man be depraved, which is improved by justice and deteriorated by injustice? Do we suppose that principle, whatever it may be in man, which has to do with justice and injustice, to be inferior to the body?

Cr. Certainly not.

Soc. More honored, then?

Cr. Far more honored.

Soc. Then, my friend, we must not regard what the many say of us: but what he, the one man who has understanding of just and unjust, will say, and what the truth will say. And therefore you begin in error when you suggest that we should regard the opinion of the many about just and unjust, good and evil, honorable and dishonorable.—Well, some one will say, "but the many can kill us."

Cr. Yes, Socrates; that will clearly be the answer.

Soc. That is true: but still I find with surprise that the old argument is, as I conceive, unshaken as ever. And I should like to know whether I may say the same of another proposition—that not life, but a good life, is to be chiefly valued?

Cr. Yes, that also remains.

Soc. And a good life is equivalent to a just and honorable one—that holds also?

Cr. Yes, that holds.

Soc. From these premisses I proceed to argue the question whether I ought or ought not to try and escape without the consent of the Athenians: and if I am clearly right in escaping, then I will make the attempt; but if not, I will abstain. The other considerations which you mention, of money and loss of character and the duty of educating children, are, as I fear, only the doctrines of the multitude, who would be as ready to call people to life, if they were able, as they are to put them to death—and with as little reason. But now, since the argument has thus far prevailed, the only question which remains to be considered is, whether we shall do rightly either in escaping or in suffering others to aid in our escape and paying them in money and thanks, or whether we shall not do rightly; and if the latter, then death or any other calamity which may ensue on my remaining here must not be allowed to enter into the calculation.

Cr. I think that you are right, Socrates; how then shall we proceed?

Soc. Let us consider the matter together, and do you either refute me if you can, and I will be convinced; or else cease, my dear friend, from repeating to me that I ought to escape against the wishes of the Athenians: for I am extremely desirous to be persuaded by you, but not against my own better judgment. And now please to consider my first position, and do your best to answer me.

Cr. I will do my best.

Soc. Are we to say that we are never intentionally to do wrong, or that in one way we ought and in another way we ought not to do wrong, or is doing wrong always evil and dishonorable, as I was just now saying, and as has been already acknowledged by us? Are all our former admissions which were made within a few days to be thrown away? And have we, at our age, been earnestly discoursing with one another all our life long only to discover that we are no better than children? Or are we to rest assured, in spite of the opinion of the many, and in spite of consequences whether better or worse, of the truth of what was then said, that injustice is always an evil and dishonor to him who acts unjustly? Shall we affirm that?

Cr. Yes.

Soc. Then we must do no wrong?

Cr. Certainly not.

Soc. Nor when injured injure in return, as the many imagine; for we must injure no one at all?

Cr. Clearly not.

Soc. Again, Crito, may we do evil?

Cr. Surely not, Socrates.

Soc. And what of doing evil in return for evil, which is the morality of the many—is that just or not?

Cr. Not just.

Soc. For doing evil to another is the same as injuring him?

Cr. Very true.

Soc. Then we ought not to retaliate or render evil for evil to any one, whatever evil we may have suffered from him. But I would have you consider, Crito, whether you really mean what you are saying. For this opinion has never been held, and never will be held, by any considerable number of persons; and those who are agreed and those who are not agreed upon this point have no common ground, and can only despise one another when they see how widely they differ. Tell me, then, whether you agree with and assent to my first principle, that neither injury nor retaliation nor warding off evil by evil is ever right. And shall that be the premiss of our argument? Or do you decline and dissent from this? For this has been of old and is still my opinion; but, if you are of another opinion, let me hear what you have to say. If, however, you remain of the same mind as formerly, I will proceed to the next step.

Cr. You may proceed, for I have not changed my mind.

Soc. Then I will proceed to the next step, which may be put in the form of a question:—Ought a man to do what he admits to be right, or ought he to betray the right?

Cr. He ought to do what he thinks right.

Soc. But if this is true, what is the application? In leaving the prison against the will of the Athenians, do I wrong any? or rather do I not wrong those whom I ought least to wrong? Do I not desert the principles which were acknowledged by us to be just? What do you say?

Cr. I can not tell, Socrates; for I do not know.

Soc. Then consider the matter in this way:—Imagine that I am about to play truant (you may call the proceeding by any name which you like), and the laws and the government come and interrogate me: "Tell us, Socrates," they say; "what are you about? are you going by an act of yours to overturn us—the laws and the whole state, as far as in you lies? Do you imagine that a state can subsist and not be overthrown, in which the decisions of law have no power, but are set aside and overthrown by individuals?" What will be our answer, Crito, to these and the like words? Any one, and especially a clever rhetorician, will have a good deal to urge about the evil of setting aside the law which requires a sentence to be carried out; and we might reply, "Yes; but the state has injured us and given an unjust sentence." Suppose I say that?

Cr. Very good, Socrates.

Soc. "And was that our agreement with you?" the law would say; "or were you to abide by the sentence of the state?" And if I were to express astonishment at their saying this, the law would probably add: "Answer, Socrates, instead of opening your eyes: you are in the habit of asking and answering questions. Tell us what complaint you have to make against us which justifies you in attempting to destroy us and the state? In the first place did we not bring you into existence? Your father married your mother by our aid and begat you. Say whether you have any objection to urge against those of us who regulate marriage?" None, I should reply. "Or against those of us who regulate the system of nurture and education of children in which you were trained? Were not the laws, who have the charge of this, right in commanding your father to train you in music and gymnastic?" Right, I should reply. "Well then, since you were brought into the world and nurtured and educated by us, can you deny in the first place that you are our child and slave, as your fathers were before you? And if this is true you are not on equal terms with us; nor can you think that you have a right to do to us what we are doing to you. Would you have any right to strike or revile or do any other evil to a father or to your master, if you had one, when you have been struck or reviled by him, or received some other evil at his hands?—you would not say this? And because we think right to destroy you, do you think that you have any right to destroy us in return, and your country as far as in you lies? And will you, O professor of true virtue, say that you are justified in this? Has a philosopher like you failed to discover that our country is more to be valued and higher and holier far than mother or father or any ancestor, and more to be regarded in the eyes of the gods and of men of understanding? also to be soothed, and gently and reverently entreated when angry, even more than a father, and if not persuaded, obeyed? And when we are punished by her, whether with imprisonment or stripes, the punishment is to be endured in silence; and if she lead us to wounds or death in battle, thither we follow as is right; neither may any one yield or retreat or leave his rank, but whether in battle or in a court of law, or in any other place, he must do what his city and his country order him; or he must change their view of what is just: and if he may do no violence to his father or mother, much less may he do violence to his country." What answer shall we make to this, Crito? Do the laws speak truly, or do they not?

Cr. I think that they do.

Soc. Then the laws will say: "Consider, Socrates, if this is true, that in your present attempt you are going to do us wrong. For, after having brought you into the world, and nurtured and educated you, and given you and every other citizen a share in every good that we had to give, we further proclaim and give the right to every Athenian, that if he does not like us when he has come of age and has seen the ways of the city, and made our acquaintance, he may go where he pleases and take his goods with him; and none of us laws will forbid him or interfere with him. Any of you who does not like us and the city, and who wants to go to a colony or to any other city, may go where he likes, and take his goods with him. But he who has experience of the manner in which we order justice and administer the state, and still remains, has entered into an implied contract that he will do as we command him. And he who disobeys us is, as we maintain, thrice wrong; first, because in disobeying us he is disobeying his parents; secondly, because we are the authors of his education; thirdly, because he has made an agreement with us that he will duly obey our commands; and he neither obeys them nor convinces us that our commands are wrong; and we do not rudely impose them, but give them the alternative of obeying or convincing us;—that is what we offer, and he does neither. These are the sort of accusations to which, as we were saying, you, Socrates, will be exposed if you accomplish your intentions; you, above all other Athenians." Suppose I ask, why is this? they will justly retort upon me that I above all other men have acknowledged the agreement. "There is clear proof," they will say, "Socrates, that we and the city were not displeasing to you. Of all Athenians you have been the most constant resident in the city, which, as you never leave, you may be supposed to love. For you never went out of the city either to see the games, except once when you went to the Isthmus, or to any other place unless when you were on military service; nor did you travel as other men do. Nor had you any curiosity to know other states or their laws: your affections did not go beyond us and our state; we were your special favorites, and you acquiesced in our government of you; and this is the state in which you begat your children, which is a proof of your satisfaction. Moreover, you might, if you had liked, have fixed the penalty at banishment in the course of the trial—the state which refuses to let you go now would have let you go then. But you pretended that you preferred death to exile, and that you were not grieved at death. And now you have forgotten these fine sentiments, and pay no respect to us the laws, of whom you are the destroyer; and are doing what only a miserable slave would do, running away and turning your back upon the compacts and agreements which you made as a citizen. And first of all answer this very question: Are we right in saying that you agreed to be governed according to us in deed, and not in word only? Is that true or not?" How shall we answer that, Crito? Must we not agree?

Cr. There is no help, Socrates.

Soc. Then will they not say: "You, Socrates, are breaking the covenants and agreements which you made with us at your leisure, not in any haste or under any compulsion or deception, but having had seventy years to think of them, during which time you were at liberty to leave the city, if we were not to your mind, or if our covenants appeared to you to be unfair. You had your choice, and might have gone either to Lacedaemon or Crete, which you often praise for their good government, or to some other Hellenic or foreign state. Whereas you, above all other Athenians, seemed to be so fond of the state, or, in other words, of us her laws (for who would like a state that has no laws), that you never stirred out of her; the halt, the blind, the maimed were not more stationary in her than you were. And now you run away and forsake your agreements. Not so, Socrates, if you will take our advice; do not make yourself ridiculous by escaping out of the city.

"For just consider, if you transgress and err in this sort of way, what good will you do either to yourself or to your friends? That your friends will be driven into exile and deprived of citizenship, or will lose their property, is tolerably certain; and you yourself, if you fly to one of the neighboring cities, as, for example, Thebes or Megara, both of which are well-governed cities, will come to them as an enemy, Socrates, and their government will be against you, and all patriotic citizens will cast an evil eye upon you as a subverter of the laws, and you will confirm in the minds of the judges the justice of their own condemnation of you. For he who is a corruptor of the laws is more than likely to be corruptor of the young and foolish portion of mankind. Will you then flee from well-ordered cities and virtuous men? and is existence worth having on these terms? Or will you go to them without shame, and talk to them, Socrates? And what will you say to them? What you say here about virtue and justice and institutions and laws being the best things among men. Would that be decent of you? Surely not. But if you go away from well-governed states to Crito's friends in Thessaly, where there is a great disorder and license, they will be charmed to have the tale of your escape from prison, set off with ludicrous particulars of the manner in which you were wrapped in a goatskin or some other disguise, and metamorphosed as the fashion of runaways is—that is very likely; but will there be no one to remind you that in your old age you violated the most sacred laws from a miserable desire of a little more life. Perhaps not, if you keep them in a good temper; but if they are out of temper you will hear many degrading things; you will live, but how?—as the flatterer of all men, and the servant of all men; and doing what?—eating and drinking in Thessaly, having gone abroad in order that you may get a dinner. And where will be your fine sentiments about justice and virtue then? Say that you wish to live for the sake of your children, that you may bring them up and educate them—will you take them into Thessaly and deprive them of Athenian citizenship? Is that the benefit which you would confer upon them? Or are you under the impression that they will be better cared for and educated here if you are still alive, although absent from them; for that your friends will take care of them? Do you fancy that if you are an inhabitant of Thessaly they will take care of them, and if you are an inhabitant of the other world they will not take care of them? Nay; but if they who call themselves friends are truly friends, they surely will.

"Listen, then, Socrates, to us who have brought you up. Think not of life and children first, and of justice afterwards, but of justice first, that you may be justified before the princes of the world below. For neither will you nor any that belong to you be happier or holier or juster in this life, or happier in another, if you do as Crito bids. Now you depart in innocence, a sufferer and not a doer of evil; a victim, not of the laws, but of men. But if you go forth, returning evil for evil, and injury for injury, breaking the covenants and agreements which you have made with us, and wronging those whom you ought least to wrong, that is to say, yourself, your friends, your country, and us, we shall be angry with you while you live, and our brethren, the laws in the world below, will receive you as an enemy; for they will know that you have done your best to destroy us. Listen, then, to us and not to Crito."

This is the voice which I seem to hear murmuring in my ears, like the sound of the flute in the ears of the mystic; that voice, I say, is humming in my ears, and prevents me from hearing any other. And I know that anything more which you may say will be vain. Yet speak, if you have anything to say.

Cr. I have nothing to say, Socrates.

Soc. Then let me follow the intimations of the will of God.

Letter from Birmingham Jail*

MARTIN LUTHER KING JR.

April 16, 1963

My Dear Fellow Clergymen:

WHILE CONFINED HERE in the Birmingham city jail, I came across your recent statement calling my present activities 'unwise and untimely.' Seldom do I pause to answer criticism of my work and ideas. If I sought to answer all the criticisms that cross my desk, my secretaries would have little time for anything other than such correspondence in the course of the day, and I would have no time for constructive work. But since I feel that you are men of genuine good will and that your criticisms are sincerely set forth, I want to try to answer your statement in what I hope will be patient and reasonable terms.

I think I should indicate why I am here in Birmingham, since you have been influenced by the view which argues against 'outsiders coming in.' I have the honor of serving as president of the Southern Christian Leadership Conference, an organization operating in every southern state, with headquarters in Atlanta, Georgia. We have some eighty-five affiliated organizations across the South, and one of them is the Alabama Christian Movement for Human Rights. Frequently we share staff, educational and financial resources with our affiliates. Several months ago the affiliate here in Birmingham asked us to be on call to engage in a nonviolent direct-action program if such were deemed necessary. We readily consented, and when the hour came we lived up to our promise. So I, along with several members of my staff, am here because I was invited here. I am here because I have organizational ties here.

But more basically, I am in Birmingham because injustice is here. Just as the prophets of the eighth century B.C. left their villages and carried their 'thus saith the Lord' far beyond the boundaries of their home towns, and just as the Apostle Paul left his village of Tarsus and carried the gospel of Jesus Christ to the far corners of the Greco-Roman world, so am I compelled to carry the gospel of freedom beyond my own home town. Like Paul, I must constantly respond to the Macedonian call for aid.

Moreover, I am cognizant of the interrelatedness of all communities and states. I cannot sit idly by in Atlanta and not be concerned about what happens in Birmingham. Injustice anywhere is a threat to justice everywhere. We are caught in an inescapable network of mutuality, tied in a single garment of destiny. Whatever affects one directly, affects all indirectly. Never again can we afford to live with the narrow, provincial 'outside agitator' idea. Anyone who lives inside the United States can never be considered an outsider anywhere within its bounds.

You deplore the demonstrations taking place in Birmingham. But your statement, I am sorry to say, fails to express a similar concern for the conditions that brought about the demonstrations. I am sure that none of you would want to rest content with the superficial kind of social analysis that deals merely with effects and does not grapple with underlying causes. It is unfortunate that demonstrations are taking place in Birmingham, but it is even more unfortunate that the city's white power structure left the Negro community with no alternative.

In any nonviolent campaign there are four basic steps: collection of the facts to determine whether

**From* Why We Can't Wait *by Martin Luther King, Jr. Reprinted by arrangement with the heirs to the estate of Martin Luther King, Jr., in care of the John Daves Agency, as agent for the proprietor.*

injustices exist; negotiation; self-purification; and direct action. We have gone through all these steps in Birmingham. There can be no gainsaying the fact that racial injustice engulfs this community. Birmingham is probably the most thoroughly segregated city in the United States. Its ugly record of brutality is widely known. Negroes have experienced grossly unjust treatment in the courts. There have been more unsolved bombings of Negro homes and churches in Birmingham than in any other city in the nation. These are the hard, brutal facts of the case. On the basis of these conditions, Negro leaders sought to negotiate with the city fathers. But the latter consistently refused to engage in good-faith negotiation.

Then, last September, came the opportunity to talk with leaders of Birmingham's economic community. In the course of the negotiations, certain promises were made by the merchants—for example, to remove the stores' humiliating racial signs. On the basis of these promises, the Reverend Fred Shuttlesworth and the leaders of the Alabama Christian Movement for Human Rights agreed to a moratorium on all demonstrations. As the weeks and months went by, we realized that we were the victims of a broken promise. A few signs, briefly removed, returned; the others remained.

As in so many past experiences, our hopes had been blasted, and the shadow of deep disappointment settled upon us. We had no alternative except to prepare for direct action, whereby we would present our very bodies as a means of laying our case before the conscience of the local and the national community. Mindful of the difficulties involved, we decided to undertake a process of self-purification. We began a series of workshops on nonviolence, and we repeatedly asked ourselves: 'Are you able to accept blows without retaliating?' 'Are you able to endure the ordeal of jail?' We decided to schedule our direct-action program for the Easter season, realizing that except for Christmas, this is the main shopping period of the year. Knowing that a strong economic-withdrawal program would be the by-product of direct action, we felt that this would be the best time to bring pressure to bear on the merchants for the needed change.

Then it occurred to us that Birmingham's mayoral election was coming up in March, and we speedily decided to postpone action until after election day. When we discovered that the Commissioner of Public Safety, Eugene 'Bull' Connor, had piled up enough votes to be in the run-off, we decided again to postpone action until the day after the run-off so that the demonstrations could not be used to cloud the issues. Like many others, we waited to see Mr. Connor defeated, and to this end we endured postponement after postponement. Having aided in this community need, we felt that our direct-action program could be delayed no longer.

You may well ask: 'Why direct action? Why sit-ins, marches and so forth? Isn't negotiation a better path?' You are quite right in calling for negotiation. Indeed, this is the very purpose of direct action. Nonviolent direct action seeks to create such a crisis and foster such a tension that a community which has constantly refused to negotiate is forced to confront the issue. It seeks so to dramatize the issue that it can no longer be ignored. My citing the creation of tension as part of the work of the nonviolent-resister may sound rather shocking. But I must confess that I am not afraid of the word 'tension.' I have earnestly opposed violent tension, but there is a type of constructive, nonviolent tension which is necessary for growth. Just as Socrates felt that it was necessary to create a tension in the mind so that individuals could rise from the bondage of myths and half-truths to the unfettered realm of creative analysis and objective appraisal, so must we see the need for nonviolent gadflies to create the kind of tension in society that will help men rise from the dark depths of prejudice and racism to the majestic heights of understanding and brotherhood.

The purpose of our direct-action program is to create a situation so crisis-packed that it will inevitably open the door to negotiation. I therefore concur with you in your call for negotiation. Too long has our beloved Southland been bogged down in a tragic effort to live in monologue rather than dialogue.

One of the basic points in your statement is that the action that I and my associates have taken in Birmingham is untimely. Some have asked: 'Why didn't you give the new city administration time to act?' The only answer that I can give to this query is that the new Birmingham administration must be prodded about as much as the outgoing one, before it will act. We are sadly mistaken if we feel that the election of Albert Boutwell as mayor will bring the millennium to Birmingham. While Mr. Boutwell is a much more gentle person than Mr. Connor, they are both segregationists, dedicated to maintenance of the status quo. I have hope that Mr. Boutwell will be reasonable enough to see the futility of massive resistance to desegregation. But he will not see this without pressure from devotees of civil rights. My friends, I must say to you that we have not made a single gain in civil rights without determined legal and nonviolent pressure. Lamentably, it is an historical fact that privileged groups seldom give up their privileges voluntarily. Individuals may see the moral light and voluntarily give up their unjust posture; but, as Reinhold Niebuhr has reminded us, groups tend to be more immoral than individuals.

We know through painful experience that freedom is never voluntarily given by the oppressor; it must be demanded by the oppressed. Frankly, I have yet to engage in a direct-action campaign that was 'well timed' in the view of those who have not suffered unduly from the disease of segregation. For years now I have heard the word 'Wait!' It rings in the ear of every Negro with piercing familiarity. This 'Wait' has almost always meant 'Never.' We must come to see, with one of our distinguished jurists, that 'justice too long delayed is justice denied.'

We have waited for more than 340 years for our constitutional and God-given rights. The nations of Asia and Africa are moving with jetlike speed toward gaining political independence, but we still creep at horse-and-buggy pace toward gaining a cup of coffee at a lunch counter. Perhaps it is easy for those who have never felt the stinging darts of segregation to say, 'Wait.' But when you have seen vicious mobs lynch your mothers and fathers at will and drown your sisters and brothers at whim; when you have seen hate-filled policemen curse, kick and even kill your black brothers and sisters; when you see the vast majority of your twenty million Negro brothers smothering in an airtight cage of poverty in the midst of an affluent society; when you suddenly find your tongue twisted and your speech stammering as you seek to explain to your six-year-old daughter why she can't go to the public amusement park that has just been advertised on television, and see tears welling up in her eyes when she is told that Funtown is closed to colored children, and see ominous clouds of inferiority begining to form in her little mental sky, and see her begining to distort her personality by developing an unconscious bitterness toward white people; when you have to concoct an answer for a five-year-old son who is asking: 'Daddy, why do white people treat colored people so mean?'; when you take a cross-country drive and find it necessary to sleep night after night in the uncomfortable corners of your automobile because no motel will accept you; when you are humiliated day in and day out by nagging signs reading 'white' and 'colored'; when your first name becomes 'nigger,' your middle name becomes 'boy' (however old you are) and your last name becomes 'John,' and your wife and mother are never given the respected title 'Mrs.'; when you are harried by day and haunted by night by the fact that you are a Negro, living constantly at tiptoe stance, never quite knowing what to expect next, and are plagued with inner fears and outer resentments; when you are forever fighting a degenerating sense of 'nobodiness'—then you will understand why we find it difficult to wait. There comes a time when the cup of endurance runs over, and men are no longer willing to be plunged into the abyss of despair. I hope, sirs, you can understand our legitimate and unavoidable impatience.

You express a great deal of anxiety over our willingness to break laws. This is certainly a legitimate concern. Since we so diligently urge people to obey the Supreme Court's decision of 1954 outlawing segregation in the public schools, at first glance it may seem rather paradoxical for us consciously to break laws. One may well ask: 'How can you advocate breaking some laws and obeying others?' The answer lies in the fact that there are two types of laws: just and unjust. I would be the first to advocate obeying just laws. One has not only a legal but a moral responsibility to obey just laws. Conversely, one has a moral responsibility to disobey unjust laws. I would agree with St. Augustine that 'an unjust law is no law at all.'

Now, what is the difference between the two? How does one determine whether a law is just or unjust? A just law is a man-made code that squares with the moral law or the law of God. An unjust law is a code that is out of harmony with the moral law. To put it in the terms of St. Thomas Aquinas: An unjust law is a human law that is not rooted in eternal and natural law. Any law that uplifts human personality is just. Any law that degrades human personality is unjust. All segregation statutes are unjust because segregation distorts the soul and damages the personality. It gives the segregator a false sense of superiority and the segregated a false sense of inferiority. Segregation, to use the terminology of the Jewish philosopher Martin Buber, substitutes an 'I-it' relationship for an 'I-thou' relationship and ends up relegating persons to the status of things. Hence segregation is not only politically, economically and sociologically unsound, it is morally wrong and sinful. Paul Tillich has said that sin is separation. Is not segregation an existential expression of man's tragic separation, his awful estrangement, his terrible sinfulness? Thus it is that I can urge men to obey the 1954 decision of the Supreme Court, for it is morally right; and I can urge them to disobey segregation ordinances, for they are morally wrong.

Let us consider a more concrete example of just and unjust laws. An unjust law is a code that a numerical or power majority group compels a minority group to obey but does not make binding on itself. This is *difference* made legal. By the same token, a just law is a code that a majority compels a minority to follow and that it is willing to follow itself. This is *sameness* made legal.

Let me give another explanation. A law is unjust if it is inflicted on a minority that, as a result of being denied the right to vote, had no part in enacting or devising the law. Who can say that the legislature of Alabama which set up that state's segregation laws was democratically elected? Throughout Alabama all sorts of devious methods are used to prevent Negroes from becoming registered voters, and there are some counties in which, even though Negroes constitute a majority of the population, not a single Negro is registered. Can any law enacted under such circumstances be considered democratically structured?

Sometimes a law is just on its face and unjust in its application. For instance, I have been arrested on a charge of parading without a permit. Now, there is nothing wrong in having an ordinance which requires a permit for a parade. But such an ordinance becomes unjust when it is used to maintain segregation and to deny citizens the First-Amendment privilege of peaceful assembly and protest.

I hope you are able to see the distinction I am trying to point out. In no sense do I advocate evading or defying the law, as would the rabid segregationist. That would lead to anarchy. One who breaks an unjust law must do so openly, lovingly, and with a willingness to accept the penalty. I submit that an individual who breaks a law that conscience tells him is unjust, and who willingly accepts the penalty of imprisonment in order to arouse the conscience of the community over its injustice, is in reality expressing the highest respect for law.

Of course, there is nothing new about this kind of civil disobedience. It was evidenced sublimely in the refusal of Shadrach, Meshach and Abednego to obey the laws of Nebuchadnezzar, on the ground that a higher moral law was at stake. It was practiced superbly by the early Christians, who were willing to face hungry lions and the excruciating pain of chopping blocks rather than submit to certain unjust laws of the Roman Empire. To a degree, academic freedom is a reality today because Socrates practiced civil disobedience. In our own nation, the Boston Tea Party represented a massive act of civil disobedience.

We should never forget that everything Adolf Hitler did in Germany was 'legal' and everything the Hungarian freedom fighters did in Hungary was 'illegal.' It was 'illegal' to aid and comfort a Jew in Hitler's Germany. Even so, I am sure that, had I lived in Germany at the time, I would have aided and comforted my Jewish brothers. If today I lived in a Communist country where certain principles dear to the Christian faith are suppressed, I would openly advocate disobeying that country's antireligious laws.

I must make two honest confessions to you, my Christian and Jewish brothers. First, I must confess that over the past few years I have been gravely disappointed with the white moderate. I have almost reached the regrettable conclusion that the Negro's great stumbling block in his stride toward freedom is not the White Citizen's Counciler or the Ku Klux Klanner, but the white moderate, who is more devoted to 'order' than to justice; who prefers a negative peace which is the absence of tension to a positive peace which is the presence of justice; who constantly says: 'I agree with you in the goal you seek, but I cannot agree with your methods of direct action'; who paternalistically believes he can set the timetable for another man's freedom; who lives by a mythical concept of time and who constantly advises the Negro to wait for a 'more convenient season.' Shallow understanding from people of good will is more frustrating than absolute misunderstanding from people of ill will. Lukewarm acceptance is much more bewildering than outright rejection.

I had hoped that the white moderate would understand that law and order exist for the purpose of establishing justice and that when they fail in this purpose they become the dangerously structured dams that block the flow of social progress. I had hoped that the white moderate would understand that the present tension in the South is a necessary phase of the transition from an obnoxious negative peace, in which the Negro passively accepted his unjust plight, to a substantive and positive peace, in which all men will respect the dignity and worth of human personality. Actually, we who engage in nonviolent direct action are not the creators of tension. We merely bring to the surface the hidden tension that is already alive. We bring it out in the open, where it can be seen and dealt with. Like a boil that can never be cured so long as it is covered up but must be opened with all its ugliness to the natural medicines of air and light, injustice must be exposed, with all the tension its exposure creates, to the light of human conscience and the air of national opinion before it can be cured.

In your statement you assert that our actions, even though peaceful, must be condemned because they precipitate violence. But is this a logical assertion? Isn't this like condemning a robbed man because his possession of money precipitated the evil act of robbery? Isn't this like condemning Socrates because his unswerving commitment to truth and his philosophical inquiries precipitated the act by the misguided populace in which they made him drink hemlock? Isn't this like condemning Jesus because his unique God-consciousness and never-ceasing devotion to God's will precipitated the evil act of crucifixion? We must come to see that, as the federal courts have consistently affirmed, it is wrong to urge an individual to cease his efforts to gain his basic constitutional rights because the quest may precipitate violence. Society must protect the robbed and punish the robber.

I had also hoped that the white moderate would reject the myth concerning time in relation to the struggle for freedom. I have just received a letter from a white brother in Texas. He writes: 'All Christians know that the colored people will receive equal rights eventually, but it is possible that you are in too great a religious hurry. It has taken Christianity almost two thousand years to accomplish what it has. The teachings of Christ take time to come to earth.' Such an attitude stems from a tragic misconception of time, from the strangely irrational notion that there is something in the very flow of time that will inevitably cure all ills. Actually, time itself is neutral; it can be used either destructively or constructively. More and more I feel that the people of ill will have used time much more effectively than have the people of good will. We will have to repent in this generation not merely for the hateful words and actions of the bad people but for the appalling silence of the good people. Human progress never rolls in on wheels of inevitability; it comes through the tireless efforts of men willing to be co-workers with God, and without this hard work, time itself becomes an ally of the forces of social stagnation. We must use time creatively, in the knowledge that the time is always ripe to do right. Now is the time to make real the promise of democracy and transform our pending national elegy into a creative psalm of brotherhood. Now is the time to lift our national policy from the quicksand of racial injustice to the solid rock of human dignity.

You speak of our activity in Birmingham as extreme. At first I was rather disappointed that fellow clergymen would see my nonviolent efforts as those of an extremist. I began thinking about the fact that I stand in the middle of two opposing forces in the Negro community. One is a force of complacency, made up in part of Negroes who, as a result of long years of oppression, are so drained of self-respect and a sense of 'somebodiness' that they have adjusted to segregation; and in part of a few middle-class Negroes who, because of a degree of academic and economic security and because in some ways they profit by segregation, have become insensitive to the problems of the masses. The other force is one of bitterness and hatred, and it comes perilously close to advocating violence. It is expressed in the various black nationalist groups that are springing up across the nation, the largest and best-known being Elijah Muhammad's Muslim movement. Nourished by the Negro's frustration over the continued existence of racial discrimination, this movement is made up of people who have lost faith in America, who have absolutely repudiated Christianity, and who have concluded that the white man is an incorrigible 'devil.'

I have tried to stand between these two forces, saying that we need emulate neither the 'donothingism' of the complacent nor the hatred and despair of the black nationalist. For there is the more excellent way of love and nonviolent protest. I am grateful to God that, through the influence of the Negro church, the way of nonviolence became an integral part of our struggle.

If this philosophy had not emerged, by now many streets of the South would, I am convinced, be flowing with blood. And I am further convinced that if our white brothers dismiss as 'rabble-rousers' and 'outside agitators' those of us who employ nonviolent direct action, and if they refuse to support our nonviolent efforts, millions of Negroes will, out of frustration and despair, seek solace and security in black-nationalist ideologies—a development that would inevitably lead to a frightening racial nightmare.

Oppressed people cannot remain oppressed forever. The yearning for freedom eventually manifests itself, and that is what has happened to the American Negro. Something within has reminded him of his birthright of freedom, and something without has reminded him that it can be gained. Consciously or unconsciously, he has been caught up by the *Zeitgeist,* and with his black brothers of Africa and his brown and yellow brothers of Asia, South America and the Caribbean, the United States Negro is moving with a sense of great urgency toward the promised land of racial justice. If one recognizes this vital urge that has engulfed the Negro community, one should readily understand why public demonstrations are taking place. The Negro has many pent-up resentments and latent frustrations, and he must release them. So let him march; let him make prayer pilgrimages to the city hall; let him go on freedom rides—and try to understand why he must do so. If his repressed emotions are not released in nonviolent ways, they will seek expression through violence; this is not a threat but a fact of history. So I have not said to my people: 'Get rid of your discontent.' Rather, I have tried to say that this normal and healthy discontent can be channeled into the creative outlet of nonviolent direct action. And now this approach is being termed extremist.

But though I was initially disappointed at being categorized as an extremist, as I continued to think about the matter I gradually gained a measure of satisfaction from the label. Was not Jesus an extremist for love: 'Love your enemies, bless them that curse you, do good to them that hate you, and pray for them which despitefully use you, and persecute you.' Was not Amos an extremist for justice: 'Let justice roll down like waters and righteousness like an ever-flowing stream.' Was not Paul an extremist for the Christian gospel: 'I bear in my body the marks of the Lord Jesus.' Was not Martin Luther an extremist: 'Here I stand; I cannot do otherwise, so help me God.' And John Bunyan: 'I will stay in jail to the end of my days before I make a butchery of my conscience.' And Abraham Lincoln: 'This nation cannot survive half slave and half free.' And Thomas Jefferson: 'We hold these truths to be self-evident, that all men are created equal. . . .' So the question is not whether we will be extremists, but what kind of extremists we will be. Will we be extremists for hate or for love? Will we be extremists for the preservation of injustice or for the extension of justice? In that dramatic scene on Calvary's hill three men were crucified. We must never forget that all three were crucified for the same crime—the crime of extremism. Two were extremists for immorality, and thus fell below their environment. The other, Jesus Christ, was an extremist for love, truth and goodness, and thereby rose above his environment. Perhaps the South, the nation and the world are in dire need of creative extremists.

I had hoped that the white moderate would see this need. Perhaps I was too optimistic; perhaps I expected too much. I suppose I should have realized that few members of the oppressor race can understand the deep groans and passionate yearnings of the oppressed race, and still fewer have the vision to see that injustice must be rooted out by strong, persistent and determined action. I am thankful, however, that some of our white brothers in the South have grasped the meaning of this social revolution and committed themselves to it. They are still all too few in quantity, but they are big in quality. Some—such as Ralph McGill, Lillian Smith, Harry Golden, James McBride Dabbs, Ann Braden and Sarah Patton Boyle—have written about our struggle in eloquent and prophetic terms. Others have marched with us down nameless streets of the South. They have languished in filthy, roach-infested jails, suffering the abuse and brutality of policemen who view them as 'dirty nigger-lovers.' Unlike so many of their moderate brothers and sisters, they have recognized the urgency of the moment and sensed the need for powerful 'action' antidotes to combat the disease of segregation.

Let me take note of my other major disappointment. I have been so greatly disappointed with the white church and its leadership. Of course, there are some notable exceptions. I am not unmindful of the fact that each of you has taken some significant stands on this issue. I commend you, Reverend Stallings, for your Christian stand on this past Sunday, in welcoming Negroes to your worship service on a nonsegregated basis. I commend the Catholic leaders of this state for integrating Spring Hill College several years ago.

But despite these notable exceptions, I must honestly reiterate that I have been disappointed with the church. I do not say this as one of those negative critics who can always find something wrong with the church. I say this as a minister of the gospel, who loves the church; who was nurtured in its bosom; who has been sustained by its spiritual blessings and who will remain true to it as long as the cord of life shall lengthen.

When I was suddenly catapulted into the leadership of the bus protest in Montgomery, Alabama, a few years ago, I felt we would be supported by the white church. I felt that the white ministers, priests and rabbis of the South would be among our strongest allies. Instead, some have been outright opponents, refusing to understand the freedom movement and misrepresenting its leaders; all too many others have been more cautious than courageous and have remained silent behind the anesthetizing security of stained-glass windows.

In spite of my shattered dreams, I came to Birmingham with the hope that the white religious leadership of this community would see the justice of our cause and, with deep moral concern, would serve as the channel through which our just grievances could reach the power structure. I had hoped that each of you would understand. But again I have been disappointed.

I have heard numerous southern religious leaders admonish their worshippers to comply with a desegregation decision because it is the law, but I have longed to hear white ministers declare: 'Follow this decree because integration is morally right and because the Negro is your brother.' In the midst of blatant injustices inflicted upon the Negro, I have watched white churchmen stand on the sidelines and mouth pious irrelevancies and sanctimonious trivialities. In the midst of a mighty struggle to rid our nation of racial and economic injustice, I have heard many ministers say: 'Those are social issues, with which the gospel has no real concern.' And I have watched many churches commit themselves to a completely otherworldly religion which makes a strange, un-Biblical distinction between body and soul, between the sacred and the secular.

I have traveled the length and breadth of Alabama, Mississippi and all the other southern states. On sweltering summer days and crisp autumn mornings I have looked at the South's beautiful churches with their lofty spires pointing heavenward. I have beheld the impressive outlines of her massive religious-education buildings. Over and over I have found myself asking: 'What kind of people worship here? Who is their God? Where were their voices when the lips of Governor Barnett dripped with words of interposition and nullification? Where were they when Governor Wallace gave a clarion call for defiance and hatred? Where were their voices of support when bruised and weary Negro men and women decided to rise from the dark dungeons of complacency to the bright hills of creative protest?'

Yes, these questions are still in my mind. In deep disappointment I have wept over the laxity of the church. But be assured that my tears have been tears of love. There can be no deep disappointment where there is not deep love. Yes, I love the church. How could I do otherwise? I am in the rather unique position of being the son, the grandson and the great-grandson of preachers. Yes, I see the church as the body of Christ. But, oh! How we have blemished and scarred that body through social neglect and through fear of being nonconformists.

There was a time when the church was very powerful—in the time when the early Christians rejoiced at being deemed worthy to suffer for what they believed. In those days the church was not merely a thermometer that recorded the ideas and principles of popular opinion: it was a thermostat that transformed the mores of society. Whenever the early Christians entered a town, the people in power became disturbed and immediately sought to convict the Christians for being 'disturbers of the peace' and 'outside agitators.' But the Christians pressed on, in the conviction that they were 'a colony of heaven,' called to obey God rather than man. Small in number, they were big in commitment. They were too God-intoxicated to be 'astronomically intimidated.' By their effort and example they brought an end to such ancient evils as infanticide and gladiatorial contests.

Things are different now. So often the contemporary church is a weak, ineffectual voice with an uncertain sound. So often it is an archdefender of the status quo. Far from being disturbed by the presence of the church, the power structure of the average community is consoled by the church's silent—and often even vocal—sanction of things as they are.

But the judgment of God is upon the church as never before. If today's church does not recapture the sacrificial spirit of the early church, it will lose its authenticity, forfeit the loyalty of millions, and be dismissed as an irrelevant social club with no meaning for the twentieth century. Every day I meet young people whose disappointment with the church has turned into outright disgust.

Perhaps I have once again been too optimistic. Is organized religion too inextricably bound to the status quo to save our nation and the world? Perhaps I must turn my faith to the inner spiritual church, the church within the church, as the true *ekklesia* and the hope of the world. But again I am thankful to God that some noble souls from the ranks of organized religion have broken loose from the paralyzing chains of conformity and joined us as active partners in the struggle for freedom. They have left their secure congregations and walked the streets of Albany, Georgia, with us. They have gone down the highways of the South on tortuous rides for freedom. Yes, they have gone to jail with us. Some have been dismissed from their churches, have lost the support of their bishops and fellow ministers. But they have acted in the faith that right defeated is stronger than evil triumphant. Their witness has been the spiritual salt that has preserved the true meaning of the gospel in these troubled times. They have carved a tunnel of hope through the dark mountain of disappointment.

I hope the church as a whole will meet the challenge of this decisive hour. But even if the church does not come to the aid of justice, I have no despair about the future. I have no fear about the outcome of our struggle in Birmingham, even if our motives are at present misunderstood. We will reach the goal of freedom in Birmingham and all over the nation, because the goal of America is freedom. Abused and scorned though we may be, our destiny is tied up with America's destiny. Before the pilgrims landed at Plymouth, we were here. Before the pen of Jefferson etched the majestic words of the Declaration of Independence across the pages of history, we were here. For more than two centuries our forebears labored in this country without wages; they made cotton king; they built the homes of their masters while suffering gross injustice and shameful humiliation—and yet out of a bottomless vitality they continued to thrive and develop. If the inexpressible cruelties of slavery could not stop us, the opposition we now face will surely fail. We will win our freedom because the sacred heritage of our nation and the eternal will of God are embodied in our echoing demands.

Before closing I feel impelled to mention one other point in your statement that has troubled me profoundly. You warmly commended the Birmingham police force for keeping 'order' and 'preventing violence.' I doubt you would have so warmly commended the police force if you had seen its dogs sinking their teeth into unarmed, nonviolent Negroes. I doubt that you would so quickly commend the policemen if you were to observe their ugly and inhumane treatment of Negroes here in the city jail; if you were to watch them push and curse old Negro women and young Negro girls; if you were to see them slap and kick old Negro men and young boys; if you were to observe them, as they did on two occasions, refuse to give us food because we wanted to sing our grace together. I cannot join you in your praise of the Birmingham police department.

It is true that the police have exercised a degree of discipline in handling the demonstrators. In this sense they have conducted themselves rather 'nonviolently' in public. But for what purpose? To preserve the evil system of segregation. Over the past few years I have consistently preached that nonviolence demands that the means we use must be as pure as the ends we seek. I have tried to make clear that it is wrong to use immoral means to attain moral ends. But now I must affirm that it is just as wrong, or perhaps even more so, to use moral means to preserve immoral ends. Perhaps Mr. Connor and his policemen have been rather nonviolent in public, as was Chief Pritchett in Albany, Georgia, but they have used the moral means of nonviolence to maintain the immoral end of racial injustice. As T. S. Eliot has said: 'The last temptation is the greatest treason: To do the right deed for the wrong reason.'

I wish you had commended the Negro sit-inners and demonstrators of Birmingham for their sublime courage, their willingness to suffer and their amazing discipline in the midst of great provocation. One day the South will recognize its real heroes. They will be the James Merediths, with the noble sense of purpose that enables them to face jeering and hostile mobs, and with the agonizing loneliness that characterizes the life of the pioneer. They will be old, oppressed, battered Negro women, symbolized in a seventy-two-year-old woman in Montgomery, Alabama, who rose up with a sense of dignity and with her people decided not to ride segregated buses, and who responded with ungrammatical profundity to one who inquired about her weariness: 'My feets is tired, but my soul is at rest.' They will be the young high school and college students, the young ministers of the gospel and a host of their elders, courageously and nonviolently sitting in at lunch counters and willingly going to jail for conscience' sake. One day the South will know that when these disinherited children of God sat down at lunch counters, they were in reality standing up for what is best in the American dream and for the most sacred values in our Judaeo-Christian heritage, thereby bringing our nation back to those great wells of democracy which were dug deep by the founding fathers in their formulation of the Constitution and the Declaration of Independence.

Never before have I written so long a letter. I'm afraid it is much too long to take your precious time. I can assure you that it would have been much shorter if I had been writing from a comfortable desk, but what else can one do when he is alone in a narrow jail cell, other than write long letters, think long thoughts and pray long prayers?

If I have said anything in this letter that overstates the truth and indicates an unreasonable impatience, I beg you to forgive me. If I have said anything that understates the truth and indicates my having a patience that allows me to settle for anything less than brotherhood, I beg God to forgive me.

I hope this letter finds you strong in the faith. I also hope that circumstances will soon make it possible for me to meet each of you, not as an integrationist or a civil-rights leader but as a fellow clergyman and a Christian brother. Let us all hope that the dark clouds of racial prejudice will soon pass away and the deep fog of misunderstanding will be lifted from our fear-drenched communities, and in some not too distant tomorrow the radiant stars of love and brotherhood will shine over our great nation with all their scintillating beauty.

Yours for the cause of Peace and Brotherhood.

Martin Luther King, Jr.

Civil Disobedience in the Modern World*

JOEL FEINBERG

THE COMMON ELEMENT among the various kinds of actions that have been called "civilly disobedient" is, as David Daube puts it, "an offense against human authority, committed openly in a higher cause, or a cause thought to be higher."[1] The focus of the modern discussion of civil disobedience, however, is somewhat narrower, since it is restricted to disobedience of political authority, usually by acts that violate the law of the state and thereby incur criminal sanctions. In Western countries in the nineteenth and twentieth centuries the focus is narrower still. Civilly disobedient acts do not aim to overthrow whole regimes thought to be illegitimate; nor do they reject an accepted principle of legitimacy itself, like that of "the divine right of kings" or "the consent of the governed." They occur in post-revolutionary countries against a background of acknowledged just constitutions, democratic parliaments, and valid laws; and their purpose is not to undermine authority but to protest its misuse.

Closely related to civil disobedience but properly distinguishable from it are rule departures by state officials, those of police officers who do not arrest law-breakers, prosecutors who do not prosecute them, jurors who acquit obviously guilty defendants, judges who depart from judicial rules—in general, deliberate failures, often for conscientious reasons, to discharge the duties of one's office. Such official derelictions resemble civil disobedience in important ways, but they do not normally render officials liable to criminal punishment, so I shall not consider them to be civilly disobedient, even though when their intended beneficiary is himself an avowed civil disobedient, refusal to arrest, prosecute, or convict him form part of the complete treatment of our subject. In this chapter I shall not discuss the official's problem but shall concentrate on civil disobedience as a moral problem for the private citizen. My question will be, When, if ever, is there a moral right to commit civil disobedience? and not the closely related derivative question, What are the moral duties of legal officials toward civilly disobedient law-breakers?

Civil disobedience, however, is not just *any* kind of deliberate infraction of valid penal law; so it will be useful, at the outset, to distinguish it from other sorts of law-breaking with which it can be confused. First of all, the common crimes of robbers, mug-

1. David Daube, *Civil Disobedience in Antiquity* (Edinburgh: Edinburgh University Press, 1972), p. 1.

**From* Humanities in Society, *Vol. 2, no. 1 Winter 1979, pp. 37–60. Reprinted by permission of the publisher.*

gers, burglars, killers, rapists, and con artists, although they are instances of deliberate law-breaking, have no other resemblance to the acts with which we are concerned. Civil disobedience is law-breaking from certain motives only and in certain circumstances only. The common crimes are committed from such familiar motives as personal gain, malice, and hate; their specific intent is to harm the interests of others; and they are accompanied either by a desire to escape apprehension or an emotionally induced indifference to the risk of apprehension. In all of these ways they differ from civil disobedience. In other respects civil disobedience contrasts with acts of "warfare against the state"—assassination, sabotage, terrorism, riot, insurrection, avowed revolution—since civil disobedience is a kind of resistance within the accepted political structure, a violation of the law without loss of respect for law and the other basic political institutions, which are acknowledged to be, by and large, fair.

When the only alternative in the circumstances to the evil of law-breaking is to permit an evil that is greater still, a desperate choice of the illegal "lesser evil" may often look like civil disobedience, but since most modern legal systems accept the defense of "necessity" as a complete justification, it is not really "disobedience" at all. I have in mind such examples as borrowing a stranger's car without his permission in order to get a heart attack victim quickly to the hospital, destroying another's property to prevent the spread of a raging fire, violating the speed limit in pursuit of an escaping criminal, and so on. The traditional attitude of the Anglo-American law toward such actions is well expressed in the words of the judge in a sixteenth-century criminal case: "An act may break the words of the law and yet not break the law itself." The defense of necessity is a generalized justification based on two judgments: first, when the evil produced by breaking a rule is likely to be substantially less than the evil that would result in a given case from complying with it, then it is reasonable to breach it; second, it is unfair to impose criminal liability on objectively reasonable conduct. Rule departures resulting from such forced choices of a lesser evil, then, are not examples of civil disobedience. But if our legal system did not recognize the defense of necessity and remained rigidly and stupidly literalistic, then exceeding the speed limit to get a wife in labor to the maternity ward might well count as civilly disobedient, dissimilar though it may be to the acts of disinterested political protest that are the most familiar examples, in our time, of that broad genre.

Even closer to civil disobedience, but probably still worth distinguishing from it, are deliberately created test cases for statutes of doubtful validity. These phenomena are a peculiar feature of the American system, in which private citizens can get constitutionally suspect laws overthrown by the tactic of getting themselves convicted for disobeying them and then launching an appeal upward through the courts. "You pays your money and you takes your chances," as carnival barkers used to say. You violate the explicit prohibitions of the suspect law; you are found guilty; you get an expensive constitutional lawyer, and proceed through the appellate system perhaps even to the Supreme Court, arguing always that the reason why you are innocent is not that you did not do what the prosecution alleges that you did, but rather that the statute you violated was not a valid law in the first place. If you win, then you are a public benefactor, for you have effectively employed what is virtually the only way in our system to get rid of popular but unconstitutional pseudolaws, and you have paid a price in money, time, and anxiety in order to do that public service. But if you lose, and the Supreme Court does not accept your arguments, you are as unlucky as any losing gambler, and the law may treat you no differently from any common criminal. In addition to all the previously mentioned personal costs, you may be sent to prison for a while as a reward for your public service. Such test cases raise moral issues, similar to those we shall be considering, but I still wish to distinguish them from genuine civil disobedience because the "law-breaker" is not intentionally violating a law. He thinks that what he is doing is entirely within his legal rights, an opinion that happens to disagree with that of the local police, the prosecutor, and the courts. He wants the appellate courts to settle the disagreement, and "disobedience" is the only way he can get them to do so, since he must have "standing" if he is to use the courts for that purpose, and one cannot acquire standing by complying with the law in question. Of course, he may want to repeat his behavior even after the Supreme Court has declared it illegal once and for all, as an act of public protest against an unfair law, and that would begin to look like civil disobedience proper.

Three types of law-breaking remain to be discussed: conscientious evasion, conscientious refusal, and disobedience as moral protest. Many writers, following John Rawls, speak of the third of these (moral protests) as civil disobedience proper and contrast it with acts of conscientious evasion and refusal. There are differences, of course, among these three forms of disobedience, and clarity is always served by a recognition of dissimilarities among classes otherwise easily confused. But since the three types of conduct raise importantly similar moral questions, we can lump them together, along with forced choices of the lesser evil in a system that does not recognize the necessity defense, under the generic label "civil disobedience in the wide sense" and reserve the label "civil disobedience in the strict and narrow sense" for moral protests, those acts of law-breaking that Rawls thinks of as "civil disobedience proper." Our concern in the second half of this chapter will be with the moral justification of civil disobedience in the broad sense.

Acts of conscientious evasion might be thought of as borderline cases of civil disobedience since they share with covert crimes the hope of escaping apprehension and arrest. Their impelling motives, however, are strikingly different from those of most ordinary crimes. The conscientious evader genuinely believes that the law he violates is morally wrong, even though validly enacted, and personal gain is not a large element—if it is present at all—in his motivation for violating it. He thinks that he can do more good for the cause of justice by remaining free to violate the iniquitous law some more than by making a martyr of himself. The clearest historical examples of what I have in mind were the covert infractions by white Northerners of the fugitive slave laws before the Civil War.

"Conscientious refusal" is the term Rawls used to describe deliberate "noncompliance with a more or less direct legal injunction or administrative order,"[2] where one's action is assumed to be known to the authorities, however much one might wish, in some cases, to conceal it. Among the examples cited by Rawls are the refusal of Jehovah's Witnesses to salute the flag, the refusal of pacifists to serve in the armed forces, and Thoreau's famous refusal to pay his taxes during the Mexican War on the ground that payment would make him a participant in a great evil. Conscientious refusal resembles civil disobedience in the narrow sense in that its motives are conscientious. It is not done from the desire for personal gain, and there is little hope of escaping apprehension. But neither is it impelled by a desire to act as a form of public protest. Rather one acts either to avert an evil close at hand or else simply to keep one's own hands, morally speaking, clean. (Thoreau had no hope of stopping the Mexican War, but at least he could avoid having guilt on *his* hands.)

Civil disobedience (in what I call the "narrow sense") is defined by Rawls as "a public, nonviolent, conscientious yet political act contrary to law usually done with the aim of bringing about a change in the law or policies of the government."[3] Rawls here describes a kind of conduct that was frequently engaged in by moral protestors in the 1960s, first against racial discrimination and then against the Vietnam War. Let us briefly consider the defining elements of this form of protest, one by one.

Civil disobedience is *public*—engaged in openly, often even with prior notice, since the protestor wants as much publicity and attention as possible for his tactical purposes. Civil disobedience is *nonviolent* for the simple tactical reason that injury to others, harm to property, and extreme inconvenience to others are likely to be self-defeating, since they can obscure one's message, cause bitter resentment, and distract public attention from what is vital. The main reason, in short, why the civil disobedient wants his act to be nonviolent is the same as his reason for wanting it to be public—so that he can convince the majority of his fellow citizens that the act is indeed conscientious and sincere and in-

2. John Rawls, *A Theory of Justice* (Cambridge, Mass.: Harvard University Press, 1971), p. 368.
3. Ibid., p. 364.

tended to address the public's sense of justice. Indeed it is absolutely essential to civil disobedience as Rawls conceives it that it is a form of address, a symbolic way of making a statement, in his words "an expression of profound and conscientious political conviction . . . in the public forum."[4] As such it can be valued on the one hand as an end in itself, either a kind of "bearing witness" to a moral truth for its own sake, or a disavowal of responsibility, or on the other hand (what is more likely) as a tactic. When it is meant to be a method for producing reform, it must be distinguished from intimidation. It is in essential contrast to such tactics as disruption of traffic, strikes, boycotts, and political pressure. It does not say, "Give us our way or else." That sort of threat often backfires. The only pressure involved is "moral pressure"—dramatically sincere appeal to the public's sense of justice.

The third defining characteristic in Rawls' account is *deliberate unlawfulness.* Under his heading two types of civil disobedience must be distinguished. Direct civil disobedience violates the very law that is the target of the protest, whereas indirect civil disobedience violates some other law whose reasonableness is not in question. As Rawls points out, civil disobedience cannot always be direct: "If the government enacts a vague and harsh statute against treason, it would not be appropriate to commit treason as a way of objecting to it."[5] Similarly, it has been observed that one does not protest capital punishment for rape by committing rape. In fact it is surprisingly difficult to protest the most likely sorts of unjust laws and policies by direct civil disobedience. White people sitting in the black sections of segregated buses in the 1950s and war protestors burning their draft cards are good examples. But more characteristically, acts of civil disobedience in recent years have been indirect, the most familiar being those that violate local trespass ordinances, for example, "sitting in" at an atomic energy site until one must be forcibly carried away by the police in order to protest, not trespass laws, but rather the policy of building atomic power plants.

Finally, civilly disobedient acts in Rawls' conception must be *conscientious.* The main point of this part of the definition presumably is to rule out the motives of private or personal gain or malicious emotion as primary and immediate. Insofar as those motives, which are characteristic of ordinary crimes, are present at all, we should hesitate to classify an infraction as "civil disobedience." Rawls reminds us that the civil disobedient suffers inconvenience, expense, taunts, threats, real danger, and eventually punishment. His willingness, in the typical case, to suffer these consequences helps to demonstrate that his purpose is to protest an injustice or a wrong—not to achieve some immediate gain for himself. He suffers for a cause, some larger goal or principle for whose sake he breaks the law publicly and thereby sacrifices at least his short-run interests. While all of this is true, the word "conscientious," as we shall see, may be a misleading way of expressing it.

What does it mean to act conscientiously? I shall want to qualify the following answer shortly, but let me begin by giving what might be called "the strongest account of conscientiousness," namely, that to act conscientiously is to act because of one's honest and sincere conviction that what one is doing is right, not merely in the sense of "all right," but rather in the sense of "morally mandatory"—the uniquely correct thing to do, whatever the cost. "Here I stand; I can do no other," said Luther. "Here I sit; I can do no other" might have been said during the Southern sit-ins of the early 1960s. There are two important, though obvious, things to say about conscientiousness so construed: (1) people can be wrong in their conscientious convictions as in any other ones; but (2) insofar as convictions are genuinely conscientious, in this strong sense, they deserve respect from everyone and respectful treatment, insofar as that is consistent with other goals, from the law. Conscientious motives have a very special kind of moral value.

There is no denying that the motives of many acts of civil disobedience fit the above description, but if the strong account of conscientiousness is included in our definition, then many apparent examples of civil disobedience are not civil disobedience at all, because they are not "conscientious." I have in mind not acts done from a sense of duty, but rather acts done because the actor wishes to stand on his rights—to affirm them, vindicate them, and demand their recognition and enforce-

4. Ibid., p. 366.
5. Ibid., p. 365.

ment. These are acts done *in* clear conscience, but not *from* conscientiousness (in the strong sense). Publicly drinking beer during Prohibition and attending a marijuana smoke-in are examples. The drinker may well have been affirming thereby his moral right to drink beer, but he was not doing what he did because his conscience required beer-drinking. One can hardly compare him with Luther! When one is prepared to sacrifice one's short-run interests in order to secure one's rights and acts out of genuine conviction that a moral principle does indeed confer those rights, then there is a sense in which one's action is disinterested, at least more so than actions that demand, in the absence of moral deliberation or conviction, of any kind, that others simply "gimme, gimme, gimme, gimme, what I cry for." We can even call them "conscientious" in a weaker sense of that term. It is important, however, to understand that civil disobedience (in the wide sense that includes principled protest, evasion, and refusal) need not be conscientious in the usual strong sense. To persist in the contrary view may be to fall into a serious muddle about the very concept of a conscience. It is essential to the idea of a person's conscience that it is a faculty of self-address concerned only with the duties of its possessor. My conscience tells me what it is right for me to do, what I must do, what it is my duty to do, and not merely what I may do if I wish. If we say, on the contrary, that my conscience tells me what my rights are, then we are committed logically to the view that one person's conscience can tell him what other people's duties are, which is not only conceptually odd, but politically dangerous as well.

The modern discussion among philosophers of the justifiability of civil disobedience has at least a dual source, partly in democratic political theory and partly in philosophical jurisprudence. On the one hand, the problem civil disobedience raises for our moral judgments derives from the almost universal belief that every citizen in a constitutional democracy with at least approximately just institutions has a general obligation to obey the valid laws and lawful commands of his government. Civil disobedience by definition is a violation of those laws or commands. How then can it be justified? Duties of course can be overridden in particular cases by a "higher duty" or in a "higher cause." What then must these higher principles be like, and when are they strong enough to override the general moral obligation to be law-abiding? That in turn depends, at least in part, on the grounds, strength, and limits of the latter obligation. In this way the question of civil disobedience draws philosophers into the traditional problem of the nature of political obligation.

There is also a path through the philosophy of law to the same destination. The period during which civil disobedience began to challenge modern thinkers largely corresponded with the rise of the doctrine called "legal positivism" and the decline of the traditional doctrines of natural law. According to the natural law theory, the validity of humanly made coercive laws depends in part on their content, that is, on what they require or prohibit. If they are, in the appropriate way, arbitrary, unjust, cruel, pointless, or immoral, then they have no authority or force of law whatever, in which case there is no more moral obligation to obey them than there is to comply with any pseudolaw or mere masquerade as law. To the legal positivists that view was intolerably paradoxical. The validity of law, they insisted, is one thing; its injustice or morality is another; so there can be no contradiction in characterizing a statute as an unjust valid law. The validity of law, on their view, stems from its proper enactment. All valid law is enacted law. So-called laws of nature may be standards for distinguishing good from bad law, but law is law, whether good or bad. It is the pedigree of a law (where it comes from) rather than its content (what it commands) that determines its validity.

The positivist account of legal validity obviously gains much support from common sense, but historically the legal positivists have often held another doctrine that is hard to reconcile with the first, namely, that valid law as such, no matter what its content, deserves our respect and our general fidelity. Even if valid law is bad law, we have some obligation to obey it simply because it is law. But how can this be so if a law's validity has nothing to do with its content? Why ashould I have any respect or duty of fidelity toward a statute with a wicked or stupid content just because it was passed into law by a bunch of men (possibly very wicked men like the Nazi legislators) according to the accepted recipes for making law? Thus Lon Fuller, the leading American critic of legal positivism, triumphantly springs his trap: the positivist cannot explain how "laws, even bad laws, have a claim to our respect."[6] The two doctrines of validity by pedigree and respect for law as such yield in combination an unstable conception of law as "an amoral datum" that has a kind of magical capacity to generate moral obligations. One easy way out for the positivist, and I think the only way, is to abandon the second doctrine and admit that there is no moral duty whatever to obey law simply because it is valid law. To support that startlingly radical proposition the positivist must cast his skeptical eye on the variously alleged grounds for "the moral obligation to obey the law as such," and soon he is likely to encounter the political theorist exploring the possible grounds for a perfectly general moral obligation to obey the democratic state and the moralist puzzled about the moral justifiability of civil disobedience.

The standard way of characterizing the individual citizen's moral problem concerning civil disobedience is as a conflict of reasons of basically different types. According to this conception, the question, Is it ever right to disobey a law, and if so, under what conditions? is exactly the same in form as the question(s), Is it ever right to break a promise, tell a lie, inflict pain on others (and so on), and if so, under what conditions? This approach to the problem assumes that there is (to use philosophical jargon that I do not altogether like) a "prima facie obligation" to obey the law that can in principle conflict with, override, or be overridden by "prima facie obligations" of other kinds. I would prefer to speak of "reasons for" and "reasons against," but since the term "prima facie obligation" has become fixed by a strong convention, it will be well to come to terms with it. So for the moment let us see what philosophers have meant by prima facie obligation, or PFO, as I shall abbreviate it.

In explaining what they mean by a PFO, some philosophers resort to an analogy with the idea of a vector of forces that is used in physics. The analogy is useful up to a point. We do feel "pulled in both ways," as we say, when we are in situations like that which Plato describes in the *Republic,* in which we have promised a neighbor to keep a weapon for him and return it when he requests and he then comes back in a furious homicidal rage against another party and demands that we return his property to him. Thinking no doubt of cases of this sort, Carl Cohen writes:

> One's ultimate or actual obligation in any morally complex situation will require the careful weighing of several, even many, *prima facie* obligations, some of which may conflict head-on with others. We may think of such *prima facie* obligations as components, or vectors, pushing us in different directions with differing degrees of force, the morally correct outcome of the set being our resultant obligation.[7]

Despite the intuitively familiar points of resemblance between PFOs and physical forces, this analogy is more misleading than helpful. In physics, a resultant force compounded out of component forces is always a kind of splitting of the difference, not always right down the middle of course, but a result determined in some measure by each of its components. When two forces act on a body, the resultant direction and velocity of that object will be a kind of "compromise." Its resultant direction, if the two forces are equal and at right angles to one another, will be at a 45° angle, splitting the difference between where it would have gone if only the one force were acting on it and where it would have gone if only the other force were acting on it. But in morals there is often no way of splitting the difference, in which case one must do the one duty or the other, rather than do a part of each. Plato's householder could hardly solve his problem by means of a compromise between the moral demand that he keep his promise to return another's lethal weapon and the moral demand that he protect a third party from harm. It would not do, for example, to substitute a less lethal weapon—say a somewhat brittle wooden club—for the original sword.

6. Lon L. Fuller, "Positivism and Fidelity to Law: A Reply to Professor Hart," *Harvard Law Review* 71 (1958): 630.

7. Carl Cohen, *Civil Disobedience: Conscience, Tactics, and the Law* (New York: Columbia University Press, 1971), p. 6.

I think that we can avoid this difficulty and achieve greater clarity by thinking of PFOs and resultant obligations simply in terms of supporting and conclusive reasons. Then we can say that one's having promised to do an act *A* (say) is always a reason of direct relevance and at least some cogency in favor of doing *A* and one's promise not to do *B* is a reason against doing *B*, and in the absence of other reasons having a bearing on the situation, either would be a conclusive reason. Further, a PFO (general type of supporting reason) is not in every case a decisive reason, but it is always a relevant one and one that would be conclusive if no other relevant reason of greater strength applied to the situation. Thus if Jones has a PFO to do *A*, then he has a moral reason to do *A* that is such that unless he has a moral reason *not* to do *A* that is at least as strong, then not doing *A* is wrong, and he has an actual obligation to do *A*.[8]

Philosophers have differed over the question of how many general kinds of PFOs there are and over which are basic and which are derivative. The following list of basic PFOs is, I think, representative and plausible, though I can make no stronger claim for it here:

1. The PFO of fidelity: to keep promises.
2. The PFO of veracity: to tell the truth (or better—not to tell lies).
3. The PFO of fair play: not to exploit, cheat, or "free load" on others.
4. The PFO of gratitude: to return favors.
5. The PFO of nonmaleficence: not to cause pain or suffering to others.
6. The PFO of beneficence: to help others in distress when this involves no great danger to oneself or third parties.
7. The PFO of reparation: to repair harms to others that are one's own fault.
8. The PFO not to kill others (except in self-defense).
9. The PFO not to deprive others of their property.
10. The PFO to oppose injustices when this involves no great cost to oneself.
11. The PFO to promote just institutions and to work toward their establishment, maintenance, and improvement.

Insofar as a given act is an instance of one of the above eleven kinds, that is, a moral reason in favor of doing it, and if it is not, at the same time, a negative instance of one of the other categories on the list, then it is a decisive reason. If it is a positive instance of one type and a negative instance of another, say a promise that can be kept only by telling a lie, then one's actual duty will be to perform the PFO that is the more stringent in the circumstances. That is all that a moralist can say in the abstract with any degree of certainty.

In addition to the list of eleven PFOs, is there also a PFO to obey the law? Is the fact that a contemplated act would be illegal a reason against doing so? Of course it might always be a prudential reason of some weight against doing it. You might get caught, and the risk is always a consideration to be weighed carefully by any reasonable person. But that is not what we are concerned about. We wish to know whether illegality is also a type of *moral reason*, a consideration that tends to bind us morally to refrain from the act and will ground an actual obligation to refrain if no other conflicting PFOs are pulling us even harder in the opposite direction. Philosophers have differed sharply over this question. Few are tempted these days to hold the view, so effectively demolished by Richard Wasserstrom,[9] that it can *never* be right to disobey a law, that "*X* is illegal" is always a decisive moral reason against doing *X*. But a growing number of philosophers hold the very opposite and surprisingly plausible view that "*X* is illegal" is no kind of reason at all, that there is not even a PFO to obey the law. (We do, of course, have a PFO not to do many of the things prohibited by law—not to kill, steal, and the like—but because these things are *mala in se*, not because they are illegal.) These philosophers usually argue that there is no sort of reason why anyone ought to obey a rotten rule created in a rotten system under an authoritarian regime or a thoroughly

8. Compare M. B. E. Smith, "Is There a Prima Facie Obligation to Obey the Law?" *Yale Law Journal* 82 (1973): 950.

9. Richard Wasserstrom, "The Obligation to Obey the Law," *UCLA Law Review* 10 (1963).

iniquitous constitution. Nazi rules against helping Jews were "valid laws" in Germany, all right, and duly enacted by Nazi legislatures. Their ruthless enforcement, moreover, gave every German citizen a prudential reason for obeying them. But the fact that helping Jews was illegal was itself morally irrelevant, neither here nor there in the moral universe, utterly beside the point. Surely, these philosophers conclude, not just *any* legal obligation in *any* legal system imposes a moral PFO, giving us a moral reason of any strength at all for obedience.

Philosophers on the other side usually grant the point and make a small strategic retreat. If there is a PFO to obey the law as such, they concede, it can only be in a reasonably just society, under a reasonably just constitution, with fair (presumably democratic) procedures for making and changing laws. But in such a state, they insist, the fact that *X* is illegal is always a moral reason, of some discernible weight at least, against doing *X*. But even that reasonably modified position no longer gains unanimous assent, and more and more philosophers, myself included, are coming to question it.

There is a dilemma for adherents of even the weakest version of the doctrines that there is a moral PFO to obey the law. (I refer to the version that restricts the PFO to valid laws in the citizen's own legal system when that system is democratic and by and large just.) Either this alleged PFO is one of the basic ones, on the same level as the eleven on our list, or it is derivative from some one or combination of them. If basic, it can be defended only by an appeal to self-evidence, for *ex hypothesi* there is no more basic ethical principle from which it follows. But whereas that kind of appeal is plausible in the eleven other cases (who could deny, for example, that "you promised" is always *a* reason, at the very least, for doing what was promised?), it seems much less so in this case. In any event when so many astute philosophers[10] are saying, "I don't see it," it certainly lacks argumentative force to rest one's case on the insistence that it is just obviously so. But if, on the other hand, the PFO to obey the law is derivative from one or more of the basic ones, one must be able to show how it is derived, and that is a notoriously difficult undertaking, not yet successfully done.[11]

Almost all of the basic PFOs on our list have been thought by one philosopher or another to be the ground, or part of the ground, for a derivative PFO to obey the law, but the most interesting attempts to derive such a PFO, and the most popular, invoke numbers 4 (gratitude), 1 (fidelity), 3 (fair play), and 10–11 (justice). Let us examine each of these attempts briefly but critically.

The argument from gratitude proceeds as follows. In general, by accepting benefits from others we incur "debts of gratitude." Many moralists derive the PFO to help one's parents from this basic one, and indeed Socrates, in Plato's *Crito,* likens his own relations to the Athenian state to that of a son to his parents and declines to resist even a fatally unjust application of its laws on that ground. We do accept the protection of the police, the armed forces, and the Public Health Service, and the benefits of the money system, the postal service, public schools, and so on; therefore we are said to have a debt of gratitude to the state and a PFO to obey its laws. Not to do so would be ungrateful.

What are we to make of this curious argument? In the first place, it should be observed that debts of gratitude have nothing to do with gratitude in the usual sense, which is a certain motive, attitude, or feeling. There can be no duty to have a particular feeling or to act from a certain motive, for the pinpoint control over our emotions that would be

10. For example, Rolf Sartorius, *Individual Conduct and Social Norms* (Belmont, Calif.: Wadsworth, 1975), chapter 6; A. John Simmons, *Moral Principles and Political Obligations* (Princeton, N.J.: Princeton University Press, 1979), chapter 8; Smith, "Prima Facie Obligation." I have found Simmons' brilliant new book especially useful.

11. One early sketchy attempt was that of W. D. Ross, *The Right and the Good* (Oxford, 1930), pp. 27–28, who derived the PFO to obey the laws of one's country "partly (as Socrates contends in the *Crito*) from the duty of gratitude for the benefits one has received from it, partly from the implicit promise to obey which seems to be involved in permanent residence in a country whose laws we know we are *expected* to obey, and still more clearly involved when we ourselves invoke the protection of its law . . . and partly (if we are fortunate in our country) from the fact that its laws are potent instruments for the general good."

required by such a duty is beyond our powers of self-manipulation. Our only plausible duties are to do, or to omit doing, certain things (from whatever motive). A duty to repay services is less paradoxically called a "duty of reciprocation" than a duty of gratitude. Indeed, so separate are the ideas of reciprocation and gratitude that sometimes the former is taken as a sign of the absence of the latter, as was noted by St. Thomas Aquinas, who quotes with approval a passage from Seneca that "a person who wants to repay a gift too quickly with a gift in return is an unwilling debtor and an ungrateful person."[12] Nevertheless a duty of reciprocation is fully discharged by appropriate payment even when done in a grudging spirit of ungrateful resentment, and gratitude without suitable repayment, however commendable for its own sake, cannot discharge a duty of reciprocation.

A stronger and more relevant point is also yielded by the example of the gift. Unlike formal loans and contractual performances, a gift is not the sort of thing that one has a duty to "repay." Gratitude may be appropriate although it is not the sort of thing that can be exacted, but repayment is not the sort of concept that has any application at all to the gift situation. There can no more be a duty of reciprocation than a duty of gratitude to return gratuitous gifts and favors. Suppose that the Joneses, obscure acquaintances of yours, invite you to dinner, and you accept, to your later regret. Do you have a PFO to reciprocate by inviting them to dinner? Would you be blamably "ungrateful" if you did not? Would a cash payment sent later through the mails be an acceptable mode of repayment? Suppose that Jones is a rich man or the president of your university, someone who entertains others constantly and lavishly and is more than occupied by his own busy social schedule. Are you torn over your duty to reciprocate? Or, to take examples of another kind, suppose that a young woman receives flowers from an admirer, than candy, then dresses, then electrical appliances, despite her continued efforts to discourage him. Finally she begins to "doubt his motives." Is there even a trace of a moral reason here for reciprocation? cooperation? obedience? Or suppose that a college teacher gives a pretty coed a good grade when the student knows that her work is poor. She might well wonder "What is he up to anyway?" but certainly not "What should I do for him?" In the latter two cases not only is a duty of reciprocation out of the question; it is also the case that one of the psychologically necessary conditions for the emergence of the feeling of gratitude itself is absent, namely, the belief that the gratuitous gift or favor was offered from genuinely disinterested friendship or benevolence, with no "ulterior motive." In any event, even if we are grateful—let us suppose for a good dinner given us by well-meaning but very boring persons who wished only to please us—it does not follow that we have a moral PFO to reciprocate, but at most that we may feel some trace of a desire or inclination to do so. (If only they were not so boring!)

The case for deriving a PFO to obey the laws of the state from a basic PFO of "gratitude" collapses completely in the light of the above observations. If the argument is meant only to establish a ground for the feeling of gratitude, then it needs to be supplemented by a showing that the state's undoubted services and protections are genuine gifts rather than contractual performances and, further, that its motive was personal benevolence or disinterested friendship (an enviable task); and even if there is a ground for gratitude, there can be no duty to *feel* grateful; and even if there were such a duty, it could not in turn ground a duty of reciprocation. Finally, and most conclusively, even if there is some sort of duty repayment (which is most implausible), it could not take the form required by the argument, namely, faithful obedience to commands, for as M. B. E. Smith puts it, "The mere fact that a person has conferred benefits on me, even the most momentous benefits conferred from genuinely benevolent motives, doesn't establish his right to dictate all my behavior."[13] The benefits are no reason at all in support of *that* PFO. A fifty-year-old son may have numerous duties toward his eighty-year-old

12. As quoted by Josef Pieper, *Justice* (London, 1957), p. 107.

13. Smith, "Prima Facie Obligation," p. 952.

parents, but they will all be duties to help them, not to obey them. No matter how grateful he is to them for their past services, he can have no duty to let them determine, for example, at what hour he must come home at night or what foods he may eat.

Like any theory that has been defended by great philosophers in the past, the gratitude theory does have a grain of truth. There is a more plausible interpretation of something that can be called a duty of gratitude, and no doubt such a duty can yield, under very special circumstances, something like a PFO to comply with the laws of a state and even to perform certain positive services for it. If there is such a thing in ordinary interpersonal relations as a PFO of gratitude, it is not an obligation to reciprocate favor for favor, service for service, benefit for benefit, but rather an obligation to stand ready, in case one's benefactor should ever falter, to help him too. If a wealthy friend of his father gives a young person enough money to pay for his whole college education, he will appropriately feel grateful, especially if he believes that the gift was a genuine expression of benevolence or friendship without ulterior motive. But insofar as the payment was a genuine gift and not a loan, the young person will have no burdensome duty to repay a like sum during his postgraduate years. Presumably if the benefactor had intended to impose such a burden, he would have explicitly described his transfer of funds as a *loan,* not a gift. Suppose, however, that years later it comes to the attention of the younger man, now middle-aged and comfortable, that the elderly benefactor has come upon hard times, having lost all his money through unlucky investments, and now is suffering from bad health. Not to help him *now,* if he can, would indeed be ungrateful and a violation of a moral duty to reciprocate the old man's earlier favors. Similarly, an expatriate living happily abroad, although with warm feelings toward his native land and "gratitude" for having learned its language and culture and for having been shaped by its institutions, might feel morally impelled to come to the aid of his country in its time of dire need and pay taxes and bear arms in its defense. On the other hand, an Englishman at the start of the World War II or an Israeli at the outset of the Yom Kippur War who takes all of his goods and flees to Geneva or Cuernavaca would rightly be thought a morally derelict ingrate by his countrymen. In such cases one has a moral duty to come to the aid of one's country, a duty derived perhaps in part from having benefited from its laws and services in the past. But that is quite another thing than a general duty in good or hard times to obey each and every law or order.

The second way of deriving a moral PFO of obedience to law bases it on a deliberate undertaking of the citizen, a kind of formal promise to comply with laws, or at least a voluntary granting of one's consent to the law-maker's authority, which amounts to the same thing. Thus the PFO of obedience is like the obligation to discharge one's part of a bargain; the state provides its benefits *in exchange for which* the citizen provides his constant fidelity to law. (State benefits, on this view, are more like loans than gifts.) The argument can be stated simply: (1) a person can have no obligation to obey or support the state unless he has personally granted his consent to its authority, but once that consent is granted or promise made, a duty of obedience has been assumed; (2) we all have granted that consent; therefore, (3) we all have the standing duty (like all general duties, a PFO) to obey the law of the state.

The most doubtful part of the argument, of course, is its second premise. The reader might well claim that he (for one) never granted consent of the sort required by the argument. In fact, no representative of the state ever asked him to do so. His friend Angelo did so at the naturalization ceremony as part of a solemn oath with his hand on a Bible. But most native-born citizens never did anything of the kind. It will not do to say in reply to this that the reader's ancestors took the oath, either at the time of "the original contract" or at later naturalization proceedings, for there is no way to explain how a person can be bound morally by a promise made by another person at a time before he even came into existence.

A more plausible rejoinder than the "inherited obligation" ploy is that for which John Locke is famous: Of course the reader gave no explicit statement of consent; rather he granted a "tacit consent," not in language but in conduct from which the consent can be inferred. A. John Simmons has given a definitive refutation of this claim.[14] He points out first that there *is* a kind of behavior that can be called "tacit consent," but that it is not "unexpressed consent deduced from conduct," but rather "consent expressed in a certain way—by silence."[15] For an example he has us imagine a board meeting at which the chairman announces: "We will meet again next Thursday unless there are objections to that date. Does anyone have objections?" There is silence for one full minute, at the conclusion of which the chairman notes that all have agreed (consented) to his proposal. The reader will recognize this familiar notion of consent by silence but strenuously resist its application to his own case. How could anyone think that he consented to the authority of his government simply by being silent? No one in authority ever asked him if he consented. He was never presented with options and alternatives and asked to decide. He was no more aware that his silence on this question constituted consent than he is that his silence about network television scheduling constitutes an agreement to watch all the shows.

Simmons points out, however, that Locke surely did not mean by "tacit consent" the familiar notion of consent by silence. Rather Locke argued in two other ways, first, that our consent is implied by our acceptance of government benefits and, second, by our continued residence in the country of our citizenship. The odd thing about these closely interrelated arguments is that they imply that we can give our binding consent by accident, so to speak, unknowingly and unintentionally. Perhaps if I had known that I was assuming a lifelong obligation of fidelity I would at least have hesitated before accepting benefits. As it is, Locke puts me in the position that would be occupied by the lady in our earlier example if she learned belatedly that her acceptance of gifts from her suitor was a way of getting married and that he is now her husband come what may, for better or worse.

14. A. John Simmons, "Tacit Consent and Political Obligation," *Philosophy and Public Affairs* 5 (1976).
15. Ibid., p. 279.

Elsewhere Locke writes that a sure sign of consent to governmental authority (whatever the consenter's actual intentions) is one's continued residence in a country. But in the absence of a clearly presented choice and a formal convention for indicating consent (like the board meeting described above), this too would be an "unknowing or unintentional consent," which is to say an absurdity. In modern nations at the present time, at least, there is no such general procedure; no genuine choice is ever made available to most of us. The reader might complain that he did not know that he was incurring a permanent obligation of obedience when he chose to settle down in his native land until he read Locke, and by then it was too late!

Perhaps it is possible in principle, however, although not presently the case, to design a political procedure that would make residence a sign of "tacit consent" to a country's laws. Simmons reminds us that Socrates in the *Crito* claimed that such formal procedures *were* available to every Athenian on attaining the "age of manhood." The Athenian state in effect told every young man that he could take all his property and "go wherever you wish with our blessing, if you do not like it here. Your silence will be taken as an acknowledgment of a lifelong obligation to obey our laws." Assuming that this was an accurate account of things in at least one ancient Greek city-state and that young Athenians were able to make a truly voluntary choice of political allegiance, we must now ask whether it is possible to design such a procedure for the modern state.

Surely the difficulties would be formidable. Perhaps it was not very difficult, economically or psychologically, for free Hellenic Greeks to change their residence from one city-state to another. All moves are disruptive, of course, but in total impact on the lives of the movers, a change from Athens to Corinth was probably no harder than a change from New York to California today. But now, the "option" for a twenty-one-year-old American youth to say good-bye to his family and friends, pack his bags, change his money, and board a jet plane for a new life in whatever alien land would deign to receive him is hardly a genuine "choice" at all. Simmons is hardly less scathing than David Hume had been in his eighteenth-century reply to Locke[16] when he (Simmons) writes that "our most precious 'possessions' are not movable property that can be put on the boat with one's books and TV set."[17] The legal opportunity to emigrate then hardly provides a procedure for voluntarily expressing one's consent by silence. Simmons' example of the opportunity at the board meeting to express an objection, freely and knowingly, by the easy and conventionally understood device of raising one's arm in response to a question bears little analogy to the forced and dangerous expedient of emigrating. The latter, Simmons tells us, is more like the case of the boss at the board meeting inviting all those who object to so signify by lopping off their right arms or implying by his manner that objection however expressed carries a high risk of demotion or firing.[18]

The third way of basing a PFO to obey the law is to derive it from the PFO of fair play. This argument was well formulated (and first named) in an influential article of John Rawls, which was later severely qualified and even renamed in Rawls' book.[19] A PFO of fair play comes into existence not only in sports and competitive games (as its name suggests) but also in a large variety of social settings. Its principal home, in fact, is in cooperative rather than competitive joint undertakings, in voluntary rule-structured associations like clubs, teams, partnerships, political parties, and the like, and in more informal joint enterprises, like voluntary clean-up or repair work among a group of friends who possess a car in common. Each person has his own share to do if all are to gain, but it is possible for a given person to cheat, not do his share, and thus take his benefit as "free" only because the others are doing their shares. The "free rider" does not "play fair." He may not harm anybody directly, but by cheating he exploits the others' cooperativeness to his own benefit. He "takes advantage of them," as we say. A paradigmatic example is not paying one's fare on a railroad train. The others pay in full confidence that everyone will, and the free rider takes advantage of that trust. So he gains at their expense. It is not that he harms them; that is not the gravamen of the grievance. Their share of the costs of the railroad (reflected in the owners' adjusted prices) may go up only a tiny fraction of a penny because of his nonpayment. But they have voluntarily foregone the benefits he got in expectation that he would forego them too. Their grievance is that he took advantage of them.

That complaint can just as well be expressed in the language of rights and duties. Adapting one of Simmons' examples, we can consider a community scheme to preserve water pressure during a dry spell by prohibiting the watering of lawns in the evening, although the facts are such that if as many as 5 percent of the homeowners watered their lawns, there would be no lowering of the pressure. Jones waters his lawn in the evening. He causes no harm to anyone because noncompliance has not passed the 5 percent threshold. Nevertheless, his neighbors are understandably indignant. They see that Jones profits *only because they forebear.* They cooperated and discharged their duties of fair play, and they had a right that Jones do so too.

Perhaps the most apt and familiar example is drawn from one of the largest of all the collective activities of our time, the cooperative movement of automobiles in all directions through a modern nation's highway system. Suppose that there is a restricted lane reserved for emergency vehicles on the right shoulder of a multilane road. You are creeping along bumper to bumper in heavy traffic, returning from a well-attended football game. You look in your rearview mirror and see a car pull into that forbidden lane and accelerate rapidly by the line of cars jammed in the permitted lanes. Generously you infer that there is some extreme emergency that has impelled this motorist to so desperate a course. But as he passes on your right you note that his car is packed with spirited revelers; there are pennants flying from all the windows, and lusty voices are

16. David Hume, "Of the Original Contract." First published in his *Essays Moral and Political* (1748).
17. Simmons, *Moral Principles,* p. 99.
18. Ibid.
19. The earlier formulation is in John Rawls, "Legal Obligation and the Duty of Fair Play," on *Law and Philosophy,* ed. Sidney Hook (New York, 1964), pp. 3–18. Rawls' second thoughts are found in his *Theory of Justice,* pp. 342–49. In the book Rawls refers to "the principle of fairness" rather than "the principle of fair play," in part, apparently, to avoid the suggestion that all life is a game.

singing the college fight song. The other motorists have stayed out of the restricted lane and because—only because—of their obedience, the disobedient motorist profits. He has exploited their good faith for his own benefit.

If a general PFO to obey the law can be derived from the basic PFO of fair play, then each individual citizen's duty of obedience is owed ultimately, not to the state, but to the other citizens, for it is essentially a duty not to take advantage of them even in "harmless" ways. There are indeed many examples of legal disobedience that does exploit unfairly the law-abidingness of others. Traffic infractions of course provide one class of examples. Income tax evasion provides another. But there are too many counterexamples for there to be a perfectly general PFO of obedience derived from the basic PFO of fair play. There are many types of cases where violating the law does not take advantage of anyone, and since the element of exploitation is not involved *necessarily* in every instance of law-breaking, "fair play" is by no means a perfect model. In those cases where exploitation of other citizens is involved (and indeed they are common), we have a PFO to obey the law not simply because it *is* the law, but rather because it would be unfair exploitation not to, just as in other cases, we may have a duty to obey the law, not because it is the law, but because it would harm someone, or break a promise to someone, or so on, not to.

Examples of nonexploitative law-breaking may not be typical instances of crimes in a democracy, but they are not so rare as to seem exotic. Most traffic violations either endanger or take advantage of others, but particular instances even of generally dangerous or exploitative types do neither—running a red light on empty streets late at night under perfect conditions of visibility, for example, or exceeding the speed limit on an empty stretch of highway when it is perfectly safe (except for the possibility of apprehension by a traffic cop) to do so. Whatever the reasons for avoiding such conduct, there is surely no one who can complain that he has been taken advantage of by it. Such law-breaking is neither harmful nor dangerous nor exploitative. What then could be the basis of a moral PFO to abstain from it? Then there are examples of so-called victimless crimes like smoking marijuana or cohabitation that abound in almost all penal codes. Not only do they not harm (or at least not *wrong*) anyone; they do not take advantage of anyone either. Surely the models of driving in a restricted lane and cheating on one's income tax do not apply to them.

Most deliberate law-breaking is obviously harmful to someone, namely, its victims. But even much wrongful law-breaking of that class cannot be thought of as exploitative of other parties who are *not* its victims. When *A* rapes *B* may all males complain that *A* took unfair advantage of male compliance with the rape law to benefit at all males' expense? When *B* murders her husband in a fit of wrathful jealousy, may all the other married people complain that she was able to get her way only because of their forebearance, that it is unfair to *them* that she acted on her wrath when they must repress theirs? Not very likely.

It is prima facie more plausible to claim that civil disobedience in the narrow sense (political protest) does invariably have the characteristic of unfair play and that exploitation is at least one of its inevitable moral costs even when it is justified on balance. If that is so, then there is always *some* reason against that kind of disobedience (a PFO to refrain from it) even when counterbalanced by reasons on the other side. When you sit in at the atomic energy site, for example, your fellow citizens might all be entitled to say, "You are able to violate the trespass laws to further your favorite moral cause *only* because we don't do the same every time we think we have a higher moral cause. If all our moral causes were promoted in your fashion, the costs to our democratic institutions, our public civility, and our domestic tranquility would be disastrous." This is often a quite proper thing to say to the rash civil disobedient whose political anger is more like self-righteousness than genuinely disinterested indignation. Civil disobedience is often *not* justified precisely on the ground that it is not fair play and is made possible only by the self-sacrificial forebearance of others. There is in fact a moral PFO of fair play, and when civil disobedience violates that PFO, it is usually unjustified. But some disobedience does not violate that PFO, and if it also does not violate any other basic and obvious PFO, there can be no grounds for calling it unjustified, except perhaps its contravention of an alleged PFO to obey the law as such. Civil disobedience in the narrow sense can be justified, as Rawls has insisted all along,[20] only when (1) it is done sincerely for a "higher moral cause," (2) when there are no other legal means available (when all democratic remedies have been exhausted), and (3) when civil disobedience is not yet so widespread as to be self-defeating and dangerous to the survival of mutually beneficial institutions. When it is done under these conditions, it retains its character as an unusual and extreme step and is not "exploitative" of anyone. To the question, What if everyone did it? the justified civil disobedient can answer that if everyone did it (where by "it" we mean disobedience that satisfies the above condition), the results would not be bad at all.

There is one further respect in which some law-breaking departs from the unfair play models, and this too has been emphasized by Rawls, especially in his book, in which he severely qualifies his earlier view of the importance of the fair play analogy. The benefits of government and the rule of law are not as equally distributed among the citizens of a modern industrial state as the benefits of traffic laws, for example, are distributed among motorists. So long as there is economic deprivation, social discrimination, and unequal access to powerful offices, society is not a "mutually advantageous" cooperative venture. If there is a PFO of obedience derived from the basic PFO of fair play, therefore, it could apply at most to the more favored members of society.

The final argument for a PFO of obedience to law derives it from what Rawls in his more mature work calls the "natural duty to uphold just institutions."[21] This argument has the advantage over his earlier reliance on "fair play" in that the basic PFO in question is one we *all* share, regardless of our position in society and the degree to which we share the benefits of common undertakings. Rawls begins by distinguishing technical senses of *obligation* and *duty* (terms that I have treated here, for reasons of convenience, as synonyms). Obligations are incurred only by one's own voluntary acts, for example, the obligations to keep one's promises, pay one's debts, and honor one's agreements. Duties typically attach to special stations, offices, or roles, whether or not we voluntarily occupy them; but our "natural duties" are those that everyone has, regardless of jobs or roles—for example, duties to be generally friendly, helpful to those in need, and not to be cruel. Among our other natural duties, Rawls reports, is a duty to work toward the establishment of just institutions and to strengthen and support them once they are established.

Rawls' account of these matters has much to recommend it. I think that there clearly is a "natural duty," in his sense, to uphold just institutions, and that it is one of the basic PFOs in our sense. Individual justice is much less likely to be done in general in the absence of strong and reliable just institutions that are constituted by clear and reasonable rules. I have in mind especially such political institutions and constitutive rules as the jury system, the universal franchise, free speech, majority rule in legislatures, and courts organized on the principle of due process. Insofar as one damages these institutional practices, one harms the cause of justice generally. That we are morally bound not to do such harm is as self-evident, I think, as that we are bound not to harm the cause of human happiness in general. Nevertheless, I doubt that a general PFO to obey valid laws can be derived from the basic PFO to support just institutions. Much law-breaking does damage or threaten just institutions, but equally certainly much law-breaking (including much unjustified law-breaking) has no damaging effect on them whatever—for example, running a red light at three in the morning, cohabiting, playing poker at home with friends (where this is illegal). These are actions that do not generate "disrespect for law," because they are unwitnessed or done in private. Perhaps many open and public acts of civil disobedience do damage just institutions, but there is no necessity that this be so. Rawls himself writes that civil disobedience, when it satisfies certain minimal conditions of reasonableness (including the circumstantial condition that such acts have not already become so common as to threaten to poison public discourse and lower standards of civility),

20. *Theory of Justice,* pp. 371–77.
21. Ibid., pp. 333–41.

actually functions as "a final device to maintain the stability of a just constitution,"[22] because it is an escape valve for pent-up indignations and is "disobedience to law within the framework of fidelity to law, although at the outer edge thereof."[23] Warfare against the state, covert subversion, disruption, violent intimidation, and the like do always carry the high risk of weakening just institutions, but civil disobedience, paradoxically, can actually strengthen them.

There could be a derivative moral PFO to obey the law only if, of necessity, every individual instance of deliberate disobedience were a violation of some basic PFO, but that seems to be no more true of the PFO to uphold just institutions than of the PFOs of gratitude, promise-keeping, and fair play. The fact that an act would be illegal then, we may conclude, has no tendency whatever to make that act wrong. Why, in that case, does our conclusion seem, at first sight, so startling? That may be because in our legal system, as well as in many others that we can imagine, most of the actions that are legally prohibited also happen to be wrong on other grounds. The typical crimes of fraud and violence are wrong because they harm or endanger other people; they would be no less wrong if they were perfectly legal. Other prohibited acts, like driving in restricted lanes, are wrong even when harmless in the given case because they unfairly take advantage of the forebearance of others. If we knew that 90 percent of all illegal acts in our country are in similar ways wrong on the grounds independent of their illegality and all we knew of a given act is that it is illegal, then we would be entitled to infer, with a degree of confidence proportioned to the evidence, that the given act is wrong too. That is to say that illegal acts are "prima facie wrong" in a sense different from the one we have been considering, namely, that there is a *statistical presumption* that they are, in any given case, wrong. But that is not to say that it is their character as illegal that makes them wrong or contributes in any degree to their wrongness. Rather their illegality is a characteristic contingently linked to the other properties that truly make them wrong; so that its presence may be a more or less reliable index or clue to the presence of wrongness, not its ground or basis.

The conclusions of this chapter can now be stated tersely:

1. There is no general moral PFO to obey valid law, even in a democratic state with a just constitution.
2. The individual's moral problem in civil disobedience is not that of choosing between his higher moral cause and the PFO of obedience to law, but rather it is either
   a. no problem at all since his civil disobedience will not violate any PFOs but only break the law; or
   b. the problem of choosing between his higher moral cause and prudence (for example, personal safety); or
   c. the moral problem of choosing between conflicting PFOs, one that supports his loyalty to the higher moral cause and another basic PFO (such as the PFO of fair play or the PFO to support just institutions) that may in this particular case be in conflict with it.

   In case (*c*) no *general* advice from a moral philosopher is possible except to weigh sensitively the two conflicting PFOs and act in accordance with the one that seems weightier in the present circumstances.
3. Legal positivists should drop their assumption that even bad laws deserve respect simply because they are laws and that they impose some small obligation, at least, of obedience. Then, having no more problem of reconciliation, they can hold to their primary contention that all properly enacted law is valid law.
4. The ancient quest for a perfectly general ground of political obligation can be abandoned.

22. Ibid., p. 384.
23. Ibid., p. 366.

Distributive Justice

A Theory of Justice*

JOHN RAWLS

John Rawls (1921–) is the author of the influential work *A Theory of Justice.* He taught for many years at Harvard University.

THE ROLE OF JUSTICE

JUSTICE IS THE FIRST VIRTUE of social institutions, as truth is of systems of thought. A theory however elegant and economical must be rejected or revised if it is untrue; likewise laws and institutions no matter how efficient and well-arranged must be reformed or abolished if they are unjust. Each person possesses an inviolability founded on justice that even the welfare of society as a whole cannot override. For this reason justice denies that the loss of freedom for some is made right by a greater good shared by others. It does not allow that the sacrifices imposed on a few are outweighed by the larger sum of advantages enjoyed by many. Therefore in a just society the liberties of equal citizenship are taken as settled; the rights secured by justice are not subject to political bargaining or to the calculus of social interests. The only thing that permits us to acquiesce in an erroneous theory is the lack of a better one; analogously, an injustice is tolerable only when it is necessary to avoid an even greater injustice. Being first virtues of human activities, truth and justice are uncompromising.

These propositions seem to express our intuitive conviction of the primacy of justice. No doubt they are expressed too strongly. In any event I wish to inquire whether these contentions or others similar to them are sound, and if so how they can be accounted for. To this end it is necessary to work out a theory of justice in the light of which these assertions can be interpreted and assessed. I shall begin by considering the role of the principles of justice. Let us assume, to fix ideas, that a society is a more or less self-sufficient association of persons who in their relations to one another recognize certain rules of conduct as binding and who for the most part act in accordance with them. Suppose further that these rules specify a system of cooperation designed to advance the good of those taking part in it. Then, although a society is a cooperative venture for mutual advantage, it is typically marked by a conflict as well as by an identity of interests. There is an identity of interests since social cooperation makes possible a better life for all than any would have if each were to live solely by his own efforts. There is a conflict of interests since persons are not indifferent as to how the greater benefits produced by their collaboration are distributed, for in order to pursue their ends they each prefer a larger to a lesser share. A set of principles is required for choosing among the various social arrangements which determine this division of advantages and for underwriting an agreement on the proper distributive shares. These principles are the principles of social justice: they provide a way of assigning rights and duties in the basic institutions of society and they define the appropriate distribution of the benefits and burdens of social cooperation. . . .

THE MAIN IDEA OF THE THEORY OF JUSTICE

My aim is to present a conception of justice which generalizes and carries to a higher level of abstraction the familiar theory of the social contract as found, say, in Locke, Rousseau, and Kant. In order to do this we are not to think of the original contract as one to enter a particular society or to set up a particular form of government. Rather, the guiding idea is that the principles of justice for the basic structure of society are the object of the original agreement. They are the principles that free and rational persons concerned to further their own interests would accept in an initial position of equality as defining the fundamental terms of their association. These principles are to regulate all further agreements; they specify the kinds of social cooperation that can be entered into and the forms of government that can be established. This way of regarding the principles of justice I shall call justice as fairness.

Thus we are to imagine that those who engage in social cooperation choose together, in one joint act, the principles which are to assign basic rights and duties and to determine the division of social benefits. Men are to decide in advance how they are to regulate their claims against one another and what is to be the foundation charter of their society. Just as each person must decide by rational reflection what constitutes his good, that is, the system of ends which it is rational for him to pursue, so a group of persons must decide once and for all what is to count among them as just and unjust. The choice which rational men would make in this hypothetical situation of equal liberty, assuming for the present that this choice problem has a solution, determines the principles of justice.

In justice as fairness the original position of equality corresponds to the state of nature in the traditional theory of the social contract. This original position is not, of course, thought of as an actual historical state of affairs, much less as a primitive condition of culture. It is understood as a purely hypothetical situation characterized so as to lead to a certain conception of justice. Among the essential features of this situation is that no one knows his place in society, his class position or social status, nor does any one know his fortune in the distribution of natural assets and abilities, his intelligence, strength, and the like. I shall even assume that the parties do not know their conceptions of the good or their special psychological propensities. The principles of justice are chosen behind a veil of ignorance. This ensures that no one is advantaged or disadvantaged in the choice of principles by the outcome of natural chance or the contingency of social circumstances. Since all are similarly situated and no one is able to design principles to favor his particular condition, the principles of justice are the result of a fair agreement or bargain. For given the circumstances of the original position, the symmetry of everyone's relations to each other, this initial situation is fair between individuals as moral persons, that is, as rational beings with their own ends and capable, I shall assume, of a sense of justice. The original position is, one might say, the appropriate initial status quo, and thus the fundamental agreements reached in it are fair. This explains the propriety of the name "justice as fairness": it conveys the idea that the principles of justice are agreed to in an initial situation that is fair. The name does not mean that the concepts of justice and fairness are the same, any more than the phrase "poetry as metaphor" means that the concepts of poetry and metaphor are the same.

Justice as fairness begins, as I have said, with one of the most general of all choices which persons might make together, namely, with the choice of the first principles of a conception of justice which is to regulate all subsequent criticism and reform of institutions. Then, having chosen a conception of justice, we can suppose that they are to choose a constitution and a legislature to enact laws, and so on, all in accordance with the principles of justice initially agreed upon. Our social situation is just if it is such that by this sequence of hypothetical agreements we would have contracted into the general system of rules which defines it.

. . . It may be observed, however, that once the principles of justice are thought of as arising from an original agreement in a situation of equality, it is an open question whether the principle of utility would be acknowledged. Offhand it hardly seems likely that persons who view themselves as equals, entitled to press their claims upon one another, would agree to a principle which may require lesser life prospects for some simply for the sake of a greater sum of advantages enjoyed by others. Since each desires to protect his interests, his capacity to advance his conception of the good, no one has a reason to acquiesce in an enduring loss for himself in order to bring about a greater net balance of satisfaction. In the absence of strong and lasting benevolent impulses, a rational man would not accept a basic structure merely because it maximized the algebraic sum of advantages irrespective of its permanent effects on his own basic rights and interests. Thus it seems that the principle of utility is incompatible with the conception of social cooperation among equals for mutual advantage. It appears to be inconsistent with the idea of reciprocity implicit in the notion of a well-ordered society. Or, at any rate, so I shall argue.

I shall maintain instead that the persons in the initial situation would choose two rather different principles: the first requires equality in the assignment of basic rights and duties, while the second holds that social and economic inequalities, for example inequalities of wealth and authority, are just only if they result in compensating benefits for everyone, and in particular for the least advantaged members of society. These principles rule out justifying institutions on the grounds that the hardships of some are offset by a greater good in the aggregate. It may be expedient but it is not just that some should have less in order that others may prosper. But there is no injustice in the greater benefits earned by a few provided that the situation of persons not so fortunate is thereby improved. The intuitive idea is that since everyone's well-being depends upon a scheme of cooperation without which no one could have a satisfactory life, the division of advantages should be such as to draw forth the willing cooperation of everyone taking part in it, including those less well situated. Yet this can be expected only if reasonable terms are proposed. The two principles mentioned seem to be a fair agreement on the basis of which those better endowed, or more fortunate in their social position, neither of which we can be said to deserve, could expect the willing cooperation of others when some workable scheme is a necessary condition of the welfare of all. Once we decide to look for a conception of justice that nullifies the accidents of natural endowment and the contingencies of social circumstance as counters in quest for political and economic advantage, we are led to these principles. They express the result of leaving aside those aspects of the social world that seem arbitrary from a moral point of view. . . .

THE ORIGINAL POSITION AND JUSTIFICATION

. . . The idea here is simply to make vivid to ourselves the restrictions that it seems reasonable to impose on arguments for principles of justice, and therefore on these principles themselves. Thus it seems reasonable and generally acceptable that no one should be advantaged or disadvantaged by natural fortune or social circumstances in the choice of principles. It also seems widely agreed that it should be impossible to tailor principles to the circumstances of one's own case. We should insure further that particular inclinations and aspirations, and persons' conceptions of their good, do not affect the principles adopted. The aim is to rule out those principles that it would be rational to propose for acceptance, however little the chance of success, only if one knew certain things that are irrelevant from the standpoint of justice. For example, if a man knew that he was wealthy, he might find it rational to advance the principle that various taxes for welfare measures be counted unjust; if he knew that he was poor, he would most likely propose the contrary principle. To represent the desired restrictions one imagines a situation in which everyone is deprived of this sort of information. One excludes the knowledge of those contingencies which sets men at odds and allows them to be guided by their prejudices. In this manner the veil of ignorance is arrived at in a natural way. . . .

TWO PRINCIPLES OF JUSTICE

I shall now state in a provisional form the two principles of justice that I believe would be chosen in the original position. . . .

The first statement of the two principles reads as follows.

> First: each person is to have an equal right to the most extensive basic liberty compatible with a similar liberty for others.
>
> Second: social and economic inequalities are to be arranged so that they are both (a) reasonably expected to be to everyone's advantage, and (b) attached to positions and offices open to all. . . . [The Difference Principle]

By way of general comment, these principles primarily apply, as I have said, to the basic structure of society. They are to govern the assignment of rights and duties and to regulate the distribution of social and economic advantages. As their formulation suggests, these principles presuppose that the social structure can be divided into two more or less distinct parts, the first principle applying to the one, the second to the other. They distinguish between those aspects of the social system that define and secure the equal liberties of citizenship and those that specify and establish social and economic inequalities. The basic liberties of citizens are, roughly speaking, political liberty (the right to vote and to be eligible for public office) together with freedom of speech and assembly; liberty of conscience and freedom of thought; freedom of the person along with the right to hold (personal) property; and freedom from arbitrary arrest and seizure as defined by the concept of the rule of law. These liberties are all required to be equal by the first principle, since citizens of a just society are to have the same basic rights.

The second principle applies, in the first approximation, to the distribution of income and wealth and to the design of organizations that make use of differences in authority and responsibility, or chains of command. While the distribution of wealth and income need not be equal, it must be to everyone's advantage, and at the same time, positions of authority and offices of command must be accessible to all. One applies the second principle by holding positions open, and then, subject to this constraint, arranges social and economic inequalities so that everyone benefits.

These principles are to be arranged in a serial order with the first principle prior to the second. This ordering means that a departure from the institutions of equal liberty required by the first principle cannot be justified, or compensated for, by greater social and economic advantages. The distribution of wealth and income, and the hierarchies of authority, must be consistent with both the liberties of equal citizenship and equality of opportunity.

It is clear that these principles are rather specific in their content, and their acceptance rests on certain assumptions that I must eventually try to explain and justify. A theory of justice depends upon a theory of society in ways that will become evident as we proceed. For the present, it should be observed that the two principles (and this holds for all formulations) are a special case of a more general conception of justice that can be expressed as follows.

> All social values—liberty and opportunity, income and wealth, and the bases of self-respect—are to be distributed equally unless an unequal distribution of any, or all, of these values is to everyone's advantage.

Injustice, then, is simply inequalities that are not to the benefit of all. Of course, this conception is extremely vague and requires interpretation.

As a first step, suppose that the basic structure of society distributes certain primary goods, that is, things that every rational man is presumed to want. These goods normally have a use whatever a person's rational plan of life. For simplicity, assume that the chief primary goods at the disposition of society are rights and liberties, powers and opportunities, income and wealth. These are the social primary goods. Other primary goods such as health and vigor, intelligence and imagination, are natural goods; although their possession is influenced by the basic structure, they are not so directly under its control. Imagine, then, a hypothetical initial arrangement in which all the social primary goods are equally distributed: everyone has similar rights and duties, and income and wealth are evenly shared. This state of affairs provides a benchmark for judging improvements. If certain inequalities of wealth and organizational powers would make everyone better off than in this hypothetical starting situation, then they accord with the general conception.

Now it is possible, at least theoretically, that by giving up some of their fundamental liberties men are sufficiently compensated by the resulting social and economic gains. The general conception of justice imposes no restrictions on what sort of inequalities are permissible; it only requires that everyone's position be improved. . . .

Now the second principle insists that each person benefit from permissible inequalities in the basic structure. This means that it must be reasonable for each relevant representative man defined by this structure, when he views it as a going concern, to prefer his prospects with the inequality to his prospects without it. One is not allowed to justify differences in income or organizational powers on the ground that the disadvantages of those in one position are outweighed by the greater advantages of those in another. Much less can infringements of liberty be counterbalanced in this way. Applied to the basic structure, the principle of utility would have us maximize the sum of expectations of representative men (weighted by the number of persons they represent, on the classical view); and this would permit us to compensate for the losses of some by the gains of others. Instead, the two principles require that everyone benefit from economic and social inequalities. . . .

THE TENDENCY TO EQUALITY

I wish to conclude this discussion of the two principles by explaining the sense in which they express an egalitarian conception of justice. Also I should like to forestall the objection to the principle of fair opportunity that it leads to a callous meritocratic society. In order to prepare the way for doing this, I note several aspects of the conception of justice that I have set out.

First we may observe that the difference principle gives some weight to the considerations singled out by the principle of redress. This is the principle that undeserved inequalities call for redress; and since inequalities of birth and natural endowment are undeserved, these inequalities are to be somehow compensated for. Thus the principle holds that in order to treat all persons equally, to provide genuine equality of opportunity, society must give more attention to those with fewer native assets and to those born into the less favorable social positions. The idea is to redress the bias of contingencies in the direction of equality. In pursuit of this principle greater resources might be spent on the education of the less rather than the more intelligent, at least over a certain time of life, say the earlier years of school.

Now the principle of redress has not to my knowledge been proposed as the sole criterion of justice, as the single aim of the social order. It is plausible as most such principles are only as a prima facie principle, one that is to be weighed in the balance with others. For example, we are to weigh it against the principle to improve the average standard of life, or to advance the common good. But whatever other principles we hold, the claims of redress are to be taken into account. It is thought to represent one of the elements in our conception of justice. Now the difference principle is not of course the principle of redress. It does not require society to try to even out handicaps as if all were expected to compete on a fair basis in the same race. But the difference principle would allocate resources in education, say, so as to improve the long-term expectation of the least favored. If this end is attained by giving more attention to the better endowed, it is permissible; otherwise not. And in making this decision, the value of education should not be assessed solely in terms of economic efficiency and social welfare. Equally if not more important is the role of education in enabling a person to enjoy the culture of his society and to take part in its affairs, and in this way to provide for each individual a secure sense of his own worth.

Thus although the difference principle is not the same as that of redress, it does achieve some of the intent of the latter principle. It transforms the aims of the basic structure so that the total scheme of institutions no longer emphasizes social efficiency and technocratic values. . . .

The natural distribution is neither just nor unjust; nor is it unjust that persons are born into society at some particular position. These are simply natural facts. What is just and unjust is the way that institutions deal with these facts. Aristocratic and caste societies are unjust because they make these contingencies the ascriptive basis for belonging to more or less enclosed and privileged social classes. The basic structure of these societies incorporates the arbitrariness found in nature. But there is no necessity for men to resign themselves to these contingencies. The social system is not an unchangeable order beyond human control but a pattern of human action. In justice as fairness men agree to share one another's fate. In designing institutions they undertake to avail themselves of the accidents of nature and social circumstance only when doing so is for the common benefit. The two principles are a fair way of meeting the arbitrariness of fortune; and while no doubt imperfect in other ways, the institutions which satisfy these principles are just.

A further point is that the difference principle expresses a conception of reciprocity. It is a principle of mutual benefit. We have seen that, at least when chain connection holds, each representative man can accept the basic structure as designed to advance his interests. The social order can be justified to everyone, and in particular to those who are least favored; and in this sense it is egalitarian. But it seems necessary to consider in an intuitive way how the condition of mutual benefit is satisfied. Consider any two representative men A and B, and let B be the one who is less favored. Actually, since we are most interested in the comparison with the least favored man, let us assume that B is this individual. Now B can accept A's being better off since A's advantages have been gained in ways that improve B's prospects. If A were not allowed his better position, B would be even worse off than he is. The difficulty is to show that A has no grounds for complaint. Perhaps he is required to have less than he might since his having more would result in some loss to B. Now what can be said to the more favored man? To begin with, it is clear that the well-being of each depends on a scheme of social cooperation without which no one could have a satisfactory life. Secondly, we can ask for the willing cooperation of everyone only if the terms of the scheme are reasonable. The difference principle, then, seems to be a fair basis on which those better endowed, or more fortunate in their social circumstances, could expect others to collaborate with them when some workable arrangement is a necessary condition of the good of all.

There is a natural inclination to object that those better situated deserve their greater advantages whether or not they are to the benefit of others. At this point it is necessary to be clear about the notion of desert. It is perfectly true that given a just system of cooperation as a scheme of public rules and the expectations set up by it, those who, with the prospect of improving their condition, have done what the system announces that it will reward are entitled to their advantages. In this sense the more fortunate have a claim to their better situation; their claims are legitimate expectations established by social institutions, and the community is obligated to meet them. But this sense of desert presupposes the existence of the cooperative scheme; it is irrelevant to the question whether in the first place the scheme is to be designed in accordance with the difference principle or some other criterion.

Perhaps some will think that the person with greater natural endowments deserves those assets and the superior character that made their development possible. Because he is more worthy in this sense, he deserves the greater advantages that he could achieve with them. This view, however, is surely incorrect. It seems to be one of the fixed points of our considered judgments that no one deserves his place in the distribution of native endowments, any more than one deserves one's initial starting place in society. The assertion that a man deserves the superior character that enables him to make the effort to cultivate his abilities is equally problematic; for his character depends in large part upon fortunate family and social circumstances for which he can claim no credit. The notion of desert seems not to apply to these cases. Thus the more advantaged representative man cannot say that he deserves and therefore has a right to a scheme of cooperation in which he is permitted to acquire benefits in ways that do not contribute to the welfare of others. There is no basis for his making this claim. From the standpoint of common sense, then, the difference principle appears to be acceptable both to the more advantaged and to the less advantaged individual. Of course, none of this is strictly speaking an argument for the principle, since in a contract theory arguments are made from the point of view of the original position. But these intuitive considerations help to clarify the nature of the principle and the sense in which it is egalitarian.

Justice and Entitlement*

ROBERT NOZICK

Robtert Nozick (1938–) teaches philosophy at Harvard University. His many publications include *Philosophical Explanations* and *The Nature of Rationality.*

THE TERM "DISTRIBUTIVE JUSTICE" is not a neutral one. Hearing the term "distribution," most people presume that some thing or mechanism uses some principle or criterion to give out a supply of things. Into this process of distributing shares some error may have crept. So it is an open question, at least, whether *re*distribution should take place; whether we should do again what has already been done once, though poorly. However, we are not in the position of children who have been given portions of pie by someone who now makes last minute adjustments to rectify careless cutting. There is no *central* distribution, no person or group entitled to control all the resources, jointly deciding how they are to be doled out. What each person gets, he gets from others who give to him in exchange for something, or as a gift. In a free society, diverse persons control different resources, and new holdings arise out of the voluntary exchanges and actions of persons. . . .

The subject of justice in holdings consists of three major topics. The first is the *original acquisition of holdings*, the appropriation of unheld things. This includes the issues of how unheld things may come to be held, the process, or processes, by which unheld things may come to be held, the things that may come to be held by these processes, the extent of what comes to be held by a particular process, and so on. We shall refer to the complicated truth about this topic, which we shall not formulate here, as the principle of justice in acquisition. The second topic concerns the *transfer of holdings* from one person to another. By what processes may a person transfer holdings to another? How may a person acquire a holding from another who holds it? Under this topic come general descriptions of voluntary exchange, and gift and (on the other hand) fraud, as well as reference to particular conventional details fixed upon in a given society. The complicated truth about this subject (with placeholders for conventional details) we shall call the principle of justice in transfer. (And we shall suppose it also includes principles governing how a person may divest himself of a holding, passing it into an unheld state.)

If the world were wholly just, the following inductive definition would exhaustively cover the subject of justice in holdings.

1. A person who acquires a holding in accordance with the principle of justice in acquisition is entitled to that holding.
2. A person who acquires a holding in accordance with the principle of justice in transfer, from someone else entitled to the holding, is entitled to the holding.
3. No one is entitled to a holding except by (repeated) applications of 1 and 2.

The complete principle of distributive justice would say simply that a distribution is just if everyone is entitled to the holdings they possess under the distribution. . . .

Not all actual situations are generated in accordance with the two principles of justice in holdings: the principle of justice in acquisition and the principle of justice in transfer. Some people steal from others, or defraud them, or enslave them, seizing their product and preventing them from living as they choose, or forcibly exclude others from competing in exchanges. None of these are permissible modes of transition from one situation to another. And some persons acquire holdings by means not sanctioned by the principle of justice in acquisition. The existence of past injustice (previous violations of the first two principles of justice in holdings) raises the third major topic under justice in holdings: the rectification of injustice in holdings. If past injustice has shaped present holdings in various ways, some identifiable and some not, what now, if anything, ought to be done to rectify these injustices? . . .

HISTORICAL PRINCIPLES AND END-RESULT PRINCIPLES

The general outlines of the entitlement theory illuminate the nature and defects of other conceptions of distributive justice. The entitlement theory of justice in distribution is *historical;* whether a distribution is just depends upon how it came about. In contrast, *current time-slice principles* of justice hold that the justice of a distribution is determined by how things are distributed (who has what) as judged by some *structural* principle(s) of just distribution. A utilitarian who judges between any two distributions by seeing which has the greater sum of utility and, if the sums tie, applies some fixed equality criterion to choose the more equal distribution, would hold a current time-slice principle of justice. As would someone who had a fixed schedule of trade-offs between the sum of happiness and equality. According to a current time-slice principle, all that needs to be looked at, in judging the justice of a distribution, is who ends up with what; in comparing any two distributions one need look only at the matrix presenting the distributions. No further information need be fed into a principle of justice. It is a consequence of such principles of justice that any two structurally identical distributions are equally just. . . .

Most persons do not accept current time-slice principles as constituting the whole story about distributive shares. They think it relevant in assessing the justice of a situation to consider not only the distribution it embodies, but also how that distribution came about. If some persons are in prison for murder or war crimes, we do not say that to assess the justice of the distribution in the society we must look only at what this person has, and that person has, and that person has, . . . at the current time. We think it relevant to ask whether someone did something so that he *deserved* to be punished, deserved to have a lower share. . . .

PATTERNING

. . . Almost every suggested principle of distributive justice is patterned: to each according to his moral merit, or needs, or marginal product, or how hard he tries, or the weighted sum of the foregoing, and so on. The principle of entitlement we have sketched is *not* patterned. There is no one natural dimension or weighted sum or combination of a small number of natural dimensions that yields the distributions generated in accordance with the principle of entitlement. The set of holdings that results when some persons receive their marginal products, others win at gambling, others receive a share of their mate's income, others receive gifts from foundations, others receive interest on loans, others receive gifts from admirers, others receive returns on investment, others make for themselves much of what they have, others find things, and so on, will not be patterned. . . .

To think that the task of a theory of distributive justice is to fill in the blank in "to each according to his ___" is to be predisposed to search for a pattern: and the separate treatment of "from each according to his ___" treats production and distribution as two separate and independent issues. On an entitlement view these are *not* two separate questions. Whoever makes something, having bought or contracted for all other held resources used in the process (transferring some of his holdings for these cooperating factors), is entitled to it. . . .

So entrenched are maxims of the usual form that perhaps we should present the entitlement conception as a competitor. Ignoring acquisition and rectification, we might say:

> From each according to what he chooses to do, to each according to what he makes for himself (perhaps with the contracted aid of others) and what others choose to do for him and choose to give him of what they've been given previously (under this maxim) and haven't yet expended or transferred.

This, the discerning reader will have noticed, has its defects as a slogan. So as a summary and great simplification (and not as a maxim with any independent meaning) we have:

> *From each as they choose, to each as they are chosen.*

HOW LIBERTY UPSETS PATTERNS

It is not clear how those holding alternative conceptions of distributive justice can reject the entitlement conception of justice in holdings. For suppose a distribution favored by one of these non-entitlement conceptions is realized. Let us suppose it is your favorite one and let us call this distribution D_1; perhaps everyone has an equal share, perhaps shares vary in accordance with some dimension you treasure. Now suppose that Wilt Chamberlain is greatly in demand by basketball teams, being a great gate attraction. (Also suppose contracts run only for a year, with players being free agents.) He signs the following sort of contract with a team: In each home game, twenty-five cents from the price of each ticket of admission goes to him. (We ignore the question of whether he is "gouging" the owners, letting them look out for themselves.) The season starts, and people cheerfully attend his team's games; they buy their tickets, each time dropping a separate twenty-five cents of their admission price into a special box with Chamberlain's name on it. They are excited about seeing him play; it is worth the total admission price to them. Let us suppose that in one season one million persons attend his home games, and Wilt Chamberlain winds up with $250,000, a much larger sum than the average income and larger even than anyone else has. Is he entitled to this income? Is this new distribution, D_2, unjust? If so, why? There is *no* question about whether each of the people was entitled to the control over the resources they held in D_1; because that was the distribution (your favorite) that (for the purposes of argument) we assumed was acceptable. Each of these persons *chose* to give twenty-five cents of their money to Chamberlain. They could have spent it on going to the movies, or on candy bars, or on copies of *Dissent* magazine, or of *Monthly Review.* But they all, at least one million of them, converged on giving it to Wilt Chamberlain in exchange for watching him play basketball. If D_1 was a just distribution, and people voluntarily moved from it to D_2, transferring parts of their shares they were given under D_1 (what was it for if not to do something with?), isn't D_2 also just? If the people were entitled to dispose of the resources to which they were entitled (under D_1), didn't this include their being entitled to give it to, or exchange it with, Wilt Chamberlain? Can anyone else complain on grounds of justice? Each other person already has his legitimate share under D_1. Under D_1, there is nothing that anyone has that anyone else has a claim of justice against. After someone transfers something to Wilt Chamberlain, third parties *still* have their legitimate shares; *their* shares are not changed. By what process could such a transfer among two persons give a rise to a legitimate claim of distributive justice on a portion of what was transferred, by a third party who had no claim of justice on any holding of the others *before* the transfer? To cut off objections irrelevant here, we might imagine the exchanges occurring in a socialist society, after hours. After playing whatever basketball he does in his daily work, or doing whatever other daily work he does, Wilt Chamberlain decides to put in *overtime* to earn additional money. (First his work quota is set; he works time over that.) Or imagine it is a skilled juggler people like to see, who puts on shows after hours. . . .

The general point illustrated by the Wilt Chamberlain example is that no end-state principle or distributional patterned principle of justice can be continuously realized without continuous interference with people's lives. Any favored pattern would be transformed into one unfavored by the principle, by people choosing to act in various ways; for example, by people exchanging goods and services with other people, or giving things to other people, things the transferrers are entitled to under the favored distributional pattern. To maintain a pattern one must either continually interfere to stop people from transferring resources as they wish to, or continually (or periodically) interfere to take from some persons resources that others for some reason chose to transfer to them. . . .

Patterned principles of distributive justice necessitate *re*distributive activities. The likelihood is small that any actual freely-arrived-at set of holdings fits a given pattern; and the likelihood is nil that it will continue to fit the pattern as people exchange and give. From the point of view of an entitlement theory, redistribution is a serious matter indeed, involving, as it does, the violation of people's rights. (An exception is those takings that fall under the principle of the rectification of injustices.) . . .

LOCKE'S THEORY OF ACQUISITION

. . . [W]e must introduce an additional bit of complexity into the structure of the entitlement theory. This is best approached by considering Locke's attempt to specify a principle of justice in acquisition. Locke views property rights in an unowned object as originating through someone's mixing his labor with it. This gives rise to many questions. What are the boundaries of what labor is mixed with? If a private astronaut clears a place on Mars, has he mixed his labor with (so that he comes to own) the whole planet, the whole uninhabited universe, or just a particular plot? Which plot does an act bring under ownership? The minimal (possibly disconnected) area such that an act decreases entropy in that area, and not elsewhere? Can virgin land (for the purposes of ecological investigation by high-flying airplane) come under ownership by a Lockean process? Building a fence around a territory presumably would make one the owner of only the fence (and the land immediately underneath it).

Why does mixing one's labor with something make one the owner of it? Perhaps because one owns one's labor, and so one comes to own a previously unowned thing that becomes permeated with what one owns. Ownership seeps over into the rest. But why isn't mixing what I own with what I don't own a way of losing what I own rather than a way of gaining what I don't? If I own a can of tomato juice and spill it in the sea so that its molecules (made radioactive, so I can check this) mingle evenly throughout the sea, do I thereby come to own the sea, or have I foolishly dissipated my tomato juice? Perhaps the idea, instead, is that laboring on something improves it and makes it more valuable; and anyone is entitled to own a thing whose value he has created. (Reinforcing this, perhaps, is the view that laboring is unpleasant. If some people made things effortlessly, as the cartoon characters in *The Yellow Submarine* trail flowers in their wake, would they have lesser claim to their own products whose making didn't *cost* them anything?) Ignore the fact that laboring on something may make it less valuable (spraying pink enamel paint on a piece of driftwood that you have found). Why should one's entitlement extend to the whole object rather than just to the *added value* one's labor has produced? (Such reference to value might also serve to delimit the extent of ownership; for example, substitute "increases the value of" for "decreases entropy in" in the above entropy criterion.) No workable or coherent value-added property scheme has yet been devised, and any such scheme presumably would fall to objections (similar to those) that fell the theory of Henry George.

It will be implausible to view improving an object as giving full ownership to it, if the stock of unowned objects that might be improved is limited.

For an object's coming under one person's ownership changes the situation of all others. Whereas previously they were at liberty (in Hohfeld's sense) to use the object, they now no longer are. This change in the situation of others (by removing their liberty to act on a previously unowned object) need not worsen their situation. If I appropriate a grain of sand from Coney Island, no one else may now do as they will with *that* grain of sand. But there are plenty of other grains of sand left for them to do the same with. Or if not grains of sand, then other things. Alternatively, the things I do with the grain of sand I appropriate might improve the position of others, counterbalancing their loss of the liberty to use that grain. The crucial point is whether appropriation of an unowned object worsens the situation of others.

Locke's proviso that there be "enough and as good left in common for others" (sect. 27) is meant to ensure that the situation of others is not worsened.

. . . . . .

Is the situation of persons who are unable to appropriate (there being no more accessible and useful unowned objects) worsened by a system allowing appropriation and permanent property? Here enter the various familiar social considerations favoring private property: it increases the social product by putting means of production in the hands of those who can use them most efficiently (profitably): experimentation is encouraged, because with separate persons controlling resources, there is no one person or small group whom someone with a new idea must convince to try it out; private property enables people to decide on the pattern and types of risks they wish to bear, leading to specialized types of risk bearing; private property protects future persons by leading some to hold back resources from current consumption for future markets; it provides alternate sources of employment for unpopular persons who don't have to convince any one person or small group to hire them, and so on. These considerations enter a Lockean theory to support the claim that appropriation of private property satisfies the intent behind the "enough and as good left over" proviso, *not* as a utilitarian justification of property. They enter to rebut the claim that because the proviso is violated no natural right to private property can arise by a Lockean process. The difficulty in working such an argument to show that the proviso is satisfied is in fixing the appropriate baseline for comparison. Lockean appropriation makes people no worse off than they would be *how?* This question of fixing the baseline needs more detailed investigation than we are able to give it here.

. . . . . .

THE PROVISO

Whether or not Locke's particular theory of appropriation can be spelled out so as to handle various difficulties, I assume that any adequate theory of justice in acquisition will contain a proviso similar to the weaker of the ones we have attributed to Locke. A process normally giving rise to a permanent bequeathable property right in a previously unowned thing will not do so if the position of others no longer at liberty to use the thing is thereby worsened. It is important to specify *this* particular mode of worsening the situation of others, for the proviso does not encompass other modes. It does not include the worsening due to more limited opportunities to appropriate . . . , and it does not include how I "worsen" a seller's position if I appropriate materials to make some of what he is selling, and then enter into competition with him. Someone whose appropriation otherwise would violate the proviso still may appropriate provided he compensates the others so that their situation is not thereby worsened; unless he does compensate these others, his appropriation will violate the proviso of the principle of justice in acquisition and will be an illegitimate one. A theory of appropriation incorporating this Lockean proviso will handle correctly the cases (objections to the theory lacking the proviso) where someone appropriates the total supply of something necessary for life.

A theory which includes this proviso in its principle of justice in acquisition must also contain a more complex principle of justice in transfer. Some reflection of the proviso about appropriation constrains later actions. If my appropriating all of a certain substance violates the Lockean proviso, then so does my appropriating some and purchasing all the rest from others who obtained it without otherwise violating the Lockean proviso. If the proviso excludes someone's appropriating all the drinkable water in the world, it also excludes his purchasing it all. (More weakly, and messily, it may exclude his charging certain prices for some of his supply.) This proviso (almost?) never will come into effect; the more someone acquires of a scarce substance which others want, the higher the price of the rest will go, and the more difficult it will become for him to acquire it all. But still, we can imagine, at least, that something like this occurs: someone makes simultaneous secret bids to the separate owners of a substance, each of whom sells assuming he can easily purchase more from the other owners; or some natural catastrophe destroys all of the supply of something except that in one person's possession. The total supply could not be permissibly appropriated by one person at the beginning. His later acquisition of it all does not show that the original appropriation violated the proviso. . . . Rather, it is the combination of the original appropriation *plus* all the later transfers and actions that violates the Lockean proviso.

Each owner's title to his holding includes the historical shadow of the Lockean proviso on appropriation. This excludes his transferring it into an agglomeration that does violate the Lockean proviso and excludes his using it in a way, in coordination with others or independently of them, so as to violate the proviso by making the situation of others worse than their baseline situation. Once it is known that someone's ownership runs afoul of the Lockean proviso, there are stringent limits on what he may do with (what it is difficult any longer unreservedly to call) "his property." Thus a person may not appropriate the only water hole in a desert and charge what he will. Nor may he charge what he will if he possesses one, and unfortunately it happens that all the water holes in the desert dry up, except for his. This unfortunate circumstance, admittedly no fault of his, brings into operation the Lockean proviso and limits his property rights. Similarly, an owner's property right in the only island in an area does not allow him to order a castaway from a shipwreck off his island as a trespasser, for this would violate the Lockean proviso.

. . . . . .

The fact that someone owns the total supply of something necessary for others to stay alive does *not* entail that his (or anyone's) appropriation of anything left some people (immediately or later) in a situation worse than the baseline one. A medical researcher who synthesizes a new substance that effectively treats a certain disease and who refuses to sell except on his terms does not worsen the situation of others by depriving them of whatever he has appropriated. The others easily can possess the same materials he appropriated; the researcher's appropriation or purchase of chemicals didn't make those chemicals scarce in a way so as to violate the Lockean proviso. Nor would someone else's purchasing the total supply of the synthesized substance from the medical researcher. The fact that the medical researcher uses easily available chemicals to synthesize the drug no more violates the Lockean proviso than does the fact that the only surgeon able to perform a particular operation eats easily obtainable food in order to stay alive and to have the energy to work. This shows that the Lockean proviso is not an "end-state principle"; it focuses on a particular way that appropriative actions affect others, and not on the structure of the situation that results.

Intermediate between someone who takes all of the public supply and someone who makes the total supply out of easily obtainable substances is someone who appropriates the total supply of something in a way that does not deprive the others of it. For example, someone finds a new substance in an out-of-the-way place. He discovers that it effectively treats a certain disease and appropriates the total supply. He does not worsen the situation of others; if he did not stumble upon the substance no one else would have, and the others would remain without it. However, as time passes, the likelihood increases that others would have come across the substance; upon this fact might be based a limit to his property right in the substance so that others are not below their baseline position; for example, its bequest might be limited. The theme of someone worsening another's situation by depriving him of something he otherwise would possess may also illuminate the example of patents. An inventor's patent does not deprive others of an object which would not exist if not for the inventor. Yet patents would have this effect on others who independently invent the object. Therefore, these independent inventors, upon whom the burden of proving independent discovery may rest, should not be excluded from utilizing their own invention as they wish (including selling it to others). Furthermore, a known inventor drastically lessens the chances of actual independent invention. For persons who know of an invention usually will not try to reinvent it, and the notion of independent discovery here would be murky at best. Yet we may assume that in the absence of the original invention, sometime later someone else would have come up with it. This suggests placing a time limit on patents, as a rough rule of thumb to approximate how long it would have taken, in the absence of knowledge of the invention, for independent discovery.

I believe that the free operation of a market system will not actually run afoul of the Lockean proviso. . . .

Justice and Utilitarianism*

JOHN STUART MILL

In all ages of speculation, one of the strongest obstacles to the reception of the doctrine that Utility or Happiness is the criterion of right and wrong, has been drawn from the idea of Justice. The powerful sentiment, and apparently clear perception, which that word recalls with a rapidity and certainty resembling an instinct, have seemed to the majority of thinkers to point to an inherent quality in things; to show that the Just must have an existence in Nature as something absolute, generically distinct from every variety of the Expedient, and, in idea, opposed to it, though (as is commonly acknowledged) never, in the long run, disjoined from it in fact. . . .

. . . Our present object is to determine whether the reality, to which the feeling of justice corresponds, is one which needs any such special revelation; whether the justice or injustice of an action is a thing intrinsically peculiar, and distinct from all its other qualities, or only a combination of certain of those qualities, presented under a peculiar aspect. For the purpose of this inquiry it is practically important to consider whether the feeling itself, of justice and injustice, is *sui generis* like our sensations of colour and taste, or a derivative feeling, formed by a combination of others. And this it is the more essential to examine, as people are in general willing enough to allow, that objectively the dictates of Justice coincide with a part of the field of General Expediency; but inasmuch as the subjective mental feeling of Justice is different from that which commonly attaches to simple expediency, and, except in the extreme cases of the latter, is far more imperative in its demands, people find it difficult to see, in Justice, only a particular kind or branch of general utility, and think that its superior binding force requires a totally different origin.

To throw light upon this question, it is necessary to attempt to ascertain what is the distinguishing character of justice, or of injustice: what is the quality, or whether there is any quality, attributed in common to all modes of conduct designated as unjust (for justice, like many other moral attributes, is best defined by its opposite), and distinguishing them from such modes of conduct as are disapproved, but without having that particular epithet of disapprobation applied to them. If in everything which men are accustomed to characterise as just or

**From* Utilitarianism, *ch. 5, by John Stuart Mill, published in England (1863).*

unjust, some one common attribute or collection of attributes is always present, we may judge whether this particular attribute or combination of attributes would be capable of gathering round it a sentiment of that peculiar character and intensity by virtue of the general laws of our emotional constitution, or whether the sentiment is inexplicable, and requires to be regarded as a special provision of Nature. If we find the former to be the case, we shall, in resolving this question, have resolved also the main problem: if the latter, we shall have to seek for some other mode of investigating it.

To find the common attributes of a variety of objects, it is necessary to begin by surveying the objects themselves in the concrete. Let us therefore advert successively to the various modes of action, and arrangements of human affairs, which are classed, by universal or widely spread opinion, as Just or as Unjust. . . .

In the first place, it is mostly considered unjust to deprive any one of his personal liberty, his property, or any other thing which belongs to him by law. Here, therefore, is one instance of the application of the terms just and unjust in a perfectly definite sense, namely, that it is just to respect, unjust to violate, the *legal rights* of any one. . . .

Secondly; the legal rights of which he is deprived, may be rights which *ought* not to have belonged to him; in other words, the law which confers on him these rights, may be a bad law. When it is so, or when (which is the same thing for our purpose) it is supposed to be so, opinions will differ as to the justice or injustice of infringing it. Some maintain that no law, however bad, ought to be disobeyed by an individual citizen; that his opposition to it, if shown at all, should only be shown in endeavouring to get it altered by competent authority. This opinion (which condemns many of the most illustrious benefactors of mankind, and would often protect pernicious institutions against the only weapons which, in the state of things existing at the time, have any chance of succeeding against them) is defended, by those who hold it, on grounds of expediency; principally on that of the importance, to the common interest of mankind, of maintaining inviolate the sentiment of submission to law. Other persons, again, hold the directly contrary opinion, that any law, judged to be bad, may blamelessly be disobeyed, even though it be not judged to be unjust, but only inexpedient; while others would confine the licence of disobedience to the case of unjust laws: but again, some say, that all laws which are inexpedient are unjust; since every law imposes some restriction on the natural liberty of mankind, which restriction is an injustice, unless legitimated by tending to their good. Among these diversities of opinion, it seems to be universally admitted that there may be unjust laws, and that law, consequently, is not the ultimate criterion of justice, but may give to one person a benefit, or impose on another an evil, which justice condemns. When, however, a law is thought to be unjust, it seems always to be regarded as being so in the same way in which a breach of law is unjust, namely, by infringing somebody's right; which, as it cannot in this case be a legal right, receives a different appellation, and is called a moral right. We may say, therefore, that a second case of injustice consists in taking or withholding from any person that to which he has a *moral right.*

Thirdly, it is universally considered just that each person should obtain that (whether good or evil) which he *deserves;* and unjust that he should obtain a good, or be made to undergo an evil, which he does not deserve. . . . The precept of returning good for evil has never been regarded as a case of the fulfilment of justice, but as one in which the claims of justice are waived, in obedience to other considerations.

Fourthly, it is confessedly unjust to *break faith* with any one: to violate an engagement, either express or implied, or disappoint expectations raised by our own conduct, at least if we have raised those expectations knowingly and voluntarily. . . .

Fifthly, it is, by universal admission, inconsistent with justice to be *partial;* to show favour or preference to one person over another, in matters to which favour and preference do not properly apply. Impartiality, however, does not seem to be regarded as a duty in itself, but rather as instrumental to some other duty; for it is admitted that favour and preference are not always censurable, and indeed the cases in which they are condemned are rather the exception than the rule. A person would be more likely to be blamed than applauded for giving his family or friends no superiority in good offices over strangers, when he could do so without violating any other duty; and no one thinks it unjust to seek one person in preference to another as a friend, connection, or companion. . . . Impartiality, in short, as an obligation of justice, may be said to mean, being exclusively influenced by the considerations which it is supposed ought to influence the particular case in hand; and resisting the solicitation of any motives which prompt to conduct different from what those considerations would dictate.

Nearly allied to the idea of impartiality is that of *equality;* which often enters as a component part both into the conception of justice and into the practice of it, and, in the eyes of many persons, constitutes its essence. But in this, still more than in any other case, the notion of justice varies in different persons, and always conforms in its variations to their notion of utility. Each person maintains that equality is the dictate of justice, except where he thinks that expediency requires inequality. The justice of giving equal protection to the rights of all, is maintained by those who support the most outrageous inequality in the rights themselves. Even in slave countries it is theoretically admitted that the rights of the slave, such as they are, ought to be as sacred as those of the master; and that a tribunal which fails to enforce them with equal strictness is wanting in justice; while, at the same time, institutions which leave to the slave scarcely any rights to enforce, are not deemed unjust, because they are not deemed inexpedient. Those who think that utility requires distinctions of rank, do not consider it unjust that riches and social privileges should be unequally dispensed; but those who think this inequality inexpedient, think it unjust also. Whoever thinks that government is necessary, sees no injustice in as much inequality as is constituted by giving to the magistrate powers not granted to other people. Even among those who hold levelling doctrines, there are as many questions of justice as there are differences of opinion about expediency. Some Communists consider it unjust that the produce of the labour of the community should be shared on any other principle than that of exact equality; others think it just that those should receive most whose wants are greatest; while others hold that those who work harder, or who produce more, or whose services are more valuable to the community, may justly claim a larger quota in the division of the produce. And the sense of natural justice may be plausibly appealed to in behalf of every one of these opinions.

Among so many diverse applications of the term Justice, which yet is not regarded as ambiguous, it is a matter of some difficulty to seize the mental link which holds them together, and on which the moral sentiment adhering to the term essentially depends. . . .

. . . Now it is known that ethical writers divide moral duties into two classes, denoted by the ill-chosen expressions, duties of perfect and of imperfect obligation; the latter being those in which, though the act is obligatory, the particular occasions of performing it are left to our choice; as in the case of charity or beneficence, which we are indeed bound to practise, but not towards any definite person, nor at any prescribed time. In the more precise language of philosophic purists, duties of perfect obligation are those duties in virtue of which a correlative *right* resides in some person or persons; duties of imperfect obligation are those moral obligations which do not give birth to any right. I think it will be found that this distinction exactly coincides with that which exists between justice and the other obligations of morality. . . . Justice implies something which is not only right to do, and wrong not to do, but which some individual person can claim from us as his moral right. No one has a moral right to our generosity or beneficence, because we are not morally bound to practise those virtues towards any given individual. . . . Wherever there is a right, the case is one of justice, and not of the virtue of beneficence: and whoever does not place the distinction between justice and morality in general, where we have now placed it, will be found to make no distinction between them at all, but to merge all morality in justice. . . .

We have seen that the two essential ingredients in the sentiment of justice are, the desire to punish a person who has done harm, and the knowledge or belief that there is some definite individual or individuals to whom harm has been done.

Now it appears to me, that the desire to punish a person who has done harm to some individual is a spontaneous outgrowth from two sentiments, both in the highest degree natural, and which either are or resemble instincts; the impulse of self-defence, and the feeling of sympathy.

It is natural to resent, and to repel or retaliate, any harm done or attempted against ourselves, or against those with whom we sympathise. . . . By virtue of his superior intelligence, even apart from his superior range of sympathy, a human being is capable of apprehending a community of interest between himself and the human society of which he forms a part, such that any conduct which threatens the security of the society generally, is threatening to his own, and calls forth his instinct (if instinct it be) of self-defence. The same superiority of intelligence, joined to the power of sympathising with human beings generally, enables him to attach himself to the collective idea of his tribe, his country, or mankind, in such a manner that any act hurtful to them, raises his instinct of sympathy, and urges him to resistance.

The sentiment of justice, in that one of its elements which consists of the desire to punish, is thus, I conceive, the natural feeling of retaliation or vengeance, rendered by intellect and sympathy applicable to those injuries, that is, to those hurts, which wound us through, or in common with, society at large. This sentiment, in itself, has nothing moral in it; what is moral is, the exclusive subordination of it to the social sympathies, so as to wait on and obey their call. For the natural feeling would make us resent indiscriminately whatever any one does that is disagreeable to us; but when moralised by the social feeling, it only acts in the directions conformable to the general good: just persons resenting a hurt to society, though not otherwise a hurt to themselves, and not resenting a hurt to themselves, however painful, unless it be of the kind which society has a common interest with them in the repression of. . . .

To recapitulate: the idea of justice supposes two things; a rule of conduct, and a sentiment which sanctions the rule. The first must be supposed common to all mankind, and intended for their good. The other (the sentiment) is a desire that punishment may be suffered by those who infringe the rule. There is involved, in addition, the conception of some definite person who suffers by the infringement; whose rights (to use the expression appropriated to the case) are violated by it. And the sentiment of justice appears to me to be, the animal desire to repel or retaliate a hurt or damage to oneself, or to those with whom one sympathises, widened so as to include all persons, by the human capacity of enlarged sympathy, and the human conception of intelligent self-interest. From the latter elements, the feeling derives its morality; from the former, its peculiar impressiveness, and energy of self-assertion.

I have, throughout, treated the idea of a *right* residing in the injured person, and violated by the injury, not as a separate element in the composition of the idea and sentiment, but as one of the forms in which the other two elements clothe themselves. These elements are, a hurt to some assignable person or persons on the one hand, and a demand for punishment on the other. An examination of our own minds, I think, will show, that these two things include all that we mean when we speak of violation of a right. When we call anything a person's right, we mean that he has a valid claim on society to protect him in the possession of it, either by the force of law, or by that of education and opinion. If he has what we consider a sufficient claim, on whatever account, to have something guaranteed to him by society, we say that he has a right to it. If we desire to prove that anything does not belong to him by right, we think this done as soon as it is admitted that society ought not to take measures for securing it to him, but should leave him to chance, or to his own exertions. . . .

To have a right, then, is, I conceive, to have something which society ought to defend me in the possession of. If the objector goes on to ask, why it ought? I can give him no other reason than general utility. . . .

If the preceding analysis, or something resembling it, be not the correct account of the notion of justice; if justice be totally independent of utility, and be a standard *per se,* which the mind can recognise by simple introspection of itself; it is hard to understand why that internal oracle is so ambiguous, and why so many things appear either just or unjust, according to the light in which they are regarded. . . .

. . . In a co-operative industrial association, is it just or not that talent or skill should give a title to superior remuneration? On the negative side of the question it is argued, that whoever does the best he can, deserves equally well, and ought not in justice to be put in a position of inferiority for no fault of his own; that superior abilities have already advantages more than enough, in the admiration they excite, the personal influence they command, and the internal sources of satisfaction attending them, without adding to these a superior share of the world's goods; and that society is bound in justice rather to make compensation to the less favoured, for this unmerited inequality of advantages, than to aggravate it. On the contrary side it is contended, that society receives more from the more efficient labourer; that his services being more useful, society owes him a larger return for them; that a greater share of the joint result is actually his work, and not to allow his claim to it is a kind of robbery; that if he is only to receive as much as others, he can only be justly required to produce as much, and to give a smaller amount of time and exertion, proportioned to his superior efficiency. Who shall decide between these appeals to conflicting principles of justice? Justice has in this case two sides to it, which it is impossible to bring into harmony, and the two disputants have chosen opposite sides; the one looks to what it is just that the individual should receive, the other to what it is just that the community should give. Each, from his own point of view, is unanswerable; and any choice between them, on grounds of justice, must be perfectly arbitrary. Social utility alone can decide the preference.

How many . . . and how irreconcilable are the standards of justice to which reference is made in discussing the repartition of taxation? One opinion is, that payment to the State should be in numerical proportion to pecuniary means. Others think that justice dictates what they term graduated taxation; taking a higher percentage from those who have more to spare. In point of natural justice a strong case might be made for disregarding means altogether, and taking the same absolute sum (whenever it could be got) from every one: as the subscribers to a mess, or to a club, all pay the same sum for the same privileges, whether they can all equally afford it or not. Since the protection (it might be said) of law and government is afforded to, and is equally required by all, there is no injustice in making all buy it at the same price. It is reckoned justice, not injustice, that a dealer should charge to all customers the same price for the same article, not a price varying according to their means of payment. This doctrine, as applied to taxation, finds no advocates, because it conflicts so strongly with man's feelings of humanity and of social expediency; but the principle of justice which it invokes is as true and as binding as those which can be appealed to against it. Accordingly it exerts a tacit influence on the line of defence employed for other modes of assessing taxation. People feel obliged to argue that the State does more for the rich man than for the poor, as a justification for its taking more from them: though this is in reality not true, for the rich would be far better able to protect themselves, in the absence of law and government, than the poor, and indeed would probably be successful in converting the poor into their slaves. Others, again, so far defer to the same conception of justice, as to maintain that all should pay an equal capitation tax for the protection of their persons (these being of equal value to all), and an unequal tax for the protection of their property, which is unequal. To this others reply, that the all of one man is as valuable to him as the all of another. From these confusions there is no other mode of extrication than the utilitarian.

Is, then, the difference between the Just and the Expedient a merely imaginary distinction? Have mankind been under a delusion in thinking that justice is a more sacred thing than policy, and that the latter ought not to be listened to after the former has been satisfied? By no means. The exposition we have given of the nature and origin of the sentiment, recognises a real distinction; and no one of those who profess the most sublime contempt for the consequences of actions as an element in their morality, attaches more importance to the distinction than I do. While I dispute the pretensions of any theory which sets up an imaginary standard of justice not grounded on utility, I account the justice which is grounded on utility to be the chief part, and incomparably the most sacred and binding part, of all morality. Justice is a name for certain classes of moral rules, which concern the essentials of human well-being more nearly, and are therefore of more absolute obligation, than any other rules for the guidance of life; and the notion which we have found to be the essence of the idea of justice, that of a right residing in an individual, implies and testifies to this more binding obligation.

The moral rules which forbid mankind to hurt one another (in which we must never forget to include wrongful interference with each other's freedom) are more vital to human well-being than any maxims, however important, which only point out the best mode of managing some department of human affairs. They have also the peculiarity, that they are the main element in determining the whole of the social feelings of mankind. It is their observance which alone preserves peace among human beings: if obedience to them were not the rule, and disobedience the exception, every one would see in every one else an enemy, against whom he must be perpetually guarding himself. . . .

The same powerful motives which command the observance of these primary moralities, enjoin the punishment of those who violate them; and as the impulses of self-defence, of defence of others, and of vengeance, are all called forth against such persons, retribution, or evil for evil, becomes closely connected with the sentiment of justice, and is universally included in the idea. Good for good is also one of the dictates of justice; and this, though its social utility is evident, and though it carries with it a natural human feeling, has not at first sight that obvious connection with hurt or injury, which, existing in the most elementary cases of just and unjust, is the source of the characteristic intensity of the sentiment. But the connection, though less obvious, is not less real. . . . The principle, therefore, of giving to each what they deserve, that is, good for good as well as evil for evil, is not only included within the idea of Justice as we have defined it, but is a proper object of that intensity of sentiment, which places the Just, in human estimation, above the simply Expedient. . . .

That first of judicial virtues, impartiality, is an obligation of justice . . . as being a necessary condition of the fulfilment of the other obligations of justice. But this is not the only source of the exalted rank, among human obligations, of those maxims of equality and impartiality, which, both in popular estimation and in that of the most enlightened, are included among the precepts of justice. In one point of view, they may be considered as corollaries from the principles already laid down. If it is a duty to do to each according to his deserts, returning good for good as well as repressing evil by evil, it necessarily follows that we should treat all equally well (when no higher duty forbids) who have deserved equally well of *us,* and that society should treat all equally well who have deserved equally well of *it,* that is, who have deserved equally well absolutely. This is the highest abstract standard of social and distributive justice; towards which all institutions, and the efforts of all virtuous citizens, should be made in the utmost possible degree to converge. But this great moral duty rests upon a still deeper foundation, being a direct emanation from the first principle of morals, and not a mere logical corollary from secondary or derivative doctrines. It is involved in the very meaning of Utility, or the Greatest Happiness Principle. That principle is a mere form of words without rational signification, unless one person's happiness, supposed equal in degree (with the proper allowance made for kind), is counted for exactly as much as another's. Those conditions being supplied, Bentham's dictum, "everybody to count for one, nobody for more than one," might be written under the principle of utility as an explanatory commentary. The equal claim of everybody to happiness in the estimation of the moralist and of the legislator, involves an equal claim to all the means of happiness, except insofar as the inevitable conditions of human life, and the general interest, in which that of every individual is included, set limits to the maxim; and those limits ought to be strictly construed. As every other maxim of justice, so this is by no means applied or held applicable universally; on the contrary, as I have already remarked, it bends to every person's ideas of social expediency. But in whatever case it is deemed applicable at all, it is held to be the dictate of justice. All persons are deemed to have a *right* to equality of treatment, except when some recognised social expediency requires the reverse. And hence all social inequalities which have ceased to be considered expedient, assume the character not of simple inexpediency, but of injustice, and appear so tyrannical, that people are apt to wonder how they ever could have been tolerated; forgetful that they themselves perhaps tolerate other inequalities under an equally mistaken notion of expediency, the correction of which would make that which they approve seem quite as monstrous as what they have at last learnt to condemn. The entire history of social improvement has been a series of transitions, by which one custom or institution after another, from being a supposed primary necessity of social existence, has passed into the rank of a universally stigmatised injustice and tyranny. So it has been with the distinctions of slaves and freemen, nobles and serfs, patricians and plebeians; and so it will be, and in part already is, with the aristocracies of colour, race, and sex. . . .

. . . Justice remains the appropriate name for certain social utilities which are vastly more important, and therefore more absolute and imperative, than any others are as a class (though not more so than others may be in particular cases); and which, therefore, ought to be, as well as naturally are, guarded by a sentiment not only different in degree, but also in kind; distinguished from the milder feeling which attaches to the mere idea of promoting human pleasure or convenience, at once by the more definite nature of its commands, and by the sterner character of its sanctions.

Glossary

Italic terms within the definition are defined in the glossary.

academics Members of Plato's school of philosophy.

ad hoc (Latin, "for a specific purpose.") An hypothesis is ad hoc if it is adopted purely to save a theory from a difficulty without an independent motivation of its own.

ad infinitum Into infinity; endlessly.

aesthetic Belonging to the appreciation of beauty.

aesthetics Pertaining to the appreciation of beauty and other values of pictorial art, music, poetry, fiction, and drama.

a fortiori (Latin, "from the stronger.") This means "and even more so" or "all the more." For example, John owns horses of all ages; a fortiori he owns young horses.

agnosticism The view that something is not known, and perhaps cannot be known. In theology, the view that the existence or nonexistence of God is not known. Neither *theism* nor *atheism* can be justified.

akrasia (Greek, for "weakness of the will.") Not being able to make yourself do what you think it would be best for you to do.

altruism Any act that seeks to advance the good of others for their own sake and not for the sake of advancing the self-interest of the agent. (See *ethical altruism*.)

analytical behaviorism See *behaviorism, logical*.

analytic statement Originally introduced by Kant, an analytic statement is one where the concept of the predicate is contained within the concept of the subject. For example, the statement that all bachelors are unmarried is analytic. The concept "unmarried" is contained within the concept "bachelor." Frege generalized the notion to cover more than just subject-predicate statements. For Frege, an analytic statement is true solely in virtue of the meanings of the words in which it is expressed. Also known as a "tautology." (See *synthetic statement*.)

antecedent What comes before. In a statement of the form, "If *A* then *B*," *A* is the antecedent, and *B* is the consequent.

anthropomorphism Attributing human characteristics, such as human form or human thoughts and intentions, to something that is not human. For example, attributing intentions to rocks to explain why they move or attributing a human appearance to God.

a posteriori Knowledge that is not a priori. A posteriori knowledge, though it may involve the use of reason, depends upon evidence from experience.

a priori Knowledge that is based on reason, independently of experience. The *ontological argument* is an example of an a priori argument.

argument A series of one or more statements called *premises* that are meant to support another statement called *conclusion*. (See also *valid* and *sound*.)

argument from design See *teleological argument*.

argumentum ad hominem An argument that attacks the character of an opponent and not the content of the opponent's position or argument. For example, arguing that because John is a jerk or John is uneducated that he cannot be correct.

artificial intelligence (AI), strong The view that an appropriately programmed computer can have "intelligence," or, more generally, that such a computer can have a whole variety of cognitive states such as believing, wanting, intending, understanding, and so on.

artificial intelligence (AI), weak The view that computers give us a useful research tool for investigating the mind, but they do not have and cannot be programmed to have true cognitive states in the sense that humans have such states.

atheism The view that God does not exist.

automaton A self-moving mechanical being capable of simulating the behavior of a conscious agent, but itself not a conscious agent.

autonomy The capacity, right, or actual condition of self-government, or the determination of one's own actions.

Bayes's theorem A statistical theorem describing how, given an observed outcome, the conditional probability of each of a set of possible causes can be computed from knowledge of the probability of each cause and the conditional probability of the outcome, given each cause.

begging the question The logical fallacy of assuming in the premises of an argument the very conclusion which is to be proved. For example, to argue that God exists because the Bible says so, and the Bible is reliable because it is the word of God, is to assume the very proposition one set out to prove in the process of its own proof. Also called "petitio principii." (See *circular reasoning*.)

behaviorism, logical A view about the meaning of mental state terms. The view claims that mental terms such as "pain," "belief," or "desire" are equivalent in meaning to behavioral terms. This is supposed to show that mental states are dispositions to behave in certain ways. (Also called analytical behaviorism.)

behaviorism, radical The methodological claim that psychology should study only regularities exhibited in behavior—such as principles connecting stimuli and responses. (Also called methodological behaviorism.)

benevolence Desire or disposition to be good to others, kindly and charitable.

bourgeois A member of the middle class in a market economy, with its characteristic tastes and ideas. Originally, the term referred to the class of capitalists in a market economy who owned the means of production.

brute fact A fact for which there can be no explanation.

capitalism An economic system in which trade and industry are controlled by private owners. The owners provide the capital with which to produce goods and employ workers.

catastrophism The geological doctrine, prevalent well into the 18th century, that the geological features of the surface of the Earth are the result of violent cataclysms. The doctrine assumed that the Earth is only a few thousand years old, and was congenial to theological accounts of the origin and history of the Earth.

categorical imperative A moral directive from reason that is binding without condition; a command that applies to all rational beings, no matter what. Kant formulated the categorical imperative as: "Act only according to that maxim by which you can at the same time will that it should become a universal law."

causal theory of perception The theory that material objects are the causes of the ideas, appearances, or sense data we have of them. The material substance itself is distinct from its own qualities (including its *primary qualities*) and, not being directly perceivable, must simply be posited as an unknowable *substratum* for its powers and properties.

causally possible Consistent with the causal laws of nature. A statement is causally possible if it is true in at least one physically *possible world*.

causation The relationship between two events, one as cause, the other as effect. If the first event occurs, the second produces or necessitates the second.

christolatry The worship of Christ as divine.

circular reasoning When the conclusion is concealed within the premises of an argument. (See *begging the question.*)

civil disobedience A nonviolent, conscientious, public form of protest contrary to the law that is done with the aim of bringing about a change in the law or policies of the government.

cogito ergo sum This means "I think, therefore I am." This inference played a central role in Descartes' argument for the distinction between the mental and the physical and in his response to *skepticism.*

cognitive process Mental operations such as reasoning, inferring, deliberating, planning, and perceiving.

cognitive science The interdisciplinary study of cognitive processes in human beings, animals and machines. The core disciplines are psychology, computer science, linguistics, neuroscience, and philosophy.

computational theory of mind The view that mental states and processes are identical to computational states and processes. On this view, the mind is a (suitably programmed) computer.

conclusion In an *argument,* the statement that is being argued for and that the *premises* are meant to jointly establish.

conditioning A form of learning whereby new connections between stimulus and response are formed. (See also *reinforcement.*)

consequentialism A type of moral theory stating that to act morally we must base our actions on their probable results or consequences, rather than acting out of duty, in cases where duty and promoting good consequences come into conflict. It can be contrasted with *deontology.* Examples of consequentialism are *ethical egoism, utilitarianism,* and *ethical altruism.*

contiguity Contact or proximity; the state of being close together.

contingent being A being whose existence depends on something else and therefore might not have come to exist. For example, your existence was contingent on your mother having conceived. (See also *necessary being.*)

contractarianism The theory that the correct way to derive a principle of justice is to decide whether it would be chosen over any alternative principle of justice that could be proposed to a group of normally self-interested, rational persons.

conventionalism The doctrine that the truth of a proposition, or a class of propositions, is determined not by fact but by social agreement or usage. Conventionalism is opposed to versions of realism, which hold that the truth of a proposition, or a class of propositions, is determined by objective facts of nature.

copper rule, the Do unto others as they do unto you. Compare the golden rule: do unto others as you would have them do unto you.

corporeal Bodily.

cosmogony (From the Greek word "kosmogonia" for creation of the world.) Theory of the origin and development of the *cosmos.*

cosmological argument Argument for the existence of God that holds (1) every being is either a *dependent being* or a *self-existent being;* (2) not every being can be a dependent being; (3) therefore, there exists a self-existent being, who is God.

cosmos (From the Greek for "order.") The whole universe conceived as ordered and law-governed.

counterfactuals Statements describing what would have been true if something else were true. The interesting property of such statements for philosophical purposes is that they can be true even when the conditions described are not actually met. For instance, the statement that this wine glass would shatter if thrown to the ground could be true of only an unshattered glass—one that has never met the conditional part of the counterfactual. Counterfactuals are thus a good way of expressing dispositions, tendencies, and other scientifically interesting regularities.

creationism The theory in the philosophy of biology that God intervenes into the natural order to create new species and to create people.

criterion A standard of judgment that is either a sufficient condition for something being the case, or a condition that provides good evidence for something being the case.

culpable Deserving blame.

cultural relativism The view that morality is relative to a given culture; what is right in one culture may be wrong in another. For example, cannibalism might be wrong for Greeks but right for Callations. Cultural relativism goes beyond merely stating the fact that different cultures have different beliefs; it asserts that for each society, its beliefs are really right (not just believed to be right by its members). (See *moral relativism.*)

Darwinism Acceptance of the theory of *evolution* by natural selection developed originally by Charles Darwin (1809–82).

decision theory The theory of rational choices aimed at achieving an optimal outcome where the amount of information available to the agent is limited. The agent has only incomplete information about the true state of affairs and the possible consequences of each possible action.

deductive argument An argument whose *conclusion* must be true if the *premises* are all true, as long as the argument is valid.

deicide The killing of God.

deontology A type of moral theory stating that morality consists in doing one's duty, rather than in considering the probable consequences of one's actions, in cases where duty and the promotion of good consequences come into conflict. Can be contrasted to *consequentialism*. An example of a deontological theory is Kantian ethics.

dependent being A being whose existence is causally dependent on and explained by other things.

determinism The theory that all events, including human actions and choices, are, without exception, totally determined.

determinism, hard A kind of determinist view that rejects the possibility of free will and moral responsibility. Also called nonreconciling determinism.

determinism, soft The view that holds that *determinism* is true and that determinism is compatible with free will and responsibility.

deus ex machina "God from a machine." An artificial or improbable device introduced to resolve an entanglement in a plot or argument. A person invokes a *deus ex machina* when introducing some contrivance to save a theory from some large problem.

diallelus A vicious circle in a proof.

diarchal Pertaining to a joint mode of government by two independent authorities.

dilemma An argument that presents a choice between two alternatives.

doxastic (From the Greek word, "doxa," for "belief.") Theories of justification that are doxastic are those that hold that a belief can be justified only by another belief.

dualism Generally, the view that there are two kinds of stuff. More specifically, "dualism" is associated with the doctrine that mental states, events, or processes are distinct from physical or material states, events, or processes.

dualistic interactionism The view that mental states, events, and processes can causally affect physical states, events, and processes.

efficient cause The physical or mechanical cause of an effect or thing. Efficient causes are one of the four types of causes of Aristotle. Consider a table. For Aristotle, the "material" cause of the table is the material or stuff that the table is made of. The "formal" cause is the blueprint or shape that determines the form of the table. The "final" cause is the reason or purpose for which the table was built. The "efficient cause" is the actual agency or mechanical production of the table by the builder out of material. Efficient causation is often contrasted with "teleological" causation, causation that is the result of purposes or ends (Aristotelian "final" causes).

egoistic hedonism The theory that, in deciding how to act, a person ought to choose (among those acts open) the act that is likely to cause the greatest net balance of pleasure over pain for oneself.

elective freedom The freedom to do, or to forebear from doing, one's duty. (See also *rational freedom.*)

eliminative materialism The view that mental states and processes as we ordinarily conceive of them simply do not exist, in the same way as witches and phlogiston do not exist.

empirical generalization A statement of the form: All *F*s are *G*s. For example, "All the coins in my pockets are pennies." Such generalizations need not express a tendency, disposition, or natural law.

empirical hypothesis A kind of *synthetic statement* whose function is to sum up past experience and enable us to successfully predict or anticipate future experience.

empiricism The theory that all our ideas come from experience and that no proposition about any matter of fact can be known independently of experience.

Epicureanism From the views of the Greek philosopher Epicurus, 341–270 B.C. Epicureans advocated the pursuit of certain pleasures that bring tranquillity and freedom from mental anxiety in order to achieve happiness. In metaphysics, Epicurus was an atomist who attempted to avoid *determinism* by allowing for chance events due to the unpredictable "swerving" of atoms.

epiphenomenalism The view that there is only one form of interaction between the mental and the physical, that in which the physical affects the mental. In this view, the mental can never affect the physical. The mind is not itself a material thing; rather, it is a distinct but causally impotent by-product (*epiphenomenon*) of the world of physics. This is a kind of *dualism.*

epiphenomenon A mere by-product of a process that has no real effect on the process itself.

epistemic Relating to knowledge.

epistemic norm The norms governing how, from an epistemological point of view, an agent ought to reason.

epistemology The theory of knowledge. The study of the origin, nature, and limits of knowledge, including especially the study of the nature of epistemic justification.

equivocation A *fallacy of argument* whereby one uses an ambiguous word in more than one way.

eros Sexual longing or desire; love.

eschatology The development of theories relating to the end of life, as in Christian theology, or to the ultimate end of the *cosmos.*

esoteric intended only for people with special knowledge or interest. The opposite of "exoteric" (opinions or ideas suitable for the uninitiated.)

ethical altruism The theory that morality requires us to forget our own interests and selflessly devote ourselves to the interests of others.

ethical egoism The view that to act morally, individuals should act solely so as to promote their own best interests. Ethical egoism is a moral view; it states a thesis about how humans ought to act. In this it differs from *psychological egoism,* which states a thesis about how humans always do act. An ethical egoist holds that people do not always act to promote their own well-being, even though they should.

ethical relativism See *moral relativism.*

ethical skepticism The view that no moral knowledge is possible.

evolution The process by which something develops gradually from a different form. In biology, evolution is the origin and transformations of biological populations through time due to genetic variation and interaction with the environment, and not by special creation.

existentialism A loose-knit philosophical viewpoint connecting a rejection of determinism with a focus on the responsibility of the agent for making his or her own character out of his or her freely chosen actions. Existentialism rejects the rationalistic view of the universe as planned and comprehensible and consequently faces life with a feeling of dread and a sense of the absurdity of life. Major existentialists are Kierkegaard and Sartre.

ex nihilo Out of nothing.

expected utility (EU) The utility of an uncertain outcome multiplied by its probability.

fallacy A logical mistake in reasoning, especially one which often gives the appearance of being sound.

falsifiable Refutable by experience. For example, if a theory predicts that an eclipse will occur on a certain day, then experience will refute the theory if the eclipse does not occur. *Freudianism* and *Creationism* are often criticized as being unfalsifiable.

fatalism The theory that all events are fated to happen; they would have happened no matter what the person involved might have done to avoid it. This is a stronger view than *determinism.*

fideist A theist whose belief is based on faith rather than argument or reason.

final cause The end, purpose, or goal for which something is working or moving. One of Aristotle's four causes. (See *efficient cause.*)

Freudianism Relating to the views of Sigmund Freud, 1856–1939. Freud developed an elaborate psychological theory focusing on sexual desires and the subconscious. For Freud, the ego is the conscious self. The ego stands between the Id, which demands that basic sexual and physical desires be satisfied, and the superego, which represses the desires of the Id. Freud hypothesized that there exist a variety of repressive mechanisms responsible for neurotic behavior. Freud developed the therapeutic technique of psychoanalysis.

functional equivalence Two systems are functionally equivalent when they do the same tasks or when they have the same capacities. (See *strong equivalence.*)

functionalism Generally, the view that concepts should be defined according to their function. In cognitive theory, the view that mental states, events, and processes are "functional" states of the brain (or other *hardware*). Functional states of a device are those that are defined in terms of their relations to the device's input, its internal transitions, and its output. According to the functionalist, these causal relations and dispositions are what constitute the mental.

genes Biological units that carry hereditary characteristics from parent to offspring. Currently, genes are identified with lengths of DNA or RNA.

gestalt A conception of organization based on the idea that a perceived whole is not just the sum of its parts. The parts are organized into structures and derive their character from the structure of the whole. Gestalt psychology denies the atomistic theory of perception whereby perceptions of patterns or wholes arrive from constructing the whole out of its independently existing parts.

good will For Kant, a good will determines to act in accordance with universal moral law, regardless of the effects of the act in the world, selfish or otherwise.

greatest happiness principle The utilitarian principle, put forth by John Stuart Mill, stating that actions are right in proportion as they promote happiness (pleasure) and wrong in proportion as they promote pain. (See *utilitarianism.*)

hardware The physical apparatus that executes the software in programming a computer. The analog for an organism is its brain (often called its "wetware"). (See also *software.*)

hedonism The view that pleasure is the ultimate good for humans.

hedonism, universalistic The theory that in deciding how to act, I ought to choose (among those acts open to me) the act that is likely to cause the greatest net balance of pleasure over pain, counting my own interests as no less and no more important than everyone else's. The theory is universalistic because it considers everyone equally and hedonistic because it tells us to choose the act that will create the most pleasure.

heuristics Rules of thumb which are useful generalizations for problem-solving tasks, such as "get your queen out early" in chess.

hierophany Pertaining to the official expounding of sacred mysteries or ceremonies or the interpretation of *esoteric* principles.

humanism Generally, any view in which human interests and welfare play a central role. More specifically, the theory that emphasizes reason, scientific inquiry, and human welfare, often rejecting the importance of belief in God.

humanitarian theory of punishment The theory that the goal of punishment should be to mend or "cure" the offender, rather than to punish because he or she deserves it.

hypothetical imperative An action that you should do if you want to promote some goal or end you already have. For example, if you want a good grade, you have a hypothetical imperative to study; if you want some chocolate ice cream, you have a hypothetical imperative to go to the store and buy some. Can be contrasted to a *categorical imperative,* which says that you should perform an action regardless of your ends.

ideal morality Standards of moral excellence that a moral tradition or community sets up as models to aspire to and admire. Praise, honor, and respect are the rewards of those who live according to the standards of ideal morality. However, people are not in general blamed for failing to live up to the standards of ideal morality, or even for not aiming at them. (See *practice morality.*)

idealism The theory that there are only immaterial minds and their mental "contents." The body itself is nothing but a collection of actual or possible sense-data—sights, sounds, touches, and smells. By holding that there is only mind and no matter, idealism avoids the problems of causal interaction between radically different kinds of substances.

idealism, subjective The theory that matter is merely the projection of a finite mind and has no external, independent existence.

identity theory A kind of *materialism* stating that mental events are simply identical to brain processes, the same way that lightning flashes are "identical" to electrical discharges. The mental event (a thought, desire, or sensation) *is* a brain process.

ideology Any set of general ideas or system of beliefs that form the basis of an economic or political theory. The term is used pejoratively to characterize a person's set of beliefs as both false and as adopted to disguise or ignore the economic or political realities of the status quo.

ignoratio elenchi The *fallacy* of irrelevance, that is, of proving a *conclusion* that is not relevant to the matter at hand.

immaterialist One who believes that reality is not material. (See *idealism.*)

immoralist One who rejects conventional morality, arguing that it is in his or her, or even our, best interests, and therefore rational, to act against the dictates of conventional morality.

immutable Unchangeable.

imperative Command. (See also *categorical imperative; hypothetical imperative.*)

imperfect duty A duty that is not owed to any particular person or persons. For example, I have an imperfect duty to help alleviate poverty, but I do not owe it to any particular poor person to feed her, nor to each individual poor person. (See *perfect duty.*)

impersonal evil Evil that is natural and not caused by human action—for example, natural disasters and disease. Even if humans were morally perfect, there would still be impersonal evil. (Also called nonmoral evil.)

indeterminate Not fixed in extent or character. The truth value of a statement is indeterminate when the relevant facts fail to determine whether the statement is true or false.

indeterminism The view that some events are not determined.

indeterminism, simple The theory that human action is not determined; rather, it is caused by inner *volition.*

indubitable Incapable of being doubted; beyond all doubt. Descartes, for example, searched for indubitable truths to combat *skepticism.*

inductive argument An argument whose *premises* establish a probability (rather than a certainty) that its conclusion is true; for example, if no one has ever seen a green flamingo, then there probably are no green flamingos. The argument from design is an example of an inductive argument.

inductive inference An *inference* from evidence to hypothesis, where the evidence does not entail or necessitate that the hypothesis is true, but it is nevertheless reasonable to suppose that the hypothesis is true.

inference The movement from *premises* to a *conclusion.* Inferences can be *deductive* or *inductive.*

in infinitum Into infinity; endlessly.

innate idea An idea that we are born with inherited dispositions to have. *Rationalism* argues that human minds have the disposition to acquire concepts such as being, substance, duration, and even God, once a certain amount of experience is added.

intentionality The property that some mental states have of being about something. Thus, one belief might be about Caesar's crossing the Rubicon, and another might be about the first person to orbit the earth. By contrast, a mental state such as a free-floating anxiety need not be about anything in particular and thus not have intentionality.

interactionism See *dualistic interactionism.*

intertheoretic reduction See *reduction.*

intrinsic good Something that is good in and of itself.

intuition Direct knowledge or awareness of a truth or fact, independent of any reasoning process.

intuitionism Any theory in which *intuition* is appealed to as the basis of knowledge.

intuition pump A thought experiment that is used to support a view. The term is often used to denigrate the effectiveness of the thought experiment.

justification In *epistemology*, knowledge is traditionally defined as justified true belief. To know *p* you must not only believe *p*, *p* must be true and your belief that *p* is true must be justified. Epistemologists disagree about the nature of justification. Some think that a belief is justified if it is caused in the right way or if it is based on another belief that counts as knowledge or if the agent can give reasons in defense of why she holds the belief, and so forth.

kin altruism The disposition to favor the interests of one's near relatives (as distinct from one's own interests) over the interests of complete strangers. Such a disposition may have evolutionary advantages by increasing the probability that those who share many of the individual's genes will survive and reproduce.

Lamarckism In the philosophy of biology, the view that offspring may inherit the characteristics that their parents acquired during their adult lives. This view is no longer held to be credible.

lexical order In John Rawls's theory of justice, the ordering of principles that requires us to satisfy the first principle before going on to consider the second principle; once the first principle is satisfied, we can go on to attempt to satisfy the second principle. (Also called serial order.)

libertarianism In metaphysics, the theory that we possess free will and that our free will is neither determined nor the result of random chance, but instead the result of rational agency. In politics and economics, the theory that emphasizes the importance of personal liberty as opposed to state interference. Political libertarians often oppose taxation for social welfare programs as unjust intrusions into personal freedom.

liberum arbitrium indifferentiae The freedom of indifference; the ability of the will to choose independently of *antecedent* determination.

liturgy A fixed form of public worship used in churches.

logically possible Consistent with the laws of logic. A statement is logically possible if it is true in at least one logically *possible world:* for example, that the next President of the United States is a woman. A statement is logically impossible if it is inconsistent with the laws of logic. A logically impossible statement is, or entails, a contradiction. For example, that some squares are round. Since squares are, by definition, not round, it is a contradiction to say that some squares are round.

machine functionalism See *computational theory of mind.*

manslaughter The act of killing a person unlawfully but not intentionally or by negligence.

Marxism From the views of the German philosopher Karl Marx (1818–1883), on which communism is putatively based. Marxism rejects *capitalism* and predicts the development of society beyond capitalism through a revolution by the working class. Inherent to all forms of Marxism is the rejection of the exploitation of labor due to the private control of the means of production.

materialism The view that everything—every object, state, event, and process—is a material object, state, event, or process and nothing else. According to materialists, there is no immaterial mind or soul and thus no problem of interaction between radically different kinds of substances. (Also called *physicalism.*)

maxim A principle or rule of conduct.

maximin strategy A principle of decision theory for choice under uncertainty. The strategy ranks the best decision as that which is superior to the worst outcomes of other possible decisions. The strategy "maximizes" the "minimum" outcome.

mediately perceivable Perceivable indirectly, by means of something else.

Mendelian genetics The theory developed by Gregor Mendel (1822–1884) that the inheritance of any particular characteristic is controlled by the inheritance of *genes*, which occur in pairs and separate independently of each other in meiosis, a stage of cell division.

mens rea The accompanying intention to commit a crime or pursue a wrongful aim which makes the act a crime.

mentalism Originally, the term referred to idealistic doctrines such as Berkeley's, which held that only minds and their subjective states exist. In contemporary philosophy of mind, mentalism is the view that *cognitive processes* can be explained only by postulating a set of internal mental representations and rules that operate on the representations. (See *artificial intelligence* and *computational theory of mind.*)

metaphysics The study of the ultimate nature of reality. Common metaphysical views are *materialism, idealism,* and *dualism.*

methodicide The death or killing of method or methodology.

methodist Epistemologists who first answer the question, How are we to decide whether we know? What are the *criteria* of knowledge? and then use their answer to go on to answer the question, What do we know? What is the extent of our knowledge? A methodist is the opposite of a *particularist.*

methodological behaviorism See *behaviorism, radical.*

monism The view that reality is ultimately made up of only one kind of thing. *Idealism* and *materialism* are two different monistic theories. Can be contrasted to *dualism,* which holds that there are two kinds of things: mind and body.

monotheism Belief in one, and only one, God.

moral evil Evil that is caused by human action, rather than natural causes such as earthquakes. If humans were as morally perfect as God, there would be no moral evil.

moral relativism The view that the "truth" of moral judgments is always relative to a given system of beliefs that itself cannot be proven correct.

mutation Change or alteration in form.

The Myth of Gyges The story in Plato's *Republic* that is meant to show that injustice is in our self-interest; Gyges found a ring of invisibility that allowed him to act unjustly and reap the benefits. Plato argues against the *immoralist*'s challenge presented by the Myth of Gyges in the rest of the *Republic.*

narcissism A tendency to self-worship. An excessive or erotic interest in one's own personal features.

naturalism (1) The view that the universe is self-existent, self-explanatory, and self-operating, requiring no supernatural or spiritual cause or explanation. (2) The view that nature does not require a *teleological* explanation; scientific laws are adequate to cover all phenomena.

necessary being A being whose existence depends on nothing else and who necessarily has to exist. Some people have argued that God is such a being. (See also *contingent being.*)

necessary condition If *A* is a necessary condition for *B,* then *B* cannot be true unless *A* is true. For instance, being alive is a necessary condition for going golfing. If you are dead, you cannot golf. (See *sufficient condition.*)

negligence Lack of proper care or attention; carelessness.

nonmaleficence Not injuring others.

nonmoral evil See *impersonal evil.*

normative Having to do with norms or standards; regulative. In ethics, norms are standards for right conduct.

objective Something that is objective has a particular nature that is not dependent on us or our judgments of it. For example, those who hold that there are objective moral truths believe that such truths are there for us to discover and hold regardless of any of our beliefs or judgments.

occasionalism A kind of *dualism* stating that mind and body do not really interact. Being kicked does not *cause* my pain; rather, it is the occasion for God, whose infinite nature somehow encompasses both mind and matter, to cause me to feel pain. Similarly, my mental states are occasion for God to cause my body to act.

omnipotent All-powerful; able to do anything.

omniscient All-knowing.

ontological argument An *a priori* argument for the existence of God stating that the very concept or definition of God automatically entails that God exists; because of the special nature of the concept, there is no way that God could fail to exist.

ontology The theory of being, or of existence. From the Greek *ontos* (being) and *logos* (theory, account).

ontophany The appearance of being; the manifestation of existence.

oracle An ancient Greek shrine where a priest or priestess would give a response (often difficult to interpret) to an inquiry from a god or goddess.

original contract In *social contract theories,* the hypothetical contract that establishes the fundamental principles of justice and/or structure of society, to which all rational, normally self-interested persons would agree in entering society.

original position In John Rawls's contractarian theory of justice (*contractarianism*), the original position is the hypothetical gathering of people in a condition of equal power and ignorance for the purpose of determining fair principles of justice for society. (See *veil of ignorance.*)

orthodox Beliefs that are declared by a group to be true and normative. Heresy is a departure from and relative to a given orthodoxy. Of or holding correct or conventional or currently accepted beliefs, especially in religion.

paradox of hedonism This paradox is that the single-minded pursuit of happiness is necessarily self-defeating, for the way to get happiness is to forget it; then it may come to you. If you aim exclusively at pleasure itself, with no concern for the things that bring pleasure, then pleasure will never come. One must first desire something other than satisfaction to achieve satisfaction.

paradox of omnipotence Can an *omnipotent* being make things which he subsequently cannot control, or make rules which bind himself? For example, can God create a rock so heavy that even He cannot lift it? On the one hand, it seems as though he should be able to, since he is, by definition, able to do anything. But if he did make a rule that bound himself—which he could not violate—it seems as though he would not still be all-powerful.

parallelism A kind of *dualism* stating that mind and body only appear to interact because of a kind of "preestablished harmony" between them, like two clocks independently striking at the same moment. Thus, because of this harmony, when I kick the table, I also feel pain; the kicking does not cause the pain.

particular A specific example of a class of things, rather than the class itself or that which defines the class. An individual rather than a *universal.*

particularist Epistemologists who first answer the question, What do we know? What is the extent of our knowledge? and then use their answer to go on to answer the question, How are we to decide whether we know? What are the *criteria* of knowledge? A particularist is the opposite of a *methodist.*

Pascal's wager Blaise Pascal's argument that we should believe in (or "bet on") God because the stakes are infinitely high on the side of God. The rewards for believing correctly and the penalties for wrongly not believing are high, and the costs of believing mistakenly are low. (Also called a wager argument.)

patriarchy The domination or government of a social structure or institution by the fathers or male elders.

Pavlov Russian psychologist who discovered *conditioning*. In his famous experiment, he trained a dog to salivate when it heard a bell ring. The bell ringing replaced the presence of food as the stimulus.

pedagogy The art of teaching.

perceptron A device designed by Frank Rosenblatt in the 1950s to understand perceptual recognition tasks. A perceptron consists of three layers of connected units—an input layer, an associative layer, and an output layer. Additional layers of units can be added to further complicate the device.

perfect duty A duty that is owed to a particular person or persons. For example, I have a perfect duty to my banker to repay my loan and to every person not to lie to them. (See *imperfect duty*.)

personal identity The problem of explaining what constitutes both the identity of a person at a time and the identity of a person through time.

petitio principii See *begging the question* and *circular reasoning*.

phallocentric Penis centered, having to do with men or men's sexuality or male gender.

phenomenalism The theory that our only knowledge of reality is mind-dependent; the phenomena we experience are the only objects of knowledge. Phenomenalists may affirm or deny the existence of a reality of things-in-themselves behind the phenomena.

phenomenology A descriptive study of subjective processes such as consciousness, feelings, emotions, and so on. The study of "what it is like" to be in a certain mental state. (See *qualia*.)

phobia A lasting abnormal fear or dislike of something.

physicalism (1) *Materialism*. (2) The theory that every object, state, event, or process can be completely described and explained by the physical sciences. And we are to understand that some things in the physical sciences are *not* material—for instance, gravitational fields and electromagnetic radiation. According to this use of the term, one could believe that physicalism is true but *materialism* is false.

physicalism, token A version of *physicalism* that contends that being in a mental state (process, etc.) always involves being in a physical state (process, etc.). This allows for the possibility that there might be different physical states for different thinking beings. For instance, adding 2 + 2, for a human being might involve certain electrical activity in neurons located in certain areas of the brain; but adding 2 + 2 for a computer, might involve electrical activity in silicon chips.

physicalism, type A version of *physicalism* that denies that it is possible for different thinkers to have the same kind of mental state without being in the same kind of physical state. Thus, in this view, a person and a computer could both be said to be adding 2 + 2 only if there were some physical process that they were both in at the same time.

Platonism The philosophy of Plato stating that the *particular*, individual things we see are merely imperfect "copies" of perfect, unchanging, universal forms.

polytheism Belief in more than one God.

posit To assume that something is true without argument, either because it is a self-evident truth or merely as an arbitrary assumption.

possible world A complete state of affairs, and so the actual world is itself a possible world. Complete states of affairs distinct from the actual world are ways the actual world might have been. Complete states of affairs that are consistent with the laws of logic are logically possible worlds. Complete states of affairs that are consistent with both the laws of logic and the laws of nature are physically or causally possible worlds.

postulate A self-evident truth or fundamental principle.

practice morality The standards of conduct actually expected of, and generally practiced by, persons living within a given moral tradition or community. The part of morality concerned with requirements, those standards for which people are blamed, criticized, or punished for failing to live up to. See *ideal morality* and *supererogation.*

pragmatic Of or pertaining to practical considerations.

pragmatism The theory that the meaning or value of concepts should be understood in terms of their practical consequences.

predicate That which is said of a subject.

predominant egoism The claim that as a matter of fact the egoistic or self-interested motivations of human behavior tend to override their altruistic or other-regarding motivations until they have achieved a satisfactory level of security and well being. (See *altruism* and *psychological egoism.*)

premise In an *argument,* the reasons that are given to support the *conclusion.*

prima facie duty A self-evident duty, such as promise keeping, which we are required to act upon if no other, more weighty, duty intervenes.

primary qualities Intrinsic characteristics of a physical object itself, such as solidity, extension in space (size), figure (shape), motion or rest, and number. Primary qualities are ones that objects would continue to possess even if there were no perceiving beings in the world, for they are inseparable from the material object and found in every part of it. (See also *secondary qualities.*)

primeval Of the earliest times of the world; ancient.

principle of sufficient reason (PSR) For everything that happens there must be a sufficient reason for its happening and not some other thing.

privation The condition of a substance that lacks a certain quality which it is capable of possessing and normally does possess. Loss or lack of something.

problem of evil Problem posed for theists: If God is all-good, *omnipotent,* and *omniscient,* how can his existence be compatible with the existence of evil?

program A sequence of instructions, in some computer language, that causes a physical apparatus (*hardware*) to perform some task or sequence of operations.

projectible property When past instances of a property are a guide to predictions about future instances of a property. For example, if every raven I have seen is black, then it is reasonable to predict that future ravens will be black. But if every raven I have seen is alive in the twentieth century, it does not follow that it is reasonable to predict that future ravens will be alive in the twentieth century. Being black is a projectible property of ravens; being alive in the twentieth century is not.

propositional calculus (logic) Systems of logic that concern themselves with how statements can be combined—using such connectives as "and," "or," "if then," and "not"—into more complex statements and with the logical properties possessed by such statements.

prudential reasonableness When an act conforms to the norms of rationality that govern the selection and performance of actions.

psychological egoism A theory about the psychology of humans stating that the only thing anyone is capable of desiring or pursuing ultimately (as an end in itself) is one's own self-interest. According to psychological egoism, people always act selfishly. If someone appears to act altruistically, that person is doing it only because taking the interests of other people is the means to promoting his or her own good; genuinely disinterested acts of benevolence do not exist. (See also *ethical egoism.*)

psychological egoistic hedonism A common form of *psychological egoism* stating that our only kind of ultimate desire is to prolong our own pleasure and reduce our own pains.

punitive Inflicting or intending to inflict punishment.

punitive contingencies Punishments intentionally administered by people, and not naturally by environmental conditions, to induce other people *not* to behave in certain ways.

putative Reputed or supposed. For instance, a putative proof is a reputed or supposed proof. It may not in fact be a proof.

qua As; in the character or capacity of. For example, your duties *qua* student are different from your duties *qua* friend.

qualia The qualitative feels of mental experiences: the hurt of pain, the color of red, the taste of wine, the scent of a rose, the longing of love, the ecstasy of an orgasm. The qualitative character of an experience is "what it is like" to have that experience. (See *phenomenology.*)

ratiocination The process of logical reasoning.

rational freedom The freedom that a person has to the degree that her will is led by moral principles. (See also *elective freedom.*)

rationalism The theory that there are *innate ideas* and that certain general propositions (usually called necessary, or *a priori,* propositions) can be known to be true in advance of or in the absence of empirical verification.

Rawls, John, (1921–) American moral and political philosopher, author of *A Theory of Justice,* 1971.

realism The theory that the objects of our knowledge have an independent existence rather than being mind-dependent.

realism, naive The theory that *primary* and *secondary qualities* are both strictly part of physical objects and that both can exist quite independently of perceiving minds.

realism, representative The theory that our ideas are faithful representations of the real, external world.

realism, sophisticated The theory that physical substances and their *primary qualities* can exist independently of perceiving beings and only the *secondary qualities* are mind-dependent.

reciprocity A relation of mutual exchange.

reductio ad absurdum A method of demonstrating that a proposition is false by showing that its truth, along with other accepted propositions, would entail a logical contradiction.

reduction One theory (T_1) reduces to another theory (T_2) when the propositions and principles of the first are entailed by the second, then apply to the same cases, but the second theory does not contain some items (such as "light" or "belief") from the first. These items in T_1 have been reduced to something else in T_2. (Also called intertheoretic reduction.)

reify To treat a concept or idea as a thing. Reification is the philosophical mistake of treating a concept, abstraction, convention, or artificial construct as if it were a real natural thing.

reinforcement Positive reinforcement is the use of rewards in *conditioning.* Negative reinforcement is the use of punishments in conditioning.

relativism In general, the doctrine that truth is relative to the standpoint of the individual or of the community or culture.

relativism, cultural Relativism about values stems from the fact that the values or ethical principles of individuals vary widely. Cultural relativism holds that most disagreements about values or ethical principles stem from enculturation in different ethical traditions. Cultural relativism need not entail *moral relativism.*

relativism, moral The view that the truth of moral judgments is relative to the judging subject or community. We ought to do that, and only that, which we think we ought to do. The having of an opinion about what we ought to do, individually or collectively, makes it true that that is what we ought to do.

repeatable pleasure Pleasures such that you would want to repeat the pleasure again in the future. Pleasures of sex, eating great meals, seeing great art, and so on. (See *self-exhausting pleasure.*)

repentance The feeling of regret about what one has done or failed to do.

res cogitans (Latin, "thinking thing.") Used by Descartes to refer to the mind.

result theories of punishment See *utilitarian theories of punishment.*

retributive theory The theory of punishment stating that the primary justification of punishment is the fact that a committed offense deserves punishment, rather than any advantage gained through punishment.

secondary qualities Those qualities of an object (such as color, taste, smell, sound, warmth, and cold) that exist (according to some theories) only when actually sensed and then only "in the mind" of the one who senses them. (See also *primary qualities.*)

self-exhausting pleasure Pleasures such that when one experiences such pleasures one tends not to want to repeat them. Once, or perhaps a few times, is enough. Sometimes these pleasures are disappointing. Other times they are complete in themselves. For instance, climbing Mt. Everest. You may want to climb it only once, and once you have, you never have the desire to climb it again. (See *repeatable pleasure.*)

self-existent being A being whose existence is not dependent on other things, but rather is accounted for by its own nature.

self-presenting That which is directly evident to an agent. Thoughts are self-presenting if to have them is to think that you have them. So if I believe that Socrates is mortal, then if my belief is self-presenting it will be the case by that very fact that it is evident to me that I believe that Socrates is mortal.

serial order See *lexical order.*

skepticism The position that denies the possibility of knowledge. A skeptic might hold that no knowledge of any sort is possible or might confine skepticism to a particular field such as ethics.

social contract theory The theory that grounds political obligations in a hypothetical social contract to which all rational, normally self-interested persons would agree in forming a society.

sociobiology The study of the social behavior of animals, especially the role of behavior in survival and reproduction.

software Computer *program* (set of instructions) that can be loaded and executed on computer *hardware.*

sophism A piece of deceptive reasoning characteristic of the ancient Greek Sophists.

sophists Wandering teachers in ancient Greece who claimed to teach people (for a fee) how to achieve political success. Socrates objected to the way in which they argued; they would use tricks to win the argument and would argue for anything, regardless of its truth.

sound An *argument* is sound if it is *valid* and its *premises* are true.

species chauvinism The limitation of mentality and consciousness to animals physically similar to human beings, to the exclusion of machines and, perhaps, silicon-based life forms.

Spinoza Dutch Jewish Rationalist (1632–1677). He held that God is immanent in the world, and individual things are modes or modifications of God.

stoicism To be stoic is to be calm and not excitable, bearing difficulties or discomfort without complaining. A school of philosophy founded by Zeno of Citium c. 300 B.C.

strong equivalence Two systems are strongly equivalent if they are not only weakly equivalent but also produce the same outputs (given the same inputs) in the same way—that is, their internal functionings are the same. (See *weak equivalence.*)

subjectivism (1) The view that all knowledge is limited to the nature of objects as known through human experience, rather than objectively in themselves; it is impossible for us to transcend human subjectivity. (2) In ethics, the view that no objective moral truths exist; moral judgments are based on the subjective emotional or mental reactions of the individual or community.

substratum That which underlies all an object's attributes or qualities and of which the attributes are predicated.

sufficient condition If *A* is a sufficient condition for *B,* then given that *A* is true, *B* is true as well. For instance, it is a sufficient condition for being alive that you are golfing. If you are golfing, then it follows that you are alive.

summum bonum From the Latin for the supreme good. The *summum bonum* is the ultimate end of human action, the worth of which is intrinsically good (good in and of itself).

supererogation An act that would be good to do, but not wrong not to do; it is "above and beyond the call of duty." An example might be throwing yourself on a live grenade to save your friends.

synthetic statement The opposite of an *analytic* statement. A synthetic statement is true partly in virtue of the meanings of the words used to express it, but also by the nature of things. A synthetic statement can be known *a priori;* for example, the statement that every event has a cause; or a synthetic statement can be known *a posteriori;* for example, snow is wet.

tabula rasa A blank tablet. Empiricists hold that the mind at birth is a *tabula rasa;* it awaits experience and has no *innate ideas.*

tautology A statement of logic that is true under any assignment of truth values to the constituent parts of the statement. For example, either *p* or not *p,* as in it is either raining here now or it is not raining here now.

teleological argument *Inductive argument* for the existence of God that cites purported examples of design in nature as proof for the existence of a designer who is God. (Also called argument from design.)

teleology The view that there is a purpose or goal to the universe. From the Greek *telos* (goal, end) and *logos* (theory, account).

theism The view that God (or gods) exist.

theodicy An attempted justification for the existence of God despite the existence of evil.

theogony An account of the origin of the gods.

theology The study of God—his nature and his relation to the world.

theoretical entities Usually contrasted with observational entities. As the terminology suggests, observational entities can be observed by the senses, but theoretical entities are postulated to explain observable phenomena. The distinction between observation and postulation is difficult to draw.

theoretical terms The opposite of observational terms. Observational terms are the terms of a scientific theory that refer to objects that can be observed by the senses. Theoretical terms refer to the objects putatively postulated by a theory to explain the existence and nature of observed entities. The distinction between theoretical and observational terms is notoriously difficult to draw.

theory of agency The view that although human behavior is caused, not every chain of causes and effects is infinite; some causal chains begin with agents themselves.

truth tables A method of tabulating how the truth of constituent propositions of a statement in a *propositional calculus* determines the truth of the complex proposition.

turing machine Despite its name, it is not a machine but a kind of mathematical system that can be viewed as plans for a device for executing *programs* or other sequences of instructions. Turing machines are very restricted in that they can do only a limited number of basic things (such as read a 0 or a 1, write a 0 or 1, move left one step, move right one step). However, they are very flexible and can be programmed to do anything any computer can do—at least, if given enough time and memory.

type-token relations (for behavior) Relations that determine how to categorize a particular output in the vocabulary of behavior—for example, "In raising his arm, he was signaling that he knew the answer."

ultimate cause The goal or purpose toward which a thing acts or moves.

universal A general concept rather than a *particular* individual; that which is definitive of a class of individuals.

universalizable Capable of being applied universally, to everything or everyone.

utilitarianism The moral theory stating that individuals should choose the act, among those available to the agent, that is likely to create the greatest amount of happiness and the least amount of pain. Each person's (and perhaps each animal's) pleasures and pains are to count equally; you may not count your own pleasures and pains more (or less) than anyone else's. (See *greatest happiness principle.*)

utilitarian theories of punishment These theories hold that punishment is at best a necessary evil, justifiable if and only if the good of its consequences (its social utility) outweigh its own immediate and intrinsic evil. Punishment is an evil inflicted upon a person for the sake of greater future goods such as correction or reform of the offender, protection of society, and deterrence.

valid An *argument* is valid if its *conclusion* follows logically from its *premises.* Arguments are either valid or invalid, premises and conclusions are either true or false.

veil of ignorance In John Rawls's contractarian theory of justice, the veil of ignorance is what keeps the people in the (hypothetical) original position from knowing the facts (such as their race, gender, talents, and social position) about their own condition that could bias their decisions. (See *original position.*)

vengeance theory of punishment, emotional version The view that the justification of punishment is to be found in the emotions of hate and anger, allegedly felt by all normal or right-thinking people, that it expresses.

vengeance theory of punishment, escape-valve version The theory that legal punishment is an orderly outlet for aggressive feelings that would otherwise demand satisfaction in socially disruptive ways.

vengeance theory of punishment, hedonistic version The view that the justification of punishment is the pleasure that it gives people to see the criminal suffer for his or her crime.

volition The act or capacity of willing or choosing.

voluntariness The quality of having been freely chosen by an agent without compulsion or any other sort of excuse (such as insanity or intoxication) that might make the choice less than free.

wager argument See *Pascal's wager.*

weak equivalence Two systems are weakly equivalent if they both produce the same output, given the same input.

Michelle Svatos

Peter J. Graham